BUILDERS OF
AMERICAN INSTITUTIONS

BUILDERS OF AMERICAN INSTITUTIONS

READINGS IN UNITED STATES HISTORY

Edited by FRANK FREIDEL, *Harvard University*
and NORMAN POLLACK, *Yale University*

RAND McNALLY & COMPANY · *Chicago*

RAND McNALLY HISTORY SERIES

FRED HARVEY HARRINGTON, Consulting Editor

Borden, ed., AMERICA'S TEN GREATEST PRESIDENTS
Freidel and Pollack, eds., BUILDERS OF AMERICAN INSTITUTIONS
Gatzke, THE PRESENT IN PERSPECTIVE, 2nd edition
Jones, ANCIENT CIVILIZATION
Mosse, THE CULTURE OF WESTERN EUROPE: THE NINETEENTH
    AND TWENTIETH CENTURIES
Palmer, ed., ATLAS OF WORLD HISTORY
Palmer, ed., HISTORICAL ATLAS OF THE WORLD
Sellers, ed., THE BERKELEY READINGS IN AMERICAN HISTORY
Sellers and May, A SYNOPSIS OF AMERICAN
    HISTORY
Shannon, TWENTIETH CENTURY AMERICA
Starr, Nowell, Lyon, Stearns, and Hamerow, A HISTORY
    OF THE WORLD (2 vols.)
Treadgold, TWENTIETH CENTURY RUSSIA
Williams, ed., THE SHAPING OF AMERICAN DIPLOMACY
Wright, FRANCE IN MODERN TIMES: 1760 TO THE PRESENT

PREFACE

The publication explosion in American historical writing together with the profusion of paperback reprints provide far richer and more meaningful readings in American history than were available to students a few years ago. *Builders of American Institutions* supplies a core of significant readings on some of the most vital themes in American history. It can be read by itself or used as a starting point for lengthier excursions into specialized paperbacks and pamphlets. It consists of illuminating essays by present-day writers—most of them historians—and related source material, much of which is not reprinted elsewhere. The essays survey basic issues from the struggles of the first settlers to the current debates over the relationship of government to the economy and the control of nuclear weapons. The topics introduce the reader to some of the aspects of political, constitutional, social, intellectual, economic, and diplomatic history. The readings within each section are interrelated. There is also an interrelation among the topics, as several themes (such as the changing role of government) unfold from colonial beginnings into the twentieth century. The topics may serve as supplementary reading or as a basis for discussion. For several vital reasons they do not emphasize the problems approach. Too often problems collections (1) direct students toward the rather narrow questions that historians are debating rather than toward the larger themes of American history; (2) lead to a study of historiography at the expense of a grasp of history; and (3) force the student on the basis of inadequate evidence to choose among conflicting points of view or to drift to the conclusion that the truth inevitably lies between two extremes. This collection does contain some historiographical essays and at some points presents sharply conflicting viewpoints that the student will be challenged to analyze, but the emphasis is upon broad themes and trends, toward which the approach in discussions may well be less of "either-or" than of "how, why, and of what purport?"

The authors wish to thank their numerous fellow historians who suggested significant selections, especially Bernard Bailyn who gave generously from his rich knowledge of colonial sources. They also express their appreciation to the authors who so kindly granted permission for republication of their essays in this volume. They are grateful for the aid of the library and photography staffs of the Yale and the Harvard libraries. As always, they thank their wives for their encouragement and forebearance.

Frank Freidel
Norman Pollack

TABLE OF CONTENTS

TABLE OF CONTENTS

12.   THE MEN OF RECONSTRUCTION   265

13.   CAPTAINS OF INDUSTRY   286

14.   URBANITES IN THE INDUSTRIAL AGE: CHICAGO   310

15.   THE POPULISTS   335

16.   THE IMPERIALISTS AND THEIR FOES   358

TABLE OF CONTENTS

CHAPTER ONE

SEVENTEENTH-CENTURY AMERICANS

Throughout the seventeenth century, successive waves of bold, ambitious, and hardy Europeans arrived as colonizers on the shores of the vast American wilderness. Some were adventurers who came primarily to seek estates; others were men of religious conviction who wished above all to erect a new Zion. Many of the newcomers sought both material and spiritual ends. Whatever their motivations, they gradually had to adapt their preconceptions and to modify the European institutions they brought with them in ways that would meet the stringent necessities of the raw New World. They were transformed from transplanted Europeans into the first Americans.

The institutions these seventeenth-century Americans created represented an important point of evolution between those of sixteenth-century Europe and twentieth-century America. They were not precisely those of contemporary England; neither were they as close to present-day institutions in the United States as is sometimes supposed. Religious and economic freedom and political democracy were not the general rule, and class distinctions were sharp. The political, religious, and social views of one significant group of settlers, the Puritans, found lucid expression in the writings of their leader, John Winthrop. In some ways he was the greatest theoretician of the new order—a rather rigid concept of society that quickly became outmoded. The new American society was fluid compared with that of the Old World, and as successive generations of Americans reached maturity, social and economic structures rapidly changed. The evolution of the people and institutions in Virginia between 1607 and the close of the seventeenth century illustrates this fluidity.

The Puritans, coming from an English society of which they disapproved, tried to build a better order, a new Canaan, on the shores of New England in the 1630's. A group of well-to-do Puritans, disliking the religious policies of their new king, Charles I, and suffering from the depression in England, sought to protect their religious beliefs and mend their fortunes in the New World. Bringing the royal charter of the Massachusetts Bay Company with them, they endeavored upon their arrival in 1630 to establish a suitable government. They elected as their governor John Winthrop, an impressive Suffolk squire who had imbibed deeply of Puritanism at Cambridge University and had become versed in the law at one of the Inns of the Court in London. Winthrop, a humane and moderate man, struggled to set the new government upon a middle course, despite the occasional triumphs of fanatics who seemed to him to favor either too much or too little authority for the government. In his biography of Winthrop, Edmund S. Morgan analyzed the manner in which the government of Massachusetts Bay Colony came into being.

EDMUND S. MORGAN:
A DUE FORM OF GOVERNMENT*

When Winthrop and eleven other members of the Massachusetts Bay Company met at Cambridge, England, on August 26, 1629, they agreed to go to New England if the charter and headquarters of the company could be transferred with them. Ten of the twelve kept their pledge, eight of them arriving with Winthrop or shortly after. Besides these, Winthrop could count only four or five other members of the company in New England at the end of 1630. This handful of men was now the Massachusetts Bay Company and endowed with all the powers described in the charter which Winthrop guarded among his papers.

In the charter the King had granted authority "to make, ordeine, and establishe all manner of wholesome and reasonable orders, lawes, statutes, and ordinances, directions, and instructions, not contrarie to the lawes of this our realm of England, as well for setling of the forms and ceremonies of government and magistracy fitt and necessary for the said plantation, and the inhabitants there, and for nameing and stiling of all sortes of officers, both superior and inferior, which they shall finde needefull for that governement and plantation, and the distinguishing and setting forth of the severall duties, powers, and lymytts of every such office and place."

It was intended, of course, that these extensive powers should be exercised by a corporation meeting in England; but the charter did not say so, and the only actual limitation which the King placed on the company's governmental authority over Massachusetts Bay was that it should make no laws repugnant to the laws of England. Settlers going to the colony from England and their children born there were to enjoy "all liberties and immunities" that they would have had if they had been born in England. But English birth did not in 1630 confer the right to participate in government, and the charter did not specify that the consent of the settlers should be obtained for the laws made to govern them. Instead the company

had full powers to legislate for the colony and to organize a government to carry out their decrees in any way they saw fit.

With regard to the organization and government of the company itself the charter was much more specific. The members, known as "freemen," were to meet four times a year in a "Great and General Court," to make laws for both company and colony. Once a year, at one of these courts, they would elect a governor, a deputy governor, and eighteen "assistants" for the coming year, to manage affairs between meetings of the General Court. This executive council was to meet every month. The governor or deputy governor and at least six of the assistants must be present also at every meeting of the General Court, but the charter did not specify that any other members must be present to constitute a quorum, so that these seven officers, in the absence of any other members, could presumably exercise all the powers of the General Court.

In Massachusetts, therefore, Winthrop and the dozen or so members of the company who came with him had unlimited authority to exercise any kind of government they chose over the other settlers. In order to satisfy the terms of the charter they had only to meet once a month as assistants (all but one of the members who are known to have migrated the first year were assistants) and four times a year as a General Court, though the two types of meeting would now be virtually indistinguishable in membership. Provided they followed this procedure and passed no laws repugnant to the laws of England, they could govern Massachusetts in any way they saw fit. And for that matter, who was to say what law was repugnant to those of England? Who was to decide, who to correct them if they erred? Here was no King, Parliament, bishop, or judge to stand in their way.

A group of men as sure of their cause as were Winthrop and his friends must have been strongly tempted to establish themselves as a permanent aristocracy or oligarchy, holding fast the power granted in the charter and using it to enforce the special commission which they believed God had given them. They were a determined, stiff-jawed set, quick to anger and slow to laughter, as likely a group of oligarchs as ever assembled. John

* Reprinted from Edmund S. Morgan, *The Puritan Dilemma: The Story of John Winthrop* (Boston: Little, Brown and Company, 1958), pp. 84–100 by permission. Copyright © 1958, by Edmund S. Morgan.

Endecott and Thomas Dudley, after Winthrop the most influential of the group, were also the most headstrong.

Endecott had been governing the colony under instructions from the company in England before Winthrop and the others got there. Winthrop saw no need for any such subordinate officer after his own arrival on the scene, but Endecott was still a member of the company and entitled to a place in its councils. He was a soldier by past experience and by temperament, impatient of civilian impertinence, all too ready to draw his sword or strike with a fist when his commands were not obeyed with alacrity. The General Court commissioned him to keep the peace in Salem, where he continued to live, but his notion of keeping the peace was sometimes far from peaceful. On one occasion, when a man had not treated him with due respect, he felt obliged to defend his dignity with his fists. When Winthrop rebuked him, he answered, "I acknowledge I was too rash in strikeing him, understanding since that it is not lawfull for a justice of peace to strike. But if you had seene the manner of his carriadge, with such daring of mee with his armes on kembow etc. It would have provoked a very patient man." And this John Endecott was not.

Neither was Thomas Dudley, who as deputy governor was Winthrop's second-in-command. Dudley was a rigid, literal-minded type, ready to exact his pound of flesh whenever he thought it due him. As steward of the Earl of Lincoln in England he had prided himself on getting the Earl out of debt by raising the tenants' rents. In Massachusetts he engrossed quantities of corn and lent it to his poorer neighbors on credit, to receive ten bushels for seven and a half after harvest. Winthrop regarded this practice as oppressive usury, but Dudley's temper flared when his conduct was questioned in any way. He was obviously not the sort of man to diminish his own authority.

Winthrop himself was more mature than Dudley or Endecott would ever be. His long struggle with his passions had left him master of himself in a way that few men ever achieve. The fire was still there, and if blown up by other men's wrath, it would occasionally burst out, but generally it lay well below the surface, imparting a warmth and power which everyone around him sensed. Winthrop, as he himself realized, had acquired a talent for command. He never grasped for authority as Dudley or Endecott might, but he did not need to: he was the kind of man upon whom authority was inevitably thrust.

These three men, all disposed in their different ways to command those around them, were equipped also with a philosophy of government to give their commands a superhuman sanction. For more than a hundred years Protestants had been confronting the pope with declarations of the God-given authority of civil rulers. In England Anglican and Puritan alike maintained the divine right of their king against the enemy at Rome, who claimed a power to depose Protestant monarchs. Though the Puritans reserved to the people a right of resistance against tyrants who violated the laws of God, they were always ready to quote the Epistle to the Romans in support of rulers who enforced the laws of God. And the members of the Massachusetts Bay Company were all godly men; they had come with no other intention than to see God's will done at last.

Winthrop never lost an opportunity to affirm his belief that the powers that be were ordained of God and must be honored and respected accordingly. While still aboard the *Arbella,* he had reminded the other passengers that "God Almightie in his most holy and wise providence hath soe disposed of the Condicion of mankinde, as in all times some must be rich some poore, some highe and eminent in power and dignitie; others meane and in subjeccion." There was no doubt in Winthrop's mind that God intended civil governments to be in the hands of men like himself; to entrust the people at large with powers of government, as in a Greek democracy, was not only unwarranted by Scripture but dangerous to the peace and well-being of the community, for the people at large were unfit to rule. The best part of them was always the smallest part, "and of that best part the wiser part is always the lesser."

Winthrop and the other members of the Bay Company were authorized by their charter to exercise absolute powers of government; they were endowed by temperament with the inclination to exercise those powers; and they were assisted by a philosophy of government which clothed every civil ruler in the armor of divine authority. How natural, then, that they should become a ruling oligarchy. They might readily have succumbed to the lust for power, since power lay unchallenged in their hands.

But they did not succumb.

They did not even keep the powers to which the charter entitled them.

After Winthrop had explored the bay and moved the headquarters of the colony from Salem to Charlestown, he summoned the assistants for their first meeting on August 23, 1630. There were seven members present besides himself and Dudley, and they got down to the business of government at once. They provided for the maintenance of two ministers, set maximum wages for workmen in various trades, and appointed a beadle "to attend upon the Governor, and alwaies to be ready to execute his commands in publique businesses." They also ordered that there should be regular meetings, or "courts," of the assistants and of the General Court, though the difference between the two would be a formality, since their membership would be virtually identical (unless future emigration brought over other company members without the status of assistant). On September 7 and September 28 they met again as assistants and exercised their authority in a variety of actions. They forbade the sale of firearms to the Indians; they put an embargo on corn; they seized Richard Clough's strong water because he sold too much of it to other men's servants; and they fined Sir Richard Saltonstall, one of their own number, for being absent from court.

Then on October 19 Winthrop summoned at Charlestown the first meeting labeled in the records as a General Court. For this day he and the seven company members who met with him had prepared a revolution that was to affect the history of Massachusetts from that time forward. The records described the event with tantalizing brevity: "For the establishinge of the government. It was propounded if it were not the best course that the Freemen should have the power of chuseing Assistants when there are to be chosen, and the Assistants from amongst themselves to chuse a Governor and Deputy Governor, whoe with the Assistants should have the power of makeing lawes and chuseing officers to execute the same."

This was surely a strange proposal to make to a group of men all of whom were both freemen and assistants. Why, when there were no freemen but themselves in the colony, should they make provision for freemen electing the assistants and the assistants electing the other officers? One begins to get an inkling of what was happening in the next sentence of the records: "This was fully assented unto by the generall vote of the people, and ereccion of hands."

The "people" here referred to were not simply the eight company members present. This we can conclude from events that followed. Winthrop had apparently thrown open the first meeting of the General Court to the whole body of settlers assembled at Charlestown. Together they had established the first constitution of Massachusetts. It used the terminology of the charter, and presumably allowed the provisions of the charter not expressly revised to remain in effect. But by general vote of the people of Massachusetts, the assistants were transformed from an executive council into a legislative assembly; and the term "freeman" was transformed from a designation for the members of a commercial company, exercising legislative and judicial control over that company and its property, into a designation for the citizens of a state, with the right to vote and hold office. The right of the citizen freemen to vote, however, was confined to electing assistants. These assistants, and not the freemen themselves, were to make laws and appoint from their own number a governor and deputy governor.

This transformation of the Bay Company's charter into a constitution for government of the colony would scarcely have been necessary or desirable if the members of the company had intended to keep control in their own hands. The reduction of the freemen's role in the government and the securing of popular consent to this change presaged the admission to freemanship of a large proportion of settlers, men who could contribute to the joint stock nothing but godliness and good citizenship. The transformation of trading company into commonwealth was completed at the next meeting of the General Court, when one hundred and sixteen persons were admitted as freemen. (This was probably most, if not all, of the adult males, excluding servants, then in the colony.) The new freemen then voted that elections should be annual and, doubtless at the behest of Winthrop, that "for time to come noe man shalbe admitted to the freedome of this body polliticke, but such as are members of some of the churches within the lymitts of the same." Though stated in the form of a limitation, this declaration was in fact an open invitation to every future church member in Massachusetts to take up the privileges of freemanship.

Since the people had no political rights under the charter, Winthrop had given them a role to which they had had no legal claim at all. That he confined the gift to church members was not surprising: he would scarcely have wished to take into partnership all of the multitude of men who might come to his colony for the wrong reasons, and the qualified franchise might also help attract the right kind of settlers. By limiting freemanship to church members he extended political rights to a larger proportion of the people than enjoyed such rights in England—and to people who were better qualified to use them than the mere possessors of a forty-shilling freehold. The question that needs to be answered is not why he limited suffrage but why he extended it. What induced Winthrop and the other members of the Bay Company to resign voluntarily the exclusive powers which the charter conferred on them and which their political beliefs and native dispositions made congenial?

Possibly they gave way to popular demand, but there is no evidence that any such demand existed. Possibly they felt a need to keep their own ranks filled. With sickness and death whittling away at their number, they were already close to the minimum quota of seven assistants required by the charter for the holding of the Assistants Court (only six were required in the General Court). But granting their need to perpetuate themselves, they could still have filled vacancies with a few hand-picked men as the need arose. The charter gave them express permission to admit new members to the company if they chose, but it put them under no obligation to do so. Even a popular demand, if it existed, could have been met by a less drastic measure than the one they took.

The real answer as to why they opened the door to freemanship so wide is to be found in the terms of the commission with which they believed the colony entrusted. The idea of a "covenant," or contract, between God and man occupied a pre-eminent place in their thought: it was the basis of an individual's salvation; it was the origin of every true church and also of every state. "It is of the nature and essence of every society," Winthrop once wrote, "to be knitt together by some Covenant, either expressed or implyed." God's special commission to Massachusetts was an implied covenant.

But there was more than one covenant involved in the establishment of any society. After the people joined in covenant with God, agreeing to be bound by his laws, they must establish a government to see those laws enforced, for they did not have enough virtue to carry out their agreement without the compulsive force of government. They must decide among themselves what form of government they wanted and then create it by a voluntary joint compact—a second covenant.

Winthrop evidently thought that the mere act of coming to Massachusetts constituted a sufficient acceptance of the basic covenant, the special commission which God had given the colony. But the second covenant, establishing the government, required a more explicit agreement. Though the King's charter gave the Bay Company a clear and exclusive right to govern the territory, the King's authority was insufficient. The "due form of government" which Winthrop believed the special commission called for could originate only from a covenant between the settlers and the men who were to rule them. Hence the extraordinary action of October 19, with its sequel, the extension of freemanship.

Winthrop did not believe that in extending freemanship he had transformed Massachusetts into a democracy. The legislative power was lodged not in the people but in a select group where, according to his reading of the Bible, it belonged. Nor was Winthrop's action in securing the consent of the people to his government an affirmation of the principle that governments derive their just powers from the consent of the governed. He did not believe that the officers chosen under the new system would be simply the agents of the people who elected them. Rulers, however selected, received their authority from God, not from the people, and were accountable to God, not to the people. Their business was to enforce the nation's covenant with God, and during their term of office, so long as they devoted themselves to this business, they were free to act as they thought best, suiting their actions to the circumstances.

Winthrop did believe that the people, or a properly qualified portion of them, were entitled to determine the form of government to be established over them and to select the persons who should run that government. These two operations performed, their role was played out until, under the form of government they had chosen, it was time to elect new rulers. If a ruler failed in his duty to enforce the laws of God, the people would be obliged to turn him out without waiting for election time. But so long as he did his duty, his authority was absolute, and, regardless of any

errors of judgment he might make, the people were obliged to submit. Indeed, anything less than submission would be rebellion against the authority of God.

In Winthrop's view, then, he had not in any way limited or reduced the authority of government by extending to church members a voice in the selection of the men who were to exercise the authority. Rather he had given to government a practical strength which it could not otherwise have possessed, for Winthrop was enough of a politician to know that, regardless of any divine authority a ruler might claim, people would submit to him more readily if they had a voice in choosing him, especially a Puritan people well educated by their ministers in the principle of government based on covenant.

There was a danger, of course, that the people would choose the wrong kind of men to rule them. Government was a difficult business, not something that one honest man could do as well as another. It required not only virtue but learning and wisdom as well: learning because the laws of God were not so obvious that he who runs might read them, wisdom because the ruler must be able to apply the laws every day to new situations and choose the right law for the case in hand. But the limitation of freemanship to church members furnished some insurance against the wiles of demagogues. Winthrop counted on the ministers to give the people sound advice and to instruct them about the kind of men who were best fitted to rule.

The ministers must not seek public office themselves, and there was little likelihood that they would or that they would succeed if they did. Though the ministers enjoyed a powerful influence over their congregations, the shadow of Rome still lay heavily on the Puritans. None of them wanted a "theocracy" in the sense of a government by the clergy. Indeed, of all the governments in the Western world at the time, that of early Massachusetts gave the clergy least authority. As long as Winthrop lived, ministers neither sought nor obtained government office. Their advice was frequently asked and frequently given; their influence over the people was invaluable; but authority rested firmly in the hands of laymen.

Under the new constitution Winthrop and most of the original assistants were re-elected until 1634. With the explicit consent of the new body of freemen and the support of the ministers, they moved swiftly and with assurance to establish in Massachusetts the kind of society that God's commission called for. The offense which they dealt with most severely was contempt of their God-given authority. The New World, with a three-thousand-mile moat on the one hand and boundless free land on the other, offered strong temptation to adventurous spirits to kick over the traces and defy every kind of authority. The American frontiersman with his fine scorn for the restrictions of civilization had not yet emerged, but he had his prototype in men like Maverick and Blackstone, who had thought Massachusetts Bay a good enough place before the saints arrived to purify it. A number of such men were on hand when the Great Migration began, and more came with it. If the Puritan experiment was to succeed, they would have to be kept strictly in check or else removed. Blackstone removed himself to the Narragansett country, remarking that he had left England because he did not like the Lord Bishops and found the rule of the Lord Brethren no better. Maverick remained behind but moved to the comparative isolation of Noddle's Island, where his bibulous hospitality frequently annoyed the government. Others, less discreet than these two, got themselves whipped and fined and banished. John Stone, for example, the captain of a small pinnace, was suspected of adultery, and his vessel was stayed until the matter could be investigated, whereupon he went to Roger Ludlow, one of the justices, and called him "just ass." This kind of punning was dangerous, and though a grand jury could not find enough evidence to indict him for adultery, he was given a suspended fine of a hundred pounds for his contempt of authority and ordered not to enter the colony again without permission on pain of death.

In operating their new government, Winthrop and the assistants did not differentiate sharply between judicial and legislative functions. Guided by the laws of God as set down in the Bible and fortified with the absolute authority to enforce those laws in any way they saw fit, they felt little need for explicit legislation. They needed no law, for example, to tell them that Mr. Clearke was looking too longingly at the mistress of the family in which he lived, Mrs. Freeman, "concerning whome there is strong suspicion of incontinency"; they simply forbade Mr. Clearke to live with the Freemans or to keep company with Mrs. Freeman. Nor did they need any special law to justify their punishment of Nicholas Knopp by a fine of five pounds "for taekeing upon him to cure the scurvey by a water of noe worth nor value, which hee solde att a very deare rate". Since adultery, which was punishable by death under the Biblical code, had seldom been punished in England at all, the court did legislate explicitly on that subject, providing the punishment God demanded. But for the most part their general orders dealt with prudential matters, such as the times for burning land to clear it, the cutting of timber, the fixing of bounties on wolves, the fencing of corn, and the disposal of straying cattle and swine.

Because they were free to act without restraint, by enjoining good actions as well as punishing bad ones they could keep a sharp watch on every kind of heresy and nip ill weeds in the bud. They could argue men out of dangerous positions before an impasse was reached, and doubtless the effectiveness of their arguments owed much to the fact that the authority of the state could enforce them if necessary.

The way Winthrop operated this government and the kind of problem he had to deal with are both well illustrated in a case that arose in 1631 in Watertown, where Winthrop's former neighbor, George Phillips, was pastor. Phillips, about a year after he and Winthrop arrived together on the *Arbella,* voiced the opinion that not only the churches of England but those of Rome too were true churches, and he succeeded in convincing many of his congregation. This was separatism inverted: the Reformation had been put through on the assumption that the Catholic Church was incurable, was no true church; it was too late now to give up the Reformation. Winthrop went to Watertown and debated before the congregation against Phillips and Richard Brown, the ruling elder (a lay officer). All but three of the liberals concluded that their opinion was an error.

Richard Brown was one of the three, an intransigent liberal. The Watertown church, probably under Winthrop's influence, formally condemned Brown's too charitable view of Catholicism but did not proceed against him for holding it. He was not even removed from office as ruling elder. The church evidently did not consider this a fatal error, and no doubt Winthrop agreed with them.

A few months later, however, another troublesome party arose in the congregation. Since Elder Brown held an erroneous opinion, some of the members felt they could not pollute themselves by remaining as communicants in the same church with him. This was a more serious matter. Again Winthrop hurried off to Watertown and this time persuaded the purists that they were going too far. There was a general reconciliation; but one John Masters, the leader of the purist faction, apparently had second thoughts afterwards and still refused to take communion with Brown, turning his back whenever the service was performed. Masters, by his exclusiveness, was committing a very serious mistake, for when he steadfastly refused to reform, the church placed its most severe penalty, excommunication, on him, after which he came round and was restored.

This incident epitomized the problem that Winthrop had wrestled with and conquered in his own life and now faced as governor. Because he had learned so painfully and so well that there was no honorable escape from the sins and perils and temptations of the world, he determined from the beginning that New England must not be an escape. The position taken by John Masters pointed straight toward escape. It could lead to the ultimate absurdity of complete withdrawal into oneself, nobody being quite pure enough to join with. It would not only separate New England from the rest of the world but split it into a host of little communities, each repudiating the others as insufficiently holy.

The position taken by Richard Brown, on the other hand, was equally dangerous to God's commission, for it led to moral indifference, to the obliteration of the distinction between Catholic and Protestant, which for Winthrop was as much as to say the distinction between right and wrong. Neither position could be allowed, but Winthrop sensed that the colony had more to fear from Masters's error than from Brown's. The most dangerous tendency among the saints of Massachusetts was not excessive liberality but excessive purity. In either case the solution lay in early and flexible treatment. Winthrop caught the danger before it got out of hand, and he did not have to prosecute anyone. The members of the church had been reasonable. After he argued them round, they handled the problem themselves.

This was the way to deal with men who wanted to be too good, and the form of government he had established gave him the maximum freedom to deal with them in this way. Absolute authority, resting on a consent that was renewed every year—this was the formula to keep zealots and scamps alike under control.

But the happy combination, happy at least in Winthrop's eyes, was not to last.

As the temper of the American people changed during the nineteenth and twentieth centuries, the prevailing views of the Puritan political order were also modified. Perry Miller, the historian of the Puritan mind, points out that it was fashionable for nineteenth-century political orators to ascribe the blessings of the Constitution and the Bill of Rights to the institutions established by their Puritan forebears. A later generation in scholarly reaction, however, emphasized what was dour and authoritarian. The latest generation again reacted, "to dwell upon the inherent individualism, the respect for private conscience, the implications of revolution, nurtured by the Puritan doctrine." Miller, himself, presents a balanced synthesis of this thought:

The Puritan state was based on the hypothesis of original sin. Since Adam's fall, God required men to institute governments of whatever form necessary in order to restrain wickedness and preserve order. Within the Puritan system there was much individualism as men struggled to gain their personal salvation and to earn a living. But Puritans lived in groups under firm government, which supervised much of their conduct, whether religious, moral, or economic. The idea of laissez faire would have been abhorrent to them; absolute political democracy was unthinkable. "The government of Massachusetts, and of Connecticut as well, was a dictatorship, and never pretended to be anything else," Miller asserts. "It was a dictatorship, not of a single tyrant, or of an economic class, or of a political faction, but of the holy and regenerate." [1]

These are the themes that run through the writings of John Winthrop. In 1629 when Winthrop was debating with himself whether or not to leave England, he drafted and repeatedly reworked a set of arguments. The arguments, widely circulated and debated among the Puritan leaders, were an important factor in bringing about migration to Massachusetts Bay.

JOHN WINTHROP:
GENERAL OBSERVATIONS*

1. It wilbe a service to the Churche of great Consequence to carrye the Gospell into those partes of the world, and to rayse a bullwarke against the kingdom of Antichrist which the Jesuites labour to reare vp in all places of the worlde.

2. All other Churches of Europe are brought to desolation, and it cannot be, but the like Judgment is comminge vpon vs: and who knows,

[1] Perry Miller, *Errand Into the Wilderness* (Cambridge: Belknap Press of Harvard Univ. Press, 1956), pp. 141–43.

* Reprinted from *Winthrop Papers* (Boston: Massachusetts Historical Society, 1931), II, 114–17 by permission.

but that God hathe provided this place, to be a refuge for manye, whom he meanes to save out of the general destruction?

3. This lande growes wearye of her Inhabitantes, so as man which is the most pretious of all Creatures, is heere more vile and base, then the earthe they treade vpon: so as children neighbours and freindes (especi[ally] if they be poore) are rated the greatest burdens, which if things were right, would be the cheifest earthly bless[ings].

4. We are growne to that height of Intemperance in all excesse of Ryot, as no mans estate all most will suffice to keepe sayle with his equalls: and he that fayles in it, must liue in scorn and contempt: hence it comes, that all artes and trades are carried in that deceiptfull and vnrighteous course, as it is allmost imposs[ible] for a good and vpright man to maintaine his charge and liue comfortably in any of them.

5. The fountains of learninge and Relig[ion] are so corrupted, as (besides the vnsupport[able] chardge of their educat[ion]) most Children, even the best wittes and of fayrest hopes, are perverted corrupted and vtterly overthrowne by the multitude of evill examples and the licentious government of those seminaryes.

6. The whole earthe is the Lordes garden: and he hathe given it to the sons of men to be tilld and improved by them: why then should we stand striving heere for places of habitation etc. (many men spending as muche labor and cost to recover or keepe sometyme an Acre or 2 of lande, as would procure him many C [hundred] acres as good or better in another place) and in the mene tyme suffer whole countrys as fruitfull and convenient for the vse of man, to lye waste without any improvement?

7. What can be a better worke and more honorable and worthy [a Christian then to helpe] rayse and supporte a partic[ular] Churche while it is in the infancye, and to ioine our forces with suche a Companye of faithfull people, as [one word cancelled] by a tymely assistance maye growe stronge and prosper, and for want of it may be putt to great hazard, if not wholly ruined?

8. If suche as are knowne to be godly and liue in wealthe and prosperitye heere, shall forsake all this to ioine themselues to this Churche, and to runne the hazard with them of a harde and meane condition, it wilbe an example of great vse, bothe for removinge the schandale of worldly and sinister respectes to give more life to the Faithe of Godes people in their prayers for the plantation, and allso to incourage others to ioyne the more willingly in it.

Ob. 1: It wilbe a great wronge to our owne Churche and Countrye, to take awaye the good people, and we shall laye it the more open to the Judgment feared.

Ans. 1: the number wilbe nothing in respecte of those that are lefte: 2 many that liue to no vse heere, more then for their owne private familys, may be imployed to a more com[mon] good in another place: 3: suche as are of noe

vse heere, may yet be so imployed, as the Church shall receive no losse: and since Christes tyme the Chur[ch] is to be considered as vniversall, without distinction of countrys, so as he that dothe good in any one place serves the Church in all places in regarde of the vnitye. lastly it is the revealed will of God, that the Gospell should be preached to all nations: and thoughe we knowe not, whither the Indians will receive it or not, yet it is a good worke, to observe Godes will in offering it to them, for God shall haue Glory by it, though they refuse it.

Ob. 2. We have feared a Judgement a longe tyme, but yet we are safe, soe it were better to staye till it come, and either we may flye then, or if we be overtaken in it we may well contente our selues to suffer with suche a Churche as ours is.

Ans. It is like that this consideration made the Churches beyonde the seas (as the Pal[atinate] Rochell etc.) to sitt still at home, and not look out for shelter while they might have founde it: but the woefull spectacle of their ruine, may teache vs more wisdome, to avoyde the plague when it is foreseene, and not to tarrye, as they did, till it overtake vs: if they were now at their former libertye, we may be sure, they would take other Course for their safety: and though most of them had misca[rried] in their escape, yet it had not been halfe so miserable to suche selues, nor scandalous to Religion, as this desperate backslidinge, and abiuringe the truethe, which many of the auncient professors amonge them, and the whole posteryty that remaine [have *cancelled*] are now plunged into.

Ob. 3. We have heere a fruitfull lande with peace and plenty of all thinges etc.

Ans. our superfluities excepted we are like to be followed with as good con[sequences] remaininge there in a shorte tyme, and be far from many temptations [*illegible*] meet with here. yet we must leave all this abondance, if it be not taken from vs: and when we are in our graves it wilbe all one to have liued in plentye or penurye, whither we had dyed in a bedd of downe, or a lock of strawe, and onely this is the advantage of a meane condition, that it is at more freedom [to dye and the lesse comfort any hathe in the things of this world, the more] liberty and desire he may have to laye vp treasure in heaven.

Ob. 4. But we may perishe by the waye or when we come there, either hanginge hunger or the sworde etc., and how vncomfortable it would be to see our wiues children and friendes come to suche misery by our occasion?

Ans. Suche ob[jection] savours to muche of the flesh: who can saue him selfe or his familye from calamitys heere? if this course be warrantable we must trust Godes providence for these thinges, either he will keepe these evills from vs, or will dispose them for our good, and enable vs to beare them.

Ob. 5: But what warrant haue we to take that lande which is and hathe been of longe tyme possessed by other sonnes of Adam?

sol. That which is com[mon] to all is proper

to none, these saluadge peoples ramble over muche lande without title or propertye: 2: there is more then enough for them and vs; 3: God hathe consumed the natives with a miraculous plague, wherby a great parte of the Country is left voyde of Inh[abita]ntes. 4. We shall come in with good leave of the natiues.

Ob. 6. we should yet send yonge ones, and suche as may best be spared, and not of our best min[isters] and magistrates.

sol. It is a greater worke and requires more skillful artizans, to laye the foundation of a newe building, then to vphould or repaire one that is ready built: if great things be attempted by weake instrum[en]tes, the effectes willbe answerable:

Ob. 7. We see those plantations, which have been formerly made, succeeded ill.

Ans. the fruit of any publ[ick] designe is not to be discerned by the im[me]diate successe, [2: *cancelled*] it may appeare in tyme, that they were all to good vse. 2: there were great and fundamentall errors in the other, which are like to be avoyded in this: for 1: their maine ende [*two words cancelled*] [and] purpose was carnall and not religious; they aymed cheifly at profitt, and not the propagating of Religion. 2: they vsed vnfitt instrumentes, a multitude of Rude and misgoverned persons the verye scomme of the lande. 3: they did not establish a right forme of Gover[n]ment.

[*Endorsed, in a later hand:*] For Newe Englande May 1629.

During the religious controversy over the doctrines of Antinomianism, Governor Winthrop sponsored an order of court intended to restrict the immigration of those holding such views. When he was denounced for exceeding his powers, he delivered the following speech, remarkable for the clarity with which it presents Puritan political theories, to the General Court.

JOHN WINTHROP:
A DECLARATION IN DEFENSE
OF AN ORDER OF COURT MADE IN MAY, 1637*

A DECLARATION OF THE INTENT AND EQUITYE OF THE ORDER MADE AT THE LAST COURT, TO THIS EFFECT, THAT NONE SHOULD BE RECEIVED TO INHABITE WITHIN THIS JURISDICTION BUT SUCH AS SHOULD BE ALLOWED BY SOME OF THE MAGISTRATES

For clearing of such scruples as have arisen about this order, it is to be considered, first, what is the essentiall forme of a common weale or body politic such as this is, which I conceive to be this —The consent of a certaine companie of people, to cohabite together, under one government for their mutual safety and welfare.

In this description all these things doe concurre to the well being of such a body, 1 Persons, 2 Place, 3 Consent, 4 Government or Order, 5 Wellfare.

It is clearly agreed, by all, that the care of safety and wellfare was the original cause or occasion of common weales and of many familyes subjecting themselves to rules and laws; for no man hath lawfull power over another, but by birth or consent, so likewise, by the law of pro-

prietye, no man can have just interest in that which belongeth to another, without his consent.

From the premises will arise these conclusions.

1. No common weale can be founded but by free consent.

2. The persons so incorporating have a public and relative interest each in other, and in the place of their co-habitation and goods, and laws etc. and in all the means of their wellfare so as none other can claime priviledge with them but by free consent.

3. The nature of such an incorporation tyes every member thereof to seeke out and entertaine all means that may conduce to the wellfare of the bodye, and to keepe off whatsoever doth appeare to tend to theire damage.

4. The wellfare of the whole is [not] to be put to apparent hazard for the advantage of any particular members.

From these conclusions I thus reason.

1. If we heere be a corporation established by free consent, if the place of our cohabitation be our owne, then no man hath right to come into us etc. without our consent.

2. If no man hath right to our lands, our government priviledges etc., but by our consent, then it is reason we should take notice of before we conferre any such upon them.

3. If we are bound to keepe off whatsoever appears to tend to our ruine or damage, then we

*Reprinted from *Winthrop Papers* (Boston: Massachusetts Historical Society), III, 422–26 by permission.

may lawfully refuse to receive such whose dispositions suite not with ours and whose society (we know) will be hurtfull to us, and therefore it is lawfull to take knowledge of all men before we receive them.

4. The churches take liberty (as lawfully they may) to receive or reject at their discretion; yea particular towns make orders to the like effect; why then should the common weale be denied the like liberty, and the whole more restrained than any parte?

5. If it be sinne in us to deny some men place etc. amongst us, then it is because of some right they have to this place etc. for to deny a man that which he hath no right unto, is neither sinne nor injury.

6. If strangers have right to our houses or lands etc., then it is either of justice or of mercye; if of justice let them plead it, and we shall know what to answer: but if it be only in way of mercye, or by the rule of hospitality etc., then I answer 1st a man is not a fit object of mercye except he be in miserye. 2d. We are not bound to exercise mercye to others to the ruine of ourselves. 3d. There are few that stand in neede of mercye at their first coming hither. As for hospitality, that rule doth not bind further than for some present occasion, not for continual residence.

7. A family is a little common wealth, and a common wealth is a greate family. Now as a family is not bound to entertaine all comers, no not every good man (otherwise than by way of hospitality) no more is a common weale.

8. It is a generall received rule, *turpius ejicitur quam non admittitur hospes,* it is worse to receive a man whom we must cast out againe, than to denye him admittance.

9. The rule of the Apostle, John 2. 10. is, that such as come and bring not the true doctrine with them should not be received to house, and by the same reason not into the common weale.

10. Seeing it must be granted that there may come such persons (suppose Jesuits etc.) which by consent of all ought to be rejected, it will follow that by this law (being only for notice to be taken of all that come to us, without which we cannot avoyd such as indeed are to be kept out) is no other but just and needfull, and if any should be rejected that ought to be received, that is not to be imputed to the law, but to those who are betrusted with the execution of it. And herein is to be considered, what the intent of the law is, and by consequence, by what rule they are to walke, who are betrusted with the keeping of it. The intent of the law is to preserve the wellfare of the body; and for this ende to have none received into any fellowship with it who are likely to disturbe the same, and this intent (I am sure) is lawful and good. Now then, if such to whom the keeping of this law is committed, be persuaded in theire judgments that such a man is likely to disturbe and hinder the publick weale, but some others who are not in the same trust,

judge otherwise, yet they are to follow their owne judgments, rather than the judgments of others who are not alike interested: As in tryall of an offender by jury; the twelve men are satisfied in their consciences, upon the evidence given, that the party deserves death: but there are 20 or 40 standers by, who conceive otherwise, yet is the jury bound to condemn him according to their owne consciences, and not to acquit him upon the different opinion of other men, except theire reasons can convince them of the errour of their consciences, and this is according to the rule of the Apostle. Rom. 14. 5. Let every man be fully persuaded in his own mynde.

If it be objected, that some prophane persons are received and others who are religious are rejected, I answer 1st, It is not knowne that any such thinge has as yet fallen out. 2. Such a practice may be justifiable as the case may be, for younger persons (even prophane ones) may be of lesse danger to the common weale (and to the churches also) than some older persons, though professors of religion: for our Saviour Christ when he conversed with publicans etc. sayeth that such were nearer the Kingdom of heaven than the religious pharisees, and one that is of large parts and confirmed in some erroneous way, is likely to doe more harme to church and common weale, and is of lesse hope to be reclaymed, than 10 prophane persons, who have not yet become hardened, in the contempt of the meanes of grace.

Lastly, Whereas it is objected that by this law, we reject good christians and so consequently Christ himselfe: I answer 1st. It is not knowne that any christian man hath been rejected. 2. a man that is a true christian, may be denyed residence among us, in some cases, without rejecting Christ, as admitt a true christian should come over, and should maintain community of goods, or that magistrates ought not to punish the breakers of the first table, or the members of churches for criminal offences: or that no man were bound to be subject to those lawes or magistrates to which they should not give an explicite consent, etc. I hope no man will say, that not to receive such an one were to reject Christ; for such opinions (though being maintained in simple ignorance, they might stand with a state of grace yet) they may be so dangerous to the publick weale in many respects, as it would be our sinne and unfaithfulness to receive such among us, except it were for tryall of theire reformation. I would demand then in the case in question (for it is bootlesse curiosity to refrayne openesse in things publick) whereas it is sayd that this law was made of purpose to keepe away such as are of Mr. Wheelwright his judgment (admitt it were so which yet I cannot confesse) where is the evill of it? If we conceive and finde by sadd experience that his opinions are such, as by his own profession cannot stand with externall peace, may we not provide for our peace, by keeping of such as would strengthen him and infect others with such dangerous tenets? and if we finde his opinions such as will cause divisions, and make people looke at their magistrates, ministers and brethren as enemies to Christ and Antichrists etc., were it not sinne and unfaithfullness in us, to receive more of those opinions, which we already finde the evill fruite of: Nay, why doe not those who now complayne joyne with us in keeping out of such, as well as formerly they did in expelling Mr. Williams for the like, though lesse dangerous? Where this change of theire judgments should arise I leave them to themselves to examine, and I earnestly entreat them so to doe, and for this law let the equally mynded judge, what evill they finde in it, or in the practice of those who are betrusted with the execution of it.

The seventeenth century brought numerous innovations in the social, the economic, and the political structure of all of the colonies. Well before the end of the century, as Bernard Bailyn points out, rebellions in several of the colonies were "symptomatic of a profound disorganization of European society in its American setting." New forces were at work creating new systems of American politics. Bernard Bailyn analyzed these forces and demonstrated their effect in shaping the political institutions of seventeenth-century Virginia in the following essay.

BERNARD BAILYN:
POLITICS AND SOCIAL STRUCTURE IN VIRGINIA*

By the end of the seventeenth century the American colonists faced an array of disturbing problems in the conduct of public affairs. Settlers from England and Holland, reconstructing familiar institutions on American shores, had become participants in what would appear to have been a wave of civil disobedience. Constituted authority was confronted with repeated challenges. Indeed, a veritable anarchy seems to have prevailed at the center of colonial society, erupting in a series of insurrections that began as early as 1635 with the "thrusting out" of Governor Harvey in Virginia. Culpeper's Rebellion in Carolina, the Protestant Association in Maryland, Bacon's Rebellion in Virginia, Leisler's seizure of power in New York, the resistance to and finally the overthrow of Andros in New England—every colony was affected.

These outbursts were not merely isolated local affairs. Although their immediate causes were rooted in the particular circumstances of the separate colonies, they nevertheless had common characteristics. They were, in fact, symptomatic of a profound disorganization of European society in its American setting. Seen in a broad view, they reveal a new configuration of forces which shaped the origins of American politics.

In a letter written from Virginia in 1623, George Sandys, the resident treasurer, reported despondently on the character and condition of the leading settlers. Some of the councilors were "no more then Ciphers," he wrote; others were "miserablie poore"; and the few substantial planters lived apart, taking no responsibility for public concerns. There was, in fact, among all those "worthie the mencioninge" only one person deserving of full approval. Lieutenant William Peirce "refuses no labour, nor sticks at anie expences that may aduantage the publique." Indeed, Sandys added, Peirce was "of a Capacitie that is not to bee expected in a man of his breeding." [1]

The afterthought was penetrating. It cut below the usual complaints of the time that many of the settlers were lazy malcontents hardly to be preferred to the Italian glassworkers, than whom, Sandys wrote, "a more damned crew hell never vomited." [2] What lay behind Sandys' remark was not so much that wretched specimens were arriving in the shipments of servants nor even that the quality of public leadership was declining but that the social foundations of political power were being strangely altered.

All of the settlers in whatever colony presumed a fundamental relationship between social structure and political authority. Drawing on a common medieval heritage, continuing to conceive of society as a hierarchical unit, its parts justly and

---

* Reprinted from James M. Smith, ed., *Seventeenth-Century America: Essays in Colonial History* (Chapel Hill: Univ. of North Carolina Press, 1959), pp. 90–115 by permission.

[1] Sandys to John Ferrar, April 11, 1623, Susan M. Kingsbury, ed., *The Records of the Virginia Company of London* (4 vols.; Washington, D.C., 1906–35), IV, 110–11.

[2] Sandys to "Mr. Farrer," March 1622/23, *ibid.*, 23.

naturally separated into inferior and superior levels, they assumed that superiority was indivisible; there was not one hierarchy for political matters, another for social purposes. John Winthrop's famous explanation of God's intent that "in all times some must be rich some poore, some highe and eminent in power and dignitie; others meane and in subieccion" could not have been more carefully worded. Riches, dignity, and power were properly placed in apposition; they pertained to the same individuals.[3]

So closely related were social leadership and political leadership that experience if not theory justified an identification between state and society. To the average English colonist the state was not an abstraction existing above men's lives, justifying itself in its own terms, taking occasional human embodiment. However glorified in monarchy, the state in ordinary form was indistinguishable from a more general social authority; it was woven into the texture of everyday life. It was the same squire or manorial lord who in his various capacities collated to the benefice, set the rents, and enforced the statutes of Parliament and the royal decrees. Nothing could have been more alien to the settlers than the idea that competition for political leadership should be open to all levels of society or that obscure social origins or technical skills should be considered valuable qualifications for office. The proper response to new technical demands on public servants was not to give power to the skilled but to give skills to the powerful.[4] The English gentry and landed aristocracy remained politically adaptable and hence politically competent, assuming when necessary new public functions, eliminating the need for a professional state bureaucracy. By their amateur competence they made possible a continuing identification between political and social authority.

In the first years of settlement no one had reason to expect that this characteristic of public life would fail to transfer itself to the colonies. For at least a decade and a half after its founding there had been in the Jamestown settlement a small group of leaders drawn from the higher echelons of English society. Besides well-born soldiers of fortune like George Percy, son of the Earl of Northumberland, there were among them four sons of the West family—children of Lord de la Warr and his wife, a second cousin of Queen Elizabeth. In Virginia the West brothers held appropriately high positions; three of them served as governors.[5] Christopher Davison, the colony's

secretary, was the son of Queen Elizabeth's secretary, William Davison, M.P. and Privy Councilor.[6] The troublesome John Martin, of Martin's Brandon, was the son of Sir Richard Martin, twice Lord Mayor of London, and also the brother-in-law of Sir Julius Caesar, Master of the Rolls and Privy Councilor.[7] Sir Francis and Haute Wyatt were sons of substantial Kent gentry and grandsons of the Sir Thomas Wyatt who led the rebellion of 1554 against Queen Mary.[8] George Sandys' father was the Archbishop of York; of his three older brothers, all knights and M.P.'s, two were eminent country gentlemen, and the third, Edwin, of Virginia Company fame, was a man of great influence in the city.[9] George Thorpe was a former M.P. and Gentlemen of the Privy Chamber.[10]

More impressive than such positions and relationships was the cultural level represented. For until the very end of the Company period, Virginia remained to the literary and scientific an exotic attraction, its settlement an important moment in Christian history.[11] Its original magnetism for those in touch with intellectual currents affected the early immigration. Of the twenty councilors of 1621, eight had been educated at Oxford, Cambridge, or the Inns of Court. Davison, like Martin trained in the law, was a poet in a family of poets. Thorpe was a "student of Indian views on religion and astronomy." Francis Wyatt wrote verses and was something of a student of political theory. Alexander Whitaker, M.A., author of Good Newes from Virginia, was the worthy heir "of a good part of the learning of his renowned father," the master of St. John's College and Regius Professor of Divinity at Cambridge. John Pory, known to history mainly as the speaker of the first representative assembly in America, was a Master of Arts, "protege and disciple of Hakluyt," diplomat, scholar, and traveler, whose writings from and about America have a rightful place in literary history. Above all there was George Sandys, "poet, traveller, and scholar," a member of Lord Falkland's literary

[3] John Winthrop, "Modell of Christian Charity," *Winthrop Papers* (5 vols.; Boston, 1929–47), II, 282.

[4] Cf. J. H. Hexter, "The Education of the Aristocracy in the Renaissance," *Jour. of Modern Hist.*, 22 (1950), 1–20.

[5] *Dictionary of National Biography*, 1908–9 edn. (New York), XV, 836–37; Annie L. Jester and Martha W. Hiden, comps. and eds., *Adven-*

turers of Purse and Person: Virginia 1607–1625 ([Princeton, N.J.], 1956), 349–50.

[6] *D.N.B.*, V, 632; Richard B. Davis, *George Sandys: Poet-Adventurer* (London, 1955), 112–13n.

[7] Alexander Brown, *Genesis of the United States* (Boston, 1890), II, 943–44.

[8] Jester and Hiden, comps., *Adventurers*, 372; *D.N.B.*, XXI, 1092–93, 1102–4.

[9] Davis, *Sandys,* Chap. I.

[10] Brown, *Genesis,* II, 1031.

[11] Perry Miller, *Errand into the Wilderness* (Cambridge, Mass., 1956), 99–140; Howard Mumford Jones, *The Literature of Virginia in the Seventeenth Century* (*Memoirs of the American Academy of Arts and Sciences,* XIX, Part 2, Boston, 1946), 3–7.

circle; while in Jamestown he continued as a matter of course to work on his notable translation of Ovid's *Metamorphoses*.[12]

There was, in other words, during the first years of settlement a direct transference to Virginia of the upper levels of the English social hierarchy as well as of the lower. If the great majority of the settlers were recruited from the yeoman class and below, there was nevertheless a reasonable representation from those upper groups acknowledged to be the rightful rulers of society.

It is a fact of some importance, however, that this governing elite did not survive a single generation, at least in its original form. By the thirties their number had declined to insignificance. Percy, for example, left in 1612. Whitaker drowned in 1617. Sandys and Francis Wyatt arrived only in 1621, but their enthusiasm cooled quickly; they were both gone by 1626. Of the Wests, only John was alive and resident in the colony a decade after the collapse of the Company. Davison, who returned to England in 1622 after only a year's stay, was sent back in 1623 but died within a year of his return. Thorpe was one of the six councilors slain in the massacre of 1622. Pory left for England in 1622; his return as investigating commissioner in 1624 was temporary, lasting only a few months. And the cantankerous Martin graced the Virginia scene by his absence after 1625; he is last heard from in the early 1630's petitioning for release from a London debtor's prison.[13]

To be sure, a few representatives of important English families, like John West and Edmund Scarborough, remained. There were also one or two additions from the same social level.[14] But there were few indeed of such individuals, and the basis of their authority had changed. The group of gentlemen and illuminati that had dominated the scene during the Company era had been dispersed. Their disappearance created a political void which was filled soon enough, but from a different area of recruitment, from below, from the toughest and most fortunate of the surviving planters whose eminence by the end of the thirties had very little to do with the transplantation of social status.[15]

The position of the new leaders rested on their ability to wring material gain from the wilderness. Some, like Samuel Mathews, started with large initial advantages,[16] but more typical were George Menefie and John Utie, who began as independent landowners by right of transporting themselves and only one or two servants. Abraham Wood, famous for his explorations and like Menefie and Utie the future possessor of large estates and important offices, appears first as a servant boy on Mathews' plantation. Adam Thoroughgood, the son of a country vicar, also started in Virginia as a servant, aged fourteen. William Spencer is first recorded as a yeoman farmer without servants.[17]

Such men as these—Spencer, Wood, Menefie, Utie, Mathews—were the most important figures in Virginia politics up to the Restoration, en-

---

[12] Davis, *Sandys*, especially 190–92; Harry C. Porter, "Alexander Whitaker," *Wm. and Mary Qtly.*, 3rd ser., 14 (1957), 336; Jones, *Literature of Virginia*, 14n, 5–6, 26–28.

[13] Davis, *Sandys*, 195–97, 112–13n; Jester and Hiden, comps., *Adventurers*, 350–51; Brown, *Genesis*, II, 1031, 970; *Va. Mag. of Hist. and Biog.*, 54 (1946), 60–61; Jones, *Literature of Virginia*, 14n.

[14] Scarborough was a well-educated younger son of an armigerous Norfolk family. Among the additions were Charles Harmar (who died in 1640), nephew of the warden of Winchester College and brother of the Greek Reader, later the Greek Professor, at Oxford; and Nathaniel Littleton, whose father was Chief Justice of North Wales, two of whose brothers were Fellows of All Souls and a third Chief Justice of Common Pleas and Lord Keeper of the Great Seal. Susie M. Ames, ed., *County Court Records of Accomack-Northampton, Virginia, 1632–1640* (Washington, D.C., 1954), xxvii, xxix–xxx, xxxv.

[15] The difficulty of maintaining in Virginia the traditional relationship between social and political authority became in 1620 the basis of an attack by a group of "ancient planters," including Francis West, on the newly appointed governor, Sir George Yeardley. Although Yeardley had been knighted two years earlier in an effort to enhance his personal authority, the petitioners argued that his lack of eminence was discouraging settlement. "Great Actions," they wrote, "are carryed wth best successe by such Comanders who haue personall Aucthoritye & greatness answerable to the Action, Sithence itt is nott easye to swaye a vulgar and seruile Nature by vulgar & seruile Spiritts." Leadership should devolve on commanders whose "Eminence or Nobillitye" is such that "euerye man subordinate is ready to yeild a willing submission wthowt contempt or repyning." The ordinary settlers, they said, would not obey the same authority "conferrd vpon a meane man . . . no bettar than selected owt of their owne Ranke." If, therefore, the Company hoped to attract and hold colonists, especially of "the bettar sorte," it should select as leaders in Virginia "some eythar Noble or little lesse in Honor or Dower . . . to mantayne & hold vp the dignitye of so Great and good a cawse." Kingsbury, ed., *Records of the Virginia Company*, III, 231–32.

[16] For Mathews' twenty-three servants and his "Denbigh" plantation, described in 1649 as a self-sufficient village, see John C. Hotten, ed., *Original List of Persons of Quality . . .* (London, 1874), 233–34; Jester and Hiden, comps., *Adventurers*, 244–45; *A Perfect Description of Virginia . . .*, in Peter Force, comp., *Tracts and Other Papers Relating Principally to the Origin, Settlement, and Progress of the Colonies in North America* (4 vols., Washington, D.C., 1836–46), II, no. 8, 14–15.

[17] Jester and Hiden, comps., *Adventurers*, 248–49, 321, 329, 339–40; Hotten, ed., *Persons of Quality*, 226, 237, 233, 253, 228; Clarence W. Alvord and Lee Bidgood, *The First Explorations of the Trans-Alleghany Region . . . 1650–1674* (Cleveland, 1912), 34 ff.

13

grossing large tracts of land, dominating the Council, unseating Sir John Harvey from the governorship. But in no traditional sense were they a ruling class. They lacked the attributes of social authority, and their political dominance was a continuous achievement. Only with the greatest difficulty, if at all, could distinction be expressed in a genteel style of life, for existence in this generation was necessarily crude. Mathews may have created a flourishing estate and Menefie had splendid fruit gardens, but the great tracts of land such men claimed were almost entirely raw wilderness. They had risen to their positions, with few exceptions, by brute labor and shrewd manipulation; they had personally shared the burdens of settlement. They succeeded not because of, but despite, whatever gentility they may have had. William Claiborne may have been educated at the Middle Temple; Peirce could not sign his name; but what counted was their common capacity to survive and flourish in frontier settlements.[18] They were tough, unsentimental, quick-tempered, crudely ambitious men concerned with profits and increased landholdings, not the grace of life. They roared curses, drank exuberantly, and gambled (at least according to deVries) for their servants when other commodities were lacking.[19] If the worst of Governor Harvey's offenses had been to knock out the teeth of an offending councilor with a cudgel, as he did on one occasion, no one would have questioned his right to the governorship.[20] Rank had its privileges, and these men were the first to claim them, but rank itself was unstable and the lines of class or status were fluid. There was no insulation for even the most elevated from the rude impact of frontier life.

As in style of life so in politics, these leaders of the first permanently settled generation did not re-create the characteristics of a stable gentry. They had had little opportunity to acquire the sense of public responsibility that rests on deep identification with the land and its people. They performed in some manner the duties expected of leaders, but often public office was found simply burdensome. Reports such as Sandys' that Yeardley, the councilor and former governor, was wholly absorbed in his private affairs and scarcely glanced at public matters and that Mathews "will rather hazard the payment of fforfeitures then performe our Injunctions" were echoed by Harvey throughout his tenure of office. Charles Harmar, justice of the peace on the Eastern Shore, attended the court once in eight years, and Claiborne's record was only slightly better. Attendance to public duties had to be specifically enjoined, and privileges were of necessity accorded provincial officeholders. The members of the Council were particularly favored by the gift of tax exemption.[21]

The private interests of this group, which had assumed control of public office by virtue not of inherited status but of newly achieved and strenuously maintained economic eminence, were pursued with little interference from the traditional restraints imposed on a responsible ruling class. Engaged in an effort to establish themselves in the land, they sought as specific ends: autonomous local jurisdiction, an aggressive expansion of settlement and trading enterprises, unrestricted access to land, and, at every stage, the legal endorsement of acquisitions. Most of the major public events for thirty years after the dissolution of the Company—and especially the overthrow of Harvey—were incidents in the pursuit of these goals.

From his first appearance in Virginia, Sir John Harvey threatened the interests of this emerging planter group. While still in England he had identified himself with the faction that had successfully sought the collapse of the Company, and thus his mere presence in Virginia was a threat to the legal basis of land grants made under the Company's charter. His demands for the return as public property of goods that had once belonged to the Company specifically jeopardized the planters' holdings. His insistence that the governorship was more than a mere chairmanship of the Council tended to undermine local autonomy. His conservative Indian policy not only weakened the settlers' hand in what already seemed an irreconcilable enmity with the natives but also restricted the expansion of settlement. His opposition to Claiborne's claim to Kent Island threatened to kill off the lucrative Chesapeake Bay trade, and his attempt to ban the Dutch ships from the colony endangered commerce more generally. His support of the official policy of economic diversification, together with his endorsement of the English schemes of to-

[18] *Wm. and Mary Qtly.*, 2nd ser., 19 (1939), 475n; Davis, *Sandys*, 158n.

[19] Ames, ed., *Accomack-Northampton Recs.*, xxxiv, xxxix–xl; Susie M. Ames, *Studies of the Virginia Eastern Shore in the Seventeenth Century* (Richmond, Va., 1940), 181, 183. DeVries wrote of his astonishment at seeing servants gambled away: "I told them that I had never seen such work in Turk or Barbarian, and that it was not becoming Christians." David P. deVries, *Short Historical . . . Notes of several Voyages . . .* (Hoorn, 1655), reprinted in the New York Hist. Soc., *Collections*, 2nd ser., 3 (1857), 36, 125.

[20] Harvey readily confessed to the deed, offering as an official justification the fact that it had all taken place outside the Council chamber, and anyhow the fellow had "assailed him with ill language." *The Aspinwall Papers*, Mass. Hist. Soc., *Collections*, 4th ser., 9 (1871), 133n.

[21] Kingsbury, ed., *Records of the Virginia Company*, IV, 110–11; *Va. Mag. of Hist. and Biog.*, 8 (1900–1), 30; Ames, ed., *Accomack-Northampton Recs.*, xxv, xxix; William W. Hening, ed., *The Statutes-at-Large . . . of Virginia (1619–1792)* (New York, 1823), I, 350, 454; Philip A. Bruce, *Institutional History of Virginia in the Seventeenth Century* (2 vols.; New York, 1910), II, Chaps. XV, XXIX.

bacco monopoly, alienated him finally and completely from the Council group.[22]

Within a few months of his assuming the governorship, Harvey wrote home with indignation of the "waywardnes and oppositions" of the councilors and condemned them for factiously seeking "rather for their owne endes then either seekinge the generall good or doinge right to particuler men." Before a year was out the antagonisms had become so intense that a formal peace treaty had to be drawn up between Harvey and the Council. But both sides were adamant, and conflict was inescapable. It exploded in 1635 amid comic opera scenes of "extreame coller and passion" complete with dark references to Richard the Third and musketeers "running with their peices presented." The conclusion was Harvey's enraged arrest of George Menefie "of suspicion of Treason to his Majestie"; Utie's response, "And wee the like to you sir"; and the governor's forced return to England.[23]

Behind these richly heroic "passings and repassings to and fro" lies not a victory of democracy or representative institutions or anything of the sort. Democracy, in fact, was identified in the Virginians' minds with the "popular and tumultuary government" that had prevailed in the old Company's quarter courts, and they wanted none of it; the Assembly as a representative institution was neither greatly sought after nor hotly resisted.[24] The victory of 1635 was that of resolute leaders of settlement stubbornly fighting for individual establishment. With the reappointment of Sir Francis Wyatt as governor, their victory was assured and in the Commonwealth period it was completely realized. By 1658, when Mathews was elected governor, effective interference from outside had disappeared and the supreme authority had been assumed by an Assembly which was in effect a league of local magnates secure in their control of county institutions.[25]

One might at that point have projected the situation forward into a picture of dominant county families dating from the 1620's and 1630's, growing in identification with the land and people, ruling with increasing responsibility from increasingly eminent positions. But such a projection would be false. The fact is that with a few notable exceptions like the Scarboroughs and the Wormeleys, these struggling planters of the first generation failed to perpetuate their leadership into the second generation. Such families as the Woods, the Uties, the Mathews, and the Peirces faded from dominant positions of authority after the deaths of their founders. To some extent this was the result of the general insecurity of life that created odds against the physical survival in the male line of any given family. But even if male heirs had remained in these families after the death of the first generation, undisputed eminence would not. For a new emigration had begun in the forties, continuing for close to thirty years, from which was drawn a new ruling group that had greater possibilities for permanent dominance than Harvey's opponents had had. These newcomers absorbed and subordinated the older group, forming the basis of the most celebrated oligarchy in American history.

Most of Virginia's great eighteenth-century names, such as Bland, Burwell, Byrd, Carter, Digges, Ludwell, and Mason, appear in the colony for the first time within ten years either side of 1655. These progenitors of the eighteenth-century aristocracy arrived in remarkably similar circumstances. The most important of these immigrants were younger sons of substantial families well connected in London business and governmental circles and long associated with Virginia; family claims to land in the colony or inherited shares of the original Company stock were now brought forward as a basis for establishment in the New World.

Thus the Bland family interests in Virginia date from a 1618 investment in the Virginia Company by the London merchant John Bland, supplemented in 1622 by another in Martin's Hundred. The merchant never touched foot in America, but three of his sons did come to Virginia in the forties and fifties to exploit these investments. The Burwell fortunes derive from the early subscription to the Company of Edward Burwell, which was inherited in the late forties by his son, Lewis I. The first William Byrd arrived about 1670 to assume the Virginia properties of his mother's family, the Steggs, which dated back to the early days of the Company. The Digges's interests in Virginia stem from the original investments of Sir Dudley Digges and two of his sons in the Company, but it was a third son, Edward, who emigrated in 1650 and established the American branch of the family. Similarly, the Masons had been financially interested in Virginia thirty-two years before 1652, when the first immigrant of that family appeared in the colony. The Culpeper clan, whose private affairs enclose much of the history of the South in the second half of the seventeenth century, was first represented in Virginia by Thomas Culpeper, who arrived in 1649; but the family interests in Virginia

---

[22] The charges and countercharges are summarized, together with supporting documents, in the profuse footnotes of *Aspinwall Papers*, 131–52.

[23] *Va. Mag. of Hist. and Biog.*, 8 (1900–1), 30, 43–45; 1 (1893–94), 418, 419, 427, 420.

[24] *Ibid.*, 1 (1893–94), 418; Hening, ed., *Va. Stat. at L.*, I, 232–33. For a balanced statement of the importance attached by contemporaries to Virginia's representative Assembly, see Wesley Frank Craven, *Dissolution of the Virginia Company* (New York, 1932), 71 ff., 330 ff. Cf. Charles M. Andrews, *The Colonial Period of American History* (4 vols.; New Haven, Conn., 1934–38), I, 181 ff., and Davis, " 'Liberalism' in the Virginia Company and Colony," *Sandys*, Appendix G.

[25] Wesley Frank Craven, *The Southern Colonies in the Seventeenth Century, 1607–1689* (Baton Rouge, La., 1949), 288–94.

had been established a full generation earlier: Thomas' father, uncle, and cousin had all been members of the original Virginia Company and their shares had descended in the family. Even Governor Berkeley fits the pattern. There is no mystery about his sudden exchange in 1642 of the life of a dilettante courtier for that of a colonial administrator and estate manager. He was a younger son without prospects, and his family's interests in Virginia, dating from investments in the Company made twenty years earlier, as well as his appointment held out the promise of an independent establishment in America.[26]

Claims on the colony such as these were only one, though the most important, of a variety of forms of capital that might provide the basis for secure family fortunes. One might simply bring over enough of a merchant family's resources to begin immediately building up an imposing estate, as, presumably, did that ambitious draper's son, William Fitzhugh. The benefits that accrued from such advantages were quickly translated into landholdings in the development of which these settlers were favored by the chronology of their arrival. For though they extended the area of cultivation in developing their landholdings, they were not obliged to initiate settlement. They fell heirs to large areas of the tidewater region that had already been brought under cultivation. "Westover" was not the creation of William Byrd; it had originally been part of the De la Warr estate, passing, with improvements, to Captain Thomas Pawlett, thence to Theodorick Bland, and finally to Byrd. Lewis Burwell inherited not only his father's land, but also the developed estate of his stepfather, Wingate. Some of the Carters' lands may be traced back through John Utie to a John Jefferson, who left Virginia as early as 1628. Abraham Wood's entire Fort Henry property ended in the hands of the Jones family. The Blands' estate in Charles City County, which later became the Harrisons' "Berkeley" plantation, was cleared for settlement in 1619 by servants of the "particular" plantation of Berkeley's Hundred.[27]

Favored thus by circumstance, a small group within the second generation migration moved toward setting itself off in a permanent way as a ruling landed gentry. That they succeeded was

due not only to their material advantages but also to the force of their motivation. For these individuals were in social origins just close enough to establishment in gentility to feel the pangs of deprivation most acutely. It is not the totally but the partially dispossessed who build up the most propulsive aspirations, and behind the zestful lunging at propriety and status of a William Fitzhugh lay not the narcotic yearnings of the disinherited but the pent-up ambitions of the gentleman *manqué*. These were neither hardhanded pioneers nor dilettante romantics, but ambitious younger sons of middle-class families who knew well enough what gentility was and sought it as a specific objective.[28]

The establishment of this group was rapid. Within a decade of their arrival they could claim, together with a fortunate few of the first generation, a marked social eminence and full political authority at the county level. But their rise was not uniform. Indeed, by the seventies a new circumstance had introduced an effective principle of social differentiation among the colony's leaders. A hierarchy of position within the newly risen gentry was created by the Restoration government's efforts to extend its control more effectively over its mercantile empire. Demanding of its colonial executives and their advisors closer supervision over the external aspects of the economy, it offered a measure of patronage necessary for enforcement. Public offices dealing with matters that profoundly affected the basis of economic life—tax collection, customs regulation, and the bestowal of land grants—fell within the gift of the governor and tended to form an inner circle of privilege. One can note in Berkeley's administration the growing importance of this barrier of officialdom. Around its privileges there formed the "Green Spring" faction, named after Berkeley's plantation near Jamestown, a group bound to the governor not by royalist sympathies so much as by ties of kinship and patronage.

Thus Colonel Henry Norwood, related to Berkeley by a "near affinity in blood," was given the treasurership of the colony in 1650, which he held for more than two decades. During this time Thomas Ludwell, cousin and Somerset neighbor of the governor, was secretary of state, in which post he was succeeded in 1678 by his brother Philip, who shortly thereafter married Berkeley's widow. This Lady Berkeley, it should be noted, was the daughter of Thomas Culpeper, the immigrant of 1649 and a cousin of Thomas Lord Culpeper who became governor in 1680. Immediately after her marriage to Berkeley, her brother Alexander requested and received from the governor the nomination to the surveyor-generalship of Virginia, a post he filled for twenty-three years while resident in England, appointing as successive deputies the brothers Ludwell, to whom by

---

[26] Nell M. Nugent, *Cavaliers and Pioneers* (Richmond, Va., 1934), I, 160; Jester and Hiden, comps., *Adventurers*, 97, 108, 154–55, 288; Louis B. Wright, *The First Gentlemen of Virginia* (San Marino, Calif., 1940), 312–13; *Va. Mag. of Hist. and Biog.*, 35 (1927), 227–28; Helen Hill, *George Mason, Constitutionalist* (Cambridge, Mass., 1938), 3–4; Fairfax Harrison, "A Key Chart of the . . . Culpepers . . . ," *Va. Mag. of Hist. and Biog.*, 33 (1925), f. 113, 339, 344; *D.N.B.*, II, 368; Kingsbury, ed., *Records of the Virginia Company*, II, 75, 90, 391.

[27] Wright, *First Gentlemen*, 155 ff.; Jester and Hiden, comps., *Adventurers*, 98, 108, 339–41, 363–64, 97, 99.

[28] Fitzhugh's letters, scattered through the *Va. Mag. of Hist. and Biog.*, I–VI, cannot be equalled as sources for the motivation of this group.

1680 he was twice related by marriage. Lady Berkeley was also related through her mother to William Byrd's wife, a fact that explains much about Byrd's prolific office-holding.[29]

The growing distinctiveness of provincial officialdom within the landed gentry may also be traced in the transformation of the Council. Originally, this body had been expected to comprise the entire effective government, central and local; councilors were to serve, individually or in committees, as local magistrates. But the spread of settlement upset this expectation, and at the same time as the local offices were falling into the hands of autonomous local powers representing leading county families, the Council, appointed by the governor and hence associated with official patronage, increasingly realized the separate, lucrative privileges available to it.[30]

As the distinction between local and central authority became clear, the county magistrates sought their own distinct voice in the management of the colony, and they found it in developing the possibilities of burgess representatation. In the beginning there was no House of Burgesses; representation from the burghs and hundreds was conceived of not as a branch of government separate from the Council but as a periodic

supplement to it.[31] Until the fifties the burgesses, meeting in the Assemblies with the councilors, felt little need to form themselves into a separate house, for until that decade there was little evidence of a conflict of interests between the two groups. But when, after the Restoration, the privileged status of the Council became unmistakable and the county magnates found control of the increasingly important provincial administration pre-empted by this body, the burgess part of the Assembly took on a new meaning in contrast to that of the Council. Burgess representation now became vital to the county leaders if they were to share in any consistent way in affairs larger than those of the counties. They looked to the franchise, hitherto broad not by design but by neglect, introducing qualifications that would ensure their control of the Assembly. Their interest in provincial government could no longer be expressed in the conglomerate Assembly, and at least by 1663 the House of Burgesses began to meet separately as a distinct body voicing interests potentially in conflict with those of the Council.[32]

Thus by the eighth decade the ruling class in Virginia was broadly based on leading county families and dominated at the provincial level by a privileged officialdom. But this social and political structure was too new, too lacking in the sanctions of time and custom, its leaders too close to humbler origins and as yet too undistinguished in style of life, to be accepted without a struggle. A period of adjustment was necessary, of which Bacon's Rebellion was the climactic episode.

Bacon's Rebellion began as an unauthorized frontier war against the Indians and ended as an upheaval that threatened the entire basis of social and political authority. Its immediate causes have to do with race relations and settlement policy, but behind these issues lay deeper elements related to resistance against the maturing shape of a new social order. These elements explain the dimensions the conflict reached.

There was, first, resistance by substantial planters to the privileges and policies of the inner provincial clique led by Berkeley and composed of those directly dependent on his patronage. These dissidents, among whom were the leaders of the Rebellion, represented neither the downtrodden masses nor a principle of opposition to privilege as such. Their discontent stemmed to a large extent from their own exclusion from privileges they sought. Most often their grievances were based on personal rebuffs they had received as they reached for entry into provincial officialdom. Thus—to speak of the leaders of the Rebellion—Giles Bland arrived in Virginia in 1671

[29] Colonel [Henry] Norwood, *A Voyage to Virginia* (1649), in Force, ed., *Tracts*, III, 49, 50; *Va. Mag. of Hist. and Biog.*, 33 (1925), 5, 8; Harrison, "Key Chart," *ibid.*, 351–55, 348; *Wm. and Mary Qtly.*, 1st ser., 19 (1910–11), 209–10. It was after Culpeper's appointment to the governorship that Byrd was elevated to the Council and acquired the auditor- and receiver-generalships. William G. and Mary N. Stanard, comps., *The Colonial Virginia Register* (Albany, N.Y., 1902), 22–23.

The Berkeley-Norwood connection may be followed out in other directions. Thus the Colonel Francis Moryson mentioned by Norwood as his friend and traveling companion and whom he introduced to the governor was given command of the fort at Point Comfort upon his arrival in 1649, replacing his brother, Major Richard Moryson, whose son Charles was given the same post in the 1660's. Francis, who found the command of the fort "profitable to him," was elevated by Berkeley to the Council and temporarily to the deputy-governorship, "wherein he got a competent estate"; he finally returned to England in the position of colony agent. Norwood, *Voyage*, 50; *Va. Mag. of Hist. and Biog.*, 9 (1900–1), 122–23; Ella Lonn, *The Colonial Agents of the Southern Colonies* (Chapel Hill, 1945), 21 ff.

The inner kinship core of the group enclosed the major provincial positions mentioned above. But the wider reaches of the clique extended over the Council, the collectorships, and the naval offices as well as minor positions within the influence of the governor. On these posts and their holders, see Stanard and Stanard, comps., *Va. Register*, 38–40; Bruce, *Institutional History*, II, Chaps. XXXVIII–XLII. On the limitations of the gubernatorial influence after 1660, see Craven, *Southern Colonies*, 293.

[30] Craven, *Southern Colonies*, 167–69, 270, 288; Bruce, *Institutional History*, II, Chap. XV.

[31] For the Assembly as "the other Counsell," see the "Ordinance and Constitution" of 1621 in Kingsbury, ed., *Records of the Virginia Company*, III, 483–84.

[32] Andrews, *Colonial Period*, I, 184–85; Craven, *Southern Colonies*, 289 ff.

to take over the agency of his late uncle in the management of his father's extensive landholdings, assuming at the same time the lucrative position of customs collector which he had obtained in London. But, amid angry cries of *"pittyfull fellow, puppy* and *Sonn of a Whore,"* he fell out first with Berkeley's cousin and favorite, Thomas Ludwell, and finally with the governor himself; for his "Barbarous and Insolent Behaviors" Bland was fined, arrested, and finally removed from the collectorship.[33] Of the two "chiefe Incendiarys," William Drummond and Richard Lawrence, the former had been quarreling with Berkeley since 1664, first over land claims in Carolina, then over a contract for building a fort near James City, and repeatedly over lesser issues in the General Court; Lawrence "some Years before . . . had been partially treated at Law, for a considerable Estate on behalfe of a Corrupt favorite." Giles Brent, for his depredations against the Indians in violation of official policy, had not only been severely fined but barred from public office.[34] Bacon himself could not have appeared under more favorable circumstances. A cousin both of Lady Berkeley and of the councilor Nathaniel Bacon, Sr., and by general agreement "a Gent:man of a Liberall education" if of a somewhat tarnished reputation, he had quickly staked out land for himself and had been elevated, for reasons "best known to the Governour," to the Council. But being "of a most imperious and dangerous hidden Pride of heart . . . very ambitious and arrogant," he wanted more, and quickly. His alienation from and violent opposition to Berkeley were wound in among the animosities created by the Indian problem and were further complicated by his own unstable personality; they were related also to the fact that Berkeley finally turned down the secret offer Bacon and Byrd made in 1675 for the purchase from the governor of a monopoly of the Indian trade.[35]

These specific disputes have a more general aspect. It was three decades since Berkeley had assumed the governorship and begun rallying a favored group, and it was over a decade since the Restoration had given this group unconfined sway over the provincial government. In those years much of the choice tidewater land as well as the choice offices had been spoken for, and the tendency of the highly placed was to hold firm. Berkeley's Indian policy—one of stabilizing the borders between Indians and whites and protecting the natives from depredation by land-hungry settlers—although a sincere attempt to deal with an extremely difficult problem, was also conservative, favoring the established. Newcomers like Bacon and Bland and particularly landholders on the frontiers felt victimized by a stabilization of the situation or by a controlled expansion that maintained on an extended basis the existing power structure. They were logically drawn to aggressive positions. In an atmosphere charged with violence, their interests constituted a challenge to provincial authority. Bacon's primary appeal in his "Manifesto" played up the threat of this challenge: "Let us trace these men in Authority and Favour to whose hands the dispensation of the Countries wealth has been commited; let us observe the sudden Rise of their Estates [compared] with the Quality in wch they first entered this Country. . . And lett us see wither their extractions and Education have not bin vile, And by what pretence of learning and vertue they could [enter] soe soon into Imployments of so great Trust and consequence, let us. . .see what spounges have suckt up the Publique Treasure and wither it hath not bin privately contrived away by unworthy Favourites and juggling Parasites whose tottering Fortunes have bin repaired and supported at the Publique chardg." Such a threat to the basis of authority was not lost on Berkeley or his followers. Bacon's merits, a contemporary wrote, "thretned an eclips to there riseing gloryes. . . . (if he should continue in the Governours favour) of Seniours they might becom juniours, while there younger Brother . . . might steale away that blessing, which they accounted there owne by birthright."[36]

But these challengers were themselves challenged, for another main element in the upheaval was the discontent among the ordinary settlers at the local privileges of the same newly risen county magnates who assailed the privileges of the Green Spring faction. The specific Charles City County grievances were directed as much at the locally dominant family, the Hills, as they were at Berkeley and his clique. Similarly, Surry County

[33] Jester and Hiden, comps., *Adventurers,* 98–99; H. R. McIlwaine, ed., *Minutes of the Council and General Court . . . 1622–1632, 1670–1676* (Richmond, Va., 1924), 399, 423.

[34] Charles M. Andrews, ed., *Narratives of the Insurrections, 1675–1690* (New York, 1915), 96, 27; Wilcomb E. Washburn, "The Humble Petition of Sarah Drummond," *Wm. and Mary Qtly.,* 3rd ser., 13 (1956), 368–69; H. R. McIlwaine, ed., *Journals of the House of Burgesses of Virginia 1659/60–1693* (Richmond, Va., 1914), 14.

[35] Wilcomb E. Washburn, *The Governor and the Rebel, A History of Bacon's Rebellion in Virginia* (Chapel Hill, 1957), 17–19; Andrews, ed., *Narratives,* 74, 110. For the offer to buy the monopoly and Berkeley's initial interest in it, see Bacon to Berkeley, September 18, 1675, and William and Frances Berkeley to Bacon, September 21, 1675, Coventry Papers, Longleat Library of the Marquises of Bath, LXXVII, 6, 8 (microfilm copy, Library of Congress); for the refusal, see *Aspinwall Papers,* 166. Mr. Washburn, who first called

attention to these Bacon letters at Longleat, is editing them for publication by the Virginia Historical Society.

[36] Craven, *Southern Colonies,* 362–73; *Va. Mag. of Hist. and Biog.,* 1 (1893–94), 56–57; Andrews, ed., *Narratives,* 53.

complained of its county court's highhanded and secretive manner of levying taxes on "the poore people" and of setting the sheriffs' and clerks' fees; they petitioned for the removal of these abuses and for the right to elect the vestry and to limit the tenure of the sheriffs. At all levels the Rebellion challenged the stability of newly secured authority.[37]

It is this double aspect of discontent behind the violence of the Rebellion that explains the legislation passed in June, 1676, by the so-called "Bacon's Assembly." At first glance these laws seem difficult to interpret because they express disparate if not contradictory interests. But they yield readily to analysis if they are seen not as the reforms of a single group but as efforts to express the desires of two levels of discontent with the way the political and social hierarchy was becoming stabilized. On the one hand, the laws include measures designed by the numerically predominant ordinary settlers throughout the colony as protests against the recently acquired superiority of the leading county families. These were popular protests and they relate not to provincial affairs but to the situation within the local areas of jurisdiction. Thus the statute restricting the franchise to freeholders was repealed; freemen were given the right to elect the parish vestrymen; and the county courts were supplemented by elected freemen to serve with the regularly appointed county magistrates.

On the other hand, there was a large number of measures expressing the dissatisfactions not so much of the ordinary planter but of the local leaders against the prerogatives recently acquired by the provincial elite, prerogatives linked to officialdom and centered in the Council. Thus the law barring office-holding to newcomers of less than three years' residence struck at the arbitrary elevation of the governor's favorites, including Bacon; and the acts forbidding councilors to join the county courts, outlawing the governor's appointment of sheriffs and tax collectors, and nullifying tax exemption for councilors all voiced objections of the local chieftains to privileges enjoyed by others. From both levels there was objection to profiteering in public office.[38]

Thus the wave of rebellion broke and spread. But why did it subside? One might have expected that the momentary flood would have become a steady tide, its rhythms governed by a fixed political constellation. But in fact it did not; stable political alignments did not result. The conclusion to this controversy was characteristic of all the insurrections. The attempted purges and counterpurges by the leaders of the two sides were followed by a rapid submerging of factional identity. Occasional references were later made to the episode, and there were individuals who found an interest in keeping its memory alive. Also, the specific grievances behind certain of the attempted legal reforms of 1676 were later revived. But of stable parties or factions around these issues there were none.

It was not merely that in the late years of the century no more than in the early was there to be found a justification for permanently organized political opposition or party machinery, that persistent, organized dissent was still indistinguishable from sedition; more important was the fact that at the end of the century as in 1630 there was agreement that some must be "highe and eminent in power and dignitie; others meane and in subieccion."[39] Protests and upheaval had resulted from the discomforts of discovering who was, in fact, which, and what the particular consequences of "power and dignitie" were.

But by the end of the century the most difficult period of adjustment had passed and there was an acceptance of the fact that certain families were distinguished from others in riches, in dignity, and in access to political authority. The establishment of these families marks the emergence of Virginia's colonial aristocracy.

It was a remarkable governing group. Its members were soberly responsible, alive to the implications of power; they performed their public obligations with notable skill.[40] Indeed, the glare of their accomplishments is so bright as occasionally to blind us to the conditions that limited them. As a ruling class the Virginian aristocracy of the eighteenth century was unlike other contemporary nobilities or aristocracies, including the English. The differences, bound up with the special characteristics of the society it ruled, had become clear at the turn of the seventeenth century.

Certain of these characteristics are elusive, difficult to grasp and analyze. The leaders of early eighteenth-century Virginia were, for example, in a particular sense, cultural provincials. They were provincial not in the way of Polish *szlachta* isolated on their estates by poverty and impassable roads, nor in the way of sunken *seigneurs* grown rustic and old-fashioned in lonely Norman chateaux. The Virginians were far from uninformed or unaware of the greater world; they were in fact deeply and continuously involved in the cultural life of the Atlantic community. But they knew themselves to be provincials in the

---

[37] *Va. Mag. of Hist. and Biog.*, 3 (1895–96), 132 ff. (esp. 142–46), 239–52, 341–49; IV, 1–15; II, 172.

[38] Hening, ed., *Va. Stat. at L.*, II, 341–65.

[39] Thus the Burgesses, proposing in 1706 that the vestries be made elective, did not dispute the Council's assertion that the "men of Note & Estates" should have authority and assured them that the people would voluntarily elect the "best" men in the parish. H. R. McIlwaine, ed., *Legislative Journals of the Council of Colonial Virginia* (Richmond, Va., 1918–19), I, 468.

[40] Charles S. Sydnor, *Gentlemen Freeholders: Political Practices in Washington's Virginia* (Chapel Hill, 1952), Chaps. I, VI–IX.

sense that their culture was not self-contained; its sources and superior expressions were to be found elsewhere than in their own land. They must seek it from afar; it must be acquired, and once acquired be maintained according to standards externally imposed, in the creation of which they had not participated. The most cultivated of them read much, purposefully, with a diligence the opposite of that essential requisite of aristocracy, uncontending ease. William Byrd's diary with its daily records of stints of study is a stolid testimonial to the virtues of regularity and effort in maintaining standards of civilization set abroad.[41]

In more evident ways also the Virginia planters were denied an uncontending ease of life. They were not *rentiers*. Tenancy, when it appeared late in the colonial period, was useful to the landowners mainly as a cheap way of improving lands held in reserve for future development. The Virginia aristocrat was an active manager of his estate, drawn continuously into the most intimate contacts with the soil and its cultivation. This circumstance limited his ease, one might even say bound him to the soil, but it also strengthened his identity with the land and its problems and saved him from the temptation to create of his privileges an artificial world of self-indulgence.[42]

But more important in distinguishing the emerging aristocracy of Virginia from other contemporary social and political elites were two very specific circumstances. The first concerns the relationship between the integrity of the family unit and the descent of real property. "The English political family," Sir Lewis Namier writes with particular reference to the eighteenth-century aristocracy, "is a compound of 'blood,' name, and estate, this last . . . being the most important of the three. . . . The name is a weighty symbol, but liable to variations. . . . the estate . . . is, in the long run, the most potent factor in securing continuity through identification. . . . Primogeniture and entails psychically preserve the family in that they tend to fix its position through the successive generations, and thereby favour conscious identification." The descent of landed estates in eighteenth-century England was controlled by the complicated device known as the strict settlement which provided that the heir at his marriage received the estate as a life tenant, entailing its descent to his unborn eldest son

and specifying the limitations of the encumbrances upon the land that might be made in behalf of his daughters and younger sons.[43]

It was the strict settlement, in which in the eighteenth century perhaps half the land of England was bound, that provided continuity over generations for the landed aristocracy. This permanent identification of the family with a specific estate and with the status and offices that pertained to it was achieved at the cost of sacrificing the younger sons. It was a single stem of the family only that retained its superiority; it alone controlled the material basis for political dominance.

This basic condition of aristocratic governance in England was never present in the American colonies, and not for lack of familiarity with legal forms. The economic necessity that had prompted the widespread adoption of the strict settlement in England was absent in the colonies. Land was cheap and easily available, the more so as one rose on the social and political ladder. There was no need to deprive the younger sons or even daughters of landed inheritances in order to keep the original family estate intact. Provision could be made for endowing each of them with plantations, and they in turn could provide similarly for their children. Moreover, to confine the stem family's fortune to a single plot of land, however extensive, was in the Virginia economy to condemn it to swift decline. Since the land was quickly worn out and since it was cheaper to acquire new land than to rejuvenate the worked soil by careful husbandry, geographical mobility, not stability, was the key to prosperity. Finally, since land was only as valuable as the labor available to work it, a great estate was worth passing intact from generation to generation only if it had annexed to it a sufficient population of slaves. Yet this condition imposed severe rigidities in a plantation's economy—for a labor force bound to a particular plot was immobilized—besides creating bewildering confusions in law.

The result, evident before the end of the seventeenth century, was a particular relationship between the family and the descent of property. There was in the beginning no intent on the part of the Virginians to alter the traditional forms; the continued vitality of the ancient statutes specifying primogeniture in certain cases was assumed.[44] The first clear indication of a new trend came in the third quarter of the century, when the leading gentry, rapidly accumulating large estates, faced for the first time the problem of

[41] Albert Goodwin, ed., *The European Nobility in the Eighteenth Century* (London, 1953), *passim;* John Clive and Bernard Bailyn, "England's Cultural Provinces: Scotland and America," *Wm. and Mary Qtly.*, 3rd ser., 9 (1954), 200–13; Louis B. Wright and Marion Tinling, eds., *The Secret Diary of William Byrd of Westover 1709–1712* (Richmond, Va., 1941).

[42] Willard F. Bliss, "The Rise of Tenancy in Virginia," *Va. Mag. of Hist. and Biog.*, 58 (1950), 427 ff.; Louis B. Wright, *Cultural Life of the American Colonies, 1607–1763* (New York, 1957), 5–11.

[43] Lewis B. Namier, *England in the Age of the American Revolution* (London, 1930), 22–23; H. J. Habakkuk, "Marriage Settlements in the Eighteenth Century," Royal Hist. Soc., *Transactions,* 4th ser., 32 (1950), 15–30.

[44] Clarence R. Keim, Influence of Primogeniture and Entail in the Development of Virginia (unpublished Ph.D. dissertation, University of Chicago, 1926), Chap. I.

the transfer of property. The result was the subdivision of the great holdings and the multiplication of smaller plots while the net amount of land held by the leading families continued to rise.[45]

This trend continued. Primogeniture neither at the end of the seventeenth century nor after prevailed in Virginia. It was never popular even among the most heavily endowed of the tidewater families. The most common form of bequest was a grant to the eldest son of the undivided home plantation and gifts of other tracts outside the home county to the younger sons and daughters. Thus by his will of 1686 Robert Beverley, Sr., bequeathed to his eldest son, Peter, all his land in Gloucester County lying between "Chiescake" and "Hoccadey's" creeks (an unspecified acreage); to Robert, the second son, another portion of the Gloucester lands amounting to 920 acres; to Harry, 1,600 acres in Rappahannock County; to John, 3,000 acres in the same county; to William, two plantations in Middlesex County; to Thomas, 3,000 acres in Rappahannock and New Kent counties; to his wife, three plantations including those "whereon I now live" for use during her lifetime, after which they were to descend to his daughter Catherine, who was also to receive £200 sterling; to his daughter Mary, £150 sterling, to "the childe that my wife goeth with, be it male or female," all the rest of his real property; and the residue of his personal property was "to be divided and disposed in equall part & portion betwix my wife and children." Among the bequests of Ralph Wormeley, Jr., in 1700 was an estate of 1,500 acres to his daughter Judith as well as separate plantations to his two sons.

Entail proved no more popular than primogeniture. Only a small minority of estates, even in the tidewater region, were ever entailed. In fact, despite the extension of developed land in the course of the eighteenth century, more tidewater estates were docked of entails than were newly entailed.[46]

Every indication points to continuous and increasing difficulty in reproducing even pale replicas of the strict settlement. In 1705 a law was passed requiring a special act of the Assembly to break an entail; the law stood, but between 1711 and 1776 no fewer than 125 such private acts were passed, and in 1734 estates of under £200 were exempted from the law altogether.

The labor problem alone was an insuperable barrier to perpetuating the traditional forms. A statute of 1727, clarifying the confused legislation of earlier years, had attempted to ensure a labor force on entailed land by classifying slaves as real property and permitting them to be bound together with land into bequests. But by 1748 this stipulation had resulted in such bewildering "doubts, variety of opinions, and confusions" that it was repealed. The repeal was disallowed in London, and in the course of a defense of its action the Assembly made vividly clear the utter impracticality of entailment in Virginia's economy. Slaves, the Assembly explained, were essential to the success of a plantation, but "slaves could not be kept on the lands to which they were annexed without manifest prejudice to the tenant in tail. . . . often the tenant was the proprietor of fee simple land much fitter for cultivation than his intailed lands, where he could work his slaves to a much greater advantage." On the other hand, if a plantation owner did send entailed slaves where they might be employed most economically the result was equally disastrous: "the frequent removing and settling them on other lands in other counties and parts of the colony far distant from the county court where the deeds or wills which annexed them were recorded and the intail lands lay; the confusion occasioned by their mixture with fee simple slaves of the same name and sex and belonging to the same owner; the uncertainty of distinguishing one from another after several generations, no register of their genealogy being kept and none of them having surnames, were great mischiefs to purchasers, strangers, and creditors, who were often unavoidably deceived in their purchases and hindered in the recovery of their just debts. It also lessened the credit of the country; it being dangerous for the merchants of Great Britain to trust possessors of many slaves for fear the slaves might be intailed."[47]

A mobile labor force free from legal entanglements and a rapid turnover of lands, not a permanent hereditary estate, were prerequisites of family prosperity. This condition greatly influenced social and political life. Since younger sons and even daughters inherited extensive landed properties, equal often to those of the eldest son, concentration of authority in the stem family was precluded. Third generation collateral descendants of the original immigrant were as important in their own right as the eldest son's eldest son. Great clans like the Carters and the

---

[45] E.g., Ames, *Eastern Shore,* 29–32.

[46] Keim, Primogeniture and Entail, 44 ff., 113–14. Keim found that only 1 of a sample of 72 wills in Westmoreland (1653–72) contained provisions for entailing; by 1756–61 the proportions had risen to 14 out of 39, but these entails covered only small parts of the total estates. Typical of his other tidewater samples are Middlesex, 1698–1703, 16 out of 65, and 1759–72, 7 out of 48; Henrico, 1677–87, 2 out of 29, and no increase for the later periods. The piedmont samples show even smaller proportions; *ibid.,* 54–62. The Beverley will is printed in *Va. Mag. of Hist. and Biog.,* 3 (1895–96), 47–51; on Wormeley, see *ibid.,* 36 (1928), 101.

[47] Hening, ed., *Va. Stat. at L.,* III, 320, IV, 399–400, 222 ff., V, 441–42n (quoted). In 1765 the legal rigors of entailment were permanently relaxed by a law permitting the leasing of entailed land for up to three lives, a move made necessary, the Assembly said, because "many large tracts of entailed lands remain uncultivated, the owners not having slaves to work them. . . ." *Ibid.,* VIII, 183. For a striking example of the difficulties of maintaining entailed lands, see *ibid.,* VI, 297–99; Keim, Primogeniture and Entail, 108.

Lees, though they may have acknowledged a central family seat, were scattered throughout the province on estates of equal influence. The four male Carters of the third generation were identified by contemporaries by the names of their separate estates, and, indistinguishable in style of life, they had an equal access to political power.[48]

Since material wealth was the basis of the status which made one eligible for public office, there was a notable diffusion of political influence throughout a broadening group of leading families. No one son was predestined to represent the family interest in politics, but as many as birth and temperament might provide. In the 1750's there were no fewer than seven Lees of the same generation sitting together in the Virginia Assembly; in the Burgesses they spoke for five separate counties. To the eldest, Philip Ludwell Lee, they conceded a certain social superiority that made it natural for him to sit in the Council. But he did not speak alone for the family; by virtue of inheritance he had no unique authority over his brothers and cousins.

The leveling at the top of the social and political hierarchy, creating an evenness of status and influence, was intensified by continuous intermarriage within the group. The unpruned branches of these flourishing family trees, growing freely, met and intertwined until by the Revolution the aristocracy appeared to be one great tangled cousinry.[49]

As political power became increasingly diffused throughout the upper stratum of society, the Council, still at the end of the seventeenth century a repository of unique privileges, lost its effective superiority. Increasingly through the successive decades its authority had to be exerted through alignments with the Burgesses—alignments made easier as well as more necessary by the criss-crossing network of kinship that united the two houses. Increasingly the Council's distinctions became social and ceremonial.[50]

The contours of Virginia's political hierarchy were also affected by a second main conditioning element, besides the manner of descent of family property. Not only was the structure unusually level and broad at the top, but it was incomplete in itself. Its apex, the ultimate source of legal decision and control, lay in the quite different society of England, amid the distant embroilments of London, the court, and Parliament. The levers of control in that realm were for the most part hidden from the planters; yet the powers that ruled this remote region could impose an arbitrary authority directly into the midst of Virginia's affairs.

One consequence was the introduction of instabilities in the tenure and transfer of the highest offices. Tenure could be arbitrarily interrupted, and the transfer to kin of such positions at death or resignation—uncertain in any case because of the diffusion of family authority—could be quite difficult or even impossible. Thus William Byrd II returned from England at the death of his father in 1704 to take over the family properties, but though he was the sole heir he did not automatically or completely succeed to the elder Byrd's provincial offices. He did, indeed, become auditor of Virginia after his father, but only because he had carefully arranged for the succession while still in London; his father's Council seat went to someone else, and it took three years of patient maneuvering through his main London contact, Micajah Perry, to secure another; he never did take over the receivership. Even such a power as "King" Carter, the reputed owner at his death of 300,000 acres and 1,000 slaves, was rebuffed by the resident deputy governor and had to deploy forces in England in order to transfer a Virginia naval office post from one of his sons to another. There was family continuity in public office, but at the highest level it was uncertain, the result of place-hunting rather than of absolute prerogative of birth.[51]

Instability resulted not only from the difficulty of securing and transferring high appointive positions but also and more immediately from the presence in Virginia of total strangers to the scene, particularly governors and their deputies, armed with extensive jurisdiction and powers of enforcement. The dangers of this element in public life became clear only after Berkeley's return to England in 1677, for after thirty-five years of residence in the colony Sir William had become a leader in the land independent of his royal authority. But Howard, Andros, and Nicholson were governors with full legal powers but with at best only slight connections with local society. In them, social leadership and political leadership had ceased to be identical.

In the generation that followed Berkeley's departure, this separation between the two spheres created the bitterest of political controversies. Firmly entrenched behind their control of the colony's government, the leading families battled with every weapon available to reduce the power of the executives and thus to eliminate what appeared to be an external and arbitrary authority. Repeated complaints by the governors of the intractable opposition of a league of local oligarchs marked the Virginians' success. Efforts by the executives to discipline the indigenous leaders could only be mildly successful. Patronage was a useful weapon, but its effectiveness diminished steadily,

---

[48] Louis Morton, *Robert Carter of Nomini Hall* (Williamsburg, 1941), 11.

[49] Burton J. Hendrick, *The Lees of Virginia* (Boston, 1935), 97.

[50] Percy S. Flippin, *The Royal Government in Virginia, 1624–1775* (New York, 1919), 166–67, 169; Herbert L. Osgood, *The American Colonies in the Eighteenth Century* (4 vols.; New York, 1924–25), IV, 231–32.

[51] John S. Bassett, ed., *The Writings of "Colonel William Byrd of Westover in Virginia Esqr"* (New York, 1901), xlviii–ix; Morton, *Carter*, 28n.

ground down between a resistant Assembly and an office-hungry bureaucracy in England. The possibility of exploiting divisions among the resident powers also declined as kinship lines bound the leading families closer together and as group interests became clearer with the passage of time. No faction built around the gubernatorial power could survive independently; ultimately its adherents would fall away and it would weaken. It was a clear logic of the situation that led the same individuals who had promoted Nicholson as a replacement for Andros to work against him once he assumed office.[52]

Stability could be reached only by the complete identification of external and internal authority through permanent commitment by the appointees to local interests. Commissary Blair's extraordinary success in Virginia politics was based not only on his excellent connections in England but also on his marriage into the Harrison family, which gave him the support of an influential kinship faction. There was more than hurt pride and thwarted affection behind Nicholson's reported insane rage at being spurned by the highly marriageable Lucy Burwell; and later the astute Spotswood, for all his success in imposing official policy, fully quieted the controversies of his administration only by succumbing completely and joining as a resident Virginia landowner the powers aligned against him.[53]

But there was more involved than instability and conflict in the discontinuity between social and political organization at the topmost level. The state itself had changed its meaning. To a Virginia planter of the early eighteenth century the highest public authority was no longer merely one expression of a general social authority. It had become something abstract, external to his life and society, an ultimate power whose purposes were obscure, whose direction could neither be consistently influenced nor accurately plotted, and whose human embodiments were alien and antagonistic.

The native gentry of the early eighteenth century had neither the need nor the ability to fashion a new political theory to comprehend their experience, but their successors would find in the writings of John Locke on state and society not merely a reasonable theoretical position but a statement of self-evident fact.

I have spoken exclusively of Virginia, but though the histories of each of the colonies in the seventeenth century are different, they exhibit common characteristics. These features one might least have expected to find present in Virginia, and their presence there is, consequently, most worth indicating.

In all of the colonies the original transference of an ordered European society was succeeded by the rise to authority of resident settlers whose influence was rooted in their ability to deal with the problems of life in wilderness settlements. These individuals attempted to stabilize their positions, but in each case they were challenged by others arriving after the initial settlements, seeking to exploit certain advantages of position, wealth, or influence. These newcomers, securing after the Restoration governmental appointments in the colonies and drawn together by personal ties, especially those of kinship and patronage, came to constitute colonial officialdom. This group introduced a new principle of social organization; it also gave rise to new instabilities in a society in which the traditional forms of authority were already being subjected to severe pressures. By the eighth decade of the seventeenth century the social basis of public life had become uncertain and insecure, its stability delicate and sensitive to disturbance. Indian warfare, personal quarrels, and particularly the temporary confusion in external control caused by the Glorious Revolution became the occasions for violent challenges to constituted authority.

By the end of the century a degree of harmony had been achieved, but the divergence between political and social leadership at the topmost level created an area of permanent conflict. The political and social structures that emerged were by European standards strangely shaped. Everywhere as the bonds of empire drew tighter the meaning of the state was changing. Herein lay the origins of a new political system.

---

[52] For the classic outcry against "the party of Malecontents," see Spotswood's letter to the Board of Trade, March 25, 1719, in R. A. Brock, ed., *The Official Letters of Alexander Spotswood* (Richmond, Va., 1882–85), II, 308 ff.; cf. 285. On patronage, see Flippin, *Royal Government,* 208–214; Leonard W. Labaree, *Royal Government in America* (New Haven, Conn., 1930), 102; Worthington C. Ford, "A Sketch of Sir Francis Nicholson," *Mag. of Amer. Hist.,* 29 (1893), 508–12.

[53] Peter Laslett, "John Locke . . . ," *Wm. and Mary Qtly.,* 3rd ser., 14 (1957), 398; Daniel E. Motley, *Life of Commissary James Blair* . . . (Baltimore, 1901), 10, 43 ff.; William S. Perry, ed., *Historical Collections Relating to the . . . Church* ([Hartford], 1870–78), I, 69, 72–73, 88, 90, 102, 135; Leonidas Dodson, *Alexander Spotswood* (Philadelphia, 1932), 251 ff.

Nathaniel Bacon has generally been hailed as the patriotic leader of a popular rebellion against tyranny. Thus, in 1893, the *Virginia Magazine of History and Biography* when publishing his proclamation of 1676 declared, "The spirit breathing through the Declaration of the People is the spirit of the Declaration of Independence written a hundred years later."

NATHANIEL BACON:
MANIFESTO CONCERNING THE PRESENT TROUBLES IN VIRGINIA, 1676*

If vertue be a sin, if Piety be giult, all the Principles of morality goodness and Justice be perverted, Wee must confesse That those who are now called Rebells may be in danger of those high imputations, Those loud and severall Bulls would affright Innocents and render the defense of o^r Brethren and the enquiry into o^r sad and heavy oppressions, Treason. But if there bee as sure there is, a just God to appeal too, if Religion and Justice be a sanctuary here, If to plead ye cause of the oppressed, If sincerely to aime at his Mat^{ies} Honour and the Publick good without any reservation or by Interest, If to stand in the Gap after soe much blood of o^r dear Brethren bought and sold, If after the losse of a great part of his Maties Colony deserted and dispeopled, freely with o^r lives and estates to indeavor to save the remaynders bee Treason God Almighty Judge and lett guilty dye, But since wee cannot in o^r hearts find one single spott of Rebellion or Treason or that wee have in any manner aimed at the subverting ye setled Government or attempting of the Person of any either magistrate or private man not with standing the severall Reproaches and Threats of some who for sinister ends were disaffected to us and censured o^r ino[cent] and honest designes, and since all people in all places where wee have yet bin can attest o^r civill quiet peaseable behaviour farre different from that of Rebellion and tumultuous persons let Trueth be bold and all the world know the real Foundations of pretended giult, Wee appeale to the Country itselfe what and of what nature their Oppressions have bin or by what Caball and mistery the designes of many of those whom wee call great men have bin transacted and caryed on, but let us trace these men in Authority and Favour to whose hands the dispensation of the Countries wealth has been commited; let us observe the sudden Rise of their Estates composed with the Quality in wch they first entered this Country Or the Reputation they have held here amongst wise and discerning men, And lett us see wither their extractions and Education have not bin vile, And by what pretence of learning and vertue they could soe soon into Imployments of so great Trust and consequence, let us consider their sud-

den advancement and let us also consider wither any Publick work for o^r safety and defence or for the Advancem^t and propogation of Trade, liberall Arts or sciences is here Extant in any [way] adaquate to o^r vast chardg, now let us compare these things togit[her] and see what spounges have suckt up the Publique Treasure and wither it hath not bin privately contrived away by unworthy Favourites and juggling Parasites whose tottering Fortunes have bin repaired and supported at the Publique chardg, now if it be so Judg what greater giult can bee then to offer to pry into these and to unriddle the misterious wiles of a powerfull Cabal let all people Judge what can be of more dangerous Import then to suspect the soe long Safe proceedings of Some of o^r Grandees and wither People may with safety open their Eyes in soe nice a Concerne.

Another main article of o^r Giult is o^r open and manifest aversion of all, not onely the Foreign but the protected and Darling Indians, this wee are informed is Rebellion of a deep dye For that both the Governour and Councell are by Colonell Coales Assertion bound to defend the Queen and the Appamatocks with their blood Now whereas we doe declare and can prove that they have bin for these Many years enemies to the King and Country, Robbers and Theeves and Invaders of his Maties Right and o^r Interest and Estates, but yet have by persons in Authority bin defended and protected even against His Maties loyall Subjects and that in soe high a Nature that even the Complaints and oaths of his Maties Most loyall Subjects in a lawfull Manner proffered by them against tho^s barborous Outlawes have bin by ye right honourable Governour rejected and ye Delinquents from his presence dismissed not only with pardon and indemnitye but with all incouragement and favour, Their Fire Arms soe destructfull to us and by o^r lawes prohibited, Commanded to be restored them, and open Declaration before Witness made That they must have Ammunition although directly contrary to o^r law, Now what greater giult can be then to oppose and indeavour the destruction of these Honest quiet neighbours of ours.

Another main article of our Giult is o^r Design not only to ruine and extirpate all Indians in Generall but all Manner of Trade and Commerce with them, Judge who can be innocent

* Reprinted from *The Virginia Magazine of History and Biography*, I (July, 1893), 55–58.

that strike at this tender Eye of Interest; Since the Right honourable the Governour hath bin pleased by his Commission to warrant this Trade who dare oppose it, or opposing it can be innocent, Although Plantations be deserted, the blood of oʳ dear Brethren Spilt, on all Sides oʳ complaints, continually Murder upon Murder renewed upon us, who may or dare think of the generall Subversion of all Mannor of Trade and Commerce with oʳ enemies who can or dare impeach any of * * * Traders at the Heades of the Rivers if contrary to the wholesome provision made by lawes for the countries safety, they dare continue their illegall practises and dare asperse ye right honourable Governours wisdome and Justice soe highly to pretend to have his warrant to break that law wᶜʰ himself made, who dare say That these Men at the Heads of the Rivers buy and sell oʳ blood, and doe still notwithstanding the late Act made to the contrary, admit Indians painted and continue to Commerce, although these things can be proved yet who dare bee soe giulty as to doe it.

Another Article of oʳ Giult is To Assert all those neighbour Indians as well as others to be outlawed, wholly unqualifyed for the benefitt and Protection of the law, For that the law does reciprocally protect and punish, and that all people offending must either in person or Estate make equivalent satisfaction or Restitution ac-

cording to the manner and merit of yᵉ Offences Debts or Trespasses; Now since the Indians cannot according to the tenure and forme of any law to us known be prosecuted, Seised or Complained against, Their Persons being difficulty distinguished or known, Their many nations languages, and their subterfuges such as makes them incapeable to make us Restitution or satisfaction would it not be very giulty to say They have bin unjustly defended and protected these many years.

If it should be said that the very foundation of all these disasters the Grant of the Beaver trade to the Right Honourable Governour was illegall and not granteable by any power here present as being a monopoly, were not this to deserve the name of Rebell and Traytor.

Judge therefore all wise and unprejudiced men who may or can faithfully or truely with an honest heart attempt yᵉ country's good, their vindication and libertie without the aspersion of Traitor and Rebell, since as soe doing they must of necessity gall such tender and dear concernes, But to manifest Sincerity [sic] and loyalty to the World, and how much wee abhorre those bitter names, may all the world know that we doe unanimously desire to represent oʳ sad and heavy grievances to his most sacred Maᵗⁱᵉ as oʳ Refuge and Sanctuary, where wee doe well know that all oʳ Causes will be impartially heard and Equall Justice administred to all men.

A critical view of Bacon's Rebellion appeared in 1705 in Robert Beverley's *History and Present State of Virginia*. Beverley was only three years old in 1676, too young to be an eyewitness, but he grew up among men who were, and his father had been one of Governor Berkeley's stanchest supporters. Beverley regarded Bacon as a demagogue eager to destroy the Indians. His analysis of the causes of the rebellion has been praised by Wilcomb E. Washburn as being as near to a successful interpretation as that of anyone since.[1]

ROBERT BEVERLEY: CAUSES OF BACON'S REBELLION, 1705*

92. The Occasion of this Rebellion is not easie to be discover'd: But 'tis certain there were many Things that concurr'd towards it. For it cannot be imagined, that upon the Instigation of Two or Three Traders only, who aim'd at a Monopoly of the *Indian* Trade, as some pretend to say, the whole Country would have fallen into so much Distraction; in which People did not only hazard

[1] Wilcomb E. Washburn, *The Governor and the Rebel: A History of Bacon's Rebellion in Virginia* (Chapel Hill: Univ. of North Carolina Press, 1957), pp. 4, 154.

* Reprinted from *The History and Present State of Virginia* (1705).

their Necks by Rebellion: But endeavor'd to ruine a Governour, whom they all entirely loved, and had unanimously chosen; a Gentleman who had devoted his whole Life and Estate to the Service of the Country; and against whom in Thirty Five Years Experience, there had never been one single Complaint. Neither can it be supposed, that upon so slight Grounds, they would make Choice of a Leader they hardly knew, to oppose a Gentleman, that had been so long, and so deservedly the Darling of the People. So that in all Probability there was something else in the Wind, without which the Body of the Country had never been engaged in that Insurrection.

Four Things may be reckon'd to have been

the main Ingredients towards this intestine Commotion, *viz.* First, The extream low Price of Tobacco, and the ill Usage of the Planters in the Exchange of Goods for it, which the Country, with all their earnest Endeavours, could not remedy. Secondly, The Splitting the Colony into Proprieties, contrary to the original Charters; and the extravagant Taxes they were forced to undergo, to relieve themselves from those Grants. Thirdly, The heavy Restraints and Burdens laid upon their Trade by Act of Parliament in *England*. Fourthly, The Disturbance given by the *Indians*. Of all which I beg Leave to speak in their Order.

93. First, Of the low Price of Tobacco, and the Disappointment of all sort of Remedy, I have spoken sufficiently before. Secondly, Of splitting the Country into Proprieties.

King *Charles* the Second, to gratifie some Nobles about him, made Two great Grants out of that Country. These Grants were not of the uncultivated Wood-Land only, but also of Plantations, which for many Years had been seated and improv'd, under the Encouragement of several Charters granted by his Royal Ancestors to that Colony. Those Grants were distinguished by the Names of the Northern and Southern Grants of *Virginia*, and the same Men were concern'd in both. They were kept dormant some Years after they were made, and in the Year 1674 begun to be put in Execution. As soon as ever the Country came to know this, they remonstrated against them; and the Assembly drew up an humble Address to his Majesty, complaining of the said Grants, as derogatory to the previous Charters and Privileges granted to that Colony, by his Majesty and his Royal Progenitors. They sent to *England* Mr. Secretary *Ludwell* and Colonel *Park,* as their Agents to address the King to vacate those Grants. And the better to defray that Charge, they laid a Tax of Fifty Pounds of Tobacco *per* Poll, for Two Years together, over and above all other Taxes, which was an excessive Burden. They likewise laid Amercements of Seventy, Fifty, and Thirty Pounds of Tobacco on every Cause tried throughout the Country. Besides all this, they applied the Ballance, remaining due upon Account of the Two Shilling *per* Hogshead, and Fort Duties, to this Use. Which Taxes and Amercements fell heaviest on the poor People, the Effect of whose Labour wou'd not cloath their Wives and Children. This made them desperately uneasie, especially when, after a whole Year's Patience under all these Pressures, they had no Encouragement from their Agents in *England*, to hope for Remedy; nor any Certainty when they should be eased of those heavy Impositions.

94. Thirdly, Upon the Back of all these Misfortunes came out the Act of 25 *Car. II.* for better securing the Plantation Trade. By this Act several Duties were laid on the Trade from one Plantation to another. This was a new Hardship, and the rather, because the Revenue arising

by this Act, was not applied to the Use of the Plantation wherein it was raised: But given clear away; nay, in that Country it seem'd to be of no other Use, but to create a good Income to the Officers; for the Collector had Half, the Comptroller a Quarter, and the remaining Quarter was subdivided into Salaries, till it was lost.

By the same Act also very great Duties were laid on the Fisheries of the Plantations, if manufactured by the *English* Inhabitants there; while the People of *England* were absolutely free from all Customs. Nay, tho' the Oil, Blubber, and Whale-Bone, which were made by the Inhabitants of the Plantations, were carried to *England* by *English* Men, and in *English* built Ships, yet it was held to a considerable Duty.

95. These were the Afflictions that Country labour'd under, when the Fourth Accident happen'd, *viz.* The Disturbance offer'd by the *Indians* to the Frontiers.

This was occasion'd, First, By the *Indians* on the Head of the Bay. Secondly, By the *Indians* on their own Frontiers.

First, The *Indians* at the Head of the Bay drove a constant Trade with the *Dutch* in *Monadas*, now call'd *New-York;* and, to carry on this, they used to come and return every Year by their Frontiers of *Virginia*, to purchase Skins and Furs of the *Indians* to the Southward. This Trade was carried on peaceably while the *Dutch* held *Monadas;* and the *Indians* used to call on the *English,* to whom they would sell part of their Furs, and with the rest go on to *Monadas*. But after the *English* came to possess that Place, and understood the Advantages the *Virginians* made by the Trade of their *Indians*, they inspired them with such a Hatred to the Inhabitants of *Virginia*, that, instead of coming peaceably to trade with them, as they had done for several Years before, they afterwards never came, but only to commit Robberies and Murders upon the People.

Secondly, The *Indians* upon their own Frontiers were likewise inspir'd with ill Thoughts of 'em. For their *Indian* Merchants had lost a considerable Branch of their Trade they knew not how; and apprehended the Consequences of Sir *William Berkeley's* intended Discoveries, which were espoused by the Assembly, might take away the remaining Part of their Profit. This made them very troublesome to the Neighbour *Indians;* who on their part, observing an unusual Uneasiness in the *English*, and being terrified by their rough Usage, immediately suspected some wicked Design against their Lives, and so fled to their remoter Habitations. This confirm'd the *English* in the Belief, that they had been the Murderers, till at last they provoked them to be so in Earnest.

96. This Addition of Mischief to Minds already full of Discontent, made People ready to vent all their Resentment against the poor *Indians*. There was nothing to be got by Tobacco; neither could they turn any other Manufacture to Advantage; so that most of the poorer Sort were willing to quit their unprofitable Employ-

ments, and go Volunteers against the *Indians*.

At first they flock'd together tumultuously, running in Troops from one Plantation to another without a Head; till at last the seditious Humour of Colonel *Nath. Bacon*, led him to be of the Party. This Gentleman had been brought up at one of the Inns of Court in *England*, and had a moderate Fortune. He was young, bold, active, of an inviting Aspect, and powerful Elocution. In a Word, he was every way qualified to head a giddy and unthinking Multitude. Before he had been Three Years in the Country, he was, for his extraordinary Qualifications, made one of the Council, and in great Honour and Esteem among the People. For this Reason he no sooner gave Countenance to this riotous Mob, but they all presently fix'd their Eyes upon him for their General, and accordingly made their Addresses to him. As soon as he found this, he harangued them publickly. He aggravated the *Indian* Mischiefs, complaining, that they were occasion'd for want of a due Regulation of their Trade. He recounted particularly the other Grievances and Pressures they lay under; and pretended, that he accepted of their Command with no other Intention, but to do them and the Country Service, in which he was willing to encounter the greatest Difficulties and Dangers. He farther assured them, he would never lay down his Arms, till he had revenged their Sufferings upon the *Indians*, and redress'd all their other Grievances.

97. By these Insinuations he wrought his Men into so perfect a Unanimity, that they were one and all at his Devotion. He took care to exasperate them to the utmost, by representing all their Misfortunes. After he had begun to muster them, he dispatch'd a Messenger to the Governour, by whom he aggravated the Mischiefs done by the *Indians*, and desired a Commission of General to go out against them. This Gentleman was in so great Esteem at that Time with the Council, that the Governour did not think fit to give him a flat Refusal: But sent him Word, he would consult the Council, and return him a further Answer.

98. In the mean time, *Bacon* was expeditious in his Preparations, and having all Things in Readiness, began his March, depending on the Authority the People had given him. He would not lose so much Time, as to stay for his Commission; but dispatched several Messengers to the Governour to hasten it. On the other Hand, the Governour, instead of a Commission, sent positive Orders to him to disperse his Men, and come down in Person to him, upon Pain of being declared a Rebel.

99. This unexpected Order, was a great Surprize to *Bacon*, and not a little Trouble to his Men. However, he was resolved to prosecute his first Intentions, depending upon his Strength, and Interest with the People. Nevertheless, he intended to wait upon the Governour, but not altogether defenceless. Pursuant to this Resolution, he took about Forty of his Men down with

him in a Sloop to *James-Town*, where the Governour was with his Council.

100. Matters did not succeed there to Mr. *Bacon's* Satisfaction; wherefore he express'd himself a little too freely. For which being suspended from the Council, he went away again in a Huff with his Sloop and Followers. The Governour fill'd a Long-Boat with Men, and pursued the Sloop so close, that Colonel *Bacon* removed into his Boat to make more Haste. But the Governour had sent up by Land to the Ships at *Sandy-Point*, where he was stopp'd, and sent down again. Upon his Return he was kindly received by the Governour, who, knowing he had gone a Step beyond his Instructions in having suspended him, was glad to admit him again of the Council; after which he hoped all Things might be pacified.

101. Notwithstanding this, Col. *Bacon* still insisted upon a Commission to be General of the Voluntiers, and to go out against the *Indians;* from which the Governour endeavour'd to disswade him, but to no Purpose, because he had some secret Project in View. He had the Luck to be countenanced in his Importunities, by the News of fresh Murder and Robberies committed by the *Indians*. However, not being able to accomplish his Ends by fair Means, he stole privately out of Town; and having put himself at the Head of Six Hundred Voluntiers, marched directly to *James-Town*, where the Assembly was then sitting. He presented himself before the Assembly, and drew up his Men in Battalia before the House wherein they sat. He urged to them his Preparations; and alledged, that if the Commission had not been delay'd so long, the War against the *Indians* might have been finish'd.

102. The Governour resented this insolent Usage worst of all, and now obstinately refused to grant him any thing, offering his naked Breast against the presented Arms of his Followers. But the Assembly, fearing the fatal Consequence of provoking a discontented Multitude ready arm'd, who had the Governour, Council and Assembly entirely in their Power, address'd the Governour to grant *Bacon* his Request. They prepar'd themselves the Commission, constituting him General of the Forces of *Virginia*, and brought it to the Governour to be sign'd.

With much Reluctancy his Excellency sign'd it, and thereby put the Power of War and Peace into *Bacon's* Hands. Upon this he march'd away immediately, having gain'd his End, which was in effect a Power to secure a Monopoly of the *Indian* Trade to himself and his Friends.

103. As soon as General *Bacon* had march'd to such a convenient Distance from *James-Town*, that the Assembly thought they might deliberate with Safety, the Governour, by their Advice, issued a Proclamation of Rebellion against him, commanding his Followers to surrender him, and forthwith disperse themselves. Not contented with this, he likewise gave Orders at the same time, for raising the Militia of the Country against him.

CHAPTER TWO

EDWARDS, WHITEFIELD, AND THE GREAT AWAKENING

As had people in Europe of the sixteenth century and earlier, men in seventeenth-century America had to submit to authority imposed upon them by the state and the church. They did not always submit complacently, and throughout the colonies there were rumblings of discontent and occasional upheavals. Viewed in this context, the sweeping religious revivalism of the 1740's, known as the Great Awakening, marked a defiance of religious authority, the first permanent break from the established order. It signified, says Perry Miller, "the end of the reign over the New England and American mind of a European and scholastic conception of an authority put over men because men were incapable of recognizing their own welfare."

Revivalism came to America from England with John and Charles Wesley, who became the founders of Methodism. Associated with them for a while was the most spellbinding of the revivalists, George Whitefield, who drew enormous crowds wherever he preached, from Georgia to New Hampshire. Revivalism spread rapidly through all of the colonies, especially along the southern frontier and particularly among poorer and less well-educated farmers and artisans. It split the Presbyterian church, planted Methodism, and propagated several Baptist sects. It stimulated humanitarianism (for a short while at least) toward orphans, Indians, and Negro slaves. It led to the founding of four new colleges which in time came to flourish: Brown (Baptist), Princeton (Presbyterian), Rutgers (Dutch Reformed), and Dartmouth (Congregationalist).

In addition to the Wesleys and Whitefield, several evangelists won wide followings. William Tennent, born in Ireland, preached among the Scotch-Irish Presbyterians pouring into the backcountry. Tennent's son, Gilbert, cooperated with a pietist Dutch Reformed revivalist, Theodore Frelinghuysen. In 1740, when the younger Tennent conducted a revival in Boston, a scandalized conservative minister complained that in the "dreadfullest winter I ever saw, people wallowed in the snow night and day for the benefit of his beastly braying." To most orthodox Congregationalists, Tennent and his followers seemed to advocate the antithesis of what religion meant in New England; the revivalists proclaimed that men could attain salvation through conversion rather than works and that even unlettered men could find truth for themselves in the Bible.

Yet it was one of the most ardently Calvinistic adherents to the old Puritan code, Jonathan Edwards, pastor at Northampton, Massachusetts, who became the intellectual leader of the Great Awakening. Edwards is best known as a mystic who could frighten his listeners to repentance through vivid descriptions of hellfire and damnation, but there was more to his thought. His ideas were, as Perry Miller demonstrates in the essay that follows, an important link between the Puritans and the Transcendentalists.

PERRY MILLER:
JONATHAN EDWARDS AND THE GREAT AWAKENING*

[The social historian, if he keeps strictly within the limits of his commitment, has difficulty in dealing with the Great Awakening of 1740. On the surface it seems an inexplicable outburst of neurotic energies which, in most if not all of the colonies, had not been bottled up, which assuredly needed no such spectacular vent. By the time the hysteria died down in the middle of the decade (except for sporadic heavings in Virginia and the Carolinas), it does not appear to have accomplished much in the history of America other than producing acrimonious divisions within the churches—generating "separatists" in New England and a split (ultimately healed) between the "Old" and the "New" sides in the Presbyterian synods of the middle colonies. Efforts have been made to identify the commotion with agrarian protest, with an uprising of debtors against creditors, of the common man against the gentry, or even with the sheer panic resulting from a sore-throat epidemic. None of these accounts offers an "explanation," either of the causes or of the consequences, that strikes one as more than peripheral.

Wherefore I am obliged to argue that this eruption came from sources that elude a merely sociological analysis. At the risk of sacrificing every pretense to scientific respectability, but out of respect for the theme of this volume, I am ready to say that the Great Awakening was the point at which the wilderness took over the task of defining the objectives of the Puritan errand. I am the more prepared to say this because Jonathan Edwards was a child of the wilderness as well as of Puritanism.

Thus there is a certain satisfaction in standing beside the greatest American leader of the Awakening, and trying to make out what he thought he was doing, or what he himself conceived that he had wrought, particularly because in 1750 he became the victim of whatever it was he had done.

Edwards is a mysterious being, and any effort to interpret the Awakening through his view of

it comes to a dead stop before his reticence. This is true, even though in his revival tracts, above all in *A Treatise Concerning Religious Affections,* he analyzed the phenomenon in ultrascientific terms. Still, whatever light we can get upon the cataclysm from the enigmatic Edwards is worth having. This effort at a statement about his relation to the mysterious convulsion was the first in a series delivered at Bennington College in 1949, under the comprehensive title of "American Response to Crisis." My contribution is here reprinted from *America in Crisis,* edited by Daniel Aaron, copyrighted 1952 by Alfred A. Knopf, Inc.

Two or three of my colleagues objected that the Great Awakening was not, in historical terms, a "crisis," such as Nullification, John Brown's raid, or the closing of the banks in 1933. In that sense, it was not. Wherefore it remains something deeper than a specific event: it was a transformation, a blaze that consumed the theological universe of the seventeenth century, and left the American wilderness to rake the embers for a new concept of meaning. Jonathan Edwards survived the holocaust to put his final meditations on the social revolution into the subtle comment of *The Nature of True Virtue.* In the relation of that essay to the story I here briefly recount, we might say that *True Virtue* is almost a satire, utterly opposite in technique to Dr. Johnson's *Vanity of Human Wishes,* but oddly coincident in the lesson. If the absolute validity of the good, just, and honest would no longer prevail, in the wilderness of the Valley no less than in the turmoil of London, how then is modern man to find even the semblance of moral universality?

I have endeavored herein to point out a corollary of Edwards' thinking, though I do not for a moment suppose that he, could he read it, would agree.]

I

Although in the year 1740 some fairly flagrant scenes of emotional religion were being enacted in Boston, it was mainly in the Connecticut Valley that the frenzy raged and whence it spread like a pestilence to the civilized East. The Harvard faculty of that time would indeed have con-

*Reprinted from *Errand Into the Wilderness* (Cambridge: Belknap Press of Harvard Univ. Press, 1956), pp. 153–66 by permission.

sidered the Great Awakening a "crisis," because to them it threatened everything they meant by culture or religion or just common decency. It was a horrible business that should be suppressed and altogether forgotten. Certainly they would not have approved its being dignified as a starting point in a series of great American crises.

As far as they could see, it was nothing but an orgy of the emotions. They called it—in the lexicon of the Harvard faculty this word conveyed the utmost contempt—"enthusiasm." It was not a religious persuasion: it was an excitement of overstimulated passions that understandably slopped over into activities other than the ecclesiastical and increased the number of bastards in the Valley, where already there were too many. And above all, in the Valley lived their archenemy, the deliberate instigator of this crime, who not only fomented the frenzy but was so lost to shame that he brazenly defended it as a positive advance in American culture. To add insult to injury, he justified the Awakening by employing a science and a psychological conception with which nothing they had learned at Harvard had prepared them to cope.

It was certainly a weird performance. Edwards delivered his revival sermons—for example the goriest, the one at Enfield that goes by the title "Sinners in the Hands of an Angry God" and is all that most people nowadays associate with his name—to small audiences in country churches. In these rude structures (few towns had yet prospered enough to afford the Georgian churches of the later eighteenth century which are now the charm of the landscape) the people yelled and shrieked, they rolled in the aisles, they crowded up to the pulpit and begged him to stop, they cried for mercy. One who heard him described his method of preaching: he looked all the time at the bell rope (hanging down from the roof at the other end of the church) as though he would look it in two; he did not stoop to regard the screaming mass, much less to console them.

Of course, in a short time the opinion of the Harvard faculty appeared to be vindicated. In 1740 Edwards had writhing in the churches not only his own people but every congregation he spoke to, and he dominated the entire region. Ten years later he was exiled, thrown out of his church and town after a vicious squabble (the fight against him being instigated by certain of the first citizens, some of them his cousins, who by adroit propaganda mobilized "the people" against him), and no pulpit in New England would invite this terrifying figure. He had no choice but to escape to the frontier, as did so many misfits in American history. He went to Stockbridge, where he eked out his last years as a missionary to a lot of moth-eaten Indians. Because of the works he produced under these—shall we call them untoward?—circumstances, and because he was still the acknowledged leader of the revival movement, he was invited in 1758 to become president of the College of New Jersey (the present-day Princeton), but he died a few weeks after his inauguration, so that his life really belongs to the Connecticut Valley.

One may well ask what makes such a chronicle of frenzy and defeat a "crisis" in American history. From the point of view of the social historian and still more from that of the sociologist it was a phenomenon of mass behavior, of which poor Mr. Edwards was the deluded victim. No sociologically trained historian will for a moment accept it on Edwards' terms—which were, simply, that it was an outpouring of the Spirit of God upon the land. And so why should we, today, mark it as a turning point in our history, especially since thereafter religious revivals became a part of the American social pattern, while our intellctual life developed, on the whole, apart from these vulgar eruptions? The answer is that this first occurrence did actually involve all the interests of the community, and the definitions that arose out of it were profoundly decisive and meaningful. In that perspective Jonathan Edwards, being the most acute definer of the terms on which the revival was conducted and the issues on which it went astray, should be regarded— even by the social historian—as a formulator of propositions that the American society, having been shaken by this experience, was henceforth consciously to observe.

There is not space enough here to survey the Awakening through the vast reaches of the South and the Middle Colonies, nor even to list the intricate consequences for the social ordering of New England. The splintering of the churches and the increase of sectarianism suggest one way in which Americans "responded" to this crisis, and the impulse it gave to education, most notably in the founding of Princeton, is another. Such discussions, however valuable, are external and statistical. We come to a deeper understanding of what this crisis meant by examining more closely a revelation or two from the most self-conscious —not to say the most literate—theorist of the Awakening.

The theme I would here isolate is one with which Edwards dealt only by indirection. He was skilled in the art of presenting ideas not so much by expounding as by vivifying them, and he achieved his ends not only by explicit statement but more often by a subtle shift in emphasis. In this case, it is entirely a matter of divining nuances. Nevertheless, the issue was present throughout the Awakening and, after the temporary manifestations had abated, on this proposition a revolution was found to have been wrought that is one of the enduring responses of the American mind to crisis.

I mean specifically what it did to the conception of the relation of the ruler—political or ecclesiastical—to the body politic. However, before we can pin down this somewhat illusive development, we are confronted with the problem of whether the Great Awakening is properly to be viewed as a peculiarly American phenomenon at all. It would be possible to write about it—as has been done—as merely one variant of a universal occurrence in Western culture. Between about 1730 and 1760 practically all of Western Europe was swept by some kind of religious emotionalism. It was present in Germany, Holland, Switzerland, and France, and in Catholic circles there was an analogous movement that can be interpreted as an outcropping of the same thing: this the textbooks call "Quietism." And most dramatically, it was present in England with the Wesleys, Whitefield, and Methodism.

Once this international viewpoint is assumed, the American outburst becomes merely one among many—a colonial one at that—and we hesitate to speak about it as a crisis in a history specifically American. What was at work throughout the Western world is fairly obvious: the upper or the educated classes were tired of the religious squabbling of the seventeenth century, and turned to the more pleasing and not at all contentious generalities of eighteenth-century rationalism; the spiritual hungers of the lower classes or of what, for shorthand purposes, we may call "ordinary" folk were not satisfied by Newtonian demonstrations that design in the universe proved the existence of God. Their aspirations finally found vent in the revivals, and in each country we may date the end of a Calvinist or scholastic or, in short, a theological era by the appearance of these movements, and thereupon mark what is by now called the era of Pietism or Evangelicalism.

In this frame of reference, the Great Awakening was only incidentally American. It is merely necessary to translate the European language into the local terminology to have an adequate account. In this phraseology, the Great Awakening in New England was an uprising of the common people who declared that what Harvard and Yale graduates were teaching was too academic. This sort of rebellion has subsequently proved so continuous that one can hardly speak of it as a crisis. It is rather a chronic state of affairs. And in this view of it, the uprising of 1740 belongs to the international history of the eighteenth century rather than to any account of forces at work only on this continent.

Told in this way, the story will be perfectly true. Because we talk so much today of the unity of Western European culture, maybe we ought to tell it in these terms, and then stop. But on the other hand there is a curiously double aspect to the business. If we forget about Germany and Holland and even England—if we examine in detail the local history of Virginia, Pennsylvania, and New England—we will find that a coherent narrative can be constructed out of the cultural developments in each particular area. This Awakening can be seen as the culmination of factors long at work in each society, and as constituting, in that sense, a veritable crisis in the indigenous civilization.

II

The church polity established in New England was what today we call congregational. This meant, to put it crudely, that a church was conceived as being composed of people who could certify before other people that they had a religious experience, that they were qualified to become what the founders called "visible saints." The founders were never so foolish as to suppose that everybody who pretended to be a saint *was* a saint, but they believed that a rough approximation of the membership to the covenant of grace could be worked out. A church was composed of the congregation, but these were only the professing Christians. The rest of the community were to be rigorously excluded; the civil magistrate would, of course, compel them to come to the church and listen to the sermon, collect from them a tax to support the preacher, but they could not be actual members. Those who qualified were supposed to have had something happen to them that made them capable—as the reprobate was not—of swearing to the covenant of the church. They were able, as the others were not, *physically* to perform the act.

The basic contention of the founders was that a church is based upon the covenant. Isolated individuals might be Christians in their heart of hearts, but a corporate body could not come into being unless there was this preliminary clasping of hands, this taking of the official oath in the open and before all the community, saying in effect: "We abide by this faith, by this covenant." In scholastic language, the congregation were the "matter" but the covenant was the "form" of the church. They objected above all things to the practice in England whereby churches were made by geography; that a lot of people, merely because they resided in Little Willingdon, should make the church of Little Willingdon, seemed to them blasphemy. That principle was mechanical and unreal; there was no spiritual participation in it—no covenant.

That was why they (or at any rate the leaders and the theorists) came to New England. On the voyage over, in 1630, John Winthrop said to them: "For wee must Consider that wee shall be as a citty vppon a Hill, the eies of all people are vppon us." They had been attempting in England to lead a revolution; after the King's dismissal of Parliament in 1629 it looked as though there was no longer any hope of revolution there, and so they migrated to New England, to build the revolutionary city, where they could exhibit to Englishmen an England that would be as all England should be.

The essence of this conception was the covenant. As soon as they were disembarked, as soon as they could collect in one spot enough people to examine each other and acknowledge that each seemed visibly capable of taking the oath, they incorporated churches—in Boston, Charlestown, and Watertown, and, even in the first decade, in the Connecticut Valley. But we must always remember that even in those first days, when conviction was at its height, and among so highly selected and dedicated numbers as made up the Great Migration, only about one fifth of the population were found able, or could find themselves able, to take the covenant. The rest of them—with astonishingly few exceptions—accepted their exclusion from the churches, knowing that they were not "enabled" and praying for the grace that might yet empower them.

From that point on, the story may seem somewhat peculiar, but after a little scrutiny it becomes an old and a familiar one: it is what happens to a successful revolution. The New Englanders did not have to fight on the barricades or at Marston Moor; by the act of migrating, they *had* their revolution. Obeying the Biblical command to increase and multiply, they had children—hordes of them. Despite the high rate of infant mortality, numbers of these children grew up in New England knowing nothing, except by hearsay and rumor, of the struggles in Europe, never having lived amid the tensions of England. This second generation were, for the most part, good people; but they simply did not have—they could not have—the kind of emotional experience that made them ready to stand up before the whole community and say: "On Friday the 19th, I was smitten while plowing Deacon Jones's meadow; I fell to the earth, and I knew that the grace of God was upon me." They were honest people, and they found it difficult to romanticize about themselves—even when they desperately wanted to.

In 1662 the churches of New England convoked a synod and announced that the children of the primitive church members were included in the covenant by the promise of God to Abraham. This solution was called at the time the halfway covenant, and the very phrase itself is an instructive demonstration of the New Englanders' awareness that their revolution was no longer revolutionary. These children, they decided, must be treated as members of the church, although they had not had the kind of experience that qualified their fathers. They must be subject to discipline and censures, because the body of the saints must be preserved. But just in case the authorities might be mistaken, they compromised by giving to these children only a "halfway" status, which made them members but did not admit them to the Lord's Supper.

This provision can easily be described as a pathetic, where it is not a ridiculous, device. It becomes more comprehensible when we realize that it was an accommodation to the successful revolution. Second and third generations grow up inheritors of a revolution, but are not themselves revolutionaries.

For the moment, in the 1660's and 1670's, the compromise worked, but the situation got worse. For one thing, New England suffered in King Philip's War, when the male population was deci-

mated. Then, in 1684, the charter of Massachusetts was revoked, and after 1691 the colony had to adjust itself to the notion that its governor was imposed by the royal whim, not by the election of the saints. Furthermore, after 1715 all the colonies were prospering economically; inevitably they became more and more concerned with earthly things—rum, land, furs. On the whole they remained a pious people. Could one go back to Boston of 1710 or 1720—when the ministers were asserting that it was as profligate as Babylon—I am sure that one would find it, compared with modern Hollywood, a strict and moral community. Nevertheless, everybody was convinced that the cause of religion had declined. Something had to be done.

As early as the 1670's the ministers had found something they could do: they could work upon the halfway members. They could say to these hesitants: "You were baptized in this church, and if you will now come before the body and 'own' the covenant, then your children can in turn be baptized." Gradually a whole segment of doctrine was formulated that was not in the original theory—which made it possible to address these citizens who were neither outside the pale nor yet snugly inside, which told them that however dubious they might be as saints, visible or invisible, they yet had sufficient will power to perform the public act of "owning the covenant."

With the increasing pressures of the late seventeenth and early eighteenth centuries, the practice of owning the covenant gradually became a communal rite. It was not enough that the minister labored separately with John or Elizabeth to make an acknowledgement the next Sunday: a day was appointed when all the Johns and Elizabeths would come to church and do it in unison, the whole town looking on. It is not difficult to trace through the increasing reënactments of this ceremony a mounting crescendo of communal action that was, to say the least, wholly foreign to the original Puritanism. The theology of the founders conceived of man as single and alone, apart in a corner or in an empty field, wrestling with his sins; only after he had survived this experience in solitude could he walk into the church and by telling about it prove his right to the covenant. But this communal confession—with everybody doing it together, under the urgencies of an organized moment—this was something new, emerging so imperceptibly that nobody recognized it as an innovation (or rather I should say that some did, but they were shouted down) that by the turn of the century was rapidly becoming the focus for the ordering of the spiritual life of the town.

The grandfather of Jonathan Edwards, Solomon Stoddard of Northampton, was the first man who openly extended the practice or renewal of covenant to those who had never been in it at all. In short, when these occasions arose, or when he could precipitate them, he simply took into the church and up to the Lord's Supper everyone who would or could come. He called the periods when the community responded en masse his "harvests," of which he had five: 1679, 1683, 1696, 1712, 1718. The Mathers attacked him for so completely letting down the bars, but in the Connecticut Valley his success was envied and imitated.

The Great Awakening of 1740, seen in the light of this development, was nothing more than an inevitable culmination. It was the point at which the method of owning the covenant became most widely and exultingly extended, in which the momentum of the appeal got out of hand, and the ministers, led by Jonathan Edwards, were forced by the logic of evolution not only to admit all those who would come, but to excite and to drive as many as possible, by such rhetorical stimulations as "Sinners in the Hands of an Angry God," into demanding entrance.

All of this, traced historically, seems natural enough. What 1740 did was present a number of leading citizens, like the Harvard faculty, with the results of a process that had been going on for decades but of which they were utterly unaware until the explosion. Then they found themselves trying to control it or censure it by standards that had in fact been out of date for a century, although they had all that while professed them. In this sense—which I regret to state has generally eluded the social historian—the Great Awakening was a crisis in the New England society.

Professional patriots, especially those of New England descent, are fond of celebrating the Puritans as the founders of the American tradition of rugged individualism, freedom of conscience, popular education, and democracy. The Puritans were not rugged individualists; they did indeed believe in education of a sort, but not in the "progressive" sense; they abhorred freedom of conscience; and they did not believe at all in democracy. They advertised again and again that their church polity was not democratic. The fact that a church was founded on a covenant and that the minister happened to be elected by the mass of the church—this emphatically did not constitute a democracy. John Cotton made the position of the founders crystal clear when he told Lord Say and Seal that God never ordained democracy as a fit government for either church or commonwealth; although at first sight one might suppose that a congregational church was one, in that the people chose their governors, the truth was that "the government is not a democracy, if it be administered, not by the people, but by the governors." He meant, in short, that even though the people did select the person, the office was prescribed; they did not define its functions, nor was it responsible to the will or the whim of the electors. "In which respect it is, that church government is justly denied . . . to be democratical, though the people choose their owne officers and rulers."

The conception ran through every department of the social thinking of New England in the seventeenth century, and persisted in the eighteenth up to the very outbreak of the Awakening. The essence of it always was that though officers may come into their office by the choice of the people, nevertheless the definition of the function, dignity, and prerogatives of the position does not depend upon the intentions or wishes of the electorate, but upon an abstract, divinely given, absolute prescription, which has nothing —in theory—to do with such practical or utilitarian considerations as may, at the moment of the election, be at work among the people.

The divine and immutable pattern of church government was set, once and for all, in the New Testament; likewise, the principles of political justice were given in an eternal and definitive form. The machinery by which a particular man was chosen to fulfill these directives (as the minister was elected by the vote of a congregation, or as John Winthrop was made governor of the Massachusetts Bay Company by a vote of the stockholders) was irrelevant. The existence of such machinery did not mean that the elected officer was in any sense responsible to the electorate. He knew what was expected of him from an entirely other source than their temporary passions; he knew what he, upon becoming such a being, should do—as such!

The classic statement, as is widely known, was the speech that John Winthrop delivered before the General Court on July 3, 1645. He informed the people that the liberty of the subject may sometimes include, as happily it did in Massachusetts, the privilege of selecting this or that person for office, but that it did not therefore mean the right to tell the officer what he should do once he was installed. The liberty that men enjoy in civil society, he said, "is the proper end and object of authority, and cannot subsist without it." It is not a liberty to do what you will, or to require the authority to do what you want: "It is a liberty to do that only which is good, just, and honest." Who defines the good, the just, and the honest? Obviously, the authority does.

In other words, the theory of early New England was basically medieval. Behind it lay the conception of an authoritative scheme of things, in which basic principles are set down once and for all, entirely antecedent to, and utterly without regard for, political experience. The formulation of social wisdom had nothing to do with the specific problems of any one society. It was not devised by a committee on ways and means. Policy was not to be arrived at by a discussion of strategy—for example (in modern terms), shouldn't we use the atomic bomb now? This sort of argument was unavailing, because the function of government was to maintain by authority that which was inherently—and definably —the true, just, and honest.

In Hartford, Connecticut, Samuel Stone, colleague of the great Thomas Hooker, summarized the argument by declaring that congregationalism meant a silent democracy in the face of a speaking aristocracy. There might be something which we call democracy in the form of the church, but the congregation had to keep silent when the minister spoke. And yet, for a hundred years after the death of Hooker, this strange alteration went on inside the institution. The official theory remained, down to the time of Edwards, that the spokesman for the society—be he governor or minister—told the society, by right divine, what it should or should not do, without any regard to its immediate interests, whether emotional or economic. He had laid upon him, in fact, the duty of forgetting such wisdom as he might have accumulated by living as a particular person in that very community or having shared the hopes and qualities of precisely these people.

What actually came about, through the device of renewing the covenant, was something that in fact completely contradicted the theory. (We must remember that the church was, during this century, not merely something "spiritual," but the institutional center of the organized life.) Instead of the minister standing in his pulpit, saying: "I speak; you keep quiet," he found himself, bit by bit, assuming the posture of pleading with the people: "Come, and speak up." He did not know what was happening. He began to find out only in the Great Awakening, when the people at last and multitudinously spoke up.

III

The greatness of Jonathan Edwards is that he understood what had happened. But note this carefully. He was not Thomas Jefferson: he did not preach democracy, and he had no interest whatsoever in any social revolution. He was the child of this aristocratic, medieval system; he was born to the purple, to ecclesiastical authority. Yet he was the man who hammered it home to the people that they *had* to speak up, or else they were lost.

Edwards was a Puritan and a Calvinist. He believed in predestination and original sin and all those dogmas which modern students hold to be outworn stuff until they get excited about them as slightly disguised by Franz Kafka. Edwards did not submit these doctrines to majority vote, and he did not put his theology to the test of utility. But none of this was, in his existing situation, an issue. Granting all that, the question he had to decide was: What does a man do who leads the people? Does he, in 1740, say with the Winthrop of 1645 that they submit to what he as an ontologist tells them is good, just, and honest?

What he realized (lesser leaders of the Awakening, like Gilbert Tennent, also grasped the point, but none with the fine precision of Edwards) was that a leader could no longer stand before the people giving them mathematically or logically impregnable postulates of the eternally good, just, and honest. That might

work in 1640, or in Europe (where to an astonishing extent it still works), but it would not work in the American wilderness. By 1740 the leader had to get down amongst them, and bring them by actual participation into an experience that was no longer private and privileged, but social and communal.

In other words, Edwards carried to its ultimate implication—this constitutes his "relation to his times," which no purely social historian can begin to diagnose—that slowly forming tendency which had been steadily pressing through enlargements of the ceremonial owning of the covenant. He carried it so far that at last everybody could see what it really did mean. Then the Harvard faculty lifted their hands in horror—because this ritual, which they had thought was a segment of the cosmology of John Winthrop, was proved by Edwards' use to flow from entirely alien principles. For this reason, his own Yale disowned him.

IV

In the year 1748 Edwards' revolutionary effort —his leadership of the Awakening must be seen as a resumption of the revolutionary thrust that had been allowed to dwindle in the halfway covenant—was almost at an end. The opposition was mobilizing, and he knew, even before they did, that they would force him out. When the fight had only begun, his patron and friend, his one bulwark in the civil society, Colonel John Stoddard, chief of the militia and warden of the marches, died. There was now no civil power that could protect him against the hatred of the "river gods." Out of all New England, Stoddard had been really *the* outstanding magistrate in that tradition of aristocratic leadership which had begun with Winthrop and had been sustained through a massive succession. As was the custom in New England, the minister gave a funeral sermon; Edwards preached over the corpse of the town's greatest citizen—who happened, in this case, to be also his uncle and his protector. Those who were now certain, with Colonel Stoddard in the ground, that they could get Edwards' scalp were in the audience.

Edwards delivered a discourse that at first sight seems merely one more Puritan eulogy. He told the people that when great and good men like Stoddard are taken away, this is a frown of God's displeasure, which indicates that they ought to reform their vices. This much was sheer convention. But before he came, at the end, to the traditional berating of the populace, Edwards devoted the major part of his oration to an analysis of the function and meaning of authority.

It should be remembered that Winthrop had commenced the New England tradition by telling the people that they had the liberty to do only that which is in itself good, just, and honest; that their liberty was the proper end and object of authority thus defined; that the approbation of the people is no more than the machinery by which God calls certain people to the exercise of the designated powers. And it should also be borne in mind that these powers are given apart from any consideration of the social welfare, that they derive from ethical, theological—a priori—considerations.

Jonathan Edwards says that the supreme qualification of a ruler is that he be a man of "great ability for the management of public affairs." This is his first and basic definition! Let us follow his very words, underlining those which carry revolutionary significance. Rulers are men "of great *natural* abilities" who are versed in discerning "those things wherein the *public welfare or calamity consists,* and the proper *means* to avoid the one and promote the other." They must have lived among men long enough to discover how the mass of them disguise their motives, must have learned how to "unravel the false, subtle arguments and cunning sophistry that is often made use of to defend *iniquity.*" They must be men who have improved their talents by—here are his great criteria—*study, learning, observation,* and *experience.* By these means they must have acquired "skill" in public affairs, "a great understanding of *men and things,* a great *knowledge of human nature,* and of the way of *accommodating* themselves to it." Men are qualified to be rulers if and when they have this "very extensive knowledge of men with whom they are concerned," and when also they have a full and particular understanding "of the *state and circumstances* of the country or people that they have the care of." These are the things—not scholastical articles—that make those in authority "fit" to be rulers!

Look closely at those words and phrases: skill, observation, men and things, state and circumstances—above all, experience! Is this the great Puritan revivalist? It is. And what is he saying, out of the revival? He is telling what in political terms the revival really meant: that the leader has the job of accommodating himself to the realities of human and, in any particular situation, of social, experience. No matter what he may have as an assured creed, as a dogma—no matter what he may be able to pronounce, in the terms of abstract theology, concerning predestination and original sin—as a public leader he must adapt himself to public welfare and calamity. He cannot trust himself to a priori rules of an eternal and uncircumstanced good, just, and honest. There are requirements imposed by the office; authority does indeed consist of propositions that pertain to it, but what are they? They are the need for knowing the people, the knack of properly manipulating and operating them, the wit to estimate their welfare, and the cunning to foresee what may become their calamity.

When we are dealing with so highly conscious an artist as Edwards, we not only are justified in submitting this crucial paragraph to close analysis,

we are criminally obtuse if we do not. So it becomes significant to note what Edwards says immediately after his radically new definition of the ruler. Following his own logic, he is prepared at once to attack what, in the state and circumstances of the Connecticut Valley, constituted the primary iniquity, from which the greatest social calamity might be expected.

He says it without, as we might say, pulling punches: a ruler must, on these considerations of welfare, be unalterably opposed to all persons of "a mean spirit," to those "of a narrow, private spirit that may be found in little tricks and intrigues to promote their private interest, [who] will shamefully defile their hands to gain a few pounds, are not ashamed to hip and bite others, grind the faces of the poor, and screw upon their neighbors; and will take advantage of their authority or commission to line their own pockets with what is fraudulently taken or withheld from others." At the time he spoke, there sat before him the merchants, the sharp traders, the land speculators of Northampton; with the prompt publication of the sermon, his words reached similar gentlemen in the neighboring towns. Within two years, they hounded him out of his pulpit.

The more one studies Edwards, the more one finds that much of his preaching is his condemnation, in this language of welfare and calamity rather than of "morality," of the rising and now rampant businessmen of the Valley. It was Edwards' great perception—and possibly his greatest value for us today is precisely here—that the get-rich-quick schemes of his contemporaries were wrong not from the point of view of the eternal values but from that of the public welfare. The ruler, he said, must know the "theory" of government in such a way that it becomes "natural" to him, and he must apply the knowledge he has obtained by study and observation "to that business, so as to perform it most advantageously and effectually." Here he was, at the moment his protector was gone, when he knew that he was lost, telling those about to destroy him that the great man is he who leads the people by skill and experiential wisdom, and not by making money.

It is further revealing that, after Edwards had portrayed the ruler in this frame of utility and calculation, as he came to his fourth point, he then for the first time said that the authority ought to be a pious man, and only in his fifth and last did he suggest the desirability of a good family. For Winthrop these qualifications had been essentials of the office; for Edwards they were radically submitted to a criterion of utility. "It also contributes to the strength of a man in authority . . . when he is in such circumstances as give him advantage for the exercise of his strength, for the public good; as his being a person of honorable descent, of a distinguished education, his being a man of estate." But note—these are all "useful" because they "add to his strength, and increase his ability and advantage to serve his generation." They serve "in some respect" to make him more effective. It had never occurred to John Winthrop that the silent democracy should imagine for a moment that the elected ruler, in church or state, would be anyone but a pious, educated, honorably descended person, of adequate economic substance. Edwards (who was pious, educated, and very well descended, but not wealthy) says that in some respects these advantages are helps to efficiency.

From one point of view, then, this was what actually was at work inside the hysterical agonies of the Great Awakening. This is one thing they meant: the end of the reign over the New England and American mind of a European and scholastical conception of an authority put over men because men were incapable of recognizing their own welfare. This insight may assist us somewhat in comprehending why the pundits of Boston and Cambridge, all of whom were rational and tolerant and decent, shuddered with a horror that was deeper than mere dislike of the antics of the yokels. To some extent, they sensed that the religious screaming had implications in the realm of society, and those implications they—being businessmen and speculators, as were the plutocracy of Northampton—did not like.

Again, I would not claim too much for Edwards, and I have no design of inscribing him among the prophets of democracy or the New Deal. What he marks—and what he alone could make clear—is the crisis of the wilderness' Awakening, in which the social problem was taken out of the arcana of abstract morality and put into the arena of skill, observation, and accommodation. In this episode, the Americans were indeed participating in an international movement; even so, they came—or Edwards brought them—to sharper formulations of American experience. What the Awakening really meant for Americans was not that they too were behaving like Dutchmen or Germans or Lancashire workmen, but that in the ecstasy of the revival they were discovering, especially on the frontier, where life was the toughest, that they rejected imported European philosophies of society. They were now of themselves prepared to contend that the guiding rule of this society will be its welfare, and the most valuable knowledge will be that which can say what threatens calamity for the state.

When Jonathan Edwards, barely twenty-three years old, was ordained and installed as pastor in the little Connecticut River village of Northampton, the community had long been known for its periodic revivals or spells of "attention to religion." But the last of these had waned away nine years before Edwards arrived in 1727, and he was by no means satisfied with the moral and spiritual level of his flock. By 1734 Edwards had succeeded in generating among his parishioners such a spectacular and contagious revival spirit that Northampton became the fountainhead of the Great Awakening. In a letter, subsequently revised and enlarged, to Benjamin Colman, Edwards described the remarkable occurrences of 1734.

JONATHAN EDWARDS:
NARRATIVE OF SURPRISING CONVERSIONS*

TO THE REV. DR. COLMAN

Reverend and Honored Sir,

Having seen your letter to my honored uncle Williams, of Hatfield, of July 20, wherein you inform him of the notice that has been taken of the late wonderful work of God in this, and some other towns in this county, by the Rev. Dr. Watts and Dr. Guyse of London, and the congregation to which the last of these preached on a monthly day of solemn prayer; as also of your desire to be more perfectly acquainted with it, by

some of us on the spot: And having been since informed by my uncle Williams, that you desire me to undertake it; I would now do it in as just and faithful a manner as in me lies.

The people of the county in general, I suppose are as sober, and orderly, and good sort of people, as in any part of Newengland; and I believe they have been preserved the freest by far, of any part of the country from error, and variety of sects and opinions. Our being so far within the land, at a distance from seaports, and in a corner of the country, has doubtless been one reason why we have not been so much corrupted with vice, as most other parts. But without question the religion, and good order of the country, and their purity in doctrine, has, under

---

* Reprinted from *The Works of President Edwards* (Worcester, Mass.: Isaiah Thomas, 1808), III, 9–18.

God, been very much owing to the great abilities, and eminent piety, of my venerable and honored grandfather Stoddard. I suppose we have been the freest of any part of the land from unhappy divisions, and quarrels in our ecclesiastical and religious affairs, till the late lamentable Springfield contention.

We being much separated from other parts of the province, and having comparatively but little intercourse with them, have from the beginning, till now, always managed our ecclesiastical affairs within ourselves; it is the way in which the country, from its infancy, has gone on by the practical agreement of all, and the way in which our peace and good order has hitherto been maintained.

The town of Northampton is of about eighty-two years standing, and has now about two hundred families; which mostly dwell more compactly together than any town of such a bigness in these parts of the country; which probably has been an occasion that both our corruptions and reformations have been, from time to time, the more swiftly propagated, from one to another, through the town. Take the town in general, and so far as I can judge, they are as rational and understanding a people as most I have been acquainted with: Many of them have been noted for religion, and particularly, have been remarkable for their distinct knowledge in things that relate to heart religion, and Christian experience, and their great regards thereto.

I am the third minister that has been settled in the town: The Reverend Mr. Eleazar Mather, who was the first, was ordained in July 1669. He was one whose heart was much in his work, abundant in labors for the good of precious souls; he had the high esteem and great love of his people, and was blessed with no small success. The Rev. Mr. Stoddard who succeeded him, came first to the town the November after his death, but was not ordained till September 11, 1672, and died February 11, 1728-9. So that he continued in the work of the ministry here from his first coming to town, near sixty years. And as he was eminent and renowned for his gifts and grace; so he was blessed, from the beginning, with extraordinary success in his ministry, in the conversion of many souls. He had five harvests as he called them: The first was about fiftyseven years ago; the second about fiftythree years; the third about forty; the fourth about twentyfour; the fifth and last about eighteen years ago. Some of these times were much more remarkable than others, and the ingathering of souls more plentiful. Those that were about fiftythree, and forty, and twentyfour years ago, were much greater than either the first or the last: But in each of them, I have heard my grandfather say, the greater part of the young people in the town, seemed to be mainly concerned for their eternal salvation.

After the last of these, came a far more degenerate time, (at least among young people) I suppose, than ever before. Mr. Stoddard, indeed, had the comfort before he died, of seeing a time when there was no small appearance of a divine work amongst some, and a considerable ingathering of souls, even after I was settled with him in the ministry, which was about two years before his death; and I have reason to bless God for the great advantage I had by it. In these two years there were near twenty that Mr. Stoddard hoped to be savingly converted; but there was nothing of any general awakening. The greater part seemed to be at that time very insensible of the things of religion, and engaged in other cares and pursuits. Just after my grandfather's death, it seemed to be a time of extraordinary dullness in religion: Licentiousness for some years greatly prevailed among the youth of the town; they were many of them very much addicted to night walking, and frequenting the tavern, and lewd practices, wherein some by their example exceedingly corrupted others. It was their manner very frequently to get together in conventions of both sexes, for mirth and jollity, which they called frolics; and they would often spend the greater part of the night in them, without any regard to order in the families they belonged to: And indeed family government did too much fail in the town. It was become very customary with many of our young people to be indecent in their carriage at meeting, which doubtless would not have prevailed to such a degree, had it not been that my grandfather, through his great age, (though he retained his powers surprisingly to the last) was not so able to observe them. There had also long prevailed in the town a spirit of contention between two parties, into which they had for many years been divided, by which was maintained a jealousy one of the other, and they were prepared to oppose one another in all public affairs.

But in two or three years after Mr. Stoddard's death, there began to be a sensible amendment of these evils; the young people shewed more of a disposition to hearken to counsel, and by degrees left off their frolicing, and grew observably more decent in their attendance on the public worship, and there were more that manifested a religious concern than there used to be.

At the latter end of the year 1733, there appeared a very unusual flexibleness, and yielding to advice, in our young people. It had been too long their manner to make the evening after the sabbath,* and after our public lecture, to be especially the times of their mirth, and company keeping. But a sermon was now preached on the sabbath before the lecture, to shew the evil tendency of the practice, and to persuade them to reform it; and it was urged on heads of families, that it should be a thing agreed upon

---

* It must be noted, that it has never been our manner to observe the evening that follows the sabbath, but that which precedes it, as part of holy time.

among them, to govern their families, and keep their children at home, at these times;...and withal it was more privately moved, that they should meet together the next day, in their several neighborhoods, to know each other's minds: Which was accordingly done, and the motion complied with throughout the town. But parents found little or no occasion for the exercise of government in the case; the young people declared themselves convinced by what they had heard from the pulpit, and were willing of themselves to comply with the counsel that had been given: And it was immediately, and, I suppose, almost universally complied with; and there was a thorough reformation of these disorders thenceforward, which has continued ever since.

Presently after this, there began to appear a remarkable religious concern at a little village belonging to the congregation, called Pascommuck, where a few families were settled, at about three miles distance from the main body of the town. At this place a number of persons seemed to be savingly wrought upon. In the April following, Anno 1734, there happened a very sudden and awful death of a young man in the bloom of his youth; who being violently seized with a pleurisy, and taken immediately very delirious, died in about two days; which (together with what was preached publicly on that occasion) much affected many young people. This was followed with another death of a young married woman, who had been considerably exercised in mind, about the salvation of her soul, before she was ill, and was in great distress, in the beginning of her illness; but seemed to have satisfying evidences of God's saving mercy to her, before her death; so that she died very full of comfort, in a most earnest and moving manner, warning and counselling others. This seemed much to contribute to the solemnizing of the spirits of many young persons; and there began evidently to appear more of a religious concern on people's minds.

In the fall of the year, I proposed it to the young people, that they should agree among themselves to spend the evenings after lectures, in social religion, and to that end to divide themselves into several companies to meet in various parts of the town; which was accordingly done, and those meetings have been since continued, and the example imitated by elder people. This was followed with the death of an elderly person, which was attended with many unusual circumstances, by which many were much moved and affected.

About this time began the great noise that was in this part of the country, about Arminianism, which seemed to appear with a very threatening aspect upon the interest of religion here. The friends of vital piety trembled for fear of the issue; but it seemed, contrary to their fear, strongly to be overruled for the promoting of religion. Many who looked on themselves as in a Christless condition seemed to be awakened by it, with

fear that God was about to withdraw from the land, and that we should be given up to heterodoxy, and corrupt principles; and that then their opportunity for obtaining salvation would be past; and many who were brought a little to doubt about the truth of the doctrines they had hitherto been taught, seemed to have a kind of a trembling fear with their doubts, lest they should be led into bypaths, to their eternal undoing: And they seemed with much concern and engagedness of mind to inquire what was indeed the way in which they must come to be accepted with God. There were then some things said publicly on that occasion, concerning justification by faith alone.

Although great fault was found with meddling with the controversy in the pulpit, by such a person, at that time, and though it was ridiculed by many elsewhere; yet it proved a word spoken in season here; and was most evidently attended with a very remarkable blessing of heaven to the souls of the people in this town. They received thence a general satisfaction with respect to the main thing in question, which they had in trembling doubts and concern about; and their minds were engaged the more earnestly to seek that they might come to be accepted of God, and saved in the way of the gospel, which had been made evident to them to be the true and only way. And then it was, in the latter part of December, that the spirit of God began extraordinarily to set in, and wonderfully to work amongst us; and there were, very suddenly, one after another, five or six persons, who were, to all appearance, savingly converted, and some of them wrought upon in a very remarkable manner.

Particularly, I was surprised with the relation of a young woman, who had been one of the greatest company keepers in the whole town: When she came to me, I had never heard that she was become in any wise serious, but by the conversation I then had with her, it appeared to me, that what she gave an account of, was a glorious work of God's infinite power and sovereign grace; and that God had given her a new heart, truly broken and sanctified. I could not then doubt of it, and have seen much in my acquaintance with her since to confirm it.

Though the work was glorious, yet I was filled with concern about the effect it might have upon others: I was ready to conclude (though too rashly) that some would be hardened by it, in carelessness and looseness of life; and would take occasion from it to open their mouths, in reproaches of religion. But the event was the reverse, to a wonderful degree; God made it, I suppose, the greatest occasion of awakening to others, of any thing that ever came to pass in the town. I have had abundant opportunity to know the effect it had, by my private conversation with many. The news of it seemed to be almost like a flash of lightning, upon the hearts of young people, all over the town, and upon many others. Those persons amongst us, who used to be farthest from seriousness, and that I most feared would make an ill improvement of it, seemed greatly to be awakened with it; many went to talk with her, concerning what she had met with; and what appeared in her seemed to be to the satisfaction of all that did so.

Presently upon this, a great and earnest concern about the great things of religion, and the eternal world, became universal in all parts of the town, and among persons of all degrees, and all ages; the noise amongst the dry bones waxed louder and louder: All other talk but about spiritual and eternal things was soon thrown by; all the conversation in all companies, and upon all occasions, was upon these things only, unless so much as was necessary for people carrying on their ordinary secular business. Other discourse than of the things of religion, would scarcely be tolerated in any company. The minds of people were wonderfully taken off from the world; it was treated amongst us as a thing of very little consequence: They seemed to follow their worldly business, more as a part of their duty, than from any disposition they had to it; the temptation now seemed to lie on that hand, to neglect worldly affairs too much, and to spend too much time in the immediate exercise of religion: Which thing was exceedingly misrepresented by reports that were spread in distant parts of the land, as though the people here had wholly thrown by all worldly business, and betook themselves entirely to reading and praying, and such like religious exercises.

But though the people did not ordinarily neglect their worldly business, yet there then was the reverse of what commonly is: Religion was with all sorts the great concern, and the world was a thing only by the bye. The only thing in their view was to get the kingdom of heaven, and every one appeared pressing into it: The engagedness of their hearts in this great concern could not be hid; it appeared in their very countenances. It then was a dreadful thing amongst us to lie out of Christ, in danger every day of dropping into hell; and what persons, minds were intent upon was to escape for their lives, and to *fly from the wrath to come.* All would eagerly lay hold of opportunities for their souls; and were wont very often to meet together in private houses for religious purposes: And such meetings, when appointed, were wont greatly to be thronged.

There was scarcely a single person in the town, either old or young, that was left unconcerned about the great things of the eternal world. Those that were wont to be the vainest, and loosest, and those that had been most disposed to think and speak slightly of vital and experimental religion, were now generally subject to great awakenings. And the work of conversion was carried on in a most astonishing manner, and increased more and more; souls did, as it were, come by flocks to Jesus Christ. From day to day, for many months together, might be seen evident instances of sinners brought *out of darkness into marvellous light,* and delivered *out of an horrible pit, and from the miry clay, and set upon a rock* with a *new song of praise to God in their mouths.*

This work of God, as it was carried on, and the number of true saints multiplied, soon made a glorious alteration in the town; so that in the spring and summer following, Anno 1735, the town seemed to be full of the presence of God: It never was so full of love, nor so full of joy; and yet so full of distress as it was then. There were remarkable tokens of God's presence in almost every house. It was a time of joy in families on the account of salvation's being brought unto them; parents rejoicing over their children as new born, and husbands over their wives, and wives overtheir husbands. *The goings of God were then seen in his sanctuary, God's day was a delight, and his tabernacles were amiable.* Our public assemblies were then beautiful; the congregation was alive in God's service, every one earnestly intent on the public worship, every hearer eager to drink in the words of the minister as they came from his mouth; the assembly in general were, from time to time, in tears while the word was preached; some weeping with sorrow and distress, others with joy and love, others with pity and concern for the souls of their neighbors.

Our public praises were then greatly enlivened; God was then served in our psalmody, in some measure, in the beauty of holiness. It has been observable, that there has been scarce any part of divine worship, wherein good men amongst us have had grace so drawn forth, and their hearts so lifted up in the ways of God, as in singing his praises: Our congregation excelled all that ever I knew in the external part of the duty before, the men generally carrying regularly, and well, three parts of music, and the women a part by themselves: But now they were evidently wont to sing with unusual elevation of heart and voice, which made the duty pleasant indeed.

In all companies, on other days, on whatever occasions persons met together, Christ was to be heard of, and seen in the midst of them. Our young people, when they met, were wont to spend the time in talking of the excellency and dying love of Jesus Christ, the gloriousness of the way of salvation, the wonderful, free, and sovereign grace of God, his glorious work in the conversion of a soul, the truth and certainty of the great things of God's word, the sweetness of the views of his perfections, &c. And even at weddings, which formerly were merely occasions of mirth and jollity, there was now no discourse of any thing but the things of religion, and no appearance of any but spiritual mirth.

Those amongst us that had been formerly converted, were greatly enlivened and renewed with fresh and extraordinary incomes of the spirit of God; though some much more than others, according to the measure of the gift of Christ:

Many that before had labored under difficulties about their own state, had now their doubts removed by more satisfying experience, and more clear discoveries of God's love.

When this work of God first appeared, and was so extraordinarily carried on amongst us in the winter, others round about us, seemed not to know what to make of it; and there were many that scoffed at, and ridiculed it; and some compared what we called conversion to certain distempers. But it was very observable of many, that occasionally came amongst us from abroad, with disregardful hearts, that what they saw here cured them of such a temper of mind: Strangers were generally surprised to find things so much beyond what they had heard, and were wont to tell others that the state of the town could not be conceived of by those that had not seen it. The notice that was taken of it by the people that came to town on occasion of the court, that sat

here in the beginning of March, was very observable. And those that came from the neighborhood to our public lectures, were for the most part remarkably affected. Many that came to town, on one occasion or other, had their consciences smitten, and awakened, and went home with wounded hearts, and with those impressions that never wore off till they had hopefully a saving issue; and those that before had serious thoughts, had their awakenings and convictions greatly increased. And there were many instances of persons that came from abroad, on visits, or on business, that had not been long here before, to all appearance, they were savingly wrought upon, and partook of that shower of divine blessing that God rained down here, and went home rejoicing; till at length the same work began evidently to appear and prevail in several other towns in the county. . . .

The most famous of Edwards' revival sermons was "Sinners in the Hands of an Angry God," preached at Enfield, Massachusetts, July 8, 1741. One of the congregation present reported, "The assembly appeared deeply impressed and bowed down with an awful conviction of their sin and danger. There was such a breathing of distress and weeping, that the preacher was obliged to speak to the people and desire silence, that he might be heard."

JONATHAN EDWARDS:
SINNERS IN THE HANDS OF AN ANGRY GOD*

DEUTERONOMY XXXII. 35.

. . . Their Foot Shall Slide in Due Time . . .

In this verse is threatened the vengeance of God on the wicked unbelieving Israelites, that were God's visible people, and lived under means of grace; and that notwithstanding all God's wonderful works that he had wrought towards that people, yet remained, as is expressed verse 28, void of counsel, having no understanding in them; and that, under all the cultivations of heaven, brought forth bitter and poisonous fruit; as in the two verses next preceding the text.

The expression that I have chosen for my text, *Their foot shall slide in due time,* seems to imply the following things relating to the punishment and destruction that these wicked Israelites were exposed to.

1. That they were always exposed to destruction; as one that stands or walks in slippery places is always exposed to fall. This is implied

in the manner of their destruction's coming upon them, being represented by their foot's sliding. The same is expressed, Psalm lxxiii. 18 "Surely thou didst set them in slippery places; thou castedst them down into destruction."

2. It implies, that they were always exposed to sudden unexpected destruction. As he that walks in slippery places is every moment liable to fall, he cannot foresee one moment whether he shall stand or fall the next; and when he does fall, he falls at once without warning: Which is also expressed in that Psalm lxxiii. 18, 19. "Surely thou didst set them in slippery places; thou castedst them down into destruction: How are they brought into desolation as in a moment?

3. Another thing implied is, that they are liable to fall of themselves, without being thrown down by the hand of another; as he that stands or walks on slippery ground needs nothing but his own weight to throw him down.

4. That the reason why they are not fallen already, and do not fall now, is only that God's appointed time is not come. For it is said, that when that due time, or appointed time comes, *their foot shall slide.* Then they shall be left to

* Reprinted from *The Works of President Edwards* (Worcester, Mass.: Isaiah Thomas, 1809), VII, 486–97.

fall, as they are inclined by their own weight. God will not hold them up in these slippery places any longer, but will let them go; and then, at that very instant, they shall fall into destruction; as he that stands in such slippery declining ground on the edge of a pit that he cannot stand alone, when he is let go he immediately falls and is lost.

The observation from the words that I would now insist upon is this,

"There is nothing that keeps wicked men at any one moment out of hell, but the mere pleasure of God."

By the mere pleasure of God, I mean his sovereign pleasure, his arbitrary will, restrained by no obligation, hindered by no manner of difficulty, any more than if nothing else but God's mere will had in the least degree or in any respect whatsoever, any hand in the preservation of wicked men one moment.

The truth of this observation may appear by the following considerations.

1. There is no want of power in God to cast wicked men into hell at any moment. Men's hands cannot be strong when God rises up: The strongest have no power to resist him, nor can any deliver out of his hands.

He is not only able to cast wicked men into hell, but he can most easily do it. Sometimes an earthly prince meets with a great deal of difficulty to subdue a rebel, that has found means to fortify himself, and has made himself strong by the numbers of his followers. But it is not so with God. There is no fortress that is any defence from the power of God. Though hand join in hand, and vast multitudes of God's enemies combine and associate themselves, they are easily broken in pieces: They are as great heaps of light chaff before the whirlwind; or large quantities of dry stubble before devouring flames. We find it easy to tread on and crush a worm that we see crawling on the earth; so it is easy for us to cut or singe a slender thread that any thing hangs by; thus easy is it for God, when he pleases, to cast his enemies down to hell. What are we, that we should think to stand before him, at whose rebuke the earth trembles, and before whom the rocks are thrown down?

2. They deserve to be cast into hell; so that divine justice never stands in the way, it makes no objection against God's using his power at any moment to destroy them. Yea, on the contrary, justice calls aloud for an infinite punishment of their sins. Divine justice says of the tree that brings forth such grapes of Sodom, "Cut it down, why cumbereth it the ground?" Luke xiii.7. The sword of divine justice is every moment brandished over their heads, and it is nothing but the hand of arbitrary mercy, and God's mere will, that holds it back.

3. They are already under a sentence of condemnation to hell. They do not only justly deserve to be cast down thither, but the sentence of the law of God, that eternal and immutable rule of righteousness that God has fixed between him and mankind, is gone out against them, and stands against them; so that they are bound over already to hell. John iii. 18. "He that believeth not is condemned already." So that every unconverted man properly belongs to hell; that is his place; from thence he is. John viii. 23. "Ye are from beneath:" And thither he is bound; it is the place that justice, and God's word, and the sentence of his unchangeable law, assign to him.

4. They are now the objects of that very same anger and wrath of God, that is expressed in the torments of hell: And the reason why they do not go down to hell at each moment, is not because God, in whose power they are, is not then very angry with them; as angry, as he is with many of those miserable creatures that he is now tormenting in hell, and do there feel and bear the fierceness of his wrath. Yea, God is a great deal more angry with great numbers that are now on earth; yea, doubtless, with many that are now in this congregation, that, it may be, are at ease and quiet, than he is with many of those that are now in the flames of hell.

So that it is not because God is unmindful of their wickedness, and does not resent it, that he does not let loose his hand and cut them off. God is not altogether such an one as themselves, though they may imagine him to be so. The wrath of God burns against them; their damnation does not slumber; the pit is prepared; the fire is made ready; the furnace is now hot; ready to receive them; the flames do now rage and glow. The glittering sword is whet, and held over them, and the pit hath opened her mouth under them.

5. The devil stands ready to fall upon them, and seize them as his own, at what moment God shall permit him. They belong to him; he has their souls in his possession, and under his dominion. The scripture represents them as his goods, Luke xi. 21. The devils watch them; they are ever by them, at their right hand; they stand waiting for them, like greedy, hungry lions that see their prey, and expect to have it, but are for the present kept back; if God should withdraw his hand by which they are restrained, they would in one moment fly upon their poor souls. The old serpent is gaping for them; hell opens its mouth wide to receive them; and if God should permit it, they would be hastily swallowed up and lost.

6. There are in the souls of wicked men those hellish principles reigning, that would presently kindle and flame out into hell fire, if it were not for God's restraints. There is laid in the very nature of carnal men, a foundation for the torments of hell: There are those corrupt principles, in reigning power in them, and in full possession of them, that are the beginnings of hell fire. These principles are active and powerful, exceeding violent in their nature, and if it were not for the restraining hand of God upon them, they would soon break out, they would flame out after the same manner as the same corruptions, the

same enmity does in the hearts of damned souls, and would beget the same torments in them as they do in them. The souls of the wicked are in scripture compared to the troubled sea, Isaiah lvii. 20. For the present God restrains their wickedness by his mighty power, as he does the raging waves of the troubled sea, saying, "Hitherto shalt thou come, and no further;" but if God should withdraw that restraining power, it would soon carry all before it. Sin is the ruin and misery of the soul; it is destructive in its nature; and if God should leave it without restraint, there would need nothing else to make the soul perfectly miserable. The corruption of the heart of man is a thing that is immoderate and boundless in its fury; and while wicked men live here, it is like fire pent up by God's restraints, whereas if it were let loose, it would set on fire the course of nature; and as the heart is now a sink of sin, so, if sin was not restrained, it would immediately turn the soul into a fiery oven, or a furnace of fire and brimstone.

7. It is no security to wicked men for one moment, that there are no visible means of death at hand. It is no security to a natural man, that he is now in health, and that he does not see which way he should now immediately go out of the world by any accident, and that there is no visible danger in any respect in his circumstances. The manifold and continual experience of the world in all ages, shews that this is no evidence that a man is not on the very brink of eternity, and that the next step will not be into another world. The unseen, unthought of ways and means of persons' going suddenly out of the world are innumerable and inconceivable. Unconverted men walk over the pit of hell on a rotten covering, and there are innumerable places in this covering so weak that they will not bear their weight, and these places are not seen. The arrows of death fly unseen at noonday; the sharpest sight cannot discern them. God has so many different, unsearchable ways of taking wicked men out of the world and sending them to hell, that there is nothing to make it appear, that God had need to be at the expense of a miracle, or go out of the ordinary course of his providence, to destroy any wicked man, at any moment. All the means that there are of sinners' going out of the world, are so in God's hands, and so absolutely subject to his power and determination, that it does not depend at all less on the mere will of God, whether sinners shall at any moment go to hell, than if means were never made use of, or at all concerned in the case.

8. Natural men's prudence and care to preserve their own lives, or the care of others to preserve them, do not secure them a moment. This, divine providence and universal experience do also bear testimony to. There is this clear evidence that men's own wisdom is no security to them from death; that if it were otherwise we should see some difference between the wise and politic men of the world, and others, with regard to their liableness to early and unexpected death; but how is it in fact? Eccles. ii. 16. "How dieth the wise man? As the fool."

9. All wicked men's pains and contrivance they use to escape hell, while they continue to reject Christ, and so remain wicked men, do not secure them from hell one moment. Almost every natural man that hears of hell, flatters himself that he shall escape it; he depends upon himself for his own security; he flatters himself in what he has done, in what he is now doing, or what he intends to do; every one lays out matters in his own mind how he shall avoid damnation, and flatters himself that he contrives well for himself, and that his schemes will not fail. They hear indeed that there are but few saved, and that the bigger part of men that have died heretofore are gone to hell; but each one imagines that he lays out matters better for his own escape than others have done: He does not intend to come to that place of torment; he says within himself, that he intends to take care that shall be effectual, and to order matters so for himself as not to fail.

But the foolish children of men do miserably delude themselves in their own schemes, and in their confidence in their own strength and wisdom, they trust to nothing but a shadow. The bigger part of those that heretofore have lived under the same means of grace, and are now dead, are undoubtedly gone to hell; and it was not because they were not as wise as those that are now alive; it was not because they did not lay out matters as well for themselves to secure their own escape. If it were so that we could come to speak with them, and could enquire of them, one by one, whether they expected, when alive, and when they used to hear about hell, ever to be subjects of that misery, we, doubtless, should hear one and another reply, "No, I never intended to come here: I had laid out matters otherwise in my mind; I thought I should contrive well for myself: I thought my scheme good: I intended to take effectual care; but it came upon me unexpectedly; I did not look for it at that time, and in that manner; it came as a thief: Death outwitted me: God's wrath was too quick for me: O my cursed foolishness! I was flattering myself, and pleasing myself with vain dreams of what I would do hereafter; and when I was saying peace and safety, then sudden destruction came upon me."

10. God has laid himself under no obligation, by any promise, to keep any natural man out of hell one moment: God certainly has made no promises either of eternal life, or of any deliverance or preservation from eternal death, but what are contained in the covenant of grace, the promises that are given in Christ, in whom all the promises are yea and amen. But surely they have no interest in the promises of the covenant of grace that are not the children of the covenant, and that do not believe in any of the promises of the covenant, and have no interest in the Mediator of the covenant.

So that, whatever some have imagined and pretended about promises made to natural mens' earnest seeking and knocking, it is plain and manifest, that whatever pains a natural man takes in religion, whatever prayers he makes, till he believes in Christ, God is under no manner of obligation to keep him a moment from eternal destruction.

So that thus it is, that natural men are held in the hand of God over the pit of hell; they have deserved the fiery pit, and are already sentenced to it; and God is dreadfully provoked, his anger is as great towards them as to those that are actually suffering the executions of the fierceness of his wrath in hell, and they have done nothing in the least, to appease or abate that anger, neither is God in the least bound by any promise to hold them up one moment; the devil is waiting for them, hell is gaping for them, the flames gather and flash about them, and would fain lay hold on them and swallow them up; the fire pent up in their own hearts is struggling to break out; and they have no interest in any Mediator, there are no means within reach that can be any security to them. In short, they have no refuge, nothing to take hold of; all that preserves them every moment is the mere arbitrary will, and uncovenanted, unobliged forbearance of an incensed God.

APPLICATION

The use may be of awakening to unconverted persons in this congregation. This that you have heard is the case of every one of you that are out of Christ. That world of misery, that lake of burning brimstone, is extended abroad under you. There is the dreadful pit of the glowing flames of the wrath of God; there is hell's wide gaping mouth open; and you have nothing to stand upon, nor anything to take hold of: There is nothing between you and hell but the air; it is only the power and mere pleasure of God that holds you up.

You probably are not sensible of this; you find you are kept out of hell, but do not see the hand of God in it; but look at other things, as the good state of your bodily constitution, your care of your own life, and the means you use for your own preservation. But indeed these things are nothing; if God should withdraw his hand, they would avail no more to keep you from falling, than the thin air to hold up a person that is suspended in it.

Your wickedness makes you as it were heavy as lead, and to tend downwards with great weight and pressure towards hell; and if God should let you go, you would immediately sink and swiftly descend and plunge into the bottomless gulf, and your healthy constitution, and your own care and prudence, and best contrivance, and all your righteousness, would have no more influence to uphold you and keep you out of hell, than a spider's web would have to stop a falling

rock. Were it not that so is the sovereign pleasure of God, the earth would not bear you one moment; for you are a burden to it; the creation groans with you; the creature is made subject to the bondage of your corruption, not willingly; the sun does not willingly shine upon you to give you light to serve sin and Satan; the earth does not willingly yield her increase to satisfy your lusts; nor is it willingly a stage for your wickedness to be acted upon; the air does not willingly serve you for breath to maintain the flame of life in your vitals, while you spend your life in the service of God's enemies. God's creatures are good, and were made for men to serve God with, and do not willingly subserve to any other purpose, and groan when they are abused to purposes so directly contrary to their nature and end. And the world would spew you out, were it not for the sovereign hand of him who hath subjected it in hope. There are the black clouds of God's wrath now hanging directly over your heads, full of the dreadful storm, and big with thunder; and were it not for the restraining hand of God, it would immediately burst forth upon you. The sovereign pleasure of God, for the present, stays his rough wind; otherwise it would come with fury, and your destruction would come like a whirlwind, and you would be like the chaff of the summer threshing floor.

The wrath of God is like great waters that are dammed for the present; they increase more and more, and rise higher and higher, till an outlet is given; and the longer the stream is stopped, the more rapid and mighty is its course, when once it is let loose. It is true, that judgment against your evil work has not been executed hitherto; the floods of God's vengeance have been withheld; but your guilt in the mean time is constantly increasing, and you are every day treasuring up more wrath; the waters are continually rising, and waxing more and more mighty; and there is nothing but the mere pleasure of God, that holds the waters back, that are unwilling to be stopped, and press hard to go forward. If God should only withdraw his hand from the flood gate, it would immediately fly open, and the fiery floods of the fierceness and wrath of God, would rush forth with inconceivable fury, and would come upon you with omnipotent power; and if your strength were ten thousand times greater than it is, yea, ten thousand times greater than the strength of the stoutest, sturdiest devil in hell, it would be nothing to withstand or endure it.

The bow of God's wrath is bent, and the arrow made ready on the string, and justice bends the arrow at your heart, and strains the bow, and it is nothing but the mere pleasure of God, and that of an angry God, without any promise or obligation at all, that keeps the arrow one moment from being made drunk with your blood.

Thus are all you that never passed under a great change of heart, by the mighty power of the Spirit of God upon your souls; all that were never born again, and made new creatures, and raised from being dead in sin, to a state of new, and before altogether unexperienced light and life, (however you may have reformed your life in many things, and may have had religious affections, and may keep up a form of religion in your families and closets, and in the houses of God, and may be strict in it) you are thus in the hands of an angry God; it is nothing but his mere pleasure that keeps you from being this moment swallowed up in everlasting destruction.

However unconvinced you may now be of the truth of what you hear, by and by you will be fully convinced of it. Those that are gone from being in the like circumstances with you, see that it was so with them; for destruction came suddenly upon most of them; when they expected nothing of it, and while they were saying, Peace and safety: Now they see, that those things that they depended on for peace and safety were nothing but thin air and empty shadows.

The God that holds you over the pit of hell, much as one holds a spider, or some loathsome insect, over the fire, abhors you, and is dreadfully provoked; his wrath towards you burns like fire; he looks upon you as worthy of nothing else, but to be cast into the fire; he is of purer eyes than to bear to have you in his sight; you are ten thousand times so abominable in his eyes, as the most hateful and venomous serpent is in ours. You have offended him infinitely more than ever a stubborn rebel did his prince: And yet, it is nothing but his hand that holds you from falling into the fire every moment: It is to be ascribed to nothing else, that you did not go to hell the last night; that you was suffered to awake again in this world, after you closed your eyes to sleep: And there is no other reason to be given, why you have not dropped into hell since you arose in the morning, but that God's hand has held you up: There is no other reason to be given why you have not gone to hell, since you have sat here in the house of God, provoking his pure eyes by your sinful wicked manner of attending his solemn worship: Yea, there is nothing else that is to be given as a reason why you do not this very moment drop down into hell.

O sinner! Consider the fearful danger you are in: It is a great furnace of wrath, a wide and bottomless pit, full of the fire of wrath, that you are held over in the hand of that God, whose wrath is provoked and incensed as much against you, as against many of the damned in hell: You hang by a slender thread, with the flames of divine wrath flashing about it, and ready every moment to singe it, and burn it asunder; and you have no interest in any Meditator, and nothing to lay hold of to save yourself, nothing to keep off the flames of wrath, nothing of your own, nothing that you ever have done, nothing that you can do, to induce God to spare you one moment....

Even Benjamin Franklin, not notable for his religiosity, fell under the spell of George Whitefield when the evangelist spent November, 1739, in Philadelphia. In 1788, Franklin, writing as an ailing old man of eighty-two, penned the following recollections.

BENJAMIN FRANKLIN:
WHITEFIELD IN PHILADELPHIA*

In 1739 arriv'd among us from England the Rev. Mr Whitefiel, who had made himself remarkable there as an itinerant Preacher. He was at first permitted to preach in some of our Churches; but the Clergy taking a Dislike to him, soon refus'd him their Pulpits and he was oblig'd to preach in the Fields. The Multitudes of all Sects and Denominations that attended his Sermons were enormous, and it was matter of Speculation to me who was one of the Number, to observe the extraordinary Influence of his Oratory on his Hearers, and how much they admir'd & respected him, notwithstanding his common Abuse of them, by assuring them they were naturally *half Beasts and half Devils*. It was wonderful to see the Change soon made in the Manners of our Inhabitants; from being thoughtless or indifferent about Religion, it seem'd as if all the World were growing Religious; so that one could not walk thro' the Town in an Evening without Hearing Psalms sung in different Families of every Street. And it being found inconvenient to assemble in the open Air, subject to its Inclemencies, the Building of a House to meet in was no sooner propos'd and Persons appointed to receive Contributions, but sufficient Sums were soon receiv'd to procure the Ground and erect the Building which was 100 feet long & 70 broad, about the Size of Westminster-hall; and the Work was car-

* Reprinted from Max Farrand, ed., *Benjamin Franklin's Memoirs* (parallel text edition; Berkeley: Univ. of California Press, 1949), pp. 264–74 by permission.

ried on with such Spirit as to be finished in a much shorter time than could have been expected. Both House and Ground were vested in Trustees, expressly for the Use of any Preacher of any religious Persuasion who might desire to say something to the People of Philadelphia, the Design in building not being to accommodate any particular Sect, but the Inhabitants in general, so that even if the Mufti of Constantinople were to send a Missionary to preach Mahometanism to us, he would find a Pulpit at his Service. (The Contributions being made by People of different Sects promiscuously, Care was taken in the Nomination of Trustees to avoid giving a Predominancy to any Sect, so that one of each was appointed, viz. one Church of England-man, one Presbyterian, one Baptist, one Moravian, &c.). Mr Whitfield, in leaving us, went preaching all the Way thro' the Colonies to Georgia. The Settlement of that Province had lately been begun; but instead of being made with hardy industrious Husbandmen accustomed to Labour, the only People fit for such an Enterprise, it was with Families of broken Shopkeepers and other insolvent Debtors, many of indolent & idle habits, taken out of the Goals, who being set down in the Woods, unqualified for clearing Land, & unable to endure the Hardships of a new Settlement, perished in Numbers, leaving many helpless Children unprovided for. The Sight of their miserable Situation inspired the benevolent Heart of Mr Whitefield with the Idea of building an Orphan House there, in which they might be supported and educated. Returning northward he preach'd up this Charity, & made large Collections; for his Eloquence had a wonderful Power over the Hearts and Purses of his Hearers, of which I myself was an Instance. I did not disapprove of the Design, but as Georgia was then destitute of Materials & Workmen, and it was propos'd to send them from Philadelphia at a great Expence, I thought it would have been better to have built the House here & Brought the Children to it. This I advis'd, but he was resolute in his first Project, and rejected my Counsel, and I thereupon refus'd to contribute. I happened soon after to attend one of his Sermons, in the Course of which I perceived he intended to finish with a Collection, & I silently resolved he should get nothing from me. I had in my Pocket a Handful of Copper Money, three or four silver Dollars, and five Pistoles in Gold. As he proceeded I began to soften, and concluded to give the Coppers. Another Stroke of his Oratory made me asham'd of that, and determined me to give the Silver; & he finish'd so admirably, that I empty'd my Pocket wholly into the Collector's Dish, Gold and all. At this Sermon there was also one of our Club, who being of my Sentiments respecting the Building in Georgia, and suspecting a Collection might be intended, had by Precaution emptied his Pockets before he came from home; towards the Conclusion of the Discourse however, he felt a strong Desire to give, and apply'd to a Neighbour who stood near him to borrow some Money for the Purpose. The Application was unfortunately to perhaps the only Man in the Company who had the firmness not to be affected by the Preacher. His Answer was, *At any other time, Friend Hopkinson, I would lend to thee freely; but not now; for thee seems to be out of thy right Senses.*

Some of Mr Whitfield's Enemies affected to suppose that he would apply these Collections to his own private Emolument; but I, who was intimately acquainted with him, (being employ'd in printing his Sermons and Journals, &c.) never had the least Suspicion of his Integrity, but am to this day decidedly of Opinion that he was in all his Conduct, a perfectly *honest Man.* And methinks my Testimony in his Favour ought to have the more Weight, as we had no religious Connection. He us'd indeed sometimes to pray for my Conversion, but never had the Satisfaction of believing that his Prayers were heard. Ours was a mere civil Friendship, sincere on both Sides, and lasted to his Death.

The following Instance will show something of the Terms on which we stood. Upon one of his Arrivals from England at Boston, he wrote to me that he should come soon to Philadelphia, but knew not where he could lodge when there, as he understood his old kind Host Mr Benezet was remov'd to Germantown. My Answer was; You know my House, if you can make shift with its scanty Accommodations you will be most heartily welcome. He reply'd, that if I made that kind Offer for Christ's sake, I should not miss of a Reward. And I return'd, *Don't let me be mistaken; it was not for Christ sake, but for your sake.* One of our common Acquaintance jocosely remark'd, that knowing it to be the Custom of the Saints, when they receiv'd any favour, to shift the Burthen of the Obligation from off their own Shoulders, and place it in Heaven, I had contriv'd to fix it on Earth.

The last time I saw Mr Whitefield was in London, when he consulted me about his Orphan House Concern, and his Purpose of appropriating it to the Establishment of a College.

He had a loud and clear Voice, and articulated his Words & Sentences so perfectly that he might be heard and understood at a great Distance, especially as his Auditories, however numerous, observ'd the most exact Silence. He preach'd one Evening from the Top of the Court House Steps, which are in the Middle of Market Street, and on the West Side of Second Street which crosses it at right angles. Both Streets were fill'd with his Hearers to a considerable Distance. Being among the hindmost in Market Street, I had the Curiosity to learn how far he could be heard, by retiring backwards down the Street towards the River, and I found his Voice distinct till I came near Front-Street, when some Noise in that Street, obscur'd it. Imagining then a Semi-Circle, of which my Distance should be the Radius, and that it were fill'd with Auditors, to each of whom I allow'd two square feet, I computed that he might well be heard by more than

Thirty-Thousand. This reconcil'd me to the Newspaper Accounts of his having preach'd to 25000 People in the Fields, and to the antient Histories of Generals haranguing whole Armies, of which I had sometimes doubted.

By hearing him often I came to distinguish easily between Sermons newly compos'd, & those which he had often preach'd in the Course of his Travels. His Delivery of the latter was so improv'd by frequent Repetitions, that every Accent, every Emphasis, every Modulation of Voice, was so perfectly well turn'd and well plac'd, that without being interested in the Subject, one could not help being pleas'd with the Discourse, a Pleasure of much the same kind with that receiv'd from an excellent Piece of Musick. This is an Advantage itinerant Preachers have over those who are stationary: as the latter cannot well improve their Delivery of a Sermon by so many Rehearsals.

His Writing and Printing from time to time gave great Advantage to his Enemies. Unguarded Expressions and even erroneous Opinions del[ivere]d in Preaching might have been afterwards explain'd, or qualify'd by supposing others that might have accompany'd them; or they might have been deny'd; But *litera scripta manet*. Critics attack'd his Writings violently, and with so much Appearance of Reason as to diminish the Number of his Votaries, and prevent their Encrease. So that I am of Opinion, if he had never written any thing he would have left behind him a much more numerous and important Sect. And his Reputation might in that case have been still growing, even after his Death; as there being nothing of his Writing on which to found a censure; and give him a lower Character, his Proselites would be left at liberty to feign for him as great a Variety of Excellencies, as their enthusiastic Admiration might wish him to have possessed.

On October 23, 1740, Nathan Cole, an unlettered farmer and carpenter of Kensington parish, Connecticut, heard that Whitefield would preach in Middletown that day. He later wrote:

NATHAN COLE:
WHITEFIELD PREACHES IN MIDDLETOWN*

Now it pleased god to send mr. whitfeld into this land & my hearing of his preaching at philadelphia like one of the old aposels, & many thousands floocking after him to hear ye gospel and great numbers were converted to Christ, i felt the spirit of god drawing me by conviction i longed to see & hear him & wished he would come this way and i soon heard he was come to new york & ye jases [Jerseys] & great multitudes flocking after him under great concern for their Soule & many converted wich brought on my concern more & more hoping soon to see him but next i herd he was on long iland & next at boston & next at northampton & then one morning all on a Suding about 8 or 9 o Clock there came a messenger & said mr. whitfeld preached at hartford & weathersfield yesterday & is to preach at middeltown this morning at 10 o clock i was in my field at work i dropt my tool that i had in my hand & run home & run throu my house & bad my wife get ready quick to goo and hear mr. whitfeld preach at middeltown & run to my pasture for my hors with all my might fearing i should be too late to hear him i brought my hors

home & soon mounted & took my wife up & went forward as fast as i thought ye hors could bear, & when my hors began to be out of breath i would get down & put my wife on ye Saddel & bid her ride as fast as she could & not Stop or Slak for except i bad her & so i would run untill i was almost out of breth & then mount my hors again & so i did severel times to favour my hors we improved every moment to get along as if we was fleeing for our lives all this while fearing we should be too late to hear ye Sarmon for we had twelve miles to ride dubble in littel more then an hour & we went round by the upper housen parish & when we came within about half a mile of ye road that comes down from hartford weathersfield & stepney to middeltown on high land i saw before me a Cloud or fog rising i first thought off from ye great river but as i came nearer ye road i heard a noise something like a low rumbling thunder & i presently found it was ye rumbling of horses feet coming down ye road & this Cloud was a Cloud of dust made by ye running of horses feet it arose some rods into ye air over the tops of ye hills & trees & when i came within about twenty rods of ye road i could see men & horses Sliping along in ye Cloud like shadows & when i came nearer it was like a stedy streem of horses & their riders scarcely a horse more then his length behind another all of

* Reprinted from George Leon Walker, *Some Aspects of the Religious Life of New England with Special Reference to Congregationalists* (New York: Silver, Burdett and Company, 1897), pp. 89–92.

a lather and fome with swet ther breth rooling out of their noistrels in ye cloud of dust every jump every hors semed to go with all his might to carry his rider to hear ye news from heaven for ye saving of their Souls it made me trembel to see ye Sight how ye world was in a strugle i found a vacance between two horses to Slip in my hors & my wife said law our cloaths will be all spoiled see how they look for they was so covered with dust that thay looked allmost all of a color coats & hats & shirts & horses We went down in ye Streem i herd no man speak a word all ye way three mile but evry one presing forward in great hast & when we gat down to ye old meating house thare was a great multitude it was said to be 3 or 4000 of people asembled together we gat of from our horses & shook off ye dust and ye ministers was then coming to the meating house i turned and looked toward ye great river & saw the fery boats running swift forward & backward bringing over loads of people ye ores roed nimble & quick every thing men horses & boats all seamed to be struglin for life ye land & ye banks over ye river lookt black with people & horses all along ye 12 miles i see no man at work in his field but all seamed to be gone—when i see mr. whitfeld come up upon ye Scaffil he looked almost angellical a young slim slender youth before some thousands of people & with a bold undainted countenance & my hearing how god was with him every where as he came along it solumnized my mind & put me in a trembling fear before he began to preach for he looked as if he was Cloathed with authority from ye great god, & a sweet sollome Solemnity sat upon his brow & my hearing him preach gave me a heart wound by gods blessing my old foundation was broken up & i saw that my righteousness would not save me then i was convinced of ye doctrine of Election & went right to quareling with god about it because all that i could do would not save me & he had decreed from Eternity who should be saved & who not i began to think i was not Elected & that god made some for heaven & me for hell & i thought god was not Just in so doing i thought i did not stand on even Ground with others if as i thought i was made to be damned my heart then rose against god exceedigly for his making me for hell now this distress lasted almost two years.

CHAPTER THREE

THE REVOLUTIONARIES

The revolutionary process in America began with the first settlements and continued long after the establishment of independence. Many of the institutional reforms that earlier generations of historians have ascribed to the Revolutionary War actually were on their way to realization early in the eighteenth century; there are a number of historical monographs published in recent years to substantiate the theory. These studies have so revised earlier interpretations that they make an over-all reappraisal of colonial governmental and social institutions and of the role of Enlightenment thought in bringing on the Revolution necessary. Bernard Bailyn, in the essay that follows, undertakes this reappraisal. He suggests that in the quarrel with England, the American leaders sought, by making use of the powerful doctrines of the European Enlightenment, to legitimize both the changes they had already achieved and other changes they still wished to obtain. "In behalf of Enlightenment liberalism," Bailyn concluded, "the Revolutionary leaders undertook to complete, formalize, systematize, and symbolize, what previously had been only partially realized, confused, and disputed matters of fact."

Viewed from this perspective of recent historical research, the great debate between the American leaders and the British takes on new dimensions. The Americans, adept in Enlightenment thought, frequently demonstrated their skill as pamphleteers and polemicists in defending the institutions and practices they so ardently cherished. The struggle went on at many levels, from the sophisticated pamphleteering of the most erudite to the crude outbursts of the Sons of Liberty. As the debate forced the Americans into more and more radical positions, they moved slowly toward the ultimate natural-rights view which in 1776 they proclaimed so boldly and eloquently in the Declaration of Independence.

BERNARD BAILYN: POLITICAL EXPERIENCE AND ENLIGHTENMENT IDEAS IN EIGHTEENTH-CENTURY AMERICA*

The political and social ideas of the European Enlightenment have had a peculiar importance in American history. More universally accepted in eighteenth century America than in Europe, they were more completely and more permanently embodied in the formal arrangements of state and society; and, less controverted, less subject to criticism and dispute, they have lived on more vigorously into later periods, more continuous and more intact. The peculiar force of these ideas in America resulted from many causes. But originally, and basically, it resulted from the circumstances of the pre-Revolutionary period and from the bearing of these ideas on the political experience of the American colonists.

What this bearing was—the nature of the relationship between Enlightenment ideas and early American political experience—is a matter of particular interest at the present time because it is centrally involved in what amounts to a fundamental revision of early American history now under way. By implication if not direct evidence and argument, a number of recent writings have undermined much of the structure of historical thought by which, for a generation or more, we have understood our eighteenth century origins, and in particular have placed new and insupportable pressures on its central assumption concerning the political significance of Enlightenment thought. Yet the need for rather extensive rebuilding has not been felt, in part because the architecture has not commonly been seen as a whole—as a unit, that is, of mutually dependent parts related to a central premise—, in part because the damage has been piecemeal, uncoordinated: here a beam destroyed, there a stone dislodged, the inner supports only slowly weakened and the balance only gradually thrown off. The edifice still stands, mainly, it seems, by habit and by the force of inertia. A brief consideration of the whole, consequently, a survey from a position far enough above the details to see the outlines of the overall architecture, and an attempt, however tentative, to sketch a line—a principle—of reconstruction would seem to be in order.

1

A basic, organizing assumption of the group of ideas that dominated the earlier interpretation of eighteenth century American history is the belief that previous to the Revolution the political experience of the colonial Americans had been roughly analogous to that of the English. Control of public authority had been firmly held by a native aristocracy—merchants and landlords in the north, planters in the south—allied, commonly, with British officialdom. By restricting representation in the provincial assemblies, limiting the franchise, and invoking the restrictive power of the English state, this aristocracy had dominated the governmental machinery of the mainland colonies. Their political control, together with legal devices such as primogeniture and entail, had allowed them to dominate the economy as well. Not only were they successful in engrossing landed estates and mercantile fortunes, but they were for the most part able also to fight off the clamor of yeoman debtors for cheap paper currency, and of depressed tenants for freehold property. But the control of this colonial counterpart of a traditional aristocracy, with its Old World ideas of privilege and hierarchy, orthodoxy in religious establishment, and economic inequality, was progressively threatened by the growing strength of a native, frontier-bred democracy that expressed itself most forcefully in the lower houses of the "rising" provincial assemblies. A conflict between the two groups and ways of life was building up, and it broke out in fury after 1765.

The outbreak of the Revolution, the argument runs, fundamentally altered the old regime. The Revolution destroyed the power of this traditional aristocracy, for the movement of opposition to Parliamentary taxation, 1760–1776, originally controlled by conservative elements, had been taken over by extremists nourished on Enlightenment radicalism, and the once dominant conservative groups had gradually been alienated. The break with England over the question of home rule was part of a general struggle, as Carl Becker put it, over who shall rule at home. Independence gave control to the radicals, who, imposing their advanced doctrines on a traditional society, transformed a rebellious secession into a social revolution. They created a new regime, a reformed society, based on enlightened political and social theory.

But that is not the end of the story; the sequel is important. The success of the enlightened radicals during the early years of the Revolution was notable; but, the argument continues, it was not wholly unqualified. The remnants of the earlier aristocracy, though defeated, had not been eliminated: they were able to reassert themselves in the post-war years. In the 1780's they gradually regained power until, in what amounted to a counter-revolution, they impressed their views indelibly on history in the

* Reprinted from Bernard Bailyn, "Political Experience and Enlightenment Ideas in Eighteenth-Century America," *American Historical Review,* LXVII (January, 1962), 339–51 by permission. This paper was read at the Massachusetts Historical Society, January 12, 1961, and presented in briefer form to the Eleventh International Congress of Historical Sciences, Stockholm, 1960.

new federal constitution, in the revocation of some of the more enthusiastic actions of the earlier Revolutionary period, and in the Hamiltonian program for the new government. This was not, of course, merely the old regime resurrected. In a new age whose institutions and ideals had been born of Revolutionary radicalism, the old conservative elements made adjustments and concessions by which to survive and periodically to flourish as a force in American life.

The importance of this formulation derived not merely from its usefulness in interpreting eighteenth century history. It provided a key also for understanding the entire course of American politics. By its light, politics in America, from the very beginning, could be seen to have been a dialectical process in which an aristocracy of wealth and power struggled with the People, who, ordinarily ill-organized and inarticulate, rose upon provocation armed with powerful institutional and ideological weapons, to reform a periodically corrupt and oppressive polity.

In all of this the underlying assumption is the belief that Enlightenment thought—the reforming ideas of advanced thinkers in eighteenth century England and on the continent—had been the effective lever by which native American radicals had turned a dispute on imperial relations into a sweeping reformation of public institutions and thereby laid the basis for American democracy.

2

For some time, now, and particularly during the last decade, this interpretation has been fundamentally weakened by the work of many scholars working from different approaches and on different problems. Almost every important point has been challenged in one way or another.[1] All arguments concerning politics during the pre-Revolutionary years have been affected by an exhaustive demonstration for one colony, which might well be duplicated for others, that the

franchise, far from having been restricted in behalf of a borough-mongering aristocracy, was widely available for popular use. Indeed, it was more widespread than the desire to use it—a fact which in itself calls into question a whole range of traditional arguments and assumptions. Similarly, the Populist terms in which economic elements of pre-Revolutionary history have most often been discussed may no longer be used with the same confidence. For it has been shown that paper money, long believed to have been the inflationary instrument of a depressed and desperate debtor yeomanry, was in general a fiscally sound and successful means—whether issued directly by the governments or through land banks —not only of providing a medium of exchange but also of creating sources of credit necessary for the growth of an underdeveloped economy and a stable system of public finance for otherwise resourceless governments. Merchants and creditors commonly supported the issuance of paper, and many of the debtors who did so turn out to have been substantial property owners.

Equally, the key writings extending the interpretation into the Revolutionary years have come under question. The first and still classic monograph detailing the inner social struggle of the decade before 1776—Carl Becker's *History of Political Parties in the Province of New York* (1909)—has been subjected to sharp criticism on points of validation and consistency. And, because Becker's book, like other studies of the movement towards revolution, rests upon a belief in the continuity of "radical" and "conservative" groupings, it has been weakened by an analysis proving such terminology to be deceptive in that it fails to define consistently identifiable groups of people. Similarly, the "class" characteristics of the merchant group in the northern colonies, a presupposition of important studies of the merchants in the Revolutionary movement, has been questioned, and along with it the belief that there was an economic or occupational basis for positions taken on the Revolutionary con-

---

[1] The revisionist writings on eighteenth-century America that have recently appeared are voluminous. The main points of reinterpretation will be found in the following books and articles, to which specific reference is made in the paragraphs that follow: Robert E. Brown, *Middle-Class Democracy and the Revolution in Massachusetts, 1691–1780* (Ithaca, 1955); E. James Ferguson, "Currency Finance: An Interpretation of Colonial Monetary Practices," *William and Mary Quarterly*, 3d ser., X (1953), 153–80; Theodore Thayer, "The Land Bank System in the American Colonies," *Journal of Economic History*, XIII (1953), 145–59; Bray Hammond, *Banks and Politics in America from the Revolution to the Civil War* (Princeton, 1957); George A. Billias, *The Massachusetts Land Bankers of 1740* (*University of Maine Studies*, Second Series, No. 74 [Orono, Maine, 1959]); Milton M. Klein, "Democracy and Politics in Colonial New York," *New York History*, XL (1959), 221–46; Oscar and Mary F. Handlin, "Radicals and Conservatives in Massachusetts after Independence," *New England Quarterly*, XVII (1944), 343–55; Bernard Bailyn, "The Blount Papers: Notes on the Merchant 'Class' in the Revolutionary Period," *William and Mary Quarterly*, 3d ser., XI (1954), 98–104; Frederick B. Tolles, "The American Revolution Considered as a Social Movement: A Re-Evaluation," *American Historical Review*, LX (1954–55), 1–12; Robert E. Brown, *Charles Beard and the Constitution: A Critical Analysis of "An Economic Interpretation of the Constitution"* (Princeton, 1956); Forrest McDonald, *We the People: The Economic Origins of the Constitution* (Chicago, 1958); Daniel J. Boorstin, *The Genius of American Politics* (Chicago, 1953), and *The Americans: The Colonial Experience* (N.Y., 1958). References to other writings, and other points of view, will be found in Edmund S. Morgan, "The American Revolution: Revisions in Need of Revising," *William and Mary Quarterly*, 3d ser., XIV (1957), 3–15; and Richard B. Morris, "The Confederation Period and the American Historian," *ibid.*, XIII (1956), 139–56.

troversy. More important, a recent survey of the writings following up J. F. Jameson's classic essay, *The American Revolution Considered as a Social Movement* (1926), has shown how little has been written in the last twenty-five years to substantiate that famous statement of the Revolution as a movement of social reform. Most dramatic of all has been the demolition of Charles Beard's *Economic Interpretation of the Constitution* (1913), which stood solidly for over forty years as the central pillar of the counter-revolution argument: the idea, that is, that the Constitution was a "conservative" document, the polar opposite of the "radical" Articles of Confederation, embodying the interests and desires of public creditors and other moneyed conservatives, and marking the Thermidorian conclusion to the enlightened radicalism of the early Revolutionary years.

Finally, there are arguments of another sort, assertions to the effect that not only did Enlightenment ideas not provoke native American radicals to undertake serious reform during the Revolution, but that ideas have never played an important role in American public life, in the eighteenth century or after, and that the political "genius" of the American people, during the Revolution as later, has lain in their brute pragmatism, their successful resistance to the "distant example and teachings of the European Enlightenment", the maunderings of "garret-spawned European illuminati."

Thus from several directions at once have come evidence and arguments that cloud if they do not totally obscure the picture of eighteenth century American history composed by a generation of scholars. These recent critical writings are of course of unequal weight and validity; but few of them are totally unsubstantiated, almost all of them have some point and substance, and taken together they are sufficient to raise serious doubts about the organization of thought within which we have become accustomed to view the eighteenth century. A full reconsideration of the problems raised by these findings and ideas would of course be out of the question here even if sufficient facts were now available. But one might make at least an approach to the task and a first approximation to some answers to the problems by isolating the central premise concerning the relationship between Enlightenment ideas and political experience and reconsidering it in view of the evidence that is now available.

3

Considering the material at hand, old and new, that bears on this question, one discovers an apparent paradox. There appear to be two primary and contradictory sets of facts. The first and more obvious is the undeniable evidence of the seriousness with which colonial and Revolutionary leaders took ideas, and the deliberateness of their efforts during the Revolution to reshape institutions in their pattern. The more we know about these American provincials the clearer it is that among them were remarkably well informed students of contemporary social and political theory. There never was a dark age that destroyed the cultural contacts between Europe and America. The sources of transmission had been numerous in the seventeenth century; they increased in the eighteenth. There were not only the impersonal agencies of newspapers, books and pamphlets, but also continuous personal contact through travel and correspondence. Above all there were Pan-Atlantic, mainly Anglo-America, interest groups that occasioned a continuous flow of fresh information and ideas between Europe and the mainland colonies in America. Of these, the most important were the English dissenters and their numerous co-denominationalists in America. Located perforce on the left of the English political spectrum, acutely alive to ideas of reform that might increase their security in England, they were, for the almost endemically nonconformist colonists, a rich source of political and social theory. It was largely through nonconformist connections, as Caroline Robbins' recent book, *The Eighteenth-Century Commonwealthman,* suggests, that the commonwealth radicalism of seventeenth century England continued to flow to the colonists, blending, ultimately, with other strains of thought to form a common body of advanced theory.

In every colony and in every legislature there were people who knew Locke and Beccaria, Montesquieu and Voltaire; but perhaps more important, there was in every village of every colony someone who knew such transmitters of English nonconformist thought as Watts, Neal, and Burgh; later Priestly and Price—lesser writers, no doubt, but staunch opponents of traditional authority, and they spoke in a familiar idiom. In the bitterly contentious pamphlet literature of mid-eighteenth century American politics, the most frequently cited authority on matters of principle and theory was not Locke or Montesquieu but *Cato's Letters,* a series of radically libertarian essays written in London in 1720–1723 by two supporters of the dissenting interest, John Trenchard and Thomas Gordon. Through such writers, as well as through the major authors, leading colonists kept contact with a powerful tradition of enlightened thought.

This body of doctrine fell naturally into play in the controversy over the power of the imperial government. For the Revolutionary leaders it supplied a common vocabulary and a common pattern of thought, and, when the time came, common principles of political reform. That reform was sought and seriously if unevenly undertaken, there can be no doubt. Institutions were remodelled, laws altered, practices questioned all in accordance with advanced doctrine on the nature of liberty and of the institutions needed to achieve it. The Americans were acutely aware of being innovators, of bringing mankind a long step forward. They believed that they had so far succeeded in their effort to reshape circumstances to conform to enlightened ideas and ideals that they had introduced a new era in human affairs. And they were supported in this by the opinion of informed thinkers in Europe. The contemporary image of the American Revolution at home and abroad was complex; but no one doubted that a revolution that threatened the existing order and portended new social and political arrangements had been made, and made in the name of reason.

4

Thus, throughout the eighteenth century there were prominent, politically active Americans who were well aware of the development of European thinking, took ideas seriously, and during the Revolution deliberately used them in an effort to reform the institutional basis of society. This much seems obvious. But paradoxically, and less obviously, it is equally true that many, indeed most, of what these leaders considered to be their greatest achievements during the Revolution—reforms that made America seem to half the world like the veritable heavenly city of the eighteenth century philosophers—had been matters of fact before they were matters of theory and Revolutionary doctrine.

No reform in the entire Revolution appeared of greater importance to Jefferson than the Virginia acts abolishing primogeniture and entail. This action, he later wrote, was part of "a system by which every fibre would be eradicated of antient or future aristocracy; and a foundation laid for a government truly republican." But primogeniture and entail had never taken deep roots in America, not even in tidewater Virginia. Where land was cheap and easily available such legal restrictions proved to be encumbrances profiting few. Often they tended to threaten rather than secure the survival of the family, as Jefferson himself realized when in 1774 he petitioned the Assembly to break an entail on his wife's estate on the very practical, untheoretical, and common ground that to do so would be "greatly to their [the petitioners'] interest and that of their Families." The legal abolition of primogeniture and entail during and after the Revolution was of little material consequence. Their demise had been effectively decreed years before by the circumstances of life in a wilderness environment.

Similarly, the disestablishment of religion—a major goal of Revolutionary reform—was carried out, to the extent that it was, in circumstances so favorable to it that one wonders not how it was done but why it was not done more thoroughly. There is no more eloquent, moving testimony to Revolutionary idealism than the Virginia Act for Establishing Religious Freedom: it is the essence of Enlightenment faith. But what did it, and the disestablishment legislation that had preceded it, reform? What had the establishment of

religion meant in pre-Revolutionary Virginia? The Church of England was the state church, but dissent was tolerated well beyond the limits of the English Acts of Toleration. The law required nonconformist organizations to be licensed by the government, but dissenters were not barred from their own worship nor penalized for failure to attend the Anglican communion, and they were commonly exempted from parish taxes. Noncomformity excluded no one from voting and only the very few Catholics from enjoying public office. And when the itinerary of revivalist preachers led the establishment to contemplate more restrictive measures, the Baptists and Presbyterians advanced to the point of arguing publicly, and pragmatically, that the toleration they had so far enjoyed was an encumbrance, and that the only proper solution was total liberty: in effect, disestablishment.

Virginia was if anything more conservative than most colonies. The legal establishment of the Church of England was in fact no more rigorous in South Carolina and Georgia: it was considerably weaker in North Carolina. It hardly existed at all in the middle colonies (there was of course no vestige of it in Pennsylvania), and where it did, as in four counties of New York, it was either ignored or had become embattled by violent opposition well before the Revolution. And in Massachusetts and Connecticut, where the establishment, being nonconformist according to English law, was legally tenuous to begin with, tolerance in worship and relief from church taxation had been extended to the major dissenting groups early in the century, resulting well before the Revolution in what was, in effect if not in law, a multiple establishment. And this had been further weakened by the splintering effect of the Great Awakening. Almost everywhere the Church of England, the established church of the highest state authority, was embattled and defensive —driven to rely more and more on its missionary arm, the Society for the Propagation of the Gospel, to sustain it against the cohorts of dissent.

None of this had resulted from Enlightenment theory; it had been created by the mundane exigencies of the situation: by the distance that separated Americans from ecclesiastical centers in England and the continent; by the never-ending need to encourage immigration to the colonies; by the variety, the mere numbers, of religious groups, each by itself a minority, forced to live together; and by the weakness of the coercive powers of the state: its inability to control the social forces within it.

Even more gradual and less contested had been the process by which government in the colonies had become government by the consent of the governed. What has been proved about the franchise in early Massachusetts—that it was open for practically the entire free adult male population—can be proved to a lesser or greater extent for all the colonies. But the extraordinary breadth of the franchise in the American colonies had not resulted from popular demands: there had been no cries for universal manhood suffrage, nor were there popular theories claiming, or even justifying, general participation in politics. Nowhere in eighteenth century America was there "democracy"—middle-class or otherwise—as we use the term. The main reason for the wide franchise was that the traditional English laws limiting suffrage to freeholders of certain competences proved in the colonies, where freehold property was almost universal, to be not restrictive but widely permissive.

Representation would seem to be different, since before the Revolution complaints had been voiced against the inequity of its apportioning, especially in the Pennsylvania and North Carolina assemblies. But these complaints were based on an assumption that would have seemed natural and reasonable almost nowhere else in the western world: the assumption that representation in governing assemblages was a proper and rightful attribute of people as such—of regular units of population, or of populated land—rather than the privilege of particular groups, institutions, or regions. Complaints there were, bitter ones. But they were complaints claiming injury and deprivation, not abstract ideals or unfamiliar desires. They assumed from common experience the normalcy of regular and systematic representation. And how should it have been otherwise? The colonial assemblies had not, like ancient parliaments, grown to satisfy a monarch's need for the support of particular groups or individuals or to protect the interests of a social order, and they had not developed insensibly from precedent to precedent. They had been created at a stroke, and they were in their composition necessarily regular and systematic. Nor did the process, the character, of representation as it was known in the colonies derive from theory. For colonial Americans, representation had none of the symbolic and little of the purely deliberative qualities which, as a result of the Revolutionary debates and of Burke's speeches, would become celebrated as "virtual." To the colonists it was direct and actual: it was, most often, a kind of agency, a delegation of powers, to individuals commonly required to be residents of their constituencies and, often, bound by instructions from them—with the result that eighteenth-century American legislatures frequently resembled, in spirit if not otherwise, those "ancient assemblies" of New York, composed, the contemporary historian William Smith wrote, "of plain, illiterate husbandmen, whose views seldom extended farther than to the regulation of highways, the destruction of wolves, wild cats, and foxes, and the advancement of the other little interests of the particular counties which they were chosen to represent." There was no theoretical basis for such direct and actual representation. It had been created and was continuously reinforced by the pressure of local politics in the colonies and by the political circumstances in England, to which the colonists had found it necessary to send closely instructed, paid representatives—agents, so called—from the very beginning.

But franchise and representation are mere mechanisms of government by consent. At its heart lies freedom from executive power, from the independent action of state authority, and the concentration of power in representative bodies and elected officials. The greatest achievement of the Revolution was of course the repudiation of just such state authority and the transfer of power to popular legislatures. No one will deny that this action was taken in accordance with the highest principles of Enlightenment theory. But the way had been paved by fifty years of grinding factionalism in colonial politics. In the details of pre-Revolutionary American politics, in the complicated maneuverings of provincial politicians seeking the benefits of government, in the patterns of local patronage and the forms of factional groupings, there lies a history of progressive alienation from the state which resulted, at least by the 1750's, in what Professor Robert Palmer has lucidly described as a revolutionary situation: a condition ". . . in which confidence in the justice or reasonableness of existing authority is undermined; where old loyalties fade, obligations are felt as impositions, law seems arbitrary, and respect for superiors is felt as a form of humiliation; where existing sources of prestige seem undeserved . . . and government is sensed as distant, apart from the governed and not really 'representing' them." Such a situation had developed in mid-eighteenth century America, not from theories of government or Enlightenment ideas but from the factional opposition that had grown up against a succession of legally powerful, but often cynically self-seeking, inept, and above all politically weak officers of state.

Surrounding all of these circumstances and in various ways controlling them is the fact that that great goal of the European revolutions of the late eighteenth century, equality of status before the law—the abolition of legal privilege—had been reached almost everywhere in the American colonies at least by the early years of the eighteenth century. Analogies between the upper strata of colonial society and the European aristocracies are misleading. Social stratification existed, of course; but the differences between aristocracies in eighteenth century Europe and in America are more important than the similarities. So far was legal privilege, or even distinction, absent in the colonies that where it existed it was an open sore of festering discontent, leading not merely, as in the case of the Penn family's hereditary claims to tax exemption, to formal protests, but, as in the case of the powers enjoyed by the Hudson River land magnates, to violent opposition as well. More important, the colonial aristocracy, such as it was, had no formal, institutional role in government. No public office or function was legally a prerogative of birth. As there were no social orders in the eyes of the law, so there were no governmental bodies to represent them. The only claim that has been made to the contrary is that, in effect, the governors' Councils constituted political institutions in the service of the aristocracy. But this claim—of dubious value in any case because of the steadily declining political importance of the Councils in the eighteenth century—cannot be substantiated. It is true that certain families tended to dominate the Councils, but they had less legal claim to places in those bodies than certain royal officials who, though hardly members of an American aristocracy, sat on the Councils by virtue of their office. Councillors could be and were removed by simple political maneuver. Council seats were filled either by appointment or election: when appointive, they were vulnerable to political pressure in England; when elective, to the vagaries of public opinion at home. Thus on the one hand it took William Byrd II three years of maneuvering in London to get himself appointed to the seat on the Virginia Council vacated by his father's death in 1704, and on the other, when in 1766 the Hutchinson faction's control of the Massachusetts Council proved unpopular it was simply removed wholesale by being voted out of office at the next election. As there were no special privileges, no peculiar group possessions, manners, or attitudes to distinguish Councillors from other affluent Americans, so there were no separate political interests expressed in the Councils as such. Councillors joined as directly as others in the factional disputes of the time, associating with groups of all sorts, from minute and transient American opposition parties to massive English-centered political syndicates. A century before the Revolution and not as the result of anti-aristocratic ideas, the colonial aristocracy had become a vaguely defined, fluid group whose power—in no way guaranteed, buttressed, or even recognized in law—was competitively maintained and dependent on continuous, popular support.

Other examples could be given. Were written constitutions felt to be particular guarantees of liberty in enlightened states? Americans had known them in the form of colonial charters and governors' instructions for a century before the Revolution; and after 1763, seeking a basis for their claims against the constitutionality of specific acts of Parliament, they had been driven, out of sheer logical necessity and not out of principle, to generalize that experience. But the point is perhaps clear enough. Major attributes of enlightened politics had developed naturally, spontaneously, early in the history of the American colonies, and they existed as simple matters of social and political fact on the eve of the Revolution.

5

But if all of this is true, what did the Revolution accomplish? Of what real significance were the ideals and ideas? What was the bearing of Enlightenment thought on the political experience of eighteenth century Americans?

Perhaps this much may be said. What had evolved spontaneously from the demands of place and time was not self-justifying, nor was it universally welcomed. New developments, however gradual, were suspect by some, resisted in part, and confined in their effects. If it was true that the establishment of religion was everywhere weak in the colonies and that in some places it was even difficult to know what was orthodoxy and what was not, it was nevertheless also true that faith in the idea of orthodoxy persisted and with it belief in the propriety of a privileged state religion. If, as a matter of fact, the spread of freehold tenure qualified large populations for voting, it did not create new reasons for using that power nor make the victims of its use content with what, in terms of the dominant ideal of balance in the state, seemed a disproportionate influence of "the democracy." If many colonists came naturally to assume that representation should be direct and actual, growing with the population and bearing some relation to its distribution, crown officials did not, and they had the weight of precedent and theory as well as of authority with them and hence justification for resistance. If state authority was seen increasingly as alien and hostile and was forced to fight for survival within an abrasive, kaleidoscopic factionalism, the traditional idea nevertheless persisted that the common good was somehow defined by the state and that political parties or factions—organized opposition to established government—were seditious. A traditional aristocracy did not in fact exist; but the assumption that superiority was indivisible, that social eminence and political influence had a natural affinity to each other, did. The colonists instinctively conceded to the claims of the well-born and rich to exercise public office, and in this sense politics remained aristocratic. Behavior had changed—had had to change—with the circumstances of everyday life; but habits of mind and the sense of rightness lagged behind. Many felt the changes to be *away from,* not *towards,* something: that they represented deviance; that they lacked, in a word, legitimacy.

This divergence between habits of mind and belief on the one hand and experience and behavior on the other was ended at the Revolution. A rebellion that destroyed the traditional sources of public authority called forth the full range of advanced ideas. Long settled attitudes were jolted and loosened. The grounds of legitimacy suddenly shifted. What had happened was seen to have been good and proper, steps in the right direction. The glass was half full, not half empty; and to complete the work of fate and nature, further thought must be taken, theories tested, ideas applied. Precisely because so many social and institutional reforms had already taken place in America, the Revolutionary movement there, more than elsewhere, was a matter of doctrine, ideas, and comprehension.

And so it remained. Social change and social conflict of course took place during the Revolutionary years; but the essential developments of the period lay elsewhere, in the effort to think through and to apply under the most favorable, permissive, circumstances enlightened ideas of government and society. The problems were many, often unexpected and difficult; some were only gradually perceived. Social and personal privilege, for example, could easily be eliminated —it hardly existed; but what of the impersonal privileges of corporate bodies? Legal orders and ranks within society could be outlawed without creating the slightest tremor, and executive power with equal ease subordinated to the legislative: but how was balance within a polity to be achieved? What were the elements to be balanced and how were they to be separated? It was not even necessary formally to abolish the interest of state as a symbol and determinant of the common good; it simply dissolved: but what was left to keep clashing factions from tearing a government apart? The problems were pressing, and the efforts to solve them mark the stages of Revolutionary history.

In behalf of Enlightenment liberalism the Revolutionary leaders undertook to complete, formalize, systematize, and symbolize, what previously had been only partially realized, confused, and disputed matters of fact. Enlightenment ideas were not instruments of a particular social group, nor did they destroy a social order. They did not create new social and political forces in America. They released those that had long existed, and vastly increased their power. This completion, this rationalization, this symbolization, this lifting into consciousness and endowing with high moral purpose inchoate, confused elements of social and political change— this was the American Revolution.

Parliament, by imposing new taxes upon the colonies after 1763, precipitated a sharp exchange of constitutional arguments. James Otis, the moderate spokesman for the Boston merchants, argued in *The Rights of British Colonists* (1764) that Parliament was exceeding its authority. Soame Jenyns, a member both of Parliament and of the Board of Trade and Plantations, penned a vigorous British answer.

SOAME JENYNS:
OBJECTIONS TO THE TAXATION . . . BRIEFLY CONSIDER'D*

The right of the Legislature of Great Britain to impose taxes on her American colonies, and the expediency of exerting that right in the present conjuncture, are propositions so indisputably clear that I should never have thought it necessary to have undertaken their defence, had not many arguments been lately flung out both in papers and conversation, which with insolence equal to their absurdity deny them both. As these are usually mixt up with several patriotic and favorite words such as liberty, property, Englishmen, etc., which are apt to make strong impressions on that more numerous part of mankind who have ears but no understanding, it will not, I think, be improper to give them some answers. To this, therefore, I shall singly confine myself, and do it in as few words as possible, being sensible that the fewest will give least trouble to myself, and probably most information to my reader.

The great capital argument which I find on this subject, and which, like an elephant at the head of a Nabob's army, being once overthrown must put the whole into confusion, is this; that no Englishman is, or can be taxed, but by his own consent: by which must be meant one of these three propositions; either that no Englishman can be taxed without his own consent as an individual; or that no Englishman can be taxed without the consent of the persons he chuses to represent him; or that no Englishman can be taxed without the consent of the majority of all those who are elected by himself and others of his fellow subjects to represent them. Now let us impartially consider whether any one of these propositions are in fact true: if not, then this wonderful structure which has been erected upon them falls at once to the ground, and like another Babel, perishes by a confusion of words, which the builders themselves are unable to understand.

First then, that no Englishman is or can be taxed but by his own consent as an individual: this is so far from being true, that it is the very reverse of truth; for no man that I know of is taxed by his own consent, and an Englishman, I believe, is as little likely to be so taxed as any man in the world.

Secondly, that no Englishman is or can be taxed but by the consent of those persons whom he has chose to represent him. For the truth of

* Reprinted from [Soame Jenyns], *The objections to the taxation of our American colonies, by the legislature of Great Britain, briefly consider'd* (London: 1765).

this I shall appeal only to the candid representatives of those unfortunate counties which produce cyder, and shall willingly acquiesce under their determination.

Lastly, that no Englishman is or can be taxed without the consent of the majority of those who are elected by himself and others of his fellow subjects to represent them. This is certainly as false as the other two; for every Englishman is taxed, and not one in twenty represented: copyholders, leaseholders, and all men possessed of personal property only, chuse no representatives; Manchester, Birmingham, and many more of our richest and most flourishing trading towns send no members to Parliament, consequently cannot consent by their representatives, because they chuse none to represent them; yet are they not Englishmen? or are they not taxed?

I am well aware that I shall hear Lock, Sidney, Selden, and many other great names quoted to prove that every Englishman, whether he has a right to vote for a representative or not, is still represented in the British Parliament, in which opinion they all agree. On what principle of commonsense this opinion is founded I comprehend not, but on the authority of such respectable names I shall acknowledge its truth; but then I will ask one question, and on that I will rest the whole merits of the cause. Why does not this imaginary representation extend to America as well as over the whole Island of Great Britain? If it can travel three hundred miles, why not three thousand? if it can jump over rivers and mountains, why cannot it sail over the ocean? . . . Are they not alike British subjects? are they not Englishmen? or are they only Englishmen when they sollicit for protection, but not Englishmen when taxes are required to enable this country to protect them?

But it is urged that the colonies are by their charters placed under distinct Governments each of which has a legislative power within itself, by which alone it ought to be taxed; that if this privilege is once given up, that liberty which every Englishman has a right to, is torn from them, they are all slaves, and all is lost.

The liberty of an Englishman is a phrase of so various a signification, having within these few years been used as a synonymous term for blasphemy, bawdy, treason, libels, strong beer, and cyder, that I shall not here presume to define its meaning; but I shall venture to assert what it cannot mean; that is, an exemption from taxes imposed by the authority of the Parliament of Great Britain; nor is there any charter that ever pretended to grant such a privilege to any colony in America; and had they granted it, it could have had no force; their charters being derived from the Crown, and no charter from the Crown can possibly supersede the right of the whole legislature. Their charters are undoubtedly no more than those of all corporations, which impower them to make bye-laws, and raise duties for the purposes of their own police, for ever subject to the superior authority of Parliament; and in some of their charters the manner of exercising these powers is specifyed in these express words, 'according to the course of other corporations in Great Britain'. And therefore they can have no more pretence to plead an exemption from this parliamentary authority, than any other corporation in England.

It has been moreover alledged, that though Parliament may have power to impose taxes on the colonies, they have no right to use it, because it would be an unjust tax; and no supreme or legislative power can have a right to enact any law in its nature unjust. To this, I shall only make this short reply, that if Parliament can impose no taxes but what are equitable, and if the persons taxed are to be the judges of that equity, they will in effect have no power to lay any tax at all. No tax can be imposed exactly equal on all, and if it is not equal it cannot be just, and if it is not just, no power whatever can impose it; by which short syllogism all taxation is at end; but why it should not be used by Englishmen on this side the Atlantic as well as by those on the other, I do not comprehend.

Thus much for the right. Let us now a little inquire into the expediency of this measure, to which two objections have been made; that the time is improper, and the manner wrong.

As to the first, can any time be more proper to require some assistance from our colonies, to preserve to themselves their present safety, than when this country is almost undone by procuring it? Can any time be more proper to impose some tax upon their trade, than when they are enabled to rival us in our manufactures, by the encouragement and protection which we have given them? Can any time be more proper to oblige them to settle handsome incomes on their Governors, than when we find them unable to procure a subsistence on any other terms than those of breaking all their instructions, and betraying the rights of their sovereign? Can there be a more proper time to compel them to fix certain salaries on their judges, than when we see them so dependent on the humours of their Assemblies, that they can obtain a livelihood no longer than *quam diu se male gesserint?* Can there be a more proper time to force them to maintain an army at their expence, than when that army is necessary for their own protection, and we are utterly unable to support it? Lastly; can there be a more proper time for this mother country to leave off feeding out of her own vitals these children whom she has nursed up, than when they are arrived at such strength and maturity as to be well able to provide for themselves, and ought rather with filial duty to give some assistance to her distresses?

As to the manner; that is, the imposing taxes on the colonies by the authority of Parliament, it is said to be harsh and arbitrary; and that it would have been more consistent with justice, at least with maternal tenderness, for administration here to have settled quotas on each of the colonies, and have then transmitted them with injunctions that the sums allotted should be immediately raised by their respective legislatures, on the penalty of their being imposed by Parliament in case of their non-compliance. But was this to be done, what would be the consequence? Have their Assemblies shewn so much obedience to the orders of the Crown, that we could reasonably expect that they would immediately tax themselves on the arbitrary command of a minister? Would it be possible here to settle those quotas with justice, or would any one of the colonies submit to them, were they ever so just? Should we not be compared to those Roman tyrants, who used to send orders to their subjects to murder themselves within so many hours, most obligingly leaving the method to their own choice, but on their disobedience threatening a more severe fate from the hands of an executioner? And should we not receive votes, speeches, resolutions, petitions, and remonstrances in abundance, instead of taxes? In short, we either have a right to tax the colonies, or we have not. If Parliament is possessed of this right, why should it be exercised with more delicacy in America than it has ever been even in Great Britain itself? If on the other hand, they have no such right, sure it is below the dignity as well as justice of the Legislature to intimidate the colonies with vain threats, which they have really no right to put in execution.

One method indeed has been hinted at, and but one, that might render the exercise of this power in a British Parliament just and legal, which is the introduction of representatives from the several colonies into that body; but as this has never seriously been proposed, I shall not here consider the impracticability of this method, nor the effects of it if it could be practised; but only say that I have lately seen so many specimens of the great powers of speech of which these American gentlemen are possessed, that I should be much afraid that the sudden importation of so much eloquence at once, would greatly endanger the safety and government of this country; or in terms more fashionable, though less understood, this our most excellent Constitution. If we can avail ourselves of these taxes on no other condition, I shall never look upon it as a measure of frugality; being perfectly satisfyed that in the end it will be much cheaper for us to pay their army than their orators.

I cannot omit taking notice of one prudential reason which I have heard frequently urged against this taxation of the colonies, which is this: That if they are by this means impoverished, they will be unable to purchase our manufactures, and consequently we shall lose that trade from which the principal benefit which we receive from them must arise. But surely, it requires but little sagacity to see the weakness of this argument; for should the colonies raise taxes for the purposes of their own government and protection, would the money so raised be immediately annihilated?

What some pay, would not others receive? Would not those who so receive it, stand in need of as many of our manufactures, as those who pay? Was the army there maintained at the expence of the Americans, would the soldiers want fewer coats, hats, shirts, or shoes than at present? Had the judges salaries ascertained to them, would they not have occasion for as costly perriwigs, or robes of as expensive scarlet, as marks of their legal abilities, as they now wear in their present state of dependency? Or had their Governors better incomes settled on them for observing their instructions, than they can now with difficulty obtain for disobeying them, would they expend less money in their several Governments, or bring home at their return less riches to lay out in the manufactories of their native country?

It has been likewise asserted that every shilling which our colonies can raise either by cultivation or commerce, finally centers in this country; and therefore it is argued we can acquire nothing by their taxation, since we can have no more than their all; and whether this comes in by taxes or by trade, the consequence is the same. But allowing this assertion to be true, which it is not, yet the reasoning upon it is glaringly false: for surely it is not the same whether the wealth derived from these colonies flows immediately into the coffers of the public, or into the pockets of individuals from whence it must be squeezed by various domestic taxes before it can be rendered of any service to the nation. Surely it is by no means the same, whether this money brought in by taxes enables us to diminish part of that enormous debt contracted by the last expensive war, or whether coming in by trade it enables the merchant, by augmenting his influence together with his wealth, to plunge us into new wars and new debts for his private advantage.

From what has been here said, I think that not only the right of the legislature of Great Britain to impose taxes on her colonies, not only the expediency, but the absolute necessity of exercising that right in the present conjuncture, has been so clearly though concisely proved, that it is to be hoped that in this great and important question all parties and factions, or in the more polite and fashionable term, all connections will most cordially unite; that every member of the British Parliament, whether in or out of humour with Administration, whether he has been turned out because he has opposed, or whether he opposes because he has been turned out, will endeavour to the utmost of his power to support this measure. A measure which must not only be approved by every man who has any property or common sense, but which ought to be required by every English subject of an English Administration.

FINIS

Upon receiving Jenyns' pamphlet, James Otis authored a sharp and witty rebuttal which he published in London.

JAMES OTIS:
CONSIDERATIONS ON BEHALF OF THE COLONISTS*

My Lord,

I have read the *Opusculum* of the celebrated Mr. J——s, called "Objections to the taxation of the colonies by the legislature of Great-Britain, briefly considered." In obedience to your lordships commands, I have thrown a few thoughts on paper, all indeed that I have patience on this melancholy occasion to collect. The gentleman thinks it is "absurd and insolent" to question the expediency and utility of a public measure. He seems to be an utter enemy to the freedom of enquiry after truth, justice and equity. He is not only a zealous advocate for pusilanimous and passive obedience, but for the most implicit faith in the dictatorial mandates of power. The "several patriotic favorite words *liberty, property, Englishmen,* &c." are in his opinion of no use but to "make strong impressions on the more numerous part of mankind who have ears but no understanding." The times have been when the favorite terms *places, pensions,* French *louis d'ors* and English *guineas,* have made very undue impressions on those who have had votes and voices, but neither honor nor conscience—who have deserved of their country an ax, a gibbet or a halter, much better than a star or garter. The grand aphorism of the British constitution, that *"no Englishman is or can be taxed but by his own consent in person or by his deputy"* is absurdly denied. In a *vain* and most *insolent* attempt to disprove this fundamental principle he exhibits a curious specimen of his talent at chicanery and quibbling. He says that "no man that he knows of is taxed by his own consent." It is a maxim at this day, that the crown by royal prerogative alone can levy no taxes on the subject. One who had any "understanding as well as ears" would from thence be led to conclude that some men must consent to their taxes before they can be imposed. It has been commonly understood, at least since the glorious revolution, that the consent of the British Lords and Commons, i. e. of all men within the realm, must be obtained to make a tax legal there. The consent of the lords and commons of his majesty's ancient and very respectable kingdom of Ireland, has also been deemed necessary to a taxation of the subjects there. The consent of the two houses of assembly in the colonies has till lately been also thought requisite for the taxation of his majesty's most dutiful and loyal subjects, the colonists. *Sed tempora mutantur.*

I would ask Mr. J——s, if when a knight of a shire, or burgess of a borough, civil military, or errant, possessed of a real estate, votes for a land tax, he does not tax himself and consent to such tax? And does he not by thus voting, tax himself as an *identic* individual, as well as some of his silly neighbours, who "may have ears but no understanding", and be therefore in great danger at a future election of chusing an empty *individuum vagum* to manage their highest concerns. Tis much to be lamented that these people with "ears but without understanding" by certain vulgar low arts, may be as easily led to elect a state auctioneer or a vote seller as the wisest and most upright man in the three kingdoms. We have known some of them cry Hosanna to the man who under God and his King had been their saviour, and the next day appear ready to crucify him. However, when a man in Europe or America, votes a tax on his constituents, if he has any estate, he is at the same time taxing himself, and that by *his own consent;* and of all this he must be conscious, unless we suppose him to be void of common sense.

No one ever contended that "the consent of the very person he chuses to represent him," nor that "the consent of the majority of those who are chosen by himself, *and* others of his fellow subjects to represent them," should be obtained before a tax can be rightfully levied. The pitiful chicanery here, consists wholly in substituting *and* for *or.* If for *and,* we read *or,* as the great Mr. J——s himself inadvertently reads it a little afterwards, the same proposition will be as strictly true, as any political aphorism or other general maxim whatever, the theorems of Euclid not excepted; namely, *"that no Englishman, nor indeed any other freeman, is or can be rightfully taxed, but by his own actual consent in person, or by the majority of those who are chosen by himself or others his fellow subjects to represent the whole people."*

Right reason and the spirit of a free constitution require that the representation of the whole people should be as equal as possible. A perfect equality of representation has been thought impracticable; perhaps the nature of human affairs will not admit of it. But it most certainly might and ought to be more equal than it is at present in any state. The difficulties in the way of a perfectly equal representation are such that in most countries the poor people can

* [James Otis], *Considerations on Behalf of the Colonists in a Letter to a Noble Lord* (London: 1765).

obtain none. The lust of power and unreasonable domination are, have been, and I fear ever will be not only impatient of, but above, controul. The Great love pillows of down for their own heads, and chains for those below them. Hence 'tis pretty easy to see how it has been brought about, that in all ages despotism has been the general tho' not quite universal government of the world. No good reason however can be given in any country why every man of a sound mind should not have his vote in the election of a representative. If a man has but little property to protect and defend, yet his life and liberty are things of some importance. Mr. J——s argues only from the vile abuses of power to the continuance and increase of such abuses. This it must be confessed is the common logic of modern politicians and vote sellers. To what purpose is it to ring everlasting changes to the colonists on the cases of Manchester, Birmingham and Sheffield, who return no members? If those now so considerable places are not represented, they ought to be. Besides the counties in which those respectable abodes of tinkers, tinmen, and pedlars lie, return members, so do all the neighbouring cities and boroughs. In the choice of the former, if they have no vote, they must naturally and necessarily have a great influence. I believe every gentlemen of a landed estate, near a flourishing manufactory, will be careful enough of its interests. Tho' the great India company, as such, returns no members, yet many of the company are returned, and their interests have been ever very carefully attended to.

Mr. J——s says, "by far the major part of the inhabitants of Great Britain are non electors." The more is the pity. "Every Englishman, he tells us, is taxed, and yet not one in twenty is represented." To be consistent, he must here mean that not one in twenty, votes for a representative. So a small minority rules and governs the majority. This may for those in the saddle be clever enough, but can never be right in theory. What *ab initio* could give an absolute unlimitted right to one twentieth of a community, to govern the other nineteen by their sovereign will and pleasure? Let him, if his intellects will admit of the research, discover how in any age or country this came to be the fact. Some favourite modern systems must be given up or maintained by a clear open avowal of these *Hobbeian* maxims, viz. That dominion is rightfully founded on force and fraud.—That power universally confers right. —That war, bloody war, is the real and natural state of man—and that he who can find means to buy, sell, enslave, or destroy, the greatest number of his own species, is right worthy to be dubbed a modern politician and an hero. Mr. J——s has a little contemptible flirt at the sacred names of Selden, Locke, and Sidney. But their ideas will not quadrate with the half-born sentiments of a courtier. Their views will never center in the *paricranium* of a modern politician. The characters of their writings cannot be affected by the crudities of a ministerial mercenary pamphleteer. He next proceeds to give us a specimen of his agility in leaping hedge and ditch, and of paddling through thick and thin. He has proved himself greatly skilled in the ancient and honourable sciences of horse-racing, bruising, boxing, and cock-fighting. He offers to "risk the merits of the whole cause on a single question." For this one question he proposes a string of five or six.—To all which I say he may be a very great statesman, but must be a very indifferent lawyer. A good lawyer might risque the merit of a cause on answers, but never would rest it on mere interrogatories. A multiplicity of questions, especially such as most of Mr. J——s's, only prove the folly and impertinence of the querist. Answers may be evidence, but none results from questions only. Further, to all his queries, let him take it for a full answer, that his way of reasoning would as well prove that the British house of commons, in fact, represent all the people on the globe, as those in America. True it is, that from the nature of the British constitution, and also from the idea and nature of a supreme legislature, the parliament represents the whole community or empire, and have an undoubted power, authority, and jurisdiction, over the whole; and to their final decisions the whole must and ought peaceably to submit. They have an undoubted right also to unite to all intents and purposes, for benefits and burthens, a dominion, or subordinate jurisdiction to the mother state, if the good of the whole requires it. But great tenderness has been shown to the customs of particular cities and boroughs, and surely as much indulgence might be reasonably expected towards large provinces, the inhabitants of which have been born and grown up under the modes and customs of a subordinate jurisdiction. But in a case of necessity, the good of the whole requires, that not only private interests, but private passions, should give way to the public. But all this will not convince me of the reasonableness of imposing heavy taxes on the colonists, while their trade and commerce are every day more than ever restricted. Much less will it follow, that the colonists are, in fact, represented in the house of commons. Should the British empire one day be extended round the whole world, would it be reasonable that all mankind should have their concerns managed by the electors of old Sarum, and the "occupants of the Cornish barns and ale-houses," we sometimes read of? We who are in the colonies, are by common law, and by act of parliament, declared entitled to all the privileges of the subjects within the realm. Yet we are heavily taxed, without being, in fact, represented.—In all trials here relating to the revenue, the admiralty courts have jurisdiction given them, and the subject may, at the pleasure of the informer, be deprived of a trial by his peers. To do as one would be done by, is a divine rule. Remember Britons, when you shall be taxed without your consent, and tried without a jury, and have an army quartered in private families, you will have little to hope or to fear! But I must not lose sight of my man, who sagaciously asks "if the colonists are English when they solicit protection, but not Englishmen when taxes are required to enable *this country* to protect them?" I ask in my turn, when did the colonies solicit for protection? They have had no occasion to solicit for protection since the happy accession of our gracious Sovereign's illustrious family to the British diadem. His Majesty, the father of all his people, protects all his loyal subjects of every complexion and language, without any particular solicitation. But before the ever memorable revolution, the Northern Colonists were so far from receiving protection from Britain, that every thing was done from the throne to the footstool, to cramp, betray, and ruin them: yet against the combined power of France, Indian savages, and the corrupt administration of those times, they carried on their settlements, and under a mild government for these eighty years past, have made them the wonder and envy of the world.

These colonies may, if truly understood, be one day the last resource, and best barrier of Great Britain herself. Be that as it may, sure I am that the colonists never in any reign received protection but from the king and parliament. From most others they had nothing to ask, but every thing to fear. Fellow subjects in every age, have been the temporal and spiritual persecutors of fellow subjects. The Creoles follow the example of some politicians and ever employ a negroe to whip negroes. As to "that country," and "protection from that country," what can Mr. J——s mean? I ever thought the territories of the same prince made one country. But if, according to Mr. J——s, Great Britain is a distinct country from the British colonies, what is that *country* in nature more than this country? The same sun warms the people of Great Britain and us; the same summer chears, and the same winter chills.

Mr. J——s says, "the liberty of an Englishman is a phrase of so various a signification, having, within these few years, been used as synonymous terms for *blasphemy, bawdy, treason, libels, strong beer,* and *cyder,* that he shall not here presume to define its meaning." I commend his prudence in avoiding the definition of *English Liberty;* he has no idea of the thing.

But your lordship may, if you please, look back to the most infamous times of the Stuarts, ransack the history of all their reigns, examine the conduct of every debauchee who counted for one in that parliament, which Sidney says, "drunk or sober," passed the five mile act, and you will not find any expressions equal in absurdity to those of Mr. J——s. He sagely affirms, "that there can be no pretence to plead any exemption from parliamentary authority." I know of no man in America who understands himself, that ever pleaded or pretended any such exemption. I think it our greatest happiness in the true and genuine sense of law and the constitution, to be subject to, and controulable by, parliamentary

authority. But Mr. J——s will scribble about *"our American colonies."* Whose colonies can the creature mean? The minister's colonies? No surely. Whose then, his own? I never heard he had any colonies. *Nec gladio noc arcu, nec astu vicerunt.* He must mean his Majesty's American colonies. His Majesty's colonies they are, and I hope and trust ever will be; and that the true native inhabitants, as they ever have been, will continue to be, his Majesty's most dutiful and loyal subjects. Every garetteer, from the environs of Grubstreet, to the purlieus of St. James's, has lately talked of *his* and *my* and *our* colonies, and of the *rascally colonists,* and of *yokeing* and *curbing* the *cattle,* as they are by some politely called, at "this present now and very nascent crisis."*

I cannot see why the American peasants may not with as much propriety speak of their cities of London and Westminster, of their isles, of Britain, Ireland, Jersey, Guernsey, Sark, and the Orcades, and of the "rivulets and runlets thereof,"† and consider them all but as appendages to their sheep-cots and goose-pens. But land is land, and men should be men. The property of the former God hath given to the possessor. These are *sui juris,* or slaves and vassals; there neither is nor can be any medium. Mr. J——s would do well once in his life to reflect that were it not for *our* American colonies, he might at this "present crisis," been but the driver of a baggage cart, on a crusade to the holy sepulchre, or sketching caracatura's, while the brave were bleeding and dying for their country. He gives us three or four sophistical arguments, to prove that "no taxes can be exactly equal." "If not exactly equal on all, then not just." "Therefore no taxes at all can be justly imposed." This is arch. But who before ever dreamt that no taxes could be imposed, because a mathematical exactness or inequality is impracticable. . . .

Mr. J——s asks, if "any time can be more proper to impose taxes on their *trade,* than when they are enabled to rival us in our manufactures, by the encouragement and protection *we* have given them?" Who are WE? It is a miracle he had not affirmed, that the colonies rival Great Britain in trade also. His not asserting this, is the only glimmering of modesty or regard to truth, discoverable through his notable performance. As the colonists are British subjects, and confessedly on all hands entitled to the same rights and privileges, with the subjects born within the realm, I challenge Mr. J——s or any one else to give even the colour of a conclusive reason, why the colonists are not entitled to the same means and methods of obtaining a living with their fellow-subjects in the islands.

Can any one tell me why trade, commerce, arts, sciences and manufactures, should not be as free for an American as for an European? Is there

---

* Pownall's Administration of the Colonies. Second edition.

† Terms used in our obsolete charters.

any thing in the laws of nature and nations, any thing in the nature of our allegiance that forbids a colonist to push the manufacture of iron much beyond the making a horse-shoe or a hob nail? We have indeed "files for our mattocks, and for our coulters, and for our forks, and for our axes, to sharpen our goads," and to break our teeth; but they are of the manufacture of Europe: I never heard of one made here. Neither the refinements of Montesquieu nor the imitations of the servile Frenchified half thinking mortals, who are so fond of quoting him, to prove, that it is a law of Europe, to confine the trade and manufactures to the mother state, "to prohibit the colonists erecting manufactories," and "to interdict all commerce between them and other countries," will pass with me for any evidence of the rectitude of this custom and procedure. The *Administrator* has worked these principles up to "fundamental maxims of police at this crisis." The *Regulator* hath followed him, and given broad hints that all kinds of American manufactures will not only be discountenanced, but even prohibited, as fast as they are found to interfere with those of Britain. That is, in plain English, we shall do nothing that they can do for us. This is kind!—And what they cannot do for us, we are permitted to do for ourselves. Generous! . . . .

The reaction of the Newport, Rhode Island, populace to the Stamp Act was described by William Almy in a letter to a Boston friend.

WILLIAM ALMY:
THE STAMP AFFAIR IN NEWPORT*

NEWPORT Aug't 29th 1765. Thursday My Worthy Friend,—In my Last I Promis'd to give you the Particulars of Our Transactions here, Concerning the Stamp Affair, Which I now shall Endeavour to do. In the First Place I'll Just Inform you Concerning Mr. Martin Howard Jun'r and Doct'r Moffatt, who was hung in Efigy with the Stamp Master. Mr. Howard and the Doctor you must know have made themselves very Busy with their Pen (By all accounts) In Writing Against the Colonies and in Favour of the Stamp Act etc.

In the Morning of the 27th Inst. between five and six a Mob Assembled and Erected a Gallows near the Town House and then Dispers'd, and about Ten A Clock Reassembled and took the Effigys of the Above Men and the Stamp Master and Carted them up Thames Street, then up King Street to the said Gallows where they was hung up by the Neck and Suspended near 15 feet in the Air, And on the Breast of the Stamp Master, was this Inscription THE STAMP MAN, and holding in his Right hand the Stamp Act, And upon the Breast of the Doct'r was wrote, THAT INFAMOUS, MISCREATED, LEERING JACOBITE DOCT'R MURFY. In his Right hand was a folded Letter with this Direction To that Mawgazeene of Knowledge Doct'r Muffy in Rhode Island, And on the Same Arm was Wrote, If I had but Rec'd this Letter from the Earl of Bute But One Week sooner. And upon a strip of paper hanging out of his Mouth was wrote It is too late Martinius to Retract, for we are all Aground.

And upon Mr. Howard's Breast was wrote, THAT FAWNING, INSIDIOUS, INFAMOUS MISCREANT AND PARACIDE MARTINIUS SCRIBLERIUS, and upon his Right Arm was wrote, THE ONLY FILIAL PEN. Upon his left Arm was wrote, CURS'D AMBITION AND YOUR CURSED CLAN HAS RUIN'D ME and upon the Same Arm a little Below was this, WHAT THO' I BOAST OF INDEPENDANCE POSTERITY WILL CURSE MY MEMORY. And upon one of the Posts of the Gallows was wrote, We have an Heriditary Indefeasible Right to a Halter, Besides we Encourag'd the Growth of Hemp you know. And Underneath that, was a New Song (made upon the Occasion) which I have here Inclos'd. And upon the other Post was wrote That Person who shall Efface this Publick Mark of Resentment will be Deem'd an Enemy to liberty and Accordingly meet with Proper Chastisement. And about five A Clock in the Afternoon they made a Fire under the Gallows which Consum'd the Effigy's, Gallows and all, to Ashes. I forgot to tell you that a Boot hung over the Doctor's Shoulder with the Devil Peeping out of it etc. I've Inclos'd you a piece that was Stuck up in the Town House at the Same time. And after the Effigys were Burnt the Mob Dispers'd and we thought it was all Over. But last Night about Dusk they all Muster'd again, and first they went to Martin Howard's, and Broke Every Window in his house Frames and all, likewise Chairs Tables, Pictures and every thing they cou'd come across. they also Saw'd down two Trees which Stood before his door and Bro't them and Stuck them up in two Great Guns which have been

* Reprinted from Massachusetts Historical Society, *Proceedings* (Boston: Massachusetts Historical Society, 1923), LV, 235–37 by permission.

fix'd at the Bottom of the Parade some Years as Posts. when they found they had Entirely Demolish'd all his Furniture and done what damage they Cou'd, They left his house, and Proceeded to Doctor Moffatts where they Behav'd much in the Same Manner. I Can't say which Came off the Worst, For all the Furniture of Both Houses were Entirely Destroy'd, Petitions of the houses broke down, Fences Level'd with the Ground and all the Liquors which were in Both Houses were Entirely Lost. Dear Doctor this Moment I've Rec'd a Peace of News which Effects me so Much that I Cant write any More, which is the Demolition of your worthy Daddy's house and Furniture etc. But I must Just let you know that the Stamp Master has Resign'd, the Copy of His Resignation and Oath I now Send you. I hope, my Friend You'll Send me the Particulars of your daddy's Misfortune. Yours for Ever.

W. Almy.

[Addressed] To Doctor Elisha Story, Boston.

A NEW SONG

He who for a Post or Base sordid Pelf
His Country Betrays, Makes a Rope for himself.
Of this an Example, Before you we Bring

In these Infamous Rogues, Who in Effigy Swing.

Huzza my Brave Boys, Ev'ry man Stand his Ground
With Liberty's Praise, Let the Welkin Resound
Eternal Disgrace On those Miscreants Fall
Who Through Pride or for Wealth, Wou'd Ruin us All.

Let us Make wise Resolves and to them stand strong
Your Puffs and your Vapours will Ne'er last Long
To Ma[i]ntain Our Just Rights, Every Measure Pursue
To Our King we'll be Loyal, To Ourselves we'll be True.

Those Blessings Our Fathers, Obtain'd by their Blood
We are Justly Oblig'd to Our sons to make Good
All Internal Taxes let us then Nobly spurn
These Effigy's First, The Next The Stamp Papers Burn.

CHORUS

Sing Tantarara, Burn All, Burn All
Sing Tantarara, Burn All.

The crisis that was to culminate in the American Revolution unfolded rapidly in December, 1773, when colonists reacted vigorously against the shipping into their ports of cheap, but taxed, British East India Company tea. On December 15, the following document was drafted in New York; a mass meeting of the Sons of Liberty ratified it the next day.

THE ASSOCIATION OF THE SONS OF LIBERTY OF NEW YORK*

The following association is signed by a great number of the principal gentlemen of the city, merchants, lawyers, and other inhabitants of all ranks, and it is still carried about the city to give an opportunity to those who have not yet signed, to unite with their fellow citizens, to testify their abhorrence to the diabolical project of enslaving America.

THE ASSOCIATION OF THE SONS OF LIBERTY OF NEW YORK

It is essential to the freedom and security of a free people, that no taxes be imposed upon them but by their own consent, or their representatives. For "What property have they in that which another may, by right, take when he pleases to himself?" The former is the undoubted right of Englishmen, to secure which they expended millions and sacrificed the lives of thousands. And yet, to the astonishment of all the world, and the grief of America, the Commons of Great Britain, after the repeal of the memorable and detestable Stamp Act, reassumed the power of imposing taxes on the American colonies; and insisting on it as a necessary badge of parliamentary supremacy, passed a bill, in the seventh year of his present Majesty's reign, imposing duties on all glass, painters' colours, paper, and teas, that should, after the 20th of November, 1767, be "imported from Great Britain into any colony or plantation in America". This bill, after

* Reprinted from Hezekiah Niles, *Principles and Acts of the Revolution in America* (Baltimore: 1822), pp. 169–70.

the concurrence of the Lords, obtained the royal assent. And thus they who, from time immemorial, have exercised the right of giving to, or withholding from the crown, their aids and subsidies, according to their *own free will and pleasure,* signified by their representatives in Parliament, do, by the Act in question, deny us, their brethren in America, the enjoyment of the same right. As this denial, and the execution of that Act, involves our slavery, and would sap the foundation of our freedom, whereby we should become slaves to our brethren and fellow subjects, born to no greater stock of freedom than the Americans—the merchants and inhabitants of this city, in conjunction with the merchants and inhabitants of the ancient American colonies, entered into an agreement to decline a part of their commerce with Great Britain, until the above mentioned Act should be totally repealed. This agreement operated so powerfully to the disadvantage of the manufacturers of England that many of them were unemployed. To appease their clamours, and to provide the subsistence for them, which the non-importation had deprived them of, the Parliament, in 1770, repealed so much of the Revenue Act as imposed a duty on glass, painters' colours, and paper, and left the duty on tea, as *a test of the parliamentary right to tax us.* The merchants of the cities of New York and Philadelphia, having strictly adhered to the agreement, so far as it is related to the importation of articles subject to an American duty, have convinced the ministry, that some other measures must be adopted to execute parliamentary supremacy over this country, and to remove the distress brought on the East India Company, by the ill policy of that Act. Accordingly, to increase the temptation to the shippers of tea from England, an Act of Parliament passed the last session, which gives the whole duty on tea, the company were subject to pay, upon the importation of it into England, to the purchasers and exporters; and when the company have ten millions of pounds of tea in their warehouses exclusive of the quantity they may want to ship, they are allowed to export tea, discharged from the payment of that duty with which they were before chargeable. In hopes of aid in the execution of this project, by the influence of the owners of the American ships, application was made by the company to the captains of those ships to take the tea on freight; but they virtuously rejected it. Still determined on the scheme, they have chartered ships to bring the tea to this country, which may be hourly expected, to make an important trial of our virtue. If they succeed in the sale of that tea, we shall have no property that we can call our own, and then we may bid adieu to American liberty. Therefore, to prevent a calamity which, of all others, is the most to be dreaded—slavery and its terrible concomitants—we, the subscribers, being influenced from a regard to liberty, and disposed to use all lawful endeavours in our power, to defeat the pernicious project, and to transmit to our posterity those blessings of freedom which our ancestors have handed down to us; and to contribute to the support of the common liberties of America, which are in danger to be subverted, *do,* for those important purposes, agree to associate together, under the name and style of the *sons of New York,* and engage our honour to, and with each other faithfully to observe and perform the following resolutions, viz.

1st. Resolved, that whoever shall aid or abet, or in any manner assist, in the introduction of tea from any place whatsoever, into this colony, while it is subject, by a British Act of Parliament, to the payment of a duty, for the purpose of raising a revenue in America, he shall be deemed an enemy to the liberties of America.

2d. Resolved, that whoever shall be aiding, or assisting, in the landing, or carting of such tea, from any ship, or vessel, or shall hire any house, storehouse, or cellar or any place whatsoever, to deposit the tea, subject to a duty as aforesaid, he shall be deemed an enemy to the liberties of America.

3d. Resolved, that whoever shall sell, or buy, or in any manner contribute to the sale, or purchase of tea, subject to a duty as aforesaid, or shall aid, or abet, in transporting such tea, by land or water, from this city, until the 7th George III, chap. 46, commonly called the Revenue Act, shall be totally and clearly repealed, he shall be deemed an enemy to the liberties of America.

4th. Resolved, that whether the duties on tea, imposed by this Act, be paid in Great Britain or in America, our liberties are equally affected.

5th. Resolved, that whoever shall transgress any of these resolutions, we will not deal with, or employ, or have any connection with him.

On the evening of December 16, 1773, a number of men dressed as Indians boarded three tea ships in Boston harbor and emptied 342 chests of tea into the water. When the British government retaliated by passing the Intolerable Acts, three of which punished Massachusetts Bay Colony, Samuel Adams helped rally the support of other colonies through correspondence. Joseph Galloway once described Adams as "a man, who though by no means remarkable for brilliant abilities, yet is equal to most men in popular intrigue, and the management of a faction. He eats little, drinks little, sleeps little, thinks much, and is most decisive and indefatigable in the pursuit of his objects."

SAMUEL ADAMS RALLIES SUPPORT FOR MASSACHUSETTS*

SAMUEL ADAMS TO ARTHUR LEE

Jan 25 1774

The sending the East India Companies Tea into America appears evidently to have been with Design of the British Administration, and to complete the favorite plan of establishing a Revenue in America. The People of Boston and the other adjacent Towns endeavored to have the Tea sent back to the place from whence it came & then to prevent the Design from taking Effect. Had this been done in Boston, as it was done in New York & Philadelphia, the Design of the Ministry would have been as effectually prevented here as in those Colonies and the property would have been saved. Governor Hutchinson & the other Crown officers having the Command of the Castle by which the Ships must have passed, & other powers in their Hands, made use of these Powers to defeat the Intentions of the people & succeeded; in short the Governor who for Art & Cunning as well as an inveterate hatred of the people was inferior to no one of the Cabal; both encouraged & provoked the people to destroy the Tea. By refusing to grant a Passport he held up to them the alternative of destroying the property of the East India Company or suffering that to be the sure means of unhinging the Security of property in general in America, and by delaying to call on the naval power to protect the Tea, he led them to determine their Choice of Difficulties. In this View of the Matter the Question is easily decided who ought in Justice to pay for the Tea if it ought to be paid for at all.

The Destruction of the Tea is the pretence for the unprecedented Severity shown to the Town of Boston but the real Cause is the opposition to Tyranny for which the people of that Town have always made themselves remarkeable & for which I think this Country is much obliged

to them. They are suffering the Vengeance of Administration in the Common Cause of America.

THE TOWN OF BOSTON
TO THE COLONIES

Boston May 13th: 1774

I am desired by the Freeholders and other Inhabitants of this Town to inclose you an Attested Copy of their Vote passed in Town Meeting legally assembled this day. The Occasion of this Meeting is most alarming: We have receivd the Copy of an Act of the British Parliament (which is also inclos'd) wherein it appears that the Inhabitants of this Town have been tryed and condemned and are to be punished by the shutting up of the Harbour, and other Ways, without their having been called to answer for, nay, for aught that appears without their having been even accused of any crime committed by them; for no such Crime is alledgd in the Act.

The Town of Boston is now Suffering the Stroke of Vengeance in the Common Cause of America. I hope they will sustain the Blow with a becoming fortitude; and that the Effects of this cruel Act, intended to intimidate and subdue the Spirits of all America will by the joynt Efforts of all be frustrated.

The People receive this Edict with Indignation. It is expected by their Enemies and feard by some of their Friends, that this Town singly will not be able to support the Cause under so severe a Tryal. As the very being of every Colony, considerd as a free People depends upon the Event, a Thought so dishonorable to our Brethren cannot be entertained, as that this Town will now be left to struggle alone.

General Gage is just arrivd here, with a Commission to supercede Govr Hutchinson. It is said that the Town of Salem about twenty Miles East of this Metropolis is to be the Seat of Government—that the Commissioners of the Customs and their numerous Retinue are to remove to the Town of Marblehead a Town contiguous to Salem and that this if the General shall think

---

* Reprinted from Harry Alonzo Cushing, ed., *The Writings of Samuel Adams* (New York: Putnam, 1907), III, 78–79, 107–9, 157–59 by permission.

proper is to be a Garrisond Town. Reports are various and contradictory.

I am &c.

Sent to the Com^e of Correspondence for

by Mr Revere—and in that sent to Philadelphia there

Connecticutt
New York
New Jersey
& Philadelphia

} were Copies of the Vote of the Town inclosd for the Colonies to the Southward of them which they were desired to forward with all possible Dispatch with their own Sentiments.

SAMUEL ADAMS TO JOSEPH WARREN

PHILADELPHIA, September 25, 1774. MY DEAR SIR,—I wrote you yesterday by the post. A frequent communication at this critical conjuncture is necessary. As the all-important American cause so much depends upon each colony's acting agreeably to the sentiments of the whole, it must be useful to you to know the sentiments which are entertained here of the temper and conduct of our province. Heretofore we have been accounted by many, intemperate and rash; but now we are universally applauded as cool and judicious, as well as spirited and brave. This is the character we sustain in congress. There is, however, a certain degree of jealousy in the minds of some, that we aim at a total independency, not only of the mother-country, but of the colonies too; and that, as we are a hardy and brave people, we shall in time overrun them all. However groundless this jealousy may be, it ought to be attended to, and is of weight in your deliberations on the subject of your last letter. I spent yesterday afternoon and evening with Mr. Dickinson. He is a true Bostonian. It is his opinion, that, if Boston can safely remain on the defensive, the liberties of America, which that town has so nobly contended for, will be secured. The congress have, in their resolve of the 17th instant, given their sanction to the resolutions of the county of Suffolk, one of which is to act merely on the defensive, so long as such conduct may be justified by reason and the principles of self-preservation, but *no longer*. They have great dependence upon your tried patience and fortitude. They suppose you mean to defend your civil constitution. They strongly recommend perseverance in a firm and temperate conduct, and give you a full pledge of their united efforts in your behalf. They have not yet come to final resolutions. It becomes them to be deliberate. I have been assured, in private conversation with individuals, that, if you should be driven to the necessity of acting in the defence of your lives or liberty, you would be justified by their constituents, and openly supported by all the means in their power; but whether they will ever be prevailed upon to think it necessary for you to set up another form of government, I very much question, for the reason I have before suggested. It is of the greatest importance, that the American opposition should be united, and that it should be conducted so as to concur with the opposition of our friends in England. Adieu,

In response to the repression of Massachusetts, the Virginia House of Burgesses called for a Continental Congress at which delegates from every colony but Georgia assembled. On September 6, 1774, the day after it opened in Philadelphia, the Congress appointed a committee "to State the rights of the Colonies." One of its members, John Adams, took notes on the members' sharp disagreement concerning the nature of these rights.

JOHN ADAMS:
NOTES ON THE DEBATE IN THE COMMITTEE TO STATE THE RIGHTS OF THE COLONIES*

Coll. Lee. The Rights are built on a fourfold foundation—on Nature, on the british Constitution, on Charters, and on immemorial usage. The Navigation Act, a Capital Violation.

Mr. Jay. It is necessary to recur to the Law of Nature, and the british Constitution to ascertain our Rights.

The Constitution of G.B. will not apply to some of the Charter Rights.

A Mother Country surcharged with Inhabitants, they have a Right to emigrate. It may be

* Reprinted by permission of the publishers from Lyman H. Butterfield, editor, *Diary and Autobiography of John Adams. The Adams Papers.* Cambridge, Mass.: The Belknap Press of Harvard University Press, Copyright, 1961, by The Massachusetts Historical Society.

said, if We leave our Country, We cannot leave our Allegiance. But there is no Allegiance without Protection. And Emigrants have a Right, to erect what Government they please.

Mr. J. Rutledge. An Emigrant would not have a Right to set up what constitution they please. A Subject could not alienate his Allegiance.

Lee. Cant see why We should not lay our Rights upon the broadest Bottom, the Ground of Nature. Our Ancestors found here no Government.

Mr. Pendleton. Consider how far We have a Right to interfere, with Regard to the Canada Constitution.

If the Majority of the People there should be pleased with the new Constitution, would not the People of America and of England have a Right to oppose it, and prevent such a Constitution being established in our Neighbourhood.

Lee. It is contended that the Crown had no Right to grant such Charters as it has to the Colonies—and therefore We shall rest our Rights on a feeble foundation, if we rest em only on Charters—nor will it weaken our Objections to the Canada Bill.

Mr. Rutledge. Our Claims I think are well founded on the british Constitution, and not on the Law of Nature.

Coll. Dyer. Part of the Country within the Canada Bill, is a conquered Country, and part not. It is said to be a Rule that the King can give a Conquered Country what Law he pleases.

Mr. Jay. I cant think the british Constitution inseperably attached to the Person of every Subject. Whence did the Constitution derive its Authority? From compact. Might not that Authority be given up by Compact.

Mr. Wm. Livingston. A Corporation cannot make a Corporation. Charter Governments have done it. K[ing] cant appoint a Person to make a Justice of Peace. All Governors do it. Therefore it will not do for America to rest wholly on the Laws of England.

Mr. Sherman. The Ministry contend, that the Colonies are only like Corporations in England, and therefore subordinate to the Legislature of the Kingdom.—The Colonies not bound to the King or Crown by the Act of Settlement, but by their consent to it.

There is no other Legislative over the Colonies but their respective Assemblies.

The Colonies adopt the common Law, not as the common Law, but as the highest Reason.

Mr. Duane. Upon the whole for grounding our Rights on the Laws and Constitution of the Country from whence We sprung, and Charters, without recurring to the Law of Nature—because this will be a feeble Support. Charters are Compacts between the Crown and the People and I think on this foundation the Charter Governments stand firm.

England is Governed by a limited Monarchy and free Constitution.

Priviledges of Englishmen were inherent, their Birthright and Inheritance, and cannot be deprived of them, without their Consent.

Objection. That all the Rights of Englishmen will make us independent.

I hope a Line may be drawn to obviate this Objection.

James was against Parliaments interfering with the Colonies. In the Reign of Charles 2d. the Sentiments of the Crown seem to have been changed. The Navigation Act was made. Massachusetts denied the Authority—but made a Law to inforce it in the Colony.

Lee. Life and Liberty, which is necessary for the Security of Life, cannot be given up when We enter into Society.

Mr. Rutledge. The first Emigrants could not be considered as in a State of Nature—they had no Right to elect a new King.

Mr. Jay. I have always withheld my Assent from the Position that every Subject discovering Land [does so] for the State to which they belong.

Mr. Galloway. I never could find the Rights of Americans, in the Distinctions between Taxation and Legislation, nor in the Distinction between Laws for Revenue and for the Regulation of Trade. I have looked for our Rights in the Laws of Nature—but could not find them in a State of Nature, but always in a State of political Society.

I have looked for them in the Constitution of the English Government, and there found them. We may draw them from this Soursce securely.

Power results from the Real Property, of the Society.

The States of Greece, Macedon, Rome, were founded on this Plan. None but Landholders could vote in the Comitia, or stand for Offices.

English Constitution founded on the same Principle. Among the Saxons the Landholders were obliged to attend and shared among them the Power. In the Norman Period the same. When the Landholders could not all attend, the Representation of the freeholders, came in. Before the Reign of H[enry] 4., an Attempt was made to give the Tenants in Capite a Right to vote. Magna Charta. Archbishops, Bishops, Abbots, Earls and Barons and Tenants in Capite held all the Lands in England.

It is of the Essence of the English Constitution, that no Law shall be binding, but such as are made by the Consent of the Proprietors in England.

How then did it stand with our Ancestors, when they came over here? They could not be bound by any Laws made by the British Parliament—excepting those made before. I never could see any Reason to allow that we are bound to any Law made since—nor could I ever make any Distinction between the Sorts of Laws.

I have ever thought We might reduce our Rights to one. An Exemption from all Laws made by British Parliament, made since the Emigration of our Ancestors. It follows therefore that all the Acts of Parliament made since, are Violations of our Rights.

These Claims are all defensible upon the Principles even of our Enemies—Ld. North himself when he shall inform himself of the true Principles of the Constitution, &c.

I am well aware that my Arguments tend to an Independency of the Colonies, and militate against the Maxim that there must be some absolute Power to draw together all the Wills and strength of the Empire.

War broke out on April 19, 1775, when British troops fought colonists at Lexington and Concord, Massachusetts. As other colonies hastened to raise troops, they proclaimed their grievances against the British. One such statement was the preamble to the Connecticut Act for the regulating and ordering of troops.

CONNECTICUT ACT FOR REGULATING AND ORDERING THE TROOPS, MAY, 1775*

Whereas God in his providence hath been pleased in great mercy to bestow upon the inhabitants of this Colony all the rights, liberties and immunities of the free and natural born subjects of the realm of England, which have been established and confirmed by a sacred compact and secured by a Royal Charter; which rights, liberties and immunities were the birthright of our brave, virtuous and religious ancestors whilst in England, who rather than submit to religious or civil tyranny chose to leave their pleasant seats and all their happy prospects in their native country, bravely encountered the danger of untried seas and coasts of a howling wilderness, barbarous men and savage beasts, at the expence of their ease and safety of their blood, their treasure and their lives, transplanted and reared the English constitution in these wilds upon the strong pillars of civil and religious liberty, and having led the way by their great example bequeathed their inestimable purchase as a sacred and unalienable legacy to their posterity, who have ever since united the sincerest loyalty to their sovereign and the warmest affection for their elder brethren in England with the enjoyment of their aforesaid rights, liberties and immunities, nor have they till lately been thought incompatible.

And whereas since the close of the last war the British Parliament claiming a power of right to bind the people of America by statute in all cases whatsoever, hath in some acts expressly imposed taxes upon them, and in others, under various pretences but in fact for the purpose of raising a revenue, hath imposed rates and duties payable in these Colonies, established a Board of Commissioners with unconstitutional powers, and extended the jurisdiction of Courts of Admiralty not only for collecting said duties but also for the tryal of causes merely arising within the body of a county.

And whereas in consequence of other statutes, judges who before held only estates at will in their offices have been made to depend on the crown alone for their salaries, and standing armies kept in time of peace; and it has been lately resolved in Parliament that by force of a statute made in the thirty-fifth year of the reign of King Henry the eighth, colonists may be transported to England and tryed there upon accusations for treasons and misprisions, or concealment of treasons, committed, or alledged to be committed, in the Colonies; and by a late statute such tryals have been directed in cases therein mentioned.

And whereas three acts of Parliament have been passed, by one of which the Port of Boston is shut up and thousands reduced from affluence to poverty and distress; by another the charter of the Province of the Massachusets Bay is subverted and destroyed; and by the third, under pretence of the impartial administration of justice, all hope of justice is taken away in certain cases.

And whereas another statute hath been made by which the Roman Catholic Religion is established, the equitable system of English laws are abolished, and a tyranny erected, in the Province of Quebec, to the great danger of the neighbouring Colonies; and also in the present session of Parliament another act is passed by which the New England Colonies are in a great measure deprived of their trade and fishery, the blessings which God and nature have indulged them being thus attempted by force to be wrested from them.

And whereas all our humble, dutifull and loyal petitions to the throne for redress of grievances have been treated with contempt, or passed

---

* Reprinted from Charles J. Hoadly, ed., *The Public Records of the Colony of Connecticut* (Hartford: 1890), XV, 18–21.

by in silence by his Majesty's ministers of state, and the refusal to surrender our just rights, liberties and immunities, hath been stiled Rebellion, and fleets and armies have been sent into a neighbouring Colony to force them to submit to slavery and awe the other Colonies to submission by the example of vengeance inflicted on her, who have, besides the usual calamities and insults that proceed from standing armies, fortified the town of Boston, driven the peaceable inhabitants from their dwellings, and imbrued their hands in the blood of our countrymen; all which acts and measures have relation to all the British Colonies in the principles from which they flow, and are evidently intended to force or terrify them into a submission to Parliamentary taxation, or at least into a surrender of their property at the pleasure of the British Parliament, and in such proportion as they shall please to prescribe, with which we must comply or lye at the mercy of those who cannot know our situation and circumstances, and will be interested to oppress and enslave us. Our liberty, our lives and property, will become precarious and dependant upon the will of men over whom we can have no check or controul. Religion, property, personal safety, learning, arts, public and private virtue, social happiness and every blessing attendant on liberty, will fall victims to the principles and measures advanced and pursued against us, whilst shameless vice, infidelity, irreligion, abject dependance, ignorance, superstition, meanness, servility and the whole train of despotism, present themselves to our view in melancholy prospect.

And whereas, although this Assembly wish for no new rights and privileges, and desire only to preserve their antient constitution as it has been understood and practiced upon from the beginning, freely yielding to the British Parliament the regulation of our external commerce, for the purpose of securing the commercial advantages of all the dominions of our sovereign to the mother country, and the commercial benefits of its several members excluding every idea of taxation for raising a revenue without our consent, and claiming only a right to regulate our internal police and government, and are most earnestly desirous of peace and deprecate the horrors of war: Yet, when they see military preparations against them at hand, and the hopes of peace and harmony placed at a greater distance, being fully determined never to make a voluntary sacrifice of their rights, not knowing how soon parliamentary and ministerial vengeance may be directed against them immediately, as it is now against the Province of Massachusets Bay, who are suffering in the common cause of British America, trusting in the justice of their cause and the righteous providence of Almighty God, for the restoration of quiet and peace, or for success in their efforts for their defence, have thought it their duty to raise troops for the defence of this Colony.

And whereas it is necessary that such troops, both officers and soldiers, should be made acquainted with their duty, and that articles, rules and regulations should be established to preserve order, good government and discipline in the army, agreeable to the mild spirit of our constitution, and not according to the severities practiced in standing armies. . . [the regulations for the troops follow].

The final great debate on the rights of the colonists took place at the Second Continental Congress in the early summer of 1776. The Virginia Resolution on Independence of June 7, 1776, led to a debate on June 8 and 10 and the momentous Declaration in July. Jefferson's notes, although not entirely accurate, are the only important account of the proceedings.

THOMAS JEFFERSON: NOTES ON THE DEBATES ON THE VIRGINIA RESOLUTION OF INDEPENDENCE*

In Congress, Friday, June 7, 1776

The delegates from Virginia moved in obedience to instructions from their constituents that the Congress should declare that these United Colonies are and of right ought to be free and independent states; that they are absolved from all obedience to the British Crown, and that all political connection between them and the state of Great Britain is and ought to be totally dissolved; that measures should be immediately taken for procuring the assistance of foreign powers, and a confederation be formed to bind the colonies more closely together.

The house being obliged to attend at that time to some other business, the proposition was referred to the next day when the members were ordered to attend punctually at ten o'clock.

Saturday June 8th they proceeded to take it into consideration, and referred it to a committee

* Reprinted from Worthington C. Ford, *et al.,* eds., *Journals of the Continental Congress, 1774–1789* (Washington, D.C.: Government Printing Office, 1904–1937), VI, 1087–93.

of the whole, into which they immediately resolved themselves, and passed that day and Monday the 10th in debating on the subject.

It was argued by [James] Wilson, Robert R. Livingston, E[dward] Rutledge, [John] Dickinson, and others:

That though they were friends to the measures themselves and saw the impossibility that we should ever again be united with Great Britain, yet they were against adopting them at this time;

That the conduct we had formerly observed was wise and proper now, of deferring to take any capital step till the voice of the people drove us into it;

That they were our power and without them our declarations could not be carried into effect;

That the people of the middle colonies (Maryland, Delaware, Pennsylvania, the Jersies, and N[ew] York) were not yet ripe for bidding adieu to British connection; but that they were fast ripening and in a short time would join in the general voice of America;

That the resolution entered into by this house on the 15th of May for suppressing the exercise of all powers derived from the Crown had shown, by the ferment into which it had thrown these middle colonies, that they had not yet accommodated their minds to a separation from the mother country;

That some of them had expressly forbidden their delegates to consent to such a declaration, and others had given no instructions, and consequently no powers to give such consent;

That if the delegates of any particular colony had no power to declare such colony independent, certain they were the others could not declare it for them, the colonies being as yet perfectly independent of each other;

That the Assembly of Pennsylvania was now sitting above stairs, their convention would sit within a few days; the convention of New York was now sitting, and those of the Jersies and Deleware counties would meet on the Monday following, and it was probable these bodies would take up the question of independence, and would declare to their delegates the voice of their state;

That if such a declaration should now be agreed to, these delegates must retire and possibly their colonies might secede from the union;

That such a secession would weaken us more than could be compensated by any foreign alliance;

That in the event of such a division foreign powers would either refuse to join themselves to our fortunes, or having us so much in their power as that desperate declaration would place us, they would insist on terms proportionably more hard and prejudicial;

That we had little reason to expect an alliance with those to whom alone as yet we had cast our eyes;

That France and Spain had reason to be jealous of that rising power which would one day certainly strip them of all their American possessions;

That it was more likely they should form a connection with the British court who, if they should find themselves unable otherwise to extricate themselves from their difficulties, would agree to a partition of our territories, restoring Canada to France and the Floridas to Spain to accomplish for themselves a recovery of these colonies;

That it would not be long before we should receive certain information of the disposition of the French court from the agent whom we had sent to Paris for that purpose;

That if this disposition should be favourable, by waiting the event of the present campaign, which we all hoped would be successful, we should have reason to expect an alliance on better terms;

That this would in fact work no delay of any effectual aid from such ally, as, from the advance of the season and distance of our situation, it was impossible we could receive any assistance during this campaign;

That it was prudent to fix among ourselves the terms on which we would form alliance before we declared we would form one at all events;

And that if these were agreed on and our declaration of independence ready by the time our ambassador should be ready to sail, it would be as well as to go into that declaration at this day.

On the other side it was urged by J[ohn] Adams, [Richard Henry] Lee, [George] Wythe, and others:

That no gentleman had argued against the policy or the right of separation from Britain, nor had supposed it possible we should ever renew our connection; that they had only opposed its being now declared;

That the question was not whether, by a declaration of independence we should make ourselves what we are not, but whether we should declare a fact which already exists;

That as to the people or Parliament of England, we had always been independent of them, their restraints on our trade deriving efficacy from our acquiescence only and not from any rights they possessed of imposing them, and that so far our connection had been federal only and was now dissolved by the commencement of hostilities;

That as to the king, we had been bound to him by allegiance, but that this bond was now dissolved by his assent to the late Act of Parliament by which he declares us out of his protection and by his levying war on us, a fact which had long ago proved us out of his protection, it being a certain position in law that allegiance and protection are reciprocal, the one ceasing when the other is withdrawn;

That James II never declared the people of England out of his protection; yet his actions proved it, and the Parliament declared it;

No delegates then can be denied, or ever want a power of declaring an existent truth;

That the delegates from the Delaware counties having declared their constituents ready to join, there are only two colonies, Pennsylvania and Maryland, whose delegates are absolutely tied up, and that these had by their instructions only reserved a right of confirming or rejecting the measure;

That the instructions from Pennsylvania might be accounted for from the times in which they were drawn, near a twelvemonth ago, since which the face of affairs has totally changed;

That within that time it had become apparent that Britain was determined to accept nothing less than a carte blanche, and that the king's answer to the lord mayor, aldermen, and common council of London, which had come to hand four days ago, must have satisfied everyone of this point;

That the people wait for us to lead the way;

That *they* are in favour of the measure, though the instructions given by some of their *representatives* are not;

That the voice of the representatives is not always consonant with the voice of the people, and that this is remarkably the case in these middle colonies;

That the effect of the resolution of the 15th of May has proved this, which, raising the murmurs of some in the colonies of Pennsylvania and Maryland, called forth the opposing voice of the freer part of the people and proved them to be the majority, even in these colonies;

That the backwardness of these two colonies might be ascribed partly to the influence of proprietary power and connections, and partly to their having not yet been attacked by the enemy;

That these causes were not likely to be soon removed, as there seemed no probability that the enemy would make either of these the seat of this summer's war;

That it would be vain to wait either weeks or months for perfect unanimity, since it was impossible that all men should ever become of one sentiment on any question;

That the conduct of some colonies from the beginning of this contest had given reason to suspect it was their settled policy to keep in the rear of the confederacy, that their particular prospect might be better, even in the worst event;

That therefore it was necessary for those colonies who had thrown themselves forward and hazarded all from the beginning to come forward now also and put all again to their own hazard;

That the history of the Dutch revolution, of whom three states only confederated at first, proved that a secession of some colonies would not be so dangerous as some apprehended;

That a declaration of independence alone could render it consistent with European delicacy for European powers to treat with us, or even to receive an ambassador from us;

That till this they would not receive our vessels into their ports nor acknowledge the adjudications of our courts of admiralty to be legitimate in cases of capture of British vessels;

That though France and Spain may be jealous of our rising power, they must think it will be much more formidable with the addition of Great Britain and will therefore see it their interest to prevent a coalition; but should they refuse, we shall be but where we are; whereas without trying we shall never know whether they will aid us or not;

That the present campaign may be unsuccessful, and therefore we had better propose an alliance while our affairs wear a hopeful aspect;

That to wait the event of this campaign will certainly work delay because during this summer France may assist us effectually by cutting off those supplies of provisions from England and Ireland on which the enemy's armies here are to depend, or by setting in motion the great power they have collected in the West Indies and calling our enemy to the defence of the possessions they have there;

That it would be idle to lose time in settling the terms of alliance, till we had first determined we would enter into alliance;

That it is necessary to lose no time in opening a trade for our people, who will want clothes and will want money too for the payment of taxes;

And that the only misfortune is that we did not enter into alliance with France six months sooner, as, besides opening their ports for the vent of our last year's produce, they might have marched an army into Germany and prevented the petty princes there from selling their unhappy subjects to subdue us.

It appearing in the course of these debates that the colonies of N[ew] York, N[ew] Jersey, Pennsylvania, Delaware, and Maryland were not yet matured for falling from the parent stem, but that they were fast advancing to that state, it was thought most prudent to wait a while for them, and to postpone the final decision to July 1. But that this might occasion as little delay as possible, a committee was appointed to prepare a declaration of independence. The committee were J[ohn] Adams, Dr. Franklin, Roger Sherman, Robert R. Livingston, and myself. Committees were also appointed at the same time to prepare a plan of confederation for the colonies, and to state the terms proper to be proposed for foreign alliance. The committee for drawing the declaration of independence desired me to do it. It was accordingly done, and being approved by them, I reported it to the house on Friday the 28th of June, when it was read and ordered to lie on the table. On Monday the 1st of July the house resolved itself into a committee of the whole and resumed the consideration of the original motion made by the delegates of Virginia, which being again debated through the day, was carried in the affirmative by the votes of N[ew] Hampshire, Connecticut, Massachusetts, Rhode Island, N[ew] Jersey, Maryland, Virginia, N[orth] Carolina, and Georgia. S[outh] Carolina and Pennsylvania voted against it. Delaware having but two members present, they were divided. The delegates for N[ew] York declared they were for it themselves and were assured their constituents were for it but that their instructions, having been drawn near a twelvemonth before, when reconciliation was still the general object, they were enjoined by them to do nothing which should impede that object. They therefore thought themselves not justifiable in voting on either side and asked leave to withdraw from the question which was given them. The committee rose and reported their resolution to the house. Mr. Rutledge of S[outh] Carolina then requested the determination might be put off to the next day as he believed his colleagues, though they disapproved of the resolution, would then join in it for the sake of unanimity. The ultimate question whether the house would agree to the resolution of the committee, was accordingly postponed to the next day, when it was again moved and S[outh] Carolina concurred in voting for it. In the meantime a third member had come post from the Delaware counties and turned the vote of that colony in favour of the resolution. Members of a different sentiment attending that morning from Pennsylvania also, their vote was changed so that the whole twelve colonies who were authorized to vote at all gave their voices for it; and within a few days the convention of N[ew] York approved of it, and thus supplied the void occasioned by the withdrawing of their delegates from the vote.

CHAPTER FOUR

THE FOUNDING FATHERS

With independence won, the American people faced the crucial problem of developing a workable plan of government. Their success was astounding. Who could have predicted in 1787 that the little group assembled in Philadelphia, representatives of a thinly-populated string of agricultural states stretched along the eastern seaboard, could draft a Constitution so practical and so flexible that in the twentieth century it would still fit the needs of a vast industrial nation? Surely the transcending factor about the founding fathers was their consummate blending of theory and realism to produce such an effective frame of government. They were men of the Enlightenment, and they were equally men of everyday affairs. They had strong ideas concerning the nature of man and the forms of government under which he could successfully carry out his enterprises. On the basis of the long experience of self-government in individual colonies combined with over-all imperial controls, they evolved a formula for federalism, a dividing of power and responsibilities between the states and the central government. Out of their floundering experiences during the Confederation came their quest for a stronger central government.

Few historians would question these basic facts. But many of them have sharply queried the motivations of the Federalists and debated whether or not the years of the Confederation were actually such a critical period during which the American nation was on the verge of disaster. Merrill Jensen in *The New Nation* (1950) asserts in eloquent detail that the Articles of Confederation were indeed a success and that the founding fathers were more intent upon their own aggrandizement than the rescue of the Republic. Richard B. Morris, whose essay follows, was skeptical of Jensen's arguments. In reviewing the debate that has been going on for many decades, Morris, in common with a number of present-day historians, places less emphasis upon economic caution and more upon the remarkable achievement that the new machinery of government represented. "The imposition of a vitalized federalism and the tightening of the bonds of union," he concluded, "precipitated a greater revolution in American life than did separation from England."

RICHARD B. MORRIS: THE CONFEDERATION PERIOD AND THE AMERICAN HISTORIAN*

Plautus tells us that "one eyewitness is worth ten hearsays," but I am not sure that he would have left us this counsel if he had lived during the Confederation period of American history. In this era the eyewitnesses themselves failed to see eye to eye. In fact, the two opposing views of the post-Revolutionary years which are held by historians of the twentieth century can be traced directly to the Founding Fathers. The first we might call the Washington-Madison-Hamilton approach, accepted by most historians of the post-Revolutionary generation, and developed by George Bancroft, John Fiske, John B. McMaster, and with some reservations by Andrew C. McLaughlin. The other is the approach of certain Antifederalist leaders, an approach adopted by Henry B. Dawson, by J. Allen Smith, by the early Charles A. Beard, and by the more recent Merrill Jensen.

If one could read the minds of the majority of the Founding Fathers in 1787—and an abundant and ever-increasing quantity of first-hand documentation makes this a less formidable effort than it seems on its face—he might be very much surprised indeed that any issue should have arisen in historiography about the years of the Confederation. The majority of the Founders saw a clear drift toward anarchy culminating in a crisis. Constantly needled by such correspondents as Henry Knox and David Humphreys, Washington's alarm at the weaknesses of the Confederacy was deepened as the disorders in Massachusetts in the fall of 1786 seemed to portend a crisis for the nation. "I predict the worst consequences from a half-starved, limping government, always moving upon crutches and tottering at every step," he wrote. On August 1, 1786, he asserted: "I do not conceive we can long exist as a nation without having lodged somewhere a power which will pervade the whole Union in as energetic a manner as the authority of the State governments extends over the several states." On October 22 he wrote David Humphreys: "But for God's sake tell me what is the cause of all these commotions? . . . I am mortified beyond expression that in the moment of our acknowledged independence we should by our conduct verify the predictions of our transatlantic foe, and render ourselves ridiculous and contemptible in the eyes of all Europe." Nine days later he wrote Henry Lee, "To be more exposed in the eyes of the world, and more contemptible than we already are, is hardly possible."[1] On November 5 he told James Madison, "We are fast verging to anarchy and confusion!"[2]

Others than the New England Federalists, who were closest to Shays' Rebellion and understandably perturbed, shared Washington's views about the state of the nation. Henry Lee declared: "We are all in dire apprehension that a beginning of anarchy with all its calamitys has approached, and have no means to stop the dreadful work."[3] In December of 1786 Madison wrote Jefferson of "dangerous defects" in the Confederation.[4] During the fall of 1786 John Jay kept writing Jefferson that "the inefficacy of our Government becomes daily more and more apparent," and intimated that the Shaysites had more "extensive" objectives than the immediate redress of grievances.[5] Edmund Randolph, who oscillated between Federalism and Antifederalism, wrote Washington in March of 1787, "Every day brings forth some new crisis"; and he expressed doubt whether Congress could survive beyond the current year.[6] No one at the Constitutional Convention was more explicit than Randolph in spelling out the defects of the government, which he considered "totally inadequate to the peace, safety, and security of the Confederation" and which he repeatedly denounced for its "imbecility."[7]

For the classic contemporary view of the alarming weaknesses of the Confederation we must turn to *The Federalist*. Therein Hamilton, a consistent viewer-with-alarm during this period, attacks the Confederation government as inefficient, asserts that the country had "reached almost the last stage of national humiliation," speaks disparagingly of "the present shadow of a federal government," views the Confederacy as dying, and urges ratification of the Constitution to prevent anarchy, civil war, and "perhaps the military despotism of a victorious demagogue."[8]

---

* Reprinted from Richard B. Morris, "The Confederation Period and the American Historian," *William and Mary Quarterly*, XIII (April, 1956), 139–56 by permission.

[1] *The Writings of George Washington from the*

Original Manuscript Sources, 1745–1799, ed. J. C. Fitzpatrick (Washington, 1931–44), XXVIII, 502; XXIX, 27, 34.

[2] *Ibid.*, XXIX, 51.

[3] Henry Lee to George Washington, Oct. 17, 1786, *Letters of Members of the Continental Congress*, ed. E. C. Burnett (Washington, 1921–33), VIII, 486.

[4] *The Papers of Thomas Jefferson*, ed. Julian P. Boyd (Princeton, 1950–   ), X, 574.

[5] *Ibid.*, p. 489.

[6] *The Writings of George Washington . . . ,* ed. Jared Sparks (Boston, 1834–37), IX, 243 n.

[7] *Records of the Federal Convention of 1787*, ed. Max Farrand (New Haven, 1911–37), I, 19, 24, 25.

[8] See especially *Federalist* 1, 15, 16, and 85.

It would be easy to pile up assertions in similar vein from the pens of Knox and the two Morrises.

These Federalist worthies were in general agreement that the weaknesses of the Confederation could be attributed to financial muddling by the states; to English dumping; to the loss of the British West Indian market; to paper money; to stay laws; to state tariffs; but, above all, to a lack of coercive power by a central authority. Observers in charge of foreign affairs, notably Jay and John Adams, felt that this was the most critical spot in the American system of government. "I may reason till I die to no purpose," declared Adams in June 1785. "It is unanimity in America which will produce a fair treaty of commerce." [9]

In eloquence, prestige, and even in numbers among the leadership the Federalist view of conditions had impressive support, but it was far from universally held. George Clinton, the bête noire of the nationalist leaders, was quoted as intimating that the calling of a Constitutional Convention was "calculated to impress the people with an idea of evils which do not exist." [10] At the Convention, Gunning Bedford of Delaware expressed a complacent view of the government of the Confederacy, and at the Pennsylvania ratifying convention Antifederalists under the leadership of William Findley, Robert Whitehill, and John Smilie asserted that the people along with the legislature had been frightened into consenting to a state convention by unfounded talk of impending anarchy.

Thus there was a division of opinion in 1787 about conditions in the Confederation, and there never has ceased to be down to the present day. More recent writers who look at the Confederation through Antifederalist spectacles are buoyed up by the fact that Franklin and Jefferson were not as disturbed about conditions as other contemporaries. Yet Jefferson, as he was passing through Boston on his way to France, found "the conviction growing strongly that nothing could preserve the confederacy unless the bond of union, their common council, should be strengthened." [11] It is perhaps especially significant that when Franklin, Jefferson, and Robert R. Livingston expressed in writing a more roseate view of conditions than other Founding Fathers, they were making these observations to foreigners—to Frenchmen or to Englishmen. They were seeking to reassure friends and well-wishers of America abroad that this country was not headed for a collapse. Such assertions must be discounted as skillful propaganda. In France, for example, Jefferson reassured Démeunier that the United States was

in no danger of bankruptcy and that, with certain minor exceptions, "the Confederation is a wonderfully perfect instrument." [12] Similarly, when Franklin wrote to M. Le Veillard on March 6, 1786, that "America never was in higher prosperity," [13] commodity prices had steadily dropped —they were to decline thirty per cent between 1785 and 1789; farm wages were shrinking and were to fall to a low of forty cents a day by 1787; mortgage foreclosures and judgments for debts in central and western Massachusetts had reached an all-time high; and in the Valley of Virginia, as Freeman Hart has pointed out, executions more than doubled between 1784 and 1788. [14] In fact, the only economic index that showed an upturn was that for foreign trade, for in commerce the worst of the depression set in a bit earlier than in other lines and showed a more complete recovery by 1788. Again, when Livingston wrote Lafayette in April 1787 that commodity prices and wages were higher than before the war, he was evading the real issue of how far they had dropped since the coming of the peace. [15]

This double standard of correspondence—one line for Americans, the other for foreign well-wishers—is revealed in the writings of that arch-pessimist, George Washington. It is true that he was somewhat more candid with his old friend Lafayette, whom he wrote on August 15, 1786, that he chose to remain silent on domestic affairs "since I could not disguise or palliate, where I might think them erroneous." [16] Yet two weeks earlier he had written two letters which are very nearly contradictory to each other. On August 1 he wrote the Chevalier de la Luzerne a reassuring letter to counteract reports of the American situation circulating in Europe. "In short," he concluded his picture of domestic America, "the foundation of a great empire is laid, and I please myself with a persuasion, that Providence will not leave its work imperfect." On the same day, however, he wrote John Jay, then Secretary for Foreign Affairs, expressing the doubt that the nation

[12] *Jefferson Papers*, X, 14 ff.

[13] *Complete Works of Benjamin Franklin*, ed. John Bigelow (New York, 1887–88), IX, 300–301.

[14] Freeman H. Hart, *The Valley of Virginia in the American Revolution* (Chapel Hill, 1942), pp. 123–125. For evidence from the court records of sharply mounting indebtedness in central and western Massachusetts, see R. B. Morris, "Insurrection in Massachusetts," in *America in Crisis*, ed. Daniel Aaron (New York, 1952), p. 24. On the steady upsurge of insolvency in Connecticut during the entire Confederation period, see *Public Records of the State of Connecticut (1776–1796)*, eds. C. J. Hoadly and L. W. Labaree (Hartford, 1894–1951), VII, xv, xvi.

[15] R. R. Livingston Papers, Bancroft Transcripts, New York Public Library.

[16] Washington, *Writings*, ed. Fitzpatrick, XXVIII, 521.

[9] Adams to Jay, June 26, 1785, *Works of John Adams,* ed. C. F. Adams (Boston, 1850–56), VIII, 276.

[10] *Advertiser,* New York, July 21, 1787.

[11] Jefferson to Madison, July 1, 1784, *Jefferson Papers,* VII, 356.

could exist much longer unless stronger powers were lodged with the central government.[17]

Even the younger generation, men who could scarcely be accused of strong Federalist attachments, accepted the Federalist view of the glaring weaknesses of the Confederation. Consider, for example, Andrew Jackson, who was admitted to practice law the year the Constitutional Convention met in Philadelphia. In his Proclamation against Nullification Jackson declared in 1832: "But the defects of the Confederation need not be detailed. Under its operation we could scarcely be called a nation. We had neither prosperity at home nor consideration abroad. This state of things could not be endured, and our present happy Constitution was formed, but formed in vain if this fatal doctrine prevails." [18]

Jackson's view of the Confederation period was the view of the nationalist commentators on the Constitution and of the nationalist historians. It was expounded by James Wilson and Nathaniel Chipman, by Nathan Dane, and most notably by Joseph Story and George Ticknor Curtis, who gave formal expression to the views of Daniel Webster. In his History of the Origin, Formation, and Adoption of the Constitution, first published in 1854, Curtis begins by declaring: "The Constitution of the United States was the means by which republican liberty was saved from the consequences of impending anarchy...." Paraphrasing the Founding Fathers, Curtis saw the Confederation as "a great shadow without the substance of a government...." He saw the whole period as replete with "dangers and difficulties," full of "suffering and peril." [19]

Curtis' view of the Confederation interlude was fully shared by the nationalist historians writing in the generation or two following the adoption of the Constitution. Most distinguished of this group, George Bancroft—whose literary career spans the period from the Age of Jackson to the Age of Chester A. Arthur—put off writing about the post-Revolutionary era until the closing years of his life. His History of the Formation of the Constitution of the United States of America was not published until 1882. As might be expected, Bancroft viewed the period from a nationalist or continental point of view. He stressed the "helplessness" of Congress, whose "perpetual failures" he considered "inherent and incurable." To Bancroft, "no ray of hope remained" but from the convention summoned at Annapolis. [20] Neverthe-

less, he treats the Massachusetts debtors with sympathy and understanding, approves of Bowdoin's lenity toward the Shaysites, and reviews the economic decline which set in at the start of the period in sober language, in sharp contrast with the more intemperate treatment of the insurrection by his contemporary Richard Hildreth, who had surveyed the period many years earlier. [21]

Perhaps the historian who coined the term "critical period" to describe the Confederation interlude was William Henry Trescot. In his rather temperate and fair-minded Diplomatic History of the Administrations of Washington and Adams, published in 1857, he asserted: "Indeed, it would be more correct to say, that the most critical period of the country's history embraced the time between the peace of 1783 and the adoption of the constitution in 1788." [22] This point of view was adopted by Frothingham, by Schouler, and by von Holst. The last-named spoke of "the contemptible impotence of congress...." This was strong language, but Washington had used it before him. [23]

The classic exposition of the Federalist approach is found in John Fiske's The Critical Period of American History, 1783–1789. His title has fastened upon an epoch in American history a popular nomenclature that dies hard. The first edition appeared in 1888, not too long after the appearance of Bancroft's Last Revision. The title and theme of the book were suggested by the fact of Tom Paine's stopping the publication of the "Crisis," on hearing the news of the treaty of peace in 1783. Now, Paine said, "the times that tried men's souls are over." Fiske does not agree with Paine. The next five years, he contends, were to be the most critical time of all. Fiske used the term "critical" first to settle the question whether there was to be a national government or a group

---

[17] Ibid., pp. 501, 502.

[18] Compilation of the Messages and Papers of the Presidents, 1789–1902, ed. J. D. Richardson (Washington, 1903), II, 643.

[19] George Ticknor Curtis, History of the Origin, Formation, and Adoption of the Constitution of the United States . . . (New York, 1854), I, xi, 233, 234, 330.

[20] George Bancroft, History of the Formation

of the Constitution of the United States of America (New York, 1885), I, 262–266.

[21] Ibid., pp. 274–275; Richard Hildreth, The History of the United States of America (New (New York, 1885), I, 262–266.

[22] William Henry Trescot, The Diplomatic History of the Administrations of Washington and Adams: 1789–1801 (Boston, 1857), p. 9. Long before Trescot, however, Richard Henry Lee, a leading Antifederalist, wrote, Oct. 8, 1787: "I know our situation is critical, and it behoves us to make the best of it." "Letters of the Federal Farmer," Letter I, in Pamphlets on the Constitution of the United States, ed. P. L. Ford (Brooklyn, 1888), p. 280.

[23] Richard Frothingham, The Rise of the Republic of the United States (Boston, 1910. First published in 1872), pp. 583 ff.; James Schouler, History of the United States of America under the Constitution (revised ed., New York, 1894), I, 13 ff.; H. von Holst, The Constitutional and Political History of the United States, trans. John J. Lalor and Alfred B. Mason (Chicago, 1889–92), I, 37.

of small city-states. Secondly, he used the term to describe what he regarded to be the utter incompetence of the states and the federal government to deal with the problem of postwar reconstruction. To Fiske the drift "toward anarchy" was only checked by the eleventh-hour ratification of the federal Constitution.[24]

It has become the fashion of latter-day historians to criticize Fiske's scholarship. McLaughlin concedes that "there are not many errors in fact in the book," but insists that "as an authority the work is altogether without scientific standing, because it is little more than a remarkably skilful adaptation of a very few secondary authorities, showing almost no evidence of first-hand acquaintance with the sources."[25] Yet McLaughlin himself shows surprisingly little acquaintance with the sources when he describes economic conditions in the Confederation and gives the reader a string of generalizations entirely unsupported by statistical evidence or other business documentation. But the issue is not whether Fiske used first-hand sources, but whether he produced a valid synthesis. As one who has conducted graduate seminars for some time, I am not unaware of the fact that a good many people saturate themselves in the primary sources but are utterly unable to interpret them intelligently. Whether or not William Macdonald's appraisal of Fiske's book as "the best comprehensive account of the period"[26] still stands today, John Fiske's approach to the era had an enormous impact both upon the public and upon fellow historians. John Bach McMaster adopts it without reservations. In his *History of the People of the United States* he refers to the "disaffected," meaning the Shaysites, "associating for evil purposes," as opposed to "the better-minded," equally active in forming societies "for good purposes."[27] His treatment might well have been written by George R. Minot, clerk of the Massachusetts lower house, whose contemporary account of Shays' Rebellion betrays the fears of the conservative element as to the broader implications of the insurrection.[28] McMaster excoriates Clinton and New York for particularist tendencies. Save for Rhode Island, no state behaved worse than New York, McMaster contends.[29]

Other writers, while generally accepting the nationalist synthesis of the period, have approached the Confederation years in a somewhat more objective spirit than did Fiske and most of his predecessors. In the editor's introduction to Andrew C. McLaughlin's volume in the old *American Nation* series, Albert Bushnell Hart expresses doubt whether Fiske's "critical period" was "really a time of such danger of national dissolution as people then and since have supposed." He views the McLaughlin volume as showing "a more orderly, logical, and inevitable march of events than has commonly been described."[30] McLaughlin sees little or no justification for the constant lament about poverty in this period. "Some tribulation there was," he concedes, "but that the country was forlorn, destitute, and poverty-stricken is far from the truth." He sees indications of an upturn in trade by 1786. However, on the constitutional and diplomatic aspects of the period there is little difference between McLaughlin and Fiske. Referring to the humiliating relations with the Barbary states, McLaughlin asserts: "All this, like everything else one touches during the dismal period, discloses the helplessness of the confederacy." Toward the Shaysites he is far less sympathetic than Bancroft. "The vicious, the restless, the ignorant, the foolish—and there were plenty of each class—were coming together to test the strength of the newly established government of Massachusetts." The result, as he sees it, was "nothing short of civil war," but its virtue was that it disclosed the dangers, helped to bring about a reaction, discredited extreme democratic tendencies, and thereby aided the men who sought to inject vigor into the union.[31] Thus, those who were led by the editor of the series to believe that they were going to read a revisionist book were to find that it was essentially conventional in interpretation. Similarly, Edward Channing, in his *History of the United States,* published some years after McLaughlin, stresses the "helplessness" of the existing government and its failure to win respect either at home or abroad, but finds evidence of a business upthrust before the new Constitution went into operation.[32]

The Antifederalist or pro-democratic interpretation (and I need hardly say that the two terms are not necessarily equated) was perhaps first, among nineteenth-century historians, expounded by Henry B. Dawson, a learned military historian of the American Revolution, who also devoted

[24] John Fiske, *The Critical Period of American History, 1783–1789* (Boston and New York, 1888), pp. 55–57, and Chap. IV, *passim.*

[25] Andrew C. McLaughlin, *The Confederation and the Constitution, 1783–1789,* in *The American Nation: A History,* ed. Albert Bushnell Hart, X (New York and London, 1905), 319–320.

[26] William Macdonald, in *The Literature of American History: A Bibliographical Guide . . . ,* ed. J. N. Larned (Boston, 1902), p. 156.

[27] John Bach McMaster, *A History of the People of the United States, From the Revolution to the Civil War* (New York 1883–1913), I, 313.

[28] *History of the Insurrection in Massachusetts in 1786 . . .* (Worcester, 1788).

[29] *History,* I, 369–370.

[30] McLaughlin, *The Confederation and the Constitution,* p. xv.

[31] *Ibid.,* pp. 71, 107, 156, 161.

[32] Edward Channing, *A History of the United States* (New York, 1916–26), III, 491, 414–415, 426–427.

himself to studying the role of the masses in that war, and had a penchant for picking controversial issues which he fought with relish and passion. In an article in the *Historical Magazine* in 1871, Dawson attempted to refute John Lothrop Motley, who, in a celebrated letter to the London *Times* written during the Civil War, had asserted that the Confederation was a period of "chaos," in which the absence of law, order, and security for life and property was "as absolute as could be well conceived in a civilized land." These were reckless and false accusations, Dawson charged. He traced their origin to distinguished men of the Confederation period who had spread them "for selfish or partisan motives." He accused these leaders of having "nullified the established law of the Confederacy and violently and corruptly substituted for it what they styled the Constitution of the United States." Dawson had made extreme and curiously unbalanced charges but failed to substantiate them. The significance of the attack, however, lies far less in the kind of evidence adduced than in its formulation of the notion that the Federalists conspired to falsify the true conditions of the period in a deliberate effort to create panic and undermine the government of the Confederation. Oddly enough, the criminal statistics Dawson cites for New York State not only are inconclusive regarding lawlessness, but point directly opposite to what Dawson believed. They indicate that in New York City and County there were almost twice as many indictments between 1784 and 1789 as there were for the first five years under the new federal government. [33] Concerning law and order, Dawson may very well have been on the right track, but somewhere along the path he lost the scent.

Despite the intemperate character of his attack, Dawson had touched off certain doubts as to the reportorial objectivity both of the Founding Fathers and of later historians. These were again raised in 1907, when J. Allen Smith in his *The Spirit of American Government,* attacked on a second front, contending that the Constitution was the result of a counterrevolution. To him the Declaration of Independence spelled sweeping changes in the American form of government, changes manifest in an omnipotent legislature and the overthrow of the system of checks and balances which had been derived from the English constitution, with its characteristic blending of monarchical, aristocratic, and democratic elements. To Smith the chief feature of the Articles of Confederation was the entire absence of checks and balances, the vesting of all power in a single legislative body, unchecked by a distinct executive or judiciary. The fact that the power which was vested in the continental legislature was ineffectual did not disturb him. His main point, though,

was that such democratic changes had been wrought by radical forces and that the conservatives, once they had a chance to assess the situation, set about, in more or less conspiratorial fashion, to redress the balance. The Constitutional Convention was called, according to Smith, not only to impart vigor to the government but to institute an elaborate system of constitutional checks. The adoption of this system he calls a "triumph of a skillfully directed reactionary movement." [34] The idea that the adoption of the Constitution was the result of a struggle among interest groups was pressed by Arthur F. Bentley in *The Process of Government* (1908), in language which stemmed from Madison's *Federalist 10,* and in a more naked form by A. M. Simons' *Social Forces in American History* (1911).

The most significant amplification of the Smith-Bentley-Simons approach came in 1913 from the pen of Charles A. Beard. In his *An Economic Interpretation of the Constitution of the United States* Beard concedes that "interpretative schools seem always to originate in social antagonism," but he prefers the road which explains proximate or remote causes and relations to the so-called "impartial" history which surveys outward events and classifies and orders phenomena. [35] Beard was profoundly influenced by the Turnerian school, which substituted for the states'-rights interpretation of our history a recognition of social and economic areas, independent of state lines, which acted as units in political history. For the period of the Confederation the most important Turnerian contribution was Orin G. Libby's *Geographical Distribution of the Vote of the Thirteen States on the Federal Constitution,* an original and searching study published as far back as 1894. Beard found that nationalism cut across state lines, that it was created by a welding of economic interests of creditors, holders of personalty—especially public securities—, manufacturers, shippers, commercial groups, and speculators in western lands. While this majestic formula helped explain why people were Federalists, it has failed dismally in explaining differences between Federalists and Antifederalists. Recent studies by Robert Thomas of the property interests of members of the ratifying convention in Virginia have failed to turn up any significant differences between the two parties either in the kind and quantity of their property-holding or in their relative status as creditors or debtors. On the other hand, Jackson T. Main asserts that the Virginians who favored greater centralization were found in pro-creditor areas, the Northern Neck and much

---

[33] Henry B. Dawson, "The Motley Letter," *Historical Magazine,* 2nd Ser., IX (Mar., 1871), 157 ff.

[34] J. Allen Smith, *The Spirit of American Government: A Study of the Constitution, Its Origin, Influence, and Relation to Democracy* (Chautauqua, 1911), p. 37.

[35] Charles A. Beard, *An Economic Interpretation of the Constitution of the United States* (New York, 1949), pp. 3–4.

of the Tidewater, while the opposition came from the debtor Piedmont. After 1785, Main contends, the Shenandoah Valley counties, which had previously voted with the Piedmont on most issues, now supported a grant to Congress of power over commerce. But the picture is at best hardly clean-cut or conclusive.[36]

Beard suggested that general social conditions were prosperous and that the defects of the Articles did not justify the "loud complaints" of the advocates of change. In short, Beard found that the "critical period" was really not so critical after all, but, drawing upon Dawson's article, "a phantom of the imagination produced by some undoubted evils which could have been remedied without a political revolution."[37] Save for a quotation from Franklin, Beard fails to document this crucial generalization.

Lest anyone should carry away with him the view that Beard opposed the Constitution, as did J. Allen Smith, it might be well to point out that in his *Supreme Court and the Constitution,* published the previous year, he praised the Constitution and furnished historical precedents for judicial review. In later years he drew further and further away from any monolithic economic interpretation of the period. Although his *Rise of American Civilization* adhered to the approach of his *Economic Interpretation,* as did Parrington's treatment in *Main Currents in American Thought,* Beard by 1935 completely repudiated economic determinism. In *The Republic* (1943) he considered the adoption of the Constitution as the alternative to military dictatorship. In his *Basic History of the United States* (1944) he defended checks and balances as curbs on despotic powers, whereas in his earlier *Rise of American Civilization* he insists that checks and balances dissolved "the energy of the democratic majority."[38] In *The Enduring Federalist,* published in 1948, he refers to the Congress of the Confederation as "a kind of debating society," and describes conditions in the Confederation period in language which would have gratified Fiske and perhaps shocked Bancroft.[39] In short, by the end of his career, Beard, the confirmed nationalist and isolationist, had moved a long way from the Beard of pre-World War I days.

But it is the unreconstructed Beard who still captures the imagination of our younger scholars.

Today the chief disciple of J. Allen Smith and the early Beard is Merrill Jensen. In two significant books, *The Articles of Confederation,* published in 1940, and a more amplified treatment of the same problem, *The New Nation,* which appeared in 1950, Professor Jensen expounds learnedly and at length the argument that the Federalist party was organized to destroy the kind of democratic government and economic practice made possible by the Articles of Confederation.[40] Jensen sees the Articles as a constitutional expression of the philosophy of the Declaration of Independence, the Constitution as a betrayal of those principles. To Jensen the Articles were designed to prevent the central government from infringing upon the rights of the states, whereas the Constitution was designed to check both the states and the democracy that found expression within state bounds. As Jensen sees it, the Confederation government failed, not because it was inadequate, but because the radicals failed to maintain the organization they had created to bring about the American Revolution. He speaks of the radicals as having won *"their* war," but the fact remains that it was as much the war of the conservatives; probably a good deal more so.

Mr. Jensen finds conspiracy and betrayal at various levels. He suggests that the conservatives might well have betrayed the diplomatic objectives of the Revolution were it not for the integrity of Jay and Adams. He deplores the fact that radical leaders of the Thomas Burke-Richard Henry Lee-Sam Adams vintage quit the field and left it to what General Horatio Gates, scarcely an objective or disinterested patriot, called "the rapacious graspers of power and profit." Gates was one grasper of power who just missed the brass ring. Mr. Jensen sees this revolutionary group outnumbered by 1781, and worn down by defeat. Then from 1781 to 1783 the government revolved around Robert Morris and his satellites, for all practical purposes a dictatorship in Mr. Jensen's eyes. But when we look more closely at these counterrevolutionaries, the sharp line between radicals and conservatives seems to fade away. Who was more radical than Alexander McDougall in Sons-of-Liberty days? Yet it was he who headed a delegation of officers to Congress in the winter of 1783. Perhaps Hamilton was not far wrong when he defended the Morris faction as not only "the most liberal," but as "the men who think continentally." The issue does not seem to have been one between radicals and conservatives, but between extreme particularists of the Clinton stripe and continental nationalists of varying shades and degrees.

Mr. Jensen is most effective in recounting the

[36] Robert E. Thomas, "The Virginia Convention of 1788: A Criticism of Beard's *An Economic Interpretation of the Constitution,*" *Journal of Southern History,* XIX (1953), 63–72. Jackson T. Main, "Sections and Politics in Virginia, 1781–1787," *William and Mary Quarterly,* 3rd Ser., XII (1955), 96–112.

[37] Beard, *An Economic Interpretation of the Constitution,* pp. 47–48.

[38] Charles A. Beard and Mary R. Beard, *The Rise of American Civilization* (New York, 1930. First published in 1927), I, 326.

[39] Beard, *The Enduring Federalist* (New York, 1948), pp. 27–30.

[40] *The Articles of Confederation: An Interpretation of The Social-Constitutional History of the American Revolution, 1774–1781* (University of Wisconsin, 1940. Second printing with additional foreword, 1948). *The New Nation: A History of the United States During the Confederation, 1781–1789* (New York, 1950).

constructive steps taken in the Confederation period to repair federal and state finances. He points out that the Confederation actually managed to reduce the principal of its debt, and praises the states for their role in paying the national debt. Mr. Jensen points to the rapid amortization of state debts as evidence of the ability of the states to put their financial houses in order without much help from a central government. There is no doubt whatsoever that the states had now largely assumed the debt-funding function that the federal government had proven incapable of shouldering. Dr. E. J. Ferguson's studies of the assumption of the federal debts by the states reveal the considerable progress that was made in that direction in the Confederation period.[41] But, in terms of more recent ideas of economic planning, it would now seem that states like Massachusetts made the mistake of a too rapid amortization of the state debt, thereby initiating a sharp deflationary thrust. Even a conservative like Governor Bowdoin urged in 1786 a more gradual plan of amortization than that which the property-conscious legislature had enacted.

In short, the Beard-Jensen approach has served to present the Confederation period in a more constructive light, to give greater recognition to signs of economic expansion in the period and to the stabilizing role of the states, particularly in financial matters. As Allan Nevins has pointed out, when the new federal government went into effect, in no state was the debt appallingly high, and in some it was already low.[42] Mr. Jensen is doubtless correct in arguing that in most states the forces of law and order never lost the upper hand. In New York that arch-Antifederalist George Clinton personally led the troops of the state against the insurrectionary Shays. In most cases—and Maryland is an excellent example—the disgruntled elements confined their efforts to obtaining relief in a legal manner through legislative action.

In truth, the real difference between the nationalist and Antifederalist schools of historiography turns neither on the extent of the depression nor on the amount of anarchy in the "critical period," but springs from a deep divergence in interpreting the American Revolution and the issues for which it was fought. Mr. Jensen sees the radical party in the Revolution as comprising the town masses and the frontier groups. As he views it, the radicals fought for an internal revolution; those conservatives who reluctantly supported the war merely wanted independence from England. In fact, this school of historiography depicts the American Revolution as essentially a civil war among the Whigs. In this version there seems to be little or no room for Tories, for redcoats, or for

Hessians. This formula fails to explain why New York City and Philadelphia were hotbeds of Loyalism, why the regulators of Carolina and the levelers of upstate New York were Tories, or why debtors and creditors, hard-money men and paper-money men, suffrage expansionists and suffrage restrictionists were arrayed on the same side. It fails to explain the prominent role of the Whig conservative elite in bringing about the Revolution or to lay the foundation for understanding why in so many areas the radicalism of the leadership was that of the Gironde, not the Mountain.[43]

In the last analysis the view that the course of the Confederation period was determined by a counterrevolutionary movement, which, through the instrumentality of the Constitutional Convention, nipped democracy in the bud, hinges upon one's ideas about the American Revolution. Unless one is ready to accept the thesis that the group that started the war were libertarians and democrats and were supplanted by a conservative authoritarian party, one cannot give uncritical adherence to the Smith-Beard-Jensen approach to the Confederation period. The facts simply will not support the argument that the democratic forces originally seized control of the movement in the states. Even in the short run, these forces were unsuccessful in every state save Pennsylvania and Georgia. In New Jersey, then as now hospitable to democracy, the Constitution, as Mr. McCormick has demonstrated,[44] was welcomed by all classes because it promised needed financial relief. In that state a western conservative coalition brought about deflationary policies, but not until the very end of the period under review. But the counterrevolution, if the halting of the leftward swing of the pendulum deserves that appellation, was gradual and mild. States like Delaware and Maryland, as John A. Munroe[45] and Philip Crowl[46] have shown us, did not have a counterrevolution, be-

---

[41] E. J. Ferguson, "State Assumption of Federal Debt During the Confederation," *Mississippi Valley Historical Review*, XXXVIII (1951), 403.

[42] Allan Nevins, *The American States During and After the American Revolution* (New York, 1927), p. 541.

[43] For examples from New England, see Lee N. Newcomer, *The Embattled Farmers: A Massachusetts Countryside in the American Revolution* (New York, 1953); Oscar Zeichner, *Connecticut's Years of Controversy, 1750–1776* (Chapel Hill, 1949). Robert E. Brown, *Middle-Class Democracy and the Revolution in Massachusetts, 1691–1780* (Ithaca, N.Y., 1955), demonstrates that in Massachusetts the property qualification for voting did not bar the majority of adult males from taking part in elections. He opposes the view of an "internal revolution" on the ground that democracy was already established. It is unlikely, however, that a re-examination of the nature and extent of the franchise and other so-called democratic indices in most of the remaining twelve states will support his concluding speculation that the "common man . . . had come into his own long before the era of Jacksonian Democracy."

[44] Richard P. McCormick, *Experiment in Independence: New Jersey in the Critical Period, 1781–1789* (New Brunswick, 1950).

[45] *Federalist Delaware, 1775–1815* (New Brunswick, 1954).

[46] *Maryland During and After the Revolution* (Baltimore, 1942).

cause there never was the kind of democratic upthrust that characterized the early Revolutionary years in Pennsylvania.

The failure of the so-called democratic forces, as Elisha P. Douglass has recently restated for us,[47] is a tribute to the vigorous Revolutionary leadership of the Whig conservative forces and their awareness of the fundamental issues at stake. It was the Whig conservatives, not the regulators in North Carolina or the back-country insurgents in Massachusetts, who took the lead in the movement toward independence. Only where the Whig elite seemed timorous and unwilling to move from protest to revolution did the democratic and backcountry forces have any chance of seizing power. That was the case in Pennsylvania, where the conservatives had abdicated their political leadership, and to a lesser degree in Georgia, where the story still remains to be spelled out and where the democratic victory was by no means as clear-cut as in Pennsylvania.

The Burke-Bryan-Lee-Clinton forces that comprised the so-called "democratic" party in the Revolutionary years—just what did they stand for? What kind of democracy did they want? The touchstone of their democracy seems to have been an advocacy of a unicameral legislature, a popularly elected judiciary, and a weak executive—and very little else. In some respects the Whig conservatives held more advanced views than did the radicals. Judged by present-day standards the majoritarians were not always liberal. Backcountry enthusiasts of the Great Awakening, they were by no means as ready to tolerate non-Protestant religious beliefs as were the deistically-minded Whig leaders. In fact, some of the most revealing evidence presented by Mr. Douglass is that which indicates that left-wing Protestants of Pietist or evangelical inclinations were fundamentalists in outlook and often basically conservative on political issues. It was they who tried to curb the political rights of non-Protestants, and in Pennsylvania it was the so-called radicals who enacted a law restricting freedom of expression. No, the majoritarians did not always act in democratic ways, nor did they seem always willing to abide by the will of the majority. Witness the shocking abuse of power by the radicals in Pennsylvania who established the state constitution by fiat and did not dare submit it to the people. In fact, they went so far as to require the people to take an oath to support the constitution as a prerequisite to exercising the franchise.

Much has been made of the distrust of the masses held by the Whig conservatives, of the views of men like Jay that "the mass of men are neither wise nor good." But many of the Antifederalists shared similar views. Take Samuel Chase, who, as Philip Crowl has shown us, was instrumental in framing Maryland's ultraconservative constitution, and is alleged to have been unstinting in his praise of the aristocratic features of that document, particularly of the electoral college for choosing senators. His desertion to the Antifederalist camp is perhaps best explained by his financial reverses, but he did not linger in it too long. In the federal Convention the Antifederalist John F. Mercer had opposed allowing the people to participate, declaring, "The people cannot know and judge of the characters of Candidates. The worst possible choice will be made."[48] Elbridge Gerry, who refused to sign the Constitution, asserted that "the evils we experience flow from the excess of democracy" and expressed concern at "the danger of the levilling [sic] spirit."[49] In New York the bulwark of Antifederalism was the landowner, with his rural isolation, his dread of the federal impost, and his jealousy of sharing political power. True, he was supported in his opposition to the Constitution by tenants and small farmers, but the Antifederalist leaders of that state had little faith in the people. At the New York Convention George Clinton criticized the people for their fickleness, their tendency "to vibrate from one extreme to another." It was this very disposition, Clinton confessed, against which he wished to guard.[50]

The Antifederalists were not poured out of one democratic mold,[51] any more than the Federalists represented a unitary point of view about how to strengthen the central government. As Robert East has demonstrated,[52] there was a wide breach between the Bowdoin-Adams kind of federalism in Massachusetts and the Cabot-Pickering stripe of particularism, with its strong sectional and anti-Southern overtones. There was an even wider gulf between the democratic nationalism of Franklin and the authoritarian nationalism of Hamilton.

On the pro-democratic side of the Federalist ledger must be credited the position of the Whig conservatives in support of certain basic human rights which they conceived as fundamental and not subject to change at the caprice of majority rule. Fortunately for the evolution of American democracy, the principles of the conservative revolutionaries and their so-called democratic opponents were largely complementary to each other. Although almost everywhere the radicals were defeated in their efforts to seize the ma-

---

[48] *Records of the Federal Convention of 1787*, ed. Max Farrand (New Haven, 1911–37) II, 205.

[49] *Ibid.,* I, 48.

[50] *Debates in the Several State Conventions on the Adoption of the Federal Constitution, . . . Together with the Journal of the Federal Convention . . . ,* ed. Jonathan Elliot (Philadelphia, 1881), II, 359.

[51] The reader is referred to the provocative article by Cecelia M. Kenyon, "Men of Little Faith: The Anti-Federalists on the Nature of Representative Government," *William and Mary Quarterly,* 3rd Ser., XII (1955), 3–43.

[52] "The Massachusetts Conservatives in the Critical Period," in *The Era of the American Revolution,* ed. R. B. Morris (New York, 1939), pp. 349–391.

---

[47] *Rebels and Democrats* (Chapel Hill, 1955).

chinery of Revolution, the liberative effects of the war proved a deterrent to the kind of social revolution which would have enshrined class hatreds and ensured violent reaction. [53]

Yes, the American Whigs were divided in the years of the Revolution on almost all issues except that of political independence from Great Britain. Since diverse and even divergent interests forged the Whig alliance, it was only to be expected that the victory of the patriots would settle no single social or economic issue except freedom from British mercantilist controls, hardly an unmixed blessing in the years of the Confederation. Despite the efforts of J. Franklin Jameson to consider the American Revolution as a social movement, the fact is that the great internal social reforms lay ahead. As Harrison Gray Otis once wrote to a friend of Revolutionary days: "You and I did not imagine when the first war with Britain was over

that the revolution was just begun." [54] Similar sentiments were expressed by Dr. Benjamin Rush on an earlier occasion. In his "Address to the People of the United States on the Defects of the Confederation" Rush declared: "The American war is over; but this is far from being the case with the American Revolution." [55]

Indeed, the imposition of a vitalized federalism and the tightening of the bonds of union precipitated a greater revolution in American life than did separation from England. To those who view the adoption of a system of republican federalism as constituting a more thoroughgoing break with the political system of the past than did that earlier severing of the tenuous bonds of empire—and there is impressive evidence in the Confederation interlude of our history to substantiate this interpretation—the Federalists, not the Antifederalists, were the real radicals of their day.

In 1787 and 1788, a lengthy interchange of letters passed between two leaders of the Virginia gentry, James Madison, who had been one of the chief framers of the Constitution, and Thomas Jefferson, Minister to France. Jefferson viewed the Convention as "an assembly of demigods," but, when he first received a copy of the Constitution, he wrote to John Adams, "I confess there are things in it which stagger all my dispositions to subscribe to what such an Assembly has proposed." Madison, whose thinking on constitutional problems had been deeper and more precise, labored skilfully to overcome many of Jefferson's misgivings. In turn, Jefferson impressed Madison with arguments in favor of a bill of rights. The letters which follow (which are only part of the total correspondence) present the constitutional views of both men and some account of the struggles for its ratification. Madison was not entirely candid with Jefferson; he did not mention *The Federalist,* to which he contributed so substantially, until months after the New York ratifying convention was over.[1] Nevertheless, these letters offer remarkable views of the Constitution and the debates over its ratification by two of the greatest American political figures.

MADISON AND JEFFERSON DISCUSS
THE PROPOSED CONSTITUTION*

[53] "Was there ever a revolution brought about, especially so important as this, without great internal tumults and violent convulsions!" Sam Adams asked rhetorically. *The Writings of Samuel Adams,* ed. H. A. Cushing (New York, 1904–08), III, 304.

[54] Samuel Eliot Morison, *The Life and Letters of Harrison Gray Otis* (Boston and New York, 1913), I, 49.

[55] Reprinted in H. Niles, *Principles and Acts of the Revolution in America* (Baltimore, 1822), p. 402.

[1] For analyses of the correspondence, its background, and Jefferson's attitudes, see Dumas Malone, *Jefferson and the Rights of Man* (Boston: Little, Brown, 1951), ch. 9 and Adrienne Koch,

MADISON TO JEFFERSON

Dear Sir   New York Octr. 24. 1787.
... You will herewith receive the result of the Convention, which continued its session till the 17th of September. I take the liberty of making some observations on the subject which will help to make up a letter, if they should answer no other purpose.

Jefferson and Madison: The Great Collaboration (New York: Knopf, 1950), ch. 4.

* Reprinted from Julian P. Boyd, *et al.,* eds., *The Papers of Thomas Jefferson* (Princeton, N.J.: Princeton Univ. Press, 1950———), XII, 271–84, 409–12, 439–42; XIII, 98–99, 412–13, 442–43; XIV, 17–21, 187–88, 339–42, 659–62 by permission.

It appeared to be the sincere and unanimous wish of the Convention to cherish and preserve the Union of the States. No proposition was made, no suggestion was thrown out in favor of a partition of the Empire into two or more Confederacies.

It was generally agreed that the objects of the Union could not be secured by any system founded on the principle of a confederation of sovereign States. A voluntary observance of the federal law by all the members could never be hoped for. A compulsive one could evidently never be reduced to practice, and if it could, involved equal calamities to the innocent and the guilty, the necessity of a military force both obnoxious and dangerous, and in general, a scene resembling much more a civil war, than the administration of a regular Government.

Hence was embraced the alternative of a government which instead of operating, on the States, should operate without their intervention on the individuals composing them: and hence the change in the principle and proportion of representation.

This ground-work being laid, the great objects which presented themselves were 1. to unite a proper energy in the Executive and a proper stability in the Legislative departments, with the essential characters of Republican Government. 2. To draw a line of demarkation which would give to the General Government every power requisite for general purposes, and leave to the States every power which might be most beneficially administered by them. 3. To provide for the different interests of different parts of the Union. 4. To adjust the clashing pretensions of the large and small States. Each of these objects was pregnant with difficulties. The whole of them together formed a task more difficult than can be well conceived by those who were not concerned in the execution of it. Adding to these considerations the natural diversity of human opinions on all new and complicated subjects, it is impossible to consider the degree of concord which ultimately prevailed as less than a miracle.

The first of these objects as it respects the Executive, was peculiarly embarrassing. On the question whether it should consist of a single person, or a plurality of co-ordinate members, on the mode of appointment, on the duration in office, on the degree of power, on the re-eligibility, tedious and reiterated discussions took place. The plurality of co-ordinate members had finally but few advocates. Governour Randolph was at the head of them. The modes of appointment proposed were various, as by the people at large—by electors chosen by the people—by the Executives of the States—by the Congress, some preferring a joint ballot of the two Houses—some a separate concurrent ballot allowing to each a negative on the other house—some a nomination of several candidates by one House, out of whom a choice should be made by the other. Several other modifications were started. The expedient at length adopted seemed to give pretty general satisfaction to the members. As to the duration in office, a few would have preferred a tenure during good behaviour—a considerable number would have done so in case an easy and effectual removal by impeachment could be settled. It was much agitated whether a long term, seven years for example, with a subsequent and perpetual ineligibility, or a short term with a capacity to be re-elected, should be fixed. In favor of the first opinion were urged the danger of a gradual degeneracy of re-elections from time to time, into first a life and then a hereditary tenure, and the favorable effect of an incapacity to be reappointed, on the independent exercise of the Executive authority. On the other side it was contended that the prospect of necessary degradation would discourage the most dignified characters from aspiring to the office, would take away the principal motive to the faithful discharge of its duties. The hope of being rewarded with a reappointment, would stimulate ambition to violent efforts for holding over the constitutional term, and instead of producing an independent administration, and a firmer defence of the constitutional rights of the department, would render the officer more indifferent to the importance of a place which he would soon be obliged to quit for ever, and more ready to yield to the incroachments of the Legislature of which he might again be a member.—The questions concerning the degree of power turned chiefly on the appointment to offices, and the controul on the Legislature. An *absolute* appointment to all offices —to some offices—to no offices, formed the scale of opinions on the first point. On the second, some contended for an absolute negative, as the only possible mean of reducing to practice, the theory of a free government which forbids a mixture of the Legislative and Executive powers. Others would be content with a revisionary power to be overruled by three fourths of both Houses. It was warmly urged that the judiciary department should be associated in the revision. The idea of some was that a separate revision should be given to the two departments—that if either objected two thirds; if both three fourths, should be necessary to overrule.

In forming the Senate, the great anchor of the Government, the questions as they came within the first object turned mostly on the mode of appointment, and the duration of it. The different modes proposed were, 1. by the House of Representatives, 2. by the Executive, 3 by electors chosen by the people for the purpose, 4. by the State Legislatures. On the point of duration, the propositions descended from good behavior to four years, through the intermediate terms of nine, seven, six and five years. The election of the other branch was first determined to be triennial, and afterwards reduced to biennial.

The second object, the due partition of power, between the General and local Governments, was perhaps of all, the most nice and difficult. A few contended for an entire abolition of the States;

Some for indefinite power of Legislation in the Congress, with a negative on the laws of the States, some for such a power without a negative, some for a limited power of legislation, with such a negative: the majority finally for a limited power without the negative. The question with regard to the Negative underwent repeated discussions, and was finally rejected by a bare majority. As I formerly intimated to you my opinion in favor of this ingredient, I will take this occasion of explaining myself on the subject. [1] [Such a check on the States appears to me necessary 1. to prevent encroachments on the General authority, 2. to prevent instability and injustice in the legislation of the States.

1. Without such a check in the whole over the parts, our system involves the evil of imperia in imperio. If a compleat supremacy some where is not necessary in every Society, a controuling power at least is so, by which the general authority may be defended against encroachments of the subordinate authorities, and by which the latter may be restrained from encroachments on each other. If the supremacy of the British Parliament is not necessary as has been contended, for the harmony of that Empire, it is evident I think that without the royal negative or some equivalent controul, the unity of the system would be destroyed. The want of some such provision seems to have been mortal to the antient Confederacies, and to be the disease of the modern. Of the Lycian Confederacy little is known. That of the Amphyctions is well known to have been rendered of little use whilst it lasted, and in the end to have been destroyed by the predominance of the local over the federal authority. The same observation may be made, on the authority of Polybius, with regard to the Achæan League. The Helvetic System scarcely amounts to a confederacy and is distinguished by too many peculiarities to be a ground of comparison. The case of the United Netherlands is in point. The authority of a Statholder, the influence of a standing army, the common interest in the conquered possessions, the pressure of surrounding danger, the guarantee of foreign powers, are not sufficient to secure the authority and interests of the generality, against the antifederal tendency of the provincial sovereignties. The German Empire is another example. A Hereditary chief with vast independent resources of wealth and power, a federal Diet, with ample parchment authority, a regular Judiciary establishment, the influence of the neighbourhood of great and formidable Nations, have been found unable either to maintain the

subordination of the members, or to prevent their mutual contests and encroachments. Still more to the purpose is our own experience both during the war and since the peace. Encroachments of the States on the general authority, sacrifices of national to local interests, interferences of the measures of different States, form a great part of the history of our political system. It may be said that the new Constitution is founded on different principles, and will have a different operation. I admit the difference to be material. It presents the aspect rather of a feudal system of republics, if such a phrase may be used, than of a Confederacy of independent States. And what has been the progress and event of the feudal Constitutions? In all of them a continual struggle between the head and the inferior members, until a final victory has been gained in some instances by one, in others, by the other of them. In one respect indeed there is a remarkable variance between the two cases. In the feudal system the sovereign, though limited, was independent; and having no particular sympathy of interests with the great Barons, his ambition had as full play as theirs in the mutual projects of usurpation. In the American Constitution The general authority will be derived entirely from the subordinate authorities. The Senate will represent the States in their political capacity, the other House will represent the people of the States in their individual capacity. The former will be accountable to their constituents at moderate, the latter at short periods. The President also derives his appointment from the States, and is periodically accountable to them. This dependence of the General, on the local authorities seems effectually to guard the latter against any dangerous encroachments of the former: Whilst the latter within their respective limits, will be continually sensible of the abridgment of their power, and be stimulated by ambition to resume the surrendered portion of it. We find the representatives of counties and corporations in the Legislatures of the States, much more disposed to sacrifice the aggregate interest, and even authority, to the local views of their Constituents, than the latter to the former. I mean not by these remarks to insinuate that an esprit de corps will not exist in the national Government, that opportunities may not occur of extending its jurisdiction in some points. I mean only that the danger of encroachments is much greater from the other side, and that the impossibility of dividing powers of legislation, in such a manner, as to be free from different constructions by different interests, or even from ambiguity in the judgment of the impartial, requires some such expedient as I contend for. Many illustrations might be given of this impossibility. How long has it taken to fix, and how imperfectly is yet fixed the legislative power of corporations, though that power is subordinate in the most compleat manner? The line of distinction between the power of regulating trade and that of drawing revenue from it, which was once considered as the barrier of our liberties, was found on fair discussion, to be ab-

---

[1] In a letter of March 19, 1787, Madison had argued that a properly revised federal government would have to have "a negative *in all cases whatsoever* on the local legislatures." Jefferson had disagreed strongly in a letter of June 20, suggesting instead that federal jurisdiction over state legislation be strictly limited to matters that "concern the confederacy," and that the exercise of this federal veto power be handled only by the federal courts.

solutely undefinable. No distinction seems to be more obvious than that between spiritual and temporal matters. Yet wherever they have been made objects of Legislation, they have clashed and contended with each other, till one or the other has gained the supremacy. Even the boundaries between the Executive, Legislative and Judiciary powers, though in general so strongly marked in themselves, consist in many instances of mere shades of difference. It may be said that the Judicial authority under our new system will keep the States within their proper limits, and supply the place of a negative on their laws. The answer is that it is more convenient to prevent the passage of a law, than to declare it void after it is passed; that this will be particularly the case where the law aggrieves individuals, who may be unable to support an appeal against a State to the supreme Judiciary, that a State which would violate the Legislative rights of the Union, would not be very ready to obey a Judicial decree in support of them, and that a recurrence to force, which in the event of disobedience would be necessary, is an evil which the new Constitution meant to exclude as far as possible.

2. A Constitutional negative on the laws of the States seems equally necessary to secure individuals against encroachments on their rights. The mutability of the laws of the States is found to be a serious evil. The injustice of them has been so frequent and so flagrant as to alarm the most stedfast friends of Republicanism. I am persuaded I do not err in saying that the evils issuing from these sources contributed more to that uneasiness which produced the Convention, and prepared the public mind for a general reform, than those which accrued to our national character and interest from the inadequacy of the Confederation to its immediate objects. A reform therefore which does not make provision for private rights, must be materially defective. The restraints against paper emissions, and violations of contracts are not sufficient. Supposing them to be effectual as far as they go, they are short of the mark. Injustice may be effected by such an infinitude of legislative expedients, that where the disposition exists it can only be controuled by some provision which reaches all cases whatsoever. The partial provision made, supposes the disposition which will evade it. It may be asked how private rights will be more secure under the Guardianship of the General Government than under the State Governments, since they are both founded on the republican principle which refers the ultimate decision to the will of the majority, and are distinguished rather by the extent within which they will operate, than by any material difference in their structure. A full discussion of this question would, if I mistake not, unfold the true principles of Republican Government, and prove in contradiction to the concurrent opinions of theoretical writers, that this form of Government, in order to effect its purposes must operate not within a small but an extensive sphere. I will state some of the ideas which have occurred to me on this subject. Those who contend for a simple Democracy, or a pure republic, actuated by the sense of the majority, and operating within narrow limits, assume or suppose a case which is altogether fictitious. They found their reasoning on the idea, that the people composing the Society enjoy not only an equality of political rights; but that they have all precisely the same interests and the same feelings in every respect. Were this in reality the case, their reasoning would be conclusive. The interest of the majority would be that of the minority also; the decisions could only turn on mere opinion concerning the good of the whole of which the major voice would be the safest criterion; and within a small sphere, this voice could be most easily collected and the public affairs most accurately managed. We know however that no Society ever did or can consist of so homogeneous a mass of Citizens. In the savage State indeed, an approach is made towards it; but in that state little or no Government is necessary. In all civilized Societies, distinctions are various and unavoidable. A distinction of property results from that very protection which a free Government gives to unequal faculties of acquiring it. There will be rich and poor; creditors and debtors; a landed interest, a monied interest, a mercantile interest, a manufacturing interest. These classes may again be subdivided according to the different productions of different situations and soils, and according to different branches of commerce and of manufactures. In addition to these natural distinctions, artificial ones will be founded on accidental differences in political, religious and other opinions, or an attachment to the persons of leading individuals. However erroneous or ridiculous these grounds of dissention and faction may appear to the enlightened Statesman, or the benevolent philosopher, the bulk of mankind who are neither Statesmen nor Philosophers, will continue to view them in a different light. It remains then to be enquired whether a majority having any common interest, or feeling any common passion, will find sufficient motives to restrain them from oppressing the minority. An individual is never allowed to be a judge or even a witness in his own cause. If two individuals are under the biass of interest or enmity against a third, the rights of the latter could never be safely referred to the majority of the three. Will two thousand individuals be less apt to oppress one thousand, or two hundred thousand, one hundred thousand? Three motives only can restrain in such cases. 1. A prudent regard to private or partial good, as essentially involved in the general and permanent good of the whole. This ought no doubt to be sufficient of itself. Experience however shews that it has little effect on individuals, and perhaps still less on a collection of individuals, and least of all on a majority with the public authority in their hands. If the former are ready to forget that honesty is the best policy; the last do more. They often proceed on the converse of the maxim: that whatever is politic is

honest. 2. Respect for character. This motive is not found sufficient to restrain individuals from injustice, and loses its efficacy in proportion to the number which is to divide the praise or the blame. Besides as it has reference to public opinion, which is that of the majority, the standard is fixed by those whose conduct is to be measured by it. 3. Religion. The inefficacy of this restraint on individuals is well known. The conduct of every popular assembly, acting on oath, the strongest of religious ties, shews that individuals join without remorse in acts against which their consciences would revolt, if proposed to them separately in their closets. When Indeed Religion is kindled into enthusiasm, its force like that of other passions is increased by the sympathy of a multitude. But enthusiasm is only a temporary state of Religion, and whilst it lasts will hardly be seen with pleasure at the helm. Even in its coolest state, it has been much oftener a motive to oppression than a restraint from it. If then there must be different interests and parties in Society; and a majority when united by a common interest or passion can not be restrained from oppressing the minority, what remedy can be found in a republican Government, where the majority must ultimately decide, but that of giving such an extent to its sphere, that no common interest or passion will be likely to unite a majority of the whole number in an unjust pursuit. In a large Society, the people are broken into so many interests and parties, that a common sentiment is less likely to be felt, and the requisite concert less likely to be formed, by a majority of the whole. The same security seems requisite for the civil as for the religious rights of individuals. If the same sect form a majority and have the power, other sects will be sure to be depressed. Divide et impera, the reprobated axiom of tyranny, is under certain qualifications, the only policy, by which a republic can be administered on just principles. It must be observed however that this doctrine can only hold within a sphere of a mean extent. As in too small a sphere oppressive combinations may be too easily formed against the weaker party; so in too extensive a one a defensive concert may be rendered too difficult against the oppression of those entrusted with the administration. The great desideratum in Government is, so to modify the sovereignty as that it may be sufficiently neutral between different parts of the Society to controul one part from invading the rights of another, and at the same time sufficiently controuled itself, from setting up an interest adverse to that of the entire Society. In absolute monarchies, the Prince may be tolerably neutral towards different classes of his subjects, but may sacrifice the happiness of all to his personal ambition or avarice. In small republics, the sovereign will is controuled from such a sacrifice of the entire Society, but it is not sufficiently neutral towards the parts composing it. In the extended Republic of the United States, the General Government would hold a pretty even balance between the parties of particular States, and be at the same time sufficiently restrained by its dependence on the community, from betraying its general interests.]

Begging pardon for this immoderate digression, I return to the third object abovementioned, the adjustment of the different interests of different parts of the Continent. Some contended for an unlimited power over trade including exports as well as imports, and over slaves as well as other imports; some for such a power, provided the concurrence of two thirds of both Houses were required; some for such a qualification of the power, with an exemption of exports and slaves, others for an exemption of exports only. The result is seen in the Constitution. S. Carolina and Georgia were inflexible on the point of the slaves.

The remaining object, created more embarrassment, and a greater alarm for the issue of the Convention than all the rest put together. The little States insisted on retaining their equality in both branches, unless a compleat abolition of the State Governments should take place; and made an equality in the Senate a sine qua non. The large States on the other hand urged that as the new Government was to be drawn principally from the people immediately and was to operate directly on them, not on the States; and consequently as the States would lose that importance which is now proportioned to the importance of their voluntary compliances with the requisitions of Congress, it was necessary that the representation in both Houses should be in proportion to their size. It ended in the compromise which you will see, but very much to the dissatisfaction of several members from the large States.

It will not escape you that three names only from Virginia are subscribed to the Act. Mr. Wythe did not return after the death of his lady. Docr. McClurg left the Convention some time before the adjournment. The Governour and Col. Mason refused to be parties to it. Mr. Gerry was the only other member who refused. The objections of the Govr. turn principally on the latitude of the general powers, and on the connection established between the President and the Senate. He wished that the plan should be proposed to the States with liberty to them to suggest alterations which should all be referred to another general Convention to be incorporated into the plan as far as might be judged expedient. He was not inveterate in his opposition, and grounded his refusal to subscribe pretty much on his unwillingness to commit himself so as not to be at liberty to be governed by further lights on the subject. Col. Mason left Philada. in an exceeding ill humour indeed. A number of little circumstances arising in part from the impatience which prevailed towards the close of the business, conspired to whet his acrimony. He returned to Virginia with a fixed disposition to prevent the adoption of the plan if possible. He considers the want of a Bill of Rights as a fatal objection. His other objections are to the substitution of the Senate in place of an Executive Council and to the powers vested in that body—to the powers of the Judiciary—to the vice President being made President of the Senate—to the smallness of the number of Representatives—to the restriction on the States with regard to ex post facto laws—and most of all probably to the power of regulating trade, by a majority only of each House. He has some other lesser objections. Being now under the necessity of justifying his refusal to sign, he will of course, muster every possible one. His conduct has given great umbrage to the County of Fairfax, and particularly to the Town of Alexandria. He is already instructed to promote in the Assembly the calling a Convention, and will probably be either not deputed to the Convention, or be tied up by express instructions. He did not object in general to the powers vested in the National Government, so much as to the modification. In some respects he admitted that some further powers could have improved the system. He acknowledged in particular that a negative on the State laws, and the appointment of the State Executives ought to be ingredients; but supposed that the public mind would not now bear them and that experience would hereafter produce these amendments.

The final reception which will be given by the people at large to this proposed System can not yet be decided. The Legislature of N. Hampshire was sitting when it reached that State and was well pleased with it. As far as the sense of the people there has been expressed, it is equally favorable. Boston is warm and almost unanimous in embracing it. The impression on the country is not yet known. No symptoms of disapprobation have appeared. The Legislature of that State is now sitting, through which the sense of the people at large will soon be promulged with tolerable certainty. The paper money faction in Rh. Island is hostile. The other party zealously attached to it. Its passage through Connecticut is likely to be very smooth and easy. There seems to be less agitation in this state than any where. The discussion of the subject seems confined to the newspapers. The principal characters are known to be friendly. The Governour's party which has hitherto been the popular and most numerous one, is supposed to be on the opposite side; but considerable reserve is practiced, of which he sets the example. N. Jersey takes the affirmative side of course. Meetings of the people are declaring their approbation, and instructing their representatives. Penna. will be divided. The City of Philada., the Republican party, the Quakers, and most of the Germans espouse the Constitution. Some of the Constitutional leaders, backed by the western Country will oppose. An unlucky ferment on the subject in their assembly just before its late adjournment has irritated both sides, particularly the opposition, and by redoubling the exertions of that party may render the event doubtful. The voice of Maryland I understand from pretty good authority, is, as far as it has been declared, strongly in favor of the Constitution. Mr. Chase is an enemy, but the Town of Baltimore which

he now represents, is warmly attached to it, and will shackle him as far as they can. Mr. Paca will probably be, as usually, in the politics of Chase. My information from Virginia is as yet extremely imperfect. I have a letter from Genl. Washington which speaks favorably of the impression within a circle of some extent, and another from Chancellor Pendleton which expresses his full acceptance of the plan, and the popularity of it in his district. I am told also that Innis and Marshall are patrons of it. In the opposite scale are Mr. James Mercer, Mr. R. H. Lee, Docr. Lee and their connections of course, Mr. M. Page according to Report, and most of the Judges and Bar of the general Court. The part which Mr. Henry will take is unknown here. Much will depend on it. I had taken it for granted from a variety of circumstances that he would be in the opposition, and still think that will be the case. There are reports however which favor a contrary supposition. From the States South of Virginia nothing has been heard. As the deputation from S. Carolina consisted of some of its weightiest characters, who have returned unanimously zealous in favor of the Constitution, it is probable that State will readily embrace it. It is not less probable, that N. Carolina will follow the example unless that of Virginia should counterbalance it. Upon the whole, although, the public mind will not be fully known, nor finally settled for a considerable time, appearances at present augur a more prompt, and general adoption of the plan than could have been well expected.

When the plan came before Congress for their sanction, a very serious report was made by R. H. Lee and Mr. Dane from Masts. to embarrass it. It was first contended that Congress could not properly give any positive countenance to a measure which had for its object the subversion of the Constitution under which they acted. This ground of attack failing, the former gentleman urged the expediency of sending out the plan with amendments, and proposed a number of them corresponding with the objections of Col. Mason. This experiment had still less effect. In order however to obtain unanimity it was necessary to couch the resolution in very moderate terms....

Novr. 1. Commodore Jones having preferred another vessel to the packet, has remained here till this time. The interval has produced little necessary to be added to the above. The Legislature of Massts. has it seems taken up the Act of the Convention and have appointed or probably will appoint an early day for its State Convention. There are letters also from Georgia which denote a favorable disposition. I am informed from Richmond that the new Election-law from the Revised Code produced a pretty full House of Delegates, as well as a Senate, on the first day. It had previously had equal effect in producing full meetings of the freeholders for the County elections. A very decided majority of the Assembly is said to be zealous in favor of the New Constitution. The same is said of the Country at large. It appears however that individuals of great weight both within and without the Legislature are opposed to it. A letter I just have from Mr. A. Stuart names Mr. Henry, Genl. Nelson, W. Nelson, the family of Cabels, St. George Tucker, John Taylor and the Judges of the General Court except P. Carrington. The other opponents he described as of too little note to be mentioned, which gives a negative information of the Characters on the other side. All are agreed that the plan must be submitted to a Convention. . . .

With the most affectionate attachment I remain Dear Sr. Your obed friend & servant,

Js. Madison Jr.

MADISON TO JEFFERSON

Dear Sir   New York. Decr. 9th. 1787.
. . . The Constitution proposed by the late Convention engrosses almost the whole political attention of America. All the Legislatures except that of R. Island, which have been assembled, have agreed in submitting it to State Conventions. Virginia has set the example of opening a door for amendments, if the Convention there should chuse to propose them. Maryland has copied it. The States which preceded, referred the Constitution as recommended by the General Convention, to be ratified or rejected as it stands. The Convention of Pennsylvania, is now sitting. There are about 44 or 45, on the affirmative and about half that number on the opposite side; A considerable number of the Constitutional party as it was called, having joined the other party in espousing the federal Constitution. The returns of deputies for the Convention of Connecticut are known, and prove, as is said by those who know the men that a very great majority will adopt it in that State. The event in Massachusetts lies in greater uncertainty. The friends of the New Government continue to be sanguine. N. Hampshire from every account, as well as from some general inducements felt there, will pretty certainly be on the affirmative side. So will New Jersey and Delaware. N. York is much divided. She will hardly dissent from N. England, particularly if the conduct of the latter should coincide with that of N. Jersey and Pennsylva. A more formidable opposition is likely to be made in Maryland than was at first conjectured. Mr. Mercer, it seems, who was a member of the Convention, though his attendance was but for a short time, is become an auxiliary to Chace. Johnson the Carrolls, Govr. Lee, and most of the other characters of weight are on the other side. Mr. T. Stone died a little before the Government was promulged. The body of the people in Virginia. particularly in the upper and lower Country, and in the Northern Neck, are as far as I can gather, much disposed to adopt the new Constitution. The middle Country, and the South side of James River are principally in the opposition to it. As yet a large majority of the people are under the first description. As yet also are a majority of the Assembly. What change

may be produced by the united influence of exertions of Mr. Henry, Mr. Mason, and the Governor with some pretty able auxiliaries, is uncertain. My information leads me to suppose there must be three parties in Virginia. The first for adopting without attempting amendments. This includes Genl. W and the other deputies who signed the Constitution, Mr. Pendleton (Mr. Marshal I believe), Mr. Nicholas, Mr. Corbin, Mr. Zachy. Johnson, Col. Innis, (Mr. B. Randolph as I understand) Mr. Harvey, Mr. Gabl. Jones, Docr. Jones, &c. &c. At the head of the 2d. party which urges amendments are the Governor and Mr. Mason. These do not object to the substance of the Government but contend for a few additional guards in favor of the Rights of the States and of the people. I am not able to enumerate the characters which fall in with their ideas, as distinguished from those of a third Class, at the head of which is Mr. Henry. This class concurs at present with the patrons of amendments, but will probably contend for such as strike at the essence of the System, and must lead to an adherence to the principle of the existing Confederation, which most thinking men are convinced is a visionary one, or to a partition of the Union into several Confederacies. Mr. Harrison the late Governor is with Mr. Henry. So are a number of others. The General and Admiralty Courts with most of the Bar, oppose the Constitution, but on what particular grounds I am unable to say. Genl. Nelson, Mr. Jno. Page, Col. Bland, &c. are also opponents, but on what principle and to what extent, I am equally at a loss to say. In general I must note, that I speak with respect to many of these names, from information that may not be accurate, and merely as I should do in a free and confidential conversation with you. I have not yet heard Mr. Wythe's sentiments on the subject. Docr. McClurg the other absent deputy, is a very strenuous defender of the new Government. Mr. Henry is the great adversary who will render the event precarious. He is I find with his usual address, working up every possible interest, into a spirit of opposition. It is worthy of remark that whilst in Virga. and some of the other States in the middle and Southern Districts of the Union, the men of intelligence, patriotism, property, and independent circumstances, are thus divided; all of this description, with a few exceptions, in the Eastern States, and most of the middle States, are zealously attached to the proposed Constitution. In N. England, the men of letters, the principal officers of Government, the Judges and Lawyers, the Clergy, and men of property, furnish only here and there an adversary. It is not less worthy of remark that in Virginia where the mass of the people have been so much accustomed to be guided by their rulers on all new and intricate questions, they should on the present [question], which certainly surpasses the judgment of the greater part of them, not only go before, but contrary to, their most popular leaders. And the phenomenon is the more wonderful, as a popular ground is taken by all the adversaries to the new Constitution. Perhaps the solution in both these cases, would not be very difficult; but it would lead to observations too diffusive; and to you unnecessary. I will barely observe that the case in Virga. seems to prove that the body of sober and steady people, even of the lower order, are tired of the vicisitudes, injustice and follies which have so much characterised public measures, and are impatient for some change which promises stability and repose. The proceedings of the present assembly are more likely to cherish than remove this disposition. I find Mr. Henry has carried a Resolution for *prohibiting* the importation of Rum, brandy, and other ardent spirits; and if I am not misinformed all manufactured leather, hats and sundry other articles are included in the *prohibition*. Enormous duties at least are likely to take place on the last and many other articles. A project of this sort without the concurrence of the other States, is little short of madness. With such concurrence, it is not practicable without resorting to expedients equally noxious to liberty and œconomy. The consequences of the experiment in a single State, as unprepared for manufactures as Virginia may easily be preconceived. . . .

We have no certain information from the three Southern States concerning the temper relative to the New Government. It is in general favorable according to the vague accounts we have. Opposition however will be made in each. Mr. Wiley Jones, and Governour Caswell have been named as opponents in N. Carolina.

So few particulars have come to hand concerning the State of things in Georgia that I have nothing to add on that subject, to the contents of my last by Commodore Jones.

We have two or three States only yet met for Congress. As many more can be called in when their attendance will make a quorum. It continues to be problematical, whether the interregnum will not be spun out through the winter. . . .

I remain Dear Sir with the most sincere esteem & affection, Your Obedt. Servt.

JEFFERSON TO MADISON

Dear Sir   Paris Dec. 20. 1787.
. . . The season admitting only of operations in the Cabinet, and these being in a great measure secret, I have little to fill a letter. I will therefore make up the deficiency by adding a few words on the Constitution proposed by our Convention. I like much the general idea of framing a government which should go on of itself peaceably, without needing continual recurrence to the state legislatures. I like the organization of the government into Legislative, Judiciary and Executive. I like the power given the Legislature to levy taxes; and for that reason solely approve of the greater house being chosen by the people directly. For tho' I think a house chosen by them will be very illy qualified to legislate for the Union, for foreign nations &c. yet this evil does not weigh against the

good of preserving inviolate the fundamental principle that the people are not to be taxed but by representatives chosen immediately by themselves. I am captivated by the compromise of the opposite claims of the great and little states, of the latter to equal, and the former to proportional influence. I am much pleased too with the substitution of the method of voting by persons, instead of that of voting by states: and I like the negative given to the Executive with a third of either house, though I should have liked it better had the Judiciary been associated for that purpose, or invested with a similar and separate power. There are other good things of less moment. I will now add what I do not like. First the omission of a bill of rights providing clearly and without the aid of sophisms for freedom of religion, freedom of the press, protection against standing armies, restriction against monopolies, the eternal and unremitting force of the habeas corpus laws, and trials by jury in all matters of fact triable by the laws of the land and not by the law of Nations. To say, as Mr. Wilson does that a bill of rights was not necessary because all is reserved in the case of the general government which is not given, while in the particular ones all is given which is not reserved might do for the Audience to whom it was addressed, but is surely gratis dictum, opposed by strong inferences from the body of the instrument, as well as from the omission of the clause of our present confederation which had declared that in express terms. It was a hard conclusion to say because there has been no uniformity among the states as to the cases triable by jury, because some have been so incautious as to abandon this mode of trial, therefore the more prudent states shall be reduced to the same level of calamity. It would have been much more just and wise to have concluded the other way that as most of the states had judiciously preserved this palladium, those who had wandered should be brought back to it, and to have established general right instead of general wrong. Let me add that a bill of rights is what the people are entitled to against every government on earth, general or particular, and what no just government should refuse, or rest on inference. The second feature I dislike, and greatly dislike, is the abandonment in every instance of the necessity of rotation in office, and most particularly in the case of the President. Experience concurs with reason in concluding that the first magistrate will always be re-elected if the constitution permits it. He is then an officer for life. This once observed it becomes of so much consequence to certain nations to have a friend or a foe at the head of our affairs that they will interfere with money and with arms. A Galloman or an Angloman will be supported by the nation he befriends. If once elected, and at a second or third election outvoted by one or two votes, he will pretend false votes, foul play, hold possession of the reins of government, be supported by the states voting for him, especially if they are the central ones lying in a compact body themselves and separating their opponents: and they will be aided by one nation of Europe, while the majority are aided by another. The election of a President of America some years hence will be much more interesting to certain nations of Europe than ever the election of a king of Poland was. Reflect on all the instances in history antient and modern, of elective monarchies, and say if they do not give foundation for my fears, the Roman emperors, the popes, while they were of any importance, the German emperors till they became hereditary in practice, the kings of Poland, the Deys of the Ottoman dependancies. It may be said that if elections are to be attended with these disorders, the seldomer they are renewed the better. But experience shews that the only way to prevent disorder is to render them uninteresting by frequent changes. An incapacity to be elected a second time would have been the only effectual preventative. The power of removing him every fourth year by the vote of the people is a power which will not be exercised. The king of Poland is removeable every day by the Diet, yet he is never removed.—Smaller objections are the Appeal in fact as well as law, and the binding all persons Legislative, Executive and Judiciary by oath to maintain that constitution. I do not pretend to decide what would be the best method of procuring the establishment of the manifold good things in this constitution, and of getting rid of the bad. Whether by adopting it in hopes of future amendment, or, after it has been duly weighed and canvassed by the people, after seeing the parts they generally dislike, and those they generally approve, to say to them 'We see now what you wish. Send together your deputies again, let them frame a constitution for you omitting what you have condemned, and establishing the powers you approve. Even these will be a great addition to the energy of your government.'—At all events I hope you will not be discouraged from other trials, if the present one should fail of it's full effect.—I have thus told you freely what I like and dislike: merely as a matter of curiosity for I know your own judgment has been formed on all these points after having heard every thing which could be urged on them. I own I am not a friend to a very energetic government. It is always oppressive. The late rebellion in Massachusets has given more alarm than I think it should have done. Calculate that one rebellion in 13 states in the course of 11 years, is but one for each state in a century and a half. No country should be so long without one. Nor will any degree of power in the hands of government prevent insurrections. France with all it's despotism, and two or three hundred thousand men always in arms has had three insurrections in the three years I have been here in every one of which greater numbers were engaged than in Massachusets and a great deal more blood was spilt. In Turkey, which Montesquieu supposes more despotic, insurrections are the events of every day. In England, where the hand of power is lighter than here, but heavier than with us they

happen every half dozen years. Compare again the ferocious depredations of their insurgents with the order, the moderation and the almost self extinguishment of ours.—After all, it is my principle that the will of the Majority should always prevail. If they approve the proposed Convention in all it's parts, I shall concur in it chearfully, in hopes that they will amend it whenever they shall find it work wrong. I think our governments will remain virtuous for many centuries; as long as they are chiefly agricultural; and this will be as long as there shall be vacant lands in any part of America. When they get piled upon one another in large cities, as in Europe, they will become corrupt as in Europe. Above all things I hope the education of the common people will be attended to; convinced that on their good sense we may rely with the most security for the preservation of a due degree of liberty. I have tired you by this time with my disquisitions and will therefore only add assurances of the sincerity of those sentiments of esteem and attachment with which I am Dear Sir your affectionate friend & servant,

Th: Jefferson

P. S. The instability of our laws is really an immense evil. I think it would be well to provide in our constitutions that there shall always be a twelvemonth between the ingrossing a bill and passing it: that it should then be offered to it's passage without changing a word: and that if circumstances should be thought to require a speedier passage, it should take two thirds of both houses instead of a bare majority.

MADISON TO JEFFERSON

Dear Sir   Virginia Orange April 22. 1788
... The proposed Constitution still engrosses the public attention. The elections for the Convention here are but just over and promulged. From the returns (excluding those from Kentucky which are not yet known) it seems probable, though not absolutely certain that a majority of the members elect are friends to the Constitution. The superiority of abilities at least seems to lie on that side. The characters of most note which occur to me, are marshalled thus. For the Constitution, Pendleton, Wythe, Blair, Innis, Marshal, Doctr. W. Jones, G. Nicholas, Wilson Nicholas, Gabl. Jones, Thos. Lewis, F. Corbin, Ralph Wormley Jr. White of Frederik, Genl. Gates, Genl. A. Stephens, Archd. Stuart, Zachy. Johnson, Docr. Stuart, Parson Andrews, H. Lee Jr. Bushrod Washington considered as a young Gentleman of talents: against the Constitution, Mr. Henry, Mason, Harrison, Grayson, Tyler, M. Smith, W. Ronald, Lawson, Bland, Wm. Cabell, Dawson.

The Governor is so temperate in his opposition and goes so far with the friends of the Constitution that he cannot properly be classed with its enemies. Monroe is considered by some as an enemy, but I believe him to be a friend though a cool one. There are other individuals of weight whose opinions are unknown to me. R. H. Lee is not elected. His brother F. L. Lee is a warm friend to the Constitution, as I am told, but also is not elected. So are Jno. and Man Page.

The adversaries take very different grounds of opposition. Some are opposed to the substance of the plan; others to particular modifications only. Mr. H[enr]y is supposed to aim at disunion. Col. M[ason]n is growing every day more bitter, and outrageous in his efforts to carry his point; and will probably in the end be thrown by the violence of his passions into the politics of Mr. H[enr]y. The preliminary question will be whether previous alterations shall be insisted on or not? Should this be carried in the affirmative, either a condiional ratification, or a proposal for a new Convention will ensue. In either event, I think the Constitution and the Union will be both endangered. It is not to be expected that the States which have ratified will reconsider their determinations, and submit to the alterations prescribed by Virga. and if a second Convention should be formed, it is as little to be expected that the same spirit of compromise will prevail in it as produced an amicable result to the first. It will be easy also for those who have latent views of disunion, to carry them on under the mask of contending for alterations popular in some but inadmissible in other parts of the U. States.

The real sense of the people of this State cannot be easily ascertained. They are certainly attached and with warmth to a continuance of the Union; and I believe a large majority of the most intelligent and independent are equally so to the plan under consideration. On a geographical view of them, almost all the counties in the N. Neck have elected fœderal deputies. The Counties on the South side of James River have pretty generally elected adversaries to the Constitution. The intermediate district is much chequered in this respect. The Counties between the blue ridge and the Alleghany have chosen friends to the Constitution without a single exception. Those Westward of the latter, have as I am informed, generally though not universally pursued the same rule. Kentucky it is supposed will be divided....

I am Dear Sir your affect. friend & Servt.,

Js. Madison Jr.

MADISON TO JEFFERSON

Dear Sir   New York 24. July 1788
... I returned here about ten days ago from Richmond which I left a day or two after the dissolution of the convention. The final question on the new plan of government was put on the 25th of June. It was twofold: 1. whether previous amendments should be made a condition of ratification; 2. directly on the Constitution in the form it bore. On the first the decision was in the negative, 88 being no, 80 only aye. On the second and definitive question, the ratification was affirmed by 89 ayes against 79 noes. A number of alterations were then recommended to be con-

sidered in the mode pointed out in the Constitution itself. The meeting was remarkably full, two members only being absent and those known to be on the opposite sides of the question. The debates also were conducted on the whole with very laudable moderation and decorum, and continued until both sides declared themselves ready for the question. And it may be safely concluded that no irregular opposition to the system will follow in that state, at least with the countenance of the leaders on that side. What local eruptions may be occasioned by ill-timed or rigorous executions of the treaty of peace against British debtors, I will not pretend to say. But altho' the leaders, particularly [Henry] and [Mason], will give no countenance to popular violences, it is not to be inferred that they are reconciled to the event, or will give it a positive support. On the contrary both of them declared they could not go that length, and an attempt was made under their auspices to induce the minority to sign an address to the people which if it had not been defeated by the general moderation of the party, would probably have done mischief.

Among a variety of expedients employed by the opponents to gain proselytes, Mr. *Henry first and after him Col. Mason introduced the opinions, expressed in a letter from a correspondent (Mr. Donald or Skipwith I believe)* and endeavored to turn the influence of your *name even against parts of which I knew you approved. In this situation I thought it due to truth* as well as that it would be most agreeable to *yourself* and *accordingly took the liberty to state some of your opinions on the favorable side.* I am informed that copies or extracts of a letter *from you were handed about at the Maryld. Convention with a like view of impeding the ratification.*

New Hampshire ratified the Constitution on the 21st ult. and made the ninth state. The votes stood 57 for and 46 against the measure. South Carolina had previously ratified by a very great majority. The convention of North Carolina is now sitting. At one moment the sense of that state was considered as strongly opposed to the system. It is now said that the tide has been for some time turning, which with the example of other states and particularly of Virginia, prognosticates a ratification there also. The convention of New York has been in session ever since the 17th ult. without having yet arrived at any final vote. Two thirds of the members assembled with a determination to reject the Constitution, and are still opposed to it in their hearts. The local situation of New York, the number of ratifying states and the hope of retaining the federal government in this city afford however powerful arguments to such men as Jay, Hamilton, the Chancellor Duane and several others; and it is not improbable that some form of ratification will yet be devised by which the dislike of the opposition may be gratified, and the state notwithstanding made a member of the new Union....

July 26. We just hear that the convention of this state have determined by a small majority to exclude from the ratification everything involving a condition and to content themselves with recommending the alterations wished for. . . .

I remain with the sincerest affection your friend and servant,

Js. Madison, Jr.

JEFFERSON TO MADISON

Dear Sir   Paris. July 31. 1788.
. . . I sincerely rejoice at the acceptance of our new constitution by nine states. It is a good canvas, on which some strokes only want retouching. What these are, I think are sufficiently manifested by the general voice from North to South, which calls for a bill of rights. It seems pretty generally understood that this should go to Juries, Habeas corpus, Standing armies, Printing, Religion and Monopolies. I conceive there may be difficulty in finding general modification of these suited to the habits of all the states. But if such cannot be found then it is better to establish trials by jury, the right of Habeas corpus, freedom of the press and freedom of religion in all cases, and to abolish standing armies in time of peace, and Monopolies, in all cases, than not to do it in any. The few cases wherein these things may do evil, cannot be weighed against the multitude wherein the want of them will do evil. In disputes between a foreigner and a native, a trial by jury may be improper. But if this exception cannot be agreed to, the remedy will be to model the jury by giving the medietas linguae in civil as well as criminal cases. Why suspend the Hab. corp. in insurrections and rebellions? The parties who may be arrested may be charged instantly with a well defined crime. Of course the judge will remand them. If the publick safety requires that the government should have a man imprisoned on less probable testimony in those than in other emergencies; let him be taken and tried, retaken and retried, while the necessity continues, only giving him redress against the government for damages. Examine the history of England: see how few of the cases of the suspension of the Habeas corpus law have been worthy of that suspension. They have been either real treasons wherein the parties might as well have been charged at once, or sham-plots where it was shameful they should ever have been suspected. Yet for the few cases wherein the suspension of the hab. corp. has done real good, that operation is now become habitual, and the minds of the nation almost prepared to live under its constant suspension. A declaration that the federal government will never restrain the presses from printing any thing they please, will not take away the liability of the printers for false facts printed. The declaration that religious faith shall be unpunished, does not give impunity to criminal acts dictated by religious error. The saying there shall be no monopolies lessens the incitements to ingenuity, which is spurred on by the hope of a monopoly for a limited time, as of 14. years; but the benefit even of limited monopolies is too doubtful to be opposed to that of their general suppression. If no check can be found to keep the number of standing troops within safe bounds, while they are tolerated as far as necessary, abandon them altogether, discipline well the militia, and guard the magazines with them. More than magazine-guards will be useless if few, and dangerous if many. No European nation can ever send against us such a regular army as we need fear, and it is hard if our militia are not equal to those of Canada or Florida. My idea then is, that tho' proper exceptions to these general rules are desireable and probably practicable, yet if the exceptions cannot be agreed on, the establishment of the rules in all cases will do ill in very few. I hope therefore a bill of rights will be formed to guard the people against the federal government, as they are already guarded against their state governments in most instances.

The abandoning the principle of necessary rotation in the Senate, has I see been disapproved by many; in the case of the President, by none. I readily therefore suppose my opinion wrong, when opposed by the majority as in the former instance, and the totality as in the latter. In this however I should have done it with more complete satisfaction, had we all judged from the same position. . . .

I am with very sincere esteem Dear Sir Your affectionate friend & servt.,   Th: Jefferson

MADISON TO JEFFERSON

Dear Sir   New York Ocr. 17. 1788
. . . The States which have adopted the new Constitution are all proceeding to the arrangements for putting it into action in March next. Pennsylva. alone has as yet actually appointed deputies; and that only for the Senate. My last mentioned that these were Mr. R. Morris and a Mr. McClay. How the other elections there and elsewhere will run is matter of uncertainty. The Presidency alone unites the conjectures of the public. The vice president is not at all marked out by the general voice. As the President will be from a Southern State, it falls almost of course for the other part of the Continent to supply the next in rank. South Carolina may however think of Mr. Rutledge unless it should be previously discovered that votes will be wasted on him. The only candidates in the Northern States brought forward with their known consent are *Hancock and Adams* and *between these it seems probable the question will lie.* Both of them *are objectionable and would I think be postponed* by the *general suffrage to several others* if they *would accept the place. Hancock is weak, ambitious, a courtier of popularity given to low intrigue* and *lately reunited by a factious friend-*

ship with S. Adams.—J. Adams has made himself obnoxious to many particularly in the Southern states by the political principles avowed in his book.[1] *Others recolecting his cabal during the war against General Washington, knowing his extravagant self importance and considering his preference of an unprofitable dignity to some place of emolument better adapted to private fortune as a proof of his having an eye to the presidency conclude that he would not be a very cordial second to the General and that an impatient ambition might even intrigue for a premature advancement. The danger would be the greater if particular factious characters, as may be the case, should get into the public councils. Adams it appears, is not unaware of some of the obstacles to his wish and thro a letter to Smith has thrown out popular sentiments as to the proposed president.*

The little pamphlet herewith inclosed[2] will give you a collective view of the alterations which have been proposed for the new Constitution. Various and numerous as they appear they certainly omit many of the true grounds of opposition. The articles relating to Treaties, to paper money, and to contracts, created more enemies than all the errors in the System positive and negative put together. It is true nevertheless that not a few, particularly in Virginia have contended for the proposed alterations from the most honorable and patriotic motives; and that among the advocates for the Constitution there are some who wish for further guards to public liberty and individual rights. As far as these may consist of a constitutional declaration of the most essential rights, it is probable they will be added; though there are many who think such addition unnecessary, and not a few who think it misplaced in such a Constitution. There is scarce any point on which the party in opposition is so much divided as to its importance and its propriety. My own opinion has always been in favor of a bill of rights; provided it be so framed as not to imply powers not meant to be included in the enumeration. At the same time I have never thought the omission a material defect, nor been anxious to supply it even by subsequent amendment, for any other reason than that it is anxiously desired by others. I have favored it because I supposed it might be of use, and if properly executed could not be of disservice. I have not viewed it in an important light 1. Because I conceive that in a certain degree, though not in the extent argued by Mr. Wilson, the rights in question are reserved

by the manner in which the federal powers are granted. 2. Because there is great reason to fear that a positive declaration of some of the most essential rights could not be obtained in the requisite latitude. I am sure that the rights of conscience in particular, if submitted to public definition would be narrowed much more than they are likely ever to be by an assumed power. One of the objections in New England was that the Constitution by prohibiting religious tests opened a door for Jews Turks and infidels. 3. Because the limited powers of the federal Government and the jealousy of the subordinate Governments, afford a security which has not existed in the case of the State Governments, and exists in no other. 4. Because experience proves the inefficacy of a bill of rights on those occasions when its controul is most needed. Repeated violations of these parchment barriers have been committed by overbearing majorities in every State. In Virginia I have seen the bill of rights violated in every instance where it has been opposed to a popular current. Notwithstanding the explicit provision contained in that instrument for the rights of Conscience it is well known that a religious establishment would have taken place in that State, if the legislative majority had found as they expected, a majority of the people in favor of the measure; and I am persuaded that if a majority of the people were now of one sect, the measure would still take place and on narrower ground than was then proposed, notwithstanding the additional obstacle which the law has since created. Wherever the real power in a Government lies, there is the danger of oppression. In our Governments the real power lies in the majority of the Community, and the invasion of private rights is *chiefly* to be apprehended, not from acts of Government contrary to the sense of its constituents, but from acts in which the Government is the mere instrument of the major number of the constituents. This is a truth of great importance, but not yet sufficiently attended to: and is probably more strongly impressed on my mind by facts, and reflections suggested by them, than on yours which has contemplated abuses of power issuing from a very different quarter. Wherever there is an interest and power to do wrong, wrong will generally be done, and not less readily by a powerful and interested party than by a powerful and interested prince. The difference, so far as it relates to the superiority of republics over monarchies, lies in the less degree of probability that interest may prompt abuses of power in the former than in the latter; and in the security in the former against oppression of more than the smaller part of the Society, whereas in the former it may be extended in a manner to the whole. The difference so far as it relates to the point in question—the efficacy of a bill of rights in controuling abuses of power—lies in this: that in a monarchy the latent force of the nation is superior to that of the Sovereign, and a solemn charter of popular rights must have a great effect, as a standard for trying the validity of public acts,

---

[1] The three volume *Defense of the Constitutions of Government of the United States of America* . . . (London: 1787–88), which, as Madison had explained earlier to Jefferson (June 6, 1787), struck many Americans as "unfriendly to republicanism" and prejudiced in favor of the British Constitution.

[2] *The Ratifications of the New Federal Constitution, together with the Amendments, proposed by the Several States* (Richmond: 1788).

and a signal for rousing and uniting the superior force of the community; whereas in a popular Government, the political and physical power may be considered as vested in the same hands, that is in a majority of the people, and consequently the tyrannical will of the sovereign is not to be controuled by the dread of an appeal to any other force within the community. What use then it may be asked can a bill of rights serve in popular Governments? I answer the two following which though less essential than in other Governments, sufficiently recommend the precaution. 1. The political truths declared in that solemn manner acquire by degrees the character of fundamental maxims of free Government, and as they become incorporated with the national sentiment, counteract the impulses of interest and passion. 2. Altho' it be generally true as above stated that the danger of oppression lies in the interested majorities of the people rather than in usurped acts of the Government, yet there may be occasions on which the evil may spring from the latter sources; and on such, a bill of rights will be a good ground for an appeal to the sense of the community. Perhaps too there may be a certain degree of danger, that a succession of artful and ambitious rulers, may by gradual and well-timed advances, finally erect an independent Government on the subversion of liberty. Should this danger exist at all, it is prudent to guard against it, especially when the precaution can do no injury. At the same time I must own that I see no tendency in our governments to danger on that side. It has been remarked that there is a tendency in all Governments to an augmentation of power at the expence of liberty. But the remark as usually understood does not appear to me well founded. Power when it has attained a certain degree of energy and independence goes on generally to further degrees. But when below that degree, the direct tendency is to further degrees of relaxation, until the abuses of liberty beget a sudden transition to an undue degree of power. With this explanation the remark may be true; and in the latter sense only is it in my opinion applicable to the Governments in America. It is a melancholy reflection that liberty should be equally exposed to danger whether the Government have too much or too little power; and that the line which divides these extremes should be so inaccurately defined by experience.

Supposing a bill of rights to be proper the articles which ought to compose it, admit of much discussion. I am inclined to think that absolute restrictions in cases that are doubtful, or where emergencies may overrule them, ought to be avoided. The restrictions however strongly marked on paper will never be regarded when opposed to the decided sense of the public; and after repeated violations in extraordinary cases, they will lose even their ordinary efficacy. Should a Rebellion or insurrection alarm the people as well as the Government, and a suspension of the Hab. Corp. be dictated by the alarm, no written prohibitions on earth would prevent the measure. Should an army in time of peace be gradually established in our neighbourhood by Britn: or Spain, declarations on paper would have as little effect in preventing a standing force for the public safety. The best security against these evils is to remove the pretext for them. With regard to Monopolies they are justly classed among the greatest nusances in Government. But is it clear that as encouragements to literary works and ingenious discoveries, they are not too valuable to be wholly renounced? Would it not suffice to reserve in all cases a right to the public to abolish the privilege at a price to be specified in the grant of it? Is there not also infinitely less danger of this abuse in our Governments than in most others? Monopolies are sacrifices of the many to the few. Where the power is in the few it is natural for them to sacrifice the many to their own partialities and corruptions. Where the power, as with us, is in the many not in the few, the danger can not be very great that the few will be thus favored. It is much more to be dreaded that the few will be unnecessarily sacrificed to the many. . . .

I am Dr. Sir with the sincerest esteem & affectn. Yours,

Js. Madison Jr

JEFFERSON TO MADISON

Dear Sir   Paris Nov. 18. 1788
. . . I am to thank you for another copy of the federalist. . . . With respect to the Federalist, the three authors had been named to me. I read it with care, pleasure and improvement, and was satisfied there was nothing in it by one of those hands, and not a great deal by a second. It does the highest honor to the third, as being, in my opinion, the best commentary on the principles of government which ever was written. In some parts it is discoverable that the author means only to say what may be best said in defence of opinions in which he did not concur. But in general it establishes firmly the plan of government. I confess it has rectified me in several points. As to the bill of rights however I still think it should be added, and I am glad to see that three states have at length considered the perpetual reeligibility of the president as an article which should be amended. I should deprecate with you indeed the meeting of a new convention. I hope they will adopt the mode of amendment by Congress and the Assemblies, in which case I should not fear any dangerous innovation in the plan. But the minorities are too respectable not to be entitled to some sacrifice of opinion in the majority. Especially when a great proportion of them would be contented with a bill of rights. . . .

Th: Jefferson

MADISON TO JEFFERSON

Dear Sir   Philadelphia Decr. 8. 1788
. . . Notwithstanding the formidable opposition made to the new federal government, first in

order to prevent its adoption, and since in order to place its administration in the hands of disaffected men, there is now both a certainty of its peaceable commencement in March next, and a flattering prospect that it will be administred by men who will give it a fair trial. General Washington will certainly be called to the Executive department. Mr. Adams who is *pledged to support him* will probably be the vice president. The enemies to the Government, at the head and the most inveterate of whom, is Mr. Henry are laying a train for the election of Governour Clinton, but it cannot succeed unless the federal votes be more dispersed than can well happen. Of the seven States which have appointed their Senators, Virginia alone will have antifederal members in that branch. Those of N. Hampshire are President Langdon and Judge Bartlett, of Massachusetts Mr. Strong and Mr. Dalton, of Connecticut Docr. Johnson and Mr. Elseworth, of N. Jersey Mr. Patterson and Mr. Elmer, of Penna. Mr. R. Morris and Mr. McClay, of Delaware Mr. Geo: Reed and Mr. Bassett, of Virginia Mr. R. H. Lee and Col. Grayson. Here is already a majority of the ratifying States on the side of the Constitution. And it is not doubted that it will be reinforced by the appointments of Maryland, S. Carolina and Georgia. As one branch of the Legislature of N. York is attached to the Constitution, it is not improbable that one of the Senators from that State also will be added to the majority.—In the House of Representatives the proportion of antifederal members will of course be greater, but can not if present appearances are to be trusted amount to a majority or even a very formidable minority. The election for this branch has taken place as yet no where except in Penna. and here the returns are not yet come in from all the Counties. It is certain however that seven out of the eight, and probable that the whole eight representatives will bear the federal stamp. Even in Virginia where the enemies to the Government form ⅔ of the *legislature* it is computed that more than half the number of Representatives, who will be elected by the *people,* formed into districts for the purpose, will be of the same stamp. By some it is computed that 7 out of the 10 allotted to that State will be opposed to the politics of the present Legislature.

The questions which divide the public at present relate 1. to the extent of the amendments that ought to be made to the Constitution, 2. to the mode in which they ought to be made. The friends of the Constitution, some from an approbation of particular amendments, others from a spirit of conciliation, are generally agreed that the System should be revised. But they wish the revisal to be carried no farther than to supply additional guards for liberty, without abridging the sum of power transferred from the States to the general Government, or altering previous to trial, the particular structure of the latter and are fixed in opposition to the risk of another Convention, whilst the purpose can be as well answered, by the other mode provided for introducing amendments. Those who have opposed the Constitution, are on the other hand, zealous for a second Convention, and for a revisal which may either not be restrained at all, or extend at least as far as alterations have been proposed by any State. Some of this class are, no doubt, friends to an effective Government, and even to the substance of the particular Government in question. It is equally certain that there are others who urge a second Convention with the insidious hope of throwing all things into Confusion, and of subverting the fabric just established, if not the Union itself. If the first Congress embrace the policy which circumstances mark out, they will not fail to propose of themselves, every desireable safeguard for popular rights; and by thus separating the well meaning from the designing opponents fix on the latter their true character, and give to the Government its due popularity and stability. . . .

I shall leave this place in a day or two for Virga. where my friends who wish me to cooperate in putting our political machine into activity as a member of the House of Representatives, press me to attend. They made me a candidate for the Senate, for which I had not allotted my pretensions. The attempt was defeated by Mr. Henry who is omnipotent in the present legislature and who added to the expedients common on such occasions, a public philippic against my federal principles. He has taken equal pains in forming the Counties into districts for the election of Representatives to associate with Orange such as are most devoted to his politics, and most likely to be swayed by the prejudices excited against me. From the best information I have of the prevailing temper of the district, I conclude that my going to Virga. will answer no other purpose than to satisfy the Opinions and intreaties of my friends. The trip is in itself very disagreeable both on account of its electioneering appearance, and the sacrifice of the winter for which I had assigned a task which the intermission of Congressional business would have made convenient at New York.

With the sincerest affection & the highest esteem I am Dear Sir yrs.   Js. Madison Jr.

JEFFERSON TO MADISON

Dear Sir   Paris Mar. 15. 1789.
. . . Your thoughts on the subject of the Declaration of rights in the letter of Oct. 17. I have weighed with great satisfaction. Some of them had not occurred to me before, but were acknoleged just in the moment they were presented to my mind. In the arguments in favor of a declaration of rights, you omit one which has great weight with me, the legal check which it puts into the hands of the judiciary. This is a body, which if rendered independent, and kept strictly to their own department merits great confidence for their learning and integrity. In fact what degree of

confidence would be too much for a body composed of such men as Wythe, Blair, and Pendleton? On characters like these the 'civium ardor prava jubentium' would make no impression. I am happy to find that on the whole you are a friend to this amendment. The Declaration of rights is like all other human blessings alloyed with some inconveniences, and not accomplishing fully it's object. But the good in this instance vastly overweighs the evil. I cannot refrain from making short answers to the objections which your letter states to have been raised. 1. That the rights in question are reserved by the manner in which the federal powers are granted. Answer. A constitutive act may certainly be so formed as to need no declaration of rights. The act itself has the force of a declaration as far as it goes: and if it goes to all material points nothing more is wanting. In the draught of a constitution which I had once a thought of proposing in Virginia, and printed afterwards, I endeavored to reach all the great objects of public liberty, and did not mean to add a declaration of rights. Probably the object was imperfectly executed: but the deficiencies would have been supplied by others in the course of discussion. But in a constitutive act which leaves some precious articles unnoticed, and raises implications against others, a declaration of rights becomes necessary by way of supplement. This is the case of our new federal constitution. This instrument forms us into one state as to certain objects, and gives us a legislative and executive body for these objects. It should therefore guard us against their abuses of power within the feild submitted to them. 2. A positive declaration of some essential rights could not be obtained in the requisite latitude. Answer. Half a loaf is better than no bread. If we cannot secure all our rights, let us secure what we can. 3. The limited powers of the federal government and jealousy of the subordinate governments afford a security which exists in no other instance. Answer. The first member of this seems resolvable into the 1st. objection before stated. The jealousy of the subordinate governments is a precious reliance. But observe that those governments are only agents. They must have principles furnished them whereon to found their opposition. The

declaration of rights will be the text whereby they will try all the acts of the federal government. In this view it is necessary to the federal government also: as by the same text they may try the opposition of the subordinate governments. 4. Experience proves the inefficacy of a bill of rights. True. But tho it is not absolutely efficacious under all circumstances, it is of great potency always, and rarely inefficacious. A brace the more will often keep up the building which would have fallen with that brace the less. There is a remarkeable difference between the characters of the Inconveniencies which attend a Declaration of rights, and those which attend the want of it. The inconveniences of the Declaration are that it may cramp government in it's useful exertions. But the evil of this is shortlived, moderate, and reparable. The inconveniencies of the want of a Declaration are permanent, afflicting and irreparable: they are in constant progression from bad to worse. The executive in our governments is not the sole, it is scarcely the principal object of my jealousy. The tyranny of the legislatures is the most formidable dread at present, and will be for long years. That of the executive will come in it's turn, but it will be at a remote period. I know there are some among us who would now establish a monarchy. But they are inconsiderable in number and weight of character. The rising race are all republicans. We were educated in royalism: no wonder if some of us retain that idolatry still. Our young people are educated in republicanism. An apostacy from that to royalism is unprecedented and impossible. I am much pleased with the prospect that a declaration of rights will be added: and hope it will be done in that way which will not endanger the whole frame of the government, or any essential part of it. . . .

As you will be in a situation to know when the leave of absence will be granted me which I have asked, will you be so good as to communicate it by a line to Mr. Lewis and Mr. Eppes? I hope to see you in the summer, and that if you are not otherwise engaged, you will encamp with me at Monticello for a while. I am with great and sincere attachment Dear sir Your affectionate friend & servt,
Th: Jefferson

CHAPTER FIVE

HAMILTON AND JEFFERSON

One of the most significant and stirring aspects of the Federalist era was the debates between Hamilton and Jefferson over the nature of the new Constitution. There was, in essence, the Hamiltonian or broad construction and the Jeffersonian or narrow construction. Hamilton would add to the powers and prestige of the federal government; Jefferson would protect the rights of the states. Two great traditions in American history thus got their start.[1] In time each was to become so amplified and exaggerated that it would be easy to overlook what Hamilton and Jefferson stood for during their own lifetimes; historians would be likely to forget that each was a product of the Enlightenment and that, despite their differences, they had much in common.

Several recent historians have pointed to these common bases, and others have suggested that despite the theoretical differences separating the two men, as political leaders Hamilton's policies tended to be divisive while Jefferson's were basically nationalistic. Thus, John C. Miller, in *Alexander Hamilton: Portrait in Paradox,* points out that Hamilton realized "to a greater degree than any American of his generation that the republic must draw its strength from union." Nevertheless, "he, more than any other individual, was responsible for the policies which divided the American people." As for Jefferson, Julian Boyd, editor of *The Papers of Thomas Jefferson,* points out in an essay that follows, "His devotion to the union, his belief in its strength and immense potentialities, his wholehearted and undeviating acceptance of the idea and meaning of nationhood were characterized by a faith, a vision, and an elevation of purpose that made him all but unique among the Founding Fathers." Obviously both men deserve honor; more than that they both merit understanding.

The pages that follow present Miller's over-all estimate and analysis of some of the political effects of the Hamiltonian program.

---

[1] See especially Merrill D. Peterson, *The Jefferson Image in the American Mind* (New York: Oxford University Press, 1960).

JOHN C. MILLER:
HAMILTON: A PARADOX*

The period in which Alexander Hamilton lived was an age of great men and great events. In the United States, besides Hamilton himself, George Washington, Thomas Jefferson, James Madison and John Marshall held the center of the stage; while the European scene was dominated by William Pitt, Charles James Fox and Napoleon Bonaparte. And yet, Talleyrand, whose career is a convincing testimonial of his astuteness in judging men and measures and who was intimately acquainted with the leaders on both sides of the Atlantic, pronounced Alexander Hamilton to be the greatest of these "choice and master spirits of the age."

Probably no American statesman has displayed more constructive imagination than did Hamilton. Prodigal of ideas, bursting with plans for diversifying the American economy and obsessed by a determination to make the United States a powerful nation under a centralized government, he left an imprint upon this country that time has not yet effaced. Of some of our institutions it may be justly said that they are the lengthened shadow of one man—Alexander Hamilton.

In Hamilton's comparatively brief span, he lived through three great wars, in two of which he was an active participant. Whenever he looked abroad he found wars or rumors of wars. As a result, the conviction was implanted in him that the survival of the United States depended to a great degree upon its warmaking potential. If this was a harsh and unattractive philosophy, at least it could be said to have been based upon the facts of international life as Hamilton knew them.

Everything depended, he believed, upon strengthening the union: if it perished, Americans would never attain the liberty, material well-being and happiness to which they aspired. Even his financial and economic plans were but means to the great end of solidifying the union; in his hands, capitalism became a barrier against the strong centrifugal forces that threatened to reduce the central government to impotence.

Paradoxically enough, the abounding love of the American union that actuated Hamilton was partly owing to the fact that he was born outside the continental boundaries of what later became the United States. He was thereby preserved against the corroding effects of state loyalty which in most of his contemporaries seriously weakened the springs of nationalism. Even more important, Hamilton's service in the Revolutionary Army impressed upon him the necessity of strong central government capable of acting upon Americans directly rather than through the states. Above all,

he realized to a greater degree than any American of his generation that the republic must draw its strength from union. The source of American greatness, he perceived, was continental, not provincial. From first to last, he "thought continentally."

Hamilton's was a strange career—and no one was more conscious of its strangeness than was Hamilton himself. A West Indian by birth and of antecedents that provided his enemies with a never-failing source of scurrility—John Adams called him "the bastard brat of a Scotch pedlar" —he rose to high social, political and military position in the United States. To the cause of American union he gave unstintingly of his energy and devotion, and yet he had little love for the people whose power and material well-being he sought to advance. Never, he said, had he expected to find a people born to greatness who more stubbornly resisted their destiny than did Americans. He confessed that he did not understand them and on one occasion he cried out in anguish of spirit that "this American world" was not made for him. Frequently he asked himself to what end he was laboring; but he never ceased to strive to mold the United States in accord with the vision that had been granted him.

The supreme irony of Hamilton's achievement is that the methods by which he sought to lay the economic foundations of the American union actually aggravated political sectionalism in the United States—the very eventuality he most dreaded. There are few instances in history that demonstrate more strikingly how the best-laid plans of statesmen can go awry. Hamilton dedicated himself to the cause of union; yet when he retired from the office of Secretary of the Treasury, the fissures between North and South had begun to assume menacing proportions. True, Hamilton did not bear the sole responsibility for this untoward and, for him, wholly unexpected development; and yet he, more than any other individual, was responsible for the policies which divided the American people and which led to the creation of political parties. It was his archrival, Thomas Jefferson, who united Americans and, until the imposition of the embargo of 1808, seemed on the point of making the United States a one-party state. If the American world were made for Thomas Jefferson, then Alexander Hamilton felt that he stood on foreign ground indeed. . . .

Had Alexander Hamilton been content to be the spokesman of the majority of the people of the United States and to reflect faithfully their ideals and aspirations, he would never have written his reports or, had they been written, they would have been dedicated to furthering the immediate interests of agriculture. The prevailing ideas of the day were hostile to the kind of finan-

* Reprinted from *Alexander Hamilton: Portrait in Paradox* by John C. Miller. Copyright © 1959 by John C. Miller. Reprinted by permission of Harper & Row, Publishers.

cial and economic planning that emanated from the office of the Secretary of the Treasury: Hamilton's plans were conceived by a minority, designed to benefit a minority and carried into execution by a minority. With characteristic audacity, he undertook to run a farmers' republic for the immediate profit of businessmen.

No wonder, therefore, as the planters and farmers beheld the landmarks of agricultural America slipping away, to be replaced by monuments to the "greed and cunning" of businessmen, speculators and bankers, they became increasingly distrustful of the federal government. The "energy" displayed by that government under the direction of the Secretary of the Treasury seemed directed wholly to the furtherance of commerce, manufacturing and the "fiscal faction."

For southern planters, the enemy was essentially the same antagonist that they had always faced. In place of British merchants and manufacturers, they were now obliged to do battle with northern merchants and manufacturers—which could hardly be accounted a victory, they lamented, for men who had fought a seven years' war for freedom. And, as they quickly learned, the "fiscal interest" led by Hamilton was an overmatch for the "agrarian interest." "The Bank has a flush of trumps," exclaimed John Taylor of Caroline. Since Taylor did not credit the farmers with holding more than a pair of deuces, he predicted that the Bank would take over the country—at which time it would presumably be known as the "United States of the Bank."

In some degree, this was a struggle between different kinds of aristocrats. The planters of the South represented the old, established, landed wealth of the country, whereas Hamilton's capitalists and speculators were to a large extent nouveaux riches. Moreover, their wealth was acquired in commerce, trade, banking and speculation in paper—methods of money-getting that a true gentleman of the South held in utter disdain. Many of the so-called "gentlemen" of the North who rode in coaches and whose servants wore livery "would appear more in character," it was said in Virginia, "if they were to parade the streets in buttermilk-carts, or at the arms of bakers' wheelbarrows." In the eyes of southern patricians, Hamiltonianism threatened to saddle the republic with a governing class of parvenus—"the most repulsive of all, as it would have embraced the pride of distinction without its refinements." It therefore struck Hamilton as highly ironical that southern planters should fulminate against the "privileged orders" quite as though they themselves were not conspicuous members of that order. William Giles of Virginia, Hamilton's most vituperative critic in the House of Representatives, declared that "he should view the banishment of the privileged orders from the world as the surest harbinger of the approach of the millennium"—but it is plain that Giles was thinking only of the French, British and Federalist aristocrats, not of the goodly company of southern slaveowners to which he belonged.

If his enemies could be believed, Hamilton's objective was totally to overthrow the "landed interest" and reduce the farmers to the status of slaves to the overlords of business and finance. Since the planters knew from firsthand experience the degradation of slavery, they spoke with peculiar authority about their future lot at the hands of northern masters. Hamilton, on the other hand, although he never professed to any love for Negro slavery, did not admit to any intention of inflicting servitude upon the white slaveowners or, indeed, upon anyone else. Nor did he acknowledge that his plan for the advancement of commerce and manufactures would depress agriculture. On the contrary, he conceded that agriculture was "the best basis of the prosperity" of every other form of industry and that it merited the fostering care of government. Because of the wasteful methods used by American farmers and planters, he thought that the most effective aid the government could give agriculture was to create a Board of Agriculture to instruct farmers in scientific knowledge. He contended that the interests of agriculture, commerce and manufacturing were indissolubly united and that measures which directly benefited one indirectly benefited the others. But he never departed from the position he had taken in 1790—that since commerce and manufacturing had been far outstripped by agriculture, the attention of the government ought to be chiefly directed toward stimulating the lagging branches of the economy.

Considered solely from the viewpoint of theory, republicanism seemed to Hamilton to be an excellent system of government. "I am affectionately attached to the republican theory," he declared. "I desire above all things to see the equality of political rights, exclusive of all hereditary distinction, firmly established by a practical demonstration of its being consistent with the order and happiness of society." Had he been given to building castles in the air, he would have given them at least a republican façade. He was not a believer in monarchy because of any theoretical preference for that form; a king, lords and commons appeared to him to be the most practical way of coping with the notorious shortcomings of human nature. As an empiricist and pragmatist, he gave his allegiance to monarchy; republicanism always seemed to him to be more suited to a community of angels than of human beings. Still, he recognized that the American people would have no other form of government.

Monarchism, then, was a red herring, but Jefferson and Madison succeeded in hanging it round Hamilton's neck. And there, despite everything Hamilton might say or do, it remained. Nevertheless, it was clear that if Hamilton actually intended to subvert the republican order in the United States, he chose an exceedingly devious method of reaching his objective. By attaching the capitalists to the federal government, he virtually ensured that they would support the established system. As a newspaper writer observed: "It would be a queer blunder for a man of six per cent to join in a plot against a free government, which pays his income. Liberty, therefore, has gained new friends rather than foes in the funding system." Even Jefferson, when he appraised Hamilton's work in a more judicious frame of mind, admitted that "creditors will never, of their own accord, fly off entirely from their debtors."

According to his own lights, Hamilton was engaged in doing the things that had to be done if republicanism were to endure. Since he never supposed that a republican form of government had received special approval from God and that there were preordained forces working toward its triumph, he was the more determined to take measures to ensure its survival in a hostile world. By declaring its independence and establishing a republican form of government, the United States in effect had flung down a challenge to the monarchies of Europe. And, equally important in Hamilton's mind, it had challenged human nature by raising the question whether or not men were capable of maintaining law and order at the same time that they were given almost unprecedented freedom. Hamilton acted upon the premise that a nation which so recklessly defied the laws of probability could not afford to overlook any means of strengthening its defenses.

If republicanism miscarried in the United States, Hamilton felt sure that it would be through no fault of his; but he could not say as much for Thomas Jefferson. He thought that Jefferson would end by killing republicanism, whereas he himself, having diagnosed the causes of its periodic breakdowns, was trying to keep the patient alive. If he wished to destroy republicanism, Hamilton said, he would play the demagogue: "I would mount the hobby horse of popularity; I would cry out 'usurpation,' 'danger to liberty,' etc; I would endeavor to prostrate the national government, raise a ferment, and then ride the whirlwind and direct the storm." He suspected that Jefferson and Madison were planning to do that very thing.

One of the consequences of the struggle over the funding of the debt, the assumption of state debts, the organization of the Bank of the United States and the implementation of the Report on Manufactures was the emergence of a political party dedicated to the support of the policies of the Secretary of the Treasury. It had not been generally expected that parties would disturb the felicity of Americans under the new Constitution; thanks presumably to the wisdom of the Founding Fathers, these particular serpents had been excluded from the republican paradise. But, as the Founding Fathers soon learned, they had not sufficiently reckoned with Alexander Hamilton.

Hamilton himself had been one of the foremost in deploring political parties. Although in *The Federalist* he had acknowledged the utility and, indeed, the indispensability of parties in a free government, most of his pronouncements on this subject deal with the evil wrought by parties.

He recoiled from "the tempestuous waves of sedition and party rage" and he prayed that the Constitution would deliver the United States from their malign influence. His ideal was government not by parties but by superior persons—an ideal which perhaps came closest to attainment in the rule of the merchant-bankers of Venice and Florence. By means of indirect election and tenure during good behavior, he clearly hoped to put the President and Senate above party; these exalted personages were expected to concern themselves only with the national welfare. In the New York ratifying convention he declared that "we are attempting, by this Constitution, to abolish factions, and to unite all parties for the general welfare."

Pernicious as Hamilton considered parties to be, he admitted that there was an even more iniquitous by-product of political freedom—faction. According to the definition generally accepted in the eighteenth century, a faction was a group of ambitious and unscrupulous men whose sole objective was self-aggrandizement. Hamilton did not always distinguish between faction and party—in his opinion, both stemmed from the same infirmity in human nature—but he never said of faction what he said of party, that under some circumstances it might serve a useful purpose. In his papers he preserved a quotation with which he no doubt was fully in agreement: "The demon [faction] can no more be banished the earth than human depravity, of which it is at once the parent & the offspring."

What compelled Hamilton, contrary to his intentions, to make himself the head and front of a political party was the fact that his program could not be carried through Congress without strong leadership from the Executive Branch. He recognized that Congress had to be given direction lest it dissipate its energy in the kind of hauling and pulling that had rendered nugatory so much of the work of the old Continental Congress. This executive impulse was not forthcoming from Washington during the early period of his presidency. As a man above party, it neither comported with his dignity nor with his views of the strict separation of powers established by the Constitution for the President to descend into the political arena. As a result of Washington's self-imposed abstention from the kind of leadership practiced by present-day Presidents, a vacuum of power was created. Before Congress itself could fill this vacuum, Hamilton rushed in and the air was soon filled with the tumult of party war cries.

In all likelihood, the breakup of the Federalist party would have occurred without the instrumentality of Alexander Hamilton. A party based upon an alliance of northern businessmen and southern planters contained the seeds of dissolution; only by the constant exercise of moderation and compromise could a coalition of such antagonistic elements have been preserved. Nevertheless, it was the Secretary of the Treasury whose policies provided the catalyst that split the Federalist party. As a result of his reports, the political heats and animosities that had been thought dead and buried were suddenly resurrected. It was Hamilton's peculiar contribution to the history of American politics that he made two parties grow where only one had grown before. As was observed at the time, "Whoever forms *one* party, necessarily forms *two,* for he forms an antagonistic party."

These parties were not organized along the lines of modern political parties, with such appurtenances as nominating conventions, campaign chests and party platforms. But even though their organization was embryonic, they did have a set of political doctrines; their objective was to secure or to retain for their leaders the control of the government, and from such control individuals in both parties hoped to win material benefits and advantages.

The party that challenged the ascendancy of the Hamiltonian "phalanx" called itself the Republican party. It was largely the creation of two Virginians, James Madison and Thomas Jefferson, two of the shrewdest political strategists that ever graced the American scene. As the Federalists ruefully admitted, the choice of the name "Republican" was a stroke of genius worthy of the old master himself, Alexander Hamilton. The name became "a powerful instrument in the process of making proselytes to the party," lamented Noah Webster. "The influence of *names* on the mass of mankind, was never more distinctly exhibited, than in the increase of the democratic party in the United States. The popularity of the denomination of the *republican party,* was more than a match for the popularity of Washington's character and services, and contributed to overthrow his administration."

Initially called the "Madison party," the opponents of Hamiltonianism owed more at first to the leadership of James Madison than to that of Thomas Jefferson. Indeed, the Secretary of State seemingly possessed few of the qualifications usually considered necessary for political success: he could not make a moving speech to a crowd;

he always tried to avoid quarrels; and he professed himself to be disinterested in politics and eager to get back to his library at Monticello. This mild, disarming and scholarly man bore none of the marks of the demagogue, but Hamilton was not deceived: he had found demagogues in strange places—including the Grove of Academe. When Hamilton observed a party arising in opposition to his policies, his first thought was that the old leaven of Antifederalism was at work. Since he believed that his policies were sanctioned in every respect by the Constitution, it followed that opposition to these policies was opposition to the Constitution. This implied—as Hamilton intended it should—that Republicanism was Antifederalism masquerading under a new name and that its objective was to destroy the frame of government established in 1788. Casting himself in the role of guardian of the flame that had been lighted at Philadelphia, he solicitously watched its flaring and flickerings, fearful that every breeze would snuff out this brief candle of union.

Contrary to his wishes, Hamilton seemed to have succeeded in making Americans a race of politicians to whom party slogans and polemics were the breath of life. An English traveler observed that Americans of all classes "are for ever cavilling at some of the public measures; something or other is always wrong, and they never appear perfectly satisfied. . . . Party spirit is for ever creating dissentions amongst them, and one man is continually endeavoring to obtrude his political creed upon another." Banks, taverns and shops were patronized by those who shared the political sympathies of the proprietors and were shunned by political opponents; doctors, clergymen and teachers were rated according to their political orthodoxy. Indeed, it was to be feared that these contentious republicans would raise up parties in Heaven, provided they attained that high place; and Hamilton felt certain that they would find fault with the Administration.

President Jefferson asserted in his first inaugural address, "I know, indeed, that some honest men fear that a republican government cannot be strong; that this government is not strong enough. . . . I believe this, on the contrary, the strongest government on earth. I believe it is the only one where every man, at the call of the laws, would fly to the standard of the law, and would meet invasions of the public order as his own personal concern." Julian Boyd suggests that Chief Justice John Marshall, who had just administered Jefferson's oath, must have been skeptical about these words. Both Marshall and history have viewed the states' rights aspects of Jefferson's thought. But Boyd, in contrast, traces throughout Jefferson's public career an impressive record of concern both for his nation and for humanity.

JULIAN P. BOYD:
THOMAS JEFFERSON'S "EMPIRE OF LIBERTY"*

. . . If Marshall wondered, doubted, and frowned in disagreement as he listened to the haunting phrases of the First Inaugural, he was not alone. History, too, has doubted. Less by historians, more by popular legend, and most of all by partisan claims, Jefferson has been regarded not as the staunch advocate of a strong, indissoluble union but as the zealous champion of States Rights. Opposing the ends for which Hamilton and Marshall sought to mobilize the national power, he has become for many the foe of national power itself. In 1788 Hector St. John de Crèvecoeur, writing to Jefferson, expressed the hope that "the destructive jealousy, the fatal influence of local prepossessions" would be at least partly extinguished by the adoption of the Federal Constitution and that "one great national prevailing sentiment" would operate throughout the nation. De Crèvecoeur, knowing Jefferson's political principles and public acts, wrote with the confidence of one who felt that his hope was deeply shared. But he little dreamed that the great spokesman for national ideals to whom he addressed these remarks would become to many of his countrymen a spokesman also for these local jealousies and prepossessions and, even worse, would find the principles that he employed to protect human rights turned against them. Macaulay in 1857, in the first of four remarkable letters that he addressed to H. S. Randall, noted —and deplored—the fact that during the first half of the nineteenth century American institutions had been "constantly becoming more Jeffersonian and less Washingtonian. It is surely strange that, while this process has been going on, Washington should have been exalted into a god, and Jefferson degraded into a demon." A demon, that is, who advocated principles of human right that the mid-nineteenth century called glittering generalities and who advanced the doctrine of the rights of "sovereign" states. The process that Macaulay noted has been enormously accelerated since he wrote. Extension of the popular control of political institutions has proceeded inexorably. This much is admittedly Jeffersonian. But at the same time, parallel to this development, national power has grown in gigantic measure, reducing the doctrine of States Rights almost to the ignominious status of a shibboleth. This, according to the generally accepted view, is Hamiltonian and Marshallian.

Such a view, I venture to suggest, has done both Jefferson and his country a disservice. It has obscured the great end he labored to achieve and has magnified unduly the means he employed, means which the passage of time rather than the conditions of his day made irrelevant. His was a constructive achievement, grounded upon an enlarged view of man in relation to his potentialities and to the society in which he moves. His devotion to the union, his belief in its strength and immense potentialities, his wholehearted and undeviating acceptance of the idea and meaning of nationhood were characterized by a faith, a vision, and an elevation of purpose that made him all but unique among the Founding Fathers. Only Franklin was his peer as an embodiment of the Enlightenment which provided the intellectual climate for this new and unprecedented nation and even Franklin was not his peer in grandeur of moral purpose.

Methods of arranging and distributing political power were not among Jefferson's absolutes. His advocacy of an agrarian commonwealth, its greatest concentrations of political power localized within the immediate purview of the citizen, its distant agencies of government restricted to foreign affairs and such domestic concerns as were specifically delegated to it, its executive, legislative and judicial functions carefully compartmented, was a realistic, effective arrangement

* Reprinted from Julian P. Boyd, "Thomas Jefferson's 'Empire of Liberty,'" *The Virginia Quarterly Review*, XXIV (Autumn, 1948), 541–54 by permission.

under the social and economic conditions of his day. He did not believe that those conditions would continue unchanged and unchangeable; still less did he expect succeeding generations to be bound by the contractual commitments of his generation. "Nothing, then," he declared in 1824, "is unchangeable but the inherent and inalienable rights of man" and to protect these, as he had expressed it half a century earlier, the people had the right to change their government, "laying its foundations on such principles, and organizing its powers in such form, as to them shall seem most likely to effect their Safety and Happiness." Believing the people to be the ultimate source of power and constitutions and laws merely their instruments, he believed unfalteringly in the destiny of a nation whose only immutable foundation was the rights of its citizens. Perhaps better than any other contemporary he sensed the fact that the people, too, believed in their own national destiny. This was the irresistible force, the abundant source of national strength and unity; that he understood and voiced.

Understanding history, he perceived that laws and constitutions merely codify and do not create the elements of nationhood. The monumental achievements of American constitutionalism—the Declaration of Independence, the Articles of Confederation, the Northwest Ordinance, the Federal Constitution—were the written expressions of a people already unified in ideals, as Jefferson clearly perceived. History offered abundant evidence of the futility of attempting to reverse this process. John Locke's Fundamental Constitutions of Carolina, as Jefferson must have known, endeavored to establish centralized power in the hands of a ruling class far exceeding anything proposed by Hamilton or his contemporaries, but these were merely acts of intellectual virtuosity and not a crystallization of national aspirations. Lacking the cementing force of an ideal sprung from human hearts and minds, they were cast upon history's intellectual rubbish heap along with scores of written charters of the past century and a half that have tried to imitate the act of drafting a document without matching a people's act of faith. Funding acts, national bank charters, theories of inherent sovereignty, and doctrines of judicial review might organize the credit of the nation and enlarge its powers but these, important as they were, could not in themselves create enduring bonds of nationality. The great fiscal measures of Hamilton and the judicial statecraft of Marshall, universally regarded as achievements by advocates of a strong national government, rest at bottom upon an abstraction phrased by Jefferson in the opening paragraphs of the Declaration of Independence and upon its validity as an expression of the mind of the people. It was this exalted statement of the national ideal and Jefferson's undeviating pursuit of it that entitle him to rank not with those who employ an outworn doctrine to oppose the national will, but among the foremost advocates of "the strongest government on earth." Those who feared this ultimate force

or sought to circumscribe it stood in uncomprehending resentment at their defeat by one whose political principles seemed to them to reveal more of inconsistency than of firm conviction. Historians and political scientists, no less than contemporary partisans, have mislabeled his adherence to the national ideals as political opportunism if not constitutional hypocrisy. But Jefferson's devotion to a nation based on the unchanging rights of men and his concept of a readily changeable distribution of national power were not conceived for the comfort of political opponents or for the accommodation of scholars' generalizations. They were intended for the support of a self-governing people in their pursuit of an ideal. Many of his contemporaries, of whom Hamilton and Marshall are conspicuous because of their stature, embraced this ideal in youth, faltered in mid-course, and came at last to oppose its implications if not its terms. Theirs was the ultimate opportunism, his the settled and unchanging course.

Jefferson's assertion of belief in the strength of republican government was, therefore, not a rhetorical gesture but an expression of a profound conviction. His daring to mention in the First Inaugural the possibility that some honest patriots might be induced to abandon the great experiment in the full tide of success was evidence that he knew quite well many had indeed considered its abandonment. He must have remembered how, in the debates of June, 1776, even before the Declaration of Independence was proclaimed to the world, the threat of disunion had been voiced, paradoxically making disunionism older than the union itself. A year after his inauguration, during the thunderous debate over the repeal of the Judiciary Act of 1801, the threat of separation would again be made. In another decade and a half the men of the Essex Junto against whom he had declared implacable hostility would come near to the establishment of their New England Confederacy. These assertions of the right of secession, as historians have long since pointed out, were repeated in many forms and in many causes by different political parties from the earliest days of the Republic. For, as the twentieth century would rediscover, this was the central problem of all politics—that of balancing and adjusting the rights and claims of conflicting sovereignties. If the solution to this problem were to be that of Calhoun, logic if not the dynamic of history would lead inevitably down the path to disunion or, as phrased by another great Southerner, to self-determination. If the solution were to be of the sort linked with the names of Hamilton and Marshall, the steady flow of centripetal forces would create an ever-growing vortex of power at the center and an ever-diminishing area of authority at the periphery. In our own pragmatic way we have disposed of the issue for ourselves without solving the problem at all. Perhaps it is one of those problems we refuse to recognize as insoluble. Certainly the Founding Fathers, as astute and as disinterested a group of men as ever faced the fundamental issues of government, could only dispose of the enigma by passing it on to a later generation, trusting to its wisdom, forbearance, and skill in adjustment to keep the greatest of experiments going.

But to Jefferson, upon whom fell the first great crisis calling for statesmanlike adjustment, the issue was one lying far deeper than those that might be arranged by harmonious political manipulations. It lay deeper even than an intellectual acceptance of the philosophy of self-government. It lay so deep as to reach the innermost loyalties. The salient fact that we have too long overlooked is that the cardinal principle of Jefferson's life was his uncompromising devotion to the union because of its identity with human rights. It was a compact with the future of man, not with his past errors. Jefferson knew the world and its imperfections too well not to be aware of the immense obstacles that needed to be removed before a government based on reason and justice could realize its promise. In this respect we must except him from the generalization made in Carl Becker's profound work, "The Heavenly City of the Eighteenth Century Philosophers," that the faith of the Enlightenment in man's capacity for rational and just behavior was a naïve faith, engaging and humane though it might be. Jefferson was too great a humanist, too much the embodiment of the universal man of the eighteenth century, to place his reliance solely upon the intellect. His devotion to liberty, to freedom of inquiry, to an educational system that would enlarge moral and intellectual capacities, to the idea of the destiny of the American people was a passionate loyalty. In this respect we must except him from the generalizations of those modern philosophers—Niebuhr, for example—whose reaction to eighteenth-century rationalism and secularism has led them to minimize its moral content and to attribute contemporary ills to the supposed "shallowness of a liberalism based on illusions of reason." Because this republican experiment held forth a promise for all men everywhere, Jefferson believed with overwhelming conviction that it would endure. "I own," he declared in 1801, "that the day which should convince me of the contrary doctrine would be the bitterest of my life." The second number of "The Federalist" declared that "politicians now appear, who insist that . . . instead of looking for safety and happiness in union, we ought to seek it in a division of the States into distinct confederacies or sovereignties." This was a doctrine of Patrick Henry, George Mason, and many other stalwart Americans in 1788, but it was never a doctrine of Thomas Jefferson. Its acceptance would have meant a denial of the ideal for which the nation had been founded.

The "Empire of Liberty" that Jefferson envisaged was one with that described in the same number of "The Federalist"—"a people descended from the same ancestors, speaking the same language, professing the same religion, attached to the same principles of government, very similar in their manners and customs, and who, by their joint counsels, arms, and efforts, fighting side by side throughout a long and bloody war, have nobly established general liberty and independence." But the Jeffersonian Empire of Liberty was also more than this. Language, religion, customs, and traditions shared in common indubitably provided the sense of commonalty essential to nationhood, but an insistence upon uniformity might also be equated with tyranny. Toward tyranny in any form Jefferson had vowed eternal hostility and in his Empire of Liberty, therefore, tolerance of diversity was implicit. His devotion to this nation was not the narrow patriotism of the Greeks nor the barbaric sense of fatherland that Goethe and Lessing abhorred. Though he called it an Empire of Liberty, it was to be neither an isolated political entity nor an imperialistic force for compulsory extension of ideals of liberty: its domain and compulsions would be in the realm of the mind and spirit of man, freely and inexorably transcending political boundaries, incapable of being restrained, and holding imperial sway not by arms or political power but by the sheer majesty of ideas and ideals. The great republican experiment would be an example and a beacon, unsheltered and unafraid of the light of truth. Its own people would be at once its greatest strength and its most searching critics.

To this task of remolding ancient institutions, stripping away the incongruous heritages of the past, and planning the route to the future, Jefferson dedicated himself with the urgent industry of a zealot. His great legal and political reforms in Virginia during the Revolution provide the first comprehensive index to his concept of the Empire of Liberty. Privilege was at war with the principles of this new nation and so he aimed a destructive blow at primogeniture and other pillars of what he considered an artificial and unnatural aristocracy. So great was the weight of custom that Rochefoucauld-Liancourt, two decades after the abolition of primogeniture in Virginia, found testators still favoring the eldest son with their inheritances, but the privilege was no longer protected legally and in time the force of an idea destroyed the inherited custom. An established religion was also an incongruity in a society dedicated to freedom of conscience and the protecting barriers surrounding it were removed. Education in such an Empire of Liberty was of the utmost importance if the people in general were to understand their rights and responsibilities, if the superior talents scattered by nature through all parts of society were to be improved, and if the geniuses so necessary to the development of man's potentialities were to be encouraged. Hence Jefferson envisaged a system of education not to accommodate an average mediocrity but to give every individual the privilege of unlimited opportunities for development—an aristocratic system of education equated with the natural aristocracy of virtue and talent. These and other enactments in Jefferson's political reforms in Virginia, which he hoped to see duplicated in all parts of the nation, he conceived "as forming a system by which every fibre would be eradicated of ancient or future aristocracy; and a foundation laid for a government truly republican." As a legislator, as governor, as chief executive, and as private citizen, Jefferson guided his entire conduct by these concepts of his Empire of Liberty. His angry rejection of the theories of Buffon and Abbé Raynal concerning the degenerative quality of all life in America was not the chauvinism of a narrow patriot: it was a rejection made with passion because such a theory struck at the roots of his profound belief in the destiny of the American people and in the endurance of their nation.

Next to his rôle as spokesman for the national ideal, Jefferson perhaps made his greatest contribution to the number, strength, and duration of the bonds of union by his understanding of the relation of a people to its land. Brought up on the fringes of settlement in the Virginia piedmont, son of an explorer and cartographer, he early realized the vast potentialities awaiting the American nation in the West. The letter that he addressed to George Rogers Clark on December 25, 1779, was one of the earliest of his statesmanlike expressions concerning westward expansion. Its essence was that military conquest should be so conducted, and conquered people so treated in respect to their enjoyment of religion and customs, that there should be added "to the empire of liberty an extensive and fertile country, thereby converting dangerous enemies into valuable friends." During the years immediately following the Revolution when leaders along the Western frontier, drawing their arguments from the Declaration of Independence itself, began organizing movements for separate, independent states, Jefferson deplored this "Vermont doctrine" as an abrogation of the compact of the states. "I wish to see," he wrote in 1788, "the Western Country in the hands of people well disposed, who know the value of the connection between that and the maritime states and who wish to cultivate it. I consider their happiness as bound up together, and that every measure should be taken which may draw the bands of union tighter."

Both in his public duty and in his private capacity, Jefferson acted consistently upon this policy. He was one of the first and most zealous advocates of a surrender of claims to Western territory by Virginia and other states, moving resolutely against this great obstacle to the consolidation of the union. He was assiduous in his efforts to persuade legislators that it was individual pioneers and settlers, not great Eastern land capitalists, who would develop the West and cause it to add strength to the union. While Robert Morris, George Washington, James Wilson, Benjamin Franklin, and many other Founders of the Republic were heavily engaged in this favorite form of investment in eighteenth-century America and saw no necessary conflict between their private acts and public policy, Jefferson refrained. Just as he refused to become involved in the engrossment

of vast tracts of land for private gain, so he stood fast against state rivalries and claims that jeopardized the union in its most critical years. He advocated, moreover, such a system of sale and tenure of land—low costs and allodial titles—as would protect the "great bulk of his countrymen" who were not always in a position to protect themselves. But these were attitudes toward the extension of the Empire of Liberty westward that Jefferson could not always implement as legislator or executive. Jealousies among states because of conflicting territorial claims came all too close to disrupting the union and land speculators commanded a voice in the Continental Congress that sometimes drowned the voice of statesmanship.

Yet on two great occasions Jefferson's constructive acts leading to the expansion and solidarity of the union were unparalleled in their importance. The first was the enactment of the Northwest Ordinance of 1784 and the second was the Purchase of Louisiana of 1803. Both, be it noted, were based upon the doctrine of implied powers of the national government, a doctrine usually more closely linked to the names of Hamilton, Wilson, and Marshall than to that of Jefferson.

Scarcely had the final act of separation from the British Empire been completed before the Continental Congress was obliged to face this central problem of balancing the sovereign rights of the whole against those of the parts—the same problem that had troubled the statesmen of Whitehall for a generation. Were the new sovereignties proposed by leaders in the West to be tolerated and encouraged to set up such forms of government as would "seem most likely to effect their Safety and Happiness"? The arguments concerning the natural rights of the conquerors of a wilderness that Jefferson had stated in his "Summary View" and in the Declaration of Independence were as valid here as they had been in 1776. Or, since these Western areas lay within the territory ceded to the United States by the Treaty of Paris—territory won by the joint efforts of the States in their bid for nationhood—were they to be regarded as colonial dependencies of the older Confederation? Neither extreme was acceptable. Though American constitutional lawyers in the early days of the Revolution had argued that there was no "Middle Doctrine" for this perennial problem, Jefferson and his colleagues in Congress now proceeded to act upon such a middle doctrine and to lay the foundations for an indefinite expansion of the Empire of Liberty. The new governments in the West would be neither colonial dependencies nor independent sovereignties: they would be admitted to the union on a plane of equality with the original states. Their governments would be republican in form, they would share in the public debt, they would participate as equals in the authority exercised by the general government. This much the Continental Congress would accept. But two other propositions advocated by Jefferson were so far-seeing, so wise, so statesmanlike in their implications that he stood almost alone in advancing them. One would have riveted the bonds of union so firmly as to make national dissolution impossible, since it provided that the new governments should "forever remain a part of the United States of America." The other provided that slavery should cease to exist in the new governments established in all territory ceded or to be ceded. The tragic events of the succeeding century would reveal, too late, the wisdom of Jefferson's attempt to strengthen the bonds of union by disallowing the right of secession and by prohibiting the extension of the institution that helped to bring separatism to its final stage. It was with complete truth that Jefferson, in closing his legislative career in Congress in 1784, could report to the Virginia legislature: "I have made the just rights of my country and the cement of that union in which her happiness and security is bound up, the leading objects of my conduct."

The Louisiana Purchase of 1803, fortuitous as it was, unconstitutional as Jefferson thought it to be, was another vast extension of the Empire of Liberty. By this one stroke, Jefferson added to the union a domain whose influence upon the solidarity, the achievements, the cultural and material richness of this nation is incalculable. The Constitution made no specific authorization of the acquisition of new territory by purchase, nor did the principle established in the Northwest Ordinance apply. Though Jefferson seriously considered the idea of proposing an amendment to the Constitution that would remove all doubt as to the legitimacy of the purchase, he allowed his executive act to stand by itself even though, as he unquestionably knew, he would thereby expose himself to the charge of inconsistency in his constitutional principles. But inconsistency, if it were such, was in this instance only another name for statesmanship.

Yet there were other voices whose inconsistency at this juncture in American history has not been so closely noticed. "Adopt this Western World into the Union," warned one Federalist senator, "and you destroy at once the weight and importance of the Eastern States and compel them to establish a separate and independent empire." "Our country," mourned Fisher Ames, "is too big for union, too sordid for patriotism, too democratic for liberty." Uriah Tracy, in grammar that matched the faultiness of his vision, solemnly proclaimed: "I am convinced that the accession of Louisiana will accelerate a division of these States: whose whenabouts is uncertain, but somewhen is inevitable." And Timothy Pickering, dour and querulous even when in office, declared: "I do not believe in the practicability of a long-continued union." These were the voices of believers in the theory of a strong, centralized government, the voices of a party whose leaders feared that the republican principles advocated by Jefferson would produce a weak, decentralized government

and would ultimately "add the name of America to the melancholy catalogue of fallen Republics."

Nowhere in the entire legislative and executive career of the man who believed a government of republican principles the strongest on earth can one find comparable doubts, threats, and prophecies of disunion. Even in the disillusioning postwar period, when many stouthearted Americans yielded to doubt and despair and replaced the high hopes of the Revolutionary cause with the promotion of local interests, Jefferson never wavered. To have consented to the proposition that the country was too large for union and too sordid for patriotism would have been to deny the possibility and the hope of establishing a free society of free men. This he could never do. "I hope," he wrote to John Dickinson two days after his inauguration in 1801, "to see shortly a perfect consolidation, to effect which nothing shall be spared on my part, short of the abandonment of the principles of our revolution. A just & solid republican government maintained here will be a standing monument & example for the aim & imitation of the people of other countries; and I join with you in the hope and belief that they will see from our example that a free government is of all others the most energetic, that the enquiry which has been excited among the mass of mankind by our revolution & it's consequences will ameliorate the condition of man over a great portion of the globe. What a satisfaction have we in the contemplation of the benevolent effects of our efforts, compared with those of the leaders of the other side, who have discountenanced all advances in science as dangerous innovations, have endeavored to render philosophy & republicanism terms of reproach, to persuade us that man cannot be governed but by the rod &c. I shall have the happiness of living & dying in the contrary hope."

Such was the Empire of Liberty to which, unceasingly and unselfishly, he devoted his life. If the Heavenly City of this eighteenth-century philosopher was founded on a belief that we, in our superior enlightenment and in our skepticism of the power of reason and justice, begin to consider naïve, what of the promises and prophecies of those in Jefferson's day who thought with Gouverneur Morris that "To save the people from their most dangerous enemy: to save them from themselves" was the purpose and end of the national government? If the bright promise of his Heavenly City has become tarnished in the eyes of some, what of theirs? They spoke for the past, not of a Heavenly City to come. "Jefferson aspired," wrote Henry Adams, "beyond the ambition of a nationality and embraced in his view the whole future of man." That future still stretches before us and we have the privilege of facing it under the guidance of his ennobling example. But, lest we become complacent, we also have before us those who yet repeat the cynical distrust voiced by the Gouverneur Morrises of an earlier day.

As Secretary of the Treasury, Hamilton's first great proposal was a funding of the national debt and an assumption of state debts in such a fashion as to strengthen the federal government. As had been achieved in Great Britain, he wished to use the debt as a basis for credit and, thus, capitalistic development. Also he wished to bind the creditors, "generally speaking, enlightened men," to the central government.

ALEXANDER HAMILTON:
FIRST REPORT ON THE PUBLIC CREDIT*

Treasury Department, January 9, 1790.

The Secretary of the Treasury, in obedience to the resolution of the House of Representatives of the twenty-first day of September last, has, during the recess of Congress, applied himself to the consideration of a proper plan for the support of the public credit, with all the attention which was due to the authority of the House, and to the magnitude of the object.

In the discharge of this duty, he has felt, in no small degree, the anxieties which naturally flow from a just estimate of the difficulty of the task, from a well-founded diffidence of his own qualifications for executing it with success, and from a deep and solemn conviction of the momentous nature of the truth contained in the resolution under which his investigations have been conducted,—"That an adequate provision for the support of the public credit is a matter of high importance to the honor and prosperity of the United States."

With an ardent desire that his well-meant endeavors may be conducive to the real advantage of the nation, and with the utmost deference to the superior judgment of the House, he now respectfully submits the result of his inquiries and reflections to their indulgent construction.

In the opinion of the Secretary, the wisdom of the House, in giving their explicit sanction to the proposition which has been stated, cannot but be applauded by all who will seriously consider and trace, through their obvious consequences, these plain and undeniable truths:

That exigencies are to be expected to occur, in the affairs of nations, in which there will be a necessity for borrowing.

That loans in time of public danger, especially from foreign war, are found an indispensable resource, even to the wealthiest of them.

And that, in a country which, like this, is possessed of little active wealth, or, in other words, little moneyed capital, the necessity for that resource must, in such emergencies, be proportionably urgent.

And as, on the one hand, the necessity for borrowing in particular emergencies cannot be doubted, so, on the other, it is equally evident that, to be able to borrow upon good terms, it is essential that the credit of a nation should be well established.

For, when the credit of a country is in any degree questionable, it never fails to give an extravagant premium, in one shape or another, upon all the loans it has occasion to make. Nor does the evil end here; the same disadvantage must be sustained on whatever is to be bought on terms of future payment.

From this constant necessity of borrowing and buying dear, it is easy to conceive how immensely the expenses of a nation, in a course of time, will be augmented by an unsound state of the public credit.

To attempt to enumerate the complicated variety of mischiefs, in the whole system of the social economy, which proceed from a neglect of the maxims that uphold public credit, and justify the solicitude manifested by the House on this point, would be an improper intrusion on their time and patience.

In so strong a light, nevertheless, do they appear to the Secretary, that, on their due observance, at the present critical juncture, materially depends, in his judgment, the individual and aggregate prosperity of the citizens of the United States; their relief from the embarrassments they now experience; their character as a people; the cause of good government.

If the maintenance of public credit, then, be truly so important, the next inquiry which suggests itself is: By what means is it to be effected? The ready answer to which question is, by good faith; by a punctual performance of contracts. States, like individuals, who observe their engagements are respected and trusted, while the reverse is the fate of those who pursue an opposite conduct.

Every breach of the public engagements, whether from choice or necessity, is, in different degrees, hurtful to public credit. When such a necessity does truly exist, the evils of it are only to be palliated by a scrupulous attention, on the part of the Government, to carry the violation no further than the necessity absolutely requires, and to manifest, if the nature of the case admit of it, a sincere disposition to make reparation whenever circumstances shall permit. But, with every pos-

---

* Reprinted from Henry Cabot Lodge, ed., *The Works of Alexander Hamilton* (Federal Edition; New York: Putnam, 1904), II, 227–89, *passim.* Transmitted to the House of Representatives, January 14, 1790.

sible mitigation, credit must suffer, and numerous mischiefs ensue. It is, therefore, highly important, when an appearance of necessity seems to press upon the public councils, that they should examine well its reality, and be perfectly assured that there is no method of escaping from it, before they yield to its suggestions. For, though it cannot safely be affirmed that occasions have never existed, or may not exist, in which violations of the public faith, in this respect, are inevitable; yet there is great reason to believe that they exist far less frequently than precedents indicate, and are oftenest either pretended, through levity or want of firmness; or supposed, through want of knowledge. Expedients often have been devised to effect, consistently with good faith, what has been done in contravention of it. Those who are most commonly creditors of a nation are, generally speaking, enlightened men; and there are signal examples to warrant a conclusion that, when a candid and fair appeal is made to them, they will understand their true interest too well to refuse their concurrence in such modifications of their claims as any real necessity may demand.

While the observance of that good faith, which is the basis of public credit, is recommended by the strongest inducements of political expediency, it is enforced by considerations of still greater authority. There are arguments for it which rest on the immutable principles of moral obligation. And in proportion as the mind is disposed to contemplate, in the order of Providence, an intimate connection between public virtue and public happiness, will be its repugnancy to a violation of those principles.

This reflection derives additional strength from the nature of the debt of the United States. It was the price of liberty. The faith of America has been repeatedly pledged for it, and with solemnities that give peculiar force to the obligation. There is, indeed, reason to regret that it has not hitherto been kept; that the necessities of the war, conspiring with inexperience in the subjects of finance, produced direct infractions; and that the subsequent period has been a continued scene of negative violation or non-compliance. But a diminution of this regret arises from the reflection, that the last seven years have exhibited an earnest and uniform effort, on the part of the Government of the Union, to retrieve the national credit, by doing justice to the creditors of the nation; and that the embarrassments of a defective Constitution, which defeated this laudable effort, have ceased.

From this evidence of a favorable disposition given by the former Government, the institution of a new one, clothed with powers competent to calling forth the resources of the community, has excited correspondent expectations. A general belief accordingly prevails, that the credit of the United States will quickly be established on the firm foundation of an effectual provision for the existing debt. The influence which this has had at home is witnessed by the rapid increase that has taken place in the market value of the public securities. From January to November, they rose thirty-three and a third per cent.; and, from that period to this time, they have risen fifty per cent. more; and the intelligence from abroad announces effects proportionably favorable to our national credit and consequence.

It cannot but merit particular attention, that, among ourselves, the most enlightened friends of good government are those whose expectations are the highest.

To justify and preserve their confidence; to promote the increasing respectability of the American name, to answer the calls of justice; to restore landed property to its due value; to furnish new resources, both to agriculture and commerce; to cement more closely the union of the States, to add to their security against foreign attack; to establish public order on the basis of an upright and liberal policy;—these are the great and invaluable ends to be secured by a proper and adequate provision, at the present period, for the support of public credit.

To this provision we are invited, not only by the general considerations which have been noticed, but by others of a more particular nature. It will procure, to every class of the community, some important advantages, and remove some no less important disadvantages.

The advantage to the public creditors, from the increased value of that part of their property which constitutes the public debt, needs no explanation.

But there is a consequence of this, less obvious, though not less true, in which every other citizen is interested. It is a well-known fact, that, in countries in which the national debt is properly funded, and an object of established confidence, it answers most of the purposes of money. Transfers of stock or public debt are there equivalent to payments in specie; or, in other words, stock, in the principal transactions of business, passes current as specie. The same thing would, in all probability, happen here under the like circumstances.

The benefits of this are various and obvious:

First.—Trade is extended by it, because there is a larger capital to carry it on, and the merchant can, at the same time, afford to trade for smaller profits; as his stock, which, when unemployed, brings him an interest from the Government, serves him also as money when he has a call for it in his commercial operations.

Secondly.—Agriculture and manufactures are also promoted by it, for the like reason, that more capital can be commanded to be employed in both; and because the merchant, whose enterprise in foreign trade gives to them activity and extension, has greater means for enterprise.

Thirdly.—The interest of money will be lowered by it; for this is always in a ratio to the quantity of money, and to the quickness of circulation. This circumstance will enable both the public and individuals to borrow on easier and cheaper terms.

And from the combination of these effects, additional aids will be furnished to labor, to industry, and to arts of every kind. But these good effects of a public debt are only to be looked for, when, by being well funded, it has acquired an adequate and stable value; till then, it has rather a contrary tendency. The fluctuation and insecurity incident to it, in an unfunded state, render it a mere commodity, and a precarious one. As such, being only an object of occasional and particular speculation, all the money applied to it is so much diverted from the more useful channels of circulation, for which the thing itself affords no substitute; so that, in fact, one serious inconvenience of an unfunded debt is, that it contributes to the scarcity of money.

This distinction, which has been little if at all attended to, is of the greatest moment; it involves a question immediately interesting to every part of the community, which is no other than this: Whether the public debt, by a provision for it on true principles, shall be rendered a substitute for money; or whether, by being left as it is, or by being provided for in such a manner as will wound those principles and destroy confidence, it shall be suffered to continue as it is, a pernicious drain of our cash from the channels of productive industry?

The effect which the funding of the public debt, on right principles, would have upon landed property, is one of the circumstances attending such an arrangement, which has been least adverted to, though it deserves the most particular attention. The present depreciated state of that species of property is a serious calamity. The value of cultivated lands, in most of the States, has fallen, since the Revolution, from twenty-five to fifty per cent. In those farther south, the decrease is still more considerable. Indeed, if the representations continually received from that quarter may be credited, lands there will command no price which may not be deemed an almost total sacrifice. This decrease in the value of lands ought, in a great measure, to be attributed to the scarcity of money; consequently, whatever produces an augmentation of the moneyed capital of the country must have a proportional effect in raising that value. The beneficial tendency of a funded debt, in this respect, has been manifested by the most decisive experience in Great Britain.

The proprietors of lands would not only feel the benefit of this increase in the value of their property, and of a more prompt and better sale, when they had occasion to sell, but the necessity of selling would be itself greatly diminished. As the same cause would contribute to the facility of loans, there is reason to believe that such of them as are indebted would be able, through that resource, to satisfy their more urgent creditors.

It ought not, however, to be expected that the advantages described as likely to result from funding the public debt would be instantaneous. It might require some time to bring the value of stock to its natural level, and to attach to it that fixed confidence which is necessary to its quality as money. Yet the late rapid rise of the public securities encourages an expectation that the progress of stock, to the desirable point, will be much more expeditious than could have been foreseen. And as, in the meantime, it will be increasing in value, there is room to conclude that it will, from the outset, answer many of the purposes in contemplation. . . .

Having now taken a concise view of the inducements to a proper provision for the public debt, the next inquiry which presents itself is: What ought to be the nature of such a provision? This requires some preliminary discussions.

It is agreed, on all hands, that that part of the debt which has been contracted abroad, and is denominated the foreign debt, ought to be provided for according to the precise terms of the contracts relating to it. The discussions which can arise, therefore, will have reference essentially to the domestic part of it, or to that which has been contracted at home. It is to be regretted that there is not the same unanimity of sentiment on this part as on the other.

The Secretary has too much deference for the opinions of every part of the community not to have observed one, which has more than once made its appearance in the public prints, and which is occasionally to be met with in conversation. It involves this question: Whether a discrimination ought not to be made between original holders of the public securities, and present possessors, by purchase? Those who advocate a discrimination are for making a full provision for the securities of the former at their nominal value, but contend that the latter ought to receive no more than the cost to them, and the interest. And the idea is sometimes suggested of making good the difference to the primitive possessor.

In favor of this scheme it is alleged that it would be unreasonable to pay twenty shillings in the pound to one who had not given more for it than three or four. And it is added that it would be hard to aggravate the misfortune of the first owner, who, probably through necessity, parted with his property at so great a loss, by obliging him to contribute to the profit of the person who had speculated on his distresses.

The Secretary, after the most mature reflection on the force of this argument, is induced to reject the doctrine it contains, as equally unjust and impolitic; as highly injurious, even to the original holders of public securities; as ruinous to public credit.

It is inconsistent with justice, because, in the first place, it is a breach of contract—a violation of the rights of a fair purchaser. . . .

It will be perceived, at first sight, that the transferable quality of stock is essential to its operation as money, and that this depends on the idea of complete security to the transferee, and a firm persuasion that no distinction can, in any circumstances, be made between him and the original proprietor. . . .

The Secretary, concluding that a discrimination between the different classes of creditors of the United States cannot, with propriety, be made, proceeds to examine whether a difference ought to be permitted to remain between them and another description of public creditors—those of the States individually. The Secretary, after mature reflection on this point, entertains a full conviction that an assumption of the debts of the particular States by the Union, and a like provision for them as for those of the Union, will be a measure of sound policy and substantial justice.

It would, in the opinion of the Secretary, contribute, in an eminent degree, to an orderly, stable, and satisfactory arrangement of the national finances. Admitting, as ought to be the case, that a provision must be made, in some way or other, for the entire debt, it will follow that no greater revenues will be required whether that provision be made wholly by the United States, or partly by them and partly by the States separately. . . .

If all the public creditors receive their dues from one source, distributed with an equal hand, their interest will be the same. And, having the same interests, they will unite in the support of the fiscal arrangements of the Government—as these, too, can be made with more convenience where there is no competition. These circumstances combined will insure to the revenue laws a more ready and more satisfactory execution. . . .

The result of the foregoing discussion is this: That there ought to be no discrimination between the original holders of the debt, and present possessors by purchase; that it is expedient there should be an assumption of the State debts by the Union; and that the arrears of interest should be provided for on an equal footing with the principal. . . .

The interesting problem now occurs: Is it in the power of the United States, consistently with those prudential considerations which ought not to be overlooked, to make a provision equal to the purpose of funding the whole debt, at the rates of interest which it now bears, in addition to the sum which will be necessary for the current service of the Government?

The Secretary will not say that such a provision would exceed the abilities of the country, but he is clearly of opinion that to make it would require the extension of taxation to a degree and to objects which the true interest of the public creditors forbids. It is, therefore, to be hoped, and even to be expected, that they will cheerfully concur in such modifications of their claims, on fair and equitable principles, as will facilitate to the Government an arrangement substantial, durable, and satisfactory to the community. The importance of the last characteristic will strike every discerning mind. No plan, however flattering in appearance, to which it did not belong, could be truly entitled to confidence. . . .

Persuaded, as the Secretary is, that the proper funding of the present debt will render it a national blessing, yet he is so far from acceding to the position, in the latitude in which it is sometimes laid down, that "public debts are public benefits"—a position inviting to prodigality and liable to dangerous abuse—that he ardently wishes to see it incorporated as a fundamental maxim in the system of public credit of the United States, that the creation of debt should always be accompanied with the means of extinguishment. . . .

Secretary Hamilton's proposal that the federal government take over the state debts ran into serious opposition in Congress. Since the debt of some states like Massachusetts was larger than that of others like Virginia, the Virginians did not like the prospect of helping to pay for the troubles of Massachusetts. With the aid of Jefferson, who had just returned from France, Hamilton obtained the Virginia votes in exchange for agreeing that after ten years the nation's capital would be relocated on the banks of the Potomac. In 1818, Jefferson, revising the notes or Anas that he had kept at the time, set forth his version of the bargain and launched into a general criticism of the Hamiltonian system and its effect upon politics.

THOMAS JEFFERSON:
THE POLITICAL CONSEQUENCES OF HAMILTON'S SYSTEM*

I returned from that mission [to France] in the 1st. year of the new government, having landed in Virginia in Dec. 89. & proceeded to N. York in

* Reprinted from Paul Leicester Ford, ed., *The Works of Thomas Jefferson* (New York: Putnam, 1904), I, 171–78.

March 90. to enter on the office of Secretary of State. Here certainly I found a state of things which, of all I had ever contemplated, I the least expected. I had left France in the first year of its revolution, in the fervor of natural rights, and zeal for reformation. My conscientious devotion to these rights could not be heightened, but it had been aroused and excited by daily exercise. The President received me cordially, and my Colleagues & the circle of principal citizens, apparently, with welcome. The courtesies of dinner parties given me as a stranger newly arrived among them, placed me at once in their familiar society. But I cannot describe the wonder and mortification with which the table conversations filled me. Politics were the chief topic, and a preference of kingly, over republican, government, was evidently the favorite sentiment. An apostate I could not be; nor yet a hypocrite: and I found myself, for the most part, the only advocate on the republican side of the question, unless, among the guests, there chanced to be some member of that party from the legislative Houses. Hamilton's financial system had then past. It had two objects. 1st as a puzzle, to exclude popular understanding & inquiry. 2dly, as a machine for the corruption of the legislature; for he avowed the opinion that man could be governed by one of two motives only, force or interest: force he observed, in this country, was out of the question; and the interests therefore of the members must be laid hold of, to keep the legislature in unison with the Executive. And with grief and shame it must be acknowledged that his machine was not without effect. That even in this, the birth of our government, some members were found sordid enough to bend their duty to their interests, and to look after personal, rather than public good. It is well known that, during the war, the greatest difficulty we encountered was the want of money or means, to pay our souldiers who fought, or our farmers, manufacturers & merchants who furnished the necessary supplies of food & clothing for them. After the expedient of paper money had exhausted itself, certificates of debt were given to the individual creditors, with assurance of payment, so soon as the U.S. should be able. But the distresses of these people often obliged them to part with these for the half, the fifth, and even a tenth of their value; and Speculators had made a trade of cozening them from the holders, by the most fraudulent practices and persuasions that they would never be paid. In the bill for funding & paying these, Hamilton made no difference between the original holders, & the fraudulent purchasers of this paper. Great & just repugnance arose at putting these two classes of creditors on the same footing, and great exertions were used to pay to the former the full value, and to the latter the price only which he had paid, with interest. But this would have prevented the game which was to be played, & for which the minds of greedy members were already tutored and prepared. When the trial of strength on these several efforts had indicated the form in which the bill would finally pass, this being known within doors sooner than without, and especially than to those who were in distant parts of the Union, the base scramble began. Couriers & relay horses by land, and swift sailing pilot boats by sea, were flying in all directions. Active part[n]ers & agents were as-

sociated & employed in every state, town and country, neighborhood, and this paper was bought up at 5/ and even as low as 2/ in the pound, before the holder knew that Congress had already provided for it's redemption at par. Immense sums were thus filched from the poor & ignorant, and fortunes accumulated by those who had themselves been poor enough before. Men thus enriched by the dexterity of a leader, would follow of course the chief who was leading them to fortune, and become the zealous instruments of all his enterprises. This game was over, and another was on the carpet at the moment of my arrival; and to this I was most ignorantly & innocently made to hold the candle. This fiscal maneuvre is well known by the name of the Assumption. Independantly of the debts of Congress, the states had, during the war, contracted separate and heavy debts; and Massachusetts particularly in an absurd attempt, absurdly conducted, on the British post of Penobscot: and the more debt Hamilton could rake up, the more plunder for his mercenaries. This money, whether wisely or foolishly spent, was pretended to have been spent for general purposes, and ought therefore to be paid from the general purse. But it was objected that nobody knew what these debts were, what their amount, or what their proofs. No matter; we will guess them to be 20. millions. But of these 20. millions we do not know how much should be reimbursed to one state, nor how much to another. No matter; we will guess. And so another scramble was set on foot among the several states, and some got much, some little, some nothing. But the main object was obtained, the phalanx of the treasury was reinforced by additional recruits. This measure produced the most bitter & angry contests ever known in Congress, before or since the union of the states. I arrived in the midst of it. But a stranger to the ground, a stranger to the actors on it, so long absent as to have lost all familiarity with the subject, and as yet unaware of it's object, I took no concern in it. The great and trying question however was lost in the H. of Representatives. So high were the feuds excited by this subject, that on it's rejection business was suspended. Congress met and adjourned from day to day without doing any thing, the parties being too much out of temper to do business together. The Eastern members particularly, who, with [William] Smith from South Carolina, were the principal gamblers in these scenes, threatened a secession and dissolution. Hamilton was in despair. As I was going to the President's one day, I met him in the street. He walked me backwards & forwards before the President's door for half an hour. He painted pathetically the temper into which the legislature had been wrought, the disgust of those who were called the Creditor states, the danger of the secession of their members, and the separation of the states. He observed that the members of the administration ought to act in concert, that tho' this question was not of my department, yet a common duty should make it a common concern; that the President was the center on which all administrative questions ultimately rested, and that all of us should rally around him, and support with joint efforts measures approved by him; and that the question having been lost by a small majority only, it was probable that an appeal from me to the judgment and discretion of some of my friends might effect a change in the vote, and the machine of government, now suspended, might be again set into motion. I told him that I was really a stranger to the whole subject; not having yet informed myself of the system of finances adopted, I knew not how far this was a necessary sequence; that undoubtedly if it's rejection endangered a dissolution of our union at this incipient stage, I should deem that the most unfortunate of all consequences, to avert which all partial and temporary evils should be yielded. I proposed to him however to dine with me the next day, and I would invite another friend or two, bring them into conference together, and I thought it impossible that reasonable men, consulting together coolly, could fail, by some mutual sacrifices of opinion, to form a compromise which was to save the union. The discussion took place. I could take no part in it, but an exhortatory one, because I was a stranger to the circumstances which should govern it. But it was finally agreed that, whatever importance had been attached to the rejection of this proposition, the preservation of the union, & of concord among the states was more important, and that therefore it would be better that the vote of rejection should be rescinded, to effect which some members should change their votes. But it was observed that this pill would be peculiarly bitter to the Southern States, and that some concomitant measure should be adopted to sweeten it a little to them. There had before been propositions to fix the seat of government either at Philadelphia, or at Georgetown on the Potomac; and it was thought that by giving it to Philadelphia for ten years, and to Georgetown permanently afterwards, this might, as an anodyne, calm in some degree the ferment which might be excited by the other measure alone. So two of the Potomac members ([Alexander] White & [Richard Bland] Lee, but White with a revulsion of stomach almost convulsive) agreed to change their votes, & Hamilton undertook to carry the other point. In doing this the influence he had established over the Eastern

members, with the agency of Robert Morris with those of the middle states, effected his side of the engagement, and so the assumption was passed, and 20. millions of stock divided among favored states, and thrown in as pabulum to the stockjobbing herd. This added to the number of votaries to the treasury and made its Chief the master of every vote in the legislature which might give to the government the direction suited to his political views. I know well, and so must be understood, that nothing like a majority in Congress had yielded to this corruption. Far from it. But a division, not very unequal, had already taken place in the honest part of that body, between the parties styled republican and federal. The latter being monarchists in principle, adhered to Hamilton of course, as their leader in that principle, and this mercenary phalanx added to them ensured him always a majority in both houses: so that the whole action of the legislature was now under the direction of the treasury. Still the machine was not compleat. The effect of the funding system, & of the assumption, would be temporary. It would be lost with the loss of the individual members whom it had enriched, and some engine of influence more permanent must be contrived, while these myrmidons were yet in place to carry it thro' all opposition. This engine was the Bank of the U. S. All that history is known; so I shall say nothing about it. While the government remained at Philadelphia, a selection of members of both houses were constantly kept as Directors, who, on every question interesting to that institution, or to the views of the federal head, voted at the will of that head; and, together with the stockholding members, could always make the federal vote that of the majority. By this combination, legislative expositions were given to the constitution, and all the administrative laws were shaped on the model of England, & so passed. And from this influence we were not relieved until the removal from the precincts of the bank, to Washington. Here then was the real ground of the opposition which was made to the course of administration. It's object was to preserve the legislature pure and independant of the Executive, to restrain the administration to republican forms and principles, and not permit the constitution to be construed into a monarchy, and to be warped in practice into all the principles and pollutions of their favorite English model. . . .

Jefferson's objections to the Bank of the United States were more than just political ones. When President Washington asked him for his opinion of its constitutionality, Jefferson quickly replied with a vigorous statement, narrowly interpreting the Constitution to place the proposed Bank outside of its scope.

THOMAS JEFFERSON:
CONSTITUTIONAL ARGUMENTS
AGAINST THE BANK OF THE UNITED STATES*

February 15, 1791.

The bill for establishing a National Bank undertakes among other things:

1. To form the subscribers into a corporation.

2. To enable them in their corporate capacities to receive grants of land; and so far is against the laws of *Mortmain*.[1]

3. To make alien subscribers capable of holding lands; and so far is against the laws of *Alienage*.

4. To transmit these lands, on the death of a proprietor, to a certain line of successors; and so far changes the course of *Descents*.

5. To put the lands out of the reach of forfeiture or escheat; and so far is against the laws of *Forfeiture and Escheat*.

6. To transmit personal chattels to successors in a certain line; and so far is against the laws of *Distribution*.

7. To give them the sole and exclusive right of banking under the national authority; and so far is against the laws of *Monopoly*.

8. To communicate to them a power to make laws paramount to the laws of the States; for so they must be construed, to protect the institution from the control of the State legislatures; and so, probably, they will be construed.

I consider the foundation of the Constitution as laid on this ground: That "all powers not delegated to the United States, by the Constitution, nor prohibited by it to the States, are reserved to the States or to the people." [XIIth amendment.] To take a single step beyond the boundaries thus specially drawn around the powers of Congress is to take possession of a boundless field of power, no longer susceptible of any definition.

The incorporation of a bank, and the powers assumed by this bill, have not, in my opinion, been delegated to the United States, by the Constitution.

I. They are not among the powers specially enumerated; for these are: 1st. A power to lay taxes for the purpose of paying the debts of the United States; but no debt is paid by this bill, nor any tax laid. Were it a bill to raise money, its origination in the Senate would condemn it by the Constitution.

2d. "To borrow money." But this bill neither borrows money nor ensures the borrowing it. The proprietors of the bank will be just as free as any other money-holders, to lend or not to lend their money to the public. The operation proposed in the bill, first, to lend them two millions, and then to borrow them back again, cannot change the nature of the latter act, which will still be a payment, and not a loan, call it by what name you please.

3d. To "regulate commerce with foreign nations, and among the States, and with the Indian tribes." To erect a bank, and to regulate commerce, are very different acts. He who erects a bank creates a subject of commerce in its bills; so does he who makes a bushel of wheat, or digs a dollar out of the mines; yet neither of these persons regulates commerce thereby. To make a thing which may be bought and sold is not to prescribe regulations for buying and selling. Besides, if this was an exercise of the power of regulating commerce, it would be void, as extending as much to the internal commerce of every State, as to its external. For the power given to Congress by the Constitution does not extend to the internal regulation of the commerce of a State (that is to say of the commerce between citizen and citizen), which remains exclusively with its own legislature; but to its external commerce only, that is to say, its commerce with another State, or with foreign nations, or with the Indian tribes. Accordingly the bill does not propose the measure as a regulation of trade, but as "productive of considerable advantages to trade." Still less are these powers covered by any other of the special enumerations.

II. Nor are they within either of the general phrases, which are the two following:

1. To lay taxes to provide for the general welfare of the United States, that is to say, "to lay taxes for *the purpose* of providing for the general welfare." For the laying of taxes is the *power,* and the general welfare the *purpose* for which the power is to be exercised. They are not to lay taxes

* Reprinted from Paul Leicester Ford, ed., *The Works of Thomas Jefferson* (New York: Putnam, 1904), VI, 197–204.

[1] Though the Constitution controls the laws of Mortmain so far as to permit Congress itself to hold land for certain purposes, yet not so far as to permit them to communicate a similar right to other corporate bodies.—T.J.

ad libitum for any purpose they please; but only *to pay the debts or provide for the welfare of the Union.* In like manner, they are not *to do anything they please* to provide for the general welfare, but only to *lay taxes* for that purpose. To consider the latter phrase, not as describing the purpose of the first, but as giving a distinct and independent power to do any act they please, which might be for the good of the Union, would render all the preceding and subsequent enumerations of power completely useless.

It would reduce the whole instrument to a single phrase, that of instituting a Congress with power to do whatever would be for the good of the United States; and, as they would be the sole judges of the good or evil, it would be also a power to do whatever evil they please.

It is an established rule of construction where a phrase will bear either of two meanings, to give it that which will allow some meaning to the other parts of the instrument, and not that which would render all the others useless. Certainly no such universal power was meant to be given them. It was intended to lace them up straitly within the enumerated powers, and those without which, as means, these powers could not be carried into effect. It is known that the very power now proposed *as a means* was rejected as *an end* by the Convention which formed the Constitution. A proposition was made to them to authorize Congress to open canals, and an amendatory one to empower them to incorporate. But the whole was rejected, and one of the reasons for rejection urged in debate was that then they would have a power to erect a bank, which would render the great cities, where there were prejudices and jealousies on the subject, adverse to the reception of the Constitution.

2. The second general phrase is, "to make all laws *necessary* and proper for carrying into execution the enumerated powers." But they can all be carried into execution without a bank. A bank therefore is not *necessary,* and consequently not authorized by this phrase.

It has been urged that a bank will give great facility or convenience in the collection of taxes. Suppose this were true; yet the Constitution allows only the means which are *"necessary,"* not those which are merely "convenient" for effecting the enumerated powers. If such a latitude of construction be allowed to this phrase as to give any non-enumerated power, it will go to every one, for there is not one which ingenuity may not torture into a *convenience* in some instance *or other,* to *some one* of so long a list of enumerated powers. It would swallow up all the delegated powers, and reduce the whole to one power, as before observed. Therefore it was that the Constitution restrained them to the *necessary* means, that is to say, to those means without which the grant of power would be nugatory.

But let us examine this convenience and see what it is. The report on this subject, page 3,

states the only *general* convenience to be, the preventing the transportation and re-transportation of money between the States and the Treasury (for I pass over the increase of circulating medium, ascribed to it as a want, and which, according to my ideas of paper money, is clearly a demerit). Every State will have to pay a sum of tax money into the Treasury; and the Treasury will have to pay, in every State, a part of the interest on the public debt, and salaries to the officers of government resident in that State. In most of the States there will still be a surplus of tax money to come up to the seat of government for the officers residing there. The payments of interest and salary in each State may be made by Treasury orders on the State collector. This will take up the greater part of the money he has collected in his State, and consequently prevent the great mass of it from being drawn out of the State. If there be a balance of commerce in favor of that State against the one in which the government resides, the surplus of taxes will be remitted by the bills of exchange drawn for that commercial balance. And so it must be if there was a bank. But if there be no balance of commerce, either direct or circuitous, all the banks in the world could not bring up the surplus of taxes, but in the form of money. Treasury orders then, and bills of exchange may prevent the displacement of the main mass of the money collected, without the aid of any bank; and where these fail, it cannot be prevented even with that aid.

Perhaps, indeed, bank bills may be a more *convenient* vehicle than treasury orders. But a little *difference* in the degree of *convenience* cannot constitute the necessity which the constitution makes the ground for assuming any non-enumerated power.

Besides; the existing banks will, without a doubt, enter into arrangements for lending their agency, and the more favorable, as there will be a competition among them for it; whereas the bill delivers us up bound to the national bank, who are free to refuse all arrangement, but on their own terms, and the public not free, on such refusal, to employ any other bank. That of Philadelphia, I believe, now does this business, by their post-notes, which, by an arrangement with the Treasury, are paid by any State collector to whom they are presented. This expedient alone suffices to prevent the existence of that *necessity* which may justify the assumption of a non-enumerated power as a means for carrying into effect an enumerated one. The thing may be done, and has been done, and well done, without this assumption; therefore, it does not stand on that degree of *necessity* which can honestly justify it.

It may be said that a bank whose bills would have a currency all over the States, would be more convenient than one whose currency is limited to a single State. So it would be still more convenient that there should be a bank whose bills should have a currency all over the world. But it does not follow from this superior conveniency, that there exists anywhere a power to establish such a bank; or that the world may not go on very well without it.

Can it be thought that the Constitution intended that for a shade or two of *convenience,* more or less, Congress should be authorized to break down the most ancient and fundamental laws of the several States; such as those against mortmain, the laws of alienage, the rules of descent, the acts of distribution, the laws of escheat and forfeiture, the laws of monopoly? Nothing but a necessity invincible by any other means can justify such a prostitution of laws, which constitute the pillars of our whole system of jurisprudence. Will Congress be too strait-laced to carry the Constitution into honest effect, unless they may pass over the foundation-laws of the State government for the slightest convenience of theirs?

The negative of the President is the shield provided by the Constitution to protect against the invasions of the legislature: 1. The right of the Executive. 2. Of the Judiciary. 3. Of the States and State legislatures. The present is the case of a right remaining exclusively with the States, and consequently one of those intended by the Constitution to be placed under its protection.

It must be added, however, that unless the President's mind, on a view of everything which is urged for and against this bill, is tolerably clear that it is unauthorized by the Constitution; if the pro and the con hang so even as to balance his judgment, a just respect for the wisdom of the legislature would naturally decide the balance in favor of their opinion. It is chiefly for cases where they are clearly misled by error, ambition, or interest, that the Constitution has placed a check in the negative of the President.

Secretary Hamilton, writing with Jefferson's opinion before him (and also an equivocal one by Attorney General Edmund Randolph), prepared an opinion strongly defending the constitutionality of the proposed Bank for President Washington. Hamilton's reasoning, broadly construing the implied powers bestowed upon Congress by the Constitution, was so cogent that Chief Justice John Marshall followed it twenty-eight years later in the McCulloch decision which upheld the constitutionality of the Bank.

ALEXANDER HAMILTON:
THE CONSTITUTIONALITY
OF THE BANK OF THE UNITED STATES*

February 23, 1791.

The Secretary of the Treasury having perused with attention the papers containing the opinions of the Secretary of State and the Attorney-General, concerning the constitutionality of the bill for establishing a national bank, proceeds, according to the order of the President, to submit the reasons which have induced him to entertain a different opinion.

It will naturally have been anticipated, that in performing this task he would feel uncommon solicitude. Personal considerations alone, arising from the reflection that the measure originated with him, would be sufficient to produce it. The sense which he has manifested of the great importance of such an institution to the successful administration of the department under his particular care, and an expectation of serious ill consequences to result from a failure of the measure, do not permit him to be without anxiety on public accounts. But the chief solicitude arises from a firm persuasion, that principles of construction like those espoused by the Secretary of State and the Attorney-General would be fatal to the just and indispensable authority of the United States.

In entering upon the argument, it ought to be premised that the objections of the Secretary of State and the Attorney-General are founded on a general denial of the authority of the United States to erect corporations. The latter, indeed, expressly admits, that if there be anything in the bill which is not warranted by the Constitution, it is the clause of incorporation.

Now it appears to the Secretary of the Treasury that this *general principle* is *inherent* in the very *definition* of government, and *essential* to every step of the progress to be made by that of the United States, namely: That every power vested in a government is in its nature *sovereign,* and includes, by *force* of the *term,* a right to employ all the *means* requisite and fairly applicable to the attainment of the *ends* of such power,

* Reprinted from Henry Cabot Lodge, ed., *The Works of Alexander Hamilton* (Federal Edition; New York: Putnam, 1904), III, 445–93, *passim.*

and which are not precluded by restrictions and exceptions specified in the Constitution, or not immoral, or not contrary to the *essential ends* of political society.

This principle, in its application to government in general, would be admitted as an axiom; and it will be incumbent upon those who may incline to deny it, to prove a distinction, and to show that a rule which, in the general system of things, is essential to the preservation of the social order, is inapplicable to the United States.

The circumstance that the powers of sovereignty are in this country divided between the National and State governments, does not afford the distinction required. It does not follow from this, that each of the portion of *powers* delegated to the one or to the other, is not sovereign with *regard to its proper objects.* It will only *follow* from it, that each has sovereign power, as to its declared purposes and trusts, because its power does not extend to all cases, would be equally to deny that the State governments have sovereign power in any case, because their power does not extend to every case. The tenth section of the first article of the Constitution exhibits a long list of very important things which they may not do. And thus the United States would furnish the singular spectacle of a *political society* without *sovereignty,* or of a *people governed,* without *government.*

If it would be necessary to bring proof to a proposition so clear, as that which affirms that the powers of the federal government, as to *its objects,* were sovereign, there is a clause of its Constitution which would be decisive. It is that which declares that the Constitution, and the laws of the United States made in pursuance of it, . . . shall be the *supreme law of the land.* The power which can create the *supreme law of the land,* in any case, is doubtless *sovereign* as to such case.

This general and indisputable principle puts at once an end to the *abstract* question, whether the United States have power to erect a corporation; that is to say, to give a *legal* or *artificial capacity* to one or more persons, distinct from the *natural.* For it is unquestionably incident to *sovereign power* to erect corporations, and consequently to *that* of the United States, in *relation* to the *objects* intrusted to the management of the government. The difference is this: where the authority of the government is general, it can create corporations in *all cases;* where it is confined to certain branches of legislation, it can create corporations *only* in those cases.

It is not denied that there are *implied* as well as *express powers,* and that the *former* are as effectually delegated as the *latter.* And for the sake of accuracy it shall be mentioned, that there is another class of powers, which may be properly denominated *resulting powers.* It will not be doubted, that if the United States should make a conquest of any of the territories of its neighbours, they would possess sovereign jurisdiction over the conquered territory. This would be rather a result from the whole mass of the powers of the government, and from the nature of political society, than a consequence of either of the powers specially enumerated. . . .

It is conceded that *implied powers* are to be considered as delegated equally with *express ones.* Then it follows, that as a power of erecting a corporation may as well be *implied* as any other thing, it may as well be employed as an *instrument* or *means* of carrying into execution any of the specified powers, as any other *instrument* or *means* whatever. The only question must be, in this, as in every other case, whether the means to be employed, or, in this instance, the corporation to be erected, has a natural relation to any of the acknowledged objects or lawful ends of the government. Thus a corporation may not be erected by Congress for superintending the police of the city of Philadelphia, because they are not authorized to *regulate* the *police* of that city. But one may be erected in relation to the collection of taxes, or to the trade with foreign countries, or to the trade between the States, or with the Indian tribes; because it is the province of the federal government to *regulate* those objects, and because it is incident to a general *sovereign* or *legislative* power to *regulate* a thing, to employ all the means which relate to its regulation to the best and greatest advantage.

Through this mode of reasoning respecting the right of employing all the means requisite to the execution of the specified powers of the government, it is to be objected, that none but necessary and proper means are to be employed; and the Secretary of State maintains, that no means are to be considered *necessary* but those without which the grant of the power would be *nugatory.* . . .

It is essential to the being of the national government, that so erroneous a conception of the meaning of the word *necessary* should be exploded.

It is certain, that neither the grammatical nor popular sense of the term requires that construction. According to both, *necessary* often means no more than *needful, requisite, incidental, useful,* or *conducive to.* . . . And it is the true one in which it is to be understood as used in the Constitution. The whole turn of the clause containing it indicates, that it was the intent of the Convention, by that clause, to give a liberal latitude to the exercise of the specified powers. The expressions have peculiar comprehensiveness. They are, "to make all *laws* necessary and proper for *carrying into execution* the *foregoing powers,* and *all other powers,* vested by the Constitution in the *government* of the United States, or in any *department* or *officer* thereof."

To understand the word as the Secretary of State does, would be to depart from its obvious and popular sense, and to give it a restrictive operation, an idea never before entertained. It would be to give it the same force as if the word *absolutely* or *indispensably* had been prefixed to it. . . .

The *degree* in which a measure is necessary, can never be a *test* of the legal right to adopt it; that must be a matter of opinion, and can only be a *test* of expediency. The *relation* between the *measure* and the *end;* between the *nature* of the *means* employed towards the execution of a power, and the object of that power, must be the criterion of constitutionality, not the more or less of *necessity* or *utility.* . . .

This restrictive interpretation of the word *necessary* is also contrary to this sound maxim of construction; namely, that the powers contained in a constitution of government, especially those which concern the general administration of the affairs of a country, its finances, trade, defence &c., ought to be construed liberally in advancement of the public good. . . . The means by which national exigencies are to be provided for, national inconveniences obviated, national prosperity promoted, are of such infinite variety, extent, and complexity, that there must of necessity be great latitude of discretion in the selection and application of those means. Hence, consequently, the necessity and propriety of exercising the authorities intrusted to a government on principles of liberal construction. . . .

But the doctrine which is contended for is not chargeable with the consequences imputed to it. It does not affirm that the National Government is sovereign in all respects, but that it is sovereign to a certain extent; that it is, to the extent of the objects of its specified powers.

It leaves, therefore, a criterion of what is constitutional, and of what is not so. This criterion is the *end,* to which the measure relates as a *means.* If the *end* be clearly comprehended within any of the specified powers, and if the measure have an obvious relation to that *end,* and is not forbidden by any particular provision of the Constitution, it may safely be deemed to come within the compass of the national authority. There is also this further criterion, which may materially assist the decision; Does the proposed measure abridge a pre-existing right of any State or of any individual? If it does not, there is a strong presumption in favor of its constitutionality, and slighter relations to any declared object of the Constitution may be permitted to turn the scale. . . .

It is presumed to have been satisfactorily shown in the course of the preceding observations:

1. That the power of the government, as to the objects intrusted to its management, is, in its nature, sovereign.

2. That the right of erecting corporations is one inherent in, and inseparable from, the idea of sovereign power.

3. That the position, that the government of the United States can exercise no power but such as is delegated to it by its Constitution, does not militate against this principle.

4. That the word *necessary,* in the general clause, can have no *restrictive* operation derogating from the force of this principle; indeed, that the degree in which a measure is or is not *necessary,* cannot be a *test* of *constitutional right,* but of *expediency only.*

5. That the power to erect corporations is not to be considered as an *independent* or *substantive* power, but as an *incidental* and *auxiliary* one, and was therefore more properly left to implication than expressly granted.

6. That the principle in question does not extend the power of the government beyond the prescribed limits, because it only affirms a power to *incorporate* for purposes *within the sphere* of the *specified powers.*

And lastly, that the right to exercise such a power in certain cases is unequivocally granted in the most *positive* and *comprehensive* terms. . . .

A hope is entertained that it has, by this time, been made to appear, to the satisfaction of the President, that a bank has a natural relation to the power of collecting taxes—to that of regulating trade—to that of providing for the common defence—and that, as the bill under consideration contemplates the government in the light of a joint proprietor of the stock of the bank, it brings the case within the provision of the clause of the Constitution which immediately respects the property of the United States.

Under a conviction that such a relation subsists, the Secretary of the Treasury, with all deference, conceives, that it will result as a necessary consequence from the position, that all the specified powers of government are sovereign, as to the proper objects; that the incorporation of a bank is a constitutional measure; and that the objections taken to the bill, in this respect, are illfounded. . . .

In the election of 1800, due to a flaw in the Constitution (subsequently remedied by the Twelfth Amendment), Thomas Jefferson and Aaron Burr technically tied for president in the electoral college. Consequently, the election had to be decided by the Federalist-dominated House of Representatives. Many Federalist representatives favored Burr, who had been the Republican candidate for vice president, but Hamilton threw his influence behind Jefferson, the eventual winner. Hamilton's reasons for favoring Jefferson follow.

ALEXANDER HAMILTON:
AN ESTIMATE OF JEFFERSON*

HAMILTON TO JAMES A. BAYARD

New York, Jan. 16, 1801

. . . Among the letters which I receive assigning the reasons *pro* and *con* for preferring Burr to J., I observe no small exaggeration to the prejudice of the latter, and some things taken for granted as to the former, which are at least questionable. Perhaps myself the first, at some expense of popularity, to unfold the true character of Jefferson, it is too late for me to become his apologist; nor can I have any disposition to do it.

I admit that his politics are tinctured with fanaticism; that he is too much in earnest in his democracy; that he has been a mischievous enemy to the principal measures of our past administration; that he is crafty and persevering in his objects; that he is not scrupulous about the means of success, nor very mindful of truth, and that he is a contemptible hypocrite. But it is not true, as is alleged, that he is an enemy to the power of the Executive, or that he is for confounding all the powers in the House of Representatives. It is a fact which I have frequently mentioned, that, while we were in the administration together, he was generally for a large construction of the Executive authority and not backward to act upon it in cases which coincided with his views. Let it be added that in his theoretic ideas he has considered as improper the participations of the Senate in the Executive authority. I have more than once made the reflection that, viewing himself as the reversioner, he was solicitous to come into the possession of a good estate. Nor is it true that Jefferson is zealot enough to do any thing in pursuance of his principles which will contravene his popularity or his interest. He is as likely as any man I know to temporize—to calculate what will be likely to promote his own reputation and advantage; and the probable result of such a temper is the preservation of systems, though originally opposed, which, being once established, could not be overturned without danger to the person who did it. To my mind a true estimate of Mr. Jefferson's character warrants the expectation of a temporizing rather than a violent system. That Jefferson has manifested a culpable predilection for France is certainly true; but I think it a question whether it did not proceed quite as much from her *popularity* among us as from sentiment, and, in proportion as that popularity is diminished, his zeal will cool. Add to this that there is no fair reason to suppose him capable of being corrupted, which is a security that he will not go beyond certain limits. . . .

* Reprinted from Henry Cabot Lodge, ed., *The Works of Alexander Hamilton* (Federal Edition; New York: Putnam, 1904), X, 412–14.

Despite the bitterness of his political quarrels with the Federalists, President Jefferson's first inaugural address was a model of conciliation as well as a great exposition of Republican principles. "We are all Republicans, we are all Federalists," he asserted. He also called for "a wise and frugal Government, which shall restrain men from injuring one another, [and] shall leave them otherwise free to regulate their own pursuits of industry and improvement."

THOMAS JEFFERSON:
FIRST INAUGURAL ADDRESS*

FRIENDS AND FELLOW-CITIZENS:

Called upon to undertake the duties of the first executive office of our country, I avail myself of the presence of that portion of my fellow-citizens which is here assembled to express my grateful thanks for the favor with which they have been pleased to look toward me, to declare a sincere consciousness that the task is above my talents, and that I approach it with those anxious and awful presentiments which the greatness of the charge and the weakness of my powers so justly inspire. A rising nation, spread over a wide and fruitful land, traversing all the seas with the rich productions of their industry, engaged in commerce with nations who feel power and forget right, advancing rapidly to destinies beyond the reach of mortal eye—when I contemplate these transcendent objects, and see the honor, the happiness, and the hopes of this beloved country committed to the issue and the auspices of this day, I shrink from the contemplation, and humble myself before the magnitude of the undertaking. Utterly, indeed, should I despair did not the presence of many whom I here see remind me that in the other high authorities provided by our Constitution I shall find resources of wisdom, of virtue, and of zeal on which to rely under all difficulties. To you, then, gentlemen, who are charged with the sovereign functions of legislation, and to those associated with you, I look with encouragement for that guidance and support which may enable us to steer with safety the vessel in which we are all embarked amidst the conflicting elements of a troubled world.

During the contest of opinion through which we have passed the animation of discussions and of exertions has sometimes worn an aspect which might impose on strangers unused to think freely and to speak and to write what they think; but this being now decided by the voice of the nation, announced according to the rules of the Constitution, all will, of course, arrange themselves under the will of the law, and unite in common efforts for the common good. All, too, will bear in mind this sacred principle, that though the will of the majority is in all cases to prevail, that will to be rightful must be reasonable; that the minority possess their equal rights, which equal law must protect, and to violate would be oppression. Let us, then, fellow-citizens, unite with one heart and one mind. Let us restore to social intercourse that harmony and affection without which liberty and even life itself are but dreary things. And let us reflect that, having banished from our land that religious intolerance under which mankind so long bled and suffered, we have yet gained little if we countenance a political intolerance as despotic, as wicked, and capable of as bitter and bloody persecutions. During the throes and convulsions of the ancient world, during the agonizing spasms of infuriated man, seeking through blood and slaughter his long-lost liberty, it was not wonderful that the agitation of the billows should reach even this distant and peaceful shore; that this should be more felt and feared by some and less by others, and should divide opinions as to measures of safety. But every difference of opinion is not a difference of principle. We have called by different names brethren of the same principle. We are all Republicans, we are all Federalists. If there be any among us who would wish to dissolve this Union or to change its republican form, let them stand undisturbed as monuments of the safety with which error of opinion may be tolerated where reason is left free to combat it. I know, indeed, that some honest men fear that a republican government can not be strong, that this Government is not strong enough; but would the honest patriot, in the full tide of successful experiment, abandon a government which has so far kept us free and firm on the theoretic and visionary fear that this Government, the world's best hope, may by possibility want energy to preserve itself? I trust not. I believe this, on the contrary, the strongest Government on earth. I believe it the only one where every man, at the call of the law, would fly to the standard of the law, and would meet invasions of the public order as his own personal concern. Sometimes it is said that man can not be trusted with the government of him-

* Reprinted from James D. Richardson, ed., *A Compilation of the Messages and Papers of the Presidents, 1789–1897* (Washington: 1896), I, 321–24.

self. Can he, then, be trusted with the government of others? Or have we found angels in the forms of kings to govern him? Let history answer this question.

Let us, then, with courage and confidence pursue our own Federal and Republican principles, our attachment to union and representative government. Kindly separated by nature and a wide ocean from the exterminating havoc of one quarter of the globe; too high-minded to endure the degradations of the others; possessing a chosen country, with room enough for our descendants to the thousandth and thousandth generation; entertaining a due sense of our equal right to the use of our own faculties, to the acquisitions of our own industry, to honor and confidence from our fellow-citizens, resulting not from birth, but from our actions and their sense of them; enlightened by a benign religion, professed, indeed, and practiced in various forms, yet all of them inculcating honesty, truth, temperance, gratitude, and the love of man; acknowledging and adoring an overruling Providence, which by all its dispensations proves that it delights in the happiness of man here and his greater happiness hereafter—with all these blessings, what more is necessary to make us a happy and a prosperous people? Still one thing more, fellow-citizens—a wise and frugal Government, which shall restrain men from injuring one another, shall leave them otherwise free to regulate their own pursuits of industry and improvement, and shall not take from the mouth of labor the bread it has earned. This is the sum of good government, and this is necessary to close the circle of our felicities.

About to enter, fellow-citizens, on the exercise of duties which comprehend everything dear and valuable to you, it is proper you should understand what I deem the essential principles of our Government, and consequently those which ought to shape its Administration. I will compress them within the narrowest compass they will bear, stating the general principle, but not all its limitations. Equal and exact justice to all men, of whatever state or persuasion, religious or political; peace, commerce, and honest friendship with all nations, entangling alliances with none; the support of the State governments in all their rights, as the most competent administrations for our domestic concerns and the surest bulwarks against antirepublican tendencies; the preservation of the General Government in its whole constitutional vigor, as the sheet anchor of our peace at home and safety abroad; a jealous care of the right of election by the people—a mild and safe corrective of abuses which are lopped by the sword of revolution where peaceable remedies are unprovided; absolute acquiescence in the decisions of the majority, the vital principle of republics, from which is no appeal but to force, the vital principle and immediate parent of despotism; a well-disciplined militia, our best reliance in peace and for the first moments of war, till regulars may relieve them; the supremacy of the civil over the military authority; economy in the public expense, that labor may be lightly burthened; the honest payment of our debts and sacred preservation of the public faith; encouragement of agriculture, and of commerce as its handmaid; the diffusion of information and arraignment of all abuses at the bar of the public reason; freedom of religion; freedom of the press, and freedom of person under the protection of the habeas corpus, and trial by juries impartially selected. These principles form the bright constellation which has gone before us and guided our steps through an age of revolution and reformation. The wisdom of our sages and blood of our heroes have been devoted to their attainment. They should be the creed of our political faith, the text of civic instruction, the touchstone by which to try the services of those we trust; and should we wander from them in moments of error or of alarm, let us hasten to retrace our steps and to regain the road which alone leads to peace, liberty, and safety.

I repair, then, fellow-citizens, to the post you have assigned me. With experience enough in subordinate offices to have seen the difficulties of this the greatest of all, I have learnt to expect that it will rarely fall to the lot of imperfect man to retire from this station with the reputation and the favor which bring him into it. Without pretensions to that high confidence you reposed in our first and greatest revolutionary character, whose preëminent services had entitled him to the first place in his country's love and destined for him the fairest page in the volume of faithful history, I ask so much confidence only as may give firmness and effect to the legal administration of your affairs. I shall often go wrong through defect of judgment. When right, I shall often be thought wrong by those whose positions will not command a view of the whole ground. I ask your indulgence for my own errors, which will never be intentional, and your support against the errors of others, who may condemn what they would not if seen in all its parts. The approbation implied by your suffrage is a great consolation to me for the past, and my future solicitude will be to retain the good opinion of those who have bestowed it in advance, to conciliate that of others by doing them all the good in my power, and to be instrumental to the happiness and freedom of all.

Relying, then, on the patronage of your good will, I advance with obedience to the work, ready to retire from it whenever you become sensible how much better choice it is in your power to make. And may that Infinite Power which rules the destinies of the universe lead our councils to what is best, and give them a favorable issue for your peace and prosperity.

CHAPTER SIX

CHIEF JUSTICE JOHN MARSHALL
AND THE JUDICIAL TRADITION

Chief Justice John Marshall erected a strong judicial tradition as a capstone on the Federal structure which had been so long abuilding. In powerfully reasoned decisions, he heralded the triumph of American nationalism; his work seemed to bring to a successful conclusion the long colonial struggle, the plans of the founding fathers, and the legislative and administrative handiwork of the Federalists in creating an American nation. Marshall established first, through the logic of Marbury *vs*. Madison (1803), what most lawyers had assumed but what had previously been untested by the Supreme Court—the doctrine of judicial review. The decision, invalidating a portion of an act of Congress as being in conflict with the Constitution, was repugnant to President Jefferson and the Republicans, but they could not negate it. In the two decades that followed, Marshall, in decision after decision, gave steadfast protection to the rights of property, even where they conflicted with the public interest. Concurrently, he established the right of the Supreme Court to decide upon the constitutionality not only of acts of Congress but also those of state legislatures and to review the decisions of state courts. In the dual Federal system, Marshall exalted the central government wherever the states came into conflict with it, and through judicial review he reserved the ultimate power within the Federal structure for the Supreme Court.

Marshall bequeathed a legacy of nationalism which has endured into the twentieth century, but in his time it received sharp challenge from the defenders of state and sectional interests. In his own state of Virginia, he came under vitriolic attack from his cousin, Thomas Jefferson; and especially from Judge Spencer Roane, head of the Virginia Supreme Court of Appeals; and an indefatigable planter pamphleteer, John Taylor of Caroline. Their attack was unavailing at the time, but set forth many of the states' rights doctrines which ultimately were to receive their testing on the battlefields of the Civil War. Consequently, not only Marshall's judicial nationalism, but also the Virginia confutation has been of continuing significance.

In a trying time in the twentieth century when the Supreme Court was again under attack, this time for decisions invalidating much of the New Deal legislation, Max Lerner penned an appraisal of Marshall's significance both for the Chief Justice's own times and the crisis developing in 1935. Marshall's background, Lerner began, scarcely seemed to indicate that he had been "earmarked by fate to play his great role."

MAX LERNER:
JOHN MARSHALL'S LONG SHADOW*

. . . [Marshall] was a frontier boy, but of good proprietary stock. He had been brought up in a high-minded and conventional home, his formal schooling was fragmentary, his legal training casual. Pope, Blackstone, and Burke formed his mind; Hamilton's *Federalist* was his American Bible; George Washington was his archetypal hero. In such an education the Revolutionary War was a curious interlude, a sort of shadow-play in which Marshall went gallantly through all the motions of a minor young hero, experienced Valley Forge and came home to Virginia to be idolized by the girls. But that did not keep him, later in life, from repudiating "the wild and enthusiastic notions" of his youth. In the turbulent years of the Confederation he was dismayed at the agrarian unrest; as a member of the Virginia legislature he fought for ratification; he served a term in Congress; went to France on the famous XYZ mission; was Secretary of State in the closing years of John Adams's administration. For a time it looked as if Marshall were only a second-string Federalist politician, caught like the other Federalists in a blind alley of history.

His class roots were theirs. His disarming democratic ways, casting a spell over his biographers, have tended to conceal this fact. An entire mythology has grown up around all the little tender and mildly heterodox ways in which the great Chief Justice half outraged and half titillated his friends by forgetting the dignity of his position. But while Marshall was no New England Brahmin or New York fashionable, he was actually a man of substance, with a deep personal and psychological stake in property. His business and political connections were with the men of funds and funded income, the lawyers and *rentiers,* the landowners and speculators, the shipbuilders, the merchants and manufacturers. He was himself a large landowner, up to the neck in suits over land titles. You have here only the lag that you will find in any man between his boyhood conditionings and his manhood maturities. The boyhood patterns linger on, outliving their utility or even their congruity, like the college-boy folkways in the chairman of a finance board, or a debutante whimsey in a dowager of fifty.

Much has been made also of Marshall's nationalist feeling, especially by his biographer Senator Beveridge, who uses it to pattern Marshall's entire career. But it must be remembered that Marshall was to show himself, on the bench, as the best of the Federalist political strategists. And nationalism, however fatefully it may have been rooted in Marshall's personality, was also good strategy. After the XYZ affair Marshall came home to find himself a national hero, toasted everywhere. He saw that the common man, who would not respond to Federalist aristocratic theory, would respond to the same property interests when they were clothed in the rhetoric of the national interest. It was a crucial discovery and Marshall was to make the most of it on the judicial front, where he was to fight the battles of business enterprise.

For his mind was not that of the great lawyers, with their heavy erudition, their tortuousness, their narrow legalism, but the mind of a captain of industry with its powerful concentration on a single purpose. Like the elder Pierpont Morgan, he had mastered the art of finality; like him, he possessed a footloose opportunism in the service of a singular tenacity; like him, he was to be a magnificent dictator, dwarfing and intimidating his colleagues, polarizing around himself as a dominant personality the forces that were later to be institutionalized in the Court.

This was Marshall—a man who was not really to find himself until he reached the Court, and who seems miraculously to have turned up in American history at just the point where a rising capitalism most needed him. So near a miracle does this seem that I am ready to pardon Senator Beveridge his four volumes of ecstasy and hosannas. Yet Justice Holmes seems nearer the truth. "A great man," he writes of Marshall, "represents a great ganglion in the nerves of society, or, to vary the figure, a strategic point in the campaign of history, and part of his greatness consists of his being *there*." Marshall's role was to effect a nexus between the property interests under an expanding industrialism and the judicial power under a federal system of government. He was to be the strategic link between capitalism and constitutionalism. And for occupying that position in the campaign of history his experience and the nature of his mind fitted him superbly. Rarely in American history has the exterior tension of events been matched so completely by an interior tension of preparation and purpose on the part of the exactly right man.

Marbury v. Madison (1803) showed Marshall's daring and his mastery. He was seizing the first occasion to affirm the power of judicial re-

* Reprinted from Max Lerner, *Ideas Are Weapons* (New York: Viking Press, 1939), pp. 28–37 by permission.

121

view. Nor was his urgency either accidental or whimsical. It was the last-ditch necessity of the Federalist property groups when confronted by Jefferson's victory at the polls. The question of judicial review had been allowed only a few volcanic rumbles at the Constitutional Convention and after. Fearing the common man, the Federalists had not forced the issue. But when they were swept out of the presidency and Congress by the "revolutionary" wave of 1800, there was nothing to do but seek refuge in the judiciary, affirm its supremacy, and claim for the Court the final right to pass on the constitutionality of legislation and the distribution of powers.

Marbury, one of the "midnight appointments" as justice of the peace, had not had his commission delivered. He now sought from the Court a writ of mandamus commanding the Secretary of State to give it up. Marshall was faced by a dilemma. If he denied Marbury's claim it would be an admission of judicial powerlessness. If he upheld it, Jefferson would undoubtedly say what Jackson is reputed to have said thirty years later: "John Marshall has made his decision, now let him enforce it." But Marshall, by a maneuver, managed to administer a public spanking to the new administration, assert judicial supremacy, yet leave Jefferson helpless to strike back. Marbury's commission, he said, was a valid one and Marbury had a vested right in it which it was the function of "a government of laws and not of men" to protect; having a right he had also a remedy, which was mandamus. *But* the Supreme Court, by its reading of the Constitution, could not have jurisdiction over such cases; and the section of the Judiciary Act that sought to confer such jurisdiction was therefore unconstitutional.

It mattered little to Marshall that if his conclusion was valid and the Court had no jurisdiction, then his whole opinion up to that point was superfluous as law—an *obiter dictum* that was sheer political maneuver. Nor did it matter that to declare the section of the Judiciary Act unconstitutional he had to wrench it beyond all principles of statutory interpretation. He was setting the classic example for "judicial statesmanship." It was the formative period of American political life, when every important move was decisive for later power configurations. Legalisms did not count; what counted was the daring, decisive coup. From a legalistic point of view alone, *Marbury v. Madison* has a nightmarish fascination. If ever the history of the Court is written with the proper cosmic irony here will be the cream of the jest. Upon this case, as precedent, rests the power of judicial review. Yet every part of its reasoning has been repudiated by commentators and decisions of later courts which none the less continue to exercise the power it established. "Nothing remains of *Marbury v. Madison*," writes Professor Grant, "except its influence." And its influence continues to grin at us from the Cimmerian darkness like the disembodied smile of the Cheshire cat.

What is the nature of Marshall's contribution to judicial review? He did not originate it, nor did he single-handed establish it beyond all dislodgment. He added nothing substantial to the argument of the Federalists in the "great judiciary debate" in the Senate in 1802. Ultimately, the whole of the theory is in No. 78 of the Federalist Papers; in fact, much of Marshall's career may be viewed as a process of reading Hamilton's state papers into the Constitution. And yet his having translated these ideas into judicial action is Marshall's decisive achievement.

As to the permanence of his work, I find much in Louis B. Boudin's forceful contention that judicial review as we know it is primarily a post-Civil War creation, and that *Marbury v. Madison* actually decided only the Court's power to determine its own jurisdiction. And yet the prestige of the case went far beyond its strict legal effect; everything the Court drew upon after the Civil War in completing judicial review is already to be found in Marshall's opinion. And while the Court did not use judicial review against Congress again until the Dred Scott case a half-century later, it was because in all economic matters the property interests wanted to expand the national power. Where judicial review *was* used effectively during this period was with reference to state power. Marshall's role in this entire process was to give judicial review a foothold, use it for the immediate interests of the capitalism of his day, tie it up with the powerful appeal of nationalism, and entrench it where a later stage of capitalism could take it up and carry it further for its own purposes.

The state legislatures in Marshall's day had an unseemly habit of being responsive to the economic plight of the common man. What was needed was a way of using judicial review to keep them in check. Marshall's "contract clause" opinions were the answer. They stretched contract far beyond its contemporary meaning and gave it a sanctity overriding every consideration of public policy or economic control. Next to judicial review this doctrine of vested rights, as Professor Corwin has called it, was probably the most important invention in the history of the Court. It dominated the constitutional scene up to the Civil War, and it served as a model after which later doctrines, such as due process of law and liberty of contract, could be fashioned.

The first of these "contract cases," *Fletcher v. Peck* (1810), has been described as "a cornerstone of legal structure laid in mud." Behind it is one of the most malodorous episodes in American history, the Yazoo land frauds. Georgia had sold a strip of Indian lands half the size of New England to a land-speculation company for a cent and a half an acre. And every legislator save one had received a large bribe of land stock which could be disposed of for cash. The scandal broke, the people of Georgia, in a fury, elected a new legislature and rescinded the corrupt act. But meanwhile the speculators had sold their stock to

Northerners, who now brought a trumped-up suit before the Court. Marshall's decision is breathtaking. He held that the Court could not concern itself with the alleged corruption of the Georgia legislature, and that the original grant was a contract that could not be impaired.

In the context of the land speculation of the day, the decision takes on meaning. Gambling in land values represented the principal financial activity in expansionist America at the turn of the nineteenth century, before industrialism came to overshadow everything else. Some of the most prominent men of the day had been involved in the Yazoo land transactions. Marshall himself knew land and loved land; land speculation was the breath of life in the circles that he moved in. The Fletcher case served as model during the next quarter-century for a series of important decisions in which Marshall and Story led the Court in holding the flimsiest of land titles legal. While hoping to encourage stability through the enforcement of contract, Marshall was actually encouraging the reckless development of economic resources and flagrant corruption in politics. The decisions were decidedly in harmony with the progress of an exploitative capitalism.

The contract cases made Marshall the best-hated man in the country. State bankruptcy laws, squatter laws, tax laws fell under the interdict of "vested rights." Marshall made clearest the philosophy underlying all these decisions in *Ogden v. Saunders* (1827), in which a revolt of his colleagues had for once forced him into a solitary dissent. In an opinion breathing a weird Rousseauist natural-rights mysticism he insisted that "the obligations created by contract . . . exist anterior to and independent of society." But the case that comes closest home to us is the famous Dartmouth College case (1819), in which the issue was whether New Hampshire could make any changes in the charter it had granted the college. Every schoolboy knows Webster's eloquent plea ("It is, sir, as I have said, a small college. Yet there are those who love it.") and how Marshall, whom the Yazoo land scandals had left cold, wept over it. But few schoolboys know that the case had ultimately less to do with colleges than with the charters of business corporations; that sanctity of contract was invoked to give them immunity against legislative control; and that business enterprise in America has never had more useful mercenaries than the tears Daniel Webster and John Marshall shed so copiously that day. Later developments have stripped the decision of some of its starkness, yet the overmastering fact is that it set up an inviolability of corporate charters that has had slowly to be qualified, instead of starting at the opposite pole with a rule of legislative discretion and control.

It is, however, not with the states but on the national judicial-economic front that Marshall's greatest meaning for today lies. I can say this without succumbing uncritically to the elements of sheer rhetoric in Marshall's nationalism. That rhetoric, like the rhetoric of sanctity of contract, is best cleaved by the sundering blade of the logic of business interests. Its hollowness is most shockingly revealed by Marshall's serious negotiations with the New England secession movement on the eve of (and even during) the War of 1812. In the face of a war that was being fought for the agricultural rather than for the industrial and mercantile groups, his principles of nationalism were dangerously shaken. Marshall had little of the deeper national consciousness of the common man, based on national expansion and adventure and on the promise of American life. His was a theoretical, a strictly judicial nationalism.

Its guiding logic was the relation of the national power to the scope of industrial development. This is brought out clearly in his two famous nationalist decisions, *McCulloch v. Maryland* (1819) and *Gibbons v. Ogden* (1824). The first involved the constitutionality of the Second United States Bank. Marshall made it the occasion of his most resounding opinion, building a doctrine of implied national powers on the "necessary and proper" clause, and waving away Maryland's attempt to tax the bank with "the power to tax involves the power to destroy." Thus Marshall showed himself master of the two-way stretch, interpreting national powers broadly and state powers narrowly. In *Gibbons v. Ogden,* the steamboat case (Marshall's only popular decision), he construed the power of Congress to regulate commerce among the states so broadly that it became one of the most effective elastic clauses of the Constitution. These decisions were part of the upswing of a rising capitalism. Through them Marshall sought to strengthen congressional jurisdiction over the two main lines of business expansion of the day—a national banking system and a national transportation system. In the early stages of industrial capitalism, the function of a central government was to ensure favorable conditions for the development of business enterprise.

Marshall here had the advantage of working with the course of history. He had vision enough to see that political power had to be coterminous with the scale of economic activity. He saw it only dimly, and it was obscured in his mind by a hatred of states' rights and of the common man, and by a protective obsession about the rights of property. But his historical meaning for us lies none the less in this dim insight of his. The position of his opponents, such as Jefferson and John Taylor, embodied an archaic economic vision, whatever the merits of their political views. They dreamed the Physiocratic dream of a society that was even then beyond recall—a republic of small farmers. They failed to see that technology was settling that question for them, and that the issue was now not between states' rights and national power, but between some form of control and no control at all. If, instead of following a policy of states'-rights obstructionism, they had come out frankly for national legislative control of the developing industrial system, Marshall's much vaunted nationalism would quickly have changed to a different tune. What it amounted to was aid and tolerance for business enterprise, both of them on a national scale.

As American capitalism developed, it was inevitable that the mere absence of restraint over private property should no longer be adequate to resolve the deepening contradictions of economic life. In the search for new methods of economic control through the federal government, Marshall's judicial nationalism proved a memorable instrument. The Marshall technique of interpretation became a tradition that created new uses not only for the commerce power, but for the taxing and spending power of Congress as well. It is this technique which, since the eighteen-seventies, has formed one facet of judicial liberalism. And it was upon the continuation of this technique that the administration laid its hope for the New Deal legislation. Indeed, a very good case could have been made out, on the basis of continuous precedents since the Swift case in 1905, when the nature of our market economy had already become clear to some of the Justices, that all important business enterprise today is interstate commerce, that the whole industrial process is an unbroken chain flung out over a national market, and that every important link in that chain is therefore a link in interstate commerce.

But the important question, as we have since learned, is not whether the Court *could if it would* interpret the commerce clause broadly enough to validate legislative control of industry, but whether it *would if it could*. And to explain its unwillingness we have to go back to Marshall as surely as we do when we wish to explain its competence. Marshall's class interest took two forms in his own thinking: the doctrine of the vested rights of property and the doctrine of judicial nationalism. Each of these has given rise to a tradition that has been followed in the later history of the Court, the first principally by the conservatives, the second principally by the liberals. And it need scarcely be added that the dominant one has been not the broad interpretation of the Constitution in the interests of federal jurisdiction over industry, but the setting up of the Supreme Court as the guardian of the vested interests. In Marshall's thought, in the period of a rising capitalism, these two streams could flow together smoothly and feed each other. But the movement of economic events has caused a deepening cleavage between them.

Today, in a period of capitalist crisis, to follow Marshall's vested-rights tradition means to entrench further the hegemony of Big Ownership; to follow his tradition of judicial nationalism means for a time to salvage capitalism, but to salvage it by stripping it of some of its powers; and, more important, it means to maintain tolerable standards of wages and working conditions. Today, even more than in Marshall's time, the issue is one between national control of business enterprise and no control at all. What the Court thus far has done has been to turn its back on everything in the Marshall tradition that was worth following, everything that was an abiding part of the campaign of history. And it has chosen to cling to that part of his tradition which was narrow, immediate, and actuated chiefly by a jealous and exclusive class interest.

For the liberals on the Court this was no easy choice. Nor did they make it as a deliberate preference for the interests of business enterprise. And here, for explanation, we must turn to a third element in Marshall's thought—that of constitutonalism, the supremacy and sanctity of the Constitution and of the Supreme Court as its exclusive interpreter and guardian. A potential liberal minority on the Court, far removed from a defense of reactionary capitalism, is none the less fearful of what may lie ahead in the unexplored vistas of hitherto unparalleled federal control of industry. And they find nothing to fall back upon except an austere constitutionalism and Marshall's doctrine of judicial supremacy. Like *Marbury v. Madison,* the Hot Oil and Schechter decisions express (for some of the Justices) a jealousy of the executive power and the insistence of the judiciary that it alone can apportion powers among government departments. That is the meaning of the contentions about the delegation of congressional powers to the Executive.

Unfortunately the Court liberals do not see that the constitutionalism which they regard as the safeguard of the polity is, in the hands of the Court majority, not the expression of a tortured and sensitive conscience, but a stubborn defense of the *status quo*. And on the part of many people outside the Court this heritage from Marshall becomes a militant vigilantism that is violently opposed to any form of social change, is fed by Hearstian poisons, and is one of our peculiarly American forms of supernationalism. It defeats the very purposes that Marshall's real judicial nationalism stood for. And it promises to form a considerable part of whatever fascist future the unkind gods may have in store for us.

Thus there are three Marshalls alive today—a hundred years after his death: the Marshall of expanded national power, the Marshall of the protection of the vested interests, and the Marshall of a sacred constitutional fetishism. And it is the great irony of his place in the campaign of history that the last two have combined to kill their brother.

In his sweeping decision in the case involving the Bank of the United States, Marshall held that the Congress under the Constitution had the implied power to establish a bank. Thus far he retraced the familiar arguments of Hamilton. But he went much farther. The case involved a heavy tax that the State of Maryland was trying to impose upon paper money that the Bank issued in order to drive a branch of the Bank out of Maryland. Marshall, arguing that the Constitution and laws of the federal government were supreme over those of state governments, held that "the power to tax involves the power to destroy," and that "the power to destroy may defeat and render useless the power to create." Therefore, the Court held that the Maryland tax measure was unconstitutional.

McCULLOCH vs. MARYLAND*

MARSHALL, C. J., delivered the opinion of the Court.

In the case now to be determined, the defendant, a sovereign state, denies the obligation of a law enacted by the legislature of the Union, and the plaintiff, on his part, contests the validity of an act which has been passed by the legislature of that state. The constitution of our country, in its most interesting and vital parts, is to be considered; the conflicting powers of the government of the Union and of its members, as marked in that constitution, are to be discussed; and an opinion given, which may essentially influence the great operations of the government. No tribunal can approach such a question without a deep sense of its importance, and of the awful responsiblity involved in its decision. But it must be decided peacefully, or remain a source of hostile legislation, perhaps of hostility of a still more serious nature; and if it is to be so decided, by this tribunal alone can the decision be made. On the supreme court of the United States has the constitution of our country devolved this important duty.

The first question made in the cause is—has congress power to incorporate a bank?

It has been truly said, that this can scarcely be considered as an open question, entirely unprejudiced by the former proceedings of the nation respecting it. The principle now contested was introduced at a very early period of our history, has been recognized by many successive legislatures, and has been acted upon by the judicial department, in cases of peculiar delicacy, as a law of undoubted obligation.

It will not be denied that a bold and daring usurpation might be resisted, after an acquiescence still longer and more complete than this. But it is conceived that a doubtful question, one on which human reason may pause, and the human judgment be suspended, in the decision of which the great principles of liberty are not concerned, but the respective powers of those who are equally the

representatives of the people, are to be adjusted; if not put at rest by the practice of the government, ought to receive a considerable impression from that practice. An exposition of the constitution, deliberately established by legislative acts, on the faith of which an immense property has been advanced, ought not to be lightly disregarded. . . .

In discussing this question, the counsel for the State of Maryland have deemed it of some importance, in the construction of the constitution, to consider that instrument not as emanating from the people, but as the act of sovereign and independent States. The powers of the general government, it has been said, are delegated by the States, who alone are truly sovereign; and must be exercised in subordination to the States, who alone possess supreme dominion.

It would be difficult to sustain this proposition. The convention which framed the constitution was, indeed, elected by the State legislatures. But the instrument, when it came from their hands, was a mere proposal, without obligation, or pretensions to it. It was reported to the then existing Congress of the United States, with a request that it might "be submitted to a convention of Delegates, chosen in each State, by the people thereof, under the recommendation of its legislature, for their assent and ratification." This mode of proceeding was adopted; and by the Convention, by Congress, and by the State Legislatures, the instrument was submitted to the people. They acted upon it, in the only manner in which they can act safely, effectively, and wisely, on such a subject, by assembling in Convention. It is true, they assembled in their several States; and where else should they have assembled? No political dreamer was ever wild enough to think of breaking down the lines which separate the States, and of compounding the American people into one common mass. Of consequence, when they act, they act in their States. But the measures they adopt do not, on that account cease to be the measures of the people themselves, or become the measures of the state governments.

* Reprinted from 4 Wheaton 316 (1819).

From these Conventions the constitution derives its whole authority. The government proceeds directly from the people; is "ordained and established" in the name of the people; and is declared to be ordained, "in order to form a more perfect union, establish justice, insure domestic tranquillity, and secure the blessings of liberty to themselves and to their posterity." The assent of the States, in their sovereign capacity, is implied in calling a Convention, and thus submitting that instrument to the people. But the people were at perfect liberty to accept or reject it; and their act was final. It required not the affirmance, and could not be negatived, by the State governments. The constitution, when thus adopted, was of complete obligation, and bound the State sovereignties. . . .

. . . The government of the Union, then (whatever may be the influence of this fact on the case), is emphatically and truly a government of the people. In form and in substance it emanates from them, its powers are granted by them, and are to be exercised directly on them, and for their benefit.

This government is acknowledged by all to be one of enumerated powers. The principle, that it can exercise only the powers granted to it, would seem too apparent to have required to be enforced by all those arguments which its enlightened friends, while it was depending before the people, found it necessary to urge. That principle is now universally admitted. But the question respecting the extent of the powers actually granted, is perpetually arising, and will probably continue to arise, as long as our system shall exist. In discussing these questions, the conflicting powers of the State and general governments must be brought into view, and the supremacy of their respective laws, when they are in opposition, must be settled.

If any one proposition could command the universal assent of mankind, we might expect it would be this: that the government of the Union, though limited in its powers, is supreme within its sphere of action. This would seem to result necessarily from its nature. It is the government of all; its powers are delegated by all; it represents all, and acts for all. Though any one State may be willing to control its operations, no State is willing to allow others to control them. The nation, on those subjects on which it can act, must necessarily bind its component parts. But this question is not left to mere reason: the people have, in express terms, decided it, by saying, "this constitution, and the laws of the United States, which shall be made in pursuance thereof," "shall be the supreme law of the land," and by requiring that the members of the State legislatures, and the officers of the executive and judicial departments of the States, shall take the oath of fidelity to it.

The government of the United States, then, though limited in its powers, is supreme; and its laws, when made in pursuance of the constitution, form the supreme law of the land, "anything in the constitution or laws of any State, to the contrary, notwithstanding."

Among the enumerated powers, we do not find that of establishing a bank or creating a corporation. But there is no phrase in the instrument which, like the articles of confederation, excludes incidental or implied powers; and which requires that everything granted shall be expressly and minutely described. Even the 10th amendment, which was framed for the purpose of quieting the excessive jealousies which had been excited, omits the word "expressly," and declares only that the powers "not delegated to the United States, nor prohibited to the states are reserved to the states or to the people"; thus leaving the question whether the particular power which may become the subject of contest has been delegated to the one government, or prohibited to the other, to depend on a fair construction of the whole instrument. The men who drew and adopted this amendment had experienced the embarrassments resulting from the insertion of this word in the articles of confederation, and probably omitted it to avoid those embarrassments. A constitution, to contain an accurate detail of all the subdivisions of which its great powers will admit, and of all the means by which they may be carried into execution, would partake of the prolixity of a legal code, and could scarcely be embraced by the human mind. It would, probably, never be understood by the public. Its nature, therefore, requires, that only its great outlines should be marked, its important objects designated, and the minor ingredients which compose those objects be deduced from the nature of the objects themselves. . . .

Although, among the enumerated powers of government, we do not find the word "bank" or "incorporation," we find the great powers, to lay and collect taxes; to borrow money; to regulate commerce; to declare and conduct a war; and to raise and support armies and navies. The sword and the purse, all the external relations, and no inconsiderable portion of the industry of the nation, are entrusted to its government. It can never be pretended that these vast powers draw after them others of inferior importance, merely because they are inferior. Such an idea can never be advanced. But it may with great reason, be contended, that a government, intrusted with such ample powers, on the due execution of which the happiness and prosperity of the nation so vitally depends, must also be intrusted with ample means for their execution. The power being given, it is the interest of the nation to facilitate its execution. It can never be their interest, and cannot be presumed to have been their intention, to clog and embarrass its execution by withholding the most appropriate means. Throughout this vast republic, from the St. Croix to the Gulph of Mexico, from the Atlantic to the Pacific, revenue is to be collected and expended, armies are to be marched and supported. The exigencies of the nation may require, that the treasure raised in the north should be transported to the south, *that* raised in the east conveyed to the west, or that this order should be reversed. Is that construction of the constitution to be preferred which would render these operations difficult, hazardous, and expensive? Can we adopt that construction (unless the words imperiously require it) which would impute to the framers of that instrument, when granting these powers for the public good, the intention of impeding their exercise by withholding a choice of means? If, indeed, such be the mandate of the constitution, we have only to obey; but that instrument does not profess to enumerate the means by which the powers it confers may be executed; nor does it prohibit the creation of a corporation, if the existence of such a being be essential to the beneficial exercise of those powers. It is, then, the subject of fair inquiry, how far such means may be employed.

It is not denied that the powers given to the government imply the ordinary means of execution. That, for example, of raising revenue and applying it to national purposes, is admitted to imply the power of conveying money from place to place, as the exigencies of the nation may require, and of employing the usual means of conveyance. But it is denied that the government has its choice of means, or that it may employ the most convenient means, if to employ them it be necessary to erect a corporation. . . .

The government which has a right to do an act, and has imposed on it the duty of performing that act, must, according to the dictates of reason, be allowed to select the means; and those who contend that it may not select any appropriate means, that one particular mode of effecting the object is expected, take upon themselves the burden of establishing that exception. . . .

But the constitution of the United States has not left the right of congress to employ the necessary means, for the execution of the powers conferred on the government, to general reasoning. To its enumeration of powers is added that of making "all laws which shall be necessary and proper, for carrying into execution the foregoing powers, and all other powers vested by this constitution, in the government of the United States, or in any department thereof."

The counsel for the State of Maryland have urged various arguments, to prove that this clause, though in terms a grant of power, is not so in effect; but is really restrictive of the general right, which might otherwise be implied, of selecting means of executing the enumerated powers. . . .

But the argument on which most reliance is placed, is drawn from the peculiar language of this clause. Congress is not empowered by it to make all laws, which may have relation to the powers conferred on the government, but such only as may be *"necessary and proper"* for carrying them into execution. The word *"necessary"* is considered as controlling the whole sentence, and as limiting the right to pass laws for the execution of the granted powers, to such as are indispensable, and without which the power would be nugatory. That it excludes the choice of means, and leaves to Congress, in each case, that only which is most direct and simple.

Is it true, that this is the sense in which the word "necessary" is always used? Does it always import an absolute physical necessity, so strong, that one thing, to which another may be termed necessary cannot exist without that other? We think it does not. If reference be had to its use, in the common affairs of the world, or in approved authors, we find that it frequently imports no more than that one thing is convenient, or useful, or essential to another. To employ the means necessary to an end, is generally understood as employing any means calculated to produce the end, and not as being confined to those single means, without which the end would be entirely unattainable. Such is the character of human language, that no word conveys to the mind, in all situations one single definite idea; and nothing is more common than to use words in a figurative sense. Almost all compositions contain words, which, taken in their rigorous sense, would convey a meaning different from that which is obviously intended. It is essential to just construction, that many words which import something excessive, should be understood in a more mitigated sense—in that sense which common usage justifies. The word "necessary" is of this description. It has not a fixed character peculiar to itself. It admits of all degrees of comparison; and is often connected with other words, which increase or diminish the impression the mind receives of the urgency it imports. A thing may be necessary, very necessary, absolutely or indispensably necessary. To no mind would the same idea be conveyed, by these several phrases. . . . This word, then, like others, is used in various senses; and, in its construction, the subject, the context, the intention of the person using them, are all to be taken into view.

Let this be done in the case under consideration. The subject is the execution of those great powers on which the welfare of a nation essentially depends. It must have been the intention of those who gave these powers, to insure, as far as human prudence could insure, their beneficial execution. This could not be done by confiding the choice of means to such narrow limits as not to leave it in the power of Congress to adopt any which might be appropriate, and which were conducive to the end. This provision is made in a constitution intended to endure for ages to come, and, consequently, to be adapted to the various crises of human affairs. To have prescribed the means by which government should, in all future time, execute its powers, would have been to change, entirely, the character of the instrument, and give it the properties of a legal code. It would have been an unwise attempt to provide, by immutable rules, for exigencies which, if foreseen at all, must have been seen dimly, and which can be best provided for as they occur. To have declared that the best means shall not be used, but those alone without which the power given would be nugatory, would have been to deprive the legislature of the capacity to avail itself of experience, to exercise its reason, and to accommodate its legislation to circumstances. . . . This clause, as construed by the State of Maryland, would abridge and almost annihilate this useful and necessary right of the legislature to select its means. That this could not be intended is, we should think, had it not been already controverted, too apparent for controversy. . . .

The result of the most careful and attentive consideration bestowed upon this clause is, that if it does not enlarge, it cannot be construed to restrain the powers of Congress, or to impair the right of the legislature to exercise its best judgment in the section of measures to carry into execution the constitutional powers of the government. If no other motive for its insertion can be suggested, a sufficient one is found in the desire to remove all doubts respecting the right to legislate on that vast mass of incidental powers which must be involved in the constitution, if that instrument be not a splendid bauble.

We admit, as all must admit, that the powers of the government are limited, and that its limits are not to be transcended. But we think the sound construction of the constitution must allow to the national legislature that discretion, with respect to the means by which the powers it confers are to be carried into execution, which will enable that body to perform the high duties assigned to it, in the manner most beneficial to the people. Let the end be legitimate, let it be within the scope of the constitution, and all means which are appropriate, which are plainly adapted to that end, which are not prohibited, but consist with the letter and spirit of the constitution, are constitutional. . . .

If a corporation may be employed indiscriminately with other means to carry into execution the powers of the government, no particular reason can be assigned for excluding the use of a bank, if required for its fiscal operations. To use one, must be within the discretion of congress, if it be an appropriate mode of executing the powers of government. That it is a convenient, a useful, and essential instrument in the prosecution of its fiscal operations, is not now a subject of controversy. All those who have been concerned in the administration of our finances, have concurred in representing its importance and necessity; and so strongly have they been felt, that statesmen of the first class, whose previous opinions against it had been confirmed by every circumstance which can fix the human judgment, have yielded those opinions to the exigencies of the nation. . . .

But were its necessity less apparent, none can deny its being an appropriate measure; and if it is, the degree of its necessity, as has been very justly observed, is to be discussed in another place. Should congress, in the execution of its powers, adopt measures which are prohibited by the constitution; or should congress, under the pretext of executing its powers, pass laws for the accomplishment of objects not intrusted to the government, it would become the painful duty of this tribunal, should a case requiring such a deci-

sion come before it, to say, that such an act was not the law of the land. But where the law is not prohibited, and is really calculated to effect any of the objects intrusted to the government, to undertake here to inquire into the degree of its necessity, would be to pass the line which circumscribes the judicial department, and to tread on legislative ground. This court disclaims all pretensions to such a power. . . .

After the most deliberate consideration, it is the unanimous and decided opinion of this court, that the act to incorporate the Bank of the United States is a law made in pursuance of the constitution, and is a part of the supreme law of the land. . . .

It being the opinion of the Court, that the act incorporating the bank is constitutional; and that the power of establishing a branch in the State of Maryland might be properly exercised by the bank itself, we proceed to inquire—

2. Whether the State of Maryland may, without violating the constitution, tax that branch?

That the power of taxation is one of vital importance; that it is retained by the States; that it is not abridged by the grant of a similar power to the government of the Union; that it is to be concurrently exercised by the two governments: are truths which have never been denied. But, such is the paramount character of the constitution, that its capacity to withdraw any subject from the action of even this power, is admitted. The States are expressly forbidden to lay any duties on imports or exports, except what may be absolutely necessary for executing their inspection laws. If the obligation of this prohibition must be conceded—if it may restrain a state from the exercise of its taxing power on imports and exports, the same paramount character would seem to restrain, as it certainly may restrain, a state from such other exercise of this power, as is in its nature incompatible with, and repugnant to, the constitutional laws of the Union. A law, absolutely repugnant to another, as entirely repeals that other as if express terms of repeal were used.

On this ground the counsel for the bank place its claim to be exempted from the power of a State to tax its operations. There is no express provision for the case, but the claim has been sustained on a principle which so entirely pervades the constitution, is so intermixed with the materials which compose it, so interwoven with its web, so blended with its texture, as to be incapable of being separated from it, without rending it into shreds.

This great principle is, that the constitution and the laws made in pursuance thereof are supreme; that they control the constitution and laws of the respective States, and cannot be controlled by them. From this, which may be almost termed an axiom, other propositions are deduced as corollaries, on the truth or error of which, and on their application to this case, the cause has been supposed to depend. These are, 1. That a power to create implies a power to preserve. 2. That a power to destroy, if wielded by a different hand, is hostile to, and incompatible with, these powers to create and preserve. 3. That where this repugnancy exists, that authority which is supreme must control, not yield to that over which it is supreme. . . .

The argument on the part of the State of Maryland is not that the states may directly resist a law of congress, but that they may exercise their acknowledged powers upon it, and that the constitution leaves them this right, in the confidence that they will not abuse it. . . .

It may be objected . . . , that the power of taxation is not confined to the people and property of a state. It may be exercised upon every object brought within its jurisdiction. This is true. But to what source do we trace this right? It is obvious, that it is an incident of sovereignty, and is co-extensive with that to which it is an incident. All subjects over which the sovereign power of a state extends, are objects of taxation; but those over which it does not extend, are, upon the soundest principles, exempt from taxation. This proposition may almost be pronounced self-evident.

The sovereignty of a state extends to everything which exists by its own authority, or is introduced by its permission; but does it extend to those means which are employed by congress to carry into execution powers conferred on that body by the people of the United States? We think it demonstrable, that it does not. Those powers are not given by the people of a single state. They are given by the people of the United States, to a government whose laws, made in pursuance of the constitution, are declared to be supreme. Consequently, the people of a single state cannot confer a sovereignty which will extend over them.

If we measure the power of taxation residing in a state, by the extent of sovereignty which the people of a single state possess, and can confer on its government, we have an intelligible standard, applicable to every case to which the power may be applied. We have a principle which leaves the power of taxing the people and property of a state unimpaired; which leaves to a state the command of all its resources, and which places beyond its reach, all those powers which are conferred by the people of the United States on the government of the Union, and all those means which are given for the purpose of carrying those powers into execution. We have a principle which is safe for the states, and safe for the Union. We are relieved, as we ought to be, from clashing sovereignty; from interfering powers; from a repugnancy between a right in one government to pull down, what there is an acknowledged right in another to build up; from the incompatibility of a right in one government to destroy, what there is a right in another to preserve. We are not driven to the perplexing inquiry, so unfit for the judicial

department, what degree of taxation is the legitimate use, and what degree may amount to the abuse of the power. The attempt to use it on the means employed by the government of the Union, in pursuance of the constitution, is itself an abuse, because it is the usurpation of a power which the people of a single state cannot give.

We find, then, on just theory, a total failure of this original right to tax the means employed by the government of the Union, for the execution of its powers. The right never existed, and the question whether it has been surrendered, cannot arise.

But, waiving this theory for the present, let us resume the inquiry, whether this power can be exercised by the respective states, consistently with a fair construction of the constitution? That the power to tax involves the power to destroy; that the power to destroy may defeat and render useless the power to create; that there is a plain repugnance in conferring on one government a power to control the constitutional measures of another, which other, with respect to those very measures, is declared to be supreme over that which exerts the control, are propositions not to be denied. But all inconsistencies are to be reconciled by the magic of the word *confidence*. Taxation, it is said, does not necessarily and unavoidably destroy. To carry it to the excess of destruction, would be an abuse, to presume which, would banish that confidence which is essential to all government.

But is this a case of confidence? Would the people of any one state trust those of another with a power to control the most insignificant operations of their state government? We know they would not. Why, then, should we suppose that the people of any one state should be willing to trust those of another with a power to control the operations of a government to which they have confided their most important and most valuable interests? In the legislature of the Union alone, are all represented. The legislature of the Union alone, therefore, can be trusted by the people with the power of controlling measures which concern all, in the confidence that it will not be abused. This, then, is not a case of confidence, and we must consider it as it really is. . . If the controlling power of the states be established; if their supremacy as to taxation be acknowledged; what is to restrain their exercising control in any shape they may please to give it? Their sovereignty is not confined to taxation. That is not the only mode in which it might be displayed. The question is, in truth, a question of supremacy; and if the right of the states to tax the means employed by the general government be conceded, the declaration that the constitution, and the laws made in pursuance thereof, shall be the supreme law of the land, is empty and unmeaning declamation. . .

It has also been insisted, that, as the power of taxation in the general and state governments is acknowledged to be concurrent, every argument which would sustain the right of the general government to tax banks chartered by the states, will equally sustain the right of the states to tax banks chartered by the general government. But the two cases are not on the same reason. The people of all the states have created the general government, and have conferred upon it the general power of taxation. The people of all the states, and the states themselves, are represented in congress, and, by their representatives, exercise this power. When they tax the chartered institutions of the states, they tax their constituents; and these taxes must be uniform. But when a state taxes the operations of the government of the United States, it acts upon institutions created, not by their own constituents, but by people over whom they claim no control. It acts upon the measures of a government created by others as well as themselves, for the benefit of others in common with themselves. The difference is that which always exists, and always must exist, between the action of the whole on a part, and the action of a part on the whole—between the laws of a government declared to be supreme, and those of a government which, when in opposition to those laws, is not supreme.

But if the full application of this argument could be admitted, it might bring into question the right of congress to tax the state banks, and could not prove the right of the states to tax the Bank of the United States.

The court has bestowed on this subject its most deliberate consideration. The result is a conviction that the States have no power, by taxation or otherwise, to retard, impede, burden, or in any manner control, the operations of the constitutional laws enacted by Congress to carry into execution the powers vested in the general government. This is, we think, the unavoidable consequence of that supremacy which the constitution has declared. We are unanimously of opinion, that the law passed by the legislature of Maryland, imposing a tax on the Bank of the United States, is unconstitutional and void. . . .

Judgment Reversed.

Marshall's Bank decision was one of a series that drew vehement protest from states' rights advocates, especially a group of militant Virginians. The Virginians had already been aroused by Martin vs. Hunter's Lessee (1816) in which Justice Joseph Story asserted that the Supreme Court had the right to review decisions of state courts. (Marshall had disassociated himself from this case because his family had been involved in the litigation.) In 1821, in a second Virginia case (Cohens vs. Virginia), Marshall himself emphatically held that the Supreme Court had the right to hear appeals from state courts. These decisions especially evoked the ire of Spencer Roane, head of the Virginia court system, who would have been Jefferson's choice for Chief Justice of the United States. A son-in-law of Patrick Henry, Roane, writing under pseudonyms in the Richmond *Enquirer*, attacked each of the decisions as being contrary to the common law, the intent of the founding fathers and writers of the Federalist essays, and the doctrines of the Virginia and Kentucky Resolutions of 1799. The first of his articles against the McCulloch decision follows.

SPENCER ROANE:
THE RIGHTS OF THE STATES AND OF THE PEOPLE*

*TO THE EDITOR OF
THE ENQUIRER:[1]*

By means of a letter to you, sir, I beg leave to address my fellow citizens. I address them on a momentous subject. I address them with diffidence, and with the respect; the respect which is due the most favored, if not the most respectable

---

* Reprinted from *John P. Branch Historical Papers of Randolph-Macon College* (Richmond: Johnson Publishing Company, 1905), II, 77–83. Originally published in Richmond *Enquirer* (June 11, 1819).

[1] We cannot too earnestly press upon our readers the following exposition of the alarming errors of the Supreme Court of the United States in their late interpretation of the Constitution. We conceive the errors to be most alarming, and this exposition most satisfactory. Whenever State rights are threatened or invaded, Virginia will not be the last to sound the tocsin. Again, we earnestly recommend the following to the attention of the reader.
—Editor *Richmond Enquirer*

section of the human race: and with the diffidence which I ought to feel, when I compare the smallness of my means with the greatness of my undertaking. I address my fellow citizens without any distinction of parties. Although some of them will, doubtless, lend a more willing ear than others, to the important truths I shall endeavor to articulate, none can hear them with indifference. None of them can be prepared to give a *carte blanche* to our federal rulers, and to obliterate the State governments, forever, from our political system.

It has been the happiness of the American people to be connected together in a confederate republic; to be united by a system, which extends the sphere of popular government, and reconciles the advantages of monarchy with those of a republic; a system which combines all the internal advantages of the latter, with all the force of the former. It has been our happiness to believe, that in the partition of powers between the general and State governments, the former possessed only such as were expressly granted, or passed therewith as necessary incidents, while all the residuary powers were reserved by the latter. It was deemed by the enlightened founders of the Constitution, as essential to the internal happiness and welfare of their constituents, to reserve some powers to the State governments; as to their external safety, to grant others to the government of the union. This, it is believed, was done by the Constitution, in its original shape; but such were the natural fears and jealousies of our citizens, in relation to this all-important subject, that it was deemed necessary to quiet those fears by the tenth amendment to the Constitution. It is not easy to devise stronger terms to effect that object than those used in that amendment.

Such, however, is the proneness of all men to extend and abuse their power—to "feel power and forget right"—that even this article has afforded us no security. That legislative power which is everywhere extending the sphere of its activity and drawing all power into its impetuous vortex, has blinked even the strong words of this amendment. That judicial power, which, according to Montesquieu is, "in some measure, next to nothing;" and whose province this great writer limits to "punishing criminals and determining the disputes which arise between individuals"; that judiciary which, in Rome, according to the same author, was not entrusted to decide questions which concerned "the interests of the State, in the relation which it bears to its citizens"; and which, in England, has only invaded the Constitution in the worst of times, and then, always, on the side of arbitrary power, has also deemed its interference necessary, in our country. It will readily be perceived that I allude to the decision of the Supreme Court of the United States, in the case of M'Culloh against the State of Maryland.

The warfare carried on by the legislature of the Union, against the rights of "the States" and of "the people" has been with various success and always by detachment. *They* have not dared to break down the barriers of the Constitution by a *general* act declaratory of their power. That measure was too bold for these ephemeral duties of the people. The people hold them in check by a short rein, and would consign them to merited infamy, at the next election. . . . A new mode of amending the Constitution has been added to the ample ones provided in that instrument, and the strongest checks established in it have been made to yield to the force of precedents! The time will soon arrive, if it is not already at hand, when the Constitution may be expounded without ever looking into it!—by merely reading the acts of a renegade Congress. . . .

The warfare waged by the judicial body has been of a bolder tone and character. It was not enough for them to sanction, in former times, the detestable doctrines of Pickering & Co., as aforesaid: it was not enough for them to annihilate the freedom of the press, by incarcerating all those who dare, with a manly freedom, to canvass the conduct of their public agents; it was not enough for the predecessors of the present judges to preach political sermons from the bench of justice and bolster up the most unconstitutional measures of the most abandoned of our rulers; it did not suffice to do the business in detail, and ratify, one by one, the legislative infractions of the Constitution. That process would have been too slow, and perhaps too troublesome. It was possible, also, that some *Hampden* might make a stand against some ship-money measure of the government, and although he would lose his cause with the court, might ultimately gain it with the *people*.[2] They resolved, therefore, to put down all discussions of the kind, in future, by a judicial *coup de main*; to give a *general* letter of attorney to the future legislators of the Union; and to tread under foot all those parts and articles of the Constitution which had been, heretofore, deemed to set limits to the power of the federal legislature. That man must be a deplorable idiot who does not see that there is no earthly difference between an *unlimited* grant of power and a grant limited in its terms, but accompanied with *unlimited* means of carrying it into execution.

The Supreme Court of the United States have not only granted this *general* power of attorney to Congress, but they have gone out of the record to do it, in the case in question. It was only necessary, in that case, to decide whether or not the bank law was "necessary and proper," within the meaning of the Constitution, for carrying into effect some of the granted powers; but the court have, in effect, expunged those words from the Constitution. There is no essential difference between expunging words from an instrument, by erasure, and reading them in a sense entirely arbitrary with the reader, and which they do not

[2] John Hampden, an English Puritan, who in 1634 went to court rather than pay a tax he claimed Charles I was illegally imposing.

naturally bear. Great as is the confidence of the nation in all its tribunals, they are not at liberty to change the meaning of our language. I might, therefore, justly contend that this opinion of the court, in so far as it outgoes the actual case depending before it, and so far as it established a *general* and *abstract* doctrine, was entirely extra-judicial and without authority. I shall not, however, press this point, as it is entirely merged in another, which I believe will be found conclusive—namely, that that court had no power to adjudicate away the *reserved* rights of a sovereign member of the confederacy, and vest them in the general government.

It results from these remarks, Mr. Editor, that my opinion is, that the Supreme Court had no jurisdiction justifying the judgment which it gave, and that it decided the question wrongly. The power of the Supreme Court is indeed great, but it does not extend to everything; it is not great enough to *change* the Constitution. . . . These points I shall endeavor to maintain in one or more subsequent numbers. I shall also briefly touch upon the bank law of the United States. That law is neither justified by the Constitution, nor ratified by any acquiescence.

Had this opinion of the Supreme Court, however, not been pronounced, I should not have deemed it necessary to address the public on the subject. I should not have been moved by any *particular* measure of aggression. I know full well that however guarded our Constitution may be, we must submit to particular infractions of it. I know that our forefathers, of glorious and revolutionary memory, submitted to many particular acts of oppression, inflicted upon them by the British parliament. I know that "all experience hath shown that mankind are more disposed to suffer while evils are sufferable, than to right themselves by abolishing the forms to which they are accustomed"; and I know that it was only the *general* declaration by the British parliament of their right "to legislate for us in all cases whatsoever," that combined the American people, as one man, against the oppressions of the British tyrant.

Such a declaration is now at hand. It exists, in the opinion of the Supreme Court. If the limits imposed on the general government, by the Constitution, are stricken off, they have, *literally,* the power to legislate for us "in all cases whatsoever"; and then we may bid a last adieu to the State governments.

In discussing these momentous questions, I shall not hesitate to speak with the spirit of a freeman. I shall not be overawed by the parasites of a government gigantic in itself, and inflated with recent victories. I love the honor, and, if you please, the glory of my country, but I love its liberty better. Truth and liberty are dearer to me than Plato or Socrates. I speak only of the measures of our public functionaries, but of them I shall speak freely. I am not a political surgeon; but this I know, that a wound which threatens to be mortal must be probed to the bottom. The crisis is one which portends destruction to the liberties of the American people.

I address you, Mr. Editor, on this great subject with no sanguine presage of success. I must say to my fellow citizens that they are sunk in apathy, and that a torpor has fallen upon them. Instead of that noble and magnanimous spirit which achieved our independence, and has often preserved us since, we are sodden in the *luxuries* of banking. A money-loving, funding, stock-jobbing spirit has taken foothold among us. We are almost prepared to sell our liberties for a "mess of pottage." If Mason or Henry could lift their patriot heads from the grave, while they mourned the complete fulfillment of their prophecies, they would almost exclaim, with Jugurtha, "Venal people! you will soon perish if you can find a purchaser." . . .

I shall commence, in the next number, *some* examination of the opinion of the Supreme Court. . . . I am provided with a sling and a stone, but I fear the inspiration will be wanting. I consider that opinion as the "*Alpha* and *Omega,* the beginning and the *end,* the first and the *last,* of federal usurpations."

HAMPDEN.

Jefferson, in retirement, complimented Roane upon his series of articles. Not wishing to take public part in the controversy, he wrote a letter to William Jarvis in 1820 which nevertheless found its way into print. Writing privately also in 1821, he recommended that Virginia not force the Supreme Court issue for fear that the states would divide as they just had over the slavery issue in the Missouri Compromise. "She had better lie by therefore," he recommended, "until the shoe shall pinch an Eastern state."

THOMAS JEFFERSON:
"THE CONSTITUTION . . . IS A MERE THING OF WAX IN THE HANDS OF THE JUDICIARY"*

JEFFERSON TO SPENCER ROANE

Poplar Forest, September 6, 1819.
Dear Sir,—I had read in the Enquirer, and with great approbation, the pieces signed Hampden, and have read them again with redoubled approbation, in the copies you have been so kind as to send me. I subscribe to every tittle of them. They contain the true principles of the revolution of 1800, for that was as real a revolution in the principles of our government as that of 1776 was in its form; not effected indeed by the sword, as that, but by the rational and peaceable instrument of reform, the suffrage of the people. The nation declared its will by dismissing functionaries of one principle, and electing those of another, in the two branches, executive and legislative, submitted to their election. Over the judiciary department, the constitution had deprived them of their control. That, therefore, has continued the reprobated system, and although new matter has been occasionally incorporated into the old, yet the leaven of the old mass seems to assimilate to itself the new, and after twenty years' confirmation of the federal system by the voice of the nation, declared through the medium of elections, we find the judiciary on every occasion, still driving us into consolidation.

In denying the right they usurp of exclusively explaining the constitution, I go further than you do, if I understand rightly your quotation from the *Federalist*, of an opinion that "the judiciary is the last resort in relation *to the other departments* of the government, but not in relation to the rights of the parties to the compact under which the judiciary is derived." If this opinion[1] be sound, then indeed is our constitution a complete *felo de se*. For intending to establish three departments, co-ordinate and independent, that they might check and balance one another, it has given, according to this opinion, to one of them alone, the right to prescribe rules for the government of the others, and to that one too, which is

unelected by, and independent of the nation. For experience has already shown that the impeachment it has provided is not even a scarecrow; that such opinions as the one you combat, sent cautiously out, as you observe also, by detachment, not belonging to the case often, but sought for out of it, as if to rally the public opinion beforehand to their views, and to indicate the line they are to walk in, have been so quietly passed over as never to have excited animadversion, even in a speech of any one of the body entrusted with impeachment. The constitution, on this hypothesis, is a mere thing of wax in the hands of the judiciary, which they may twist, and shape into any form they please. It should be remembered, as an axiom of eternal truth in politics, that whatever power in any government is independent, is absolute also; in theory only, at first, while the spirit of the people is up, but in practice, as fast as that relaxes. Independence can be trusted nowhere but with the people in mass. They are inherently independent of all but moral law. My construction of the constitution is very different from that you quote. It is that each department is truly independent of the others, and has an equal right to decide for itself what is the meaning of the constitution in the cases submitted to its action; and especially, where it is to act ultimately and without appeal. I will explain myself by examples, which, having occurred while I was in office, are better known to me, and the principles which governed them.

A legislature had passed the sedition law. The federal courts had subjected certain individuals to its penalties of fine and imprisonment. On coming into office, I released these individuals by the power of pardon committed to executive discretion, which could never be more properly exercised than where citizens were suffering without the authority of law, or, which was equivalent, under a law unauthorized by the constitution, and therefore null. In the case of Marbury and Madison, the federal judges declared that commissions, signed and sealed by the President, were valid, although not delivered. I deemed delivery essential to complete a deed, which, as long as it remains in the hands of the party, is as yet no deed, it is in *posse* only, but not in *esse*,

---

* Reprinted from Paul Leicester Ford, ed., *The Works of Thomas Jefferson* (New York: Putnam, 1905), XII, 135–39, 162–63, 214–17.

[1] The McCulloch decision.

and I withheld delivery of the commissions. They cannot issue a mandamus to the President or legislature, or to any of their officers.[2] When the British treaty of —— arrived, without any provision against the impressment of our seamen, I determined not to ratify it. The Senate thought I should ask their advice. I thought that would be a mockery of them, when I was predetermined against following it, should they advise its ratification. The constitution had made their advice necessary to confirm a treaty, but not to reject it. This has been blamed by some; but I have never doubted its soundness. In the cases of two persons, *antenati,* under exactly similar circumstances, the federal court had determined that one of them (Duane) was not a citizen; the House of Representatives nevertheless determined that the other (Smith, of South Carolina) was a citizen, and admitted him to his seat in their body. Duane was a republican, and Smith a federalist, and these decisions were made during the federal ascendancy.

These are examples of my position, that each of the three departments has equally the right to decide for itself what is its duty under the constitution, without any regard to what the others may have decided for themselves under a similar question. But you intimate a wish that my opinion should be known on this subject. No, dear Sir, I withdraw from all contests of opinion, and resign everything cheerfully to the generation now in place. They are wiser than we were, and their successors will be wiser than they, from the progressive advance of science. Tranquillity is the *summum bonum* of age. I wish, therefore, to offend no man's opinion, nor to draw disquieting animadversions on my own. While duty required it, I met opposition with a firm and fearless step. But loving mankind in my individual relations with them, I pray to be permitted to depart in their peace; and like the superannuated soldier, *"quadragenis stipendiis emeritis,"* to hang my arms on the post. . . .

JEFFERSON TO
WILLIAM CHARLES JARVIS

Monticello, September 28, 1820.
. . . You seem. . . to consider the judges as the ultimate arbiters of all constitutional questions; a very dangerous doctrine indeed, and one which would place us under the despotism of an oligarchy. Our judges are as honest as other men, and not more so. They have, with others, the same passions for party, for power, and the privilege of their corps. Their maxim is *"boni judicis est ampliare jurisdictionem,"* and their power the more dangerous as they are in office for life, and are not responsible, as the other functionaries are, to the elective control. The constitution has erected no such single tribunal, knowing that to

whatever hands confided, with the corruptions of time and party, its members would become despots. It has more wisely made all the departments co-equal and co-sovereign within themselves. If the legislature fails to pass laws for a census, for paying the judges and other officers of government, for establishing a militia, for naturalization as prescribed by the constitution, or if they fail to meet in congress, the judges cannot issue their mandamus to them; if the President fails to supply the place of a judge, to appoint other civil or military officers, to issue requisite commissions, the judges cannot force him. They can issue their mandamus or distringas to no executive or legislative officer to enforce the fulfilment of their official duties, any more than the president or legislature may issue orders to the judges or their officers. Betrayed by the English example, and unaware, as it should seem, of the control of our constitution in this particular, they have at times overstepped their limit by undertaking to command executive officers in the discharge of their executive duties; but the constitution, in keeping three departments distinct and independent, restrains the authority of the judges to judiciary organs, as it does the executive and legislative to executive and legislative organs. The judges certainly have more frequent occasion to act on constitutional questions, because the laws of *meum* and *tuum* and of criminal action, forming the great mass of the system of law, constitute their particular department. When the legislative or executive functionaries act unconstitutionally, they are responsible to the people in their elective capacity. The exemption of the judges from that is quite dangerous enough. I know no safe depository of the ultimate powers of the society but the people themselves; and if we think them not enlightened enough to exercise their control with a wholesome discretion, the remedy is not to take it from them, but to inform their discretion by education. This is the true corrective of abuses of constitutional power. . . .

JEFFERSON TO
JAMES PLEASANTS

Monticello, Dec. 26. 21.
Dear Sir,—
. . . But you will have a more difficult task in curbing the Judiciary in their enterprises on the constitution. I doubt whether the erection of the Senate into an appellate court on Constitutional questions would be deemed an unexceptionable reliance; because it would enable the judiciary, with the representatives in Senate of one third only of our citizens, and that in a single house, to make *by construction* what they should please of the constitution, and thus bind in a double knot the other two thirds, for I believe that one third of our citizens chuse a majority of the Senate, and these too of the smaller states whose interests lead to lessen state influence, & strengthen that of the general government. A better remedy I

---

[2] The constitution controlling the common law in this particular,—T. J.

think, and indeed the best I can devise would be to give future commissions to judges for six years (the Senatorial term) with a re-appointment-ability by the president with the approbation of *both* houses. That of the H. of Repr. imports a majority of citizens, that of the Senate a majority of states and that of both a majority of the three sovereign departments of the existing government, to wit, of it's Executive & legislative branches. If this would not be independance enough, I know not what would be such, short of the total irresponsibility under which we are acting and sinning now. The independance of the judges in England on the King alone is good; but even there they are not independant on the Parliament; being removable on the joint address of both houses, by a vote of a majority of each, but we require a majority of one house and ⅔ of the other, a concurrence which, in practice, has been and ever will be found impossible; for the judiciary perversions of the constitution will forever be protected under the pretext of errors of judgment, which by principle are exempt from punishment. Impeachment therefore is a bugbear which they fear not at all. But they would be under some awe of the canvas of their conduct which would be open to both houses regularly every 6th year. It is a misnomer to call a government republican, in which a branch of the supreme power is independant of the nation. By this change of tenure a remedy would be held up to the states, which altho' very distant, would probably keep them quiet. In aid of this a more immediate effect would be produced by a joint protestation of both Houses of Congress, that the doctrines of the judges in the case of Cohens, adjudging a state amenable to their tribunal, and that Congress can authorize a corporation of the district of Columbia to pass any act which shall have the force of law within a state, are contrary to the provisions of the Constitution of the US. This would be effectual; as with such an avowal of Congress, no state would permit such a sentence to be carried into execution, within it's limits. If, by the distribution of the sovereign powers among three branches, they were intended to be checks on one another, the present case calls loudly for the exercise of that duty, and such a counter declaration, while proper in form, would be most salutary as a precedent.

Another most condemnable practice of the supreme court to be corrected is that of cooking up a decision in Caucus & delivering it by one of their members as the opinion of the court, without the possibility of our knowing how many, who, and for what reasons each member concurred. This compleatly defeats the possibility of impeachment by smothering evidence. A regard for character in each being now the only hold we can have of them, we should hold fast to it. They would, were they to give their opinions seriatim and publicly, endeavor to justify themselves to the world by explaining the reasons which led to their opinion. While Edmd Randolph was attorney general, he was charged on a particular occasion by the H. of R. to prepare a digest and some amendments to the judiciary law. One of the amendments he proposed was that every judge should give his individual opinion, and reasons in open court, which opinions and reasons should be recorded in a separate book to be published occasionally in the nature of Reports. Other business prevented Congress from acting then on the bill. Such a provision would produce valuable effect and emulation in forming an opinion and correctly reasoning on it; and would give us Reports, unswelled by the arguments of counsel and within the compass of our reading and book shelves. But these things belong to the present generation, who are to live under them. The machine, as it is, will, I believe, last my time, and those coming after will know how to repair it to their own minds. I cannot help sometimes yielding to senile garrulity on matters not belonging to me, yet I pray not to be quoted, but pardoned for this weakness of age. With my prayers that our constitution may *perpetuum durare per aevum* accept the assurances of my affectionate esteem and respect.

Roane's articles and Jefferson's letter which appeared in print sharply irritated Marshall. He launched an angry, anonymous rebuttal at Roane and over a period of several years confided to his New England colleague, Story, his alarm over the continuing attacks.

JOHN MARSHALL:
"THE ATTACK . . . IS A MASKED BATTERY AIMED AT THE GOVERNMENT ITSELF."*

MARSHALL TO STORY

Richmond, March 24th, 1819.
Dear Sir,— . . . Our opinion in the Bank case has aroused the sleeping spirit of Virginia, if indeed it ever sleeps. It will, I understand, be attacked in the papers with some asperity, and as those who favor it never write for the publick it will remain undefended & of course be considered as *damnably heretical.*
Yours truely.
J. Marshall.

Richmond, May 27th, 1819.
My Dear Sir,— . . . I am much obliged by the alterations you have made in the opinion in the Dartmouth College case, & am highly gratified by what you say respecting it. The opinion in the Bank case continues to be denounced by the democracy in Virginia. An effort is certainly making to induce the legislature which will meet in December to take up the subject & to pass resolutions not very unlike those which were called forth by the alien & sedition laws in 1799. Whether the effort will be successful or not may perhaps depend in some measure on the sentiments of our sister states. To excite this ferment the opinion has been grossly misrepresented; and where its argument has been truely stated it has been met by principles one would think too palpably absurd for inteligent men. But prejudice will swallow anything. If the principles which have been advanced on this occasion were to prevail the constitution would be converted into the old confederation. The piece to which you allude was not published in Virginia. Our patriotic papers admit no such political heresies. It contained, I think, a complete demonstration of the fallacies & errors contained in those attacks on the opinion of the Court which have most credit here & are supposed to proceed from a high source, but was so mangled in the publication that those only who had bestowed close attention to the subject could understand it. There were two numbers & the editor of the Union in Philadelphia, the paper in which it was published, had mixed the different numbers together so as in several instances to place the reasoning intended to demonstrate one

proposition under another. The points & the arguments were so separated from each other, & so strangely mixed as to constitute a labyrinth to which those only who understood the whole subject perfectly could find a clue. . . .
With great regard and esteem, I am, dear Sir, your obed[t]
J. Marshall.

Richmond, June 15th, 1821.
Dear Sir,—
. . . The opinion of the Supreme Court in the Lottery case[1] has been assaulted with a degree of virulence transcending what has appeared on any former occasion. Algernon Sidney is written by the gentleman who is so much distinguished for his feelings towards the Supreme Court,[2] & if you have not an opportunity of seeing the Enquirer I will send it to you. There are other minor gentry who seek to curry favor & get into office by adding their mite of abuse, but I think for coarseness & malignity of invention Algernon Sidney surpasses all party writers who have ever made pretensions to any decency of character. There is on this subject no such thing as a free press in Virginia, and of consequence the calumnies and misrepresentations of this gentleman will remain uncontradicted & will by many be believed to be true. He will be supposed to be the champion of state rights, instead of being what he really is, the champion of dismemberment.
With great regard & esteem
I am, dear Sir, yours, &c.
J. Marshall.

Richmond, July 13th, 1821.
My dear Sir,— . . . .
What you say of M[r] Jefferson's letter rather grieves than surprizes me.[3] It grieves me because his influence is still so great that many, very many will adopt his opinions, however unsound they may be, & however contradictory to their own reason. I cannot describe the surprize & mortification I have felt at hearing that M[r] Madison has embraced them with respect to the judicial department.

---

[1] Cohens *vs.* Virginia, which involved the sale of lottery tickets.

[2] Another of the pseudonyms of Spencer Roane.

[3] The letter here commented on was probably the letter to William C. Jarvis.

---

* Reprinted from *Proceedings of the Massachusetts Historical Society, 1900, 1901* (2nd series; Boston: 1901), XIV, 324–31.

For Mr Jefferson's opinion as respects this department it is not difficult to assign the cause. He is among the most ambitious, & I suspect among the most unforgiving of men. His great power is over the mass of the people, & this power is chiefly acquired by professions of democracy. Every check on the wild impulse of the moment is a check on his own power, & he is unfriendly to the source from which it flows. He looks of course with ill will at an independent judiciary.

That in a free country with a written constitution any inteligent man should wish a dependent judiciary, or should think that the constitution is not a law for the court as well as the legislature would astonish me, if I had not learnt from observation that with many men the judgement is completely controuled by the passions. The case of the mandamus may be the cloak, but the batture[4] is recollected with still more resentment.

I send you the papers containing the essays of Algernon Sidney. Their coarseness & malignity would designate the author if he was not avowed. The argument, if it may be called one, is, I think, as weak as its language is violent & prolix. Two other gentlemen have appeared in the papers on this subject, one of them is deeply concerned in pillaging the purchasers of the Fairfax estate in which goodly work he fears no other obstruction than what arises from the appellate power of the Supreme Court, & the other is a hunter after office who hopes by his violent hostility to the Union, which in Virginia assumes the name of regard for state rights, & by his devotion to Algernon Sidney, to obtain one. In support of the sound principles of the constitution & of the Union of the States, not a pen is drawn. In Virginia the tendency of things verges rapidly to the destruction of the government & the re-establishment of a league of sovereign states. I look elsewhere for safety.

With very much esteem & affection
I am, dear Sir, your
J. Marshall.

Richmond, Septr 18th, 1821.

My dear Sir,—I had yesterday the pleasure of receiving your favor of the 9th. I thank you for your quintal of fish, & shall try my possibles to observe your instructions in the cooking department. I hope to succeed; but be this as it may I promise to feed on the fish with an appetite which would not disgrace a genuine descendant of one of the Pilgrims.

I am a little surprized at the request which you say has been made to Mr Hall,[5] although there is no reason for my being so. The settled hostility of the gentleman who has made that request to the judicial department will show itself in that & in every other form which he believes will conduce to its object. For this he has several motives, & it is not among the weakest that the department would never lend itself as a tool to work for his political power. The Batture will never be forgotten. Indeed, there is some reason to believe that the essays written against the Supreme Court were, in a degree at least, stimulated by this gentleman, and that although the coarseness of the language belongs exclusively to the author, its acerbity has been increased by his communications with the great Lama of the mountains. He may therefore feel himself in some measure required to obtain its republication in some place of distinction. But what does Mr Hall purpose to do? I do not suppose you would willingly interfere so as to prevent his making the publication, although I really think it is in form & substance totally unfit to be placed in his law journal. I really think a proper reply to the request would be to say that no objection existed to the publication of any law argument against the opinion of the Supreme Court, but that the coarseness of its language, its personal & official abuse & its tedious prolixity constituted objections to the insertion of Algernon Sidney which were insuperable. If, however, Mr Hall determines to comply with this request, I think he ought, unless he means to make himself a party militant, to say that he published that piece by particular request, & ought to subjoin the masterly answer of Mr Wheaton. I shall wish to know what course Mr Hall will pursue. . . .

A deep design to convert our government into a mere league of states has taken strong hold of a powerful & violent party in Virginia. The attack upon the judiciary is in fact an attack upon the union. The judicial department is well understood to be that through which the government may be attacked most successfully, because it is without patronage, & of course without power. And it is equally well understood that every subtraction from its jurisdiction is a vital wound to the government itself. The attack upon it therefore is a masked battery aimed at the government itself. The whole attack, if not originating with Mr Jefferson, is obviously approved & guided by him. It is therefore formidable in other states as well as in this, & it behoves the friends of the union to be more on the alert than they have been. An effort will certainly be made to repeal the 25th sec. of the judicial act. . . .

Yours truely & sincerely.
J. Marshall.

---

[4] The first of these references is to *Marbury v. Madison*. The second reference is to the protracted litigation which involved the title to what was known as the batture, near New Orleans, and in which Jefferson took a strong personal interest.

[5] Mr. John E. Hall, editor of a law journal published in Philadelphia. From 1808 to 1817 he published "The American Law Journal." In 1821 he published one volume of "The Journal of Jurisprudence," which was intended to be a continuation of the former periodical, but it did not reach a second volume. It does not contain the article against the Supreme Court to which reference is here made.

The Virginians were not able, as Marshall had feared, to gain the support of a requisite number of states to add an amendment to the Constitution limiting the powers of the Supreme Court. But the states' rights arguments that the controversy had evoked were beginning, with the debate over the Missouri Compromise, to serve larger and more serious ends which would culminate in secession. One of the most effective of Marshall's critics, John Taylor of Caroline, was equally ready to train his diffuse barrage of aphorisms against anyone who would tamper with the slavery system within the states. Thus his lengthy treatise, *Construction Construed,* published under the aegis of the Richmond *Enquirer* in 1801, concluded with observations on the Missouri question. The Missouri controversy frightened Jefferson like "a fire-bell in the night," yet he endorsed *Construction Construed* as "the most effectual retraction of our government to its original principles which has ever yet been sent by heaven to our aid."

JOHN TAYLOR OF CAROLINE:
CONSTRUCTION CONSTRUED*

THE BANK DECISION.—SUPREMACY

The attempt made by the court . . . to transplant sovereignty from the people of each state, by whom it has been and may be exercised, to the people of the United States, by whom it never has been nor can be exercised, under our present system of government, might fail of success; and therefore a new mode of destroying the sovereignty of the people is resorted to. Its jealousy is first appeased by the acknowledgment of spherical sovereignties [state and national sovereignty], and then its degradation is finished by subjecting these sovereignties to supremacy. If the ground is a good one, all the states of the union took bad ground both in establishing and sustaining their independence. Supremacy was the literal claim of the British parliament over the colonies. . . .

"The *constitution,* and the laws of the United States which shall be made *in pursuance thereof,* and *all treaties made* or which shall be made, *under the authority* of the United States shall be the supreme law of the land, and *the judges,* in every state, shall be bound thereby, any thing in the constitution or laws of any state to the contrary notwithstanding." This is the clause of the constitution supposed by the court to confer on congress a power over the state governments and state sovereignties. These state sovereignties made, may revoke, or can alter the constitution itself, and therefore the supremacy bestowed upon the constitution, being some power subservient to the state sovereignties, demonstrates that the word "supreme" was used in a sense subordinate to these sovereignties. . . .

The United States have no authority, except that which is given by the constitution. Both the laws and treaties to be supreme must, therefore, be made in conformity with the powers bestowed, limited and reserved by the constitution, and by these we must determine whether a law or a treaty has been constitutionally made, before the question of its supremacy can occur. The judges are expressly referred to, as the curators or executors of this moral supremacy, and no other department is by the least hint recognized, as being able to impair or enforce it. And finally, all officers, legislative, executive and judicial, take on oath to support the constitution, which is a moral sanction in favour of a moral system; and none take an oath to acknowledge any species of personal or spherical supremacy. This clause then amounts to no more, than that the constitution shall be the supreme law of the land. As proceeding from the sovereignty of the people, the highest political authority, the term was proper; because it was paramount and supreme over whatever should proceed from any inferior authority; and as the constitution embraced our whole system of government, both state and federal, by delegating and reserving powers, the supremacy bestowed on it was intended equally and coextensively to protect and secure the powers delegated to the federal government, and those reserved to the states. In this construction of the word "supreme," the court itself has literally concurred, in asserting "that it would be its duty to declare an unconstitutional law void." The right of doing this arises from the supremacy of the constitution over law; from the restriction it imposes upon political departments or spheres to confine themselves within their limited orbits; and from its intention that each department or sphere should controul another, if it transgresses its boundary. Upon this ground the court has asserted this constitutional power in its own sphere. It can be defended upon

* Reprinted from John Taylor, *Construction Construed, and Constitutions Vindicated* (Richmond: 1820), pp. 121–30, 144–45, 194–99, 300–301.

no other; because the constitution does not say, that their judgments shall be the supreme law of the land. If the ground be solid in relation to the judicial sphere, it is equally solid in relation to the limited federal and state spheres. If the legislative federal sphere have no supreme power over the judicial federal sphere; because its power is limited by the constitution, and not extended beyond these limitations by the clause of the constitution under consideration; it follows, that neither the federal nor state spheres derive any supremacy over the other from the same clause, whilst acting within their limited boundaries. . . .

Power in the exercise of verbal construction, and in deducing inferences from particular phrases, like a fine lady admiring a casket of jewels, very easily discovers whatever it wishes for, to be right, convenient, useful and necessary. Particular texts are often tortured to appease conscience, or to gratify prejudice; and good or bad intentions are equally fertile in expedients for surmounting obstacles. A single word is often so indefinite, that its meaning is controuled by another. A single sentence may generally be twisted into an enmity with principles plainly asserted, in any book; but the defects of language do not equally extend to an entire treatise. Thus the imperfections of isolated words and sentences, and the frailties of mankind unite to teach us, that the licentiousness of construction can only be controuled by an impartial estimate of a whole, and a candid comparison of its parts. If the reader shall examine the federal constitution by this rule, and should discover that it delegates a power to the federal government "so to *modify every power* vested in the state governments as to exempt its own operations from their influence," he must conclude, that the decision of the court, founded upon the existence of this power in the federal government, is correct; but if the constitution invests the federal government with no such power, then it follows, that this decision, founded upon a supposition that it did, must be unconstitutional. This is in fact the very essence of the question; as interferences by the federal or state governments with powers delegated to the other, are in truth modifications of those powers; and it is extremely important to ascertain, whether a power so enormous and unspecified is common to both, or exclusively conferred upon the former. The latter is asserted by the court for the purpose of modifying the state right of taxation; by those members of congress who supported a bill for prohibiting slavery in a particular state, and is the ground upon which alone all interfering with the police of states can be defended.

It will be allowed, that the people of each state had, and exercised the right of modifying the powers vested in the state governments. If the federal government now have it, the most unexpected consequences will ensue. The people can no longer exercise the right, because they have given it away. If it be a concurrent right, should they exercise it, the federal government may re-modify their modifications. The state govern-

ments will be responsible either to the federal government singly, or both to this government and the people for their conduct. It was quite idle to reserve to the state governments the powers previously bestowed, if they were at the same time subjected to the subsequent modifications of the federal government. And the meditated check upon the federal government by the powers reserved to the state governments would be equally insignificant. These consequences of the construction given to the word "supreme" by the court, so completely subversive of the essential principles of our system of government, are a sufficient exposition of its incorrectness.

But the argument becomes stronger, when we resort to the provisions of the constitution. I shall venture to test the position relied on by the court, by the mode before practised of confronting it with a contradictory position; so that one or the other must be disallowed. It is a question of supremacy; the constitution has invested the states with a complete, and the state governments with a limited supremacy, over the federal government, and expressly subjected its *operations to the influence* of the latter, in sundry important instances. The states by common consent may dissolve or modify the union, over which, by the natural right of self-government, which they have never relinquished, they retain a complete supremacy. By the constitution, the state governments are invested with the rights of appointing senators and electors of a president, for the very purpose of influencing the operations of the federal government for their own security. They may forbear to exercise this right, and thus dissolve the federal government. They may elect the members of the house of representatives by a general ticket, and thereby very considerably influence its operations. They may compel congress to call a convention. They may ratify changes of the federal government, without its consent. They may affirm or reject amendments proposed by congress. They have a concurrent right of internal taxation with the federal government, and these concurrent rights may deeply influence each other; and they are exclusively invested with the appointment of all the officers of that force, upon which the safety and liberty of the nation depend. These powers seem to me, to invest the state governments with a limited supremacy over the federal government; at least it must be admitted, that they are such as may and do deeply influence its operations. The constitution gives no authority to the federal government to exercise such powers over the state governments. Can it then be true, as the position of the court declares, that the federal government have a right so *to modify every power vested in the state governments, as to exempt its own operations from their influence?* Upon the ground of this doctrine, the supreme court of the federal government has attempted so to modify the concurrent right of taxation reserved to the states, as to exempt the incorporating power assumed by congress, from its influence. This is one of the enumerated powers invested in the states, by which it was certainly foreseen and intended, that they might influence the operations of the federal government; and if in this case such an influence justifies a modification of the state power of taxation by the federal government, and even by one of its departments, the same reason will justify a modification of all the rest of the enumerated influencing state powers. The supreme court might by the same principle, appoint senators, electors, and militia officers, should the states neglect to do it; in order, by modifying these powers of the state governments, as being subordinate to the supposed supremacy of the federal government, *to exempt the latter from their influence.*

If, therefore, it should have been proved, that the federal government is not invested with a power of modifying the powers bestowed by the people on the state governments, the pretended supremacy, supposed to bestow a right so unlimited, does not exist; the modification on the state power of taxation was of course unconstitutional; and the question would seem to be settled. But it starts up again in a new form; and though it should be allowed that the entire federal government do not possess a right to modify the state constitutions, yet it is still contended, that one of its subordinate departments does possess it; and its supreme court have accordingly modified and restricted the power of internal taxation bestowed by the state constitutions on their governments. This power under the state constitutions was unlimited. It is not limited by the federal constitution. But the federal court have adjudged, that it is either necessary or convenient that it should be limited; and for that reason they have modified it by a precedent sufficient to justify other modifications of state powers to any extent, upon the ground of possessing an unlimited supremacy over the legislative and judicial power of the states.

The supremacy we have examined is confined to the constitution, the laws, and treaties. It is not extended to judicial decisions. Suppose congress should pass a law declaring such state laws as they pleased, to be unconstitutional and void. An excessive interpretation of the word "supreme," might give some countenance to so evident an usurpation; and as one branch of the federal legislature is elected by the people, it would afford some security, however imperfect, against such a prostration of the state governments at the feet of the federal legislative power. But neither this excessive supremacy, nor this defective security, plead for lodging the same unlimited power in the federal courts. Were they to possess it, they might modify the state governments, in a mode, contrary to the will of congress, as is exemplified in the case under consideration. In creating the bank of the United States, congress did not endeavour to prohibit the states from taxing the property employed in that speculation. Had the state right to do so been considered in that body, its constitutionality might have been decided in the affirmative. The court, therefore, in assuming a power to restrain this state right, may have violated the

will both of the federal and state legislature, and modified the state constitutions, contrary to the judgment of both. The state law asserted the right, the federal law is silent, and the court imposes a constitutional rule on both (as if it were itself a constituent or elemental power,) objected to by one, and never assented to by the other. This outstrips even the arbitrary principle laid down by the court itself "that the supreme government may modify every power vested in subordinate governments, to exempt its own operations from their influence." It will not be asserted that the federal court is the supreme government, or that it has operations to carry on, which ought to be exempted from the influence of the subordinate state governments. If these governments are not subordinate to that court, it cannot modify their powers, even under its own principle; and if the federal government possesses this modifying power, it ought to be exercised by congress, before it can be enforced by the court. The court at most can only execute, and have no power to pronounce the modification. Congress might have intended, that the power of taxing the United States bank, like that of taxing state banks, should remain as a concurrent power, like the other concurrent powers of taxation. If that body conceived itself possessed of a power to modify the state power of taxation, it could only do so by its own act, and that act ought to have been explicit, that the people might, by election, have expressed their opinion concerning it. But when the modification is expressed by the court, the chief remedy for deciding spherical collisions, and for restraining each division of power within its own orbit, is wholly evaded, and completely transferred from the people to the judges. . . .

. . . If federal legislatures do not possess an absolute supremacy, federal judiciaries cannot possess it, since judgments cannot enforce that which is not law. In conformity with this reasoning, neither federal legislative majorities, nor a majority of the states, can amend the constitution, because it was a compact by which each state delegated for itself only limited powers to the federal government; attended by a supremacy not of any political sphere, but of the constitution, limited and confined to the powers delegated, and not extending to the portion of primitive state supremacy, never delegated. Thus it happened, that no state was bound by the constitution, until it had acceded individually to that compact. And hence it results, that the right of construing the constitution within their respective spheres, is mutual between the state and general governments, because the latter have no supremacy over the state powers retained, and the former no supremacy over the federal powers delegated, except that which provides the stipulated mode for amending the constitution.

It is objected, that if the supreme federal court do not possess an unlimited or unchecked supremacy in construing the constitution, clashing constructions will ensue. This is true; and yet it is not a good reason for overturning our system for dividing, limiting and checking power, if that system be a good one; and if it be even a bad one, the people only, and neither one of their departments separately, nor all united, can alter or amend it. The objection applies as strongly to the other departments of our government, as to the judicial. If the federal legislature and executive do not possess an absolute supremacy over the state legislatures and executives, clashing constitutional constructions will ensue. The jurisdiction of the federal judicial power is as expressly limited, as the legislative and executive federal powers. There is no judicial supremacy recognized in the supreme federal court, except that over inferior federal courts. And, if the supremacy of the constitution bestows upon any federal department a supremacy over the correspondent state department, it must bestow upon every federal department, a similar supremacy over the other correspondent state departments.

It is therefore obvious, that the subject proposed by the objection for consideration is, whether it is better to abandon our primary division of powers between the state and federal governments, to prevent clashing constructions; or to retain this chief security against a gradual introduction of oppression, trusting to the mutual prudence of these governments, and the supreme authority of the people, for meeting the inconvenience, as it appears. The greatest scope of human wisdom is, to compare evils and choose the least. I cannot discern the wisdom of one who cuts off his head, lest his face should be scratched occasionally as he journeys through life. Montesquieu has somewhere said, that when the savage of America wants fruit, he cuts down the tree to obtain it. Shall we act with still less foresight, by cutting down the division of power between the general and state governments, calculated to produce the fruit of moderation in both, that one may cram us with the fruits of supremacy? . . .

THE BANK DECISION.—PRECEDENTS

I shall conclude this subject, by an examination of an argument with which the court began. It remarks, that "banking was introduced at a very early period of our history, has been recognized by many successive legislatures, and has been acted upon by the judicial department in cases of peculiar delicacy, as a law of undoubted obligation." This remark must either furnish the conclusion, that precedents may change the federal constitution, or it has no weight. As it was intended to have weight, it deserves an attentive consideration. . . .

Judicial precedents are commonly the work of one man or a very few men. An opinion becomes an authority, and as it rolls along, it magnifies by others which adhere to it, not because it is right, but because it is authority. In my view, it bears no resemblance to the species of consent by which we make constitutions.

The submission of the people is one argument of little or no weight to prove the constitutionality of laws. The influence of government, and not the approbation of the people, generally causes a submission to laws; and therefore, it is but a bad argument for sanctifying precedents. But under the federal constitution, the argument has moreover a fraudulent aspect, because its provisions for amendment have taught the people to believe, that there are no other modes by which the constitution can be altered; and lulled them into security against precedents. . . . Suppose, it had been proposed to amend the constitution in either of the prescribed modes, by investing congress with powers to create banks, to bestow bounties, to grant exclusive privileges, to make roads and canals, to annex conditions to the admission of new states into the union, and to prohibit the state governments from taxing the persons or property it should invest with exclusive privileges; would all these powers have been as quietly and silently obtained in the constitutional mode, as by precedents? There is no fair way of deciding the doubt, except one, which I wish to see resorted to, namely, a formal proposal in congress for conferring all these powers upon itself, by a positive amendment of the constitution. The inconsistency between limiting a government attended with prescribed modes of amendment, and the doctrine that this same government might extend its powers by its own precedents, is sufficient to have deluded the people into an opinion, if it be a delusion, that the constitution was not liable to be altered by precedents; and that whatever law could do, law could undo. . . .

Veneration for our constitutions is the best security for the endurance of our free form of government, and the best infusion for elevating the national character. But, how can a nation love an embryo litter of fluctuating precedents, concealed in the womb of time, each of which as it grows, hustles some principle out of the constitution, as the cuckoo does the sparrow out of its own nest? . . . What should we say to a husband, who should surrender the custody of his wife to a set of professed rakes? That which ought to be said of a nation, which entrusts its constitution to the care of precedents. They are only the projects or opinions of successive legislators, presidents, judges, generals or statesmen, none of whom will acknowledge that their laws, actions, decisions, orders or schemes are unconstitutional, though they will be forever as various and contradictory as the characters from which they proceed. Mankind have generally, however, confided in this chance medley current of governmental promulgation, for the preservation of their happiness; but we have preferred principles, maturely considered, carefully selected, cautiously approved, and distinctly defined, as a better security. . . . By surrendering its constitution to precedents, a nation would surrender its strongest fortress to its strongest enemy; and would subscribe to the opinion, that the best mode of defending itself, is to throw down its arms. . . .

The finest effort of ingenuity to be found in the opinion of the court, is, that of availing itself of precedents in a point only incidental, and of passing them by altogether in reference to the true question to be decided. The state of Maryland had not disputed the constitutionality of the bank, but had exercised its concurrent right of taxation; and the court refers to the multiplicity of precedents as a proof of its constitutionality, and forgets the same species of multiplicity as a proof of the constitutionality of the concurrent right. There was a sound reason for doing so. The intended decision was to make a new precedent, to overthrow the whole multitude of precedents establishing the concurrent right of taxation, and therefore it was wise to transfer our attention from the precedents applying to the question, intended to be destroyed, to make a shew the back ground, as some generals have gained a victory by formally arraying the scullions of their army, and deceiving their adversaries into an opinion, that they were really soldiers. Besides, it held out an aspect of paying respect to precedents, under cover of which they were actually to be overturned. There was no precedent at all by which the court could abridge or modify the concurrent powers of taxation established by the constitution; but a multitude of precedents in favour of the constitutionality of this concurrency, had arisen from its mutual exercise. Congress had established it by many laws, especially in taxing the state banks by a stamp act. If the establishment of state banks was within the state spheres, congress had no right to throw *obstacles in the way of their sphere of action*, except by virtue of the concurrent power of taxation; and if this power justified congress in taxing state banks, the same power justified the states in taxing the banks of congress, though these latter were also constitutional. But, the court, instead of considering the precedents in relation to the concurrent right of taxation, have insisted at large upon those which relate to the constitutionality of banking, and adhered to the precedent of searching for a goose, when the thing lost was a cow. . . .

THE MISSOURI QUESTION

. . . A southern majority in congress has no right to compel the northern states to permit slavery, nor a northern majority to compel the southern states to abolish it, because it is a subject of internal state regulation prohibited to congress, and reserved to the states. One and the same principle applies to the two rights of suffering or abolishing slavery, and to assert and deny its efficacy, will never operate any conviction upon the party whose rights under it are invaded, by a party who claims and uses its protection. It has been handled as a religious question, and zeal, even in these modern times, has forgotten the freedom of conscience, and adopted the antiquated plan of effecting conversion by violence. The French nation, actuated at first by an honest but intemperate enthusiasm, attempted to compel the other nations of Europe to be free and happy; and the events produced by the fanatical undertaking were such as may be expected, should a combination of states attempt to administer by force the same medicines to another combination of states. Nothing can be more offensive than such attempts, because they assail natural rights; nor more presumptuous, because the dictators are infinitely worse informed upon the subject, than those who have the right of determination. To prevent this dictatorial and absurd exercise of power by a majority of states, as being an infallible cause of civil war and disunion, congress was not made a representation of any internal powers, those few excepted necessary for common safety; and all internal powers, except a few specified prohibitions, were reserved to the states. The reasons for this policy which then existed, still exist, and will exist forever. The members of congress could never be well informed of local concerns, and therefore could never decide upon them correctly. Vanity cannot supply the place of knowledge. They would not feel the effects of their local laws, and therefore congress as to local subjects would not possess the best quality of a representative body. Above all, they would not decide like local representatives; this is so true, that if all the members of congress now opposed to slavery in Missouri, should emigrate to that state, there is no doubt but that most of them would soon change their opinion. Indeed, this is the reason of the difference of opinion between the eastern and southern states upon the question; and if either placed in the circumstances of the others, would have adopted opinions the reverse of those now held, it forcibly displays the injustice of a dictatorial power to be exercised by either party. . . .

CHAPTER SEVEN

THE JACKSONIANS

The Jacksonian movement in the United States expressed the emergence of liberal, middle-class capitalism. Historians differ on who should be regarded as the representative figure of Jacksonian democracy (the small western and southern farmer, the wage worker in eastern seaboard cities, or the businessman opposed to the Bank of the United States) but they are in substantial agreement that this was an expanding economy of the rising middle classes. Recent scholars have sharpened our focus even more, contending that the age was not, as had been generally assumed, one of laissez faire in thought or practice. Thus, the most basic question confronting the student of Jacksonian democracy is: What was the relationship between government and the economy during the 1830's and 1840's? This makes such traditional topics as the influence of the frontier and individualism, or the effect of the spoils system, of lesser interest to the modern student of this period.

Oscar Handlin in the first essay discussed what the prevailing American attitudes toward the role of government in economic life were. Basing his analysis on an intensive look at Massachusetts, Handlin contended that laissez faire was not the influential doctrine it was commonly supposed to be. "From the very first organization of the Commonwealth in 1780," Handlin stated, "the state actively and vigorously engaged in all the economic affairs of the area, sometimes as participant, sometimes as regulator." Further, the lack of laissez faire in America was not reflected in a comparable situation, the parallel economic stage in England, because the United States did not have a well-defined mercantilist system or guild and manorial restrictions. Handlin concluded that "the relative newness of the country, and the comparative swiftness of economic developments precluded legal formalism and rigidity in institutions."

The second major development of the Jacksonian period, the rise of a national political party system, is reflected both directly and indirectly in the remaining selections. The buoyancy of hope, the partisan definitions of democracy, and the optimism of a new age all helped to shape the Jacksonian spirit. In many respects, said William N. Chambers in his interpretive essay included here, Jackson symbolized all of these forces.

OSCAR HANDLIN:
LAISSEZ-FAIRE THOUGHT IN MASSACHUSETTS, 1790–1880*

I

This paper will deal not with the development, but rather with the lack of development of laissez-faire thought in Massachusetts during most of the nineteenth century. A common misconception of American economic thought, as of American economy, ascribes a continuous laissez-faire bent to policy in the United States. This misconception will be found not only in the pretty publications of the National Association of Manufacturers where it might be expected, but also in the serious works of our most careful scholars into which it obtrudes almost automatically. Thus Mr. Nef recently referred to laissez faire as "part of our national heritage." [1] Yet, in general, and specifically as applied to Massachusetts, this is completely erroneous.

One source of misunderstanding lies in the circumstance that discussion of American policy has often revolved about the powers of the national government as contrasted with those of the states. But arguments which denied powers to the federal government on the ground that they belonged to the states hardly betoken laissez faire. Federalism is a red herring which only confuses the issues involved. Nor should this discussion take stock of debates concerning the advisability or expediency of particular measures; whether the government would regulate banks by a board of commissioners or by a single commissioner did not involve the question of the power to regulate. In this paper the conception of laissez faire will be limited to the abstention by government from interference with or participation in economic processes and the restriction of its functions to certain narrow police powers, mainly the protection of life and property. [2]

In the realm of the practical there never was a period in Massachusetts history when this conception was of the slightest consequence. From the very first organization of the Commonwealth in 1780, the state actively and vigorously engaged in all the economic affairs of the area, sometimes as participant, sometimes as regulator. But that is not the subject of a paper devoted to ideas. These do not always follow practice; sometimes, indeed, they are evoked to counter it. Nevertheless, it is worth remembering that whatever the ideas, practice was never laissez faire.

The rejection of that doctrine was not unconscious. The writings of the English liberals were well-known and appreciated in Massachusetts. Adam Smith was widely read and the works of his successors circulated on this side of the Atlantic soon after they appeared in England. Even the French exponents of Smith found a sympathetic audience here; J. B. Say, for instance, was known by 1820 and translated a year later. For a long time there were close ties between Bay State thinkers and the leaders of the Manchester school. But, though all these were read and understood in Massachusetts, their essential ideas were never espoused. [3]

II

Laissez-faire conceptions failed to develop because there was nowhere they could take root. No large group or section of the state found them compatible with its interests. The merchants—the most powerful segment of the community—were, throughout the period, more than willing to foster interference from the government. They rarely indulged in abnegation. On the contrary, they eagerly accepted bounties for their venturesome enterprises, monopolies for the turnpikes, bridges, and canals in which they invested their funds, and inspection laws which guaranteed the security of their export markets.

At the beginning, it is true, they were dubious about protection. Some importers like Henry Lee were always free-traders and consistently questioned the virtues of the tariff. [4] Until the 1820's though, that issue affected the general run of traders little and they were rarely dogmatic on the subject. As far as their commercial interests were concerned, they generally felt the impost was a tax on consumers with little influence on their own profits so long as drawbacks and rebates safeguarded trade. [5] As for manufacturing, artificial stimuli could have only a slight effect, and, in any case, the particular enterprises in

---

* Reprinted from *Tasks of Economic History*, 1943, pp. 55–65 by permission.

[1] John U. Nef, *The United States and Civilization* (Chicago: The University of Chicago Press, 1942), 319, 345.

[2] For the origin of the phrase, cf. August Oncken, *Die Maxime Laissez faire et Laissez passer, ihr Ursprung, ihr Werden* (Bern, 1886). A brief classical statement may be found in J. R. M'Culloch, *Discourse on the Rise, Progress, Peculiar Objects, and Importance, of Political Economy* (Edinburgh, 1824), 53 ff. Cf. also Roberto Michels, *Introduzione alla storia delle dottrine economiche e politiche* (Bologna, 1932), 2–22.

[3] E. R. A. Seligman, "Economists," *Cambridge History of American Literature* (New York, 1921), IV, 431.

[4] Henry Lee, *Report of a Committee of the Citizens of Boston and Vicinity* (Boston, 1827); J. T. Morse, Jr., *Memoir of Colonel Henry Lee* (Boston, 1905), 114, 115.

[5] On the importance of drawbacks, cf. J. T. Austin in *North American Review*, 1821, XII, 61 ff.

which the traders invested needed little assistance.[6] Frequently their attitude towards specific bills was based on political rather than economic considerations. Thus they supported the earliest tariff measures as part of Hamilton's general scheme. They opposed those of 1816 because of their antipathy to the national government. But in any case, they were never doctrinaire. The merits of each bill were considered on an *ad hoc* basis in the light of immediate interests. Webster made this point bluntly in 1824:

"There may be good reasons for favoring some of the provisions of the bill, and equally strong reasons for opposing others; and these provisions do not stand to each other in the relation of principal and incident."[7]

That is why the same line of reasoning led him to vote against the Act of 1824 and for that of 1828. In both cases, he wanted duties on woolen and cotton cloth; in both he opposed those on raw cotton, raw wool, molasses, tallow, hemp, and iron.[8] The balance of advantages and disadvantages, not a general attitude towards protection or free trade, was important.

During the third decade of the nineteenth century, the expansion of trade with England convinced many that their interests as merchants rested on the maintenance of a protective tariff. In the free exchange of English manufactures for American staples, Boston fell far behind New York, New Orleans, Philadelphia, and Baltimore, for the Massachusetts city never acquired the direct communications with the South and the West on which the prosperity of her rivals rested. Because of the niggardliness of her hinterland, Boston's trade whether with Russia, the East Indies, China, the West Indies, or the Mediterranean was largely triangular. The essential problem of her merchants was how to import without exporting, how to build up a surplus of specie or London credits to serve her world-wide trade.

Like their European contemporaries, Boston merchants recognized the existence of a fixed balance of trade in which imports always equalled exports. But they also believed, as A. H. Everett explained, that the United States "forms a sort of exception to the general rule." For American cotton was free of competition and its flow was limited solely by the needs of the English market.[9]

A protective tariff which stood in the way of imports from England would not affect the amount of cotton that crossed the Atlantic. Needing as much as before, and prevented by the tariff from paying entirely with their own products, the British would simply have to make up the difference by balancing American exports with specie or with credits on London.[10] Sound or not, these doctrines carried undoubted weight in the counting houses of State Street and pushed important elements in the mercantile community solidly behind the tariff.

Protection was, of course, only one facet of the merchants' attitude against laissez faire. As exporters of specie in the normal course of trade, they needed a flexible but sound circulating medium and they looked for strict control by the state to keep the value of bank notes constant and to regulate banking practices in general. Also as traders, they demanded constant improvement in the communications between the seaport and the interior markets. Here too they looked to the state for leadership in planning, for monopolies to encourage private enterprise, and for outright assistance by grants and guarantees. With B. R. Curtis they incredulously asked, "What people has ever doubted, that the building of roads and bridges was a subject not only fit for the action of government, but necessarily under its *exclusive control?*" and added, "We suppose no one will be so hardy as to attempt to make a distinction between a ferry and a canal, or a bridge and a railroad."[11]

After the middle of the century, as the industrial stake of many merchants increased in importance, their protectionist leanings grew more pronounced. And now they could ally themselves with the small manufacturers and petty industrialists all over New England whose demands for higher tariffs for higher profits found ultimate expression in the writings of E. B. Bigelow.[12] Merchants and industrialists generally worked together. But on the rare occasions when their interests diverged, both looked to the state for asssistance. Thus when financial stringency after

---

[6] F. C. Gray, *ibid.*, 1820, X, 317 ff.; *ibid.*, 1823, XVII, 188 ff.; Edward Everett, *ibid.*, XIX, 223 ff.

[7] Speech of April 1, 1824, Daniel Webster, *Works* (Boston, 1853), III, 95.

[8] Cf. the speeches of April 1, 1824 and May 9, 1828, *ibid.*, III, 94 ff., 228 ff. Cf. also F. W. Taussig, *Tariff History of the United States* (New York, 1923), 72, 75, 101.

[9] A. H. Everett, "American System," *North American Review*, 1831, XXXII, 146; Amasa Walker, *Science of Wealth* (Boston, 1866), 327; Lee, *Report*, 155.

[10] Francis Bowen, *Principles of Political Economy Applied to . . . the American People* (Boston, 1856), 306 ff., 457 ff. For Boston trade, in general, cf. Oscar Handlin, *Boston's Immigrants* (Cambridge, 1941), ch. 1; for the character of London credits, cf. Ralph W. Hidy, "Organization and Function of Anglo-American Merchant Bankers, 1815–1860," *The Tasks of Economic History*, Supplement to *The Journal of Economic History*, December, 1941, 59, 60. For the export of specie, cf. Willard Phillips, *North American Review*, 1819, IX, 224 ff.

[11] B. R. Curtis, "Debts of the States," *North American Review*, 1844, LVIII, 128, 129; cf. also Loammi Baldwin and Jared Sparks, *ibid.*, 1818, 1821, VIII, 3 ff., XII, 17, 18.

[12] Cf., e.g., Erastus B. Bigelow, *Tariff Policy of England and the United States Contrasted* (Boston, 1877).

the panic of 1857 aroused the resentment of many manufacturers against financial control by Boston merchants, they sought governmental intervention.[13] Even when it was to their interest to do so, the owners of industry rarely troubled to invoke laissez-faire arguments. Thus in opposing the ten-hour movement, they stressed the rights of contract, but admitted, "if it should ever appear . . . that the social well-being of society were endangered" the state could act. Their opposition was based on inexpediency, the relatively good conditions in the mills, and the bad effect on business, rather than on more theoretical grounds.[14] The general opinion of both merchants and industrialists, as expressed by Abbott Lawrence, was that laissez faire was "a transcendental philosophy, which is not likely to be adopted by any government on the face of the globe."[15]

Equally unlikely to find in this source a pattern for state policy was the other large, politically conscious group, the yeomen farmers. It is true that many state activities—bank regulation, the grant of monopolies, for instance—countered their interests and were opposed. Hildreth and Morton thus spoke for them in their demand for "free banking," and when they reached power in 1843 they did abolish the state commission which had till then exerted a dampening influence upon the exuberant finance of some of the country banks.[16] But again opposition was primarily on the grounds of immediate expediency, rather than of general theory. And where their own interests dictated they never hesitated to invoke the machinery of the state. Thus, at the insistence of this element, many bank charters between 1792 and 1812 carried provisions for a fixed percentage of loans to the "agricultural interests."[17] For many years the same group fought for a state board to encourage farming by bounties, education, and other methods. Therein they sought only to extend long-standing practices; the Massachusetts Society for the Promotion of Agriculture had administered state aid since 1792, helped by a crop of local societies which sprang up in the next two

decades.[18] Throughout the period, rural communities were among the most active in getting the state to put its resources behind internal improvements so long as they were to their interest,[19] and the younger Theodore Sedgwick, who spoke for the rural communities, was active in the effort to have the state build the railroad from Boston to Albany.[20]

Other groups had less interest in the status quo and in the existing tendencies of state action; but when they thought of changes, they couched their ideas in terms of new state activities. Thus the artisans and handicraftsmen displaced by new industrial techniques opposed corporate monopolies, but asked the government to pass a ten-hour law, and to restrict immigration. And as a proletariat developed in the new factories, it too sought legislation in its own interest.[21]

Finally, the whole movement for humanitarian reform, so powerful in the two decades before the Civil War, espoused causes which infringed upon economic matters, and took for granted that the government could act in such spheres.[22] The receptive ground for laissez-faire thought was thus meagre indeed. Some reformers, like Amasa Walker, became free-traders on the score of their internationalism,[23] and isolated figures like A. L. Perry of Williams College, a follower of Bastiat, held liberal doctrines to a greater or lesser extent, but they were clearly exotic, without influence on the thought or action of the state.[24] Willard Phillips, criticizing Henry Carey's *Political Economy*, summarized Massachusetts opinion when he argued that it was useless to attempt to delimit the sphere of the state, for every action of government affected the economy: "Is it not evident to every man, that a vast proportion of the legislation and administra-

---

[13] Cf., e.g., E. B. Bigelow's demand for a new kind of stock company (*Remarks on the Depressed Condition of Manufactures in Massachusetts* [Boston, 1858]).

[14] *Mass. House Docs., 1845*, No. 50; *Mass. Senate Docs., 1846*, No. 81.

[15] Hamilton A. Hill, *Memoir of Abbott Lawrence* (Boston, 1884), 169.

[16] St. 1843, ch. 43, *Acts and Resolves . . .* (Boston, 1845), 26, 66; Arthur B. Darling, *Political Changes in Massachusetts . . .* (New Haven, 1925), 253; Harry E. Miller, *Banking Theories in the United States before 1860* (Cambridge, 1927), 148, 160, 161; W. S. Lake, History of Banking Regulation in Massachusetts, 1784–1860 (H. U. A., Ms., 1932), 175 ff.

[17] Miller, *Banking Theories*, 173.

[18] *Mass. Senate Docs., 1854*, No. 7, p. 10.

[19] Cf., e.g., J. H. Lockwood, ed., *Western Massachusetts* (New York, 1926), I, 207–224.

[20] *Dictionary of American Biography*, XVI, 551.

[21] Darling, *Political Changes in Massachusetts*, 198; John R. Commons, et al., *History of Labour in the United States* (New York, 1926), I, 291 ff., 302 ff., 493 ff., 536 ff., Seligman, "Economists," *Cambridge History of American Literature*, IV, 436 ff.

[22] Darling, *Political Changes in Massachusetts*, 157 ff.

[23] A. Walker, *Science of Wealth*, 5, 70, 90 ff., 269 ff., 318, 403 ff.; A. Walker, *Nature and Uses of Money and Mixed Currency* (Boston, 1857), 52; A. Walker, *Le Monde . . .* (London, 1859); A. Walker, *Suicidal Folly of the War-System* (Boston, 1863); Francis A. Walker, *Memoir of Hon. Amasa Walker, Ll.D.* (Boston, 1888), 6, 8–12.

[24] Carroll Perry, *Professor of Life, a Sketch of Arthur Latham Perry* (Boston, 1923), ch. 1; *Dictionary of American Biography*, XIV, 482; Walker, *Science of Wealth*, viii, 9.

tion of the laws, and the police regulations, have a prodigious effect, direct and indirect, upon productive activity. . . . Upon this subject we shall find the British economists most meagre and unsatisfactory. Only the newest and greenest legislators think of looking into their works for principles. The invocation of their authority excites the smile of men experienced in affairs." [25] And the cautious Governor Washburn in his legislative message of 1854 concluded that there was an "intimate connection . . . between the administration of a government and the business prosperity of its citizens." [26]

Already however there were tendencies which, after 1880, were to furnish the nourishment for the development of these scorned ideas. Influential elements in the state no longer needed the intervention of government and found state activities, hitherto an aid, now a hindrance. They sought in a new phrasing of laissez faire justifications for their own attitudes. To name these tendencies will throw light on the failure of the concept to flourish sooner.

As the scope of business widened, as the former merchants of Massachusetts became full-fledged industrial capitalists, their interests became national and international. In the field of railroading, for instance, while the Commonwealth still poured its funds into the Hoosac Tunnel in the vain attempt to wed its languishing seaport to the golden west, railroad men already preferred the New York route. For the sake of secure profits, the Boston and Albany passed by an opportunity to control the New York Central. The whole struggle over the management of the tunnel through the Berkshires and for control of the Boston, Hartford, and Erie Railroad showed the divergence between the objectives of the state and of those who owned the roads.[27] On a wider scale, the desire of some industrialists, like Edward Atkinson, to develop export markets in the 1870's led to dissatisfaction with restrictive tariffs and produced an embryonic free-trade movement, eventually organized formally in the Society for Political Education.[28]

No longer needing the state, business could now make use of the laissez-faire argument in repelling the attacks that mounted in bitterness after 1880. Criticism was not intellectual only, but, in Massachusetts, at least, was translated into action by effective legislation. There, for instance, restrictions on sweat shops drove the factory manufacture of ready-made clothing from Boston to New York in the 1890's. Such measures made converts to laissez-faire ideas among those who became convinced that the state could no longer aid but only obstruct their interests.

A number of intellectual changes implemented mounting laissez-faire feeling. First came a transformation in the character of the economic discipline. As late as 1880, Cliffe Leslie had noted that economics in the United States was written largely by practical men interested in specific and immediate problems.[29] After that date the science became increasingly academic, a trend marked by the establishment of numerous chairs in American colleges, by the founding of the American Economic Association in 1883, and by the publication of professional journals.[30] As the science grew professional and academic, economists lost their local ties and their connections with local interests. One could hardly speak of Dunbar or Carver or Taussig as Massachusetts men in the same sense as one could of Bowen, or Phillips, or the Walkers. In addition, as the science learned to stand on its own feet, there was a tendency to play down the role of government in order to take the political out of political economy.

Finally, new ideas had influence. After the Civil War the impact of Social Darwinism as expressed by such men as Fiske became felt. The extent of its real influence is still uncertain; but there is no doubt that for many groups the concept of survival of the fittest furnished a fresh philosophical foundation for laissez faire.[31] Similarly a new economic basis was supplied by the doctrines of marginal utility developed towards the end of the century partly independently and partly through the influence of the Austrian school.[32] In America, the concept of the vigilant consumer seeking the ultimate measure of marginal utility replaced the classical concept of benevolently selfish producers competing against each other. All these factors encouraged the spread of laissez-faire ideas as the century drew to a close. But until then the dominant tendencies were negative.

[25] *North American Review*, 1838, XLVII, 89 ff.

[26] *Mass. Senate Docs.*, 1854, No. 3, p. 5.

[27] C. F. Adams' chapter in Justin Winsor, *Memorial History of Boston* (Boston, 1881), IV, 111 ff., itself an example of the new attitude; also Matthew Josephson, *Robber Barons* (New York, 1934), 123 ff.; G. S. Merriam, *Life and Times of Samuel Bowles* (New York, 1885), II, 103 ff.; Harold F. Williamson, *Edward Atkinson* (Boston, 1934), 40 ff.

[28] F. B. Joyner, *David Ames Wells . . .* (Cedar Rapids, 1939), 147 ff.; Williamson, *Atkinson*, 37, 74 ff., 88, 148.

[29] Quoted in L. H. Haney, *History of Economic Thought* (New York, 1920), 614.

[30] Seligman, "Economists," *Cambridge History of American Literature*, IV, 441.

[31] T. C. Cochran and William Miller, *Age of Enterprise* (New York, 1942), 119 ff.; B. J. Loewenberg, "Darwinism Comes to America, 1859–1900," *Mississippi Valley Historical Review*, XXVIII (1941–1942), 339 ff.

[32] Gaétan Pirou, *L'utilité marginale de C. Menger à J.-B. Clark* (Paris, 1938), 229–281; F. A. Fetter, "Amerika," Hans Mayer, ed., *Die Wirtschaftstheorie der Gegenwart* (Wien, 1927), I, 41 ff.

III

The influence of adverse factors may be measured in the work of the most typical Massachusetts economist, Francis Bowen. There were some who went further than he in the rejection of laissez faire. John Rae, for instance, who came to Boston to publish his *Statement of Some New Principles . . .* (1834) because he felt its intellectual milieu most receptive to his ideas, denied completely the identity established by Adam Smith between public and private interests and public and private wealth, and thus undermined the whole laissez-faire doctrine. But Bowen was more typical; he accepted the basic premises of the classical thinkers and rejected their laissez-faire implications.

Long editor of the *North American Review* and professor of political economy at Harvard, Bowen was a prolific writer of articles on many subjects. His chief economic work, *Principles of Political Economy Applied to the Condition, the Resources, and the Institutions of the American People* (Boston, 1856) was first delivered in a series of popular lectures, and then published as a textbook, dedicated to Nathan Appleton, one of "the Merchant Princes of Boston." It represents accurately the dominant trend in the economic thinking of Massachusetts.[33]

Starting with fundamentals essentially the same as those of the English writers, Bowen reached conclusions essentially different. With the most optimistic, he believed in a natural order, in "a wise and benevolent arrangement of Providence" that converted individual selfishness into a public good. Consequently he could, *a priori*, and, in theory, accept the whole liberal argument. Government action only marred the perfection of the natural order. The function of legislation was "not to meddle with the general laws of the universe" but "to remove all casual and unnatural impediments from that path which society instinctively chooses for itself."[34]

In the abstract, however, this theory was meaningless to Bowen. It acquired significance only in the application to the concrete, practical configuration of the entire economy. English ideas grew out of English circumstances. "Such theories as those of Malthus upon population, Ricardo upon rent and profits, Adam Smith upon free trade, and McCulloch upon . . . the succession to property . . . originated from experience in an anomalous state of society, from observation of the laws of wealth as exemplified in their operation under very peculiar circumstances."[35] To arrive at an American system, the general laws of wealth had to be tailored to fit American circumstances.[36]

In the application, Bowen transformed the general laws. Thus, the ideal system of free trade was impractical because imperfections in the law of nations made it necessary that each country be independent economically as well as politically and justified tariffs to protect infant industries, an argument for a national economy repeated endlessly by publicists like Everett and Phillips.[37] Also on the count of inconsistency with American conditions, Bowen rejected the Malthusian view on population. He used against it an argument developed earlier by A. H. Everett who attempted to show in *New Ideas on Population* (1823) that a rise in numbers led to greater division of labor and therefore to greater abundance.[38] Ricardo's theory of rent was set aside on the familiar grounds that in the United States increases in population produced lower prices for lands first settled as frontier areas were brought under cultivation.[39] The theory of gluts and crises was similarly modified, and the classical concepts of a "natural" rate of wages at the subsistence level and of a wage fund were refuted by a line of reasoning which anticipated Francis Walker.[40]

In these applications of general theory to American conditions Bowen found that, in practice, private and public interests were not identical and therefore that state interference was sometimes necessary. Consistently, he belabored the point that laissez-faire doctrines were made to fit a special set of English circumstances; in the United States they could not be applied unchanged.[41] Logical or not, his contentions convinced his contemporaries.

IV

At this point an inevitable question rises: Why was American experience, as exemplified in Massachusetts, so different from that of European countries at a similar economic level? Perhaps not many students of English history would still agree with the well-known work which affirmed that after Waterloo: "Nothing remained which could possibly check the advent of laissez faire. Free competition became universal. The state re-

---

[33] Bowen, *Principles*, iii, vi. The work passed through five editions, 1856–1868, and was rewritten in 1870. The basic features of his system remained unchanged however.

[34] *Ibid.*, 20, 22, 23; *North American Review*, 1851, LXXII, 419.

[35] Bowen, *Principles*, 522.

[36] Bowen, *Principles*, 13 ff.

[37] *Ibid.*, 24, 25, 457 ff.; *North American Review*, 1851, LXXII, 414; also A. H. Everett, *ibid.*, XXX, 160 ff., XXXII, 127 ff.; Willard Phillips, *Protection and Free Trade* (Boston, 1850).

[38] Bowen, *Principles*, 131 ff. Cf. also Walker, *Science of Wealth*, 452 ff.

[39] Bowen, *Principles*, 164 ff. This became the basis for an ingenious, if unconvincing, tariff argument (*ibid.*, 192).

[40] *Ibid.*, 193 ff., 237 ff., 271.

[41] *Ibid.*, vi, vii, 457 ff.

nounced all rights of interference either with the organization of production or with the relations between masters and men." [42] Undoubtedly the old picture of bright and sturdy liberal ideas marching forth from Manchester to sweep English politics before them, needs considerable modification.[43] But England did produce a consistent and well-developed body of laissez-faire thought from which, whatever the degree of their real influence, justifications for policy could be drawn. The United States had not even a von Thünen or a Bastiat.

European laissez faire had no counterpart here because in England and on the continent it filled a need which did not exist in America. Across the ocean, thoughtful men concerned with economic problems found a large body of practice and law standing in the way of swiftly moving economic developments. These obstacles and restrictions stemmed from the government and, often thrown together under the general designation mercantilism, were uniformly fought. That is why it was always easier to say what laissez faire opposed than what it favored. In America, this body of ideas was never needed because the practices and laws it was designed to combat never existed, or were early eliminated. Some, like guild or manorial restrictions, never were successfully transplanted to the new world; others, like the acts of trade and navigation, were liquidated by the War for Independence; and still

others, like primogeniture, entail, and quit rents, were wiped out by revolutions within the new states. Frontier conditions also stood in the way; thus the Northwest Ordinance of 1787 decided that the United States would have no colonies for more than a century. And finally, the relative newness of the country, and the comparative swiftness of economic developments precluded legal formalism and rigidity in institutions. The corporation, for instance, was a much more flexible institution than in Adam Smith's England, and the laws of mills and roads were susceptible of innumerable adaptations to new circumstances. Laissez-faire thought failed to develop because there was no place for it in the life of Massachusetts as of the rest of the nation.

If this paper has proved its subject not worth talking about, it has served its function. Discussion of the development of economic policy in terms of laissez faire is hardly meaningful. The issues in the determination of American economic policy through most of the nineteenth century were not whether the government had or had not a role in the economy, but, what was to be the character of its role, what agencies were to exercise it, who was to control it, and in whose interests it was to operate. As for theory, ideas phrased in terms of laissez faire were so rare and so thoroughly divorced from reality and practice that they remained almost completely sterile.

William N. Chambers, in sketching Jackson's career, evaluated his significance in American history. "At the core of Jackson's importance for the American tradition," he wrote, "are four great themes or issues: equalitarianism, democracy, and—as instruments —strong presidential leadership and party action."

WILLIAM N. CHAMBERS: JACKSON: REPRESENTATIVE MAN OF AN ERA*

The evil lay in schemes to make "rich men . . . richer by act of Congress," and deny the fundamental principle of "equal protection and

[42] Charles Gide and Charles Rist, *History of Economic Doctrines,* 170; Paul Mombert, *Geschichte der Nationalökonomie* (Jena, 1927), 277 ff., 307 ff.; Gerald Berkeley Hertz, *British Imperialism* (London, 1908), 123.

[43] G. B. Hertz, *Manchester Politician 1750–1912* (London, 1912), 27–56; Kenneth O. Walker, "Classical Economists and the Factory Acts," *The Journal of Economic History,* 1941, I, 168 ff.

* Reprinted from Morton Borden, ed., *America's Ten Greatest Presidents* (Chicago: Rand McNally & Company, 1961), pp. 81–84, 105–6, 107–12 by permission.

equal benefits," Andrew Jackson proclaimed. He was defending in July, 1832, his veto of a bill to recharter the Bank of the United States for another twenty years. Privately, his confidante and later vice president recalled, he had exclaimed in the midst of a wasting illness, "The bank, Mr. Van Buren, is trying to kill me, *but I will kill it!*" The rhetoric, and Jackson's dogged conviction of his own rectitude as the voice of the popular will against sinister forces, suggest a key to his controversial presidency. Under scrutiny, they also point to ambiguities in the movement Jackson led.

Some presidents attain stature chiefly by their specific achievements; others, significantly by their symbolic representation of important national values. Among the first we find a Polk or a Truman; among the second a Jefferson, an Abraham

Lincoln, or a Franklin D. Roosevelt—and Jackson. Some presidents, of course, are significant in both ways, but in the case of Old Hickory it is certainly less his accomplishments that make him memorable than what he stood for. The Bank issue and other acrid controversies of his two terms from 1829 to 1837 are dry dust. His basic moral and political perspective, and his political style, however, retain relevance a century and a quarter later. In short, Jackson was *the* complex, even contradictory, representative man of an era that was not only colorful and contradictory in itself, but formative of the nation as well. Not only his presidency, but substantially his whole career, symbolize deep forces in his America.

At the core of Jackson's importance for the American tradition are four great themes or issues: equalitarianism, democracy, and—as instruments—strong presidential leadership and political party action. Each was the product of earlier history; yet each also bore the imprint of Jackson's commitment and purpose. Finally, each contained the seeds of unresolved problems. Thus, Jackson has been subject to hero-worship and demonology not only in his own time, but at the hands of historians down to our own day.

Stresses toward broadened liberal democracy and equalitarianism were central elements in the Jacksonian perspective. A liberal tradition, in the sense of emphasis on the value of the individual, and a pervading equalitarian ethos as an aspect of the tradition, have been practically indigenous in American soil. In contrast with European nations with their feudal tradition, new America quickly achieved substantial democracy in the form of open competition of groups and parties, free elections, and representative government, together with substantial consensus on settling controversies by vote, not revolt. In addition, "this American, this new man," as Crèvecoeur called him, enjoyed relative freedom from fixed class and social distinctions, and relatively widely-diffused opportunity and welfare. This was the case well before Jackson's presidency. What Jackson as the leader of a many-faceted movement did, was to represent the impulses of equality and democracy at a critical juncture, and *extend* them in idea and action.

These impulses of equality and democracy were embroiled, in the context of the era, with conflicting views of the good life. To Jackson in certain moods, and to purist Jacksonians, one view represented welfare for the many; another, the interests of a few; but other forces in the Jacksonian complex saw the issue differently. The nation had begun as an agricultural domain of farmers and planters, with commerce and manufactures subordinate. As Jefferson, John Tyler, and other prophets of pristine democracy saw it, an agrarian base of small property-holding farmers in a rough equality of condition was the best of all soils for nurturing a simple, republican way of life.

The forces of trade, industry, and finance were not so easily contained, however. Factors from normal economic growth to the strenuous efforts of Hamilton and of Henry Clay in his "American System" to promote hothouse capitalist development through a national bank, protective tariffs, and "internal improvements," produced an economic expansion which was happily embraced by venturesome Americans with their eyes on economic gain. As one of Jackson's chief disciples put it, Americans were a "go-ahead people." In the 1830's opportunities to "go ahead" in making money seemed nearly everywhere.

Thus, the eighteenth-century dream of a simple, equalitarian freeholder's republic came into conflict with a new nineteenth-century vision of enterprise unlimited, in which "equality" would mean equality in chances for economic acquisition and advancement. This issue, the conflict of perspectives of Enterprise and perspectives of Arcadia, with all of the questions it posed for the meaning of equality in the American way of life, was the ordeal of the Jacksonian experience. Not only Jackson himself, but many of his disciples were torn by tensions between these two sets of values.

Old Hickory was always perceived by his followers as a "people's president." As one of them put it on the occasion of his first inauguration in 1829, a marshalling of popular fervor typical of his presidency, "It was a proud day for the *people*—General Jackson is *their own* president!" Repeatedly, Jackson drew on this reservoir of popular excitement to support a style of presidential leadership which was bold, dramatic, and aggressive. He performed in the office in a fashion hardly conceived by Washington and scarcely touched by Jefferson, to say nothing of such *roisfainéants* among Jackson's immediate predecessors as the bedevilled Madison and the feckless Monroe. Jackson's presidential practice suggests the twentieth-century Roosevelts in manner, though not in content or policy. It was exhibited in his dramatic and often polemical messages to Congress and in his direct appeals to public opinion—in his frequent showdowns with the legislative branch, as well as in repeated instances of decisive executive action. Unquestionably, Jackson contributed powerfully to establishing the pattern of strong presidential leadership as a force for coherence in American government, fragmented as it is through the separation of powers and federalism.

He also played a catalytic role in party development, particularly as a folk hero and dramatic leader around whom party forces could combine. The decade previous to Jackson's advent was a period of party collapse. In the late 1820's, however, a new party began to grow around him as a "people's candidate." And during his presidency the work of party formation was carried forward through organization and patronage and through partisan issues his policies produced. Thus Jackson stands as the saint and symbol of the founding of the modern Democratic party—and also as the spur to the Whig opposition of 1834 and after. By 1840 the United States could at last claim a mass-based, institutionalized two-party system.

A nation, like a man, *is* in large degree what it *became* in its formative years. Thus Jackson and the American themes he symbolized at a crucial stage in national development possess immediacy today—not just on the ritual occasions of his party, but in our whole confrontation of public problems. He was not an intellectual in the sense Jefferson was; he left us no significant philosophy or reflections on fundamentals of politics. What Jackson did bequeath was an example of energy, and a perspective, a broad pattern of faiths, commitments, and loyalties. . . .

In the 1830's Jackson and his cohorts were generally triumphant in rhetoric and politics. As a dramatic, charismatic leader and president he did much to shape the outlook and character of the age. In succeeding decades the capitalist development and spirit of Enterprise which also cut channels across the 1830's, sometimes in cross-current to Jacksonian directions, sometimes in a parallel stream, surged to new high-water marks. The dream of Arcadia—in the age of Jackson already part myth, part nostalgia—became in the age of Carnegie the pathos of a lost cause. Long after Jackson died at the Hermitage in 1845, however, already in the process of being canonized as a popular saint, his essence lived on. It survived in the broad perspective he symbolized and bequeathed to the American tradition. . . .

National self-discovery is never-ending, and reflective reconsideration of the themes of Jackson's presidency may help promote the quest. We can never in an age of organization recapture the simple, atomistic democracy he spoke for; his nineteenth-century policy prescriptions provide no specifics for the health of the twentieth-century body politic. Yet his larger perspective is relevant today—in part because it contained the seeds of still unresolved problems.

The equalitarian urge gives rise to a tangle of complex questions. Under Jackson, it was bent against economic and social privilege; life's good things were to go not only to "the few, the rich, and the well-born," as a Federalist ideologist put it, but to the "many" or "majority." Today the "many" no longer own the property from which they derive their living. Concentration in great corporations employing vast thousands sets an economic and bureaucratic climate for gradations of status and power. Supplemented by insensitivity to personal distinction, this atmosphere generates a compensatory scramble for materially-based status and recognition. How, then, can the equalitarian impulse be sustained as a living force? Unless we are indeed doomed to invidious rule by a "power elite"—in the dubious hypothesis of C. Wright Mills—the hope of equality may lie in further diffusion of economic well-being and social acceptance, and in a calmer climate which reduces the anxieties of status-seeking through greater assurance in individual identities

and roles. Over-all, lacking a Jacksonian base of self-sufficient freeholders, equality today may depend on a pattern in which nineteenth-century economic individualism is circumscribed, and concentrated economic power is met by countervailing powers of Government, union organization, regulation for public purposes of both business and unions, and of group associations of many kinds. Equality and well-being may also be promoted by a more purposeful balance of expenditure in the public sector of the economy, from schools to housing and parks, as compared with the private sector. Such possibilities hardly revive the pristine, individualistic equalitarianism of Jackson, but any attempt at such revival can only be a form of nostalgia. They may, however, constitute contemporary applications of his basic theme.

The still-unconquered frontier of minimum equalitarianism, of course, is in overt discrimination and unspoken prejudice against racial and religious minorities—a problem that requires not only good will but energy (public and private) and time for solution.

Yet, other questions remain. A latent danger in being born equal, which de Tocqueville noted in Jackson's era, lurks in the potentiality of negation of the exceptional by the mediocre, of conformist leveling of individual personality. To our own day, such stresses have prompted ambivalent denigrations of intellect, judgment, and meaningful leaders-in-action, while we exalt organization-age "smooth dealers" or special heroes. Such figures, particularly as they may be shaped by Madison Avenue image-mongering, can deceive us. The charisma of Old Hickory pointed the way to hurrahs for meaningless Old Tippecanoe in a cynically-contrived bandwagon campaign in 1840 and to future triumphs for hero-images from Grant to Eisenhower. It is easy to see as "great men" figures whose aura is commanding but whose creativity and boldness in leadership is at least debatable. The problem, which Jackson only touched in a more inner-directed age, lies in reshaping the equalitarian perspective to accept personal individuality, encourage variety, cherish the exceptional, and extend intellect and critical judgment. In this connection, Jackson's personality and address have something to offer for our day in his very individuality, ahead-of-the-crowd leadership and dogged commitment.

Such questions, together with much of Jackson's political style, also raise problems for democratic functioning. To an important degree, his appeal evoked mass emotive identifications with Jackson-hero and with ambiguous rhetoric. Thus, the satisfactions he provided were composed as much or more of cathexis and symbolism as of fulfillment of concrete interests. This is often the way in politics—we may find warm gratification in seeing *our* men, and thus *our* perspectives or *our* hopes, ascendent in public symbolism. So reformers could enjoy happy identification with Franklin Roosevelt, innumerable middle-class

Americans with the likeable image of "Ike" Eisenhower, and intellectuals with Adlai Stevenson, because each seemed to speak in *their* way—whatever they meant to others. A crucial distinction remains for democracy, however. It is the extent to which appeal-and-response involves not only personality images, but also some measure of popular choice on concrete issues—some chance to judge candidates on the grounds of policies they espouse. As Jackson became a spokesman for significant policies, he, with his party, helped to extend such choice. Successor hero-candidates have not always undertaken such commitments. When elections are left to revolve around candidate-orientation to the detriment of issue-orientation, the meaning of electoral choices is smudged, the effect of elections on public decisions is attenuated.

Strong presidential leadership, by shaping policy and clarifying alternatives, may further democratic values. A president who seeks to harness the wonderful three-horse shay of the separated executive, legislative, and judicial branches, who grasps the whip of party leadership, may make much of the potential scope and weight of presidential power as an agent of purposes of the "many," even of a "majority." He may use it, as Jackson largely did, in a negative fashion to restrain impulses he and the preponderant opinion oppose. He may make it, as Franklin Roosevelt did, a majority-based force for positive Government intervention through policy innovation. If he does so, he is bound to provoke counterappeals to the deeply-ingrained American fear of concentrations of political power, such as the Whig cry of "executive despotism." In fact, strong presidents from Jackson and Lincoln to the two Roosevelts have not subverted our liberties. Furthermore, an age of complex problems, massive economic organization, and nuclear threat seems particularly to require energetic presidential leadership as a force for coherence. Yet, how much dependence do we want to place on one man, or more properly on one office? and how may we hold him responsible? There is no ready answer; presumably proximate solutions will evolve, as they did in Jackson's era, as different men take the presidential reins. One answer, however, which can be argued as an extension of the Jacksonian sense-of-purpose in our less-individualistic, organized contemporary context, may lie in efforts to strengthen tendencies toward coherence at other points of power. These would include parties, Congress, Federal-state-municipal relationships, and administration.

Such considerations inevitably raise continuing problems of party structure and action, again taking us back to Jacksonian origins. At the outset, the Jackson party was a democratic instrument, not only in terms of interparty democratic competition, but of intraparty democracy in its structure. Internally it was broadly representative of its popular power-base. Yet it was also a party of organization, and a "party of politicians"—who became more and more like Disraeli's contemporaneous fictional characters, Tadpole and Taper, who swam in the muddy waters of opinion and lined up votes. As the professionalization of politicians spread, the party was increasingly vulnerable to domination by the cadre who managed it and who saw the chance to make their own purposes the party purposes. *Hoi polloi* symbolism derived from Jackson's ascendency, gradually emptied of all but residual meaning, became a cover for manipulation. Thus, both Democrats and Whigs tended to what Ostrogorski called "democratic formalism," in which party organs, particularly conventions, often spoke in the name of "the people," without significant interaction between that "people" and party managers. Thus by the 1850's the party of Jackson had spawned prototypes of the classical boss and machine depending on patronage, other spoils, corruption, and coercion. The old-style boss and his graft-greased behemoth are practically extinct, but problems rooted in organization and professionalization remain. By its very nature, the party structure Jackson and his followers bequeathed to us entails a continuing tension between tendencies to oligarchy and self-serving manipulation on the one hand and impulses to intraparty democracy on the other. The result depends on popular attitudes and participation, as well as on the conduct of professional politicians. The issue marks another point at which unresolved problems of the Jacksonian perspective intersect our own times.

Finally, as the broadest link between the public on one side and public decisions on the other, parties offer potentialities of mobilizing support for coherent policy. Furthermore, the intraparty democracy of electoral competition and continuing criticism may provide some check over presidential power. Thus the radical Jackson, like the conservative Burke before him, could see party action as "a situation of power and energy," though Jackson left the notion of party as a check-rein mostly to his Whig opposition. Today, however, we may wonder if our parties will develop the requisite power and energy. Despite organization superior to that of Jackson's day, American parties are still relatively loose-jointed, federal, and heterogeneous—ill-equipped to channel the pluralistic swirl of groups and opinions into coherent action. This is the structure many party figures believe the parties ought to maintain, to be sure, though some tendencies toward articulation and nationalization are discernible. The complex tensions of the twentieth century, meanwhile, make the job simply bigger than it was in Jackson's easier era. Finally, the 1950's, somewhat like the span of the Monroe years, have shown signs of decline in party standing with the electorate. This decline is evidenced in negative attitudes toward parties and in more independent or "floating" voters, or ticket-splitters and "switchers." Whether our parties will enjoy a new resurgence as instruments of democracy, as they did under Jackson, is an open question.

"A second-class intellect," Mr. Justice Holmes remarked, *"but a first-class temperament."* Though he was speaking of Franklin Roosevelt, the comment might well have been made of Jackson, who offered little in the way of philosophy but much in energy, perspective, and example. The themes of democracy and equalitarianism he symbolized remain with us—as presidential leadership and party action continue to be our best public hopes for implementing them.

Andrew Jackson in his Farewell Address, March 4, 1837, proclaimed that the government must act within its proper constitutional limits and not engage in heavy taxation for "lavish expenditures." Directing his gaze to the monetary and banking system, Jackson warned that these factors were responsible for the "spirit of monopoly."

ANDREW JACKSON:
FAREWELL ADDRESS*

It is well known that there have always been those amongst us who wish to enlarge the powers of the General Government, and experience would seem to indicate that there is a tendency on the part of this Government to overstep the boundaries marked out for it by the Constitution. Its legitimate authority is abundantly sufficient for all the purposes for which it was created, and its powers being expressly enumerated, there can be no justification for claiming anything beyond them. Every attempt to exercise power beyond these limits should be promptly and firmly opposed, for one evil example will lead to other measures still more mischievous; and if the principle of constructive powers or supposed advantages or temporary circumstances shall ever be permitted to justify the assumption of a power not given by the Constitution, the General Government will before long absorb all the powers of legislation, and you will have in effect but one consolidated government. From the extent of our country, its diversified interests, different pursuits, and different habits, it is too obvious for argument that a single consolidated government would be wholly inadequate to watch over and protect its interests; and every friend of our free institutions should be always prepared to maintain unimpaired and in full vigor the rights and sovereignty of the States and to confine the action of the General Government strictly to the sphere of its appropriate duties.

There is, perhaps, no one of the powers conferred on the Federal Government so liable to abuse as the taxing power. The most productive and convenient sources of revenue were necessarily given to it, that it might be able to perform the important duties imposed upon it; and the taxes which it lays upon commerce being concealed from the real payer in the price of the article, they do not so readily attract the attention of the people as smaller sums demanded from them directly by the taxgatherer. But the tax imposed on goods enhances by so much the price of the commodity to the consumer, and as many of these duties are imposed on articles of necessity which are daily used by the great body of the people, the money raised by these imposts is drawn from their pockets. Congress has no right under the Constitution to take money from the people unless it is required to execute some one of the specific powers intrusted to the Government; and if they raise more than is necessary for such purposes, it is an abuse of the power of taxation, and unjust and oppressive. It may indeed happen that the revenue will sometimes exceed the amount anticipated when the taxes were laid. When, however, this is ascertained, it is easy to reduce them, and in such a case it is unquestionably the duty of the Government to reduce them, for no circumstances can justify it in assuming a power not given to it by the Constitution nor in taking away the money of the people when it is not needed for the legitimate wants of the Government.

Plain as these principles appear to be, you will yet find there is a constant effort to induce the General Government to go beyond the limits of its taxing power and to impose unnecessary burdens upon the people. Many powerful interests are continually at work to procure heavy duties on commerce and to swell the revenue beyond the real necessities of the public service, and the country has already felt the injurious effects of their combined influence. They succeeded in obtaining a tariff of duties bearing most oppressively on the agricultural and laboring classes of society and producing a revenue that could not be usefully employed within the range of the powers conferred upon Congress, and in order to fasten

* Reprinted from James D. Richardson, ed., *A Compilation of the Messages and Papers of the Presidents, 1789–1897* (Washington, D.C.: 1900), III, 298–306.

upon the people this unjust and unequal system of taxation extravagant schemes of internal improvement were got up in various quarters to squander the money and to purchase support. Thus one unconstitutional measure was intended to be upheld by another, and the abuse of the power of taxation was to be maintained by usurping the power of expending the money in internal improvements. You can not have forgotten the severe and doubtful struggle through which we passed when the executive department of the Government by its veto endeavored to arrest this prodigal scheme of injustice and to bring back the legislation of Congress to the boundaries prescribed by the Constitution. The good sense and practical judgment of the people when the subject was brought before them sustained the course of the Executive, and this plan of unconstitutional expenditures for the purposes of corrupt influence is, I trust, finally overthrown.

The result of this decision has been felt in the rapid extinguishment of the public debt and the large accumulation of a surplus in the Treasury, notwithstanding the tariff was reduced and is now very far below the amount originally contemplated by its advocates. But, rely upon it, the design to collect an extravagant revenue and to burden you with taxes beyond the economical wants of the Government is not yet abandoned. The various interests which have combined together to impose a heavy tariff and to produce an overflowing Treasury are too strong and have too much at stake to surrender the contest. The corporations and wealthy individuals who are engaged in large manufacturing establishments desire a high tariff to increase their gains. Designing politicians will support it to conciliate their favor and to obtain the means of profuse expenditure for the purpose of purchasing influence in other quarters; and since the people have decided that the Federal Government can not be permitted to employ its income in internal improvements, efforts will be made to seduce and mislead the citizens of the several States by holding out to them the deceitful prospect of benefits to be derived from a surplus revenue collected by the General Government and annually divided among the States; and if, encouraged by these fallacious hopes, the States should disregard the principles of economy which ought to characterize every republican government, and should indulge in lavish expenditures exceeding their resources, they will before long find themselves oppressed with debts which they are unable to pay, and the temptation will become irresistible to support a high tariff in order to obtain a surplus for distribution. Do not allow yourselves, my fellow-citizens, to be misled on this subject. The Federal Government can not collect a surplus for such purposes without violating the principles of the Constitution and assuming powers which have not been granted. It is, moreover, a system of injustice, and if persisted in will inevitably lead to corruption, and must end in ruin. The surplus reve-nue will be drawn from the pockets of the people —from the farmer, the mechanic, and the laboring classes of society; but who will receive it when distributed among the States, where it is to be disposed of by leading State politicians, who have friends to favor and political partisans to gratify? It will certainly not be returned to those who paid it and who have most need of it and are honestly entitled to it. There is but one safe rule, and that is to confine the General Government rigidly within the sphere of its appropriate duties. It has no power to raise a revenue or impose taxes except for the purposes enumerated in the Constitution, and if its income is found to exceed these wants it should be forthwith reduced and the burden of the people so far lightened.

In reviewing the conflicts which have taken place between different interests in the United States and the policy pursued since the adoption of our present form of Government, we find nothing that has produced such deep-seated evil as the course of legislation in relation to the currency. The Constitution of the United States unquestionably intended to secure to the people a circulating medium of gold and silver. But the establishment of a national bank by Congress, with the privilege of issuing paper money receivable in the payment of the public dues, and the unfortunate course of legislation in the several States upon the same subject, drove from general circulation the constitutional currency and substituted one of paper in its place.

It was not easy for men engaged in the ordinary pursuits of business, whose attention had not been particularly drawn to the subject, to foresee all the consequences of a currency exclusively of paper, and we ought not on that account to be surprised at the facility with which laws were obtained to carry into effect the paper system. Honest and even enlightened men are sometimes misled by the specious and plausible statements of the designing. But experience has now proved the mischiefs and dangers of a paper currency, and it rests with you to determine whether the proper remedy shall be applied.

The paper system being founded on public confidence and having of itself no intrinsic value, it is liable to great and sudden fluctuations, thereby rendering property insecure and the wages of labor unsteady and uncertain. The corporations which create the paper money can not be relied upon to keep the circulating medium uniform in amount. In times of prosperity, when confidence is high, they are tempted by the prospect of gain or by the influence of those who hope to profit by it to extend their issues of paper beyond the bounds of discretion and the reasonable demands of business; and when these issues have been pushed on from day to day, until public confidence is at length shaken, then a reaction takes place, and they immediately withdraw the credits they have given, suddenly curtail their issues, and produce an unexpected and ruinous contraction of the circulating medium, which is felt by the whole community. The banks by this means save themselves, and the mischievous consequences of their imprudence or cupidity are visited upon the public. Nor does the evil stop here. These ebbs and flows in the currency and these indiscreet extensions of credit naturally engender a spirit of speculation injurious to the habits and character of the people. We have already seen its effects in the wild spirit of speculation in the public lands and various kinds of stock which within the last year or two seized upon such a multitude of our citizens and threatened to pervade all classes of society and to withdraw their attention from the sober pursuits of honest industry. It is not by encouraging this spirit that we shall best preserve public virtue and promote the true interests of our country; but if your currency continues as exclusively paper as it now is, it will foster this eager desire to amass wealth without labor; it will multiply the number of dependents on bank accommodations and bank favors; the temptation to obtain money at any sacrifice will become stronger and stronger, and inevitably lead to corruption, which will find its way into your public councils and destroy at no distant day the purity of your Government. Some of the evils which arise from this system of paper press with peculiar hardship upon the class of society least able to bear it. A portion of this currency frequently becomes depreciated or worthless, and all of it is easily counterfeited in such a manner as to require peculiar skill and much experience to distinguish the counterfeit from the genuine note. These frauds are most generally perpetrated in the smaller notes, which are used in the daily transactions of ordinary business, and the losses occasioned by them are commonly thrown upon the laboring classes of society, whose situation and pursuits put it out of their power to guard themselves from these impositions, and whose daily wages are necessary for their subsistence. It is the duty of every government so to regulate its currency as to protect this numerous class, as far as practicable, from the impositions of avarice and fraud. It is more especially the duty of the United States, where the Government is emphatically the Government of the people, and where this respectable portion of our citizens are so proudly distinguished from the laboring classes of all other nations by their independent spirit, their love of liberty, their intelligence, and their high tone of moral character. Their industry in peace is the source of our wealth and their bravery in war has covered us with glory; and the Government of the United States will but ill discharge its duties if it leaves them a prey to such dishonest impositions. Yet it is evident that their interests can not be effectually protected unless silver and gold are restored to circulation.

These views alone of the paper currency are sufficient to call for immediate reform; but there is another consideration which should still more strongly press it upon your attention.

Recent events have proved that the paper money system of this country may be used as an engine to undermine your free institutions, and that those who desire to engross all power in the hands of the few and to govern by corruption or force are aware of its power and prepared to employ it. Your banks now furnish your only circulating medium, and money is plenty or scarce according to the quantity of notes issued by them. While they have capitals not greatly disproportioned to each other, they are competitors in business, and no one of them can exercise dominion over the rest; and although in the present state of the currency these banks may and do operate injuriously upon the habits of business, the pecuniary concerns, and the moral tone of society, yet, from their number and dispersed situation, they can not combine for the purposes of political influence, and whatever may be the dispositions of some of them their power of mischief must necessarily be confined to a narrow space and felt only in their immediate neighborhoods.

But when the charter for the Bank of the United States was obtained from Congress it perfected the schemes of the paper system and gave to its advocates the position they have struggled to obtain from the commencement of the Federal Government to the present hour. The immense capital and peculiar privileges bestowed upon it enabled it to exercise despotic sway over the other banks in every part of the country. From its superior strength it could seriously injure, if not destroy, the business of any one of them which might incur its resentment; and it openly claimed for itself the power of regulating the currency throughout the United States. In other words, it asserted (and it undoubtedly possessed) the power to make money plenty or scarce at its pleasure, at any time and in any quarter of the Union, by controlling the issues of other banks and permitting an expansion or compelling a general contraction of the circulating medium, according to its own will. The other banking institutions were sensible of its strength, and they soon generally became its obedient instruments, ready at all times to execute its mandates; and with the banks necessarily went also that numerous class of persons in our commercial cities who depend altogether on bank credits for their solvency and means of business, and who are therefore obliged, for their own safety, to propitiate the favor of the money power by distinguished zeal and devotion in its service. The result of the ill-advised legislation which established this great monopoly was to concentrate the whole moneyed power of the Union, with its boundless means of corruption and its numerous dependents, under the direction and command of one acknowledged head, thus organizing this particular interest as one body and securing to it unity and concert of action throughout the United States, and enabling it to bring forward upon any occasion its entire and undivided strength to support or defeat any measure of the Government. In the hands of this formidable power, thus perfectly organized, was also placed unlimited dominion over the amount of the circulating medium, giving it the power to regulate the value of property and the fruits of labor in every quarter of the Union, and to bestow prosperity or bring ruin upon any city or section of the country as might best comport with its own interest or policy.

We are not left to conjecture how the moneyed power, thus organized and with such a weapon in its hands, would be likely to use it. The distress and alarm which pervaded and agitated the whole country when the Bank of the United States waged war upon the people in order to compel them to submit to its demands can not yet be forgotten. The ruthless and unsparing temper with which whole cities and communities were oppressed, individuals impoverished and ruined, and a scene of cheerful prosperity suddenly changed into one of gloom and despondency ought to be indelibly impressed on the memory of the people of the United States. If such was its power in a time of peace, what would it not have been in a season of war, with an enemy at your doors? No nation but the freemen of the United States could have come out victorious from such a contest; yet, if you had not conquered, the Government would have passed from the hands of the many to the hands of the few, and this organized money power from its secret conclave would have dictated the choice of your highest officers and compelled you to make peace or war, as best suited their own wishes. The forms of your Government might for a time have remained, but its living spirit would have departed from it.

The distress and sufferings inflicted on the people by the bank are some of the fruits of that system of policy which is continually striving to enlarge the authority of the Federal Government beyond the limits fixed by the Constitution. The powers enumerated in that instrument do not confer on Congress the right to establish such a corporation as the Bank of the United States, and the evil consequences which followed may warn us of the danger of departing from the true rule of construction and of permitting temporary circumstances or the hope of better promoting the public welfare to influence in any degree our decisions upon the extent of the authority of the General Government. Let us abide by the Constitution as it is written, or amend it in the constitutional mode if it is found to be defective.

The severe lessons of experience will, I doubt not, be sufficient to prevent Congress from again chartering such a monopoly, even if the Constitution did not present an insuperable objection to it. But you must remember, my fellow-citizens, that eternal vigilance by the people is the price of liberty, and that you must pay the price if you wish to secure the blessing. It behooves you, therefore, to be watchful in your States as well as in the Federal Government. The power which the moneyed interest can exercise, when concentrated under a single head and with our present system

of currency, was sufficiently demonstrated in the struggle made by the Bank of the United States. Defeated in the General Government, the same class of intriguers and politicians will now resort to the States and endeavor to obtain there the same organization which they failed to perpetuate in the Union; and with specious and deceitful plans of public advantages and State interests and State pride they will endeavor to establish in the different States one moneyed institution with overgrown capital and exclusive privileges sufficient to enable it to control the operations of the other banks. Such an institution will be pregnant with the same evils produced by the Bank of the United States, although its sphere of action is more confined, and in the State in which it is chartered the money power will be able to embody its whole strength and to move together with undivided force to accomplish any object it may wish to attain. You have already had abundant evidence of its power to inflict injury upon the agricultural, mechanical, and laboring classes of society, and over those whose engagements in trade or speculation render them dependent on bank facilities the dominion of the State monopoly will be absolute and their obedience unlimited. With such a bank and a paper currency the money power would in a few years govern the State and control its measures, and if a sufficient number of States can be induced to create such establishments the time will soon come when it will again take the field against the United States and succeed in perfecting and perpetuating its organization by a charter from Congress.

It is one of the serious evils of our present system of banking that it enables one class of society—and that by no means a numerous one—by its control over the currency, to act injuriously upon the interests of all the others and to exercise more than its just proportion of influence in political affairs. The agricultural, the mechanical, and the laboring classes have little or no share in the direction of the great moneyed corporations, and from their habits and the nature of their pursuits they are incapable of forming extensive combinations to act together with united force. Such concert of action may sometimes be produced in a single city or in a small district of country by means of personal communications with each other, but they have no regular or active correspondence with those who are engaged in similar pursuits in distant places; they have but little patronage to give to the press, and exercise but a small share of influence over it; they have no crowd of dependents about them who hope to grow rich without labor by their countenance and favor, and who are therefore always ready to execute their wishes. The planter, the farmer, the mechanic, and the laborer all know that their success depends upon their own industry and economy, and that they must not expect to become suddenly rich by the fruits of their toil. Yet these classes of society form the great body of the people of the United States; they are the bone and sinew of the country—men who love liberty and desire nothing but equal rights and equal laws, and who, moreover, hold the great mass of our national wealth, although it is distributed in moderate amounts among the millions of freemen who possess it. But with overwhelming numbers and wealth on their side they are in constant danger of losing their fair influence in the Government, and with difficulty maintain their just rights against the incessant efforts daily made to encroach upon them. The mischief springs from the power which the moneyed interest derives from a paper currency which they are able to control, from the multitude of corporations with exclusive privileges which they have succeeded in obtaining in the different States, and which are employed altogether for their benefit; and unless you become more watchful in your States and check this spirit of monopoly and thirst for exclusive privileges you will in the end find that the most important powers of Government have been given or bartered away, and the control over your dearest interests has passed into the hands of these corporations.

The paper-money system and its natural associations—monopoly and exclusive privileges—have already struck their roots too deep in the soil, and it will require all your efforts to check its further growth and to eradicate the evil. The men who profit by the abuses and desire to perpetuate them will continue to besiege the halls of legislation in the General Government as well as in the States, and will seek by every artifice to mislead and deceive the public servants. It is to yourselves that you must look for safety and the means of guarding and perpetuating your free institutions. In your hands is rightfully placed the sovereignty of the country, and to you everyone placed in authority is ultimately responsible. It is always in your power to see that the wishes of the people are carried into faithful execution, and their will, when once made known, must sooner or later be obeyed; and while the people remain, as I trust they ever will, uncorrupted and incorruptible, and continue watchful and jealous of their rights, the Government is safe, and the cause of freedom will continue to triumph over all its enemies.

But it will require steady and persevering exertions on your part to rid yourselves of the iniquities and mischiefs of the paper system and to check the spirit of monopoly and other abuses which have sprung up with it, and of which it is the main support. So many interests are united to resist all reform on this subject that you must not hope the conflict will be a short one nor success easy. My humble efforts have not been spared during my administration of the Government to restore the constitutional currency of gold and silver, and something, I trust, has been done toward the accomplishment of this most desirable object; but enough yet remains to require all your energy and perseverance. The power, however, is in your hands, and the remedy must and will be applied if you determine upon it.

William Leggett, editor of the New York *Evening Post,* was identified with the Equal Rights, or Locofoco, section of the Jacksonian movement. In the following editorial he wrote on the fundamental equality of the common man. As with Jackson, this theme signified not pure equalitarianism, but the plea for equal opportunity in the face of "monopoly and a great paper system."

WILLIAM LEGGETT:
EQUALITY*

The rich perceive, acknowledge, and act upon a common interest, and why not the poor? Yet the moment the latter are called upon to combine for the preservation of their rights, forsooth the community is in danger. Property is no longer secure and life in jeopardy. This cant has descended to us from those times when the poor and laboring classes had no stake in the community and no rights except such as they could acquire by force. But the times have changed though the cant remains the same. The scrip nobility of this Republic have adopted towards the free people of this Republic the same language which the feudal barons and the despot who contested with them the power of oppressing the people used towards their serfs and villains, as they were opprobriously called.

These would-be lordlings of the Paper Dynasty cannot or will not perceive that there is some difference in the situation and feelings of the people of the United States and those of the despotic governments of Europe. They forget that at this moment our people—we mean emphatically the class which labors with its own hands—is in possession of a greater portion of the property and intelligence of this country, ay, ten times over, than all the creatures of the "paper credit

---

* Reprinted from New York *Evening Post,* December 6, 1834.

system" put together. This property is indeed more widely and equally distributed among the people than among the phantoms of the paper system, and so much the better. And as to their intelligence, let any man talk with them, and if he does not learn something it is his own fault. They are as well acquainted with the rights of person and property and have as just a regard for them as the most illustrious lordling of the scrip nobility. And why should they not? Who and what are the great majority of the wealthy people of this city, we may say of this country? Are they not—we say it not in disparagement, but in high commendation—are they not men who began the world comparatively poor with ordinary education and ordinary means? And what should make them so much wiser than their neighbors? Is it because they live in better style, ride in carriages, and have more money or at least more credit than their poorer neighbors? Does a man become wiser, stronger, or more virtuous and patriotic because he has a fine house over his head? Does he love his country the better because he has a French cook and a box at the opera? Or does he grow more learned, logical, and profound by intense study of the daybook, ledger, bills of exchange, bank promises, and notes of hand?

Of all the countries on the face of the earth or that ever existed on the face of the earth, this is the one where the claims of wealth and aristocracy are the most unfounded, absurd, and ridiculous. With no claim to hereditary distinctions, with no exclusive rights except what they derive from monopolies, and no power of perpetuating their estates in their posterity, the assumption of aristocratic airs and claims is supremely ridiculous. Tomorrow they themselves may be beggars for aught they know, or at all events their children may become so. Their posterity in the second generation will have to begin the world again and work for a living as did their forefathers. And yet the moment a man becomes rich among us, he sets up for wisdom; he despises the poor and ignorant; he sets up for patriotism; he is your only man who has a stake in the community and therefore the only one who ought to have a voice in the state. What folly is this? And how contemptible his presumption? He is not a whit wiser, better, or more patriotic than when he commenced the world, a wagon driver. Nay, not half so patriotic, for he would see his country disgraced a thousand times rather than see one fall of the stocks, unless perhaps he had been speculating on such a contingency. To him a victory is only of consequence as it raises, and a defeat only to be lamented as it depresses a loan. His soul is wrapped up in a certificate of scrip or a bank note. Witness the conduct of these pure patriots during the late war, when they, at least a large proportion of them, not only withheld all their support from the Government but used all their influence to prevent others from giving their assistance. Yet these are the people who alone have a stake in the community

and, of course, exclusively monopolize patriotism.

But let us ask what and where is the danger of a combination of the laboring classes in vindication of their political principles or in defense of their menaced rights? Have they not the right to act in concert when their opponents act in concert? Nay, is it not their bounden duty to combine against the only enemy they have to fear as yet in this free country: monopoly and a great paper system that grinds them to the dust? Truly, this is strange republican doctrine, and this is a strange republican country, where men cannot unite in one common effort, in one common cause, without rousing the cry of danger to the rights of person and property. Is not this a government of the people, founded on the rights of the people, and instituted for the express object of guarding them against the encroachments and usurpations of power? And if they are not permitted the possession of common interest, the exercise of a common feeling, if they cannot combine to resist by constitutional means these encroachments, to what purpose were they declared free to exercise the right of suffrage in the choice of rulers and the making of laws?

And what, we ask, is the power against which the people not only of this country but of almost all Europe are called upon to array themselves, and the encroachment on their rights they are summoned to resist? Is it not emphatically the power of monopoly and the encroachments of corporate privileges of every kind which the cupidity of the rich engenders to the injury of the poor?

It was to guard against the encroachments of power, the insatiate ambition of wealth, that this government was instituted by the people themselves. But the objects which call for the peculiar jealousy and watchfulness of the people are not now what they once were. The cautions of the early writers in favor of the liberties of mankind have in some measure become obsolete and inapplicable. We are menaced by our old enemies, avarice and ambition, under a new name and form. The tyrant is changed from a steel-clad feudal baron or a minor despot, at the head of thousands of ruffian followers, to a mighty civil gentleman who comes mincing and bowing to the people with a quill behind his ear, at the head of countless millions of magnificent *promises*. He promises to make everybody rich; he promises to pave cities with gold; and he promises to pay. In short he is made up of promises. He will do wonders such as never were seen or heard of, provided the people will only allow him to make his promises equal to silver and gold and human labor, and grant him the exclusive benefits of all the great blessings he intends to confer on them. He is the sly, selfish, grasping, and insatiable tyrant the people are now to guard against. *A concentrated money power; a usurper in the disguise of a benefactor; an agent exercising privileges which his principal never possessed; an* imposter who, while he affects to wear chains, is placed above those who are free; a chartered libertine that pretends to be manacled only that he may the more safely pick our pockets and lord it over our rights. This is the enemy we are now to encounter and overcome before we can expect to enjoy the substantial realities of freedom.

George Bancroft, noted historian and political figure, was probably the most renowned philosopher of Jacksonian democracy. Not only did he complete a ten-volume *History of the United States,* but he penned many tributes to the rationality and essential goodness of the masses.

GEORGE BANCROFT:
OFFICE OF THE PEOPLE*

If it be true, that the gifts of mind and heart are universally diffused, if the sentiment of truth, justice, love, and beauty exists in every one, then it follows, as a necessary consequence, that the common judgment in taste, politics, and religion, is the highest authority on earth, and the nearest possible approach to an infallible decision. From the consideration of individual powers I turn to the action of the human mind in masses.

If reason is a universal faculty, the universal decision is the nearest criterion of truth. The common mind winnows opinions; it is the sieve which separates error from certainty. The exercise by many of the same faculty on the same subject would naturally lead to the same conclusions. But if not, the very differences of opinion that arise prove the supreme judgment of the general mind. Truth is one. It never contradicts itself. One truth cannot contradict another truth. Hence truth is a bond of union. But error not only contradicts truth, but may contradict itself; so that there may be many errors, and each at variance with the rest. Truth is therefore of necessity an element of harmony; error as necessarily an element of discord. Thus there can be no continuing universal judgment but a right one. Men cannot agree in an absurdity; neither can they agree in a falsehood.

If wrong opinions have often been cherished by the masses, the cause always lies in the complexity of the ideas presented. Error finds its way into the soul of a nation, only through the channel of truth. It is to a truth that men listen; and if they accept error also, it is only because the error is for the time so closely interwoven with the truth, that the one cannot readily be separated from the other.

Unmixed error can have no existence in the public mind. Wherever you see men clustering together to form a party, you may be sure that however much error may be there, truth is there also. Apply this principle boldly; for it contains a lesson of candor, and a voice of encouragement. There never was a school of philosophy, nor a clan in the realm of opinion, but carried along with it some important truth. And therefore every sect that has ever flourished has benefited Humanity; for the errors of a sect pass away and are forgotten; its truths are received into the common inheritance. To know the seminal thought of every prophet and leader of a sect, is to gather all the wisdom of mankind. . . .

In like manner the best government rests on the people and not on the few, on persons and not on property, on the free development of public opinion and not on authority; because the munificent Author of our being has conferred the gifts of mind upon every member of the human race without distinction of outward circumstances. Whatever of other possessions may be engrossed, mind asserts its own independence. Lands, estates, the produce of mines, the prolific abundance of the seas, may be usurped by a privileged class. Avarice, assuming the form of ambitious power, may grasp realm after realm, subdue continents, compass the earth in its schemes of aggrandizement, and sigh after other worlds; but mind eludes the power of appropriation; it exists only in its own individuality; it is a property which cannot be confiscated and cannot be torn away; it laughs at chains; it bursts from imprisonment; it defies monopoly. A government of equal rights must, therefore, rest upon mind; not wealth, not brute force, the sum of the moral intelligence of the community should rule the State. Prescription can no more assume to be a valid plea for political injustice; society studies to eradicate established abuses, and to bring social institutions and laws into harmony with moral right; not dismayed by the natural and necessary imperfections of all human effort, and not giving way to despair, because every hope does not at once ripen into fruit.

* Reprinted from George Bancroft, *Literary and Historical Miscellanies* (New York, 1855), pp. 415–16, 421–26.

The public happiness is the true object of legislation, and can be secured only by the masses of mankind themselves awakening to the knowledge and the care of their own interests. Our free institutions have reversed the false and ignoble distinctions between men; and refusing to gratify the pride of caste, have acknowledged the common mind to be the true material for a commonwealth. Every thing has hitherto been done for the happy few. It is not possible to endow an aristocracy with greater benefits than they have already enjoyed; there is no room to hope that individuals will be more highly gifted or more fully developed than the greatest sages of past times. The world can advance only through the culture of the moral and intellectual powers of the people. To accomplish this end by means of the people themselves, is the highest purpose of government. If it be the duty of the individual to strive after a perfection like the perfection of God, how much more ought a nation to be the image of Deity. The common mind is the true Parian marble, fit to be wrought into likeness to a God. The duty of America is to secure the culture and the happiness of the masses by their reliance on themselves.

The absence of the prejudices of the old world leaves us here the opportunity of consulting independent truth; and man is left to apply the instinct of freedom to every social relation and public interest. We have approached so near to nature, that we can hear her gentlest whispers; we have made Humanity our lawgiver and our oracle; and, therefore, the nation receives, vivifies and applies principles, which in Europe the wisest accept with distrust. Freedom of mind and of conscience, freedom of the seas, freedom of industry, equality of franchises, each great truth is firmly grasped, comprehended and enforced; for the multitude is neither rash nor fickle. In truth, it is less fickle than those who profess to be its guides. Its natural dialectics surpass the logic of the schools. Political action has never been so consistent and so unwavering, as when it results from a feeling or a principle, diffused through society. The people is firm and tranquil in its movements, and necessarily acts with moderation, because it becomes but slowly impregnated with new ideas; and effects no changes, except in harmony with the knowledge which it has acquired. Besides, where it is permanently possessed of power, there exists neither the occasion nor the desire for frequent change. It is not the parent of tumult; sedition is bred in the lap of luxury, and its chosen emissaries are the beggared spendthrift and the impoverished libertine. The government by the people is in very truth the strongest government in the world. Discarding the implements of terror, it dares to rule by moral force, and has its citadel in the heart.

Such is the political system which rests on reason, reflection, and the free expression of deliberate choice. There may be those who scoff at the suggestion, that the decision of the whole is to be preferred to the judgment of the enlightened few. They say in their hearts that the masses are ignorant; that farmers know nothing of legislation; that mechanics should not quit their workshops to join in forming public opinion. But true political science does indeed venerate the masses. It maintains, not as has been perversely asserted, that "the people can make right," but that the people can DISCERN right. Individuals are but shadows, too often engrossed by the pursuit of shadows; the race is immortal: individuals are of limited sagacity; the common mind is infinite in its experience: individuals are languid and blind; the many are ever wakeful: individuals are corrupt; the race has been redeemed: individuals are time-serving; the masses are fearless: individuals may be false, the masses are ingenuous and sincere: individuals claim the divine sanction of truth for the deceitful conceptions of their own fancies; the Spirit of God breathes through the combined intelligence of the people. Truth is not to be ascertained by the impulses of an individual; it emerges from the contradictions of personal opinions; it raises itself in majestic serenity above the strifes of parties and the conflict of sects; it acknowledges neither the solitary mind, nor the separate faction as its oracle; but owns as its only faithful interpreter the dictates of pure reason itself, proclaimed by the general voice of mankind. The decrees of the universal conscience are the nearest approach to the presence of God in the soul of man.

Thus the opinion which we respect is, indeed, not the opinion of one or of a few, but the sagacity of the many. It is hard for the pride of cultivated philosophy to put its ear to the ground, and listen reverently to the voice of lowly humanity; yet the people collectively are wiser than the most gifted individual, for all his wisdom constitutes but a part of theirs. When the great sculptor of Greece was endeavoring to fashion the perfect model of beauty, he did not passively imitate the form of the loveliest woman of his age; but he gleaned the several lineaments of his faultless work from the many. And so it is, that a perfect judgment is the result of comparison, when error eliminates error, and truth is established by concurring witnesses. The organ of truth is the invisible decision of the unbiased world; she pleads before no tribunal but public opinion; she owns no safe interpreter but the common mind; she knows no court of appeals but the soul of humanity. It is when the multitude give counsel, that right purposes find safety; theirs is the fixedness that cannot be shaken; theirs is the understanding which exceeds in wisdom; theirs is the heart, of which the largeness is as the sand on the sea-shore.

It is not by vast armies, by immense natural resources, by accumulations of treasure, that the greatest results in modern civilization have been accomplished. The traces of the career of conquest pass away, hardly leaving a scar on the national intelligence. The famous battle grounds of victory are, most of them, comparatively indifferent to the human race; barren fields of blood, the scourges of their times, but affecting the social condition as little as the raging of a pestilence. Not one benevolent institution, not one ameliorating principle in the Roman state, was a voluntary concession of the aristocracy; each useful element was borrowed from the Democracies of Greece, or was a reluctant concession to the demands of the people. The same is true in modern political life. It is the confession of an enemy to Democracy, that "ALL THE GREAT AND NOBLE INSTITUTIONS OF THE WORLD HAVE COME FROM POPULAR EFFORTS."

John L. O'Sullivan, editor of the *Democratic Review,* articulated in his magazine the expansionist and humanitarian impulses of the Jacksonian period. Placing confidence in the unlimited vistas of the mind, he sought a society where man would "employ his productive means" to the best of his ability.

JOHN L. O'SULLIVAN: DEMOCRACY*

Democracy must finally triumph in human reason, because its foundations are deep in the human heart. The great mass, whose souls are bound by a strong fraternal sympathy, once relieved from ancient prejudice, will stand forth as its moveless champions. It fastens the affections of men, as the shield of their present liberties and the ground of their future hopes. They perceive in it a saving faith, a redeeming truth, a regenerating power. It is the only creed which does justice to man, or that can bind the entire race in eternal chains of brotherhood and love. Nothing sinks so deep into the hearts of the multitude, for nothing else is so identified with their moral and social good. Though the high and mighty of the earth may deride its simple truths, these are willing to die in their defence. Those truths are blended too closely with all for which it is worthy to live and glorious to perish, to be relinquished without a struggle or a pang. They are too firmly allied to the imperishable hopes, the deathless aspirations, the onward triumphant march of humanity, ever to be deserted. The fortunes of individuals may change—empires be born and blotted out—kings rise and fall—wealth, honor, distinction, fade as the dying pageant of a dream —but Democracy must live. While man lasts it must live. Its origin is among the necessary relations of things, and it can only cease to be when eternal truth is no more.

It is the principle of this Democracy we wish to unfold. Our design is to expound in our own way its nature, tendency, beauty, and end. We are drawn to it by strong cords, and cannot but explain the grounds of our love. In doing so, our business shall be mainly with great truths. Party names and distinctions shall have little influence over our thoughts. In every party there is much to approve, but much also to condemn. The duty of man—the preëminent duty of Americans—is to seek truth; to pursue it through every difficulty, wherever it lurks, with restless zeal. There is a clear region of philosophic inquiry above the clouds of party strife. To procure exemption from common errors and ordinary modes of thought, one must breathe its pure and wholesome air. He must retire from the din of daily warfare; he must live in the calm study of his own soul—in the silent observation of man. Freedom from prejudice is the indispensable condition of free thought. It is not from the hustings or the arena, we can send forth the strongest voice to our fellow men. In the sacred depths of retirement the soul alone is free—for there it roams gladly over the universe—communes with its own deep experience— consults the sublime spirits of the past—casts aside the trammels of the present—indulges glorious visions of the future, and comes in contact with truth. We speak, therefore, not to parties, but to men. The interests of party fluctuate like the ceaseless flowings of the sea, while the interests of humanity are as permanent and eternal as the hills. Yet, if there be associations of men which, above others, recognize the principles we shall maintain; if there be a party, how obscure or dejected soever, which holds the truths we hold, as the distinctive ground of their political faith, as the badge of their fraternity—we hail them as brothers—extend the right hand of fellowship—unite with them in the great cause, and, from the last depth of our souls, bid them a right hearty God-speed.

Democracy, in its true sense, is the last best revelation of human thought. We speak, of course, of that true and genuine Democracy which breathes the air and lives in the light of Christianity—whose essence is justice, and whose object is human progress. We have no sympathy with that which usurps the name, like that fierce and turbulent spirit of ancient Greece, which was only the monstrous misgrowth of faction and fraud, or that Democracy whose only distinction

* Reprinted from John L. O'Sullivan, "Democracy," *The United States Magazine and Democratic Review,* VII (March, 1840), 215–19, 222–28.

is the slavelike observance of party usages—the dumb repetition of party creeds; and still less for that wild, reckless spirit of mobism which triumphs, with remorseless and fiendish exultation, over all lawful authority, all constituted restraint. The object of our worship is far different from these; the present offering is made to a spirit which asserts a virtuous freedom of act and thought—which insists on the rights of men—demands the equal diffusion of every social advantage—asks the impartial participation of every gift of God—sympathizes with the down-trodden—rejoices in their elevation—and proclaims to the world the sovereignty, not of the people barely, but of immutable justice and truth.

The subject, in every aspect it may be regarded, is obviously important. It involves questions of the highest moment, which have engaged and baffled the greatest minds, from the days of Aristotle to those of Sidney and Locke—which have tasked the loftiest energies of the loftiest intellects, and furnished themes of earnest discussion in each successive age of the world. The inquiry into human rights is the fundamental preliminary question of political science; it is the source of a thousand controversies—the centre of numberless great universal truths. As men view it, they determine the complexion of their political lives, their notions of government, their position in civil contests, their influence on the degradation or progress of mankind. Accordingly as we extend this doctrine of human rights, we become the upholders of tyranny, or the true friends of man—we become the contemptible adherents of the cherished few, or the noble champions of the oppressed many—we are identified with the rotten abuses of past misgovernment, or the healthful spirit of modern reform. The condition of society is modified by every change in this doctrine of rights. No other doctrine exerts a mightier power over the weal or woe of the whole human race. In times which are gone, it has been the moving-spring of revolutions—has aroused the ferocious energies of oppressed nations—has sounded into the ears of despots and dynasties the fearful moanings of coming storms—has crimsoned fields of blood—has numbered troops of martyrs—has accelerated the downfall of empires—has moved the foundations of mighty thrones. Even now, millions of imprisoned spirits await its march with anxious solicitude and hope. It must go forth, like a bright angel of God, to unbar the prison-doors, to succour the needy, heal the sick, relieve the distressed, and pour a flood of light and love into the darkened intellects and dreary hearts of the sons of man.

As in the consciousness of moral truths all hearts confess their distinctions, though all are not agreed as to their precise number or force, so in the conviction of rights all acknowledge their reality, though they differ as to their nature and extent. The simple fact that man has rights seems unquestionable, and is accordingly admitted by almost unanimous suffrage, to the rank of a standard truth. Controversy commences with the attempted verbal definition or statement of what is contained in the fact. Man has rights, is every where the exclamation—but what are they?—how are they defined—what is their extent—where their limitation? What are the actual characteristics of the fact—whither does it lead—and what relation has it to the social arrangements of life? The problem is not without its difficulty, as toppling piles of fiery disputations, essays, tracts, and speeches may prove; yet it is not surrounded by that dark mist which should drive us despairingly away. Perhaps the labors of our fathers—certainly the eternal instincts of our own souls—will throw light into the gloom, so that all around may not partake of that Cimmerian night in which the pale ghost of thought wanders sightless and cheerless. Let us appeal to the reason and conscience and heart of man; for there is our only appeal—there is the only tribunal which can be called upon legitimately to decide. On this question there is no long line of authorities to cite, or despotic precedents to consult. If reason and conscience are incompetent guides, the whole inquiry is impracticable and absurd; we are thrown into the void, uncertain darkness, abandoned to dim conjecture and still dimmer hope.

That man has some rights, we say, is a fact beyond the limits of a lawful doubt; it is a fact presupposed in some sense in all political ratiocination; it is a fact of universal consciousness, which can no more be disbelieved than the existence of self; it is a fact which admits no formal demonstration, for itself is the groundwork and first-truth of demonstration. The best proof of its legitimacy is the appeal to each individual truth. It rests on instincts which are broad, bursting manifestations of Nature—on convictions which spring up spontaneously with the earliest as well as mightiest unfoldings of human thought which are developed in the child and the savage, and ever wield, under every sky, despotic influence over the volitions of human will. The spirit of resistance is never more instantly or violently aroused, than when these spontaneous convictions of right are infringed. No people, how stupid in mind or degraded in morals soever, which has not felt their might—so inseparable are they from human existence, so powerfully active over all the movings of human impulse. Years of oppression cannot wholly eradicate or dim their force, whilst they grow stronger and firmer with intellectual progress and moral elevation. Man has rights. To every faculty of his organization there is annexed the consciousness of a right to its use, of a right to invigorate and expand it, to multiply its objects and unfold its power. As a being of flesh and blood, of appetite and passions, of organs and limbs, he feels he has a right to their gratification and use. He may eat and drink whatever is adapted to his taste, and accumulate whatever means will increase his happiness or content. He may employ his corporeal powers in any occupation for which they were designed; he may exercise his labour and skill in the direction which may best contribute to his comfort; he may fix his habitation, and adjust his modes of life, as private necessity or pleasure shall control. In all these dispositions, none on earth can say, what doest thou? As an intellectual being, he may use that capacity of intellectual growth with which he is endowed. He has a right to expand and invigorate every mental power, to cultivate every mental gift, to lay up knowledge in stores, to investigate every science, to comprehend all arts, to exhaust literature, to penetrate nature, to unfold past records, to commune with great minds, to sympathize with heroic deeds, to delight in virtuous achievement, to revel amid the magnificent creations of genius. Who shall restrain thought in its free passage over the broad universe—who shall clip the restless wings of imagination, or imprison the giant energies of the will? Man has the right to think—not only to think, but to utter. Thank Heaven, no chains can bind the viewless thought—no tyranny can reach the immaterial mind. Whatever his mind in the "wide circuit of its musings" may conceive, his mouth in the presence of the world may speak; what his noble spirit feels, he has the right to express. He may send forth his "truths of power in words immortal;" he may seek to convince and persuade his fellow men; to make known his convictions; to declare his aspirations; to unfold the truth; to discover new relations of thought; to promulge novel doctrine; to question error; and, if he be able, to move men towards a triumphant assault on evil institutions and corrupt laws. As a moral being, he has a right to decide on the duties of the sphere in which he is placed; he has the right to indulge the tenderest as well as loftiest sensibilities of the heart; to sigh with the sorrowful; to commiserate the oppressed, and to weep the bitter tears of a broken heart over misplaced confidence or wounded love. He has the right to nourish the sense of duty, the power of endurance, the energies of self-command; to conquer passion with manly force; to throw back temptation with lusty arm; to resist the myriad fascinations of deceitful life with iron heart and iron will. He has the right to act according to that conscience which his God has given; to oppose vice, though millions swell the ranks of its worshippers; to espouse and uphold truth, despised as it may be, and even when the prospect reveals only the faggot and flame.

These rights of man belong to him as man— they are neither gifts or grants, or privileges, but rights. He traces them to no concessions of a parliament which may have assembled far back in the darkness of time; to no constitution which his forefathers may have sanctioned or framed; to no royal assent unwillingly yielded to the stubborn requisitions of a sturdy people; to no concessions granted in the plenitude of aristocratic generosity; to no revolutions nor battles; but to a higher and greater source than these—the God of his spirit, the Creator of the worlds. They are the primary, absolute, imprescriptible rights of his nature, derived through the laws of his being, as an immediate gift from Him that is over all. They belong to man as an individual, and are higher than human constitutions or human laws. The charter on which they depend was drawn from the skies, and bears the signet and stamp of Heaven. To fetter the freedom of man is not only to act the part of tyranny, but to inflict a gross wrong, to outrage a high gift, to trample on a creation of God.

As rights, then, are the possession of the whole race, equality of right is predicable of its constituent members. Identity of nature involves a community of attributes, and a parity of moral claims. Inequality of condition, it is obvious, can effect no transfer of rights. The strong, the rich, the gifted, the good, are only equal, in respect to rights, to those less abundantly endowed. Supremacy in one shape confers no supremacy in others; and if it did, as the roads to excellence are infinitely varied, there could be no mode of adjusting the diversity of conflicting claims. . . .

Government is the agent of society, the organ through which its purposes are declared and its will executed. It is the instrument by which the few exert the delegated power of the many. Its origin is in the weakness or wickedness of men. To protect the feeble from the strong, the good from the bad, each from all and all from each, is its prominent design. Would all conform to the natural laws of their being, its functions would be exceedingly simple and few. Vice, intolerance, precipitancy, crime of all sorts, create the necessity for complex forms and strong powers of government. The best government is that whose rule of action is simple justice to all. Justice is the supreme, sovereign arbiter of the world—of higher authority than either the edict of royalty, the decrees of party, or the injunctions of law. The state's most indispensable duty is to provide for its impartial administration. Thus fastening to it, by indissoluble bonds, the affinities of every individual and class, it will establish a social union more stable than the hills, and more harmonious than the spheres.

If it be true, then, that men are equal in respect to their rights—that they enter society on common ground—that government is the agent of all—there are momentous inferences which the truth plainly involves.

I. The basis of representation is the person. Neither birth, wisdom nor wealth confers on its possessor an exclusive right to legislative control, or, what is the same thing, an exclusive right to select those in whom the legislation is placed. Power emanates from the people: it is transiently delegated by society to be wielded for its benefit. It is transferred to representatives to guard and facilitate its exercise. Every individual is interested in its use or abuse; for it is his own power relinquished for a moment, with a view to his higher security and good. Property qualifications are but little regarded in these States. The prevailing theoretical doctrine is, the majority of the whole number must rule. Objections to this principle, however sturdily advanced, have fallen, one after another, before the triumphant experiment of our free people. The assertion that the majority will absorb the rights of the minority is about to share the same fate. It will be urged a little while by the adherents of "privileged classes," and will die. It is wholly destitute of foundation or strength. There is no danger to be apprehended from the people, if left to themselves. Though the majority is not always right, probability is in its favor. Its ability to decide in matters of state is more than equal to that of those "better classes" which affect all wisdom and knowledge. It is a common error to overrate our own capacities, and underrate those of others. There is a vulgar pride gratified in depreciating the integrity and information of the great mass. The arrogant vanity of the rich, the haughty pretension of the privileged, the insolence of the unprincipled, the pomposity of the learned, and the inflated conceit of the selfish and superficial "business man" delight to disparage the intellectual or moral claims of "the multitude." They are stigmatized as the lower orders, but a little, if any, removed from the brute; they are spoken of as the wild, ferocious herd; passed by with the rude jest or the scornful look, or at times crushed in the dust like crawling, loathsome earthworms. But there is a native instinct in the general mind more unerring in its decisions than prejudiced instruction—a practical sagacity, which sets the most subtle or far-reaching intellect at naught—the conviction of great truths, which sink deep, deep into the heart, and guide its sympathies and movements aright. So long as the many shall know their rights—while they can distinguish moral rectitude from guilt—while they are judges of the means most conducive to their happiness and growth—and while they may be addressed by every variety of persuasion and appeal, it is no frightful absurdity to rely confidently on their will. Most especially may they be trusted when government is confined by its legitimate bounds. The details of a consolidated government based on unwritten laws, perpetually changing—comprehending an infinity of functions—fettered by a vast variety of checks, balances and restrictions—connected directly with every interest of society—mingling in all the gambling and speculation of trade—entrenching itself behind immense civil, ecclesiastical and military establishments, and operating through a machinery as intricate as the differential calculus, it is true, would puzzle their heads, as they do the most experienced statesmen themselves. But the Democratic creed contemplates no such complicated arrangement. That creed is consistent with itself throughout. It does not construct an engine of adjustments and relations so multiplied and abstruse, that the most practised wisdom is alone adequate to their comprehension. It does not abuse the people for not controlling what is beyond their capacity to understand. It does not hang laws far above their heads, and then Draco like, execute a terrible penalty upon every infringement. While it asserts the competency of the whole to govern themselves, it restricts government to its natural uses; it curtails the number of its functions; separates its action from partial interests; simplifies the mode of its operation, and reduces the principles of legislation to the simplest expression compatible with some form of national organization. It insists strenuously on popular rights, because it believes the popular body sufficient to the discharge of its public duties. There is intelligence enough abroad to answer the purposes required of it. On this point we wish to be understood. Our desire is not to magnify the intelligence of the people; we would rate it at its worth. We admit that men may be deceived, misled, prejudiced, corrupted by flattery, inflamed by eloquence, or aroused by designing leaders into all the excess of tumultous passion; yet, in the conflict of free thought and free discussion, the evil will cure itself. There is ever in the great mass a power of self-rectification. There is ever intelligence enough to conduct a government rightly framed; to appreciate public measures; to distinguish good and evil; to reward patriotism and virtue, and to rebuke tyranny and vice. Nothing but long outrage and oppression can drive a whole people into insubordination and discord. The convulsions which shake civilized nations are the accumulated results of dreary years of crimes. They are the spasms of distorted and wrenched limbs—the explosion of volcanic fire long pent up, but at last finding vent. Freedom and justice are conservative in all their influence. The majority of a free populace has no inducement to go wrong. They cannot be long deluded. They have no exclusive affinities to cloud their perceptions or warp their judgments. Their whole interest is on the side of order and right. They have no partial or unjust laws to sustain, no privileges to perpetuate, no selfish relations to protect, and no corrupting ambition to gratify. They cannot live at the expense of the few. Their dependence must be upon themselves. Their resources and strength must be drawn from themselves; whilst their frantic excesses, if any, must fall with full severity upon their own heads. Privileged classes, on the other hand, whether their exclusiveness be founded on birth or acquisition of any sort, have always plans of their own to accomplish. Their very existence depends upon the maintenance of their assumed superiority. Their entire interest is centred in the retention of power already possessed, and the usurpation of as much more as can be gained. To this object every effort, open and secret, must be addressed. In this way alone can they live. Their growth is ever an under-current, running counter to the great currents of society. Let them enlarge their sympathies, extend the landmarks of their dominion, and they resolve sooner or later into the general mass, like bubbles into the yesty waves of the sea. Every concession to the multitude without opens broader channels to the escape of power—is a stimulus to additional encroachment —deepens the inroads of aggression. Their safety depends upon their bigoted and unflinching resistance of popular influence. Their wisest policy is uncompromising hostility to innovation in every guise. To retain their integrity unbroken, they must strangle the spirit of reform in the womb; they must crush in the bud every manifestation of liberal feeling; they must chain the wings of thought; muzzle the press; organize a government of the sternest, strongest materials; expand, by corruption and fraud, the ranks of their dependents; draw around them an immense armed force; shut up human speech by the bayonet and sword; and thus add power to power, and heap wrong upon wrong, until the adverse mass, wearied of its burdens and maddened by the agony of long years, bursts every restraint, and dashes in tempestuous billows over the land. Restriction and injustice, in proportion to their degree, are fruitful sources of tumult and distress. The stability and safety of a people corresponds with the extent of their freedom from unequal legislation or unjust control.

II. Again: As government is the agent of society, its operation must be directed to the good of all its members. In this we include more than is commonly meant by that very indefinite phrase, "the general good"—a phrase to which the lives and fortunes of millions have been wantonly sacrificed. The great object of government is to secure every man in the enjoyment of his rights. Beyond this, it should not meddle with the affairs of men. There is provision for the existence and growth of society in our very constitution. It seems to be imagined by many that human nature must be fostered, fondled, or stimulated to exertion by legislative interposition. They forget those great principles at the bottom of that nature which compel the use of every faculty. The injunction to labor there written is far more imperative than human law could make it; for its motives are ever vigilant and active. While a thousand clamorous desires reign in the human breast; while man shall seek his highest happiness; while he shall delight in advancement and conquest; while industry will add to his comfort, and indolence prove the inevitable source of misery and death; no mode of exertion, no means of production, no road to improvement, will be left untried. The movements of human thought are not more tireless than the springs of human action. A curiosity which is never satisfied, an instinct ever effective, appetites more importunate than death, impulses like steeds restlessly panting and champing for the race, are ever urging the human being to additional, accumulated effort. Under this influence, no benefit will be allowed to elude his grasp; every prospect of personal advantage will be readily embraced; every hope of gain will be realized; he will traverse distant seas, explore the wildest woods, face every difficulty, and only cease to act when he has ceased to live. We may rest assured that labor will be put forth whenever it will meet with success, and capital will be applied where it shall command the best return. The agency of government is obviously not required here. The movings of self-interest are too powerful to need extraneous aid. The interference of legislation will only blind its eyes, and diminish its strength. It will infallibly prove a burden and a curse. From the necessity of the case, it must ever be partial; and if so, it is an infringement of natural right, an abandonment of the first principles of social union, a perversion of the clearest doctrines of science, a usurpation of power, and the infliction of the grossest wrong. The form in which it is manifested cannot alter the fact. Whether it be done by granting monopolies of any branch of trade, by conferring reward and distinction on a chosen few, by deputing privileges of an honorable or commercial sort, by yielding facilities to any department of business, by forcing industry into unusual channels, by imposing restraints on particular interests, by subjecting certain men to liabilities from which other men are exempt, or by fostering the wealth of some classes at the expense of the rest, it is equally odious and unjust. In every shape, these restrictions are hostile to the plainest rights of person and property, prejudicial to the growth and destructive of the peace of society. We conceive that every man has a right to employ his productive means, in whatever they consist, in a mode to ensure the largest returns, or most consistent with his notions of propriety. His only limit is the regard which is due to the rights of his fellow men. The faculties of both body and mind were given for this purpose. The strongest laws of his nature, and every condition of his being, have reference to this result. To labor in the vocation in which he is most apt, to apply his agency where it may purchase the best recompense, or to choose that form of exertion most consistent with his highest good—the enjoyment of physical comfort and the gratification of mental and moral wants—it is evident to the commonest sense, is the chief design of the economy in which he is placed. The interposition of authority may be called government, but is in fact robbery and fraud. It despoils him of property to which he has the firmest claim which reason or justice can give. In form of law, it abrogates the highest law, and makes the grossest tyranny the daily duty of the State. It strips industry of its motive, by disturbing the amount and certainty of its reward. It takes from enterprise half its energy, by forcing it into those unnatural channels where its efforts are fruitless, or, if successful, invariably spasmodic and shortlived. The spirit of commerce is crushed by the mountains of weight which are laid upon it; all its departments lumber sluggishly along, or waste their strength in ineffectual struggles for relief; or, excited by unhealthy stimulus, the body politic staggers under intoxication, to fall the weak, miserable victim of debauchery and excess. One portion of the community is bled to the last stages of depletion—another is pampered to the point of plethora and apoplexy; or both, shaking under the inconstant attacks of alternate health and disease, are soon exhausted of strength, and die. Thus it creates unnecessary distinctions. In the one case, it raises a class to an unnatural elevation; in the other, depresses it far below the position it was destined to attain. It fixes one portion of society in forced dependence upon another—makes over the prosperity of the many to the arbitrary disposal of the few, and frequently hangs the necessaries of life on the wings of speculation and chance. Overgrown wealth, with its ever attendant miseries of luxury, oppression, and vice, shoots up in rank luxuriance, amidst the barrenest poverty and distress. The splendid palace, glittering in gold, vocal with the shouts of merriment, looks proudly down on hovels where sit cheerless, haggard hunger and heart-withering care. An aristocracy of wealth most odious of all—proud, overbearing, insolent, and ignorant—strikes deep root into the soil. The poor, through bleak days of wretchedness, are filled with jealousy and discontent. The opposition of mutually dependent classes festers into hate. Party contests, which should ever be the conflict of great principles, degenerates into the acrimonious strife of personal interest; and society is dissevered and rent, whilst its morals perish in the same common catastrophe which sinks its prosperity and peace.

III. As the will of the whole people is the source, and their good the end, of government, it is manifest they may at any time effect its change. They may accomplish any revolution which their growing civilization demands. They may adapt the structure of all its departments to whatever state public morality and intelligence requires. Their naked right none but the sturdiest adherents of unrelenting despotism will deny. But in the practical determination of a change, parties will inevitably arise; they will arrange themselves under the operation of necessary influences and principles springing from the diversity of human nature. The interests fostered by established systems, through the natural instinct of selfishness, will speedily form themselves into conservative bands. Their dependents, through all the ramifications of society, will hasten to swell the same ranks; while the naturally timid, dubious as to the virtue of their fellow-men, averse to change, conjuring up dismal prospects of future anarchy and misrule, will enlist under the same banners. To these will be gathered the wealth and fashion which draws its existence from old customs and laws—the privilege which subsists on ancient error—and the talent which, accustomed to profound veneration, never travels beyond a beaten track. They will be met, on the other hand, by the untutored yet unsophisticated mass, and those bold, independent men of genius who intuitively seize the right, and labor with fearless self-denying energy for human progress. The contest will be intense, as the interests and principles involved are great. As it embraces the great doctrines of science, the first-truths of government, the welfare of nations, and the destinies of a race, a long warfare will infringe on the civilities of life, will break the restraints of law, will estrange friends, will throw the sword into families, and give rein to the wildest excesses of passion. Yet it is not difficult to tell where victory will perch. The rights and happiness of the many will prevail. Democracy must finally reign. There is in man an eternal principle of progress which no power on earth may resist. Every custom, law, science, or religion, which obstructs its course, will fall as leaves before the wind. Already it has done much, but will do more. The despotism of force, the absolutism of religion, the feudalism of wealth, it has laid on the crimson field; while the principle, alive, unwounded, vigorous, is still battling against nobility and privilege with unrelaxing strength. It is contending for the extinction of tyranny, for the abolition of prerogative, for the reform of abuse, for the amelioration of government, for the destruction of monopoly, for the establishment of justice, for the elevation of the masses, for the progress of humanity, and for the dignity and worth of the individual man.

CHAPTER EIGHT

THE EXPANSIONISTS

With the Texas and Oregon questions attracting national attention, there was widespread enthusiasm in the 1840's for America to enlarge its boundaries. It was America's "Manifest Destiny" to occupy the entire continent, and indeed beyond in both southern and western directions. But, as Albert K. Weinberg pointed out in the first selection, expansion was not regarded as an end in itself: "The conception of expansion as a destiny meant primarily that it was a means to the fulfilment of a certain social ideal the preservation and perfection of which was America's providential mission or destiny." This ideal—democracy—signified a new confluence in American thought: the merging of expansion and freedom. That this was not the case prior to the 1840's becomes clear from Weinberg's analysis. By this date, however, when expansionism was believed to be the means to the achievement of democracy, the concept's appeal exercised a profound influence on American thought and policies.

Turning to manifest destiny in the Pacific, Dan E. Clark presented examples of "genuine idealism" as well as "the all too evident jingoism" in our past. Expansionism is seen in the second article as compounded of many faiths, chiefly "the chosen-people, beacon-to-mankind interpretation of America's mission and duty." Other strands are also evident: the doctrine of inevitability governing westward progress, the "ceaseless inward urge . . . impelling Anglo-saxon peoples westward," the belief that America must occupy its natural boundaries, and, not to be overlooked, the proclamation of commercial supremacy over underdeveloped areas. In these utterances one sees the unbounded confidence and enthusiasm of a dynamic country beginning to enter the world arena.

ALBERT K. WEINBERG:
EXTENSION OF THE AREA OF FREEDOM*

In the "roaring 'forties," a decade thus designated because the spirit of American life

* Reprinted from Albert K. Weinberg, *Manifest Destiny: A Study of Nationalist Expansionism in American History* (Baltimore: The Johns Hopkins Press, 1935), pp. 100–12 by permission.

rose into high and turbulent flame, there was welded an association of two ideals which gave a new integration to the American's consciousness of national destiny. One of the two ideals was territorial expansion. After several decades of relative quiescence, expansionism was rekindled by the issues of Texas and Oregon and was fanned to white heat by the oratory of Democrats in the presidential election of 1844. For the first time the wish of numerous Americans fathered the thought that their eventual possession of no less a domain than the entire North American continent was "manifest destiny"—a phrase which now passed into the national vocabulary.

The central implication of "manifest destiny" in the 'forties, however, was less a matter of the scope of expansion than of its purpose. The conception of expansion as a destiny meant primarily that it was a means to the fufilment of a certain social ideal the preservation and perfection of which was America's providential mission or destiny. This ideal, conceived as "the last best revelation of human thought," was democracy—a theory of mass sovereignty but in a more important aspect a complex of individualistic values which, despite Fisher Ames's observation that America was too democratic for liberty,[1] Americans most frequently summarized by the inspiring word "freedom." It was because of the association of expansion and freedom in a means-end relationship that expansion now came to seem most manifestly a destiny.

While the championship of the rights of man appeared from the beginning of national life to be America's special destiny, expansion had not seemed in general to be a necessary element in this preeminent national purpose. It is true that expansionists of the Revolution and the War of 1812 tendered "liberty"[2] to the "oppressed" Canadians, and that Jefferson once included not only Canada but Cuba and Florida as well in America's "empire for liberty."[3] Yet in all these instances . . . the extension of democracy was probably neither a primary motive of any expansionists nor even a secondary motive of many of them. It was not until the 'forties that the popular ideology of expansionism centered in democracy. The new importance of this ideal to the expansionist was shown by the words which rang through the land as his slogan, "extension of the area of freedom."

It was because of its infusion with this ideal that American expansionism of the middle 'forties became possessed, as Professor Adams says in his valuable essay on "Manifest Destiny," of a "spiritual exaltation" in contemplation of the assumed superiority of American institutions. A recognition of the rôle played by idealistic American nationalism in this expansion movement has led to an explanation which is very different from that of most early American historians. Writers close to the passions of the Civil War attributed

expansionism to "the glut of our slaveholders,"[4] the desire of the Southern States to extend the system of slavery. More objective contemporary historians believe that the intensity and extensity of expansionism, while due partly to sectional interests, were caused primarily by nationalistic attitudes resting not merely upon practical interests but also upon the "emotion" of "manifest destiny"[5] and its correlate, the "idealism"[6] of the spirit of democracy.

However, it is as yet more common to refer to democracy as an explanation of American expansionism than to attempt an explanation of expansionist democratic idealism itself. The zeal for extending the area of freedom raises several interesting and important problems. Why is it that, despite the fact that neither expansionism nor the attachment to democracy was new, the two did not come into fusion before? What were the historical circumstances which overcame the previous estrangement of these pieties? Most important of all, what was the true meaning of the ideal described vaguely as extension of the area of freedom?

The point of the last question is made sharper by the fact that the most usual connotation of such words as "extension of the area of freedom" does not make sense in the light of the historical context. The phrase was used primarily by those who urged the annexation of Texas. But Texas already had a republican government, as was pointed out by anti-expansionists attacking the slogan. Thus Representative McIlvain asked "how, if freedom mean republican liberty, can its area be extended by the union of the two governments?"[7] Perplexed by the same question, Representative Marsh characterized "extension of the area of freedom" as "an argument addressed to the ear and not the understanding—a mere jingle of words without meaning, or, if significant, false in the only sense which the words will fairly bear."[8]

Unfortunately the matter cannot be so quickly dismissed. The popular slogan is often vapid, but in this case it did have a meaningful content. Only, it was very different from the significance which contemporary anti-expansionists and even later historians attached to the shibboleth. To understand its rather surprising implication, it will be necessary to turn first to the historical background of the expansionist ideal in order to

---

[1] *Works of Fisher Ames*, I, 328.

[2] Representative Johnson, *Annals of Cong.*, 12th Cong., 1st sess., col. 458.

[3] *The Writings of Thomas Jefferson*, ed. H. A. Washington (Philadelphia, 1854), V, 444.

[4] James Schouler, *History of the United States of America* (Washington, 1889), IV, 519.

[5] Ephraim Douglass Adams, *The Power of Ideals in American History* (New Haven, 1926), p. 93.

[6] William Archibald Dunning, *The British Empire and the United States* (New York, 1914), p. 138.

[7] *Cong. Globe*, 28th Cong., 2d sess., App., p. 373.

[8] *Ibid.*, p. 316.

survey briefly the previous development of the relationship between the ideas of democracy and expansion.

When Representative Severance urged in the 'forties that Americans "rather extend the 'area of freedom' by . . . our bright and shining example as a pattern republic,"[9] he was reverting to the conception which had been held by the founders of the nation. Originally "the extension of the area of freedom" signified extension of freedom regardless of political connection. Moreover the chief method chosen for extending freedom was the purely passive one of radiating democratic influence through impressive example. Thus Joel Barlow said in 1787 that "the example of political wisdom and felicity, here to be displayed, will excite emulation throughout the kingdoms of the earth, and meliorate the condition of the human race."[10] Thomas Jefferson spoke of America as "a standing monument and example" which would "ameliorate the condition of man over a great portion of the globe."[11] Jefferson also suggested another non-expansionist method of extending freedom. It was the pioneer migration covering even the Western Coast "with free and independent Americans, unconnected with us but by the ties of blood and interest, and employing like us the rights of self-government."[12] It is clear from many such utterances that Americans at first perceived no necessary logical relationship between the extension of democracy and the extension of America's boundaries.

Why did early Americans see no logical nexus between the two ideals which were firmly associated by their descendants? One reason for the original disassociation of democracy and expansion was the internationalist orientation of many of the founders of the Republic. Early idealists, as the nationalistic Gouverneur Morris complained, had a *penchant* for referring to themselves as "citizens of the world."[13] Associated with this internationalism was a devotion to democracy for its own sake. If only the offshoots of the American Republic blossomed into freedom, the retention of political connection seemed to Jefferson "not very important to the happiness of either part."[14]

Yet it is doubtful whether these magnanimous attitudes account fundamentally for the non-expansionist character of early democratic philosophy. Indifference to the national label of expansive democracy may be explicable basically by the aspect in which expansion of territory presented itself from the viewpoint of self-interest. It did not seem originally that wide extent of territory was needful to the American democracy. Its original domain appeared, Thomas Paine said, as a world; as late as 1801 Jefferson thought that it would suffice unto the thousandth generation. But in addition to those who thought territorial expansion unnecessary there were many who believed it dangerous to democracy. Thus a large group attached to State sovereignty opposed the Constitution on the ground, largely derived from the theory of Montesquieu, that the existing domain even of the thirteen States was too large for one national government. The authors of the *Federalist* countered by distinguishing between a pure democracy and a representative republic and by assuming the greater immunity of the large republic to faction. Even they, however, had reference not to expansion but only to the amalgamation of the thirteen States.

After adjusting themselves to the new Federal Union the small-territory party took renewed alarm from the proposal to purchase the "vast new world" of Louisiana. A republican government, declared Fisher Ames on this occasion, could not be practicable, honest, or free, if applied to the government of a third of God's earth.[15] The anti-expansionist arguments in this and the later issue of Orleans Territory reveal clearly the ideas which made democracy and expansion seem incompatible. The chief objection to expansion was that it would cause, sooner or later, the very destruction of a republican government. The reasons for this view were set forth by Representative Griswold: "The vast and unmanageable extent which the accession of Louisiana will give to the United States; the consequent dispersion of our population; and the destruction of that balance which it is so important to maintain between the Eastern and Western States, threatens, at no very distant day, the subversion of our Union."[16] Eight years later Josiah Quincy, opposing the incorporation of Orleans Territory, asserted similarly that the bill contained "a principle incompatible with the liberties and safety of my country," and if passed would be "a death-blow to the Constitution."[17]

A second objection, felt by some more keenly than the first, was that expansion endangered the rights and liberties of the individual States. This objection was offered in the Louisiana discussion, and again in Josiah Quincy's speech opposing the creation of Orleans Territory. Quincy avowed

---

[9] *Ibid.*, p. 371.

[10] Joel Barlow, *An Oration, Delivered . . . July 4, 1787* (Hartford, 1787), p. 20.

[11] *Writings of Thomas Jefferson*, Memorial ed., X, 217.

[12] *Writings of Thomas Jefferson*, IX, 351.

[13] S. E. Morison, ed., *Sources and Documents Illustrating the American Revolution, 1764–1788, and the Formation of the Federal Constitution* (Oxford, 1923), pp. 281–82.

[14] *Writings of Thomas Jefferson*, VIII, 295.

[15] *Works of Fisher Ames*, I, 329.

[16] *Annals of Cong.*, 8th Cong., 1st sess., col. 465.

[17] *Ibid.*, 11th Cong., 3d sess., col. 542.

frankly that his first public love was the Commonwealth of Massachusetts, whereas his love of the Union was merely devotion to a safeguard of the prosperity and security of his State. He opposed expansion because it introduced a new power to overbalance the political weight of any one State. He decried as an "effective despotism" that condition of things in which the original States must lose their political control to the new States, which, taking advantage of a conflict of interests, would throw themselves into the scale most conformable to their purposes.[18]

A third type of criticism alleged the danger of expansion to the liberties of individual citizens. Representative Griswold opposed the Louisiana Purchase because of fear that "additional territory might overbalance the existing territory, and thereby the rights of the present citizens of the United States be swallowed up and lost."[19] Certain Americans, like Josiah Quincy, not merely feared to throw their "rights and liberties" into "hotchpot" with those of an alien race.[20] They even feared, as Senator White declared in the Louisiana debate, that their own citizens who roved so far from the capital would lose their affection for the center and develop antagonistic interests.[21] Both fears motivated John Randolph's words of 1813: "We are the first people that ever acquired provinces . . . not for us to govern, but that they might *govern us*—that we might be ruled to our ruin by people bound to us by no common tie of interest or sentiment."[22]

Thus the original failure to relate democracy and expansion was due not merely to altruism, but also, and perhaps primarily, to egoistic fear for the liberties of the American nation, States, and individual citizens. A general tendency to associate democracy and expansion could not possibly develop before these fears had disappeared.

The years following America's first territorial acquisition did in fact witness the gradual dissipation of one after another of the anti-expansionist's apprehensions. The first to pass was the morbid notion that the Union itself could be destroyed through plethora of territory. Louisiana was scarcely incorporated before it seemed an increment of natural growth rather than of elephantiasis. In his oration of 1804 on the acquisition, Dr. David Ramsay taunted those who had phophesied that the Constitution would never answer for a large territory.[23] Jefferson's

inaugural address of 1805 reminded those once fearful of Louisiana that "the larger our association the less will it be shaken by local passions."[24]

The fear that extended territory would prove injurious to the liberties of the individual States also quickly evaporated. By 1822 President Monroe could say with an expectation of general approbation: "The expansion of our Union over a vast territory can not operate unfavorably to the States individually. . . . With governments separate, vigorous, and efficient for all local purposes, their distance from each other can have no injurious effect upon their respective interests."[25] State anti-expansionism was lessened not only by the defeat of the particularists in the War of 1812 but also by the rise of the political theory which Monroe's words intimated. The years following the War of 1812 witnessed the increasing popularity of the view that the United States Government was based upon a distinctive principle of federation dividing power between State and Federal Government in a manner safe and efficacious for both. The encouraging implication of this theory for expansion was stated by Edward Everett in an address of 1824: " . . . by the wise and happy partition of powers between the national and state governments, in virtue of which the national government is relieved from all the odium of internal administration, and the state governments are spared the conflicts of foreign politics, all bounds seem removed from the possible extension of our country, but the geographical limits of the continent. Instead of growing cumbrous, as it increases in size, there never was a moment, since the first settlement in Virginia, when the political system of America moved with so firm and bold a step, as at the present day."[26]

The fear that the inhabitants of the distant sections would subvert the liberties of their eastern fellow citizens also proved unfounded. The Eastern States learned that their western kinsmen were not only the strongest of Unionists but also the most democratic of the democrats. One may again turn to an address by Everett, who, though of the same State as the particularist Josiah Quincy, spoke in 1829 to citizens of Tennessee with utmost friendliness. After prophesying that the sceptre of political power would depart from Judah, the East, to the multiplying States of the West, he said: "We look forward to that event without alarm, as in the order of the natural growth of this great Republic. We have a firm faith that our interests are mutually consistent; that if you prosper, we shall prosper; if you suffer, we shall suffer; . . . and that our children's welfare, honor, and prosperity

[18] *Ibid.*, col., 536.

[19] *Ibid.*, 8th Cong., 1st sess., col. 433.

[20] *Ibid.*, 11th Cong., 3d sess., col. 538.

[21] *Ibid.*, 8th Cong., 1st sess., col. 34.

[22] Quoted by William Cabell Bruce, *John Randolph of Roanoke 1773–1833* (New York, 1922), I, 402.

[23] David Ramsay, *An Oration on the Cession of Louisiana to the United States, Delivered on the 12th May, 1804 . . .* (Charleston, 1804), pp. 20–21.

[24] Richardson, *Messages*, I, 379.

[25] *Ibid.*, II, 177.

[26] Edward Everett, *Orations and Speeches on Various Occasions* (2d ed.; Boston, 1850–1868), I, 33.

will not suffer in the preponderance, which, in the next generation, the west must possess in the balance of the country." [27] Not only did Everett trust the West but he regarded westward migration as the *"principle* of our institutions" going forth to take possession of the land.[28]

By the decade of the 'thirties there had disappeared every apprehension of incompatibility between the principle of democracy and America's existing domain; the course of this decade was to witness the beginnings of the belief in the compatibility of democracy and future increased domain. One factor in this development was a growing confidence in the flexibility of the federative principle. Thus a writer in the *Democratic Review* of 1838 affirmed that "the peculiar characteristic of our system . . . is, that it may, if its theory is maintained pure in practice, be extended, with equal safety and efficiency, over any indefinite number of millions of population and territory." [29] Favorable contemplation of indefinite future expansion was also induced by the fact that the self-consciousness and spiritual inflammability of Jacksonian equalitarianism brought to most intense fervor, not only the appreciation of democracy, but also the belief that, as Jackson's Farewell Message asserted, Providence had chosen Americans as "the guardians of freedom to preserve it for the benefit of the human race." [30] So grandiose a status seemed to some to demand as its symbol a grandiosity of territorial extent. Thus an essay in the *Democratic Review* of 1838, depicting America as "The Great Nation of Futurity," not only foreshadowed its editor's later coinage of the phrase "manifest destiny" but also exemplified the incipient transition of the idea of manifest destiny from its non-expansionist to its expansionist form: "The far-reaching, the boundless future will be the era of American greatness. In its magnificent domain of space and time, the nation of many nations is *destined to manifest* [italics mine] to mankind the excellence of divine principles; to establish on earth the noblest temple ever dedicated to the worship of the Most High—the Sacred and the True. Its floor shall be a hemisphere—its roof the firmament of the star-studded heavens, and its congregation an Union of many Republics, comprising hundreds of happy millions, calling, owning no man master, but governed by God's natural and moral law of equality, the law of brotherhood—of 'peace and good will amongst men.' " [31]

While the conception of the United States as

embracing an entire hemisphere outdid even the ambition of the 'forties, the very ambitiousness of the vision indicates the relegation of its fulfillment to the distant future. With respect to the present, the 'thirties were not a decade of active expansionism. Like others the *Democratic Review* was cool toward the vague possibility of annexation raised by the Canadian revolts.[32] The definite proffers of annexation by Texas after its successful rebellion were successively rebuffed, despite the recognition by Senator Niles and other Americans that "destiny had established intimate political connexion between the United States and Texas." [33] In some measure the apathy regarding immediate expansion was due to the persistence of the sedentary ideal of radiating freedom by example—an ideal expressed by a writer in the *North American Review* of 1832 when he affirmed that "we can wait the peaceful progress of our own principles." [34] But this attitude is an inadequate explanation of the fact that Americans rejected an opportunity to render greatly needed assistance in the progress of their democratic principles. Such assistance was refused the Texans when they appealed for annexation after falling into deplorable difficulties. The reserve of Americans toward their former compatriots was caused not only by the fear of difficulty over annexation with both Mexico and American abolitionists, but also by the absence of any belief in the urgent need for expansion. The speeches of Jackson as president exude the complacency and sense of self-sufficiency of this decade. Especially noteworthy is his confident observation concerning an issue always highly determinative of the attitude toward expansion: "You have no longer any cause to fear danger from abroad . . ." [35]

One finally comes to the task of explaining the sudden rise in the 'forties of the ideal of extending the area of freedom by expansion. Is it conceivable that, after having been cold to the sufferings of the Texans for seven years, Americans quite spontaneously developed an overwhelming desire to enfold them with their protective democracy? Such a conception is the more difficult because the expansionists themselves made no pretension to undiluted altruism. On the other hand, only a priori cynicism would suppose that the democratic ideology was merely a hypocritical grace whereby the American appeased conscience before indulging the land-hunger of this decade. An examination of the circumstances and ideas attending the inception of the expansionist movement reveals that a

---

[27] *Ibid.*, p. 196.

[28] *Ibid.*, p. 210.

[29] *Democratic Review*, "The Canada Question," I (1838), 217.

[30] Richardson, *Messages*, III, 308.

[31] *Democratic Review*, "The Great Nation of Futurity," VI (1839), 427.

[32] *Ibid.*, I (1838), 216–17.

[33] *Reg. of Debates*, 24th Cong., 1st sess., col. 1918.

[34] *North American Review*, "North-Eastern Boundary," XXXIV (1832), 563.

[35] Richardson, *Messages*, III, 307.

definite international development, suddenly placing new problems in the center of the American's political horizon, was the factor which brought into play the spirit of democracy as well as other motives of expansionism.

The development was the emergence of that "danger from abroad" which Jackson had declared to be absent in the 'thirties. "In Texas, in California, and in Oregon," as Professor Perkins writes with reference to the years following 1841, "the ambition or the intrigue of European nations seemed to the dominant political generation of Americans to threaten fundamental American interests." [36] British and French attempts to establish sovereignty or political influence in adjacent countries appeared to threaten not merely economic and strategic interests but also the security of democracy. The expansionism of the 'forties arose as a defensive effort to forestall the encroachment of Europe in North America. So too, as one can see in the most numerous utterances, the conception of an "extension of the area of freedom" became general as an ideal of preventing absolutistic Europe from lessening the area open to American democracy; extension of the area of "freedom" was the defiant answer to extension of the area of "absolutism."

The European scare started with Texas and at least as early as 1843. In the early months of that year President Tyler was brought by information about British influence in Texas to the fear which was reflected in the reference of his annual message to "interference on the part of stronger and more powerful nations." [37] In 1843, also, Andrew Jackson wrote his famous letter on Texas to Aaron V. Brown, in which, amid warnings of British intrigue, he coined a famous phrase by advocacy of "extending the area of freedom." [38] The year 1844, which witnessed the negotiation of Tyler's unratified treaty of annexation, saw also the publication of Jackson's letter, and the popularization of his felicitous phrase. Although many Southerners wished for annexation primarily to forestall British abolitionist efforts, they also used, without sense of inconsistency, the democratic argument of Andrew Jackson. Texas, Senator Lewis of Alabama wrote to his constituents, was the "great Heritage of Freedom," to be held "in defiance of that power which has well-nigh enslaved the world." [39] The New Orleans *Jeffersonian Republican* represented press economico-ethical sentiment in arguing that unless American supremacy were extended to the Rio Del Norte a few years would suffice for the establishment of an influence near us "highly dangerous to our prosperity, and inimical to the spread of Republican institutions." [40] The discussions of annexation in the congressional debates gave rise to numerous similar observations, and the passage by the Senate of the resolution for annexation of Texas was acclaimed by the New Orleans *Picayune* as "the triumph of republican energy over royal finesse; as the triumph of free minds over the diplomacy of foreign taskmaster." [41] President Polk's message announcing the acceptance of annexation by Texas gave prominent place to an attack upon the attempted application of the European doctrine of the balance of power to America—an application which he attributed to hostility to "the expansion of free principles." [42]

No less frequently did the ideal of defending democracy figure in the Oregon issue, in which the claims of the United States were again pitted against those of Great Britain. This question seemed to Senator Dickinson to be "a question between two great systems; between monarchy and republicanism." [43] The annexation of Oregon, Representative Sawyer declared, would rid the continent of British power and thereby "hand down to posterity, pure and unadulterated, that freedom we received from the fathers of the Revolution." [44] For it seemed, as Representative Levin said, that the spirit of republicanism "permits not the contaminating proximity of monarchies upon the soil that we have consecrated to the rights of man." [45] Such an attitude toward the Oregon issue also occasioned Senator Allen's resolution affirming that European political interference or colonization upon this hemisphere would be "dangerous to the liberties of the people of America." [46]

With justification Americans also feared the British lion in the wilderness of California. The Whig *American Review* spoke typically in accusing Great Britain of seeking sovereignty over California in order to interpose a barrier to the general growth of the American Union and thereby to "the progress of republican liberty, by which she believes her own institutions and the position of the family of European sovereigns, to be seriously menaced." [47] Such interposition, it declared, was dangerous to the self-preservation

[36] Dexter Perkins, *The Monroe Doctrine 1826–1867* (Baltimore, 1933), p. 64.

[37] Richardson, *Messages,* IV, 261.

[38] James Parton, *Life of Andrew Jackson* (New York, 1860), III, 658.

[39] *A Letter of the Hon. Dixon H. Lewis, to His Constituents of the Third Congressional District of Alabama* (n. p., 1844), p. 8.

[40] New Orleans *Jeffersonian Republican,* reprinted in *Richmond Enquirer,* January 7, 1845.

[41] New Orleans *Daily Picayune,* reprinted in *Nashville Union,* March 25, 1845.

[42] Richardson, *Messages,* IV, 398.

[43] *Cong. Globe,* 29th Cong., 1st sess., p. 424.

[44] *Ibid.,* App., p. 229.

[45] *Ibid.,* p. 95.

[46] *Ibid.,* 29th Cong., 1st sess., p. 197.

[47] *American Review,* "California," III (1846), 98.

of the United States and therefore unallowable. Secretary of State Buchanan's despatch of 1845 to Consul Larkin, indicating the favorable view which a petition of the colonists for annexation would receive, spoke of Great Britain's designs as conflicting with the desire of the colonists for republican institutions.[48] The *New York Herald,* calling likewise for protection of free institutions, wished to annex the whole of Mexico instead of merely California.[49] Stephen Douglas hoped to check absolutism by annexing Canada. Representative Cary stated his constituents' broader doctrine: "Their doctrine was, that this continent was intended by Providence as a vast theatre on which to work out the grand experiment of Republican government, under the auspices of the Anglo-Saxon race. If the worn-out and corrupt monarchies of the Old World had colonies here; let them be kept within the narrowest limits, consistent with justice and the faith of treaties. Let all which remains be preserved for the growth and spread of the free principles of American democracy." [50]

However, the toleration of existent European colonies seemed to still bolder spirits to be contrary to the true purpose of Providence. In the July number of the *Democratic Review* of 1845 an article on the Texas question affirmed nothing less than continental dominion to be America's "manifest destiny." The historic phrase, as the researches of Professor Pratt indicate, seems to have been used for the first time in this article. The article is attributed by Professor Pratt[51] on the ground of internal evidence to John L.

O'Sullivan, editor of the *Democratic Review* and the *New York Morning News,* later Minister to Portugal, who was called by John St. Tammany rather fulsomely "one of the ablest writers and most accomplished scholars and gentlemen of the times." [52] The passage using the later famous phrase is as follows: "Why, were other reasons wanting, in favor of now elevating this question of the reception of Texas into the Union, out of the lower region of our past party dissensions, up to its proper level of a high and broad nationality, it surely is to be found, found abundantly, in the manner in which other nations have undertaken to intrude themselves into it, between us and the proper parties to the case, in a spirit of hostile interference against us, for the avowed object of thwarting our policy and hampering our power, limiting our greatness and checking the fulfilment of our manifest destiny to overspread the continent allotted by Providence for the free development of our yearly multiplying millions." [53] European encroachment must thus be thanked for making manifest the destiny of continental dominion. With truth Professor Rippy remarks that "manifest destiny never pointed to the acquisition of a region so unmistakably as when undemocratic, conservative Europe revealed an inclination to interfere or to absorb." [54] What was not manifest to Americans was the vicious circle which their defensive expansion created; for Europe's inclination to interfere in North America was caused chiefly by fear of the growing economic and political ambition of the United States.

DAN E. CLARK:
MANIFEST DESTINY AND THE PACIFIC*

. . . The term Manifest Destiny is here used in a broad sense. It includes, in the first place, the emotion which prompted Elkanah Watson, prophesying in 1778 for the year 1900, to speak of "the decrees of the Almighty, who has evidently raised up this nation to become a lamp to guide degraded and oppressed humanity";[2] or Albert J. Beveridge in 1900 to call America

"trustee, under God, of the civilization of the world." [3] This is the chosen-people, beacon-to-mankind interpretation of America's mission and duty. This is the view of which Carl Schurz wrote, although without adding his approval, when he referred to the "youthful optimism . . . inspiring the minds of many Americans with the idea that this republic, being charged with the mission of bearing the banner of freedom over the whole civilized world, could transform any country, inhabited by any kind of population, into something like itself simply by extending over it the magic charm of its political institutions." [4]

[48] *The Works of James Buchanan,* ed. J. B. Moore (Philadelphia, 1908–1911), VI, 276.

[49] *New York Herald,* January 6, 1846.

[50] *Cong. Globe,* 28th Cong., 2d sess., App., pp. 161–62.

[51] Julius W. Pratt, "The Origin of 'Manifest Destiny,'" *American Historical Review,* XXXII (1927), 795–98.

* Reprinted from Dan E. Clark, "Manifest Destiny and the Pacific," *Pacific Historical Review,* I (March, 1932), 1–17 by permission.

[2] Quoted in Jesse Lee Bennett, *The Essential American Tradition* (New York, 1925), 296.

[52] *Tri-Weekly Nashville Union,* January 28, 1845.

[53] *Democratic Review,* "Annexation," XVII (1845), 5.

[54] Rippy, *The United States and Mexico,* p. 29.

[3] *Congressional Record,* 56 cong., 1 sess., 704.

[4] Carl Schurz, "Manifest Destiny" in *Harper's Monthly,* LXXXVII, 737 (1893).

Then there is the doctrine of pre-ordination or inevitability governing the westward progress of the "star of empire." For some it was divine command and the superintending guidance of Providence that furnished the irresistible impulse. Others based their prophecies on the ceaseless inward urge which had for so long been impelling Anglo-saxon peoples westward. Still others referred to the certainty that American dominion and American enterprise must seek their natural boundaries, as water seeks its level. All these are included in the meaning of Manifest Destiny as here used.

The writer feels no necessity to pass judgment on the sincerity or motives of those who eloquently propounded the views, hereafter mentioned or quoted, in regard to the unavoidable rôle which America was destined to play on both shores of the Pacific. Most of these men lived long before the day of the modern cynic and debunker. If there was dross mingled with the gold in their exaltation and enthusiasm, few of them were conscious of it. America was still the land of the free and the home of the brave. At the same time it is true that there were always those who denied the force of predestinarian logic; and at the close of the last century there were many critics who exposed selfish economic imperialism lurking behind fine-sounding phrases.

The definite formulation of the doctrine of Manifest Destiny no doubt belongs to the decade of the roaring forties. With respect to the Pacific Coast and the Pacific, however, it seems certain that the essential features of that idea were in men's minds at a considerably earlier date. Even Coleridge in his later years was constrained to say: "The possible destiny of the United States of America, as a nation of a hundred millions of freemen, stretching from the Atlantic to the Pacific, living under the laws of Alfred, and speaking the language of Shakespeare and Milton, is an august conception."[5]

The writer will not pretend to say when the idea of the possibility or desirability or certainty of American control on the Pacific first entered men's minds. Some part of it no doubt occurred to the hardy New England sea captains who sailed around the Horn and up the western coast after the close of the Revolution. Some such vision probably animated the restless John Ledyard. Apparently it was in the thought of John Adams when, in his *Defense* of the American Constitution in 1787, he wrote: "Thirteen governments thus founded on the natural authority of the people alone . . . and which are destined to spread over the northern part of that whole quarter of the globe, are a great point gained in favor of the rights of mankind."[6] Whatever may have

been the hopes and purposes of Thomas Jefferson in his long-continued efforts to promote far western exploration, he apparently went no further than to look forward, as he wrote to John Jacob Astor, to the time when the descendants of the first settlers on the Pacific slope should "spread themselves through the whole length of that coast, covering it with free and independent Americans, unconnected with us but by the ties of blood and interest."[7]

Before Jefferson passed from the stage, however, others were to express views that were far less hesitating. "Nothing can or will limit the immigration westward, but the Western Ocean," declared Timothy Flint in 1825. "Alas! for the moving generation of the day, when the tide of advancing backwoodsmen shall have met the surge of the Pacific. They may then set themselves down and weep for other worlds."[8] The accumulating information in regard to the Oregon country and the Treaty of 1818 with Great Britain providing for joint occupancy directed attention to the importance of the mouth of the Columbia. "Upon the people of Eastern Asia," said that ardent advocate of western measures, Thomas Hart Benton, in 1820, "the establishment of a civilized power on the opposite coast of America, could not fail to produce great and wonderful benefits. Science, liberal principles in government, and the true religion, might cast their lights across the intervening sea."[9]

The debate in the House in 1822-3 on Floyd's bill to occupy the mouth of the Columbia brought out from rather unexpected sources the full idea of Manifest Destiny, even if the actual words were not used. Although George Tucker of Virginia opposed the bill, he was bound to admit that "we cannot arrest the progress of our population to the West. In vain may the Government attempt to set limits to its course. It marches on, with the increasing rapidity of a fire, and nothing will stop it until it reaches the shores of the Pacific."[10] But it was Francis Baylies of Massachusetts who preached the doctrine most fully and eloquently. Even, said he, if the settlers who went to Oregon should later decide to form their own separate government,

---

years later, in his speech on the Alaska treaty, Charles Sumner referred to this statement by Adams, and interpreted it to predict the spread of the United States to the Pacific. "Thus," said Sumner, "according to the prophetic minister, even at that early day was the destiny of the Republic manifest." *The Works of Charles Sumner* (Boston, 1874–83), XI, 222.

[7] Paul Leicester Ford (ed.), *The Writings of Thomas Jefferson* (New York, 1892–99), IX, 351.

[8] Timothy Flint, *Recollections of the Last Ten Years* (Boston, 1826), 203.

[9] Thomas Hart Benton, *Thirty Years' View* (New York, 1854–56), I, 13.

[10] *Annals of Congress*, 17 cong., 2 sess., 422.

---

[5] Coleridge's *Table Talk*, quoted on the title page of Robert Greenhow, *The History of Oregon and California* (Boston, 1845).

[6] Charles Francis Adams (ed.), *The Works of John Adams* (Boston, 1850–56), IV, 293. Eighty

"with a nation of kindred blood, governed by laws similar to yours, cherishing your principles, speaking your language, and worshipping your God, you may rear a monument more magnificent than the Arch of Trajan, more durable than the pyramids; a living, animated, and everlasting monument of your glory and your greatness." Addressing the timid and reluctant, he predicted that if they passed the bill they might in later life "cherish delightful recollections of this day, when America, almost shrinking from the 'shadows of coming events,' first placed her feet upon untrodden ground, scarcely daring to anticipate the grandeur which awaited her." Returning to the discussion at a later point in the debate, he said: "Gentlemen are talking of natural boundaries. Sir, our natural boundary is the Pacific ocean. The swelling tide of our population must and will roll on until that mighty ocean interposes its waters, and limits our territorial empire." Finally, to conclude these rather extended excerpts from this early apostle of Manifest Destiny, Baylies reached his climax when, in his peroration, he exclaimed: "To diffuse the arts of life, the light of science, and the blessings of the gospel over a wilderness, is no violation of the laws of God; it is no invasion of the rights of man to occupy a territory over which the savage roams, but which he never cultivates. . . The stream of bounty which perpetually flows from the throne of the Almighty ought not to be obstructed in its course, nor is it right that his benevolent designs should be defeated by the perversity of man."[11]

During the ensuing two decades, little happened to elicit similar exuberant predictions regarding the Pacific Coast and its destiny. And yet the idea lay not far below the current of thought and appeared occasionally on the surface in western newspapers. For instance, in 1825 the *Ohio State Journal,* speaking of the Oregon country, said: "One fourth part of this territory, that part which contains the Oregon harbor, will, at a future day, enter the Republican Confederacy as Oregon State; and the City of Oregon, will arise on its banks, which shall rival New York or Philadelphia in their wealth and population. Then the busy hum of commerce and the shouts of freemen, shall re-echo from the Atlantic to the Pacific oceans."[12] Five years later the *Buffalo Journal* reviewed the irresistible westward march of American pioneers. "This course of empire," said the editor, "may—must be stayed, when the shore of the Pacific has been reached."[13] In a speech in the House of Representatives Caleb Cushing rejoiced in "the

spectacle of the Anglo-American stock extending itself into the heart of the Continent . . . advancing with, as it were, the preordination of inevitable progress, like the sun moving westerly in the heavens, or the ascending tide on the seashore, or, in the striking language of a foreign traveller, as a deluge of civilized men rising unabatedly and driven onwards by the hand of God." When the settlers should reach the Pacific he desired them to "carry along with them the laws, education, and social improvements, which belong to the older states . . . worthily fulfilling the great destiny reserved for this exemplar American Republic."[14]

Then came the "fabulous forties" when American buoyancy reached its highest point. Now it was that the desire for territorial expansion came out into the open, unashamed and aggressive. During this decade the Oregon question was settled, after there had been set up that "redoubtable line" of 54° 40', up to which, in the words of Benton, "all true patriots were to march! and marching, fight! and fighting, die! if need be! singing all the while, with Horace— *'Dulce et decorum est pro patria mori.'* "[15] Before the ownership of Oregon was determined there were abundant opportunities for enthusiasts to portray the inevitability of our possession and the wonders that were to follow. Benton, himself, though scorning our claim up to 54° 40', was an ardent advocate of our right to the entire valley of the Columbia. "Such a country is formed for union, wealth, and strength," he said in a speech in 1842, which dims into dullness the most glowing prognostications of the modern chamber of commerce promoter. "It can have but one capital, and that will be a Thebes; but one commercial emporium, and that will be a Tyre, queen of cities. Such a country can have but one people, one interest, one government: and that people should be American—that interest ours— and that government republican. . . Accursed and infamous be the man that divides or alienates it!"[16] A year later he declared that the white race had always gone for land and, said he, "they will continue to go for it, and will go where they can get it. Europe, Asia, and America have been settled by them in this way. All the States of this Union have been so settled. The principle is founded in their nature and in God's command; and it will continue to be obeyed."[17]

It was in the debate on the termination of joint occupancy in Oregon in January, 1846, according to J. W. Pratt, that Congress first heard the doctrine of Manifest Destiny expressed in those exact words. Robert C. Winthrop of

[11] *Annals of Congress,* 17 cong., 2 sess., 421, 422, 682–3, 688.

[12] Quoted from the *Ohio State Journal* in the *Detroit Gazette,* January 3, 1826.

[13] Quoted from the *Buffalo Journal* in *The Arkansas Advocate,* June 9, 1830.

[14] Claude Moore Fuess, *The Life of Caleb Cushing* (New York, 1923), I, 246–7.

[15] Benton, *Thirty Years' View,* II, 669.

[16] Benton, *Thirty Years' View,* II, 430.

[17] Benton, *Thirty Years' View,* II, 474.

Massachusetts spoke of this "new revelation of right" justifying expansion over the whole continent. He apparently referred to an editorial which had recently appeared in the New York *Morning News*. The editor pushed aside all the time-honored rights to territorial possession and based our claim to Oregon on a manifest destiny originating in a divine purpose and command that we should extend far and wide the blessings of liberty and self-government.[18] This concise and convenient formula met with ready acceptance. We may well imagine with what gratitude it was seized upon by some of those advocates of expansion who had been troubled by secret misgivings that national aggrandizement was not a wholly altruistic ambition.

Oregon was not the only Pacific project during the forties to which this formula or a similar viewpoint might be applied. Caleb Cushing's mission to China in 1843 was undertaken, according to his own words, "in behalf of civilization." The amazing letter from President Tyler, attributed to Webster, which he bore to the Emperor of China, breathed condescension and cited "the will of Heaven" that a treaty should be the outcome of the mission.[19]

During this decade also the pioneer promoters of a railroad to the Pacific, like John Plumbe and Asa Whitney, were painting alluring pictures of the great development of commerce with the orient that would follow the fruition of their plans. They did not neglect to call attention to the attendant opportunities for the dissemination of the light of American civilization. Benton became a convert to the plan and made his famous speech in which he suggested that the completed line should "be adorned with its crowning honor, the colossal statue of the great Columbus, whose design it accomplishes, hewn from the granite mass of a peak of the Rocky Mountains, overlooking the road, the mountain itself the pedestal, and the statue a part of the mountain, pointing with outstretched arm to the western horizon, and saying to the flying passenger, 'There is the East! There is India!'"[20]

Last, but not least, it was during this decade that California came within the scope of practical politics and Manifest Destiny. "California," declared Benton in 1846, "become independent of Mexico by the revolt of the Picos, and independent of them by the revolt of the American settlers, had its destiny to fulfill—which was, to be handed over to the United States. So that its incorporation with the American Republic was equally sure in any and every event."[21] In a political letter in the same year, William H. Seward announced his belief that "Our population is destined to roll its resistless waves to the icy barriers of the North, and to encounter oriental civilization on the shores of the Pacific."[22]

Thus early did Seward enter upon his grandiloquent career as perhaps the most persistent exponent of the doctrine of America's unescapable and all-including destiny. To him no prospect was more exhilarating than that offered by the opportunities on the shores of the Pacific and across its waters. "The Atlantic states, through their commercial, social, and political affinities and sympathies," said he, during the debate on the admission of California in 1850, "are steadily renovating the governments and the social constitutions of Europe and of Africa. The Pacific states must necessarily perform the same sublime and beneficent functions in Asia. If, then, the American people shall remain an undivided nation, the ripening civilization of the West, after a separation growing wider and wider for four thousand years, will, in its circuit of the world, meet again and mingle with the declining civilization of the East on our own free soil, and a new and more perfect civilization will arise to bless the earth, under the sway of our own cherished and beneficent democratic institutions."[23] Later in the same debate, speaking of California, he said: "She has brought us to the banks of streams which flow over precious sands, and, at the base of mountains which yield massive gold, she delivers into our hand the key that unlocks the long-coveted treasures of the eastern world. . . She invites us . . . to extend the sway of peace, of arts, and of freedom, over nations beyond the seas, still slumbering under the mingled reign of barbarian superstition and unalleviated despotism."[24]

Most men ceased to talk of expansion during the timid years immediately following the achievement of the great compromise, and during the troublous times after the enactment of the Kansas-Nebraska bill. The emotion of Manifest Destiny was satisfied for most Americans by the extension of our national domains to the southwest and to the Pacific. It was not so with Seward. The Pacific railroad bill, measures for the encouragement of commerce on the Pacific—any and every pertinent project was seized by him as the occasion for a panegyric on his favorite subject. He was equally capable of making his own occasion. In the Senate in 1852 he delivered

---

[18] Julius W. Pratt, "The Origin of Manifest Destiny" in *American Historical Review*, XXXII, 795-6.

[19] Fuess, *The Life of Caleb Cushing*, I, 414–415, 419–420.

[20] J. P. Davis, *The Union Pacific Railway* (Chicago, 1894), 136.

[21] Benton, *Thirty Years' View*, II, 693.

[22] Frederic Bancroft, *The Life of William H. Seward* (New York, 1900), II, 470.

[23] G. E. Baker (ed.), *The Works of William H. Seward* (New York, 1853–1884), I, 58.

[24] Baker, *The Works of William H. Seward*, I, 94.

his most famous prophecy concerning our destiny in the Pacific. "Even the discovery of this continent and its islands," he declared, "and the organization of society and government upon them, grand and important as these events have been, were but conditional, preliminary, and ancillary to the more sublime result, now in the act of consummation—the reunion of the two civilizations, which, having parted on the plains of Asia four thousand years ago, and having travelled ever afterward in opposite directions around the world, now meet again on the coasts and islands of the Pacific Ocean." This movement was no delusion; it was inevitable, and the benefits to Asia would be profound. "Who does not see, then," he continued, "that every year hereafter, European commerce, European politics, European thoughts, and European activity, although actually gaining greater force—and European connections, although actually becoming more intimate—will, nevertheless, relatively sink in importance; while the Pacific Ocean, its shores, its islands, and the vast regions beyond, will become the chief theatre of events in the world's great hereafter." [25]

In 1860 neither the gathering clouds of civil conflict nor the approach of the Republican nominating convention was sufficient wholly to divert Seward's gaze from the constantly enlarging vision which his crystal revealed. By this time he saw a United States covering at least all the continent of North America, with its capital in the valley of Mexico. It was in a speech at St. Paul that he presaged an event in which he was to play a leading role seven years later. "Standing here and looking far off into the northwest," he said, "I see the Russian as he busily occupies himself in establishing seaports and towns and fortifications, on the verge of the continent, as the outposts of St. Petersburg, and I can say 'Go on and build up your outposts all along the coast, up even to the Arctic Ocean—they will yet become the outposts of my own country—monuments of the civilization of the United States in the northwest." [26] Opponents of Seward at this time claimed that he was even in favor of the annexation of a part of China. One of his biographers suggests that something of the kind may have been in Seward's mind when he wrote to Cassius M. Clay in 1861 suggesting that Russia and the United States might remain good friends until they met "in regions where civilization first began." [27]

Professor Golder furnished us with an illustration of the impression which American push

and optimism made about this time upon at least one European—one whom he identified as Rear-admiral Popov of Russia, who had been in California and Alaska. Whether this observer had read Seward's St. Paul speech or whether he merely absorbed his ideas from the spirit of the people, he wrote to his home government that Europeans might sneer at the Monroe Doctrine and Manifest Destiny, but that these doctrines were in the blood of Americans and in the air they breathed. "There are twenty millions of Americans," he wrote, in substance, "every one of them a free man and filled with the idea that America is for Americans. They have taken California, Oregon, and sooner or later they will get Alaska. It is inevitable. It cannot be prevented; and it would be better to yield with good grace and cede the territory to them." [28]

Seven years later the destiny foretold by Seward and Admiral Popov was fulfilled and Alaska came into the possession of the United States as if by magic and in spite of the sneers of the skeptical. One of the defenders of the purchase treaty in the Senate was Charles Sumner. He was concerned that the treaty should not be "a precedent for a system of indiscriminate and costly annexation." Nevertheless, he sincerely believed "that republican institutions under the primacy of the United States must embrace this whole continent." At another point in his long speech he spoke of the republic as "something more than a local policy; it is a general principle not to be forgotten when the opportunity is presented of bringing an immense region within its influence. The present treaty," he continued, "is a visible step in the occupation of the whole North American continent. As such it will be recognized by the world and accepted by the American people. But the treaty involves something more. We dismiss one other monarch from the continent. One by one they have retired—first France, then Spain, then France again, and now Russia—all giving way to the absorbing Unity declared in the national motto, *E pluribus unum*." [29]

No sooner was Alaska acquired than Seward's active mind was contemplating new realms of destiny. The ink on the treaty was scarcely dry when he was talking of Hawaii and complaining that people were too much engrossed in domestic questions "to entertain the higher, but more remote, questions of national extension." [30] But that engrossment in domestic affairs was too deep to be seriously disturbed. To be sure, the completion of the Union Pacific Railroad in

[25] Baker, *The Works of William H. Seward*, I, 248–250.

[26] Bancroft, *The Life of William H. Seward*, II, 471.

[27] Bancroft, *The Life of William H. Seward*, II, 471.

[28] Frank A. Golder, "The Purchase of Alaska" in *American Historical Review*, XXV, 416.

[29] *The Works of Charles Sumner*, XI, 222–223, 233.

[30] Bancroft, *The Life of William H. Seward*, II, 489.

1869 occasioned a burst of national enthusiasm. Appreciation of the significance of that achievement as far as the Pacific was concerned was best expressed by Bret Harte when he had the western engine say to the one from the east as they met at Promontory Point:

> You brag of your East! You do?
> Why, I bring the East to you!
> All the Orient, all Cathay,
> Find through me the shortest way;
> And the sun you follow here
> Rises in my hemisphere.[31]

Then for more than two decades the American people were willing to let their further destiny wait while they frenziedly exploited the resources already within their reach, and while they enjoyed the new toys introduced by the industrial revolution. It was not until the decade of the nineties that there seemed a need for more worlds to conquer. Then again the islands of the Pacific became very alluring. Among the early proponents of this recrudescence of Manifest Destiny was that great expositor of the dominance of sea power, Captain A. T. Mahan. "That which we have received of the true spirit of freedom we have kept—liberty and law—not the one or the other, but both," he wrote in 1893 in an article on the importance of Hawaii to us. "In that spirit we not only have occupied our original inheritance, but also, step by step, as Rome incorporated the other nations of the peninsula, we have added to it, spreading and perpetuating everywhere the same foundation principles of free and good government. . . And now, arrested on the south by the rights of a race wholly alien to us, and on the north by a body of states of like traditions to our own, whose freedom to choose their own affiliations we respect, we have come to the sea. . . Have we no right or call to progress farther in any direction?" The real direction of his thoughts appeared when he said that "the annexation, even, of Hawaii would be no mere sporadic effort, irrational because disconnected from an adequate motive, but a first-fruit and a token that the nation in its evolution has aroused itself to the necessity of carrying its life—that has been the happiness of those under its influence—beyond the borders which heretofore have sufficed for its activities."

In order to safeguard and make useful an acquisition so evidently ordained, it was likewise inevitable that the United States should build an Isthmian Canal. "Land-carriage, always restricted and therefore always slow," explained Mahan, "toils enviously but hopelessly behind, vainly seeking to replace and supplant the royal highway of Nature's own making. Corporate interests, vigorous in that power of concentration which is the strength of armies and of minorities, may here for a while withstand the

ill-organized strivings of the multitude, only dimly conscious of its wants; yet the latter, however temporarily opposed and baffled, is sure at last, like the blind force of nature, to overwhelm all that stand in the way of its necessary progress. So the Isthmian Canal is an inevitable part in the future of the United States." [32]

Four years later the captain's views had expanded and an even more glorious destiny and mission had been unfolded to him. It appeared to him then "that in the ebb and flow of human affairs, under those mysterious impulses the origin of which is sought by some in a personal Providence, by some in laws not yet fully understood, we stand at the opening of a period when the question is to be settled" whether eastern or western civilization was to dominate the world. "The great task now before the world of civilized Christianity," he declared, "its great mission, which it must fulfil or perish, is to receive into its own bosom and raise to its own ideals those ancient and different civilizations . . . at the head of which stand China, India, and Japan." [33]

Even more persuasive and literary, but less sweeping in his vision, was Mahan's brother naval officer, Commodore George W. Melville. The dignified pages of the *North American Review* for March, 1898, carried his glowing exhortation: "But little more than a century has gone by since on the winter wind at Valley Forge, there streamed a ragged flag, the star of hope to the stern soldiery whose bare and bleeding feet reddened the snow as they guarded it there. In the generations that have passed, that flag, with the clustering memories not only of victory by land and sea, but of many a year of happy peace, has swept from ocean to ocean.

> Shall a noble destiny lead it still farther on, as
> Bright on the banner of lily and rose,
> Lo, the last sun of our century sets?

Shall its purpose hold," he further inquired, "to follow the pathway of the stars, 'to sail beyond the sunset,' and floating over Hawaii to guard the golden shore of the Republic and to win a new glory on that wide sea?" [34]

Contemporaneously Charles Denby Jr. sounded a similar note concerning the Orient, with his major emphasis less disguised. "America may attempt to evade the responsibility thrust upon her," he asserted. "She may, with shortsighted resolution, turn her face away from her great future, but she will not succeed. The markets of the Orient are the heritage of her merchants, and the time will inevitably come when

---

[31] See Davis, *The Union Pacific Railway*, 155.

[32] Alfred T. Mahan, "Hawaii and our Future Sea Power" in *Forum*, XV, I–II.

[33] Alfred T. Mahan, "A Twentieth-Century Outlook" in *Harper's Monthly*, XCV, 527.

[34] George W. Melville, "Our Duty on the Pacific—What We Have There to Hold and Win" in *North American Review*, CLXVI, 296.

the voice of the Republic will be heard in oriental courts with the same accent of authority as in the commonwealths of South America. It would be well if the certainty of this destiny could be recognized before European statesmanship has barred the way with 'vested interests'." [35]

Within a few months after the last two exhortations were printed, war with Spain was declared and the United States was launched on her career as a world power, with island dominions in both great oceans. It needs not to be shown in this presence how Manifest Destiny was now pressed into the service of imperial policy, especially with regard to the Philippines. "The war has brought us new duties and responsibilities," proclaimed President McKinley, "which we must meet and discharge as becomes a great nation on whose growth and career from the beginning the Ruler of Nations has plainly written the high command and pledge of civilization. Incidental to our tenure in the Philippines is the commercial opportunity to which American statesmanship cannot be indifferent." Our own E. D. Adams slyly paraphrased this sentiment to read "God directs us—perhaps it will pay." [36] William Allen White seems to have been caught up in the emotional fervor of the period. In his *Emporia Gazette* he exclaimed: "It is the Anglo-saxon's manifest destiny to go forth as a world conqueror. He will take possession of the islands of the sea. . . This is what fate holds for the chosen people. It is so written. . . It is so to be." [37]

Even this sketchy recital would be inadequate if it neglected to quote more fully from that classic gem—Albert J. Beveridge's maiden speech in the United States Senate on January 9, 1900—from which an excerpt was read at the beginning of this paper. "We will not renounce our part in the mission of the race, trustee, under God, of the civilization of the world," he insisted, speaking of our retention of control in the Philippines. "He has made us adepts in government that we may administer government among savages and senile peoples. . . And of all our race He has marked the American people as His chosen nation to finally lead in the regeneration of the world. This is the divine mission of America, and it holds for us all the profit, all the glory, all the happiness possible to man. . . What shall history say of us? Shall it say that we renounced that holy trust, left the savage to his base condition, the wilderness to the reign of waste, deserted duty, abandoned glory, forgot our

sordid profit even, because we feared our strength and read the charter of our powers with the doubter's eye and the quibbler's mind? Shall it say that, called by events to captain and command the proudest, ablest, purest race in history in history's noblest work, we declined that great commission?" [38]

This survey of the application of the doctrine of Manifest Destiny to the Pacific would seem to demand a fervid peroration. Such a task is beyond the powers or imagination of the writer. Let him who wishes speculate as to the next occasion that shall cause this emotion to find expression in the halls of Congress and the pages of our press. Let him who can tell us whether the American's sense of humor or his fairness to Providence will make such utterances less probable in the future.

It is perhaps fitting that we should close with reverential words written two decades ago by the great historian of our Pacific Coast, Hubert Howe Bancroft. "Were we as ready as were our forefathers to see the hand of Providence in the affairs of men, some things might be accounted for which must now await further accession of wisdom," he wrote in his time of retrospection, as he surveyed the course of events on these western shores. "In our ignorance we might ask, for example, what possible connection could there be between a Yankee fur-trader on the Northwest Coast of America in the year 1792, the federal congress at Philadelphia, and a Corsican adventurer seeking advancement in the streets of Paris. Or, again, what could black cannibals in the jungles of Africa, or whilom importations thence in Georgia and Alabama, or the visit of a future president to Florida have to do with the late possessions of the king of Spain, or in establishing the southern limits and frontage on the Pacific of an Anglo-saxon commonwealth in the wilds of America. And yet, enlightened by wisdom from on high, one might answer, It is the Invisible Architect of the Republic, his finger pointing out where the corner stones shall be laid, corners so wide apart, so utterly at variance, that only the eye of omniscience may trace the lines of their connection."

Again Bancroft said: "The star of empire leading westward; the star of empire which we have followed, from Holland, from England, across the continent, across the Pacific sinks now as we approach the threshold of the ancient East, while we find ourselves still holding fast to our traditions." [39] While we may lack something of his faith, these words hold for us a challenge to separate the genuine idealism from the all too evident jingoism in our great American emotion of Manifest Destiny.

---

[35] C. Denby Jr., "America's Opportunity in Asia" in *North American Review*, CLXVI, 35.

[36] Ephraim D. Adams, *The Power of Ideals in American History* (New Haven, 1913), 92.

[37] Helen O. Mahin (ed.), *The Editor and his People* (New York, 1924), 305. In a footnote supplied by Mr. White his comment in 1924 is: "The squawk of the hard-boiled chicken that has not pipped the shell."

[38] *Congressional Record*, 56 cong., 1 sess., 704, 711.

[39] Hubert Howe Bancroft, *Retrospection, Political and Personal* (New York, 1912), I, 13.

Commodore Robert F. Stockton, fresh from his California adventures, spoke enthusiastically about territorial expansion to a Philadelphia audience in 1847. In this selection he impassionately asked, "Do we not indeed present an example of the beneficent care of Providence for which we can find no parallel in the history of man?"

ROBERT F. STOCKTON:
CALIFORNIA*

Annexation, nay acquisition, is not a necessary consequence of conquest—and, therefore, it is not on that account that I would offer my congratulations here today—oh, no!

I care not for the beautiful fields and healthful skies of California. I care not for her leagues of land and her mines of silver. The glory of the achievements there—if any glory there be, is in the establishment of the first free press, in California—(Great applause)—in having built the first school house in California—in having established religious toleration as well as civil liberty in California—(Tremendous applause)—May the torch grow brighter and brighter, until from Cape Mendocino to Cape St. Lucas, it illumines the dark path of the victim of religious intolerance and political despotism. (Thunders of applause.)

The inhabitants of California, number, I believe about 12 or 15000. A large portion of them, if not all of them, prefer the institutions of the US; and it is much to be hoped, may I not say, fervently, devoutly to be prayed for, that they shall in some way or other be secured in the permanent enjoyment of civil and religious liberty—(great applause)—and that our friends there may not pay the dreadful penalty the Mexican always demands—his life for his fidelity to us! (Great applause.) Well, however this may turn out, if it should be otherwise—if these pleasing anticipations should not be realized—other hands must tear down the school houses—other hands must put out the light of liberty! (Great cheers.) For me and mine, before God, we'll take no part in such a business! (Enthusiastic applause.)

California has within herself the elements of wealth and power; and when art, and science, and religion—when all the genial influences of civilization, which in our day is advancing with such marvellous rapidity, are brought to bear upon her, may we not reasonably assert that the years will be but few, before we behold her standing erect in the attitude of a free and independent nation. (Great applause.") . . .

"No thoughtful observer of the progress of the U. States, can fail to be impressed with the conviction that we enjoy a degree of happiness and prosperity never heretofore vouchsafed to the nations of mankind. With an unexampled measure of political liberty; unbroken social order; extraordinary growth of the arts and sciences—philanthropic and benevolent institutions, the fair offspring of the christian faith, extending their blessed agency, in all directions—unbounded religious toleration, heaven's best gift; for which our fathers risked and suffered most—with all these rich endowments, do we not indeed present an example of the beneficent care of Providence for which we can find no parallel in the history of man? And now when engaged in war, we find ourselves, followed by the same blessed influences. Wherever our soldiers have carried our arms, victory has awaited them. We see them rushing against walls, bristling with bayonets and artillery, and lined with legions of armed men;—we see our youthful heroes precipitating themselves from parapet to parapet, and charging from bastion to bastion—we hear the crash of grape and canister, and amid the smoke and thunder of the battle, we behold the flag of our country, waiving—(the remainder of the sentence was lost in the tremendous cheering which here burst forth from the assemblage.) We behold the flag of civil and religious freedom waiving over what had been regarded as impregnable fortresses and the remains of armies fleeing to the mountains.

Gentlemen, how has all this been accomplished? Whence those achievements? I speak to intellectual men. All in the hearing of my voice entertain, I doubt not, a just and abiding sense of their deep responsibility not only on this earth, but in time hereafter. I ask you, then, how has all this happened? Is it to be attributed exclusively to the wisdom of our cabinet and the powers of our armies? These are all well—admirably well. But our successes have overleaped the bounds of all human calculation and the most sanguine hope. Therefore we must look beyond all this for the secret of our successes and the source of our remarkable prosperity. It is because the spirit of our pilgrim fathers is with us.—It is because the God of armies and the Lord of hosts is with us. (Tremendous applause.) And how is it with poor, unfortunate, wretched Mexico? Ever since the day of the last of the Montezumas, intestine broils have disturbed her peace. Her whole territory has been drenched with the blood of her own children. Within the last quar-

* Reprinted from *Niles National Register,* January 22, 1848.

ter of a century, revolution has succeeded revolution. Now in the encounter with us she has been beaten in every field. She has been driven from fortress to fortress—from town to town, until the scattered remnants of her broken armies are fleeing to the mountains and calling upon the rocks to hide them. (Applause.) Is it not, therefore, in this disposition of public affairs, proper to rise superior to the consideration of party influences, and in true philosophical spirit and patriotic fidelity, take an honest view of our condition, in the sight of God and beneath the scrutiny of the christian and civilized world?

What you may think of it, I know not; and you must permit me to add, I care not; but for myself I speak not to you as a party man. Remember, gentlemen, that I go for my country. I cannot be bound, I cannot be kept within the restraints of party discipline when my country calls me forth. [Tremendous cheering, which lasted several minutes.] I go for my country—my whole country and nothing but my country. I desire to address you now in the spirit of the father of a large family, desirous to transmit to his latest posterity the blessings of civil and religious liberty. I speak to you as a christian man—as a son, perhaps an unworthy son of this great republic, but one whose heart burns with an ardent deire to transmit, not only to his own immediate descendants, the blessings of which I speak, but to extend them to our neighbors on this continent. [Great applause.]

But do not mistake me. Do not misunderstand me. I am no propagandist in the common reception of the term. In my judgment, principles depend much upon relations and circumstances, and that which in the abstract may be well enough, often wastes itself in fanaticism. All things must bide their time.

I have no respect for the man or set of men who will recklessly disturb the social order of any community and produce civil war for the purpose of hastening such a result, no matter how beneficial in the abstract it may seem to be. [Cheers.] And I am bound to say farther, that I have quite as little respect for the man or set of men, who have in the Providence of God been placed in stations, when the great questions of civil and religious liberty are to be determined, who will shrink from the responsibilities of that station. [Cheers.] In the application of these principles to the future policy of this country, let it not be supposed for a moment that I would presume to censure the great men of this nation.—Nor would I attempt to instruct the most humble of my countrymen. I present these views merely for the purpose of rendering more distinct and clear the remarks which I have offered, and which I may not have stated with sufficient explicitness.

I suppose the war with Mexico was caused by the repeated insults which time after time had been heaped upon this nation. [Great applause.] I regard this much talked of indemnity as merely collateral or incidental, arising out of the circumstances of the war. In my opinion, that question will be set aside, if not wholly lost sight of in the pressure of the great considerations which are to grow out of the high responsibilities and delicate duties crowding upon us, and the unexampled victories which have attended our arms. [Cheers.] In pursuing a legitimate object of war —in the providence of God we are placed, or are likely so to be placed, in a position where by a fair and legitimate construction of the law of nations, the fate of Mexico and the peace of this continent, to a greater or less extent, will devolve upon the virtue, the wisdom, and the humanity of our rulers. [Applause.] In these rulers I have the greatest confidence, and for them I entertain the most profound respect. [Applause.]

I tell you again gentlemen, this matter of indemnity, in money or any thing else, will be secondary, altogether secondary, in comparison with the considerations which I have no doubt will be presented to this nation in the farther prosecution of this war. The insults have been resented—nobly resented—they have been wiped out—they have been washed out with blood. [Enthusiastic applause.] If, then, indemnity, means money, any financier will tell you that in *that* is what you seek as the only object of the war, you had better withdraw your troops as soon as possible, and you will *save* money. [A laugh.]

But indemnity is not the object of the war. No man here or elsewhere will consent to weigh blood against money. [Great applause.] I do not care who presents the proposition—when it is presented; or to whom it is presented, whig or democrat; no man will weigh blood for money. (Loud applause) But this is not, I repeat, our condition. Higher and nobler objects present themselves for the attainment of which you must increase your armies in Mexico, *cost* what it may. [Great applause.] Fifty thousand men must go to Mexico. [Renewed applause.]—Let me then state the objects for the attainment of which, in my judgment, this augmentation of our force in Mexico, is required.

Mexico is poor and wretched. Why? Misgovernment—insatiable avarice—unintermitted wrong unsparing cruelty and unbending insolence —these have inflicted their curse on the unhappy country, and made her what she is. But as the darkest hour is that which just precedes the advent of the morning sun, so let us hope that a better and happier day is now about to dawn upon unfortunate Mexico. Be it ours, now to forgive her all her trespasses, and returning good for evil, make her free and happy!—[Enthusiastic applause which lasted several minutes.]

If I were now the sovereign authority, as I was once the viceroy—[laughter.]—I would prosecute this war for the express purpose of redeeming Mexico from misrule and civil strife. If, however, such a treaty were offered me as that offered to the government of the United States, before God, I would consider it my bounden duty to reject it. [Loud applause]—I would say to them, we can pay the indemnity ourselves. But we have a duty before God which we cannot—we must not evade. The priceless boon of civil and religious liberty has been confided to us as trustees—[cheers.]—I would insist, if the war were to be prolonged for fifty years, and cost money enough to demand from us each year the half of all that we possess, I would still insist that the inestimable blessings of civil and religious liberty should be guaranteed to Mexico. We must not shrink from the solemn duty. We dare not shrink from it. We cannot lose sight of the great truth that nations are accountable as well as individuals, and that they too must meet the stern responsibilities of their moral character—they too must encounter the penalty of violated law in the more extended sphere adapted to their physical condition.

Let the solemn question come home to the bosom and business of every citizen of this great republic: "What have I done—what has this generation done for the advancement of civil and religious liberty!—(Applause.]

It is in view of this responsibility—of our obligations to the infinite source of all our peace, prosperity and happiness—of our duty to fulfil the great mission of liberty committed to our hands, that I would insist, cost what it may, on the establishment of a permanent, independent republic in Mexico.—[Cheers] I would insist that the great principle of religious toleration should be secured to all—that the Protestant in Mexico should be guaranteed the enjoyment of all the immunities and privileges enjoyed by Mexicans in the United States: [Loud cheers.] These great and benevolent objects I would accomplish by sending into Mexico a force adequate to maintain all the posts which we now occupy, to defend them against any assaults that might be made against them, and to keep open our communications. I would seize upon Paredes, Arista, and other military chieftains, and send them to St. Helena, if you please. [Laughter and applause.] I would declare an armistice; and the executive should be called upon to issue a proclamation, and send six or more commissioners to meet Mexico in a liberal and generous spirit.

We have vanquished Mexico. She is prostrate at our feet—we can afford to be magnanimous. Let us act so that we need not fear the strictest scrutiny of the christian and civilized word. I would with a magnanimous and kindly hand gather these wretched people within the fold of republicanism. [Loud applause.] This I would accomplish at any cost.

Proclaiming "Texas is now ours," John L. O'Sullivan stated in the following selection the classic argument for Manifest Destiny. In fact, the very term, "Manifest Destiny," was first coined in print in this article from the *Democratic Review*.

JOHN L. O'SULLIVAN:
ANNEXATION OF TEXAS*

It is time now for opposition to the Annexation of Texas to cease, all further agitation of the waters of bitterness and strife, at least in connexion with this question,—even though it may perhaps be required of us as a necessary condition of the freedom of our institutions, that we must live on for ever in a state of unpausing struggle and excitement upon some subject of party division or other. But, in regard to Texas, enough has now been given to party. It is time for the common duty of Patriotism to the Country to succeed;—or if this claim will not be recognized, it is at least time for common sense to acquiesce with decent grace in the inevitable and the irrevocable.

Texas is now ours. Already, before these words are written, her Convention has undoubtedly ratified the acceptance, by her Congress, of our proffered invitation into the Union; and made the requisite changes in her already republican form of constitution to adapt it to its future federal relations. Her star and her stripe may already be said to have taken their place in the glorious blazon of our common nationality; and the sweep of our eagle's wing already includes within its circuit the wide extent of her fair and fertile land. She is no longer to us a mere geographical space—a certain combination of coast, plain, mountain, valley, forest and stream. She is no longer to us a mere country on the map. She comes within the dear and sacred designation of Our Country; no longer a "*pays*," she is a part of "*la patrie*;" and that which is at once a sentiment and a virtue, Patriotism, already begins to thrill for her too within the national heart. It is time then that all should cease to treat her as alien, and even adverse—cease to denounce and

* Reprinted from John L. O'Sullivan, "Annexation of Texas," *The United States Magazine and Democratic Review*, XVII (July and August, 1845), 5–10.

vilify all and everything connected with her accession—cease to thwart and oppose the remaining steps for its consummation; or where such efforts are felt to be unavailing, at least to embitter the hour of reception by all the most ungracious frowns of aversion and words of unwelcome. There has been enough of all this. It has had its fitting day during the period when, in common with every other possible question of practical policy that can arise, it unfortunately became one of the leading topics of party division, of presidential electioneering. But that period has passed, and with it let its prejudices and its passions, its discords and its denunciations, pass away too. The next session of Congress will see the representatives of the new young State in their places in both our halls of national legislation, side by side with those of the old Thirteen. Let their reception into "the family" be frank, kindly, and cheerful, as befits such an occasion, as comports not less with our own self-respect than patriotic duty towards them. Ill betide those foul birds that delight to file their own nest, and disgust the ear with perpetual discord of ill-omened croak.

Why, were other reasoning wanting, in favor of now elevating this question of the reception of Texas into the Union, out of the lower region of our past party dissensions, up to its proper level of a high and broad nationality, it surely is to be found, found abundantly, in the manner in which other nations have undertaken to intrude themselves into it, between us and the proper parties to the case, in a spirit of hostile interference against us, for the avowed object of thwarting our policy and hampering our power, limiting our greatness and checking the fulfilment of our manifest destiny to overspread the continent allotted by Providence for the free development of our yearly multiplying millions. This we have seen done by England, our old rival and enemy; and by France, strangely coupled with her against us, under the influence of the Anglicism strongly tinging the policy of her present prime minister, Guizot. The zealous activity with which this effort to defeat us was pushed by the representatives of those governments, together with the character of intrigue accompanying it, fully constituted that case of foreign interference, which Mr. Clay himself declared should, and would unite us all in maintaining the common cause of our country against the foreigner and the foe. We are only astonished that this effect has not been more fully and strongly produced, and that the burst of indignation against this unauthorized, insolent and hostile interference against us, has not been more general even among the party before opposed to Annexation, and has not rallied the national spirit and national pride unanimously upon that policy. We are very sure that if Mr. Clay himself were now to add another letter to his former Texas correspondence, he would express this sentiment, and carry out the idea already strongly stated in one of them, in a manner which would tax all the powers of blushing belonging to some of his party adherents.

It is wholly untrue, and unjust to ourselves, the pretence that the Annexation has been a measure of spoilation, unrightful and unrighteous—of military conquest under forms of peace and law—of territorial aggrandizement at the expense of justice, and justice due by a double sanctity to the weak. This view of the question is wholly unfounded, and has been before so amply refuted in these pages, as well as in a thousand other modes, that we shall not again dwell upon it. The independence of Texas was complete and absolute. It was an independence, not only in fact, but of right. No obligation of duty towards Mexico tended in the least degree to restrain our right to effect the desired recovery of the fair province once our own—whatever motives of policy might have prompted a more deferential consideration of her feelings and her pride, as involved in the question. If Texas became peopled with an American population, it was by no contrivance of our government, but on the express invitation of that of Mexico herself; accompanied with such guaranties of State independence, and the maintenance of a federal system analogous to our own, as constituted a compact fully justifying the strongest measures of redress on the part of those afterwards deceived in this guaranty, and sought to be enslaved under the yoke imposed by its violation. She was released, rightfully and absolutely released, from all Mexican allegiance, or duty of cohesion to the Mexican political body, by the acts and fault of Mexico herself, and Mexico alone. There never was a clearer case. It was not revolution; it was resistance to revolution: and resistance under such circumstances as left independence the necessary resulting state, caused by the abandonment of those with whom her former federal association had existed. What then can be more preposterous than all this clamor by Mexico and the Mexican interest, against Annexation, as a violation of any rights of hers, any duties of ours?

We would not be understood as approving in all its features the expediency or propriety of the mode in which the measure, rightful and wise as it is in itself, has been carried into effect. Its history has been a sad tissue of diplomatic blundering. How much better it might have been managed—how much more smoothly, satisfactorily, and successfully! Instead of our present relations with Mexico—instead of the serious risks which have been run, and those plausibilities of opprobrium which we have had to combat, not without great difficulty, nor with entire success—instead of the difficulties which now throng the path to a satisfactory settlement of all our unsettled questions with Mexico—Texas might, by a more judicious and conciliatory diplomacy, have been as securely in the Union as she is now—her boundaries defined—California probably ours—and Mexico and ourselves united by closer ties than ever; of mutual friendship and mutual support in resistance to the intrusion of European interference in the affairs of the American republics. All this might have been, we little doubt, already secured, had counsels less violent, less rude, less one-sided, less eager in precipitation from motives widely foreign to the national question, presided over the earlier stages of its history. We cannot too deeply regret the mismanagement which has disfigured the history of this question; and especially the neglect of the means which would have been so easy of satisfying even the unreasonable pretensions and the excited pride and passion of Mexico. The singular result has been produced, that while our neighbor has, in truth, no real right to blame or complain—when all the wrong is on her side, and there has been on ours a degree of delay and forbearance, in deference to her pretensions, which is to be paralleled by few precedents in the history of other nations—we have yet laid ourselves open to a great deal of denunciation hard to repel, and impossible to silence; and all history will carry it down as a certain fact, that Mexico would have declared war against us, and would have waged it seriously, if she had not been prevented by that very weakness which should have constituted her best defence.

We plead guilty to a degree of sensitive annoyance—for the sake of the honor of our country, and its estimation in the public opinion of the world—which does not find even in satisfied conscience full consolation for the very necessity of seeking consolation there. And it is for this state of things that we hold responsible that gratuitous mismanagement—wholly apart from the main substantial rights and merits of the question, to which alone it is to be ascribed; and which had its origin in its earlier stages, before the accession of Mr. Calhoun to the department of State.

Nor is there any just foundation for the charge that Annexation is a great pro-slavery measure—calculated to increase and perpetuate that institution. Slavery had nothing to do with it. Opinions were and are greatly divided, both at the North and South, as to the influence to be exerted by it on Slavery and the Slave States. That it will tend to facilitate and hasten the disappearance of Slavery from all the northern tier of the present Slave States, cannot surely admit of serious question. The greater value in Texas of the slave labor now employed in those States, must soon produce the effect of draining off that labor southwardly, by the same unvarying law that bids water descend the slope that invites it. Every new Slave State in Texas will make at least one Free State from among those in which that institution now exists—to say nothing of those portions of Texas on which slavery cannot spring and grow—to say nothing of the far more rapid growth of new States in the free West and North-west, as these fine regions are overspread by the emigration fast flowing over them from Europe, as well as from the Northern and Eastern

States of the Union as it exists. On the other hand, it is undeniably much gained for the cause of the eventual voluntary abolition of slavery, that it should have been thus drained off towards the only outlet which appeared to furnish much probability of the ultimate disappearance of the negro race from our borders. The Spanish-Indian-American populations of Mexico, Central America and South America, afford the only receptacle capable of absorbing that race whenever we shall be prepared to slough it off—to emancipate it from slavery, and (simultaneously necessary) to remove it from the midst of our own. Themselves already of mixed and confused blood, and free from the "prejudices" which among us so insuperably forbid the social amalgamation which can alone elevate the Negro race out of a virtually servile degradation, even though legally free, the regions occupied by those populations must strongly attract the black race in that direction; and as soon as the destined hour of emancipation shall arrive, will relieve the question of one of its worst difficulties, if not absolutely the greatest.

No—Mr. Clay was right when he declared that Annexation was a question with which slavery had nothing to do. The country which was the subject of Annexation in this case, from its geographical position and relations, happens to be—or rather the portion of it now actually settled, happens to be—a slave country. But a similar process might have taken place in proximity to a different section of our Union; and indeed there is a great deal of Annexation yet to take place, within the life of the present generation, along the whole line of our northern border. Texas has been absorbed into the Union in the inevitable fulfilment of the general law which is rolling our population westward; the connexion of which with that ratio of growth in population which is destined within a hundred years to swell our numbers to the enormous population of *two hundred and fifty millions* (if not more), is too evident to leave us in doubt of the manifest design of Providence in regard to the occupation of this continent. It was disintegrated from Mexico in the natural course of events, by a process perfectly legitimate on its own part, blameless on ours; and in which all the censures due to wrong, perfidy and folly, rest on Mexico alone. And possessed as it was by a population which was in truth but a colonial detachment from our own, and which was still bound by myriad ties of the very heart-strings to its old relations, domestic and political, their incorporation into the Union was not only inevitable, but the most natural, right and proper thing in the world—and it is only astonishing that there should be any among ourselves to say it nay.

In respect to the institution of slavery itself, we have not designed, in what has been said above, to express any judgment of its merits or demerits, *pro* or *con*. National in its character and aims, this Review abstains from the discussion of a topic pregnant with embarrassment and danger—intricate and double-sided—exciting and embittering—and necessarily excluded from a work circulating equally in the South as in the North. It is unquestionably one of the most difficult of the various social problems which at the present day so deeply agitate the thoughts of the civilized world. Is the negro race, or is it not, of equal attributes and capacities with our own? Can they, on a large scale, co-exist side by side in the same country on a footing of civil and social equality with the white race? In a free competition of labor with the latter, will they or will they not be ground down to a degradation and misery worse than slavery? When we view the condition of the operative masses of the population in England and other European countries, and feel all the difficulties of the great problem, of the distribution of the fruits of production between capital, skill, and labor, can our confidence be undoubting that in the present condition of society, the conferring of sudden freedom upon our negro race would be a boon to be grateful for? Is it certain that competitive wages are very much better, for a race so situated, than guarantied support and protection? Until a still deeper problem shall have been solved than that of slavery, the slavery of an inferior to a superior race—a relation reciprocal in certain important duties and obligations—is it certain that the cause of true wisdom and philanthropy is not rather, for the present, to aim to meliorate that institution as it exists, to guard against its abuses, to mitigate its evils, to modify it when it may contravene sacred principles and rights of humanity, by prohibiting the separation of families, excessive severities, subjection to the licentiousness of mastership, &c.? Great as may be its present evils, is it certain that we would not plunge the unhappy Helot race which has been entailed upon us, into still greater ones, by surrendering their fate into the rash hands of those fanatic zealots of a single idea, who claim to be their special friends and champions? Many of the most ardent social reformers of the present day are looking towards the idea of *Associated Industry* as containing the germ of such a regeneration of society as will relieve its masses from the hideous weight of evil which now depresses and degrades them to a condition which these reformers often describe as no improvement upon any form of legal slavery—is it certain, then, that the institution in question, as a mode of society, as a relation between the two races, and between capital and labor,—does not contain some dim undeveloped germ of that very principle of reform thus aimed at, out of which proceeds some compensation at least for its other evils, making it the duty of true reform to cultivate and develope the good, and remove the evils?

To all these, and the similar questions which spring out of any intelligent reflection on the subject, we attempt no answer. Strong as are our sympathies in behalf of liberty, universal liberty,

in all applications of the principle not forbidden by great and manifest evils, we confess ourselves not prepared with any satisfactory solution to the great problem of which these questions present various aspects. Far from us to say that either of the antagonist fanaticisms to be found on either side of the Potomac is right. Profoundly embarrassed amidst the conflicting elements entering into the question, much and anxious reflection upon it brings us as yet to no other conclusion than to the duty of a liberal tolerance of the honest differences of both sides; together with the certainty that whatever good is to be done in the case is to be done only by the adoption of very different modes of action, prompted by a very different spirit, from those which have thus far, among us, characterized the labors of most of those who claim the peculiar title of "friends of the slave" and "champions of the rights of man." With no friendship for slavery, though unprepared to excommunicate to eternal damnation, with bell, book, and candle, those who are, we see nothing in the bearing of the Annexation of Texas on that institution to awaken a doubt of the wisdom of that measure, or a compunction for the humble part contributed by us towards its consummation.

California will, probably, next fall away from the loose adhesion which, in such a country as Mexico, holds a remote province in a slight equivocal kind of dependence on the metropolis. Imbecile and distracted, Mexico never can exert any real governmental authority over such a country. The impotence of the one and the distance of the other, must make the relation one of virtual independence; unless, by stunting the province of all natural growth, and forbidding that immigration which can alone develope its capabilities and fulfil the purposes of its creation, tyranny may retain a military dominion, which is no government in the legitimate sense of the term. In the case of California this is now impossible. The Anglo-Saxon foot is already on its borders. Already the advance guard of the irresistible army of Anglo-Saxon emigration has begun to pour down upon it, armed with the plough and the rifle, and marking its trail with schools and colleges, courts and representative halls, mills and meeting-houses. A population will soon be in actual occupation of California, over which it will be idle for Mexico to dream of dominion. They will necessarily become independent. All this without agency of our government, without responsibility of our people—in the natural flow of events, the spontaneous working of principles, and the adaptation of the tendencies and wants of the human race to the elemental circumstances in the midst of which they find themselves placed. And they will have a right to independence—to self-government—to the possession of the homes conquered from the wilderness by their own labors and dangers, sufferings and sacrifices—a better and a truer right than the artificial title of sovereignty in

Mexico, a thousand miles distant, inheriting from Spain a title good only against those who have none better. Their right to independence will be the natural right of self-government belonging to any community strong enough to maintain it—distinct in position, origin and character, and free from any mutual obligations of membership of a common political body, binding it to others by the duty of loyalty and compact of public faith. This will be their title to independence; and by this title, there can be no doubt that the population now fast streaming down upon California will both assert and maintain that independence. Whether they will then attach themselves to our Union or not, is not to be predicted with any certainty. Unless the projected railroad across the continent to the Pacific be carried into effect, perhaps they may not; though even in that case, the day is not distant when the Empires of the Atlantic and Pacific would again flow together into one, as soon as their inland border should approach each other. But that great work, colossal as appears the plan on its first suggestion, cannot remain long unbuilt. Its necessity for this very purpose of binding and holding together in its iron clasp our fast-settling Pacific region with that of the Mississippi valley—the natural facility of the route—the ease with which any amount of labor for the construction can be drawn in from the over-crowded populations of Europe, to be paid in the lands made valuable by the progress of the work itself—and its immense utility to the commerce of the world with the whole eastern coast of Asia, alone almost sufficient for the support of such a road—these considerations give assurance that the day cannot be distant which shall witness the conveyance of the representatives from Oregon and California to Washington within less time than a few years ago was devoted to a similar journey by those from Ohio; while the magnetic telegraph will enable the editors of the "San Francisco Union," the "Astoria Evening Post," or the "Nootka Morning News," to set up in type the first half of the President's Inaugural before the echoes of the latter half shall have died away beneath the lofty porch of the Capitol, as spoken from his lips.

Away, then, with all idle French talk of *balances of power* on the American Continent. There is no growth in Spanish America! Whatever progress of population there may be in the British Canadas, is only for their own early severance of their present colonial relation to the little island three thousand miles across the Atlantic; soon to be followed by Annexation, and destined to swell the still accumulating momentum of our progress. And whosoever may hold the balance, though they should cast into the opposite scale all the bayonets and cannon, not only of France and England, but of Europe entire, how would it kick the beam against the simple, solid weight of the two hundred and fifty, or three hundred millions—and American millions—destined to gather beneath the flutter of the stripes and stars, in the fast hastening year of the Lord 1945!

Even the staid emigrant guides, giving descriptions on what routes to follow west and the type of equipment to take, often contained outbursts of enthusiasm for the new land. Lansford Hastings concluded his own 1845 guide to the Pacific Coast on the following optimistic note.

LANSFORD W. HASTINGS: EMIGRANTS' GUIDE TO OREGON AND CALIFORNIA*

In leaving this subject it is natural for us, not only to review what we have just seen, in reference to those countries, and to contemplate their present, prosperous condition, but also, to anticipate their condition, in reference to the progressive future. In view of their increasing population, accumulating wealth, and growing prosperity, I can not but believe, that the time is not distant, when those wild forests, trackless plains, untrodden valleys, and the unbounded ocean, will present one grand scene, of continuous improvements, universal enterprise, and unparalleled commerce: when those vast forests, shall have disappeared, before the hardy pioneer; those extensive plains, shall abound with innumerable herds, of domestic animals; those fertile valleys, shall groan under the immense weight of their abundant products: when those numerous rivers, shall team with countless steam-boats, steam-ships, ships, barques and brigs; when the entire country, will be everywhere intersected, with turnpike roads, rail-roads and canals; and when,

---

* Reprinted from Lansford W. Hastings, *The Emigrants' Guide to Oregon and California* (Cincinnati: 1845), pp. 151–52.

all the vastly numerous, and rich resources, of that now, almost unknown region, will be fully and advantageously developed. To complete this picture, we may fancy to ourselves, a Boston, a New York, a Philadelphia and a Baltimore, growing up in a day, as it were, both in Oregon and California; crowded with a vast population, and affording all the enjoyments and luxuries, of civilized life. And to this we may add, numerous churches, magnificent edifices, spacious colleges, and stupendous monuments and observatories, all of Grecian architecture, rearing their majestic heads, high in the ærial region, amid those towering pyramids of perpetual snow, looking down upon all the busy, bustling scenes, of tumultuous civilization, amid the eternal verdure of perennial spring. And in fine, we are also led to contemplate the time, as fast approaching, when the supreme darkness of ignorance, superstition, and despotism, which now, so entirely pervade many portions of those remote regions, will have fled forever, before the march of civilization, and the blazing light, of civil and religious liberty; when genuine *republicanism,* and unsophisticated *democracy,* shall be reared up, and tower aloft, even upon the now wild shores, of the great Pacific; where they shall forever stand forth, as enduring monuments, to the increasing wisdom of *man,* and the infinite kindness and protection, of an all-wise, and overruling *Providence.*

Congressman Cathcart of Indiana, in boldly denouncing England on the Oregon Question, saw the westward movement as bringing more and more states "into this great temple of freedom, and burning their incense upon an alter consecrated to the enjoyment of civil and religious liberty." This speech was made on the floor of Congress, February 6, 1846.

CHARLES W. CATHCART:
EXPANSION AND LIBERTY*

The spirit of the West, its enthusiastic devotion to the glory and grandeur of our common country, and the enlargement of the bounds of civilization, and the expansion of our republican institutions, has been called a war spirit; and we have been read lectures upon the horrors of war, and the blessings of peace; and told that by the decisive action which we are about taking we hazard everything and can gain nothing; that wisdom dictates a course of "masterly inactivity."

Sir, was it by this supine course that we gained our present independent existence as the freest and happiest people on earth? Was it by inactivity that we sealed our title to be considered one of the first, and greatest, and bravest people under heaven's sun?—in a word, was it by masterly inactivity that we acquired Texas? No, sir, no! But by action—energetic action! . . .

We are asked how we expect to dispossess the Hudson Bay Company of her pallisade forts in Oregon? Is it possible that an American can doubt upon this point? Prepare yourself and demand their surrender, as Ethan Allen did the surrender of Ticonderoga, "in the name of the Great Jehovah and the Continental Congress." And this reminds me of the sneers of some gentlemen in relation to what they call our "western doctrine of manifest destiny." Do gentlemen reflect where they place themselves by these sneers? Do they forget that the Savior of mankind has said that a "sparrow shall not fall to the ground without your Father?" And yet we are asked, where is the clause in Adam's will which gives us this territory? Apart from the "book-title," which is "clear and unquestionable," we see it written in letters of living light in everything which surrounds us—in that merciful dispensation, full of charity and love, towards the fallen children of Adam—of a just and omniscient God, who has given to man that control of the elements, the effect of which is to bring the remotest parts of our vast country into practical propinquity. The iron horse, (the steam-car,) with the wings of the wind, his nostrils distended with flame, salamander-like vomiting fire and smoke, trembling with power, but submissive to the steel curb imposed upon him by the hand of man, flies from one end of the continent to the other in less time than our ancestry required to visit a neighboring city; while by the magnetic telegraph the lightning of heaven is made subservient to the will of man in annihilating space. In storm and in darkness, in the heat of a torrid sun or the chilling blasts of a Siberian winter, this mystical symbol of man's intelligence speeds its onward way. Truly it may be said, that with the social influence of these two great inventions, all the people of this continent may be moulded to one

* Reprinted from *Congressional Globe,* 29th Cong., 1st sess. (Washington, D.C.: 1846), pp. 323–24.

mind. And what heart does not leap at the vision presented of this great territory peopled by one republican family? Would it be saying too much, that the magnetic telegraph may be compared, when extended, as extended it will be, over the length and breadth of our land, to the nervous system of the human body? The sensations of its remotest parts will vibrate upon a common sensorium, communicating its ray of intelligence to a common centre, to be sent to all other portions of our Republic.

Who, then, shall measure the limits of a confederacy of States like ours? Who, then, shall perpetrate that almost sacrilegious imputation upon the mercy of Heaven, and say that the blessings of this Union are spreading too far? What, then, will become of the cry that we do not want Oregon, because of its great distance? How agreeable the vision of State after State coming into this great temple of freedom, and burning their incense upon an altar consecrated to the enjoyment of civil and religious liberty.

The cry of some is that we are not prepared; and some gentlemen, in deprecating our weakness, and in eulogizing the greatness of England's power, have, in my humble opinion, made speeches much better suited to the longitude of Westminster Hall than to that of the floor of the American House of Representatives. I assert boldly, and without fear of contradiction, that we are now better prepared to wage a successful war than if we had been frittering away our substance during the long period which has intervened since the treaty of Ghent, in keeping afloat an immense navy, and a great and splendid military establishment. Why, sir, it can be established—I might almost say mathematically —that by husbanding our means, we aggregate our capacity for any emergency; and when that emergency arises, that this preparation in time of peace, constitutes the best, the strongest, and most reliable foundation for effective military defensive and aggressive operations.

Let the shrill bugle-blast break upon our ears, and from the mountain side, and valley's depth, prairie and wood, as if touched by the hand of magic, you will see the true sons of Columbia springing responsive to their country's call. The shrill whistle of the Scottish chieftain never called as ready and as determined a clan around his standard, as would rally under the Oregon banner. The people, the great masses, those whose servants we are, and whose orders the genius of our institutions demands that we should obey, are heaving, I might say, like the waves of that great ócean, to whose confines they demand the extension of the American republic. And, sir, as wave after wave of public opinion culminates and

breaks into foam, when I look around me and see the danger into which some gentlemen here have placed themselves of being engulfed and buried deep, deep beneath the turgid waters, I would warn them, while there is yet time, to spring aboard the ark of political safety.

Canute was so exalted by the flattery of his courtiers that he foolishly believed that he could, by his lordly command, stay the waves of the sea, and bid them, "thus far shalt thou come, and no farther."

As well might you attempt to roll back the tidal wave of the great Pacific ocean, as it comes thundering on the coast of the Oregon, as to stay this great movement, this progressive movement, if you please, of the American millions; and as a friend, I would here warn the "Canutes" of this House to cast their eyes upon land before the waves shall dash with spray their chariot wheels.

Great Britain founded her first pretensions to the northwest coast in an outrageous attack upon the rights of Spain; and, taking advantage of her weakness, bleeding from the effects of a disastrous war, she, under the lash of her superior power, extorted from Spain the Nootka sound convention, as the treaty is called, upon which her main reliance is placed in her claim to the Oregon territory.

The value of this claim, even in the eyes of *her own statesmen,* is shown by one of my colleagues [Mr. OWEN] to be such as to justify the charge that she has been guilty of the most unmitigated rapacity in the assertion of her claims to territory in all her negotiations with us. And it remains to be seen if American freemen will agree to be despoiled with the tame submission of the effeminate Spaniard. Hers is the robber's title, and thus it has ever been with her. This vaunted circle of British military posts, which some gentlemen have brought in review before us, with a view "to frighten us from our propriety," are but monuments of her rapacity and lust of power.

She yet lacks one link in the chain which is destined, if secured, to bind the world in her commercial fetters. That link is the key to the Pacific, washing, as it does, the shores of both great continents; and the command of this ocean is hers, and hers alone, if she is permitted to occupy the harbors which she has studiously claimed in every proffer of settlement which she has made of this question. It remains to be seen whether the cowardice of the descendants of the men of Bunker's Hill, and of those gallant spirits who conquered in our war of the Revolution, and of our second independence, shall permit her to grasp it. I blush at the bare suggestion of the possibility.

CHAPTER NINE

THE ABOLITIONISTS AND SLAVERY ADVOCATES

Fundamentally a moral protest against human degradation, abolitionism was also a social and economic critique of the institution of slavery itself. Abolitionists, combining these strands, strongly urged the position that human bondage in any form violated the natural rights of man. Thus this movement was an intensified form and a direct outgrowth of the broader humanitarian currents of American thought during the first half of the nineteenth century. In 1831, William Lloyd Garrison, in the first issue of the *Liberator,* sounded the keynote for "immediate and unconditional emancipation." He was soon joined by such men as Wendell Phillips, John Greenleaf Whittier, and James Russell Lowell in denouncing slavery as a crime against humanity. Public opinion was aroused through antislavery societies, the distribution of tracts and newspapers, and the activities of underground railroads to aid escaping slaves. Yet the abolitionists were, in the last analysis, numerically weak, receiving only sixty-five thousand votes in the 1844 election under the Liberty party banner. "Nevertheless," as Charles and Mary Beard observed, "it appears that the influence of the abolition agitation far outran the measurements that were taken at the polls."

The defenders of slavery struck back. Not only was dissent in behalf of antislavery all but crushed in the South, but elaborate arguments from the Bible and other sources were used to defend the "peculiar institution." John C. Calhoun saw slavery as exercising a civilizing influence on the Negro and argued that exploitation was justifiable because cultured people must live on the labor of others. Abolition literature sent through the mails was destroyed, textbooks were purged, and other evidence of increasing intransigence was manifested in the South. Slavery, by the 1840's, was no longer on the way out in the South. Nor was the lot of the abolitionists easy even in the North. Garrison was mobbed and beaten in Boston in 1835, and at Alton, Illinois, Elijah P. Lovejoy was killed while protecting his printing press. But, as Dwight L. Dumond suggested in the first selection, "Slavery and free discussion were incompatible, but the attempt to suppress the latter served mightily to hasten the former's destruction."

DWIGHT L. DUMOND:
THE ABOLITION INDICTMENT OF SLAVERY*

No other reform movement is quite like the anti-slavery crusade, because it was based upon an appeal to the consciences of men; yet the sinners were almost wholly insulated from the preachment, and the anxious seat was crowded with saints, so that the historian is tempted to agree with Pascal, that "There are but two classes of men, the righteous, who think themselves to be sinners, and the sinners, who think themselves righteous." One *expects* to find the contemporary literature of the great controversy strongly biased, but race prejudice still lives, and the writings of trained historians, also, have such an overtone of moralizing or apology as to leave the impression their wishes determined what they should accept as truth. Fortunately, we do not need to agree on the precise nature of American Negro slavery. Historians have too long focused their attention upon that controversial point, to the neglect of more important things. One can no more describe the life of the slave than describe a typical plantation. There was too much diversity, and the human element entered in too largely to permit even a highly centralized picture. To attempt it is to become lost in a labyrinth of qualifications. Abolitionists omitted the qualifications and strengthened their case accordingly, but weakened it in the light of historical research.

One may find in abolition literature, not here and there but in dreary succession, charges of vilest depravity. . . .

The weakness of this sort of propaganda lay in the necessity (1) for a constant increase in the enormity of the offense charged; (2) for variation, since attention was more easily arrested by the novelty of the guilt than by its degree; and (3) for unimpeachable supporting evidence to satisfy the skeptic. Some of the pornographic calendar is so stereotyped in form as to bear the impress of legend. Some of it was hearsay, undoubtedly magnified in the telling. The more repulsive incidents were of uncommon occurrence and were no more authentic criteria by which to judge the institution as a whole than was Jefferson Davis' experiment in self-government for his slaves. It was the sort of stuff that warms the heart of the true propagandist and fascinates the sanctimonious pietist as well as the irreligious miscreant. But such aspects of slavery as miscegenation, separation of families, cruel punishments, and barbarous treatment of fugitives cannot be minimized either by one who seeks a true picture of slavery or by one who seeks the causes of the Civil War. Historians have no justification

* Reprinted from *Antislavery Origins of the Civil War* by Dwight L. Dumond by permission of The University of Michigan Press. Copyright 1939 by The University of Michigan Press.

for ignoring abolition literature in their work on slavery. The great bulk of this part of it was written by high-minded men and women who were either born and reared in the South or had lived there many years. One would hardly expect to find mention of these sordid aspects of the institution in plantation records, in private diaries or letters, or in treatises written in defense of slavery. The fact that Southerners who did write about them were living at the time in states where there was no slavery does not detract from, but rather increases, the probability of their accuracy. Supported, as they were, by certain other indisputable facts we shall shortly refer to, they would have given all but the most obdurate champions of slavery cause for serious reflection; but the generality of Southerners had not the slightest conception of abolition arguments or of the principles for which they were contending.

The restlessness of slaveholders over colonization activities crystallized into a militant defense of slavery as anti-slavery agitation increased in the North—a defense which denied freedom of speech and of the press, excluded abolition literature from the mails, and drove everyone suspected of heresy out of the South, and hence closed the public forums to all antislavery doctrine. At the same time the fulminations of those abolitionists who allowed their opposition to slavery to lead them along the psychopathic trail to a hatred of slaveholders and who took special delight in foul invective and ribald abuse of everyone connected with the institution were copied into the Southern newspapers as a warning of the impending Northern plague. Perhaps it was inevitable that men who hated slavery should hate slaveholders. Perhaps it is just to lump the sinner with the sin. That is a matter of opinion. In any case it was not conducive to calm reflection or sympathetic understanding or a peaceable solution of the question. Year after year the Southerners went on enduring these charges of moral turpitude, with their holier-than-thou implications, nursing their wrath, and finding consolation in self-justification.

This catalogue of specific wrongs was also a part of the more general indictment of slavery as a sin. The antislavery movement was a powerful religious crusade, and religion played a far more important part in American life then than it does today. The Bible was presented as irrefutable proof that Jesus taught a doctrine of universal brotherhood; that man was created in the image of God; and that slavery reduced him to a piece of merchandise to be bought and sold in the market place. Said Theodore Weld, when the American Anti-Slavery Society was organized: "God has committed to every moral agent the privilege, the right and the responsibility of personal ownership. This is God's plan. Slavery annihilates it, and surrenders to avarice, passion and lust, all that makes life a blessing. It crushes the body, tramples into the dust the upward tendencies of the intellect, breaks the heart and kills the soul." [1] Said the Central Executive Committee: "Every man who has put on the armor of Jesus Christ is under the paramount pledge to do all in his power for the salvation of the souls for which He died. How can you, my brother, do more than by *now* espousing the cause of those for whose souls there are *no men* to care." [2] Slavery was denounced as a sin, "always, everywhere and only sin," *aside* from the evils of its administration. Abolitionists demanded that slaveholders be excluded from the pulpits of Northern churches and from the privileges of the sacraments, and those Southerners who finally championed the cause of secession lingered long on this aspect of the cause for action. Said the distinguished John S. Preston of South Carolina before the Virginia Convention: "This diversity at this moment is appearing not in forms of denominational polemics, but in shapes as bloody and terrible as religion has ever assumed since Christ came to earth. Its representative, the Church, has bared her arm for the conflict—her sword is already flashing in the glare of the torch of fanaticism—and the history of the world tells us that when that sword cleaves asunder, no human surgery can heal the wound. There is not one Christian slaveholder here, no matter how near he may be to his meek and lowly master, who does not feel in his heart that from the point of that sword is now dripping the last drop of sympathy which bound him to his brethren at the North. With demoniac rage they have set the Lamb of God between their seed and our seed." [3]

In support of their charge that these violations of the standards of contemporary civilization were far more prevalent than Southerners were willing to admit, were inherent in slavery, and were indicative of the general moral tone of the institution, abolitionists presented a line of argument which was not easily contradicted. Slaves were property. They were bought and sold. The purchase price alone determined who might be a slaveholder. Society set no standards of intelligence, character, or integrity for slaveholding. There were no public or private agencies charged with responsibility for the slave's welfare. Human

nature being what it is or, better still, what it then was, what security was there for the individual slave against abuse of arbitrary power? Said Weld: "Arbitrary power is to the mind what alcohol is to the body; it intoxicates. It is perhaps the strongest human passion; and the more absolute the power, the stronger the desire for it; and the more it is desired, the more its exercise is enjoyed. . . . The fact that a person intensely desires power over others, *without restraint,* shows the absolute necessity of restraint." [4] This condition was greatly aggravated by the fact that slaves were subject not only to the will of their owner, but to the authority of every white person with whom they came in contact off the owner's property, and to the slightest whim of the owner's family, even of children too immature to have disciplined themselves; and by the further fact that, in spite of abject servility and personal desire to suppress emotions, evidences of resentment must have been a common occurrence. "The idea of *property* having a will," said Weld, "and that too in opposition to the will of its *owner,* and counteracting it, is a stimulant of terrible power to the most relentless human passions." [5] In support of his logic he brought together in *American Slavery As It Is* what he chose to call the "testimony of a thousand witnesses," the most devastating arraignment of slavery ever published. Hundreds of thousands of copies of the pamphlet were distributed, and its influence was incalculable. There was no effective reply to it, nor could there have been.

Not only did abolitionists examine slavery in the light of the Scriptures and of the moral standards prevailing in contemporary civilization; they also pronounced it contrary to the fundamental principles of the American way of life because it plundered the slaves of their inalienable rights as men: ownership of their own bodies; freedom of choice as to use of time and to occupation; the rights of marriage, family life, and paternal authority; the right to worship according to conscience; the right to cultivate their minds, utilize their peculiar talents and influence their fellow men; the right to protect themselves, their homes, and their families against violence; the right to the protection of the law. These were things which, especially in those days of rugged individualism, made a powerful impression upon the average American.

The lack of legal protection for the slave constituted the greatest single indictment against the slaveholding states. The slave owner had no restraint but his own will over the type and amount of labor assigned to the slave. He might hire him out to other men; he might permit him to labor on his own account and claim his wages; he might inflict any kind or degree of

---

[1] Theodore D. Weld to Arthur Tappan, Joshua Leavitt, and Elizur Wright, Jr., November 22, 1833, *Weld-Grimké Letters,* I, 120.

[2] Elizur Wright, Jr., to Theodore D. Weld, December 31, 1833, *ibid.,* p. 122.

[3] *Addresses Delivered by Hon. Fulton Anderson, Commissioner from Mississippi, Hon. Henry L. Benning, Commissioner from Georgia, and Hon. John S. Preston, Commissioner from South Carolina, before the Virginia State Convention, February 1, 1861* (Charleston, 1861), p. 61.

[4] [Weld, Theodore D.], *American Slavery As It Is* (New York, 1839), p. 115.

[5] *Ibid.,* p. 111.

punishment without fear of redress; he might assign absolute authority over the slave to any agent. He might sell the slave at will. The slave was both a chattel and real estate and liable to be sold in satisfaction of debts. He could not testify in court in any case involving a white man. If he raised his hand against a white man in any circumstances whatsoever, the penalty was death. He had no recourse against intolerable conditions but perilous flight. He could own no property, make no contracts, receive no education, claim no religious instruction. Whatever legislation had been passed with respect to slaves was purely for protection of property rights and the security of the institution. One may find, only rarely, feeble recognition by legislatures and courts of slaves as human beings. This was slavery's most vulnerable spot and was so considered by the abolitionists.

The practical application of the law, said the apologists for slavery, was far less rigorous than the provisions of the law, which was simply ignoring the point at issue. When they spoke of the slave codes as being unenforced except at rare intervals when mass hysteria followed attempted insurrections, a particularly brutal murder, or the apprehension of a suspected incendiary, they were speaking of laws passed for the protection of society, i.e. laws forbidding slaves to assemble without the presence of a white person; forbidding slaves to leave their owners' premises without a written permit; forbidding slaves to preach or masters to teach them to read; and requiring the regular patrol of all public highways. The important point is that that great body of law, both common and statute, and the courts, the instrument of its operation, to which men have looked since time immemorial for the administration of justice and for the protection of their most elementary human rights simply did not exist for three million slaves. Privileges they might have and no doubt did enjoy in generous measure from indulgent masters, but they had no more semblance of rights than the beasts of the field.

More difficult to evaluate with respect to its place in the Northern educational program was the abolition argument concerning the effect of slavery upon the two races and upon the South from the viewpoint of general culture and economy. This was in the nature of a rebuttal to the positive-good argument, the development of which preceded the abolition crusade of the thirties. The positive-good dogma embraced four theses: (1) that slave labor was essential to the development and continued prosperity of the southern country; (2) that the Negro race was inferior and destined by nature to a subordinate position; (3) that slavery had lifted a savage people from barbarism to Christian civilization; and (4) that the white race had not degenerated as a consequence, but, on the contrary, had developed a unique and high degree of culture. Ancillary to these there were, of course, a number of supporting theses. Divine sanction was invoked for the institution with the Bible as evidence. Historical precedent of the existence of slavery in every age was cited. Culture, it was said, could thrive only if the few enjoyed leisure from exploitation of the many, and Negro slavery threw wide the door of opportunity to all white men by substituting race exploitation for class exploitation. Southern bond slavery was compared to Northern wage slavery to prove that the Negro slave shared more abundantly in the necessaries of life than the Northern wage earner.

Much of the abolitionists' reply to the Southern claims of cultural superiority and the defense of slavery as a humane and civilizing institution is to be found in the general indictments of slavery as a sin and as incompatible with the standards of contemporary civilization. They did not hesitate, however, to meet the argument on specific points, twitting the slaveholders about their lack of a common school system, their resort to murder under the *code duello* for the satisfaction of every fancied wrong, their compulsory diversion of all mixed blood back into the Negro race to hide the shame of their immorality, and their propensity for gambling and hard drinking. They ridiculed the idea that a system which made the happiness of a defenseless people "the sport of every whim, and the prey of every passion that may . . . infest the master's bosom" could possibly develop a profound sense of responsibility in the slaveholder, holding that the "daily practice of forcibly robbing others and habitually living on the plunder can not but beget in the mind the *habit* of regarding the interests and happiness of those whom it robs, as of no sort of consequence in comparison with its own."[6] As for the slave, his very dependence impaired his manliness and independence of character, crushed his soul, and destroyed his ability to distinguish right from wrong. It cultivated immorality, placed a premium upon deception, and made lying and stealing acts of self-preservation.

The Bible argument waxed long and furiously, with perhaps a slight advantage to the abolitionists. Over the long view it appears to have been a rather fruitless discussion, without much influence one way or the other. Slavery's rôle in history was assessed as a liability rather than as a contribution to the glory and stability of Rome. It was condemned as an impediment to a balanced economy in the South, absorbing the capital necessary to industrial enterprise, denying the entrepreneur the public coöperation essential to the development of manufacturing, destroying the fertility of the soil through forced and incompetent labor, driving the non-slaveholder to the free states or ever farther back upon the margin of a bare subsistence level, turning the

---

[6] "Testimony of the Presbyterian Synod of Kentucky," *ibid.*, p. 61.

stream of foreign immigration elsewhere, and creating a contempt for manual labor on the part of the whites, the fruits of which were indolence on the one hand and arrogant snobbery on the other.

Finally, slavery was condemned as a menace to the peace and safety of the nation. Concentration of Negroes in the Black Belt entered into every phase of the slavery question. From the earliest days the champions of slavery had admitted the necessity of maintaining a proper ratio between the two races. The subject arose in connection with colonization. Southern pamphleteers conceded the desirability of diffusion as an aid to the alleviation of the system's harsher features. Fear of insurrection increased as the center of the slave population moved steadily toward the Southwest. It was advanced in defense of the prohibition against teaching slaves to read, permitting them to assemble without the presence of whites, etc. It played an important part in the discussion over the expansion of slave territory and in the Confederate Constitutional Convention with respect to the non-seceding states in 1861.

Abolitionists took particular delight, it would seem, in playing upon this fear of the South by exposing it as a national weakness, calling attention to the vulnerability of the southern coast to attack, chiding the South for dependence upon the great strength of the nation to protect from outside interference and from internal combustion an institution it insisted upon regarding as its own domestic concern, lashing out with bitter invective against the slavocracy for involving the whole nation in a war of conquest, and bringing all the pressure at their command against the state department's representations to Great Britain in the *Creole* and other cases.

The particular emphasis placed upon each of these several indictments depended upon the time, the occasion, and the person discussing the subject. It is essential to remember that the antislavery movement was almost completely unorganized until the founding of the American Anti-Slavery Society in December, 1833. There were the New York City Manumission Society, organized by John Jay and Alexander Hamilton in 1785; the Pennsylvania Abolition Society, organized by Benjamin Franklin in 1789; and scattered local societies in North Carolina, Tennessee, and southern Ohio; but the organized movement for the entire abolition of slavery in the United States began in the early thirties. From 1833 to 1840 it was under the direction of a powerful executive committee of the American Anti-Slavery Society, located in New York City. After 1839 there were two national organizations: the American Anti-Slavery Society, under the control of William Lloyd Garrison at Boston, and the American and Foreign Anti-Slavery Society, under the control of Lewis Tappan in New York City. During the first period work was carried on largely through local and travel-ing agents and was predominantly religious, with churches the forums, the sin of slavery the theme, and the organization of state and local auxiliary societies and the founding of antislavery newspapers an important function of the agents. After 1840 neither of the national organizations exercised much influence or control over the movement; but, so far as they did, the American and Foreign Anti-Slavery Society was the functional continuation of the original American Anti-Slavery Society, distinctly religious and friendly to the churches and promoting the old policy of seeking the abolition of slavery by moral suasion. The real work of maintaining agencies and newspapers and depositories for antislavery literature, however, was carried on by the powerful state societies. The function of giving direction to the movement and defining its objectives was now under the control of a small group of politically minded abolitionists, and state societies shortly became almost identical with state antislavery political parties. The American Anti-Slavery Society under Garrison at Boston—the old society name without the substance—was distinctly antichurch, antipolitical, and strongly flavored with peace, no-human-government, and woman's rights.

The sin of slavery and the Bible argument were first emphasized in the Lane Seminary debate and by the agents in opening the churches and securing the support of the clergy. Thenceforth noted theologians, North and South, published elaborate treatises in the religious journals of the day; thousands of copies of sermons on the subject by such men as John Rankin, Beriah Green, and Samuel Crothers, were distributed among the clergy; and a few books were circulated by the hundred thousand, including Birney's *Letter to the Ministers and Elders* (1834), Weld's *The Bible against Slavery* (1837), and La Roy Sunderland's *The Testimony of God against Slavery* (1835); but their influence was as nothing compared with the Bible quotations, usually accompanied by appropriate etchings, impressed upon the letterheads used by the officials of the societies or embroidered upon all sorts of fancy work by the female abolitionists:

"Thou shalt not steal."

"Thou shalt love thy neighbor as thyself."

"All things whatsoever ye would that men should do to you, do you even so to them."

"First, be reconciled to thy brother, and then come and offer thy gift."

"He hath sent me to heal the broken-hearted, to preach deliverance to the captives, to set at liberty them that are bruised."

"Woe unto him that buildeth his house by unrighteousness, and his chambers by wrong; that useth his neighbor's service without wages, and giveth him not for his work."

"And he that stealeth a man, and selleth him, or if he be found in his hand, he shall surely be put to death."

"Open thy mouth for the dumb in the cause

of all such as are appointed to destruction. Open thy mouth, judge righteously, and plead the cause of the poor and needy."

"This is my commandment, That ye love one another, as I have loved you."

This phase of the antislavery crusade is inseparable from the pioneering efforts of three Southern Presbyterian clergymen: George Bourne, whose book caused him to be convicted of heresy by the Virginia Synod and to be driven out of the state to the more friendly environment of Philadelphia; Samuel Doak, of Little Limestone, Tennessee, who sent one student after another into the ministry, with antislavery doctrines, in the region which later became the first battleground; and John Rankin, one of Doak's students, who carried the fight into one Presbyterian general assembly after another; but the organization of the movement on the principle of preaching the sin of slavery was Theodore Weld's great contribution, and it was the dominant note in antislavery effort while he retained direction of it, i.e. until 1840.

Weld and his wife, Angelina Grimké Weld, did more than anyone else to create the highly centralized picture of slavery as a barbaric institution. Their *American Slavery As It Is* was a complete anthology of horrors, and its sale probably equaled the combined sales of all other books of the sort before the publication of *Uncle Tom's Cabin*. It was published in 1839 and thenceforth there was no cessation of slave narratives, novels, etc., emphasizing one or another of slavery's sordid aspects.

Between 1834 and 1838 the challenge of slavery to civil rights in the North was made. Weld and the Lane Seminary boys who went out as agents met mob violence and overcame it by Christian meekness. Others, particularly the Cincinnati group of Levi Coffin, David Burnett, and William Birney, the Illinois group who defended Lovejoy's press, and the delegates to the first Ohio state convention, met violence with violence, and eventually forced the civil authorities to assume their responsibilities. It was Birney, however, who first saw the full significance of the denial of free enquiry and discussion, developed the thesis that slavery was incompatible with the fundamental principles of Americanism, and expanded the movement to free the Negro into a movement to preserve the essence of freedom for the white man. Edward Beecher, president of Illinois College, and Wendell Phillips of Boston were probably the two outstanding men induced to join the crusade by this contest over civil rights, and both were towers of strength. . . .

After 1840 the antislavery movement was political; the hustings were the forums; every candidate for office in an antislavery community was an antislavery lecturer; and the halls of Congress were the battleground. Myron Holley was the father of political action. Birney, Joshua Leavitt, and Alvan Stewart carried the burden after Holley's untimely death. The forties were the transition period, culminating in a Northern sectional party, but the central themes of the movement after 1840 were the withering influence of slavery upon the welfare and progress of the nation and the necessity of purging all branches of the federal government of its influence.

The scope of the abolition indictment of slavery, its widespread organization and skilful direction, and the length of time required to achieve its objective would seemingly indicate either a weak case or a strongly entrenched institution. Neither is correct. The weakness of the attack upon slavery and the strength of its defense lay not at all in one or the other per se, but in the fact that slavery was so inextricably bound up with the nation's political philosophy that the two were inseparable; and the indictment of slavery, because it was not allowed to operate upon the minds and hearts of the Southern people, embraced and came to be identified with a new political philosophy, unsupported by precedent or tradition and hostile to the genius of the people.

Although the attendance at the abolitionist national convention in 1833 was small, this body exercised an influence far out of proportion to its number. The following declaration can be taken as a manifesto of the abolitionist position.

WILLIAM LLOYD GARRISON: DECLARATION OF THE ANTI-SLAVERY CONVENTION*

The Convention, assembled in the City of Philadelphia to organize a National Anti-Slavery Society, promptly seize the opportunity to promulgate the following DECLARATION OF SENTIMENTS, as cherished by them in relation to the enslavement of one-sixth portion of the American people.

More than fifty-seven years have elapsed since a band of patriots convened in this place, to devise measures for the deliverance of this country from a foreign yoke. The cornerstone upon which they founded the TEMPLE OF FREEDOM was broadly this—'that all men are created equal; that they are endowed by their Creator with certain inalienable rights; that among these are life, LIBERTY, and the pursuit of happiness.' At the sound of their trumpet-call, three millions of people rose up as from the sleep of death, and rushed to the strife of blood; deeming it more glorious to die instantly as freemen, than desirable to live one hour as slaves. They were few in number—poor in resources; but the honest conviction that TRUTH, JUSTICE and RIGHT were on their side, made them invincible.

We have met together for the achievement of an enterprise, without which, that of our fathers is incomplete, and which, for its magnitude, solemnity, and probable results upon the destiny of the world, as far transcends theirs, as moral truth does physical force.

In purity of motive, in earnestness of zeal, in decision of purpose, in intrepidity of action, in steadfastness of faith, in sincerity of spirit, we would not be inferior to them.

Their principles led them to wage war against their oppressors, and to spill human blood like water, in order to be free. *Ours* forbid the doing of evil that good may come, and lead us to reject, and to entreat the oppressed to reject, the use of all carnal weapons for deliverance from bondage—relying solely upon those which are spiritual, and mighty through God to the pulling down of strong holds.

Their measures were physical resistance—the marshalling in arms—the hostile array—the mortal encounter. *Ours* shall be such only as the opposition of moral purity to moral corruption—the destruction of error by the potency of truth—the overthrow of prejudice by the power of love—and the abolition of slavery by the spirit of repentance.

Their grievances, great as they were, were trifling in comparison with the wrongs and sufferings of those for whom we plead. Our fathers were never slaves—never bought and sold like cattle—never shut out from the light of knowledge and religion—never subjected to the lash of brutal taskmasters.

But those, for whose emancipation we are striving,—constituting at the present time at least one-sixth part of our countrymen,—are recognized by the laws, and treated by their fellow beings, as marketable commodities—as good and chattels—as brute beasts;—are plundered daily of the fruits of their toil without redress;—really enjoy no constitutional nor legal protection from licentious and murderous outrages upon their persons;—are ruthlessly torn asunder—the tender babe from the arms of its frantic mother—the heart-broken wife from her weeping husband—at the caprice or pleasure of irresponsible tyrants;—and, for the crime of having a dark complexion, suffer the pangs of hunger, the infliction of stripes, and the ignominy of brutal servitude. They are kept in heathenish darkness by laws expressly enacted to make their instruction a criminal offence.

These are the prominent circumstances in the condition of more than TWO MILLIONS of our people, the proof of which may be found in thousands of indisputable facts, and in the laws of the slaveholding States.

Hence we maintain—

That in view of the civil and religious privileges of this nation, the guilt of its oppression is unequalled by any other on the face of the earth;—and, therefore,

That it is bound to repent instantly, to undo the heavy burden, to break every yoke, and to let the oppressed go free.

We further maintain—

That no man has a right to enslave or imbrute his brother—to hold or acknowledge him, for one moment, as a piece of merchandise—to keep back his hire by fraud—or to brutalize his mind by denying him the means of intellectual, social and moral improvement.

The right to enjoy liberty is inalienable. To invade it, is to usurp the prerogative of Jehovah. Every man has a right to his own body—to the

* Reprinted from *Abolitionist,* I (December, 1833), 178–80.

products of his own labor—to the protection of law—and to the common advantages of society. It is piracy to buy or steal a native African, and subject him to servitude. Surely the sin is as great to enslave an AMERICAN as an AFRICAN.

Therefore we believe and affirm—

That there is no difference, *in principle,* between the African slave trade and American slavery;

That every American citizen, who retains a human being in involuntary bondage, as his property, is [according to Scripture] a MAN-STEALER.

That the slaves ought instantly to be set free, and brought under the protection of law;

That if they had lived from the time of Pharaoh down to the present period, and had been entailed through successive generations, their right to be free could never have been alienated, but their claims would have constantly risen in solemnity;

That all those laws which are now in force, admitting the right of slavery, are therefore before God utterly null and void; being an audacious usurpation of the Divine prerogative, a daring infringement on the law of nature, a base overthrow of the very foundations of the social compact, a complete extinction of all the relations, endearments and obligations of mankind, and a presumptuous transgression of all the holy commandments—and that therefore they ought to be instantly abrogated.

We further believe and affirm—

That all persons of color who possess the qualifications which are demanded of others, ought to be admitted forthwith to the enjoyment of the same privileges, and the exercise of the same prerogatives, as others; and that the paths of preferment, of wealth, and of intelligence, should be opened as widely to them as to persons of a white complexion.

We maintain that no compensation should be given to the planters emancipating their slaves—

Because it would be a surrender of the great fundamental principle, that man cannot hold property in man;

Because SLAVERY IS A CRIME, AND THEREFORE IT IS NOT AN ARTICLE TO BE SOLD;

Because the holders of slaves are not the just proprietors of what they claim;—freeing the slaves is not depriving them of property, but restoring it to the right owner;—it is not wronging the master, but righting the slave—restoring him to himself;

Because immediate and general emancipation would only destroy nominal, not real property: it would not amputate a limb or break a bone of the slaves, but by infusing motives into their breasts, would make them doubly valuable to the masters as free laborers; and

Because if compensation is to be given at all, it should be given to the outraged and guiltless slaves, and not to those who have plundered and abused them.

We regard, as delusive, cruel and dangerous, any scheme of expatriation which pretends to aid, either directly or indirectly, in the emancipation of the slaves, or to be a substitute for the immediate and total abolition of slavery.

We fully and unanimously recognize the sovereignty of each State, to legislate exclusively on the subject of the slavery which is tolerated within its limits. We concede that Congress, *under the present national compact,* has no right to interfere with any of the slave States, in relation to this momentous subject.

But we maintain that Congress has a right, and is solemnly bound, to suppress the domestic slave trade between the several States, and to abolish slavery in those portions of our territory which the Constitution has placed under its jurisdiction.

We also maintain that there are, at the present time, the highest obligations resting upon the people of the free States to remove slavery by moral and political action, as prescribed in the Constitution of the United States. They are now living under a pledge of their tremendous physical force to fasten the galling fetters of tyranny upon the limbs of millions in the southern States;—they are liable to be called at any moment to suppress a general insurrection of the slaves;—they authorise the slave owner to vote for three-fifths of his slaves as property, and thus enable him to perpetuate his oppression;—they support a standing army at the south for its protection;—and they seize the slave who has escaped into their territories, and send him back to be tortured by an enraged master or a brutal driver.

This relation to slavery is criminal and full of danger: IT MUST BE BROKEN UP.

These are our views and principles—these, our designs and measures. With entire confidence in the overruling justice of God, we plant ourselves upon the Declaration of our Independence, and upon the truths of Divine Revelation, as upon the EVERLASTING ROCK.

We shall organize Anti-Slavery Societies, if possible, in every city, town and village in our land.

We shall send forth Agents to lift up the voice of remonstrance, of warning, of entreaty and rebuke.

We shall circulate, unsparingly and extensively, anti-slavery tracts and periodicals.

We shall enlist the PULPIT and the PRESS in the cause of the suffering and the dumb.

We shall aim at a purification of the churches from all participation in the guilt of slavery.

We shall encourage the labor of freemen over that of the slaves, by giving a preference to their productions;—and

We shall spare no exertions nor means to bring the whole nation to speedy repentance.

Our trust for victory is solely in GOD. *We* may be personally defeated, but our principles never. TRUTH, JUSTICE, REASON, HUMANITY, must and will gloriously triumph. Already a host is coming up to the help of the Lord against the mighty, and the prospect before us is full of encouragement.

Submitting this DECLARATION to the candid examination of the people of this country, and of the friends of liberty all over the world, we hereby affix our signatures to it;—pledging ourselves that, under the guidance and by the help of Almighty God, we will do all that in us lies, consistently with this Declaration of our principles, to overthrow the most execrable system of slavery that has ever been witnessed upon earth—to deliver our land from its deadliest curse—to wipe out the foulest stain which rests upon our national escutcheon—and to secure to the colored population of the United States, all the rights and privileges which belong to them as men and as Americans—come what may to our persons, our interests, or our reputations—whether we live to witness the triumph of JUSTICE, LIBERTY and HUMANITY, or perish untimely as martyrs in this great, benevolent and holy cause.

The conception abolitionists held of slavery was in a great part derived from the data gathered by Theodore Dwight Weld. His findings, published in 1839, constitute a significant landmark in abolitionist tracts.

THEODORE DWIGHT WELD: NARRATIVE OF NEHEMIAH CAULKINS*

I feel it my duty to tell some things that I know about slavery, in order, if possible, to awaken more feeling at the North in behalf of the slave. The treatment of the slaves on the plantation where I had the greatest opportunity of getting knowledge, *was not so bad* as that on some neighboring estates, where the owners were noted for their cruelty. There were, however, other estates in the vicinity, where the treatment was better; the slaves were better clothed and fed, were not worked so hard, and more attention was paid to their quarters.

The scenes that I have witnessed are enough to harrow up the soul; but could the slave be permitted to tell the story of his sufferings, which no white man, not linked with slavery, *is allowed to know,* the land would vomit out the horrible system, slaveholders and all, if they would not unclinch their grasp upon their defenceless victims.

I spent eleven winters, between the years of 1820 and 1835, in the state of North Carolina, mostly in the vicinity of Wilmington; and four out of the eleven on the estate of Mr. John Swan, five or six miles from that place. There were on his plantation about seventy slaves, male and female: some were married, and others lived together as man and wife, without even a mock ceremony. With their owners generally, it is a matter of indifference; the marriage of slaves not being recognized by the slave code. The slaves, however, think much of being married by a clergyman.

The cabins or huts of the slaves were small, and were built principally by the slaves themselves, as they could find time on Sundays and moonlight nights; they went into the swamps, cut the logs, backed or *hauled* them to the quarters, and put up their cabins. . . .

It is customary in that part of the country, to let the hogs run in the woods. On one occasion a slave caught a pig about two months old, which he carried to his quarters. The overseer, getting information of the fact, went to the field where he was at work, and ordered him to come to him. The slave at once suspected it was something about the pig, and fearing punishment, dropped his hoe and ran for the woods. He had got but a few rods, when the overseer raised his gun, loaded with duck shot, and brought him down. It is a common practice for overseers to go into the field armed with a gun or pistols, and sometimes both. He was taken up by the slaves and carried to the plantation hospital, and the physician sent for. A physician was employed by the year to take care of the sick or wounded slaves. In about six weeks this slave got better, and was able to come out of the hospital. He came to the mill where I was at work, and asked me to examine his body, which I did, and counted twenty-six duck shot still remaining in his flesh, though the doctor had removed a number while he was laid up.

There was a slave on Mr. Swan's plantation, by the name of Harry, who, during the absence of his master, ran away and secreted himself in the woods. This the slaves sometimes do, when the master is absent for several weeks, to escape the cruel treatment of the overseer. It is common for them to make preparations, by secreting a

* Reprinted from Theodore Dwight Weld, *American Slavery as It Is: Testimony of a Thousand Witnesses* (New York: 1839), pp. 11–13.

mortar, a hatchet, some cooking utensils, and whatever things they can get that will enable them to live while they are in the woods or swamps. Harry staid about three months, and lived by robbing the rice grounds, and by such other means as came in his way. The slaves generally know where the runaway is secreted, and visit him at night and on Sundays. On the return of his master, some of the slaves were sent for Harry. When he came home he was seized and confined in the stocks. The stocks were built in the barn, and consisted of two heavy pieces of timber, ten or more feet in length, and about seven inches wide; the lower one, on the floor, has a number of holes or places cut in it, for the ancles; the upper piece, being of the same dimensions, is fastened at one end by a hinge, and is brought down after the ancles are placed in the holes, and secured by a clasp and padlock at the other end. In this manner the person is left to sit on the floor. Harry was kept in the stocks *day and night for a week,* and flogged *every morning.* After this, he was taken out one morning, a log chain fastened around his neck, the two ends dragging on the ground, and he sent to the field, to do his task with the other slaves. At night he was again put in the stocks, in the morning he was sent to the field in the same manner, and thus dragged out another week.

The overseer was a very miserly fellow, and restricted his wife in what are considered the comforts of life—such as tea, sugar, &c. To make up for this, she set her wits to work, and, by the help of a slave, named Joe, used to take from the plantation whatever she could conveniently, and watch her opportunity during her husband's absence, and send Joe to sell them and buy for her such things as she directed. Once when her husband was away, she told Joe to kill and dress one of the pigs, sell it, and get her some tea, sugar, &c. Joe did as he was bid, and she gave him the offal for his services. When Galloway returned, not suspecting his wife, he asked her if she knew what had become of his pig. She told him she suspected one of the slaves, naming him, had stolen it, for she had heard a pig squeal the evening before. The overseer called the slave up, and charged him with the theft. He denied it, and said he knew nothing about it. The overseer still charged him with it, and told him he would give him one week to think of it, and if he did not confess the theft, or find out who did steal the pig, he would flog every negro on the plantation; before the week was up it was ascertained that Joe had killed the pig. He was called up and questioned, and admitted that he had done so, and told the overseer that he did it by the order of Mrs. Galloway, and that she directed him to buy some sugar, &c. with the money. Mrs. Galloway gave Joe the lie; and he was terribly flogged. Joe told me he had been several times to the smoke-house with Mrs. G, and taken hams

and sold them, which her husband told me he supposed were stolen by the negroes on a neighboring plantation. Mr. Swan, hearing of the circumstance, told me he believed Joe's story, but that his statement would not be taken as proof; and if every slave on the plantation told the same story it could not be received as evidence against a white person.

To show the manner in which old and worn-out slaves are sometimes treated, I will state a fact. Galloway owned a man about seventy years of age. The old man was sick and went to his hut; laid himself down on some straw with his feet to the fire, covered by a piece of an old blanket, and there lay four or five days, groaning in great distress, without any attention being paid him by his master, until death ended his miseries; he was then taken out and buried with as little ceremony and respect as would be paid to a brute.

There is a practice prevalent among the planters, of letting a negro off from severe and long-continued punishment on account of the intercession of some white person, who pleads in his behalf, that he believes the negro will behave better; that he promises well, and he believes he will keep his promise, &c. The planters sometimes get tired of punishing a negro, and, wanting his services in the field, they get some white person to come in, and, in the presence of the slave, intercede for him. At one time a negro, named Charles, was confined in the stocks in the building where I was at work, and had been severely whipped several times. He begged me to intercede for him and try to get him released. I told him I would; and when his master came in to whip him again, I went up to him and told him I had been talking with Charles, and he had promised to behave better, &c., and requested him not to punish him any more, but to let him go. He then said to Charles, "As Mr. Caulkins has been pleading for you, I will let you go on his account;" and accordingly released him.

Women are generally shown some little indulgence for three or four weeks previous to child birth; they are at such times not often punished if they do not finish the task assigned them; it is, in some cases, passed over with a severe reprimand, and sometimes without any notice being taken of it. They are generally allowed four weeks after the birth of a child, before they are compelled to go into the field, they then take the child with them, attended sometimes by a little girl or boy, from the age of four to six, to take care of it while the mother is at work. When there is no child that can be spared, or not young enough for this service, the mother, after nursing, lays it under a tree, or by the side of a fence, and goes to her task, returning at stated intervals to nurse it. While I was on this plantation, a little negro girl, six years of age, destroyed the life of a child about two months old, which was left in her care. It seems this little nurse, so called, got tired of her charge and the labor of carrying it to the quarters at night, the mother being obliged to work as long as she could see. One evening she nursed the infant at sunset as usual, and sent it to the quarters. The little girl, on her way home, had to cross a run, or brook, which led down into the swamp; when she came to the brook she followed it into the swamp, then took the infant and plunged it head foremost into the water and mud, where it stuck fast; she there left it and went to the negro quarters. When the mother came in from the field, she asked the girl where the child was; she told her she had brought it home, but did not know where it was; the overseer was immediately informed, search was made, and it was found as above stated, and dead. The little girl was shut up in the barn, and confined there two or three weeks, when a speculator came along and bought her for two hundred dollars.

The slaves are obliged to work from daylight till dark, as long as they can see. When they have tasks assigned, which is often the case, a few of the strongest and most expert, sometimes finish them before sunset; others will be obliged to work till eight or nine o'clock in the evening. All must finish their tasks or take a flogging. The whip and gun, or pistol, are companions of the overseer; the former he uses very frequently upon the negroes, during their hours of labor, without regard to age or sex. Scarcely a day passed while I was on the plantation, in which some of the slaves were not whipped; I do not mean that they were *struck a few blows* merely, but had a *set flogging*. The same labor is commonly assigned to men and women,—such as digging ditches in the rice marshes, clearing up land, chopping cord-wood, threshing, &c. I have known the women go into the barn as soon as they could see in the morning, and work as late as they could see at night, threshing rice with the flail, (they now have a threshing machine,) and when they could see to thresh no longer, they had to gather up the rice, carry it up stairs, and deposit it in the granary.

William Ellery Channing, a Unitarian minister, was perhaps the most eloquent philosopher of the abolitionist movement. Voicing the humanistic sentiments of the 1830's and 1840's, Channing found slavery contrary to the natural rights of the individual.

WILLIAM ELLERY CHANNING: CRITIQUE OF MAN AS PROPERTY*

The slave-holder claims the slave as his property. The very idea of a slave is, that he belongs to another, that he is bound to live and labor for another, to be another's instrument, and to make another's will his habitual law, however adverse to his own. Another owns him, and of course has a right to his time and strength, a right to the fruits of his labor, a right to task him without his consent, and to determine the kind and duration of his toil, a right to confine him to any bounds, a right to extort the required work by stripes,—a right, in a word, to use him as a tool, without contract, against his will, and in denial of his right to dispose of himself, or to use his power for his own good. "A slave," says the Louisiana code, "is in the power of the master to whom he belongs. The master may sell him, dispose of his person, his industry, his labor; he can do nothing, possess nothing, nor acquire any thing, but which must belong to his master." "Slaves shall be deemed, taken, reputed, and adjudged," say the South Carolina laws, "to be chattels personal in the hands of their masters, and possessions to all intents and purposes whatsoever." Such is slavery, —a claim to man as property.

Now this claim of property in a human being is altogether false, groundless. No such right of man in man can exist. A human being cannot be justly owned. To hold and treat him as property is to inflict a great wrong, to incur the guilt of oppression.

This position there is a difficulty in maintaining, on account of its exceeding obviousness. It is too plain for proof. To defend it is like trying to confirm a self-evident truth. To find arguments is not easy, because an argument is something clearer than the proposition to be sustained. The man who, on hearing the claim to property in man, does not see and feel distinctly that it is a cruel usurpation, is hardly to be reached by reasoning, for it is hard to find any plainer principles than what he begins with denying. I will endeavor, however, to illustrate the truth which I have stated.

1. It is plain that if one man may be held as property, then every other man may be so held. If there be nothing in human nature, in our common nature, which excludes and forbids the con-

* Reprinted from William E. Channing, *The Works of William E. Channing* (Boston: 1880), pp. 692–97.

version of him who possesses it into an article of property; if the right of the free to liberty is founded, not on their essential attributes as rational and moral beings, but on certain adventitious, accidental circumstances, into which they have been thrown; then every human being, by a change of circumstances, may justly be held and treated by another as property. If one man may be rightfully reduced to slavery, then there is not a human being on whom the same chain may not be imposed. Now, let every reader ask himself this plain question: Could I, can I, be rightfully seized, and made an article of property; be made a passive instrument of another's will and pleasure; be subjected to another's irresponsible power; be subjected to stripes at another's will; be denied the control and use of my own limbs and faculties for my own good? Does any man, so questioned, doubt, waver, look about him for an answer? Is not the reply given immediately, intuitively, by his whole inward being? Does not an unhesitating, unerring conviction spring up in my breast, that no other man can acquire such a right in myself? Do we not repel, indignantly and with horror, the thought of being reduced to the condition of tools and chattels to a fellow-creature? Is there any moral truth more deeply rooted in us, than that such a degradation would be an infinite wrong? And, if this impression be a delusion, on what single moral conviction can we rely? This deep assurance, that we cannot be rightfully made another's property, does not rest on the hue of our skins, or the place of our birth, or our strength, or wealth. These things do not enter our thoughts. The consciousness of indestructible rights is a part of our moral being. The consciousness of our humanity involves the persuasion that we cannot be owned as a tree or a brute. As men, we cannot justly be made slaves. Then no man can be rightfully enslaved. In casting the yoke from ourselves as an unspeakable wrong, we condemn ourselves as wrong-doers and oppressors in laying it on any who share our nature. It is not necessary to inquire whether a man, by extreme guilt, may not forfeit the rights of his nature, and be justly punished with slavery. On this point crude notions prevail. But the discussion would be foreign to the present subject. We are now not speaking of criminals. We speak of innocent men, who have given us no hold on them by guilt; and our own consciousness is a proof that such cannot rightfully be seized as property by a fellow-creature.

2. A man cannot be seized and held as property, because he has rights. What these rights are, whether few or many, or whether all men have the same, are questions for future discussion. All that is assumed now is, that every human being has *some* rights. This truth cannot be denied, but by denying to a portion of the race that moral nature which is the sure and only foundation of rights. This truth has never, I believe, been disputed. It is even recognized in the very codes of slave legislation, which, while they strip a man of liberty, affirm his right to life, and threaten his murderer with punishment. Now, I say, a being having rights cannot justly be made property; for this claim over him virtually annuls all his rights. It strips him of all power to assert them. It makes it a crime to assert them. The very essence of slavery is to put a man defenceless into the hands of another. The right claimed by the master to task, to force, to imprison, to whip, and to punish the slave, at discretion, and especially to prevent the least resistance to his will, is a virtual denial and subversion of all the rights of the victim of his power. The two cannot stand together. Can we doubt which of them ought to fall?

3. Another argument against property is to be found in the essential equality of men. I know that this doctrine, so venerable in the eyes of our fathers, has lately been denied. Verbal logicians have told us that men are "born equal" only in the sense of being equally born. They have asked whether all are equally tall, strong, or beautiful; or whether nature, Procrustes-like, reduces all her children to one standard of intellect and virtue. By such arguments it is attempted to set aside the principle of equality, on which the soundest moralists have reared the structure of social duty; and in these ways the old foundations of despotic power, which our fathers in their simplicity thought they had subverted, are laid again by their sons.

It is freely granted that there are innumerable diversities among men; but be it remembered, they are ordained to bind men together, and not to subdue one to the other; ordained to give means and occasions of mutual aid, and to carry forward each and all, so that the good of all is equally intended in this distribution of various gifts. Be it also remembered, that these diversities among men are as nothing in comparison with the attributes in which they agree; and it is this which constitutes their essential equality. All men have the same rational nature and the same power of conscience, and all are equally made for indefinite improvement of these divine faculties, and for the happiness to be found in their virtuous use. Who, that comprehends these gifts, does not see that the diversities of the race vanish before them? Let it be added, that the natural advantages which distinguish one man from another, are so bestowed as to counterbalance one another, and bestowed without regard to rank or condition in life. Whoever surpasses in one endowment is inferior in others. Even genius, the greatest gift, is found in union with strange infirmities, and often places its possessors below ordinary men in the conduct of life. Great learning is often put to shame by the mother-wit and keen good sense of uneducated men. Nature, indeed, pays no heed to birth or condition in bestowing her favors. The noblest spirits sometimes grow up in the obscurest spheres. Thus equal are men; and among these equals, who can substantiate his claim to make others his property, his tools, the mere instruments of his private interest and gratification? Let this claim begin, and where will it stop? If one may assert it, why not all? Among these partakers of the same rational and moral nature, who can make good a right over others, which others may not establish over himself? Does he insist on superior strength of body or mind? Who of us has no superior in one or the other of these endowments? Is it sure that the slave or the slave's child may not surpass his master in intellectual energy, or in moral worth? Has nature conferred distinctions which tell us plainly who shall be owners and who be owned? Who of us can unblushingly lift his head and say that God has written "Master" there? or who can show the word "Slave" engraven on his brother's brow? The equality of nature makes slavery a wrong. Nature's seal is affixed to no instrument by which property in a single human being is conveyed.

4. That a human being cannot be justly held and used as property, is apparent from the very nature of property. Property is an exclusive right. It shuts out all claim but that of the possessor. What one man owns cannot belong to another. What, then, is the consequence of holding a human being as property? Plainly this. He can have no right to himself. His limbs are, in truth, not morally his own. He has not a right to his own strength. It belongs to another. His will, intellect, and muscles, all the powers of body and mind which are exercised in labor, he is bound to regard as another's. Now, if there be property in any thing, it is that of a man in his own person, mind, and strength. All other rights are weak, unmeaning, compared with this, and in denying this all right is denied. It is true that an individual may forfeit by crime his right to the use of his limbs, perhaps to his limbs, and even to life. But the very idea of forfeiture implies that the right was originally possessed. It is true that a man may by contract give to another a limited right to his strength. But he gives only because he possesses it, and gives it for considerations which he deems beneficial to himself; and the right conferred ceases at once on violation of the conditions on which it was bestowed. To deny the right of a human being to himself, to his own limbs and faculties, to his energy of body and mind, is an absurdity too gross to be confuted by any thing but a simple statement. Yet this absurdity is involved in the idea of his belonging to another.

5. We have a plain recognition of the principle now laid down, in the universal indignation excited towards a man who makes another his slave. Our laws know no higher crime than that of reducing a man to slavery. To steal or to buy an African on his own shores is piracy. In this act the greatest wrong is inflicted, the most sacred right violated. But if a human being cannot without infinite injustice be seized as property, then he cannot without equal wrong be held and used as such. The wrong in the first seizure lies in the destination of a human being to future bondage, to the criminal use of him as a chattel or brute. Can that very use, which makes the original seizure an enormous wrong, become gradually innocent? If the slave receive injury without measure at the first moment of the outrage, is he less injured by being held fast the second or the third? Does the duration of wrong, the increase of it by continuance, convert it into right? It is true, in many cases, that length of possession is considered as giving a right, where the goods were acquired by unlawful means. But in these cases the goods were such as might justly be appropriated to individual use. They were intended by the Creator to be owned. They fulfil their purpose by passing into the hands of an exclusive possessor. It is essential to rightful property in a thing, that the thing from its nature may be rightfully appropriated. If it cannot originally be made one's own without crime, it certainly cannot be continued as such without guilt. Now, the ground on which the seizure of the African on his own shore is condemned is, that he is a man who has by his nature a right to be free. Ought not, then, the same condemnation to light on the continuance of his yoke? Still more. Whence is it that length of possession is considered by the law as conferring a right? I answer, from the difficulty of determining the original proprietor, and from the apprehension of unsettling all property by carrying back inquiry beyond a certain time. Suppose, however, an article of property to be of such a nature that it could bear the name of the true original owner stamped on it in bright and indelible characters. In this case, the whole ground on which length of possession bars other claims would fail. The proprietor would not be concealed, or rendered doubtful by the lapse of time. Would not he, who should receive such an article from a robber, or a succession of robbers, be involved in their guilt? Now the true owner of a human being is made manifest to all. It is himself. No brand on the slave was ever so conspicuous as the mark of property which God has set on him. God, in making him a rational and moral being, has put a glorious stamp on him, which all the slave legislation and slave markets of worlds cannot efface. Hence no right accrues to the master from the length of the wrong which has been done to the slave.

6. Another argument against the right of property in man may be drawn from a very obvious principle of moral science. It is a plain truth, universally received, that every right supposes or involves a corresponding obligation. If, then, a man has a right to another's person or powers, the latter is under obligation to give himself up as a chattel to the former. This is his duty. He is bound to be a slave; and bound not merely by the Christian law, which enjoins submission to injury, not merely by prudential con-

siderations, or by the claims of public order and peace; but bound because another has a right of ownership, has a moral claim to him, so that he would be guilty of dishonesty, of robbery, in withdrawing himself from this other's service. It is his duty to work for his master, though all compulsion were withdrawn; and in deserting him he would commit the crime of taking away another man's property as truly as if he were to carry off his owner's purse. Now, do we not instantly feel, can we help feeling, that this is false? Is the slave thus morally bound? When the African was first brought to these shores, would he have violated a solemn obligation by slipping his chain, and flying back to his native home? Would he not have been bound to seize the precious opportunity of escape? Is the slave under a moral obligation to confine himself, his wife, and children, to a spot where their union in a moment may be forcibly dissolved? Ought he not, if he can, to place himself and his family under the guardianship of equal laws? Should we blame him for leaving his yoke? Do we not feel that, in the same condition, a sense of duty would quicken our flying steps? Where, then, is the obligation which would necessarily be imposed, if the right existed which the master claims? The absence of obligation proves the want of the right. The claim is groundless. It is a cruel wrong.

7. I come now to what is to my own mind the great argument against seizing and using a man as property. He cannot be property in the sight of God and justice, because he is a rational, moral, immortal being; because created in God's image, and therefore in the highest sense his child; because created to unfold godlike faculties, and to govern himself by a divine law written on his heart, and republished in God's word. His whole nature forbids that he should be seized as property. From his very nature it follows that so to seize him is to offer an insult to his Maker, and to inflict aggravated social wrong. Into every human being God has breathed an immortal spirit, more precious than the whole outward creation. No earthly or celestial language can exaggerate the worth of a human being. No matter how obscure his condition. Thought, reason, conscience, the capacity of virtue, the capacity of Christian love, an immortal destiny, an intimate moral connection with God,—here are attributes of our common humanity which reduce to insignificance all outward distinctions, and make every human being unspeakably dear to his Maker. No matter how ignorant he may be. The capacity of improvement allies him to the more instructed of his race and places within his reach the knowledge and happiness of higher worlds. Every human being has in him the germ of the greatest idea in the universe, the idea of God; and to unfold this is the end of his existence. Every human being has in his breast the elements of that divine, everlasting law, which the highest orders of the creation obey. He has the idea of duty; and to unfold, revere, obey this is the very purpose for which life was given. Every human being has the idea of what is meant by that word, truth; that is, he sees, however dimly, the great object of divine and created intelligence, and is capable of ever-enlarging perceptions of truth. Every human being has affections, which may be purified and expanded into a sublime love. He has, too, the idea of happiness, and a thirst for it which cannot be appeased. Such is our nature. Wherever we see a man, we see the possessor of these great capacities. Did God make such a being to be owned as a tree or a brute? How plainly was he made to exercise, unfold, improve his highest powers, made for a moral, spiritual good! and how is he wronged, and his Creator opposed, when he is forced and broken into a tool to another's physical enjoyment!

Such a being was plainly made for an end in himself. He is a person, not a thing. He is an end, not a mere instrument or means. He was made for his own virtue and happiness. Is this end reconcilable with his being held and used as a chattel? The sacrifice of such a being to another's will, to another's present, outward, ill-comprehended good, is the greatest violence which can be offered to any creature of God. It is to degrade him from his rank in the universe, to make him a means, not an end, to cast him out from God's spiritual family into the brutal herd.

Such a being was plainly made to obey a law within himself. This is the essence of a moral being. He possesses, as a part of his nature, and the most essential part, a sense of duty, which he is to reverence and follow, in opposition to all pleasure or pain, to all interfering human wills. The great purpose of all good education and discipline is, to make a man master of himself, to excite him to act from a principle in his own mind, to lead him to propose his own perfection as his supreme law and end. And is this highest purpose of man's nature to be reconciled with entire subjection to a foreign will, to an outward, overwhelming force, which is satisfied with nothing but complete submission?

The end of such a being as we have described is, manifestly, improvement. Now, it is the fundamental law of our nature that all our powers are to improve by free exertion. Action is the indispensable condition of progress to the intellect, conscience, and heart. Is it not plain, then, that a human being cannot, without wrong, be owned by another, who claims, as proprietor, the right to repress the powers of his slaves, to withhold from them the means of development, to keep them within the limits which are necessary to contentment in chains, to shut out every ray of light and every generous sentiment which may interfere with entire subjection to his will?

No man who seriously considers what human nature is, and what it was made for, can think of setting up a claim to a fellow-creature. What! own a spiritual being, a being made to know and adore God, and who is to outlive the sun and stars! What! chain to our lowest uses a being made for truth and virtue! convert into a brute instrument that intelligent nature on which the idea of duty has dawned, and which is a nobler type of God than all outward creation! Should we not deem it a wrong which no punishment could expiate, were one of our children seized as property and driven by the whip to toil? And shall God's child, dearer to him than an only son to a human parent, be thus degraded? Every thing else may be owned in the universe; but a moral, rational being cannot be property. Suns and stars may be owned, but not the lowest spirit. Touch any thing but this. Lay not your hand on God's rational offspring. The whole spiritual world cries out, Forbear! The highest intelligences recognize their own nature, their own rights, in the humblest human being. By that priceless, immortal spirit which dwells in him, by that likeness of God which he wears, tread him not in the dust, confound him not with the brute.

We have thus seen that a human being cannot rightfully be held and used as property. No legislation, not that of all countries or worlds, could make him so. Let this be laid down as a first fundamental truth. Let us hold it fast as a most sacred, precious truth. Let us hold it fast

against all customs, all laws, all rank, wealth, and power. Let it be armed with the whole authority of the civilized and Christian world.

I have taken it for granted that no reader would be so wanting in moral discrimination and moral feeling as to urge that men may rightfully be seized and held as property, because various governments have so ordained. What! is human legislation the measure of right? Are God's laws to be repealed by man's? Can government do no wrong? To what a mournful extent is the history of human governments a record of wrongs! How much does the progress of civilization consist in the substitution of just and humane for barbarous and oppressive laws! The individual, indeed, is never authorized to oppose physical force to unrighteous ordinances of government, as long as the community choose to sustain them. But criminal legislation ought to be freely and earnestly exposed. Injustice is never so terrible, and never so corrupting, as when armed with the sanctions of law. The authority of government, instead of being a reason for silence under wrongs, is a reason for protesting against wrong with the undivided energy of argument, entreaty, and solemn admonition.

George Fitzhugh, Southern polemicist for slavery, argued just before the Civil War that all private property, including slaves, was sacred and that plantation labor was far better treated than Northern wage workers. Fitzhugh contended, in pointing to the alleged beneficence of slavery, "Capital exercises a more perfect compulsion over free laborers, than human masters over slaves: for free laborers must at all times work or starve, and slaves are supported whether they work or not."

GEORGE FITZHUGH: CANNIBALS ALL!*

We are, all, North and South, engaged in the White Slave Trade, and he who succeeds best, is esteemed most respectable. It is far more cruel than the Black Slave Trade, because it exacts more of its slaves, and neither protects nor governs them. . . But we not only boast that the White Slave Trade is more exacting and fraudulent (in fact, though not in intention,) than Black Slavery, but we also boast, that it is more cruel, in leaving the laborer to take care of himself and family out of the pittance which skill or capital have allowed him to retain. When the day's labor is ended, he is free, but is overburdened with the cares of family and household,

which make his freedom an empty and delusive mockery. But his employer is really free, and may enjoy the profits made by others' labor, without a care, or a trouble, as to their wellbeing. The Negro slave is free, too, when the labors of the day are over, and free in mind as well as body; for the master provides food, raiment, house fuel, and everything else necessary to the physical well-being of himself and family. The master's labors commence just when the slave's end. No wonder men should prefer white slavery to capital, to Negro slavery, since it is more profitable, and is free from all the cares and labors of black slave-holding.

Now, reader, if you wish to know yourself—to 'descant on your own deformity'—read on. But if you would cherish self-conceit, self-esteem, or self-appreciation, throw down our book; for we

* Reprinted from George Fitzhugh, *Cannibals All!* (Richmond: 1857), pp. 25–32, 48–49, 323–26, 353–57.

203

will dispel illusions which have promoted your happiness, and shew you that what you have considered and practiced as virtue, is little better than moral Cannibalism. But you will find yourself in numerous and respectable company; for all good and respectable people are 'Cannibals all,' who do not labor, or who are successfully trying to live without labor, on the unrequited labor of other people. . .

But, reader, we do not wish to fire into the flock. 'Thou art the man!' You are a Cannibal! and if a successful one, pride yourself on the number of your victims, quite as much as any Feejee chieftain, who breakfasts, dines and sups on human flesh.—And your conscience smites you, if you have failed to succeed, quite as much as his, when he returns from an unsuccessful foray.

Probably, you are a lawyer, or a merchant, or a doctor, who have made by your business fifty thousand dollars, and retired to live on your capital. But, mark! not to spend your capital. That would be vulgar, disreputable, criminal. That would be, to live by your own labor; for your capital is your amassed labor. That would be, to do as common working men do; for they take the pittance which their employers leave them, to live on. They live by labor; for they exchange the results of their own labor for the products of other people's labor. It is, no doubt, an honest, vulgar way of living; but not at all a respectable way. The respectable way of living is, to make other people work for you, and to pay them nothing for so doing—and to have no concern about them after their work is done. Hence, white slave-holding is much more respectable than Negro slavery—for the master works nearly as hard for the Negro, as he for the master. But you, my virtuous, respectable reader, exact three thousand dollars per annum from white labor, (for your income is the product of white labor,) and make not one cent of return in any form. You retain your capital, and never labor, and yet live in luxury on the labor of others. Capital commands labor, as the master does the slave. Neither pays for labor; but the master permits the slave to retain a larger allowance from the proceeds of his own labor, and hence 'free labor is cheaper than slave labor.' You, with the command over labor which your capital gives you, are a slave owner—a master, without the obligations of a master. They who work for you, who create your income, are slaves, without the rights of slaves. Slaves without a master! Whilst you were engaged in amassing your capital, in seeking to become independent, you were in the White Slave Trade. To become independent, is to be able to make other people support you, without being obliged to labor for *them*. Now, what man in society is not seeking to attain this situation? He who attains it, is a slave owner, in the worst sense. He who is in pursuit of it, is engaged in the slave trade. You,

reader, belong to the one or other class. The men without property, in free society, are theoretically in a worse condition than slaves. Practically, their condition corresponds with this theory, as history and statistics every where demonstrate. The capitalists, in a free society, live in ten times the luxury and show that Southern masters do, because the slaves to capital work harder and cost less, than negro slaves.

The Negro slaves of the South are the happiest, and, in some sense, the freest people in the world. The children and the aged and infirm work not at all, and yet have all the comforts and necessaries of life provided for them. They enjoy liberty, because they are oppressed neither by care nor labor. The women do little hard work, and are protected from the despotism of their husbands by their masters. The Negro men and stout boys work, on the average, in good weather, not more than nine hours a day. The balance of their time is spent in perfect abandon. Besides, they have their Sabbaths and holidays. White men, with so much of license and liberty, would die of ennui; but Negroes luxuriate in corporeal and mental repose. With their faces upturned to the sun, they can sleep at any hour; and quiet sleep is the greatest of human enjoyments. . . .

Free laborers have not a thousandth part of the rights and liberties of negro slaves. Indeed, they have not a single right or a single liberty, unless it be the right or liberty to die. But the reader may think that he and other capitalists and employers are freer than negro slaves. Your capital would soon vanish, if you dared indulge in the liberty and abandon of Negroes. You hold your wealth and position by the tenure of constant watchfulness, care and circumspection. You never labor; but you are never free.

Where a few own the soil, they have unlimited power over the balance of society, until domestic slavery comes in, to compel them to permit this balance of society to draw a sufficient and comfortable living from 'terra mater.' Free society, asserts the right of a few to the earth—slavery, maintains that it belongs, in different degrees, to all. . .

'Property in man' is what all are struggling to obtain. Why should they not be obliged to take care of man, their property, as they do of their horses and their hounds, their cattle and their sheep. Now, under the delusive name of liberty, you work him, 'from morn to dewy eve'—from infancy to old age—then turn him out to starve. You treat your horses and hounds better. Capital is a cruel master. The free slave trade, the commonest, yet the cruelest of trades. . . .

It is impossible to place labor and capital in harmonious and friendly relations, except by the means of slavery, which identifies their interests. Would that gentleman lay his capital out in land and negroes, he might be sure, in whatever hands it came, that it would be employed to protect laborers, not to oppress them; for when slaves are worth near a thousand dollars a head, they will be carefully and well provided for. In any other investment he may make of it, it will be used as an engine to squeeze the largest amount of labor from the poor, for the least amount of allowance. We say allowance, not wages; for neither slaves nor free laborers get wages, in the popular sense of the term: that is, the employer or capitalist pays them from nothing of his own but allows them a part, generally a very small part, of the proceeds of their own labor. Free laborers pay one another, for labor creates all values and capital, after taking the lion's share by its taxing power, but pays the so-called wages of one laborer from the proceeds of the labor of another. Capital does not breed, yet remains undiminished. Its profits are but its taxing power. Men seek to become independent, in order to cease to pay labor; in order to become masters, without the cares, duties and responsibilities of masters. Capital exercises a more perfect compulsion over free laborers, than human masters over slaves: for free laborers must at all times work or starve, and slaves are supported whether they work or not. Free laborers have less liberty than slaves, are worse paid and provided for, and have no valuable rights. Slaves, with more of actual practical liberty, with ampler allowance, and constant protection, are secure in the enjoyment of all the rights, which provide for their physical comfort at all times and under all circumstances. The free laborer must be employed or starve, yet no one is obliged to employ him. The slave is taken care of, whether employed or not. Though each free laborer has no particular master, his wants and other men's capital, make him a slave without a master, or with too many masters, which is as bad as none. It were often better than he had an ascertained master, instead of an irresponsible and unascertained one. . . .

The Abolitionists and Socialists, who, alone, have explored the recesses of social science, well understand that they can never establish their Utopia until private property is abolished or equalized. The man without property is theoretically, and, too often, practically, without a single right. Air and water, 'tis generally believed, are the common property of mankind; but nothing is falser in fact as well as theory. The ownership of land gives to the proprietor the exclusive right to every thing above and beneath the soil. The lands are all appropriated, and with them the air above them, the waters on them, and the mines beneath them. The pauper, to breathe the air or drink the waters, must first find a place where he may rightfully enjoy them. He can find, at all times, no such place, and is compelled, by his necessities, to inhale the close and putrid air of small rooms, damp cellars and crowded factories, and to drink insufficient quantities of impure water, furnished to him at a price he can ill afford. He pays for the water which he drinks, because it has ceased to be common property. He

is not free, because he has no where that he may rightfully lay his head. Private property has monopolized the earth, and destroyed both his liberty and equality. He has no security for his life, for he cannot live without employment and adequate wages, and none are bound to employ him. If the earth were in common, he could always enjoy not only air and water, but by his industry might earn the means of subsistence. His situation is theoretically and practically desperate and intolerable. Were he a slave, he would enjoy in fact as well as in legal fiction, all necessary and essential rights. Pure air and water, a house, sufficient food, fire, and clothing, would be his at all times. Slavery is a form of communism, and as the Abolitionists and Socialists have resolved to adopt a new social system, we recommend it to their consideration. The manner in which the change shall be made from the present form of society to that system of communism which we propose is very simple. Negro slaves are now worth seven hundred dollars a-head. As whites work harder, they are worth about a thousand. Make the man who owns a thousand dollars of capital the guardian (the term master is objectionable) of one white pauper of average value; give the man who is worth ten thousand dollars ten paupers, and the millionaire a thousand. This would be an act of simple mercy and justice; for the capitalists now live entirely by the proceeds of poor men's labor, which capital enables them to command; and they command and enjoy it in almost the exact proportions which we have designated. Thus, a family of poor laborers, men, women and children, ten in number can support themselves, and make about six hundred dollars, for their employer, which is the interest on ten thousand. They would work no harder than they do now, would be under no greater necessity to work, would be relieved of most of the cares of life, and let into the enjoyment of all valuable and necessary rights. What would they lose in liberty and equality? Just nothing. Having more rights, they would have more liberty than now, and approach nearer to equality. It might be, that their security and exemption from care would render their situation preferable to that of their employers. We suspect it would be easier to find wards or slaves than guardians or masters —for the gain would be all on the laborer's side, and the loss all on that of the capitalist.

Set your miscalled free laborers actually free, by giving them enough property or capital to live on, and then call on us at the South to free our negroes. At present, you Abolitionists know our negro slaves are much the freer of the two; and it would be a great advance towards freeing your laborers, to give them guardians, bound, like our masters, to take care of them, and entitled, in consideration thereof, to the proceeds of their labor. . . .

In the Liberator of the 19th December, we observe that the editor narrows down the slavery contest to the mere question, whether "Man may rightfully hold property in man?"

We think we can dispose of this objection to domestic slavery in a very few words.

Man is a social and gregarious animal, and all such animals hold property in each other. Nature imposes upon them slavery as a law and necessity of their existence. They live together to aid each other, and are slaves under Mr. Garrison's higher law. Slavery arises under the higher law, and is, and ever must be, coëval and coëxtensive with human nature.

We will enumerate a few of its ten thousand modifications.

The husband has a legally recognized property in his wife's services, and may legally control, in some measure, her personal liberty. She is his property and his slave.

The wife has also a legally recognized property in the husband's services. He is her property, but not her slave.

The father has property in the services and persons of his children till they are twenty-one years of age. They are his property and his slaves.

Children have property, during infancy, in the services of each parent.

Infant negroes, sick, infirm and superannuated negroes, hold most valuable property in the services and capital of their masters. The masters hold no property in such slaves, because, for the time, they are of no value.

Owners and captains of vessels own property in the services of sailors, and may control their personal liberty. They (the sailors) are property, and slaves also.

The services and persons, lives and liberty of soldiers and of officers, belong to the Government; they are, whilst in service, both property and slaves.

Every white working man, be he clerk, carpenter, mechanic, printer, common laborer, or what else, who contracts to serve for a term of days, months, or years, is, for such term, the property of his employer. He is not a slave, like the wife, child, apprentice, sailor or soldier, because, although the employer's right to his services be equally perfect, his remedy to enforce such right is very different. In the one case, he may resort to force to compel compliance; in the other, he is driven to a suit for damages.

Again: Every capitalist holds property in his fellow men to the extent of the profits of his capital, or income. The only income possibly resulting from capital, is the result of the property which capital bestows on its owners, in the labor of other people. In our first three chapters we attempt to explain this.

All civilized society recognizes, and, in some measure, performs the obligation to support and provide for all human beings, whether natives or foreigners, who are unable to provide for themselves. Hence poor-houses, &c.

Hence all men hold valuable property, actual or contingent, in the services of each other.

If, Mr. Garrison, this be the only difficulty to be adjusted between North and South, we are sure that your little pet, Disunion, "living will linger, and lingering will die."

When Mr. Andrews and you have quite "expelled human nature," dissolved and disintegrated society, and reduced mankind to separate, independent, but conflicting monads, or human atoms—then, and not till then, will you establish the 'sovereignty of the individual,' and destroy the property of man in man. . . .

We do not agree with the authors of the Declaration of Independence, that governments "derive their just powers from the consent of the governed." The women, the children, the negroes, and but few of the non-property holders were consulted, or consented to the Revolution, or the governments that ensued from its success. As to these, the new governments were self-elected despotisms, and the governing class self-elected despots. Those governments originated in force, and have been continued by force. All governments must originate in force, and be continued by force. The very term, government, implies that it is carried on against the consent of the governed. Fathers do not derive their authority, as heads of families, from the consent of wife and children, nor do they govern their families by their consent. They never take the vote of the family as to the labors to be performed, the moneys to be expended, or as to anything else. Masters dare not take the vote of slaves, as to their government. If they did, constant holiday, dissipation and extravagance would be the result. Captains of ships are not appointed by the consent of the crew, and never take their vote, even in "doubling Cape Horn." If they did, the crew would generally vote to get drunk, and the ship would never weather the cape. Not even in the most democratic countries are soldiers governed by their consent, nor is their vote taken on the eve of battle. They have some how lost (or never had) the "inalienable rights of life, liberty and the pursuit of happiness;" and, whether Americans or Russians, are forced into battle, without and often against their consent. The ancient republics were governed by a small class of adult male citizens, who assumed and exercised the government, without the consent of the governed. The South is governed just as those ancient republics were. In the county in which we live, there are eighteen thousand souls, and only twelve hundred voters. But we twelve hundred, the governors, never ask and never intend to ask the consent of the sixteen thousand eight hundred whom we govern. Were we to do so, we should soon have an "organized anarchy." The governments of Europe could not exist a week without the positive force of standing armies.

They are all governments of force, not of consent. Even in our North, the women, children, and free negroes, constitute four-fifths of the population; and they are all governed without their consent. But they mean to correct this gross and glaring iniquity at the North. They hold that all men, women, and negroes, and smart children, are equals, and entitled to equal rights. The widows and free negroes begin to vote in some of those States, and they will have to let all colors and sexes and ages vote soon, or give up the glorious principles of human equality and universal emancipation.

The experiment which they will make, we fear, is absurd in theory, and the symptoms of approaching anarchy and agrarianism among them, leave no doubt that its practical operation will be no better than its theory. Anti-rentism, "vote-myself-a-farm" ism, and all the other isms, are but the spattering drops that precede a social deluge.

Abolition ultimates in "Consent Government;" Consent Government in Anarchy, Free Love, Agrarianism, &c., &c., and "Self-elected despotism," winds up the play.

If the interests of the governors, or governing class, be not conservative, they certainly will not conserve institutions injurious to their interests. There never was and never can be an old society, in which the immediate interests of a majority of human souls do not conflict with all established order, all right of property, and all existing institutions. Immediate interest is all the mass look to; and they would be sure to revolutionize government, as often as the situation of the majority was worse than that of the minority. Divide all property to-day, and a year hence the inequalities of property would provoke a re-division.

In the South, the interest of the governing class is eminently conservative, and the South is fast becoming the most conservative of nations.

Already, at the North, government vibrates and oscillates between Radicalism and Conservatism; at present, Radicalism or Black Republicanism is in the ascendant.

The number of paupers is rapidly increasing; radical and agrarian doctrines are spreading; the women and the children, and the negroes, will soon be let in to vote; and then they will try the experiment of "Consent Government and Constituted Anarchy."

It is falsely said, that revolutions never go backwards. They always go backwards, and generally farther back than where they started. The Social Revolution now going on at the North, must some day go backwards. Shall it do so now, ere it has perpetrated an infinitude of mischief, shed oceans of blood, and occasioned endless human misery; or will the Conservatives of the North let it run the length of its leather, inflict all these evils, and then rectify itself by issuing into military despotism? We think that by a kind of alliance, offensive and defensive, with the South, Northern Conservatism may now arrest and turn back the tide of Radicalism and Agrarianism. We will not presume to point out the whole means and modus operandi. They on the field of action will best see what is necessary to be done.

William Harper, a South Carolina judge, wrote an 1837 *Memoir* defending slavery as part of the natural order of civilized societies and a definite indication of progress. Referring to the Declaration of Independence, Harper asks, "Is it not palpably nearer the truth to say that no man was ever born free, and that no two men were ever born equal?"

WILLIAM HARPER:
MEMOIR ON SLAVERY*

The institution of domestic slavery exists over far the greater portion of the inhabited earth. Until within a very few centuries, it may be said to have existed over the whole earth—at least in all those portions of it which had made any advances towards civilization. We might safely conclude then that it is deeply founded in the nature of man and the exigencies of human society. Yet, in the few countries in which it has

* Reprinted from William Harper, *Memoir on Slavery* (Charleston: 1838), pp. 3–11.

been abolished—claiming, perhaps justly, to be farthest advanced in civilization and intelligence, but which have had the smallest opportunity of observing its true character and effects—it is denounced as the most intolerable of social and political evils. Its existence, and every hour of its continuance, is regarded as the crime of the communities in which it is found. Even by those in the countries alluded to, who regard it with the most indulgence or the least abhorrence—who attribute no criminality to the present generation —who found it in existence, and have not yet

207

been able to devise the means of abolishing it, it is pronounced a misfortune and a curse injurious and dangerous always, and which must be finally fatal to the societies which admit it. This is no longer regarded as a subject of argument and investigation. The opinions referred to are assumed as settled, or the truth of them as self-evident. If any voice is raised among ourselves to extenuate or to vindicate, it is unheard. The judgment is made up. We can have no hearing before the tribunal of the civilized world.

Yet, on this very account, it is more important that we, the inhabitants of the slave holding States of America, insulated as we are, by this institution, and cut off, in some degree, from the communion and sympathies of the world by which we are surrounded, or with which we have intercourse, and exposed continually to their animadversions and attacks, should thoroughly understand this subject and our strength and weakness in relation to it. If it be thus criminal, dangerous and fatal; and if it be possible to devise means of freeing ourselves from it, we ought at once to set about the employing of those means. It would be the most wretched and imbecile fatuity, to shut our eyes to the impending dangers and horrors, and "drive darkling down the current of our fate," till we are overwhelmed in the final destruction. If we are tyrants, cruel, unjust, oppressive, let us humble ourselves and repent in the sight of Heaven, that the foul stain may be cleansed, and we enabled to stand erect as having common claims to humanity with our fellow men.

But if we are nothing of all this; if we commit no injustice or cruelty; if the maintenance of our institutions be essential to our prosperity, our character, our safety, and the safety of all that is dear to us, let us enlighten our minds and fortify our hearts to defend them.

It is a somewhat singular evidence of the indisposition of the rest of the world to hear any thing more on this subject, that perhaps the most profound, original and truly philosophical treatise, which has appeared within the time of my recollection,* seems not to have attracted the slightest attention out of the limits of the slave holding States themselves. If truth, reason and conclusive argument, propounded with admirable temper and perfect candour, might be supposed to have an effect on the minds of men, we should think this work would have put an end to agitation on the subject. The author has rendered inappreciable service to the South in enlightening them on the subject of their own institutions, and turning back that monstrous tide of folly and madness which, if it had rolled on, would have involved his own great State along with the rest of the slave holding States in a common ruin. But beyond these, he seems to have produced no effect

whatever. The denouncers of Slavery, with whose productions the press groans, seem to be unaware of his existence—unaware that there is reason to be encountered, or argument to be answered. They assume that the truth is known and settled, and only requires to be enforced by denunciation.

Another vindicator of the South has appeared in an individual who is among those that have done honour to American literature.† With conclusive argument, and great force of expression he has defended Slavery from the charge of injustice or immorality, and shewn clearly the unspeakable cruelty and mischief which must result from any scheme of abolition. He does not live among slave holders, and it cannot be said of him as of others, that his mind is warped by interest, or his moral sense blunted by habit and familiarity with abuse. These circumstances, it might be supposed, would have secured him hearing and consideration. He seems to be equally unheeded, and the work of denunciation disdaining argument, still goes on.

President Dew has shewn that the institution of Slavery is a principal cause of civilization. Perhaps nothing can be more evident than that it is the sole cause. If any thing can be predicated as universally true of uncultivated man, it is that he will not labour beyond what is absolutely necessary to maintain his existence. Labour is pain to those who are unaccustomed to it, and the nature of man is averse to pain. Even with all the training, the helps and motives of civilization, we find that this aversion cannot be overcome in many individuals of the most cultivated societies. The coercion of Slavery alone is adequate to form man to habits of labour. Without it, there can be no accumulation of property, no providence for the future, no taste for comforts or elegancies, which are the characteristics and essentials of civilization. He who has obtained the command of another's labour, first begins to accumulate and provide for the future, and the foundations of civilization are laid. We find confirmed by experience that which is so evident in theory. Since the existence of man upon the earth, with no exception whatever, either of ancient or modern times, every society which has attained civilization, has advanced to it through this process.

Will those who regard Slavery as immoral, or crime in itself, tell us that man was not intended for civilization, but to roam the earth as a biped brute? That he was not to raise his eyes to Heaven, or be conformed in his nobler faculties to the image of his Maker? Or will they say that the Judge of all the earth has done wrong in ordaining the means by which alone that end can be attained? It is true that the Creator can make the wickedness as well as the wrath of man to praise him, and bring forth the most benevolent results from the most atrocious actions. But in

---

* President Dew's Review of the Virginia Debates on the subject of Slavery.

† Paulding on Slavery.

such cases, it is the motive of the actor alone which condemns the action. The act itself is good, if it promotes the good purposes of God, and would be approved by him, if that result only were intended. Do they not blaspheme the providence of God who denounce as wickedness and outrage, that which is rendered indispensable to his purposes in the government of the world? Or at what stage of the progress of society will they say that Slavery ceases to be necessary, and its very existence becomes sin and crime? I am aware that such argument would have little effect on those with whom it would be degrading to contend—who pervert the inspired writings—which in some parts expressly sanction Slavery, and throughout indicate most clearly that it is a civil institution, with which religion has no concern—with a shallowness and presumption not less flagrant and shameless than his, who would justify murder from the text, "and Phineas arose and executed judgment."

There seems to be something in this subject, which blunts the perceptions, and darkens and confuses the understandings and moral feelings of men. Tell them that, of necessity, in every civilized society, there must be an infinite variety of conditions and employments, from the most eminent and intellectual, to the most servile and laborious; that the negro race, from their temperament and capacity, are peculiarly suited to the situation which they occupy, and not less happy in it than any corresponding class to be found in the world; prove incontestably that no scheme of emancipation could be carried into effect without the most intolerable mischiefs and calamities to both master and slave, or without probably throwing a large and fertile portion of the earth's surface out of the pale of civilization—and you have done nothing. They reply, that whatever may be the consequence, you are bound to do *right;* that man has a right to himself, and man cannot have a property in man; that if the negro race be naturally inferior in mind and character, they are not less entitled to the rights of humanity; that if they are happy in their condition, it affords but the stronger evidence of their degradation, and renders them still more objects of commiseration. They repeat, as the fundamental maxim of our civil policy, that all men are born free and equal, and quote from our Declaration of Independence, "that men are endowed by their Creator with certain inalienable *rights,* among which are life, liberty, and the pursuit of happiness."

It is not the first time that I have had occasion to observe that men may repeat with the utmost confidence, some maxim or sentimental phrase, as self-evident or admitted truth, which is either palpably false or to which, upon examination, it will be found that they attach no definite idea. Notwithstanding our respect for the important document which declared our independence, yet if any thing be found in it, and

especially in what may be regarded rather as its ornament than its substance—false, sophistical or unmeaning, that respect should not screen it from the freest examination.

All men are born free and equal. Is it not palpably nearer the truth to say that no man was ever born free, and that no two men were ever born equal? Man is born in a state of the most helpless dependence on others. He continues subject to the absolute control of others, and remains without many of the civil, and all of the political privileges of his society, until the period which the laws have fixed, as that at which he is supposed to attain the maturity of his faculties. Then equality is further developed, and becomes infinite in every society, and under whatever form of government. Wealth and poverty, fame or obscurity, strength or weakness, knowledge or ignorance, ease or labor, power or subjection, make the endless diversity in the condition of men.

But we have not arrived at the profundity of the maxim. This inequality is in a great measure the result of abuses in the institutions of society. They do not speak of what exists, but of what ought to exist. Every one should be left at liberty to obtain all the advantages of society which he can compass, by the free exertion of his faculties, unimpeded by civil restraints. It may be said that this would not remedy the evils of society which are complained of. The inequalities to which I have referred, with the misery resulting from them, would exist in fact under the freest and most popular form of government that man would devise. But what is the foundation of the bold dogma so confidently announced? Females are human and rational beings. They may be found of better faculties and better qualified to exercise political privileges and to attain the distinctions of society than many men; yet who complains of the order of society by which they are excluded from them? For I do not speak of the few who would desecrate them; do violence to the nature which their Creator has impressed upon them; drag them from the position which they necessarily occupy for the existence of civilized society, and in which they constitute its blessing and ornament—the only position which they have ever occupied in any human society—to place them in a situation in which they would be alike miserable and degraded. Low as we descend in combatting the theories of presumptuous dogmatists, it cannot be necessary to stoop to this. A youth of eighteen may have powers which cast into the shade those of any of his more advanced co[n]temporaries. He may be capable of serving or saving his country, and if not permitted to do so now, the occasion may have been lost forever. But he can exercise no political privilege or aspire to any political distinction. It is said that of necessity, society must exclude from some civil and political privileges those who are unfitted to exercise them, by infirmity, unsuitableness of character, or defect of discretion; that of necessity there must be some general rule on the subject, and that any rule which can be devised will operate with hardship and injustice on individuals. This is all that can be said and all that need be said. It is saying, in other words, that the privileges in question are no matter of natural right, but to be settled by convention, as the good and safety of society may require. If society should disfranchise individuals convicted of infamous crimes, would this be an invasion of natural right? Yet this would not be justified on the score of their moral guilt, but that the good of society required, or would be promoted by it. We admit the existence of a moral law, binding on societies as on individuals. Society must act in good faith. No man or body of men has a right to inflict pain or privation on others, unless with a view, after full and impartial deliberation, to prevent a greater evil. If this deliberation be had, and the decision made in good faith, there can be no imputation of moral guilt. Has any politician contended that the very existence of governments in which there are orders privileged by law, constitutes a violation of morality; that their continuance is a crime, which men are bound to put an end to without any consideration of the good or evil to result from the change? Yet this is the natural inference from the dogma of the natural equality of men as applied to our institution of slavery—an equality not to be invaded without injustice and wrong, and requiring to be restored instantly, unqualifiedly, and without reference to consequences.

This is sufficiently common-place, but we are sometimes driven to common-place. It is no less a false and shallow than a presumptuous philosophy, which theorizes on the affairs of men as of a problem to be solved by some unerring rule of human reason, without reference to the designs of a superior intelligence, so far as he has been pleased to indicate them, in their creation and destiny. Man is born to subjection. Not only during infancy is he dependant and under the control of others; at all ages, it is the very bias of his nature, that the strong and the wise should control the weak and the ignorant. So it has been since the days of Nimrod. The existence of some form of Slavery in all ages and countries, is proof enough of this. He is born to subjection as he is born in sin and ignorance. To make any considerable progress in knowledge, the continued efforts of successive generations, and the diligent training and unwearied exertions of the individual are requisite. To make progress in moral virtue, not less time and effort, aided by superior help, are necessary; and it is only by the matured exercise of his knowledge and his virtue, that he can attain to civil freedom. Of all things, the existence of civil liberty is most the result of artificial institution. The proclivity of the natural man is to domineer or to be subservient. A noble result indeed, but in the attaining of which, as in the instances of knowledge and virtue, the Crea-

tor, for his own purposes, has set a limit beyond which he cannot go.

But he who is most advanced in knowledge, is most sensible of his own ignorance, and how much must forever be unknown to man in his present condition. As I have heard it expressed, the further you extend the circle of light, the wider is the horizon of darkness. He who has made the greatest progress in moral purity, is most sensible of the depravity, not only of the world around him, but of his own heart and the imperfection of his best motives, and this he knows that men must feel and lament so long as they continue men. So when the greatest progress in civil liberty has been made, the enlightened lover of liberty will know that there must remain much inequality, much injustice, much *Slavery,* which no human wisdom or virtue will ever be able wholly to prevent or redress. As I have before had the honor to say to this Society, the condition of our whole existence is but to struggle with evils—to compare them—to choose between them, and so far as we can, to mitigate them. To say that there is evil in any institution, is only to say that it is human.

And can we doubt but that this long discipline and laborious process, by which men are required to work out the elevation and improvement of their individual nature and their social condition, is imposed for a great and benevolent end? Our faculties are not adequate to the solution of the mystery, why it should be so; but the truth is clear, that the world was not intended for the seat of universal knowledge or goodness or happiness or freedom.

Man has been endowed by his Creator with certain inalienable rights, among which are life, liberty and the pursuit of happiness. What is meant by the *inalienable* right of liberty? Has any one who has used the words ever asked himself this question? Does it mean that a man has no right to alienate his own liberty—to sell himself and his posterity for slaves? This would seem to be the more obvious meaning. When the word *right* is used, it has reference to some law which sanctions it, and would be violated by its invasion. It must refer either to the general law of morality or the law of the country—the law of God or the law of man. If the law of any country permitted it, it would of course be absurd to say that the law of that country was violated by such alienation. If it have any meaning in this respect, it must mean that though the law of the country permitted it, the man would be guilty of an immoral act who should thus alienate his liberty. A fit question for schoolmen to discuss, and the consequences resulting from its decision as important as from any of theirs. Yet who will say that the man pressed by famine and in prospect of death, would be criminal for such an act? Self-preservation as is truly said, is the first law of nature. High and peculiar characters, by elaborate cultivation, may be taught to prefer death to Slavery, but it would be folly to prescribe this as a duty to the mass of mankind.

If any rational meaning can be attributed to the sentence I have quoted, it is this:—That the society, or the individuals who exercise the powers of government, are guilty of a violation of the law of God or of morality, when by any law or public act, they deprive men of life or liberty, or restrain them in the pursuit of happiness. Yet every government does, and of necessity must, deprive men of life and liberty for offences against society. Restrain them in the pursuit of happiness! Why all the laws of society are intended for nothing else but to restrain men from the pursuit of happiness, according to their own ideas of happiness or advantage—which the phrase must mean if it means any thing. And by what right does society punish by the loss of life or liberty? Not on account of the moral guilt of the criminal—not by impiously and arrogantly assuming the prerogative of the Almighty, to dispense justice or suffering, according to moral desert. It is for its own protection—it is the right of self-defence. If there existed the blackest moral turpitude, which by its example or consequences, could be of no evil to society, government would have nothing to do with that. If an action, the most harmless in its moral character, could be dangerous to the security of society, society would have the perfect right to punish it. If the possession of a black skin would be otherwise dangerous to society, society has the same right to protect itself by disfranchising the possessor of civil privileges, and to continue the disability to his posterity, if the same danger would be incurred by its removal. Society inflicts these forfeitures for the security of the lives of its members; it inflicts them for the security of their property, the great essential of civilization; it inflicts them also for the protection of its political institutions; the forcible attempt to overturn which, has always been justly regarded as the greatest crime; and who has questioned its right so to inflict? "Man cannot have property in man"—a phrase as full of meaning as, "who slays fat oxen should himself be fat." Certainly he may, if the laws of society allow it, and if it be on sufficient grounds, neither he nor society do wrong.

And is it by this—as we must call it, however recommended to our higher feelings by its associations—well-sounding, but unmeaning verbiage of natural equality and inalienable rights, that our lives are to be put in jeopardy, our property destroyed, and our political institutions overturned or endangered? If a people had on its borders a tribe of barbarians, whom no treaties or faith could bind, and by whose attacks they were constantly endangered, against whom they could devise no security, but that they should be exterminated or enslaved; would they not have the right to enslave them, and keep them in slavery so long as the same danger would be incurred by their manumission? If a civilized man and a savage were by chance placed together on a desolate island, and the former, by the superior power of civilization, would reduce the latter to subjection, would he not have the same right? Would this not be the strictest self-defence? I do not now consider, how far we can make out a similar case to justify our enslaving of the negroes. I speak to those who contend for inalienable rights, and that the existence of slavery always, and under all circumstances, involves injustice and crime.

As I have said, we acknowledge the existence of a moral law. It is not necessary for us to resort to the theory which resolves all right into force. The existence of such a law is imprinted on the hearts of all human beings. But though its existence be acknowledged, the mind of man has hitherto been tasked in vain to discover an unerring standard of morality. It is a common and undoubted maxim of morality, that you shall not do evil that good may come. You shall not do injustice or commit an invasion of the rights of others, for the sake of a greater ulterior good. But what is injustice, and what are the rights of others? And why are we not to commit the one or invade the others? It is because it inflicts pain or suffering, present or prospective, or cuts them off from enjoyment which they might otherwise attain. The Creator has sufficiently revealed to us that *happiness* is the great end of existence, the sole object of all animated and sentient beings. To this he has directed their aspirations and efforts, and we feel that we thwart his benevolent purposes when we destroy or impede that happiness. This is the only *natural* right of man. All other rights result from the conventions of society, and these, to be sure, we are not to invade, whatever good may appear to us likely to follow. Yet are we in no instance to inflict pain or suffering, or disturb enjoyment for the sake of producing a greater good? Is the madman not to be restrained who would bring destruction on himself or others? Is pain not to be inflicted on the child, when it is the only means by which he can be effectually instructed to provide for his own future happiness? Is the surgeon guilty of wrong who amputates a limb to preserve life? Is it not the object of all penal legislation, to inflict suffering for the sake of greater good to be secured to society?

By what right is it that man exercises dominion over the beasts of the field; subdues them to painful labour, or deprives them of life for his sustenance or enjoyment? They are not rational beings. No, but they are the creatures of God, sentient beings, capable of suffering and enjoyment, and entitled to enjoy according to the measure of their capacities. Does not the voice of nature inform every one, that he is guilty of wrong when he inflicts on them pain without necessity or object? If their existence be limited to the present life, it affords the stronger argument for affording them the brief enjoyment of which it is capable. It is because the greater good is effected; not only to man but to the inferior animals themselves. The care of man gives the boon of existence to myriads who would never otherwise have enjoyed it, and the enjoyment of their existence is better provided for while it lasts. It belongs to the being of superior faculties to judge of the relations which shall subsist between himself and inferior animals, and the use he shall make of them; and he may justly consider himself, who has the greater capacity of enjoyment, in the first instance. Yet he must do this conscientiously, and no doubt, moral guilt has been incurred by the infliction of pain on these animals, with no adequate benefit to be expected. I do no disparagement to the dignity of human nature, even in its humblest form, when I say that on the very same foundation, with the difference only of circumstance and degree, rests the right of the civilized and cultivated man, over the savage and ignorant. It is the order of nature and of God, that the being of superior faculties and knowledge, and therefore of superior power, should control and dispose of those who are inferior. It is as much in the order of nature, that men should enslave each other, as that other animals should prey upon each other.

CHAPTER TEN

SECESSIONISTS *vs.* UNIONISTS

Although historians disagree on many aspects concerning the coming of the Civil War, recent scholars nonetheless see the theme of continuity and change running through this period. Whether the moral absolutes raised were freedom and national unity or self-government and states' rights, Unionists and Secessionists alike appealed to tradition and expressed the desire to build toward a golden age. These parallel feelings were the result of the long-range growth of sectionalism, in which both North and South developed antagonistic cultural nationalisms. It is open to dispute, however, that the ensuing differences were sufficient to lead to war. One school of historical thought contends that the Civil War was not an irrepressible conflict. Rather, war was brought on by the intensification of emotional factors accomplished through the agitation of extremists, particularly the abolitionists. Critics of this thesis point out, on the other hand, that the War cannot be blamed on a "blundering generation," for such a view obscures the significance of the moral issue of slavery.

Kenneth M. Stampp, in the first selection, rejected the notion that agitators on both sides explain the resort to war. Instead, he holds, that the existence of slavery made agitation possible in the first place. Thus Stampp observed, "The northern attack on slavery was a logical product of nineteenth-century liberal capitalism. The southern defense of slavery—by planters deeply concerned about both their profits and their capital investment—was just as understandable." Stampp provided in this selection numerous examples of the prevailing opinions on both sides, as well as the confusion and apprehensiveness surrounding the question of secession. In the last analysis, he believed, "Disaster came because these men accepted as God-given the social institutions and political standards which generated and shaped the forces making for war."

KENNETH M. STAMPP:
THE ROOTS OF THE SECESSION CRISIS*

"Sir, disguise the fact as you will, there is an enmity between the northern and southern people that is deep and enduring, and you never can eradicate it—never!" Alfred Iverson of Georgia, accomplished fire-eating orator, was addressing his senatorial colleagues a month after the election of Abraham Lincoln. Recasting ominous phrases which had become trite to the Americans of 1860, Iverson looked squarely at the Republicans in the Senate chamber: "You sit upon your side, silent and gloomy; we sit upon ours with knit brows and portentous scowls. . . . We are enemies as much as if we were hostile States. I believe that the northern people hate the South worse than ever the English people hated France; and I can tell my brethren over there that there is no love lost upon the part of the South."[1]

Perhaps, in his eagerness to carry the South out of the Union, Senator Iverson overstated his case. Yet there was much truth in what he said. The hostility between northern Republicans and southern Democrats in Congress, which he so eloquently described, was a fact. Real enmity existed between a host of Yankees and countless sons of Dixie; even moderate men, North and South, looked upon the rival section with suspicion. There were numerous apostles of "irrepressible conflict," besides Senator Iverson himself. Abolitionists, fire-eating politicians, and malignantly partisan editors had long been preparing the secession crisis now at hand.

The propaganda of northern and southern agitators is often considered one of the prime causes of the American Civil War. William Lloyd Garrison, Horace Greeley, and Wendell Phillips, it is said, exaggerated the barbarities of slavery and the cruelties of slave masters; William L. Yancey, Robert Barnwell Rhett, and Edmund Ruffin misrepresented the North and maligned its citizens. In both sections propagandists distorted public opinion and so, it is argued, eventually brought on disunion and war.

There is an element of truth in this view. Before a bloody war could be waged, there had to be a systematic molding of mental attitudes. But this was not the whole story. Beneath all the propaganda there was the fact of Negro slavery.[2] Without the "peculiar institution" there could have been no proslavery or antislavery agitators,

no division on the issue (whether real or fictitious) of the extension of slave territory. The northern attack on slavery was a logical product of nineteenth-century liberal capitalism. The southern defense of slavery—by planters deeply concerned about both their profits and their capital investment—was just as understandable.

Enmeshed with slavery were other economic differences which contributed to sectional hate. The South was a static, agrarian, debtor section, tied to an economy of staple crops. The North was a dynamic, commercialized, industrializing, creditor section. The South was exploited and the North was the exploiter. Spokesmen for the two sections could never agree upon the wisdom of protective tariffs, navigation acts, shipping and fishing subsidies, national banks, or Federal appropriations for internal improvements. These matters, together with slavery, were always back of the tirades of the agitators. And these matters, rather than the tirades, were at the roots of things. Without them there could have been no sectional agitation and no civil war. Between North and South there did exist a profound and irrepressible clash of material interests.

All this did not make a civil war necessary or inevitable. Actually the question of "inevitability" is not within the historian's province, for it is something that can never be solved by research. It should be left to the philosopher. But William H. Seward, the author of the phrase "irrepressible conflict," himself vigorously denied the inevitability of war when the final crisis came. Social and economic differences need not always be referred to battlefields. The Civil War was no more necessary or inevitable than any other war. Neither was it any less so. Unfortunately the issues were the sort that often produce hatreds that, in turn, drive men to mortal combat. Some wars have grown out of less serious causes.

One should not deal too harshly with the men who failed to prevent war in 1861. It is unfair to judge them by more than the common standards of statesmanship. There was nothing unique about the problem they faced, nor about the way they elected to "solve" it. The statesmen of 1861 were thinking in terms of "national interest." Unless the concept of "national interest" is reevaluated, their decision, their choice of war rather than peace, must be accepted as just and right.

The politicians did have an alternative. They might have agreed that the price of war was too high, that a peaceful solution was worth any sacrifice. Southerners might have yielded to northern political supremacy and prepared to see their "peculiar institution" go sooner or later. Northerners might have agreed to southern independence. From either decision sectional leaders

---

* Reprinted from Kenneth M. Stampp, *And the War Came* (Baton Rouge: Louisiana State Univ. Press, 1950), pp. 1–12 by permission.

[1] *Congressional Globe,* 36 Cong., 2 Sess., 12. Hereinafter, unless otherwise stated, all references to the *Globe* will be to this session.

[2] For an evaluation of the slavery issue in the sectional conflict see Dwight L. Dumond, *Antislavery Origins of the Civil War in the United States* (Ann Arbor, 1939).

would have gained a fame unique in the history of statesmanship. The choice they actually made was the usual one. It was nevertheless tragic.

2

The economic development of the United States, from the very beginning, had the effect of variously strengthening or weakening the national loyalties of its citizens. Public men who lived through this development found their views changing as the interests of their sections changed. It was hard for politicians to keep up an appearance of consistency. Actually they had to entertain extremely flexible opinions regarding the comparative merits of nationalism and state rights. A man could begin his public life by glorifying the grand destiny of the nation and close it by "calculating the value of the Union." Or he might reverse the process. The political philosophy prevailing in a state or section at a given time would depend upon the current policies of the Federal government and upon the advantages or injuries which important economic groups seemed at the moment to derive from those policies.[3]

So it was from the start. Federalist merchants under the benevolence of Hamilton began as nationalists, and Republican farmers under the leadership of Jefferson began as state-rights men, who even flirted with nullification in the Kentucky and Virginia Resolutions. A few years later, when the South and West were in power, New England Federalists toyed with secession schemes while Jeffersonians were outdoing Hamilton in augmenting the powers of Congress. When Daniel Webster and Josiah Quincy, of Massachusetts, took refuge in the Constitution, it was John C. Calhoun of South Carolina who sneered at their crabbed sophistries, while the Richmond *Enquirer* screamed "Treason!"[4] Two decades afterward, when South Carolina under a reformed Calhoun sought to nullify a tariff close to the hearts of New England manufacturers, it was Webster's turn to take national grounds and warn solemnly of the perils of disunion.

In the 1830's and after, the state-rights concept was the dogma of the South, and national doctrines were entrenched in the North; but there were always qualifications and exceptions. Thirteen northern members of Congress signed a declaration that the annexation of Texas would justify a dissolution of the Union.[5] A coterie of Garrisonian abolitionists openly advocated separation from the slaveholders. Various northern states found enough virtue in state rights to justify their personal-liberty laws, which in a sense nullified a Federal law, the fugitive-slave act of 1850. Defying the United States Supreme Court, the Wisconsin legislature resolved that the Federal government was not the final judge of the powers delegated to it. Rather, "as in all other cases of compact among parties having no common judge, each has an equal right to judge for itself as well of infractions as of the mode and measure of redress."[6] That may have been the Calhoun gospel, but Southerners howled in protest when a northern state applied it to northern ends. Likewise, Southerners disregarded Calhoun's strictures upon judicial usurpation when the Supreme Court, in the Dred Scott decision, favored southern interests by opening all the territories to slavery.

These, perhaps, were mere aberrations. In the North, where population and economic and political power were growing fast, most statesmen became champions of the Union. In the South, where economic development was lagging, politicians came more and more to espouse defensive doctrines of localism.[7] As early as the 1820's a faction of South Carolinians looked to secession as their only recourse against northern encroachments. Thereafter Southerners repeatedly threatened to secede. They did so after the Mexican War when sectional leaders were debating the question of slavery expansion into the newly acquired territories. By the Compromise of 1850 the politicians set up a new equilibrium, but it was a precarious one. Within a few years they found the balance again upset, following the passage of the Kansas-Nebraska Act and the formation of the Republican party, a strictly sectional organization. During the presidential campaign of 1856 southern politicians repeatedly warned that a "Black" Republican victory would mean immediate dissolution of the Union.[8] During the next four years this cry became a commonplace of southern rhetoric.

Giving an ear to this cry, northern nationalists warned of the consequences of disunion. Daniel Webster insisted that the Union could never be dissolved without bloodshed. Henry Clay, during the Senate debates in 1850, replied to a secessionist from Georgia by avowing his readiness to try the strength of the nation, to ascertain "whether we have a government or not." "Nor, sir," he said, "am I to be alarmed or dissuaded from any such course by intimations of the spilling of blood."[9] Nine years later Edward Bates, the

---

[3] For an excellent, brief discussion of the state-rights issue in American History see Arthur M. Schlesinger, *New Viewpoints in American History* (New York, 1922), 220–44.

[4] Richmond *Enquirer,* quoted in Charles A. and Mary R. Beard, *The Rise of American Civilization* (New York, 1927), I, 428.

[5] William B. Hesseltine, *The South in American History* (New York, 1943), 250.

[6] Dwight L. Dumond, *The Secession Movement 1860–1861* (New York, 1931), 5 n.

[7] Jesse T. Carpenter, *The South as a Conscious Minority, 1789–1861* (New York, 1930).

[8] David M. Potter, *Lincoln and His Party in the Secession Crisis* (New Haven, 1942), 1–3.

[9] *Congressional Globe,* 31 Cong., 1 Sess., 1486.

venerable St. Louis Whig, recorded his conviction that control of the lower Mississippi River would never be surrendered to a foreign power. Southerners needed to know that this was "a *fighting* question, and not fit to be debated." [10]

After the execution of John Brown for treason against Virginia, Senator Zachariah Chandler of Michigan drew from Brown's fate a lesson for the South. He wanted that episode to go on the records as a "warning to traitors" from any section: ". . . dare to raise your impious hands against this Government, against our Constitution and laws and you hang." [11] And in the same month Abraham Lincoln, speaking at Leavenworth, Kansas, echoed those sentiments: "So, if constitutionally we elect a president, and therefore you undertake to destroy the Union, it will be our duty to deal with you as old John Brown was dealt with. We can only do our duty." [12]

Americans had become accustomed to threats and counterthreats when the presidential election of 1860 got under way. Political sophisticates could hardly have been surprised when southern newspapers and orators once more raised the old cry of impending disunion.

3

The visions of politicians facing defeat at the ballot boxes are generally etched in black. In October, 1860, the Democratic New York *Herald* saw a fearful "spirit of violence and unreason . . . abroad in the land." Southern fire-eaters talked of fighting to preserve their rights. Youthful supporters of Lincoln, the "Wide-Awakes," engaged in military drills with "simulated muskets and lances, real cannon, [and] a regular battle cry." The *Herald's* editor, James Gordon Bennett, believed these demonstrations were "but the thunder mutterings of the coming tempest." [13] But editor Bennett might well have had some inward doubts about the accuracy of his melancholy forecast. He would have had doubts if his thinking had harmonized with that of the majority of Northerners.

True, the southern threats that disunion would be the consequence of a Republican victory were more widespread and serious than ever before. The legislatures of South Carolina, Alabama, and Mississippi were actually taking preliminary steps toward secession. [14] In the North nearly

every Democratic or Constitutional Union newspaper printed generous excerpts from the letters, speeches, and editorials emanating from the South. [15] A pro-Douglas paper thought the people should see the peril from "the unanimous tone of the Southern press; the plain business-like statements, . . . showing the utter impossibility of the South's remaining in the Union should our National Government pass under the control of Black Republican fanatics." [16]

After Republicans swept the October state elections in Pennsylvania, Ohio, and Indiana, the other parties redoubled their prophecies of approaching doom. "Fanaticism and treachery have triumphed," wailed a Douglas partisan. "The 'irrepressible conflict' of Seward and Lincoln has commenced. No human foresight can see the end." [17] Another Democrat foresaw "State after State declaring its independence . . . panic and confusion on all sides . . . banks suspending, business men failing, commerce languishing, industry starving." [18] A New York opponent of the Republicans feared the prosperity of Wall Street merchants was hanging in the balance, for with the South out of the Union, "New York ceases to be the Empire State, this city becomes no more a great national metropolis." [19]

Some of this was doubtless written in good faith, but much of it was probably considered by its authors as a legitimate electioneering device. Most Republicans dismissed it all as scaremongering, and the secession flurry in the South as a colossal game of bluff. [20] "*Who's afraid*," mocked Seward. "*Nobody's afraid; nobody can be bought.*" [21] The simple fact was that the disunion alarm had been sounded so often that only a few were willing to heed it any longer. To Republicans it was "the last desperate resort of the pro-slavery democracy," "the idlest gossip imaginable," "too absurd either for discussion or ridicule," an "effort to bully the people out of their

---

Editorials on Secession (New York, 1931); Ollinger Crenshaw, *The Slave States in the Presidential Election of 1860* (Baltimore, 1945).

[15] New York *Herald*, October 3, 11, 23, 24, 27, 1860; New York *Journal of Commerce*, October 23, 30; November 3, 1860; Boston *Daily Courier*, October 25, 1860.

[16] New York *Leader*, October 13, 1860.

[17] Indianapolis *Indiana Daily State Sentinel*, October 10, 1860.

[18] Providence *Daily Post*, October 31, 1860.

[19] New York *Herald*, October 18, 25; November 4, 1860.

[20] Lawrence T. Lowery, *Northern Opinion of Approaching Secession, October, 1859–November, 1860* (Northampton, Mass., 1918), 247–49; Potter, *Lincoln and His Party in the Secession Crisis*, 9–19.

[21] New York *Daily Tribune*, December 4, 1860.

---

[10] Howard K. Beale (ed.), *The Diary of Edward Bates, 1859–1866*, in American Historical Association, *Annual Report*, 1930, IV (Washington, 1933), 20.

[11] *Congressional Globe*, 36 Cong., 1 Sess., 34.

[12] New York *Evening Post*, October 31, 1860.

[13] New York *Herald*, October 6, 1860.

[14] Potter, *Lincoln and His Party in the Secession Crisis*, 3–9; Dwight L. Dumond, *Southern*

choice." [22] Quoting strong Union sentiments from the southern press, Republicans found abundant evidence that the small clique of secessionists would be put down by the people at home. The sooner this "game" ceased to be profitable, "the sooner shall we be delivered from these periodical soundings of the Disunion gong." [23]

How, indeed, could the South survive without the Union when it was more vital to her than it was to the North? How could her stormy politicians live without the rich plums of Federal patronage? The Providence *Journal* was sure that if the Union survived "as long as the applicants for office in any southern State exceed the whole number at the disposal of the President in all the States," it would be perpetual. [24] Some Republicans went so far as to promise the beginning of a new era of good feeling after the inauguration of Lincoln. His wise and conservative policies would benefit all sections, and "we venture to predict a time of actual repose and peace . . . quite unheard of for the last ten years." [25] It was clearly in the interest of Republicans to minimize the danger from the South.

There was reason, then, to doubt the entire sincerity of northern Democrats and Bell men who seemed so pessimistic. But there was also reason to doubt the complete sincerity of Republicans who wore, some of them almost gaily, an air of optimism. While giving calm assurances that the South was only bluffing, Republican papers sometimes issued stern and disquieting appeals to the northern people to see the issue through, to try at last the "policy of courage and firmness." They said that Lincoln deserved to be elected simply "to have this question of disunion . . . settled . . . [and] to see the matter tested and decided." [26] Among the propertied classes there were, according to the independent New York *World*, some who were ready "to let worst come to worst, so that now and finally there may be an end of this quadrennial disunion clamor." [27] Was

it not time, asked others, to find out whether the constitutional election of a President would provide sufficient cause for dissolving the Union? [28]

By their nervous impatience to face the issue, some Republican editors and politicians revealed their uncertainty as to its outcome. Conversely, the majority of eastern merchants, whose prosperity hinged upon the southern trade, revealed their uncertainty by a fear of risking the test. Partly for this reason they were overwhelmingly opposed to Lincoln's election. [29] Right after the Republican victories in October, a panic occurred on the New York stock exchange, railroad shares and southern state bonds declined rapidly, and credit became stringent. [30] Evidently the men of Wall Street anticipated a political crisis, and the parties opposing Lincoln exploited their terror to the utmost.

Republicans, however, were ready with their own explanations of the panic. They said it stemmed from a mixture of cowardice and conspiracy. The "Dry Goods party," the "dear old ladies" who marketed their "patriotism in packages," were once more bending the knee to their southern masters and letting themselves be bullied and frightened. [31] In an editorial entitled "Wanted—A First-Rate Panic!" the New York *Times* developed the thesis that the whole thing was a fraud, the last desperate effort to defeat Lincoln. [32] The New York *World* asserted that the fall of stocks was "a purely fictitious operation, conducted in pursuance of an atrocious plot concocted by leading political and financial gamblers." [33] A few eastern businessmen, feeling that the scare campaign had gone too far, ultimately supported the Republicans. [34] But most businessmen were too preoccupied with the dangers of the immediate future to be able to appreciate the more remote economic possibilities of a Republican victory.

[22] *Ibid.,* October 12, 22, 1860; Philadelphia *Public Ledger,* October 31, 1860; Bangor *Daily Whig and Courier,* October 30, 1860.

[23] New York *Times,* October 10, 1860; New York *Evening Post,* October 20, 1860; New York *World,* October 19, 1860; Philadelphia *North American and United States Gazette,* October 20; November 3, 1860; Boston *Daily Journal,* October 26, 1860; Springfield (Mass.) *Daily Republican,* October 31, 1860.

[24] Providence *Daily Journal,* October 16, 1860; New York *Daily Tribune,* October 22, 1860; Philadelphia *North American and United States Gazette,* October 6, 1860.

[25] Philadelphia *North American and United States Gazette,* October 6, 19, 1860; *Morning Courier and New-York Enquirer,* October 11, 1860.

[26] Boston *Daily Advertiser,* October 9, 1860; Providence *Daily Journal,* October 31, 1860.

[27] New York *World,* November 1, 1860.

[28] Philadelphia *North American and United States Gazette,* November 2, 1860; Providence *Daily Journal,* November 5, 1860.

[29] Philip S. Foner, *Business & Slavery: The New York Merchants & the Irrepressible Conflict* (Chapel Hill, 1941), 169–207.

[30] See files of New York *Herald* for October, 1860; *Morning Courier and New-York Enquirer,* November 1, 1860.

[31] New York *Evening Post,* October 9, 1860; New York *Daily Tribune,* October 5, 9, 12, 17, 1860.

[32] New York *Times,* October 10, 1860.

[33] New York *World,* October 27, 31, 1860. See also New York *Evening Post,* October 24, 26, 1860; New York *Daily Tribune,* October 26, 1860; Boston *Evening Transcript,* October 27, 1860.

[34] New York *Daily Tribune,* October 29, 1860; *Morning Courier and New-York Enquirer,* November 2, 3, 5, 6, 1860; New York *Evening Post,* November 6, 1860; Foner, *Business & Slavery,* 169–207.

The merchants' fears increased when some of Lincoln's followers gave renewed warnings that, once in power, the Republicans would resist with force any attempt at secession. Some of the bolder spirits openly, defiantly, challenged the secessionists to proceed at their own peril. Carl Schurz, the fiery German-American orator, told Southerners that the Yankees would "fight now, if need be." "There is a great column of Germans and Scandinavians," Schurz said, "who can handle a musket, who stand ready to aid them." [35] At a Brooklyn rally late in October one Republican spokesman vowed that if Lincoln were not inaugurated the following March, 200,000 Wide-Awakes would "know the reason why." Another speaker, Senator Benjamin F. Wade of Ohio, added gruffly that secessionists would find "a sleeping lion in their path." [36] The day before the election William Curtis Noyes informed a gathering of New York merchants that seceders would "share the fate of all traitors." [37] Meanwhile the New York *Evening Post,* finding lessons in history, recounted President Washington's suppression of the Whiskey Rebellion and President Jackson's forceful handling of the nullification crisis. There was no reason now for treating rebels any differently, said the *Evening Post;* President Buchanan, like his illustrious predecessors, should do his duty and execute the laws. [38] There were enough expressions of this kind to prompt the New York *World* to caution against any further irritation of the South. [39]

To be sure, these belligerent sentiments were often combined with expressions of doubt that there would be need for drastic action. They nevertheless reflect a certain apprehensiveness.

Though the majority in all parties doubted that the South was in earnest, some were not quite sure, and a few credited their senses and expected the worst. As usual, one could not always determine a man's beliefs by the things he said in public—nor even by the things he wrote in private.

All this pre-election talk of secession and force indicated that the elements of a crisis were already present. The Republicans, with their sectional platform, threatened to upset the balance of power which had prevailed between the two sections for a generation. Inevitably this would challenge the South to seek some new security for its peculiar interests, perhaps through political independence. If the North found its own interests endangered thereby, it would have the choice of a political retreat or direct intervention to prevent secession. The latter alternative would force the South in turn to choose between surrender and resistance. And, finally, if Southerners elected a trial of strength, the verdict ultimately would go to the side with superior physical and human resources.

This was neither the first nor the last time that two peoples were driven to hostilities by essentially similar forces. On this as on other occasions disaster resulted not because the leaders on either side failed to show greater wisdom after the crisis was upon them. Disaster came because these men accepted as God-given the social institutions and political standards which generated and shaped the forces making for war. The five months following Lincoln's election were to show that, once released, these forces became too powerful for human resistance.

This monumental speech of John C. Calhoun contains the fully-matured statement of the Southern position on the nature of the Union. Speaking in the Senate on March 4, 1850, Calhoun traced his section's discontent to the destruction of a long-standing political and economic equilibrium.

JOHN C. CALHOUN:
ON THE SLAVERY QUESTION*

I have, Senators, believed from the first that the agitation of the subject of slavery would, if

not prevented by some timely and effective measure, end in disunion. Entertaining this opinion, I have, on all proper occasions, endeavored to call the attention of both the two great parties which divide the country to adopt some measure to prevent so great a disaster, but without success. The agitation has been permitted to proceed, with almost no attempt to resist it, until it has reached a point when it can no longer be disguised or denied that the Union is in danger. You have thus had forced upon you the greatest and the gravest question that can ever come under your

[35] *Daily Boston Traveller,* October 22, 1860.

[36] New York *Herald,* October 30, 1860.

[37] *Morning Courier and New-York Enquirer,* November 6, 1860.

[38] New York *Evening Post,* October 20, 31, 1860.

[39] New York *World,* October 22, 1860.

* Reprinted from Richard K. Crallé, ed., *Speeches of John C. Calhoun* (New York: 1854), IV, 542–59.

consideration—How can the Union be preserved?

To give a satisfactory answer to this mighty question, it is indispensable to have an accurate and thorough knowledge of the nature and the character of the cause by which the Union is endangered. Without such knowledge it is impossible to pronounce, with any certainty, by what measure it can be saved; just as it would be impossible for a physician to pronounce, in the case of some dangerous disease, with any certainty, by what remedy the patient could be saved, without similar knowledge of the nature and character of the cause which produced it. The first question, then, presented for consideration, in the investigation I propose to make, in order to obtain such knowledge, is—What is it that has endangered the Union?

To this question there can be but one answer, —that the immediate cause is the almost universal discontent which pervades all the States composing the Southern section of the Union. This widely-extended discontent is not of recent origin. It commenced with the agitation of the slavery question, and has been increasing ever since. The next question, going one step further back, is— What has caused this widely diffused and almost universal discontent?

It is a great mistake to suppose, as is by some, that it originated with demagogues, who excited the discontent with the intention of aiding their personal advancement, or with the disappointed ambition of certain politicians, who resorted to it as the means of retrieving their fortunes. On the contrary, all the great political influences of the section were arrayed against excitement, and exerted to the utmost to keep the people quiet. The great mass of the people of the South were divided, as in the other section, into Whigs and Democrats. The leaders and the presses of both parties in the South were very solicitous to prevent excitement and to preserve quiet; because it was seen that the effects of the former would necessarily tend to weaken, if not destroy, the political ties which united them with their respective parties in the other section. Those who know the strength of party ties will readily appreciate the immense force which this cause exerted against agitation, and in favor of preserving quiet. But, great as it was, it was not sufficient to prevent the wide-spread discontent which now pervades the section. No; some cause, far deeper and more powerful than the one supposed, must exist, to account for discontent so wide and deep. The question then recurs—What is the cause of this discontent? It will be found in the belief of the people of the Southern States, as prevalent as the discontent itself, that they cannot remain, as things now are, consistently with honor and safety, in the Union. The next question to be considered is—What has caused this belief?

One of the causes is, undoubtedly, to be traced to the long-continued agitation of the slave question on the part of the North, and the many aggressions which they have made on the rights of the South during the time. I will not enumerate them at present, as it will be done hereafter in its proper place.

There is another lying back of it—with which this is intimately connected—that may be regarded as the great and primary cause. This is to be found in the fact that the equilibrium between the two sections, in the Government as it stood when the constitution was ratified and the Government put in action, has been destroyed. At that time there was nearly a perfect equilibrium between the two, which afforded ample means to each to protect itself against the aggression of the other; but, as it now stands, one section has the exclusive power of controlling the Government, which leaves the other without any adequate means of protecting itself against its encroachment and oppression. To place this subject distinctly before you, I have, Senators, prepared a brief statistical statement, showing the relative weight of the two sections in the Government under the first census of 1790 and the last census of 1840.

According to the former, the population of the United States, including Vermont, Kentucky, and Tennessee, which then were in their incipient condition of becoming States, but were not actually admitted, amounted to 3,929,827. Of this number the Northern States had 1,997,899, and the Southern 1,952,072, making a difference of only 45,827 in favor of the former States. The number of States, including Vermont, Kentucky, and Tennessee, were sixteen; of which eight, including Vermont, belonged to the Northern section, and eight, including Kentucky and Tennessee, to the Southern,—making an equal division of the States between the two sections under the first census. There was a small preponderance in the House of Representatives, and in the Electoral College, in favor of the Northern, owing to the fact that, according to the provisions of the constitution, in estimating federal numbers five slaves count but three; but it was too small to affect sensibly the perfect equilibrium which, with that exception, existed at the time. Such was the equality of the two sections when the States composing them agreed to enter into a Federal Union. Since then the equilibrium between them has been greatly disturbed.

According to the last census the aggregate population of the United States amounted to 17,063,357, of which the Northern section contained 9,728,920, and the Southern 7,334,437, making a difference, in round numbers of 2,400,000. The number of States had increased from sixteen to twenty-six, making an addition of ten States. In the mean time the position of Delaware had become doubtful as to which section she properly belonged. Considering her as neutral, the Northern States will have thirteen and the Southern States twelve, making a difference in the Senate of two Senators in favor of the former. According to the apportionment under the census of 1840, there were two hundred and twenty-three members of the House of Representatives, of which the Northern States had one hundred and thirty-five, and the Southern States (considering Delaware as neutral) eighty-seven, making a difference in favor of the former in the House of Representatives of forty-eight. The difference in the Senate of two members, added to this, gives to the North, in the electoral college, a majority of fifty. Since the census of 1840, four States have been added to the Union—Iowa, Wisconsin, Florida, and Texas. They leave the difference in the Senate as it stood when the census was taken; but add two to the side of the North in the House, making the present majority in the House in its favor fifty, and in the electoral college fifty-two.

The result of the whole is to give the Northern section a predominance in every department of the Government, and thereby concentrate in it the two elements which constitute the Federal Government,—majority of States, and a majority of their population, estimated in federal numbers. Whatever section concentrates the two in itself possesses the control of the entire Government.

But we are just at the close of the sixth decade, and the commencement of the seventh. The census is to be taken this year, which must add greatly to the decided preponderance of the North in the House of Representatives and in the electoral college. The prospect is, also, that a great increase will be added to its present preponderance in the Senate, during the period of the decade, by the addition of new States. Two territories, Oregon and Minnesota, are already in progress, and strenuous efforts are making to bring in three additional States from the territory recently conquered from Mexico; which, if successful, will add three other States in a short time to the Northern section, making five States; and increasing the present number of its States from fifteen to twenty, and of its Senators from thirty to forty. On the contrary, there is not a single territory in progress in the Southern section, and no certainty that any additional State will be added to it during the decade. The prospect then is, that the two sections in the Senate, should the efforts now made to exclude the South from the newly acquired territories succeed, will stand, before the end of the decade, twenty Northern States to fourteen Southern (considering Delaware as neutral), and forty Northern Senators to twenty-eight Southern. This great increase of Senators, added to the great increase of members of the House of Representatives and the electoral college on the part of the North, which must take place under the next decade, will effectually and irretrievably destroy the equilibrium which existed when the Government commenced.

Had this destruction been the operation of time, without the interference of Government, the South would have had no reason to complain; but such was not the fact. It was caused by the legislation of this Government, which was appointed, as the common agent of all, and charged with the protection of the interests and security of all. The legislation by which it has been effected, may be classed under three heads. The first is, that series of acts by which the South has been excluded from the common territory belonging to all the States as members of the Federal Union—which have had the effect of extending vastly the portion allotted to the Northern section, and restricting within narrow limits the portion left the South. The next consists in adopting a system of revenue and disbursements, by which an undue proportion of the burden of taxation has been imposed upon the South, and an undue proportion of its proceeds appropriated to the North; and the last is a system of political measures, by which the original character of the Government has been radically changed. I propose to bestow upon each of these, in the order they stand, a few remarks, with the view of showing that it is owing to the action of this Government, that the equilibrium between the two sections has been destroyed, and the whole powers of the system centered in a sectional majority.

The first of the series of acts by which the South was deprived of its due share of the territories, originated with the confederacy which preceded the existence of this Government. It is to be found in the provision of the ordinance of 1787. Its effect was to exclude the South entirely from that vast and fertile region which lies between the Ohio and the Mississippi rivers, now embracing five States and one territory. The next of the series is the Missouri compromise, which excluded the South from that large portion of Louisiana which lies north of 36° 30', excepting what is included in the State of Missouri. The last of the series excluded the South from the whole of the Oregon Territory. All these, in the slang of the day, were what are called slave territories, and not free soil; that is, territories belonging to slaveholding powers and open to the emigration of masters with their slaves. By these several acts, the South was excluded from 1,238,025 square miles—an extent of country considerably exceeding the entire valley of the Mississippi. To the South was left the portion of the Territory of Louisiana lying south of 36° 30', and the portion north of it included in the State of Missouri, with the portion lying south of 36° 30', including the States of Louisiana and Arkansas, and the territory lying west of the latter, and south of 36° 30', called the Indian country. These, with the Territory of Florida, now the State, make, in the whole, 283,503 square miles. To this must be added the territory acquired with Texas. If the whole should be added to the Southern section, it would make an increase of 325,520, which would make the whole left to the South, 609,023. But a large part of Texas is still in contest between the two sections, which leaves it uncertain what will be the real extent of the portion of territory that may be left to the South.

I have not included the territory recently acquired by the treaty with Mexico. The North is making the most strenuous efforts to appropriate the whole to herself, by excluding the South from every foot of it. If she should succeed, it will add to that from which the South has already been excluded, 526,078 square miles, and would increase the whole which the North has appropriated to herself, to 1,764,023, not including the portion that she may succeed in excluding us from in Texas. To sum up the whole, the United States, since they declared their independence, have acquired 2,373,046 square miles of territory, from which the North will have excluded the South, if she should succeed in monopolizing the newly acquired territories, about three-fourths of the whole, leaving to the South but about one-fourth.

Such is the first and great cause that has destroyed the equilibrium between the two sections in the Government.

The next is the system of revenue and disbursements which has been adopted by the Government. It is well known that the Government has derived its revenue mainly from duties on imports. I shall not undertake to show that such duties must necessarily fall mainly on the exporting States, and that the South, as the great exporting portion of the Union, has in reality paid vastly more than her due proportion of the revenue; because I deem it unnecessary, as the subject has on so many occasions been fully discussed. Nor shall I, for the same reason, undertake to show that a far greater portion of the revenue has been disbursed at the North, than its due share; and that the joint effect of these causes has been, to transfer a vast amount from South to North, which, under an equal system of revenue and disbursements, would not have been lost to her. If to this be added, that many of the duties were imposed, not for revenue, but for protection,—that is, intended to put money, not in the treasury, but directly into the pocket of the manufacturers,—some conception may be formed of the immense amount which, in the long course of sixty years, has been transferred from South to North. There are no data by which it can be estimated with any certainty; but it is safe to say, that it amounts to hundreds of millions of dollars. Under the most moderate estimate, it would be sufficient to add greatly to the wealth of the North, and thus greatly increase her population by attracting emigration from all quarters to that section.

This, combined with the great primary cause, amply explains why the North has acquired a preponderance in every department of the Government by its disproportionate increase of population and States. The former, as has been shown, has increased, in fifty years, 2,400,000 over that of the South. This increase of population, during so long a period, is satisfactorily accounted for, by the number of emigrants, and the increase of their descendants, which have been attracted to the Northern section from Europe and the South, in consequence of the advantages derived from the causes assigned. If they had not existed—if the South had retained all the capital which has been extracted from her by the fiscal action of the Government; and, if it had not been excluded by the ordinance of 1787 and the Missouri compromise, from the region lying between the Ohio and the Mississippi rivers, and between the Mississippi and the Rocky Mountains north of 36° 30′ —it scarcely admits of a doubt, that it would have divided the emigration with the North, and by retaining her own people, would have at least equalled the North in population under the census of 1840, and probably under that about to be taken. She would also, if she had retained her equal rights in those territories, have maintained an equality in the number of States with the North, and have preserved the equilibrium between the two sections that existed at the commencement of the Government. The loss, then, of the equilibrium is to be attributed to the action of this Government.

But while these measures were destroying the equilibrium between the two sections, the action of the Government was leading to a radical change in its character, by concentrating all the power of the system in itself. [The occasion will not permit me to trace the measures by which this great change has been consummated. If it did, it would not be difficult to show that the process commenced at an early period of the Government; and that it proceeded, almost without interruption, step by step, until it absorbed virtually its entire powers; but without going through the whole process to establish the fact, it may be done satisfactorily by a very short statement.]

That the Government claims, and practically maintains the right to decide in the last resort, as to the extent of its powers, will scarcely be denied by any one conversant with the political history of the country. That it also claims the right to resort to force to maintain whatever power it claims, against all opposition, is equally certain. Indeed it is apparent, from what we daily hear, that this has become the prevailing and fixed opinion of a great majority of the community. Now, I ask, what limitation can possibly be placed upon the powers of a government claiming and exercising such rights? And, if none can be, how can the separate governments of the States maintain and protect the powers reserved to them by the constitution—or the people of the several States maintain those which are reserved to them, and among others, the sovereign powers by which they ordained and established, not only their separate State Constitutions and Governments, but also the Constitution and Government of the United States? But, if they have no constitutional means of maintaining them against the right claimed by this Government, it necessarily follows, that they hold them at its pleasure and discretion, and that all the powers of the system are in reality concentrated in it. It also follows, that the character of the Government has been changed in consequence, from a federal republic, as it originally came from the hands of its framers, into a great national consolidated democracy. It has indeed, at present, all the characteristics of the latter, and not one of the former, although it still retains its outward form.

The result of the whole of these causes combined is—that the North has acquired a decided ascendency over every department of this Government, and through it a control over all the powers of the system. A single section governed by the will of the numerical majority, has now, in fact, the control of the Government and the entire powers of the system. What was once a constitutional federal republic, is now converted, in reality, into one as absolute as that of the Autocrat of Russia, and as despotic in its tendency as any absolute government that ever existed.

As, then, the North has the absolute control over the Government, it is manifest, that on all questions between it and the South, where there is a diversity of interests, the interest of the latter will be sacrificed to the former, however oppressive the effects may be; as the South possesses no means by which it can resist, through the action of the Government. But if there was no question of vital importance to the South, in reference to which there was a diversity of views between the two sections, this state of things might be endured, without the hazard of destruction to the South. But such is not the fact. There is a question of vital importance to the Southern section, in reference to which the views and feelings of the two sections are as opposite and hostile as they can possibly be.

I refer to the relation between the two races in the Southern section, which constitutes a vital portion of her social organization. Every portion of the North entertains views and feelings more or less hostile to it. Those most opposed and hostile, regard it as a sin, and consider themselves under the most sacred obligation to use every effort to destroy it. Indeed, to the extent that they conceive they have power, they regard themselves as implicated in the sin, and responsible for not suppressing it by the use of all and every means. Those less opposed and hostile, regard it as a crime—an offence against humanity, as they call it; and, although not so fanatical, feel themselves bound to use all efforts to effect the same object; while those who are least opposed and hostile, regard it as a blot and a stain on the character of what they call the Nation, and feel themselves accordingly bound to give it no countenance or support. On the contrary, the Southern section regards the relation as one which cannot be destroyed without subjecting the two races to the greatest calamity, and the section to poverty, desolation, and wretchedness; and accordingly they feel bound, by every consideration of interest and safety, to defend it.

This hostile feeling on the part of the North towards the social organization of the South long lay dormant, but it only required some cause to act on those who felt most intensely that they were responsible for its continuance, to call it into action. The increasing power of this Government, and of the control of the Northern section over all its departments, furnished the cause. It was this which made an impression on the minds of many, that there was little or no restraint to prevent the Government from doing whatever it might choose to do. This was sufficient of itself to put the most fanatical portion of the North in action, for the purpose of destroying the existing relation between the two races in the South.

The first organized movement towards it commenced in 1835. Then, for the first time, societies were organized, presses established, lecturers sent forth to excite the people of the North, and incendiary publications scattered over the whole South, through the mail. The South was thoroughly aroused. Meetings were held every where, and resolutions adopted, calling upon the North to apply a remedy to arrest the threatened evil, and pledging themselves to adopt measures for their own protection, if it was not arrested. At the meeting of Congress, petitions poured in from the North, calling upon Congress to abolish slavery in the District of Columbia, and to prohibit, what they called, the internal slave trade between the States—announcing at the same time, that their ultimate object was to abolish slavery, not only in the District, but in the States and throughout the Union. At this period, the number engaged in the agitation was small, and possessed little or no personal influence.

Neither party in Congress had, at that time, any sympathy with them or their cause. The members of each party presented their petitions with great reluctance. Nevertheless, small and contemptible as the party then was, both of the great parties of the North dreaded them. They felt, that though small, they were organized in reference to a subject which had a great and a commanding influence over the Northern mind. Each party, on that account, feared to oppose their petitions, lest the opposite party should take advantage of the one who might do so, by favoring them. The effect was, that both united in insisting that the petitions should be received, and that Congress should take jurisdiction over the subject. To justify their course, they took the extraordinary ground, that Congress was bound to receive petitions on every subject, however objectionable they might be, and whether they had, or had not, jurisdiction over the subject. These views prevailed in the House of Representatives, and partially in the Senate; and thus the party succeeded in their first movements, in gaining what they proposed—a position in Congress, from which agitation could be extended over the whole Union. This was the commencement of the agitation, which has ever since continued, and which, as is now acknowledged, has endangered the Union itself.

As for myself, I believed at that early period, if the party who got up the petitions should succeed in getting Congress to take jurisdiction, that agitation would follow, and that it would in the end, if not arrested, destroy the Union. I then so expressed myself in debate, and called upon both parties to take grounds against assuming jurisdiction; but in vain. Had my voice been heeded, and had Congress refused to take jurisdiction, by the united votes of all parties, the agitation which followed would have been prevented, and the fanatical zeal that gives impulse to the agitation, and which has brought us to our present perilous condition, would have become extinguished, from the want of fuel to feed the flame. *That* was the time for the North to have shown her devotion to the Union; but, unfortunately, both of the great parties of that section were so intent on obtaining or retaining party ascendency, that all other considerations were overlooked or forgotten.

What has since followed are but natural consequences. With the success of their first movement, this small fanatical party began to acquire strength; and with that, to become an object of courtship to both the great parties. The necessary consequence was, a further increase of power, and a gradual tainting of the opinions of both of the other parties with their doctrines, until the infection has extended over both; and the great mass of the population of the North, who, whatever may be their opinion of the original abolition party, which still preserves its distinctive organization, hardly ever fail, when it comes to acting, to co-operate in carrying out their measures. With the increase of their influence, they extended the sphere of their action. In a short time after the commencement of their first movement, they had acquired sufficient influence to induce the legislatures of most of the Northern States to pass acts, which in effect abrogated the clause of the constitution that provides for the delivery up of fugitive slaves. Not long after, petitions followed to abolish slavery in forts, magazines, and dockyards, and all other places where Congress had exclusive power of legislation. This was followed by petitions and resolutions of legislatures of the Northern States, and popular meetings, to exclude the Southern States from all territories acquired, or to be acquired, and to prevent the admission of any State hereafter into the Union, which, by its constitution, does not prohibit slavery. And Congress is invoked to do all this, expressly with the view to the final abolition of slavery in the States. That has been avowed to be the ultimate object from the beginning of the agitation until the present time; and yet the great body of both parties of the North, with the full knowledge of the fact, although disavowing the abolitionists, have co-operated with them in almost all their measures.

Such is a brief history of the agitation, as far as it has yet advanced. Now I ask, Senators, what is there to prevent its further progress, until it fulfils the ultimate end proposed, unless some decisive measure should be adopted to prevent it? Has any one of the causes, which has added to its increase from its original small and contemptible beginning until it has attained its present magnitude, diminished in force? Is the original cause of the movement—that slavery is a sin, and ought to be suppressed—weaker now than at the commencement? Or is the abolition party less numerous or influential, or have they less influence with, or control over the two great parties of the North in elections? Or has the South greater means of influencing or controlling the movements of this Government now, than it had when the agitation commenced? To all these questions but one answer can be given: No—no— no. The very reverse is true. Instead of being weaker, all the elements in favor of agitation are stronger now than they were in 1835, when it first commenced, while all the elements of influence on the part of the South are weaker. Unless something decisive is done, I again ask, what is to stop this agitation, before the great and final object at which it aims—the abolition of slavery in the States—is consummated? Is it, then, not certain, that if something is not done to arrest it, the South will be forced to choose between abolition and secession? Indeed, as events are now moving, it will not require the South to secede, in order to dissolve the Union. Agitation will of itself effect it, of which its past history furnishes abundant proof—as I shall next proceed to show.

It is a great mistake to suppose that disunion can be effected by a single blow. The cords which bound these States together in one common Union, are far too numerous and powerful for that. Disunion must be the work of time. It is only through a long process, and successively, that the cords can be snapped, until the whole fabric falls asunder. Already the agitation of the slavery question has snapped some of the most important, and has greatly weakened all the others, as I shall proceed to show.

The cords that bind the States together are not only many, but various in character. Some are spiritual or ecclesiastical; some political; others social. Some appertain to the benefit conferred by the Union, and others to the feeling of duty and obligation.

The strongest of those of a spiritual and ecclesiastical nature, consisted in the unity of the great religious denominations, all of which originally embraced the whole Union. All these denominations, with the exception, perhaps, of the Catholics, were organized very much upon the principle of our political institutions. Beginning with smaller meetings, corresponding with the political divisions of the country, their organization terminated in one great central assemblage, corresponding very much with the character of Congress. At these meetings the principal clergymen and lay members of the respective denominations, from all parts of the Union, met to transact business relating to their common concerns. It was not confined to what appertained to the doctrines and discipline of the respective denominations, but extended to plans for disseminating the Bible—establishing missions, distributing tracts—and of establishing presses for the publication of tracts, newspapers, and periodicals, with a view of diffusing religious information—and for the support of their respective doctrines and creeds. All this combined contributed greatly to strengthen the bonds of the Union. The ties which held each denomination together formed a strong cord to hold the whole Union together; but, powerful as they were, they have not been able to resist the explosive effect of slavery agitation.

The first of these cords which snapped, under its explosive force, was that of the powerful Methodist Episcopal Church. The numerous and strong ties which held it together, are all broken, and its unity gone. They now form separate churches; and, instead of that feeling of attachment and devotion to the interests of the whole church which was formerly felt, they are now arrayed into two hostile bodies, engaged in litigation about what was formerly their common property.

The next cord that snapped was that of the Baptists—one of the largest and most respectable of the denominations. That of the Presbyterian is not entirely snapped, but some of its strands have given way. That of the Episcopal Church is the only one of the four great Protestant denominations which remains unbroken and entire.

The strongest cord, of a political character, consists of the many and powerful ties that have held together the two great parties which have, with some modifications, existed from the beginning of the Government. They both extended to every portion of the Union, and strongly contributed to hold all its parts together. But this powerful cord has fared no better than the spiritual. It resisted, for a long time, the explosive tendency of the agitation, but has finally snapped under its force—if not entirely, in a great measure. Nor is there one of the remaining cords which has not been greatly weakened. To this extent the Union has already been destroyed by agitation, in the only way it can be, by sundering and weakening the cords which bind it together.

If the agitation goes on, the same force, acting with increased intensity, as has been shown, will finally snap every cord, when nothing will be left to hold the States together except force. But, surely, that can, with no propriety of language, be called a Union, when the only means by which the weaker is held connected with the stronger portion is *force*. It may, indeed, keep them connected; but the connection will partake much more of the character of subjugation, on the part of the weaker to the stronger, than the union of free, independent, and sovereign States, in one confederation, as they stood in the early stages of the Government, and which only is worthy of the sacred name of Union.

Having now, Senators, explained what it is that endangers the Union, and traced it to its cause, and explained its nature and character, the question again recurs—How can the Union be saved? To this I answer, there is but one way by which it can be—and that is—by adopting such measures as will satisfy the States belonging to the Southern section, that they can remain in the Union consistently with their honor and their safety. There is, again, only one way by which this can be effected, and that is—by removing the causes by which this belief has been produced. Do *this*, and discontent will cease—harmony and kind feelings between the sections be restored—and every apprehension of danger to the Union removed.

On December 21, 1860, South Carolina proclaimed its reasons for secession. Here the intermixture of the constitutional theory of Calhoun and South Carolina's criticism of recent events is revealed.

SOUTH CAROLINA DECLARATION OF THE CAUSES INDUCING SECESSION*

The people of the State of South Carolina in Convention assembled, on the 2d day of April, A.D. 1852, declared that the frequent violations of the Constitution of the United States by the Federal Government, and its encroachments upon the reserved rights of the States, fully justified this State in their withdrawal from the Federal Union; but in deference to the opinions and wishes of the other Slaveholding States, she forbore at that time to exercise this right. Since that time these encroachments have continued

---

* Reprinted from Frank Moore, ed., *The Rebellion Record* (New York: 1861), pp. 3–4.

to increase, and further forbearance ceases to be a virtue.

And now the State of South Carolina having resumed her separate and equal place among nations, deems it due to herself, to the remaining United States of America, and to the nations of the world, that she should declare the immediate causes which have led to this act.

In the year 1765, that portion of the British Empire embracing Great Britain undertook to make laws for the Government of that portion composed of the thirteen American Colonies. A struggle for the right of self-government ensued, which resulted, on the 4th of July, 1776, in a Declaration, by the Colonies, "that they are, and of right ought to be, FREE AND INDEPENDENT STATES; and that, as free and independent States, they have full power to levy war, conclude peace, contract alliances, establish commerce, and do all other acts and things which independent States may of right do."

They further solemnly declared that whenever any "form of government becomes destructive of the ends for which it was established, it is the right of the people to alter or abolish it, and to institute a new government." Deeming the Government of Great Britain to have become destructive of these ends, they declared that the Colonies "are absolved from all allegiance to the British Crown, and that all political connection between them and the State of Great Britain is, and ought to be, totally dissolved."

In pursuance of this Declaration of Independence, each of the thirteen States proceeded to exercise its separate sovereignty; adopted for itself a Constitution, and appointed officers for the administration of government in all its departments—Legislative, Executive and Judicial. For purposes of defence they united their arms and their counsels; and, in 1778, they entered into a League known as the Articles of Confederation, whereby they agreed to intrust the administration of their external relations to a common agent, known as the Congress of the United States, expressly declaring, in the first article, "that each State retains its sovereignty, freedom and independence, and every power, jurisdiction and right which is not, by this Confederation, expressly delegated to the United States in Congress assembled."

Under this Confederation the War of the Revolution was carried on; and on the 3d of September, 1783, the contest ended, and a definite Treaty was signed by Great Britain, in which she acknowledged the Independence of the Colonies in the following terms:

"ARTICLE 1. His Britannic Majesty acknowledges the said United States, viz.: New Hampshire, Massachusetts Bay, Rhode Island and Providence Plantations, Connecticut, New York, New Jersey, Pennsylvania, Delaware, Maryland, Virginia, North Carolina, South Carolina and Georgia, to be FREE, SOVEREIGN, AND INDEPENDENT STATES; that he treats with them as such;

and, for himself, his heirs and successors, relinquishes all claims to the government, property, and territorial rights of the same and every part thereof."

Thus were established the two great principles asserted by the Colonies, namely, the right of a State to govern itself; and the right of a people to abolish a Government when it becomes destructive of the ends for which it was instituted. And concurrent with the establishment of these principles, was the fact, that each Colony became and was recognized by the mother country as a FREE, SOVEREIGN AND INDEPENDENT STATE.

In 1787, Deputies were appointed by the States to revise the articles of Confederation; and on 17th September, 1787, these Deputies recommended, for the adoption of the States, the Articles of Union, known as the Constitution of the United States.

The parties to whom this constitution was submitted were the several sovereign States; they were to agree or disagree, and when nine of them agreed, the compact was to take effect among those concurring; and the General Government, as the common agent, was then to be invested with their authority.

If only nine of the thirteen States had concurred, the other four would have remained as they then were—separate, sovereign States, independent of any of the provisions of the Constitution. In fact, two of the States did not accede to the Constitution until long after it had gone into operation among the other eleven; and during that interval, they each exercised the functions of an independent nation.

By this Constitution, certain duties were imposed upon the several States, and the exercise of certain of their powers was restrained, which necessarily impelled their continued existence as sovereign states. But, to remove all doubt, an amendment was added, which declared that the powers not delegated to the United States by the Constitution, nor prohibited by it to the States, are reserved to the States respectively, or to the people. On the 23d May, 1788, South Carolina, by a Convention of her people, passed an ordinance assenting to this Constitution, and afterwards altered her own Constitution to conform herself to the obligations she had undertaken.

Thus was established, by compact between the States, a Government with defined objects and powers, limited to the express words of the grant. This limitation left the whole remaining mass of power subject to the clause reserving it to the States or the people, and rendered unnecessary any specification of reserved rights. We hold that the Government thus established is subject to the two great principles asserted in the Declaration of Independence; and we hold further, that the mode of its formation subjects it to a third fundamental principle, namely, the law of compact. We maintain that in every compact between two or more parties, the obligation is mutual; that the failure of one of the contracting parties to perform a material part of the agreement, entirely releases the obligation of the other; and that, where no arbiter is provided, each party is remitted to his own judgment to determine the fact of failure, with all its consequences.

In the present case, that fact is established with certainty. We assert that fourteen of the States have deliberately refused for years past to fulfil their constitutional obligations, and we refer to their own statutes for the proof.

The Constitution of the United States, in its fourth Article, provides as follows: "No person held to service or labor in one State under the laws thereof, escaping into another, shall, in consequence of any law or regulation therein, be discharged from such service or labor, but shall be delivered up, on claim of the party to whom such service or labor may be due."

This stipulation was so material to the compact that without it that compact would not have been made. The greater number of the contracting parties held slaves, and they had previously evinced their estimate of the value of such a stipulation by making it a condition in the Ordinance for the government of the territory ceded by Virginia, which obligations, and the laws of the General Government, have ceased to effect the objects of the Constitution. The States of Maine, New Hampshire, Vermont, Massachusetts, Connecticut, Rhode Island, New York, Pennsylvania, Illinois, Indiana, Michigan, Wisconsin, and Iowa, have enacted laws which either nullify the acts of Congress, or render useless any attempt to execute them. In many of these States the fugitive is discharged from the service of labor claimed, and in none of them has the State Government complied with the stipulation made in the Constitution. The State of New Jersey, at an early day, passed a law in conformity with her constitutional obligation; but the current of Anti-Slavery feeling has led her more recently to enact laws which render inoperative the remedies provided by her own laws and by the laws of Congress. In the State of New York even the right of transit for a slave has been denied by her tribunals; and the States of Ohio and Iowa have refused to surrender to justice fugitives charged with murder, and with inciting servile insurrection in the State of Virginia. Thus the constitutional compact has been deliberately broken and disregarded by the non-slaveholding States; and the consequence follows that South Carolina is released from her obligation.

The ends for which this Constitution was framed are declared by itself to be "to form a more perfect union, to establish justice, insure domestic tranquility, provide for the common defence, promote the general welfare, and secure the blessings of liberty to ourselves and our posterity."

These ends it endeavored to accomplish by a Federal Government, in which each State was recognized as an equal, and had separate control over its own institutions. The right of property in slaves was recognized by giving to free persons distinct political rights; by giving them the right to represent, and burdening them with direct taxes for, three-fifths of their slaves; by authorizing the importation of slaves for twenty years; and by stipulating for the rendition of fugitives from labor.

We affirm that these ends for which this Government was instituted have been defeated, and the Government itself has been destructive of them by the action of the non-slaveholding States. Those States have assumed the right of deciding upon the propriety of our domestic institutions; and have denied the rights of property established in fifteen of the States and recognized by the Constitution; they have denounced as sinful the institution of Slavery; they have permitted the open establishment among them of societies, whose avowed object is to disturb the peace of and eloin the property of the citizens of other States. They have encouraged and assisted thousands of our slaves to leave their homes; and those who remain, have been incited by emissaries, books, and pictures, to servile insurrection.

For twenty-five years this agitation has been steadily increasing, until it has now secured to its aid the power of the common Government. Observing the *forms* of the Constitution, a sectional party has found within that article establishing the Executive Department, the means of subverting the Constitution itself. A geographical line has been drawn across the Union, and all the States north of that line have united in the election of a man to the high office of President of the United States whose opinions and purposes are hostile to Slavery. He is to be intrusted with the administration of the common Government, because he has declared that that "Government cannot endure permanently half slave, half free," and that the public mind must rest in the belief that Slavery is in the course of ultimate extinction.

This sectional combination for the subversion of the Constitution has been aided, in some of the States, by elevating to citizenship persons who, by the supreme law of the land, are incapable of becoming citizens; and their votes have been used to inaugurate a new policy, hostile to the South, and destructive of its peace and safety.

On the 4th of March next this party will take possession of the Government. It has announced that the South shall be excluded from the common territory, that the Judicial tribunal shall be made sectional, and that a war must be waged against Slavery until it shall cease throughout the United States.

The guarantees of the Constitution will then no longer exist; the equal rights of the States will be lost. The Slaveholding States will no longer have the power of self-government, or self-protection, and the Federal Government will have become their enemy.

Sectional interest and animosity will deepen

the irritation; and all hope of remedy is rendered vain, by the fact that the public opinion at the North has invested a great political error with the sanctions of a more erroneous religious belief.

We, therefore, the people of South Carolina by our delegates in Convention assembled, appealing to the Supreme Judge of the world for the rectitude of our intentions, have solemnly declared that the Union heretofore existing between this State and the other States of North America is dissolved, and that the State of South Carolina has resumed her position among the nations of the world, as separate and independent state, with full power to levy war, conclude peace, contract alliances, establish commerce, and to do all other acts and things which independent States may of right do.

Writing two decades later, Jefferson Davis voiced the same sentiments he held while President of the Confederacy. He stated that the purpose of his history was "to show that the Southern States had rightfully the power to withdraw from a Union into which they had, as sovereign communities, voluntarily entered; that the denial of that right was a violation of the letter and spirit of the compact between the States; and that the war waged by the Federal Government against the seceding States was in disregard of the limitations of the Constitution, and destructive of the principles of the Declaration of Independence."

JEFFERSON DAVIS:
RISE AND FALL OF THE CONFEDERACY*

When, at the close of the war of the revolution, each of the thirteen colonies that had been engaged in that contest was severally acknowledged by the mother-country, Great Britain, to be a free and independent State, the confederation of those States embraced an area so extensive, with climate and products so various, that rivalries and conflicts of interest soon began to be manifested. It required all the power of wisdom and patriotism, animated by the affection engendered by common sufferings and dangers, to keep these rivalries under restraint, and to effect those compromises which it was fondly hoped would insure the harmony and mutual good offices of each for the benefit of all. It was in this spirit of patriotism and confidence in the continuance of such abiding good will as would for all time preclude hostile aggression, that Virginia ceded, for the use of the confederated States, all that vast extent of territory lying north of the Ohio River, out of which have since been formed five States and part of a sixth. The addition of these States has accrued entirely to the preponderance of the Northern section over that from which the donation proceeded, and to the disturbance of that equilibrium which existed at the close of the war of the Revolution.

It may not be out of place here to refer to the fact that the grievances which led to that war were directly inflicted upon the Northern colonies. Those of the South had no material cause of complaint; but, actuated by sympathy for their Northern brethren, and a devotion to the principles of civil liberty and community independence, which they had inherited from their Anglo-Saxon ancestry, and which were set forth in the Declaration of Independence, they made common cause with their neighbors, and may, at least, claim to have done their full share in the war that ensued.

By the exclusion of the South, in 1820, from all that part of the Louisiana purchase lying north of the parallel of thirty-six degrees thirty minutes, and not included in the State of Missouri; by the extension of that line of exclusion to embrace the territory acquired from Texas; and by the appropriation of *all* the territory obtained from Mexico under the Treaty of Guadalupe Hidalgo, both north and south of that line, it may be stated with approximate accuracy that the North had monopolized to herself more than three fourths of all that had been added to the domain of the United States since the Declaration of Independence. This inequality, which began, as has been shown, in the more generous than wise confidence of the South, was employed to obtain for the North the lion's share of what was afterward added at the cost of the public treasure and the blood of patriots. I do not care to estimate the relative proportion contributed by each of the two sections.

Nor was this the only cause that operated

---

* Reprinted from Jefferson Davis, *The Rise and Fall of the Confederate Government* (New York: 1881), I, 47–57.

to disappoint the reasonable hopes and to blight the fair prospects under which the original compact was formed. The effects of discriminating duties upon imports have been referred to in a former chapter—favoring the manufacturing region, which was the North; burdening the exporting region, which was the South; and so imposing upon the latter a double tax: one, by the increased price of articles of consumption, which, so far as they were of home production, went into the pockets of the manufacturer; the other, by the diminished value of articles of export, which was so much withheld from the pockets of the agriculturist. In like manner the power of the majority section was employed to appropriate to itself an unequal share of the public disbursements. These combined causes—the possession of more territory, more money, and a wider field for the employment of special labor—all served to attract immigration; and, with increasing population, the greed grew by what it fed on.

This became distinctly manifest when the so-called "Republican" Convention assembled in Chicago, on May 16, 1860, to nominate a candidate for the Presidency. It was a purely sectional body. There were a few delegates present, representing an insignificant minority in the "border States," Delaware, Maryland, Virginia, Kentucky, and Missouri; but not one from any State south of the celebrated political line of thirty-six degrees thirty minutes. It had been the invariable usage with nominating conventions of all parties to select candidates for the Presidency and Vice-Presidency, one from the North and the other from the South; but this assemblage nominated Mr. Lincoln, of Illinois, for the first office, and for the second, Mr. Hamlin, of Maine—both Northerners. Mr. Lincoln, its nominee for the Presidency, had publicly announced that the Union "could not permanently endure, half slave and half free." The resolutions adopted contained some carefully worded declarations, well adapted to deceive the credulous who were opposed to hostile aggressions upon the rights of the States. In order to accomplish this purpose, they were compelled to create a fictitious issue, in denouncing what they described as "the new dogma that the Constitution, of its own force, carries slavery into any or all of the Territories of the United States"—a "dogma" which had never been held or declared by anybody, and which had no existence outside of their own assertion. There was enough in connection with the nomination to assure the most fanatical foes of the Constitution that their ideas would be the rule and guide of the party. . . .

The people of the United States now had four rival tickets presented to them by as many contending parties, whose respective position and principles on the great and absorbing question at issue may be briefly recapitulated as follows:

1. The "Constitutional-Union" party, as it was now termed, led by Messrs. Bell and Everett, which ignored the territorial controversy altogether, and contended itself, as above stated, with a simple declaration of adherence to "the Constitution, the Union, and the enforcement of the laws."

2. The party of "popular sovereignty," headed by Douglas and Johnson, who affirmed the right of the people of the Territories, in their territorial condition, to determine their own organic institutions, independently of the control of Congress; denying the power or duty of Congress to protect the persons or property of individuals or minorities in such Territories against the action of majorities.

3. The State-Rights party, supporting Breckinridge and Lane, who held that the Territories were open to citizens of all the States, with their property, without any inequality or discrimination, and that it was the duty of the General Government to protect both persons and property from aggression in the Territories subject to its control. At the same time they admitted and asserted the right of the people of a Territory, on emerging from their territorial condition to that of a State, to determine what should then be their domestic institutions, as well as all other questions of personal or proprietary right, without interference by Congress, and subject only to the limitations and restrictions prescribed by the Constitution of the United States.

4. The so-called "Republicans," presenting the names of Lincoln and Hamlin, who held, in the language of one of their leaders, that "slavery can exist only by virtue of municipal law"; that there was "no law for it in the Territories, and no power to enact one"; and that Congress was "bound to prohibit it in or exclude it from any and every Federal Territory." In other words, they asserted the right and duty of Congress to exclude the citizens of half the States of the Union from the territory belonging in common to all, unless on condition of the sacrifice or abandonment of their property recognized by the Constitution—indeed, of the *only* species of their property distinctly and specifically recognized as such by that instrument.

On the vital question underlying the whole controversy—that is, whether the Federal Government should be a Government of the whole for the benefit of all its equal members, or (if it should continue to exist at all) a sectional Government for the benefit of a part—the first three of the parties above described were in substantial accord as against the fourth. If they could or would have acted unitedly, they could certainly have carried the election, and averted the catastrophe which followed. Nor were efforts wanting to effect such a union.

Mr. Bell, the Whig candidate, was a highly respectable and experienced statesman, who had filled many important offices, both State and Federal. He was not ambitious to the extent of coveting the Presidency, and he was profoundly impressed by the danger which threatened the country. Mr. Breckinridge had not anticipated, and it may safely be said did not eagerly desire, the nomination. He was young enough to wait, and patriotic enough to be willing to do so, if the weal of the country required it. Thus much I may confidently assert of both those gentlemen; for each of them authorized me to say that he was willing to withdraw, if an arrangement could be effected by which the divided forces of the friends of the Constitution could be concentrated upon some one more generally acceptable than either of the three who had been presented to the country. When I made this announcement to Mr. Douglas—with whom my relations had always been such as to authorize the assurance that he could not consider it as made in an unfriendly spirit—he replied that the scheme proposed was impracticable, because his friends, mainly Northern Democrats, if he were withdrawn, would join in the support of Mr. Lincoln, rather than of any one that should supplant *him* (Douglas); that he was in the hands of his friends, and was sure they would not accept the proposition.

It needed little knowledge of the *status* of parties in the several States to foresee a probable defeat if the conservatives were to continue divided into three parts, and the aggressives were to be held in solid column. But angry passions, which are always bad counselors, had been aroused, and hopes were still cherished, which proved to be illusory. The result was the election, by a minority, of a President whose avowed principles were necessarily fatal to the harmony of the Union.

Of 303 *electoral* votes, Mr. Lincoln received 180, but of the *popular* suffrage of 4,676,853 votes, which the electors represented, he obtained only 1,866,352—something over a third of the votes. This discrepancy was owing to the system of voting by "general ticket"— that is, casting the States votes as a unit, whether unanimous or nearly equally divided. Thus, in New York, the total popular vote was 675,156, of which 362,646 were cast for the so-called Republican (or Lincoln) electors, and 312,510 against them. New York was entitled to 35 electoral votes. Divided on the basis of the popular vote, 19 of these would have been cast for Mr. Lincoln, and 16 against him. But under the "general ticket" system the entire 35 votes were cast for the Republican candidates, thus giving them not only the full strength of the majority in their favor, but that of the great minority against them superadded. So of other Northern States, in which the small majorities on one side operated with the weight of entire unanimity, while the virtual unanimity in the Southern States, on the other side, counted nothing more than a mere majority would have done.

The manifestations which followed this result, in the Southern States, did not proceed, as has been unjustly charged, from chagrin at their defeat in the election, or from any personal hostility to the President-elect, but from the fact that they recognized in him the representative of a party professing principles destructive to "their peace, their prosperity, and their domestic tranquillity." The long-suppressed fire burst into frequent flame, but it was still controlled by that love of the Union which the South had illustrated in every battle-field, from Boston to New Orleans. Still it was hoped, against hope, that some adjustment might be made to avert the calamities of a practical application of the theory of an "irrepressible conflict." Few, if any, then doubted the right of a State to withdraw its grants delegated to the Federal Government, or, in other words, to secede from the Union; but in the South this was generally regarded as the remedy of last resort, to be applied only when ruin or dishonor was the alternative. No rash or revolutionary action was taken by the Southern States, but the measures adopted were considerate, and executed advisedly and deliberately. The Presidential election occurred (as far as the popular vote, which determined the result, was concerned) in November, 1860. Most of the State Legislatures convened soon afterward in regular session. In some cases special sessions were convoked for the purpose of calling State Conventions—the recognized representatives of the sovereign will of the people— to be elected expressly for the purpose of taking such action as should be considered needful and proper under the existing circumstances.

These conventions, as it was always held and understood, possessed all the power of the people assembled in mass; and therefore it was conceded that they, and they only, could take action for the withdrawal of a State from the Union. The consent of the respective States to the formation of the Union had been given through such conventions, and it was only by the same authority that it could properly be revoked. The time required for this deliberate and formal process precludes the idea of hasty or passionate action, and none who admit the primary power of the people to govern themselves can consistently deny its validity and binding obligation upon every citizen of the several States. Not only was there ample time for calm consideration among the people of the South, but for due reflection by the General Government and the people of the Northern States.

President Buchanan was in the last year of his administration. His freedom from sectional asperity, his long life in the public service, and his peace-loving and conciliatory character, were all guarantees against his precipitating a conflict between the Federal Government and any of the States; but the feeble power that he possessed in the closing months of his term to mold the policy of the future was painfully evident. Like all who had intelligently and impartially studied the history of the formation of the Constitution, he held that the Federal Government had no rightful power to coerce a State. Like the sages and patriots who had preceded him in the high office that he filled, he believed that "our Union rests upon public opinion, and can never be cemented by the blood of its citizens shed in civil war. If it can not live in the affections of the people, it must one day perish. Congress may possess many means of preserving it by conciliation, but the sword was not placed in their hand to preserve it by force."—(Message of December 3, 1860.)

Ten years before, Mr. Calhoun, addressing the Senate with all the earnestness of his nature, and with that sincere desire to avert the danger of disunion which those who knew him best never doubted, had asked the emphatic question, "How can the Union be saved?" He answered his question thus: "There is but one way by which it can be [saved] with any certainty; and that is by a full and final settlement, on the principles of justice, of all the questions at issue between the sections. The South asks for justice—simple justice—and less she ought not to take. She has no compromise to offer but the Constitution, and no concession or surrender to make. . . .

"Can this be done? Yes, easily! Not by the weaker party; for it can of itself do nothing—not even protect itself—but by the stronger. . . . But will the North agree to do this? It is for her to answer this question. But, I will say, she can not refuse if she has half the love of the Union which she professes to have, nor without exposing herself to the charge that her love of power and aggrandizement is far greater than her love of the Union."

During the ten years that intervened between the date of this speech and the message of Mr. Buchanan cited above, the progress of sectional discord and the tendency of the stronger section to unconstitutional aggression had been fearfully rapid. With very rare exceptions, there were none in 1850 who claimed the right of the Federal Government to apply coercion to a State. In 1860 men had grown to be familiar with threats of driving the South into submission to any act that the Government, in the hands of a Northern majority, might see fit to perform. During the canvass of that year, demonstrations had been made by quasi-military organizations in various parts of the North, which looked unmistakably to purposes widely different from those enunciated in the preamble to the Constitution, and to the employment of means not authorized by the powers which the States had delegated to the Federal Government.

Well-informed men still remembered that, in the Convention which framed the Constitution, a proposition was made to authorize the employment of force against a delinquent State, on which Mr. Madison remarked that "the use of force against a State would look more like a declaration of war than an infliction of punishment, and would probably be considered by the party attacked as a dissolution of all previous compacts by which it might have been bound." The Convention expressly refused to confer the power proposed, and the clause was lost. While, therefore, in 1860, many violent men, appealing to passion and the lust of power, were inciting the multitude, and preparing Northern opinion to support a war waged against the Southern States in the event of their secession, there were others who took a different view of the case. Notable among such was the "New York Tribune," which had been the organ of the abolitionists, and which now declared that, "if the cotton States wished to withdraw from the Union, they should be allowed to do so"; that "any attempt to compel them to remain, by force, would be contrary to the principles of the Declaration of Independence and to the fundamental ideas upon which human liberty is based"; and that, "if the Declaration of Independence justified the secession from the British Empire of three millions of subjects in 1776, it was not seen why it would not justify the secession of five millions of Southerners from the Union in 1861." Again, it was said by the same journal that, "sooner than compromise with the South and abandon the Chicago platform," they would "let the Union slide." Taunting expressions were freely used— as, for example, "If the Southern people wish to leave the Union, we will do our best to forward their views."

All this, it must be admitted, was quite consistent with the oft-repeated declaration that the Constitution was a "covenant with hell," which stood as the caption of a leading abolitionist paper of Boston. That signs of coming danger so visible, evidences of hostility so unmistakable, disregard of constitutional obligations so wanton, taunts and jeers so bitter and insulting, should serve to increase excitement in the South, was a consequence flowing as much from reason and patriotism as from sentiment. He must have been ignorant of human nature who did not expect such a tree to bear fruits of discord and division.

Speaking on October 28, 1858, in Rochester, New York, William H. Seward first used the term, "the irrepressible conflict." The issue, Seward maintained, was between a slave and a free labor system, with the former seeking to extend itself to all people: "The white laboring man, whether native or foreigner, is not enslaved, only because he cannot, as yet, be reduced to bondage."

WILLIAM H. SEWARD:
THE IRREPRESSIBLE CONFLICT*

The unmistakable outbreaks of zeal which occur all around me, show that you are earnest men—and such a man am I. Let us therefore, at least for a time, pass by all secondary and collateral questions, whether of a personal or of a general nature, and consider the main subject of the present canvass. The democratic party—or, to speak more accurately, the party which wears that attractive name—is in possession of the federal government. The republicans propose to dislodge that party, and dismiss it from its high trust.

The main subject, then, is, whether the democratic party deserves to retain the confidence of the American people. In attempting to prove it unworthy, I think that I am not actuated by prejudices against that party, or by prepossessions in favor of its adversary; for I have learned, by some experience, that virtue and patriotism, vice and selfishness, are found in all parties, and that they differ less in their motives than in the policies they pursue.

Our country is a theatre, which exhibits, in full operation, two radically different political systems; the one resting on the basis of servile or slave labor, the other on the basis of voluntary labor of freemen.

The laborers who are enslaved are all negroes, or persons more or less purely of African derivation. But this is only accidental. The principle of the system is, that labor in every society, by whomsoever performed, is necessarily unintellectual, groveling and base; and that the laborer, equally for his own good and for the welfare of the state, ought to be enslaved. The white laboring man, whether native or foreigner, is not enslaved, only because he cannot, as yet, be reduced to bondage.

You need not be told now that the slave system is the older of the two, and that once it was universal.

The emancipation of our own ancestors, Caucasians and Europeans as they were, hardly dates beyond a period of five hundred years. The great melioration of human society which modern times exhibit, is mainly due to the incomplete

substitution of the system of voluntary labor for the old one of servile labor, which has already taken place. This African slave system is one which, in its origin and in its growth, has been altogether foreign from the habits of the races which colonized these states, and established civilization here. It was introduced on this new continent as an engine of conquest, and for the establishment of monarchical power, by the Portuguese and the Spaniards, and was rapidly extended by them all over South America, Central America, Louisiana and Mexico. Its legitimate fruits are seen in the poverty, imbecility, and anarchy, which now pervade all Portuguese and Spanish America. The free-labor system is of German extraction, and it was established in our country by emigrants from Sweden, Holland, Germany, Great Britain and Ireland.

We justly ascribe to its influences the strength, wealth, greatness, intelligence, and freedom, which the whole American people now enjoy. One of the chief elements of the value of human life is freedom in the pursuit of happiness. The slave system is not only intolerable, unjust, and inhuman, towards the laborer, whom, only because he is a laborer, it loads down with chains and converts into merchandise, but is scarcely less severe upon the freeman, to whom, only because he is a laborer from necessity, it denies facilities for employment, and whom it expels from the community because it cannot enslave and convert him into merchandise also. It is necessarily improvident and ruinous, because, as a general truth, communities prosper and flourish or droop and decline in just the degree that they practise or neglect to practise the primary duties of justice and humanity. The free-labor system conforms to the divine law of equality, which is written in the hearts and consciences of man, and therefore is always and everywhere beneficent.

The slave system is one of constant danger, distrust, suspicion, and watchfulness. It debases those whose toil alone can produce wealth and resources for defense, to the lowest degree of which human nature is capable, to guard against mutiny and insurrection, and thus wastes energies which otherwise might be employed in national development and aggrandizement.

The free-labor system educates all alike, and by opening all the fields of industrial employ-

* Reprinted from George E. Baker, ed., *Works of William H. Seward* (New York: 1861), IV, 289–97, 299–302.

ment, and all the departments of authority, to the unchecked and equal rivalry of all classes of men, at once secures universal contentment, and brings into the highest possible activity all the physical, moral and social energies of the whole state. In states where the slave system prevails, the masters, directly or indirectly, secure all political power, and constitute a ruling aristocracy. In states where the free-labor system prevails, universal suffrage necessarily obtains, and the state inevitably becomes, sooner or later, a republic or democracy.

Russia yet maintains slavery, and is a despotism. Most of the other European states have abolished slavery, and adopted the system of free labor. It was the antagonistic political tendencies of the two systems which the first Napoleon was contemplating when he predicted that Europe would ultimately be either all Cossack or all republican. Never did human sagacity utter a more pregnant truth. The two systems are at once perceived to be incongruous. But they are more than incongruous—they are incompatible. They never have permanently existed together in one country, and they never can. It would be easy to demonstrate this impossibility, from the irreconcilable contrast between their great principles and characteristics. But the experience of mankind has conclusively established it. Slavery, as I have already intimated, existed in every state in Europe. Free labor has supplanted it everywhere except in Russia and Turkey. State necessities developed in modern times, are now obliging even those two nations to encourage and employ free labor; and already, despotic as they are, we find them engaged in abolishing slavery. In the United States, slavery came into collision with free labor at the close of the last century, and fell before it in New England, New York, New Jersey and Pennsylvania, but triumphed over it effectually, and excluded it for a period yet undetermined, from Virginia, the Carolinas and Georgia. Indeed, so incompatible are the two systems, that every new state which is organized within our ever extending domain makes its first political act a choice of the one and the exclusion of the other, even at the cost of civil war, if necessary. The slave states, without law, at the last national election, successfully forbade, within their own limits, even the casting of votes for a candidate for president of the United States supposed to be favorable to the establishment of the free-labor system in new states.

Hitherto, the two systems have existed in different states, but side by side within the American Union. This has happened because the Union is a confederation of states. But in another aspect the United States constitute only one nation. Increase of population, which is filling the states out to their very borders, together with a new and extended net-work of railroads and other avenues, and an internal commerce which daily becomes more intimate, is rapidly bringing the states into a higher and more perfect social unity or consolidation. Thus, these antagonistic systems are continually coming into closer contact, and collision results.

Shall I tell you what this collision means? They who think that it is accidental, unnecessary, the work of interested or fanatical agitators, and therefore ephemeral, mistake the case altogether. It is an irrepressible conflict between opposing and enduring forces, and it means that the United States must and will, sooner or later, become either entirely a slaveholding nation, or entirely a free-labor nation. Either the cotton and rice-fields of South Carolina and the sugar plantations of Louisiana will ultimately be tilled by free labor, and Charleston and New Orleans become marts for legitimate merchandise alone, or else the rye-fields and wheat-fields of Massachusetts and New York must again be surrendered by their farmers to slave culture and to the production of slaves, and Boston and New York become once more markets for trade in the bodies and souls of men. It is the failure to apprehend this great truth that induces so many unsuccessful attempts at final compromise between the slave and free states, and it is the existence of this great fact that renders all such pretended compromises, when made, vain and ephemeral. Startling as this saying may appear to you, fellow citizens, it is by no means an original or even a moderate one. Our forefathers knew it to be true, and unanimously acted upon it when they framed the constitution of the United States. They regarded the existence of the servile system in so many of the states with sorrow and shame, which they openly confessed, and they looked upon the collision between them, which was then just revealing itself, and which we are now accustomed to deplore, with favor and hope. They knew that either the one or the other system must exclusively prevail.

Unlike too many of those who in modern time invoke their authority, they had a choice between the two. They preferred the system of free labor, and they determined to organize the government, and so to direct its activity, that that system should surely and certainly prevail. For this purpose, and no other, they based the whole structure of government broadly on the principle that all men are created equal, and therefore free—little dreaming that, within the short period of one hundred years, their descendants would bear to be told by any orator, however popular, that the utterance of that principle was merely a rhetorical rhapsody; or by any judge, however venerated, that it was attended by mental reservations, which rendered it hypocritical and false. By the ordinance of 1787, they dedicated all of the national domain not yet polluted by slavery to free labor immediately, thenceforth and forever; while by the new constitution and laws they invited foreign free labor from all lands under the sun, and interdicted the importation of African slave labor, at all times, in all places, and under all circumstances whatsoever. It is true that they necessarily and wisely modified this policy of freedom, by leaving it to the several states, affected as they were by differing circumstances, to abolish slavery in their own way and at their own pleasure, instead of confiding that duty to congress; and that they secured to the slave states, while yet retaining the system of slavery, a three-fifths representation of slaves in the federal government, until they should find themselves able to relinquish it with safety. But the very nature of these modifications fortifies my position that the fathers knew that the two systems could not endure within the Union, and expected that within a short period slavery would disappear forever. Moreover, in order that these modifications might not altogether defeat their grand design of a republic maintaining universal equality, they provided that two-thirds of the states might amend the constitution.

It remains to say on this point only one word, to guard against misapprehension. If these states are to again become universally slaveholding, I do not pretend to say with what violations of the constitution that end shall be accomplished. On the other hand, while I do confidently believe and hope that my country will yet become a land of universal freedom, I do not expect that it will be made so otherwise than through the action of the several states coöperating with the federal government, and all acting in strict conformity with their respective constitutions.

The strife and contentions concerning slavery, which gently-disposed persons so habitually deprecate, are nothing more than the ripening of the conflict which the fathers themselves not only thus regarded with favor, but which they may be said to have instituted.

It is not to be denied, however, that thus far the course of that contest has not been according to their humane anticipations and wishes. In the field of federal politics, slavery, deriving unlooked-for advantages from commercial changes, and energies unforeseen from the facilities of combination between members of the slaveholding class and between that class and other property classes, early rallied, and has at length made a stand, not merely to retain its original defensive position, but to extend its sway throughout the whole Union. It is certain that the slaveholding class of American citizens indulge this high ambition, and that they derive encouragement for it from the rapid and effective political successes which they have already obtained. The plan of operation is this: By continued appliances of patronage and threats of disunion, they will keep a majority favorable to these designs in the senate, where each state has an equal representation. Through that majority they will defeat, as they best can, the admission of free states and secure the admission of slave states. Under the protection of the judiciary, they will, on the principle of the Dred Scott case, carry slavery into all the territories of the United States now existing and hereafter to be organized. By the action of the

president and the senate, using the treaty-making power, they will annex foreign slaveholding states. In a favorable conjuncture they will induce congress to repeal the act of 1808, which prohibits the foreign slave trade, and so they will import from Africa, at the cost of only twenty dollars a head, slaves enough to fill up the interior of the continent. Thus relatively increasing the number of slave states, they will allow no amendment to the constitution prejudicial to their interest; and so, having permanently established their power, they expect the federal judiciary to nullify all state laws which shall interfere with internal or foreign commerce in slaves. When the free states shall be sufficiently demoralized to tolerate these designs, they reasonably conclude that slavery will be accepted by those states themselves. I shall not stop to show how speedy or how complete would be the ruin which the accomplishment of these slaveholding schemes would bring upon the country. For one, I should not remain in the country to test the sad experiment. Having spent my manhood, though not my whole life, in a free state, no aristocracy of any kind, much less an aristocracy of slaveholders, shall ever make the laws of the land in which I shall be content to live. Having seen the society around me universally engaged in agriculture, manufactures and trade, which were innocent and beneficent, I shall never be a denizen of a state where men and women are reared as cattle, and bought and sold as merchandise. When that evil day shall come, and all further effort at resistance shall be impossible, then, if there shall be no better hope for redemption than I can now foresee, I shall say with Franklin, while looking abroad over the whole earth for a new and more congenial home, "Where liberty dwells, there is my country."

You will tell me that these fears are extravagant and chimerical. I answer, they are so; but they are so only because the designs of the slaveholders must and can be defeated. But it is only the possibility of defeat that renders them so. They cannot be defeated by inactivity. There is no escape from them, compatible with non-resistance. How, then, and in what way, shall the necessary resistance be made. There is only one way. The democratic party must be permanently dislodged from the government. The reason is, that the democratic party is inextricably committed to the designs of the slaveholders, which I have described. Let me be well understood. I do not charge that the democratic candidates for public office now before the people are pledged to—much less that the democratic masses who support them really adopt—those atrocious and dangerous designs. Candidates may, and generally do, mean to act justly, wisely and patriotically, when they shall be elected; but they become the ministers and servants, not the dictators, of the power which elects them. The policy which a party shall pursue at a future period is only gradually developed, depending on the occurrence of events never fully foreknown. The motives of men, whether acting as electors or in any other capacity, are generally pure. Nevertheless, it is not more true that "hell is paved with good intentions," than it is that earth is covered with wrecks resulting from innocent and amiable motives.

The very constitution of the democratic party commits it to execute all the designs of the slaveholders, whatever they may be. It is not a party of the whole Union, of all the free states and of all the slave states; nor yet is it a party of the free states in the north and in the northwest; but it is a sectional and local party, having practically its seat within the slave states, and counting its constituency chiefly and almost exclusively there. Of all its representatives in congress and in the electoral colleges, two-thirds uniformly come from these states. Its great element of strength lies in the vote of the slaveholders, augmented by the representation of three-fifths of the slaves. Deprive the democratic party of this strength, and it would be a helpless and hopeless minority, incapable of continued organization. The democratic party, being thus local and sectional, acquires new strength from the admission of every new slave state, and loses relatively by the admission of every new free state into the Union.

A party is in one sense a joint stock association, in which those who contribute most direct the action and management of the concern. The slaveholders contributing in an overwhelming proportion to the capital strength of the democratic party, they necessarily dictate and prescribe its policy. The inevitable caucus system enables them to do so with a show of fairness and justice. If it were possible to conceive for a moment that the democratic party should disobey the behests of the slaveholders, we should then see a withdrawal of the slaveholders, which would leave the party to perish. The portion of the party which is found in the free states is a mere appendage, convenient to modify its sectional character, without impairing its sectional constitution, and is less effective in regulating its movement than the nebulous tail of the comet is in determining the appointed though apparently eccentric course of the fiery sphere from which it emanates.

To expect the democratic party to resist slavery and favor freedom, is as unreasonable as to look for protestant missionaries to the catholic propaganda of Rome. The history of the democratic party commits it to the policy of slavery. It has been the democratic party, and no other agency, which has carried that policy up to its present alarming culmination. Without stopping to ascertain, critically, the origin of the present democratic party, we may concede its claim to date from the era of good feeling which occurred under the administration of President Monroe. At that time, in this state, and about that time in many others of the free states, the democratic party deliberately disfranchised the free colored or African citizen, and it has pertinaciously continued this disfranchisement ever since. This was an effective aid to slavery; for, while the slaveholder votes for his slaves against freedom, the freed slave in the free states is prohibited from voting against slavery. . . .

Now, I know very well that the democratic party has, at every stage of these proceedings, disavowed the motive and the policy of fortifying and extending slavery, and has excused them on entirely different and more plausible grounds. But the inconsistency and frivolity of these pleas prove still more conclusively the guilt I charge upon that party. It must, indeed, try to excuse such guilt before mankind, and even to the consciences of its own adherents. There is an instinctive abhorrence of slavery, and an inborn and inhering love of freedom in the human heart, which render palliation of such gross misconduct indispensable. It disfranchised the free African on the ground of a fear that, if left to enjoy the right of suffrage, he might seduce the free white citizens into amalgamation with his wronged and despised race. The democratic party condemned and deposed John Quincy Adams, because he expended twelve millions a year, while it justifies his favored successor in spending seventy, eighty and even one hundred millions, a year. It denies emancipation in the District of Columbia, even with compensation to masters and the consent of the people, on the ground of an implied constitutional inhibition, although the constitution expressly confers upon congress sovereign legislative power in that district, and although the democratic party is tenacious of the principle of strict construction. It violated the express provisions of the constitution in suppressing petition and debate on the subject of slavery, through fear of disturbance of the public harmony, although it claims that the electors have a right to instruct their representatives, and even demand their resignation in cases of contumacy. It extended slavery over Texas, and connived at the attempt to spread it across the Mexican territories, even to the shores of the Pacific ocean, under a plea of enlarging the area of freedom. It abrogated the Mexican slave law and the Missouri compromise prohibition of slavery in Kansas, not to open the new territories to slavery, but to try therein the new and fascinating theories of non-intervention and popular sovereignty; and, finally, it overthrew both these new and elegant systems by the English Lecompton bill and the Dred Scott decision, on the ground that the free states ought not to enter the Union without a population equal to the representative basis of one member of congress, although slave states might come in without inspection as to their numbers.

Will any member of the democratic party now here claim that the authorities chosen by the suffrages of the party transcended their partisan platforms, and so misrepresented the party in the various transactions, I have recited? Then I ask him to name one democratic statesman or legislator, from Van Buren to Walker, who, either timidly or cautiously like them, or boldly and defiantly like Douglas, ever refused to execute a behest of the slaveholders and was not therefor, and for no other cause, immediately denounced, and deposed from his trust, and repudiated by the democratic party for that contumacy.

I think, fellow citizens, that I have shown you that it is high time for the friends of freedom to rush to the rescue of the constitution, and that their very first duty is to dismiss the democratic party from the administration of the government.

Why shall it not be done? All agree that it ought to be done. What, then, shall prevent its being done? Nothing but timidity or division of the opponents of the democratic party.

Some of these opponents start one objection, and some another. Let us notice these objections briefly. One class say that they cannot trust the republican party; that it has not avowed its hostility to slavery boldly enough, or its affection for freedom earnestly enough.

I ask, in reply, is there any other party which can be more safely trusted? Every one knows that it is the republican party, or none, that shall displace the democratic party. But I answer, further, that the character and fidelity of any party are determined, necessarily, not by its pledges, programmes, and platforms, but by the public exigencies, and the temper of the people when they call it into activity. Subserviency to slavery is a law written not only on the forehead of the democratic party, but also in its very soul—so resistance to slavery, and devotion to freedom, the popular elements now actively working for the republican party among the people, must and will be the resources for its ever-renewing strength and constant invigoration.

Others cannot support the republican party, because it has not sufficiently exposed its platform, and determined what it will do, and what it will not do, when triumphant. It may prove too progressive for some, and too conservative for others. As if any party ever foresaw so clearly the course of future events as to plan a universal scheme of future action, adapted to all possible emergencies. Who would ever have joined even the whig party of the revolution, if it had been obliged to answer, in 1775, whether it would declare for independence in 1776, and for this noble federal constitution of ours in 1787, and not a year earlier or later? The people will be as wise next year, and even ten years hence, as we are now. They will oblige the republican party to act as the public welfare and the interests of justice and humanity shall require, through all the stages of its career, whether of trial or triumph.

Others will not venture an effort, because they fear that the Union would not endure the change. Will such objectors tell me how long a constitution can bear a strain directly along the fibres of which it is composed? This is a constitution of freedom. It is being converted into a constitution of slavery. It is a republican constitu-

tion. It is being made an aristocratic one. Others wish to wait until some collateral questions concerning temperance, or the exercise of the elective franchise are properly settled. Let me ask all such persons, whether time enough has not been wasted on these points already, without gaining any other than this single advantage, namely, the discovery that only one thing can be effectually done at one time, and that the one thing which must and will be done at any one time is just that thing which is most urgent, and will no longer admit of postponement or delay. Finally, we are told by faint-hearted men that they despond; the democratic party, they say is unconquerable, and the dominion of slavery is consequently inevitable. I reply that the complete and universal dominion of slavery would be intolerable enough, when it should have come, after the last possible effort to escape should have been made. There would then be left to us the consoling reflection of fidelity to duty.

But I reply further, that I know—few, I think, know better than I—the resources and energies of the democratic party, which is identical with the slave power. I do ample prestige to its traditional popularity. I know, further—few, I think, know better than I—the difficulties and disadvantages of organizing a new political force, like the republican party, and the obstacles it must encounter in laboring without prestige and without patronage. But, understanding all this, I know that the democratic party must go down, and that the republican party must rise into its place. The democratic party derived its strength, originally, from its adoption of the principles of equal and exact justice to all men. So long as it practised this principle faithfully, it was invulnerable. It became vulnerable when it renounced the principle, and since that time it has maintained itself, not by virtue of its own strength, or even of its traditional merits, but because there as yet had appeared in the political field no other party that had the conscience and the courage to take up, and avow, and practice the life-inspiring principle which the democratic party had surrendered. At last, the republican party has appeared. It avows, now, as the republican party of 1800 did, in one word, its faith and its works, "Equal and exact justice to all men." Even when it first entered the field, only half organized, it struck a blow which only just failed to secure complete and triumphant victory. In this, its second campaign, it has already won advantages which render that triumph now both easy and certain.

The secret of its assured success lies in that very characteristic which, in the mouth of scoffers, constitutes its great and lasting imbecility and reproach. It lies in the fact that it is a party of one idea; but that idea is a noble one—an idea that fills and expands all generous souls; the idea of equality—the equality of all men before human tribunals and human laws, as they all are equal before the Divine tribunal and Divine laws.

I know, and you know, that a revolution has begun. I know, and all the world knows, that revolutions never go backward. Twenty senators and a hundred representatives proclaim boldly in congress to-day sentiments and opinions and principles of freedom which hardly so many men, even in this free state, dared to utter in their own homes twenty years ago. While the government of the United States, under the conduct of the democratic party, has been all that time surrendering one plain and castle after another to slavery, the people of the United States have been no less steadily and perseveringly gathering together the forces with which to recover back again all the fields and all the castles which have been lost, and to confound and overthrow, by one decisive blow, the betrayers of the constitution and freedom forever.

The famous "House Divided" speech was given by Lincoln on June 17, 1858, at Springfield, Illinois. In analyzing the Dred Scott decision, which revealed his acute yet homespun logic, Lincoln warned the Republican state convention that the legal foundations for extending slavery to the States may well be in a process of realization.

ABRAHAM LINCOLN:
A HOUSE DIVIDED AGAINST ITSELF
CANNOT STAND*

MR. PRESIDENT, AND GENTLEMEN OF THE CONVENTION: If we could first know where we are, and whither we are tending, we could better judge what to do, and how to do it. We are now far into the fifth year, since a policy was initiated with the avowed object, and confident promise, of putting an end to slavery agitation. Under the operation of that policy, that agitation has not only not ceased, but has constantly augmented. In my opinion, it will not cease, until a crisis shall have been reached and passed. "A house divided against itself cannot stand." I believe this government cannot endure permanently half slave and half free. I do not expect the Union to be dissolved—I do not expect the house to fall—but I do expect it will cease to be divided. It will become all one thing, or all the other. Either the opponents of slavery will arrest the further spread of it, and place it where the public mind shall rest in the belief that it is in the course of ultimate extinction; or its advocates will push it forward, till it shall become alike lawful in all the States, old as well as new—North as well as South.

Have we no tendency to the latter condition?

Let any one who doubts, carefully contemplate that now almost complete legal combination—piece of machinery, so to speak—compounded of the Nebraska doctrine, and the Dred Scott decision. Let him consider not only what work the machinery is adapted to do, and how well adapted; but also, let him study the history of its construction, and trace, if he can, or rather fail, if he can, to trace the evidences of design, and concert of action, among its chief architects, from the beginning.

The new year of 1854 found slavery excluded from more than half the States by State Constitutions, and from most of the national territory by Congressional prohibition. Four days later, commenced the struggle which ended in repealing that Congressional prohibition. This opened all the national territory to slavery, and was the first point gained.

But, so far, Congress only had acted; and an indorsement by the people, real or apparent, was indispensable, to save the point already gained, and give chance for more.

This necessity had not been overlooked; but had been provided for, as well as might be, in the notable argument of "squatter sovereignty," otherwise called "sacred right of self-government," which latter phrase, though expressive of the only rightful basis of any government, was so perverted in this attempted use of it as to amount to just this: That if any *one* man choose to enslave *another*, no *third* man shall be allowed to object. That argument was incorporated into the Nebraska bill itself, in the language which follows: "It being the true intent and meaning of this act not to legislate slavery into any Territory or State, nor to exclude it therefrom; but to leave the people thereof perfectly free to form and regulate their domestic institutions in their own way, subject only to the Constitution of the United States." Then opened the roar of loose declamation in favor of "Squatter Sovereignty," and "sacred right of self-government." "But," said opposition members, "let us amend the bill so as to expressly declare that the people of the

* Reprinted from *Political Debates Between Hon. Abraham Lincoln and Hon. Stephen A. Douglas* (Columbus, Ohio: 1860), pp. 1–5.

Territory may exclude slavery." "Not we," said the friends of the measure; and down they voted the amendment.

While the Nebraska bill was passing through Congress, a *law case* involving the question of a negro's freedom, by reason of his owner having voluntarily taken him first into a free State and then into a Territory covered by the Congressional prohibition, and held him as a slave for a long time in each, was passing through the U. S. Circuit Court for the District of Missouri; and both Nebraska bill and law suit were brought to a decision in the same month of May, 1854. The negro's name was "Dred Scott," which name now designates the decision finally made in the case. Before the then next Presidential election, the law case came to, and was argued in, the Supreme Court of the United States; but the decision of it was deferred until after the election. Still, before the election, Senator Trumbull, on the floor of the Senate, requested the leading advocate of the Nebraska bill to state *his opinion* whether the people of a Territory can constitutionally exclude slavery from their limits; and the latter answers: "That is a question for the Supreme Court."

The election came. Mr. Buchanan was elected, and the indorsement, such as it was, secured. That was the second point gained. The indorsement, however, fell short of a clear popular majority by nearly four hundred thousand votes, and so, perhaps, was not overwhelmingly reliable and satisfactory. The outgoing President, in his last annual message, as impressively as possible echoed back upon the people the weight and authority of the indorsement. The Supreme Court met again; did not announce their decision, but ordered a re-argument. The Presidential inauguration came, and still no decision of the court; but the incoming President in his inaugural address, fervently exhorted the people to abide by the forthcoming decision, whatever it might be. Then, in a few days, came the decision.

The reputed author of the Nebraska bill finds an early occasion to make a speech at this capital indorsing the Dred Scott decision, and vehemently denouncing all opposition to it. The new President, too, seizes the early occasion of the Silliman letter to indorse and strongly construe that decision, and to express his astonishment that any different view had ever been entertained!

At length a squabble springs up between the President and the author of the Nebraska bill, on the mere question of *fact,* whether the Lecompton Constitution was or was not, in any just sense, made by the people of Kansas; and in that quarrel the latter declares that all he wants is a fair vote for the people, and that he cares not whether slavery be voted *down* or voted *up.* I do not understand his declaration that he cares not whether slavery be voted down or voted up, to be intended by him other than as an apt definition of the policy he would impress upon the public mind—the principle for which he declares he has

suffered so much, and is ready to suffer to the end. And well may he cling to that principle. If he has any parental feeling, well may he cling to it. That principle is the only shred left of his original Nebraska doctrine. Under the Dred Scott decision "squatter sovereignty" squatted out of existence, tumbled down like temporary scaffolding—like the mould at the foundry served through one blast and fell back into loose sand—helped to carry an election, and then was kicked to the winds. His late joint struggle with the Republicans, against the Lecompton Constitution, involves nothing of the original Nebraska doctrine. That struggle was made on a point—the right of a people to make their own constitution—upon which he and the Republicans have never differed.

The several points of the Dred Scott decision, in connection with Senator Douglas's "care not" policy, constitute the piece of machinery, in its present state of advancement. This was the third point gained. The working points of that machinery are:

First, That no negro slave, imported as such from Africa, and no descendant of such slave, can ever be a citizen of any State, in the sense of that term as used in the Constitution of the United States. This point is made in order to deprive the negro, in every possible event, of the benefit of that provision of the United States Constitution, which declares that "The citizens of each State shall be entitled to all privileges and immunities of citizens in the several States."

Secondly, That "subject to the Constitution of the United States," neither Congress nor a Territorial Legislature can exclude slavery from any United States territory. This point is made in order that individual men may fill up the Territories with slaves, without danger of losing them as property, and thus to enhance the chances of permanency to the institution through all the future.

Thirdly, That whether the holding a negro in actual slavery in a free State, makes him free, as against the holder, the United States courts will not decide, but will leave to be decided by the courts of any slave State the negro may be forced into by the master. This point is made, not to be pressed immediately; but, if acquiesced in for awhile, and apparently indorsed by the people at an election, then to sustain the logical conclusion that what Dred Scott's master might lawfully do with Dred Scott, in the free State of Illinois, every other master may lawfully do with any other one, or one thousand slaves, in Illinois, or in any other free State.

Auxiliary to all this, and working hand in hand with it, the Nebraska doctrine, or what is left of it, is to educate and mould public opinion, at least Northern public opinion, not to care whether slavery is voted down or voted up. This shows exactly where we now are; and partially, also, whither we are tending.

It will throw additional light on the latter, to go back, and run the mind over the string of historical facts already stated. Several things will now appear less dark and mysterious than they did when they were transpiring. The people were to be left "perfectly free," "subject only to the Constitution." What the Constitution had to do with it, outsiders could not then see. Plainly enough now, it was an exactly fitted niche, for the Dred Scott decision to afterward come in, and declare the perfect freedom of the people to be just no freedom at all. Why was the amendment, expressly declaring the right of the people, voted down? Plainly enough now: the adoption of it would have spoiled the niche for the Dred Scott decision. Why was the court decision held up? Why even a Senator's individual opinion withheld, till after the Presidential election? Plainly enough now: the speaking out then would have damaged the perfectly free argument upon which the election was to be carried. Why the outgoing President's felicitation on the indorsement? Why the delay of a reargument? Why the incoming President's advance exhortation in favor of the decision? These things look like the cautious patting and petting of a spirited horse preparatory to mounting him, when it is dreaded that he may give the rider a fall. And why the hasty after-indorsement of the decision by the President and others?

We cannot absolutely know that all these exact adaptations are the result of preconcert. But when we see a lot of framed timbers, different portions of which we know have been gotten out at different times and places and by different workmen—Stephen, Franklin, Roger and James, for instance—and when we see these timbers joined together, and see they exactly make the frame of a house or a mill, all the tenons and mortices exactly fitting, and all the lengths and proportions of the different pieces exactly adapted to their respective places, and not a piece too many or too few—not omitting even scaffolding—or, if a single piece be lacking, we see the place in the frame exactly fitted and prepared yet to bring such piece in—in such a case, we find it impossible not to believe that Stephen and Franklin and Roger and James all understood one another from the beginning, and all worked upon a common plan or draft drawn up before the first blow was struck.

It should not be overlooked that, by the Nebraska bill, the people of a *State* as well as Territory, were to be left "perfectly free," "subject only to the Constitution." Why mention a State? They were legislating for Territories, and not for or about States. Certainly the people of a State are and ought to be subject to the Constitution of the United States; but why is mention of this lugged into this merely Territorial law? Why are the people of a Territory and the people of a State therein lumped together, and their relation to the Constitution therein treated as being precisely the same? While the opinion of the court, by Chief Justice Taney, in the Dred Scott case, and the separate opinions of all the

concurring Judges, expressly declare that the Constitution of the United States neither permits Congress nor a Territorial Legislature to exclude slavery from any United States Territory, they all omit to declare whether or not the same Constitution permits a State, or the people of a State, to exclude it. *Possibly,* this is a mere omission; but who can be quite sure, if McLean or Curtis had sought to get into the opinion a declaration of unlimited power in the people of a State to exclude slavery from their limits, just as Chase and Mace sought to get such declaration, in behalf of the people of a Territory, into the Nebraska bill;—I ask, who can be quite sure that it would not have been voted down in the one case as it had been in the other? The nearest approach to the point of declaring the power of a State over slavery, is made by Judge Nelson. He approaches it more than once, using the precise idea, and almost the language, too, of the Nebraska act. On one occasion, his exact language is, "except in cases where the power is restrained by the Constitution of the United States, the law of the State is supreme over the subject of slavery within its jurisdiction." In what cases the power of the States is so restrained by the United States Constitution, is left an open question, precisely as the same question, as to the restraint on the power of the Territories, was left open in the Nebraska act. Put this and that together, and we have another nice little niche, which we may, ere long, see filled with another Supreme Court decision, declaring that the Constitution of the United States does not permit a *State* to exclude slavery from its limits. And this may especially be expected if the doctrine of "care not whether slavery be voted down or voted up," shall gain upon the public mind sufficiently to give promise that such a decision can be maintained when made.

Such a decision is all that slavery now lacks of being alike lawful in all the States. Welcome, or unwelcome, such decision is probably coming, and will soon be upon us, unless the power of the present political dynasty shall be met and overthrown. We shall lie down pleasantly dreaming that the people of Missouri are on the verge of making their State free, and we shall awake to the reality instead, that the Supreme Court has made Illinois a slave State. To meet and overthrow the power of that dynasty, is the work now before all those who would prevent that consummation. That is what we have to do. How can we best do it?

There are those who denounce us openly to their own friends, and yet whisper us softly, that Senator Douglas is the aptest instrument there is with which to affect that object. They wish us to *infer* all, from the fact that he now has a little quarrel with the present head of the dynasty; and that he has regularly voted with us on a single point, upon which he and we have never differed. They remind us that he is a great man, and that the largest of us are very small ones. Let this be granted. But "a living dog is better than a dead lion." Judge Douglas, if not a dead lion, for this work, is at least a caged and toothless one. How can he oppose the advances of slavery? He don't care anything about it. His avowed mission is impressing the "public heart" to *care nothing about it*. A leading Douglas democratic newspaper thinks Douglas's superior talent will be needed to resist the revival of the African slave trade. Does Douglas believe an effort to revive that trade is approaching? He has not said so. Does he really think so? But if it is, how can he resist it? For years he has labored to prove it a sacred right of white men to take negro slaves into the new Territories. Can he possibly show that it is less a sacred right to buy them where they can be bought cheapest? And unquestionably they can be bought cheaper in Africa than in Virginia. He has done all in his power to reduce the whole question of slavery to one of a mere right of property; and as such, how can he oppose the foreign slave trade—how can he refuse that trade in that "property" shall be "perfectly free" —unless he does it as a protection to the home production? And as the home producers will probably not ask the protection, he will be wholly without a ground of opposition.

Senator Douglas holds, we know, that a man may rightfully be wiser to-day than he was yesterday—that he may rightfully change when he finds himself wrong. But can we, for that reason, run ahead, and infer that he will make any particular change, of which he, himself, has given no intimation? Can we safely base our action upon any such vague inference? Now, as ever, I wish not to misrepresent Judge Douglas's position, question his motives, or do aught that can be personally offensive to him. Whenever, if ever, he and we can come together on principle so that our cause may have assistance from his great ability, I hope to have interposed no adventitious obstacle. But clearly, he is not now with us—he does not pretend to be—he does not promise ever to be.

Our cause, then, must be intrusted to, and conducted by, its own undoubted friends—those whose hands are free, whose hearts are in the work—who *do care* for the result. Two years ago the Republicans of the nation mustered over thirteen hundred thousand strong. We did this under the single impulse of resistance to a common danger, with every external circumstance against us. Of strange, discordant, and even hostile elements, we gathered from the four winds, and formed and fought the battle through, under the constant hot fire of a disciplined, proud and pampered enemy. Did we brave all then, to falter now?—now, when that same enemy is wavering, dissevered and belligerent? The result is not doubtful. We shall not fail—if we stand firm, we *shall not fail*. Wise counsels may accelerate, or mistakes delay it, but, sooner or later, the victory is sure to come.

CHAPTER ELEVEN

LINCOLN AS PRESIDENTIAL LEADER

The presidential career of Abraham Lincoln is characterized by seeming contradictions and ambiguities. This is readily seen in two major areas: Lincoln's attitude toward the Negro and emancipation, and his extension of the presidential sphere of authority without at the same time exerting control over Congress. Despite the vast scholarship on Lincoln and the Civil War, he still remains an enigma to the historian. On the issue of Negro freedom, Richard N. Current, in the first selection, examined Lincoln's record in the prepresidential years and found that "the conclusion to be drawn is not clear." During this period Lincoln called merely for the containment of slavery and the need for gradual schemes of compensated emancipation. As President, he still lagged behind Congress, offering a plan of state initiative, compensation, Federal grants-in-aid, gradualism, and Negro colonization. Even the issuance of the Emancipation Proclamation reflects an ambivalence in Lincoln. Current observed, "Maybe he meant to hasten freedom, maybe to delay it. Nobody knows." Yet, Current concluded, Lincoln does merit his reputation as the Great Emancipator through the "example he set his fellow Americans by treating all men as human beings, regardless of the pigment of their skin." This paradox then in Lincoln's conduct is resolvable: the product of a Negrophobic environment, he revealed "tremendous power of growth," moving in a truly equalitarian direction.

David Donald in the second selection pointed out still another paradox: Lincoln's extension of the range of executive power, but his lack of control over Congress and the executive departments. For Donald, Lincoln's Whig background helped explain the phenomenon of a president "who simultaneously expanded and abdicated his powers." This Whig heritage stood for opposition to a strong executive, whether in relation to Congress or the administrative offices, and the belief that Congress was the supreme policy-making agency. Lincoln did not regard his actions as contradicting these principles. Rather, "necessity, not political theory, caused him to make his first sweeping assertions of executive authority during the secession crisis." This need to adopt war-time powers, a practice not denied by Whig doctrine, suggests an explanation of the inconsistencies in Lincoln's conduct. Donald concluded, "Both in strongly asserting his war powers and in weakly deferring to Congress, he was following the Whig creed in which he was raised."

240

RICHARD N. CURRENT:
ABRAHAM LINCOLN: THE FRIEND OF FREEDOM*

His hand trembled as he held the gold pen, ready to sign. He hesitated. Before him lay the broad sheet of paper on which was written the proclamation, complete except for his signature.

"Now, therefore I, Abraham Lincoln . . . on this first day of January, in the year of our Lord one thousand eight hundred and sixty-three . . . do order and declare that all persons held as slaves . . . are, and henceforward shall be free. . . ."

Finally, with several men about him in his office witnessing the act, he signed, writing out his full name (rather than the usual *A. Lincoln*). For all the care he took, his signature was noticeably uneven and infirm.

This, he insisted, was due to no hesitation or uncertainty about the policy he was proclaming. For three hours he had been shaking hands with the visitors who trooped into the White House from the mud and slush of a dismal, overcast New Year's Day. His hand was tired, swollen, hard to control.

Though, as he said, *he* had no doubt about the policy he was confirming, others since have disagreed as to what that policy actually was. Supposedly, of course, it was emancipation. Supposedly, with the trembling movement of his pen, he prepared the way for universal freedom even if he did not strike the shackles from the millions of bondsmen all at once. But possibly he was doing the opposite of what he seemed to do. Possibly he had adopted the idea of an Emancipation Proclamation as a stratagem to delay rather than to hasten the freeing of the slaves.

2

Some of the admirers of Lincoln, viewing the Emancipation Proclamation as the grand climax of his career, have thought of him as at heart an abolitionist, one who from early manhood had been awaiting his chance to put an end to slavery. This notion can be made to seem plausible enough if only a part of the record is revealed.

There is, for instance, the story of his second flatboat voyage down the Mississippi. He was then twenty-two. In New Orleans (the story goes) he with his companions attended a slave auction at which a "vigorous and comely" mulatto girl was being offered for sale. She was treated like a mare, the prospective bidders inspecting her up and down, pinching and feeling, and then watching while she was made to trot back and forth. To Lincoln the spectacle was so shameful it aroused in him at once an "unconquerable

hate" toward the whole institution of slavery. "If I ever get a chance to hit that thing," he swore as he walked away, "I'll hit it hard."

Lincoln perhaps took a stand for freedom as a member of the Illinois Legislature in 1837, when resolutions were introduced in response to the mob murder of Elijah Lovejoy, the antislavery newspaperman of Alton. These resolutions, instead of denouncing lynch law, condemned abolitionist societies and upheld slavery within the Southern States as "sacred" by virtue of the Federal Constitution. Lincoln refused to vote for the resolutions. Not only that. Together with a fellow member he drew up a protest against them, declaring that slavery was "founded on both injustice and bad policy."

Interesting also are his reflections on his experience of 1841, when with his friend Joshua Speed he was returning from a Kentucky visit. He made part of the trip by steamboat down the Ohio. "You may remember, as I well do," he wrote to Speed fourteen years later, in 1855, "that from Louisville to the mouth of the Ohio there were, on board, ten or a dozen slaves, shackled together with irons. That sight was a continual torment to me; and I see something like it every time I touch the Ohio, or any other slave-border." Speed, having resettled in Kentucky, had come to differ with Lincoln on the slavery question, and Lincoln now was defending his own point of view. "It is hardly fair for you to assume," he wrote, "that I have no interest in a thing which has, and continually exercises, the power of making me miserable."

As a member of Congress, in 1850, Lincoln drafted and introduced a bill for the abolition of slavery in the District of Columbia.

During the 1850s, in his arguments with Stephen A. Douglas, Lincoln spoke often and with eloquence against slavery. On one occasion, in 1854, he said he hated Douglas's attitude of indifference toward the spread of slavery to new areas. "I hate it because of the monstrous injustice of slavery itself," he declared. "I hate it because it deprives our republican example of its just influence in the world—enables the enemies of free institutions, with plausibility, to taunt us as hypocrites. . . ." On another occasion Lincoln made his oft-quoted remark that the nation could not long endure half slave and half free. No wonder many Southerners considered him "all broke out" with abolitionism at the time he was elected President.

After he was in the White House, Lincoln continued to express himself eloquently for freedom. In a published reply to Horace Greeley, who was demanding action against slavery, he said (1862) it was his "oft-expressed *personal* wish that all men every where could be free." He confided in a private letter (1864): "I am naturally anti-

* Reprinted with permission of McGraw-Hill Book Co., from *The Lincoln Nobody Knows* by Richard N. Current. Copyright © 1958 by Richard N. Current.

slavery. If slavery is not wrong, nothing is wrong. I can not remember when I did not so think, and feel." And in a talk to Indiana soldiers (1865) he remarked: "Whenever I hear anyone arguing for slavery I feel a strong impulse to see it tried on him personally."

On the basis of these and other items from the record, Lincoln appears to have been a long-confirmed advocate of freedom, if not an outright abolitionist. But when the whole of the evidence is considered, the conclusion to be drawn is not so clear.

It is not even clear whether in fact Lincoln ever underwent the New Orleans experience which was supposed to have made him an eternal foe of slavery. John Hanks told the anecdote to Herndon in 1865. Hanks had been one of Lincoln's fellow voyagers on the flatboat, but did not go all the way with the others to New Orleans. So he could not have seen with his own eyes what happened at the slave auction he later described. Herndon said he also heard the story from Lincoln himself. In the account of the journey he gave in his autobiography of 1860, however, Lincoln made no mention of slaves or the slave trade (though of course he intended the autobiography for campaign purposes and could not have been so indiscreet as to emphasize any abolitionist convictions). In the autobiography he also spoke of a previous trip to New Orleans. With regard to this trip, he said nothing about slaves but did refer to Negroes, recalling that he and his one companion "were attacked by seven Negroes with intent to kill and rob them" and were "hurt some in the melee, but succeeded in driving the Negroes from the boat."

As for his stand against the 1837 resolutions of the Illinois Legislature, it is enough to point out that he actually took a position against *both sides* of the controversy. Slavery was bad, he held, but he also contended that "the promulgation of abolition doctrines tends rather to increase than to abate its evils.

Regarding the shackled slaves on the Ohio river boat, he gave at the time, in 1841, an account very different from the one he gave fourteen years afterward to Joshua Speed. Writing to Speed's sister Mary (September 27, 1841) he described the scene on board the boat quite philosophically as exemplifying "the effect of *condition* upon human happiness." Here were a dozen slaves, "strung together like so many fish upon a trotline," who were being taken from their old Kentucky homes to be sold down the river, who were being separated from families and friends and carried off where slavery was reputed to be at its harshest. Yet, as Lincoln saw them, "they were the most cheerful and apparently happy creatures on board." He concluded that God "renders the worst of human conditions tolerable, while He permits the best, to be nothing better than tolerable."

The point is not that Lincoln was falsifying his emotions when, in the much later account to

Speed, he wrote of the sight of those slaves in chains as having been a "continual torment" to him. Certainly he had not forgotten the scene, and very likely he had come to view it in retrospect with heightened feeling. His attitude toward slaves and slavery might well have changed with the passing years—especially the years after 1850, when the issue of slavery extension engrossed national politics.

As late as 1847 his torment apparently was not troublesome enough to deter him from accepting a slaveholder as a law client and arguing against a slave's claim to freedom. Though Illinois presumably was a free state, its laws still provided for Negro servitude of a sort. Under the laws slave labor could be used, provided the slaves were not kept permanently in the state. Slaves worked the Coles County farm of Robert Matson, who brought his blacks from Kentucky every spring and took them back to Kentucky every fall. One of them, Jane Bryant, aroused the ire of Matson's housekeeper and mistress, who demanded that she be sold and sent to the Deep South. Jane fled, enlisted the aid of antislavery people, was taken from them, and, lacking the required certificate of freedom, was held in accordance with the Illinois laws. Matson, claiming her as his property, appealed to Lincoln for legal aid. Lincoln took the case and lost.

In Congress, despite his bill for abolition in the District of Columbia, he took a yes-and-no attitude toward slavery. His bill was carefully hedged about, so as to offend no slaveholder. It provided for gradual emancipation, with payment to owners, and it was not to go into effect unless approved by the "free white citizens" of the District, in a referendum. The bill did not please abolitionists. One of them, Wendell Phillips, called Lincoln "the slave hound of Illinois."

As for his remarks on slavery during the 1850s, it should be borne in mind that Lincoln always was opposing the spread of the institution into the territories. He was not advocating its destruction in the Southern states. When he said the nation could not long remain half slave and half free, but must eventually become all one or the other, he doubtless was thinking of the real danger that the country might become *all slave*—if slavery were allowed to spread. He resisted the aggressive proslavery forces not only because of his concern for the sufferings of the black man, but also because of his concern for the welfare of the white man. Again and again he indicated that the civil liberties of every American, white as well as black, were at stake. He insisted upon "keeping the territories free for the settlement of free laborers." He was a free-soil man.

"You enquire where I now stand," he wrote in his letter of 1854 to Joshua Speed. "That is a disputed point. I think I am a Whig; but others say there are no Whigs, and that I am an abolitionist." And then he stated the limits of his antislavery zeal as precisely as he could: "I now do no more than oppose the *extension* of slavery."

That was where he stood in 1854, and there is no convincing evidence that he had moved beyond that position by 1860 or 1861.

In fact, in the most widely read of his pre-nomination speeches, the one at Cooper Union in New York on February 27, 1860, Lincoln said he agreed with Thomas Jefferson and other founding fathers that slavery should be merely contained, not directly attacked. *"This is all Republicans ask —all Republicans desire—in relation to slavery,"* he emphasized, underlining the words. *"As those fathers marked it, so let it be again marked, as an evil not to be extended, but to be tolerated and protected only because of and so far as its actual presence among us makes that toleration and protection a necessity."* Lincoln further said that emancipation should be most gradual and should be accompanied by deportation of the freed slaves. "In the language of Mr. Jefferson, uttered many years ago, 'It is still in our power to direct the process of emancipation, and deportation, peaceably, and in such slow degrees, as that the evil will wear off insensibly; and their places be, *pari passu,* filled up by free white laborers. If, on the contrary, it is left to force itself on, human nature must shudder at the prospect held up.' "

3

As President, even if he personally had desired immediate emancipation, Lincoln had reasons of policy for going slow with regard to slavery. At the outset of the war the border slave states—Maryland, Delaware, Missouri, and above all Kentucky—hung in the balance. It seemed to Lincoln essential that these states be kept loyal to the Union, and it also seemed to him that a forthright antislavery program might incline them toward the Confederacy.

Whatever the reasons, Lincoln in the beginning was most reluctant to use his Presidential powers against slavery. During his first year and more in office he lagged well behind the majority of his party in the cause of freedom. If, as he said, General McClellan had "the slows" when it came to advancing against the Confederate army, he himself had the same affliction when it was a matter of attacking the institution which Alexander H. Stephens called the cornerstone of the Confederacy.

Lincoln held back while Congress and some of his generals went ahead. General John C. Frémont proclaimed freedom for the slaves of disloyal masters in Missouri, and General David Hunter did the same for those in Georgia, South Carolina, and Florida. Lincoln revoked the proclamations of Frémont and Hunter, much to the disgust of all antislavery people, who were growing fast in numbers and in earnestness throughout the North. In the summer of 1861 Congress passed a confiscation act which freed such slaves as the foe put to military use. The next summer Congress passed a second confiscation act, which declared "forever free" all slaves whose owners were in rebellion, whether or not the slaves were being used for military purposes. Lincoln did not veto these laws, but neither did he see that they faithfully were carried out. He considered vetoing the second one, because in his judgment it amounted to an unconstitutional bill of attainder. He did not sign it until it had been amended, and even then he expressed to Congress his dissatisfaction with it.

While hesitating to enforce these laws, Lincoln responded in his own way to the rising sentiment in favor of emancipation. He came forth with a characteristically Lincolnian solution to the slavery problem. His plan contained five elements. First, the states themselves must emancipate the slaves, for in his opinion slavery was a "domestic" institution, the concern of the states alone. Second, slaveowners must be paid for the chattels of which they were to be deprived. Third, the Federal government must share the financial burden by providing Federal bonds as grants-in-aid to the states. Fourth, the actual freeing of the slaves must not be hurried; the states must be given plenty of time, delaying final freedom until as late as 1900 if they wished. Fifth, the freed Negroes must be shipped out of the country and colonized abroad, but they must be persuaded to go willingly. State action, compensation, Federal aid, gradual emancipation, and voluntary colonization—these were the indispensable features of the Lincoln plan.

To carry out this plan he had to gain the approval of Congress, the border slave states, and the leaders of the Negro race. Congress responded affirmatively but without enthusiasm, indicating its willingness to vote the necessary funds. None of the border politicians were won over to the scheme, however, and very few Negroes could be persuaded to leave their native land, the United States.

Three times in the spring of 1862 Lincoln appealed to the border-state congressmen. He told them that, if their states would only act, the war soon would be over, for the Confederacy lived upon the hope of winning the border states, and, once these had declared for freedom, that hope would be gone. He warned the congressmen that, if their states refused to act, slavery in time would disappear anyhow. It would be destroyed "by mere friction and abrasion—by the mere incidents of war." The border states, he eloquently said, had before them the grand opportunity of saving the Union. But he made no headway whatsoever; again and again they turned the opportunity down.

Meanwhile he did not let up in his efforts to talk the free Negroes into leaving the country. Some of their own leaders advocated starting life anew in the Negro republic of Liberia or Haiti. Lincoln preferred Central America as their new home. In his eagerness he was taken in by a group of land speculators who offered to sell the Chiriqui territory on the Isthmus of Panama. They pictured Chiriqui as a land rich in coal, among other things, but eventually became so effusive in their praises of this tropical paradise it became clear that their title was dubious and the resources nonexistent.

He was nevertheless loath to give up the colonization idea itself. He invited to the White House a group of five prominent Negroes—the first of their race a President ever so honored—and he honored them further by saying frankly that there was no place for them and their people in the United States. Though they might be treated better in the North than in the South, they would suffer discrimination everywhere so long as they remained in this country. "The ban," he said, "is still upon you." From Negroes who heard of this interview, the response was most unfavorable. One wrote to Lincoln: "Pray tell us is our right to a home in this country less than your own?"

If, in the summer of 1862, Lincoln had had his way, the later history of this country would have been radically changed. For instance, if the states had adopted his plan, there would probably be few Negroes left in the country, North or South. By 1900 the slaves of the border states would have been set free and sent abroad. The slaves of the Confederate states, if these states too had chosen to adopt the Lincoln plan, would have enjoyed the same fortune or suffered the same fate.

If, on the other hand, the war had come to an early end, as Lincoln hoped, the slaves of the Confederate states could have been left in bondage indefinitely, or at least until they were freed by some hand other than his. Even in the border states, after emancipation, slavery might have been reestablished by action of the states. What these states had done, they could undo, according to Lincoln's conception of State rights. Indeed, in order to discourage this contingency, he drafted an emancipation bill containing the proviso that, if any state should abolish and then reintroduce the institution, it would have to return to the Federal government the Federal funds it had received as a grant-in-aid!

4

President Lincoln did not behave like a great emancipator during the first year-and-a-half of his term of office. The question is, did he change his mind and his policy after that? More particularly, did he intend—with the preliminary proclamation of September 21, 1862, and the final one of January 1, 1863—to free the slaves?

According to most accounts, he did. Despite his campaign pledges and the constraints of the Constitution, argue supporters of this position, he decided that he must strike at slavery for reasons of military necessity. He came to this conclusion, and drafted a fitting proclamation, in July of 1862. When he read this draft to his Cabinet, Seward advised him to withhold the announcement till the Union armies had won a victory on the battlefield. Otherwise, Seward cautioned, the proclamation might sound like a confession of military failure, like "the last *shriek* on our retreat." So Lincoln stalled, awaiting the hoped-for victory. When a delegation of Chicago churchmen appealed to him, he asked them whether a proclamation would do any good, whether it would not be as futile as the Pope's legendary bull against the comet. Before they left, he assured them that he had not decided against a proclamation, but held the matter under advisement. When Horace Greeley in the *New York Tribune* called upon him to make freedom a reality, he patiently replied (August 22, 1862): "My paramount object in this struggle *is* to save the Union, and is *not* either to save or to destroy slavery. If I could save the Union without freeing *any* slave I would do it, and if I could save it by freeing *all* the slaves I would do it; and if I could do it by freeing some and leaving others alone I would also do that." At last McClellan's checking of Lee at Antietam gave Lincoln at least a substitute for victory, and a few days later he accordingly issued the document he long since had decided upon.

This is a familiar story, and there is a certain amount of evidence to give it historical substance. There is, for example, the record Welles made of a conversation Lincoln had with him and Seward on Sunday, July 13, while on a carriage ride to a funeral. "It was on this occasion and on this ride that he first mentioned to Mr. Seward and myself the subject of emancipating the slaves by proclamation in case the Rebels did not cease to persist in their war on the Government and the Union, of which he saw no evidence," Wells wrote afterward. "He dwelt earnestly on the gravity, importance, and delicacy of the movement, said he had given it much thought and had about come to the conclusion that it was a military necessity absolutely essential for the salvation of the Union, that we must free the slaves or be ourselves subdued, etc., etc." Welles added this comment: "It was a new departure for the President, for until this time, in all our previous interviews, whenever the question of emancipation or the mitigation of slavery had been in any way alluded to, he had been prompt and emphatic in denouncing any interference by the General Government with the subject."

Welles may have remembered accurately what the President said on that Sunday, though the record of the conversation is not a regular diary entry but a reminiscence that the diarist put down after the lapse of considerable time. And Lincoln, if Welles summarized his sentiments accurately, may have meant what he said. Yet in the ensuing weeks others who saw Lincoln reported him as saying things that seemed to belie his determination to proclaim freedom for the slaves. When Greeley visited the White House to repeat the plea of his *Tribune* editorial, Lincoln protested that he dared not antagonize Kentuckians and impel them to desert to the rebel side.

He expressed this same concern to others, including the Chicago religious group. If he really had made his decision and only was waiting for the auspicious moment to proclaim it, he might have put off his tormenters by frankly telling them so. As it was, he left even some of his official advisers to wonder whether he ever would issue the proclamation he had read to the cabinet.

These inconsistencies of his have led to the suspicion that, till after the battle of Antietam, he made no irrevocable commitment, even to himself. Here and there he dropped hints that he might issue the proclamation—and then again might not. Apparently his purpose was to prepare his hearers for the possibility that he might call the whole thing off. He was waiting for a decisive victory, but if that kind of victory had come, he might have forgotten about the proclamation. Some historians claim that he dusted it off and gave it to the world only when he learned the true proportions of Antietam. McClellan, though he turned Lee back, had let him get away. If McClellan had administered a crushing defeat, the proclamation might have stayed in its pigeonhole.

This theory depends on the supposition that Lincoln at the time was not so much concerned about military necessity as about political necessity. He had to contend with a strong bloc of Republicans in Congress, headed by Thaddeus Stevens in the House and Charles Sumner and Henry Wilson in the Senate, backed by a majority of the party, who had become Radicals on the slave question. They were demanding that the President carry out the laws, the confiscation acts, the act for the enrolment of Negro troops. They held the firm conviction that, to win the war, the government must free the slaves and use them against their former masters. As their strongest argument, the Radicals cited the succession of Union defeats on the Virginia front. The way the war was being fought, it was not being won, and it therefore must be fought another way. There was even the possibility that they might try to stop the flow of money and supplies if Lincoln did not give in. Only a conclusive victory, only a dramatic refutation of the Radical argument, would restore his freedom of action. He prayed for such a victory, and then came the disappointing news of Antietam.

To pursue this argument to its logical conclusion, Lincoln then pulled out the proclamation as his trump. In issuing it he did not really yield to the Radicals. Rather, he outfoxed them. At first they hailed the document as a triumph for them and their cause, but soon they were disillusioned, since the proclamation had as its purpose and effect the checking of the Radical program. Having announced in September that he would make a final proclamation the first of the following year, Lincoln had an excuse for disregarding the laws about confiscation and Negro troops throughout the intervening months. He also had a policy with which to frustrate Stevens's drive for legislation to make soldiers and freemen out of slaves from the border states. During the months of delay he hoped at last to gain approval for his own plan, the familiar plan of gradual emancipation by the states themselves, with Federal funds to pay to slaveowners and to rid the country of the freed slaves.

There is testimony, from some of the men who knew Lincoln, to give credence to this view. There is, for instance, the testimony of Edward Stanly, a proslavery, State-rights, Unionist North Carolinian whom Lincoln had appointed as military governor of the occupied North Carolina coast. Stanly had taken the job with the understanding that Lincoln would not interfere with slavery in the states. Once the proclamation had been issued, Stanly went to Washington intending to resign. After several talks with Lincoln, however, Stanly was satisfied. He returned to his job, but first he called at the office of James C. Welling, editor of the *National Intelligencer*. Welling wrote in his diary: "Mr. Stanly said that the President had stated to him that the proclamation had become a civil necessity to prevent the Radicals from openly embarrassing the government in the conduct of the war."

Quite apart from testimony such as this, a fairly strong inference of Lincoln's delaying tactics can be drawn from the text of the proclamation. The preliminary announcement said that after January 1, 1863, the slaves in states then still in rebellion would be considered free. The final proclamation excluded from the area of freedom not only the loyal border states but all the Confederate states and parts of states that the Union forces had occupied. As cynics pointed out at the time, Lincoln was leaving the slaves untouched in places where he had the ability to free them, and he was offering liberty only to those he had no power to reach. Congress already had enabled him to do more than this. The second confiscation act provided for the liberation of all slaves belonging to disloyal masters, regardless of the masters' residence. Instead of issuing the kind of proclamation that he did, Lincoln needed only to proclaim that he was enforcing the second confiscation act, and then he could have proceeded to order the seizure of enemy-owned slaves in every place where the Union armies got control—if his object truly had been to weaken the enemy by making inroads into his Negro manpower.

Lincoln himself gave indisputable proof that, after the preliminary proclamation, he remained as passionately devoted as ever to his own gradual-emancipation scheme. In his message to Congress of December 1, 1862, just one month before the final proclamation, he had little to say about that forthcoming pronouncement and much to say about his favored plan. He proposed a constitutional amendment to put the plan into effect. On this subject he reached one of the peaks of his eloquence. "Fellow-citizens, *we* cannot escape history," he said. "We of this Congress and this administration, will be remembered in spite of ourselves. The fiery trial through which we pass, will light us down, in honor or dishonor, to the latest generation." These words are justly famous. What is often forgotten is the fact that they were conceived as part of a plea for deporting American-born Negroes from America. Lincoln in this message actually used the word *deportation,* as if he had in the back of his mind the thought of resorting, if necessary, to the compulsion which that word implies.

No inspired phrases were to be found in the paper that Lincoln signed with the gold pen, in the quavering hand, on January 1, 1863. In itself this proclamation was a dull and prosaic document—no ringing call to freedom. The proclamation had some effect in attracting slaves out of rebeldom and into the Union lines, where they were set free, but the existing laws of Congress provided for that much and more. After two years, when the war was ending, Lincoln estimated that some 200,000 slaves had gained their liberty under his edict. That was only about one in twenty of the total number of slaves, which amounted to nearly four million. And even that minority had no sure hold on freedom. Lincoln himself doubted the constitutionality of his step, except as a temporary war measure. After the war the freedmen would have risked reenslavement, had nothing else been done to confirm their liberty.

All this does not necessarily disprove the commonly accepted story of what Lincoln did or tried to do in signing his famous proclamation. Maybe he meant to hasten freedom, maybe to delay it. Nobody knows.

5

Actually freedom for the Negroes—or at least the end of chattel slavery—came in consequence of the Thirteenth Amendment. President Lincoln played a part in bringing about this constitutional change, yet he was slow to take an out-and-out antislavery stand, and indeed he gave some indications that his conversion never was complete.

He did not claim to have originated the idea of such an amendment, though the abolitionists did. At Cleveland in May 1864 a group of these extreme Republicans nominated John C. Frémont for the Presidency and adopted a platform with a Thirteenth Amendment as the key plank.

When the regular Republicans met in convention the following month, Lincoln was aware of the need for winning the dissidents back to the party fold. He called to the White House the chairman of the Republican National Committee, Senator E. D. Morgan, and gave him instructions for his speech opening the convention. "Senator Morgan," he is reported to have said, "I want you to mention in your speech when you call the convention to order, as its keynote, and to put into the platform as the keystone, the amendment of the Constitution abolishing and prohibiting slavery forever." Senator Morgan did as the President wished. That platform included a plank stating that slavery was the cause of the rebellion, that the President's proclamations had aimed "a death blow at this gigantic evil," and that a constitutional amendment was necessary to "terminate and forever prohibit" it. Undoubtedly the delegates would have adopted such a plank whether or not Lincoln, through Senator Morgan, had urged it.

When Lincoln was reelected on this platform, and the Republican majority in Congress was increased, he was justified in feeling, as he apparently did, that he had a mandate from the people for the Thirteenth Amendment. The newly chosen Congress, with its overwhelming Republican majority, would not meet until after the Lame Duck Session of the old Congress during the winter of 1864–1865. But Lincoln did not wait. Using all his resources of patronage and persuasion on certain of the Democrats, he managed to get the necessary two-thirds vote before the session's end. He rejoiced as the amendment went out to the states for ratification, and he rejoiced again and again as his own Illinois led off and other states followed one by one in acting favorably upon it. He did not live to rejoice in its ultimate adoption.

Yet, for all he did to see that freedom finally was written into the fundamental law, Lincoln to the last seemed to have a lingering preference for another kind of amendment, another kind of plan. He still clung to his old ideas of postponing final emancipation, compensating slaveholders, and colonizing freedmen. Or so it would appear. As late as March of 1865, if the somewhat dubious Ben Butler is to be believed, Lincoln summoned him to the White House to discuss with him the feasibility of removing the colored population of the United States.

6

Lincoln is a paradoxical hero. His name has been lighted down from generation to generation as a synonym for liberty and equality. His name also has been made to symbolize the opposite doctrine of white supremacy and black oppression.

Lincoln the friend of freedom is well and widely known. For most liberals, he occupies a place beside that of Thomas Jefferson. For many Negroes, he long has held a lone position as a kind of folk god.

His exaltation dates back to January 1, 1863, when throughout the North and the conquered areas of the South the colored people held proclamation meetings to celebrate his deed in their behalf. At a Washington meeting, which began on New Year's Eve, a pastor told each member of his flock to "get down on *both knees* to thank Almighty God for his freedom and President Lincoln too." To people such as these the proclamation, whatever its inward meaning, was the outward sign of an answer to their prayers.

Most of the abolitionists joined in honoring

Lincoln at the time of his emancipation edict, but some of them qualified their praise, still doubting his sincerity. At last, when he had won Congressional approval for the Thirteenth Amendment, almost all the lingering doubts were dispelled and almost all the doubters satisfied. Even William Lloyd Garrison no longer could contain himself. To a Boston meeting of celebrators Garrison said: "And to whom is the country more immediately indebted for this vital and saving amendment of the Constitution than, perhaps, to any other man? I believe I may confidently answer—to the humble rail splitter of Illinois— to the Presidential chainbreaker for millions of the oppressed—to Abraham Lincoln!"

Less well known than Lincoln the slaves' chainbreaker is Lincoln the hero of Negro-baiters and white supremacists. Yet he has been that kind of image also. Few Negroes or friends of the Negro ever admired him more or praised him oftener than did a certain Mississippi advocate of white supremacy, James K. Vardaman . . . .

Vardaman never tired of praising "the immortal Lincoln," never tired of quoting "the wise words of this wondrous man." He insisted that he and Lincoln saw eye to eye. "I have made a very careful study of Mr. Lincoln's ideas on this question," he declared in a Senate speech, "and I have said often, and I repeat here, that my views and his on the race question are substantially identical." Next to Thomas Jefferson, he thought, Lincoln understood the Negro problem better than anyone else of former days. To prove his point, Vardaman cited Lincoln's advocacy of Negro colonization. He explained the Lincoln policy thus:

"Up to the very time of Mr. Lincoln's death he told the Negroes who came to see him here in Washington, 'You will not be permitted to share in the government of this country, and I am not prepared to say that you ought to be, if I had the power to give you that right.'

"He said further: 'The shackles of slavery will be stricken from your arms. You, the educated and more fortunate members of your race, take the others and go to some country'—his idea was the same that Jefferson's was—'and there work out your own salvation.' I do not pretend to quote Mr. Lincoln literally. The great desire of his patriotic heart was that the friction might be avoided by deportation."

The words of Lincoln that Vardaman repeated oftenest, the words he knew almost by heart, came from the debate with Douglas at Charleston, Illinois, on September 18, 1858. These words formed for Vardaman a sort of golden text. Here they are, exactly as Lincoln uttered them:

"I will say then that I am not, nor ever have been in favor of bringing about in any way the social and political equality of the white and black races, [applause]—that I am not nor ever have been in favor of making voters or jurors of Negroes, nor of qualifying them to hold office, nor to intermarry with white people; and I will say in addition to this that there is a physical difference between the white and black races which I believe will forever forbid the two races living together on terms of social and political equality. And inasmuch as they cannot so live, while they do remain together there must be the position of superior and inferior, and I as much as any other man am in favor of having the superior position assigned to the white race."

7

Yet, despite these contradictions, Lincoln does deserve his reputation as emancipator. True, his claim to the honor is supported very uncertainly, if at all, by the proclamation itself. The honor has a better basis in the support he gave to the Thirteenth Amendment. It is well founded also in his greatness as the war leader, who carried the nation safely through the four-year struggle that brought freedom in its train. But the best reason for his reputation is, perhaps, to be discovered in something else. Consider the example he set his fellow Americans by treating all men as human beings, regardless of the pigment of their skin.

The real and final emancipation of the Negro may depend more upon attitudes than upon laws. The laws, the constitutional amendments, are important, even indispensable. But, as the abolitionist Henry Wilson observed, many of those who voted for the Thirteenth Amendment and other antislavery measures did so without conversion or conviction. Many acted from a desire to hurt the slaveholder rather than to help the slave. Within their hearts still lurked the "foul spirit of caste," the spirit of race prejudice. Until this prejudice was overcome, the Negroes, though no longer the slaves of individual masters, would continue to be in a sense the slaves of the community as a whole.

Now, Lincoln himself was one of those who veered to an actively antislavery line for reasons of wartime expediency. He did not pretend to do otherwise. And he was well aware of race prejudice as an existing fact in the United States. Hence his pathetic eagerness to find new homes for freedmen in foreign lands. Yet he had the capacity to rise above prejudice, and he grandly rose above it. Again and again, during the last two years of his life, he made the White House a scene of practical demonstrations of respect for human worth and dignity. He proved that whites and Negroes, without the master-servant tie, could get along together happily in his own official home, no matter what the antagonisms that might trouble the nation at large. A kindly, unself-conscious host, he greeted Negro visitors as no President had done before.

The distinguished former slave Frederick Douglass called upon Lincoln several times at his summer cottage at the Soldiers' Home. Douglass made at least three visits to the White House. On the final occasion, when he tried to enter as an invited guest at the inaugural reception in

1865, policemen manhandled him and forced him out. Making his way in again, he managed to catch Lincoln's eye. "Here comes my friend Douglass," the President exclaimed, and, leaving the circle of guests he had been conversing with, he took Douglass by the hand and began to chat with him. Years later Douglass wrote: "In all my interviews with Mr. Lincoln I was impressed with his entire freedom from popular prejudice against the colored race. He was the first great man that I talked with in the United States freely, who in no single instance reminded me of the difference between himself and myself, of the difference of color, and I thought that all the more remarkable because he came from a state where there were black laws."

There were black laws in Illinois indeed— laws that denied the Negro the vote and deprived him of other rights. Illinois in those days was a Jim Crow state. That was where Lincoln had spent most of the years of his manhood, among people who had migrated from slave country farther south, as he himself had done. Naturally he had shared some of the Negrophobic feeling of his neighbors in Kentucky, in southern Indiana, in central Illinois. That was where, in geography and in sentiment, he came from.

But he did not stay there. The most remarkable thing about him was his tremendous power of growth. He grew in sympathy, in the breadth of his humaneness, as he grew in other aspects of the mind and spirit. In more ways than one he succeeded in breaking through the narrow bounds of his early environment.

This helps to explain and to reconcile those conflicting images of Lincoln—on the one hand, the racist; on the other, the champion of the common man, black as well as white. The one view reflects the position he started from, the other the position he was moving toward. There is confusion regarding particular phases of his Presidential career because nobody knows for sure just what point he had reached at any given moment. But there should be little question as to which way he was going.

To see Lincoln in this light is to make him more than ever relevant, more than ever inspiring, for us in the stormy present, in the fiery trial through which we too must pass. Lincoln, as a symbol of man's ability to outgrow his prejudices, still serves the cause of human freedom. He will go on serving so long as boundaries of color hem in and hinder any man, any woman, any child.

DAVID DONALD:
ABRAHAM LINCOLN: WHIG IN THE WHITE HOUSE*

The presidency of Abraham Lincoln poses a peculiar paradox to students of the American government. The most careful historian of the Civil War period, J. G. Randall, concluded that Lincoln extended the President's "sphere of activity throughout the whole government—civil and military, state and Federal, legislative and judicial as well as executive." A distinguished political scientist, W. E. Binkley, agrees that Lincoln unquestionably set "the high-water mark of the exercise of executive power in the United States." On the other hand, Edward S. Corwin, who has made a lifelong study of the American presidency, notes that Lincoln, "a spoilsman" with no conception of the requirements of sound administration, failed to exert much influence over Congress and permitted the Civil War to be fought "by a kind diarchy," with each end of Pennsylvania Avenue carrying on its own campaign against the Confederates. Recognizing that Lincoln "added a new dimension to the Presidency in the presence of national emergency," Professor Corwin concludes that his incumbency was "in certain other respects a calamity for the

office." The paradox has been most neatly posed in an able book, *The American Presidency*, by Clinton Rossiter, who asserts on one page that "Lincoln pushed the powers of the Presidency to a new plateau high above any conception of executive authority hitherto imagined in this country," but adds on the next that "Lincoln . . . left the Presidency temporarily enfeebled."

I

For the view that Lincoln dramatically extended the range of executive power there is certainly abundant evidence. In 1861 when the Confederates fired upon Fort Sumter he acted with such vigorous promptness that his critics cried out against his "dictatorship." Without consulting Congress, he decided that a state of war existed, summoned the militia to defeat this combination "too powerful to be suppressed by the ordinary course of judicial proceedings," and enlarged the size of the regular United States army. Without congressional appropriation or approval he entrusted two million dollars of government funds to his private agents in New York in order to pay for "military and naval measures necessary for the defense and support of the government." Directing General Winfield Scott "to suspend the writ of Habeas Corpus for the public safety," he authorized the arbitrary arrest

---

* Reprinted from David Donald, "Abraham Lincoln: Whig in the White House," in Norman A. Graebner, ed., *The Enduring Lincoln* (Urbana: Univ. of Illinois Press, 1959), pp. 47–66 by permission.

of suspected secessionists and other enemies of the government.

As the war progressed Lincoln further extended his executive powers, even in the loyal states of the Union. "[B]y degrees," as he explained in 1863, he had come to feel that "strong measures" were "indispensable to the public Safety." Civil rights throughout the North were drastically curbed. Both Secretary of State William H. Seward, who was in charge of the arbitrary arrests made during 1861, and Secretary of War Edwin M. Stanton, who took control in the following year, exercised power "almost as free from restraint as a dictator or a sultan." Nobody knows how many Northern civilians were imprisoned without due process of law; estimates range from fifteen thousand to thirty-eight thousand. It required but a line from the President to close down a censorious newspaper, to banish a Democratic politician, or to arrest suspected members of a state legislature.

Over the Union armed forces, too, Lincoln exercised unprecedented authority. Presidential order, not congressional enactment, instituted in 1862 the first national program of conscription in United States history. Disregarding the explicit constitutional provision that Congress should "make Rules for the Government and Regulation of the land and naval Forces," Lincoln authorized Professor Francis Lieber to draw up and General Henry W. Halleck to proclaim General Orders No. 100, spelling out the legal rules for the conduct of the war.

Lincoln took quite literally the constitutional provision that "The President shall be Commander in Chief of the Army and Navy of the United States." He not merely appointed and removed generals; he attempted to plan their campaigns. At his insistence General Irvin McDowell advanced to First Bull Run and to defeat in July, 1861. Lincoln's unsolicited strategic advice drove General George B. McClellan, McDowell's successor, into hiding at the house of a friend so as to escape "browsing presidents." During the winter of 1861 when McClellan, ill with typhoid, did not advance, Lincoln issued his unprecedented President's General War Order No. 1, taking personal direction of five Union armies and two naval flotillas and ordering them simultaneously to advance on February 22. The fact that General McClellan, upon recovering, persuaded Lincoln to abandon his plan did not mean the end of presidential war-making. In fact, even at the end of the war, after Lincoln had named U. S. Grant general-in-chief, the President continued to have a personal hand in shaping Union strategy. Lincoln himself bluntly declared that should he think any plan of campaign ill-advised, he "would scarcely allow the attempt to be made, if the general in command should desire to make it."

To an even greater extent Lincoln asserted his presidential powers over the rebellious South. His Emancipation Proclamation, which Charles A. Beard called "the most stupendous act of sequestration in the history of Anglo-Saxon jurisprudence," was a presidential act, performed without authorization from Congress—performed, indeed, when the President thought Congress had no power to authorize it. Lincoln's December, 1863, proclamation of amnesty and pardon marked another major expansion of presidential powers. Without the approval of Congress he established provisional courts in conquered Southern states and gave them "the unlimited power of determining every question that could be the subject of judicial decision." In naming military governors for the states of Louisiana, Arkansas, and Tennessee, the President, again without congressional authorization, created offices unknown to the American Constitution. In establishing new and securely loyal administrations in these ex-Confederate states, the military governors were not obliged to observe normal constitutional procedures. Lincoln himself directed them: "Follow forms of law as far as convenient. . . ."

Lincoln's record, then, abundantly justifies the conclusion of George Fort Milton that no other President in American history has "found so many new sources of executive power, nor so expanded and perfected those others already had used."

II

But there is another aspect of the Lincoln administration. Less than any other major American President did Lincoln control or even influence the Congress. Noting that many of the Civil War congressmen were his seniors and humbly declaring "that many of you have more experience than I, in the conduct of public affairs," Lincoln bowed not merely to the will but to the caprice of the legislators. In making appointments, he regularly deferred to the Republican delegation from each state. He acquiesced in the Senate's right to veto appointments by refusing to resubmit any nomination which the Senate had rejected. Even upon a matter so clearly within presidential prerogative as extending recognition to Haiti and Liberia, Lincoln declined to act until Congress assented, because, he declared, he was "Unwilling . . . to inaugurate a novel policy . . . without the approbation of Congress."

The President had remarkably little connection with the legislation passed during the Civil War. He proposed few specific laws to Congress; his bill for compensated emancipation is notably exceptional. He exerted little influence in securing the adoption of bills that were introduced. In some of the most significant legislation enacted during his administration Lincoln showed little interest. The laws providing for the construction of a Pacific railroad, for the creation of the Department of Agriculture, for the importation of "contract laborers" from Europe, for the tariff protection of American manufacturers, and for the establishment of land-grant colleges had little connection with Lincoln aside from his formal approval of them. That approval was usually granted without hesitation. Less than any other important American President did Lincoln use his veto power. He vetoed only two measures outright, an unimportant bill concerning bank notes in the District of Columbia and an act dealing with army medical officers which carelessly duplicated another he had already signed. One of his two pocket vetoes was equally trivial. The other, his highly significant refusal to sign the Wade-Davis Bill, indicated that the President thought that reconstruction was an executive, not a legislative, responsibility. Within the area of what he considered legitimate congressional power Lincoln was careful never to interfere.

Lincoln was also ineffectual in controlling the executive departments of the government. He and his cabinet never formed a unified administration. During his first months as President, Lincoln did not schedule regular cabinet meetings at all. When he later did so, at the request of the cabinet members themselves, he rarely discussed major policy decisions with his constitutional advisers. Sometimes the President himself was not present at these meetings, and soon the department heads became lax in attendance. The Secretary of State preferred to meet with the President privately—to regale him, enemies said, with vulgar stories; the Secretary of War declined to discuss his plans in cabinet meeting because he thought, with some justice, that his colleagues could not be trusted with military secrets; Salmon P. Chase, the Secretary of the Treasury, refused to waste his time attending sessions of this "so-called Cabinet." "We . . . are called members of the Cabinet," Chase indignantly protested, "but are in reality only separate heads of departments, meeting now and then for talk on whatever happens to come uppermost, not for grave consultation on matters concerning the salvation of the country."

To most of his departmental chiefs Lincoln gave a completely free hand. His Attorney-General, Postmaster-General, Secretary of the Interior, and Secretary of the Navy conducted their departmental affairs virtually without oversight or interference from the President. Even over a critical area like the Treasury Department Lincoln exerted little control. Though some of the most important financial legislation in American history was adopted during the Civil War years, Lincoln had little interest in floating bond issues, creating an internal revenue system, inaugurating the first income tax, or establishing a national banking system. Repeatedly Chase tried to bring such weighty issues to the President's attention, but Lincoln brushed him aside, saying: "You understand these matters: I do not."

Even in the conduct of foreign relations the President himself played a minor role. It is a charming fancy to think of Lincoln as a "diplomat in carpet slippers," applying homely common sense and frontier wisdom to the preservation of international peace. In fact, however, after curbing Seward's belligerent tendencies early in 1861, the President willingly left diplomacy to his able Secretary of State. In Lincoln's *Collected Works* there is notably little about foreign affairs, aside from routine diplomatic communications, which were of course written by Seward, extending congratulations to Alexander II of Russia upon the birth of a son named "Pierre to Madame the Grand Duchess Alexandra Petrovna, Spouse of Your Imperial Majestys well beloved brother His Imperial Highness Monseigneur the Grand Duke Nicholas Nicolaewitch" or offering condolences upon the demise of "His Royal Hig[h]ness the Hereditary Prince Frederick Ferdinand, of Denmark."

Even over the War Department, in which Lincoln took such a direct, personal interest, the President did not exercise unrestricted authority. Secretary Stanton, who resented Lincoln's meddling in his department, ran his affairs for the most part quite independently of executive control and often in close co-operation with the anti-Lincoln Congressional Committee on the Conduct of the War. Lincoln could, of course, have removed Stanton or any other recalcitrant subordinate, but, having put up with Simon Cameron in the War Department for nearly a year, the President was reluctant to lose a secretary who might be prickly and independent-minded but who was also honest and efficient. To an impatient friend who felt Stanton had treated him unjustly, Lincoln explained his problem succinctly: "Of course I can over rule his decision if I will, but I cannot well administer the War Department independent of the Secretary of War." Indeed, instead of Lincoln's running his own War Department, it sometimes seemed that Stanton exercised a veto power upon the President. There was rueful humor in Lincoln's offhand refusal in 1862 to discuss military matters in a public speech: "The Secretary of War, you know, holds a pretty tight rein on the Press, so that they shall not tell more than they ought to, and I'm afraid that if I blab too much he might draw a tight rein on me."

Thus the same President who so drastically expanded the scope of his office by the assertion of his war powers under the Constitution was an executive who had singularly little impact either upon Congress or upon his own administrative aides. Just after his triumphant reelection in 1864, Lincoln remarked, with as much insight as wit, that he hoped he could exercise some influence with the incoming administration.

III

It is not easy to reconcile these conflicting aspects of Lincoln's presidency. The common, and kind, explanation is that the wartime President, being a very busy man, had to concentrate upon the more essential aspects of his job and to slight the others. This argument would be more convincing if Lincoln had not devoted a quite extraordinary amount of his time to really trivial matters. He found it possible, for instance, to write an endorsement of his chiropodist on the same day he issued the Emancipation Proclamation. Nor does it solve the problem to say, with Professor Corwin, that Lincoln had a "temperamental indifference to problems of administration." In certain areas such as the discovery and testing of new arms and explosives, the President exhibited a keen interest in the most routine administrative details.

Perhaps an analysis of what Lincoln himself thought about the presidency may help resolve this paradox of a Chief Executive who simultaneously expanded and abdicated his powers. For more than a quarter of a century before his first election Lincoln had vigorously participated in every presidential canvass, and his campaign speeches show that he had developed very definite ideas about the proper role of the Chief Executive. During most of this time he was a Whig, and he always remained proud of his Whig record. During the Lincoln-Douglas debates he reminded his hearers of his Whig past: "In '32, I voted for Henry Clay, in '36 for the Hugh L. White ticket, in '40 for 'Tip and Tyler.' In '44 I made the last great effort for 'Old Harry of the West.' . . . Taylor was elected in '48, and we fought nobly for Scott in '52." The leaders of the Whig party were his heroes; Henry Clay, in particular, he "loved and revered as a teacher and leader." Proud of his Whig principles, Lincoln boasted that he "had stood by the party as long as it had a being." He did not like the idea of being "un-whigged," and only after the death of his old party did he, rather reluctantly, join the Republicans.

The party to which Lincoln belonged for most of his life originated in objections to the "executive usurpation" of Andrew Jackson. Whig leaders concealed their economic motives and personal aspirations under denunciation of Jackson as "a detestable, ignorant, reckless, vain and malignant tyrant." Just as their ancestors of 1776 had stood against another executive usurper, so the Whigs of the 1830's fought against the "dictator" in the White House. Henry Clay and Daniel Webster bewailed the policy of the Democrats, which was tending rapidly toward "a total change of the pure republican character of our government, and to the concentration of all power in the hands of one man." William Henry Harrison, the first Whig President, made his inaugural address a classic exposition of his party's creed: ". . . it is preposterous to suppose that . . . the President, placed at the capital, in the center of the country could better understand the wants and wishes of the people than their own immediate representatives who spend a part of every year among them . . . and [are] bound to them by the triple tie of interest, duty, and affection." Zachary Taylor, the only other President elected by the Whig party, held the same views: "The Executive . . . has authority to recommend (not to

dictate) measures to Congress. Having performed that duty, the Executive department of the Government cannot rightfully control the decision of Congress on any subject of legislation . . . the . . . veto will never be exercised by me except . . . as an extreme measure, to be resorted to only in extraordinary cases. . . ."

Abraham Lincoln, a young Whig campaigner who regularly supported his party's ticket and platform, shared these fears of a strong executive. In 1838, in one of his earliest public lectures, he expressed concern lest "some man possessed of the loftiest genius, coupled with ambition sufficient to push it to its utmost stretch," some man belonging "*to the family of the lion, or the tribe of the eagle*," seize executive leadership and "set boldly to the task of pulling down" the institutions of the free republic. Consequently he opposed all aggrandizement of the President's powers. The Democratic tendency to allow the President "to take the whole of legislation into his own hands" he branded "a most pernicious deception." He argued against President James K. Polk's "high-handed and despotic exercise of the veto power, and . . . utter disregard of the will of the people, in refusing to give assent to measures which their representatives passed for the good and prosperity of the country." Congress should make policy and the President should execute it. That was "the best sort of principle"; that was the basic democratic "principle of allowing the people to do as they please with their own business."

These arguments were not just campaign oratory, for Lincoln clung to them throughout his life. In 1861 on his way to Washington as President Elect, he announced that he did not believe the Chief Executive should recommend legislation to Congress, veto bills already passed, or exert "indirect influence" to affect the action of congress." "My political education," he declared, "strongly inclines me against a very free use of any of these means, by the Executive, to control the legislation of the country. As a rule, I think it better that congress should originate, as well as perfect its measures, without external bias." On the controversial tariff issue, for instance, he thought the President should "neither seek to force a tariff-law by Executive influence; nor yet to arrest a reasonable one, by a veto, or otherwise." Throughout the war he kept reminding his subordinates that the executive branch must not "expressly or impliedly seize and exercise the permanent legislative functions of the government."

Lincoln's curious failure to assert his control over his cabinet also derived from his basic Whig view of the presidency. The Whig party was originally founded not only to oppose executive pressures upon the Congress but to combat the President's complete domination of the administrative offices. When President Jackson abruptly removed two successive Secretaries of the Treasury in order to install a malleable third secretary who followed the President's will and removed federal deposits from the Bank of the United States, the Whigs howled that he was subjecting the entire government to "*one responsibility, one discretion, one will.*" Whig President Harrison declared that the Founding Fathers should have made the head of the Treasury Department "entirely independent of the Executive," since the President should "never be looked to for schemes of finance." Other Whigs extended this reasoning to cover the rest of the cabinet. Webster was only carrying Whig principles to their logical conclusion when he asserted that all measures of an administration should be brought before the cabinet, where "their settlement was to be decided by the majority of votes, each member of the Cabinet and the President having but one vote."

Lincoln was, of course, too strong a personality to submit to such dictation. Indeed, even during the Taylor administration he had realized that the Whig theory of cabinet responsibility gave "The President the . . . ruinous character of being a mere man of straw." Consequently when Seward in April, 1861, proposed to become virtual premier of the new administration in order to lead it on a daring new policy of foreign embroilments, Lincoln quietly squelched him, declaring: ". . . if this must be done, *I* must do it." Similarly, when preparing to issue the Emancipation Proclamation, Lincoln told his cabinet advisers: "I have got you together to hear what I have written down. I do not wish your advice about the main matter—for that I have determined for myself. . . . If there is anything in the expressions I use, or in any other minor matter, which anyone of you thinks had best be changed, I shall be glad to receive the suggestions."

On key policies, therefore, especially those involving the use of the war power, Lincoln, like Harrison and Taylor before him, departed from the Whig theory of cabinet responsibility, but he could not rid himself of the political ideas with which he had been raised. Given the alternatives of imposing his own will upon his cabinet or of submitting to their majority opinion, Lincoln evaded the decision by treating the cabinet as an unnecessary nuisance, allowing it to consider only insignificant matters. Since there was no real consultation to formulate common policy and since the President could not personally oversee the details of everyday administration, each secretary, however disagreeable, self-promoting, or even conspiratorial, had a free hand in conducting his own department's affairs.

IV

These weaknesses of Lincoln's administration seem to stand in sharp contrast with the President's energetic assertion of his powers over civil liberties, over the military forces, and over the rebellious South, but there is no evidence that Lincoln himself was troubled by any inconsistency in his roles. Necessity, not political theory, caused

him to make his first sweeping assertions of executive authority during the secession crisis. The onset of civil war posed the immediate, practical dilemma, he declared later, "whether, using only the existing means, agencies, and processes which Congress had provided, I should let the government fall at once into ruin, or whether, availing myself of the broader powers conferred by the Constitution in cases of insurrection, I would make an effort to save it with all its blessings for the present age and for posterity." When the question was so posed, the answer became simple. "Necessity knows no law," he thought; consequently it was obligatory for him in this crisis to take strong measures, "some of which," he admitted, "were without any authority of law," in order to save the government.

When it did become necessary for Lincoln to justify his actions, he found his defense in the war powers granted him under the Constitution. ". . . as commander-in-chief of the army and navy, in time of war," he asserted, "I suppose I have a right to take any measure which may best subdue the enemy." Though critics claimed that the President was asserting dictatorial authority, it is clear that Lincoln himself took a narrower view of his powers. For example, he rejected the application of a general to construct a railroad in Missouri, which, it was claimed, would have some military utility. Since real military necessity was not shown Lincoln felt this was an unwarranted extension of executive power. ". . . I have been," he assured Congress, "unwilling to go beyond the pressure of necessity in the unusual exercise of power."

The complex problem of emancipation shows the degree to which Lincoln's conception of his war powers served both as a source for executive action and as a restriction upon such action. His personal preferences, the expediencies of politics, the thundering pressure from Northern governors, and the growing sentiment that emancipation would aid the Union cause abroad all urged him during 1861 and 1862 to move against slavery. He delayed, not because he doubted his constitutional power but because he questioned the necessity. "The truth is," he told a Louisiana loyalist, "that what is done, and omitted, about slaves, is done and omitted on the same military necessity." By late 1862 when necessity clearly demanded the abolition of slavery, Lincoln issued his proclamation of freedom, "as Commander-in-Chief, of the Army and Navy of the United States in time of actual armed rebellion against authority and government of the United States, and as a fit and necessary war measure for suppressing said rebellion." The Emancipation Proclamation, he declared later, had "no constitutional or legal justification, except as a military measure."

This view that the Chief Executive possesses vast war powers is not necessarily in conflict with the Whig view of the presidency. To be sure, the Whiggish origins of Lincoln's thought on this problem are not so clearly demonstrable. The

Whig party had originated in opposition to a strong President. Only two Presidents were ever elected by the Whig party, and neither of them was in the White House during time of war. Consequently, men like Webster and Clay spoke more of the limitation of presidential power in peacetime than they did of its possible wartime expansion. Lincoln himself had shared these pre-occupations of his party leaders. Vigorously he denounced Democratic President Polk, who, he believed, had unjustly and unconstitutionally started the Mexican War by invading foreign territory. The argument "that if it shall become *necessary, to repel invasion,* the President, may without violation of the Constitution . . . *invade* the territory of another country" Lincoln rejected as permitting the Chief Executive "to make war at pleasure" and as subjecting the American people to "the most oppressive of all Kingly oppressions." But though he opposed the Mexican War, neither Lincoln nor his party leaders made serious objections to President Polk's vigorous assertion of his war powers once the conflict had begun.

Whigs were inhibited from making such an objection. Heirs of the Federalists, they were at heart strong nationalists. One important current of Whig thought in fact justified the broadest assertion of presidential powers in wartime. Its most articulate exponent was John Quincy Adams, who, though far too independent and cantankerous to give his undivided allegiance to any party, acted generally with the Whigs in his distinguished post-presidential career in the House of Representatives. In congressional debates in 1836, 1841, and 1842, Adams, as he proudly recorded in his diary, "stung the slaveocracy to madness" by sketching in sweeping terms the power of the President as commander-in-chief. "[B]y the laws of war," he reminded his listeners, "an invaded country has all its laws and municipal institutions swept by the board, and martial law takes the place of them." In case of "actual war, whether servile, civil, or foreign," he grimly told Congress, the South's "municipal institutions" would be entirely subject to these laws of war, which permitted the confiscation of enemy property, including slaves. Consequently, in such an event, "not only the President of the United States but the commander of the army has the power to order the universal emancipation of the slaves."

Though John Quincy Adams could never have been considered the spokesman for any party, a respectable body of Whig thinkers endorsed these views. It is significant that the strongest defender of Lincoln's power to suspend the writ of habeas corpus was the venerable Whig lawyer, Horace Binney of Philadelphia, who saw no inconsistency between this position and his condemnation of Jackson's "tyranny" during the 1830's. Another former Whig, William Whiting of Massachusetts, provided in 1862 an even broader defense of the President's powers as commander-in-chief. His booklet on *The War Powers of the President,* which went through forty-three editions during the decade after its publication, leaned heavily upon Adams' argument, which he claimed proved "in the amplest terms the powers of Congress, and the authority of the President, to free enemy's slaves, as a legitimate act of war." An old Democrat like Gideon Welles distrusted Whiting's ideas and sneered at him as "self-sufficient but superficial, with many words, some reading, but no very sound or well-founded political views," but Lincoln, who shared the lawyer's Whig background, said flatly, "I like Mr. Whiting very much . . . ," and made him Solicitor of the War Department.

Since the Whigs were generally out of office and always on the defensive, John Quincy Adams' doctrine of presidential war powers never became an official part of the party's creed, but it was not forgotten. When the Civil War came, it was the ex-Whig Horace Greeley who revived Adams' speech on the presidential power of emancipation and gave it generous space in his *New York Tribune.* Another former Whig, Senator Charles Sumner of Massachusetts, who regarded Adams' argument "as a towering landmark and beacon," welcomed the firing on Fort Sumter because it introduced just the contingency the ex-President had forecast. As soon as he heard the news, Sumner said, "I went at once to Mr. Lincoln . . . and told him I was with him now heart and soul; that under the war power the right had come to him to emancipate the slaves."

V

Thus what Lincoln called his "political education" helps explain the puzzling ambiguity of his presidency. Both in strongly asserting his war powers and in weakly deferring to Congress, he was following the Whig creed in which he was raised.

So to interpret Lincoln's course is to give more significance to the Whig party and its ideology than is fashionable among historians today. Concerned with showing that our major political parties have generally shared most of their basic ideas, recent scholars have belittled the political rivalries of the 1830's and 1840's as inconsequential struggles between conflicting economic interest groups or contests between ambitious politicians. Doubtless, in the backward glance of history, there is much justification for such an interpretation. But it must be remembered that what men think to be true often has more influence upon the course of history than actuality itself.

To the generation of American politicians who reached maturity about 1840 the difference between the Whig party and the Democratic party was a real and vital thing. Young and aspiring leaders like Abraham Lincoln who shouted themselves hoarse for rival party candidates convinced themselves, even if they convinced nobody else, that the principles which they advocated were both true and important. Rhetoric has a way of imprisoning those who use it, and the politicians of the Civil War era were never quite able to discard the party creeds of their youth. Lincoln, in other connections, recognized the danger of letting past experience dictate present action. "As our case is new," he argued, "so we must think anew, and act anew." But the President was never able to disenthrall himself from his own political education. It is ironical that the Whig party, which had a sorry record of failure during its lifetime, should have achieved its greatest success, years after its official demise, in the presidency of Abraham Lincoln.

In his first inaugural address, March 4, 1861, Lincoln sought to reassure the South that he would not interfere with slavery in the southern states. He warned, however, that "the Union is much older than the Constitution," and, hence, that the states could not terminate their contract.

ABRAHAM LINCOLN:
FIRST INAUGURAL ADDRESS*

Fellow-citizens of the United States: In compliance with a custom as old as the government itself, I appear before you to address you briefly, and to take in your presence the oath prescribed by the Constitution of the United States to be taken by the President "before he enters on the execution of his office."

I do not consider it necessary at present for me to discuss those matters of administration about which there is no special anxiety or excitement.

Apprehension seems to exist among the people of the Southern States that by the accession of a Republican administration their property and their peace and personal security are to be endangered. There has never been any reasonable cause for such apprehension. Indeed, the most ample evidence to the contrary has all the while existed and been open to their inspection. It is found in nearly all the published speeches of him who now addresses you. I do but quote from one of those speeches when I declare that "I have no purpose, directly or indirectly, to interfere with the institution of slavery in the States where it exists. I believe I have no lawful right to do so, and I have no inclination to do so." Those who nominated and elected me did so with full knowledge that I had made this and many similar declarations, and had never recanted them.

And, more than this, they placed in the platform for my acceptance, and as a law to themselves and to me, the clear and emphatic resolution which I now read: "*Resolved*, That the maintenance inviolate of the rights of the States,

and especially the right of each State to order and control its own domestic institutions according to its own judgment exclusively, is essential to that balance of power on which the perfection and endurance of our political fabric depend, and we denounce the lawless invasion by armed force of the soil of any State or Territory, no matter under what pretext, as among the gravest of crimes."

I now reiterate these sentiments; and, in doing so, I only press upon the public attention the most conclusive evidence of which the case is susceptible, that the property, peace, and security of no section are to be in any wise endangered by the now incoming administration. I add, too, that all the protection which, consistently with the Constitution and the laws, can be given, will be cheerfully given to all the States when lawfully demanded, for whatever cause—as cheerfully to one section as to another.

There is much controversy about the delivering up of fugitives from service or labor. The clause I now read is as plainly written in the Constitution as any other of its provisions: "No person held to service or labor in one State, under the laws thereof, escaping into another, shall in consequence of any law or regulation therein be discharged from such service or labor, but shall be delivered up on claim of the party to whom such service or labor may be due."

It is scarcely questioned that this provision was intended by those who made it for the reclaiming of what we call fugitive slaves; and the intention of the lawgiver is the law. All members of Congress swear their support to the whole Constitution—to this provision as much as to any other. To the proposition, then, that slaves whose cases come within the terms of this clause "shall be delivered up," their oaths are unanimous. Now, if they would make the effort in good

* Reprinted from John G. Nicolay and John Hay, eds., *Complete Works of Abraham Lincoln* (Lincoln Memorial Univ. edition, n.p., 1894), VI, 169–85.

temper, could they not with nearly equal unanimity frame and pass a law by means of which to keep good that unanimous oath?

There is some difference of opinion whether this clause should be enforced by national or by State authority; but surely that difference is not a very material one. If the slave is to be surrendered, it can be of but little consequence to him or to others by which authority it is done. And should any one in any case be content that his oath shall go unkept on a merely unsubstantial controversy as to how it shall be kept?

Again, in any law upon this subject, ought not all the safeguards of liberty known in civilized and humane jurisprudence to be introduced, so that a free man be not, in any case, surrendered as a slave? And might it not be well at the same time to provide by law for the enforcement of that clause in the Constitution which guarantees that "the citizen of each State shall be entitled to all privileges and immunities of citizens in the several States"?

I take the official oath to-day with no mental reservations, and with no purpose to construe the Constitution or laws by any hypercritical rules. And while I do not choose now to specify particular acts of Congress as proper to be enforced, I do suggest that it will be much safer for all, both in official and private stations, to conform to and abide by all those acts which stand unrepealed, than to violate any of them, trusting to find impunity in having them held to be unconstitutional.

It is seventy-two years since the first inauguration of a President under our National Constitution. During that period fifteen different and greatly distinguished citizens have, in succession, administered the executive branch of the government. They have conducted it through many perils, and generally with great success. Yet, with all this scope of precedent, I now enter upon the same task for the brief constitutional term of four years under great and peculiar difficulty. A disruption of the Federal Union, heretofore only menaced, is now formidably attempted.

I hold that, in contemplation of universal law and of the Constitution, the Union of these States is perpetual. Perpetuity is implied, if not expressed, in the fundamental law of all national governments. It is safe to assert that no government proper ever had a provision in its organic law for its own termination.

Continue to execute all the express provisions of our National Constitution, and the Union will endure forever—it being impossible to destroy it except by some action not provided for in the instrument itself.

Again, if the United States be not a government proper, but an association of States in the nature of contract merely, can it, as a contract, be peaceably unmade by less than all the parties who made it? One party to a contract may violate it—break it, so to speak; but does it not require all to lawfully rescind it?

Descending from these general principles, we find the proposition that, in legal contemplation the Union is perpetual confirmed by the history of the Union itself. The Union is much older than the Constitution. It was formed, in fact, by the Articles of Association in 1774. It was matured and continued by the Declaration of Independence in 1776. It was further matured, and the faith of all the then thirteen States expressly plighted and engaged that it should be perpetual, by the Articles of Confederation in 1778. And, finally, in 1787 one of the declared objects for ordaining and establishing the Constitution was "to form a more perfect Union."

But if the destruction of the Union by one or by a part only of the States be lawfully possible, the Union is less perfect than before the Constitution, having lost the vital element of perpetuity.

It follows from these views that no State upon its own mere motion can lawfully get out of the Union; that resolves and ordinances to that effect are legally void; and that acts of violence, within any State or States, against the authority of the United States, are insurrectionary or revolutionary, according to circumstances.

I therefore consider that, in view of the Constitution and the laws, the Union is unbroken; and to the extent of my ability I shall take care, as the Constitution itself expressly enjoins upon me, that the laws of the Union be faithfully executed in all the States. Doing this I deem to be only a simple duty on my part; and I shall perform it so far as practicable, unless my rightful masters, the American people, shall withhold the requisite means, or in some authoritative manner direct the contrary. I trust this will not be regarded as a menace, but only as the declared purpose of the Union that it will constitutionally defend and maintain itself.

In doing this there needs to be no bloodshed or violence; and there shall be none, unless it be forced upon the national authority. The power confided to me will be used to hold, occupy, and possess the property and places belonging to the government, and to collect the duties and imposts; but beyond what may be necessary for these objects, there will be no invasion, no using of force against or among the people anywhere. Where hostility to the United States, in any interior locality, shall be so great and universal as to prevent competent resident citizens from holding the Federal offices, there will be no attempt to force obnoxious strangers among the people for that object. While the strict legal right may exist in the government to enforce the exercise of these offices, the attempt to do so would be so irritating, and so nearly impracticable withal, that I deem it better to forego for the time the uses of such offices.

The mails, unless repelled, will continue to be furnished in all parts of the Union. So far as possible, the people everywhere shall have that sense of perfect security which is most favorable to calm thought and reflection. The course here indicated will be followed unless current events and experience shall show a modification or change to be proper, and in every case and exigency my best discretion will be exercised according to circumstances actually existing, and with a view and a hope of a peaceful solution of the national troubles and the restoration of fraternal sympathies and affections.

That there are persons in one section or another who seek to destroy the Union at all events, and are glad of any pretext to do it, I will neither affirm nor deny; but if there be such, I need address no word to them. To those, however, who really love the Union may I not speak?

Before entering upon so grave a matter as the destruction of our national fabric, with all its benefits, its memories, and its hopes, would it not be wise to ascertain precisely why we do it? Will you hazard so desperate a step while there is any possibility that any portion of the ills you fly from have no real existence? Will you, while the certain ills you fly to are greater than all the real ones you fly from—will you risk the commission of so fearful a mistake?

All profess to be content in the Union if all constitutional rights can be maintained. Is it true, then, that any right, plainly written in the Constitution, has been denied? I think not. Happily the human mind is so constituted that no party can reach to the audacity of doing this. Think, if you can, of a single instance in which a plainly written provision of the Constitution has ever been denied. If by the mere force of numbers a majority should deprive a minority of any clearly written constitutional right, it might, in a moral point of view, justify revolution—certainly would if such a right were a vital one. But such is not our case. All the vital rights of minorities and of individuals are so plainly assured to them by affirmations and negations, guarantees and prohibitions, in the Constitution, that controversies never arise concerning them. But no organic law can ever be framed with a provision specifically applicable to every question which may occur in practical administration. No foresight can anticipate, nor any document of reasonable length contain, express provisions for all possible questions. Shall fugitives from labor be surrendered by national or by State authority? The Constitution does not expressly say. *May* Congress prohibit slavery in the Territories? The Constitution does not expressly say. *Must* Congress protect slavery in the Territories? The Constitution does not expressly say.

From questions of this class spring all our constitutional controversies, and we divide upon them into majorities and minorities. If the minority will not acquiesce, the majority must, or the government must cease. There is no other alternative; for continuing the government is acquiescence on one side or the other.

If a minority in such case will secede rather than acquiesce, they make a precedent which in turn will divide and ruin them; for a minority of their own will secede from them whenever a majority refuses to be controlled by such minority. For instance, why may not any portion of a new confederacy a year or two hence arbitrarily secede again, precisely as portions of the present Union now claim to secede from it? All who cherish disunion sentiments are now being educated to the exact temper of doing this.

Is there such perfect identity of interests among the States to compose a new Union, as to produce harmony only, and prevent renewed secession?

Plainly, the central idea of secession is the essence of anarchy. A majority held in restraint by constitutional checks and limitations, and always changing easily with deliberate changes of popular opinions and sentiments, is the only true sovereign of a free people. Whoever rejects it does, of necessity, fly to anarchy or to despotism. Unanimity is impossible; the rule of a minority, as a permanent arrangement, is wholly inadmissible; so that, rejecting the majority principle, anarchy or despotism in some form is all that is left.

I do not forget the position, assumed by some, that constitutional questions are to be decided by the Supreme Court; nor do I deny that such decisions must be binding, in any case, upon the parties to a suit, as to the object of that suit, while they are also entitled to very high respect and consideration in all parallel cases by all other departments of the government. And while it is obviously possible that such decision may be erroneous in any given case, still the evil effect following it, being limited to that particular case, with the chance that it may be overruled and never become a precedent for other cases, can better be borne than could the evils of a different practice.

At the same time, the candid citizen must confess that if the policy of the government, upon vital questions affecting the whole people, is to be irrevocably fixed by decisions of the Supreme Court, the instant they are made, in ordinary litigation between parties in personal actions, the people will have ceased to be their own rulers, having to that extent practically resigned their government into the hands of that eminent tribunal. Nor is there in this view any assault upon the court or the judges. It is a duty from which they may not shrink to decide cases properly brought before them, and it is no fault of theirs if others seek to turn their decisions to political purposes.

One section of our country believes slavery is right, and ought to be extended, while the other believes it is wrong, and ought not to be extended. This is the only substantial dispute. The fugitive-slave clause of the Constitution, and the law for the suppression of the foreign slave-trade, are each as well enforced, perhaps, as any law can ever be in a community where the moral sense of the people imperfectly supports the law itself.

The great body of the people abide by the dry legal obligation in both cases, and a few break over in each. This, I think, cannot be perfectly cured; and it would be worse in both cases after the separation of the sections than before. The foreign slave-trade, now imperfectly suppressed, would be ultimately revived, without restriction, in one section, while fugitive slaves, now only partially surrendered, would not be surrendered at all by the other.

Physically speaking, we cannot separate. We cannot remove our respective sections from each other, nor build an impassable wall between them. A husband and wife may be divorced, and go out of the presence and beyond the reach of each other; but the different parts of our country cannot do this. They cannot but remain face to face, and intercourse, either amicable or hostile, must continue between them. Is it possible, then, to make that intercourse more advantageous or more satisfactory after separation than before? Can aliens make treaties easier than friends can make laws? Can treaties be more faithfully enforced between aliens than laws can among friends? Suppose you go to war, you cannot fight always; and when, after much loss on both sides, and no gain on either, you cease fighting, the identical old questions as to terms of intercourse are again upon you.

This country, with its institutions, belongs to the people who inhabit it. Whenever they shall grow weary of the existing government, they can exercise their constitutional right of amending it, or their revolutionary right to dismember or overthrow it. I cannot be ignorant of the fact that many worthy and patriotic citizens are desirous of having the National Constitution amended. While I make no recommendation of amendments, I fully recognize the rightful authority of the people over the whole subject, to be exercised in either of the modes prescribed in the instrument itself; and I should, under existing circumstances, favor rather than oppose a fair opportunity being afforded the people to act upon it. I will venture to add that to me the convention mode seems preferable, in that it allows amendments to originate with the people themselves, instead of only permitting them to take or reject propositions originated by others not specially chosen for the purpose, and which might not be precisely such as they would wish to either accept or refuse. I understand a proposed amendment to the Constitution—which amendment, however, I have not seen—has passed Congress, to the effect that the Federal Government shall never interfere with the domestic institutions of the States, including that of persons held to service. To avoid misconstruction of what I have said, I depart from my purpose not to speak of particular amendments so far as to say that, holding such a provision to now be implied constitutional law, I have no objection to its being made express and irrevocable.

The chief magistrate derives all his authority from the people, and they have conferred none upon him to fix terms for the separation of the States. The people themselves can do this also if they choose; but the executive, as such, has nothing to do with it. His duty is to administer the present government, as it came to his hands, and to transmit it, unimpaired by him, to his successor.

Why should there not be a patient confidence in the ultimate justice of the people? Is there any better or equal hope in the world? In our present differences is either party without faith of being in the right? If the Almighty Ruler of Nations, with his eternal truth and justice, be on your side of the North, or on yours of the South, that truth and that justice will surely prevail by the judgment of this great tribunal of the American people.

By the frame of the government under which we live, this same people have wisely given their public servants but little power for mischief; and have, with equal wisdom, provided for the return of that little to their own hands at very short intervals. While the people retain their virtue and vigilance, no administration, by any extreme of wickedness or folly, can very seriously injure the government in the short space of four years.

My countrymen, one and all, think calmly and well upon this whole subject. Nothing valuable can be lost by taking time. If there be an object to hurry any of you in hot haste to a step which you would never take deliberately, that object will be frustrated by taking time; but no good object can be frustrated by it. Such of you as are now dissatisfied, still have the old Constitution unimpaired, and, on the sensitive point, the laws of your own framing under it; while the new administration will have no immediate power, if it would, to change either. If it were admitted that you who are dissatisfied hold the right side in the dispute, there still is no single good reason for precipitate action. Intelligence, patriotism, Christianity, and a firm reliance on Him who has never yet forsaken this favored land, are still competent to adjust in the best way all our present difficulty.

In your hands, my dissatisfied fellow-countrymen, and not in mine, is the momentous issue of civil war. The government will not assail you. You can have no conflict without being yourselves the aggressors. You have no oath registered in heaven to destroy the government, while I shall have the most solemn one to "preserve, protect, and defend it."

I am loath to close. We are not enemies, but friends. We must not be enemies. Though passion may have strained, it must not break our bonds of affection. The mystic chords of memory, stretching from every battle-field and patriot grave to every living heart and hearthstone all over this broad land, will yet swell the chorus of the Union when again touched, as surely they will be, by the better angels of our nature.

A significant milestone in the achievement of human rights, the Emancipation Proclamation announced the abolition of slavery in certain areas of the South. From this point on, the Union cause was linked with the freedom of the Negro.

ABRAHAM LINCOLN:
THE EMANCIPATION PROCLAMATION*

Whereas on the 22d day of September, A.D. 1862, a proclamation was issued by the President of the United States, containing, among other things, the following, to wit:

"That on the 1st day of January, A.D. 1863, all persons held as slaves within any State or designated part of a State the people whereof shall then be in rebellion against the United States shall be then, thenceforward, and forever free; and the executive government of the United States, including the military and naval authority thereof, will recognize and maintain the freedom of such persons and will do no act or acts to repress such persons, or any of them, in any efforts they may make for their actual freedom.

"That the executive will on the 1st day of January aforesaid, by proclamation, designate the States and parts of States, if any, in which the people thereof, respectively, shall then be in rebellion against the United States; and the fact that any State or the people thereof shall on that day be in good faith represented in the Congress of the United States by members chosen thereto at elections wherein a majority of the qualified voters of such States shall have participated shall, in the absence of strong countervailing testimony, be deemed conclusive evidence that such State and the people thereof are not then in rebellion against the United States."

Now, therefore, I, Abraham Lincoln, President of the United States, by virtue of the power in me vested as Commander-in-Chief of the Army and Navy of the United States in time of actual armed rebellion against the authority and government of the United States, and as a fit and necessary war measure for suppressing said rebellion, do, on this 1st day of January, A.D. 1863, and in accordance with my purpose so to do, publicly proclaimed for the full period of one hundred days from the first day above mentioned, order and designate as the States and parts of States wherein the people thereof, respectively, are this day in rebellion against the United States the following, to wit:

Arkansas, Texas, Louisiana (except the parishes of St. Bernard, Plaquemines, Jefferson, St. John, St. Charles, St. James, Ascension, Assumption, Terrebonne, Lafourche, St. Mary, St. Martin, and Orleans, including the city of New Orleans), Mississippi, Alabama, Florida, Georgia, South Carolina, North Carolina, and Virginia (except the forty-eight counties designated as West Virginia, and also the counties of Berkeley, Accomac, Northhampton, Elizabeth City, York, Princess Anne, and Norfolk, including the cities of Norfolk and Portsmouth), and which excepted parts are for the present left precisely as if this proclamation were not issued.

And by virtue of the power and for the purpose aforesaid, I do order and declare that all persons held as slaves within said designated States and parts of States are, and henceforward shall be, free; and that the Executive Government of the United States, including the military and naval authorities thereof, will recognize and maintain the freedom of said persons.

And I hereby enjoin upon the people so declared to be free to abstain from all violence, unless in necessary self-defense; and I recommend to them that, in all cases when allowed, they labor faithfully for reasonable wages.

And I further declare and make known that such persons of suitable condition will be received into the armed service of the United States to garrison forts, positions, stations, and other places, and to man vessels of all sorts in said service.

And upon this act, sincerely believed to be an act of justice, warranted by the Constitution upon military necessity, I invoke the considerate judgment of mankind and the gracious favor of Almighty God.

---

* Reprinted from John G. Nicolay and John Hay, eds., *Complete Works of Abraham Lincoln* (Lincoln Memorial Univ. edition, n.p., 1894), VIII, 161–64.

Lincoln in this selection explained his reasons for resorting to such war-time policies as military arrests. Answering his critics among the Peace Democrats, Lincoln asserted that the suspension of habeas corpus is justifiable in times of rebellion.

ABRAHAM LINCOLN:
LETTER TO ERASTUS CORNING*

Gentlemen: Your letter of May 19, inclosing the resolutions of a public meeting held at Albany, New York, on the 16th of the same month, was received several days ago.

The resolutions, as I understand them, are resolvable into two propositions—first, the expression of a purpose to sustain the cause of the Union, to secure peace through victory, and to support the administration in every constitutional and lawful measure to suppress the rebellion; and, secondly, a declaration of censure upon the administration for supposed unconstitutional action, such as the making of military arrests. And from the two propositions a third is deduced, which is that the gentlemen composing the meeting are resolved on doing their part to maintain our common government and country, despite the folly or wickedness, as they may conceive, of any administration. This position is eminently patriotic and as such I thank the meeting, and congratulate the nation for it. My own purpose is the same; so that the meeting and myself have a common object, and can have no difference, except in the choice of means or measures for effecting that object.

And here I ought to close this paper, and would close it, if there were no apprehension that more injurious consequences than any merely personal to myself might follow the censures systematically cast upon me for doing what, in my view of duty, I could not forbear. The resolutions promise to support me in every constitutional and lawful measure to suppress the rebellion; and I have not knowingly employed, nor shall knowingly employ, any other. But the meeting, by their resolutions, assert and argue that certain military arrests and proceedings following them, for which I am ultimately responsible are unconstitutional. I think they are not. The resolutions quote from the Constitution the definition of treason, and also the limiting safeguards and guarantees therein provided for the citizen on trials for treason, and on his being held to answer for capital or otherwise infamous crimes, and in criminal prosecutions his right to a speedy and public trial by an impartial jury. They proceed to resolve "that these safeguards of the rights of the citizen against the pretensions of arbitrary power were intended more especially for his protection in times of civil commotion." And, apparently to demonstrate the proposition, the resolutions proceed: "They were secured substantially to the English people after years of protracted civil war, and were adopted into our Constitution at the close of the revolution." Would not the demonstration have been better if it could have been truly said that these safeguards had been adopted and applied during the civil wars and during our revolution, instead of after the one and at the close of the other? I, too, am devotedly for them after civil war and before civil war, and at all times, "except when, in cases of rebellion or invasion, the public safety may require" their suspension. The resolutions proceed to tell us that these safeguards "have stood the test of seventy-six years of trial under our republican system under circumstances which show that while they constitute the foundation of all free government, they are the elements of the enduring stability of the republic." No one denies that they have so stood the test up to the beginning of the present rebellion, if we except a certain occurrence at New Orleans hereafter to be mentioned; nor does any one question that they will stand the same test much longer after the rebellion closes. But these provisions of the Constitution have no application to the case we have in hand, because the arrests complained of were not made for treason—that is, not for the treason defined in the Constitution, and upon the conviction of which the punishment is death—nor yet were they made to hold persons to answer for any capital or otherwise infamous crimes; nor were the proceedings following, in any constitutional or legal sense, "criminal prosecutions." The arrests were made on totally different grounds, and the proceedings following accorded with the grounds of the arrests. Let us consider the real case with which we are dealing, and apply to it the parts of the Constitution plainly made for such cases.

Prior to my installation here it had been inculcated that any State had a lawful right to secede from the national Union, and that it would be expedient to exercise the right whenever the devotees of the doctrine should fail to elect a president to their own liking. I was elected contrary to their liking; and, accordingly, so far as it was legally possible, they had taken seven

* Reprinted from John G. Nicolay and John Hay, eds., *Complete Works of Abraham Lincoln* (Lincoln Memorial Univ. edition, n.p., 1894), VIII, 298–309.

States out of the Union, had seized many of the United States forts, and had fired upon the United States flag, all before I was inaugurated, and, of course, before I had done any official act whatever. The rebellion thus begun soon ran into the present civil war; and, in certain respects, it began on very unequal terms between the parties. The insurgents had been preparing for it more than thirty years, while the government had taken no steps to resist them. The former had carefully considered all the means which could be turned to their account. It undoubtedly was a well-pondered reliance with them that in their own unrestricted effort to destroy Union, Constitution and law, all together, the government would, in great degree, be restrained by the same Constitution and law from arresting their progress. Their sympathizers pervaded all departments of the government and nearly all communities of the people. From this material, under cover of "liberty of speech," "liberty of the press," and "habeas corpus," they hoped to keep on foot amongst us a most efficient corps of spies, informers, suppliers and aiders and abettors of their cause in a thousand ways. They knew that in times such as they were inaugurating, by the Constitution itself the "habeas corpus" might be suspended; but they also knew they had friends who would make a question as to who was to suspend it; meanwhile their spies and others might remain at large to help on their cause. Or if, as has happened, the Executive should suspend the writ without ruinous waste of time, instances of arresting innocent persons might occur, as are always likely to occur in such cases; and then a clamor could be raised in regard to this, which might be at least of some service to the insurgent cause. It needed no very keen perception to discover this part of the enemy's program, so soon as by open hostilities their machinery was fairly put in motion. Yet, thoroughly imbued with a reverence for the guaranteed rights of individuals, I was slow to adopt the strong measures which by degrees I have been forced to regard as being within the exceptions of the Constitution, and as indispensable to the public safety. Nothing is better known to history than that courts of justice are utterly incompetent to such cases. Civil courts are organized chiefly for trials of individuals, or, at most, a few individuals acting in concert—and this in quiet times, and on charges of crimes well defined in the law. Even in times of peace bands of horse-thieves and robbers frequently grow too numerous and powerful for the ordinary courts of justice. But what comparison, in numbers, have such bands ever borne to the insurgent sympathizers even in many of the loyal States? Again, a jury too frequently has at least one member more ready to hang the panel than to hang the traitor. And yet again, he who dissuades one man from volunteering, or induces one soldier to desert, weakens the Union cause as much as he who kills a Union soldier in battle. Yet this dissuasion or inducement may be

so conducted as to be no defined crime of which any civil court would take cognizance.

Ours is a case of rebellion—so called by the resolutions before me—in fact, a clear, flagrant, and gigantic case of rebellion; and the provision of the Constitution that "the privilege of the writ of *habeas corpus* shall not be suspended unless when, in cases of rebellion or invasion, the public safety may require it," is the provision which specially applies to our present case. This provision plainly attests the understanding of those who made the Constitution that ordinary courts of justice are inadequate to "cases of rebellion" —attests their purpose that, in such cases, men may be held in custody whom the courts, acting on ordinary rules, would discharge. *Habeas corpus* does not discharge men who are proved to be guilty of defined crime; and its suspension is allowed by the Constitution on purpose that men may be arrested and held who cannot be proved to be guilty of defined crime, "when, in cases of rebellion or invasion, the public safety may require it."

This is precisely our present case—a case of rebellion wherein the public safety does require the suspension. Indeed, arrests by process of courts and arrests in cases of rebellion do not proceed altogether upon the same basis. The former is directed at the small percentage of ordinary and continuous perpetration of crime, while the latter is directed at sudden and extensive uprisings against the government, which, at most, will succeed or fail in no great length of time. In the latter case arrests are made not so much for what has been done, as for what probably would be done. The latter is more for the preventive and less for the vindictive than the former. In such cases the purposes of men are much more easily understood than in cases of ordinary crime. The man who stands by and says nothing when the peril of his government is discussed, cannot be misunderstood. If not hindered, he is sure to help the enemy; much more if he talks ambiguously—talks for his country with "buts," and "ifs" and "ands." Of how little value the constitutional provision I have quoted will be rendered if arrests shall never be made until defined crimes shall have been committed, may be illustrated by a few notable examples: General John C. Breckinridge, General Robert E. Lee, General Joseph E. Johnson, General John B. Magruder, General William B. Preston, General Simon B. Buckner, and Commodore Franklin Buchanan, now occupying the very highest places in the rebel war service, were all within the power of the government since the rebellion began, and were nearly as well known to be traitors then as now. Unquestionably if we had seized and held them, the insurgent cause would be much weaker. But no one of them had then committed any crime defined in the law. Every one of them, if arrested, would have been discharged on *habeas corpus* were the writ allowed to operate. In view of these and similar cases, I think the time not unlikely to come when I shall be blamed for having made too few arrests rather than too many.

By the third resolution the meeting indicate their opinion that military arrests may be constitutional in localities where rebellion actually exists, but that such arrests are unconstitutional in localities where rebellion or insurrection does not actually exist. They insist that such arrests shall not be made "outside of the lines of necessary military occupation and the scenes of insurrection." Inasmuch, however, as the Constitution itself makes no such distinction, I am unable to believe that there is any such constitutional distinction. I concede that the class of arrests complained of can be constitutional only when, in cases of rebellion or invasion, the public safety may require them; and I insist that in such cases they are constitutional wherever the public safety does require them, as well in places to which they may prevent the rebellion extending, as in those where it may be already prevailing; as well where they may restrain mischievous interference with the raising and supplying of armies to suppress the rebellion, as where the rebellion may actually be; as well where they may restrain the enticing men out of the army, as where they would prevent mutiny in the army; equally constitutional at all places where they will conduce to the public safety, as against the danger of rebellion or invasion. Take the particular case mentioned by the meeting. It is asserted in substance, that Mr. Vallandigham was, by a military commander, seized and tried "for no other reason than words addressed to a public meeting in criticism of the course of the administration, and in condemnation of the military orders of the general." Now, if there be no mistake about this, if this assertion is the truth and the whole truth, if there was no other reason for the arrest, then I concede that the arrest was wrong. But the arrest, as I understand, was made for a very different reason. Mr. Vallandigham avows his hostility to the war on the part of the Union; and his arrest was made because he was laboring, with some effect, to prevent the raising of troops, to encourage desertions from the army, and to leave the rebellion without an adequate military force to suppress it. He was not arrested because he was damaging the political prospects of the administration or the personal interests of the commanding general but because he was damaging the army, upon the existence and vigor of which the life of the nation depends. He was warring upon the military, and this gave the military constitutional jurisdiction to lay hands upon him. If Mr. Vallandigham was not damaging the military power of the country, then his arrest was made on mistake of fact, which I would be glad to correct on reasonably satisfactory evidence.

I understand the meeting whose resolutions I am considering to be in favor of suppressing the rebellion by military force—by armies. Long experience has shown that armies cannot be maintained unless desertion shall be punished by the severe penalty of death. The case requires, and the law and the Constitution sanction, this punishment. Must I shoot a simple-minded soldier boy who deserts, while I must not touch a hair of a wily agitator who induces him to desert? This is none the less injurious when effected by getting a father, or brother, or friend into a public meeting, and there working upon his feelings till he is persuaded to write the soldier boy that he is fighting in a bad cause, for a wicked administration of a contemptible government, too weak to arrest and punish him if he shall desert. I think that, in such a case, to silence the agitator and save the boy is not only constitutional, but withal a great mercy.

If I be wrong on this question of constitutional power, my error lies in believing that certain proceedings are constitutional when, in cases of rebellion or invasion, the public safety requires them, which would not be constitutional when, in absence of rebellion or invasion, the public safety does not require them: in other words, that the Constitution is not in its application in all respects the same in cases of rebellion or invasion involving the public safety, as it is in times of profound peace and public security. . . .

Asserting that slavery "was, somehow, the cause of the war," Lincoln saw a divine purpose in the tremendous slaughter on both sides. The second inaugural address, given March 4, 1865, reflected Lincoln's brooding mood, his sense of the tragic proportions of the conflict, after four long years of war.

ABRAHAM LINCOLN:
SECOND INAUGURAL ADDRESS*

Fellow-countrymen: At this second appearing to take the oath of the presidential office, there is less occasion for an extended address than there was at the first. Then a statement, somewhat in detail, of a course to be pursued, seemed fitting and proper. Now, at the expiration of four years, during which public declarations have been constantly called forth on every point and phase of the great contest which still absorbs the attention and engrosses the energies of the nation, little that is new could be presented. The progress of our arms, upon which all else chiefly depends, is as well known to the public as to myself; and it is, I trust, reasonably satisfactory and encouraging to all. With high hope for the future, no prediction in regard to it is ventured.

On the occasion corresponding to this four years ago, all thoughts were anxiously directed to an impending civil war. All dreaded it—all sought to avert it. While the inaugural address was being delivered from this place, devoted altogether to saving the Union without war, insurgent agents were in the city seeking to destroy it without war—seeking to dissolve the Union, and divide effects, by negotiation. Both parties deprecated war; but one of them would make war rather than let the nation survive; and the other would accept war rather than let it perish. And the war came.

One-eighth of the whole population were colored slaves, not distributed generally over the Union, but localized in the Southern part of it. These slaves constituted a peculiar and powerful interest. All knew that this interest was, somehow, the cause of the war. To strengthen, perpetuate, and extend this interest was the object for which the insurgents would rend the Union, even by war; while the government claimed no right to do more than to restrict the territorial enlargement of it.

Neither party expected for the war the magnitude or the duration which it has already attained. Neither anticipated that the cause of the conflict might cease with, or even before, the conflict itself should cease. Each looked for an easier triumph, and a result less fundamental and astounding. Both read the same Bible, and pray to the same God; and each invokes his aid against the other. It may seem strange that any men should dare to ask a just God's assistance in wringing their bread from the sweat of other men's faces; but let us judge not, that we be not judged. The prayers of both could not be answered—that of neither has been answered fully.

The Almighty has his own purposes. "Woe unto the world because of offenses! for it must needs be that offenses come; but woe to that man by whom the offense cometh." If we shall suppose that American slavery is one of those offenses which, in the providence of God, must needs come, but which, having continued through his appointed time, he now wills to remove, and that he gives to both North and South this terrible war, as the woe due to those by whom the offense came, shall we discern therein any departure from those divine attributes which the believers in a living God always ascribe to him? Fondly do we hope—fervently do we pray—that this mighty scourge of war may speedily pass away. Yet, if God wills that it continue until all the wealth piled by the bondsman's two hundred and fifty years of unrequited toil shall be sunk, and until every drop of blood drawn with the lash shall be paid by another drawn with the sword, as was said three thousand years ago, so still it must be said, "The judgments of the Lord are true and righteous altogether."

With malice toward none; with charity for all; with firmness in the right, as God gives us to see the right, let us strive on to finsh the work we are in; to bind up the nation's wounds; to care for him who shall have borne the battle, and for his widow, and his orphan—to do all which may achieve and cherish a just and lasting peace among ourselves, and with all nations.

* Reprinted from John G. Nicolay and John Hay, eds., *Complete Works of Abraham Lincoln* (Lincoln Memorial Univ. edition, n.p., 1894), XI, 44–47.

Shortly before his death, with victory now assured, Lincoln turned his thoughts to Reconstruction. In his last public address, April 11, 1865, Lincoln revealed the basis for a moderate approach to the post-war period, one seeking to bring Southern states "into proper practical relations" with the rest of the nation.

ABRAHAM LINCOLN:
LAST PUBLIC ADDRESS*

We meet this evening not in sorrow, but in gladness of heart. The evacuation of Petersburg and Richmond, and the surrender of the principal insurgent army, give hope of a righteous and speedy peace, whose joyous expression cannot be restrained. In the midst of this, however, He from whom all blessings flow must not be forgotten. A call for a national thanksgiving is being prepared, and will be duly promulgated. Nor must those whose harder part give us the cause of rejoicing be overlooked. Their honors must not be parceled out with others. I myself was near the front, and had the high pleasure of transmitting much of the good news to you; but no part of the honor for plan or execution is mine. To General Grant, his skilful officers and brave men, all belongs. The gallant navy stood ready, but was not in reach to take active part.

By these recent successes the reinauguration of the national authority—reconstruction—which has had a large share of thought from the first, is pressed much more closely upon our attention. It is fraught with great difficulty. Unlike a case of war between independent nations, there is no authorized organ for us to treat with—no one man has authority to give up the rebellion for any other man. We simply must begin with and mold from disorganized and discordant elements. Nor is it a small additional embarrassment that we, the loyal people, differ among ourselves as to the mode, manner, and measure of reconstruction. As a general rule, I abstain from reading the reports of attacks upon myself, wishing not to be provoked by that to which I cannot properly offer an answer. In spite of this precaution, however, it comes to my knowledge that I am much censured for some supposed agency in setting up and seeking to sustain the new State government of Louisiana.

In this I have done just so much, and no more than, the public knows. In the annual message of December, 1863, and in the accompanying proclamation, I presented a plan of reconstruction as the phrase goes, which I promised, if adopted by any State, should be acceptable to and sustained by the executive government of the nation. I distinctly stated that this was not the only plan which might possibly be acceptable, and I also distinctly protested that the executive claimed no right to say when or whether members should be admitted to seats in Congress from such States. This plan was in advance submitted to the then Cabinet, and distinctly approved by every member of it. One of them suggested that I should then and in that connection apply the Emancipation Proclamation to the theretofore excepted parts of Virginia and Louisiana; that I should drop the suggestion about apprenticeship for freed people, and that I should omit the protest against my own power in regard to the admission of members to Congress. But even he approved every part and parcel of the plan which has since been employed or touched by the action of Louisiana.

The new constitution of Louisiana, declaring emancipation for the whole State, practically applies the proclamation to the part previously excepted. It does not adopt apprenticeship for freed people, and it is silent, as it could not well be otherwise, about the admission of members to Congress. So that, as it applies to Louisiana, every member of the Cabinet fully approved the plan. The message went to Congress, and I received many commendations of the plan, written and verbal, and not a single objection to it from any professed emancipationist came to my knowledge until after the news reached Washington that the people of Louisiana had begun to move in accordance with it. From about July, 1862, I had corresponded with different persons supposed to be interested [in] seeking a reconstruction of a State government for Louisiana. When the message of 1863, with the plan before mentioned, reached New Orleans, General Banks wrote me that he was confident that the people, with his military coöperation, would reconstruct substantially on that plan. I wrote to him and some of them to try it. They tried it, and the result is known. Such has been my only agency in getting up the Louisiana government.

As to sustaining it, my promise is out, as before stated. But as bad promises are better broken than kept, I shall treat this as a bad promise, and break it whenever I shall be convinced that keeping it is adverse to the public interest; but I have not yet been so convinced. I have been shown a letter on this subject, supposed to be an able one, in which the writer expresses regret that my mind has not seemed to be definitely

* Reprinted from John G. Nicolay and John Hay, eds., *Complete Works of Abraham Lincoln* (Lincoln Memorial Univ. edition, n.p., 1894), XI, 84–92.

fixed on the question whether the seceded States, so called, are in the Union or out of it. It would perhaps add astonishment to his regret were he to learn that since I have found professed Union men endeavoring to make that question, I have purposely forborne any public expression upon it. As appears to me, that question has not been, nor yet is, a practically material one, and that any discussion of it, while it thus remains practically immaterial, could have no effect other than the mischievous one of dividing our friends. As yet, whatever it may hereafter become, that question is bad as the basis of a controversy, and good for nothing at all—a merely pernicious abstraction.

We all agree that the seceded States, so called, are out of their proper practical relation with the Union, and that the sole object of the government, civil and military, in regard to those States, is to again get them into that proper practical relation. I believe that it is not only possible, but in fact easier, to do this without deciding or even considering whether these States have ever been out of the Union, than with it. Finding themselves safely at home, it would be utterly immaterial whether they had ever been abroad. Let us all join in doing the acts necessary to restoring the proper practical relations between these States and the Union, and each forever after innocently indulge his own opinion whether in doing the acts he brought the States from without into the Union, or only gave them proper assistance, they never having been out of it. The amount of constituency, so to speak, on which the new Louisiana government rests, would be more satisfactory to all if it contained 50,000 or 30,000, or even 20,000, instead of only about 12,000, as it does. It is also unsatisfactory to some that the elective franchise is not given to the colored man. I would myself prefer that it were now conferred on the very intelligent, and on those who serve our cause as soldiers.

Still, the question is not whether the Louisiana government, as it stands, is quite all that is desirable. The question is, will it be wiser to take it as it is and help to improve it, or to reject and disperse it? Can Louisiana be brought into proper practical relation with the Union sooner by sustaining or by discarding her new State government? Some twelve thousand voters in the heretofore slave State of Louisiana have sworn allegiance to the Union, assumed to be the rightful political power of the State, held elections, organized a State government, adopted a free-State constitution, giving the benefit of public schools equally to black and white, and empowering the legislature to confer the elective franchise upon the colored man. Their legislature has already voted to ratify the constitutional amendment recently passed by Congress, abolishing slavery throughout the nation. These 12,000 persons are thus fully committed to the Union and to perpetual freedom in the State—committed to the very things, and nearly all the things, the nation wants—and they ask the nation's recognition and its assistance to make good their committal.

Now, if we reject and spurn them, we do our utmost to disorganize and disperse them. We, in effect, say to the white man: You are worthless or worse; we will neither help you, nor be helped by you. To the blacks we say: This cup of liberty which these, your old masters, hold to your lips we will dash from you, and leave you to the chances of gathering the spilled and scattered contents in some vague and undefined when, where, and how. If this course, discouraging and paralyzing both white and black, has any tendency to bring Louisiana into proper practical relations with the Union, I have so far been unable to perceive it. If, on the contrary, we recognize and sustain the new government of Louisiana, the converse of all this is made true. We encourage the hearts and nerve the arms of the 12,000 to adhere to their work, and argue for it, and proselyte for it, and fight for it, and feed it, and grow it, and ripen it to a complete success. The colored man, too, in seeing all united for him, is inspired with vigilance, and energy, and daring, to the same end. Grant that he desires the elective franchise, will he not attain it sooner by saving the already advanced steps toward it than by running backward over them? Concede that the new government of Louisiana is only what it should be as the egg is to the fowl, we shall sooner have the fowl by hatching the egg than by smashing it.

Again, if we reject Louisiana we also reject one vote in favor of the proposed amendment to the national Constitution. To meet this proposition it has been argued that no more than three-fourths of those States which have not attempted secession are necessary to validly ratify the amendment. I do not commit myself against this further than to say that such a ratification would be questionable, and sure to be persistently questioned, while a ratification by three-fourths of all the States would be unquestioned and unquestionable. I repeat the question: Can Louisiana be brought into proper practical relation with the Union sooner by sustaining or by discarding her new State government? What has been said of Louisiana will apply generally to other States. And yet so great peculiarities pertain to each State, and such important and sudden changes occur in the same State, and withal so new and unprecedented is the whole case that no exclusive and inflexible plan can safely be prescribed as to details and collaterals. Such exclusive and inflexible plan would surely become a new entanglement. Important principles may and must be inflexible. In the present situation, as the phrase goes, it may be my duty to make some new announcement to the people of the South. I am considering, and shall not fail to act when satisfied that action will be proper.

CHAPTER TWELVE

THE MEN OF RECONSTRUCTION

Reconstruction was national and not merely sectional in character. The problems of freedom for the Negro, restoration of the South to the Union, and rehabilitation of the southern economy had to be solved within the larger context of a rising industrial society in the North determined to institute policies consolidating its newly-won economic gains. The situation was further complicated by political considerations, notably the desire of the Republican party to maintain political control and the attempt of Congress to assert its supremacy over the executive branch. Thus, there were numerous and conflicting philosophies involved in the unfolding of Reconstruction, ranging from humanitarian to narrowly economic and political goals. Recent scholars agree that the older stereotypes surrounding this period are inadequate and that it is now necessary to distinguish the main groups and what each one was trying to achieve. In this revisionist stage, historians have already shown the constructive side of Reconstruction governments, especially in the field of public education, and have shed new light on the perplexing questions of corruption and the size of expenditures.

T. Harry Williams discussed in the first selection the motives of people in the North and South during Reconstruction. He accepted the view that northern business was concerned with economic and political gain; cared little for abolition-democracy; and enlisted the support of the Midwest through free land, internal improvement policies, and the use of the bloody shirt. In the South, Williams suggested, "the overwhelming mass of the people—the yeoman farmers, middle-class whites, and poor whites—were fiercely opposed to Negro suffrage and to any condition of equality for the Negro." The planter-business class, on the other hand, opposed Negro suffrage "for economic rather than racial reasons." Yet, confronted by high taxation, this group was prepared to encourage the Negro in return for economic favors. And while such a coalition did not succeed, the evidence clearly indicates that white opinion in the South was far from being monolithic. As Williams concluded, "economic, social, and political stimuli affected groups in the South in different ways, and Southerners differed among themselves on the issues of Reconstruction in about the same degree as did groups in the North."

T. HARRY WILLIAMS: AN ANALYSIS OF SOME
RECONSTRUCTION ATTITUDES*

In late years revisionist historians have done much to correct the existing and often distorted picture of the Reconstruction period in American history. Earlier writers on Reconstruction, whether they were Republican politicians or southern polemicists, journalists, or historians, exhibited a number of historical deficiencies, but in general it may be said that they told a story that was too simple and naïve. It was simple in that the terrible complexities of Reconstruction were presented in the easy terms of stereotypes— the good white Southern Democrats fighting against the bad colored Republicans and their insidious northern allies, or vice versa. It was naïve in that virtually no analysis was made to explain why people acted as they did. Thus carpetbaggers were dishonest because they were bad men or Republicans, but no attempt was made to describe the forces which contributed to their dishonesty. The revisionists have forced several modifications in the Reconstruction story. They have demonstrated, among other things, that the corruption of the Reconstruction state governments has been exaggerated and that in any case corruption was a national, not a purely southern, phenomenon, with an expanding capitalism as the chief corrupting agent; that Democrats were quite as willing as Republicans to be bought by business; that the supposed astronomically high appropriations of the Reconstruction governments seem so only in comparison with the niggardly budgets of the planter-controlled governments of the ante-bellum period; that although the Reconstruction governments were corrupt and dishonest, they must be credited with definite progress in the fields of popular education and internal improvements; and that the national reconstruction program was radical only in a superficial sense in that it gave political power to the Negro but failed to provide economic power through the promised confiscation and ownership of land, and thus that because the position of the Negro had no lasting basis his rule was easily overthrown.[1]

These new viewpoints have provided a desirable balance and proportion to the traditional historical treatment of Reconstruction. Still debated and in part unexplored in research are the motives of the northern and southern people during this period. Who supported Reconstruction and why; and who opposed it, and why? In analyzing the motivation of Reconstruction, historians have devoted most of their attention to northern political and economic groups and have produced certain conclusions which have been generally accepted. What may be termed the Beale thesis, because it has been most competently developed by Professor Howard K. Beale, offers a sectional-class explanation of Reconstruction. According to this thesis, Reconstruction was a successful attempt by northeastern business, acting through the Republican party, to control the national government for its own economic ends: notably, the protective tariff, the national banks, a "sound" currency. To accomplish its program, the business class had to overthrow from the seats of power the old ruling agrarian class of the South and West. This it did by inaugurating Reconstruction, which made the South Republican, and by selling its policies to the voters wrapped up in such attractive vote-getting packages as northern patriotism or the bloody shirt.[2] Another student of the period, while accepting the Beale thesis, points out that northern business men supported Reconstruction not only because of national issues but also because they thought it would enable them to exploit the South through protected capital investments, and that Republican bosses supported Reconstruction because they believed that if the South could be made Republican they could stay in power.[3]

The Negro author, W. E. Burghardt Du Bois, conceding the part played by industry in formulating the Reconstruction program contends that there was in the North a substantial mass opinion of liberal idealism, which he calls "abolition-democracy," that stood for a democratic reconstruction plan, including equal rights for Negroes. This group, he insists, represented in politics by men like Thaddeus Stevens, was

* Reprinted from the *Journal of Southern History*, XII (November 1946), 469–86, by permission of the Managing Editor.

[1] Francis B. Simkins, "New Viewpoints of Southern Reconstruction," in *Journal of Southern History* (Baton Rouge, 1935–   ), V (1939), 49–61; Howard K. Beale, "On Rewriting Reconstruction History," in *American Historical Review* (New York, 1895–   ), XLV (1940), 807–27; Horace Mann Bond, "Social and Economic Forces in Alabama Reconstruction," in *Journal of Negro History* (Washington, 1916–   ), XXIII (1938), 290–348. These writers do two things that so many writers on the subject have not done: they treat Reconstruction as a national development rather than as something happening in an insulated South,

and they relate it to southern forces before and after Reconstruction.

[2] Howard K. Beale, *The Critical Year: A Study of Andrew Johnson and Reconstruction* (New York, 1930), 1, 8, 115, 143–45; Beale, "On Rewriting Reconstruction History," *loc. cit.*, 813.

[3] William B. Hesseltine, "Economic Factors in the Abandonment of Reconstruction," in *Mississippi Valley Historical Review* (Cedar Rapids, 1914–   ), XXII (1935), 191–210. See also, Hesseltine, *The South in American History* (New York, 1943), 488–89.

equally influential with business in determining the nature of Reconstruction.[4] The existence of such a body of opinion cannot be disputed. That it was as extensive as Du Bois thinks or that it was animated by as much idealism for the Negro may well be doubted; unfortunately there is no way to document accurately its numbers or influence. One thing is certain. The leaders of abolition-democracy did not succeed in incorporating their ideas into the Republican reconstruction scheme. They demanded universal suffrage, universal amnesty, and confiscation of the land of rich Southerners and its distribution among the freedmen. The Republican politicos, being economic reactionaries, discarded confiscation because they had no interest in bringing about a social revolution, and they rejected universal amnesty because it would have made a Republican South improbable. It would seem that the party bosses, instead of being influenced to any considerable degree by abolition-democracy, used it for whatever it was worth to marshal support for a program designed to benefit a plutocratic minority.

An interpretation of northern motivation that differs in part from both Beale and Du Bois has come from Marxist historians and writers.[5] The Marxian thesis has been elaborately presented by James S. Allen,[6] who regards Reconstruction as a plan formulated and carried through by big business to enable it to dominate the nation. Up to a point, this is only the Beale thesis dressed up in Marxian jargon. Allen, however, proceeds to advance the claim that the business program was "democratic," because industry, in achieving power, smashed the old, feudal planter class of the South and thus helped prepare the way for the coming of the industrial state which, after business itself was smashed, would evolve into a perfect democracy of the Marxist variety.[7] In recent years writers of Marxist persuasion have dropped Allen's emphasis on the class struggle,

and have presented Reconstruction as a straight-out plan of equalitarian democracy. The new departure has been most strikingly expressed, in fictional form, by Howard Fast, who flatly states that the Reconstruction acts of 1867 were intended "to create a new democracy in the South."[8] The Marxian thesis in any of these forms has little validity. No amount of historical legerdemain can transform the economic reactionaries of the Republican Party into great liberals or make the protective tariff and the gold standard into items of the democratic faith. Furthermore, as will be shown, the Marxists are wrong when they try to develop the corollary that Reconstruction was also a democratic process in the South.[9]

The sectional-class thesis of Beale would seem to be the most nearly correct analysis of northern motivation, although Beale did not fully explain how northeastern business persuaded agrarian Republicans from the Middle West to support industrial measures and a reconstruction policy designed to insure the rule of business in the South. It has since been demonstrated that this was done in part by giving the Middle West exceptionally generous appropriations for internal improvements and in effect buying its support;[10] and to this should be added such other inducements as free land, pensions, and railroads, as well as such emotional and psychological appeals as habitual use of the bloody shirt. Du Bois was also undoubtedly correct in contending that idealistic forces played a part in shaping reconstruction policy, and his point is a good, although minor, corrective to the purely economic analysis. But the major fact remains that the men who made Reconstruction were moved by issues of economic and political power far more than by democratic idealism.

While the question of northern motivation has been fairly well established, there has been little attempt to prepare a systematic analysis of southern attitudes toward Reconstruction. Most of the

[4] W. E. Burghardt Du Bois, *Black Reconstruction: An Essay toward a History of the Part which Black Folk Played in the Attempt to Reconstruct Democracy in America, 1860–1880* (New York, 1938), 182, 185–87. Beale, in his article, "On Rewriting Reconstruction History," *loc. cit.,* 818–19, admitted that there were minority elements of democratic idealism in the Republican party and that Stevens and Charles Sumner were representatives of these elements. For the contrary view that Stevens thought solely in terms of power for his class and party, see Richard N. Current, *Old Thad Stevens: A Story of Ambition* (Madison, 1942).

[5] The term Marxist is here applied to those writers who frankly state that they are interpreting history according to the laws and predictions of Karl Marx and to those who without acknowledging Marx write history that conforms to the Marxian pattern.

[6] James S. Allen, *Reconstruction: The Battle for Democracy, 1865–1867* (New York, 1937).

[7] *Ibid.,* 18, 22, 81, 89.

[8] Howard Fast, *Freedom Road* (New York, 1944), 71.

[9] It is significant that those Negroes who envisioned Reconstruction as a real social revolution for their people saw little idealism in the Republican party. Thus the New Orleans *Tribune,* a Negro newspaper, said: "The Republican party of the North was not formed upon the true basis of justice and equality, as the history of abolition and slavery plainly shows; and it has only the right to claim credit for having abolished slavery as a political necessity and of having given the ballot to the black men as an arm of defence to the loyal white men. Emergency, nay necessity, had more to do with the abolition of slavery and the passage of the Military Bill than had philanthropy and love for the negro." Quoted in New Orleans *Times,* July 4, 1873.

[10] Helen J. and T. Harry Williams, "Wisconsin Republicans and Reconstruction, 1865–1870," in *Wisconsin Magazine of History* (Madison, 1917–), XXIII (1939), 17–39.

professional historians writing on southern reconstruction have been members of or followers of the so-called Dunning school. They are largely responsible for the familiar stereotypes of Reconstruction. According to their interpretation, Reconstruction was a battle between two extremes: the Democrats, as the group which included the vast majority of the whites, standing for decent government and racial supremacy, versus the Republicans, the Negroes, alien carpetbaggers, and renegade scalawags, standing for dishonest government and alien ideals. These historians wrote literally in terms of white and black. This is not to say that they did not recognize the fact that there were differences between Southerners on such issues as Negro suffrage. But they explained the differences in terms of individual motivation. Thus Southerners who advocated the vote for Negroes were either bad men, or wartime Unionists who hated "rebels," or kindly planters who knew Negroes well and wanted to control their votes in the right direction. Although the Dunning writers sensed an apparent disagreement between the planter-business class and the small farmers on the Negro question, with the planters being willing to accept a position of greater equality for the Negro, they did not explore the difference or try to ascertain whether there were economic and social causes for its existence.[11]

No such reluctance characterizes Du Bois. He boldly proclaims that Reconstruction was a labor movement, an attempt by the white and black proletariat to control the South, "a vision of democracy across racial lines."[12] A basic error invalidates most of his thesis. There was no white proletariat of any significant numbers; the great mass of the whites were yeoman farmers who thought in terms of racial supremacy instead of class solidarity. Furthermore, he exaggerates the readiness of the former non-slaveholding whites to unite with the Negroes. He himself recognizes that there are factual weaknesses in his theory. He knows that the common whites furnished the power by which the Republican state governments were overthrown; but he explains this

disturbing fact by claiming that the planters cut off the developing interracial co-operation of the proletariat by appealing to the prejudices of the poorer whites and organizing them on the color line.[13] Closely paralleling Du Bois' interpretation, and even going beyond it, is that of the Marxists. They, too, present Reconstruction as a biracial movement of the laboring class which was finally destroyed by a counter-revolution of the planters.[14] According to Howard Fast, the Negroes and poor whites joined hands in the Republican party and created "a fine, a just, and a truly democratic civilization," but the reactionary planter class refused to permit this experiment in social democracy and wiped it out with force.[15] That the validity of such assertions is open to serious question can be shown by examining the attitude of the planters and business men in Louisiana toward Reconstruction and the Negro and placing the results in the larger setting of what is known about the general attitudes of the southern whites in other parts of the region.

First of all, despite the opinions of the Marxists, the overwhelming mass of the people—the yeoman farmers, middle class whites, and poor whites—were fiercely opposed to Negro suffrage and to any condition of equality for the Negro. The evidence on this point, while not voluminous because of the general inarticulateness of the common whites, is strong; it is best expressed by the fact that the small-farmer, white-belt areas of the southern states voted heavily against Republicans and Republican measures in election after election.[16] As Horace Mann Bond puts it, the farmers hated equally slavery, planters, and Negroes.[17] The attitude of the common whites of

---

[11] The views of the Dunning school are in William A. Dunning, *Reconstruction: Political and Economic, 1865–1877* (New York, 1907), especially pp. 116–17, 213; Walter L. Fleming, *The Sequel of Appomattox: A Chronicle of the Reunion of the States* (New Haven, 1921), especially pp. 47–48, 50–52, 87–88. These criticisms of Dunning and Fleming are not made in any carping spirit. It is recognized that they and other members of the Dunning school were pioneers in the study of Reconstruction and made important factual contributions to its history. It should also be noted that Fleming was aware that many planters were for Negro suffrage and that most farmers were against it. See his *Civil War and Reconstruction in Alabama* (New York, 1905), 387–88. But he ascribed the planters' attitude merely to a desire to control the Negro vote in order to maintain their power in the legislature.

[12] Du Bois, *Black Reconstruction*, 346–47, 350.

[13] *Ibid.*, 130–31. These criticisms of Du Bois do not detract from the fact that his book was a valuable contribution to Reconstruction history. In some respects he got closer to the truth of Reconstruction than any other writer.

[14] Allen, *Reconstruction*, 111–15, 126, 183–84, 193. On different pages Allen states that a significant portion of the common whites joined the Republican party and again that practically all of them did. The book as a whole gives the impression that the poorer whites as a class became Republicans.

[15] Fast, *Freedom Road*, 263.

[16] Paul Lewinson, *Race, Class, and Party: A History of Negro Suffrage in the South* (New York, 1932), 23, 37, 52; Roger W. Shugg, *Origins of Class Struggle in Louisiana: A Social History of White Farmers and Laborers during Slavery and After, 1840–1875* (Baton Rouge, 1939), 230; Hesseltine, *South in American History*, 485; Dunning, *Reconstruction*, 213; Fleming, *Sequel of Appomattox*, 47–48, 50, 87–88; Fleming, *Civil War and Reconstruction in Alabama*, 387–88.

[17] Bond, "Social and Economic Factors in Alabama Reconstruction," *loc. cit.*, 294–95. Bond finds that at the beginning of Reconstruction there was some political co-operation between poor whites and Negroes.

Reconstruction is consonant with the known attitude of the poorest whites, economically, today; that is, racial antipathy toward Negroes is always sharpest when accentuated by economic competition. The teachings of social psychology can be adduced to support the generalization concerning the reaction of the whites. In a caste system based on a fixed status for groups, any attempt by a subordinated element—in this case the Negroes—to achieve a higher status unlooses feelings of tension and fear in the next higher group, which will exert itself, often violently, to keep the subordinated group down.[18]

The most powerful group in the South was the planter-business class and its professional allies; its position on Reconstruction was of decisive importance. In the beginning days of Reconstruction, the planters and business men strongly opposed the central proposal of the Radical Republican program—suffrage for the Negro. But they opposed it for economic rather than racial reasons. This fact is crucially important in understanding their reactions. To use modern terms, they feared that the grant of the ballot to the Negro would add to the strength of the liberal or progressive vote. This is not to say that they did not regard the Negro as an inferior being of an entirely separate race. But it is to say that they reacted to a proposal to enfranchise a laboring class as would any propertied minority in any society—they opposed it because they believed it would lead to an attack upon property.[19] A few quotations selected from many statements appearing in conservative New Orleans newspapers which were spokesmen of the planter-business interests will demonstrate the point. Terming universal suffrage a menace to property, the New Orleans *Times* said: "The right to vote should be given to those only who can use it with discretion and sound judgment, and as our electoral privileges are already too wide, it would be the maddest folly to extend them at once to a class who have always been under control, and who—without the ability to form a correct judgment for themselves—would be left to the tender mercies of party tricksters." Let the Negro wait until he acquired property before he became a

voter.[20] In a fuller and more philosophical exposition of its views, the *Times* stated: "Wherever voters greatly outnumber property holders, property will assuredly be unsafe. When voters have property and intelligence, there is some hope that they may 'find their interest in the interest of the community' and be anxious to secure a consistent, honest, economical and straight-forward administration. But the selfish interest of the non-property holding voter lies in an altogether different direction. He wishes to secure rich pickings, and, too frequently, soils his fingers by base bribes. Were universal negro suffrage to be added to the white universal suffrage now existing in the South, the security of both life and property would be greatly weakened. . . . With our present too widely extended suffrage it is difficult even now to steer between the rocks of the political Scylla and the whirlpool of its Charybdis, and with universal negro suffrage added, the task would be wholly hopeless."[21]

Becoming frankly specific, the *Times* later declared that "If representative institutions are to be preserved in this country, the control of taxes must be left to those who pay them, and the protection of property to those who own it."[22] The New Orleans *Crescent*, endorsing the proposal of South Carolina's planter leader, Wade Hampton, to extend the vote to Negroes who had acquired property and an education,[23] asserted: "Southern conservatives ask nothing more on the subject of suffrage than that its distribution shall be determined by the test of character and intelligence. They have asked for nothing more from the time that, by one of the irreversible results of war, the Southern negroes became a part of the free population of the country. It is not their fault if such a test has been rejected in favor of another that proscribes a large proportion of the highest intelligence on the one hand, and opens all political functions to the maximum of ignorance on the other."[24] Expressing the conservatives' fear of the economic implications of Negro suffrage, the *Crescent* said: "It seems to be practically absurd and dangerous to commit the decisions of those difficult questions to numbers of extemporized citizens incapable of forming any accurate or rational opinions; and likely to

---

[18] Kimball Young, *Social Psychology* (New York, 1944), 262–63, 269.

[19] There was logic in this position. Many of the Negro leaders were exponents of radical agrarianism. Said the New Orleans *Tribune*: "There is no more room in the organization of our society, for an oligarchy of slaveholders, or property holders"; and again, "There is in fact, no true republican government, unless the land, and wealth in general, are distributed among the great mass of the inhabitants." Quoted in Du Bois, *Black Reconstruction*, 458–59. This agrarianism never secured any significant victories because the carpetbaggers, scalawags, and professional Negro politicians, interested mainly in corruption and power, choked it off. See Shugg, *Origins of Class Struggle in Louisiana*, 243–44.

[20] New Orleans *Times,* August 13, 1865.

[21] *Ibid.,* December 24, 1866.

[22] *Ibid.,* February 2, 1868. There are similar statements in the issues of November 26, 30, 1866, January 26, 1867.

[23] Hampton, Alexander H. Stephens, Benjamin F. Perry, and other leaders had suggested a limited Negro suffrage based on property and education, thus permitting only those Negroes to vote who were conscious of property rights. Hampton believed the planters could easily control such voters. Lewinson, *Race, Class, and Party,* 37–39; Fleming, *Sequel of Appomattox,* 50–52.

[24] New Orleans *Crescent,* October 23, 1867.

imagine that the right to vote means the right to live without work, and to rob the industrious classes for the benefit of the idle and thriftless." [25] The *Picayune* denounced Negro suffrage because it did not believe that common men of any color should vote; manhood suffrage was "the unlimited suffrage of the ignorant, landless and lawless." [26] "We look upon it [voting] as a duty rather than a right," said the *Picayune*, "and regret that there is so much of it among the whites." [27] To the *Picayune*, Reconstruction was a process that proscribed "intelligence, probity and property" and elevated propertyless nobodies to power. [28]

To the testimony of conservative newspapers can be added representative statements of conservative planter-business leaders. In 1867, when Congress was considering the radical reconstruction acts, various southern newspapers asked prominent individuals to give their reactions to the proposed measures. More frank and philosophical than most was J. W. Robb of Mississippi. He warned conservatives that all republics in history had fallen when they had extended the ballot to a laboring class, "an ignorant horde of stupid and besotted men." "I believe," he continued, "that from the introduction of negro suffrage, the worst form and spirit of agrarianism will arise to disturb the peace and order of the State, and that it will require our utmost exertions to keep it down, and retain for ourselves political existence and individual security." [29] Francis T. Nicholls, who became governor of Louisiana in 1877 when white supremacy supposedly was restored, told a Congressional committee that conservatives were opposed to Reconstruction because it had endangered property interests by placing ignorance in power. Before Reconstruction, he said, there had been a relatively small group of ignorant white voters whom the rich could control, but Reconstruction had made ignorance "the dominating power." He favored a law that in the interest of property would disfranchise the ignorant of both races. [30]

Congress ignored the opposition to Negro suffrage of the planter-business class, based primarily on economic grounds, and of the common whites, based primarily on racial grounds. In 1867 it passed the reconstruction laws of the Radical Republicans; and Negro suffrage and, in many states, Negro rule became a reality. There followed a period of years, varying in different states, in which the Republican party, led by white carpetbaggers and scalawags and composed predominantly of the Negro masses, controlled the South. The political record of its rule was a compound of blatant corruption and forward social legislation. It was an expensive program. Money was needed to gratify the desires of the white and colored politicians for graft and of the colored masses for social services furnished by the state. The Republicans had to resort to higher and higher taxation, and necessarily they laid the heaviest taxes upon real property. While taxation affected all property holders, large and small, the brunt of it fell upon the large holders. This, as Du Bois points out, is a crucial fact in Reconstruction history—a war-impoverished propertied class was being compelled by the votes of poor men to bear an almost confiscatory tax burden. [31]

Faced with extinction by taxation, the planter-business class reacted again and characteristically in economic rather than racial terms. Negro votes had imposed the tax burden. Negro votes could lift it. If in order to persuade the Negroes to do so it was necessary to grant them political and civil equality or even to let them run the state, well and good. Get the tax rate down, cried one New Orleans conservative, "even if every office in the State, from Governor to the most insignificant constable, were filled by a negro." [32] Urged another: "We must get rid of party hacks and political jobbers, and satisfy the reasonable demands of the negroes. This accomplished, Louisiana will again blossom as the rose. It is our only salvation." [33] A prominent merchant declared: "I am in favor, in case we ever have another election, of giving to the colored people the bulk of the lucrative positions. . . . I am not afraid that they will, in any considerable degree abuse their privileges, and, for ourselves, we want nothing but peaceful government." [34] "You want civil equality; you shall have it," a leading business man pledged the Negroes, "if you forsake the Northern adventurer who has plundered poor Louisiana until she is penniless." [35] On with political cooperation with Negroes, exclaimed a property holder, "for God's sake if it will give us an honest government; our present lot is insupportable." [36] A blunt Natchitoches planter asserted that it was imperative that the whites detach the Negroes from the Republicans: "When the war was over we wouldn't have anything to do with the niggers, and let the Radicals gobble them up. . . . I am in favor of anything to get them. Drop the name of Democracy, I say, and go in for the niggers." [37]

[25] *Ibid.*, May 14, 1868.

[26] New Orleans *Daily Picayune,* May 10, 1868.

[27] *Ibid.*, May 23, 1868.

[28] *Ibid.*, May 24, 1868.

[29] J. W. Robb, in Jackson *Clarion,* March 19, 1868, quoted in New Orleans *Times,* March 22.

[30] *House Reports,* 43 Cong., 2 Sess., No. 261, Part 3, pp. 646–47.

[31] Du Bois, *Black Reconstruction,* 590–91.

[32] Letter of Archibald Mitchell, in New Orleans *Picayune,* June 18, 1873.

[33] New Orleans *Times,* May 29, 1873.

[34] *Ibid.*, May 30, 1873.

[35] *Ibid.*, June 6, 1873.

[36] *Ibid.*, June 23, 1873.

[37] *Ibid.*, June 9, 1873.

THE MEN OF RECONSTRUCTION

What practical political action did the planter-business class take during Reconstruction to protect itself from excessive taxation and to foster its economic interests? In local elections in New Orleans, for example, the business men contemplated putting up Negro candidates for Congressional and city offices to compete with white Republicans. On Carondelet Street, the city's great business center, it was planned to nominate a colored foreman of one of the leading cotton presses for Congress. Such a man, asserted the business reporter of the New Orleans *Times,* "Will protect and do more for the South than any white Radical which can be selected to run against him. Carondelet street will go for the gentlemen with the cotton press." [38] The business men, this journalist explained, "are taking an unusual interest in being represented in Congress by a representative born in the South. The nearer approach to a real African, black in color, the more confidence will be placed in him." [39] Since the records do not show that the Carondelet magnates got their foreman nominated, it is probable that the Democratic leaders in New Orleans refused to take a Negro candidate, or even more probable that the cotton press gentleman, if he had political ambitions and an eye for the future, became a Republican. Regardless of the outcome, however, the episode demonstrated that these hardheaded business men placed their economic interests above racial differences and that they preferred to entrust those interests to an understanding and amenable Negro rather than to an untried white.

A second device adopted by the conservatives was to enter the Republican party and seek to control it. A recent study by David H. Donald illustrates how this was done in Mississippi. [40] After Radical Reconstruction went into effect most of the former Whigs, in antebellum times the party of the big slaveholders, became Republicans. "Such action is not hard to understand," writes Donald. "The Whigs were wealthy men—the large planters and the railroad and industrial promoters—who naturally turned to the party which in the state as in the nation was dominated by business interests." [41] At first these planters, or scalawags, to use a familiar term, dominated the party, but they lost their leadership to the carpetbaggers who, in the struggles for power within the party, were willing to promise more to the Ne-

groes. Donald points to the planters' fruitless opposition to the Republican program of big budgets and high taxes and their revulsion against the social equality claimed by the Negroes as sources of their difficulties. Finally, repudiated by people they could not control, they drifted "slowly and reluctantly over to the Democratic camp." [42]

Still a third device employed by the planters and business men was to invite the Negroes to leave the Republicans and join with them in a new political organization separate from the Democratic party. The conservatives promised in such case to respect the Negro's civil equality and his right to vote and to hold office. Such movements were tried in several states, [43] the most elaborate being the so-called "Louisiana Unification Movement." [44] Inaugurated in 1873, this movement was headed by General Pierre G. T. Beauregard and was supported by the flower of the wealth and culture of New Orleans and South Louisiana. [45] Its platform advocated complete political equality for the Negro, an equal division of state offices between the races, and a plan whereby Negroes would become landowners. The unifiers denounced discrimination because of color in hiring laborers or in selecting directors of corporations, and called for the abandonment of segregation in public conveyances, public places, railroads, steamboats, and the public schools. [46] The Louisiana movement, like the others, failed for lack of support from the white masses. The unification program was popular in New Orleans and in the plantation belt of South Louisiana, but in the

---

[38] *Ibid.,* August 13, 1867. "On 'Change" column. The business columns of the newspapers contain much information about the activities of business men in Reconstruction. Historians have overlooked this important source.

[39] *Ibid.,* August 17, 1867. See also issue of September 5.

[40] David H. Donald, "The Scalawag in Mississippi Reconstruction," in *Journal of Southern History,* X (1944), 447–60.

[41] *Ibid.,* 449–50.

[42] *Ibid.,* 453–55.

[43] Francis B. Simkins and Robert H. Woody, *South Carolina during Reconstruction* (Chapel Hill, 1932), 447–54; Alrutheus A. Taylor, *The Negro in South Carolina during the Reconstruction* (Washington, 1924), 195–97; John S. Reynolds, *Reconstruction in South Carolina, 1865–1877* (Columbia, 1905), 139–43; James W. Garner, *Reconstruction in Mississippi* (New York, 1901), 238–43.

[44] T. Harry Williams, "The Louisiana Unification Movement of 1873," in *Journal of Southern History,* XI (1945), 349–69.

[45] Beauregard believed that in the long run Negro suffrage would increase the political power of the South. The whites could control the Negroes "with a little education and some property qualifications" and "defeat our adversaries with their own weapon." Quoted in New York *Tribune,* April 1, 1867. For other expressions of a similar view, see *ibid.,* April 4, 1867, quoting Mobile *Tribune* and Wilmington (N.C.) *Dispatch.*

[46] Williams, "Louisiana Unification Movement," *loc. cit.,* 359–61. It is to be noted that rich whites could ask for the destruction of segregation without having to encounter many of the results of non-segregation. This was particularly true in education. As a North Louisiana newspaper pointed out, the rich sent their children to private white schools; the poorer whites had to send theirs to public schools which the rich proposed to make biracial. Shreveport *Times,* quoted in Monroe *Ouachita Telegraph,* June 28, 1873.

small-farmer areas of other parts of the state it was received with loathing and execration.

It is evident that a basis existed for an alliance of the planter-business class and the Negroes. "If they [the planters] had wished," writes Du Bois, "they could have held the Negro vote in the palm of their hands." [47] Why did such an alliance fail to materialize? In the first place, the leaders of the unification movements could not persuade any significant number of whites to support the concessions which the planters were willing to accord the colored people. The common whites, animated by racial motives, refused to follow planter leadership, and without any mass white support the unification movements could not succeed. In Louisiana the movement failed to develop much mass support even from the Negroes because professional Negro politicians, secure in their place in the Republican party, advised their followers to shun co-operation and because those Negro leaders who favored co-operation could not suppress their suspicion of the sincerity of the planter-business class. "We know that, by an alliance with you, we can have more privileges than we now enjoy," one Negro spokesman told the conservatives. "We will not then have to cling to the carpet-baggers for protection, but can ourselves take whatever share of office and representation falls to us fairly. Still, we have *some* rights now, and we don't intend to give them up. Rather than do that, we will cling to the carpet-bagger forever, and let him share our power." [48]

In the second place, the planters and business men, while willing to make far-reaching concessions to the Negroes, did not make them because they believed in the principles of racial equality. They made them because of pressing economic reasons and because they wanted to control the Negro vote. They never ceased to regard the Negroes as inferior creatures who by an unfortunate turn of fate had become politically powerful in the state. Hence there was a limit to their concessions, its line marked by anything that seemed to suggest social equality. The carpetbaggers, unhampered by such reservations, could always outbid the conservatives. Thus in states like Mississippi, where the planter tried to dominate the Republican party, the carpetbaggers took the leadership of the Negroes away from the scalawags. Finally, the differing economic aspirations of the wealthy whites and the Negroes prevented any lasting alliance of the two. The Negroes demanded a program of social services financed by the state, which meant high taxes. The planters wanted to control the colored vote in order to reduce these services and lower taxes which they considered almost confiscatory. The Negroes wanted higher wages and shorter hours; the planters wanted a serf-like system of sharecropping. The planters simply lacked the capital to finance the Negro's social or labor program; [49] but in view of the obvious conflict between the desires of the two groups it is doubtful whether such a program would have received support from the planters even if they had possessed the necessary means for financing it.

And so the planters and business men, unable to prevent the establishment of Negro suffrage and unable to control it after it was established, joined with the common whites to overthrow the Republican state governments. By 1877 the Democrats controlled every southern state, and what the textbooks call white supremacy was restored. Actually, Negroes continued to vote, although in reduced numbers, and white supremacy was not restored until the 1890's. As Professor C. Vann Woodward has ably demonstrated, the men who came to power after Reconstruction were not in the old agrarian, planter tradition. They were often of the planter class, but in reality they were industrialists or would-be industrialists. They preached the industrialization of the South through the importation of Yankee capital, a policy of low taxes to attract business, and a political alliance with the Northeast instead of with the South's traditional ally, the West. [50] These men reacted to Negro suffrage as had men of their class during Reconstruction. As the vote of labor, it was something to be feared and kept in hand, but as the vote of an inferior people, it was also something that might be manipulated for the benefit of the wealthy. As events developed, the bosses of the New South sometimes found that they could use the colored vote to beat down attempts of the farmers to take over control of the Democratic party. In the election of 1880 in Georgia, for example, the rich defeated the farmers through a combination of a minority of the white votes and a majority of the colored ones. [51] The southern champions of indus-

---

[47] Du Bois, *Black Reconstruction,* 611.

[48] New Orleans *Times,* May 28, 1873.

---

[49] This point is well developed in Du Bois, *Black Reconstruction,* 611–12.

[50] C. Vann Woodward, *Tom Watson: Agrarian Rebel* (New York, 1938), 58–72. For similar developments in other states, see Francis B. Simkins, *Pitchfork Ben Tillman, South Carolinian* (Baton Rouge, 1944), 79–80; Willie D. Halsell, "The Bourbon Period in Mississippi Politics, 1875–1890," in *Journal of Southern History,* XI (1945), 519–37.

[51] Woodward, *Tom Watson,* 80–81; Judson C. Ward, "The Republican Party in Bourbon Georgia, 1872–1890," in *Journal of Southern History,* IX (1943), 200. See, also, Simkins, *Pitchfork Ben Tillman,* 164, 167. The planters also employed the Negro vote against the Republicans. In 1884 Edward Gay, Democrat, was running for Congress from a South Louisiana district against Republican William P. Kellogg. Edward N. Pugh, Democratic leader of Ascension Parish, outlined for the sugar planters methods of swinging the colored vote behind Gay. Let owners and managers tell the Negro workers to vote for Gay, he advised: "They naturally receive with deference the expression of opinion by their employers on all subjects. . . .

trialism, therefore, took no action to disfranchise the Negro; they used him to maintain the supremacy of a few white men over other white men. Disfranchisement finally came as a result of the efforts of small-farmer leaders like Ben Tillman.[52]

Placed in the general setting, therefore, the interests and activities of the Louisiana planter-capitalist group serve to confirm the fact that the Reconstruction period was one of the most complex in American history. It witnessed the ending of a great civil struggle and the travail of post-war adjustment, the consummation of a momentous economic revolution, and a wrenching change in race relations. No less complex than the times were the motives that impelled people —northern and southern, white and black, rich and poor—to act as they did. No simple or generic explanation cast in the form of sectional stereotypes will supply the key to what happened. Economic, social, and political stimuli affected groups in the South in different ways, and Southerners differed among themselves on the issues of Reconstruction in about the same degree as did groups in the North. The planter-capitalist class of the South thought and acted in terms of economic self-interest in a fashion similar to the industrial magnates of the North. The important difference was that the business men carried the northern people with them while the planters were unable to convince the white masses in the South that economics transcended racial supremacy.

Speaking on December 18, 1865, Thaddeus Stevens urged Congress to adopt a firm policy toward the Southern states: "The future condition of the conquered power depends on the will of the conqueror." This meant the reversion to territorial status, for in that way the South "can learn the principles of freedom and eat the fruit of foul rebellion." Stevens closed on a strongly humanitarian note, insisting that the government was not a white man's government, but "the Government of all men alike."

THADDEUS STEVENS:
THE FUTURE CONDITION
OF THE CONQUERED POWER*

The President assumes, what no one doubts, that the late rebel States have lost their constitutional relations to the Union, and are incapable of representation in Congress, except by permission of the Government. It matters but little, with this admission, whether you call them States out of the Union, and now conquered territories, or assert that because the Constitution forbids them to do what they did do, that they are therefore only dead as to all national and political action, and will remain so until the Government shall breathe into them the breath of life anew and permit them to occupy their former position. In other words, that they are not out of the Union, but are only dead carcasses lying within the Union. In either case, it is very plain that it requires the action of Congress to enable them to form a State government and send representatives to Congress. Nobody, I believe, pretends that with their old constitutions and frames of government

---

Nearly all the leading colored men are with us and they need only the offer of substantial moral support from the employers to swell the number of the supporters of Mr. Gay from the ranks of the colored employees." Edward N. Pugh to William Porcher Miles, October 30, 1884, in W. P. Miles Papers (Southern Historical Collection, University of North Carolina).

[52] Although the impetus for disfranchisement generally came from farmer leaders, the rich whites acquiesced in the movement. They did so partly out of a desire to placate the white masses and partly because the farmers, particularly during the agrarian unrest of the 1890's, sometimes tried to vote the Negroes on their side. The competition for the colored vote frightened many whites and forced the wealthy whites to pay out large monetary sums to retain their Negro supporters. Undoubtedly the planter-business class saw in disfranchisement a chance to eliminate a purchasable vote that was steadily becoming more expensive. See George M. Reynolds, *Machine Politics in New Orleans, 1897–1926* (New York, 1936), 21, 26–27, 29–30, 35. "As the situation had developed," writes Reynolds, "it seemed best to take the Negro vote off the market and leave only the white electorate with its comparatively small venal vote to be traded in on election day" (p. 26). For an itemized account of how much it cost the planters in one Louisiana parish to buy Negro votes in the election of 1892, and a complaint about the price, see Henry McCall to William Porcher Miles, May 4, 1892, in Miles Papers.

* Reprinted from *Congressional Globe*, 39th Cong., 1st sess., (Washington, D.C.: 1865), pp. 72–75.

they can be permitted to claim their old rights under the Constitution. They have torn their constitutional States into atoms, and built on their foundations fabrics of a totally different character. Dead men cannot raise themselves. Dead States cannot restore their own existence "as it was." Whose especial duty is it to do it? In whom does the Constitution place the power? Not in the judicial branch of Government, for it only adjudicates and does not prescribe laws. Not in the Executive, for he only executes and cannot make laws. Not in the Commander-in-Chief of the armies, for he can only hold them under military rule until the sovereign legislative power of the conqueror shall give them law.

There is fortunately no difficulty in solving the question. There are two provisions in the Constitution, under one of which the case must fall. The fourth article says: "New States may be admitted by the Congress into this Union."

In my judgment this is the controlling provision in this case. Unless the law of nations is a dead letter, the late war between two acknowledged belligerents severed their original compacts, and broke all the ties that bound them together. The future condition of the conquered power depends on the will of the conqueror. They must come in as new States or remain as conquered provinces. Congress—the Senate and House of Representatives, with the concurrence of the President—is the only power that can act in the matter. But suppose, as some dreaming theorists imagine, that these States have never been out of the Union, but have only destroyed their State governments so as to be incapable of political action; then the fourth section of the fourth article applies, which says: "The United States shall guaranty to every State in this Union republican form of government."

Who is the United States? Not the judiciary; not the President; but the sovereign power of the people, exercised through their representatives in Congress, with the concurrence of the Executive. It means the political Government—the concurrent action of both branches of Congress and the Executive. The separate action of each amounts to nothing, either in admitting new States or guarantying republican governments to lapsed or outlawed States. . . .

It is obvious from all this that the first duty of Congress is to pass a law declaring the condition of these outside or defunct States, and providing proper civil governments for them. Since the conquest they have been governed by martial law. Military rule is necessarily despotic, and ought not to exist longer than is absolutely necessary. As there are no symptoms that the people of these provinces will be prepared to participate in constitutional government for some years, I know of no arrangement so proper for them as territorial governments. There they can learn the principles of freedom and eat the fruit of foul rebellion. Under such governments, while electing members to the Territorial Legislatures, they will

necessarily mingle with those to whom Congress shall extend the right of suffrage. In Territories Congress fixes the qualifications of electors; and I know of no better place nor better occasion for the conquered rebels and the conqueror to practice justice to all men, and accustom themselves to make and to obey equal laws.

As these fallen rebels cannot at their option reënter the heaven which they have disturbed, the garden of Eden which they have deserted, and flaming swords are set at the gates to secure their exclusion, it becomes important to the welfare of the nation to inquire when the doors shall be reopened for their admission.

According to my judgment they ought never to be recognized as capable of acting in the Union, or of being counted as valid States, until the Constitution shall have been so amended as to make it what its framers intended; and so as to secure perpetual ascendency to the party of the Union; and so as to render our republican Government firm and stable forever. The first of those amendments is to change the basis of representation among the States from Federal numbers to actual voters. Now all the colored freemen in the slave States, and three fifths of the slaves, are represented, though none of them have votes. The States have nineteen representatives of colored slaves. If the slaves are now free then they can add, for the other two fifths, thirteen more, making the slave representation thirty-two. I suppose the free blacks in those States will give at least five more, making the representation of non-voting people of color about thirty-seven. The whole number of representatives now from the slave States is seventy. Add the other two fifths and it will be eighty-three.

If the amendment prevails, and those States withhold the right of suffrage from persons of color, it will deduct about thirty-seven, leaving them but forty-six. With the basis unchanged, the eighty-three southern members, with the Democrats that will in the best times be elected from the North, will always give them a majority in Congress and in the Electoral College. They will at the very first election take posession of the White House and the halls of Congress. I need not depict the ruin that would follow. Assumption of the rebel debt or repudiation of the Federal debt would be sure to follow. The oppression of the freedmen; the reamendment of their State constitutions, and the reëstablishment of slavery would be the inevitable result. That they would scorn and disregard their present constitutions, forced upon them in the midst of martial law, would be both natural and just. No one who has any regard for freedom of elections can look upon those governments, forced upon them in duress, with any favor. If they should grant the right of suffrage to persons of color, I think there would always be Union white men enough in the South, aided by the blacks, to divide the representation, and thus continue the Republican ascendency. If they should refuse to thus alter their election laws it would reduce the representatives of the late slave States to about forty-five and render them powerless for evil.

It is plain that this amendment must be consummated before the defunct States are admitted to be capable of State action, or it never can be.

The proposed amendment to allow Congress to lay a duty on exports is precisely in the same situation. Its importance cannot well be overstated. It is very obvious that for many years the South will not pay much under our internal revenue laws. The only article on which we can raise any considerable amount is cotton. It will be grown largely at once. With ten cents a pound export duty it would be furnished cheaper to foreign markets than they could obtain it from any other part of the world. The late war has shown that. Two million bales exported, at five hundred pounds to the bale, would yield $100,000,000. This seems to be the chief revenue we shall ever derive from the South. Besides, it would be a protection to that amount to our domestic manufactures. Other proposed amendments—to make all laws uniform; to prohibit the assumption of the rebel debt—are of vital importance, and the only thing that can prevent the combined forces of copperheads and secessionists from legislating against the interests of the Union whenever they may obtain an accidental majority.

But this is not all that we ought to do before these inveterate rebels are invited to participate in our legislation. We have turned, or are about to turn, loose four million slaves without a hut to shelter them or a cent in their pockets. The infernal laws of slavery have prevented them from acquiring an education, understanding the commonest laws of contract, or of managing the ordinary business of life. This Congress is bound to provide for them until they can take care of themselves. If we do not furnish them with homesteads, and hedge them around with protective laws; if we leave them to the legislation of their late masters, we had better have left them in bondage. Their condition would be worse than that of our prisoners at Andersonville. If we fail in this great duty now, when we have the power, we shall deserve and receive the execration of history and of all future ages. . . .

This Congress owes it to its own character to set the seal of reprobation upon a doctrine which is becoming too fashionable, and unless rebuked will be the recognized principle of our Government. Governor Perry and other provisional governors and orators proclaim that "this is the white man's Government." The whole copperhead party, pandering to the lowest prejudices of the ignorant, repeat the cuckoo cry, "This is the white man's Government." Demagogues of all parties, even some high in authority, gravely shout, "This is the white man's Government." What is implied by this? That one race of men are to have the exclusive right forever to rule this nation, and to exercise all acts of sovereignty, while all other races and nations and colors are to be their subjects, and have no voice in making the laws and choosing the rulers by whom they are to be governed. Wherein does this differ from slavery except in degree? Does not this contradict all the distinctive principles of the Declaration of Independence? When the great and good men promulgated that instrument, and pledged their lives and sacred honors to defend it, it was supposed to form an epoch in civil government. Before that time it was held that the right to rule was vested in families, dynasties, or races, not because of superior intelligence or virtue, but because of a divine right to enjoy exclusive privileges.

Our fathers repudiated the whole doctrine of the legal superiority of families or races, and proclaimed the equality of men before the law. Upon that they created a revolution and built the Republic. They were prevented by slavery from perfecting the superstructure whose foundation they had thus broadly laid. For the sake of the Union they consented to wait, but never relinquished the idea of its final completion. The time to which they looked forward with anxiety has come. It is our duty to complete their work. If this Republic is not now made to stand on their great principles, it has no honest foundation, and the Father of all men will still shake it to its center. If we have not yet been sufficiently scourged for our national sin to teach us to do justice to all God's creatures, without distinction of race or color, we must expect the still more heavy vengeance of an offended Father, still increasing his inflictions as he increased the severity of the plagues of Egypt until the tyrant consented to do justice. And when that tyrant repented of his reluctant consent, and attempted to re-enslave the people, as our southern tyrants are attempting to do now, he filled the Red sea with broken chariots and drowned horses, and strewed the shores with dead carcasses.

Mr. Chairman, I trust the Republican party will not be alarmed at what I am saying. I do not profess to speak their sentiments, nor must they be held responsible for them. I speak for myself, and take the responsibility, and will settle with my intelligent constituents.

This is not a "white man's Government," in the exclusive sense in which it is used. To say so is political blasphemy, for it violates the fundamental principles of our gospel of liberty. This is man's Government; the Government of all men alike; not that all men will have equal power and sway within it. Accidental circumstances, natural and acquired endowment and ability, will vary their fortunes. But equal rights to all the privileges of the Government is innate in every immortal being, no matter what the shape or color of the tabernacle which it inhabits.

If equal privileges were granted to all, I should not expect any but white men to be elected to office for long ages to come. The prejudice engendered by slavery would not soon permit merit to be preferred to color. But it would still be beneficial to the weaker races. In a country where political divisions will always exist, their power, joined with just white men, would greatly modify, if it did not entirely prevent, the injustice of majorities. Without the right of suffrage in the late slave States, (I do not speak of the free States,) I believe the slaves had far better been left in bondage. I see it stated that very distinguished advocates of the right of suffrage lately declared in this city that they do not expect to obtain it by congressional legislation, but only by administrative action, because, as one gallant gentleman said, the States had not been out of the Union. Then they will never get it. The President is far sounder than they. He sees that administrative action has nothing to do with

it. If it ever is to come, it must be constitutional amendments or congressional action in the Territories, and in enabling acts.

How shameful that men of influence should mislead and miseducate the public mind! They proclaim, "This is the white man's Government," and the whole coil of copperheads echo the same sentiment, and upstart, jealous Republicans join the cry. Is it any wonder ignorant foreigners and illiterate natives should learn this doctrine, and be led to despise and maltreat a whole race of their fellow-men?

Sir, this doctrine of a white man's Government is as atrocious as the infamous sentiment that damned the late Chief Justice to everlasting fame; and, I fear, to everlasting fire.

In his third annual message to Congress, December 3, 1867, Andrew Johnson expressed his strong disapproval of the sentiments and reasoning behind the Congressional Reconstruction proposals. Asserting that "the Union is not only undissolved, but indissoluble," Johnson, in sharp disagreement with Stevens, maintained that the South could not be treated as a conquered territory.

ANDREW JOHNSON:
THE UNION: UNDISSOLVED AND INDISSOLUBLE*

FELLOW-CITIZENS OF THE SENATE AND HOUSE OF REPRESENTATIVES:

The continued disorganization of the Union, to which the President has so often called the attention of Congress, is yet a subject of profound and patriotic concern. We may, however, find some relief from that anxiety in the reflection that the painful political situation, although before untried by ourselves, is not new in the experience of nations. Political science, perhaps as highly perfected in our own time and country as in any other, has not yet disclosed any means by which civil wars can be absolutely prevented. An enlightened nation, however, with a wise and beneficent constitution of free government, may diminish their frequency and mitigate their severity by directing all its proceedings in accordance with its fundamental law.

When a civil war has been brought to a close, it is manifestly the first interest and duty of the state to repair the injuries which the war has inflicted, and to secure the benefit of the lessons it teaches as fully and as speedily as possible. This duty was, upon the termination of the rebellion,

promptly accepted, not only by the executive department, but by the insurrectionary States themselves, and restoration in the first moment of peace was believed to be as easy and certain as it was indispensable. The expectations, however, then so reasonably and confidently entertained were disappointed by legislation from which I felt constrained by my obligations to the Constitution to withhold my assent.

It is therefore a source of profound regret that in complying with the obligation imposed upon the President by the Constitution to give to Congress from time to time information of the state of the Union I am unable to communicate any definitive adjustment, satisfactory to the American people, of the questions which since the close of the rebellion have agitated the public mind. On the contrary, candor compels me to declare that at this time there is no Union as our fathers understood the term, and as they meant it to be understood by us. The Union which they established can exist only where all the States are represented in both Houses of Congress; where one State is as free as another to regulate its internal concerns according to its own will, and where the laws of the central Government, strictly confined to matters of national jurisdiction, apply with equal force to all the people of every section. That such is not the

* Reprinted from James D. Richardson, ed., *A Compilation of the Messages and Papers of the Presidents* (Washington, D.C.: 1897), VI, 558–65.

present "state of the Union" is a melancholy fact, and we must all acknowledge that the restoration of the States to their proper legal relations with the Federal Government and with one another, according to the terms of the original compact, would be the greatest temporal blessing which God, in His kindest providence, could bestow upon this nation. It becomes our imperative duty to consider whether or not it is impossible to effect this most desirable consummation.

The Union and the Constitution are inseparable. As long as one is obeyed by all parties, the other will be preserved; and if one is destroyed, both must perish together. The destruction of the Constitution will be followed by other and still greater calamities. It was ordained not only to form a more perfect union between the States, but to "establish justice, insure domestic tranquillity, provide for the common defense, promote the general welfare, and secure the blessings of liberty to ourselves and our posterity." Nothing but implicit obedience to its requirements in all parts of the country will accomplish these great ends. Without that obedience we can look forward only to continual outrages upon individual rights, incessant breaches of the public peace, national weakness, financial dishonor, the total loss of our prosperity, the general corruption of morals, and the final extinction of popular freedom. To save our country from evils so appalling as these, we should renew our efforts again and again.

To me the process of restoration seems perfectly plain and simple. It consists merely in a faithful application of the Constitution and laws. The execution of the laws is not now obstructed or opposed by physical force. There is no military or other necessity, real or pretended, which can prevent obedience to the Constitution, either North or South. All the rights and all the obligations of States and individuals can be protected and enforced by means perfectly consistent with the fundamental law. The courts may be everywhere open, and if open their process would be unimpeded. Crimes against the United States can be prevented or punished by the proper judicial authorities in a manner entirely practicable and legal. There is therefore no reason why the Constitution should not be obeyed, unless those who exercise its powers have determined that it shall be disregarded and violated. The mere naked will of this Government, or of some one or more of its branches, is the only obstacle that can exist to a perfect union of all the States.

On this momentous question and some of the measures growing out of it I have had the misfortune to differ from Congress, and have expressed my convictions without reserve, though with becoming deference to the opinion of the legislative department. Those convictions are not only unchanged, but strengthened by subsequent events and further reflection. The transcendent importance of the subject will be a sufficient excuse for calling your attention to some of the reasons which have so strongly influenced my own judgment. The hope that we may all finally concur in a mode of settlement consistent at once with our true interests and with our sworn duties to the Constitution is too natural and too just to be easily relinquished.

It is clear to my apprehension that the States lately in rebellion are still members of the National Union. When did they cease to be so? The "ordinances of secession" adopted by a portion (in most of them a very small portion) of their citizens were mere nullities. If we admit now that they were valid and effectual for the purpose intended by their authors, we sweep from under our feet the whole ground upon which we justified the war. Were those States afterwards expelled from the Union by the war? The direct contrary was averred by this Government to be its purpose, and was so understood by all those who gave their blood and treasure to aid in its prosecution. It can not be that a successful war, waged for the preservation of the Union, had the legal effect of dissolving it. The victory of the nation's arms was not the disgrace of her policy; the defeat of secession on the battlefield was not the triumph of its lawless principle. Nor could Congress, with or without the consent of the Executive, do anything which would have the effect, directly or indirectly, of separating the States from each other. To dissolve the Union is to repeal the Constitution which holds it together, and that is a power which does not belong to any department of this Government, or to all of them united.

This is so plain that it has been acknowledged by all branches of the Federal Government. The Executive (my predecessor as well as myself) and the heads of all the Departments have uniformly acted upon the principle that the Union is not only undissolved, but indissoluble. Congress submitted an amendment of the Constitution to be ratified by the Southern States, and accepted their acts of ratification as a necessary and lawful exercise of their highest function. If they were not States, or were States out of the Union, their consent to a change in the fundamental law of the Union would have been nugatory, and Congress in asking it committed a political absurdity. The judiciary has also given the solemn sanction of its authority to the same view of the case. The judges of the Supreme Court have included the Southern States in their circuits, and they are constantly, in banc and elsewhere, exercising jurisdiction which does not belong to them unless those States are States of the Union.

If the Southern States are component parts of the Union, the Constitution is the supreme law for them, as it is for all the other States. They are bound to obey it, and so are we. The right of the Federal Government, which is clear and unquestionable, to enforce the Constitution upon them implies the correlative obligation on our part to observe its limitations and execute its guaranties. Without the Constitution we are nothing; by, through, and under the Constitution we are what it makes us. We may doubt the wisdom of the law, we may not approve of its provisions, but we can not violate it merely because it seems to confine our powers within limits narrower than we could wish. It is not a question of individual or class or sectional interest, much less of party predominance, but of duty—of high and sacred duty—which we are all sworn to perform. If we can not support the Constitution with the cheerful alacrity of those who love and believe in it, we must give to it at least the fidelity of public servants who act under solemn obligations and commands which they dare not disregard.

The constitutional duty is not the only one which requires the States to be restored. There is another consideration which, though of minor importance, is yet of great weight. On the 22d day of July, 1861, Congress declared by an almost unanimous vote of both Houses that the war should be conducted solely for the purpose of preserving the Union and maintaining the supremacy of the Federal Constitution and laws, without impairing the dignity, equality, and rights of the States or of individuals, and that when this was done the war should cease. I do not say that this declaration is personally binding on those who joined in making it, any more than individual members of Congress are personally bound to pay a public debt created under a law for which they voted. But it was a solemn, public, official pledge of the national honor, and I can not imagine upon what grounds the repudiation of it is to be justified. If it be said that we are not bound to keep faith with rebels, let it be remembered that this promise was not made to rebels only. Thousands of true men in the South were drawn to our standard by it, and hundreds of thousands in the North gave their lives in the belief that it would be carried out. It was made on the day after the first great battle of the war had been fought and lost. All patriotic and intelligent men then saw the necessity of giving such an assurance, and believed that without it the war would end in disaster to our cause. Having given that assurance in the extremity of our peril, the violation of it now, in the day of our power, would be a rude rending of that good faith which holds the moral world together; our country would cease to have any claim upon the confidence of men; it would make the war not only a failure, but a fraud.

Being sincerely convinced that these views are correct, I would be unfaithful to my duty if I did not recommend the repeal of the acts of Congress which place ten of the Southern States under the domination of military masters. If calm reflection shall satisfy a majority of your honorable bodies that the acts referred to are not only a violation of the national faith, but in direct conflict with the Constitution, I dare not permit myself to doubt that you will immediately strike them from the statute book.

To demonstrate the unconstitutional character of those acts I need do no more than refer to their general provisions. It must be seen at once that they are not authorized. To dictate what alterations shall be made in the constitutions of the several States; to control the elections of State legislators and State officers, members of Congress and electors of President and Vice-President, by arbitrarily declaring who shall vote and who shall be excluded from that privilege; to dissolve State legislatures or prevent them from assembling; to dismiss judges and other civil functionaries of the State and appoint others without regard to State law; to organize and operate all the political machinery of the States; to regulate the whole administration of their domestic and local affairs according to the mere will of strange and irresponsible agents, sent among them for that purpose—these are powers not granted to the Federal Government or to any one of its branches. Not being granted, we violate our trust by assuming them as palpably as we would by acting in the face of a positive interdict; for the Constitution forbids us to do whatever it does not affirmatively authorize, either by express words or by clear implication. If the authority we desire to use does not come to us through the Constitution, we can exercise it only by usurpation, and usurpation is the most dangerous of political crimes. By that crime the enemies of free government in all ages have worked out their designs against public liberty and private right. It leads directly and immediately to the establishment of absolute rule, for undelegated power is always unlimited and unrestrained.

The acts of Congress in question are not only objectionable for their assumption of ungranted power, but many of their provisions are in conflict with the direct prohibitions of the Constitution. The Constitution commands that a republican form of government shall be guaranteed to all the States; that no person shall be deprived of life, liberty, or property without due process of law, arrested without a judicial warrant, or punished without a fair trial before an impartial jury; that the privilege of *habeas corpus* shall not be denied in time of peace, and that no bill of attainder shall be passed even against a single individual. Yet the system of measures established by these acts of Congress does totally subvert and destroy the form as well as the substance of republican government in the ten States to which they apply. It binds them hand and foot in absolute slavery, and subjects them to a strange and hostile power, more unlimited and more likely to be abused than any other now known among civilized men. It tramples down all those rights in which the essence of liberty consists, and which a free government is always most careful to protect. It denies the *habeas corpus* and the trial by jury. Personal freedom, property, and life, if assailed by the passion, the prejudice, or the rapacity of the ruler, have no security whatever. It has the effect of a bill of attainder or bill of pains and penalties, not upon a few individuals, but upon whole masses, including the millions who inhabit the subject States, and even their unborn children. These wrongs, being expressly forbidden, can not be constitutionally inflicted upon any portion of our people, no matter how they may have come within our jurisdiction, and no matter whether they live in States, Territories, or districts.

I have no desire to save from the proper and just consequences of their great crime those who engaged in rebellion against the Government, but as a mode of punishment the measures under consideration are the most unreasonable that could be invented. Many of those people are perfectly innocent; many kept their fidelity to the Union untainted to the last; many were incapable of any legal offense; a large proportion even of the persons able to bear arms were forced into rebellion against their will, and of those who are guilty with their own consent the degrees of guilt are as various as the shades of their character and temper. But these acts of Congress confound them all together in one common doom. Indiscriminate vengeance upon classes, sects, and parties, or upon whole communities, for offenses committed by a portion of them against the governments to which they owed obedience was common in the barbarous ages of the world; but Christianity and civilization have made such progress that recourse to a punishment so cruel and unjust would meet with the condemnation of all unprejudiced and right-minded men. The punitive justice of this age, and especially of this country, does not consist in stripping whole States of their liberties and reducing all their people, without distinction, to the condition of slavery. It deals separately with each individual, confines itself to the forms of law, and vindicates its own purity by an impartial examination of every case before a competent judicial tribunal. If this does not satisfy all our desires with regard to Southern rebels, let us console ourselves by reflecting that a free Constitution, triumphant in war and unbroken in peace, is worth far more to us and our children than the gratification of any present feeling.

I am aware it is assumed that this system of government for the Southern States is not to be perpetual. It is true this military government is to be only provisional, but it is through this temporary evil that a greater evil is to be made perpetual. If the guaranties of the Constitution can be broken provisionally to serve a temporary purpose, and in part only of the country, we can destroy them everywhere and for all time. Arbitrary measures often change, but they generally change for the worse. It is the curse of despotism that it has no halting place. The intermitted exercise of its power brings no sense of security to its subjects, for they can never know what more they will be called to endure when its red right hand is armed to plague them again. Nor is it possible to conjecture how or where power,

unrestrained by law, may seek its next victims. The States that are still free may be enslaved at any moment; for if the Constitution does not protect all, it protects none.

It is manifestly and avowedly the object of these laws to confer upon negroes the privilege of voting and to disfranchise such a number of white citizens as will give the former a clear majority at all elections in the Southern States. This, to the minds of some persons, is so important that a violation of the Constitution is justified as a means of bringing it about. The morality is always false which excuses a wrong because it proposes to accomplish a desirable end. We are not permitted to do evil that good may come. But in this case the end itself is evil, as well as the means. The subjugation of the States to negro domination would be worse than the military despotism under which they are now suffering. It was believed beforehand that the people would endure any amount of military oppression for any length of time rather than degrade themselves by subjection to the negro race. Therefore they have been left without a choice. Negro suffrage was established by act of Congress, and the military officers were commanded to superintend the process of clothing the negro race with the political privileges torn from white men.

The blacks in the South are entitled to be well and humanely governed, and to have the protection of just laws for all their rights of person and property. If it were practicable at this time to give them a Government exclusively their own, under which they might manage their own affairs in their own way, it would become a grave question whether we ought to do so, or whether common humanity would not require us to save them from themselves. But under the circumstances this is only a speculative point. It is not proposed merely that they shall govern themselves, but that they shall rule the white race, make and administer State laws, elect Presidents and members of Congress, and shape to a greater or less extent the future destiny of the whole country. Would such a trust and power be safe in such hands?

The peculiar qualities which should characterize any people who are fit to decide upon the management of public affairs for a great state have seldom been combined. It is the glory of white men to know that they have had these qualities in sufficient measure to build upon this continent a great political fabric and to preserve its stability for more than ninety years, while in every other part of the world all similar experiments have failed. But if anything can be proved by known facts, if all reasoning upon evidence is not abandoned, it must be acknowledged that in the progress of nations negroes have shown less capacity for government than any other race of people. No independent government of any form has ever been successful in their hands. On the contrary, wherever they have been left to their own devices they have shown a constant tendency to relapse into barbarism. In the Southern States, however, Congress has undertaken to confer upon them the privilege of the ballot. Just released from slavery, it may be doubted whether as a class they know more than their ancestors how to organize and regulate civil society. Indeed, it is admitted that the blacks of the South are not only regardless of the rights of property, but so utterly ignorant of public affairs that their voting can consist in nothing more than carrying a ballot to the place where they are directed to deposit it. I need not remind you that the exercise of the elective franchise is the highest attribute of an American citizen, and that when guided by virtue, intelligence, patriotism, and a proper apprecia-tion of our free institutions it constitutes the true basis of a democratic form of government, in which the sovereign power is lodged in the body of the people. A trust artificially created, not for its own sake, but solely as a means of promoting the general welfare, its influence for good must necessarily depend upon the elevated character and true allegiance of the elector. It ought, there-fore, to be reposed in none except those who are fitted morally and mentally to administer it well; for if conferred upon persons who do not justly estimate its value and who are indifferent as to its results, it will only serve as a means of placing power in the hands of the unprincipled and ambitious, and must eventuate in the complete destruction of that liberty of which it should be the most powerful conservator. . . .

Caleb G. Forshey, testifying before the Joint Committee on Reconstruction in March, 1866, presented a white Texan's viewpoint on postwar problems. With slavery and secession abolished, Forshey believed that the people "would be restored to their for-mer relations, and things would go on as before." This meant that freedom would be reluctantly accorded the Negro, for "the highest condition the black race has ever reached or can reach, is one where he is provided for by a master race."

CALEB G. FORSHEY:
A RESTORATION TO FORMER RELATIONS*

Question. Where do you reside?

Answer. I reside in the State of Texas.

Question. How long have you been a resident of Texas?

Answer. I have resided in Texas and been a citizen of that State for nearly thirteen years.

Question. What opportunities have you had for ascertaining the temper and disposition of the people of Texas towards the government and authority of the United States?

Answer. For ten years I have been superin-tendent of the Texas Military Institute, as its founder and conductor. I have been in the con-federate service in various parts of the confeder-acy; but chiefly in the trans-Mississippi depart-ment, in Louisiana and Texas, as an officer of engineers. I have had occasion to see and know very extensively the condition of affairs in Texas, and also to a considerable extent in Louisiana. I think I am pretty well-informed, as well as anybody, perhaps, of the present state of affairs in Texas.

Question. What are the feelings and views of the people of Texas as to the late rebellion, and the future condition and circumstances of the State, and its relations to the federal government?

Answer. After our army had given up its arms and gone home, the surrender of all matters in controversy was complete, and as nearly universal, perhaps, as anything could be. Assuming the matters in controversy to have been the right to secede, and the right to hold slaves, I think they were given up teetotally, to use a strong Ameri-canism. When you speak of feeling, I should discriminate a little. The feeling was that of any party who had been cast in a suit he had staked all upon. They did not return from feeling, but from a sense of necessity, and from a judgment that it was the only and necessary thing to be done, to give up the contest. But when they gave it up, it was without reservation; with a view to look forward, and not back. That is my impres-sion of the manner in which the thing was done. There was a public expectation that in some very limited time there would be a restoration to former relations; and in such restoration they felt great interest, after the contest was given up. The expectation was, and has been up to the present time, that there would be a speedy and immediate restoration. It was the expectation of the people that, as soon as the State was organized as proposed by the President, they would be restored to their former relations, and things

---

* Reprinted from *The Reports of the Commit-tees of the House of Representatives, Made During the First Session Thirty-Ninth Congress* (Washing-ton, D.C.: 1866), Part IV, pp. 129–32.

would go on as before, with these two main issues given up wholly; that, with that as the result, there would be harmony, and that without it there would probably not be. I think there would be considerable revulsion of feeling if that is not so, as the expectation has been almost universal that that would be the result of reorganization. It is perhaps proper that I should say, in that connexion, that a considerable apprehension has been felt lately. Texas being later in her reorganization than the other States, and having had an opportunity to witness the result in the case of the other States, considerable apprehension and some revulsion of feeling have already occurred; that is, a little terror lest such should not be the result of reorganization. My impression is, that the feeling, so far as feeling is concerned, is not as good as it was three or four months ago. I want to distinguish between feeling and judgment; for good feeling was returning as fast as human nature would admit.

Question. What proportion of the people of Texas, so far as your judgment extends, were loyal to the government during the rebellion?

Answer. Scarcely enough to be called a portion; so much so that we cannot get postmasters anywhere in the State, except in the regions where the German population prevails. The Germans, not knowing the English language very well, and not knowing much of the nature of the contest, were opposed to the war; some of them were really opposed to our movement. In other portions of the State it has been extremely difficult to fill the post offices, and only women and children could be found to perform the functions, and very rarely the women.

Question. What proportion of the members of the convention lately met in Texas to form a new constitution were loyal men during the war?

Answer. I cannot tell. There are several who left the State during the war, who are now members of the convention. There are Judge Hancock, Mr. Norton, brother to Senator Norton, and several other gentlemen, who may be regarded as loyal men; but hardly of the extreme loyalty that the test-oath embraces. Men who remained in the State had to do more or less for the rebellion, although opposed to the movement. A very small portion of the population anywhere, very small, were opposed to it after secession had occurred. That was so much the case, that in my movements, which were pretty extensive, (but not on the remote frontiers, where it was claimed there was considerable opposition to us,) I met none. I have not seen the list of all the members of the convention so as to study it. But the president of the convention, General Throckmorton, was opposed to secession, and very warmly. He opposed it and voted against it in the convention of secession. But he afterwards entered the confederate service and rose to the rank of brigadier general. He was always considered a Union man, and is one.

Question. Is there or not, among the people of Texas who have been in the rebellion, a feeling of hatred towards the people of the north who were engaged in the suppression of the rebellion?

Answer. There is some antagonism towards the government movements; towards the men engaged in the war perhaps less, for we rather think those we fought with clever fellows. There is considerable feeling yet existing which was engendered by four or five years' struggle; quieting itself perhaps as fast as human nature could be expected, as I have remarked once before. But that it existed and was very bitter cannot for a moment be doubted. On the contrary, the enmity became very strong, and was nearly universal with all our southern people. If your question is asked with the view of ascertaining the present feeling in regard to persons coming into Texas to reside, I would say that this feeling of enmity has scarcely an existence towards persons who come to pursue their own business. There are thousands of such persons all over our State, persons who have migrated there from the north. They did so immediately after our surrender, without waiting for anything. Business men were all over the State bringing in goods and buying up cotton. There has been no collision with them. It was understood as one part of the result that everybody would attend to his own business in the future; and the future only was looked to. But when men have come with a censorious disposition, and have undertaken to reflect upon the past, their positions have been made very uncomfortable, by refusal to trade with them, and sometimes some bickerings and jawings; though our people have not used any violence even when they felt like it, because it was understood that would be regarded as an evidence of disloyalty to the pledge they had made. The whole people understood they had made a pledge to lay down their arms and give the thing up; and they have been very cautious not to do anything which would seem to compromise them in that respect. Within my entire knowledge there has not been any resistance to federal authority in the State of Texas, except where individuals have got drunk and committed violence. I have sometimes seen federal authority exercised when it was thought to be very harsh; but there has not been any resistance.

Question. Is it within your knowledge that men, black and white, who were supposed to be friendly to the government have been maltreated or murdered in the State of Texas on account of their views and opinions?

Answer. Not a single case of that kind has come under my personal observation.

Question. Is it within your knowledge that men in the State of Texas have been abused or mistreated in any way for raising the United States flag or exhibiting their attachment to it?

Answer. Nothing of the kind. I heard that at Fredericksburg, where the Germans raised the flag immediately, and before they had fairly heard of the surrender, some persons made some trouble;

but that was in a remote place. But I have heard of no such trouble in any other place. I must mention one circumstance: A late confederate colonel was going along intoxicated, with a companion. They rode along under a flag at a military post, and the drunken man, who was very drunk, tore it. There was an attempt made to arrest him, and his friend said: "He is drunk; I will answer for it all; it was a drunken frolic." The friend was arrested and tried, though the trouble never extended to the second individual. The friend contended that his object was to screen the drunken man, and he responded for him, though he did not mean that he would take the responsibility of tearing the flag. He was tried for that, and was in prison when I came away; I do not know the result.

Question. What is your opinion of a military force under the authority of the federal government to preserve order in Texas and to protect those who have been loyal, both white and black, from the aggressions of those who have been in the rebellion?

Answer. My judgment is well founded on that subject: that wherever such military force is and has been, it has excited the very feeling it was intended to prevent; that so far from being necessary it is very pernicious everywhere, and without exception. The local authorities and public sentiment are ample for protection. I think no occasion would occur, unless some individual case that our laws would not reach. We had an opportunity to test this after the surrender and before any authority was there. The military authorities, or the military officers, declared that we were without laws, and it was a long time before the governor appointed arrived there, and then it was some time before we could effect anything in the way of organization. We were a people without law, order, or anything; and it was a time for violence if it would occur. I think it is a great credit to our civilization that, in that state of affairs, there was nowhere any instance of violence. I am proud of it, for I expected the contrary; I expected that our soldiers on coming home, many of them, would be dissolute, and that many of them would oppress the class of men you speak of; but it did not occur. But afterwards, wherever soldiers have been sent, there have been little troubles, none of them large; but personal collisions between soldiers and citizens.

Question. What is your opinion as to the necessity and advantages of the Freedmen's Bureau, or an agency of that kind, in Texas?

Answer. My opinion is that it is not needed; my opinion is stronger than that—that the effect of it is to irritate, if nothing else. While in New York city recently I had a conversation with some friends from Texas, from five distant points in the State. We met together and compared opinions; and the opinion of each was the same, that the negroes had generally gone to work since January; that except where the Freedmen's Bureau had interfered, or rather encouraged troubles, such as little complaints, especially between negro and negro, the negro's disposition was very good, and they had generally gone to work, a vast majority of them with their former masters. I was very gratified to learn that from districts where I feared the contrary. Still this difference was made, particularly by Mr. Carpenter, from Jefferson, the editor of the Jefferson Herald. He said that in two or three counties where they had not been able to organize the Freedmen's Bureau, there had been no trouble at all; nearly all the negroes had gone to work. The impression in Texas at present is that the negroes under the influence of the Freedmen's Bureau do worse than without it.

I want to state that I believe all our former owners of negroes are the friends of the negroes; and that the antagonism paraded in the papers of the north does not exist at all. I know the fact is the very converse of that; and good feeling always prevails between the masters and the slaves. But the negroes went off and left them in the lurch; my own family was an instance of it. But they came back after a time, saying they had been free enough and wanted a home.

Question. Do you think those who employ the negroes there are willing to make contracts with them, so that they shall have fair wages for their labor?

Answer. I think so; I think they are paid liberally, more than the white men in this country get; the average compensation to negroes there is greater than the average compensation of free laboring white men in this country. It seems to have regulated itself in a great measure by what each neighborhood was doing; the negroes saying, "I can get thus and so at such a place." Men have hired from eight to fifteen dollars per month during the year, and women at about two dollars less a month; house-servants at a great deal more.

Question. Do the men who employ the negroes claim to exercise the right to enforce their contract by physical force?

Answer. Not at all; that is totally abandoned; not a single instance of it has occurred. I think they still chastise children, though. The negro parents often neglect that, and the children are still switched as we switch our own children. I know it is done in my own house; we have little house-servants that we switch just as I do our own little fellows.

Question. What is your opinion as to the respective advantages to the white and black races, of the present free system of labor and the institution of slavery?

Answer. I think freedom is very unfortunate for the negro; I think it is sad; his present helpless condition touches my heart more than anything else I ever contemplated, and I think that is the common sentiment of our slaveholders. I have seen it on the largest plantations, where the negro men had all left, and where only women and children remained, and the owners had to keep them and feed them. The beginning certainly presents a touching and sad spectacle. The poor negro is dying at a rate fearful to relate.

I have some ethnological theories that may perhaps warp my judgment; but my judgment is that the highest condition the black race has ever reached or can reach, is one where he is provided for by a master race. That is the result of a great deal of scientific investigation and observation of the negro character by me ever since I was a man. The labor question had become a most momentous one, and I was studying it. I undertook to investigate the condition of the negro from statistics under various circumstances, to treat it purely as a matter of statistics from the census tables of this country of ours. I found that the free blacks of the north decreased 8 per cent.; the free blacks of the south increased 7 or 8 per cent., while the slaves by their sides increased 34 per cent. I inferred from the doctrines of political economy that the race is in the best condition when it procreates the fastest; that, other things being equal, slavery is of vast advantage to the negro. I will mention one or two things in connexion with this as explanatory of that result. The negro will not take care of his offspring unless required to do it, as compared with the whites. The little children will die; they do die, and hence the necessity of very rigorous regulations on our plantations which we have adopted in our nursery system.

Another cause is that there is no continence among the negroes. All the continence I have ever seen among the negroes has been enforced upon plantations, where it is generally assumed there is none. For the sake of procreation, if nothing else, we compel men to live with their wives. The discipline of the plantation was more rigorous, perhaps, in regard to men staying with their wives, than in regard to anything else; and I think the procreative results, as shown by the census tables, is due in a great measure to that discipline.

I think they are very much better off in having homes than the free blacks are. The free blacks in Louisiana, where we had 34,000, with a great deal of blood of the whites in them, and therefore a great deal of white sense, were nothing like so happy and so well off as our slaves are. My observation for many years leads me to this conclusion.

Question. What is the prevailing inclination among the people of Texas in regard to giving the negroes civil or political rights and privileges?

Answer. I think they are all opposed to it. There are some men—I am not among them—who think that the basis of intelligence might be a good basis for the elective franchise. But a much larger class, perhaps nine-tenths of our people, believe that the distinctions between the races should not be broken down by any such community of interests in the management of the affairs of the State. I think there is a very common sentiment that the negro, even with education, has not a mind capable of appreciating the political institutions of the country to such an extent as would make him a good associate for the white man in the administration of the government. I think if the vote was taken on the question of admitting him to the right of suffrage there would be a very small vote in favor of it—scarcely respectable: that is my judgment.

Question. What civil rights are the people of Texas disposed to give to the negro, such as the right to testify as a witness, to hold and sell real estate and property of any kind?

Answer. They have no objection to giving them all those rights. The elective franchise is the point of difference, and there is no other. I think they would be disposed to allow him to bear testimony in any case; not that they believe he is a good witness, for he is not a reliable witness; but they would be willing to let his testimony go for what it was worth. It has been so in Louisiana, where we have seen its influence, and it has not been very pernicious. All rights in respect to contracts, to giving full force and efficiency to them, would be granted to negroes as to white persons. To that I have seen no objection.

Question. The right to sue in court?

Answer. Yes, sir.

Question. Did the negroes generally sympathize with the Union cause during the rebellion?

Answer. None of them. There has been this: a disposition on their part to try something new—to be free; and when they came within reach of the federal army a great many of them ran away to it. But there was no resistance to discipline and authority at home. That was so much the case that a single woman on a plantation with a hundred slaves carried on the place as before and without trouble.

Also testifying before the Joint Committee, Richard R. Hill, an ex-slave, stated that Negroes did not want to go to Africa: "if they could live here contented as slaves, they can live here when free." The following is a description of conditions in Virginia during Reconstruction.

RICHARD R. HILL:
THEY CAN LIVE HERE WHEN FREE*

Question. Where do you live?

Answer. Hampton, Virginia.

Question. That is where President Tyler used to live?

Answer. Yes, sir.

Question. Did you know him?

Answer. Yet, I knew him pretty well.

Question. Can you read and write?

Answer. Yes, sir.

Question. How old are you?

Answer. About thirty-four years.

Question. Were you ever a slave?

Answer. Yes, sir.

Question. When did you become free?

Answer. When the proclamation was issued. I left Richmond in 1863.

Question. Did you serve in the rebel army?

Answer. No, sir.

Question. Or in the Union army?

Answer. No, sir.

Question. How do the rebels down there, about Hampton, treat the colored people?

Answer. The returned rebels express a desire to get along in peace if they can. There have been a few outrages out upon the roadside there. One of the returned Union colored soldiers was met out there and beaten very much.

Question. By whom was he beaten?

Answer. It was said they were rebels; they had on Union overcoats, but they were not United States soldiers. Occasionally we hear of an outrage of that kind, but there are none in the little village where I live.

Question. What appears to be the feeling generally of the returned rebels towards the freedmen; is it kind or unkind?

Answer. Well, the feeling that they manifest as a general thing is kind, so far as I have heard.

Question. Are they willing to pay the freedmen fair wages for their work?

Answer. No, sir; they are not willing to pay the freedmen more than from five to eight dollars a month.

Question. Do you think that their labor is worth more than that generally?

Answer. I do, sir; because, just at this time, everything is very dear, and I do not see how people can live and support their families on those wages.

Question. State whether the black people down there are anxious to go to school?

Answer. Yes, sir; they are anxious to go to school; we have schools there every day that are very well filled; and we have night schools that are very well attended, both by children and aged people; they manifest a great desire for education.

Question. Who are the teachers; white or black?

Answer. White, sir.

Question. How are the white teachers treated by the rebels down there?

Answer. I guess they are not treated very well, because they have very little communication between each other. I have not heard of any threatening expression in regard to them.

Question. Did you ever hear any threats among the whites to reduce your race to slavery again?

Answer. They have said, and it seems to be a prevalent idea, that if their representatives were received in Congress the condition of the freedmen would be very little better than that of the slaves, and that their old laws would still exist by which they would reduce them to something like bondage. That has been expressed by a great many of them.

Question. What has become of your former master?

Answer. He is in Williamsburg.

Question. Have you seen him since the proclamation?

Answer. Yes, sir.

Question. Did he want you to go back and live with him?

Answer. No, sir; he did not ask me to go back, but he was inquiring of me about another of his slaves, who was with him at the evacuation of Williamsburg by the rebels.

Question. How do you feel about leaving the State of Virginia and going off and residing as a community somewhere else?

Answer. They do not wish to leave and go anywhere else unless they are certain that the locality where they are going is healthy and that they can get along.

* Reprinted from *The Reports of the Committees of the House of Representatives, Made During the First Session Thirty-Ninth Congress* (Washington, D.C.: 1866), Part II, pp. 55–56.

Question. Are they not willing to be sent back to Africa?

Answer. No, sir.

Question. Why not?

Answer. They say that they have lived here all their days, and there were stringent laws made to keep them here; and that if they could live here contented as slaves, they can live here when free.

Question. Do you not think that to be a very absurd notion?

Answer. No, sir; if we can get lands here and can work and support ourselves, I do not see why we should go to any place that we do not want to go to.

CHAPTER THIRTEEN

CAPTAINS OF INDUSTRY

Were the Captains of Industry in the latter nineteenth century a group of "robber barons," or were they "industrial statesmen" performing indispensible functions in the development of the economy? The former idea, made popular by the writings of Matthew Josephson in the 1930's, has given way to the revisionist view illustrated through the first two selections. Thomas C. Cochran and Edward C. Kirkland call for a greater understanding of what businessmen themselves thought, as well as an appreciation of the economic and social context in which industrial development took place. Here the concern shifts from actual business operations, and their consequences for the corporate structure and the living conditions of farmers and factory laborers, to the strides in material production, creation of a national market, rounding out the continent, and in general establishing the foundation of modern America. Thus, the dialogue among historians centers in the last analysis on the social costs of industrialism: Does rapid economic growth serve as an end in itself, outweighing political corruption, the elimination of independent business in the drive for consolidation, the vulgarity of the nouveau riche and their impact on American taste and culture, and the basically unsatisfactory state of the urban and rural poor?

Using the correspondence of railroad leaders, Cochran discussed how businessmen conceived their relations to government and the public. Concerned with their public image, these men cultivated, through free passes and other devices, the friendship of articulate groups in politics, press, and pulpit. While they had little confidence in politicians, entrepreneurs used lobbyists to secure favorable treatment, and, as Cochran pointed out, rationalized the resulting bribery in terms of the public good. More important, Cochran suggested that the railroad leaders were not bound by a laissez-faire philosophy, but were highly pragmatic in their outlook. Kirkland analyzed a further dimension, that of the compartmentalization of business thought: economic issues were divorced from "the spheres of moral and personal considerations." Whether this led to policies devoid of ethics is for the reader to decide. The debate still waxes strongly.

THOMAS C. COCHRAN:
BUSINESS AND PUBLIC OPINION*

Closely allied with successful relations with customers was the broader problem of the good will of the general public. In a given area the two groups were usually much the same. In defending the position of the railroad, the chief difference in approach was that in the one case the customer was being kept from taking his business to a competitor, and in the other from asking his representative for regulatory laws.

State representation on the boards of directors of the Boston and Worcester, the Western, and the Illinois Central made government relations a part of the role of their early presidents. But in the early days of the other roads of the group ability to create public good will does not appear, from the correspondence, to have been a much emphasized part of the executive role. Aside from land-grant troubles in the West, these executives' relations with public authorities seem to have been chiefly in regard to federal mail contracts and occasional state laws that might affect railroads.

By 1870, as many writers have shown, the public was becoming highly critical of railroad management. The long depression of the seventies heightened this feeling and gave temporary strength to the antirailroad political activities of the Patrons of Husbandry (The Grange). While the hostility to railroads waned somewhat in the prosperity of the early eighties, it remained a force to be reckoned with by managers in every section. James C. Clarke, in fact, viewed an adverse public attitude as inherent in the railroad situation: "The people are in favor of building a new road and do what they can to promote it. After it is once built and fixed then the policy of the people is usually in opposition."

Added to the popular distrust of railroad entrepreneurs was a suspicion of corporations in general and monopolistic corporations in particular. Devereux was not surprised by a certain adverse lower court verdict, "knowing as I do the extreme bias existing in the minds of Jurors in any case wherein a corporate body is the defendant." In the same vein Perkins said: "The only point with the people is that in the state courts the railroads cannot get justice, and therefore they want to put us there." Billings feared having the grain elevators of only one company along their tracks, because "there will be charges of 'ring' management and monopoly."

EDUCATING THE PUBLIC

The executives who had to deal with the militant Western feeling thought that more pub-

lic information regarding railroad problems would help. "As the question is investigated," wrote Denison, "there must be more disposition to treat the Railroads fairly." Walker, pointing out in 1874 that only four roads in Illinois were regularly paying dividends, thought that the "cry of extortion arises more from a want of information upon this subject than from any other cause." Ten years later Perkins held to similar reasoning: "Public opinion which necessarily regulates us all in the long run, is not unreasonable, but is sometimes without proper knowledge or information on which to base its judgment," although it should be noted that after a profitable year in 1881 Perkins had thought: "The less said in a public report the better!"

Informing the public could take many forms. All entrepreneurs favored letters to important citizens or customers explaining railroad affairs in general, or giving the reason for certain actions. But the most important means of reaching the public was through publication of articles or letters, or especially prepared news releases. Railroad executives were not the first businessmen to use the press to advance their cause, but, under pressure of the criticism and regulation of the seventies and eighties, they undoubtedly engaged in such public-relations work more extensively than any previous business group.

There were some early managers who were conscious of the effects of press releases. This was true of Brooks, the politically minded group who ran the New York Central, and Baker, who thought that publishing the annual report of the C. B. & Q. in the New Bedford *Mercury* raised the morale of the stockholders in that area, but the flood of correspondence on such matters came after 1873. As Ackerman put it in an Illinois Central political dispute, increasing public attack made him feel that they must "manufacture public opinion." "I want to get your aid in having you publish some articles in the interest of the State," he wrote to a prominent citizen of Fort Dodge, Iowa.

The leaders of the western roads coöperated in paying for favorable books and articles. They also favored preparing and sending articles to various periodicals, and gave wider distribution to speeches or articles that appeared convincing. For example, Cass arranged for a pamphlet signed by congressmen from the Northwest, supporting the extension of the Northern Pacific land grant, and C. B. Wright of the same road sought to strengthen their case by giving wide newspaper publicity to an increase in rates on the Union-Central Pacific.

Education involved hiring professional writers, who might well be regarded as the direct ancestors of modern public-relations men. Henry Demarest Lloyd's articles on the Standard Oil

---

* Reprinted by permission of the publishers from Thomas C. Cochran, *Railroad Leaders, 1845–1890*. Cambridge, Mass.: Harvard University Press. Copyright, 1953, by The President and Fellows of Harvard College.

Company in the *Atlantic Monthly,* for example, led Forbes to believe that all corporations needed some defending. Accordingly he wrote E. M. Cheney suggesting a series of short articles for newspapers and longer ones for magazines. "If the idea strikes you favorably," he continued, "your pay would be sure and if successful might lead to other work." Other free-lance writers offered prepared articles to the railroad leaders. Forbes suggested that they might get someone prominent politically, like Carl Schurz, to sign his name to a book on the railroad situation that was being considered as a possible publication. Harris also employed this technique of using the publicity value of a well-known name. In 1884 he wrote Schuyler Colfax, Vice-President in the first Grant administration: "Will you kindly sit down in your study and see if you cannot prepare something that you can get into the influential papers in your State [Indiana] that will support our cause."

Railroad leaders recognized the value of apparently unsolicited news interviews or letters as a means of planting opinions. Perkins wrote his vice-president to have a reporter come around and to read him a statement explaining the basis of rates. Forbes wrote: "Who should enter my den but a very nice young reporter of the Daily Advertiser, in which Journal I have the misfortune to own some worthless stock." He gave the young man some "confidential" news regarding one of their competitors. Fish, however, thought "that, as a general proposition, it is unwise for Railroad Officers to get themselves interviewed . . . It is better to put what they have to say into formal official communications." He sent Whitelaw Reid of the New York *Tribune* a letter regarding southern trade "signed as from a correspondent in New Orleans." C. P. Clark wrote to state attorney Samuel Fessenden introducing the New Haven's advertising agent who would interview him for the New York *Tribune.* Writing some ten years apart, both Ackerman and Fish thought that the Illinois Central efforts had succeeded in improving their public relations in Iowa.

The need for settling their territory and continual trouble with Congress over the retention of their enormous land grant made Northern Pacific executives particularly sensitive to public opinion. Oakes and Villard paid at least one editor a hundred dollars to publish the Northern Pacific annual report in 1882. They also encouraged favorable public letters and articles by rewarding the writers, and arranged for articles —often for advertising rather than for public relations. In 1884 Harris thanked Henry Demarest Lloyd for a friendly article in the Chicago *Tribune.*

Actual ownership or substantial support of periodicals was variously regarded. Ackerman wanted the lines entering Chicago to support a paper, *The Prairie Farmer,* to reach "the farmers by a fair representation of our case." Oakes offered to buy at least one small newspaper for the

Northern Pacific. The road also supported a magazine, *The Northwest,* by buying and distributing most of its copies. Harris regarded it "as a very valuable special journal for spreading information concerning the resources and advantages of the new States and Territories." James C. Clarke, however, wrote: "It is a humbug to talk of R.R.s owning NewsPapers [*sic*]," and Fish later called for repudiation of the insinuation "that the Illinois Central RR Co. conspired with other RR Cos. to secretly control a newspaper in Nashville."

Although Kimball remarked: "It sounds odd to talk of a Railroad President as being popular, as if he was a comedian or a politician," railroad presidents were generally sensitive to newspaper articles. After a New York Central accident, Pruyn wrote Corning: "The tone of the press is so bitter and severe . . . the effect of it must be if continued, with our large Cos especially, to make really good men avoid them." The entrepreneurs often defended themselves by trying to get the editors to change their tone through persuasion or influence. Oakes, for example, called the attention of J. Pierpont Morgan to an inaccurate article on the Northern Pacific in the New York *World.* But on some occasions press criticism was ignored. Villard, the subject of continuous newspaper discussion, wrote his close associate, William Endicott, Jr., that he made it a rule not to notice newspaper "inventions regarding our interest." "If I undertook to do so," he added, "I would absolutely have no time left for anything else." Withdrawal of the Northern Pacific advertising patronage, however, did not appear to him to violate his rule.

Conciliation of newspaper editors by free transportation became so universal that executives hesitated to refuse one a pass. Even though the Michigan Central, for example, had formed an agreement with their competitors not to issue annual press passes, Forbes wrote in 1858: "At this moment it is desirable to have the Press with us and I suggest passing them liberally by specials (if allowable under agreement)." Kimball wrote his second vice-president: "I think giving passes to newspaper men is about the cheapest form of advertising we can get," and Ledyard said: "The newspapers do, to a greater or lesser extent, mold public opinion, and the railroad companies . . . have no means of refuting these charges made against them." In general, officers limited passes to those editors along the line of the road. The Northern Pacific executives were, of course, particularly interested in newspaper opinion, and believed in going beyond transportation in aiding useful editors. Oakes, for example, gave special rates for equipment to start newspapers in Northern Pacific territories. But influential newspaper editors in any part of the state or nation were likely to be favored with free transportation. And presidents wrote letters to critical editors in efforts to meet or eliminate their objections.

Probably none of the entrepreneurs liked this system of mixed bribery and blackmail. Walker wrote: "I think the grant of a free pass to make one friend creates half a dozen enemies," and Watrous went so far as to "wish it were a capital offence to ask or give free transportation." Both Watrous and Clarke in the middle eighties refused passes to unfriendly editors. "I should not be willing to give an annual pass for the publication of the timetable," reasoned Watrous, "unless it was understood that . . . your paper would treat our Company and its interests fairly."

Ministers and missionaries were also favored with free or reduced-rate transportation. In writing Harris to issue a pass to the superintendent of the Home Missions in Iowa, Denison said: "I think it as good a use of so much value as our company can possibly make of it. We want friends of this sort in Iowa." Ackerman was liberal with clerical passes because he was "disposed to do our best towards evangelizing the road." Perkins gave Bishop Perry and his wife annual passes over the C. B. & Q. system, Ledyard sent an annual pass to a bishop in Omaha, Nebraska, and Oakes gave free carriage to the material for constructing a church. But at least Ledyard and Clarke disliked granting such favors. Ledyard thought that "railroads have been and are today too liberal, if anything in giving reduced rates to the clergy," although he doubted that they could make any change. In 1884 Clarke "cut short the issue of free passes in all classes of missionary, religious, and educational work," granting half-fare instead. . . .

REGULATION AND TAXATION BEFORE 1887

In keeping with the pragmatic character of business roles, railroad regulation was generally discussed in terms of specific situations rather than theories. Although Clarke, Ledyard, and Perkins all distinguished between "private" and corporate enterprise, executives had little to say on the key legal point of whether a railroad was or was not peculiarly "affected with a public interest." While Perkins and others admitted that the public had an interest in the Union Pacific and the Kansas Pacific, built with the aid of government bonds, Perkins did not think that action of Congress on the practices of these roads "establishes any precedent whatever for railroads except under similar conditions." A few days later he added: "The Union Pacific has so far had Congress and the Courts upon its side and two generations of speculators have grown rich out of it—one out of the construction and another out of profits of operating the Road. It is quite proper for Congress to consider all of these things." But in general, he thought: "There was never anything more absurd and ridiculous than that prosperity can be brought to a country by legislation." Only Oakes of the Northern Pacific, the road with the largest land grant, specifically recognized the public-utility character of railroads as such. "The fact that the right of eminent domain is granted is evidence," he contended, "that the railroads are for public use and that the public has certain rights therein; or in their operation, and therefore the Legislature has the power to regulate.

Regardless of what railroad men thought about the public character of the roads, the fact that many of them had received substantial public aid in their construction supported a belief by shippers and legislators that the railroad business was subject to regulation. Government subscriptions to railroad stocks and bonds, outright subsidies, and gifts of land had, as already noted, been common particularly in branch-line construction. But for western roads the most important and most criticized type of government aid was the federal land grant. The free or low-priced service given in return by railroads to federal agencies was small in those days and received little attention.

Railroad executives had a deep distrust of legislatures and government officials. With virtual unanimity they doubted the wisdom, honesty, or efficiency of politicians. Samuel Sloan scarcely exaggerated the general attitude when he wrote Corning: "The Lieut. Gov. can adjourn the Legis & thus let us home & our constituents breathe free & be thankful they are saved from mischief." Of the Illinois state senators Ackerman wrote: "They pass their nights in rollicking, will drink all you offer them, and make you any amount of wild promises, but their actions . . . give lie to the promise. In short they are utterly unreliable. The same is true of the House." Perkins did not believe, for example, that a western municipality could be trusted to service bonds issued for bridge construction.

Congress was regarded as little better than the state legislatures. Cass thought that "wise and good men get corrupt when they go to Washington." "I . . . write this letter," Stone told James A. Garfield, "simply to express my utter disgust with the character of a Congress, that . . . seems to contain many men most thoroughly versed in the art of 'addition, division, and silence.'" Fish thought that even the great champion of business, Senator Allison of Iowa, had double-crossed the Illinois Central.

It was generally assumed that legislators lacked the understanding of railroad problems necessary for good legislation. "When you see the Congress of the United States which ought to be composed of intelligent and honest men, voting for such a measure as the Reagan Bill, and passing it by a vote of two to one," complained Clarke, "what are you to expect from State Legislatures? . . . I believe I would just about as soon own chips, wet stones and dogs as an investment in Railroad stocks." Ledyard thought, however, that "if practical business men could be induced oftener to serve in our legislature, much of the fancied ill-feeling between the public and corporations would disappear."

Managers worried continually about the dangers to railroads from what they regarded as unfair or unwise taxation. Clarke wrote that "railroad property, being of a permanent character, seems to be the only species of property which the demagogues, politicians and communists can attack at all times, they knowing full well the owners cannot remove it out of their reach." In the midst of the battles over federal regulation Perkins thought that "one of the most serious dangers is in the taxing power." And Ledyard and Platt Smith expressed the general apprehension of the effects of local taxation on railroad property.

From the sixties on, regulation of rates was the most feared type of legislation. The managers, knowing the intricacy of the rate structure, and believing that it ultimately rested "on the laws of trade and commerce," were sure that blanket definitions of fair return and uniform rates would be ruinous to the roads and might ultimately lead to complete government control. "My own impressions are," wrote Stone regarding a rate act, "that such a bill would be unconstitutional and of no effect." The strongest practical argument against regulation was that it would prevent further construction of privately owned railroads. "I am now of the opinion," wrote Corning to a correspondent in Canada as early as 1860, "that if you get hold of a good thing in this state—our Legislature will . . . render it valueless—and I have made up my mind not to again take any interest in any new undertaking." Similar letters were written by executives to prominent citizens and politicians, but they also wrote to each other in the same vein.

The presidents came to see that if state regulatory laws could not be avoided, then railroad commissions elected or appointed to administer them were not an unmixed evil. Ledyard wrote in 1883: "Where there are Commissioners to stand between the railroads and the public much dissatisfaction can be avoided, and many things made plain." Similarly, if legislation was to be framed, managers preferred that the situation first be investigated by a commission.

Refusal to observe laws deemed unjust or unconstitutional was a part of American tradition shaped in the colonial struggles with Great Britain. Railroad executives, on occasion, thought it better to disregard laws and trust to their reinterpretation by the courts or repeal by subsequent legislatures. A president also hesitated to enforce a law in his own company if competitors were gaining by violation of it. In defiance of an Illinois eight-hour law, Douglas wrote: "The company's [sic] leading into this city have all decided to employ the men by the hour working ten hours a day, and we are acting with the balance." It might also seem best to "close one's eyes to what the law requires" in order to do a favor for a politician. But these instances of violation should not obscure the fact that in general the entrepreneurs conformed to legislation and commission rulings.

Railroad men generally expected more favorable consideration from courts than from legislatures or commissions, more from judges than from juries, and more from the highest courts than from the inferior ones. In their attitudes toward the Illinois and Iowa rate laws, the C. B. & Q. executives illustrate these beliefs. Walker regarded the Iowa laws as "hostile legislation" that could not be dealt with on a reasonable basis. "There is not a complaint," he wrote, "on the whole line of our road by any of our patrons or shippers." In such circumstances the hope lay in appeal to the courts. Walker was sure that the United States courts would sustain the chartered right of the road to control its own rates, particularly if a case could be brought where the decision would not be by a jury.

The decision of the Supreme Court in the Granger cases came as a shock from which Harris, then president of the C. B. & Q., only expected to "rally when the first stunning effects have been exhausted." In 1884 Clarke wrote to Fish: "It begins to look Pretty Certain that a RR entering the Supreme Court of the U. S. leaves hope behind." But this uncertainty did not alter the belief that the highest federal tribunals were more likely to grant justice to the railroads than were commissioners or state courts.

In a few circumstances railroad executives welcomed government action. Some of these were connected with the establishment of greater security by defining liabilities in cases of bankruptcy, and providing adequate policing against city thugs and hostile Indians. Like most practical believers in laissez-faire, the railroad men were not too sensitive to the principle of government restriction when it was in their own interest. Harris wrote hopefully that "sooner or later there must be Congressional action that will oblige the U. P. [Union Pacific] to be entirely impartial [in its treatment of connecting lines]." Charles P. Clark favored legislation to enforce tests for color blindness. James C. Clarke wanted a provision in the I. C. C. Act against strikes that would tie up interstate commerce.

Similarly there are no complaints against subsidies or tariffs by the entrepreneurs of the roads whose business would be benefited thereby. "The word 'subsidy' is an unpopular term," wrote Ackerman, "but it does seem to me our Government could well afford to encourage a line of steamers between South American ports and New Orleans." And Kimball was sure that, in order to keep out foreign Bessemer ores, "protection is needed for the State of Virginia."

PARTICIPATION IN POLITICS

A number of railroad men, particularly in the first half of the period, were themselves in politics. Bishop, George Bliss, Chapin, Corning, Depew, Joy, Morgan, Pruyn, Richmond, Sloan, and Twichell all held public office during or shortly after their terms as railroad presidents. But little of their political correspondence is in the railroad archives. And, while some letters of Corning, Pruyn, and Richmond are in the Corning Collection and there are a number of political letters in the Edwin D. Morgan Papers, they scarcely warrant comment on the role of the railroad entrepreneur as a professional politician.

Regardless of their personal involvements, keeping the company itself out of openly partisan positions seems to have been a generally accepted element of the executive role. Forbes said: "Throw the weight of your influence against any attempt to get the railroad mixed up any way with politics." Similarly Clarke wrote: "Any attempt of Railroads as such to enter politics . . . so as to control legislatures or politics, is in my judgment unwise, and I fear will certainly meet with disaster."

A more extreme antipolitical view applying to both the company and its employees is Walker's statement: "It is a fundamental principle with us that none of our Officers or men shall have anything to do with politics, because it cannot fail to be injurious to our interests. We can always make it a ground of dismissal to employees of the Road."

But these general principles appear to have been subject to occasional more or less open exceptions. On the New York Central in Corning's regime, the chief officers of the railroad company were the Democratic political leaders of the state. Perkins, who certainly represented what would be regarded as sound policy, wrote of Senator Paddock to Forbes: "You may remember him as a pony Senator at Washington—a sort of washer of dirty linen for Conkling. I regret to say we put him there."

Some executives thought that the company should not interfere with the political opinions or activities of its employees. Of the tense politics of the Civil War period Platt Smith wrote: "Your Directors . . . consider political matters and questions of loyalty and disloyalty to be questions between individuals and the government and not between the company and such individuals." Oakes said: "A great corporation like the Northern Pacific cannot afford to question men's motives in political matters." He saw no objection to an employee's running for office "provided he will be elected . . . In my opinion it is desirable that employes should be identified with the people in local politics."

USE OF LOBBYISTS

As the United States became a big industrial nation the citizen could make his ideas effective only through pressure groups. Twentieth-century recognition of this fact has removed most of the invidious overtones from the word "lobbyist." From 1900 on, the country grew accustomed to reform, labor, farmer, and professional-association lobbies. Social-welfare legislation no less than the tariff had required well-organized pressure groups. The lobby became an integral part of democratic government. Nineteenth-century railroad executives were among the pioneers in working out the relations between a special business interest and democratic legislatures.

As in any new area of political conflict, there was at the start a lack of rules and traditions. And railroad presidents as well as the public were inclined to accept the never-to-be-realized ideal of George Washington: a direct democratic government without political parties, run by honest and informed representatives of the public interest. A repugnance for politics and political maneuvering was widespread among the middle and upper classes of the period. "I hate, as you do, the lobby and all the cursed implications, vexations and complications thereof," Watrous wrote to a prominent man in Hartford.

In spite of the good character of some lobbyists, such as John Lord Hayes of the National Wool Manufacturers Association, the correspondence indicates a dislike of, or contempt for, "that class of men in Washington," and a dislike of paying them. Lobbies made up of corrupt legislators and ex-legislators like New York's famous "Black Horse Cavalry" were feared by legitimate interests. Cass, for example, thought that the Northern Pacific had been badly swindled by lobbyists in the early seventies. In very important matters, leading entrepreneurs urged each other to avoid reliance on lobbyists by going in person to Washington or to the state capitals.

But entrepreneurs had early recognized the need for lobbyists or legislative counselors, if only, as Pruyn put it, "to watch and guard against mischievous projects, rather than to ask for things affirmatively." This was particularly advisable where other railroads had competing legislative aims. And federal mail contracts required someone to look after each railroad's affairs in Washington. Legislative representatives were of two types: those paid an annual salary or retainer for looking after recurrent matters, such as Honorable J. Black to whom Billings wrote in 1880: "I think you ought to be content for the sum of $2,500. I do not think you will have anything particular to do"; and those paid or otherwise rewarded for doing special jobs. The men who did special jobs in turn fell into two groups: well-known, influential politicians and lawyers friendly to the roads; and hack journalists or free-lance public-relations men. Businessmen generally respected the former group, but were often uncomfortable when dealing with the latter.

Railroad executives could reward stanch political friends in many more or less substantial ways, such as letting them in on townsite planning, giving minor positions to their dependents, or special rates on their goods. While, as Fish wrote, it was "wrong as a matter of principle and also as a matter of economy, to pay for legislation," he was willing to do so if "it cannot be obtained in any other way." The implied philosophy seems to have been that sound business was supported by a higher sanction than that against influencing corrupt and incompetent legislators. "I have neither taste nor talent for such work," Kimball explained, "and nothing but the great danger to our great property, I might say ruin, which would follow the passage of that iniquitous bill— would have induced me to take a hand in the game." But Billings, at least, refused on several occasions to make direct payments for legislation.

On matters of common interest the railroad leaders sought interroad cooperation either in Washington or the state capitals. From the Civil War on, the battle in Iowa between the railroads and hostile legislators led to appeals for concerted managerial action. Platt Smith's appeals of 1865 apparently brought effective joint "measures," because he was able to write to Jesup: "Two months since, the governor was at work in the interest of parties opposed to railroads; but now he is all right." But such uniform action required continued top executive efforts. James C. Clarke advanced the interesting idea that railroad employees were so numerous in Illinois that the roads could secure more favorable commissioners by election than by appointment.

Executives devised special methods for influencing legislators. Joy noted Thayer's suggestion of 1874 that they "send some one to Kansas with authority to offer our roads there to the State." Clarke believed that if railroads gave as little service as required by law and lived up to the letter of uniform rate and other regulations it would disrupt business to such an extent that the obnoxious acts would be repealed. This was actually tried by the managers of some roads in Iowa. Ackerman thought that a donation to Illinois Wesleyan University "would doubtless touch the heart of every Methodist Member of the Legislature." Harris at first believed that letters from stockholders to their members in Congress would be helpful in protecting the Northern Pacific land grant, but he found the stock so concentrated in seven eastern states that the technique would be ineffective. Oakes suggested a plan to prevent the governor and judges of Washington Territory from chartering a rival to the Oregon Railway and Navigation Company: "With some cheap ties and light iron I can put down a cheap narrow gauge track and just before the opening of court in the spring if the road is not then submerged I will bring down from Walla Walla one of those light engines and one car and toot around until court adjourns. The track will be located on a system of curves that will effectually take up all the ground available for RRd purposes."

As in the case of newspaper editors, free passes were also used for conciliating politicians. In the early fifties Morgan learned the usefulness of the pass in gaining public and political friendship and even included four New York City coroners, writing: "They will not, or ought not, to be great travellers and I am sorry to say are quite often needed in their official capacity by our railroad." It was about this same time that Forbes also favored giving passes to the press. When the custom of political passes was well entrenched, Clarke explained to a legislator: "Please don't consider that we expect any of you . . . To be under *obligations* to us . . . All we ask is that we receive fair and considerate treatment."

By the seventies Cass characterized the free pass as "an abominable nuisance that ought to be squelched by law." Watrous shows the entrepreneur's assurance that the approved sanctions supported his side in writing: "It is a pity, in the interest of sound morality and pure legislation, that they do not prefer to pay for what they have in the way of transportation as much as for what they eat." But passes had to be continued, as Ledyard explained, because "no step the railroad companies could take would so soon bring hostile legislation, as to refuse to issue passes to members of the Legislature." . . .

THE INTERSTATE COMMERCE ACT

Discussions of the Interstate Commerce Act and its unsuccessful Congressional predecessors illustrate the maturing views of the executives regarding government regulation. As state regulatory laws multiplied in the seventies, Perkins came to think that perhaps a national Board of Commissioners to study railroad affairs, as suggested in the Rice bill of 1878, would be better than leaving the railroad question "wholly to State politicians." He confided to Forbes that "the public *will* regulate us to some extent—& we must make up our minds to it." This note of resignation featured much of the correspondence from the late seventies until the passage of the Interstate Commerce Act.

In each session from 1878 on, Representative Reagan from Texas introduced a bill in the House for the regulation of railroads. The primary aim of all these bills was to eliminate discrimination between places, persons, or commodities. By the beginning of 1885 Ledyard thought Congressional action so likely that he warned the Michigan Central agents that "contracts involving the carriage of freight to points outside the State ought not to be arranged for until we know what the probable result of the Reagan bill will be." The blocking of the Reagan bill by the Cullom bill in the Senate prevented action in 1885, and gave the railroad entrepreneurs some hope. Perkins wrote Senator Cullom a long letter in September 1885, explaining the reasons for railroad practices, and emphasizing the futility of trying to interfere with the law of supply and demand. But as far as any public action was concerned he thought that they should proceed cautiously, perhaps submitting a joint memorandum against regulation signed by six or ten railroad presidents. Both he and Forbes feared that regulation would be the first step toward government operation and that the latter would be "the sum of all folly not to say wickedness."

Because he believed regulation *must* fail in the end, Perkins was opposed to the railroads publicly trying to guide or improve such legislation. "If the railroads want to try to guide legislation," he insisted, "they should do it by agreement with their friends privately, while insisting as a matter of principle on the truth that no legislation is needed." He feared, however, that some of the eastern presidents, not realizing the ultimate danger, favored some federal action to check excessive competition. The New Haven executives, for example, hoped that if a bill was passed Charles P. Clark might be appointed as one of the Commissioners and "be on the Board long enough to assist in getting it organized on a proper basis." But to Perkins there could be no "proper basis."

In spite of their general pessimism, most presidents, including eastern ones, continued to work for the defeat of the bill, particularly through pressure on senators and representatives.

The Act passed in 1887 threatened the entire railroad rate structure. It prohibited discrimination between persons, commodities, or localities, forbade pooling, and included an ambiguous clause against charging more for a short than for a long haul. Administration of the law was placed in the hands of a five-man commission.

The railroad presidents were in considerable doubt about the precise meaning of many of the provisions. Those of the Vanderbilt lines favored a general meeting with their attorneys "in order to determine what the bill actually means, and how far it would be safe for us to act under it, provided always that our counsel agree as to what the bill means." Ledyard favored immediate test cases before the commission or the courts to determine certain details.

All five presidents from whom there is fairly full correspondence for the years 1887 and 1888 expressed vigorous disapproval of the Act. Perkins believed that it placed "too much power in the hands of five men, and is subjecting them to too much temptation," and that it was "wrong in principle" to put control of rates in the hands of Federal Commissioners. He also feared rate cutting by roads wholly within one state. Ledyard and other presidents thought that the Act should permit regulated pooling. Fish, perhaps because of his early training in banking, found that "the most objectionable requirement of the Commission relates to the financial operations of Railway corporations, that is to say, stocks and bonds owned etc . . . The connection between such purely financial transactions and 'Commerce among the States' is to me imperceptible."

But, as other writers have observed, until the courts began to demonstrate the weakness of the Act, the presidents generally favored observing its letter. Clarke wrote Fish: "The only thing left for the Rail Roads to do is to largely increase the long haul or through rates. Act honestly with each other and be patient." "If the law is not equitable," wrote Ledyard, "the best plan would be to follow out the advice of General Grant and have it repealed by obeying it." Perkins's attitude

was: "Let us ask the Commissioners to enforce the law when its violation by others hurts us." Watrous said: "We are all interested in the *bona fide* enforcement of the bill if it can be done, but none of us are willing to be sacrificed for the purpose of teaching the lessons of either its success or failure to the rest."

Ledyard's extremely detailed correspondence provides many examples of how the law was used as a club against shippers who demanded deep rate cuts, and the extent to which it was evaded. He used the law as a basis for refusing special tariffs to G. H. Hammond and Company and John P. Squire and Company, both meat shippers whose exorbitant demands had irked him for some time. He had thought on various occasions that Chicago through rates were quoted too low at times when the Michigan Central was exceeding its quota in the trunk-line pool, and he used possible action by the Interstate Commerce Commission as an added argument with his general freight agent. Where he desired business, however, Ledyard indicated that there would be ways such as official changes in classification or even cash bonus payments for avoiding the prohibitions against special rates. For example, he wrote: "I would prefer to pay a reasonable amount, say anything under one thousand dollars [to a steel company] . . . And we can get over the giving of special rates by contract."

During this period when the executives were trying to observe the letter of the Interstate Commerce Act, it appeared that it might have some important economic effects. Ledyard wrote shippers that the effect of the equal rates prescribed by law "must, necessarily, be to restrict for many manufacturers, the field in which they can distribute their goods." Perkins maintained in 1888: "The Interstate Law is responsible for the existing rate war. Pooling, or self-regulation, has been prohibited and nothing provided to take its place," and also stated: "Railroad wars and railroad legislation are just as certain to have their effects on railroad investments, in the end, as the day is to follow the night." He supported for a time the extralegal rate agreement brought about by J. Pierpont Morgan in January 1889, on the ground that "it may help us in perhaps bringing some order out of the chaos which has existed since the Interstate Law took effect."

In case the law should have continuing force, the presidents advocated three major changes: Legalization of pooling; punishment of shippers for violation; and greater flexibility in freight classifications. Perkins wrote: "How would it do to provide simply that when two or more railroads wish to form a pool they shall submit the agreement to the Interstate Commission?" Ledyard wanted it to "be made as much a violation of the law for a shipper to fraudently furnish a carrier weights less than the amount actually shipped as it is for the carrier to knowingly underbill." C. P. Clark complained to Senator Platt that "there can be no fairness in a law which subjects all roads to the same classification of freight."

SUMMARY: A ROLE AFFECTED WITH A PUBLIC INTEREST

By 1890, ability to carry on successful relations with government agencies and the public had obviously become an important part of the executive role. But, as we have seen, this aspect was inherent from the start in the situation for which the role was developed. Railroads individually or collectively controlled the economic life of most communities. Their officers could not avoid being public figures. And since certain unpopular practices were deeply imbedded in the structure of competitive railroad operation, the railroad president was more likely to be attacked than praised.

Big shippers had bargaining power and their business was cheaper to handle than that of smaller firms. In an imperfectly competitive freight market, therefore, the few big customers were almost bound to secure lower rates than the far more numerous small patrons. The same kind of dilemma alienated the shippers at the noncompetitive local points who had to pay more than the through rate. Both kinds of discrimination violated the American sanction that big and small should be treated alike. Lacking solutions for these two major causes of public ill will, the executive role was to rationalize rather than to eliminate them.

Many executives recognized that they had this handicap to overcome, and that they, more than other businessmen, should cultivate public relations. State regulation gave added force to these views, and led to campaigns to educate the public about certain phases of railroading. Underlying these campaigns was an assumption that the public was "reasonable" and would respond to logically presented evidence. While most of the leaders, recognizing the "educational" power of the press, favored using its "inspired" articles and news releases, they were divided on the desirability of newspaper or magazine ownership by railroads.

The strongest defense for their actions, in the opinion of the entrepreneurs and probably in that of much of the public, was that business was responsible for the development of the country, and this was America's most important task. These same people regarded politicians in general as parasites who for selfish or misguided reasons often sought to hinder physical progress. In such thinking it followed readily, if not logically, that the pursuit of sound business ventures was more important than preserving political honesty. Our correspondence indicates that the president who had to authorize the "fixing" of a corrupt politician felt no loss of virtue in himself. The railroad side was the moral one. The railroad alone

could open up the country. For this purpose private investment must be encouraged. Regulatory laws that discouraged investment ran counter to this sanction for progress, and were in effect immoral. As Watrous said: "It is not a public blessing to so legislate as to prevent prosperity, or discourage enterprise and good management."

Much as he might affirm his distaste for politicians, the railroad manager was inevitably in politics. Regulations in charters, bridges over navigable streams, rights of way, taxes, land grants, financial aid, and army and mail contracts all tied the railroad companies to various legislatures. But there were still strong American sanctions against party machines and lobbies, still positive sanctions in favor of the ideal of direct democracy, and the manager had an aversion, as did many other citizens, to working with the real political machinery.

Furthermore, this new and vital utility, the railroad, had grown so fast that its leaders had achieved no uniform philosophy of their proper relations to government or the public. They were willing to accept public favors like land grants or subscriptions to stocks and bonds, but were not sure what public obligations these properly entailed. In such a situation "duty to the company" dictated that the conscientious executive should get what he could, and resist political encroachment.

Even those presidents like James C. Clarke, who came to admit that railroads were "affected with a public interest" and could not altogether escape regulation, feared that legislatures lacked both the requisite knowledge of the railroad situation and honesty of purpose. Political ignoramuses, seeking to win favor with their constituents, passed regulations contrary to "natural economic laws" that would be disastrous if obeyed. Nonobservance of such laws, therefore, coincided with social morality. No law, it was thought, could justly run counter to the apparent needs of competitive survival (the corporate right to life, liberty, and the pursuit of happiness).

The discussion in this and other chapters has shown that in practice the general philosophy that government should aid but not hinder business was loosely enough conceived to cover many exceptions. The railroad businessman seems to have been first and foremost a pragmatist. The question was: what worked to the advantage of management or the company? A theory to justify the choice could be developed later. This attitude explains why Watrous could think that the Interstate Commerce Act might be made to function reasonably well, whereas Perkins thought it economically impossible; why Oakes thought competition the only basis for efficient business, but Harris thought it deadly to railroads; why legislation in general was opposed, but a law to legalize pooling was not.

EDWARD C. KIRKLAND:
DIVIDE AND RUIN*

In order to dispel at once any mystery inherent in the title, this essay is primarily about the business generation of the "robber barons." I propose to explore not so much what the businessman of that era thought as the scheme of thought with which he chose to approach the problems of his day. Since this is the Mississippi Valley Historical Association, I shall at least be gracious enough to start my remarks in the West. Charles Elliott Perkins, president of the Chicago, Burlington and Quincy Railroad, provides my text. In 1885 he wrote in one of his frequent memoranda (for this was the manner in which he liked to express himself): "The question of political economy is not, What is noble? What is good? What is generous? What are the teachings of the Gospel?—But what, if anything, is it expedient for society, for government, to do about the production, distribution, and consumption of property, of wealth?" It is true, he continued, that "heroic example and noble obligation" are essential for a nation. "But these are individual, not governmental qualities. There is nothing noble, or generous, or heroic, or christian in a rich man's involuntary submission to taxation for the benefit of those who are less rich, if society shall deem it expedient to tax him for that object. . . . This is what some of the more recent writers call the old political economy, the economic law of Adam Smith, which they denounce as too cold and heartless for a Christian People."

The utterance was exceptional in its precision and force, but its ideas were commonplace among businessmen of that generation. Not only did they exalt the individual in the economic sphere, but they attempted to divide the individual into functions or compartments, which should as a matter of right and expediency have no relation to each other. In short, economic activity stood apart from the spheres of moral and personal considerations.

Businessmen demonstrated the application of this formula in labor policy. To the assertion of reformers and labor spokesmen that labor was entitled to a "living" wage, one which entitled the laborer to a "decent" or "respectable living," Perkins replied: "To say that a man is entitled to wages sufficient to maintain his family respectably is meaningless. What is the measure? Who is to decide what is enough to keep a man and his family respectable? Shall the labourer fix his own compensation and *somebody* be found to employ him? You may say society is morally bound to see that no honest man who is willing to work shall starve, and it may be admitted that it is better to give such men work than to give money

without work. But that is public charity in either case, because if you do work which is not needed for the sake of giving employment, that is not *business*. It is easy to say that a man ought to be 'decently' paid, or 'well paid,' or 'reasonably' paid. But what is decent, or good, or reasonable pay? Is it what a man wants? Suppose two men apply for work. One says, 'I am careful, frugal, have an economical wife, can get along respectably on a dollar and a half a day, and am ready to go to work at that.' The other says, 'I am more frugal than number one. I can get along respectably on a dollar a day and am ready to go to work at that.' Both being equally capable of doing the job, which shall be taken?" The answer, according to the principles of political economy here defined, is obvious.

This response of the business community to the interrelation of wages and human considerations was automatically extended to cognate matters of labor welfare—pensions, relief societies, payments for injuries. The objections to these devices were numerous. They relived the men of the care and responsibility for themselves, and care and responsibility were developmental. "The fact that some men are unfortunate does not change the rule. If a man put his hand over the fire, by accident or misfortune, he is burnt just as much as if he put it there intentionally." The one way to deal with these matters was to deal with them through the economic relation, the way of wages. Make the latter large enough so that men who chose to do so could take care of themselves, including emergencies. "No man can decide for another what he shall give away from motives of sympathy," wrote Perkins. "Stockholders employ agents to conduct their business affairs. If such gratuities (payment for injuries) are given, it must be for business policy or business expediency and not charity." Perkins denied that this attitude regarded men as commodities. "Of course men are not commodities . . . but their labor, when offered for sale, is just as much a commodity as the thing it produces, and all sympathy which leads people to think otherwise is doing more harm than good, like unwise charity." The capitalist not only divided himself, he divided the laborer as well.

Lest these be regarded as the self-interested rationalizations of employers, perhaps we should resort to academic economists to learn what they, in their detachment, thought on the matter. Arthur Lapham Perry of Williams College, author of one of the most widely used early texts in economic theory and a devout Christian as well, wrote of the wage contract: "When A hires B to work in his factory, this new relation is economical, not moral. . . . What is the economical relation? This. A desires the personal service of B in his factory purely for his pecuniary benefit, and assumes his own ability to make all

* Reprinted from Edward C. Kirkland, "Divide and Ruin," *Mississippi Valley Historical Review*, XLIII (June, 1956), 3–17 by permission.

the calculations requisite for determining how much he can (profitably to himself) offer B for his service; and B, who knows all about his own skill . . . wants to sell his service to A for the sake of the pecuniary return or wages. There is no obligation resting upon either. Man to man, each in his own right. There is no benevolence in the heart of either, so far as this matter goes. Benevolence is now an impertinence. It is a question of honest gain in broad daylight. Benevolence is blessed in its own sphere, but there is no call for it here and now. . . . The less either (A or B) thinks and talks and acts about the other in all the other relations of life, the better hope of good success to both in this relation. Church relations and social relations and political relations are all of consequence in themselves; but when any of these begin to get mixed up with labor-relations, there is soon a muss and a mess."

In the circumstances, it was natural that the businessman should have a dubious approach to the agencies, political and religious, which were trying to introduce into business affairs values and considerations which the businessmen thought had nothing to do with business. The laws of trade, sometimes vulgarized as "business principles," governed and should govern production, distribution, and consumption; statute laws, passed by legislatures and Congress, could have no bearing and no influence in this area. If they did, they acted only to distort and delay matters. The great tide of natural law would sooner or later break through and assert itself. Consequently businessmen, as a matter of principle, sought to stand outside the political process. Early in the 1880's, Henry Varnum Poor, the railroad expert and organizer of manuals, reached the heart of the matter: "Railroad Men form no political party. They are of all shades of parties. There is no possibility that they should be combined for any political object. They reject instead of craving political influence. They are as free from sinister political bias as our farmers, merchants, or manufacturers."

A few years later, when Lyman J. Gage, president of the First National Bank of Chicago and one of the most perceptive businessmen of that city, addressed the American Bankers' Association, he admitted that the general attitude of his hearers was that they should have no concern with politics or government and that the businessman thought of himself as "a business man, pure and simple." Certainly the historians who picture the businessman of this period in politics up to his last dollar would deny the justice of either adjective. But an illustration of the possible validity of the businessman's attitude was provided by Charles Francis Adams, Jr. As railroad commissioner of Massachusetts through the 1870's he was the advocate of general rather than special legislation for the railroads: general legislation would take railroad officials and the railroad lobby out of the legislature. In the 1880's, as president of the Union Pacific, his consuming objective was

the passage by Congress "of such laws as will once and for all separate the government from the management of this or any other railroad corporation." And in the same strain, Edwin L. Godkin of the *Nation* argued for free trade to protect Congress against the lobby of manufacturers. "The way to arm them against temptation is to leave them as little as possible to sell of the things which capitalists are eager to buy."

Godkin was getting at the separation of business and politics through the back door. While individuals like Gage were urging participation by businessmen in the political process to do away with the "demagogue" and the "political trickster," the *Nation* was arguing that businessmen abjure membership in legislatures because, too "practical minded," they could not look at public issues comprehensively and they did not understand the interests of others. "Practical men will not make good laws; it demands theories." Whatever the favored approach to the matter of division, a New England banker, Henry Lee Higginson, expressed the business wish most pithily: "Let us ask Congress to do their work in their own way and let us [businessmen] do ours in our way."

The businessman on the whole was also sure that religion and business should be separated. Partly this was a result of a historic estrangement. Edward Atkinson, Boston cotton capitalist and a Unitarian—and perhaps not, therefore, a religious person—informed his readers: "For nearly fifty years I have been engaged in the practical work of this life, occupied in the functions of life which the priest in almost all churches and under all the various phases of religion has been apt to disparage and to hold in slight repute." Whether or not the antagonism between clergyman and businessman was historically inescapable, the growth of the social gospel after the Civil War and the liveliness of "ethical economists," the allies of its pastors, were sure to stimulate a reaction in the business community. The outlook of this new group was of course the exact opposite of that of the business community; it sought to introduce morals and values into economic operations, "to apply Christianity," as the phrase of one of its leaders, Washington Gladden, put it, to substitute for the word individual the concept social, as in "social justice," "social Christianity," "social gospel."

One answer of the business spokesman was that such an objective was not the business of Christianity. The business of religion was the "old theological gospel," not the "gospel of social endeavor," the saving of souls and instruction in morals, not the "industrial millennium." On matters traditionally religious, clerics were scientific experts. "When Dr. Lyman Beecher took the charge of a group of 'anxious inquirers' out of the hands of Judge Gould at Litchfield, he did so as a professional man, just as a physician would have taken a case of typhoid out of the hands of an apothecary, and the church saw clearly the overwhelming necessity of the judge's deposition." But in matters of business and political economy, clergymen were not experts but amateurs. Andrew Carnegie announced: "Ecclesiastics . . . their attention being chiefly fixed upon the other world . . . seldom shine as advisers upon affairs pertaining to this." Generally he refused to include among his philanthropies gifts to churches. He made one exception—church organs. The reason for this exceptional generosity—he gave 8,000—he explained, "You can't always trust what the pulpit says but you can always depend upon what the organ says." Carnegie's anticlericalism and rationalism were well known. But on this point John D. Rockefeller, who generally suffered Baptist clergymen gladly, agreed: "I have sometimes been tempted to say that our clergymen could gain by knowing the essentials of business life better. . . . People who have had much to do with ministers and those who hold confidential positions in our churches have at times had surprising experiences in meeting what is sometimes practiced in the way of ecclesiastical business, because these good men have had so little of business training in the work-a-day world."

So much for the true theory of the relationship between economics and religion. Departure from this theory of separation was bound to be damaging in practical affairs. A few surmises to the effect that the agitation of preachers and their lay readers, the "ethical economists," might in some way have been responsible for the Haymarket bomb outrage stiffened into certainty in the next decade. Both groups were blamed in a general way for the discontent of the 1890's and were held directly responsible for the Pullman outbursts. As Godkin wrote Charles Eliot Norton, "The labor craze fanned and promoted by 'ethical' professors and clergymen ended in the Chicago riots." Beyond the evil of particular circumstances, the social gospel weakened the qualities of character which the business world so highly esteemed. In a discussion of the morals of the future, Godkin grieved that public admiration was no longer given to "the just, austere, proud, and truthful man," but to the man of "brotherly kindness." Humanity had become more important than honesty. Whether because clerical criticism of business practices embraced a wider area or because its persistence was getting under the businessman's skin, the resentment of the latter seemed to increase as time went by. In the end Charles Elliott Perkins was reminding Henry Lee Higginson, "Without such mitigation by business of his [the workingman's] circumstances, no other kind of assistance is of the slightest use to a man—one who is hungry and cold can think of nothing else—no gospel touches him." Whatever the soundness of this observation in a historical sense, it would seem to cast some doubt on the business theory that religion and business could occupy separate spheres. Anyway, religion apparently should not bite the hand that fed it.

Just why so many members of the business community thought it feasible to isolate their various interests one from another is a problem. So pervasive an influence has been assigned in this era to phrenology that I am tempted to find here another reflection of its importance. "The mind," wrote Orson Fowler, one of the high priests of the phrenological movement, "is a plurality of innate and independent faculties—a congregate of distinct and separate powers." But probably any parallelism between the ideas of the business community and phrenology is whimsey. Somewhat more plausible is the idea that the businessman divided his interest into separate compartments because this was the correct way of logically arriving at sound conclusions. Perkins was fond of resorting to John Locke's dictum: "The greatest part of true knowledge lies in the distinct perception of things in themselves distinct." Rigorously applied, this aphorism should have restrained the habit of arguing by analogy so prevalent with Perkins and other businessmen. In their hands the statement really had another purpose. It was a method for reducing problems to their essentials, for stripping away irrelevancies. Since that business generation was confronted with the complex problems attendant upon rapid change, they had to use every device of exacting analysis to find the answers. "There is a great difference," wrote Perkins, "in attitudes and rules of conduct for an individual employer of small numbers of men and a corporation employing 10–20 thousand." The "distinct perception of things in themselves distinct" was one way of discovering the differences in these attitudes and rules.

Be that as it may, the decision to operate under the aegis of a "distinct perception of things in themselves distinct" was impossible. Chauncey M. Depew in an address before the New York State Chamber of Commerce found it was not easy for rich men to be philanthropists when they had acquired wealth under conditions which "dry up generous impulses and make the possessor hard, cold, and unsympathetic." Charles Elliott Perkins found in practice that the businessman was indivisible. Fighting his employees who had struck for higher wages in 1888, Perkins elected to stand on the high ground of principle. Faced with a delegation of workers, he wrote on a slip of paper which he passed to an associate, "As an officer, I can't sympathize with the men, but as an individual, I do sympathize with them."

Few incidents were more instructive of the impossibility of the program of a "distinct perception of things in themselves distinct" than the experience of Charles Francis Adams, Jr., when he was president of the Union Pacific. Here was a man of principle and honesty, a civil service reformer, and one who believed that it was advantageous for railroads and the state to have little to do with each other. Yet since the government had originally given the Union Pacific a land grant and financial assistance, and since representatives from the western states, especially Iowa, frequently voiced the anti-railroad feeling of their constituencies in Congress, Adams had to maintain a *de facto* office of the railroad in Washington, although "it will not do to have it suggested that we have a lobby on the spot." Nonetheless Adams and the Union Pacific's counsel, Moorfield Storey, were always going to the capital and in emergencies Adams sent General Grenville M. Dodge thither "to fix things up."

This concentrated mobilization did not work. As Adams wrote: "This gang of operators in Washington are certainly a most ingenious set of fellows. They every now and then put in a bit of work which I cannot but look upon with admiration. It is very much to me as if I were obliged to watch a set of burglars who were breaking into my vault, and unable to prevent their operations, yet from time to time deeply impressed with the skill with which the rascals went to work." Though he professed an inability to do anything about these raids, Adams was later offering to do favors in behalf of certain bills desired by the Iowa congressmen if they would vote for his, authorizing "employments to aid in procuring the passage" of legislation, and finally he was writing Dodge in Washington in a personal letter: "I wish you would see if you can do anything to expedite the matter. If you cannot do it in one way, do it in another. Anyhow let it be done. I know you are quite equal to the occasion. Simply advise me what has been done, I will remit to you." Whatever these confidences add up to, they at least reveal the pathetic, and in this case somewhat ludicrous, fate of a man bent on separating business and government. He was caught in the toils. In a later letter Adams attempted an explanation. He confided to Dodge, "Of course we do not wish to meddle in politics except in self-defence."

The policy with which the businessmen chose to approach their own problems and the problems of their day was not only impossible; it was ruinous on every score. In the field of labor relations there was bound to be an increasing degree of impersonalization as the scale of business and the size of labor forces was enlarged. The deliberate attempt to add a designed indifference and apartness to this inherent tendency simply made matters worse. Even if the relationship between employer and employee were economic and not one of benevolence, this did not mean that the employees liked it that way. Though they complained about wages and hours, a recurrent lament of the workers was that employers thought of men not as individuals but as part of the machines, that employees were known by number, not by name, and came into contact only with superintendents. The old friendly feelings were gone and society was crystallizing into classes. "Labor unions," said one of their partisans proudly, suggest remedies implying "something more than 'business principles'; they imply the subordination of what are regarded as 'business principles' to morality." In the final analysis the history of labor organization and of labor-man-

agement strife in the late decades of the nineteenth century revealed the folly of the business attitude.

The history of national legislation in the same period does not point to so sharp a failure. In spite of the common interpretation that the legislation after the Civil War was business orientated, actually business strategy in this area was directed to retaining advantages which it had won accidentally—say the tariff and the national banks during the Civil War—and to securing the veto or repeal of legislation it did not desire, such as the issue of legal tenders or the repeal of the Sherman Silver Purchase Act. A systematic reading of a business-minded journal, like the *Commercial and Financial Chronicle*, gives the impression of one long shriek on the political retreat. Commenting upon the congressional year 1874, the *Chronicle* sighed: "The season has not been a favorable one for financial wisdom, and any proposed law which does not carry with it the certainty of positive injury is regarded to a certain extent as a safety valve, by standing in the place of some other provision which would be still less propitious." For business *vis-a-vis* public legislation, these years were one long holding operation. The exhortations of Lyman Gage, toward the end of the period, advising the businessmen to organize as citizens and shopkeepers, not into "a political machine—that would be as unwise as it would be impossible, but if I could, I would make it an avenue through which should be poured in many streams over all the people the healthful influences of a better knowledge of the true laws of our politico-social-economic life," confessed the disadvantage of separating business from government.

Whether the ability of businessmen to take the church or leave it alone was equally ruinous for them, many would say was impossible to tell. It is not given to historians to see beyond the grave, nor has any arrangement yet devised bestowed infallibility in location theory upon Protestant clergymen, particularly the social gospel variety. Be that as it may, many men of the cloth were quite certain that here the theory of divide led, as it did elsewhere, to ruin. When J. P. Morgan died in 1913, an Episcopalian divine in Philadelphia preached a sermon, "Has J. P. Morgan gone to heaven? If not, why not?" and found that he had not, partly because he was neither Christian nor democrat; and somewhat more modestly the *United Mine Workers Journal* suggested an investigating committee to determine the dead financier's whereabouts. When John D. Rockefeller died in 1937, it was the labor press and spokesmen, rather than the pastors, who speculated whether the oil king had gone to heaven or hell and seemed to lean toward the latter destination. In view of the dearth of answers on the other side of this eternal question "Whither Bound?" here as elsewhere to divide was to ruin.

My exposition of the disadvantage of dividing his personality and his character, as the businessman sought to do, is in a sense a parable. In my estimation that experience carries a lesson for historians as historians. In the narrower field of writing about business and businessmen, it seems to me to be ruinous to accept the businessman's habit of division and to apply it to him. This is the defect, to my way of thinking, in much business history writing. While it is only redressing the balance to focus such narratives upon the entrepreneurial decision, written in terms of business documents, such procedure, without attention to the social and political context, ruins the picture. To segregate the criticism of a big business in separate, topical chapters near the end of a volume is a somewhat less obvious road to ruin. Such distortions are not necessarily committed only by the supporters of business enterprise as it was. The foes of business who focus upon only one aspect of what they criticize, who select opinions without attention to the whole life of the businessman and his achievements, can easily make a monster or caricature out of Stephen J. Field and William Graham Sumner, apologists for business freedom. . . .

The plight of George Rice, an independent Ohio refiner, provided a test case of business practices in the latter nineteenth century. In this selection, compiled from testimony taken before state and national investigating committees, Henry D. Lloyd described the relations between Standard Oil and the railroads, and the mechanisms developed to stifle free competition.

HENRY D. LLOYD:
STANDARD OIL CONFRONTS
THE INDEPENDENT REFINER*

George Rice, coming from the Green Mountains of Vermont, entered the oil business twenty-nine years ago, when he and it were young. He was one of the first comers. Beginning as a producer in the Pithole region, in the days of its evanescent glory, in 1865, he prospered. Escaping the ruin which overtook those who stayed too long in that too quick sand, he was one of the first to develop the new field at Macksburg, Ohio, and to see the advantages of Marietta, on the Ohio River, as a point for refining. Crude oil could easily be brought from Ohio and Pennsylvania by barge down the Ohio River. The field he entered was unoccupied. He drove no one out, but built a new industry in a new place. In 1876 he had risen to the dignity of manufacturer, and had a refinery of a capacity of 500 barrels a week, and later of 2000 barrels. Owning wells, he produced, himself, a part of the crude which he refined. His position gave him access to all the markets by river and rail. Everything promised him fortune. His family took hold with him in the work of breadwinning. "The executive part of the business is done altogether by my family," he says. "One daughter keeps the books, another daughter does nine-tenths of the correspondence, and my son-in-law is the general manager."[1] One of the daughters was a witness in one of her father's cases before the Interstate Commerce Commission. "She discussed with counsel," said the New York *World*, "the knotty points involving tank-car rates, mileage, rebates, and the long and short haul as familiarly as any general freight agent present."

Several other refiners, seeing the advantages of Marietta, had settled there. They who elected themselves to be trustees of the light of the world, thus having the advantages of the place pointed out to them by practical men, determined that Marietta must be theirs. They bought up some of the refiners. Then they stopped buying. Their representative there, afterwards a member of the trust, "told me distinctly that he had bought certain refineries in Marietta, but that he would not buy any more. . . . He had another way," he said, "of getting rid of them."[2] Of these "other ways" the independents were now to have a full exposition. In January, 1879, freight rates on oil were suddenly and without previous notice raised by the railroads leading out of Marietta, and by their connections. Some of the rates were doubled. The increase was only on oil. It was—in Ohio—only on oil shipped from Marietta; it was exacted only from the few refiners who had not been bought, because there were "other ways of getting rid of them."[3]

This freight-tariff attack on the independent refiners was arranged by their powerful rival and

---

* Reprinted from Henry D. Lloyd, *Wealth Against Commonwealth* (New York: 1899), pp. 199–218.

[1] Trusts, Congress, 1888, p. 573.

[2] Railroad Freights, Ohio House of Representatives, 1879, p. 28.

[3] Testimony, same, pp. 5, 41, 42, 124, 141, 162, 166, 170.

the railroad managers at a secret conference, as the latter admitted.

"Did you have any consultation or invite consultation with other manufacturers of oil at Marietta?"

"No, sir." [4]

When the representatives of the combination in this market were taxed by a dealer with getting the benefit of this manipulation of freight, "they laughed." All the railroads took part in the surprise. Curiously enough, the minds of the managers of a dozen roads acted simultaneously and identically, over thousands of miles of country— some, as they admitted, with suggestion, and some, as they testified, without suggestion—upon so precise a detail of their business as the rates on oil at one little point. "I did it at my own instance," said the freight agent of the Baltimore and Ohio. Freight officials of railways as far apart east, west, and south, and in interest, as the Baltimore and Ohio, and the Pennsylvania, and the Lake Shore, which had no direct connection with Marietta, and reached it only over other lines, stopped their "wars" to play their part in the move by raising the rate on oil only, and, most remarkable of all, to a figure at which neither they, nor the railroad connecting them with Marietta, nor (and this was the game they were gunning for) the independent refiners could do any business. From other points than Marietta, as Cleveland, Parkersburg, Pittsburg, and Wheeling, where the combination had refineries, but the Marietta independents had none, the railroads left the former rates unchanged. [5]

Rice was "got rid of" at Columbus just as effectually as if Ruskin's "Money-bag Baron," successor of "the Crag Baron," stood across the road with a blunderbuss. His successful rival had but to let its Marietta refineries lie idle, and transfer to its refineries at Wheeling its Marietta business—and Rice's too. By the pooling of the earnings and of the control of all its refineries—the essential features of the combination—its business could be transferred from one point to another without loss. One locality or another could be subjected to ruinous conditions for the extermination of competitors, and the combination, no matter how large its works there, would prosper without check. It gets the same profit as before, but the competitor by its side is ruined. All its refineries along a given railroad can be closed by high rates made to "overcome competition," but profits do not cease. Their business is done elsewhere by its other refineries, and all the profits go into a pool for the common benefit.

From Rice's point of view, Marietta was the storm-centre; but the evidence before the Ohio Legislative Investigation of 1879, before the Legislative Committee of New York of 1879,

before Master in Chancery Sweitzer in Pennsylvania, and in the suit against the Lake Shore Railroad, showed that the low barometer there was part of a disturbance covering a wide area. The demonstration against the independent refiners of Marietta was only part of a wider web-spinning, in which those at all points—New York, Boston, Philadelphia, Pittsburg, Oil City, Titusville, Buffalo, Rochester, [6] and Cleveland—were to be forced to "come in" as dependents, or sell out, as most of them did.

That rates were not raised from points controlled by the combination is only part of the truth. At such places rates were lowered. This, like the increase of rates, was done at a secret conference with the oil combination and at its instance. [7] Where it had refineries the rates were to be low; the high rates were for points where it had competitors to be got rid of without the expense of buying them up. The independents knew nothing of the increase of freights prepared for them by the railroad managers and their great competitor until after, some time after, it had gone into effect.

The railroad company gave notice to their rivals what the rates were to be, but withheld that information from them. [8] That was not all. Before the new rates were given all the old rates were cancelled. "For a few days," said an independent, "we could not obtain any rates at all. We had orders from our customers, but could not obtain any rates of freight."

As to many places, the withholding of rates continued. "There's many places we can't obtain any rates to. They just say we sha'n't ship to these other places at any price." [9]

When the Ohio Legislature undertook to investigate, it found that the railroad men professed a higher allegiance to their corporations than to the State. They refused to answer the questions of the committee, or evaded them. "I am working under orders from the general freight agent," said one of them, "and I don't feel authorized to answer that." The arguments of the committee that the orders of an employer could not supersede the duty of a citizen to his government, or the obligations of his oath as a witness, were wasted. "I will tell you just how I feel," said the witness to these representatives of an inferior power. "I am connected with the railroad company, and get my instructions from the general agent, and I am very careful about telling anybody else anything." The Legislature accepted the rank of "anybody else" to which it was assigned, and did not compel the witness to answer.

[6] See ch. xviii.

[7] Railroad Freights, Ohio House of Representatives, 1879, p. 129.

[8] Trusts, Congress, 1888, p. 579.

[9] Railroad Freights, Ohio House of Representatives, 1879, pp. 33, 40–42.

[4] Testimony, same, p. 129.

[5] Railroad Freights, Ohio House of Representatives, 1879, pp. 12, 34, 172.

To a question about the increase in freight: "I object," said another railroad officer, "to going into details about my own private business." [10]

One peculiar thing about the action of the railroads was that it was an injury to themselves. The Baltimore and Ohio, for instance, by raising its rate, cut off its oil business with Marietta entirely. "What advantage is it, then?" the freight agent of the road over which the Baltimore and Ohio reached Marietta was asked.

"There is no advantage. . . . We had revenue before this increase in rates, and none since."

"What would be the inducement for her (the Baltimore and Ohio) to do it, then?"

"That is a matter I am not competent to answer." [11]

The railroad men testified positively that the increase affected all alike at Marietta. It was supposed even by those who thought they saw to the bottom of the manœuvre that the combination would close its Marietta works temporarily, in order to seem to be equally affected with all the rest. It could do this with no loss whatever, since, as explained, no raise in rates had been made from Wheeling, Parkersburg, Pittsburg, Cleveland, where it was practically alone, and it could reach all its customers from those places as well as from Marietta. But the combination kept on filling orders from its refineries at Marietta at the old freight rates, while by its side the men it was hunting down sat idle because the discriminating rates of freight made it impossible for them to use the highways. It was so careless of appearances that oil ordered of its works at Parkersburg would be sent from the Marietta branch,[12] and at the old rate of 40 cents, while the other refineries could not ship because the rate to them was 65 cents; the increase at Marietta was not enforced against it, but only against the three independents—just as planned in the South Improvement scheme.

The move was far-reaching—as far as Chicago, the rate to which was made $1.20 a barrel, instead of 90 cents a barrel.

"Then they cut you off from the Western trade as well as this State?"

"Yes, sir; almost entirely. . . . I was selling in Chicago, and it cut trade entirely off." [13]

"Before the rates were changed did you run to your full capacity?"

"Yes, sir; about that." [14]

At one stroke the independents lost the business which it had cost them years of work to get. As the testimony of witness after witness showed, the merchants who had been their customers in Chicago, Columbus and other places, now had to send their orders to those for whose benefit the railroad men had raised the rates. This sweeping change was not due to any change in their desire to sell, or of their old customers to buy. They could still make oil which was still wanted. But they were the victims of a competitor who had learned the secret of a more royal road to business supremacy than making a better thing, or selling it at a better price. Their better way was not to excel but to exclude. When their "secretary" was called before the Ohio Legislature, after this freight ambuscade had transferred the bulk of the business of the independent refineries at Marietta to him and his associates, he declared that the sole cause of their success was the "large mechanical contrivances" of the combination, its "economy," and its production of the "very best oil." "With an aggregation of capital, and a business experience, and a hold upon the channels of trade such as we have, it is idle to say that the small manufacturer can compete with us; and although that is an offensive term, 'squeezing out,' yet it has never been done by the conjunction of any railroads with us." [15]

The small manufacturer did compete and flourish until these railroad men literally switched him out of the market. He competed and got his share of the business, until the men who wanted monopoly, finding that they had no monopoly of quality or price or business ability, resorted to the "large mechanical contrivance" of inducing the managers of the railroads to derail the independent, throwing him off the track by piling impassable freight tariffs in his way. The successful men secured their supremacy by preventing their competitors from entering the market at all. Instead of winning by "better" and "cheaper," they won by preventing any competitor from coming forward to test the questions of "better" and "cheaper." Their method of demonstrating superiority has been to prevent comparisons.

All the independent refiners at Marietta, except Rice, died. "Most of those we received from have gone out of the business," a Cincinnati dealer told the Legislature. Some had fled; some had sold out.[16] Rice set himself to do two things: the first, to drag into the light of day and the public view the secrets of these "better methods"; and the second, to get new business in the place of what he had lost. He succeeded in both. It was in January that he had notice served upon him that he could no longer go to market. In two months he had the Ohio Legislature at work investigating this extraordinary administration of the highways. This was a great public service. It did not yield the fruit of immediate reform, but it did work which is the indispensable prelimi-

[10] Railroad Freights, Ohio House of Representatives, 1879, pp. 49, 51, 56.

[11] Same, pp. 159, 163.

[12] Railroad Freights, Ohio House of Representatives, 1879, p. 169.

[13] Same, pp. 249–50.

[14] Same, p. 250.

[15] Railroad Freights, Ohio House of Representatives, 1879, p. 260.

[16] Same, p. 116.

nary. It roused the people who were still asleep on these new issues, and were dreaming pleasant dreams that in George III. they had escaped from all tyrants forever, and that in the emancipation of the blacks they had freed all slaves forever.

Rice knew that the Legislature were planting trees for posterity, and did not wait for help from them. He set about looking up markets where the public were free to choose and buy. He could not go West or East or North. He went South. The little family kept the refinery at Marietta running, and the father travelled about establishing new agencies in the South, and studying freight tariffs, railroad routes, and terminal facilities for loading and unloading and storing. In 1880, through all the storm and stress of these days, he was able to double the capacity of his refinery. Again he succeeded in building up a livelihood, and again his success was treated as trespass and invasion. His bitter experience in Ohio in 1879 proved to be but an apprenticeship for a still sterner struggle. Rice was getting most of his crude oil from Pennsylvania, through a little pipe line which brought it to the Alleghany. The pipe line was taken up by the oil trust.[17]

This compelled him to turn to the Macksburg, Ohio, field for most of his petroleum. He had one tank-car, and he ran this back and forth faster than ever. Then came the next blow. The railroad over which he ran his tank-car doubled his freight to 35 cents a barrel, from 17½. That was not all. The same railroad brought oil to the combination's Marietta refineries at 10 cents a barrel, while they charged him 35. That was not all. The railroad paid over to the combination 25 cents out of every 35 cents he paid for freight. If he had done all the oil business at Marietta, and his rival had put out all its fires and let its works stand empty, it would still have made 25 cents a barrel on the whole output. Rice found a just judge when he took this thing into court. "Abhorrent," "dangerous," "gross," "illegal and inexcusable abuse by a public trust," "an unparalleled wrong," are the terms in which Judge Baxter gave voice to his indignation as he ordered the removal of the receiver of the railroad who had made this arrangement with the combination, to enable it, as the judge said "to crush Rice and his business." [18]

In an interview, filling four columns of the New York *World* of March 29, 1890, the head of the trust which would receive this rebate is reported to have made this attempt to reverse the facts of this and similar occurrences: "The railroad company proposed to our agent," he said. But the judge who heard all the evidence and rendered the decision, which has never been reversed or impaired, declared that it "compelled" the railroad to make the arrangement, "under a threat of building a pipe line for the conveyance

of its oils and withdrawing its patronage." This arrangement was negotiated by the same agent of the oil combination who engineered the similar "transfer" scheme by which the trunk-line railroads gave it, in 1878, 20 to 35 cents a barrel out of the freights paid by its competitors in Pennsylvania, as already told.[19]

"I reluctantly acquiesced," the receiver said, writing in confidence to his lawyer, anxious lest so acquiescing he had made himself legally liable. The interview describes the arrangement as an innocent thing: "A joint agreement for the transportation of oil." It was an agreement to prevent the transportation of oil by anybody else. Judge Baxter shows that it was a joint agreement, procured by threats, for the transportation of "$25 per day, clear money," from Rice's pockets into the pockets of the members of the trust for no service rendered, and without his knowledge or consent, and with the transparent purpose of transporting his business to their own refineries. Judge Baxter called it "discrimination so wanton and oppressive it could hardly have been accepted by an honest man, and a judge who would tolerate such a wrong or retain a receiver capable of perpetrating it, ought to be impeached and degraded from his position." [20]

This matter was also passed upon by the Select Committee of the United States Senate on Interstate Commerce. "No comment," the committee say, "is needed upon this most impudent and outrageous proposition"—by the oil company to the railroad.[21]

"Are you going to deny that story?" a great American statesman of the latter-day type was asked by one of his friends.

"Not I," was the reply. "The story's false. When you find me taking the trouble to deny a thing, you can bet it's true!"

This "agreement for the transportation of oil" had its calculated effect. It put a stop to the transportation of oil from the Ohio field by Rice over the railroad, just as the destruction by the same hands of the pipe line to the Alleghany had cut him off from access to the Pennsylvania oil-fields. He then built his own pipe line to the Ohio field. To lay this pipe it was necessary to cross the pipe line of his great rival. Rice had the pluck to do this without asking for a consent which would never have been given. His intrepidity carried its point, for, as he foresaw, they dared not cut his pipe for fear of reprisals.

In turning to the South, after his expulsion from the Ohio and Western markets, the Mari-

---

[17] Trusts, Congress, 1888, p. 574.

[18] Trusts, Congress, 1888, pp. 577–78.

[19] See ch. viii.

[20] Trusts, Congress, 1888, p. 578. Hardy and another *vs.* Cleveland and Marietta Railroad *et al.*, Circuit Court, Ohio, E.D., 1887. *Federal Reporter,* vol. xxxi., pp. 689–93.

[21] 49th Congress, 1st Session, Report of the Senate Select Committee on Interstate Commerce, p. 199.

etta independent did but get out of one hornet's nest to sit down in another. His opponent was selling its oil there through a representative who, as he afterwards told Congress, "was very fortunate in competing." He thought it was "cheaper in the long-run to make the price cheap and be done with it, than to fritter away the time with a competitor in a little competition. I put the price down to the bone." [22] Rice, in the South, ran into the embrace of this gentleman who had the "exclusive control" of that territory, and whose method of calling the attention of trespassers to his right was to cut them "to the bone." The people and the dealers everywhere in the South were glad to see Rice. He found a deep discontent among consumers and merchants alike. They perhaps felt more clearly than they knew that business feudalism was not better, but worse, because newer, than military feudalism. This representative of the combination assured Congress that "99.9 of all the first-class merchants of the South were in close sympathetical co-operation with us in our whole history"—that is, out of every hundred "first-class merchants" only one-tenth of one merchant was not with them. This is a picturesque percentage.

Rice's welcome among the people would not verify his opponent's estimate that his vassalage included all but one-tenth of one dealer in every hundred. From all parts came word of the anxiety of the merchants to escape from the power that held them fast. From Texas: "Most of our people are anxious to get clear." From Arkansas: "The merchants here would like to buy from some other." From Tennessee: "Can we make any permanent arrangement with you by which we can baffle such monopoly?" From Kentucky: "I dislike to submit to the unreasonable and arbitrary commands." From Mississippi: "It has gouged the people to such an extent that we wish to break it down and introduce some other oils." From Georgia, from different dealers: "They have the oil-dealers in this State so completely cooped in that they cannot move." "We are afraid." [23] As Rice went about the South selling oil the agents of the cutter "to the bone" would follow, and by threats, like those revealed in the correspondence described below, would coerce the dealers to repudiate their purchases. Telegrams would pour into the discouraged office at Marietta: "Don't ship oil ordered from your agent." "We hereby countermand orders given your agent yesterday." One telegram would often be signed by all the dealers in a town, though competitors, sometimes nearly a dozen of them, showing that they were united by some outside influence they had to obey. [24]

Where the dealers were found too independent to accept dictation, belligerent and tactical

cuts in price were proclaimed, not to make oil cheap, but to prevent its becoming permanently cheaper through free competition and an open market. Rice submitted to Congress letters covering pages of the Trust Report, [25] showing how he had been tracked through Tennessee, Missouri, Nebraska, Georgia, Kansas, Kentucky, Iowa, Mississippi, Louisiana, Texas, Arkansas, Alabama. The railroads had been got to side-track and delay his cars, and the dealers terrorized into refusing to buy his oils, although they were cheaper. If the merchants in any place persisted in buying his oil they were undersold until they surrendered. When Rice was driven out prices were put back. So close was the watch kept of the battle by the generals of "co-operation" that when one of his agents got out of oil for a day or two, prices would be run up to bleed the public during the temporary opportunity. "On the strength of my not having any oil to-day," wrote one of Rice's dealers, "I am told they have popped up the price 3½ cents." [26]

The railroad officials did their best to make it true that "the poor ye have with you always." By mistake some oil meant for the combination was delivered to Rice's agent, and he discovered that it was paying only 88 cents a barrel, while he was charged $1.68, a difference of 80 cents a barrel for a distance of sixty-eight miles.

"Could you stand such competition as that?"

"No, sir. Before that I went up there and sold to every man in the place nearly. They were glad to see me in opposition. . . . I lost them, except one man who was so prejudiced that he would not buy from them."

"Your business had been on the increase up to that time?"

"Increasing rapidly. . . . I haul it in wagons now forty miles south of Manito."

"The rates against you on that railroad are so high that you can for a distance of forty miles transport your oil by wagon and meet the competition better than you can by using their own road?"

"Infinitely better." [27]

A spy at one end of an institution proves that there is a tyrant at the other. Modern liberty has put an end to the use of spies in its government only to see it reappear in its business.

Rice throughout the South was put under a surveillance which could hardly have been done better by Vidocq. One of the employés of the oil clique, having disclosed before the Interstate Commerce Commission that he knew to a barrel just how much Rice had shipped down the river to Memphis, was asked where he got the information. He got it from the agents who "attend to our business."

"What have they to do with looking after Mr.

---

[22] Trusts, Congress, 1888, pp. 534, 535.

[23] Same, pp. 730–38.

[24] Trusts, Congress, 1888, p. 743.

[25] Same, p. 729.

[26] Same, p. 732.

[27] Trusts, Congress, 1888, pp. 416–20.

Rice's business? . . . How do your agents tell the number of barrels he shipped in April, May, and June?"

"See it arrive at the depot."

"How often do your agents go to the depot to make the examination?"

"They visit the depot once a day, not only for that purpose, but to look after the shipment of our own oil."

"Do they keep a record of Mr. Rice's shipments?"

"They send us word whenever they find that Mr. Rice has shipped a car-load of oil."

"What do their statements show with respect to Mr. Rice's shipments besides that?"

"They show the number of barrels received at any point shipped by Mr. Rice, or by anybody else."

"How often are these statements sent to the company?"

"Sent in monthly, I think."

"It is from a similar monthly report that you get the statement that in July, August, and September, Mr. Rice shipped 602 barrels of oil to Nashville, is it?"

"Yes, sir."

"Have you similar agents at all points of destination?"

"Yes, sir." [28]

This has a familiar look. It is the espionage of the South Improvement Company contract, in operation sixteen years after it was "buried." When the representative of the oil combination appears in public with tabulated statements exhibiting to a barrel the business done by its competitors for any month of any year, at any place, he tells us too plainly to be mistaken that the "partly-born," completely "buried" iniquity, sired by the "sympathetical co-operation" of the trustees and their railroad associates of easy virtue, is alive and kicking—kicking a breach in the very foundations of the republic.

A letter has found the light which was sent by the Louisville man who was so "fortunate in competing," immediately after he heard that one of "his" Nashville customers had received a shipment from the Marietta independent. It was addressed to the general freight agent of the Louisville and Nashville Railroad. It complained that this shipment, of which the writer knew the exact date, quantity, destination, and charges, "slipped through on the usual fifth-class rate." "Please turn another screw," the model merchant concluded. What it meant "to turn another screw" became quickly manifest. Not daring to give the true explanation, none of the people implicated have ever been able to make a plausible explanation of the meaning of this letter. The railroad man to whom it was sent interpreted it when examined by Congress as meaning that he should equalize rates. But Congress asked him:

"Is the commercial phrase for equalizing rates

among railroad people 'turn another screw' ?"

He had to reply, helplessly, "I do not think it is."

The sender before the same committee interpreted it as a request "to tighten up the machinery of their loose office." [29] Rice found out what the letter meant. "My rates were raised on that road over 50 per cent. in five days."

"Was it necessary to turn on more than one screw in that direction to put a stop to your business?"

"One was sufficient." [30]

The rates to the combination remained unchanged. For five years—to 1886—they did not vary a mill. After the screw had been turned on, he who suggested it wrote to the offending merchants at Nashville, that if they persisted in bringing in this outside oil he would not only cut down the price of oil, but would enter into competition on all other articles sold in their grocery. He italicized this sentence: *And certainly this competition will not be limited to coal-oil or any one article, and will not be limited to any one year.* [31] "Your co-operation or your life," says he.

"Have you not frequently, as a shipper of oil, taken part in the competition with grocers and others in other business than oil, in order to force them to buy oil?"

"Almost invariably I did that always." [32]

"The expense and influence necessary for sustaining the market in this manner are altogether expended by us, and not by the representatives of outside oil," he further wrote. "Influence," as a fact of supply and demand, an element of price-making, is not mentioned in any political economy. And yet the "influence" by which certain men have got the highways shut to other shippers has made a mark as plain as the mountains of the moon on our civilization. "If we allow any one to operate in this manner," he continued, "in any one of our localities, it simply starts off others. And whatever trouble or expense it has given us in the past to prevent it we have found it to be, and still believe it to be, the only policy to pursue." [34]

They "are threatening," his Nashville agent, after the screw was turned, wrote Rice, "to ruin us in our business." [35]

The head of the Louisville "bone-cutters," when a witness before Congress during the trust investigation, stigmatized the action of his Nashville victims as "black-mail." They were "black-mailers" because they had sold a competitor's oil, and refused to continue to sell his own unless it was made as cheap or cheaper. Competition,

---

[28] Testimony, Rice cases, Interstate Commerce Commission, Nos. 51–60, 1887, pp. 442–43.

[29] Trusts, Congress, 1888, pp. 524–30.

[30] Same, p. 620.

[31] Same, pp. 534–36.

[32] Same, p. 533.

[34] Same, p. 536.

[35] Trusts, Congress, 1888, p. 729.

when he practised it on others, was "sympathetical co-operation." Tried on him, it was "blackmail." "That man wanted us to pay him more than we paid the other jobbers"—i. e., he wanted them to meet the prices of competitors—"because he thought we had the market sustained, and he could black-mail us into it. I bluffed him in language, and language is cheap." [36] The "language" that could produce an advance of freights of 50 per cent. in five days against a competitor was certainly "cheap" for the man whose rates remained unchanged, and who thereby absorbed his neighbor's vineyard. The inevitable result followed at last. Rice fought out the fight at Nashville seven years, from 1880 to 1887; then, defeated, he had to shut up his agency there. That was "evacuation day" at Nashville. It was among his oldest agencies, he told Congress, "and it was shut out entirely last year on account of the discriminations. I cannot get in there." [37]

State inspection of oil and municipal ordinances about storage have been other "screws" that have been turned to get rid of competition. City councils passed ordinances forbidding oil in barrels to be stored, while allowing oil in tanks, which is very much more dangerous, as the records of oil fires and explosions show conclusively. His New Orleans agent wrote Rice concerning the manœuvres of his pursuer: "He has been down here for some time, and has by his engineering, and in consequence of the city ordinances, cut me out of storage. As matters now stand, I would not be able to handle a single barrel of oil." [38] In Georgia the law was made so that the charge to the oil combination shipping in tank-cars was only half what it was to others who shipped in barrels. The State inspector's charge for oil in tanks was made 25 cents a barrel; for oil in barrels it was 50 cents a barrel. But as if that was not advantage enough, the inspector inspected the tanks at about two-thirds of their actual capacity. If an independent refiner sent 100 barrels of oil into the State, he would have to pay $50 for inspection, while the oil combination sending in the same would pay but 25 cents a barrel, and that on only 66⅔ barrels, or $16 in all. This difference is a large commercial profit of itself, and would alone enable the one who received it to sell without loss at a price that would cripple all others. In this State the chief inspector had the power to appoint inspectors for the towns. He would name them only for the larger places, where the combination had storage tanks. This prevented independent refiners from shipping directly to the smaller markets in barrels, as they could not be inspected there, and if not inspected could not be sold. [39] All these manœuvres of inspection

helped to force the people to buy of only one dealer, to take what he supplied, and pay what he demanded. Why should an official appointed by the people, paid by them to protect them, thus use all his powers against them? Why?

"State whether you had not in your employ the State inspector of oil and gave him a salary," the Louisville representative of the combination was asked by Congress.

"Yes, sir." [40]

Throughout the country the people of the States have been influenced to pass inspection laws to protect themselves, as they supposed, from bad oil, with its danger of explosion. But these inspection laws prove generally to be special legislation in disguise, operating directly to deprive the people of the benefit of that competition which would be a self-acting inspection. They are useful only as an additional illustration of the extent to which government is being used as an active partner by great business interests. Meanwhile any effort of the people to use their own forces through governments to better their condition, as by the ownership of municipal gas-works, street-railways, or national railroads and telegraphs, is sung to sleep with the lullaby about government best, government least.

This second campaign had been a formidable affair—a worse was to follow; but it did not overcome the independent of Marietta. With all these odds against him, he made his way. Expelled from one place and another, like Memphis and Nashville, he found markets elsewhere. This was because the Southern people gave him market support along with their moral support. Co-operation of father and son and daughter made oil cheaper than the "sympathetical co-operation" opposing them, with its high salaries, idle refineries, and dead-heads. Rice had to pay no dividends on "trust" stock capitalized for fifteen times the value of the property. He did not, like every one of the trustees, demand for himself an income of millions a year from the consumer. He found margin enough for survival, and even something more than survival, between the cost of production and the market price. "In 1886 we were increasing our business very largely. Our rates were low enough so that we could compete in the general Southern market." [41]

Upon this thrice-won prosperity fell now blow after blow from the same hand which had struck so heavily twice before. From 1886 to the present moment Rice and his family have been kept busier defending their right to live in business than in doing the business itself. Their old enemy has come at them for the third time, with every means of destruction that could be devised, from highway exclusion to attacks upon private character, given currency by all the powerful means at his command. The game of 1886 was that of 1879, but with many improvements gained

[36] Same, p. 534.

[37] Same, p. 730.

[38] Same, p. 733.

[39] Trusts, Congress, 1888, p. 735.

[40] Same, p. 535.

[41] Trusts, Congress, 1888, p. 578.

from experience and progress of desire. His rates were doubled, sometimes almost tripled; in some cases as much as 333 per cent. Rates to his adversary were not raised at all. The raise was secret. Suspecting something wrong, he called on the railroad officer July 13th, and asked what rates were going to be. The latter replied that he "had not the list made out." But the next day he sent it in full to the combination. Rice could not get them until August 23d, six weeks later, and then not all of them. As in 1879 the new tariff was arranged at a conference with the favored shippers.[42]

This was the first gun of a concerted attack. Rice was soon under fire from all parts of the field. One road after another raised his rates until it seemed as if the entire Southern market would be closed to him. While this was in progress the new Interstate Commerce Law passed by Congress—in part through the efforts of Rice—to prevent just such misuse of the highways, went into effect. But this did not halt the railway managers. A month after it was passed the

Senate Committee on Interstate Commerce was shown that discrimination was still going on, as it is still. At points as far apart as Louisville, New Orleans, Atlanta, St. Louis, and San Francisco switches were spiked against Rice, and the main lines barricaded of all the highways between the Ohio River, the Atlantic and Pacific oceans, and the Gulf of Mexico. In the face of the Interstate Commerce Act the roads raised his freights to points in Georgia, Alabama, Tennessee, Kentucky, Louisiana, and Mississippi in no case less than 29, and in some cases as high as 150, 168, and 212 per cent. more than was charged the oil combination. Where the latter would pay $100 freight, he, shipping the same amount to the same place, would sometimes pay $310—if he got it taken at all.[43]

The general freight agent of one of the roads, when before the Interstate Commerce Commission, denied this. When confronted with written proof of it he could only say, "It is simply an error."[44] . . . [The documentation continues, showing the destruction of Rice's business.]

In contrast to the foregoing selection, Andrew Carnegie saw the competitive process as producing beneficial effects. "And while the law may be sometimes hard for the individual," he contended, competition "is best for the race, because it insures the survival of the fittest in every department." The present selection is regarded among the most persuasive arguments set forth by a Captain of Industry.

ANDREW CARNEGIE:
WEALTH*

The problem of our age is the proper administration of wealth, so that the ties of brotherhood may still bind together the rich and poor in harmonious relationship. The conditions of human life have not only been changed, but revolutionized, within the past few hundred years. In former days there was little difference between the dwelling, dress, food, and environment of the chief and those of his retainers. The Indians are to-day where civilized man then was. When visiting the Sioux, I was led to the wigwam of the chief. It was just like the others in external appearance, and even within the difference was trifling between it and those of the poorest of his braves. The contrast between the palace of the millionaire and the cottage of the laborer with us to-day measures the change which has come with civilization.

This change, however, is not to be deplored, but welcomed as highly beneficial. It is well,

nay, essential for the progress of the race, that the houses of some should be homes for all that is highest and best in literature and the arts, and for all the refinements of civilization, rather than that none should be so. Much better this great irregularity than universal squalor. Without wealth there can be no Mæcenas. The "good old times" were not good old times. Neither master nor servant was as well situated then as to-day. A relapse to old conditions would be disastrous to both—not the least so to him who serves—and would sweep away civilization with it. But whether the change be for good or ill, it is upon us, beyond our power to alter, and therefore to be accepted and made the best of. It is a waste of time to criticise the inevitable.

It is easy to see how the change has come. One illustration will serve for almost every phase of the cause. In the manufacture of products we have the whole story. It applies to all combinations of human industry, as stimulated and enlarged by

---

[42] Trusts, Congress, 1888, pp. 579–80.

* Reprinted from Andrew Carnegie, "Wealth," *North American Review,* CXLVIII (June, 1889), 653–62.

[43] Same, p. 584.

[44] Testimony, Rice cases, Interstate Commerce Commission, Nos. 51–60, p. 147.

the inventions of this scientific age. Formerly articles were manufactured at the domestic hearth or in small shops which formed part of the household. The master and his apprentices worked side by side, the latter living with the master, and therefore subject to the same conditions. When these apprentices rose to be masters, there was little or no change in their mode of life, and they, in turn, educated in the same routine succeeding apprentices. There was, substantially, social equality, and even political equality, for those engaged in industrial pursuits had then little or no political voice in the State.

But the inevitable result of such a mode of manufacture was crude articles at high prices. To-day the world obtains commodities of excellent quality at prices which even the generation preceding this would have deemed incredible. In the commercial world similar causes have produced similar results, and the race is benefited thereby. The poor enjoy what the rich could not before afford. What were the luxuries have become the necessaries of life. The laborer has now more comforts than the farmer had a few generations ago. The farmer has more luxuries than the landlord had, and is more richly clad and better housed. The landlord has books and pictures rarer, and appointments more artistic, than the King could then obtain.

The price we pay for this salutary change is, no doubt, great. We assemble thousands of operatives in the factory, in the mine, and in the counting-house, of whom the employer can know little or nothing, and to whom the employer is little better than a myth. All intercourse between them is at an end. Rigid Castes are formed, and, as usual, mutual ignorance breeds mutual distrust. Each Caste is without sympathy for the other, and ready to credit anything disparaging in regard to it. Under the law of competition, the employer of thousands is forced into the strictest economies, among which the rates paid to labor figure prominently, and often there is friction between the employer and the employed, between capital and labor, between rich and poor. Human society loses homogeneity.

The price which society pays for the law of competition, like the price it pays for cheap comforts and luxuries, is also great; but the advantages of this law are also greater still, for it is to this law that we owe our wonderful material development, which brings improved conditions in its train. But, whether the law be benign or not, we must say of it, as we say of the change in the conditions of men to which we have referred: It is here; we cannot evade it; no substitutes for it have been found; and while the law may be sometimes hard for the individual, it is best for the race, because it insures the survival of the fittest in every department. We accept and welcome, therefore, as conditions to which we must accommodate ourselves, great inequality of environment, the concentration of business, industrial and commercial, in the hands of a few, and the law of competition between these, as being

not only beneficial, but essential for the future progress of the race. Having accepted these, it follows that there must be great scope for the exercise of special ability in the merchant and in the manufacturer who has to conduct affairs upon a great scale. That this talent for organization and management is rare among men is proved by the fact that it invariably secures for its possessor enormous rewards, no matter where or under what laws or conditions. The experienced in affairs always rate the MAN whose services can be obtained as a partner as not only the first consideration, but such as to render the question of his capital scarcely worth considering, for such men soon create capital; while, without the special talent required, capital soon takes wings. Such men become interested in firms or corporations using millions; and estimating only simple interest to be made upon the capital invested, it is inevitable that their income must exceed their expenditures, and that they must accumulate wealth. Nor is there any middle ground which such men can occupy, because the great manufacturing or commercial concern which does not earn at least interest upon its capital soon becomes bankrupt. It must either go forward or fall behind: to stand still is impossible. It is a condition essential for its successful operation that it should be thus far profitable, and even that, in addition to interest on capital, it should make profit. It is a law, as certain as any of the others named, that men possessed of this peculiar talent for affairs, under the free play of economic forces, must, of necessity, soon be in receipt of more revenue than can be judiciously expended upon themselves; and this law is as beneficial for the race as the others.

Objections to the foundations upon which society is based are not in order, because the condition of the race is better with these than it has been with any others which have been tried. Of the effect of any new substitutes proposed we cannot be sure. The Socialist or Anarchist who seeks to overturn present conditions is to be regarded as attacking the foundation upon which civilization itself rests, for civilization took its start from the day that the capable, industrious workman said to his incompetent and lazy fellow, "If thou dost not sow, thou shalt not reap," and thus ended primitive Communism by separating the drones from the bees. One who studies this subject will soon be brought face to face with the conclusion that upon the sacredness of property civilization itself depends—the right of the laborer to his hundred dollars in the savings bank, and equally the legal right of the millionaire to his millions. To those who propose to substitute Communism for this intense Individualism the answer, therefore, is: The race his tried that. All progress from that barbarous day to the present time has resulted from its displacement. Not evil, but good, has come to the race from the accumulation of wealth by those who have the ability and energy that produce it. But even if we admit for a moment that it might be better for the race to discard its present foundation,

Individualism,—that it is a nobler ideal that man should labor, not for himself alone, but in and for a brotherhood of his fellows, and share with them all in common, realizing Swedenborg's idea of Heaven, where, as he says, the angels derive their happiness, not from laboring for self, but for each other,—even admit all this, and a sufficient answer is, This is not evolution, but revolution. It necessitates the changing of human nature itself—a work of æons, even if it were good to change it, which we cannot know. It is not practicable in our day or in our age. Even if desirable theoretically, it belongs to another and long-succeeding sociological stratum. Our duty is with what is practicable now; with the next step possible in our day and generation. It is criminal to waste our energies in endeavoring to uproot, when all we can profitably or possibly accomplish is to bend the universal tree of humanity a little in the direction most favorable to the production of good fruit under existing circumstances. We might as well urge the destruction of the highest existing type of man because he failed to reach our ideal as to favor the destruction of Individualism, Private Property, the Law of Accumulation of Wealth, and the Law of Competition; for these are the highest results of human experience, the soil in which society so far has produced the best fruit. Unequally or unjustly, perhaps, as these laws sometimes operate, and imperfect as they appear to the Idealist, they are, nevertheless, like the highest type of man, the best and most valuable of all that humanity has yet accomplished.

We start, then, with a condition of affairs under which the best interests of the race are promoted, but which inevitably gives wealth to the few. Thus far, accepting conditions as they exist, the situation can be surveyed and pronounced good. The question then arises,—and, if the foregoing be correct, it is the only question with which we have to deal,—What is the proper mode of administering wealth after the laws upon which civilization is founded have thrown it into the hands of the few? And it is of this great question that I believe I offer the true solution. It will be understood that *fortunes* are here spoken of, not moderate sums saved by many years of effort, the returns from which are required for the comfortable maintenance and education of families. This is not *wealth,* but only *competence,* which it should be the aim of all to acquire.

There are but three modes in which surplus wealth can be disposed of. It can be left to the families of the descedents; or it can be bequeathed for public purposes; or, finally, it can be administered during their lives by its possessors. Under the first and second modes most of the wealth of the world that has reached the few has hitherto been applied. Let us in turn consider each of these modes. The first is the most injudicious. In monarchical countries, the estates and the greatest portion of the wealth are left to the first son, that the vanity of the parent may be gratified by the thought that his name and title are to descend to succeeding generations unimpaired. The condition of this class in Europe to-day teaches the futility of such hopes or ambitions. The successors have become impoverished through their follies or from the fall in the value of land. Even in Great Britain the strict law of entail has been found inadequate to maintain the status of an hereditary class. Its soil is rapidly passing into the hands of the stranger. Under republican institutions the division of property among the children is much fairer, but the question which forces itself upon thoughtful men in all lands is: Why should men leave great fortunes to their children? If this is done from affection, is it not misguided affection? Observation teaches that, generally speaking, it is not well for the children that they should be so burdened. Neither is it well for the state. Beyond providing for the wife and daughters moderate sources of income, and very moderate allowances indeed, if any, for the sons, men may well hesitate, for it is no longer questionable that great sums bequeathed oftener work more for the injury than for the good of the recipients. Wise men will soon conclude that, for the best interests of the members of their families and of the state, such bequests are an improper use of their means.

It is not suggested that men who have failed to educate their sons to earn a livelihood shall cast them adrift in poverty. If any man has seen fit to rear his sons with a view to their living idle lives, or, what is highly commendable, has instilled in them the sentiment that they are in a position to labor for public ends without reference to pecuniary considerations, then, of course, the duty of the parent is to see that such are provided for *in moderation.* There are instances of millionaires' sons unspoiled by wealth, who, being rich, still perform great services in the community. Such are the very salt of the earth, as valuable as, unfortunately, they are rare; still it is not the exception, but the rule, that men must regard, and, looking at the usual result of enormous sums conferred upon legatees, the thoughtful man must shortly say, "I would as soon leave to my son a curse as the almighty dollar," and admit to himself that it is not the welfare of the children, but family pride, which inspires these enormous legacies.

As to the second mode, that of leaving wealth at death for public uses, it may be said that this is only a means for the disposal of wealth, provided a man is content to wait until he is dead before it becomes of much good in the world. Knowledge of the results of legacies bequeathed is not calculated to inspire the brightest hopes of much posthumous good being accomplished. The cases are not few in which the real object sought by the testator is not attained, nor are they few in which his real wishes are thwarted. In many cases the bequests are so used as to become only monuments of his folly. It is well to remember that it requires the exercise of not less ability than that which acquired the wealth to use it so as to be really beneficial to the community. Besides this, it may fairly be said that no man is to be extolled for doing what he cannot help doing, nor is he to be thanked by the community to which he only leaves wealth at death. Men who leave vast sums in this way may fairly be thought men who would not have left it at all, had they been able to take it with them. The memories of such cannot be held in grateful remembrance, for there is no grace in their gifts. It is not to be wondered at that such bequests seem so generally to lack the blessing.

The growing disposition to tax more and more heavily large estates left at death is a cheering indication of the growth of a salutary change in public opinion. The State of Pennsylvania now takes—subject to some exceptions—one-tenth of the property left by its citizens. The budget presented in the British Parliament the other day proposes to increase the death-duties; and, most significant of all, the new tax is to be a graduated one. Of all forms of taxation, this seems the wisest. Men who continue hoarding great sums all their lives, the proper use of which for public ends would work good to the community, should be made to feel that the community, in the form of the state, cannot thus be deprived of its proper share. By taxing estates heavily at death the state marks its condemnation of the selfish millionaire's unworthy life.

It is desirable that nations should go much further in this direction. Indeed, it is difficult to set bounds to the share of a rich man's estate which should go at his death to the public through the agency of the state, and by all means such taxes should be graduated, beginning at nothing upon moderate sums to dependents, and increasing rapidly as the amounts swell, until of the millonaire's hoard, as of Shylock's, at least

> "———— The other half
> Comes to the privy coffer of the state."

This policy would work powerfully to induce the rich man to attend to the administration of wealth during his life, which is the end that society should always have in view, as being that by far most fruitful for the people. Nor need it be feared that this policy would sap the root of enterprise and render men less anxious to accumulate, for to the class whose ambition it is to leave great fortunes and be talked about after their death, it will attract even more attention, and, indeed, be a somewhat nobler ambition to have enormous sums paid over to the state from their fortunes.

There remains, then, only one mode of using great fortunes; but in this we have the true antidote for the temporary unequal distribution of wealth, the reconciliation of the rich and the poor—a reign of harmony—another ideal, differing, indeed, from that of the Communist in requiring only the further evolution of existing conditions, not the total overthrow of our civilization. It is founded upon the present most intense individualism, and the race is prepared to put

it in practice by degrees whenever it pleases. Under its sway we shall have an ideal state, in which the surplus wealth of the few will become, in the best sense, the property of the many, because administered for the common good, and this wealth, passing through the hands of the few, can be made a much more potent force for the elevation of our race than if it had been distributed in small sums to the people themselves. Even the poorest can be made to see this, and to agree that great sums gathered by some of their fellow-citizens and spent for public purposes, from which the masses reap the principal benefit, are more valuable to them than if scattered among them through the course of many years in trifling amounts.

If we consider what results flow from the Cooper Institute, for instance, to the best portion of the race in New York not possessed of means, and compare these with those which would have arisen for the good of the masses from an equal sum distributed by Mr. Cooper in his lifetime in the form of wages, which is the highest form of distribution, being for work done and not for charity, we can form some estimate of the possibilities for the improvement of the race which lie embedded in the present law of the accumulation of wealth. Much of this sum, if distributed in small quantities among the people, would have been wasted in the indulgence of appetite, some of it in excess, and it may be doubted whether even the part put to the best use, that of adding to the comforts of the home, would have yielded results for the race, as a race, at all comparable to those which are flowing and are to flow from the Cooper Institute from generation to generation. Let the advocate of violent or radical change ponder well this thought. . . .

This, then, is held to be the duty of the man of Wealth: First, to set an example of modest, unostentatious living, shunning display or extravagance; to provide moderately for the legitimate wants of those dependent upon him; and after doing so to consider all surplus revenues which come to him simply as trust funds, which he is called upon to administer, and strictly bound as a matter of duty to administer in the manner which, in his judgment, is best calculated to produce the most beneficial results for the community—the man of wealth thus becoming the mere agent and trustee for his poorer brethren, bringing to their service his superior wisdom, experience, and ability to administer, doing for them better than they would or could do for themselves. . . .

The best uses to which surplus wealth can be put have already been indicated. Those who would administer wisely must, indeed, be wise, for one of the serious obstacles to the improvement of our race is indiscriminate charity. It were better for mankind that the millions of the rich were thrown into the sea than so spent as to encourage the slothful, the drunken, the unworthy. . . .

CHAPTER FOURTEEN

URBANITES IN THE INDUSTRIAL AGE: CHICAGO

Inseparably interrelated with the booming industrialism of the America of the 1880's and the 1890's was the growth of cities of a size and complexity almost never before known in human history. The rise of the great metropolis created both pride and misgivings among observers. City boosters, as always, were ready to celebrate the achievements and unique virtues of every urban center (*i.e.*, Julian Ralph in a selection that follows). But, as Morton and Lucia White pointed out, American intellectuals from colonial times to the present have viewed their cities with serious mistrust if not fear (*i.e.*, William Dean Howells in the guise of the traveler from Altruria). Cities can mean a concentration of comfort and culture; they can reflect taste and beauty; they can also involve squalor, noise, disease, exploitation, and corruption.

In no American city of the era were both the problems and the promise more spectacular than in Chicago.[1] In order to demonstrate how the issues were intertwined and in some respects interacting, all of the selections in this chapter deal with this one city: its rapid growth, its commercial and industrial base, its fire, its working people, its politicians, its civic aspirations, and its Columbian Exposition. With some local variations, the history of Chicagoans is the experience of most American urbanites between the Civil War and the Spanish-American War. Constance McL. Green in her sketch of Chicago covering these years, touches upon both what is distinctive and what is universal.

CONSTANCE McL. GREEN: CHICAGO: THE RAILROAD CENTER*

. . . The war prosperity and post-war growth were partly accident—sheer geographical advant-

age. But partly they derived from the capacity for co-operation that citizens showed again and again. When a St Louis editor wrote angrily of 'Chicago, the tool of the Philistines of the East who were jealous of the strength of St Louis', he failed

---

[1] The definitive multi-volumed panoramic study of the city is Bessie L. Pierce, *A History of Chicago*, 3 vols. (New York: Knopf, 1940, 1957).

* Reprinted from Constance McL. Green, *American Cities in the Growth of the Nation* (Lon-

don: Univ. of London, The Athlone Press, 1957), pp. 111–21 by permission.

to note what was generally acknowledged, that Chicago citizens relied upon themselves as well as upon eastern capitalists. The building of the Union Stockyards illustrated perfectly that ability of Chicagoans to act together energetically to introduce an improvement. The inconvenience and expense of switching cattle cars to pens located all over the city was manifestly clear as, during the war, the incoming carloads of hogs and beef-cattle increased in numbers. By joint agreement, railroads, butchers, and meat-packers bought an area on the southwest side of the city, drained and filled it, laid out water mains and sewer pipes, threaded it with rails and stockaded it with cattle pens, and opened the yards for use on Christmas Day, 1865. Cattle, one observer remarked, got better sanitation in Chicago than humans. The few packers who had hesitated about joining in this pooling of facilities were soon won over. The Union Stockyards became the meat-packing center of the world. Later, Kansas City and other western cities would take over some of this business, but Chicago had shown how co-operation among local competitors could build up a great enterprise. Ingenious utilization of the by-products of meat-packing, a system simplified by the concentration of the industry in one spot, early gave Chicago packers command of a wide field—oil, tallow, lard, glue, fertilizers, and leather. Wheat and corn built the city to begin with; lumber and steel built it stronger; the products of the Union Stockyards built it stronger still.

Commercial and industrial strength, however, was not synonymous with structural strength, as Mrs O'Leary's cow proved. Legend has so enshrined the story of the cow that kicked over the lantern that set the shed afire that started the great Chicago fire that the historian dare not discard the tale for mere want of verification. The blaze that October Sunday night in 1871 jumped from one tinder-dry shanty to another, and a high wind carried sparks quickly to buildings in the business area. Miles of lumber yards and sawmills along the river burned in a few hours. By Tuesday morning two-thirds of the city lay in ashes. The entire United States was shocked. Rival cities laid aside their jealousies and sent carloads of supplies. St Louis gave $500,000 within the first few days. Cincinnati had raised $160,000 before the fire was out. Citizens' committees organized wholesale relief and distributed with equity and efficiency the money and supplies that came in on every train from the rest of the country; the relief fund was even stretched over several years so that a backlog remained when the panic of 1873 occured. English writers, inspired by Thomas Hughes, author of *Tom Brown's Schooldays,* sent books and Queen Victoria a contribution for a new public library. When the city was rebuilt, city ordinances stipulated only brick or stone buildings in the business district. Undaunted by staggering losses, Chicago business houses began again, and, though some companies were ruined, others by hook or crook tided over, advertising the city's resilience by the rapidity with which they recovered.

Chicago's confidence in her own prowess reached out in all directions. New railroads and extensions of old crept further into the trans-Mississippi West where they snatched trade from St Louis. Before the end of the sixties Chicago's railroads, a St Louis newspaper declared, having gobbled up the river city's commerce with all the upper Mississippi valley, were making matters progressively worse: "Not only is the trade of the Lower Mississippi in winter cut off by the same hand, using the Illinois Central Railway, but even the trade of the Ohio River at Pittsburgh is this day being clipped by the Fort Wayne and Chicago Railway.

"The Chicago capitalists are bridging the Mississippi River at Quincy and even the Missouri River at Kansas City, and propose to draw off the trade not only of our Missouri Pacific Railroad, but also of the Southwest, even daringly striking at the center of our State." In 1869 the first transcontinental railroad, the Union and Central Pacific, gave Chicago a direct line to San Francisco, while several other roads were nosing steadily westward until in the 1880's they would reach into Denver and beyond. Chicago's railroad empire indeed became seemingly self-enlarging. In the early seventies the Baltimore and Ohio, intent on competing with the Pennsylvania and the New York lines, extended its tracks into Chicago to capture a share of her growing traffic, just as small western and northwestern companies hastened to link themselves with lines into Chicago because there they could connect with any one of the five trunk lines from the eastern seaboard. The lake freighters, moreover, eight months of the year kept railroad rates lower than they were inland and tightened Chicago's commercial hold on the Mississippi valley and the Northwest. Realization that she dared not rest on past achievements kept her businessmen alert to abuses that might damage her reputation. In 1870 the Board of Trade instituted inspection and grading of meat at the stockyards. Sensing that Chicago's grain trade would have an ill-name if warehousemen were not obliged to follow grading regulations and give honest measure, the Board succeeded in 1871 in getting a state Warehousing Act passed. Paid inspectors, upheld by public opinion, were now able to enforce some degree of control over the unscrupulous.

When the panic of 1873 closed the doors of banks in almost every city in the country, Chicago bankers refused to weaken Chicago's credit by taking the same course. Their defiant stand was possible because the city's economic foundations rested on grain and hogs. The fire of 1871 had not reached the stockyards. However financially hard hit, people had to eat. European demand for Chicago pork packed in dry salt instead of the brine used elsewhere strengthened Chicago's position in the domestic market. Cities whose well-being depended upon products less essential than food suffered to an extent unknown here where processors, while selling at declining prices, could always find buyers. Chicago bankers could thus continue to pay out cash on depositors' demand until no financial crisis existed. One local booster, forgetting St Louis' generosity in 1871, rejoiced openly at her plight. Remarking upon the drop in hog-raising in Illinois, Wisconsin, Iowa, and Missouri, he gloated over the fact that St Louis' loss in 1875 was double Chicago's and that his own city had gained in cattle shipments while St Louis lost some 24,000 head.

Nevertheless, Chicago did not emerge unscathed from the five years of depression. Many firms failed, and unemployment spread. Workmen who had come to rebuild the city after the fire added to the number of unemployed. Citizens took steps to make work by public employment paid in grocery orders and fuel, but the scheme was carried out on too small a scale to do more than scratch the surface of the city's needs. The city had nearly trebled in population between 1860 and 1870, rising from 109,000 to 299,000, and, so far from losing population, gained as a result of the fire. Wealth was concentrated in the hands of a few hundred men; several thousand others were 'comfortably fixed' in small retail businesses and the professions, but the rank and file were wage-earners dependent upon the stockyards, the grain elevators, McCormick's reaper works, the lumber yards and sawmills, the railroads, and building trades. Nearly 145,000 inhabitants in 1870 were foreign-born, and it was the newcomers, unfamiliar with the American scene, who made up the poorest element here, as in every American city. Chicago had more than 53,000 Germans, as well as 6,200 Bohemians, almost 40,000 Irish, 15,000 English, Scots, and Welsh, over 13,000 Scandinavians, and a sprinkling of other Europeans. From these came the bulk of the unskilled labor force. In the skilled occupations German craftsmen were in the lead. The large admixture of skilled German artisans—their leaders men of some education and convinced socialists—encouraged the rise of radical labor groups. In 1864 the Chicago Typographical Union had staged a strike against Chicago newspapers which indicated the strength of local labor organization. The union's fight for higher wages and the protest against using women as strikebreaking, 'scab', typesetters had failed, but it had forecast some of what was to come. Energy formerly directed at the destruction of Negro slavery now began to turn upon 'wage slavery'. In the depression of the 1870's native American workmen, left jobless and as hungry and helpless as foreign-born, joined forces with the foreign 'radicals'. Here was the first move within the city to make the melting-pot melt, and it was not welcomed by Chicago's well-to-do.

In the summer of 1877 resentment turned into action. In July a railroad workers' strike in Baltimore spread to Pittsburgh and a week later aroused Chicago switchmen. Pay had already been cut 15 per cent and a further slash was impending. When the switchmen walked out, other railroad employees followed. Within twenty-four hours every railroad yard in the city was paralysed. Lumbermen and other workers struck in sympathy. Business men screamed for suppression of the 'Commune'. Hysteria seized the city as hoodlums, 'idlers, thieves, and ragamuffins', as Carter H. Harrison described the mob, destroyed railroad property and engaged in street fighting. Harrison, later elected Mayor, was determined to make frightened employers realize that these were not acts of the strikers but of all the lawless elements in the city. Twenty thousand men, one account estimated, were under arms, and a score of people were killed before the strike collapsed. Whether it simply wore out or whether the appearance of two companies of the United States army, fresh back from Indian campaigns in the Northwest, frightened the mob when they paraded through the streets is uncertain. As the strikers returned to work, sanity returned to the city. Newspapers that had castigated the strikers began to temper their judgments, declaring it nonsense to deny that there were two sides to the question and pointing to the ruthless exploitation that railroad companies had indulged in—charging whatever rates they pleased, corrupting state legislatures, city councils, and Congress itself, milking their bondholders, and finally 'raiding not only upon the general public but their own employees'. But belated conciliatory words could not dispel wage-earners' anger and distrust. The *Working Man's Advocate,* an outspoken anti-capitalist sheet published locally since 1864, became one of the most influential labor papers in the country. Socialists and international anarchists found Chicago fertile soil for their teachings, for 1877 left a bitter taste, and social inequities were spread out for anyone with eyes and fair mind to see.

Despite this undercurrent of unrest, as the depression faded at the end of the seventies, Chicago had a new boom. She had proved to the world the soundness of her credit and the flexibility of her business methods. After the greatest fire in modern history she had rebuilt substantially and, depression notwithstanding, by 1875 showed no trace of the holocaust. She even turned that disaster to account: no other city could boast of a fire like that. European immigrants, discouraged Easterners, and Southerners, ready now at the end of the harsh regime of Reconstruction to try life in a Northern city, flooded into Chicago. Citizens no longer bothered about outdoing St Louis. The Missouri city, for all her growth during the late seventies, no longer rated as a serious competitor of the 'Queen of the Lakes'. The city of 30,000 in 1850 became before the end of the 1880's a city of a million inhabitants. The horse-drawn street railway system, started in 1859 and nursed by more than the usual amount of fraud and graft between traction magnates and city Councilmen, could not begin to meet transportation needs. Insufficient housing and a growing population created crowded slums huddled alongside the 'princely structures of marble' of the rich. Neighborhoods changed character almost overnight, making real estate speculation hazardous but diminishing it no whit. Poverty and wealth, Christian concern for the needy and heartless exploitation of the working man, apprehensive efforts to adjust to this hurlyburly and passionate determination to make Chicago bigger —contradictions were the essence of Chicago. Out of the welter of conflicting aspirations came fresh corruption, a Citizens' Association for clean municipal government, new charitable institutions, a great settlement house founded by Jane Addams, and a more vigorous labor movement.

Many substantial citizens found the truth about the condition of the working classes hard to perceive. This new doctrine of socialism must be a dangerous foreign importation brought from Europe by wild-eyed agitators who had not been privileged to grow up in the land of the free. Could not anyone with sense, diligence, and patience win his way up to economic comfort or even affluence? When in 1886 a strike was called at the McCormick works and picket lines formed along the 'Black Road', the cinder path leading to the Reaper plant, half of Chicago was frightened. Some were hopeful that issues would now come into the open and be settled fairly. The city administration was ready for strike action. The strike was more than two months old when police, attempting to disperse a gathering along the Black Road, fired into the crowd and killed six men. Labor leaders called a mass meeting. The Haymarket Riot that followed, the panic fear of social revolution that swept the city, and the brutal behavior of the city police force make a story as grim as any in American history. At that protest rally in the Haymarket, a bomb thrown into the crowd killed a policeman, wounded several others, and led to the arrest of eight anarchist leaders. Though no evidence could be adduced that they had had any direct connection with the bomb-throwing, and though all asserted their innocence, all eight were convicted of murder as men dangerous to society. One man committed suicide in prison. Four were hanged. The Governor of Illinois commuted the other sentences to life imprisonment. For a generation thereafter thousands of visitors to the city made pilgrimages to the cemetery where a monument to the executed men had been raised. It took nearly two generations to sift fact from frenzied fear and to reach a reasoned analysis of the riot. A British account in the 1911 edition of the *Britannica* reveals the extent and duration of misconceptions about this outburst. The barbarity of the punishment meted out to the anarchists did not prevent other conflicts in the years ahead. The riot set back the movement for organized labor reform for nearly a decade.

As the city regained equilibrium, sober citizens began to examine more carefully the foundations of this society that they had built and had been proud of. Men tell the story of a delegation of capitalists seeking out the Mayor to urge him to suppress free speech: Marshall Field, merchant prince and multi-millionaire, opened his argument with the statement that 'we represent great interests in Chicago'; Mayor Harrison cut him off with the retort that any poor man who owned his cottage had an equal interest. Informal meetings of public-spirited men held at the home of Lyman J. Gage, a leading banker in the city, turned into public sessions to discuss the ills that bred such violence. Jane Addams and her selfless associates at Hull House in a slum area peopled by foreigners collected facts about conditions in that section of the city that shocked self-satisfied Chicagoans. Churchmen stirred uneasily. Self-analysis killed much self-congratulation and substituted determination to make the hidden places of the city liveable.

And then John D. Rockefeller, the Standard Oil millionaire, was persuaded to donate first $600,000, a little later two million more, to found a university in Chicago. It was not the first; a Baptist university had been opened in the fifties, but had gradually withered away. The idea of a new University of Chicago captured the imagination of citizens of every creed and kind. Contributions poured in, a building went up and the first students enrolled in the fall of 1892. It is doubtful whether Rockefeller looked upon this as more than a Baptist institution. The brilliant young President, William Rainey Harper, on the other hand, saw two things clearly: his faculty must be scholars as well as teachers, and the university must keep itself a part of the city whose generosity and enthusiasm had helped build it. The men who joined that first faculty were learned, but they were also young, vigorous, and enthralled by the challenge of the great city about them. Sociologists and psychologists, political economists and historians, physiologists and chemists, philologists, literary critics, and theologians, they perceived their obligation and their opportunity. The university would thus become not only one of the world's great universities but a mighty, constructive force in the city, enriching Chicago's intellectual life while it studied her social structure and drove for intelligent, concerted civic action.

With all this new soul-searching and horrified discovery of her shortcomings, Chicago at the end of the eighties was still a community proud of her achievements and sure of her destiny. If corruption reigned in her municipal council chambers and municipal courts, if poverty and ignorance engulfed some of her citizens while wickedness and depravity infested others, if her schools were not too well taught and were ill-attended, if sanitation was sketchy and medical care scanty, she could still regard herself as no worse than other American cities and, because of her rapid growth, more worthy of acclaim. Unsolved problems she could cope with when she had time. She had crudities, but she also had culture. Important European visitors, ranging in distinction from the Prince of Wales and Lord Bryce to continental counts seeking American heiresses for wives, included Chicago in their tours. One of Levi Leiter's daughters married Lord Curzon. Huge hotels gaudy with red velvet hangings and pseudo-Louis XVI furniture enticed the sightseer and served to house conventions. Theatres offered new plays, Shakespeare, burlesque, and old-style melodrama. The Art Institute's collection of paintings was growing. Citizens patronized the opera so enthusiastically that a company built an Auditorium in 1889 to seat the eager crowds. Adeline Patti 'opened' the Auditorium. People could hear symphony concerts weekly. Bookstores were multiplying. Though coal smoke cast a grimy film over lawns and shrubs, the city was planting trees and expanding a park system. Work was beginning on deepening the river and construction of the Sanitary Canal which, when finished in 1900, would make the Chicago river flow backward without the pumping that had been necessary when the lake level was low. What Chicago lacked today she would acquire tomorrow.

She had already developed a form of architecture as original as it was dignified, simple, and functional. After the fire, demand for housing had been so acute that local architects hit upon the apartment house as the answer. Its suitability to urban life inspired other cities to adopt the plan. To Chicago of the eighties and early nineties, Sigfried Giedion has attributed 'the greatest architectural vitality of the period'. William LeBaron Jenney, trained as an engineer, was the chief innovator. From him younger architects —William Holabird, Martin Roche, Louis Sullivan, and others—learned the principles of 'skeleton construction' and the use of the horizontal windows that characterized the Chicago school. Land values in the business district were high, and office space was hard to get. Jenney pointed the way to the solution of that problem when in 1885 he erected the first modern skyscraper. Built with steel girders hung with a curtain of light masonry to serve as outer walls, the ten-story office building with its bands of horizontally set windows was a new departure. Jenney used the new materials of the industrial age, structural steel and glass, to provide the primary needs of a city office building, maximum space and maximum light. Three years later, when his disciples William Holabird and Martin Roche erected the twelve-story Tacoma building, its occupants discovered that 'gain in renting area through use of skeleton rather than masonry construction was equivalent to the rent of an additional floor.' Skyscrapers rose higher and higher, to sixteen stories, then to twenty-one; part of the floor space in each was left unpartitioned, so that tenants could subdivide it to suit

themselves. Chicago's sandy soil, some of it quicksand, necessitated new types of foundations, columns going down to bedrock and the floating foundation. In all Jenney's buildings and those of his followers, in office buildings, hotels, and apartment houses, skilful fenestration and starkly simple line did duty for ornamentation. New York in adopting the skyscraper abandoned that simplicity.

As the nineties rolled round and the United States saw fit to celebrate the four-hundredth anniversary of the discovery of America, Chicago bid fiercely for the privilege of staging the World's Columbian Exposition. She had her way. The importance of that World's Fair to the Middle West cannot be overstated. A site on the lake shore on the city's southern edge offered space, though it looked depressingly bleak and swampy when the citizen's committee chose it in January 1891. A well-known Chicago architect, made Director of Construction, laid his plans on a large scale. Seduced by Daniel Burnham's persuasiveness, Chicago men financing the fair agreed to let him engage the architects he considered the most distinguished in America, the most gifted sculptors, the most imaginative designers. Unfortunately perhaps, he chose mostly conventional New York architects instead of Chicago innovators. The greatest landscape artist in the country undertook to lay out the grounds and arrange for the planting. Where, among all this talent, jealousies and clashes of artistic temperament might have been expected, Burnham and his staff maintained harmony and enthusiastic co-operation. The Columbian Exposition opened formally on 1 May 1893.

Visitors flocked from every state in the Union, but the largest crowds came from the farms of the Middle West. The white plaster of the temporary buildings gave the fair grounds their name, the White City. Its copies of classical and Renaissance architecture led Louis Sullivan, trained in Jenney's school, to declare that native American art had been put back fifty years by the passion for the imitative that the Exposition aroused. Yet the White City, brilliantly lighted by arc lights at night and by day gleaming in the summer sun, was a thing of dramatic beauty. The masterpieces of the world's painting, lent for the occasion, and the industrial exhibits opened the eyes of sophisticated people from the East and from Europe, but the effect upon the less worldly-wise of rural America was overwhelming. Chicagoans adopted the characteristically phrased slogan: 'Make Culture hum!' One foreigner proclaimed the fair a step toward 'municipalizing the prairies'. A farmer leaving the fair grounds was overheard saying to his wife, 'Well, Mother, it took the burial money, but it was worth it.' Upon Chicago herself the effect of the Exposition was greatest of all. Imagination and courage in the face of innumerable obstacles had built the White City. It vanished in a year, leaving only the park along the lake front, the Midway Plaisance and the Art Building as a permanent visible legacy to the city; the invisible legacy was beyond measurement. The sooty, sprawling city north of the Exposition grounds, ugly despite the distinction of the buildings in the business district, could be similarly transformed. The dream of Chicago, 'the City Beautiful', took shape in men's minds that year. . . .

Terrible conflagrations all too often swept through many blocks of American cities in the nineteenth century. San Francisco had suffered a succession of such fires during the Gold Rush, and in 1907 an earthquake there precipitated the most cataclysmic fire of them all. Only the Chicago fire of 1871 rivalled it in devastation and exceeded it in legend. An eyewitness account by a young newspaperman, J. E. Chamberlin, depicted the flimsily built areas in which the fire got its start on the night of October 7 and burned uncontrollably for the next two nights. The account is even more remarkable for its description of the way diverse types of Chicagoans reacted to the crisis.

J. E. CHAMBERLIN:
THE CHICAGO FIRE*

I was at the scene in a few minutes. The fire had already advanced a distance of about a single square through the frame buildings that covered the ground thickly north of De Koven Street and east of Jefferson Street—if those miserable alleys shall be dignified by being denominated streets. That neighborhood had always been a *terra incognita* to respectable Chicagoans, and during a residence of three years in the city I had never visited it. The land was thickly studded with one-story frame dwellings, cow-stables, pig-sties, corn-cribs, sheds innumerable; every wretched building within four feet of its neighbor, and every thing of wood—not a brick or a stone in the whole area. The fire was under full headway in this combustible mass before the engines arrived, and what could be done? Streams were thrown into the flame, and evaporated almost as soon as they struck it. A single fire-engine in the blazing forests of Wisconsin would have been as effective as were these machines in a forest of shanties thrice as combustible as the pine woods of the North. But still the firemen kept at work fighting the flames—stupidly and listlessly, for they had worked hard all of Saturday night and most of Sunday, and had been enervated by the whiskey which is always copiously poured on such occasions. I stepped in among some sheds south of Ewing Street; a fence by my side began to blaze; I beat a hasty retreat, and in five minutes the place where I had stood was all ablaze. Nothing could stop that conflagration there. It must sweep on until it reached a broad street, and then, every body said, it would burn itself out.

Ewing Street was quite a thoroughfare for that region. It is a mere alley, it is true, but is somewhat broader than the surrounding lanes. It has elevated board sidewalks, and is passable for teams in dry weather. On that night it was crowded with people pouring out of the thickly-settled locality between Jefferson Street and the river, and here the first panic began. The wretched female inhabitants were rushing out almost naked, imploring spectators to help them on with their burdens of bed-quilts, cane-bottomed chairs, iron kettles, etc. Drays were thundering along in the single procession which the narrowness of the street allowed, and all was confusion.

When the fire had passed Ewing Street, I hurried on to Harrison, aware of the fact that the only hope for the staying of the conflagration was in the width of that street, and hoping that some more effective measures than squirting of water would be taken at that point. The same scene of hurry and confusion was repeated at Harrison on a larger scale than at Ewing; and that same scene kept on increasing in terror all night long, as the fire moved northward. The crowd anxiously watched the flames as they approached the street, and the universal remark was: "If it passes this, nothing can stop it but last night's burned district." At length the fire reached the street, and broke out almost simultaneously for a distance of two squares. The two fire-engines which stood in Harrison Street fled in terror. Brands of fire, driven on by the gale, struck the houses on the north side of the street. Though mostly of brick, they ignited like tinder, and the fire swept northward again.

Again I passed into Jefferson Street, keeping on the flank of the fire. In a vacant square, filled

---

* Reprinted from Elias Colbert and Everett Chamberlin, *Chicago and the Great Conflagration* (Cincinnati, 1871), pp. 226–35.

with refugees from the fire and their rescued effects, I stopped a few minutes to watch the fiery ocean before me. The open lot was covered with people, and a strange sight was presented. The fire had reached a better section, and many people of the better class were among those who had gathered a few of their household goods on that open space. Half a dozen rescued pianos were watched by delicate ladies, while the crowd still surged in every direction. Two boys, themselves intoxicated, reeled about, each bearing a small cask of whisky, out of which he insisted upon treating every body he met. Soon more casks of whisky appeared, and scores of excited men drank deeply of their contents. The result was, of course, that an equal number of drunken men were soon impeding the flight of the fugitives.

When I reached Van Buren Street, the southern limit of the Saturday night fire, I paused to see the end of the conflagration. A single engine stood on Van Buren Street, doing what seemed to me good service in preventing the fire from eating its way westward, against the wind, which it was apparently determined to do. Suddenly the horses were attached to the engine, and, as soon as the hose was reeled, it disappeared, whirling northward on Jefferson Street. What did it mean? I caught the words, "Across the river," uttered doubtingly by a bystander. The words passed from mouth to mouth, and there was universal incredulity, although the suggestion was communicated through the crowd with startling rapidity. There was a general movement northward and out of the smoke, with a view to discover whether it was really possible that the fire had been blown across the river, and had started afresh on the south side. I went with the rest, crossed the burnt ground of the night before, stood on the embankment that had been Canal Street, and perceived, through the clouds of smoke, a bright light across the river. I rushed to the Adams-street viaduct and across the bridge. The Armory, the Gas-works, "Conley's Patch," and Wells Street, as far north as Monroe, were all on fire. The wind had increased to a tempest, and hurled great blazing brands over our heads.

At this point my duty called me to my home in the West Division; but within an hour I was back again to witness the doom of the blazing city, of which I then had a full presentiment. The streets on the west side were as light as broad noon. I looked at my watch and saw that it was just two o'clock. As I ran down Monroe Street, with the burning town before me I contemplated the ruin that was working, and the tears rose to my eyes. I could have wept at that saddest of sights, but I choked down the tears, and they did not rise again that night.

When I crossed the river, I made a desperate attempt to reach my office on Madison Street, beyond Clark. I pressed through the crowd on Randolph Street as far as Lasalle, and stood in front of the burning Court-house. The cupola

was in full blaze, and presented a scene of the sublimest as well as most melancholy beauty. Presently the great tower was undermined by the fire below, and fell to the bottom with a dull sound and a heavy shock that shook the earth. Somebody called out, "Explosion!" and a panic ensued, in which every thing and every body was carried westward. Then I went to Lake Street, and found a torrent of sparks sweeping down that avenue. But I pulled my hat about my eyes, buttoned up my coat-collar, and rushed eastward, determined to reach my office. I turned down Dearborn, and leaped through a maelstrom of scorching sparks. The fiery storm at length drove me into an open store, from which the occupants had fled. I seized a large blanket which they had left on the floor, wrapped it around my head and body, and sallied forth again. I went as far as Washington Street, but any attempt at further progress would have been madness. I beat a hasty retreat to Lake Street, and came down Lasalle again to the immediate neighborhood of the fire.

And now the scene of confusion had reached its height. Wagons were rushing through the streets, laden with stocks of goods, books, valuable papers, boxes of money, and every thing conceivable; scores of men were dragging trunks frantically along the sidewalks, knocking down women and children; fabulous sums of money were offered truckmen for conveyances. The scene was indescribable.

But, as large as was the number of people who were flying from the fire, the number of passive spectators was still larger. Their eyes were all diverted from the skurrying mass of people around them to the spectacle of appalling grandeur before them. They stood transfixed, with a mingled feeling of horror and admiration, and while they often exclaimed at the beauty of the scene, they all devoutly prayed that they might never see such another. The noise of the conflagration was terrific. To the roar which the simple process of combustion always makes, magnified here to so grand an extent, was added the crash of falling buildings and the constant explosions of stores of oil and other like material. The noise of the crowd was nothing compared with this chaos of sound. All these things—the great, dazzling, mounting light, the crash and roar of the conflagration, and the desperate flight of the crowd—combined to make a scene of which no intelligent idea can be conveyed in words.

When it became too hot in Randolph Street, I retired to the eastern approach of the bridge on that street. A knot of men had gathered there, from whom all signs of excitement had disappeared. It was then almost four o'clock, and whatever excitement we had felt during the night had passed away. Wearied with two nights of exertion, I sat upon the railing and looked down on the most appalling spectacle of the whole night. The Briggs House, the Metropolitan House, Peter Schuttler's wagon manufactuory, Heath &

Mulligan's oil establishment, stored five stories high with exceedingly inflammable material, the Nevada Hotel, and all the surrounding buildings, were in a simultaneous blaze. The flames, propelled by variable gusts of wind, seemed to pour down Randolph Street in a liquid torrent. Then the appearance was changed, and the fire was a mountain over our heads. The barrels of oil in Heath's store exploded with a sound like rattling musketry. The great north wall of the Nevada Hotel plunged inward with hardly a sound, so great was the din of the surrounding conflagration. The Garden City House burned like a box of matches; the rapidity of its disappearance was remarked by every body. Toward the east and north-east we looked upon a surging ocean of flame.

Meanwhile a strange scene was being enacted in the street before us. A torrent of humanity was pouring over the bridge. Madison-street bridge had long before become impassable, and Randolph was the only outlet for the entire region south of it. Drays, express-wagons, trucks, and conveyances of every conceivable species and size, crowded across in indiscriminate haste. Collisions happened almost every moment, and when one over-loaded wagon broke down, there were enough men on hand to drag it and its contents over the bridge by main force. The same long line of men dragging trunks was there, many of them tugging over the ground with loads which a horse would strain at. Women were there, looking exactly like those I had seen all night, staggering under weights upon their backs. Whole establishments of ill-fame were there, their half-dozen inmates loaded into the bottoms of express-wagons, driven, of course, by their "men." Now and then a stray schooner, which, for want of a tug, had been unable to escape earlier from the south branch, came up, and the bridge must be opened. Then arose a howl of indignation along the line, which, being near, was audible above the tumult. A brig lay above us in the stream, and the captain was often warned by the crowd that he must make his exit at once, if he wished to save his craft—a suggestion the force of which he doubtless appreciated, as he stood upon the quarter-deck calling frantically to every tug that passed.

I saw an undertaker rushing over the bridge with his mournful stock. He had taken a dray, but was unable to load all of his goods into the vehicle. So he employed half a dozen boys, gave each of them a coffin, took a large one himself, and headed the weird procession. The sight of those coffins, upright, and bobbing along just above the heads of the crowd, without any apparent help from any body else, was somewhat startling, and the unavoidable suggestion was that they were escaping across the river to be ready for use when the *debris* of the conflagration should be cleared away. But just as men in the midst of a devastating plague carouse over each new corpse, and drink to the next who dies, so we laughed quite merrily at the ominous spectacle.

At last it became too warm to be comfortable on the east side of the river. The fire was burning along Market Street, and many were the conjectures whether Lind's block would go. The buildings opposite burned with a furnace-heat, but Lind's block stands now, a monument to its own isolation.

And then the question was every-where asked, "Will Chicago ever recover from this blow?" Many suggestions were offered on this subject. The general opinion was that the city could never again obtain a foothold. Said one old gentleman, "Our capital is wiped out of existence. You never can get what money is stored up out of those vaults. There isn't one that can stand this furnace-heat. Whatever the fire consumes tonight is utterly consumed. All loss is total; for there will not be an insurance company left to-morrow. The trade of the city *must* go to St. Louis, to Cincinnati, and to New York, and we never can get hold of it again. We couldn't transact any business even if we had customers, for we haven't got anywhere to transact it. Yes, sir, this town is gone up, and we may as well get out of it at once." Thus all seemed to talk, and there was none of that earnest, hopeful language of which I have heard so much since, and have been rejoiced to hear. But what else could I expect? Those men stood facing the burning city. They saw those great hotels and warehouses toppling, one after another, to the ground. Their spirits were elastic, as subsequent events have proved, but on that terrible night they were drawn to their utmost tension, and the cord came near breaking. . . .

When I had regained a footing in the favored West Division, it was seven o'clock. Then a curious-looking crimson ball came up out of the lake, which they said was the sun; but oh how sickly and insignificant it looked! I had watched that greatest of the world's conflagrations from its beginning to almost its end; and although the fire was still blazing all over the city with undiminished luster, I could not look at it. I was almost unable to walk with exhaustion and the effects of a long season of excitement, and sought my home for an hour's sleep. As I passed up West Madison Street, I met scores of working girls on their way 'down town,' as usual, bearing their lunch-baskets as if nothing had happened. They saw the fire and smoke before them, but could not believe that the city, with their means of livelihood, had been swept away during that night.

How well did working people fare in a city like Chicago in the last two decades of the nineteenth century? Relatively well compared with workers elsewhere. Illinois workers earned slightly more and paid slightly less for the necessities of life than did workers in Massachusetts. In turn, Carroll Wright estimated, Massachusetts workingmen supported their families in a manner that was 42 per cent better than that of their counterparts in Great Britain. It is not surprising that a heavy stream of immigrants flowed into American cities from Great Britain as well as the poverty-stricken areas of Europe.

In 1883, the average Illinois worker was employed ten hours a day, six days a week for a wage of $13.87. He was laid off for eight weeks a year. Average annual wages for day laborers were $344.59; for carpenters, $552.44; and for locomotive engineers, $1,076.00. Weekly pay ranged from $6 to $53.

ILLINOIS BUREAU OF LABOR STATISTICS: CHICAGO'S WORKERS*

FOOD AND FUEL IN ILLINOIS, 1884

Articles	Average Prices	Articles	Average Prices
Family flour, per barrel	$6 26.	Mutton, per pound	12.1
Corn meal, per hundred-weight	1 54.	Poultry, per pound	12.6
Bread, white, per loaf	05.6	Salt pork, per pound	12.
Bread, brown, per loaf	05.8	Hams, smoked, per pound	15.3
Crackers, per pound	09.	Codfish, dry, per pound	09.8
Milk, per quart	05.8	Mackerel, salt, per pound	10.3
Coffee, roasted, per pound	20.5	Fresh fish, per pound	10.5
Tea, common, per pound	51.7	Potatoes, per bushel	45.8
Sugar, brown, per pound	08.7	Beans, per quart	09.7
Eggs, per dozen	17.4	Onions, per bushel	81.9
Butter, per pound	25.8	Dried apples, per pound	10.3
Cheese, per pound	17.	Dried peaches, per pound	13.4
Molasses, per gallon	62.2	Canned fruit, per can	18.2
Soap, common bar, per pound	06.	Raisins, per pound	13.4
Salt, per sack	10.6	Lard, per pound	12.4
Baking powder, per pound	38.9	Vinegar, per gallon	26.
Bacon, per pound	13.7	Kerosene, per gallon	19.6
Beef, corned, per pound	09.7	Soft coal, per ton	2 95.
Beef or pork, roast, per pound	12.3	Hard wood, per cord	4 80.

An agent of the Bureau of Labor Statistics interviewed one hundred Chicago families, whose circumstances ranged from poverty to affluence. The following are six of the families: *

NO. 2.　　　BAKER.　　　POLE.

EARNINGS—Of father $450
CONDITION—Family numbers 5—parents and three children, all girls, aged one month, eighteen months and four years. Rent a house containing three rooms, for which they pay a rental of $8 per month. Family are very ignorant, dirty and unkempt. The street is narrow and filthy; no pavement; mud knee-deep; no vaults or sewerage. Father works fifty weeks per year, and for a winter day's work he is employed

* Reprinted from *Third Annual Report, 1884* (Springfield: Illinois Bureau of Labor Statistics, 1884), pp. 342.

* Reprinted from *Third Annual Report, 1884* (Springfield: Illinois Bureau of Labor Statistics, 1884), pp. 358, 359, 369, 380, 388.

twelve hours, and in summer fourteen. He receives $1.50 for each day's labor. His house is situated so far from his place of work that he cannot go home at noon. Carries no life insurance, and belongs to no unions.

FOOD—*Breakfast*—Coffee, bread and crackers.
   Dinner—Soup, meat and potatoes.
   Supper—What is left from dinner.

COST OF LIVING—

Rent	$ 96
Fuel	15
Meat and groceries	165
Clothing, boots and shoes and dry goods	70
Books, papers, etc	3
Sickness	40
Sundries	65
Total	$454

NO. 5.   BLACKSMITH.   AMERICAN.

EARNINGS—Of father $864

CONDITION—Family numbers 5—parents and three girls aged twelve, nine and five years, and all three attend the public schools. They rent a pleasant house containing six rooms, in healthy locality, for which they pay $15 per month. House is neatly kept and nicely furnished and carpeted. Have piano and sewing machine. Family neatly dressed and members of the church. They were fortunate in not having any sickness whatever in the family during the past year. Father secures work forty-eight weeks in the year, at $3 per day.

FOOD—*Breakfast*—Bread, meat, sundries and coffee.
   Dinner—Meat, bread, vegetables, pie, tea, etc.
   Supper—Bread, cold meat, pie and tea.

COST OF LIVING—

Rent	$180
Fuel	36
Meat and groceries	345
Clothing, boots and shoes and dry goods	210
Books, papers, etc.	15
Sundries	10
Total	$796

NO. 35.   LABORER.   ITALIAN.

EARNINGS—Of father $270

CONDITION—Family numbers 5—parents and three children, all boys, aged one, three and five. Live in one room, for which they pay $4 per month rent. A very dirty and unhealthy place, everything perfectly filthy. There are about fifteen other families living in the same house. They buy the cheapest kind of meat from the neighboring slaughter houses and the children pick up fuel on the streets and rotten eatables from the commission houses. Children do not attend school. They are all ignorant in the full sense of the word. Father could not write his name.

FOOD—*Breakfast*—Coffee and bread.
   Dinner—Soups.
   Supper—Coffee and bread.

COST OF LIVING—

Rent	$ 48
Fuel	5
Meat and groceries	100
Clothing, boots and shoes and dry goods	15
Sickness	5
Total	$173

NO. 66.   PLUMBER.   IRISH.

EARNINGS—Of husband $900

CONDITION—Family numbers 2—adults. Rent 4 comfortable rooms in brick building, at $16 per month. Rooms are nicely furnished and have healthy surroundings. Husband has fifty weeks' employment in the year, which enables them to dress and live well, considerably within their annual income.

FOOD—*Breakfast*—Bread, meat and coffee.
   Dinner—Meat, vegetables, bread and tea.
   Supper—Bread, cake, cold meat and tea.

COST OF LIVING—

Rent	$192
Fuel	45
Meat and groceries	300
Clothing, boots and shoes, dry goods	130
Books, papers, etc	10
Sickness	5
Sundries	25
Total	$707

NO. 68.   PRINTER.   AMERICAN.

EARNINGS—Of father $580
   Of girl, aged sixteen 150
   Total $730

CONDITION—Family numbers 5—parents and three children, two boys and one girl, aged five, nine and sixteen, respectively. Occupy a house containing 4 rooms, and pay for same $120 per annum. Father says the reason printers in Chicago have been able thus far to keep up their wages, is the strength and unity of their organizations. The supply of men is greatly in excess of the demand, which must necessarily entail much hardship on those not fortunate enough to find steady employment.

FOOD—*Breakfast*—Coffee, meat and potatoes.
   Dinner—Lunch.
   Supper—Tea, meat, sauce, etc.

COST OF LIVING—

Rent	$120
Fuel	30
Meat and groceries	300
Clothing, boots and shoes, dry goods	100
Books, papers, etc	25
Trade unions	6
Sickness	19
Sundries	100
Total	$720

NO. 90.   *TEAMSTER.*   *DANE.*

EARNINGS—Of father $840

CONDITION—Family numbers four—father, mother and two boys. Both go to school. They occupy a house containing 4 rooms, and pay rental for same at the rate of $10 per month. Father carries some life insurance. He is only able to secure work for thirty-five weeks in the year, and considers the system of contract and convict labor detrimental to the general class of laborers and mechanics, and is also in favor of the eight-hour law, for the reason, among others, that machinery has taken the places of workmen in factories, thereby enforcing thousands of men to idleness each year. By shortening the hours of labor, many men who are now tramps would work.

FOOD—*Breakfast*—Meat, bread and coffee.
     Dinner—Meat and sundries.
     Supper—Tea and bread.

COST OF LIVING—

Rent	$120
Fuel	50
Meat	130
Groceries	200
Clothing	50
Boots and shoes	40
Dry goods	25
Books, papers, etc.	7
Life insurance	15
Sickness	10
Sundries	193
Total	$840

Increasingly, women found employment in the growing offices of Chicago businesses. In 1892, the Bureau of Labor Statistics reported on the new and desirable work open to women as stenographers, typists, and telephone operators.*

STENOGRAPHERS

These intelligent and light fingered auxilliaries to the prompt transaction of business find employment in Chicago by the scores. A well trained stenographer, being also discreet and prompt, will soon command a good salary. There are all sorts of stenographers, however, and, as the tables will show, all sorts of pay. Perhaps the conditions that obtain in this art do not differ materially from those that govern in other lines of work. The hours are ordinarily short and the work not arduous though exacting. Women now practically monopolize the work, and may be seen in court rooms, public and private offices, hotels, counting houses, banks, and in all branches of wholesale, retail and manufacturing business. As a thorough education is essential to success, there is no danger of this vocation being overrun by *débutantes* from the nursery. It is perhaps the most desirable occupation which women can enter. The practice of selling goods by sample is rapidly giving way to the illustrated catalogue, and increased correspondence opens the field for stenographers and typewriters in great numbers. The earnings of this class range from $6 to $18 a week.

TELEPHONE OPERATORS

The telephone interest in Chicago furnishes employment to about four hundred girls. There is a day force, an extra force, a night force, and a relief force. The day force goes on at 8 A.M. and works until 6 P.M. The extra force goes on at 11 A.M. and works until 2 P.M., and again at 5 P.M. and works until 10 P.M. The night force goes on at 10 P.M. and works until 8 A.M. The relief force consists of substitutes, who take the places of any of the regular force that fail to report for duty on time. A member of the relief force holds herself in readiness to report for duty when summoned by telephone call of the chief operator, and is paid for the time actually at work. The ranks of the regular force are recruited from the relief force. The day force is required to work seven hours on one Sunday in each month, and each receives therefor a day's extra pay. The work is strictly sedentary in its nature. A quick-witted, attentive girl may soon become proficient. The pay ranges from $5.50 to $8 per week, advancement being according to merit solely. The switchboard is arranged in the form of a horse shoe, and the operators are seated closely together, each facing her section, which comprises usually about sixty numbers or subscribers. She is responsible for the efficient service of her section. The work is clean, exacting but not laborious, and essentially confining, the operators not being permitted to leave their seats unless it is absolutely necessary. The novelty of talking daily at arms-length to hundreds of people of all sorts and conditions soon wears off, and the experienced attendant finds answering calls and listening to impatient remonstrances from her patrons a mere matter of routine utterly devoid of personal interest. No girl is employed by the company who is under 18 years of age. . . .

The telephone girls are among the best paid of all operatives, having average weekly earnings of $7.13; there are only four groups which have a better average. The yearly record was obtained of 105 who worked a full year, and the average of the earnings of these was $362, with an average loss of 14.8 days lost time.

* Reprinted from *Seventh Biennial Report, 1892* (Springfield: Illinois Bureau of Labor Statistics, 1893), pp. 150–51, 136–37.

In Chicago as elsewhere, the most shockingly deplorable working conditions were usually to be found among garment manufacturers operating sweat shops.

ILLINOIS BUREAU OF LABOR STATISTICS: THE SWEAT SHOP SYSTEM*

The odious but expressive name, "sweating," has been attached to the business because of its evil nature and consequences. In its worst form, and there are doubtless degrees in its development, it is simply extortion practiced upon people whose environment prevents their escape from it; in other words, it is a deliberate preying upon the necessities of the poor. In its economical aspect it is the culmination and final fruit of the competitive system in industry.

In practice, sweating consists of the farming out by competing manufacturers to competing contractors the material for garments, which, in turn, is distributed among competing men and women to be made up. The middle-man, or contractor, is the sweater, (though he also may be himself subjected to pressure from above) and his employés are the sweated or oppressed. He contracts to make up certain garments, at a given price per piece and then hires other people to do the work at a less price. His profit lies in the difference between the two prices. In the process he will furnish shop-room and machines to some, and allow others, usually the finishers, to take the work to their living and lodging-rooms in tenements.

The sweater may be compelled to under-bid his fellow contractor in order to get work, but he can count with a degree of certainty, on the eagerness of the people who work for him to also under-bid each other, so as to leave his margin of profit little impaired. The system thrives upon the increasing demand for cheap, ready-made clothing, cheap cloaks, and cheap suits for children, which demand springs in turn from the rivalry of competing dealers and producers. Thus each class preys upon the other, and all of them upon the last and weakest. . . .

IN CHICAGO

In Chicago, where it dates back scarcely a generation, the sweating system seems to be a direct outgrowth of the factory system; that is, the sweat-shops have gradually superceded the manufacturers' shops. It increases, with the demand for cheap clothing, the influx of cheap labor, and the consequent subdivision of the processes of manufacture. In the clothing trades in Chicago, three different sorts of shops have been developed, known among the employés as the "inside shops," or those conducted on the factory system by the manufacturers themselves; the "outside shops," or those conducted by the contractors; and the "home shops" or family groups.

Inside, or Manufacturers' Shops

In the inside shops the manufacturer deals with his employés through foremen and forewomen instead of contractors. These shops are in large buildings, steam is provided for motive power, the sanitary ordinances are, in a measure, observed, and the establishments, being large and permanent, are known to the municipal authorities and are subject to inspection. Even these shops, in which there is, strictly, no sub-letting, are pervaded and dominated by the influence of the sweating system. There is but little uniformity of hours, wages, rules, length of season or proportion of men to women and children. The competition of the outside contractors renders the position of employés constantly more precarious, and the inside shops which thrive are those which approximate most closely to the organization of the sweaters' shops, substituting many subdivisions of labor for the skilled workman.

Formerly these shops employed cutters, button-holers and tailors or cloakmakers who did the whole work, taking the garment from the cutter and completing it, doing both machine and hand work. To increase their speed these skilled hands now have "hand-girls" who do the simple sewing, put on buttons, draw basting threads, etc. Formerly the skilled tailors or cloakmakers constituted a large majority of the employés, but with the growth of the sweating system the cutters alone increase in number and their speed is multiplied by the use of steam machinery. All goods not needed to fill urgent orders are now given direct from the cutters to the sweaters' shops. Some manufacturers have modified their own shops to mere cutters' shops and send all their garments to the contractors; others have found it unprofitable to manufacture for themselves and have resorted to the sweaters entirely. Thus the sweating system strengthens itself and eliminates the clothing factory proper. Very few of these remain, and those which were found are not enumerated as sweating shops.

Outside, or Contractors' Shops

Substantially all manufacturers employ a number of sweaters who conduct small shops on their own account. These underbid each other to ob-

* Reprinted from *Seventh Biennial Report, 1892* (Springfield: Illinois Bureau of Labor Statistics, 1893), pp. 358, 360–61, 364–68.

tain work. They do not make common cause against the manufacturers, either by combining among themselves or by uniting with their employés. On the contrary, they exploit their employés to the utmost to compensate themselves for the exactions of the manufacturers and the competition among themselves. . . .

In the regions occupied by these, unclean and offensive conditions are not confined to the shops; they are equally features of the dwellings and persons and habits of the people. In these districts the worst of the shops are found located often in basements, and on alleys, or in wholly inadequate and unsanitary rooms in the dilapidated structures of these neighborhoods.

A few examples may be cited illustrating what some of these places are like: In one case several men were found at work pressing knee-pants in a low basement room poorly lighted and ventilated by two small windows. There was no floor in this room, and the people were living on the bare earth, which was damp and littered with every sort of rubbish. In another case seven persons were at work in a room 12 by 15 feet in dimensions and with but two windows. These people with the sewing machines of operators and the tables used by the pressers, so filled this meagre space that it was impossible to move about. Charcoal was used for heating the pressers' irons, and the air was offensive and prostrating to a degree. Separated from this shop-room by a frail partition which did not reach to the ceiling was a bedroom about 7 by 15 feet in size, containing two beds, for the use of the family of the sweater. In another instance, in a small basement room which measured only 7 feet 10 inches by 6 feet 6 inches, and without door or window opening to the outer air, a man was at work pressing knee-pants by the light of a very poor gasoline lamp and using a gasoline stove for heating his irons.

One of the principal aims of the sweater is the avoidance of rent. Hence the only requirement for a sweaters' shop is that the structure must be strong enough to sustain the jar of the machines. This condition being filled, any tenement-room is available, whether in loft, or basement, or stable. Fire-escapes in such buildings are unknown; water for flushing closets is rarely found, and the employés are equally at the mercy of fire and disease. Frequently the sweater's home is his shop, with a bed among the machines; or, the family sleeps on cots, which are removed during the day to make room for employés. Sometimes two or three employés are also boarders or lodgers, and the tenement dwelling is the shop; and cooking, sleeping, sewing and the nursing of the sick are going on simultaneously.

A shop was found in which 12 persons lived in 6 rooms, of which two were used as a shop. Knee-pants in all stages of completion filled the shop, the bed-rooms and kitchen. Nine men were employed at machines in a room 12 by 14, and there knee-pants were being manufactured by the thousand gross. This is in the rear of a swarming tenement in a wretched street. Sometimes the landlord is the sweater, using his own basement or outhouse for a shop and renting his rooms to his employés for dwellings. Only one case was found in which a tailor, not a sweater, had acquired a house. He is a skilled tailor, still doing "the whole work" at home, assisted by his wife. For nineteen years he has lived and worked in two wretched rear tenement rooms, paying by instalments for his house, which is still incumbered. All others in the trade who owned houses were found to be either sweaters or women finishers, whose able-bodied husbands follow other occupations, such as teaming, peddling, ditching, street cleaning, etc.

But the worst conditions of all prevail among the families who finish garments at home. Here the greatest squalor and filth abounds and the garments are of necessity exposed to it and a part of it during the process of finishing. A single room frequently serves as kitchen, bed-room, living-room and working-room. In the Italian quarter four families were found occupying one four-room flat, using one cook stove, and all the women and children sewing in the bed-rooms. For this flat they pay $10 a month, each family contributing $2.50 a month. Another group was found consisting of 13 persons, of whom 4 were fathers of families, and 5 were women and girls sewing on cloaks at home. These 13 people pay $8 per month rent, each family contributing $2.

A house-to-house canvas in this district establishes the fact that it is only the poorest of the poor who finish garments at home, only the worst tenements being occupied by them, or the worst rooms of the better houses. A widow, who is a finisher, and two children were found in a rear shanty, in one room, below the street grade, and with only a narrow slit in the wall for a window. For this she pays $3 a month. Another was finishing knee-pants in a room so dark that it required some time to discern her. This room was lighted by a single window obscured by an adjacent four-story building. She also pays $3 a month rent. One of the vilest tenements in Chicago is owned by a woman whose husband is an Italian street-sweeper. She lives on the premises and sews cloaks at 8 cents apiece, collects rent from 30 families under one roof, and tolerates a wretched sweat-shop on her top floor. Eight of her tenants sew cloaks or knee-pants in their living-rooms. They pay $3 a month for the worst apartments and $10 for the best.

A Word for the Sweater

The foregoing observations relate to the aspect which the sweating system presents from a consideration of its results upon the people who are employed under it. There is no question as to the character of its influence upon them; but there may be, in Chicago at least, as to the sole responsibility of the middle-man or sweater for the conditions found. The claim made by the contractors is that they are continually subjected to reductions in contract prices by the manufacturers, and that they have not and cannot exact corresponding reductions in the wages of their employés. The time was when the contractor was simply an employer, now he is very often a co-worker with his employés, and cases have come under the observation of the bureau in which the sweater has been forced out of the business, and has been compelled to take his place in the ranks of employés in other shops. During the last four years the price which the sweater receives for making overcoats has been reduced from $1.50 each to $1. In some cases the contract price for low-grade overcoats is now only 50 cents each. For sack coats the price has been reduced from 80 cents to 60 cents each. For trousers several shops report reductions from 45 to 26 cents per pair; others report a decline from 40 cents in 1885 to 22 cents at the present time; in the cheaper grades contract prices are now as low as 15 cents a pair. A man and wife were found working at home on trousers at 18 cents per pair; they could finish ten pairs a day, earning $1.80, or 90 cents each. . . .

In the better grades of goods very little reduction in contract prices is reported; this is compensated for, however, by a constant raising of the standard of finish, so that some classes of garments now require nearly twice as much work on them as formerly, though the price for making them is unchanged.

The more intelligent and independent sweaters will submit to reductions only to a certain point; when they find there is no longer a legitimate profit in the business they will abandon it. Thus competition not only reduces prices, but gradually eliminates the better class of contractors, and continually reduces the *morale* of the remainder. It drives the business into the very lowest quarters of the city where cheap tenements and cheap labor are concentrated. One evidence of this tendency is the fact that the system is chiefly spreading at present among the recently imported Russian Jews and Poles, who eagerly take in the cheapest work and execute it in the most squalid places.

On the other hand many of the still surviving older shops are conducted under conditions which compare favorably with those of work shops in other industries. In fact they can hardly be called sweat-shops in the offensive sense, that is, the employés in them are not subjected to any such hardships as the term sweating implies, and, in many cases, truly describes. They are conducted in every material respect like ordinary factories, in rooms adapted to the business and under customary regulations. Concerns of this kind keep ordinary books of account, and from them the actual earnings of operatives for extended periods of employment can easily be read. . . . 97 women employed in 7 of the shops of this class, [appear to] fare quite as well as those in some other industries, and . . . their average earnings are about the same as the average for all industries.

In their spectacular growth, the giant cities rapidly outstripped the capacity of their governments to administer them efficiently or even honestly. "New problems are confronting American municipalities, and . . . radical changes will be found needful," the Illinois Bureau of Labor Statistics reported in 1896. "Politically, economically and legally, chaos reigns in our municipal affairs." Describing all large American cities in general, and Chicago specifically, the Bureau asserted: *

Valuable grants and privileges have been conferred, not only without compensation, but without safeguards of any kind calculated to check corporate arrogance and aggression and to insure decent treatment of the public. Corruption has certainly had as much to do with the waste of the public substance as indifference and inefficiency. Many cities have practically been governed by the corporations owning franchises. Primaries, elections and appointments have been controlled and dictated, and city councils have frequently been the obedient tools of powerful corporations.

Owing to corrupt alliances between legislators and corporations to scandals, deals, sensational bribery disclosures, and shameless disregard of the public interest, a strong movement has lately arisen in favor of more rigid control and regulation of franchise-owning corporations, or of municipal operation as an alternative.

* Reprinted from *Ninth Biennial Report . . . Franchises and Taxation, 1896* (Springfield: Illinois Bureau of Labor Statistics, 1897), p. 30.

Throughout the country, one of the most lucrative sources of graft for dishonest politicians was the sale of street railway franchises. On July 1, 1883, the Chicago *Tribune* wrote concerning the pending renewal of a franchise:

It must come up before the Common Council, a thoroughly rotten and dishonest body, always for sale to the highest bidder. The very children in the streets would laugh to derision the idea that, with so big a stake before them as the renewal of the charter of the street car lines, worth hundreds of thousands of dollars, the decision of the Common Council would for a moment turn on the public interest or on anything but the bribes that the councilmen could get from the syndicate, that was willing to pay most for the possession of the franchises. The Common Council of this city is the fetid, steaming, rotting morass, in which every righteous scheme of reform, like high license for streets, is pretty sure to be overlooked.

ILLINOIS BUREAU OF LABOR STATISTICS:
THE STREET RAILWAY FRANCHISES*

The story of the rise and growth of the street railway business of Chicago reads like a romance. Certainly in few other lines have millions multiplied with greater rapidity. On about 700 miles of surface lines that could to-day be duplicated, exclusive of the franchises, for less than $40,-000,000, there has been placed a capitalization of more than twice that amount. On all of this capital, save in the case of some lines most recently constructed, good dividends are regularly declared. The elevated roads have been still more highly capitalized, but being shut out from the down-town district, they have not, thus far, in their very short history, earned enough to make their securities worth much, if any more than the cost of construction of the roads. But with the completion of the Union Loop the coming summer, the prospects point to as great a future for these as for the surface roads, but with a corresponding creation of enormous profits for their promoters and directors. This immense capitalization, without a corresponding investment, aptly illustrates to the initiated the unearned increment in such cases, but deceives the general public as to the amount of the exorbitant tribute levied by the owners of city franchises. It has been impossible to get at the actual amount of money invested in these properties, and for that reason the computations here given are based on the most reliable estimate obtainable as to the cost of duplication.

The shares of the three leading street railway companies have all sold above par during the past year, and since the panic of 1893 some of them, owing to the exorbitant dividends paid, have sold as high as 340. On the basis of the average price of their securities in 1896, the market value of the three leading street railway systems, which operate 488 miles, is approximately $90,000,000, against a valuation, measured by the cost of duplication, of about $30,000,000. The difference of $60,000,000 represents mainly the growth in the value of these properties since they began operations, less than forty years ago, due to the increase in population of the city of Chicago.

The street railway traffic of Chicago is carried on mainly by three companies—the Chicago City Railway Company, the West Chicago Street Railway Company, and the North Chicago Street Railroad Company. There are several other smaller corporations of similar character engaged in this business and four elevated street railroad companies. The three companies first referred to, however, best show how franchises, for which the municipality received little or nothing, have grown in value with the rapid development of the city, and with very little effort on the part of capitalists who obtained them for no consideration whatever. The original capitalization of the street railways was comparatively light. . . .

There is probably no better authority on the financial history of the Chicago street railways than Mr. Frank A. Vanderlip, formerly financial editor of the Tribune and later associate editor of the Chicago Economist, and who prepared for the latter journal its valuable street railway supplement.

In a recent address,[1] delivered before the Political Economy Club of the University of Chicago, Mr. Vanderlip gave a very exhaustive review of the history of these companies, which is of so great interest and importance as to warrant liberal quotations.

He says of the Chicago City Railway: "The company has issued stock from time to time which has been paid for at par, and its property really represents an investment equal to the face value of its stocks and bonds, although it could be

* Reprinted from *Ninth Biennial Report . . . Franchises and Taxation, 1896* (Springfield: Illinois Bureau of Labor Statistics, 1897), pp. 37–38, 56–58, 103–5.

[1] Since published in Rand & McNally's Banker's Monthly for February, 1897.

duplicated to-day for considerably less than such a sum."

This company, with the least "water" of any of the three great systems, has yet been allowed to do two things which are now forbidden in Massachusetts as against public policy:

1. It has been allowed to increase its stock and bonds when its existing capital was greater than the cost of duplication, by reason of depreciation. When the horse car equipment and tracks were replaced by electric the old capital was not written off as it would have to be in competitive business where a property can not long command more than the cost of duplication. The public is still paying dividends to the City Railway on much that has gone to the junk pile. Companies that have earned such profits as the railways should be forced to make enough of their extensions out of their yearly earnings so that the outstanding obligations should never exceed the value of the tangible assets.

2. The City Railway, like the others, is allowed to sell its new stock at par to its stockholders instead of in the market to the highest bidder, as now required in Massachusetts. Thus the road is given a plausible pretext for higher net earnings than the public would allow if fully aware of what was going on.

Respecting the West and North Side systems, Mr. Vanderlip declares: "It is difficult for an outsider to say what proportion of their capital is watered and what proportion is real. A history of these roads, and of the auxiliary companies which have been organized in connection with them, forms by all odds the most interesting chapter concerning watered stock in Chicago. The president of the company, Mr. Charles T. Yerkes, has a genius both for the management of street railway properties and for the creation of corporate securities, and he has introduced more improvements in both fields than any other man who has ever been identified with corporate interests in Chicago. His original scheme, by which he obtained control of the two corporations, was an extremely clever piece of financiering, if the definition current in stock exchange circles of the word be accepted—that is, that financiering is the art of borrowing money.

Mr. Yerkes was a stock broker in Chicago in 1885 with large ambitions and comparatively small personal means. The City Railway had been operated then for several years by cable. The North Chicago and West Chicago street railways were in the hands of a few ultra-conservative millionaires, who had been getting enormous dividends, and who wanted above all things to be left alone. So long as they could earn 35 per cent. dividends on the stock they were quite satisfied with horses for motive power, even if it had been proven that there was a system much cheaper to operate and superior in point of service. Mr. Yerkes perceived the possibility that lie in transforming the slow-going horse car lines into well-equipped cable roads. He had no money with

which to do that, but he had great energy, extraordinary shrewdness and a far-seeing faith in the development of the property. He secured from some of the large holders of the stocks of the two companies an option on one share over a majority of the stock of each corporation. He then organized two new corporations—the North Chicago Street Railroad Company, with a capital of $5,000,000, and the West Chicago Street Railroad Company, with a capital of $10,000,000. He had agreed to pay $600 a share for the stock of the old North Chicago City Railway Company, which called for a total payment of $1,500,600. A lease of the North Chicago City Railway property was made to the newly organized North Chicago Street Railroad Company, the company agreeing to pay 30 per cent. dividends on the stock of the old companies. As soon as this lease was executed the new company made a mortgage to secure $1,500,000 bonds and pledged the majority of the stock in the old company as a collateral security basis for the bond issue. Mr. Yerkes and his friends were now in control of the property without having expended any money whatever. They had organized a new company, which had permanently leased the property, and the new company had issued bonds to an amount sufficient to cover the expenditure in securing control of the majority of the stock in the old company. The same operation was repeated on the West Side, with the exception that the new company in that case had a capital of $10,000,000 instead of $5,000,000. A contract was then made with a construction company, which was composed of Mr. Yerkes and his immediate associates, to cable the North Side road for all its stock, and to cable the West Side road for the $10,000,000 of stock of that company. It is generally claimed by representatives of these street railway companies that the $15,000,000 of stock obtained by the construction company represented fairly the cost of cabling the lines. As a matter of fact, the building of the forty-nine miles of cable for the two companies probably cost $7,500,000, and the remainder of the capitalization issued at that time is water."

The term "water" is here used to express the excess of capital above the original cost. Another meaning, and the one usually intended in this report, is also often attached to the term—the excess of the capitalization above the present cost of duplication. In a competitive business, such as a cotton mill, a company can not long charge for its goods more than enough to earn market rates of profit on the cost of duplication, and there is no reason why a quasi public business should be permitted by the grantees of its privileges any more right to exact monopoly profits and so be able to give a market value to watered stock than competition allows to any ordinary private business which requires so little "good will," risk and skill in finding and pleasing customers as does the street railway business in large and growing cities. After the various railway lines of such a city have been consolidated, little is required of the directors except the ordinary wisdom to select and keep able superintendents and engineers and to adopt new improvements from time to time on the advice of such subordinates. . . .

CONCLUSIONS AND REMEDIES

To those who are familiar with recent municipal history and politics the facts brought out in the foregoing accounts of the status, condition and practices of the franchise-owning quasi-public corporations of Chicago will not be especially startling. Nor will the moral to which they point be particularly novel. The problem which confronts Chicago is the same which faces every large American city. The evils from which it suffers in the sphere in question are not the product of any particular local conditions. To describe the situation in one large American city, with respect to the relation between the public and the municipal government supposed to represent it, on the one hand, and the franchise-owning corporations and their management on the other, is really to describe the situation in all municipalities rich and active enough to tempt corporate capital.

In a vague and dim way, every intelligent citizen knows that under prevailing arrangements the interests of the people receive no adequate protection at the hands of their municipal rulers; that valuable gifts and franchises are conferred upon corporations which instead of faithfully serving the public and thus justifying their creation, defraud and plunder it; that consumers of gas and electricity and patrons of street railways are forced to pay unreasonably and unnecessarily high rates in order to enable the companies to pay dividends on fictitious investments; that the most modest demands of the public or of such faithful representatives as it occasionally succeeds in electing to the municipal legislature are invariably resisted and fought with extreme bitterness; that the cry of "repudiation" and "confiscation" and "attack upon vested rights" is raised by the monopolies and their agents or apologists whenever an attempt is made to secure some concession in favor of the people, and the abuses of overcapitalization and stock-watering have assumed alarming proportions. But while such general impressions have a value in helping to create a public sentiment, friendly to equitable reforms and vigorously hostile to the preservation of the existing system of oppression and fraud, the practical work of re-construction must be based on more definite, concrete and certain information. The falsehoods and sophistry of unscrupulous, franchise-grabbers must be refuted and exposed with the aid of facts and figures that can be neither denied nor explained away.

If the public were always in possession of the exact facts, there would be less difficulty in arriving at a satisfactory solution of the problem of public franchises. It is certain that there is no disposition to discourage the investment of capital in industries requiring public franchises, and that no objection is offered to the earning of fair dividends on actual investments. Theoretically, nothing can be simpler than the relation between the municipality and franchise-owning corporations. If these corporations were honest and just, if they were satisfied with a reasonable return on their capital, no mystery would surround the question of the cost of construction, equipment and operation. The public would not ask impossible things from the companies, and the companies would be safe and secure in their enjoyment of the enviable opportunities for sound and profitable investment. What do we find in practice? Confusion, ignorance, mutual suspicion, corrupt scheming on the part of the companies and agitation for public ownership operation on the part of the outraged community.

Let us study the disclosures made in the foregoing chapters. Need we dwell on the economic, moral and political effects of such a state of affairs?

Does not the payment of dividends on fictitious capital impose a heavy burden on the people of the municipality—a burden which they can not justly be asked to support? Why should we all be taxed by and for private corporations? Why should the managers, officers and stockholders of such corporations be permitted to enrich themselves at the expense of the community? We generally rely upon the natural laws of trade and the ordinary forces of the market to protect the consumers from the greed and rapacity of would-be monopolists. Competition, however, is possible only to a very limited extent in the sphere occupied by franchise-owning corporations and other safeguards become necessary. In the absence of such safe-guards, it is irrational to expect any voluntary regard for the public welfare from the corporations, as experience has abundantly demonstrated.

Even worse than the economic consequences are the political and moral consequences. Powerful corporations control municipal governments and corrupt the people's representatives. Bribery has become so common that wholesale press indictments of a city council in connection with the passage of ordinances granting charters to corporations are accepted as a matter of course, and hardly given a second thought. In our larger cities, primaries, conventions, nominations and elections are generally managed and dictated by the corporations, and public office is a source of private profit and plunder. The moral tone of the community is lowered, and people cynically regard every man identified with politics as a conspirator against the public, and a tool of as unscrupulous combination of corporate sharpers and plotters. Recently, Judge Baker, of a federal court in the state of Indiana, denounced in open court the officers of an Indianapolis street railway corporation as a gang of modern highwaymen whose swindling operations must so exasperate the people as to drive them to appeal to lynch law, and the entire press of the city warmly applauded this sentiment. When such gentry succeed in obstructing and defeating all legislation directed against them, the belief is naturally generated that the people are helpless and powerless, and that politicians prefer to serve those who can reward them politically and pecuniary.

We have seen, in the introductory article discussing the problems of modern municipalities what reforms are being most generally advocated by students of municipal government. What, in the light of the suggestions and recommendations there presented, is to be said about the situation in Chicago?

No one denies the need of a decided improvement in the quality of Chicago municipal legislators. Of late, its councils have been notoriously inefficient, untrustworthy and not above suspicion of corruption. But it does not appear that the character of the governmental organization requires any important change. Chicago enjoys a substantial measure of home rule under its charter. Its council is not bicameral, and there is no fatal division of responsibility. It is true that aldermen are elected by wards instead of on a general ticket, and that the very inadequate pay received by them insures neither proper attention to duty nor fidelity to public interests. Increasing the salaries of aldermen to a point which would induce educated, ambitious and public spirited men to seek the office, and which would enable them to devote all their time and energy to the business of the city would undoubtedly be a step in the right direction. Election on a general ticket would also tend to keep inferior men out and improve the chances of clean, independent and faithful candidates. Civil service reform has been carried farther in Chicago than in any other large American city, and the results of the new system have proved so satisfactory that no backward step would be tolerated by the people. Efforts have been made by spoilsmen to undermine and cripple it, but their signal defeat has only served to strengthen the hold of the reform upon popular favor and confidence.

It is evident that it is entirely within the power of the citizens to secure honest and faithful municipal government. No form of organization or structure can enable us to dispense with honesty, and so long as citizens will neglect their political duties and allow political machines to elect candidates and control officials, good government can not be expected.

But honesty alone can never be sufficient. Good intentions do not save officials from blunders and the neglect of public interest due to ignorance. Shrewd corporations stand ready to take advantage of the simplicity and inexperience of respectable men elected to municipal office. Skill, intelligence and experience are as essential in officials as integrity. The questions with which municipal officials have to deal are complex and difficult, and successful conduct of public affairs requires at least as much ability as the management of the business of great private industrial enterprises. . . .

At best, the lot of the reformer in urban politics was not an enviable one, and many of the reformers compounded difficulties for themselves through their own limitations. Mr. Dooley, the saloonkeeper on Archey Road (the creation of Finley Peter Dunne, himself a Chicagoan of Irish ancestry), once ruminated upon these shortcomings.

FINLEY PETER DUNNE:
ON REFORM CANDIDATES*

"That frind iv ye'ers, Dugan, is an intilligent man," said Mr. Dooley. "All he needs is an index an' a few illusthrations to make him a bicyclopedja iv useless information."

"Well," said Mr. Hennessy, judiciously, "he ain't no Soc-rates an' he ain't no answers-to-questions colum; but he's a good man that goes to his jooty, an' as handy with a pick as some people are with a cocktail spoon. What's he been doin' again ye?"

"Nawthin'," said Mr. Dooley, "but he was in

* Reprinted from Finley Peter Dunne, *Mr. Dooley in Peace and in War* (Boston: Small, 1899), pp. 111–17.

here Choosday. 'Did ye vote?' says I. 'I did,' says he. 'Which wan iv th' distinguished bunko steerers got ye'er invalu'ble suffrage?' says I. 'I didn't have none with me,' says he, 'but I voted f'r Charter Haitch,' says he. 'I've been with him in six ilictions,' says he, 'an' he's a good man,' he says. 'D'ye think ye're votin' f'r th' best?' says I. 'Why, man alive,' I says, 'Charter Haitch was assassinated three years ago,' I says. 'Was he?' says Dugan. 'Ah, well, he's lived that down be this time. He was a good man,' he says.

"Ye see, that's what thim rayform lads wint up again. If I liked rayformers, Hinnissy, an' wanted f'r to see thim win out wanst in their lifetime, I'd buy thim each a suit iv chilled steel, ar-rm thim with raypeatin' rifles, an' take thim east iv State Sthreet an' south iv Jackson Bully-vard. At prisint th' opinion that pre-vails in th' ranks iv th' gloryous ar-rmy iv ray-form is that there ain't annything worth seein' in this lar-rge an' commodyous desert but th' pest-house an' the bridewell. Me frind Willum J. O'Brien is no rayformer. But Willum J. undherstands that there's a few hundherds iv thousands iv people livin' in a part iv th' town that looks like naw-thin' but smoke fr'm th' roof iv th' Onion League Club that have on'y two pleasures in life, to wur-ruk an' to vote, both iv which they do at th' uniform rate iv wan dollar an' a half a day. That's why Willum J. O'Brien is now a sinitor an' will be an aldherman afther next Thursdah, an' it's why other people are sindin' him flowers.

"This is th' way a rayform candydate is ilicted. Th' boys down town has heerd that things ain't goin' r-right somehow. Franchises is bein' handed out to none iv thim; an' wanst in a while a mimber iv th' club, comin' home a little late an' thryin' to riconcile a pair iv r-round feet with an embroidered sidewalk, meets a sthrong ar-rm boy that pushes in his face an' takes away all his marbles. It begins to be talked that th' time has come f'r good citizens f'r to brace up an' do somethin', an' they agree to nomynate a candy-date f'r aldherman. 'Who'll we put up?' says they. 'How's Clarence Doolittle?' says wan. 'He's laid up with a coupon thumb, an' can't r-run.' 'An' how about Arthur Doheny?' 'I swore an oath whin I came out iv colledge I'd niver vote f'r a man that wore a made tie.' 'Well, thin, let's thry Willie Boye.' 'Good,' says th' comity. 'He's jus' th' man f'r our money.' An' Willie Boye, after thinkin' it over, goes to his tailor an' ordhers three dozen pairs iv pants, an' decides f'r to be th' sthandard-bearer iv th' people. Musin' over his fried eyesthers an' asparagus an' his champagne, he bets a polo pony again a box iv golf-balls he'll be ilicted unanimous; an' all th' good citizens make a vow f'r to set th' alar-rm clock f'r half-past three on th' afthernoon iv iliction day, so's to be up in time to vote f'r th' riprisintive iv pure gover'mint.

" 'Tis some time befure they comprehind that there ar-re other candydates in th' field. But th' other candydates know it. Th' sthrongest iv thim —his name is Flannigan, an' he's a re-tail dealer in wines an' liquors, an' he lives over his estab-lishment. Flannigan was nomynated enthusyas-tically at a prim'ry held in his bar-rn; an' befure

Willie Boye had picked out pants that wud match th' color iv th' Austhreelyan ballot this here Flan-nigan had put a man on th' day watch, tol' him to speak gently to anny raygistered voter that wint to sleep behind th' sthove, an' was out that night visitin' his frinds. Who was it judged th' cake walk? Flannigan. Who was it carrid th' pall? Flannigan. Who was it sthud up at th' christen-ing? Flannigan. Whose ca-ards did th' grievin' widow, th' blushin' bridegroom, or th' happy father find in th' hack? Flannigan's. Ye bet ye'er life. Ye see Flannigan wasn't out f'r th' good iv th' community. Flannigan was out f'r Flannigan an' th' stuff.

"Well, iliction day come around; an' all th' imminent frinds iv good gover'mint had special wires sthrung into th' club, an' waited f'r th' returns. Th' first precin't showed 28 votes f'r Willie Boye to 14 f'r Flannigan. 'That's my pre-cin't,' says Willie. 'I wondher who voted thim fourteen?' 'Coachmen,' says Clarence Doolittle. 'There are thirty-five precin'ts in this ward,' says th' leader iv th' rayform ilimint. 'At this rate, I'm sure iv 440 meejority. Gossoon,' he says, 'put a keg iv sherry wine on th' ice,' he says. 'Well,' he says, 'at last th' community is relieved fr'm misrule,' he says. 'To-morrah I will start in arrangin' amindmints to th' tariff schedool an' th' ar-bitra-tion threety,' he says. 'We must be up an' doin',' he says. 'Hol' on there,' says wan iv th' comity. 'There must be some mistake in this fr'm th' sixth precin't,' he says. 'Where's the sixth pre-cin't?' says Clarence. 'Over be th' dumps,' says Willie. 'I told me futman to see to that. He lives at th' cor-ner iv Desplaines an Bloo Island Av'noo on Goose's Island,' he says. 'What does it show?' 'Flannigan, three hundherd an' eighty-five; Han-sen, forty-eight; Schwartz, twinty; O'Malley, siv-inteen; Casey, ten; O'Day, eight; Larsen, five; O'Rourke, three; Mulcahy, two; Schmitt, two; Moloney, two; Riordon, two; O'Malley, two; Willie Boye, wan.' 'Gintlemin,' says Willie Boye, arisin' with a stern look in his eyes, 'th' rascal has bethrayed me. Waither, take th' sherry wine off th' ice. They'se no hope f'r sound financial legis-lation this year. I'm goin' home.'

"An', as he goes down th' sthreet, he hears a band play an' sees a procission headed be a cal-ceem light; an', in a carredge, wit his plug hat in his hand an' his di'mond makin' th' calceem look like a piece iv punk in a smoke-house, is Flannigan, payin' his first visit this side iv th' thracks."

Despite the serious problems that plagued it, Chicago was an impressive city. A New York journalist who visited there just before the opening of the Columbian Exposition of 1893 recorded in favorable terms its sights, sounds, and spirit.

JULIAN RALPH:
CHICAGO AT THE TIME OF THE FAIR*

Chicago will be the main exhibit at the Columbian Exposition of 1893. No matter what the aggregation of wonders there, no matter what the Eiffel-Tower-like chief exhibit may be, the city itself will make the most surprising presentation. Those who go to study the world's progress will find no other result of human force so wonderful, extravagant, or peculiar. Those who carry with them the prejudices begotten of political rivalry or commercial envy will discover that, however well-founded some of the criticism has been—especially as to the spirit of the Chicagoans—the development of the place has not followed the logical deductions. Those who go clear-minded, expecting to see a great city, will find one different from that which any precedent has led them to look for. . . .

The city has been thought intolerant of criticism. The amount of truth there is in this is found in its supervoluminous civicism. The bravado and bunkum of the Chicago newspapers reflect this quality but do it clumsily, because it proceeds from a sense of business policy with the editors, who laugh at it themselves. But underlying the behavior of the most able and enterprising men in the city is this motto, which they constantly quoted to me, all using the same words, "We are for Chicago first, last, and all the time." To define that sentence is, in a great measure, to account for Chicago. It explains the possession of a million inhabitants by a city that practically dates its beginning after the war of the rebellion. Its adoption by half a million men as their watchword means the forcing of trade and manufactures and wealth; the getting of the World's Fair, if you please. In order to comprehend Chicago, it is best never to lose sight of the motto of its citizens.

I have spoken of the roar and bustle and energy of Chicago. This is most noticeable in the business part of the town, where the greater number of the men are crowded together. It seems there as if the men would run over the horses if the drivers were not careful. Everybody is in such a hurry and going at such a pace that if a stranger asks his way, he is apt to have to trot along with his neighbor to gain the information, for the average Chicagoan cannot stop to talk. The whole business of life is carried on at high

* Reprinted from Julian Ralph, *Harper's Chicago and the World's Fair* (New York: 1893), pp. 1, 2–3, 5–7, 9–12, 19–21, 30–31.

pressure, and the pithy part of Chicago is like three hundred acres of New York Stock Exchange when trading is active. . . .

In the Auditorium Hotel the guests communicate with the clerk by electricity, and may flash word of their thirst to the bar-tender as lightning dances from the top to the bottom of a steeple. A sort of annunciator is used, and by turning an arrow and pressing a button, a man may in half a minute order a cocktail, towels, ice-water, stationery, dinner, a bootblack, and the evening newspapers. Our horse-cars in New York move at the rate of about six miles an hour. The cable-cars of Chicago make more than nine miles an hour in town, and more than thirteen miles an hour where the population is less dense. They go in trains of from two to four cars each, and with such a racket of gong-ringing and such a grinding and whir of grip-wheels as to make a modern vestibuled train seem to slight its opportunities for noise. But these street-cars distribute the people grandly, and while they occasionally run over a stray citizen, they far more frequently clear their way by lifting wagons and trucks bodily to one side as they whirl along. It is a rapid and a business-like city. The speed with which cattle are killed and pigs are turned into slabs of salt pork has amazed the world, but it is only the ignorant portion thereof that does not know that the celerity at the stock-yards is merely an effort of the butchers to keep up with the rest of the town. The only slow things in Chicago are the steam railway trains. Further on we will discover why they are so.

I do not know how many very tall buildings Chicago contains, but they must number nearly two dozen. Some of them are artistically designed, and hide their height in well-balanced proportions. A few are mere boxes punctured with window-holes, and stand above their neighbors like great hitching-posts. The best of them are very elegantly and completely appointed, and the communities of men inside them might almost live their lives within their walls, so multifarious are the occupations and services of the tenants. The best New York office buildings are not injured by comparison with these towering structures, except that they are not so tall as the Chicago buildings, but there is not in New York any office structure that can be compared with Chicago's so-called Chamber of Commerce office building, so far as are concerned the advantages of light and air and openness and roominess which its tenants enjoy. In these respects there is only one finer building in America, and that is in Minneapolis. It is a great mistake to think that we in New York possess all the elegant, rich, and ornamental outgrowths of taste, or that we know better than the West what are the luxuries and comforts of the age. With their floors of deftly laid mosaic-work, their walls of marble and onyx, their balustrades of copper worked into arabesquerie, their artistic lanterns, elegant electric fixtures, their costly and luxurious public rooms, these Chicago office buildings force an exclamation of praise, however unwillingly it comes.

They have adopted what they call "the Chicago method" in putting up these steepling hives. This plan is to construct the actual edifice of steel framework, to which are added thin outer walls of brick or stone masonry, and the necessary partitions of firebrick, and plaster laid on iron lathing. The buildings are therefore like enclosed bird-cages, and it is said that, like bird-cages, they cannot shake or tumble down. The exterior walls are mere envelopes. They are so treated that the buildings look like heaps of masonry, but that is homage paid to custom more than it is a material element of strength. These walls are to a building what an envelope is to a letter, or a cover is to a book. The Chicago method is expeditious, economical, and in many ways advantageous. . . . One of the foremost business men in the city asserts that he can perceive no reason why the entire business heart of the town—that square half-mile of which I have spoken—should not soon be all builded up of cloud-capped towers. There will be a need for them, he says, and the money to defray the cost of them will accompany the demand. The only trouble he foresees will be in the solution of the problem what to do with the people who will then crowd the streets as never streets were clogged before.

This prophecy relates to a little section of the city, but the city itself contains 181½ square miles. It has been said of the many annexations by which her present size was attained that Chicago reached out and took to herself farms, prairie land, and villages, and that of such material the great city now in part consists. This is true. In suburban trips, such as those I took to Fort Sheridan and Fernwood, for instance, I passed great cabbage farms, groves, houseless but plotted tracts, and long reaches of the former prairie. Even yet Hyde Park is a separated settlement, and a dozen or more villages stand out as distinctly by themselves as ever they did. If it were true, as her rivals insist, that Chicago added all this tract merely to get a high rank in the census reports of population, the folly of the action would be either ludicrous or pitiful, according to the stand-point from which it was viewed. But the true reason for her enormous extension of municipal jurisdiction is quite as peculiar. The enlargement was urged and accomplished in order to anticipate the growth and needs of the city. It was a consequence of extraordinary foresight, which recognized the necessity for a uniform system of boulevards, parks, drainage, and water provision when the city should reach limits that it was even then seen must soon bound a compact aggregation of stores, offices, factories, and dwellings. To us of the East this is surprising. It might seem incredible were there not many other evidences of the same spirit and sagacity not only in Chicago, but in the other cities of the West, especially of the North-west. What Minneapolis, St. Paul, and Duluth are doing towards a future park system reveals the same enterprise and habit of looking far ahead. And Chicago, in her park system, makes evident her intentions. In all these cities and in a hundred ways the observant traveller notes the same forehandedness, and prepares himself to understand the temper in which the greatest of the Western capitals leaned forth and absorbed the prairie. Chicago expects to become the largest city in America—a city which, in fifty years, shall be larger than the consolidated cities that may form New York at that time.

Now on what substance does Chicago feed that she should foresee herself so great? What manner of men are those of Chicago? What are the whys and the wherefores of her growth?

It seems to have ever been, as it is now, a city of young men. One Chicagoan accounts for its low death-rate on the ground that not even its leading men are yet old enough to die. The young men who drifted there from the Eastern States after the close of the war all agree that the thing which most astonished them was the youthfulness of the most active business men. Marshall Field, Potter Palmer, and the rest, heading very large mercantile establishments, were young fellows. Those who came to Chicago from England fancied, as it is said that Englishmen do, that a man may not be trusted with affairs until he has lost half his hair and all his teeth. Our own Eastern men were apt to place wealth and success at the middle of the scale of life. But, in Chicago, men under thirty were leading in commerce and industry. The sight was a spur to all the young men who came, and they also pitched in to swell the size and successes of the young men's capital. The easy making of money by the loaning of it and by handling city realty—sources which never failed with shrewd men—not only whetted the general appetite for big and quick money-making, but they provided the means for the establishment and extension of trade in other ways and with the West at large.

It is one of the peculiarities of Chicago that one finds not only the capitalists but the store-keepers discussing the whole country with a familiarity as strange to a man from the Atlantic coast as Nebraska is strange to most Philadelphians or New-Yorkers. But the well-informed and "hustling" Chicagoan is familiar with the differing districts of the entire West, North, and South, with their crops, industries, wants, financial status, and means of intercommunication. As in London we find men whose business field is the world, so in Chicago we find the business men talking not of one section or of Europe, as is largely the case in New York, but discussing the affairs of the entire country. The figures which garnish their conversation are bewildering, but if they are analyzed, or even comprehended, they will reveal to the listener how vast and how wealthy a region acknowledges Chicago as its market and its financial and trading centre. . . .

And here one is brought to reflect that Chicago is distinctly American. I know that the Chicagoans boast that theirs is the most mixed population in the country, but the makers and movers of Chicago are Americans. The streets of the city are full of strange faces of a type to which we are not used in the East—a dish-faced, soft-eyed, light-haired people. They are Scandinavians; but they are as malleable as lead, and quickly and easily follow and adopt every Americanism. In return, they ask only to be permitted to attend a host of Lutheran churches in flocks, to work hard, live temperately, save thriftily, and to pronounce every *j* as if it were a *y*. But the dominating class is of that pure and broad American type which is not controlled by New England or any other tenets, but is somewhat loosely made up of the overflow of the New England, the Middle, and the Southern States. It is as mixed and comprehensive as the West Point school of cadets. It calls its city "She-caw-ger." It inclines to soft hats, and only once in a great while does a visitor see a Chicagoan who has the leisure or patience to carry a cane. Its signs are eloquent of its habits, especially of its habit of freedom. "Take G———'s candy to the loved ones at home," stares from hundreds of walls. "Gentlemen all chew Fraxy because it sweetens the breath after drinking," one manufacturer declares; then he adds, "Ladies who play tennis chew it because it lubricates the throat." A bottler of spring water advertises it as "God's own liver remedy." On the bill-boards of a theatre is the threat that "If you miss seeing Peter Peterson, half your life will be gone." In a principal street is a characteristic sign product, "My fifteen-cent meals are world-beaters;" yet there are worse terrors for Chicago diners-out, as is shown by the sign, "Business lunch—quick and cheap."

But the visitor's heart warms to the town when he sees its parks and its homes. In them is ample assurance that not every breath is "business," and not every thought commercial. Once out of the thicket of the business and semi-business district, the dwellings of the people reach mile upon mile away along pleasant boulevards and avenues, or facing noble parks and parkways, or in a succession of villages green and gay with foliage and flowers. They are not cliff dwellings like our flats and tenements; there are no brownstone cañons like our up-town streets; there are only occasional hesitating hints there of those Philadelphian and Baltimorean mills that grind out dwellings all alike, as nature makes pease and man makes pins. There are more miles

of detached villas in Chicago than a stranger can easily account for. As they are not only found on Prairie Avenue and the boulevards, but in the populous wards and semi-suburbs, where the middle folk are congregated, it is evident that the prosperous moiety of the population enjoys living better (or better living) than the same fraction in the Atlantic cities.

Land in New York has been too costly to permit of these villa-like dwellings, but that does not alter the fact that existence in a home hemmed in by other houses is at best but a crippled living. There never has been any valid excuse for the building of these compressed houses by New York millionaires. It sounds like a Celtic bull, but, in my opinion, the poorer millionaires of Prairie Avenue are better off. A peculiarity of the buildings of Chicago is in the great variety of building-stones that are employed in their construction. Where we would build two blocks of brownstone, I have counted thirteen varieties of beautiful and differing building material. Moreover, the contrasts in architectural design evidence among Chicago house-owners a complete sway of individual taste. It is in these beautiful homes that the people, who do not know what to do with their club-houses, hold their card-parties; it is to them that they bring their visitors and friends; in short, it is at home that the Chicagoan recreates and loafs.

It is said, and I have no reason to doubt it, that the clerks and small tradesmen who live in thousands of these pretty little boxes are the owners of their homes; also that the tenements of the rich display evidence of a tasteful and costly garnering of the globe for articles of luxury and *virtu*. A sneering critic, who wounded Chicago deeply, intimated that theirs must be a primitive society where the rich sit on their doorsteps of an evening. That really is a habit there, and in the finer districts of all the Western cities. To enjoy themselves the more completely, the people bring out rugs and carpets, always of gay colors, and fling them on the steps . . . that the ladies' dresses may not be soiled. As these step clothings are as bright as the maidens' eyes and as gay as their cheeks, the effect may be imagined. For my part, I think it argues well for any society that indulges in the trick, and proves existence in such a city to be more human and hearty and far less artificial than where there is too much false pride to permit of it. In front of many of the nice hotels the boarders lug out great armchairs upon the portal platforms or beside the curbs. There the men sit in rows. . . .

It is in Chicago that we find a great number of what are called boulevarded streets, at the intersections of which are signs bearing such admonitions as these: "For pleasure driving. No traffic wagons allowed;" or, "Traffic teams are not allowed on this boulevard." Any street in the residence parts of the city may be boulevarded and turned over to the care of the park commissioners of the district, provided that it does not lie next to any other such street, and provided that a certain proportion of the property-holders along it are minded to follow a simple formula to procure the improvement. Improved road-beds are given to such streets, and they not only become neat and pretty, but enhance the value of all neighboring land. One boulevard in Chicago penetrates to the very heart of its bustling business district. By means of it men and women may drive from the southern suburbs or parks to the centre of trade, perhaps to their office doors, under the most pleasant conditions. By means of the lesser beautified avenues among the dwellings men and women may sleep of nights, and hide from the worst of the city's tumult among green lawns and flower-beds.

Chicago's park system is so truly her crown, or its diadem, that its fame may lead to the thought that enough has been said about it. That is not the case, however, for the parks change and improve so constantly that the average Chicagoan finds some of them outgrowing his knowledge, unless he goes to them as he ought to go to his prayers. It is not in extent that the city's parks are extraordinary, for, all told, they comprise less than 2000 acres. It is the energy that has given rise to them, and the taste and enthusi-asm which have been expended upon them, that cause our wonder. Sand and swamp were at the bottom of them, and if their surfaces now roll in gentle undulations, it is because the earth that was dug out for the making of ponds has been subsequently applied to the forming of hills and knolls. The people go to some of them upon the boulevards of which I have spoken, beneath trees and beside lawns and gorgeous flower-beds, having their senses sharpened in anticipation of the pleasure-grounds beyond, as the heralds in some old plays prepare us for the action that is to follow. Once the parks are reached, they are found to be literally for the use of the people who own them. I have a fancy that a people who are so largely American would not suffer them to be otherwise. There are no signs warning the public off the grass, or announcing that they "may look, but mustn't touch" whatever there is to see. The people swarm all over the grass, and yet it continues beautiful day after day and year after year. The floral displays seem unharmed; at any rate, we have none to compare with them in any Atlantic coast parks. The people even picnic on the sward, and those who can appreciate such license find, ready at hand, baskets in which to hide the litter which follows.

When William Dean Howells went west to view the Columbian Exposition in 1893, he presented his impressions as those of a visitor from Altruria, a land run according to mild Christian-socialist principles. This sketch, which first appeared in *Cosmopolitan* magazine, later formed part of *A Traveler from Altruria*.

WILLIAM DEAN HOWELLS:
AN ALTRURIAN VISITS THE FAIR*

Chicago, Sept. 28, 1893.

My dear Cyril:

When I last wrote you, I thought to have settled quietly down in New York for the rest of my stay in America, and given my time wholly to the study of its life, which seemed to me typical of the life of the whole country. I do not know, even now, that I should wish altogether to revise this impression; it still appears to me just, if not so distinct and so decisive, as it appeared before I saw Chicago, or rather the World's Fair City at Chicago, which is what I want to write you of. Chicago, one might say, was after all only a Newer York, an ultimated Manhattan, the realized ideal of that largeness, loudness and fastness, which New York has persuaded the Americans is metropolitan. But after seeing the World's Fair City here, I feel as if I had caught a glimpse of the glorious capitals which will whiten the hills and shores of the east and the borderless plains of the west, when the New York and the Newer York of today shall seem to all the future Americans as impossible as they would seem to any Altrurian now. . . .

Its story, which I need not rehearse to you at any length, records the first great triumph of Altrurian principles among this people in a work of peace; in their mighty civil war they were Altrurian enough; and more than once they have proved themselves capable of a magnificent self-sacrifice in bloodshed, but here for the first time in their pitiless economic struggle, their habitual warfare in which they neither give nor ask quarter, and take no prisoners, the interests submitted to the arts, and lent themselves as frankly to the work as if there had never been a question of money in the world. From the beginning it was

*Reprinted from *Cosmopolitan*, XVI (December, 1893), 218–223, 230.

believed that there could be no profit in the Fair; money loss was expected and accepted as a necessary part of the greater gain; and when the question passed from how much to how, in the discussion of the ways and means of creating that beauty which is the supreme use, the capitalists put themselves into the hands of the artists. They did not do it at once, and they did not all do it willingly. It is a curious trait of the American who has made money that he thinks he can make anything; and the Chicago millionaires who found themselves authorized by the nation to spend their money in the creation of the greatest marvel of the competitive world, thought themselves fully competent to work the miracle, or to choose the men who would work it according to their ideals. But their clarification, if it was not as swift as the passage of light was thorough, and I do not suppose there is now any group of rich men in Europe or America who have so luminous a sense of the true relations of the arts and the interests as they. The notion of a competition among the artists, which is the practical American's notion of the way to get the best art, was at length rejected by these most practical Americans, and one mind large enough to conceive the true means and strong enough to give its conception effect was empowered to invite the free coöperation of the arts through the foremost artists of the country. As yet the governmental function is so weak here that the national part in the work was chiefly obstructive, and finally null; and when it came to this there remained an opportunity for the arts, unlimited as to means and unhampered by conditions.

For the different buildings to be erected, different architects were chosen; and for the first time since the great ages, since the beauty of antiquity and the elegance of the renaissance, the arts were reunited. The greatest landscape gardeners, architects, sculptors and painters, gathered at Chicago for a joyous interchange of ideas and criticisms; and the miracle of beauty which they have wrought grew openly in their breath and under their hands. Each did his work and had his way with it, but in this congress of gifted minds, of sensitive spirits, each profited by the censure of all, and there were certain features of the work—as for instance, the exquisite peristyle dividing the city from the lake—which were the result of successive impulses and suggestions from so many different artists that it would be hard to divide the honor among them with exactness. No one, however, seems to have been envious of another's share, and each one gave his talent as freely as the millionaires gave their money. These great artists willingly accepted a fifth, a tenth, of the gain which they could have commanded in a private enterprise, and lavished their time upon the opportunity afforded them, for the pleasure of it, the pride of it, the pure good of it. . . .

I first saw the Fair City by night, from one of the electric launches which ply upon the la-goon; and under the dimmed heaven, in the splendor of the hundred moony arc-lamps of the esplanades, and the myriad incandescent bubbles that beaded the white quays, and defined the structural lines of dome and porch and pediment, I found myself in the midst of the Court of Honor, which you will recognize on the general plan and the photographs I enclose. We fronted the beautiful Agricultural building, which I think fitly the finest in the city, though many prefer the perfect Greek of the Art building; and on our right was the Administration building with its coroneted dome, and the magnificent sculptured fountain before it, turned silver in the radiance of the clustered electric jets at either side. On our right was the glorious peristyle, serene, pure, silent, lifting a population of statues against the night, and dividing the lagoon from the lake, whose soft moan came appealingly through the pillared spaces, and added a divine heartache to my ecstacy. Here a group of statuary showed itself prominently on quay or cornice; we caught the flamy curve of a bridge's arch; a pale column lifted its jutting prores into the light; but nothing insisted; all was harmonized to one effect of beauty, as if in symbol of the concentered impulses which had created it. For the moment I could not believe that so foul a thing as money could have been even the means of its creation. I call the effect creation because it is divinely beautiful, but no doubt suggestion would be a better word, since they have here merely sketched in stucco what we have executed in marble in each of our Regionic capitals.

In grandeur of design and freedom of expression, it is perhaps even nobler than the public edifices of some of these, as I had to acknowledge at another moment, when we rounded the shores of the Wooded Island which forms the heart of the lagoon, and the launch slowed while we got the effect of its black foliage against the vast lateral expanse of the Liberal Arts building. . . .

[The Americans] do not seem to feel as I do the exquisite simplicity with which [the city's] life is operated, the perfection with which it is policed, and the thoroughness with which it has been dedicated to health as well as beauty. In fact, I fancy that very few out of the millions who visit this gala town realize that it has its own system of drainage, lighting and transportation, and its own government, which looks as scrupulously to the general comfort and cleanliness, as if these were the private concern of each member of the government. This is, as it is with us, military in form, and the same precision and discipline which give us the ease and freedom of our civic life, proceed here from the same spirit and the same means. The Columbian Guards, as they are called, who are here at every turn, to keep order and to care for the pleasure as well as the welfare of the people, have been trained by officers of the United States army, who still command them, and they are amenable to the rules governing the only body in America whose ideal is not interest but duty. Every night, the whole place is cleansed of the rubbish which the visitors leave behind them, as thoroughly as if it were a camp. It is merely the litter of lunch-boxes and waste paper which has to be looked after, for there is little of the filth resulting in all other American cities from the use of the horse, which is still employed in them so many centuries after it has been banished from ours. . . .

When I have spoken of all this to my American friends they have not perceived the moral value of it, and when I have insisted upon the practical perfection of the scheme apparent in the whole, they have admitted it, but answered me that it would never do for a business city, where there was something going on besides the pleasure of the eyes and the edification of the mind. . . .

By still another remove the competitive life of the present epoch is relegated to the long avenue remotest from the White City, which you will find marked as the Midway Plaisance. Even this, where a hundred shows rival one another in a furious advertisement for the favor of the passer, there is so much of a high interest that I am somewhat loth to instance it as actuated by an inferior principle; and I do so only for the sake of the contrast. In the Fair City, everything is free; in the Plaisance everything must be paid for. You strike at once here the hard level of the outside western world; and the Orient, which has mainly peopled the Plaisance, with its theaters and restaurants and shops, takes the tint of the ordinary American enterprise, and puts on some-what the manners of the ordinary American hustler. It is not really so bad as that, but it is worse than American in some of the appeals it makes to the American public, which is decent if it is dull, and respectable if it is rapacious. The lascivious dances of the East are here, in the Persian and Turkish and Egyptian theaters, as well as the exquisite archaic drama of the Javanese and the Chinese in their village and temple. One could spend many days in the Plaisance, always entertainingly, whether profit-ably or unprofitably. . . .

I have tried to make my American friends see the difference, as I do, between the motive that created the Fair City, and the motive that created the Plaisance, but both seem to them alike the outcome of the principle which they still believe animates their whole life. They think both an effect of the competitive conditions in which they glory, not knowing that their conditions are now purely monopolistic, and not perceiving that the White City is the work of an armistice be-tween the commercial interests ruling them. I expressed this belief to one of them, the banker, whom I met last summer in the country, and whom I ran upon one night during the first week of my visit here; and he said there could certainly be that view of it. But, like the rest, he asked where the money would have come from without the warfare of competitive conditions. . . .

[Later] he went on to talk . . . about the Fair, and the effect that it must have upon American civilization. He said that he hoped for an æsthetic effect from it, rather than any fresh impulse in material enterprise, which he thought the country did not need. It had inventions enough, million-aires enough, prosperity enough; the great mass of the people lived as well and travelled as swiftly as they could desire. Now what they needed was some standard of taste, and this was what the Fair City would give them. He thought that it would at once have a great influence upon architecture, and sober and refine the art-ists who were to house the people; and that one might expect to see everywhere a return to the simplicity and beauty of the classic forms, after so much mere wandering and maundering in de-sign, without authority or authenticity.

I heartily agreed with him in condemning the most that had yet been done in architecture in America, but I tried to make him observe that the simplicity of Greek architecture came out of the simplicity of Greek life, and the preference given in the Greek state to the intellectual over the industrial, to art over business. I pointed out that until there was some enlightened municipal or national control of the matter, no excellence of example could avail, but that the classicism of the Fair City would become, among a wilful and undisciplined people, a fad with the rich and a folly with the poor, and not a real taste with either class.

CHAPTER FIFTEEN

THE POPULISTS

Populism, born of economic despair in the 1890's, sought solutions to a galaxy of agrarian woes. Between 1870 and 1897, farm prices had declined disastrously, farmers were deeply indebted to mortgage companies at the same time that the amount of currency in circulation was decreasing, and many farmers were actually losing their land. Almost all western and southern farmers suffered from unfavorable arrangements for marketing their crops, discriminatory railroad rates and land and tax policies. Southern farmers also suffered from the crop-lien system. In addition, farmers sold their crops at low prices on a glutted world market, and they had to buy manufactured goods at prices that they regarded as being kept artificially high by monopolistic corporations.

While primarily an agrarian movement, Populism also rallied significant support from industrial labor, social reformers, and intellectuals. It accepted the advent of industrialism but sought a more democratic form of capitalism, one providing a more equitable distribution of wealth. But Populism went further in its criticism, calling for a more humanistic social system in which industrialism would be harnessed to develop man's potentialities.

Some recent scholars take a different view of the Populist experience. By contending that Populism actually did not adjust to industrialism, they suggest that the movement occupied an untenable historical position. They claim that it looked backward, and that thus its long-range solutions were unrealistic. Populists, the critiques continue, did not comprehend the basis for their discontent so they were forced to search for oversimplified explanations and, ultimately, scapegoats. The final image of Populism becomes, in these scholars' eyes, a movement of opportunists, crackpots, and anti-Semites, whose perception of the world conformed to the dictates of a conspiracy theory of history. C. Vann Woodward challenged this newer interpretation of Populism.

C. VANN WOODWARD:
THE POPULIST HERITAGE
AND THE INTELLECTUAL*

During the long era of the New Deal one had little difficulty living in comparative congeniality with the Populist heritage. The two periods had much in common, and it was easy to exaggerate their similarities and natural to seek antecedents and analogies in the earlier era. Because of the common setting of severe depression and economic dislocation, Populism seemed even closer to the New Deal than did Progressivism, which had a setting of prosperity. Common to both Populists and New Dealers was an antagonism to the values of the dominant leaders of the business community bordering on alienation. They shared a sense of urgency and an edge of desperation about the demand for reform. And in both, so far as the South and West were concerned, agricultural problems were the most desperate, and agrarian reforms occupied the center of attention. It seemed entirely fitting that Hugo Black of Alabama and Harry Truman of Missouri—politicians whose political style and heritage were strongly Populistic—should lead New Deal reform battles. From many points of view the New Deal was neo-Populism.

The neo-Populism of the present bred a Populistic view of the past. American historiography of the 1930's and 1940's reflects a strong persuasion of this sort. The most popular college textbook in American history was written by a Midwesterner who was friendly to Populism and was himself the foremost historian of the movement. The leading competitor among textbooks shared many of the Populist leanings, even though one of its authors was a Harvard patrician and the other a Columbia urbanite. A remarkably heterogeneous assortment struck up congenial ties in the neo-Populist coalition. Small-town Southerners and big-city Northerners, Texas mavericks and Hudson River aristocrats, Chapel Hill liberals and Nashville agrarians were all able to discover some sort of identity in the heritage. The South rediscovered ties with the West, the farmer with labor. The New York-Virginia axis was revived. Jacksonians were found to have urban affiliations and origins. Not to be outdone, the Communists staked out claims to selected Populist heroes.

Many intellectuals made themselves at home in the neo-Populist coalition and embraced the Populist heritage. They had prepared the way for the affiliation in the twenties when they broke with the genteel tradition, adopted the mucker pose, and decided that conventional politics and the two major parties were the province of the

boobocracy and that professional politicians were clowns or hypocrites. In the thirties intellectuals made naïve identification with farmers and workers and supported their spokesmen with enthusiasm. The Populist affinity outlasted the New Deal, survived the war, and perhaps found its fullest expression in the spirit of indulgent affection with which intellectuals often supported Harry Truman and his administration.

Hardly had Truman left the White House, however, when the Populist identification fell into disgrace and intellectuals began to repudiate the heritage. "Populist" suddenly became a term of opprobrium, in some circles a pejorative epithet. This resulted from no transfer of affection to Truman's successor, for there was very little of that among intellectuals. It resulted instead from the shock of the encounter with McCarthyism. Liberals and intellectuals bore the brunt of the degrading McCarthyite assault upon standards of decency. They were rightly alarmed and felt themselves betrayed. Something had gone badly wrong. They were the victims of a perversion of the democracy they cherished, a seamy and sinister side of democracy to which they now guiltily realized they had all along tended to turn a blind or indulgent eye. Stung by consciousness of their own negligence or naïveté, they reacted with a healthy impulse to make up for lost time and to confront their problem boldly with all the critical resources at their command. The consequence has been a formidable and often valuable corpus of social criticism.

Not one of the critics, not even the most conservative, is prepared to repudiate democracy. There is general agreement that the fault lay in some abuse or perversion of democracy, and was not inherent in democracy itself. All the critics are aware that these abuses and perversions had historic antecedents and had appeared in various guises and with disturbing frequency in national history. These unhappy tendencies are variously described as "mobism," "direct democracy," or "plebiscitarianism," but there is a surprising and apparently spontaneous consensus of preference for "Populism." Although the word is usually capitalized, most of the critics do not limit its reference to the political party that gave currency to the term. While there is general agreement that the essential characteristics designated by the term are best illustrated by an agrarian movement in the last decade of the nineteenth century, some of the critics take the liberty of applying it to movements as early as the Jacksonians, or earlier, and to twentieth-century phenomena as well.

The reasons for this convergence from several angles upon "Populism" as the appropriate designation for an abhorred abuse are not all clear.

---

* Reprinted from C. Vann Woodward, "The Populist Heritage and the Intellectual," *American Scholar*, XXIX (Winter, 1959–1960), 55–72 by permission.

A few, however, suggest themselves. Populism is generally thought of as an entirely Western affair, Wisconsin as a seedbed of the movement, and Old Bob La Follette as a foremost exponent. None of these assumptions is historically warranted, but it is true that Senator McCarthy came from Wisconsin, that much of his support came from the Middle West, and that there are some similarities between the two movements. The impression of similarity has been enhanced by the historical echo of their own alarm that modern intellectuals have caught in the rather hysterical fright with which Eastern conservatives reacted to Populism in the nineties.

This essay is not concerned with the validity of recent analysis of the "radical right" and its fascistic manifestations in America. It is concerned only with the tendency to identify Populism with these movements and with the implied rejection of the Populist tradition. It is admittedly very difficult, without risk of misrepresentation and injustice, to generalize about the way in which numerous critics have employed the Populist identification. They differ widely in the meaning they attribute to the term and the importance they attach to the identification. Among the critics are sociologists, political scientists, poets and journalists, as well as historians, and there is naturally a diversity in the degree of historical awareness and competence they command. Among points of view represented are the New Conservative, the New Liberal, the liberal-progressive, the Jewish, the Anglophile, and the urban, with some overlapping. There are no conscious spokesmen of the West or the South, but some are more-or-less conscious representatives of the urban East. Every effort will be made not to attribute to one the views of another.[1]

Certain concessions are due at the outset. Any fair-minded historian will acknowledge the validity of some of the points scored by the new critics against the Populist tradition and its defenses. It is undoubtedly true that liberal intellectuals have in the past constructed a flattering image of Populism. They have permitted their sympathy with oppressed groups to blind them to

the delusions, myths and foibles of the people with whom they sympathized. Sharing certain political and economic doctrines and certain indignations with the Populists, they have attributed to them other values, tastes and principles that the Populists did not actually profess. It was understandably distasteful to dwell upon the irrational or retrograde traits of people who deserved one's sympathy and shared some of one's views. For undertaking this neglected and distasteful task in the spirit of civility and forbearance which, for example, Richard Hofstadter has shown, some of the new critics deserve much credit. All of them concede some measure of value in the Populist heritage, although none so handsomely as Hofstadter, who assumes that Populism and Progressivism are strongly enough established in our tradition to withstand criticism. Others are prone to make their concessions more perfunctory and to hasten on with the job of heaping upon Populism, as upon a historical scapegoat, all the ills to which democracy is heir.

The danger is that under the concentrated impact of the new criticism the risk is incurred not only of blurring a historical image but of swapping an old stereotype for a new one. The old one sometimes approached the formulation that Populism is the root of all good in democracy, while the new one sometimes suggests that Populism is the root of all evil. Uncritical repetition and occasional exaggeration of the strictures of some of the critics threaten to result in establishing a new maxim in American political thought: *Radix malorum est Populismus.*

Few of the critics engaged in the reassessment of Populism and the analysis of the New American Right would perhaps go quite so far as Peter Viereck, when he writes, "Beneath the sane economic demands of the Populists of 1880–1900 seethed a mania of xenophobia, Jew-baiting, intellectual-baiting, and thought-controlling lynch-spirit." Yet this far from exhausts the list of unhappy or repulsive aberrations of the American spirit that have been attributed to Populism. Other aberrations are not pictured as a "seething mania" by any one critic, but by one or another the Populists are charged with some degree of responsibility for Anglophobia, Negrophobia, isolationism, imperialism, jingoism, paranoidal conspiracy-hunting, anti-Constitutionalism, anti-intellectualism, and the assault upon the right of privacy, among others. The Populist virus is seen as no respecter of the barriers of time or nationality. According to Edward A. Shils, "populism has many faces. Nazi dictatorship had markedly populistic features. . . . Bolshevism has a strand of populism in it too. . . ." And there was among fellow travelers a "populistic predisposition to Stalinism." On the domestic scene the strand of populistic tradition "is so powerful that it influences reactionaries like McCarthy and left-wing radicals and great upperclass personalities like Franklin Roosevelt." And according to Viereck, populistic attitudes once "underlay Robespierre's

[1] Daniel Bell (ed.), *The New American Right* (Criterion, 1955), especially essays by Richard Hofstadter, Peter Viereck, Talcott Parsons and Seymour Martin Lipset; Edward A. Shils, *The Torment of Secrecy* (Free Press, 1956) and "The Intellectuals and the Powers: Some Perspectives for Comparative Analysis," in *Comparative Studies in Society and History* I (October, 1958); Peter Viereck, *The Unadjusted Man* (Beacon, 1956); Oscar Handlin, *Race and Nationality in American Life* (Atlantic-Little, Brown, 1957), and "American Views of the Jews at the Opening of the Twentieth Century," *Publications of the American Jewish Historical Society*, no. 40 (June, 1951); Richard Hofstadter, *The Age of Reform* (Knopf, 1955); Victor C. Ferkiss, "Ezra Pound and American Fascism," *Journal of Politics*, XVII (1955); Max Lerner, *America as a Civilization* (Simon & Schuster, 1958).

Committee of Public Safety" and later "our neo-Populist Committee on un-American Activities."

Among certain of the critics there is no hesitancy in finding a direct continuity between the nineteenth-century Populists and twentieth-century American fascism and McCarthyism. Victor C. Ferkiss states flatly that "American fascism has its roots in American populism. It pursued the same ends and even used many of the same slogans. Both despaired of achieving a just society under the joined banners of liberalism and capitalism." His assertion supports Viereck's suggestion that "Since the same impulses and resentments inspire the old Populism and the new nationalist right, let us adopt 'neo-Populism' as the proper term for the latter group." Talcott Parsons believes that "The elements of continuity between Western agrarian populism and McCarthyism are not by any means purely fortuitous," and Edward Shils thinks the two are connected by "a straight line." It remained for Viereck to fill in the gap: "The missing link between the Populism of 1880–1900 and the neo-Populism of today—the missing link between Ignatius Donnelly and the McCarthy movement —was Father Charles Coughlin."

There is a strong tendency among the critics not only to identify Populism and the New Radical Right, but to identify both with certain regions, the West and South, and particularly the Middle West. "The areas which produced the populism of the end of the nineteenth century and the early twentieth century have continued to produce them," writes Shils. Viereck puts it somewhat more colorfully: "The Bible-belt of Fundamentalism in religion mostly overlapped with the farm-belt of the Populist, Greenback, and other free-silver parties in politics. Both belts were anti-intellectual, anti-aristocratic, anti-capitalist." Talcott Parsons and Ferkiss likewise stress the regional identity of Populist-Radical Right ideology, and Viereck supplies an interesting illustration: "Out of the western Populist movement came such apostles of thought-control and racist bigotry as Tom Watson. . . ."

If so many undesirable traits are conveniently concentrated along geographical lines, it might serve as a useful purpose to straighten out the political geography of Populism a bit. In the first place, as Hofstadter and other historians of the movement have noted, Populism had negligible appeal in the Middle Western states, and so did the quasi-Populism of William Jennings Bryan. Wisconsin, Minnesota, Iowa, Illinois and states east of them went down the line for McKinley, Hanna, gold and the Old Conservatism (and so did Old Bob La Follette). Only in the plains states of the Dakotas, Nebraska and Kansas were there strong Populist leanings, and only they and the mountain states went for Bryan in 1896. At the crest of the Populist wave in 1894 only Nebraska polled a Populist vote comparable in strength to that run up in Alabama, Georgia and North Carolina.

For the dubious distinction of being the leading Populist section, the South is in fact a strong contender; and if the test is merely quasi-Populism, the pre-eminence of the former Confederacy is unchallengeable. It was easily the most solidly Bryan section of the country, and its dogged loyalty far outlasted that of the Nebraskan's native state. But a more important test was third-party Populism, the genuine article. The remarkable strength the Populists manifested in the Lower South was gained against far more formidable obstacles than any ever encountered in the West. For there they daily faced the implacable dogmas of racism, white solidarity, white supremacy and the bloody shirt. There was indeed plenty of "thought control and racist bigotry and lynch-spirit," but the Populists were far more often the victims than the perpetrators. They had to contend regularly with foreclosure of mortgages, discharge from jobs, eviction as tenants, exclusion from church, withholding of credit, boycott, social ostracism and the endlessly reiterated charge of racial disloyalty and sectional disloyalty. Suspicion of loyalty was in fact *the* major psychological problem of the Southern Populists, as much so perhaps as the problem of loyalty faced by radicals of today. They contended also against cynical use of fraud comparable with any used against Reconstruction, methods that included stuffed ballot boxes, packed courts, stacked registration and election boards, and open bribery. They saw election after election stolen from them and heard their opponents boast of the theft. They were victims of mobs and lynchers. Some fifteen Negroes and several white men were killed in the Georgia Populist compaign of 1892, and it was rare that a major election in the Lower South came off without casualties.

Having waged their revolt at such great cost, the Southern Populists were far less willing to compromise their principles than were their Western brethren. It was the Western Populists who planned and led the movement to sell out the party to the silverites, and the Southern Populists who fought and resisted the drift to quasi-Populism. The Southerners were consistently more radical, more insistent upon their economic reforms, and more stubbornly unwilling to lose their party identity in the watered-down populism of Bryan than were Western Populists.

There is some lack of understanding about *who* the Southern Populists were for and against, as well as *what* they were for and against. Edward Shils writes that the "economic and political feebleness and pretensions to breeding and culture" of the "older aristocratic ruling class" in the South provided "a fertile ground for populistic denunciation of the upper classes." Actually the Southern Populists directed their rebellion against the newer ruling class, the industrialists and businessmen of the New South instead of the old planters. A few of the quasi-Populists like Ben Tillman did divert resentment to aristocrats like Wade Hampton. But the South was still a more deferential society than the rest of the country, and the Populists were as ready as the railroads and insurance companies to borrow the prestige and name of a great family. The names of the Populist officials in Virginia sounded like a roll call of colonial assemblies or Revolutionary founding fathers: Page, Cocke, Harrison, Beverley, Ruffin. There were none more aristocratic in the Old Dominion. General Robert E. Lee, after the surrender at Appomattox, retired to the ancestral home of Edmund Randolph Cocke after his labors. His host was later Populist candidate for governor of the state. As the editor of their leading paper, the allegedly Anglophobic Populists of Virginia chose Charles H. Pierson, an ordained Anglican priest, English by birth, Cambridge graduate and theological student of Oxford. To be sure, the Populist leaders of Virginia were not typical of the movement in the South. But neither were Jefferson, Madison, Monroe and John Taylor typical of *their* movement in the South: there were never enough aristocrats to go around. Some states had to make do with cruder customers as leaders in both Jeffersonian and Populist movements, and in the states to the west there doubtless was less habitual dependence on aristocrats even if they had been more readily available.

In their analysis of the radical right of modern America, the new critics have made use of the concept of "status resentment" as the political motivation of their subjects. They distinguish between "class politics," which has to do with the correction of economic deprivations, and "status politics," which has no definite solutions and no clear-cut legislative program but responds to irrational appeals and vents aggression and resentment for status insecurity upon scapegoats— usually ethnic minorities. Seymour Martin Lipset, who appears at times to include Populism in the category, has outlined the conditions typical of periods when status politics become ascendant. These are, he writes, "periods of prosperity, especially when full employment is accompanied by inflation, and when many individuals are able to improve their economic position." But the conditions under which Populism rose were exactly the opposite: severe depression, critical unemployment and crippling currency contraction, when few were able to improve their economic position—and certainly not farmers in cash-crop staple agriculture.

The Populists may have been bitten by status anxieties, but if so they were certainly not bred of upward social mobility, and probably few by downward mobility either—for the simple reason that there was not much further downward for most Populists to go, and had not been for some time. Populism was hardly "status politics," and I should hesitate to call it "class politics." It was more nearly "interest politics," and more specifically "agricultural interest politics." Whatever concern the farmers might have had for their status was overwhelmed by desperate and immediate economic anxieties. Not only their anxieties but their proposed solutions and remedies were eco-nomic. While their legislative program may have been often naïve and inadequate, it was almost obsessively economic and, as political platforms go, little more irrational than the run of the mill.

Yet one of the most serious charges leveled against the Populists in the reassessment by the new critics is an addiction to just the sort of irrational obsession that is typical of status politics. This is the charge of anti-Semitism. It has been documented most fully by Richard Hofstadter and Oscar Handlin and advanced less critically by others. The prejudice is attributed to characteristic Populist traits—rural provinciality, and ominous credulity and obsessive fascination with conspiracy. Baffled by the complexities of monetary and banking problems, Populist ideologues simplified them into a rural melodrama with Jewish international bankers as the principal villains. Numerous writings of Western Populists are cited that illustrate the tendency to use Jewish financiers and their race as scapegoats for agrarian resentment. Hofstadter points out that Populist anti-Semitism was entirely verbal and rhetorical and cautions that it can easily be misconstrued and exaggerated. Nevertheless, he is of the opinion "that the Greenback-Populist tradition activated most of what we have of modern popular anti-Semitism in the United States."

In the voluminous literature of the nineties on currency and monetary problems—problems that were much more stressed by silverites and quasi-Populists than by radical Populists—three symbols were repetitively used for the plutocratic adversary. One was institutional, Wall Street; and two were ethnic, the British and Jewish bankers. Wall Street was by far the most popular and has remained so ever since among politicians of agrarian and Populistic tradition. Populist agitators used the ethnic symbols more or less indiscriminately, British along with Jewish, although some of them bore down with peculiar viciousness on the Semitic symbol. As the new critics have pointed out, certain Eastern intellectuals of the patrician sort, such as Henry and Brooks Adams and Henry Cabot Lodge, shared the Populist suspicion and disdain of the plutocracy and likewise shared their rhetorical anti-Semitism. John Higham has called attention to a third anti-Semitic group of the nineties, the poorer classes in urban centers. Their prejudice cannot be described as merely verbal and rhetorical. Populists were not responsible for a protest signed by fourteen Jewish societies in 1899 that "No Jew can go on the street without exposing himself to the danger of being pitilessly beaten." That was in Brooklyn. And the mob of 1902 that injured some two hundred people, mostly Jewish, went into action in Lower East Side New York.

Populist anti-Semitism is not to be excused on the ground that it was verbal, nor dismissed because the prejudice received more violent expression in urban quarters. But all would admit that the charge of anti-Semitism has taken on an infinitely more ominous and hideous significance since the Nazi genocide furnaces than it ever had before, at least in Anglo-American society. The Populists' use of the Shylock symbol was not wholly innocent, but they used it as a folk stereotype, and little had happened in the Anglo-Saxon community between the time of Shakespeare and that of the Populists that burdened the latter with additional guilt in repeating the stereotype.

The South, again, was a special instance. Much had happened there to enhance the guilt of racist propaganda and to exacerbate racism. But anti-Semitism was not the trouble, and to stress it in connection with the South of the nineties would be comparable to stressing anti-Negro feeling in the Arab states of the Middle East today. Racism there was, in alarming quantity, but it was directed against another race and it was not merely rhetorical. The Negro suffered far more discrimination and violence than the Jew did in that era or later. Moreover, there was little in the Southern tradition to restrain the political exploitation of anti-Negro prejudice and much more to encourage its use than there was in the American tradition with respect to anti-Semitism. Racism was exploited in the South with fantastic refinements and revolting excesses in the Populist period. Modern students of the dynamics of race prejudice, such as Bruno Bettelheim and Morris Janowitz, find similarities between anti-Negro feelings and anti-Semitism and in the psychological traits of those to whom both appeal. First in the list of those traits under both anti-Negro attitudes and anti-Semitism is "the feeling of deprivation," and another lower in the list but common to both, is "economic apprehensions." The Southern Populists would seem to have constituted the perfect market for Negrophobia.

But perhaps the most remarkable aspect of the whole Populist movement was the resistance its leaders in the South put up against racism and racist propaganda and the determined effort they made against incredible odds to win back political rights for the Negroes, to defend those rights against brutal aggression, and to create among their normally anti-Negro following, even temporarily, a spirit of tolerance in which the two races of the South could work together in one party for the achievement of common ends. These efforts included not only the defense of the Negro's right to vote, but also his right to hold office, serve on juries, receive justice in the courts and defense against lynchers. The Populists failed, and some of them turned bitterly against the Negro as the cause of their failure. But in the efforts they made for racial justice and political rights they went further toward extending the Negro political fellowship, recognition and equality than any native white political movement has ever gone before or since in the South. This record is of greater historical significance and deserves more emphasis and attention than any anti-Semitic tendencies the movement manifested in

that region or any other. If resistance to racism is the test of acceptability for a place in the American political heritage, Populism would seem to deserve more indulgence at the hands of its critics than it has recently enjoyed.

Two other aspects of the identification between the old Populism and the new radical right require critical modification. Talcott Parsons, Max Lerner and Victor Ferkiss, among others, find that the old regional strongholds of Populism tended to become the strongholds of isolationism in the period between the two world wars and believe there is more than a fortuitous connection between a regional proneness to Populism and isolationism. These and other critics believe also that they discern a logical connection between a regional addiction to Populism in the old days and to McCarthyism in recent times.

In both of these hypotheses the critics have neglected to take into account the experience of the South and mistakenly assumed a strong Populist heritage in the Middle West. One of the strongest centers of Populism, if not the strongest, the South in the foreign policy crisis before the Second World War was the least isolationist and the most internationalist and interventionist part of the country. And after the war, according to Nathan Glazer and Seymour Lipset, who base their statement on opinion poll studies, "the South was the most anti-McCarthy section of the country." It is perfectly possible that in rejecting isolationism and McCarthyism the South was "right" for the "wrong" reasons, traditional and historical reasons. V. O. Key has suggested that among the reasons for its position on foreign policy were centuries of dependence on world trade, the absence of any concentration of Irish or Germanic population, and the predominantly British origin of the white population. Any adequate explanation of the South's rejection of McCarthy would be complex, but part of it might be the region's peculiarly rich historical experience with its own assortment of demagogues—Populistic and other varieties—and the consequent acquirement of some degree of sophistication and some minimal standards of decency in the arts of demagoguery. No one has attempted to explain the South's anti-isolationism and anti-McCarthyism by reference to its Populist heritage—and certainly no such explanation is advanced here.

To do justice to the new critique of Populism it should be acknowledged that much of its bill of indictment is justified. It is true that the Populists were a provincial lot and that much of their thinking was provincial. It is true that they took refuge in the agrarian myth, that they denied the commercial character of agricultural enterprise and sometimes dreamed of a Golden Age. In their economic thought they overemphasized the importance of money and oversimplified the nature of their problems by claiming a harmony of interest between farmer and labor, by dividing the world into "producers" and "nonproducers," by reducing all conflict to "just two sides," and by thinking that too many ills and too many remedies of the world were purely legislative. Undoubtedly many of them were fascinated with the notion of conspiracy and advanced conspiratorial theories of history, and some of them were given to apocalyptic premonitions of direful portent.

To place these characteristics in perspective, however, one should inquire how many of them are peculiar to the Populists and how many are shared by the classes or groups or regions or by the period to which the Populists belong. The great majority of Populists were provincial, ill-educated and rural, but so were the great majority of Americans in the nineties, Republicans and Democrats as well. They were heirs to all the superstition, folklore and prejudice that is the heritage of the ill-informed. The Populists utilized and institutionalized some of this, but so did their opponents. There were a good many conspiratorial theories and economic nostrums and oversimplifications adrift in the latter part of the nineteenth century, and the Populists had no monopoly of them. They did overemphasize the importance of money, but scarcely more so than did their opponents, the Gold Bugs. The preoccupation with monetary reforms and remedies was a characteristic of the period rather than a peculiarity of the Populists. The genuine Populist, moreover, was more concerned with the "primacy of credit" than with the "primacy of money," and his insistence that the federal government was the only agency powerful enough to provide a solution for the agricultural credit problem proved to be sound. And so did his contention that the banking system was stacked against his interest and that reform in this field was overdue.

The Populist doctrine of a harmony of interest between farmer and labor, between workers and small businessmen, and the alignment of these "producers" against the parasitic "nonproducers," is not without precedent in our political history. Any party that aspires to gain power in America must strive for a coalition of conflicting interest groups. The Populist effort was no more irrational in this respect than was the Whig coalition and many others, including the New Deal coalition.

The political crises of the nineties evoked hysterical responses and apocalyptic delusions in more than one quarter. The excesses of the leaders of a protest movement of provincial, unlettered and angry farmers are actually more excusable and understandable than the rather similar responses of the spokesmen of the educated, successful and privileged classes of the urban East. There would seem to be less excuse for hysteria and conspiratorial obsessions among the latter. One thinks of the *Nation* describing the Sherman Silver Purchase Act as a "socialistic contrivance of gigantic proportions," or of Police Commissioner Theodore Roosevelt declaring in "the greatest

soberness" that the Populists were "plotting a social revolution and the subversion of the American Republic" and proposing to make an example of twelve of their leaders by "shooting them dead" against a wall. Or there was Joseph H. Choate before the Supreme Court pronouncing the income tax "the beginnings of socialism and communism" and "the destruction of the Constitution itself." For violence of rhetoric *Harper's Weekly,* the New York *Tribune* and the Springfield *Republican* could hold their own with the wool-hat press in the campaign of 1896. Hysteria was not confined to mugwump intellectuals with status problems. Mark Hanna told an assembly of his wealthy friends at the Union League Club they were acting like "a lot of scared hens."

Anarchism was almost as much a conspiracy symbol for conservatives as Wall Street was for the Populists, and conservatives responded to any waving of the symbol even more irrationally, for there was less reality in the menace of anarchism for capitalism. John Hay had a vituperative address called "The Platform of Anarchy" that he used in the campaign of 1896. The Springfield *Republican* called Bryan "the exaltation of anarchy"; Dr. Lyman Abbott labeled Bryanites "the anarchists of the Northwest," and Dr. Charles H. Parkhurst was excited about the menace of "anarchism" in the Democratic platform. It was the Populist sympathizer Governor John Peter Altgeld of Illinois who pardoned the three anarchists of Haymarket, victims of conservative hysteria, and partly corrected the gross miscarriage of justice that had resulted in the hanging of four others. The New York *Times* promptly denounced Governor Altgeld as a secret anarchist himself, and Theodore Roosevelt said that Altgeld would conspire to inaugurate "a red government of lawlessness and dishonesty as fantastic and vicious as the Paris Commune." There was more than a touch of conspiratorial ideology in the desperate conservative reaction to the agrarian revolt. An intensive study of the nineties can hardly fail to leave the impression that this decade had rather more than its share of zaniness and crankiness, and that these qualities were manifested in the higher and middling as well as the lower orders of American society.

Venturing beyond the 1890's and speaking of populists with a small *p,* some of the new critics would suggest that popular protest movements of the populistic style throughout our history have suffered from a peculiar addiction to scares, scapegoats and conspiratorial notions. It is true that such movements tend to attract the less sophisticated, the people who are likely to succumb to cranks and the appeal of their menaces and conspiratorial obsessions. But before one accepts this as a populistic or radical peculiarity, one should recall that the Jacobin Scare of the 1790's was a Federalist crusade and that the populistic elements of that era were its victims and not its perpetrators. One should remember also that A. Mitchell Palmer and the super-patriots who staged the Great Red Scare of 1919–1920 were not populistic in their outlook. One of the most successful conspiratorial theories of history in American politics was the Great Slave Conspiracy notion advanced by the abolitionists and later incorporated in the Republican Party credo for several decades.

Richard Hofstadter has put his finger on a neglected tendency of some Populists and Progressives as well, the tendency he calls "deconversion from reform to reaction," the tendency to turn cranky, illiberal and sour. This happened with disturbing frequency among leaders as well as followers of Populism. Perhaps the classic example is the Georgia Populist Tom Watson, twice his party's candidate for President and once for Vice-President. When Watson soured he went the whole way. By no means all of the Populist leaders turned sour, but there are several other valid instances. Even more disturbing is the same tendency to turn sour among the old Populist rank and file, to take off after race phobias, religious hatreds and witch hunts. The reasons for this retrograde tendency among reformers to embrace the forces they have spent years in fighting have not been sufficiently investigated. It may be that in some instances the reform movement appeals to personalities with unstable psychological traits. In the case of the Populists, however, it would seem that a very large part of the explanation lies in embittered frustration—repeated and tormenting frustration of both the leaders and the led.

Whatever the explanation, it cannot be denied that some of the offshoots of Populism are less than lovely to contemplate and rather painful to recall. Misshapen and sometimes hideous, they are caricatures of the Populist ideal, although their kinship with the genuine article is undeniable. No one in his right mind can glory in their memory, and it would at times be a welcome relief to renounce the whole Populist heritage in order to be rid of the repulsive aftermath. Repudiation of the Populist tradition presents the liberal-minded Southerner in particular with a temptation of no inconsiderable appeal, for it would unburden him of a number of embarrassing associations.

In his study of populist traits in American society, Edward Shils has some perceptive observations on the difficult relations between politicians and intellectuals. He adds a rather wistful footnote: "How painful the American situation looked to our intellectuals when they thought of Great Britain. There the cream of the graduates of the two ancient universities entered the civil service by examinations which were delightfully archaic and which had no trace of spoils patronage about them. . . . Politics, radical politics, conducted in a seemly fashion by the learned and reflective was wonderful. It was an ideal condition which was regretfully recognized as impossible to reproduce in the United States." He

himself points out many of the reasons why this is possible in Britain, the most dignified member of the parliamentary fraternity: respect for "betters," mutual trust within the ruling classes, deferential attitudes of working class and middle class, the aura of aristocracy and monarchy that still suffuses the institutions of a government no longer aristocratic, the retention of the status and the symbols of hierarchy despite economic leveling. No wonder that from some points of view, "the British system seemed an intellectual's paradise."

America has it worse—or at least different. The deferential attitude lingers only in the South, and there mainly as a quaint gesture of habit. Respect for "betters" is un-American. Glaring publicity replaces mutual trust as the *modus vivendi* among the political elite. No aura of aristocratic decorum and hierarchal sanctity surrounds our governmental institutions, even the most august of them. Neither Supreme Court nor State Department nor Army is immune from popular assault and the rude hand of suspicion. The sense of institutional identity is weak, and so are institutional loyalties. Avenues between the seats of learning and the seats of power are often blocked by mistrust and mutual embarrassment.

America has no reason to expect that it could bring off a social revolution without a breach of decorum or the public peace, nor that the revolutionary party would eventually be led by a graduate of exclusive Winchester and Oxford. American politics are not ordinarily "conducted in a seemly fashion by the learned and reflective." Such success as we have enjoyed in this respect—the instances of the Sage of Monticello and the aristocrat of Hyde Park come to mind—have to be accounted for by a large element of luck. Close investigation of popular upheavals of protest and reform in the political history of the United States has increasingly revealed of late that they have all had their seamy side and their share of the irrational, the zany and the retrograde. A few of the more successful movements have borrowed historical reputability from the memory of the worthies who led them, but others have not been so fortunate either in their leaders or their historians.

One must expect and even hope that there will be future upheavals to shock the seats of power and privilege and furnish the periodic therapy that seems necessary to the health of our democracy. But one cannot expect them to be any more decorous or seemly or rational than their predecessors. One can reasonably hope, however, that they will not all fall under the sway of the Huey Longs and Father Coughlins who will be ready to take charge. Nor need they if the tradition is maintained which enabled a Henry George to place himself in the vanguard of the antimonopoly movement in his day, which encouraged a Henry Demarest Lloyd to labor valiantly to shape the course of Populism, or which prompted an Upton Sinclair to try to make sense of a rag-tag-and-bob-tail aberration in California.

For the tradition to endure, for the way to remain open, however, the intellectual must not be alienated from the sources of revolt. It was one of the glories of the New Deal that it won the support of the intellectual and one of the tragedies of Populism that it did not. The intellectual must resist the impulse to identify all the irrational and evil forces he detests with such movements because some of them, or the aftermath or epigone of some of them, have proved so utterly repulsive. He will learn all he can from the new criticism about the irrational and illiberal side of Populism and other reform movements, but he cannot afford to repudiate the heritage.

Populism criticized industrial society not only for creating economic hardship but also for destroying man's sense of being human. An editorial in the *Farmers' Alliance* of Lincoln, Nebraska, expressed the feeling that man had become alienated from himself, his fellow men, and the productive system.

FARMERS' ALLIANCE: ALIENATED MAN*

The materialism of to-day does all the time seggregate [sic] human lives. Take a man for instance who labors hard from fourteen to sixteen hours a day to obtain the bare necessaries of life. He eats his bacon and potatoes in a place which might rather be called a den than a home; and then, worn out, lies down and sleeps. He is brutalized both morally and physically. He has no ideas, only propensities. He has no beliefs, only instincts. He does not, often cannot, read. His contact with other people is only the relation of servant to master, of a machine to its director. How can you reach this man, how kindle the divine spark which is torpid in his soul, when he knows that it is greed that enforces the material labor that is crushing him down, when he feels it is the wage system that is stealing the fruits of his toil and abasing and enslaving him? Here is Humanity's problem. It involves all other problems, and all modern life. . . . This man's name is Million. He is all about us. He constitutes half the population of the world. How is he to have more time and more energy to develop his faculties except by lessening his hours of labor and increasing his wages? Can this be done under the present system? Has there been a better system in the world? Does not the problem of humanity demand that there shall be a better system?

There *must* be a better one. . . . The tendency of the competitive system is to antagonize and disassociate men. The survival of the fittest is a satanic creed, applicable to the savage creation, perhaps, but only in the broadest sense to men.

Humanity must rise to its own needs, or the soul of man will flee, and the senses be left alone to reign.

The actual state of society to-day is a state of war, active irreconcilable war on every side, and in all things. Deny it if you can. Competition is only another name for war. It means slavery to millions—it means the sale of virtue for bread—it means for thousands upon thousands starvation, misery and death. After four thousand years of life is this the best that we can achieve? If so, who cares how soon the end may come?

---

* Reprinted from Nebraska Historical Society, *Farmers' Alliance* (Lincoln, Nebraska), May 7, 1891.

Frank Doster, a Populist leader in Kansas, argued that not industrialism but the way productive forces were organized under capitalism was responsible for economic grievances. Speaking at Topeka on Labor Day, 1894, Doster called for a society in which the machine was made to serve man.

FRANK DOSTER:
AN INDUSTRIAL SOCIETY TO SERVE MAN*

Everything which goes to sustain his physical life, which enables him to conduct his daily toil, which makes existence possible in this fierce competitive strife have become the monopoly of others—others to whom he sustains only the harshest and most exacting kind of contract relations. Formerly the tools of agriculture were the wagon and the plow; the tools of the worker in wood his plane and chisel and saw; the tools of the worker in iron his hammer and anvil and forge; and they were sufficient for all the purposes of industrial life. Now the terrible elements of physical nature which the gods can scarce bridle or control,—steam, electricity, compressed air, are utilized to do the work of man. But these, the common property of all, have been made the monopoly of the few, have been turned aside from the beneficent ends for which designed, to serve the selfish purposes of avarice and greed. In the face of the power exerted by the monopolists of these tremendous engines of industry and commerce the republican and democratic parties stand paralyzed—hypnotized as it were, unable to control it or give it direction and shape for common good.

Against the tyrannical exercise of this power the People's Party in behalf of the laborers of the land protests. The failure to adapt the legislation of the country to the strange conditions which this new life has forced upon us is the cause in greater part of our industrial ills.

. . . The Populist Party proposes as the only means to the desired end to utilize the power of the combined whole, to bring the power of the social mass to bear upon the rebellious individuals who thus menace the peace and safety of the state. It says that the subjects of those monopolies and trusts are public in their nature, and that the powers exercised through them are in reality the functions and agencies of government itself. It would have the government, that is, the people, assert their rightful dominion over the same, and as the philosophic basis of its claim it prescribes at least two political formulae: One that it is the business of the government to do that for the individual which he can not successfully do for himself, and which other individuals will not do for him upon just and equitable terms; the other, that the industrial system of a nation, like its political system, should be a government of and for and by the people alone.

The typical Populist stump speech of the 1890's raised a number of issues, ranging from a critique of social Darwinism to an endorsement of working class goals. One such speech is the following, which Governor Lorenzo D. Lewelling of Kansas delivered at Kansas City, Kansas, in July, 1894.

LORENZO D. LEWELLING:
THE LIBERTIES OF THE INDIVIDUAL*

The trouble has been, we have so much regard for the rights of property that we have forgotten the liberties of the individual. We have

---

* Reprinted from *Advocate* (Topeka, Kansas), September 19, 1894.

* Reprinted from Kansas State Historical Society, Lorenzo D. Lewelling, speech of July 28, 1894.

had some illustration of that in the great strike at Chicago and a number of other illustrations. I claim it is the business of the Government to make it possible for me to live and sustain the life of my family. If the government don't do that, what better is the Government to me than a state of barbarism and everywhere we slay, and the slayer in turn is slain and so on the great theatre of life is one vast conspiracy all creatures from the worm to man in turn rob their fellows. That my fellow citizens is the law of natural selection the survival of the fittest. Not the survival of the fittest, but the survival of the strongest. It is time that man should rise above it. . . .

Now, there are 350,000 able-bodied men in Kansas and their average individual earnings last year and the year before were $500. per man. That is what they earned on an average, but I might imagine some of you people here in this audience saying, "Well, I didn't get my share even of the $500." And I don't think you did. What has become of that $500. you were to get? It has gone where the wang-a-doodle mourneth for its first born. It went to pay excessive freight rates on commodities which we bought and sold, and then it went to pay interest on your mortgages. Why, I might tell, and I know something about it from experience, that the people of Kansas are paying 6%, 8%, 10%, and some as high as 12 and 15% per annum. Then, what is to become of us, my fellow citizens? Where are we going to? Don't you see pretty clearly we are going into a hole every year?

Now our friends have told us that the only trouble about this country and our condition is a "lack of confidence." And I saw an old farmer the other day who said he had been to market with a load of wheat. He said he got $7.50 for the 30 bushels of wheat that he had taken to town, and he bought a couple of pairs of shoes for the children, and a calico dress for his wife, and then he felt confident he had gone dead broke . . . Still he had to pay his mortgage—And when his neighbor sold another load of wheat and still another load, and put his money in the bank and kept on accumulating in order to pay off the mortgage and finally the bank broke and then he said he had lost his confidence, and his patience too, and swore by the Great Horn Spoon, that hereafter he would vote the Populist ticket and vote for the kind of bank that never breaks and that is the Postal Savings Bank that is advocated by the Populist platform. . . .

I say now, it is the duty of government to protect the weak, because the strong are able to protect themselves. . . .

I believe, and I say it freely, that the working men and women of this country, many of them, are simply today in the shackels of industrial slavery. . . .

I do not believe it is possible, ever under the shining sun, while the present financial system continues, for the debt of the people of Kansas to be paid. I do not believe it is possible that the debt of the United States Government can be paid while the present financial condition exists.

All we want is a little relief, a little remedy. . . . Why, I would take the Colorado contingent of the Industrial Army and set them out in Colorado to digging the silver from the native hills and making money out of it. Why, my Republican friends say, these men are idlers, and

vagabonds, they don't want to work, yet the fact remains that out in Colorado they actually fought each other to obtain the picks and shovels with which to do work for the city in order that they might obtain a pittance to provide for themselves and families. When the mines shut down . . . there were 30,000 men thrown out of employment in ten days in Colorado. They didn't know what to do nor where to go. They began drifting across the country, they naturally tended towards the great centers of civilization and a great many of them brought up in Chicago and there they joined the immense multitude like the sands of the sea and they gathered themselves together on the lake shore. There were 5,000 assembled together discussing their ways and means. They said to the people, the passers by, to the authorities of Chicago, "Give us bread for we are starving, give us work or give us bread", but instead of bread they did not get the proverbial stone, but they were kicked out of the way by the heavy boots of the policeman, and next day the Chicago papers came out and said, "Oh, there's nothing like leather for dispersing a mob." The mob dispersed harmless and armless, without evil intentions to anyone, driven out of the way by the kicks of the police and that too under the shadow of the statute [sic] of Liberty which overlooks the lake shore. . . .

I ask you now, what can the poor man do today that comes to you and says, I have hands to work with, I have bodily strength, I am willing to give all those for a morsel of bread . . . but you say, "I have no work to give you." What is he to do then? . . . Senator Ingles [sic] told us some two years ago, there are over a million men in the United States who are in that condition, and today the number is swelled to three million. Oh, is it any wonder there are common wealers? Is it any wonder there are anarchists? There is no greater crime breeder in the world than poverty . . . I came here this evening asking you to join with me in the organization of a great anti-poverty society. Will you do it? (Cheers, and cries of yes.). . . . They say that I am a "calamity howler." If that is so, I want to continue to howl until those conditions are improved. . . .

What do we see today? When labor is to be crucified. . . . We see the President of the U.S. throwing an armed force across the border into Illinois, and other states, without so much as inquiring whether or not it will be agreeable to the authorities of the state itself. Not only that, we find in close alliance with the power of the Executive, the Courts of the Land. . . .

While I have talked to you about the condition of the laborer, the condition of the farmers is about the same all over Kansas, and I am specially glad to know the farmers to be in hearty sympathy with the cause of labor. Down in Arkansas City, they are bringing in supplies day by day to supply the men striking on the railroad. And I understand the same thing is done here. A friend of mine who is nominated for senator on the populist ticket had the audacity, my friends, to contribute to the striking laborers of that town. Today he is arraigned by the United States Court and summoned to Topeka and placed on trial for aiding and abetting the strikers against the government of the United States.—Think of it!

And I find also that injunctions are already issued against working men to prevent them from expressing an opinion. It is not your right or privilege my fellow citizens to make proselytes, anymore. . . . Under the decision of the United States Court you have no right to convince a man to your opinion. You have no right to ask a man to quit work today, no matter what the cause. This is the position that some of the United States Courts have taken today. This is whither we are driven, my fellow citizens. . . .

[As for the condition of the farmer:] His earnings are naught. Add several ciphers together and you will have the sum of his profits this year and last. Take his wheat, which is worth twenty-five cents a bushel, and costs forty cents to raise it. How is he going to come out this year? I will tell you something: did you know that forty three per cent of the homes of Kansas have already passed into the hands of land lords? I heard a man standing up in the pulpit . . . and discoursing loud and long over the evictions of the Irish tenants across the water and I will tell you we have got in the State of Kansas 10,000 people who are made homeless every year by the foreclosure of mortgages and this has been going on for several years. . . .

One of the means of contraction of the currency is the holding of money in the bank's vaults. Why does the banker keep it in the bank vaults? Because he is afraid to loan it to you and me, because we may not pay it back. Why don't you put your money in the bank? You say you are afraid the bank will break. . . . You are both "skeered."

What is the remedy? Take the Postal Savings bank. You can put your money in there and the government is security for it. . . . The bank isn't afraid there will be a run and so the money is kept in circulation and business is stimulated. . . .

We look at the city in a mass and we forget the individual sufferer. But these have gone on multiplying in Kansas until today one-tenth of the entire population of the United States is brought face to face with poverty. Six million people in this land of plenty are today suffering for bread. And I ask you again, is it any wonder that there are common wealers. Is it any wonder that there are anarchists, and I want to say further, we are traveling in the line of past history, we are in the same condition as a nation as that ancient Rome, when the currency of the people was contracted. . . . Remember when the currency contracts, your debts remain the

same, only they get bigger, that is the law. A few years ago, a bushel of wheat would pay a dollar of your mortgage. Today it takes four bushel. . . .

And yet, the people down there in Rome said the same thing that the Republicans said to us last year . . . "Stand up for Rome." Rome was rich, and great and powerful. Rome was wonderful in her commercial importance and supremicy [sic]. Yet, remember my friends, that underneath the City of Rome in that great day of prosperity were the grinning skulls and bleaching bones of more than six millions of paupers and laborers who had been driven to despondency and death by the same conditions which seem—.

I ask you in Honor, are we not tending in the same direction? And shall the future historian say of you and me that we as a nation of free men, have you submitted to this despotism of greed until the star of our liberty has sunk into night? . . .

Relief will come, I believe this inspiration will be found in every heart. I believe the effort will be made by the people. Already great labor organizations are uniting themselves for battle, welded together in conduct and purpose and action. . . . Our path will be in conflict, but it will also be conquest. It must be so! The demands of the people will be heard. They must be heard.

It seems to me my friends that the dead sea of civilization grows wider year by year. That the yawning gulf between Dives and Lazarus becomes more and more impassable. On one side Gould and Vanderbilt—I have a list here of eighteen names ranging in wealth from twenty to a hundred and twenty five millions of dollars, and yet, I say to you my fellow citizens that no man in America ever had the genious [sic] or brain to earn a million dollars honestly. He can't do it while the sun shines. Think of a man working at a dollar a day earning a million dollars! How long do you suppose it would take him.

I say we have the Goulds and Vanderbilts and Rockafellers [sic] on the one side—Why, Vanderbilt once deposited $50,000,000 of government bonds. How much money was that? The interest amounted to $5,000. About $3.50 a minute. . . . "Money is power." That is what we are taught in school, but I tell you today "power is money." The Goulds, Rockerfellers and Vanderbilt on the one side—Mr. Rockafeller, a great man, a rich man. He owns a hundred acres over there on the Hudson River. . . . They tore the old mansion down and built in its place a private American residence that cost three million dollars. . . . And built a stable that cost thirty thousand dollars. . . . This American simplicity. I don't blame Mr. Rockafeller for doing this, he simply lives up to the custom of the times. They say Mr. Rockafeller is a good man. Down here at Hutchingson, a minister of the gospel preached to his hearers one Sunday and told them what a great man Mr. Rockafeller was because he contributed so liberally to the church, and because he had established an institution of learning in Chicago. . . .

I simply say these men are arrayed on the one hand, and on the other the industrial army. . . . 30,000 tenants annually ejected in New York City. One tenth of all who die burried [sic] in the potter's field. 10,000 farmers made homeless in Kansas every year. . . . The great throbbing centers of civilization seem to me to be dead to the instincts of humanity. . . .

The People's party has stepped into the breach between the classes to demand justice for the poor as well as to the rich and for every man.

The machinery of government has been arrayed against us. It seems to me that the Courts and Judges of this country have become the mere tools and vassals and jumping-jacks of the great corporations that pull the string while the courts and judges dance. . . . So, these great corporations are forces against which we are to contend, but I am willing . . . to place truth against the world. . . .

Men are nothing in a great contest of the people like this. It matters not who is the leader so that all the people stand together united for the great principles of humanity.

The so-called tramp, the unemployed worker who wandered through the land in the 1890's, came to stand in the Populist mind for the pervading degradation and hardship that industrial society imposed. The Populist Governor of Kansas, Lorenzo D. Lewelling, came stanchly to the defense of these unfortunate men in an executive proclamation of December, 1893, which immediately became known as the "Tramp Circular."

LORENZO D. LEWELLING: THE TRAMP CIRCULAR*

In the reign of Elizabeth, the highways were filled with throngs of the unemployed poor, who were made to "move on," and were sometimes brutally whipped, sometimes summarily hanged, as "sturdy vagrants" or "incorrigible vagabonds." In France, just previous to the revolution, the punishment of being poor and out of work was, for the first offense, a term of years in the galleys, for the second offense the galleys for life. In this country, the monopoly of labor saving machinery and its devotion to selfish instead of social use, have rendered more and more human beings superfluous, until we have a standing army of the unemployed numbering even in the most prosperous times not less than one million ablebodied men; yet, until recently it was the prevailing notion, as it is yet the notion of all but the work-people themselves and those of other classes given to thinking, that whosoever, being able-bodied and willing to work can always find work to do, and Section 571 of the General Statutes of 1889 is a disgraceful reminder how savage even in Kansas has been our treatment of the most unhappy of our human brothers.

The man out of work and penniless is, by this legislation, classed with "confidence men." Under this statute and city ordinances of similar import,

thousands of men, guilty of no crime but poverty, intent upon no crime but that of seeking employment, have languished in the city prisons of Kansas or performed unrequited toil on "rock piles" as municipal slaves, because ignorance of economic conditions had made us cruel. The victims have been the poor and humble for whom police courts are courts of last resort—they cannot give bond and appeal. They have been unheeded and uncared for by the busy world which wastes no time visiting prisoners in jail. They have been too poor to litigate with their oppressors, and thus no voice from this underworld of human woe has ever reached the ear of the appellate court, because it was nobody's business to be his brother's keeper.

But those who sit in the seats of power are bound by the highest obligation to especially regard the cause of the oppressed and helpless poor. The first duty of the government is to the weak. Power becomes fiendish if it be not the protector and sure reliance of the friendless, to whose complaints all other ears are dull. It is my duty "to see that the laws are faithfully executed," and among those laws is the constitutional provision that no instrumentality of the state "shall deny to any person within its jurisdiction the equal protection of the laws." And who needs to be told that equal protection of the laws does not prevail where this inhuman vagrancy law is enforced? It separates men into two distinct

---

* Reprinted from *Daily Capital* (Topeka, Kansas), December 5, 1893. Issued December 4, 1893.

classes, differentiated as those who are penniless and those who are not, and declares the former criminals. Only the latter are entitled to the liberty guaranteed by the constitution. To be found in a city "without some visible means of support or some legitimate business" is the involuntary condition of some millions at this moment, and we proceed to punish them for being victims of conditions which we, as a people, have forced upon them.

I have noticed in police court reports that "sleeping in a box car" is among the varieties of this heinous crime of being poor. Some police judges have usurped a sovereign power not permitted the highest functionaries of the states or of the nation, and victims of the industrial condi-tions have been peremptorily "ordered to leave town."

The right to go freely from place to place in search of employment, or even in obedience of a mere whim, is part of that personal liberty guaranteed by the Constitution of the United States to every human being on American soil. If voluntary idleness is not forbidden; if a Diogenes prefer poverty; if a Columbus choose hunger and the discovery of a new race, rather than seek personal comfort by engaging in "some legitimate business", I am aware of no power in the legislature or in city councils to deny him the right to seek happiness in his own way, so long as he harms no other, rich or poor; but let simple poverty cease to be a crime.

In its editorials, the Topeka *Advocate* emphasized the more radical economic concerns of Populism, *e.g.,* the meaning of strikes, the creation of a surplus labor force, the need for increasing paternalism, and the significance of labor-saving machinery.

TOPEKA ADVOCATE: THREE EDITORIALS*

I

The strikes at Homestead and in the mines of Idaho are only indications of the general unrest that everywhere pervades society throughout the world. In nearly every country upon the globe the rapid concentration of wealth in few hands is constantly widening the gulf between the patrician and the plebeian classes. . . . The tendency of the times is to constantly lower the standard of wages paid to labor in order to constantly add to the accumulations of the non-producing classes. The strikes that occur from time to time are merely local protests against this general policy. In every instance almost organized labor is defeated. There is always to be found a sufficient number of idle men who have either been formerly forced into idleness in consequence of the depressed condition of all industrial pursuits, or have been imported from the idle hordes of foreign countries for the purpose, to displace organized labor, always at lower wages than have been formerly paid. The Pinkerton army, or if need be the state militia or the army of the United States, under the pretense of protection to vested rights, can always be relied upon to assist in the displacement and to see that it is accomplished to the satisfaction of the employers of labor. . . . Labor is never conceded to have any rights that capital or government authorities are under any obligation to respect. . . .

How long the great producing masses will thus submit to be defeated in detail remains to be seen. The hope that the great industrial revolution now pending may be peaceably accomplished at the ballot box seems frequently to be overshadowed by serious doubt. That the revolution is to come in one form or another is as certain as that God's eternal justice must eventually prevail among men. The arrogance and greed of the Shylock classes may force a repetition of the French revolution; and should they do so, on them must rest the terrible responsibility. Of one thing they may rest assured; as sure as the blood of the patriot fathers flows in the veins of their worthy sons they will not long submit to the system of robbery that the last quarter of a century has imposed upon them.

II

The best features of our government to-day, national, state and municipal, are those which are purely socialistic. We would refer especially to our public school system and our postal system. There is not a feature of either that is not an exemplification of pure socialism. . . . Municipal ownership of waterworks, gas works, electric light plants, and other public utilities by which the people receive the maximum of service for a minimum of cost afford other examples of pure socialism, by which serious abuses are corrected and great benefits secured to the public. . . .

It is undoubtedly true that observing and studious Populists with such examples before

---

* Reprinted from *Advocate* (Topeka, Kansas), July 20, 1892, November 22, 1893, April 11, 1894.

them, have come to believe that a still wider extension of socialistic doctrines and practices would be beneficial to mankind. Looking about them they see nearly every industry monopolized by a corporation; and they are conscious of the robbery practiced upon them for private gain. . . . They have come to believe that many of the abuses to which they are subject might be remedied, and their condition be bettered by a proper exercise of the power of the government.

III

Has society, as a whole, derived the benefits from the use of labor-saving machinery that it might have done under a different system? We think not. Under the prevailing system the capitalist has been the chief beneficiary. . . .

When a labor-saving machine was invented, instead of using it to displace men it should have been used to reduce the hours of labor, thereby continuing the opportunities of all to provide the comforts and luxuries of life for every member of society. . . .

Let us admit, for our present purpose, that there is more of everything produced than the necessities of the people require. The fact that all are not supplied, then, shows that there is something wrong in our system. . . . Look at the multitudes who have been but recently thrown out of employment and whose families have been destitute in consequence. . . . It is cruel, it is inhuman, to attribute these conditions to laziness, drunkenness and incompetency. They are the natural product of a false and vicious system by which the few grow rich beyond all human need, and the many are doomed to eternal poverty and want. One of the causes of this "modern condition" is the monopoly of machinery and other means of production and distribution by which the few are benefited and the many are deprived of fair opportunities in life.

Contrast this "modern condition" with what might be attained by a proper use of the instrumentalities of modern production and distribution. Suppose, as we propose, that machinery instead of being used to displace labor were used to diminish the hours that each should be employed. This would apply to the farmer as well as to the man who works in the shop, under a proper distribution of labor. Under such a system, no one who has the disposition to work would need to be idle. . . .

Work should be so distributed that each should do his share and receive the reward of his labor. Work enough should be done to supply the demand of the whole people for every comfort and luxury of life; and the time not required for such production should be devoted to rest, to mental culture, to social intercourse, and recreation.

The Lincoln *Farmers' Alliance,* exploring the concentration of wealth and the creation of a surplus labor force, concluded, "The present cruelly unjust system . . . is fast working the hopeless pauperization and degradation of the toiling masses."

FARMERS' ALLIANCE:
THREE EDITORIALS*

I

There is now being fought in Nebraska the fiercest political battle ever known in the history of the state. Upon its decision hangs something more than the mere choice between two masters; but a choice, rather, as between principle and party, right and wrong, justice and injustice, liberty and slavery. It is a conflict between plutocracy on the one hand and the people on the other. Between millionaires and the masses. Between the money bags of the east and the corn and wheat and beef and pork of the west. Between the insatiable greed of organized wealth and the rights of the great plain people, as vouchsafed by the constitution.

* Reprinted from Nebraska Historical Society, *Farmers' Alliance* (Lincoln, Nebraska), September 6, 1890, October 22, 1891, March 3, 1892.

It is idle to educe proofs. The simple fact that, despite a generation of hard toil, the people are poor today, mortgage-ridden and distressed, is sufficient evidence that the whole system under which they have lived is a lie and an imposture. They have produced but they possess not. They have amassed wealth for other people to enjoy while they themselves are almost without the necessaries of life. They have builded palaces for the rich while they themselves live in sod houses, and so far from luxury, are denied even the common comforts of life, which no one on earth has a right to enjoy to the exclusion of him that earned them.

The present cruelly unjust system, therefore, is fast working the hopeless pauperization and degradation of the toiling masses. The great middle class, including the farmer, is gradually being undermined and destroyed. It has been boastingly said that there will yet be two classes in this country, the very rich and the very poor; in other words, the master and the servant. To this end, legislation both state and national has directly tended, consciously or unconsciously, since 1861. And in keeping herewith, whereas the farmers owned nearly three-fourths of the aggregate wealth of the whole country in 1850, they barely own one-fourth of it in 1890. . . .

At the present time, twenty-five billions of dollars, or just half the entire wealth of the nation, are in the hands of twenty-five thousand aristocrats, while three-fifths of the whole wealth is cornered by thirty thousand persons out of a total population of sixty-five millions! Comment is unnecessary. Too plain is it to the patriotic vision that our country is fast going the way of Egypt, of Greece, of Rome, that is, to the certain death that awaits all nations alike when the wealth of all falls into the hands of the grasping few. Then is liberty at an end, and then, as in all the despotisms of the past, a nation of brow-beaten slaves will produce wealth for a handful of soulless tyrants to possess and enjoy.

The impending struggle, then, not only involves the safety of our homes, but the cause of liberty as well; the preservation of our free institutions, the very existence of our beloved country. Confronted by such dangers, and with such a stake hanging in the balance, what is the duty of the present hour? . . . It is to keep our eyes unwaveringly set on the *main issue,* the rights and liberties of the people as against the arrogant encroachments of the money power. It is to firmly and persistently demand a just and adequate solution of the problems of money, land, and transportation, that industry may be fostered and all labor fully rewarded. It is to check by every lawful means the future concentration of wealth, and to destroy forever the iniquitous domination of railroad and other corporate power in the politics of our state and nation.

II

The number unemployed is made to grow constantly greater and wages less by the pressure of poverty, our employing and distributing system being an autocrat-producing, mass-enslaving, pauper-manufacturing system.

The beautiful economic law of the competitive system reduces wages by an iron rule to the lowest level (at last) on which the workers can live and rear children to recruit their ranks. Observe, by this law the profit to the idle capitalist is made to increase with the increase of the number unemployed. His wealth depends upon their destitution; his fortune grows relatively as the poverty of the poor makes them powerless. . . . To make him a millionaire thousands must be over burdened, filled with anxiety, deprived of a share that they produce, and suffer from constant deprivation.

Why is all this necessary? It is not necessary. By the aid of invention, machinery and free motive power the work of the world can be performed in about half the time, with less than half the labor that was formerly necessary. . . .

The robber must be made to disgorge. The monopolist must be forced to yield room. The money-loaner must be dethroned and driven to labor for himself. The means of production must be placed in possession of the people. And to secure these reforms the people's independent party is organized.

III

Now what is life and so-called liberty if the means of subsistence are monopolized? Hunger-scourged, the dependent laborers must accept the wages that independent employers choose to offer, and the wages are made so low that the dependent cannot become independent. More are reduced to dependence than rise to independence. The army begging work is every year increasing, the small capitalist is being crowded down into the ranks of the wage earners by bigger, richer business rivals, and capital is concentrating and drawing to itself all power. Half a million poor emigrants from Europe are also each year pressing into our work-begging dependent class and the steadily increasing competition can no longer be relieved by going west. All land which the poor can make a living on is taken.

Railroad kings have also risen with power under present law to exact slavish and impoverishing tribute from all, and gold, by devilish inventive genius, has been made to fetter and rob and rob and ruin at the will of the bankers, and the creditor and capitalist class.

The people, the producing classes, have arisen; they have spoken; and they will perform.

At the Tattersall rally, climaxing the 1894 People's party campaign in Chicago, Henry Demarest Lloyd outlined the long-range goals of Populism. For Lloyd, Populism represented "the hope of realizing and incarnating in the lives of the common people the fullness of the divinity of humanity."

HENRY DEMAREST LLOYD:
THE DIVINITY OF HUMANITY*

The People's Party is more than the organized discontent of the people. It is the organized aspiration of the people for a fuller, nobler, richer, kindlier life for every man, woman, and child in the ranks of humanity. The price of liberty is something more than eternal vigilance. There must also be eternal advance. We can save the rights we have inherited from our fathers only by winning new ones to bequeath to our children. The air of our beloved America has been heavy for many years with the weary footfalls of the people—the workingmen tramping about, to find no doors open for them in the palaces of industry they built—the farmer surrendering first the produce of the year, and then his farm itself to market riggers and usurers; one-half the clerks, the salesmen, the skilled organizers of business set adrift, and the other half made to do double duty. . . . From the mountains of Colorado, the uplands and lowlands of Georgia, and prairies of the Dakotas, Nebraska, Minnesota, Illinois, from the north, the south, the east, and the west, we can hear the march of these millions rising to join the people's party in order to make our government a people's government.

The people's party is not a passing cloud on the political sky. It is not a transient gust of popular discontent caused by bad crops or hard times. It is an uprising of principle, and the millions who have espoused these principles will not stop until they have become incorporated into the constitution of the government and the framework of society. The people's government . . . will rest on these two principles. 1) No use of public powers or public property for private profit. 2) The public have the right to use public powers for the public welfare to any extent the public demands. . . .

The first principle will put an end forever to all land grants, charters of railroads and of banks, gifts of public streets to profit-seeking gas, telephone, street railway syndicates. . . .

It [People's Party] is the only party that stands against the division of property . . . of the property of the people among the billionaires. . . .

The People's Party represents the mightiest hope that has ever stirred in the hearts of the masses—the hope of realizing and incarnating in the lives of the common people the fullness of the divinity of humanity.

Ignatius Donnelly, a Minnesota Populist leader, described existing conditions in somewhat more dramatic terms than did most other leaders in the movement. This selection is a printed address to People's party members issued in September, 1896.

IGNATIUS DONNELLY:
THIS UNPARALLELED SUFFERING*

Think of the victims of greed which have already passed before our eyes, and disappeared into the beyond.

Think of the thousands who in the past few years have done themselves to death, by their own hands, to escape conditions more terrible to them

than any the imagination could bestow upon the unknown world. Think of them stalking across the stage of life and entering the dark portals of death, hacked and bloody, with distorted faces, flying from the sunlight to escape their oppressors.

And behind these we see an array of millions who have died in poverty and despair, amid the ruins of wrecked hopes and fortunes, cast down from a high estate of prosperity and happiness, to reach the grave, possibly through the portals of the prison or the mad-house.

* Reprinted from *Times* (Chicago), November 4, 1894.

* Reprinted from Minnesota Historical Society, Ignatius Donnelly, printed address, September, 1896.

And following those we see the millions,—dispossessed, the unemployed, the poverty-stricken, the disappointed, the degraded, the hungry,—"the line stretches out to the crack of doom;" men made beast-like by want, and women shorn of the nobility of their sex and the majesty of their nature.—

And for what object has this tremendous slaughter of the human family and this unparalleled suffering of the living been inflicted upon mankind? That a few persons might riot in a senseless luxury; that they might possess more of the property of others than they could use; that they might have more food than they could eat and more clothes than they could wear; and that they might indulge in an ape-like emulation of display and vanity. Shallow-pated, sordid, unintellectual, they stand there, grabbing and grinning, while their brethren march past them to destruction. . . .

We stand for the preservation of humanity in the highest estate of which it is capable on earth. The good God, who made the universe and maintains it, gave us this grand continental arena, for the development of man—not of a metal. Every instinct of philanthropy, every teaching of religion, every impulse of wisdom, every dictate of statesmanship is with us in this mighty struggle, and urges us forward to save the republic and the human race.

A comprehensive formulation of Populist demands can be found in the Omaha Platform of the People's party, issued in July, 1892.

THE OMAHA PLATFORM*

Assembled upon the 116th anniversary of the Declaration of Independence, the People's Party of America, in their first national convention, invoking upon their action the blessing of Almighty God, puts forth, in the name and on behalf of the people of this country, the following preamble and declaration of principles:—

The conditions which surround us best justify our cooperation: we meet in the midst of a nation brought to the verge of moral, political, and material ruin. Corruption dominates the ballot-box, the legislatures, the Congress, and touches even the ermine of the bench. The people are demoralized; most of the States have been compelled to isolate the voters at the polling-places to prevent universal intimidation or bribery. The newspapers are largely subsidized or muzzled; public opinion silenced; business prostrated; our homes covered with mortgages; labor impoverished; and the land concentrating in the hands of the capitalists. The urban workmen are denied the right of organization for self-protection; imported pauperized labor beats down their wages; a hireling standing army, unrecognized by our laws, is established to shoot them down, and they are rapidly degenerating into European conditions. The fruits of the toil of millions are boldly stolen to build up colossal fortunes for a few, unprecedented in the history of mankind; and the possessors of these, in turn, despise the republic and endanger liberty. From the same prolific womb of governmental injustice we breed the two great classes—tramps and millionaires.

The national power to create money is appropriated to enrich bondholders; a vast public debt, payable in legal tender currency, has been funded into gold-bearing bonds, thereby adding millions to the burdens of the people. Silver, which has been accepted as coin since the dawn of history, has been demonetized to add to the purchasing power of gold by decreasing the value of all forms of property as well as human labor; and the supply of currency is purposely abridged to fatten usurers, bankrupt enterprise, and enslave industry. A vast conspiracy against mankind has been organized on two continents, and it is rapidly taking possession of the world. If not met and overthrown at once, it forebodes terrible social convulsions, the destruction of civilization, or the establishment of an absolute despotism.

We have witnessed for more than a quarter of a century the struggles of the two great political parties for power and plunder, while grievous wrongs have been inflicted upon the suffering people. We charge that the controlling influences dominating both these parties have permitted the existing dreadful conditions to develop without serious effort to prevent or restrain them. Neither do they now promise us any substantial reform. They have agreed together to ignore in the coming campaign every issue but one. They propose to drown the outcries of a plundered people with the uproar of a sham battle over the tariff, so that capitalists, corporations, national banks, rings, trusts, watered stock, the demonetization of silver, and the oppressions of the usurers may all be lost sight of. They propose to sacrifice our homes, lives

---

* Reprinted from *National Economist* (Washington, D.C.), July 9, 1892.

and children on the altar of mammon; to destroy the multitude in order to secure corruption funds from the millionaires.

Assembled on the anniversary of the birthday of the nation, and filled with the spirit of the grand general and chieftain who established our independence, we seek to restore the government of the Republic to the hands of "the plain people," with whose class it originated. We assert our purposes to be identical with the purposes of the National Constitution, "to form a more perfect union and establish justice, insure domestic tranquillity, provide for the common defence, promote the general welfare, and secure the blessings of liberty for ourselves and our posterity." We declare that this republic can only endure as a free government while built upon the love of the whole people for each other and for the nation; that it cannot be pinned together by bayonets; that the civil war is over, and that every passion and resentment which grew out of it must die with it; and that we must be in fact, as we are in name, one united brotherhood of freemen.

Our country finds itself confronted by conditions for which there is no precedent in the history of the world; our annual agricultural productions amount to billions of dollars in value, which must, within a few weeks or months, be exchanged for billions of dollars of commodities consumed in their production; the existing currency supply is wholly inadequate to make this exchange; the results are falling prices, the formation of combines and rings, the impoverishment of the producing class. We pledge ourselves, if given power, we will labor to correct these evils by wise and reasonable legislation, in accordance with the terms of our platform. We believe that the powers of government—in other words, of the people—should be expanded (as in the case of the postal service) as rapidly and as far as the good sense of an intelligent people and the teachings of experience shall justify, to the end that oppression, injustice, and poverty shall eventually cease in the land.

While our sympathies as a party of reform are naturally upon the side of every proposition which will tend to make men intelligent, virtuous, and temperate, we nevertheless regard these questions —important as they are—as secondary to the great issues now pressing for solution, and upon which not only our individual prosperity but the very existence of free institutions depends; and we ask all men to first help us to determine whether we are to have a republic to administer before we differ as to the conditions upon which it is to be administered; believing that the forces of reform this day organized will never cease to move forward until every wrong is remedied, and equal rights and equal privileges securely established for all the men and women of this country.

We declare, therefore,—

First. That the union of the labor forces of the United States this day consummated shall be permanent and perpetual; may its spirit enter all hearts for the salvation of the republic and the uplifting of mankind!

Second. Wealth belongs to him who creates it, and every dollar taken from industry without an equivalent is robbery. "If any will not work, neither shall he eat." The interests of rural and civic labor are the same; their enemies are identical.

Third. We believe that the time has come when the railroad corporations will either own the people or the people must own the railroads; and, should the government enter upon the work of owning and managing all railroads, we should favor an amendment to the Constitution by which all persons engaged in the government service shall be placed under a civil service regulation of the most rigid character, so as to prevent the increase of the power of the national administration by the use of such additional government employees.

First, *Money.* We demand a national currency, safe, sound, and flexible, issued by the general government only, a full legal tender for all debts, public and private, and that, without the use of banking corporations, a just, equitable, and efficient means of distribution direct to the people, at a tax not to exceed two per cent per annum, to be provided as set forth in the subtreasury plan of the Farmers' Alliance, or a better system; also, by payments in discharge of its obligations for public improvements.

(a) We demand free and unlimited coinage of silver and gold at the present legal ratio of sixteen to one.

(b) We demand that the amount of circulating medium be speedily increased to not less than fifty dollars per capita.

(c) We demand a graduated income tax.

(d) We believe that the money of the country should be kept as much as possible in the hands of the people, and hence we demand that all state and national revenues shall be limited to the necessary expenses of the government economically and honestly administered.

(e) We demand that postal savings banks be established by the government for the safe deposit of the earnings of the people and to facilitate exchange.

Second, *Transportation.* Transportation being a means of exchange and a public necessity, the government should own and operate the railroads in the interest of the people.

(a) The telegraph and telephone, like the post-office system, being a necessity for the transmission of news, should be owned and operated by the government in the interest of the people.

Third, *Land.* The land, including all the natural sources of wealth, is the heritage of the people, and should not be monopolized for speculative purposes, and alien ownership of land should be prohibited. All land now held by railroads and other corporations in excess of their actual needs, and all lands now owned by aliens, should be reclaimed by the government and held for actual settlers only.

RESOLUTIONS

Whereas, Other questions have been presented for our consideration, we hereby submit the following, not as a part of the platform of the People's party, but as resolutions expressive of the sentiment of this convention.

1. *Resolved,* That we demand a free ballot and a fair count in all elections, and pledge ourselves to secure it to every legal voter without federal intervention, through the adoption by the States of the unperverted Australian or secret ballot system.

2. *Resolved,* That the revenue derived from a graduated income tax should be applied to the reduction of the burden of taxation now resting upon the domestic industries of this country.

3. *Resolved,* That we pledge our support to fair and liberal pensions to ex-Union soldiers and sailors.

4. *Resolved,* That we condemn the fallacy of protecting American labor under the present system, which opens our ports to the pauper and criminal classes of the world, and crowds out our wage-earners; and we denounce the present ineffective laws against contract labor, and demand the further restriction of undesirable immigration.

5. *Resolved,* That we cordially sympathize with the efforts of organized workingmen to shorten the hours of labor, and demand a rigid enforcement of the existing eight-hour law on government work, and ask that a penalty clause be added to the said law.

6. *Resolved,* That we regard the maintenance of a large standing army of mercenaries, known as the Pinkerton system, as a menace to our liberties, and we demand its abolition; and we condemn the recent invasion of the Territory of Wyoming by the hired assassins of plutocracy, assisted by federal officials.

7. *Resolved,* That we commend to the favorable consideration of the people and the reform press the legislative system known as the initiative and referendum.

8. *Resolved,* That we favor a constitutional provision limiting the office of President and Vice-President to one term, and providing for the election of senators of the United States by a direct vote of the people.

9. *Resolved,* That we oppose any subsidy or national aid to any private corporation for any purpose.

10. *Resolved,* That this convention sympathizes with the Knights of Labor and their righteous contest with the tyrannical combine of clothing manufacturers of Rochester, and declares it to be the duty of all who hate tyranny and oppression to refuse to purchase the goods made by said manufacturers, or to patronize any merchants who sell such goods.

The impact of Populism in radicalizing the Democratic party can be seen through the utterances of a young Democrat, William Jennings Bryan of Nebraska. His Cross of Gold speech at the Democratic convention in 1896 won for him the presidential nomination and signalled the triumph of the western and southern agrarians within the party. Bryan later secured the Populist presidential nomination as well.

WILLIAM JENNINGS BRYAN:
THE CROSS OF GOLD*

Mr. Chairman and Gentlemen of the Convention: I would be presumptuous, indeed, to present myself against the distinguished gentlemen to whom you have listened if this were a mere measuring of abilities; but this is not a contest between persons. The humblest citizen in all the land, when clad in the armor of a righteous cause, is stronger than all the hosts of error. I come to speak to you in defense of a cause as holy as the cause of liberty—the cause of humanity.

When this debate is concluded, a motion will

be made to lay upon the table the resolution offered in commendation of the administration, and also the resolution offered in condemnation of the administration. We object to bringing this question down to the level of persons. The individual is but an atom; he is born, he acts, he dies; but principles are eternal; and this has been a contest over a principle.

Never before in the history of this country has there been witnessed such a contest as that through which we have just passed. Never before in the history of American politics has a great issue been fought out as this issue has been, by the voters of a great party. On the fourth of March,

---

* Reprinted from William J. Bryan, *The First Battle* (Chicago: 1896), pp. 199–200, 203–6.

1895, a few Democrats, most of them members of Congress, issued an address to the Democrats of the nation, asserting that the money question was the paramount issue of the hour; declaring that a majority of the Democratic party had the right to control the action of the party on this paramount issue; and concluding with the request that the believers in the free coinage of silver in the Democratic party should organize, take charge of, and control the policy of the Democratic party. Three months later, at Memphis, an organization was perfected, and the silver Democrats went forth openly and courageously proclaiming their belief, and declaring that, if successful, they would crystallize into a platform the declaration which they had made. Then began the conflict. With a zeal approaching the zeal which inspired the crusaders who followed Peter the Hermit, our silver Democrats went forth from victory unto victory until they are now assembled, not to discuss, not to debate, but to enter up the judgment already rendered by the plain people of this country. In this contest brother has been arrayed against brother, father against son. The warmest ties of love, acquaintance and association have been disregarded; old leaders have been cast aside when they have refused to give expression to the sentiments of those whom they would lead, and new leaders have sprung up to give direction to this cause of truth. Thus has the contest been waged, and we have assembled here under as binding and solemn instructions as were ever imposed upon representatives of the people.

We do not come as individuals. As individuals we might have been glad to compliment the gentleman from New York (Senator Hill), but we know that the people for whom we speak would never be willing to put him in a position where he could thwart the will of the Democratic party. I say it was not a question of persons; it was a question of principle, and it is not with gladness, my friends, that we find ourselves brought into conflict with those who are now arrayed on the other side.

The gentleman who preceded me (ex-Governor Russell) spoke of the State of Massachusetts; let me assure him that not one present in all this convention entertains the least hostility to the people of the State of Massachusetts, but we stand here representing people who are the equals, before the law, of the greatest citizens in the State of Massachusetts. When you (turning to the gold delegates) come before us and tell us that we are about to disturb your business interests, we reply that you have disturbed our business interests by your course.

We say to you that you have made the definition of a business man too limited in its application. The man who is employed for wages is as much a business man as his employer; the attorney in a country town is as much a business man as the corporation counsel in a great metropolis; the merchant at the cross-roads store is as much a business man as the merchant of New York; the farmer who goes forth in the morning and toils all day—who begins in the spring and toils all summer—and who by the application of brain and muscle to the natural resources of the country creates wealth, is as much a business man as the man who goes upon the board of trade and bets upon the price of grain; the miners who go down a thousand feet into the earth, or climb two thousand feet upon the cliffs, and bring forth from their hiding places the precious metals to be poured into the channels of trade are as much business men as the few financial magnates who, in a back room, corner the money of the world. We come to speak for this broader class of business men.

Ah, my friends, we say not one word against those who live upon the Atlantic coast, but the hardy pioneers who have braved all the dangers of the wilderness, who have made the desert to blossom as the rose—the pioneers away out there (pointing to the West), who rear their children near to Nature's heart, where they can mingle their voices with the voices of the birds—out there where they have erected schoolhouses for the education of their young, churches where they praise their Creator, and cemeteries where rest the ashes of their dead—these people, we say, are as deserving of the consideration of our party as any people in this country. It is for these that we speak. We do not come as aggressors. Our war is not a war of conquest; we are fighting in the defense of our homes, our families, and posterity. We have petitioned, and our petitions have been scorned; we have entreated, and our entreaties have been disregarded; we have begged, and they have mocked when our calamity came. We beg no longer; we entreat no more; we petition no more. We defy them.

The gentleman from Wisconsin has said that he fears a Robespierre. My friends, in this land of the free you need not fear that a tyrant will spring up from among the people. What we need is an Andrew Jackson to stand, as Jackson stood, against the encroachments of organized wealth.

They tell us that this platform was made to catch votes. We reply to them that changing conditions make new issues; that the principles upon which Democracy rests are as everlasting as the hills, but that they must be applied to new conditions as they arise. Conditions have arisen, and we are here to meet those conditions. They tell us that the income tax ought not to be brought in here; that it is a new idea. They criticise us for our criticism of the Supreme Court of the United States. My friends, we have not criticised; we have simply called attention to what you already know. If you want criticisms, read the dissenting opinions of the court. There you will find criticisms. They say that we passed an unconstitutional law; we deny it. The income tax law was not unconstitutional when it was passed; it was not unconstitutional when it went before the Supreme Court for the first time; it did not become unconstitutional until one of the judges changed his mind, and we cannot be expected to know when a judge will change his mind. The income tax is just. It simply intends to put the burdens of government justly upon the backs of the people. I am in favor of an income tax. When I find a man who is not willing to bear his share of the burdens of the government which protects him, I find a man who is unworthy to enjoy the blessings of a government like ours.

They say that we are opposing national bank currency; it is true. If you will read what Thomas Benton said, you will find he said that, in searching history, he could find but one parallel to Andrew Jackson; that was Cicero, who destroyed the conspiracy of Cataline and saved Rome. Benton said that Cicero only did for Rome what Jackson did for us when he destroyed the bank conspiracy and saved America. We say in our platform that we believe that the right to coin and issue money is a function of government. We believe it. We believe that it is a part of sovereignty, and can no more with safety be delegated to private individuals than we could afford to delegate to private individuals the power to make penal statutes or levy taxes. Mr. Jefferson, who was once regarded as good Democratic authority, seems to have differed in opinion from the gentleman who has addressed us on the part of the minority. Those who are opposed to this proposition tell us that the issue of paper money is a function of the bank, and that the Government ought to go out of the banking business. I stand with Jefferson rather than with them, and tell them, as he did, that the issue of money is a function of government, and that the banks ought to go out of the governing business.

They complain about the plank which declares against life tenure in office. They have tried to strain it to mean that which it does not mean. What we oppose by that plank is the life tenure which is being built up in Washington, and which excludes from participation in official benefits the humbler members of society.

Let me call your attention to two or three important things. The gentleman from New York says that he will propose an amendment to the platform providing that the proposed change in our monetary system shall not affect contracts already made. Let me remind you that there is no intention of affecting those contracts which according to present laws are made payable in gold; but if he means to say that we cannot change our monetary system without protecting those who have loaned money before the change was made, I desire to ask him where, in law or in morals, he can find justification for not protecting the debtors when the act of 1873 was passed, if he now insists that we must protect the creditors.

He says he will also propose an amendment which will provide for the suspension of free coinage if we fail to maintain the parity within a year. We reply that when we advocate a policy which we believe will be successful, we are not compelled to raise a doubt as to our own sincerity by suggesting what we shall do if we fail. I ask him, if he would apply his logic to us, why he does not apply it to himself. He says he wants this country to try to secure an international agreement. Why does he not tell us what he is going to do if he fails to secure an international agreement? There is more reason for him to do that than there is for us to provide against the failure to maintain the parity. Our opponents have tried for twenty years to secure an international agreement, and those are waiting for it most patiently who do not want it at all.

And now, my friends, let me come to the paramount issue. If they ask us why it is that we say more on the money question than we say upon the tariff question, I reply that, if protection has slain its thousands, the gold standard has slain its tens of thousands. If they ask us why we do not embody in our platform all the things that we believe in, we reply that when we have restored the money of the Constitution all other necessary reforms will be possible; but that until this is done there is no other reform that can be accomplished.

Why is it that within three months such a change has come over the country? Three months ago, when it was confidently asserted that those who believe in the gold standard would frame our platform and nominate our candidates, even the advocates of the gold standard did not think that we could elect a president. And they had good reason for their doubt, because there is scarcely a State here today asking for the gold standard which is not in the absolute control of the Republican party. But note the change. Mr. McKinley was nominated at St. Louis upon a platform which declared for the maintenance of the gold standard until it can be changed into bimetallism by international agreement. Mr. McKinley was the most popular man among the Republicans, and three months ago everybody in the Republican party prophesied his election. How is today? Why, the man who was once pleased to think that he looked like Napoleon— that man shudders today when he remembers that he was nominated on the anniversary of the battle of Waterloo. Not only that, but as he listens he can hear with ever-increasing distinctness the sound of the waves as they beat upon the lonely shores of St. Helena.

Why this change? Ah, my friends, is not the reason for the change evident to any one who will look at the matter? No private character, however pure, no personal popularity, however great, can protect from the avenging wrath of an indignant people a man who will declare that he is in favor of fastening the gold standard upon this country, or who is willing to surrender the right of self-government and place the legislative control of our affairs in the hands of foreign potentates and powers.

We go forth confident that we shall win. Why? Because upon the paramount issue of this campaign there is not a spot of ground upon which the enemy will dare to challenge battle. If they tell us that the gold standard is a good thing, we shall point to their platform and tell them that their platform pledges the party to get rid of the gold standard and substitute bimetallism. If the gold standard is a good thing, why try to get rid of it? I call your attention to the fact that some of the very people who are in this convention today and who tell us that we ought to declare in favor of international bimetallism—thereby declaring that the gold standard is wrong and that the principle of bimetallism is better—these very people four months ago were open and avowed advocates of the gold standard, and were then telling us that we could not legislate two metals together, even with the aid of all the world. If the gold standard is a good thing, we ought to declare in favor of its retention and not in favor of abandoning it; and if the gold standard is a bad thing why should we wait until other nations are willing to help us to let go? Here is the line of battle, and we care not upon which issue they force the fight; we are prepared to meet them on either issue or on both. If they tell us that the gold standard is the standard of civilization, we reply to them that this, the most enlightened of all the nations of the earth, has never declared for a gold standard and that both the great parties this year are declaring against it. If the gold standard is the standard of civilization, why, my friends, should we not have it? If they come to meet us on that issue we can present the history of our nation. More than that; we can tell them that they will search the pages of history in vain to find a single instance where the common people of any land have ever declared themselves in favor of the gold standard. They can find where the holders of fixed investments have declared for a gold standard, but not where the masses have.

Mr. Carlisle said in 1878 that this was a struggle between "the idle holders of idle capital" and "the struggling masses, who produce the wealth and pay the taxes of the country;" and, my friends, the question we are to decide is: Upon which side will the Democratic party fight; upon the side of "the idle holders of idle capital" or upon the side of "the struggling masses?" That is the question which the party must answer first, and then it must be answered by each individual hereafter. The sympathies of the Democratic party, as shown by the platform, are on the side of the struggling masses who have ever been the foundation of the Democratic party. There are two ideas of government. There are those who believe that, if you will only legislate to make the well-to-do prosperous, their prosperity will leak through on those below. The Democratic idea, however, has been that if you legislate to make the masses prosperous, their prosperity will find its way up through every class which rests upon them.

You come to us and tell us that the great cities are in favor of the gold standard; we reply that the great cities rest upon our broad and fertile prairies. Burn down your cities and leave our farms, and your cities will spring up again as if by magic; but destroy our farms and the grass will grow in the streets of every city in the country.

My friends, we declare that this nation is able to legislate for its own people on every question, without waiting for the aid or consent of any other nation on earth; and upon that issue we expect to carry every State in the Union. I shall not slander the inhabitants of the fair State of Massachusetts nor the inhabitants of the State of New York by saying that, when they are confronted with the proposition, they will declare that this nation is not able to attend to its own business. It is the issue of 1776 over again. Our ancestors, when but three millions in number, had the courage to declare their political independence of every other nation; shall we, their descendants, when we have grown to seventy millions, declare that we are less independent than our forefathers? No, my friends, that will never be the verdict of our people. Therefore, we care not upon what lines the battle is fought. If they say bimetallism is good, but that we cannot have it until other nations help us, we reply that, instead of having a gold standard because England has, we will restore bimetallism, and then let England have bimetallism because the United States has it. If they dare to come out in the open field and defend the gold standard as a good thing, we will fight them to the uttermost. Having behind us the producing masses of this nation and the world, supported by the commercial interests, the laboring interests, and the toilers everywhere, we will answer their demand for a gold standard by saying to them: You shall not press down upon the brow of labor this crown of thorns, you shall not crucify mankind upon a cross of gold.

CHAPTER SIXTEEN

THE IMPERIALISTS AND THEIR FOES

At the close of 1898 in the unexpected aftermath of the Spanish American War, the United States took the momentous step and became a colonial power. The reasons for this decision were numerous and complex. Julius W. Pratt summed them up in his *Expansionists of 1898* as being "the urgings of destiny, duty, religion, commercial interests, and naval strategy." Historians have debated which of these were pre-eminent; all reflected the fact that the United States had become a mature industrial nation.

Whatever the reasons why the nation entered upon an imperialist course, the significance of the decision was enormous. The country was following in the steps of Great Britain, France, Germany, Russia, Italy, and Japan and in both the Caribbean and East Asian waters had to begin developing balance-of-power policies to meet the challenge of some of these rival imperial powers.

At home the move toward imperialism touched off a debate which with many ramifications and under quite different circumstances was to recur in one form or another into the second half of the twentieth century. In the vigorous discussion centering around the acquisition of the Philippine Islands in 1899, both imperialists and anti-imperialists assumed a firmly moral stance. On the one hand, the imperialists believed, undoubtedly sincerely, in the "white man's burden," in his obligation to bring Anglo-Saxon civilization to underdeveloped areas. This racism was a basic factor in the emerging Progressive ideology. Urged on by a sense of *noblesse oblige,* many imperialists thought in terms of providing sanitation, roads, and schools for the newly acquired islands.

There was a less noble side to imperialism also; the eagerness to seize commercial advantages which, in the case of the Philippines, were more illusory than real. Later there came shocks over the brutal fashion in which the Filipino insurrectionaries were subdued.

As Fred Harvey Harrington suggests in his essay, critics of the imperialist policy were quick to denounce what they considered as basic and numerous flaws in the imperialist argument. Imperialists were equally vehement in defending their position. In the light of the several remarkable turns in events during the twentieth century, both sides merit thoughtful appraisal.

FRED HARVEY HARRINGTON:
THE ANTI-IMPERIALIST MOVEMENT
IN THE UNITED STATES*

On May 1, 1898, the Asiatic Squadron of the United States Navy, under the command of Commodore George Dewey, engaged and virtually annihilated a Spanish fleet at anchor under the batteries of Cavite in Manila Bay. This victory, which gave the United States the first foothold in the Philippines, marks a turning point in the history of American territorial expansion.[1] It marks as well the beginning of a protest movement of proportions, a movement led by a strangely assorted group of citizens who fought expansion tooth and nail, and, in the face of overwhelming odds, urged renunciation of the spoils of war. Although it failed to achieve its purposes, the movement is of importance, for it held the political stage in the United States for two full years, and attracted to its ranks such public men as Bryan and Cleveland, Reed and Carnegie, Schurz and Hoar.

In approaching the anti-imperialist[2] movement, it is well to bear in mind that it was based almost exclusively on grounds of abstract political principle. The anti-imperialists did not oppose colonial expansion for commercial, religious, constitutional, or humanitarian reasons. They opposed it because they thought that an imperialist policy ran counter to the political doctrines of the Declaration of Independence, Washington's Farewell Address, and Lincoln's Gettysburg Address—the doctrines which asserted that a government could not rule peoples without their consent, and that the United States, having been conceived as an instrument of and for its own people, should not imitate the methods or interfere in the affairs of the Old World nations in any way.

However these doctrines may be regarded today, there can be no doubt that they had a very real meaning for the citizens who organized the anti-imperialist movement. Almost to a man the anti-expansionists sincerely believed that abandonment of these "guiding principles" would mean the doom of the republic. This feeling was reflected time after time in the articles, speeches, and private correspondence of the leaders. It was proclaimed in the utterances of Carl Schurz, David Starr Jordan, William Jennings Bryan, Grover Cleveland, and Thomas B. Reed—men who represented five distinct groups in the movement. Schurz, for example, defined his position in the fall of 1898, when he wrote: "I believe that this Republic, in that sense, can endure so long as it remains true to the principles upon which it was founded, but that it will morally decay if it abandons them. I believe that this democracy, the government of, by, and for the people, is not fitted for a colonial policy, which means conquest by force, or, as President McKinley called it, 'criminal aggression'[3] and arbitrary rule over subject populations. I believe that, if it attempts such a policy on a large scale, its inevitable degeneracy will hurt the progress of civilization more than it can possibly further that progress by planting its flag upon foreign soil on which its fundamental principles of government cannot live."[4]

David Starr Jordan, one of the first of many educators to declare against expansion, voiced the same sentiment when he told a San Francisco audience that to hold Cuba or the Philippines as colonies, "our democracy must necessarily depart from its best principles and traditions." "There was great danger. . . ," he thought, "that in easy victory we might lose sight of the basal principles of the Republic, a coöperative association in which 'all just government is derived from the consent of the governed'."[5]

Nor were the words of the two great Democratic leaders different in language or tone. "Our guns destroyed a Spanish fleet," Bryan told an Omaha audience on June 14, "but can they destroy that self-evident truth, that governments derive their just powers, not from superior force, but from the consent of the governed?"[6] Just a week later, in an address at Lawrenceville, New Jersey, Cleveland asserted that "our government was formed for the express purpose of creating

---

* Reprinted from Fred Harvey Harrington, "The Anti-Imperialist Movement in the United States," *Mississippi Valley Historical Review,* XXII (1935), 211–30 by permission.

[1] The victory aroused great enthusiasm in the United States and from this date the desire for expansion (which, as Professor Pratt has pointed out, "had turned the corner somewhere in the ten years before" 1898) grew much more rapidly than before. Julius W. Pratt, "The 'Large Policy' of 1898" in *Mississippi Valley Historical Review,* XIX (1932), 237.

[2] The terms "imperialist" and "anti-imperialist" are here used as they were used in 1898, to denote, respectively, those who favored and those who opposed the colonial expansion of the United States.

[3] A reference to McKinley's message to Congress of December 6, 1897, in which the President had said, referring to Cuba, "I speak not of forcible annexation, for that cannot be thought of. That by our code of morality would be criminal aggression." This was much cited by anti-imperialists when McKinley adopted an imperialist policy.

[4] Schurz to Björnstjerne Björnson, September 22, 1898, replying to an open letter from Björnson to Schurz. Frederic Bancroft (ed.), *Speeches, Correspondence, and Political Papers of Carl Schurz* (New York, 1913), II, 514.

[5] David Starr Jordan, *The Days of a Man* (Yonkers-on-Hudson, 1922), I, 616. This speech was delivered May 2, 1898.

[6] *Bryan on Imperialism* (Chicago, 1900), 4.

in a new world a new nation, the foundation of which should be man's self-government," and that to embark on a career of colonial aggrandizement would be to "abandon . . . old landmarks and to follow the lights of monarchical hazards." [7]

Speaker Reed, the most prominent Republican to oppose expansion, made no public pronouncement on the subject. In private, however, he let it be known that he would not support his party in opposing the "foundation principles of our government." [8]

It can readily be seen that, in each instance, the whole weight of the argument is made to rest on the point of political principle. This is the case with the other anti-imperialist speeches as well. It is true that, in the later phases of the movement, economic, constitutional, military, and humanitarian arguments were advanced against expansion, but they were used to supplement the fundamental conception. Even after the Philippine atrocities had caused many anti-expansionists to stress the humanitarian aspects of their case, the leaders continued to regard the question of political ideals as the real basis for their opposition to a colonial policy.

The anti-imperialist movement began to take shape almost immediately after the Battle of Manila Bay, as a protest against the wave of expansion sentiment set in motion by Dewey's victory. Expansionists were clamoring for the annexation of Hawaii and the "retention" of the Philippines. Whitelaw Reid's New York *Tribune* was declaring editorially that "this country will be bound, in honor and in morals, either itself to assume the administration of the islands or to empower some other competent authority to do so," even before the news of the naval victory had been confirmed. [9] Other papers—the bulk of the administration press and some Democratic organs —followed the *Tribune's* lead, declaring for expansion on military, religious, commercial, humanitarian, and other grounds. [10]

Those opposed to imperialism immediately took the field in reply. They came forward as individuals, with statements similar to those quoted above, and made themselves heard through the press. From the start they enlisted the services of the independent Democratic and the Mugwump press—papers like the New York *Evening Post,* the Springfield *Republican,* the Boston *Herald,* and the Baltimore *Sun.* These papers became the mainstays of the anti-imperialist support, but they were by no means alone in their denunciation of expansion. Many regular Democratic journals—the Chicago *Chronicle,* the Kansas City *Times,* the Charleston *News and Courier,* and the Richmond *Times,* to name but a few—followed the lead of Bryan or Cleveland in opposing imperialism. They were joined by a few Republican organs of independent leanings, among them the Boston *Transcript,* the Philadelphia *Ledger,* and the Pittsburgh *Dispatch.* [11]

Despite this support, the anti-imperialist movement achieved no satisfactory organization in the early months of its existence. War feeling was still running high. It was as yet uncertain what the policy of the administration would be. And, most important of all, there was no feeling of common purpose among those opposed to a colonial policy. Cleveland and Bryan, though both anti-imperialists and both Democrats, had no love for each other, and their forces were not disposed to coöperate on short notice even in the face of common danger. Reed and Hoar and the other regular Republicans who feared expansion, recoiled at the thought of associating with Schurz and the other Mugwumps.

Thus handicapped, the anti-imperialists made slow progress at first. They were able to put up little opposition to the annexation of Hawaii, [12] which the most prominent anti-imperialist organ termed a "letting out of the waters," the first step in a definitely imperialistic policy. [13] Henry Cabot Lodge, leader of the imperialists in Congress, could dismiss the first large anti-imperialist meeting as one of the "comic incidents" of the war, [14] and the Saratoga Conference, which was

---

[7] *The Literary Digest* (New York, 1890-), XVII (1898), 2.

[8] Samuel W. McCall, *Thomas B. Reed* (Boston, 1914), 258.

[9] New York *Tribune,* May 5, 1898.

[10] Republican papers that enthusiastically declared for expansion included the New York *Sun,* the Boston *Journal,* the Philadelphia *Inquirer, Press,* and *North American,* the Baltimore *American,* the Chicago *Times-Herald* and *Interocean,* the Minneapolis *Tribune,* and the St. Louis *Globe-Democrat.* Among the Democratic and independent papers which supported expansion were the New York *Times, Journal,* and *Herald,* the Brooklyn *Eagle,* the Baltimore *Herald,* the Washington *Times,* the Atlanta *Constitution,* the Jacksonville *Times-Union,* and the Louisville *Courier-Journal. Literary Digest,* XVII (1898), 32–38; Merle E. Curti, "Bryan and World Peace," in Smith College *Studies in History* (Northampton, 1915-), XVI (1931), 125.

[11] Three of the four leading Boston papers (the *Transcript, Herald,* and *Post*) came out strongly against expansion, but only one paper in New York (the *Evening Post*), one in Philadelphia (the *Ledger*), one in Baltimore (the *Sun*), and one in Chicago (the *Chronicle*) did the same. Naturally, many papers took half-way stands. It should be added that the German-American press was solidly anti-imperialist. *Literary Digest,* XVII (1898), 32–38, 156–57.

[12] The congressional fight was led by Reed, Senator Justin Morrill (Republicans), Senator R. F. Pettigrew (Silver Republican), and a few Democrats, including Senator Stephen White and Representatives Champ Clark and John Sharp Williams. *Congressional Record,* 55 Cong., 2 Sess., *passim;* McCall, *Reed,* 234–36; Henry Cabot Lodge (ed.), *Selections from the Correspondence of Theodore Roosevelt and Henry Cabot Lodge 1884–1918* (New York: 1925), I, 302, 313, 317.

[13] New York *Evening Post,* June 16, 1898.

[14] Lodge to Roosevelt, June 15, 1898, speaking of the Boston meeting of that date, Lodge, *Roosevelt-Lodge Correspondence,* I, 311–12.

organized by Carl Schurz to impress on President McKinley the dangers of expansion, actually delivered itself into the hands of the enemy.[15]

Organization, however, came in time. By the time of the cessation of hostilities, it had become reasonably certain that the administration would adopt an imperialist policy.[16] Those opposed to expansion began to realize the absolute necessity of common action. The independents, convinced that anti-imperialism took precedence over all other reforms, led the way. In Boston, under Gamaliel Bradford and Moorfield Storey, two Mugwumps, they organized a non-partisan Committee of Correspondence, designed to unite workers for the cause irrespective of political faith.[17] Elsewhere they showed a willingness to coöperate with anti-imperialists of every political faith. As time went on, the Bryan and Cleveland Democrats found that the issue might serve as a basis for a mutual understanding,[18] and even the Republicans in the movement—strong party men most of them—displayed a tendency to draw closer to the other opponents of expansion. By January, 1899, George F. Hoar, who had called the Mugwumps the "vilest set of political assassins that ever disgraced this or any other country,"[19] was carrying on a close personal correspondence with two Mugwump leaders, Schurz and Storey.[20] Andrew Carnegie, an anti-imperialist to whom the name of Bryan had been anathema two years before, was wishing the Nebraskan "god-speed" and warmly offering him "the hand of fellowship in the new issue before us."[21]

It was this growing sense of common purpose that made possible the formation of the Anti-Imperialist Leagues in the months after November, 1898—leagues that included in their membership most of the prominent opponents of expansion, yet managed to carry on their work without much internal friction.

The first Anti-Imperialist League, like the earlier Committee of Correspondence, was brought into being by the Boston anti-imperialists.[22] The Bostonians retained control of the executive committee, but membership was open to "any citizen of the United States, irrespective of party . . . if in sympathy with the objects of the League." The forty-one vice-presidents were drawn from all sections of the country.[23]

An examination of the list of officers of this league and similar organizations (such as the New York Anti-Imperialist League) gives insight into the elements that were behind the anti-imperialist movement. In reviewing these lists, which contain the names of many of the nation's outstanding men, one is struck at first by the heterogeneous character of the league membership. A closer inspection serves to group most of the men into a few quite definite categories, the reformers, the political and economic groups, and the intellectuals.

Unquestionably the most active and enthusiastic of the anti-imperialists were those who had long fought for various political or social reforms. Included in the anti-imperialist movement were representatives of nearly every reform movement prominent in the United States in the second half of the nineteenth century. There were Liberal Republicans of 1872, Mugwumps, civil service enthusiasts—men like Carl Schurz, Charles Francis Adams, E. L. Godkin, Moorfield Storey, Edward Atkinson, and Samuel Bowles. There were municipal reformers—James Coolidge Carter, the Cuttings, and Edward M. Shepard of New York, Edwin Burritt Smith of Chicago, Hazen Pingree of Detroit, George G. Mercer and Herbert Welsh of Philadelphia, and many more. There were social welfare workers, among them Ernest Crosby, Jane Addams, Josephine Lowell, and William Potts. There were single taxers (Crosby, Charles B. Spahr, and Edward Osgood Brown), pacifists (Crosby, Atkinson, and Mercer), Prohibitionists (Senator Edward W. Carmack and John D. White), defenders of Indian rights (Mercer and Welsh), and free traders (Gamaliel Bradford and Albert S. Parsons). The remnant of the old abolition groups, represented by the son of Garrison, the son of Emerson, the son of James Birney, rallied to the cause, as did a number of clergymen, mustering in their ranks Bishop Henry Codman Potter, Henry Van Dyke, Charles H. Parkhurst, Leonard Woolsey Bacon, John White Chadwick, and Theodore Cuyler.[24]

---

[15] To secure unanimity, the anti-imperialists yielded on points of principle. New York *Evening Post*, August 22, 1898; "Memorial Presented to William McKinley, September 15, 1898," by a committee appointed at the conference held in Saratoga Springs, New York . . . (pamphlet, 1898); Bancroft, *Schurz Papers,* V, 515–16.

[16] Walter Millis, *The Martial Spirit* (New York, 1931), 372–73.

[17] Maria C. Lanzar, "The Anti-Imperialist League," in *The Philippine Social Science Review* (Manila, 1929–), III (1930), 7–12, 17.

[18] Roosevelt noted this tendency in the New York gubernatorial campaign of 1898. Lodge, *Roosevelt-Lodge Correspondence,* I, 356.

[19] Quoted in M. A. DeWolfe Howe, *Portrait of an Independent, Moorfield Storey, 1845–1929* (Boston, 1932), 217.

[20] *Ibid.,* 217–18; Bancroft, *Schurz Papers,* V, 527–29.

[21] Curti, "Bryan and World Peace," *loc. cit.,* 127.

[22] Lanzar, "The Anti-Imperialist League," *loc. cit.,* 16. The league was founded November 19, 1898, at the office of Edward Atkinson.

[23] George S. Boutwell was president. Pamphlets of the Anti-Imperialist League; Jordan, *Days of a Man,* I, 700.

[24] These and the other anti-imperialists mentioned in the following paragraphs were associated with the movement as officers of one or more of the leagues or as active workers for the cause.

The political elements represented in the movement fall into four distinct groups—the independents, the Gold Democrats, the Bryan Democrats, and the regular Republicans. The independent group, most important of all, need only be mentioned here. It included Schurz, Adams, Storey, Godkin, Bradford, Bowles, Atkinson, and many others, men who have already been mentioned in consideration of their reform activities.

The Gold Democrats also made a notable contribution to the movement. Headed by ex-President Cleveland himself, the anti-imperialists in this classification numbered most of the prominent Democrats who had bolted Bryan and Free Silver two years before. No less than eight members of Cleveland's Cabinets,—Olney, Carlisle, Endicott, Morton, Vilas, Dickinson, Fairchild, and Harmon—came out against expansion,[25] and among the leading anti-imperialists were such Gold Democrats as Bourke Cockran, A. Augustus Healy, Thomas Mott Osborne, Louis Ehrich, and Senator Donelson Caffery.

The Bryan Democrats were significant in the movement for their numbers rather than their leadership. Following Bryan, the majority of the Silverites embraced the anti-imperialist doctrine by 1900, but their advocacy of the cause noticeably lacked the enthusiasm displayed by the independents and the Cleveland men. Only one Bryan Democrat, Senator Ben Tillman, was on the roll of the forty-one vice-presidents of the Anti-Imperialist League, and a mere handful of others, among them Joe Bailey, Champ Clark, and Senator A. O. Bacon, opposed colonial expansion with more than a show of fervor.

The Republicans who joined the anti-imperialist movement were, almost without exception, Republicans of the older generation, former supporters of Fremont and Lincoln who believed they were carrying on the tradition of the party's antislavery days in opposing colonial expansion.[26] They were ably represented in the movement by the president and secretary of the Anti-Imperialist League, George S. Boutwell and Erving Winslow; by Senators Hoar, Hale, and Justin Morrill (who died in December, 1898); by ex-Senators John Sherman, George F. Edmunds, and John B. Henderson, and former President Harrison. Notwithstanding their prominence in party politics, they brought few of the rank and file of the party with them.

A number of Silver Republicans, such as Charles S. Towne and Senator R. F. Pettigrew, a very few Republicans of the younger political generation, among them Henry U. Johnson and

Governor William Larrabee, and a scattering of individuals from minor parties also were attracted to the ranks of the anti-imperialists. Few in number, they exercised no important influence on the character of the movement.

Turning from the reform and political classifications, one finds a number of intellectuals in the movement—men who cannot be classified either as reformers or as politicians. They fall into two general categories, the educators and the literary figures. A few college presidents were active anti-imperialists, David Starr Jordan of Stanford and Henry Wade Rogers of Northwestern being the leading examples. Many college professors took the same position, prominent among them being William Graham Sumner, William James, Charles Eliot Norton, Felix Adler, Adolph Cohn, Franklin Henry Giddings, Hermann E. von Holst, William Vaughn Moody, and I. J. McGinity.[27] The literary group contained an equally noteworthy group of men, including Mark Twain, William Dean Howells, Henry B. Fuller, Thomas Wentworth Higginson, Thomas Bailey Aldrich, and Finlay Peter Dunne.

To complete the picture of the anti-imperialist movement, it is necessary to call attention to three economic classifications, the business men and industrialists, the labor leaders, and the "interested groups" in the movement. Though numerically insignificant, each of these groups deserves at least passing mention.

The business and industrial group, very small in size, should be noted because its members, as individuals, did much toward financing the movement. Andrew Carnegie was particularly generous in this respect,[28] and others, including John J. Valentine, Dana Estes, Richard T. Crane, and George Foster Peabody, did their share.

Even smaller was the labor element. The anti-imperialists made great efforts to attract labor support, but, on the whole, were unsuccessful. Samuel Gompers, president of the American Federation of Labor, did show a lively interest in the question, but he was almost the only important labor leader to do so.[29]

Nor did the "interested groups"—the growers of sugar beets, cane sugar, tobacco, and other agricultural products that presumably would suffer from Philippine competition—figure very greatly in the anti-imperialist movement of 1898–1900. Although this may appear surprising in view of the activities of those same groups in the Philippine independence movement thirty years

[27] Giddings, like Bishop Potter, later reversed his position.

[28] Albert Bigelowe Paine, *Mark Twain, A Biography* (New York, 1912), III, 1113; Lanzar-Carpio, "The Anti-Imperialist League," *loc. cit.*, IV (1932), 248; Bancroft, *Schurz Papers*, V, 531.

[29] Patrick Ford and Patrick Collins, Anti-Imperialist League vice-presidents, had engaged in labor activities, but neither had much connection with labor interests in 1898.

[25] Allan Nevins, Grover Cleveland, *A Study in Courage* (New York, 1932), 745–47.

[26] It is interesting to note that the average age of these men (in November, 1898) was 71.1 years, whereas the average age of the forty-one vice-presidents of the Anti-Imperialist League was only 58.3.

later, it follows from a careful examination of the facts. Two directors of the American Sugar Beet Company were connected with the New York Anti-Imperialist League.[30] At least one farm paper, the *American Agriculturist,* opposed expansion because of the menace of Philippine products. The secretary of the Anti-Imperialist League reported in 1899 that "the tobacco, the beet-sugar and the agricultural interests in general circulated our petitions and made canvasses among their own constituents to bring out remonstrances to the Senate."[31] This, however, is virtually all that can be said of their activities. It does not appear that the "interested groups" contributed much money to the leagues, and certainly they gave the movement few leaders of note. The great majority of the anti-imperialists had no connection, direct or otherwise, with these activities.

It can be seen from this analysis that the anti-imperialists drew their support from a number of sources. This served to increase the prestige of the leagues, but it also served to limit their effectiveness. As each crisis came, in the years from 1898 to 1900, there were differences of opinion and desertions, which periodically threatened to wreck the movement, and finally did bring about its collapse. These dissensions are clearly revealed in the first great fight waged by the anti-imperialists, their struggle against ratification of the treaty of peace with Spain.

The treaty, signed on December 10, 1898, contained the very feature the opponents of expansion most dreaded and opposed—the cession of the Philippine Islands to the United States. With this stipulation, it presented a direct challenge to the anti-imperialists, a challenge that was not long ignored. Andrew Carnegie, who had become almost fanatical on the subject of territorial expansion, repaired to Washington to use his influence against the treaty,[32] and the newly-founded Anti-Imperialist League, having established a lobby in the national capital, circulated petitions and brought what pressure it could to bear on the leading Senators.[33]

Despite this show of activity, the anti-imperialists were by no means united in opposition to the treaty. A few, typified by Senator George Gray, the only anti-expansionist on the peace commission, completely deserted the movement on the issue, and took no further part in anti-imperialist activities.[34] A larger group, while not yielding opposition to expansion, differed as to the wisdom of opposing ratification. Speaker Reed, who had used all his influence in attempting to prevent the annexation of Hawaii, criticized but made no move to fight the peace treaty,[35] and such enthusiastic anti-imperialists as William Jennings Bryan and Senator George L. Wellington felt justified in declaring for ratification.[36]

In view of Bryan's great importance in the anti-imperialist movement, his stand is worth some consideration. As it has already been noted, the Commoner had been one of the first statesmen to declare against colonial expansion. Being a Colonel of Volunteers, he had not enlarged on the sentiments of his Omaha speech in the following six months, nor had he become affiliated with the Anti-Imperialist League. On December 13, 1898, however, the day after receiving his discharge from the army, he redefined his position in an interview given at Savannah, Georgia. He was still vigorously opposed to expansion because, as he said, "this nation cannot endure half republic and half colony—half free and half vassal." At the same time, he favored ratification on the ground that it would be "easier . . . to end the war at once by ratifying the treaty and then deal with the subject in our own way." "The issue," he pointed out, "can be presented directly by a resolution of Congress declaring the policy of the nation upon this subject."[37]

Bryan's statement took the anti-imperialists by surprise, and most of them put the worst possible interpretation on the Democratic leader's words. A careful examination of Bryan's statements and his correspondence leads one to conclude that the Nebraskan was sincere in his desire for peace, and that he really wanted to see the issue of imperialism disposed of (by a congressional pledge for Philippine independence) in 1899, so that, as he wrote Carnegie on December 24, 1898, "the fight against trusts and for free silver may be continued."[38] The fact remains,

---

[30] Robert Fulton Cutting and George Foster Peabody.

[31] Erving Winslow, "The Anti-Imperialist League," in *The Independent* (New York, 1848–1928), LI (1899), 1348.

[32] *Autobiography of Andrew Carnegie* (Boston, 1906), 364. For Carnegie's state of mind see William R. Thayer, *John Hay* (Boston, 1915), II, 199.

[33] Winslow, "Anti-Imperialist League," *loc. cit.,* LI (1899), 1348.

[34] George F. Hoar, *Autobiography of Seventy Years* (New York, 1903), II, 313–15.

[35] William A. Robinson, *Thomas B. Reed, Parliamentarian* (New York, 1930), 369–71; Lodge, *Roosevelt-Lodge Correspondence,* I, 370.

[36] Wellington lived to regret supporting the treaty. See *Cong. Record,* 57 Cong., 1 Sess., 2022.

[37] *Bryan on Imperialism,* 5–6.

[38] Curti, "Bryan and World Peace," *loc. cit.,* 128. See also Bryan's Washington, New York, and Lincoln, Nebraska interviews, quoted in *ibid.,* 126–27. For evidence that Bryan hoped for political gain, see letter of Clark Howell to Atlanta Constitution, December 20, 1898, *ibid.,* 124–25. For statement of Pettigrew see Richard F. Pettigrew, *Imperial Washington* (Chicago, 1922), 270–71. The *Constitution* was enthusiastically expansionist, and Pettigrew's account (written two decades later) is not altogether trustworthy.

however, that Schurz, Hoar, Carnegie, Pettigrew, and other anti-imperialists saw the Savannah declaration in quite another light. They believed and charged that Bryan was acting in bad faith, sacrificing principle for political advantage in his desire for an issue for the 1900 campaign.[39] Bryan's attempt to persuade his friends in the Senate to support the treaty[40] increased the distrust of the Democratic leader, and caused several to turn against him as a potential leader of the anti-imperialist movement.[41]

It is not necessary here to trace in detail the unsuccessful fight against ratification. For two full months, Hoar, Hale, Gorman, Bacon, Pettigrew, and others ably maintained the anti-imperialist position on the Senate floor. Developing unexpected strength in January, 1899, they seemed close to victory in spite of Bryan's stand,[42] and the supporters of the treaty finally carried the day by a margin of just two votes.[43] The Bacon resolution, carrying a pledge of Philippine independence, was defeated by the casting vote of Vice-President Hobart.[44]

The story of the anti-imperialist movement during 1899 and most of 1900 is a story of incessant activity on the part of the leaders of the movement, a story of conferences and public meetings, of an endless succession of pamphlets, magazine articles, poems, and speeches directed against colonial expansion, and of the improvement of organization through the anti-imperialist leagues. Despite the ratification of the peace treaty, the movement continued to grow. The leaders carried the fight to the country, and met with a favorable response. By May, 1899, the original Anti-Imperialist League had over thirty thousand members,[45] and it was claimed in the first annual report that "over half a million contributors" had assisted the organization in its activities.[46]

There were anti-imperialist leagues in a dozen cities before the end of 1899—Boston, Springfield, Massachusetts, New York, Philadelphia, Balti-

more, Washington, Cincinnati, Cleveland, Detroit, St. Louis, Los Angeles, and Portland, Oregon.[47] These bodies went by various names, but were strikingly similar in set-up and purposes. In October, 1899, at an anti-imperialist conference attended by delegates from thirty states, the local organizations formed a central association, the American Anti-Imperialist League, with headquarters in Chicago.[48] The national league supplemented rather than supplanted the local bodies. The latter, and the Boston league in particular,[49] continued to issue and distribute pamphlets, organize meetings, and crystallize anti-imperialist sentiment in the same manner as before.

With the outbreak of the Philippine insurrection, in February, 1899, events in the islands came to play a much greater part in the productions of the anti-imperialists. Until this time the opponents of expansion had been inclined to deride rather than praise the Filipinos. Gompers had referred to them as a "semibarbaric population, almost primitive in their habits and customs."[50] Thomas B. Reed had spoken disparagingly of "yellow-bellies" and "naked Sulus,"[51] and other anti-imperialists, believing the Filipinos unfit for self-government, had urged that the archipelago be disposed of to a European power.[52] The insurrection, however, together with the gradually unfolded story of the relationship that had existed between Aguinaldo and certain United States officials, led virtually the entire anti-expansion group to advocate independence for the islands, and to support the cause of the insurgents against the McKinley administration.[53]

Particularly useful to the anti-imperialists were the reports of outrages committed by American troops during the insurrection—instances of the burning of crops and villages, disregard of the rules of civilized warfare, of the "water cure," and orders to "take no prisoners." Ironically

[39] Ibid.; Autobiography of Andrew Carnegie, 364–65; Hoar, Autobiography, II, 322–23; Curti, "Bryan and World Peace," loc.cit., 123–30.

[40] Bryan changed few if any votes, but it is probable that he could have prevented ratification had he chosen to do so. Ibid., 121–22.

[41] Autobiography of Carnegie, 364–65; Hoar, Autobiography, 322–23.

[42] Bancroft, Schurz Papers, VI, 37; Lodge, Roosevelt-Lodge Correspondence, I, 385, 387.

[43] February 6, 1899, 57 to 27. Senate Journal, 55 Cong., 3 Sess., 216.

[44] February 14, 1899, 29 to 29. Cong. Record, 55 Cong., 3 Sess., 1845–46.

[45] Winslow, "Anti-Imperialist League," loc.cit., LI (1899), 1350.

[46] Lanzar, "Anti-Imperialist League," loc.cit., III (1930), 21.

[47] Ibid., 21–22; The Anti-Imperialist (Brookline, Mass., 1899–1900), No. 4 (August 20, 1899), 30.

[48] Lanzar, "Anti-Imperialist League," loc.cit., 24–30; Bancroft, Schurz Papers, VI, 121.

[49] The Boston organization changed its name from the Anti-Imperialist League to the New England Anti-Imperialist League when the Chicago organization was formed. It resumed the original title on November 8, 1904.

[50] New York Evening Post, August 20, 1898.

[51] Robinson, Reed, 369, 370.

[52] E.g., Nevins, Cleveland, 746; Bancroft, Schurz Papers, V, 472–73.

[53] Anti-Imperialist Address of March 13, 1899. The Philippine atrocities brought forth the best poetry of the anti-imperialist movement, such as William Vaughn Moody's great "Ode in Time of Hesitation" and his "On a Soldier Fallen in the Philippines." For other anti-imperialist verse see Liberty Poems (Boston, 1900).

enough, these were the sort of stories that had aroused the American nation against the Spaniards in Cuba. The anti-imperialists were quick to note this, and claimed that it furnished a concrete example of the inevitable consequences of denying a people the fundamental right of self-government.

The Philippine situation led to the most sensational episode in the history of the movement, the seizure of the Atkinson pamphlets. The incident occurred because of an excess of zeal on the part of one of the first and most enthusiastic opponents of Philippine annexation—Edward Atkinson of Boston and Brookline, a retired textile manufacturer in his seventies.

Long the ardent champion of a score of reforms, Atkinson began writing, publishing, and distributing violent anti-imperialist pamphlets in the fall of 1898. This, of course, was no more than was being done by a dozen other enthusiasts in the movement. In the spring of 1899, however, he wrote to the secretary of war, enclosing his three principal pamphlets, and declaring his intention of sending them to American soldiers in the Philippines. Receiving no reply, he sent copies, as a test, to eight prominent men (most of them United States officials) in the islands.

The government acted at once. On May 2, 1899, Postmaster-General Charles Emory Smith ordered the San Francisco postmaster to remove all Atkinson pamphlets from the Manila mails. A number of the offending documents were intercepted the following day.[54]

This action aroused great interest throughout the United States. The anti-imperialists rushed to Atkinson's defense, the Springfield *Republican* finding in the seizure "the mailed hand of the rule of blood and iron being gradually disclosed . . . which," it added, "will next fall heavily upon freedom of speech within the old borders of the United States."[55] The postmaster-general defended his order in sharp words, and was supported by most of the imperialist press.[56]

On the whole, the administration suffered, and the anti-imperialists profited as a result of Smith's order. Atkinson, comparatively unknown before, achieved a degree of notoriety which showed itself in an increased demand for his pamphlets.[57] What was more, the opponents of expansion had another talking point, which they proceeded to

make the most of, in speeches, pamphlets, and through the press.[58]

The question of the election of 1900 confronted the anti-imperialists from the start. There was obviously no hope of achieving success through the Republican party, so the question was narrowed down to two alternatives—the support of Bryan or the nomination of a third ticket.

Bryan's views on expansion were generally satisfactory to the anti-imperialists, and his preëminent position in the Democratic party seemed to point to the advisability of endorsing him as the anti-imperialist candidate. There were, however, two objections to this course of action. The majority of the leaders of the anti-imperialist movement were strong gold men, and Bryan clung tenaciously to free silver. In addition, many anti-imperialists were suspicious of the Nebraskan because of his stand on the ratification question.

The result was an attempt—or rather, several attempts—to form a third party, designed to split the McKinley vote as Palmer had split Bryan's in 1896. Perhaps the most serious of these attempts was that made on January 6, 1900, at a conference held in New York. Carnegie, Schurz, Bradford, Pettigrew, Edwin Burritt Smith, John B. Henderson, Franklin Henry Giddings, and Brisbane Walker were among the dozen and a half participants. According to Pettigrew, the only person to leave a written account of the meeting, a temporary organization was effected, and plans proceeded until, in February, Carnegie withdrew his financial support and the whole movement collapsed.[59]

Meanwhile, Bryan sentiment was increasing among the opponents of expansion. By 1900 the Springfield *Republican* and other anti-expansion papers that had opposed Bryan in 1896 were displaying "a growing toleration of Mr. Bryan's aspirations."[60] Many anti-imperialists who disliked the Democratic leader intensely agreed with William James, who wrote from France that "the Republican party is fattened to kill," and that it would be best to defer plans for independent action until 1904.[61] Part of this feeling was spontaneous; part was due to the untiring activities of Erving Winslow, secretary of the New England Anti-Imperialist League, a regular Republican who had determined to secure an anti-imperialist endorsement of the Nebraskan's candidacy.[62]

As 1900 wore on, it became apparent that the

[54] *Literary Digest*, XVIII (1899), 541–42, 708–709. Orders were issued "saying that their transmission through the domestic mails had also been forbidden" but this restriction apparently was lifted immediately. The three documents concerned were circulated as Senate documents as well as by Atkinson, for they had been read into the *Congressional Record*.

[55] Quoted in *Literary Digest*, XVIII (1899), 541. The Boston league did not approve of Atkinson's course.

[56] *Ibid.*, 542.

[57] *Anti-Imperialist*, No. 6 (October 1, 1900), 2.

[58] See *e.g.*, James J. Dooling, *Rhymes without Treason* (Lexington, Massachusetts, 1899), 2; Henry B. Fuller, *The New Flag* (Chicago, 1899), *passim*.

[59] Pettigrew, *Imperial Washington*, 272–73, 321–25.

[60] Henry James, *Richard Olney and his Public Service* (Boston, 1923), 309.

[61] James to Schurz, March 16, 1900, Bancroft, *Schurz Papers*, VI, 190.

[62] *Ibid.*, 191–92.

Bryan group would prevail. The Commoner was nominated by the Democrats in June, on a platform that contained a thoroughly satisfactory anti-imperialist plank dictated by Bryan himself.[63] Some anti-imperialists looked with misgivings at the free silver plank, but many of these were placated when Bryan, at the suggestion of Erving Winslow,[64] devoted his entire acceptance speech to a ringing denunciation of colonial expansion.[65]

The Liberty Congress, a convention called by the American Anti-Imperialist League to define the position of the opponents of expansion, assembled in Indianapolis on August 15 and 16, 1900. The third party group, now a mere handful, had met on the 14th in the same city, only to find organization impossible because of numerical weakness and the lack of available candidates.[66] The Liberty Congress, therefore, had only to decide whether or not it would endorse Bryan by name. This question the committee on resolutions answered in the affirmative, and the convention, adopting the report by an overwhelming majority, declared for "the direct support of Mr. Bryan as the most effective means of crushing imperialism." [67]

The declaration of the Liberty Congress clarified the position of the anti-imperialists in the campaign. On the other hand, it did not mean that all opponents of expansion gave their support to Bryan. Many old Republicans and Gold Democrats, like Hoar and Carnegie and Abram S. Hewitt, declared for McKinley, and others, including Cleveland, Reed, and Charles Francis Adams, withheld support from both candidates. This opposition, moreover, was scarcely less harmful to Bryan's cause than was much of the support accorded him. Schurz and many of the Gold Democrats issued qualified endorsements, and plainly gave the voters to understand that they were choosing the lesser of two great evils in supporting Bryan.[68]

From the standpoint of the anti-imperialists who supported the Democratic ticket, the outcome of the election was very disappointing. Bryan fell behind his 1896 showing in every respect—in the electoral college total, in popular votes, in percentage of the vote cast. Furthermore, there was little evidence of anti-imperialist strength in the returns. Bryan's New England gains may have been due in part to the Commoner's opposition to expansion—and this was almost certainly the case in Massachusetts, where the Democrats polled 37.9% of the vote as against 26.3% in 1896—but there is no reason for believing that the anti-imperialists had much influence at the polls in other states, or that their activities affected Bryan's electoral total in the slightest degree.

Bryan's defeat in 1900 marks the end of anti-imperialism as an important factor in American politics. The opponents of expansion were reluctant to admit this at first,[69] and made strenuous efforts to revive interest in the cause.[70] These efforts met with no response, and it gradually became apparent to the most sanguine of the anti-imperialists that the movement was politically dead.[71]

As time went on, the leagues began to break up. This process, once started, proceeded rapidly, and 1905 saw the original Anti-Imperialist League as the only active survivor of the dozen organizations of five years before. Led by a little group of Bostonians, this league resolutely clung to its long dead issue for more than two decades. In the face of public apathy, it continued to distribute pamphlets, organize public meetings, and urge congressmen to vote for the independence of the Philippines. Although hampered by the lack of funds, the league plunged into the work of exposing army atrocities in the Philippines, employing H. Parker Willis as a publicity agent and presenting a great mass of material to the Senate Investigating Committee in 1903–1905.[72] In many of its activities it had a valuable ally in William Jennings Bryan, who continued to fight for the cause in the Commoner, on the lecture platform, and in party councils. Bryan rendered particularly

---

[63] Bryan to William J. Stone, June 30, 1900, Curti, "Bryan and World Peace," loc.cit., 132.

[64] Ibid. August 8, 1900, at Indianapolis.

[65] Speeches of William Jennings Bryan (New York, 1909), II, 17–49. Bryan had spoken against expansion on several other occasions in 1898, 1899, and 1900. See Bryan on Imperialism.

[66] New York Evening Post, August 14, 1900; New York Times, August 14, 15, 1900; Howe, Storey, 200. A third party convention was held in New York on September 5, 1900, but the nominees refused to run, and the whole project fell through. New York Evening Post, September 5, 1900.

[67] New York Times, August 17, 1900; George S. Boutwell, Bryan or Imperialism? (Boston, 1900).

[68] J. Sterling Morton typified this attitude, when he wrote Cleveland, November 2, 1900, "It is a choice between evils, and I am going to shut my eyes, hold my nose, vote, go home, and disinfect myself." Nevins, Cleveland, 746.

[69] See Allan Nevins, The Evening Post, A Century of Journalism (New York, 1922), 568–69, for an amusing illustration of this point.

[70] Lanzar-Carpio, "Anti-Imperialist League," loc.cit., III (1930), 118–32; also Benjamin Harrison, Views of an Ex-President (Indianapolis. 1901), 185–270; Mark Twain, "To The Person Sitting in Darkness," in North American Review (New York, 1815–), CLXXII (1901), 161–76.

[71] Charles R. Codman, in speech of March 30, 1901, Free America, Free Cuba, Free Philippines (Boston, 1901), 2–3.

[72] Lanzar-Carpio, "Anti-Imperialist League," loc.cit., IV (1932), 182–98, 239–44; V (1933), 268–71. Contributions fell from $6.574 in 1900 to $2,802 in 1901. The League managed to collect about $10,000 to spend on the exposures.

valuable service in securing anti-imperialist planks in the Democratic platforms year after year.[73] It was these planks that caused the league to declare for the Democratic nominees in every presidential campaign from 1904 to 1920.[74]

The league's last great fight was for the Jones bill, with the Clark amendment, during Wilson's administration. As the contest wore on, however, the weakness of the organization became all too apparent. Wilson paid little or no attention to the league's recommendations, and the fight for the bill rested with administration congressmen and the Filipinos rather than with the men who had fought for island independence for nearly twenty years.[75] After the passage of the bill, contributions, long on the decline, fell off to the vanishing point. The league held its last official meeting on November 27, 1920.[76] With the death of the league president, Moorfield Storey, in 1929, the last vestige of organization disappeared, the league passing into history with is objects still unrealized.[77]

The tangible results achieved by the anti-imperialists were few indeed. They may have had some slight influence on the American administration in the islands,[78] by drawing attention to conditions in the Philippines, and, in the course of their long-continued battle for Philippine independence, they may have helped secure the enactment of the Jones Act of 1916. The movement also acted as the agency for restoring many Gold Democrats of party ranks, and for depriving certain Republicans of their influence in the party.

---

[73] Curti, "Bryan and World Peace," loc.cit., 134.

[74] Lanzar-Carpio, "Anti-Imperialist League," loc.cit., III (1930), 126, V (1933), 226, 230, 254, 260.

[75] Ibid., V (1933), 250–61. Storey had a share in the drafting of the Jones bill.

[76] Ibid., V (1933), 261, 270–71.

[77] Activities practically ceased in 1923, with the death of Erving Winslow, the indefatigable secretary of the organization. "As for the Anti-Imperialist League," Storey wrote at that time, "with the death of Mr. Winslow it has ceased practically to function. Almost everybody who belonged to it is dead, and the young men do not take up the work. I am still its representative, but I have no followers." Howe, Storey, 250.

[78] Erving Winslow, The Anti-Imperialist League: Apologia Pro Vita Sua (1908), 5, referring to a statement made in private by William Howard Taft.

But that is all. Beyond these incidental results, the movement seems to have left no perceptible trace in American history. The leaders never gained control of governmental machinery. They did not impress their message on more than a small fraction of the people, and when the Philippine independence bills were finally passed, more than three decades after the second defeat of Bryan, the passage was brought about by a combination of forces very different from those represented in the anti-imperialist movement of 1898–1900.

The reasons for the failure of the anti-imperialist movement are not hard to find. First was the strong position of the imperialists. In the early months of their agitation, the anti-imperialists had to contend with a widespread feeling of nationalism, a feeling engendered by the patriotism and enthusiasm incident to the war with Spain. The people were stirred by the thought of distant possessions, of an empire second to none, a "world power" on whose territories the sun would never set. In time, this feeling gave way to one of indifference, but by then expansion was an accomplished fact.

Second, the anti-imperialists were handicapped by the nature of their case. They were forced to preach abnegation rather than indulgence, to urge the pride of renunciation as against the pride of glory and possession. Their whole case rested on an abstract principle, the application of which was not altogether clear to the public at large. Although they could present a strong emotional argument based on traditions of liberty, the imperialists could more than match this with descriptions of future greatness.

Most tragic of all, however, was the failure to unite in support of a political leader. The majority of the great anti-imperialists—Cleveland and Reed and Hoar are examples—showed no disposition to head a great protest movement. The one available champion of the cause, William Jennings Bryan, was absolutely unacceptable to many anti-imperialists, and was followed by others with extreme reluctance. Men found themselves apologizing rather than fighting for the standard bearer of their cause. And in consequence, what had started as a glorious struggle for freedom ended in bickerings, dissension, and dissatisfaction, a great crusade without crusaders. The anti-imperialists, weakened by desertions and lack of morale, wavered every time they met the enemy, and, in 1900, suffered a rout from which they were never able to recover.

Alfred T. Mahan, a naval officer, was proclaiming by 1890, that the time had come for the United States to break its confining isolationist bonds. The historic requisite for national greatness, Mahan endlessly asserted, was sea power. This was what had made a small nation like England so mighty throughout the world. To obtain sea power, a country must build a strong navy, obtain colonies at strategic points, and be able to control the sea lanes in time of war. In this comparatively early article, Mahan traced many of the considerations that came to figure prominently in the expansionist ideology.

ALFRED T. MAHAN:
THE UNITED STATES LOOKING OUTWARD*

Indications are not wanting of an approaching change in the thoughts and policy of Americans as to their relations with the world outside their own borders. For the past quarter of a century, the predominant idea, which has successfully asserted itself at the polls and shaped the course of the government, has been to preserve the home market for the home industries. The employer and the workman have alike been taught to look at the various economical measures proposed from this point of view, to regard with hostility any step favoring the intrusion of the foreign producer upon their own domain, and rather to demand increasingly rigorous measures of exclusion than to acquiesce in any loosening of the chain that binds the consumer to them. The inevitable consequence has followed, as in all cases when the mind or the eye is exclusively fixed in one direction, that the danger of loss or the prospect of advantage in another quarter has been overlooked; and although the abounding resources of the country have maintained the exports at a high figure, this flattering result has been due more to the super-abundant bounty of Nature than to the demand of other nations for our protected manufactures.

For nearly the lifetime of a generation, therefore, American industries have been thus protected, until the practice has assumed the force of a tradition, and is clothed in the mail of conservatism. In their mutual relations, these industries resemble the activities of a modern ironclad that has heavy armor, but an inferior engine and no guns; mighty for defense, weak for offense. Within, the home market is secured; but outside, beyond the broad seas, there are the markets of the world, that can be entered and controlled only by a vigorous contest, to which the habit of trusting to protection by statute does not conduce.

At bottom, however, the temperament of the American people is essentially alien to such a sluggish attitude. Independently of all bias for or against protection, it is safe to predict that, when

* Reprinted from Alfred T. Mahan, "The United States Looking Outward," *Atlantic Monthly*, LXVI (December, 1890), 816–24.

the opportunities for gain abroad are understood, the course of American enterprise will cleave a channel by which to reach them. Viewed broadly, it is a most welcome as well as significant fact that a prominent and influential advocate of protection, a leader of the party committed to its support, a keen reader of the signs of the times and of the drift of opinion, has identified himself with a line of policy which looks to nothing less than such modifications of the tariff as may expand the commerce of the United States to all quarters of the globe. Men of all parties can unite on the words of Mr. Blaine, as reported in a recent speech: "It is not an ambitious destiny for so great a country as ours to manufacture only what we can consume, or produce only what we can eat." In face of this utterance of so shrewd and able a public man, even the extreme character of the recent tariff legislation seems but a sign of the coming change, and brings to mind that famous Continental System, of which our own is the analogue, to support which Napoleon added legion to legion and enterprise to enterprise, till the fabric of the Empire itself crashed beneath the weight.

The interesting and significant feature of this changing attitude is the turning of the eyes outward, instead of inward only, to seek the welfare of the country. To affirm the importance of distant markets, and the relation to them of our own immense powers of production, implies logically the recognition of the link that joins the products and the markets,—that is, the carrying trade; the three together constituting that chain of maritime power to which Great Britain owes her wealth and greatness. Further, is it too much to say that, as two of these links, the shipping and the markets, are exterior to our own borders, the acknowledgement of them carries with it a view of the relations of the United States to the world radically distinct from the simple idea of self-sufficingness? We shall not follow far this line of thought before there will dawn the realization of America's unique position, facing the older worlds of the East and West, her shores lapped by the oceans which touch the one or the other, but which are common to her alone.

Coincident with these signs of change in our own policy there is a restlessness in the world at large which is deeply significant, if not ominous. It is beside our purpose to dwell upon the internal state of Europe, whence, if disturbances arise, the effect upon us may be but partial and indirect. But the great seaboard powers there do not only stand on guard against their continental rivals; they cherish also aspirations for commercial extension, for colonies, and for influence in distant regions, which may bring, and, even under our present contracted policy, have already brought them into collision with ourselves. The affair of the Samoa Islands, trivial apparently, was nevertheless eminently suggestive of European ambitions. America then roused from sleep as to interests closely concerning her future. At this moment internal troubles are imminent in the Sandwich Islands, where it should be our fixed determination to allow no foreign influence to equal our own. All over the world German commercial and colonial push is coming into collision with other nations: witness the affair of the Caroline Islands with Spain; the partition of New Guinea with England; the yet more recent negotiation between these two powers concerning their share in Africa, viewed with deep distrust and jealousy by France; the Samoa affair; the conflict between German control and American interests in the islands of the western Pacific; and the alleged progress of German influence in Central and South America. It is noteworthy that, while these various contentions are sustained with the aggressive military spirit characteristic of the German Empire, they are credibly said to arise from the national temper more than from the deliberate policy of the government, which in this matter does not lead, but follows, the feeling of the people, a condition much more formidable.

There is no sound reason for believing that the world has passed into a period of assured peace outside the limits of Europe. Unsettled political conditions, such as exist in Hayti, Central America, and many of the Pacific islands, especially the Hawaiian group, when combined with great military or commercial importance, as is the case with most of these positions, involve, now as always, dangerous germs of quarrel, against which it is at least prudent to be prepared. Undoubtedly, the general temper of nations is more averse from war than it was of old. If no less selfish and grasping than our predecessors, we feel more dislike to the discomforts and sufferings attendant upon a breach of peace; but to retain that highly valued repose and the undisturbed enjoyment of the returns of commerce, it is necessary to argue upon somewhat equal terms of strength with an adversary. It is the preparedness of the enemy, and not acquiescence in the existing state of things, that now holds back the armies of Europe.

On the other hand, neither the sanctions of international law nor the justice of a cause can be depended upon for a fair settlement of differences, when they come into conflict with a strong political necessity on the one side opposed to comparative weakness on the other. In our still-pending dispute over the seal-fishing of Bering Sea, whatever may be thought of the strength of our argument, in view of generally admitted principles of international law, it is beyond doubt that our contention is reasonable, just, and in the interest of the world generally. But in the attempt to enforce it we have come into collision not only with national susceptibilities as to the honor of the flag, which we ourselves very strongly share, but also with a state governed by a powerful necessity, and exceedingly strong where we are particularly weak and exposed. Not only has Great Britain a mighty navy and we a long, defenseless seacoast, but it is a great commercial and political advantage to her that her larger colonies, and above all Canada, should feel that the power of the mother country is something which they need, and upon which they can count. The dispute is between the United States and Canada, not the United States and England; but it has been ably used by the latter to promote the solidarity of sympathy between herself and her colony. With the mother country alone an equitable arrangement, conducive to well-understood mutual interests, could readily be reached; but the purely local and peculiarly selfish wishes of Canadian fishermen dictate the policy of Great Britain, because Canada is the most important link uniting her to her colonies and maritime interests in the Pacific. In case of a European war, it is probable that the British navy will not be able to hold open the route through the Mediterranean to the East; but having a strong naval station at Halifax, and another at Esquimalt, on the Pacific, the two connected by the Canadian Pacific Railroad, England possesses an alternate line of communication far less exposed to maritime aggression than the former, or than the third route by the Cape of Good Hope, as well as two bases essential to the service of her commerce, or other naval operations, in the North Atlantic and the Pacific. Whatever arrangement of this question is finally reached, the fruit of Lord Salisbury's attitude can hardly fail to be a strengthening of the sentiments of attachment to, and reliance upon, the mother country, not only in Canada, but in the other great colonies. Such feelings of attachment and mutual dependence supply the living spirit, without which the nascent schemes for Imperial Federation are but dead mechanical contrivances; nor are they without influence upon such generally unsentimental considerations as those of buying and selling, and the course of trade.

This dispute, seemingly paltry, yet really serious, sudden in its appearance, and dependent for its issue upon other considerations than its own merits, may serve to convince us of many latent and yet unforeseen dangers to the peace of the western hemisphere, attendant upon the opening of a canal through the Central American Isthmus. In a general way, it is evident enough that this canal, by modifying the direction of trade routes, will induce a great increase of commercial activity and carrying trade throughout the Caribbean Sea; and that this now comparatively deserted nook of the ocean will, like the Red Sea, become a great thoroughfare of shipping, and attract, as never before in our day, the interest and ambition of maritime nations. Every position in that sea will have enhanced commercial and military value, and the canal itself will become a strategic centre of the most vital importance. Like the Canadian Pacific Railroad, it will be a link between the two oceans; but, unlike it, the use, unless most carefully guarded by treaties, will belong wholly to the belligerent which controls the sea by its naval power. In case of war, the United States will unquestionably command the Canadian Railroad, despite the deterrent force of operations by the hostile navy upon our seaboard; but no less unquestionably will she be impotent, as against any of the great maritime powers, to control the Central American canal. Militarily speaking, the piercing of the Isthmus is nothing but a disaster to the United States, in the present state of her military and naval preparation. It is especially dangerous to the Pacific coast; but the increased exposure of one part of our seaboard reacts unfavorably upon the whole military situation. Despite a certain great original superiority conferred by our geographical nearness and immense resources,—due, in other words, to our natural advantages, and not to our intelligent preparations,—the United States is wofully unready, not only in fact, but in purpose, to assert in the Caribbean and Central America a weight of influence proportioned to the extent of her interests. We have not the navy, and, what is worse, we are not willing to have the navy, that will weigh seriously in any disputes with those nations whose interests will there conflict with our own. We have not, and we are not anxious to provide, the defense of the seaboard which will leave the navy free for its work at sea. We have not, but many other powers have, positions, either within or on the borders of the Caribbean, which not only possess great natural advantages for the control of that sea, but have received and are receiving that artificial strength of fortification and armament which will make them practically inexpugnable. On the contrary, we have not on the Gulf of Mexico even the beginning of a navy yard which could serve as the base of our operations. Let me not be misunderstood. I am not regretting that we have not the means to meet on terms of equality the great navies of the Old World. I recognize, what few at least say, that, despite its great surplus revenue, this country is poor in proportion to its length of seaboard and its exposed points. That which I deplore, and which is a sober, just, and reasonable cause of deep national concern, is that the nation neither has nor cares to have its sea frontier so defended,

and its navy of such power, as shall suffice, with the advantages of our position, to weigh seriously when inevitable discussions arise,—such as we have recently had about Samoa and Bering Sea, and which may at any moment come up about the Caribbean Sea or the canal. Is the United States, for instance, prepared to allow Germany to acquire the Dutch stronghold of Curaçoa, fronting the Atlantic outlet of both the proposed canals of Panama and Nicaragua? Is she prepared to acquiesce in any foreign power purchasing from Hayti a naval station on the Windward Passage, through which pass our steamer routes to the Isthmus? Would she acquiesce in a foreign protectorate over the Sandwich Islands, that great central station of the Pacific, equidistant from San Francisco, Samoa, and the Marquesas, and an important post on our lines of communication with both Australia and China? Or will it be maintained that any one of these questions, supposing it to arise, is so exclusively one-sided, the arguments of policy and right so exclusively with us, that the other party will at once yield his eager wish, and gracefully withdraw? Was it so at Samoa? Is it so as regards Bering Sea? The motto seen on so many ancient cannon, Ultima ratio regum, is not without its message to republics.

It is perfectly reasonable and legitimate, in estimating our needs of military preparation, to take into account the remoteness of the chief naval and military nations from our shores, and the consequent difficulty of maintaining operations at such a distance. It is equally proper, in framing our policy, to consider the jealousies of the European family of states, and their consequent unwillingness to incur the enmity of a people so strong as ourselves; their dread of our revenge in the future, as well as their inability to detach more than a certain part of their forces to our shores without losing much of their own weight in the councils of Europe. In truth, a careful determination of the force that Great Britain or France could probably spare for operations against our coasts, if the latter were suitably defended, without weakening their European position or unduly exposing their colonies and commerce, is the starting-point from which to calculate the strength of our own navy. If the latter be superior to the force that can thus be sent against it, and the coast be so defended as to leave the navy free to strike where it will, we can maintain our rights; not merely the rights which international law concedes, and which the moral sense of nations now supports, but also those equally real rights which, though not conferred by law, depend upon a clear preponderance of interest, upon obviously necessary policy, upon self-preservation, either total or partial. Were we now so situated in respect of military strength, we could secure our perfectly just claim as to the seal fisheries; not by seizing foreign ships on the open sea, but by the evident fact that, our cities being protected from maritime attack, our position and superior population lay open the Canadian Pacific, as well as the frontier of the Dominion, to do with as we please. Diplomats do not flourish such disagreeable truths in each other's faces; they look for a *modus vivendi,* and find it.

While, therefore, the advantages of our own position in the western hemisphere, and the disadvantages under which the operations of a European state would labor, are undeniable and just elements in the calculations of the statesman, it is folly to look upon them as sufficient for our security. Much more needs to be cast into the scale that it may incline in favor of our strength. They are mere defensive factors, and partial at that. Though distant, our shores can be reached; being defenseless, they can detain but a short time a force sent against them. With a probability of three months' peace in Europe, no maritime power would now fear to support its demands by a number of ships with which it would be loath indeed to part for a year.

Yet, were our sea frontier as strong as it now is weak, passive self-defense, whether in trade or war, would be but a poor policy, so long as this world continues to be one of struggle and vicissitude. All around us now is strife; "the struggle of life," "the race of life," are phrases so familiar that we do not feel their significance till we stop to think about them. Everywhere nation is arrayed against nation; our own no less than others. What is our protective system but an organized warfare? In carrying it on, it is true, we have only to use certain procedures which all states now concede to be a legal exercise of the national power, even though injurious to themselves. It is lawful, they say, to do what we will with our own. Are our people, however, so unaggressive that they are likely not to want their own way in matters where their interests turn on points of disputed right, or so little sensitive as to submit quietly to encroachment by others, in quarters where they have long considered their own influence should prevail?

Our self-imposed isolation in the matter of markets, and the decline of our shipping interest in the last thirty years, have coincided singularly with an actual remoteness of this continent from the life of the rest of the world. The writer has before him a map of the North and South Atlantic oceans, showing the direction of the principal trade routes and the proportion of tonnage passing over each; and it is curious to note what deserted regions, comparatively, are the Gulf of Mexico, the Caribbean Sea, and the adjoining countries and islands. A broad band stretches from our northern Atlantic coast to the English Channel; another as broad from the British Islands to the East, through the Mediterranean and Red Sea, overflowing the borders of the latter in order to express the volume of trade. Around either cape—Good Hope and Horn—pass strips of about one fourth this width, joining near the equator, midway between Africa and South America. From the West Indies issues a thread indicating the present commerce of Great Britain with a region which once, in the Napoleonic wars, embraced one fourth of the whole trade of the Empire. The significance is unmistakable: Europe has now little interest in the Caribbean Sea.

When the Isthmus is pierced this isolation will pass away, and with it the indifference of foreign nations. From wheresoever they come and whithersoever they afterward go, all ships that use the canal will pass through the Caribbean. Whatever the effect produced upon the prosperity of the adjacent continent and islands by the thousand wants attendant upon maritime activity, around such a focus of trade will centre large commercial and political interests. To protect and develop its own, each nation will seek points of support and means of influence in a quarter where the United States has always been jealously sensitive to the intrusion of European powers. The precise value of the Monroe doctrine is very loosely understood by most Americans, but the effect of the familiar phrase has been to develop a national sensitiveness, which is a more frequent cause of war than material interests; and over disputes caused by such feelings there will preside none of the calming influence due to the moral authority of international law, with its recognized principles, for the points in dispute will be of policy, of interest, not of conceded right. Already France and England are giving to ports held by them a degree of artificial strength uncalled for by their present importance. They look to the near future. Among the islands and on the mainland there are many positions of great importance, held now by weak or unstable states. Is the United States willing to see them sold to a powerful rival? But what right will she invoke against the transfer? She can allege but one,—that of her reasonable policy supported by her might.

Whether they will or no, Americans must now begin to look outward. The growing production of the country demands it. An increasing volume of public sentiment demands it. The position of the United States, between the two Old Worlds and the two great oceans, makes the same claim, which will soon be strengthened by the creation of the new link joining the Atlantic and Pacific. The tendency will be maintained and increased by the growth of the European colonies in the Pacific, by the advancing civilization of Japan, and by the rapid peopling of our Pacific States with men who have all the aggressive spirit of the advanced line of national progress. Nowhere does a vigorous foreign policy find more favor than among the people west of the Rocky Mountains.

It has been said that, in our present state of unpreparedness, a trans-isthmian canal will be a military disaster to the United States, and especially to the Pacific coast. When the canal is finished the Atlantic seaboard will be neither more nor less exposed than it now is; it will merely share with the country at large the increased danger of foreign complications with inadequate means to meet them. The danger of the Pacific coast will be greater by so much as the way between it and Europe is shortened through a passage which the stronger maritime power can control. The danger lies not merely in the greater facility for dispatching a hostile squadron from Europe, but also in the fact that a more powerful fleet than formerly can be maintained on that coast by a European power, because it can be so much more promptly called home in case of need. The greatest weakness of the Pacific ports, however, if wisely met by our government, will go far to insure our naval superiority there. The two chief centres, San Francisco and Puget Sound, owing to the width and the great depth of the entrances, cannot be effectively protected by torpedoes; and consequently, as fleets can always pass batteries through an unobstructed channel, they cannot obtain perfect security by means of fortifications only. Valuable as such works will be to them, they must be further garrisoned by coast-defense ships, whose part in repelling an enemy will be coördinated with that of the batteries. The sphere of action of such ships should not be permitted to extend far beyond the port to which they are allotted, and of whose defense they form an essential part; but within that sweep they will always be a powerful reinforcement to the sea-going navy, when the strategic conditions of a war cause hostilities to centre around their port. By sacrificing power to go long distances, the coast-defense ships gains proportionate weight of armor and guns; that is, of defensive and offensive strength. It therefore adds an element of unique value to the fleet with which it for a time acts. No foreign states, except Great Britain, have ports so near our Pacific coast as to bring it within the radius of action of their coast-defense ships; and it is very doubtful whether even Great Britain will put such ships at Vancouver Island, the chief value of which will be lost to her when the Canadian Pacific is severed,—a blow always in the power of this country. It is upon our Atlantic seaboard that the mistress of Halifax, of Bermuda, and of Jamaica will now defend Vancouver and the Canadian Pacific. In the present state of our seaboard defense she can do so absolutely. What is all Canada compared with our exposed great cities? Even were the coast fortified, she could still do so, if our navy be no stronger than is as yet designed. What harm can we do Canada proportionate to the injury we should suffer by the interruption of our coasting trade, and by a blockade of Boston, New York, the Delaware, and the Chesapeake? Such a blockade Great Britain certainly could make technically efficient, under the somewhat loose definitions of international law. Neutrals would accept it as such.

The military needs of the Pacific States, as well as their supreme importance to the whole country, are yet a matter of the future, but of a future so near that provision should immediately begin. To weigh their importance, consider what influence in the Pacific would be attributed to a nation comprising only the States of Washington, Oregon, and California, when filled with such men as now people them and are still pouring in, and controlling such maritime centres as San Francisco, Puget Sound, and the Columbia River. Can it be counted less because they are bound by the ties of blood and close political union to the great communities of the East? But such influence, to work without jar and friction, requires underlying military readiness, like the proverbial iron hand under the velvet glove. To provide this, three things are needful: First, protection of the chief harbors by fortifications and coast-defense ships, which gives defensive strength, provides security to the community within, and supplies the bases necessary to all military operations. Secondly, naval force, the arm of offensive power, which alone enables a country to extend its influence outward. Thirdly, it should be an inviolable resolution of our national policy that no European state should henceforth acquire a coaling position within three thousand miles of San Francisco,—a distance which includes the Sandwich and Galapagos islands and the coast of Central America. For fuel is the life of modern naval war; it is the food of the ship; without it the modern monsters of the deep die of inanition. Around it, therefore, cluster some of the most important considerations of naval strategy. In the Caribbean and the Atlantic we are confronted with many a foreign coal depot, and perhaps it is not an unmitigated misfortune that we, like Rome, find Carthage at our gates bidding us stand to our arms; but let us not acquiesce in an addition to our dangers, a further diversion of our strength, by being forestalled in the North Pacific.

In conclusion, while Great Britain is undoubtedly the most formidable of our possible enemies, both by her great navy and the strong positions she holds near our coasts, it must be added that a cordial understanding with that country is one of the first of our external interests. Both nations, doubtless, and properly, seek their own advantage; but both, also, are controlled by a sense of law and justice drawn from the same sources, and deep-rooted in their instincts. Whatever temporary aberration may occur, a return to mutual standards of right will certainly follow. Formal alliance between the two is out of the question, but a cordial recognition of the similarity of character and ideas will give birth to sympathy, which in turn will facilitate a coöperation beneficial to both; for, if sentimentality is weak, sentiment is strong.

An editorial in the *Independent,* typical of the popular expansionist writings in the wake of the Spanish American War, took issue with the charge that proponents of colonies were necessarily jingoistic.

INDEPENDENT:
THE DULL LEXICON OF SENILITY*

If in the lexicon of youth, which fate reserves for a bright manhood, there is no such word as *fail,* it must be a very different lexicon which some timorous souls are opening before the country. Its pages seem to contain no words but "corruption," "bosses," "unfitted," "impossible," "failure." The Springfield *Republican* uses the same dictionary when it says that THE INDEPENDENT and *The Outlook* illustrate the "delirium" of jingoism which has seized the religious press.

Now, just what is the reason for supposing that the United States cannot govern new territories? It is said that a self-governing people are unfitted to exercise paternal functions; but the greatest example of paternal government of colonies in the world is Great Britain, which is self-governing. Of all peoples, those that have learned first to govern themselves can best govern others, as the history of the world shows.

But the corruption of our cities. How can we govern other people till we have first learned to create good government at home? Well, if we wait till we get everything perfect we shall never do anything. And who says our government at home is bad? Is Spain's government of Havana better than ours of New York? Is not Philadelphia or Chicago better governed than Manila? We declare that the misgovernment of New York under Tammany is better than the tyranny of the government of Berlin. A citizen is in better condition in Quay's Pennsylvania than in William II's Germany, freer and less taxed.

If we have to govern Porto Rico and the Philippines by military power, wherein lies the impossibility? Have we not military and naval officers enough, men trained and honest, who can do the task? But why should we govern them entirely ourselves, and not let them govern themselves? Our Territories are self-governed, and we doubt not Porto Rico and Luzon will also be self-governed.

There is no delirium, no jingoism, in the acceptance by our religious people of the responsibilities put upon us by the war. It was noticeable that at the meeting of the American Board at Grand Rapids the universal feeling was one of gratification that the area of freedom was thus spreading. It was not that they wished to hurry in and seize the islands for their missionaries, for they had no missionaries to send and asked for none. But the spirit of philanthropy controlled, not of greed. They thanked God not for themselves but for the Cubans. They were not afraid of the responsibilities; they believed we were better equal to them than are the Spaniards, and that we will give a better government, which is saying very little.

The spirit which animates us is very different from that which paralyzes our timorous croakers. We see a chance to do good to others; they see task and danger for ourselves. We are inspired by the faith and courage of altruism; they are depressed by the fear and despair of self-concern. We believe that Dr. Johnson once said that any dictionary is better than no dictionary; but if we were compelled to give up the lexicon of youth we should rather have no dictionary at all than that over which paralysis stoops to read and repeat and gibber the chill vocabulary of impotence. Pardon the figure, for those who thus shiver may be those who have been full of youthful courage in other days, even once revolutionists of '48 or heroes of Abolition, but who now "starve in ice their soft ethereal warmth." But the great Christian heart of the country keeps warm and full of courage, and accepts responsibility, and prays God to be delivered from evil, but never from opportunity to do good.

---

* Reprinted from *Independent,* L (October 20, 1898), 1137.

Upon his return from the Philippines, where American troops were fighting Filipino insurrectionaries, Albert J. Beveridge spoke on the Senate floor in January, 1900. Defending America's role, he justified expansion in a curious mixture of racist, humanitarian, economic, and military terms.

ALBERT J. BEVERIDGE:
RACIAL EXPANSION*

I address the Senate at this time because Senators and Members of the House on both sides have asked that I give to Congress and the country my observations in the Philippines and the far East, and the conclusions which those observations compel; and because of hurtful resolutions introduced and utterances made in the Senate, every word of which will cost and is costing the lives of American soldiers.

Mr. President, the times call for candor. The Philippines are ours forever, "territory belonging to the United States," as the Constitution calls them. And just beyond the Philippines are China's illimitable markets. We will not retreat from either. We will not repudiate our duty in the archipelago. We will not abandon our opportunity in the Orient. We will not renounce our part in the mission of our race, trustee, under God, of the civilization of the world. And we will move forward to our work, not howling out regrets like slaves whipped to their burdens, but with gratitude for a task worthy of our strength, and thanksgiving to Almighty God that He has marked us as His chosen people, henceforth to lead in the regeneration of the world.

PHILIPPINES COMMAND THE PACIFIC

This island empire is the last land left in all the oceans. If it should prove a mistake to abandon it, the blunder once made would be irretrievable. If it proves a mistake to hold it, the error can be corrected when we will. Every other progressive nation stands ready to relieve us.

But to hold it will be no mistake. Our largest trade henceforth must be with Asia. The Pacific is our ocean. More and more Europe will manufacture the most it needs, secure from its colonies the most it consumes. Where shall we turn for consumers of our surplus? Geography answers the question. China is our natural customer. She is nearer to us than to England, Germany, or Russia, the commercial powers of the present and the future. They have moved nearer to China by securing permanent bases on her borders. The Philippines give us a base at the door of all the East.

Lines of navigation from our ports to the Orient and Australia; from the Isthmian Canal to Asia; from all Oriental ports to Australia, converge at and separate from the Philippines. They are a self-supporting, dividend-paying fleet, permanently anchored at a spot selected by the strategy of Providence, commanding the Pacific. And the Pacific is the ocean of the commerce of the future. Most future wars will be conflicts for commerce. The power that rules the Pacific, therefore, is the power that rules the world. And, with the Philippines, that power is and will forever be the American Republic.

VALUE OF CHINA'S TRADE

China's trade is the mightiest commercial fact in our future. Her foreign commerce was $285,738,300 in 1897, of which we, her neighbor, had less than 9 per cent, of which only a little more than half was merchandise sold to China by us. We ought to have 50 per cent, and we will. And China's foreign commerce is only beginning. Her resources, her possibilities, her wants, all are undeveloped. She has only 340 miles of railway. I have seen trains loaded with natives and all the activities of modern life already appearing along the line. But she needs, and in fifty years will have, 20,000 miles of railway.

Who can estimate her commerce, then? That statesman commits a crime against American trade—against the American grower of cotton and wheat and tobacco, the American manufacturer of machinery and clothing—who fails to put America where she may command that trade. Germany's Chinese trade is increasing like magic. She has established ship lines and secured a tangible foothold on China's very soil. Russia's Chinese trade is growing beyond belief. She is spending the revenues of the Empire to finish her railroad into Pekin itself, and she is in physical possession of the imperial province of Manchuria. Japan's Chinese trade is multiplying in volume and value. She is bending her energy to her merchant marine, and is located along China's very coast; but Manila is nearer China than Yokohama is. The Philippines command the commercial situation of the entire East. Can America best trade with China from San Francisco or New York? From San Francisco, of course. But if San Francisco were closer to China than New York is to Pittsburg, what then? And Manila is nearer Hong-

---

* Reprinted from *Congressional Record*, 56th Cong., 1st sess. (Washington, D.C.: 1900), pp. 704–5, 708–9, 711–12.

kong than Habana is to Washington. And yet American statesmen plan to surrender this commercial throne of the Orient where Providence and our soldiers' lives have placed us. When history comes to write the story of that suggested treason to American supremacy and therefore to the spread of American civilization, let her in mercy write that those who so proposed were merely blind and nothing more.

RESOURCES AND IMMENSE SIZE OF THE ISLANDS

But if they did not command China, India, the Orient, the whole Pacific for purposes of offense, defense, and trade, the Philippines are so valuable in themselves that we should hold them. I have cruised more than 2,000 miles through the archipelago, every moment a surprise at its loveliness and wealth. I have ridden hundreds of miles on the islands, every foot of the way a revelation of vegetable and mineral riches. . . .

THE FILIPINOS ARE CHILDREN, UTTERLY INCAPABLE OF SELF-GOVERNMENT

But, Senators, it would be better to abandon this combined garden and Gibraltar of the Pacific, and count our blood and treasure already spent a profitable loss, than to apply any academic arrangement of self-government to these children. They are not capable of self-government. How could they be? They are not of a self-governing race. They are Orientals, Malays, instructed by Spaniards in the latter's worst estate.

They know nothing of practical government except as they have witnessed the weak, corrupt, cruel, and capricious rule of Spain. What magic will anyone employ to dissolve in their minds and characters those impressions of governors and governed which three centuries of misrule has created? What alchemy will change the oriental quality of their blood and set the self-governing currents of the American pouring through their Malay veins? How shall they, in the twinkling of an eye, be exalted to the heights of self-governing peoples which required a thousand years for us to reach, Anglo-Saxon though we are?

Let men beware how they employ the term "self-government." It is a sacred term. It is the watchword at the door of the inner temple of liberty, for liberty does not always mean self-government. Self-government is a method of liberty—the highest, simplest, best—and it is acquired only after centuries of study and struggle and experiment and instruction and all the elements of the progress of man. Self-government is no base and common thing, to be bestowed on the merely audacious. It is the degree which crowns the graduate of liberty, not the name of liberty's infant class, who have not yet mastered the alphabet of freedom. Savage blood, oriental blood, Malay blood, Spanish example—are these the elements of self-government?

We must act on the situation as it exists, not as we would wish it. I have talked with hundreds of these people, getting their views as to the practical workings of self-government. The great majority simply do not understand any participation in any government whatever. The most enlightened among them declare that self-government will succeed because the employers of labor will compel their employees to vote as their employer wills and that this will insure intelligent voting. I was assured that we could depend upon good men always being in office because the officials who constitute the government will nominate their successors, choose those among the people who will do the voting, and determine how and where elections will be held.

The most ardent advocate of self-government that I met was anxious that I should know that such a government would be tranquil because, as he said, if anyone criticised it, the government would shoot the offender. A few of them have a sort of verbal understanding of the democratic theory, but the above are the examples of the ideas of the practical workings of self-government entertained by the aristocracy, the rich planters and traders, and heavy employers of labor, the men who would run the government.

PEOPLE INDOLENT— NO COMPETITION WITH OUR LABOR

Example for decades will be necessary to instruct them in American ideas and methods of administration. Example, example; always example—this alone will teach them. As a race, their general ability is not excellent. Educators, both men and women, to whom I have talked in Cebu and Luzon, were unanimous in the opinion that in all solid and useful education they are, as a people, dull and stupid. In showy things, like carving and painting or embroidery or music, they have apparent aptitude, but even this is superficial and never thorough. They have facility of speech, too.

The three best educators on the island at different times made to me the same comparison, that the common people in their stupidity are like their caribou bulls. They are not even good agriculturists. Their waste of cane is inexcusable. Their destruction of hemp fiber is childish. They are incurably indolent. They have no continuity or thoroughness of industry. They will quit work without notice and amuse themselves until the money they have earned is spent. They are like children playing at men's work.

No one need fear their competition with our labor. No reward could beguile, no force compel, these children of indolence to leave their trifling lives for the fierce and fervid industry of high-wrought America. The very reverse is the fact. One great problem is the necessary labor to develop these islands—to build the roads, open the mines, clear the wilderness, drain the swamps, dredge the harbors. The natives will not supply it.

A lingering prejudice against the Chinese may prevent us from letting them supply it. Ultimately, when the real truth of the climate and human conditions is known, it is barely possible that our labor will go there. Even now young men with the right moral fiber and a little capital can make fortunes there as planters. . . .

THE WHOLE QUESTION ELEMENTAL

Mr. President, this question is deeper than any question of party politics; deeper than any question of the isolated policy of our country even; deeper even than any question of constitutional power. It is elemental. It is racial. God has not been preparing the English-speaking and Teutonic peoples for a thousand years for nothing but vain and idle self-contemplation and self-admiration. No! He has made us the master organizers of the world to establish system where chaos reigns. He has given us the spirit of progress to overwhelm the forces of reaction throughout the earth. He has made us adepts in government that we may administer government among savage and senile peoples. Were it not for such a force as this the world would relapse into barbarism and night. And of all our race He has marked the American people as His chosen nation to finally lead in the regeneration of the world. This is the divine mission of America, and it holds for us all the profit, all the glory, all the happiness possible to man. We are trustees of the world's progress, guardians of its righteous peace. The judgment of the Master is upon us: "Ye have been faithful over a few things; I will make you ruler over many things."

What shall history say of us? Shall it say that we renounced that holy trust, left the savage to his base condition, the wilderness to the reign of waste, deserted duty, abandoned glory, forget our sordid profit even, because we feared our strength and read the charter of our powers with the doubter's eye and the quibbler's mind? Shall it say that, called by events to captain and command the proudest, ablest, purest race of history in history's noblest work, we declined that great commission? Our fathers would not have had it so. No! They founded no paralytic government, incapable of the simplest acts of administration. They planted no sluggard people, passive while the world's work calls them. They established no reactionary nation. They unfurled no retreating flag.

GOD'S HAND IN ALL

That flag has never paused in its onward march. Who dares halt it now—now, when history's largest events are carrying it forward; now, when we are at last one people, strong enough for any task, great enough for any glory destiny can bestow? How comes it that our first century closes with the process of consolidating the American people into a unit just accomplished, and quick

upon the stroke of that great hour presses upon us our world opportunity, world duty, and world glory, which none but a people welded into an indivisible nation can achieve or perform?

Blind indeed is he who sees not the hand of God in events so vast, so harmonious, so benign. Reactionary indeed is the mind that perceives not that this vital people is the strongest of the saving forces of the world; that our place, therefore, is at the head of the constructing and redeeming nations of the earth; and that to stand aside while events march on is a surrender of our interests, a betrayal of our duty as blind as it is base. Craven indeed is the heart that fears to perform a work so golden and so noble; that dares not win a glory so immortal.

Do you tell me that it will cost us money? When did Americans ever measure duty by financial standards? Do you tell me of the tremendous toil required to overcome the vast difficulties of our task? What mighty work for the world, for humanity, even for ourselves, has ever been done with ease? Even our bread must we eat by the sweat of our faces. Why are we charged with power such as no people ever knew, if we are not to use it in a work such as no people ever wrought? Who will dispute the divine meaning of the fable of the talents?

Do you remind me of the precious blood that must be shed, the lives that must be given, the broken hearts of loved ones for their slain? And this is indeed a heavier price than all combined. And yet as a nation every historic duty we have done, every achievement we have accomplished, has been by the sacrifice of our noblest sons. Every holy memory that glorifies the flag is of those heroes who have died that its onward march might not be stayed. It is the nation's dearest lives yielded for the flag that makes it dear to us; it is the nation's most precious blood poured out for it that makes it precious to us. That flag is woven of heroism and grief, of the bravery of men and women's tears, of righteousness and battle, of sacrifice and anguish, of triumph and of glory. It is these which make our flag a holy thing. Who would tear from that sacred banner the glorious legends of a single battle where it has waved on land or sea? What son of a soldier of the flag whose father fell beneath it on any field would surrender that proud record for the heraldry of a king? In the cause of civilization, in the service of the Republic anywhere on earth, Americans consider wounds the noblest decorations man can win, and count the giving of their lives a glad and precious duty.

Pray God that spirit never fails. Pray God the time may never come when Mammon and the love of ease shall so debase our blood that we will fear to shed it for the flag and its imperial destiny. Pray God the time may never come when American heroism is but a legend like the story of the Cid, American faith in our mission and our might a dream dissolved, and the glory of our mighty race departed.

And that time will never come. We will renew our youth at the fountain of new and glorious deeds. We will exalt our reverence for the flag by carrying it to a noble future as well as by remembering its ineffable past. Its immortality will not pass, because everywhere and always we will acknowledge and discharge the solemn responsibilities our sacred flag, in its deepest meaning, puts upon us. And so, Senators, with reverent hearts, where dwells the fear of God, the American people move forward to the future of their hope and the doing of His work.

Meeting in October, 1899, the American Anti-Imperialist League expressed in its platform the common ground shared by various groups of social reformers and opponents of expansion.

AMERICAN ANTI-IMPERIALIST LEAGUE PLATFORM*

We hold that the policy known as imperialism is hostile to liberty and tends toward militarism, an evil from which it has been our glory to be free. We regret that it has become necessary in the land of Washington and Lincoln to reaffirm that all men, of whatever race or color, are entitled to life, liberty, and the pursuit of happiness. We maintain that governments derive their just powers from the consent of the governed. We insist that the subjugation of any people is "criminal aggression" and open disloyalty to the distinctive principles of our Government.

We earnestly condemn the policy of the present National Administration in the Philippines. It seeks to extinguish the spirit of 1776 in those islands. We deplore the sacrifice of our soldiers and sailors, whose bravery deserves admiration even in an unjust war. We denounce the slaughter of the Filipinos as a needless horror. We protest against the extension of American sovereignty by Spanish methods.

We demand the immediate cessation of the war against liberty, begun by Spain and continued by us. We urge that Congress be promptly convened to announce to the Filipinos our purpose to concede to them the independence for which they have so long fought and which of right is theirs.

The United States have always protested against the doctrine of international law which permits the subjugation of the weak by the strong. A self-governing state cannot accept sovereignty over an unwilling people. The United States cannot act upon the ancient heresy that might makes right.

Imperialists assume that with the destruction of self-government in the Philippines by American hands, all opposition here will cease. This is a grievous error. Much as we abhor the war of "criminal aggression" in the Philippines, greatly as we regret that the blood of the Filipinos is on American hands, we more deeply resent the betrayal of American institutions at home. The real firing line is not in the suburbs of Manila. The foe is of our own household. The attempt of 1861 was to divide the country. That of 1899 is to destroy its fundamental principles and noblest ideals.

Whether the ruthless slaughter of the Filipinos shall end next month or next year is but an incident in a contest that must go on until the Declaration of Independence and the Constitution of the United States are rescued from the hands of their betrayers. Those who dispute about standards of value while the Republic is undermined will be listened to as little as those who would wrangle about the small economies of the household while the house is on fire. The training of a great people for a century, the aspiration for liberty of a vast immigration are forces that will hurl aside those who in the delirium of conquest seek to destroy the character of our institutions.

We deny that the obligation of all citizens to support their Government in times of grave National peril applies to the present situation. If an Administration may with impunity ignore the issues upon which it was chosen, deliberately create a condition of war anywhere on the face of the globe, debauch the civil service for spoils to promote the adventure, organize a truth-suppressing censorship and demand of all citizens a suspension of judgement and their unanimous support while it chooses to continue the fighting, representative government itself is imperiled.

We propose to contribute to the defeat of any person or party that stands for the forcible subjugation of any people. We shall oppose for reëlection all who in the White House or in Congress betray American liberty in pursuit of un-American gains. We still hope that both of our great political parties will support and defend the Declaration of Independence in the closing campaign of the century.

We hold, with Abraham Lincoln, that "no

* Reprinted from Carl Schurz, *Speeches, Correspondence and Political Papers* (New York: G. P. Putnam's Sons, 1913), VI, 77–79 by permission. Copyright, 1913, by G. P. Putnam's Sons.

man is good enough to govern another man without that man's consent. When the white man governs himself, that is self-government, but when he governs himself and also governs another man, that is more than self-government—that is despotism". "Our reliance is in the love of liberty which God has planted in us. Our defense is in the spirit which prizes liberty as the heritage of all men in all lands. Those who deny freedom to others deserve it not for themselves, and under a just God cannot long retain it."

We cordially invite the coöperation of all men and women who remain loyal to the Declaration of Independence and the Constitution of the United States.

Addressing a convocation in 1899 at the University of Chicago, Carl Schurz, a well-known liberal Republican, warned against the danger to American liberty of imperialistic conquests. Schurz concluded that a democracy "cannot long play the king over subject populations, without creating within itself ways of thinking and habits of action most dangerous to its own vitality. . . ."

CARL SCHURZ: AMERICAN IMPERIALISM*

According to the solemn proclamation of our government, the war had been undertaken solely for the liberation of Cuba, as a war of humanity and not of conquest. But our easy victories had put conquest within our reach, and when our arms occupied foreign territory, a loud demand arose that, pledge or no pledge to the contrary, the conquests should be kept, even the Philippines on the other side of the globe, and that as to Cuba herself, independence would only be a provisional formality. Why not? was the cry. Has not the career of the republic almost from its very beginning been one of territorial expansion? Has it not acquired Louisiana, Florida, Texas, the vast countries that came to us through the Mexican War, and Alaska, and has it not digested them well? Were not those acquisitions much larger than those now in contemplation? If the republic could digest the old, why not the new? What is the difference?

Only look with an unclouded eye, and you will soon discover differences enough, warning you to beware. There are five of decisive importance.

1. All the former acquisitions were on this continent, and, excepting Alaska, contiguous to our borders.

2. They were situated, not in the tropical, but in the temperate zone, where democratic institutions thrive, and where our people could migrate in mass.

3. They were but very thinly peopled,—in fact, without any population that would have been in the way of new settlement.

4. They could be organized as territories in the usual manner, with the expectation that they would presently come into the Union as self-governing States, with populations substantially homogeneous to our own.

5. They did not require a material increase of our army or navy, either for their subjection to our rule, or for their defense against any probable foreign attack that might be provoked by their being in our possession.

Acquisitions of that nature we might, since the slavery trouble has been allayed, make indefinitely without in any dangerous degree imperilling our great experiment of democratic institutions on the grandest scale; without putting the peace of the republic in jeopardy, and without depriving us of the inestimable privilege of comparative unarmed security on a compact continent which may, indeed, by an enterprising enemy, be scratched on its edges, but is, with a people like ours, virtually impregnable. Even of our far-away Alaska it can be said that, although at present a possession of doubtful value, it is at least mainly on this continent, and may at some future time, when the inhabitants of the British possessions happily wish to unite with us, be within our uninterrupted boundaries.

Compare now with our old acquisitions as to all these important points those at present in view.

They are not continental, not contiguous to our present domain, but beyond seas, the Philippines many thousand miles distant from our coast. They are all situated in the tropics, where people of the northern races, such as Anglo-Saxons, or, generally speaking, people of Germanic blood, have never migrated in mass to stay; and they are more or less densely populated, parts of them as densely as Massachusetts, their populations consisting almost exclusively of races to whom the

* Reprinted from Carl Schurz, *American Imperialism* (Boston: 1899), pp. 5–10.

tropical climate is congenial,—Spanish creoles mixed with negroes in the West Indies, and Malays, Tagals, Filipinos, Chinese, Japanese, Negritos, and various more or less barbarous tribes in the Philippines.

When the question is asked whether we may hope to adapt those countries and populations to our system of government, the advocates of annexation answer cheerily, that when they belong to us, we shall soon "Americanize" them. This may mean that Americans in sufficiently large numbers will migrate there to determine the character of those populations so as to assimilate them to our own.

This is a delusion of the first magnitude. We shall, indeed, be able, if we go honestly about it, to accomplish several salutary things in those countries. But one thing we cannot do. We cannot strip the tropical climate of those qualities which have at all times deterred men of the northern races, to which we belong, from migrating to such countries in mass, and to make their homes there, as they have migrated and are still migrating to countries in the temperate zone. This is not a mere theory, but a fact of universal experience.

It is true, you will find in tropical regions a sprinkling of persons of Anglo-Saxon or other northern origin,—merchants, railroad builders, speculators, professional men, miners, and mechanics; also here and there an agriculturist. But their number is small, and most of them expect to go home again as soon as their money-making purpose is more or less accomplished.

Thus we observe now that business men with plenty of means are casting their eyes upon our "new possessions" to establish mercantile houses there, or manufactories to be worked with native labor; and moneyed syndicates and "improvement companies" to exploit the resources of those countries; and speculators and promoters to take advantage of what may turn up,—the franchise grabber, as reported, is already there,—many having perfectly legitimate ends in view, others ends not so legitimate, and all expecting to be more or less favored by the power of our government; in short, *the capitalist* is thinking of going there, or to send his agents, his enterprises in most cases to be directed from these more congenial shores. But you will find that laboring men of the northern races, as they have never done so before, will not now go there in mass to do the work of the country, agricultural or industrial, and to found there permanent homes; and this is not merely because the rate of wages in such countries is, owing to native competition, usually low, but because they cannot thrive there under the climatic conditions.

But it is the working-masses, those laboring in agriculture and the industries, that everywhere form the bulk of the population; and they are the true constituency of democratic government. And as the northern races cannot do the work of the tropical zone, they cannot furnish such constitu-

encies. It is an incontestable and very significant fact that the British, the best colonizers in history, have, indeed, established in tropical regions governments, and rather absolute ones, but they have never succeeded in establishing there democratic commonwealths of the Anglo-Saxon type, like those in America or Australia.

The scheme of Americanizing our "new possessions" in that sense is therefore absolutely hopeless. The immutable forces of nature are against it. Whatever we may do for their improvement, the people of the Spanish Antilles will remain in overwhelming numerical predominance, Spanish creoles and negroes, and the people of the Philippines, Filipinos, Malays, Tagals, and so on,—some of them quite clever in their way, but the vast majority utterly alien to us, not only in origin and language, but in habits, traditions, ways of thinking, principles, ambitions,—in short, in most things that are of the greatest importance in human intercourse and especially in political coöperation. And under the influences of their tropical climate they will prove incapable of becoming assimilated to the Anglo-Saxon. They would, therefore, remain in the population of this republic a hopelessly heterogeneous element,—in some respects more hopeless even than the colored people now living among us.

What, then, shall we do with such populations? Shall we, according, not indeed to the letter, but to the evident spirit of our constitution, organize those countries as territories with a view to their eventual admission as States? If they become States on an equal footing with the other States they will not only be permitted to govern themselves as to their home concerns, but they will take part in governing the whole republic, in governing us, by sending Senators and Representatives into our Congress to help make our laws, and by voting for President and Vice-President to give our national government its executive. The prospect of the consequences which would follow the admission of the Spanish creoles and the negroes of West India islands, and of the Malays and Tagals of the Philippines, to participation in the conduct of our government is so alarming that you instinctively pause before taking the step.

But this may be avoided, it is said, by governing the new possessions as mere dependencies, or subject provinces. I will waive the constitutional question and merely point out that this would be a most serious departure from the rule that governed our former acquisitions, which are so frequently quoted as precedents. It is useless to speak of the District of Columbia and Alaska as proof that we have done such things before and can do them again. Every candid mind will at once admit the vast difference between those cases and the *permanent* establishment of substantially arbitrary government, over large territories with many millions of inhabitants, and with a prospect of their being many more of the same kind, if we once launch out on a career of conquest. The question is not merely whether we *can* do such things, but whether, having the public good at heart, we *should* do them.

If we do adopt such a system, then we shall, for the first time since the abolition of slavery, again have two kinds of Americans: Americans of the first class, who enjoy the privilege of taking part in the government in accordance with our old constitutional principles, and Americans of the second class, who are to be ruled in a substantially arbitrary fashion by the Americans of the first class, through congressional legislation and the action of the national executive,—not to speak of individual "masters" arrogating to themselves powers beyond the law.

This will be a difference no better—nay, rather somewhat worse—than that which a century and a quarter ago still existed between Englishmen of the first and Englishmen of the second class, the first represented by King George and the British Parliament, and the second by the American colonists. This difference called forth that great pæan of human liberty, the American Declaration of Independence,—a document which, I regret to say, seems, owing to the intoxication of conquest, to have lost much of its charm among some of our fellow citizens. Its fundamental principle was that "governments derive their just powers from the consent of the governed." We are now told that we have never fully lived up to that principle, and that, therefore, in our new policy we may cast it aside alto-

gether. But I say to you that, if we are true believers in democratic government, it is our duty to move in the direction toward the full realization of that principle, and not in the direction away from it. If you tell me that we cannot govern the people of those new possessions in accordance with that principle, then I answer that this is a good reason why this democracy should not attempt to govern them at all.

If we do, we shall transform the government of the people, for the people, and by the people, for which Abraham Lincoln lived, into a government of one part of the people, the strong, over another part, the weak. Such an abandonment of a fundamental principle as a permanent policy may at first seem to bear only upon more or less distant dependencies, but it can hardly fail in its ultimate effects to disturb the rule of the same principle in the conduct of democratic government at home. And I warn the American people that a democracy cannot so deny its faith as to the vital conditions of its being, it cannot long play the king over subject populations, without creating within itself ways of thinking and habits of action most dangerous to its own vitality,—most dangerous especially to those classes of society which are the least powerful in the assertion, and the most helpless in the defence of their rights. Let the poor and the men who earn their bread by the labor of their hands pause and consider well before they give their assent to a policy so deliberately forgetful of the equality of rights.

Perhaps the most effective weapon used to publicize the anti-imperialist position was the large number of pamphlets distributed throughout the country. Joseph Henry Crooker's *The Menace to America* is representative of these.

JOSEPH HENRY CROOKER: THE MENACE TO AMERICA*

A political doctrine is now preached in our midst that is the most alarming evidence of moral decay that ever appeared in American history. Its baleful significance consists, not simply in its moral hatefulness, but in the fact that its advocates are so numerous and so prominent.

It is this: A powerful nation, representative of civilization, has the right, for the general good of humanity, to buy, conquer, subjugate, control, and govern feeble and backward races and peoples, without reference to their wishes or opinions.

This is preached from pulpits as the gospel of Christ. It is proclaimed in executive documents

as American statesmanship. It is defended in legislative halls as the beginning of a more glorious chapter in human history. It is boastfully declaimed from the platform as the first great act in the regeneration of mankind. It is published in innumerable editorials, red with cries for blood and hot with lust for gold, as the call of God to the American people.

But how came these men to know so clearly the mind of the Almighty? Was the cant of piety ever more infamously used? Was selfishness ever more wantonly arrayed in the vestments of sanctity? Is this the modern chivalry of the strong to the weak? Then let us surrender all our fair ideals and admit that might alone makes right. Is this the duty of great nations to small peoples? Then morality is a fiction. Is this the gospel of Jesus? Then let us repudiate the Golden Rule.

* Reprinted from Joseph Henry Crooker, *The Menace to America* (Chicago: 1900), pp. 3–7, 10–13.

Is this the crowning lesson of America to the world? Then let us renounce our democracy.

A HATEFUL DOCTRINE

This doctrine is the maxim of bigotry, "The end justifies the means," reshaped by the ambition of reckless politicians and enforced by the greed of selfish speculators. It is infinitely worse than the policy of the old ecclesiastics, for they had in view the salvation of others, while the advocates of this seek the subjugation of others. The colonial motive, now stirring among us, is not love for others. The mask is too thin and too black to deceive even a savage Filipino.

A similar motive and policy piled the fagots about every burning martyr. It turned every thumbscrew that tortured heretics. It laid on the lash that drew blood from the back of every suffering slave. This teaching unbars the bottomless pit and lets loose upon the world every demon that ever vexed the human race. It unchains every wild passion that has lingered in man's blood since it flowed upward from the brute. It prepares the path by which the despot will reach his throne of tyranny and it arms him with instruments of oppression.

POLITICAL ATHEISM

It was against this denial of both God and humanity that the Barons hurled themselves at Runnymede. For its overthrow Old Ironsides fought at Naseby and Marston Moor. To banish this theory of human affairs from the new world Washington suffered at Valley Forge and contended at Yorktown. To destroy the last vestige of this hateful policy, Grant conquered at Appomattox. This is not true Americanism, but the contradiction of every principle for which we have contended and in which we have gloried for over a century. This is not the upward way of civilization, but the backward descent to barbarism.

If this be Duty, let us recite no more the Master's creed of love. If this be Destiny, let us proclaim no more the rights of men. If this be Patriotism, let us sing no more "America." We must rewrite the "Star Spangled Banner," and make its theme the praise of conquest and colonization. We must erase the motto, "E Pluribus Unum," and inscribe instead: "One nation in authority over many people." We must tear up the Declaration of Independence and put in its place "A Summary of the Duties of Colonists to Their Master." But this is political atheism.

Something more than the welfare of distant peoples is at stake. We condemn this teaching and policy, not simply to secure justice for the brown man, but to insure justice and freedom for ourselves. The motive of our protest is more than friendship for him: it is devotion to principles of liberty that are the necessary conditions of universal human progress. The feelings of sympathy and justice ought to rule us in these relations. But every advocate of our present national policy outrages these sentiments whenever he makes his defense. His words ring false. And yet, the heart of the matter lies far deeper. The true glory of America is imperiled. The happiness of our descendants is assailed. The mission of America as the representative and guardian of Liberty is in question. The perpetuity of free institutions hangs in the balance.

OUR NATIONAL SHAME

We cannot worship this golden calf and go unscourged. We cannot violate the principles of our government and enjoy the blessings of those principles. We cannot deny freedom across the ocean and maintain it at home. This Nation cannot endure with part of its people citizens and part colonists. The flag will lose all its glory if it floats at once over freemen and subjects. We cannot long rule other men and keep our own liberty. In the high and holy name of humanity, we are trampling upon the rights of men. But Nemesis will wake. The mask will fall; our joy will turn to bitterness; we shall find ourselves in chains.

Most of all, we lament the stain that has come to our flag, not from the soldier carrying it, but from the policy that has compelled him to carry it in an unjust cause. On executive hands falls, not only the blood of the hunted islander, but the blood of the American murdered by the ambition that sent him to invade distant lands. What we most deplore is the surrender that we as a nation have made of our leadership in the world's great work of human emancipation. What we most bitterly mourn is that we, by our selfish dreams of mere commercialism, have piled obstacles mountain high in the way of progress.

What is most surprising and most alarming is the fact that large numbers of our people still call this national ambition for conquest and dominion a form of exalted patriotism. But we are surely under the spell of a malign influence. A false Americanism has captivated our reason and corrupted our conscience. May this hypnotic lethargy, induced by the glittering but deceptive bauble of imperialism, speedily pass away; and may these fellow citizens become again true Americans, free to labor for the liberty of all men and intent on helping the lowly of all lands to independence.

LET US FACE THE FACTS

It is time that all American citizens should look more carefully into the conditions and tendencies which constitute what may well be called, "The Menace to America." Let me discuss briefly certain phases of what rises ominously before us as the Philippine problem. It is a problem of vast importance, and yet it has not been treated as fully as its great magnitude and inherent difficulties deserve. One of the alarming indications of the hour is the popular unwillingness to admit that these new policies present any serious problem. There seems to be no general recognition that anything strange or dangerous is happening. Those who raise a cry of warning are denounced as pessimists; those who enter criticism are branded as traitors. We are told in a jaunty manner to have faith in the American people. This blind trust in "destiny" makes the triumph of the demagogue easy. This indifference to political discussion is the symptom of the paralysis of true patriotism.

INTRUDED VS. NATIVE ANARCHY

The following is one phase of the popular argument in justification of our oriental aggressions: The obligations of humanity demanded that we take possession of the Philippine Islands in order to prevent the anarchy which would certainly have followed had we taken any other course than that which we did.

But would a little native-grown anarchy have been as bad as the slaughter and destruction which we have intruded? Let us remember that we ourselves have already killed and wounded thousands of the inhabitants. We have arrayed tribe against tribe; we have desolated homes and burned villages; agriculture and commerce have been prostrated; and finally, we have created hatred of ourselves in the breasts of millions of people to remain for years to plague us and them. It is not likely that if left to themselves anything half so serious would have occurred. It is perfectly clear that some other attitude towards those Islands besides that of domination, which this Nation most unfortunately took, would have prevented these results.

And we are not yet at the end. Recurring outbreaks against us as intruders, by people desirous of independence, will undoubtedly produce more distress and disorder in the next ten years (if our present policy is maintained) than would have resulted from native incapacity. Moreover, there are no facts in evidence that warrant the assertion that anarchy would have followed had we left them more to themselves. This is wholly an unfounded assumption. It would certainly have been well to have waited and given them a chance before interfering. That we did not wait, that we did not give them a chance, is proof positive that our national policy was not shaped by considerations of humanity or a reasonable desire to benefit them, but by a spirit of selfish aggrandizement. . . .

WHOSE FINANCIAL GAIN?

It is pitiful that our people, and especially the common people, should be so carried away by wild and baseless dreams of the commercial advantage of these Islands. It is bad enough to sacrifice patriotism upon the altar of Mammon; but it is clear that in this case the sacrifice will be made without securing any benefit, even from Mammon.

The annual expense our Nation will incur by the military and naval establishment in the Philippines will be at least $100,000,000. This the taxpayer of America must pay. On the other hand, the trade profits from these Islands—from the very nature of the case—will go directly into the pockets of millionaire monopolists, the few speculators who will get possession of the business interests there, in the line of hemp, sugar, tobacco and lumber.

The proposition is a plain one. These Islands will cost us, the common people, a hundred million dollars a year. The profits from them, possibly an equal sum, will go directly to a few very rich men. This is a very sleek speculative scheme for transferring vast sums of money from the people at large to the bank accounts of a few monopolists. Can any one see anything very helpful to the common taxpayer in such a policy? This is a serious problem for consideration, in addition to the competition of American labor with cheap Asiatic workmen—in itself sufficiently serious.

The question I press is this: Can such a policy work anything but financial harm to the average American citizen? For one, I do not care to pay this tribute money every time I draw a check or buy a bottle of medicine, tribute money that means oppression to those distant islanders, unnecessary burdens to our own people, and a still larger store for speculators to be used in corrupting American politics!

WHAT IS "EXPANSION?"

A passionate demand for expansion has taken possession of the American imagination. It is contended, We must come out of our little corner and take our place on the worldstage of the nations.

But what has been the real expansion of our Nation for over a century? It has been two-fold. (1) The extension of our free institutions westward across the continent to the Pacific coast; (2) the powerful influence of our republican principles throughout the world. Our political ideals have modified the sentiments of great nations; our people have flowed over contiguous territories and planted there the same civic, social, religious and educational institutions that they possessed in their Eastern home. All this has been a normal and natural growth of true Americanism.

The policy that now popularly bears the name "expansion" is something radically different; and it is in no sense the expansion of America. Our people have been sadly deceived by something far worse than an optical illusion—a deceptive phrase has lured them into danger and toward despotism. To buy 10,000,000 distant islanders is the expansion of Jefferson Davis, not the expansion of Abraham Lincoln. To tax far-off colonists without their consent is the expansion of the policy of George III, not the expansion of the patriotism of George Washington. To rule without representation subject peoples is not the expansion of Americanism, but the triumph of imperialism.

The policy advocated is the suppression of American principles, the surrender of our sublime ideals, and the end of our beneficent ministry of liberty among the nations. Just because I want to see America expand I condemn the policy as unpatriotic. Let us not deceive ourselves; the expansion of military rule and sordid commercialism is not the expansion of our real strength or true glory. Let us not mistake the renunciation of American ideals for the expansion of American institutions.

FLAG AND CONSTITUTION

Wherever the flag goes, there the constitution must go. Wherever the flag waves, there the whole of the flag must be present. Wherever the constitution is extended, there the entire constitution must rule. If any one does not wish to accept these consequences, then let the flag be brought back to the spot where it can represent true Americanism, and Americanism in its entirety. What shall our banner be to the Filipino? A symbol of his own liberty or the hated emblem of a foreign oppressor? Shall it float over him in Manila as a mere subject and say to him when he lands in San Francisco that he is an alien? Then that flag will become the object of the world's derision!

If it does not symbolize American institutions in their fulness wherever it floats, then our starry banner becomes false to America and oppressive to those who may fear its authority, but do not share its freedom. Disgrace and harm will not come from taking the flag down, but rather from keeping it where it loses all that our statesmen, prophets and soldiers have put into it. The only way to keep "Old Glory" from becoming a falsehood is to give all under it the liberty that it represents. Nowhere must it remain simply to represent a power to be dreaded, but everywhere it must symbolize rights and privileges shared by all.

HOW THE POISON WORKS

Among the many bad things bound up with this unfortunate business none is worse than the degradation of America, sure to follow in more ways than one, if we persist in the course that we are now following. No stronger or sadder proof of the unwise and harmful character of this policy is needed than the fact that its defenders are led so quickly to part company with sober argument and truthful statement and rush into virulent abuse and deceptive sophistries. Who would have believed two years ago that any sane man would have appealed to Washington in support of a policy so abhorrent to the Father of his Country? What ignoble unveracity in twisting his words into the approval of foreign conquest! Who would have thought it possible that scholars and statesmen would so soon become mere jugglers with words, pretending that our previous territorial expansion furnishes analogy and warrant for a colonial system far across the ocean, entered upon by warfare and maintained by Congress without constitutional safeguards! These facts show how virulent a poison is at work upon the national mind. We have here already a perversion of patriotism and a loss of political sagacity and veracity.

It is bad enough to hear men exclaim: "There is money in it and that is sufficient"—but a national venture that leads men to scoff at the Declaration of Independence, to ridicule the constitution as outgrown, to denounce the wisdom of the fathers as foolishness, and to declare that American glory dates from Manila bay: Is there not something ominous in such talk? If a brief experience in the expansion of America that scoffs at American principles produces such results, is it not time to sound the alarm? If the defense of a policy compels men to take such positions, there is something infinitely dangerous in that policy.

CHAPTER SEVENTEEN

THE PROGRESSIVES

The twentieth century ushered in a new mood. Confronting the discrepancy between its productive potential and the actuality of a maldistribution of wealth, America saw the rise of a new wave of reform. But unlike Populism, the Progressive movement was essentially middle class in character, urban in orientation, and moderate in tone. Moreover, times were relatively more prosperous than in the 1890's, and problems were different. Business consolidation was an accepted fact (by 1910, 1 per cent of the firms produced over 40 per cent of America's manufacturing), and the central problem became: How should government cope with this unified economy?

The discontent of the middle class—its members felt themselves to be sandwiched between big business and city machines—was vented in a literature of exposure, ranging from novels on the urban poor to muckraking articles on business practices. The temper of the period was further reflected in the pragmatic approach to social problems. An air of skepticism rode roughshod over the shibboleths of an earlier age, culminating in the sociological jurisprudence of Holmes, the biting critique of the productive system by Veblen, and the reliance on social planning articulated by several economists.

Man was no longer held to be the passive creature of a deterministic world; instead he could rationally shape the environment to suit his needs. All things were possible. There was a political solution for every social evil. Accordingly, whether in the Progressivism of the farm, in Wisconsin or Iowa, or of the city, in New York or Toledo, a common position emerged: an opposition to corruption in politics, the attempt to regulate business and labor, and the desire to achieve material well-being for the average citizen. This took the form for such demands as initiative and referendum, city manager plans, amelioration of slum conditions, conservation, arbitration, corporation taxes, and railroad regulation.

George E. Mowry, in the first selection, provided a depth-focus into the social composition of the Progressive movement. He found that the average Progressive in California was middle class in background, a professional or self-employed man or journalist, and one who "reacted politically" to steer a middle course between monopoly and socialism. In the second selection, Robert H. Wiebe examined the relations between the national Progressive administrations and big business. Discussing the informal agreement between the President and the House of Morgan, Wiebe observed: "Roosevelt, like the Morgan men, was groping for a new definition of the government's relationship with big business."

GEORGE E. MOWRY:
THE CALIFORNIA PROGRESSIVE AND HIS RATIONALE*

Considering the fact that the origins of early twentieth-century progressivism lay in the agrarian Middle West, California in 1905 did not seem to be the logical place for the projection of the doctrines first associated with the names of William J. Bryan, Robert M. La Follette, George W. Norris, and Albert B. Cummins. For in almost every important particular, the state offered more contrasts to the land of William Allen White than it did similarities. As opposed to the relatively homogenous population of the corn and wheat belt states, there existed in California a veritable welter of first and second generation immigrants.[1] Contrasted with the middle western one-farm, one-family type of staple agriculture, the California countryside was characterized by the tremendous holdings of corporations and cattle and lumber men on the one hand, and by the smaller but intensively cultivated fruit and vegetable plats on the other. Irrigation on the latter was but one factor in producing extremely high cost land as well as a high rate of absentee ownership and an itinerant labor force. By 1905 factories in the fields had already made their appearance south of the Tehachapi and in the San Joaquin and lesser valleys of the state.[2]

By 1910, 60 per cent of California's population was urban, and to make the comparison with the progressive Middle West a little sharper, almost one half of the state's population in the same year lived in the three metropolitan counties of San Francisco, Los Angeles, and Alameda. Moreover, throughout these urban districts organized labor was on the move as it was in few other places in the nation. After the general strike of 1901, San Francisco was often called "the most closed shop city in the country." And while Harrison Gray Otis and the Los Angeles Merchants and Manufacturers Association had managed to preserve an open shop town, organized labor never gave up its fight to break through this antiunion domination. In fact, one of the two basic state-wide conflicts in California from 1905 to 1916 was the continuous and often bloody struggle between organized capital and organized labor.

The second great state-wide clash of interests in California during these years was the one between the Southern Pacific Railroad and the state's farmers, shippers, merchants, and the rate-paying public. Until Hiram Johnson's victory in 1910, the one constant and almost omnipotent factor in California politics was the railroad. So deep were the tentacles of the "Octopus" sunk into the commonwealth that its agents even selected the receiving surgeons of city hospitals to insure favorable medical evidence whenever accidents occurred on the company's property.[3] During the years before 1910, numerous economic and political groups had fought the railroad. But through its own powerful political machine, through extensive nonpartisan corruption, and through careful nurture of the state's widespread gambling, liquor, and vice interests, the Southern Pacific weathered every popular storm. Until 1910 its rule was disputed only in a few local communities and in San Francisco.

In the Paris of the West, as San Francisco proudly styled itself, the Union Labor party ruled from 1901 to 1911. But far from contributing to honest, efficient, and responsible government, the Union Labor machine, under the able but cancerously corrupt Abraham Reuf, turned out to be a partner in pelf with the railroad. Often for a cash consideration Reuf's "pack of hounds" supplied the votes for the continuing control of the Southern Pacific. The only other force in the state, with the exception of the rising progressives, capable of voicing much protest was the Socialist party. At the crest of their power in 1911, the California Socialists elected a mayor of Berkeley and came within an eyelash of winning control of the city of Los Angeles.[4] But for one reason or another the Socialists were never able to summon up the strength to win a major victory, and it remained for the progressives alone to challenge the Southern Pacific machine.

Just what was a California progressive before he took office in 1910 and before power and the exigencies of politics altered his beliefs? What were his springs of action, his personal aspirations, and his concepts of what constituted the good society? The rest of this paper is devoted to an attempt to answer these questions in the hope that it may shed some light on the origins of progressivism, not only in California but in the rest of the nation as well, and perhaps even direct a few faint rays on the class structuring of American politics before 1917.

Fortunately, the men who first organized the California progressive movement were both literate and historically minded. The nine solid collec-

* Reprinted from George E. Mowry, "The California Progressive and His Rationale: A Study in Middle Class Politics," *Mississippi Valley Historical Review*, XXXVI (September, 1949), 239–50 by permission.

[1] *Thirteenth Census of the United States*, 11 vols. and abstracts (Washington, 1913), *Population*, II, 157–58.

[2] California Commission of Immigration and Housing, *Annual Report* (Sacramento, 1916), 325–26. See also California State Tax Commission, *Annual Report* (Sacramento, 1917), 278.

[3] Frederick L. Bird and Francis M. Ryan, *The Recall of Public Officers* (New York, 1930), 23.

[4] See the Los Angeles *Express*, November 1–December 6, 1911, for details of the Socialist campaign in Los Angeles.

tions of personal manuscripts they so considerately left behind them,[5] the diaries, documents, and inumerable published articles afford the historian perhaps an unrivaled opportunity in recent American history to inquire into the origins of a grass roots movement. Moreover, this group was small. Fewer than a hundred men attended the two state-wide progressive conferences[6] in 1907 and 1909 before victory swelled the number of the organization's would-be leaders. Of this number, the author has been able to discover biographical data on forty-seven men, which produces in total a striking picture of similarity in background, economic base, and social attitudes. Compositely, the California progressive was a young man often less than forty years old.[7] A majority of them was born in the Middle West, principally in Indiana, Illinois, Wisconsin, and Iowa. A good minority was native to the state.[8] Almost all carried north European names and many of them, with two notable exceptions, were of old American stock.

The long religious hand of New England rested heavily upon California progressivism as it has on so many American movements. Of the twenty-two progressives indicating a religious affiliation in their biographies, seven were Congregationalists, two were Unitarians, and four were

Christian Scientists.[9] Three of every four had a college education, and three of the group had studied in European universities. Occupationally, the California progressive held a significant niche in the American economic structure. In the sample obtained, there were seventeen attorneys, fourteen journalists, eleven independent businessmen and real estate operators, three doctors, and three bankers. At least one half of the journalists owned their own papers or worked for a family enterprise, and the lawyers, with two exceptions, were not practicing politicians.[10] In the entire group apparently only two had any connection with a large industrial or financial corporation save for the ownership of shares. Obviously this was a group of traditional small independent free enterprisers and professional men.

While not wealthy, the average California progressive was, in the jargon of his day, "well fixed." He was more often than not a Mason, and almost invariably a member of his town's chamber of commerce. Finally, by all available evidence he usually had been, at least until 1900, a conservative Republican, satisfied with William McKinley and his Republican predecessors.[11]

Naturally, some fundamental questions arise about these fortunate sons of the upper middle class. Inheriting a secure place in society, earning a reasonably good living and certainly not radical by temperament, what prompted their political revolt and what did they want? The answer to the first of these questions, of course, is clear. The California progressive reacted politically when he felt himself and his group being hemmed in and his place in society threatened by the monopolistic corporation on one side and organized labor and socialism on the other. Proof for this general conclusion is not hard to find. The earliest manifestation of what later became progressivism in California is apparent in two local movements starting in 1906, one aimed against the Southern Pacific political machine in Los Angeles and the other against the control of the Union Labor party in San Francisco. From that time until victory in 1910, the progressive literature was full of criticism for both politically organized capital and politically organized labor.[12]

---

[5] Perhaps the most significant collection of manuscripts for the study of California progressivism are the Meyer Lissner Papers in the Borel Collection, Stanford University. Less rewarding, but still important, are the papers of John D. Works, John C. Needham, and Rufus L. Green, also in the Borel Collection. A more significant collection of the John D. Works manuscripts is to be found in the Bancroft Library, University of California, Berkeley. There also are the letters of Dr. George C. Pardee, William R. Davis, and a small but important collection of the letters of Lincoln Steffens, most of which were written to Francis J. Heney. Of major importance are the letters of Chester H. Rowell, a portion of which are now deposited in the Bancroft Library at Berkeley, and the William Kent Papers in the Yale University Library, New Haven. The voluminous Franklin Hichborn manuscripts and those of Dr. John Randolph Haynes are preserved in the John Randolph and Dora Haynes Foundation, Los Angeles, California. Edward A. Dickson and Marshall Stimson, both of Los Angeles, have preserved many of their own letters of the period, and both are more than generous in aiding the historian in his quest. The Hiram Johnson manuscripts are not yet open for inspection.

[6] The two meetings of the Lincoln Roosevelt Republican League were held in Oakland.

[7] In 1910 the average age of ten of the most prominent progressives was thirty-eight. These and the following figures were taken from biographical data found in the standard reference works, including Who's Who in California (San Francisco, 1929), in county histories, and in newspapers.

[8] Of the forty-six available places of birth, twenty-four were in the Middle West and seventeen in California.

[9] Five Catholics, three Methodists, and one Lutheran made up the total twenty-two.

[10] The total is more than the original forty-seven because some men listed two occupations. Many of the others, of course, speculated in real estate.

[11] Like William McKinley, many conservative California Republicans had been for free silver until Marcus A. Hanna spoke.

[12] See, for example, the speech of Marshall Stimson which launched the progressive campaign in Los Angeles in the spring of 1906. Preserved in Dr. John R. Haynes, Personal Clippings, John Randolph and Dora Haynes Foundation, Los Angeles.

The adverb "politically" in the last paragraph is important, for the progressive revolt was not alone a matter of economics. It might be pointed out that progressivism arose in an extremely prosperous period in California, and that the men who really organized the movement were not employers of any significance. In addition, far from beggering these lawyers, journalists, and real estate operators, a good case can be made out that the Southern Pacific Railroad actually befriended many of them economically. Moreover, the California progressives never attacked the corporate form of business organization or the labor union as such. And although they believed that the closed shop was "anti-social, dangerous and intrinsically wrong," many of them repeatedly went to the union's defense when industry organized to break the unions and create open shops.[13]

"Modern politics," Henry Adams wrote in his *Education*, "is a struggle not of men but of forces. The men become every year more and more creatures of force massed about central power houses." With the struggle for power between capital and labor penetrating to almost every level of California life in the period, and with the individual more and more ignored, the California progressive was increasingly sensitive to that drift and increasingly determined to stop it ·if possible. This was obvious in the progressive obsession with the nightmare of class consciousness and class rule. "Class government. is always bad government," the progressive Los Angeles *Express* vehemently declared as it exclaimed that "unions had no more right to usurp the management of public affairs than had the public service corporations." [14] Chester Rowell, probably the most intelligent of the California progressives, went on to gloss that statement. "Class prejudice among the business men," he wrote, "excuses bribery and sanctifies lawlessness and disorder among labor. When the spectre of class rule is raised, then all questions of truth, right, and policy disappear, and the contest is no longer over what shall be the government but wholly who shall be it." This class spirit on both sides, the editor of the Fresno *Republican* lamented, "is destroying American liberty." When it became predominant he predicted American institutions would have to be changed. "For upon that evil day reform ends and nothing but revolution is possible." [15]

Clearly what troubled these independent progressives about both organized capital and labor was not alone a matter of economics but included questions of high politics, as well as group prestige, group morality, and group power. Involved

also was the rising threat to an old American way of life which they represented and which they enthusiastically considered good.

The progressives were members of an old group in America. Whether businessmen, successful farmers, professional people, or politicians, they had engaged in extremely individualistic pursuits and had since the decline of the colonial aristocracy supplied most of the nation's intellectual, moral, and political leadership. Still confident that they possessed most of society's virtues, the California progressives were acutely aware in 1905 that many of society's rewards and badges of merit were going elsewhere. Although finely educated, they were all but excluded from politics unless they accepted either corporate or labor domination, a thing they were exceedingly loath to do. Their church, their personal morality, and their concept of law, they felt, were demeaned by the crude power struggle between capital and labor. Before the days of the Rotarians and kindred organizations they were excluded from, or did not care to participate in, either the Union League Club or the union labor hall.

On the defensive for the first time since the disappearance of the old aristocracy, this class of supreme individualists rationally enough developed a group consciousness themselves. Although generally overlooked by the historian, this consciousness had already evolved among some farming elements in the Populist period. Nothing else can be concluded from the words of the official organ of the Michigan State Farmers' Alliance. "It has been truly said," remarked that paper, "that the People's Party is the logical and only nucleus for every element of the American population that stands for social stability and constitutional rights. It is the bulwark against anarchy of the upper and lower scum of society." [16] Now in the twentieth century, flanked by organized labor on the one side and organized capital on the other, the urban California progressives took up that song. Their letters, journals, and speeches are full of the phrases, "Our crowd," "the better element," and "the good people of the state." Even their political enemies recognized their separateness as indicated by the names they conferred upon them. The phrases "Goo-goo" and "Our Set" dripped with ridicule. But they also indicated an awareness of the progressives' claim to ethical and political superiority. Finally, no clearer expression of the progressives' self-confidence in their own moral elevation and their contempt for the classes above and below them can be found than that in an editorial of their statewide organ, the *California Weekly*. "Nearly all the problems which vex society," this illuminat-

[13] Fresno *Morning Republican*, August 23, 1911; San Francisco *Labor Clarion*, April 25, 1905; Commission on Industrial Relations, *Report, Senate Document* No. 415, 64 Cong., 1 Sess., V, 4868.

[14] Los Angeles *Express*, July 31, 1907.

[15] Fresno *Republican*, March 10, 1907.

[16] Jackson (Mich.) *Industrial News*, March 8, 1894, cited in Seymour Lutzky, "Survey of the Conflict of Labor, Progressive and Radical Newspapers, 1890–1896" (M.A. Thesis, State University of Iowa, 1948), 90.

ing item ran, "have their sources above or below the middle class man. From above come the problems of predatory wealth. . . . From below come the problems of poverty and of pigheaded and of brutish criminality." [17] Despite the fact that it was made up of extremely individualistic elements, this was unmistakably an expression of a social group on the march.

The California progressive, then, was militantly opposed to class control and class consciousness when it emanated from either below or above him. This was his point of opposition. What was his positive creed? In the first place this "rank individualist," as he gladly styled himself, was in most cases an extremely religious man. His mind was freighted with problems of morality, his talk shot full of biblical allusions. He often thought of the political movement he had started as a part of the "Religion Forward Movement." [18] As early as 1903 Arthur J. Pillsbury, who was later to become a leading progressive, praised Theodore Roosevelt for coming nearer "to exemplifying the New England conscience in government than any other president in recent times." [19]

But if the religion of the California progressive was old American in its form, much of its content was a product of his recent past. Gone was the stern God of the Puritan, the abiding sense of tragedy, and the inherent evilness of man. As William Allen White later wrote, the cult of the hour was "to believe in the essential nobility of man and the wisdom of God." [20] With an Emersonian optimism, the California progressive believed that evil perished and good would triumph. Under the influence of Darwinism, the rising social sciences, and a seemingly benign world, the progressive had traded some of his old mystical religion for a new social faith. He was aware that evil still existed, but it was a man-made thing and upon earth. And what man created he could also destroy. For the then present sinful condition of man was the result of his conditioning. As Fremont Older's San Francisco *Bulletin* editorialized, "the basic idea behind this age of liberalism is the simple one that all men, prisoners and free, rich and poor are basically alike in spirit. The difference usually lies in what happens to them." [21] And from that, one could conclude that when all men were given justice most of them would return justice to society. The progressive, then, not only wanted to abolish a supernatural hell; he was intent upon secularizing heaven.

There were, of course, individual variations from these generalizations. Chester Rowell, for one, while agreeing that men should not be treated as free moral agents, protested against considering them as "mere creatures of environment." "If we try to cure the trouble by curing the environment," Rowell argued, "we shall never go far enough, for however much we protect men from temptation there will be some left and men will fall to that. . . . Dealing with society the task is to amend the system. But dealing with the individual man the task is to reiterate forever, 'thou shall not steal' and tolerate no exceptions." [22] But Rowell was more of a child of his age than even he himself realized. Despite his strictures on the sinfulness of man, one found him writing later that William H. Taft's peace treaties made international war impossible because "the moral influence on nations (for peace) would be tantamount to compulsion." [23]

"The way to have a golden age," one progressive novelist wrote, "is to elect it by an Australian ballot." This was an extreme affirmation of democracy, but it followed logically from the progressive belief in the fundamental goodness of the individual. For according to progressive thought, behind every political question was a moral question whose answer "could safely be sought in the moral law." [24] Since all men were moral agents, then public opinion was the final distillate of moral law. "It was a jury that can not be fixed," according to Lincoln Steffens, and indeed to some progressives, "God moving among men." [25] Thus Charles D. Willard objected to Theodore Roosevelt's characterization of democracy as just a means to an end. To Willard democracy was a positive moral force in operation, a good in itself. "It is," he wrote, "a soul satisfying thing." [26]

Back in the 1890's Senator John J. Ingalls of Kansas had remarked that "the purification of politics is an iridescent dream." Dream or not, that was one of the major goals of the California progressive a decade later. There was but one law for him—that of the churchgoing middle class—and he was convinced that it should be applied equally to the home, to government, and occasionally even to business. It was in this spirit that Hiram Johnson admonished his followers to forget how to make men richer and concentrate on how to make them better. [27] This attitude helps

---

[17] *California Weekly* (San Francisco), I (December 18, 1908), 51.

[18] San Francisco *Bulletin*, March 2, 1912.

[19] Oakland *Herald*, August 21, 1903.

[20] Introduction to Fremont Older, *My Own Story* (New York, 1926), 9.

[21] San Francisco *Bulletin*, May 11, 1914.

[22] Chester Rowell to Lincoln Steffens, August 1, 1908, Lincoln Steffens Papers.

[23] Fresno *Republican*, May 18, 1911.

[24] *Ibid.*, May 21, 1909.

[25] Steffens to Francis J. Heney, June 1, 1908, Steffens Papers.

[26] Charles D. Willard to Theodore Roosevelt, [?], 1911, Theodore Roosevelt Manuscripts (Division of Manuscripts, Library of Congress).

[27] San Francisco *Bulletin*, August 12, 1912.

to explain much of the progressive interest in sumptuary legislation. Individualism was a sacred thing as long as it was moral individualism; otherwise it needed to be corrected. Thus the progressive proposals for the abolition of prize fighting, "a form of social debauchery," gambling, slang, "since it is a coverup for profanity," prostitution, and the liquor traffic. And thus their demands for the censorship of literature, the drama, and social dancing.

In protest against these "holier than thou people" among his fellow progressives, Charles J. McClatchey, owner of the Sacramento *Bee,* wrote that he was his "brother's keeper only in so far as I should set him a good example." [28] And though most progressives vehemently denied the full import of this statement when applied to morality, the majority of them was not in complete disagreement with McClatchey's views when they were applied to economics. Good Christian as he was, and on the whole benevolent, the California progressive did not quarrel with the doctrine of wardship provided it was not pushed too far. Thus he stood ready in 1910 to protect obviously handicapped individuals. And he was ready and even eager to eradicate what he called "special privilege," which to his mind was the fundamental factor in limiting opportunity for the man on the bottom to make his way economically upward. A few individuals on the left of the movement, like Congressman William Kent, felt that soon "property rights were going to tumble about the heads of the men who had built themselves pyramids of money in a desert of want and suffering." [29] And Older raised the disturbing question of why men should be paid fortunes who had been lucky enough to be born with brains or in fortunate environments. One might as well go back to the feudal system, Older answered himself, because there was no more personal merit "in having talent than in having a noble lineage." [30] But for the most part, the progressive majority was content with the basic concepts of the economic system under which 1910 American capitalism awarded its profits and pains.

What the progressive did object to in the year of his triumph was not 1910 capitalism as such but rather the ideological, moral, and political manifestations arising from that system. He was confident, at least in 1910, that there was not an inevitable causal relation between them. And he felt confident that he could cure these ills of society through the political method and through preaching and legislating morality.

The California progressive, then, wanted to preserve the fundamental pattern of twentieth-century industrial society at the same time he sought to blot out the rising clash of economic

groups, and for that matter, the groups themselves as conscious economic and political entities. But he sought to do all this, at least before he had actually taken power, without profound economic reform. "The people," Rowell wrote sometime after the sweeping progressive victory in 1910, "elected Governor Johnson to get moral and political reform." The word "economic" was significantly absent from the statement. [31]

From today's dark vantage point, the progressive aim of a capitalist commonwealth,

> Where none were for a class and all were
> for the state.
> Where the rich man helped the poor and
> the poor man loved the great,

may seem incredibly naïve. His stress on individualism in a maturing industrial economy was perhaps basically archaic. His refusal or inability to see the connection between the economic institutions and the rising class consciousness indicated a severe case of social myopia. His hopes to avert class strife by political and moral reform alone were scarcely realistic. And paradoxical in extreme was his antipathy to the class consciousness of organized capital and labor without his being aware of his own intense group loyalties.

When the California progressives confidently took control of the state in 1910, the road ahead was uncertain indeed. What, for example, would happen to the fundamental beliefs of this group if they found their ends could not be achieved without substantial economic reform, or, if in spite of their efforts, labor through one program or another threatened their economic and political estate, or if many of them became economically and psychologically absorbed by the advancing corporate system, or again in a less prosperous age than 1910, if the clash between economic groups for a livelihood created an intense social friction? Would their moral calculus, their spirit of benevolence, their faith in men, and their reverence for democracy still persist? The answers to these questions, of course, lay beyond 1910 and belong to another story, another chapter.

But the composite California progressive in 1910 was perhaps the best his economic and social group produced. He was educated, intelligent, able. A man of unquestioned sincerity and public integrity, he was also benevolently aware of the underprivileged groups around him. Devoted to the extension of political democracy and civil rights, he stood as a worthy representative of that long historical lineage of Americans who had dreamed and worked for a better commonwealth. If such a small group is ever able to amend or to alter a little the drift of society, the California progressive's chances seemed better than an even bet.

---

[28] Charles J. McClatchey to Franklin Hichborn, December 25, 1915, Franklin Hichborn Papers.

[29] San Francisco *Bulletin,* September 8, 1911.

[30] *Ibid.,* April 17, 1909.

---

[31] Fresno *Republican,* August 14, 1911.

ROBERT H. WIEBE:
THE HOUSE OF MORGAN AND THE EXECUTIVE, 1905–1913*

Early in 1902, when Theodore Roosevelt's administration began antitrust proceedings against the Northern Securities Company, John Pierpont Morgan, its organizer, reputedly complained to Roosevelt, "If we have done anything wrong . . . send your man to my man and they can fix it up."[1] Several years later, in the midst of the Panic of 1907, Elbert H. Gary and Henry Clay Frick hurried to Washington to ask Roosevelt's advice. The two men, who represented Morgan interests in the United States Steel Corporation, told Roosevelt about a plan to purchase for United States Steel a controlling interest in the Tennessee Coal and Iron Company. Presenting the proposal as a bit of altruism designed to save a hard-pressed brokerage firm that owned the stock, they requested assurances that the purchase would not bring antitrust prosecution against the Steel Corporation. Roosevelt gave vague blessings, and the House of Morgan completed the transaction.[2]

Such familiar anecdotes are the material used to describe Wall Street-Washington relations during the progressive era. Contemporary reformers popularized these stories as illustrations of big business incorrigibility and unscrupulousness. Historians, denied access to most businessmen's records and primarily concerned with the course of liberal reform, have accepted them as anecdotes.

Back of these stories lay a consistent pattern, unified by Wall Street's view of the federal government. According to an official biographer, Roosevelt, after listening to Morgan's ideas on corporation control, commented, "Mr. Morgan could not help regarding me as a big rival operator, who either intended to ruin all his interests, or else could be induced to come to an agreement to ruin none."[3] That insight held the essence of Wall Street's attitude. The New York magnates included the federal government among the autonomous blocs they found in American society. Generically, the government belonged with the Standard Oil Company and the American Federation of Labor. As a corollary, each bloc enjoyed primary power within its particular sphere, which meant that relations among these units roughly paralleled diplomacy among sovereign states.

Wall Street's leaders, reflecting their own involvement, usually spoke of the government in economic language. To the railroad magnate James J. Hill, the President served as chairman of the board for the "great economic corporation known as the United States of America."[4] Applying Wall Street logic, Hill argued that government regulation equaled federal ownership. The government, through the Interstate Commerce Commission, would have the seat of power on the boards of all railroads and could then determine policy.[5] Business journals, reasoning from similar premises, hoped for a "reconciliation" between the administration and the railroads and, more generally, "a proper 'balance of power' between the government and the corporations."[6]

In this theory the government was intrinsically neither good nor evil. Its worth varied with circumstances. In the wrong hands—Bryan's, for example—the government became, like the labor unions, an enemy. With the right men in office, it operated like a friendly corporation cooperating under a community of interest agreement.

The magnates did not sharpen their ideas with precise definitions. They had a flexible approach rather than a pat theory. Yet their orientation clearly obviated a government that arises from the whole society and in turn promotes the general welfare. Nor would their approach enable the government to act as a dispenser of justice above society's units. Early in the century, in fact, Wall Street's leaders ranked the government among the second-rate powers. When speculating about a battle between Washington and Standard Oil, Wall Street odds lay with John D. Rockefeller.[7]

At no time, however, did the magnates leave the government's disposition to chance. In various ways they cultivated the political influence they

---

* Reprinted from Robert H. Wiebe, "The House of Morgan and the Executive," *American Historical Review*, LXV (October, 1959), 49–60 by permission.

[1] Quoted in Mark Sullivan, *Our Times: The United States 1900–1925* (6 vols., New York, 1927), II (*America Finding Herself*), 414. See also Joseph Bucklin Bishop, *Theodore Roosevelt and His Times* (2 vols., New York, 1920), I, 184.

[2] Frederick Lewis Allen, *The Lords of Creation* (New York, 1935), 139–40; Henry F. Pringle, *Theodore Roosevelt: A Bibliography* (New York, 1931), 441–43. As Roosevelt phrased it, "I felt it no public duty of mine to interpose any objections." Bishop, *Roosevelt*, II, 55. Gary later called this "tacit acquiescence." House Committee on Investigation of United States Steel Corporation (May 27, 1911–Apr. 13, 1912, 62 Cong., 2 sess.), *United States Steel Corporation, Hearings* (53 pts., Washington, D.C., 1911–1912), June 7, 1911, pt. 4, p. 167.

[3] Bishop, *Roosevelt*, I, 185.

[4] Quoted in George Mowry, *The Era of Theodore Roosevelt*, The New American Nation Series, ed. Henry Steele Commager and Richard B. Morris (New York, 1958), 216.

[5] "Address Delivered June 4, 1902," James J. Hill, *Addresses* (n.p., n.d.).

[6] *Railway Age*, XLIII (Mar. 22, 1907), 373; *Wall Street Journal*, Feb. 24, 1904.

[7] New York *Journal of Commerce and Commercial Bulletin*, June 25, 1906.

had inherited from the nineteenth century. Some, like the steel leader Henry Clay Frick, worked intimately with local party leaders.[8] George W. Perkins, a Morgan partner, preferred the free play of Washington, where in 1908 he lobbied simultaneously for corporation, financial, and tariff legislation.[9] Political involvement sometimes bred contempt ("I suppose," sighed J. P. Morgan, Jr., "that when one deals with politicians one must expect to be lied to."[10]), and other Wall Street men joined Frank A. Vanderlip, vice-president of the National City Bank, who sat in his office and read reports from his two Washington agents.[11] Only the elder Morgan could call Senator Nelson W. Aldrich into his office and present him with a currency bill or have Aldrich telegraph political news while he vacationed on his yacht.[12] All of them toughened the fiber of their political connections by distributing the funds that made effective campaigning possible.

With the magnates' nineteenth-century inheritance came an emphasis upon Congressional connections. Congress made the government's economic policy in the days of Benjamin Harrison and William McKinley, and at the turn of the century the Republican Big Four—Nelson W. Aldrich, Orville H. Platt, John C. Spooner, and William B. Allison—still held sway with Mark Hanna in the Senate. Then Roosevelt tipped the balance. He sprang the Northern Securities prosecution, intervened in the anthracite coal strike, and forced the Department of Commerce and Labor bill through a reluctant Congress. Both his methods and his acts transformed the executive into a formidable power. Wall Street, in order to maintain its influence, either had to remove the rambunctious Roosevelt as soon as possible, or it had to establish strong bonds with the executive. By 1904, the first alternative—if many Wall Street men ever seriously entertained it—had vanished. Roosevelt, financed by Wall Street contributions, was triumphantly returned to office with the largest percentage of the popular vote since Monroe.[13]

On January 28, 1905, Secretary of Commerce and Labor Victor Metcalf ordered Commissioner

of Corporations James R. Garfield to investigate United States Steel.[14] After some months' delay, Garfield sent a subordinate to the offices of Elbert Gary, chairman of the corporation's board, to discuss the matter. Gary used this opportunity to open negotiations for a general understanding with the executive. Through Garfield, always cordial to Morgan's men, Gary arranged a personal conference with Roosevelt.[15]

On the evening of November 2, 1905, Gary and an assistant met with Roosevelt, Metcalf, and Garfield at the White House. Gary stated "that [United States Steel] does not raise the question of the constitutionality of the law [empowering the Bureau of Corporations to investigate]; it desires to co-operate with the Government in every possible way that is consistent with the proper protection of . . . [the stockholders'] rights and property."[16] He promised to open all books and records of the corporation to the Bureau's investigators. In return for this cooperation, Gary asked that the information gleaned from the files be used "by the President alone for his guidance in making such suggestions to Congress concerning legislation as might be proper, expedient, and for the actual benefit of the general public"; and that "any questions relative to the use, publication, and disposition of material which Judge Gary might deem confidential would be considered by him and Commissioner Garfield, and that if there should be a disagreement between them the matter should be referred to Secretary Metcalf and, if necessary, ultimately to the President for determination."[17] Gary and Roosevelt read a memorandum of the conference and seemed satisfied. Gary's first gentlemen's agreement with the administration was consummated.

On December 18, 1906, Oscar S. Straus, then Secretary of Commerce and Labor, directed the Bureau to investigate the International Harvester Company.[18] The Morgan interests were almost as involved in this company as in United States Steel: Perkins had been instrumental in organiz-

---

[8] Frick to Philander C. Knox, Nov. 11, 1901, Philander C. Knox Papers, Manuscript Division, Library of Congress.

[9] Perkins to Morgan, Mar. 16, 1908, George W. Perkins Papers, Michigan State University.

[10] J. P. Morgan, Jr., to Perkins, Oct. 28, 1907, ibid.

[11] Jerome J. Wilbur and Ailes Files, Frank A. Vanderlip Papers, Butler Library, Columbia University.

[12] Vanderlip to George E. Roberts, Dec. 23, 1907, ibid.; Aldrich to Morgan (typed copy of telegram), Aug. 5, 1909, Albert J. Beveridge Papers, Manuscript Division, Library of Congress.

[13] For a good discussion of this transition, see Mowry, Era of Theodore Roosevelt, 115–40.

[14] Metcalf to Garfield, Jan. 28, 1905, File 42395, Records of the Department of Commerce, National Archives. A House resolution that day had called for the investigation.

[15] Garfield to Z. Lewis Dalby, Sept. 20, 1905, File 3641, Records of the Federal Trade Commission, National Archives (hereafter cited as Records FTC) ; Garfield to Gary, Oct. 27, 1905, File 2604–1–1, ibid. See also Garfield to Perkins, Dec. 24, 1904, Perkins Papers.

[16] White House Conference, Nov. 2, 1905, File 2605, Records FTC.

[17] Ibid. When Roosevelt brought up the subject of overcapitalization, Gary replied that, if the Bureau believed United States Steel guilty after its study, it should say so and "the Steel Corporation could not be punished in any more severe way than by such publicity." Ibid.

[18] Straus to Garfield, Dec. 18, 1906, File 64606, Records Commerce Department. A Senate resolution of December 17 asked for the study.

ing it, and Gary owned a large bloc of its stock.[19] This time the Wall Street leaders had prepared in advance. On December 8 the board of directors of International Harvester had authorized government investigators full access to its files.[20] Then, as soon as news of the investigation broke, Perkins and Cyrus H. McCormick, Harvester's president, wrote to the Department suggesting "a personal conference on the subject."[21] With a precedent established, it was not necessary to see Roosevelt. On January 18, 1907, Garfield and Deputy Commissioner of Corporations Herbert Knox Smith came to Gary's Waldorf-Astoria suite in New York for a two-day conference with representatives from International Harvester.[22] Morgan's men were meeting Roosevelt's men in order to arrange matters.

Gary praised the administration in the language of the contented customer. United States Steel "had been absolutely satisfied with the treatment it had received from the Bureau," and he hoped "that the Harvester Company would receive the same treatment."[23] In the hands of Roosevelt and the Bureau's staff, Gary said, federal supervision became "a strong safeguard . . . to the prevention of violent attacks on private rights in general that might otherwise come."[24] On that pleasant note, the negotiators completed a second gentlemen's agreement, identical with the one concerning United States Steel.

During these years the Morgan men watched other corporations run afoul of the administration. A few months after the Steel agreement, the Justice Department charged Rockefeller's Standard Oil Company with violations of the antirebate law. Perkins reported to Morgan that as a result of Gary's "wise and vigilant" policies, "we have anticipated a great many questions and situations that might have been unpleasant and . . . [United States Steel] is looked upon in Washington with more favor than perhaps any other one concerned."[25] In 1907, when the government began antitrust prosecution of James B. Duke's American Tobacco Company, Perkins again assured Morgan that this was "about the limit to which

the Government can go in the direction of trust smashing."[26] If some business interests remained vulnerable, the Morgan men felt secure behind their private arrangement with the administration.

Why was Perkins so confident? Ostensibly these agreements covered only procedural details for two government investigations, with special emphasis upon protecting the corporations' trade secrets. The answer lay in a Wall Street assumption that, in community of interest understandings, the actual words spoken carried certain automatic implications. Perkins and Gary later spelled these out. In August 1907 Roosevelt asked Perkins whether International Harvester would "be satisfied with whatever the findings [of the Bureau's investigation] were?" Perkins replied that the company expected "the Department frankly [to] come to us and point out any mistakes or technical violations of any law; then give us a chance to correct them, if we could or would, and that if we did, then we would expect the Attorney General not to bring proceedings. . . ."[27] Perkins cited a precedent. In 1904 International Harvester had asked Secretary of Commerce and Labor George B. Cortelyou to find out whether the company was breaking the law. The Interstate Commerce Commission decided that International Harvester had illegally accepted rebates. Representatives of the company then reached an understanding with Attorney General William H. Moody whereby the company stopped its improper practices and the government in turn forgot the matter.[28]

Gary's interpretation matched that of Perkins. In 1911 an agent of the Bureau of Corporations reported Gary's reconstruction of the Steel conference: "Somewhere about 1905, Judge Gary said, he had a talk with President Roosevelt. This talk seems to have been pretty general in terms. In substance, he told the President that he wished to lay before him whatever the Corporation was doing; that if anything were wrong he wished to be advised of it, and the Corporation would change it; and the President replied that this seemed to him a fair proposition."[29] Although nothing in the gentlemen's agreements said so, the

[19] Memorandum, agreement among George W. Perkins, Elbert H. Gary, John P. Wilson, and Cyrus H. McCormick, Oct. 29, 1906, File 4921–23, Records FTC. For duplication between United States Steel and International Harvester officials, see House Committee on Investigation of United States Steel Corporation, *United States Steel Corporation, Hearings,* July 26, 1911, pt. 12, p. 802.

[20] Memorandum, Aug. 23, 1907, File 4902–1, Records FTC.

[21] Perkins to Straus, Dec. 18, 1906; McCormick to Garfield, Dec. 28, 1906, in File 4902–2, *ibid.*

[22] Memorandum of First International Harvester Conference, Jan. 18, 1907, File 4902–1, *ibid.*

[23] *Ibid.*

[24] Memorandum of Second International Harvester Interview, Jan. 19, 1907, *ibid.*

[25] Perkins to Morgan, June 25, 1906, Perkins Papers.

[26] Perkins to Morgan, July 12, 1907, *ibid.*

[27] Memorandum, Aug. 28, 1907, *ibid.*

[28] *Ibid.;* memorandum, Aug. 23, 1907, Records FTC. In the latter memorandum, Perkins' assistant William C. Beer said that "the Government has but to point out in what respect it thinks the Company is not obeying the laws to have them obeyed immediately."

[29] Memorandum, interview with E. H. Gary, Oct. 6, 1911, File 1940–1, Records FTC. Needless to say, this résumé does not agree with the official memorandum of the conference. At the time of the agreement, Gary only alluded to his thoughts. He wrote to Garfield (Nov. 10, 1905, File 2605, *ibid.*) that "there has been no disposition on my part to endeavor to bind the Government to any promise or undertaking for the protection of our Corporation," but, he added, Roosevelt certainly did not want to harm the Steel Corporation, or business in

magnates pictured them as a buffer between the corporations and the courts. The executive would issue private rulings on the corporations' legality and then allow them to avoid suits by cleaning house.

Roosevelt neither accepted nor denied this construction. When Perkins presented his gloss on the International Harvester agreement, Roosevelt evaded the issue. He assured Perkins that the Justice Department would not prosecute until the Attorney General had cleared it with him—a normal procedure—and later promised to postpone all legal action until the Bureau had completed its investigation.[30]

Despite the evasion, the Morgan men had confidence in the President's intentions. A number of Roosevelt's characteristics justified their faith. The idea of blocs within society came naturally to a politician, and Roosevelt added a personal enjoyment for the game of diplomacy. Respecting the magnates' power and their importance to the Republican party, he wanted peace between Wall Street and Washington. Because he believed so firmly in his own judgment, Roosevelt gladly committed his administration once he had determined that a course of action was right.

Roosevelt, like the Morgan men, was groping for a new definition of the government's relationship with big business. Early in his administration the President had indicated his dissatisfaction with the negativism of the Sherman Act. While he welcomed the popularity of the trust buster, he also made clear his preference for a less destructive law. By 1908 he was cooperating with Wall Street in a drive behind the so-called Hepburn amendments to the Sherman Act, bills drawn up in New York that would give the executive the discretion to distinguish between good and bad trusts.[31] Four years later, Roosevelt canvassed the nation as a presidential candidate with this idea fundamental to his platform.

Behind these areas of agreement, however, lay a distinct difference between the President and the magnates. Wall Street initially regarded the government as a mediocre power and at no time recognized it as more than an equal. From the beginning Roosevelt had considered the government above the nation's private groups.[32] Under the gentlemen's agreements he expected the gov-

ernment—in this case, Roosevelt—to have a free hand in making all final decisions. This conviction showed first in the corrections Roosevelt made when he reviewed the original memorandum of the United States Steel agreement. Where the copy read, "That the general business conditions of the country would naturally be damaged if our Corporation were injured; that it was not intended to take any unnecessary action which would be calculated to be injurious . . . ," Roosevelt changed the latter part to read, "that it was not intended to take any action which would be calculated to be injurious unless it was shown to be the Government's clear duty to take it. . . ." [33] Roosevelt's equivocal answer to Perkins in August 1907 implied the same desire to judge as he saw fit.

In this light the most important development of the agreements under Roosevelt, the Tennessee Coal and Iron episode, represented a defeat for the President. The Morgan men regarded the understandings as the foundation for general cooperation with the executive, upon which they would build as new situations arose. When, during the Panic of 1907, the House of Morgan planned to purchase the Tennessee Coal and Iron Company, it naturally sent Gary and Frick to sound out Roosevelt first. The very heart of the agreements, as Gary and Perkins construed them, involved an advance executive ruling to safeguard against later court action. For the House of Morgan, Roosevelt's approval logically extended the existing agreements. But Roosevelt suffered a reverse. Caught in a politically and economically dangerous panic he did not understand, he allowed the Morgan men to assume the initiative and thereby lost control over the agreements.[34]

George Perkins, who worked so closely with Roosevelt in the campaign, had apparently accepted Roosevelt's view that the government was a power superior to the corporations.

[33] Copy in second letter Gary to Garfield, Nov. 10, 1905, Records FTC. For another example of Roosevelt's differences with the House of Morgan over the proper function of government, see Mowry, *Era of Theodore Roosevelt*, 217.

[34] For comments on the meeting by two participants, see Gary to Elihu Root, Nov. 7, 1907, and Root to Gary, Nov. 11, 1907, both in Elihu Root Papers, Manuscript Division, Library of Congress. Gary's letter included veiled references to the United States Steel agreement. Gary later claimed that early in the panic he had also requested executive approval for his plan to stabilize prices throughout the iron and steel industry and that Roosevelt had raised no objections. (Memorandum of interview with E. H. Gary, Oct. 6, 1911, File 1940–1, Records FTC). Thus Gary considered his famous "dinners" as well as the purchase of Tennessee Coal and Iron a part of the expanding Steel agreement. Perhaps encouraged by success, Frick wrote to Roosevelt, (Nov. 30, 1907, Theodore Roosevelt Papers, Manuscript Division, Library of Congress) offering his and Gary's services as mediators in the court battles between the government and Standard Oil. The

general. He repeatedly emphasized the man-to-man character of the agreement. See also second letter to Garfield, Nov. 10, 1905, *ibid.*

[30] Memoranda, Aug. 28 and Nov. 7, 1907, in Perkins Papers.

[31] The magnates continued to campaign for a federal agency that would regularize the executive cooperation they tried to achieve through the gentleman's agreements. See Robert H. Wiebe, "Business Disunity and the Progressive Movement, 1901–1914," *Mississippi Valley Historical Review,* XLIV (Mar. 1958), 681–84.

[32] The Progressive party platform in 1912 indicated that by this time Roosevelt's concept of the government as a dispenser of justice had matured.

Otherwise relations between the magnates and Washington were cordial and uneventful during the last Roosevelt years, partly because the Bureau of Corporations did little investigating. The new Commissioner Herbert Knox Smith repeatedly showed his friendliness toward the magnates. Seconded by Secretary Straus, he offered to publicize International Harvester's cooperative attitude toward the Bureau's investigation.[35] When Attorney General Charles J. Bonaparte made threatening gestures toward International Harvester, it was Smith who extracted Roosevelt's promise to withhold any prosecution until the Bureau had finished investigating.[36] At the same time he confided in Harvester's chief counsel that all available evidence pointed toward the company's legality.[37] Roosevelt, seemingly convinced that United States Steel and International Harvester were good corporations, did not press the Bureau for action.

Left in peace, the Morgan men responded in kind. Perkins chatted often with Roosevelt and always found him congenial.[38] In March 1907, when other businessmen were blaming Roosevelt for an unsettled stock market, Gary wrote the President a letter flattering his reform record.[39] Only once did Gary experience a moment of doubt. In January 1909 Roosevelt turned over nonconfidential data from the Steel investigation to the Senate Judiciary Committee. Although the Bureau dutifully sent Gary a list of the documents divulged, Gary felt impelled "to call the attention . . . of Commissioner Smith to original

correspondence between Secretary Garfield and myself. I hope our understanding will not be overlooked." Smith assured Gary that "we have in mind the matter of which you speak," and the incident passed.[40]

When Roosevelt selected William Howard Taft as his heir, Wall Street applauded;[41] he appeared far safer than Roosevelt. Asked during the 1908 campaign whether he anticipated any action against United States Steel, Taft replied that he saw no reason for an investigation, and added, "Indeed, Secretary Garfield tells me there is not [any reason for one]." [42] The candidate did not even know that the Steel Corporation, along with International Harvester, was already under investigation. Taft's victory, coinciding with court decisions favorable to big business, made the Morgan men certain that their agreements with the executive were secure.[43]

The House of Morgan, in company with much of the nation, misjudged the new President. The agreements, in order to function properly, required a strong President whose word bound his administration. Taft was a follower who diffused responsibility among his subordinates and relied upon them for much of his policy. The agreements, as the Morgan men understood them, also depended upon a pragmatic executive, willing to bend them to fit any new developments. Where Roosevelt enjoyed the leeway of private negotiations, Taft's administration lacked the necessary flexibility. Taft's mind worked in legal channels, and in revamping the cabinet he surrounded himself with lawyers who shared his outlook. Finally, the magnates needed a President who, like Roosevelt, could accept big business as a positive good for America. Neither Taft nor Attorney General George W. Wickersham qualified. Both men believed that the dissolution of overlarge corporations would bring back old-time competition. For

---

bloc approach to government had many applications.

Emphasizing the executive's retreat during the financial crisis, Secretary of the Treasury George B. Cortelyou turned over to the House of Morgan government funds which the bankers used at their discretion to fight the panic. See Cortelyou's later testimony in the House subcommittee of the Committee on Banking and Currency (62 Cong. 3 sess., May 16, 1912–Feb. 26, 1913), *Money Trust Investigation of Financial and Monetary Conditions in the United States under House Resolutions Nos. 429 and 504* (3 vols., Washington, D.C., 1912–13), June 13, 1912, I, 430–54.

[35] Smith to McCormick, Aug. 8, 1907, Perkins Papers; Straus to Redfield Proctor, Jan. 25, 1908, File 64606, Records Commerce Department.

[36] Memorandum, Nov. 7, 1907, Perkins Papers. See also Henry F. Pringle, *The Life and Times of William Howard Taft: A Biography* (2 vols., New York, 1939), II, 790–91.

[37] Edgar A. Bancroft to Perkins, Feb. 4, 1908, Perkins Papers. See also Perkins to Smith, Apr. 18, 1908, File 5589, Records FTC; Smith to Perkins, Apr. 20, 1908, Perkins Papers.

[38] Perkins to Morgan, July 31, 1908, Perkins Papers. See also Perkins to Roosevelt, June 10, 1908, *ibid.*

[39] Gary to Roosevelt, Mar. 15, 1907, Roosevelt Papers.

[40] William H. Baldwin to Gary, Jan. 30, 1909; Gary to Baldwin, Feb. 1, 1909; Baldwin to Gary, Feb. 2, 1909; Gary to Baldwin, Feb. 4, 1909; Baldwin to Gary, Feb. 5, 1909; all in File 6096, Records FTC. Later, when the Stanley Committee asked Gary if he knew whether the President had received any information from the Bureau of Corporation's investigation of United States Steel, Gary disingenuously replied, "I have no knowledge as to whether or not the Department of Commerce and Labor has furnished any of this information to the President. There is no way I could know that." House Committee on Investigation of United States Steel Corporation, *United States Steel Corporation, Hearings*, June 1, 1911, pt. 2, p. 71. See also *ibid.*, June 2, 1911, pt. 3, p. 139; July 20, 1911, pt. 9, pp. 495–98.

[41] Pringle, *Taft*, I, 347, 355.

[42] Quoted in Mowry, *Era of Theodore Roosevelt*, 288. The remark indicates that, if Taft reported him correctly, Garfield discounted the investigations as a formality.

[43] For comments on the courts, see Perkins to J. P. Morgan, Jr., Nov. 10, 1908, Perkins Papers.

Taft, who wanted to continue Roosevelt's progressivism by administering rather than innovating, the trust issue proved a godsend. With Wickersham showing the way, the government mined the Sherman Act for all it was worth.[44]

In Roosevelt's last years a Department of Commerce and Labor sympathetic to Wall Street had counterbalanced the aggressive Attorney General Charles Bonaparte. Under Taft, Secretary Charles Nagel gave the Justice Department every possible assistance. When Nagel discovered that the Steel investigation had lagged under Roosevelt and that the International Harvester study had scarcely begun, he immediately concentrated the Department's energies on those two projects.[45] Bypassing Commissioner of Corporations Herbert Knox Smith, a confirmed friend of the Morgan men, Nagel relied upon a pair of Smith's subordinates, who distrusted Gary's motives, to manage the investigations.[46] Contrary to his predecessor's policy, Nagel never insisted that the Justice Department wait for a completed investigation before prosecuting. At the same time that he placed his Department at the service of the Attorney General, Nagel turned his back on Wall Street and, by silencing Smith, cut off the magnates' main source of unofficial information.[47]

Commissioner Smith was an anachronism in the new administration. As the only participant in the original agreements still in office, he did his best to keep them operative. He prodded Nagel to destroy copies of confidential data that the Bureau had used in its investigations and reminded his superiors of the corporations' cooperativeness. Citing Roosevelt, he tried to delay antitrust suits until the Bureau had completed its studies.[48] But he cried into the wind. Although he remained in office until 1912, he wielded no power. Taft and Nagel privately rejoiced when Smith resigned to join Roosevelt's Progressive party.[49]

Meanwhile, the Morgan men could only await developments. When the Supreme Court in May 1911 ruled that the Standard Oil and American Tobacco Companies violated the Sherman Act, the magnates read the decisions as an invitation to Wickersham and Taft to try their luck with United States Steel and International Harvester.[50] Hearing rumors of imminent prosecutions, Perkins went to Wickersham in July 1911 to revitalize the agreements. He promised Wickersham that if the Justice Department uncovered any practices which "in his judgment, should be corrected, we would all meet him half way in an effort to [correct them] by agreement rather than through a suit."[51] The magnates had come full circle: Perkins' offer exactly matched the one made to Attorney General Moody seven years earlier. But what had made sense in 1904 no longer applied in 1911. Wickersham answered Perkins on October 26 when the Justice Department, without waiting for the Bureau to finish its study, began antitrust proceedings against United States Steel.

The next day Gary sadly but firmly told the Bureau's agents that United States Steel could no longer cooperate in their investigations.[52] The corporation's attorneys received no more satisfaction from the Taft administration. When they asked the government to respect the confidential information it had at its disposal, Nagel told them they would "have to trust him to use it discreetly and to publish only what [was] necessary," and Taft added, "That is right."[53] Shortly afterward, the Justice Department brought suit against the International Harvester Company. Again the Bureau had not yet issued its report, and Harvester's attorney worked to the last minute to breathe life into the second gentlemen's agreement. He reminded the Bureau of "the very fair offer" Smith had made to allow the company to correct the report for "any inadvertent errors or [to] present further information on any point upon which I may believe you to have been misinformed."[54]

---

[44] Mowry, *Era of Theodore Roosevelt*, 231–38; and Pringle, *Taft*, I, 248, 523; II, 604–606, 655–59, 669–73, 718 ff., contain suggestive information on Taft and the nature of his administration.

[45] Memorandum, Aug. 22, 1912, File 64606, Records Commerce Department.

[46] William H. Baldwin to Garfield, Nov. 28, Dec. 3, 1906, File 3641, Records FTC; Luther Conant, Jr., to Smith, Dec. 25, 1908, File 2604-1-1, *ibid*.

[47] Perkins to Smith, July 3, 1911, File 4902-2, *ibid.*; Smith to Perkins, July 8, 1911, Perkins Papers.

[48] Smith to Nagel, June 30, Oct. 27, 1910, and Conant to Nagel, Nov. 1, 1910, in File 69445, Records Commerce Department; Smith to Taft, Apr. 28, 1912, File 64606, *ibid*. See also E. A. Bancroft to Smith, Nov. 6, 1909, and Smith to Bancroft, Nov. 12, 1909, in File 6419, Records FTC.

[49] Taft to Nagel, July 17, 1912, File 64606, Records Commerce Department.

[50] Memorandum for Mr. Roosevelt, Mar. 11, 1912, Perkins Papers, shows Perkins' distaste, shared by other men from Wall Street, for the Supreme Court's so-called rule of reason, distinguishing between acceptable and unacceptable restraint of trade.

[51] Memorandum, July 13, 1911, Perkins Papers.

[52] Memorandum, conference between Gary and Bureau of Corporation officials, Oct. 27, 1911, 1940-1, Records FTC, includes Gary's emotions.

[53] Memorandum, Nov. 29, 1911, Presidential Ser. no. 2, William Howard Taft Papers, Manuscript Division, Library of Congress. Ironically, the administration's decision still followed the letter of agreement: the Secretary, then the President, arbitrated differences between the Bureau and the Steel Corporation.

[54] E. A. Bancroft to Luther Conant, Jr., Sept. 10, 1912, File 6419, Records FTC. Just before he resigned, Smith had allowed Gary's rejoinders to be included in the Bureau's report on United States Steel. Memorandum, conference at Gary's office, Oct. 13, 1911, File 1940-1, *ibid*.

Despite rebuffs from the new Commissioner of Corporations Luther Conant, Jr., the attorney persisted until Nagel had told him twice that the report's publication could not wait for his proof-reading.[55] The Taft administration left office amid bitter complaints from the prosecuted corporations.[56]

In 1911 Gary called the Steel suit "the irony of Fate."[57] Considering his misplaced faith in Taft three years before, the judgment sounded reasonable. More accurately, the Steel prosecution, marking the end of one gentlemen's agreement, was the casualty of a transition period. The Wall Street approach to the federal government, as embodied in the agreements, required more abnegation than the progressive era's administrations would accept. It fitted neither Roosevelt's view of a government above society nor Taft's legalistic administrating executive.

Before they collapsed, the gentlemen's agreements gave Wall Street valuable experience. They taught the magnates the importance of adapting their approach to new circumstances. Even before entering the agreements, the Morgan men had made an important concession. By elevating the government from secondary power to a position of equality with the House of Morgan, they extended the executive's domain to include a study of their hitherto sacred records and, in the process, partially recognized the government's right to regulate corporations. This facilitated a later concession to Woodrow Wilson's administration by which the magnates temporarily accepted the government as a superior power with unquestioned rights to regulate business. On that basis, the American Telephone and Telegraph Company and the New York, New Haven and Hartford Railroad arranged private settlements with Attorney General James C. McReynolds that forestalled prosecution.[58] Moreover, the painful changes from Roosevelt to Taft to Wilson pointed up the value of continuity in the government's personnel and philosophy to any private understandings. The progressive era's irregular course made the magnates more appreciative of Republican consistency during the 1920's, when the business of government always remained business. In defeat, Wall Street was learning.

Speaking at Osawatomie, Kansas, in the summer of 1910, Theodore Roosevelt laid down the broad outlines of the New Nationalism. In this far-sighted statement on the trends of the modern economy, Roosevelt called for a national outlook to reconcile business consolidation with individual liberty, the role of government, he believed, must be expanded to watch over the relations between capital and labor.

THEODORE ROOSEVELT: THE NEW NATIONALISM*

We come here to-day to commemorate one of the epoch-making events of the long struggle for the rights of man—the long struggle for the uplift of humanity. Our country—this great Republic—means nothing unless it means the triumph of a real democracy, the triumph of popular government, and, in the long run, of an economic system under which each man shall be guaranteed the opportunity to show the best that there is in him. That is why the history of America is now the central feature of the history of the world; for the world has set its face hopefully toward our democracy; and, O my fellow citizens, each one of you carries on your shoulders not only the burden of doing well for the sake of your own country, but the burden of doing well and of seeing that this nation does well for the sake of mankind. . . .

Practical equality of opportunity for all citizens, when we achieve it, will have two great results. First, every man will have a fair chance to make of himself all that in him lies; to reach the highest point to which his capacities, unassisted by special privilege of his own and un-

[55] Conant to Bancroft, Sept. 18, 1912, File 6419, *ibid;* Bancroft to Nagel, Feb. 21, 1913, Nagel to Bancroft, Feb. 22, 26, 1913, File 64606, Records Commerce Department.

[56] Statement of Cyrus H. McCormick, Mar. 2, 1913, File 6963–1, Records FTC.

[57] Gary to Perkins, Aug. 1, 1911, Perkins Papers. As the date shows, this comment was written just before the government suit began, when prosecution was certain.

* "The New Nationalism" is reprinted with the permission of Charles Scribner's Sons from *The Works of Theodore Roosevelt,* Memorial Edition, Vol. XIX (1925).

[58] Arthur S. Link, *Woodrow Wilson and the Progressive Era, 1910–1917,* The New American Nation Series, ed. Henry Steele Commager and Richard B. Morris (New York, 1954), 76 and fn. 56; and a slightly different presentation in Link, *Wilson: The New Freedom* (Princeton, N.J., 1956), 418–23.

hampered by the special privilege of others, can carry him, and to get for himself and his family substantially what he has earned. Second, equality of opportunity means that the commonwealth will get from every citizen the highest service of which he is capable. No man who carries the burden of the special privileges of another can give to the commonwealth that service to which it is fairly entitled.

I stand for the square deal. But when I say that I am for the square deal, I mean not merely that I stand for fair play under the present rules of the game, but that I stand for having those rules changed so as to work for a more substantial equality of opportunity and of reward for equally good service. One word of warning, which, I think, is hardly necessary in Kansas. When I say I want a square deal for the poor man, I do not mean that I want a square deal for the man who remains poor because he has not got the energy to work for himself. If a man who has had a chance will not make good, then he has got to quit. And you men of the Grand Army, you want justice for the brave man who fought, and punishment for the coward who shirked his work. Is not that so?

Now, this means that our government, National and State, must be freed from the sinister influence or control of special interests. Exactly as the special interests of cotton and slavery threatened our political integrity before the Civil War, so now the great special business interests too often control and corrupt the men and methods of government for their own profit. We must drive the special interests out of politics. That is one of our tasks to-day. Every special interest is entitled to justice—full, fair, and complete—and, now, mind you, if there were any attempt by mob-violence to plunder and work harm to the special interest, whatever it may be, that I most dislike, and the wealthy man, whomsoever he may be, for whom I have the greatest contempt, I would fight for him, and you would if you were worth your salt. He should have justice. For every special interest is entitled to justice, but not one is entitled to a vote in Congress, to a voice on the bench, or to representation in any public office. The Constitution guarantees protection to property, and we must make that promise good. But it does not give the right of suffrage to any corporation.

The true friend of property, the true conservative, is he who insists that property shall be the servant and not the master of the commonwealth; who insists that the creature of man's making shall be the servant and not the master of the man who made it. The citizens of the United States must effectively control the mighty commercial forces which they have themselves called into being.

There can be no effective control of corporations while their political activity remains. To put an end to it will be neither a short nor an easy task, but it can be done.

We must have complete and effective publicity of corporate affairs, so that the people may know beyond peradventure whether the corporations obey the law and whether their management entitles them to the confidence of the public. It is necessary that laws should be passed to prohibit the use of corporate funds directly or indirectly for political purposes; it is still more necessary that such laws should be thoroughly enforced. Corporate expenditures for political purposes, and especially such expenditures by public-service corporations, have supplied one of the principal sources of corruption in our political affairs.

It has become entirely clear that we must have government supervision of the capitalization, not only of public-service corporations, including, particularly, railways, but of all corporations doing an interstate business. I do not wish to see the nation forced into the ownership of the railways if it can possibly be avoided, and the only alternative is thoroughgoing and effective regulation, which shall be based on a full knowledge of all the facts, including a physical valuation of property. This physical valuation is not needed, or, at least, is very rarely needed, for fixing rates; but it is needed as the basis of honest capitalization.

We have come to recognize that franchises should never be granted except for a limited time, and never without proper provision for compensation to the public. It is my personal belief that the same kind and degree of control and supervision which should be exercised over public-service corporations should be extended also to combinations which control necessaries of life, such as meat, oil, and coal, or which deal in them on an important scale. I have no doubt that the ordinary man who has control of them is much like ourselves. I have no doubt he would like to do well, but I want to have enough supervision to help him realize that desire to do well.

I believe that the officers, and, especially, the directors, of corporations should be held personally responsible when any corporation breaks the law.

Combinations in industry are the result of an imperative economic law which cannot be repealed by political legislation. The effort at prohibiting all combination has substantially failed. The way out lies, not in attempting to prevent such combinations, but in completely controlling them in the interest of the public welfare. For that purpose the Federal Bureau of Corporations is an agency of first importance. Its powers, and, therefore, its efficiency, as well as that of the Interstate Commerce Commission, should be largely increased. We have a right to expect from the Bureau of Corporations and from the Interstate Commerce Commission a very high grade of public service. We should be as sure of the proper conduct of the interstate railways and the proper management of interstate business as we are now sure of the conduct and management of the national banks, and we should have as effective supervision in one case as in the other. The Hepburn Act, and the amendment to the act in the shape in which it finally passed Congress at the last session, represent a long step in advance, and we must go yet further.

There is a wide-spread belief among our people that, under the methods of making tariffs which have hitherto obtained, the special interests are too influential. Probably this is true of both the big special interests and the little special interests. These methods have put a premium on selfishness, and, naturally, the selfish big interests have gotten more than their smaller, though equally selfish, brothers. The duty of Congress is to provide a method by which the interest of the whole people shall be all that receives consideration. To this end there must be an expert tariff commission, wholly removed from the possibility of political pressure or of improper business influence. Such a commission can find the real difference between cost of production, which is mainly the difference of labor cost here and abroad. As fast as its recommendations are made, I believe in revising one schedule at a time. A general revision of the tariff almost inevitably leads to log-rolling and the subordination of the general public interest to local and special interests.

The absence of effective State, and, especially, national, restraint upon unfair money-getting has tended to create a small class of enormously wealthy and economically powerful men, whose chief object is to hold and increase their power. The prime need is to change the conditions which enable these men to accumulate power which it is not for the general welfare that they should hold or exercise. We grudge no man a fortune which represents his own power and sagacity, when exercised with entire regard to the welfare of his fellows. Again, comrades over there, take the lesson from your own experience. Not only did you not grudge, but you gloried in the promotion of the great generals who gained their promotion by leading the army to victory. So it is with us. We grudge no man a fortune in civil life if it is honorably obtained and well used. It is not even enough that it should have been gained without doing damage to the community. We should permit it to be gained only so long as the gaining represents benefit to the community. This, I know, implies a policy of a far more active governmental interference with social and economic conditions in this country than we have yet had, but I think we have got to face the fact that such an increase in governmental control is now necessary.

No man should receive a dollar unless that dollar has been fairly earned. Every dollar received should represent a dollar's worth of service rendered—not gambling in stocks, but service rendered. The really big fortune, the swollen fortune, by the mere fact of its size acquires qualities which differentiate it in kind as well as in degree from what is possessed by men of relatively small means. Therefore, I believe in a graduated income tax on big fortunes, and in another tax which is far more easily collected and far more effective—a graduated inheritance tax on big fortunes, properly safeguarded against evasion and increasing rapidly in amount with the size of the estate.

The people of the United States suffer from periodical financial panics to a degree substantially unknown among the other nations which approach us in financial strength. There is no reason why we should suffer what they escape. It is of profound importance that our financial system should be promptly investigated, and so thoroughly and effectively revised as to make it certain that hereafter our currency will no longer fail at critical times to meet our needs.

It is hardly necessary for me to repeat that I believe in an efficient army and a navy large enough to secure for us abroad that respect which is the surest guaranty of peace. A word of special warning to my fellow citizens who are as progressive as I hope I am. I want them to keep up their interest in our internal affairs; and I want them also continually to remember Uncle Sam's interests abroad. Justice and fair dealing among nations rest upon principles identical with those which control justice and fair dealing among the individuals of which nations are composed, with the vital exception that each nation must do its own part in international police work. If you get into trouble here, you can call for the police; but if Uncle Sam gets into trouble, he has got to be his own policeman, and I want to see him strong enough to encourage the peaceful aspirations of other peoples in connection with us. I believe in national friendships and heartiest good-will to all nations; but national friendships, like those between men, must be founded on respect as well as on liking, on forbearance as well as upon trust. I should be heartily ashamed of any American who did not try to make the American Government act as justly toward the other nations in international relations as he himself would act toward any individual in private relations. I should be heartily ashamed to see us wrong a weaker power, and I should hang my head forever if we tamely suffered wrong from a stronger power.

Of conservation I shall speak more at length elsewhere. Conservation means development as much as it does protection. I recognize the right and duty of this generation to develop and use the natural resources of our land; but I do not recognize the right to waste them, or to rob, by wasteful use, the generations that come after us. I ask nothing of the nation except that it so behave as each farmer here behaves with reference to his own children. That farmer is a poor creature who skins the land and leaves it worthless to his children. The farmer is a good farmer who, having enabled the land to support himself and to provide for the education of his children, leaves it to them a little better than he found it himself. I believe the same thing of a nation.

Moreover, I believe that the natural resources must be used for the benefit of all our people, and not monopolized for the benefit of the few, and here again is another case in which I am accused of taking a revolutionary attitude. People forget now that one hundred years ago there were public men of good character who advocated the nation selling its public lands in great quantities, so that the nation could get the most money out of it, and giving it to the men who could cultivate it for their own uses. We took the proper democratic ground that the land should be granted in small sections to the men who were actually to till it and live on it. Now, with the water-power, with the forests, with the mines, we are brought face to face with the fact that there are many people who will go with us in conserving the resources only if they are to be allowed to exploit them for their benefit. That is one of the fundamental reasons why the special interests should be driven out of politics. Of all the questions which can come before this nation, short of the actual preservation of its existence in a great war, there is none which compares in importance with the great central task of leaving this land even a better land for our descendants than it is for us, and training them into a better race to inhabit the land and pass it on. Conservation is a great moral issue, for it involves the patriotic duty of insuring the safety and continuance of the nation. Let me add that the health and vitality of our people are at least as well worth conserving as their forests, waters, lands, and minerals, and in this great work the national government must bear a most important part.

I have spoken elsewhere also of the great task which lies before the farmers of the country to get for themselves and their wives and children not only the benefits of better farming, but also those of better business methods and better conditions of life on the farm. The burden of this great task will fall, as it should, mainly upon the great organizations of the farmers themselves. I am glad it will, for I believe they are all well able to handle it. In particular, there are strong reasons why the Departments of Agriculture of the various States, the United States Department of Agriculture, and the agricultural colleges and experiment stations should extend their work to cover all phases of farm life, instead of limiting themselves, as they have far too often limited themselves in the past, solely to the question of the production of crops. And now a special word to the farmer. I want to see him make the farm as fine a farm as it can be made; and let him remember to see that the improvement goes on indoors as well as out; let him remember that the farmer's wife should have her share of thought and attention just as much as the farmer himself.

Nothing is more true than that excess of every kind is followed by reaction; a fact which should be pondered by reformer and reactionary alike. We are face to face with new conceptions of the relations of property to human welfare, chiefly because certain advocates of the rights of property as against the rights of men have been pushing their claims too far. The man who wrongly holds that every human right is secondary to his profit must now give way to the advocate of human welfare, who rightly maintains that every man holds his property subject to the general right of the community to regulate its use to whatever degree the public welfare may require it.

But I think we may go still further. The right to regulate the use of wealth in the public interest is universally admitted. Let us admit also the right to regulate the terms and conditions of labor, which is the chief element of wealth, directly in the interest of the common good. The fundamental thing to do for every man is to give him a chance to reach a place in which he will make the greatest possible contribution to the public welfare. Understand what I say there. Give him a chance, not push him up if he will not be pushed. Help any man who stumbles; if he lies down, it is a poor job to try to carry him; but if he is a worthy man, try your best to see that he gets a chance to show the worth that is in him. No man can be a good citizen unless he has a wage more than sufficient to cover the bare cost of living, and hours of labor short enough so that after his day's work is done he will have time and energy to bear his share in the management of the community, to help in carrying the general load. We keep countless men from being good citizens by the conditions of life with which we surround them. We need comprehensive workmen's compensation acts, both State and national laws to regulate child labor and work for women, and, especially, we need in our common schools not merely education in book-learning, but also practical training for daily life and work. We need to enforce better sanitary conditions for our workers and to extend the use of safety appliances for our workers in industry and commerce, both within and between the States. Also, friends, in the interest of the working man himself we need to set our faces like flint against mob-violence just as against corporate greed; against violence and injustice and lawlessness by wage-workers just as much as against lawless cunning and greed and selfish arrogance of employers. If I could ask but one thing of my fellow countrymen, my request would be that, whenever they go in for reform, they remember the two sides, and that they always exact justice from one side as much as from the other. I have small use for the public servant who can always see and denounce the corruption of the capitalist, but who cannot persuade himself, especially before election, to say a word about lawless mob-violence. And I have equally small use for the man, be he a judge on the bench, or editor of a great paper, or wealthy and influential private citizen, who can see clearly enough and denounce the lawlessness of mob-violence, but whose eyes are closed so that he is blind when the question is one of corruption in business on a gigantic scale. Also remember what I said about excess in reformer and reactionary alike. If the reactionary man, who thinks of nothing but the rights of property, could have his way, he would bring about a revolution; and one of my chief fears in connection with progress comes because I do not want to see our people, for lack of proper leadership, compelled to follow men whose intentions are excellent, but whose eyes are a little too wild to make it really safe to trust them. Here in Kansas there is one paper which habitually denounces me as the tool of Wall Street, and at the same time frantically repudiates the statement that I am a Socialist on the ground that that is an unwarranted slander of the Socialists.

National efficiency has many factors. It is a necessary result of the principle of conservation widely applied. In the end it will determine our failure or success as a nation. National efficiency has to do, not only with natural resources and with men, but it is equally concerned with institutions. The State must be made efficient for the work which concerns only the people of the State; and the nation for that which concerns all the people. There must remain no neutral ground to serve as a refuge for lawbreakers, and especially for lawbreakers of great wealth, who can hire the vulpine legal cunning which will teach them how to avoid both jurisdictions. It is a misfortune when the national legislature fails to do its duty in providing a national remedy, so that the only national activity is the purely negative activity of the judiciary in forbidding the State to exercise power in the premises.

I do not ask for overcentralization; but I do ask that we work in a spirit of broad and far-reaching nationalism when we work for what concerns our people as a whole. We are all Americans. Our common interests are as broad as the continent. I speak to you here in Kansas exactly as I would speak in New York or Georgia, for the most vital problems are those which affect us all alike. The National Government belongs to the whole American people, and where the whole American people are interested, that interest can be guarded effectively only by the National Government. The betterment which we seek must be accomplished, I believe, mainly through the National Government.

The American people are right in demanding that New Nationalism, without which we cannot hope to deal with new problems. The New Nationalism puts the national need before sectional or personal advantage. It is impatient of the utter confusion that results from local legislatures attempting to treat national issues as local issues. It is still more impatient of the impotence which springs from overdivision of governmental powers, the impotence which makes it possible for local selfishness or for legal cunning, hired by wealthy special interests, to bring national activities to a deadlock. This New Nationalism regards the executive power as the steward of the public welfare. It demands of the judiciary that it shall be interested primarily in human welfare rather than in property, just as it demands that the representative body shall represent all the people rather than any one class or section of the people.

I believe in shaping the ends of government to protect property as well as human welfare. Normally, and in the long run, the ends are the same; but whenever the alternative must be faced, I am for men and not for property, as you were in the Civil War. I am far from underestimating the importance of dividends; but I rank dividends below human character. Again, I do not have any sympathy with the reformer who says he does not care for dividends. Of course, economic welfare is necessary, for a man must pull his own weight and be able to support his family. I know well that the reformers must not bring upon the people economic ruin, or the reforms themselves will go down in the ruin. But we must be ready to face temporary disaster, whether or not brought on by those who will war against us to the knife. Those who oppose all reform will do well to remember that ruin in its worst form is inevitable if our national life brings us nothing better than swollen fortunes for the few and the triumph in both politics and business of a sordid and selfish materialism.

If our political institutions were perfect, they would absolutely prevent the political domination of money in any part of our affairs. We need to make our political representatives more quickly and sensitively responsive to the people whose servants they are. More direct action by the people in their own affairs under proper safeguards is vitally necessary. The direct primary is a step in this direction, if it is associated with a corrupt-practices act effective to prevent the advantage of the man willing recklessly and unscrupulously to spend money over his more honest competitor. It is particularly important that all moneys received or expended for campaign purposes should be publicly accounted for, not only after election, but before election as well. Political action must be made simpler, easier, and freer from confusion for every citizen. I believe that the prompt removal of unfaithful or incompetent public servants should be made easy and sure in whatever way experience shall show to be most expedient in any given class of cases.

One of the fundamental necessities in a representative government such as ours is to make certain that the men to whom the people delegate their power shall serve the people by whom they are elected, and not the special interests. I believe that every national officer, elected or appointed, should be forbidden to perform any service or receive any compensation, directly or indirectly, from interstate corporations; and a similar provision could not fail to be useful within the States.

The object of government is the welfare of the people. The material progress and prosperity of a nation are desirable chiefly so far as they lead to the moral and material welfare of all good citizens. Just in proportion as the average man and woman are honest, capable of sound judgment and high ideals, active in public affairs—but, first of all, sound in their home life, and the father and mother of healthy children whom they bring up well—just so far, and no farther, we may count our civilization a success. We must have—I believe we have already—a genuine and permanent moral awakening, without which no wisdom of legislation or administration really means anything; and, on the other hand, we must try to secure the social and economic legislation without which any improvement due to purely moral agitation is necessarily evanescent. Let me again illustrate by a reference to the Grand Army. You could not have won simply as a disorderly and disorganized mob. You needed generals; you needed careful administration of the most advanced type; and a good commissary—the cracker line. You well remember that success was necessary in many different lines in order to bring about general success. You had to have the administration at Washington good, just as you had to have the administration in the field; and you had to have the work of the generals good. You could not have triumphed without that administration and leadership; but it would all have been worthless if the average soldier had not had the right stuff in him. He had to have the right stuff in him, or you could not get it out of him. In the

last analysis, therefore, vitally necessary though it was to have the right kind of organization and the right kind of generalship, it was even more vitally necessary that the average soldier should have the fighting edge, the right character. So it is in our civil life. No matter how honest and decent we are in our private lives, if we do not have the right kind of law and the right kind of administration of the law, we cannot go forward as a nation. That is imperative; but it must be an addition to, and not a substitution for, the qualities that make us good citizens. In the last analysis, the most important elements in any man's career must be the sum of those qualities which, in the aggregate, we speak of as character. If he has not got it, then no law that the wit of man can devise, no administration of the law by the boldest and strongest executive, will avail to help him. We must have the right kind of character—character that makes a man, first of all, a good man in the home, a good father, a good husband—that makes a man a good neighbor. You must have that, and, then, in addition, you must have the kind of law and the kind of administration of the law which will give to those qualities in the private citizen the best possible chance for development. The prime problem of our nation is to get the right type of good citizenship, and, to get it, we must have progress, and our public men must be genuinely progressive.

Herbert Croly was one of the weightiest publicists of the New Nationalism, and indeed of the entire progressive movement. As Charles Forcey pointed out in *The Crossroads of Liberalism,* Croly was less an innovator than a codifier and expositor of the policies of Theodore Roosevelt. More than this, as can be seen in the following pages from *The Promise of American Life,* Croly was concerned with the underlying philosophic assumptions of reform.

HERBERT CROLY:
THE INDIVIDUAL AND THE NATIONAL PURPOSE*

I
INDIVIDUAL VS. COLLECTIVE EDUCATION

Hitherto we have been discussing the ways in which existing American economic and political methods and institutions should be modified in order to make towards the realization of the national democratic ideal. In course of this discussion, it has been taken for granted that the

American people under competent and responsible leadership could deliberately plan a policy of individual and social improvement, and that with the means at their collective disposal they could make headway towards its realization. These means consisted, of course, precisely in their whole outfit of political, economic, and social institutions; and the implication has been, consequently, that human nature can be raised to a higher level by an improvement in institutions and laws. The majority of my readers will probably have thought many times that such an assumption, whatever its truth, has been overworked. Admitting that some institutions may be better

* Reprinted with permission of the publisher from *The Promise of American Life* by Herbert Croly. Copyright 1909 by The Macmillan Company.

than others, it must also be admitted that human nature is composed of most rebellious material, and that the extent to which it can be modified by social and political institutions of any kind is, at best, extremely small. Such critics may, consequently, have reached the conclusion that the proposed system of reconstruction, even if desirable, would not accomplish anything really effectual or decisive towards the fulfillment of the American national Promise.

It is no doubt true that out of the preceding chapters many sentences could be selected which apparently imply a credulous faith in the possibility of improving human nature by law. It is also true that I have not ventured more than to touch upon a possible institutional reformation, which, in so far as it was successful in its purpose, would improve human nature by the most effectual of all means—that is, by improving the methods whereby men and women are bred. But if I have erred in attaching or appearing to attach too much efficacy to legal and institutional reforms, the error or its appearance was scarcely separable from an analytic reconstruction of a sufficient democratic ideal. Democracy must stand or fall on a platform of possible human perfectibility. If human nature cannot be improved by institutions, democracy is at best a more than usually safe form of political organization; and the only interesting inquiry about its future would be: How long will it continue to work? But if it is to work better as well as merely longer, it must have some leavening effect on human nature; and the sincere democrat is obliged to assume the power of the leaven. For him the practical questions are: How can the improvement best be brought about? and, How much may it amount to?

As a matter of fact, Americans have always had the liveliest and completest faith in the process of individual and social improvement and in accepting the assumption, I am merely adhering to the deepest and most influential of American traditions. The better American has continually been seeking to "uplift" himself, his neighbors, and his compatriots. But he has usually favored means of improvement very different from those suggested hereinbefore. The real vehicle of improvement is education. It is by education that the American is trained for such democracy as he possesses; and it is by better education that he proposes to better his democracy. Men are uplifted by education much more surely than they are by any tinkering with laws and institutions, because the work of education leavens the actual social substance. It helps to give the individual himself those qualities without which no institutions, however excellent, are of any use, and with which even bad institutions and laws can be made vehicles of grace.

The American faith in education has been characterized as a superstition; and superstitious in some respects it unquestionably is. But its superstitious tendency is not exhibited so much in respect to the ordinary process of primary, secondary, and higher education. Not even an American can over-emphasize the importance of proper teaching during youth; and the only wonder is that the money so freely lavished on it does not produce better results. Americans are superstitious in respect to education, rather because of the social "uplift" which they expect to achieve by so-called educational means. The credulity of the socialist in expecting to alter human nature by merely institutional and legal changes is at least equaled by the credulity of the good American in proposing to evangelize the individual by the reading of books and by the expenditure of money and words. Back of it all is the underlying assumption that the American nation by taking thought can add a cubit to its stature,—an absolute confidence in the power of the idea to create its own object and in the efficacy of good intentions.

Do we lack culture? We will "make it hum" by founding a new university in Chicago. Is American art neglected and impoverished? We will enrich it by organizing art departments in our colleges, and popularize it by lectures with lantern slides and associations for the study of its history. Is New York City ugly? Perhaps, but if we could only get the authorities to appropriate a few hundred millions for its beautification, we could make it look like a combination of Athens, Florence, and Paris. Is it desirable for the American citizen to be something of a hero? I will encourage heroes by establishing a fund whereby they shall be rewarded in cash. War is hell, is it? I will work for the abolition of hell by calling a convention and passing a resolution denouncing its iniquities. I will build at the Hague a Palace of Peace which shall be a standing rebuke to the War Lords of Europe. Here, in America, some of us have more money than we need and more good will. We will spend the money in order to establish the reign of the good, the beautiful, and the true.

This faith in a combination of good intentions, organization, words, and money is not confined to woman's clubs or to societies of amiable enthusiasts. In the state of mind which it expresses can be detected the powerful influence which American women exert over American men; but its guiding faith and illusion are shared by the most hard-headed and practical of Americans. The very men who have made their personal successes by a rigorous application of the rule that business is business—the very men who in their own careers have exhibited a shrewd and vivid sense of the realities of politics and trade; it is these men who have most faith in the practical, moral, and social power of the Subsidized Word. The most real thing which they carry over from the region of business into the region of moral and intellectual ideals is apparently their bank accounts. The fruits of their hard work and their business ability are to be applied to the purpose of "uplifting" their fellow-countrymen. A certain number of figures written on a check and signed by a familiar name, what may it not accomplish? Some years ago at the opening exercises of the Carnegie Institute in Pittsburg, Mr. Andrew Carnegie burst into an impassioned and mystical vision of the miraculously constitutive power of first mortgage steel bonds. From his point of view and from that of the average American there is scarcely anything which the combination of abundant resources and good intentions may not accomplish.

The tradition of seeking to cross the gulf between American practice and the American ideal by means of education or the Subsidized Word is not to be dismissed with a sneer. The gulf cannot be crossed without the assistance of some sort of educational discipline; and that discipline depends partly on a new exercise of the "money power" now safely reposing in the strong boxes of professional millionaires. There need be no fundamental objection taken to the national faith in the power of good intentions and re-distributed wealth. That faith is the immediate and necessary issue of the logic of our national moral situation. It should be, as it is, innocent and absolute; and if it does not remain innocent and absolute, the Promise of American Life can scarcely be fulfilled.

A faith may, however, be innocent and absolute without being inexperienced and credulous. The American faith in education is by way of being credulous and superstitious, not because it seeks individual and social amelioration by what may be called an educational process, but because the proposed means of education are too conscious, too direct, and too superficial. Let it be admitted that in any one decade the amount which can be accomplished towards individual and social amelioration by means of economic and political reorganization is comparatively small; but it is certainly as large as that which can be accomplished by subsidizing individual good intentions. Heroism is not to be encouraged by cash prizes any more than is genius; and a man's friends should not be obliged to prove that he is a hero in order that he may reap every appropriate reward. A hero officially conscious of his heroism is a mutilated hero. In the same way art cannot become a power in a community unless many of its members are possessed of a native and innocent love of beautiful things; and the extent to which such a possession can be acquired by any one or two generations of traditionally inartistic people is extremely small. Its acquisition depends not so much upon direct conscious effort, as upon the growing ability to discriminate between what is good and what is bad in their own native art. It is a matter of the training and appreciation of American artists, rather than the cultivation of art. Illustrations to the same effect might be multiplied. The popular interest in the Higher Education has not served to make Americans attach much importance to the advice of the highly educated man. He is less of a practical power in the United States than he is in any European country; and this fact is in itself a sufficient commentary

on the reality of the American faith in education. The fact is, of course, that the American tendency to disbelieve in the fulfillment of their national Promise by means of politically, economically, and socially reconstructive work has forced them into the alternative of attaching excessive importance to subsidized good intentions. They want to be "uplifted," and they want to "uplift" other people; but they will not use their social and political institutions for the purpose, because those institutions are assumed to be essentially satisfactory. The "uplifting" must be a matter of individual, or of unofficial associated effort; and the only available means are words and subsidies.

There is, however, a sense in which it is really true that the American national Promise can be fulfilled only by education; and this aspect of our desirable national education can, perhaps, best be understood by seeking its analogue in the training of the individual. An individual's education consists primarily in the discipline which he undergoes to fit him both for fruitful association with his fellows and for his own special work. Important as both the liberal and the technical aspect of this preliminary training is, it constitutes merely the beginning of a man's education. Its object is or should be to prepare him both in his will and in his intelligence to make a thoroughly illuminating use of his experience in life. His experience,—as a man of business, a husband, a father, a citizen, a friend,— has been made real to him, not merely by the zest with which he has sought it and the sincerity with which he has accepted it, but by the disinterested intelligence which he has brought to its understanding. An educational discipline which has contributed in that way to the reality of a man's experience has done as much for him as education can do; and an educational discipline which has failed to make any such contribution has failed of its essential purpose. The experience of other people acquired at second hand has little value,—except, perhaps, as a means of livelihood,—unless it really illuminates a man's personal experience.

Usually a man's ability to profit by his own personal experience depends upon the sincerity and the intelligence which he brings to his own particular occupation. The rule is not universal, because some men are, of course, born with much higher intellectual gifts than others; and to such men may be given an insight which has little foundation in any genuine personal experience. It remains true, none the less, for the great majority of men, that they gather an edifying understanding of men and things just in so far as they patiently and resolutely stick to the performance of some special and (for the most part) congenial task. Their education in life must be grounded in the persistent attempt to realize in action some kind of a purpose—a purpose usually connected with the occupation whereby they live. In the pursuit of that purpose they will be continually making experiments—opening up new lines of work, establishing new relations with other men, and taking more or less serious risks. Each of these experiments offers them an opportunity both for personal discipline and for increasing personal insight. If a man is capable of becoming wise, he will gradually be able to infer from this increasing mass of personal experience, the extent to which or the conditions under which he is capable of realizing his purpose; and his insight into the particular realities of his own life will bring with it some kind of a general philosophy—some sort of a disposition and method of appraisal of men, their actions, and their surroundings. Wherever a man reaches such a level of intelligence, he will be an educated man, even though his particular job has been that of a mechanic. On the other hand, a man who fails to make his particular task in life the substantial support of a genuine experience remains essentially an unenlightened man.

National education in its deeper aspect does not differ from individual education. Its efficiency ultimately depends upon the ability of the national consciousness to draw illuminating inferences from the course of the national experience; and its power to draw such inferences must depend upon the persistent and disinterested sincerity with which the attempt is made to realize the national purpose—the democratic ideal of individual and social improvement. So far as Americans are true to that purpose, all the different aspects of their national experience will assume meaning and momentum; while in so far as they are false thereto, no amount of "education" will ever be really edifying. The fundamental process of American education consists and must continue to consist precisely in the risks and experiments which the American nation will make in the service of its national ideal. If the American people balk at the sacrifices demanded by their experiments, or if they attach finality to any particular experiment in the distribution of political, economic, and social power, they will remain morally and intellectually at the bottom of a well, out of which they will never be "uplifted" by the most extravagant subsidizing of good intentions and noble words.

The sort of institutional and economic reorganization suggested in the preceding chapters is not, consequently, to be conceived merely as a more or less dubious proposal to improve human nature by laws. It is to be conceived as (possibly) the next step in the realization of a necessary collective purpose. Its deeper significance does not consist in the results which it may accomplish by way of immediate improvement. Such results may be worth having; but at best they will create almost as many difficulties as they remove. Far more important than any practical benefits would be the indication it afforded of national good faith. It would mean that the American nation was beginning to educate itself up to its own necessary standards. It would imply a popular realization that our first experiment in

democratic political and economic organization was founded partly on temporary conditions and partly on erroneous theories. A new experiment must consequently be made; and the great value of this new experiment would derive from the implied intellectual and moral emancipation. Its trial would demand both the sacrifice of many cherished interests, habits, and traditions for the sake of remaining true to a more fundamental responsibility and a much larger infusion of disinterested motives into the economic and political system. Thus the sincere definite decision that the experiment was necessary, would probably do more for American moral and social amelioration than would the specific measures actually adopted and tried. Public opinion can never be brought to approve any effectual measures, until it is converted to a constructive and consequently to a really educational theory of democracy.

Back of the problem of educating the individual lies the problem of collective education. On the one hand, if the nation is rendered incapable of understanding its own experience by the habit of dealing insincerely with its national purpose, the individual, just in so far as he himself has become highly educated, tends to be divided from his country and his fellow-countrymen. On the other hand, just in so far as a people is sincerely seeking the fulfillment of its national Promise, individuals of all kinds will find their most edifying individual opportunities in serving their country. In aiding the accomplishment of the collective purpose by means of increasingly constructive experiments, they will be increasing the scope and power of their own individual action. The opportunities, which during the past few years the reformers have enjoyed to make their personal lives more interesting, would be nothing compared to the opportunities for all sorts of stirring and responsible work, which would be demanded of individuals under the proposed plan of political and economic reorganization. The American nation would be more disinterestedly and sincerely fulfilling its collective purpose, partly because its more distinguished individuals had been called upon to place at the service of their country a higher degree of energy, ability, and unselfish devotion. If a nation, that is, is recreant to its deeper purpose, individuals, so far as they are well educated, are educated away from the prevailing national habits and traditions; whereas when a nation is sincerely attempting to meet its collective responsibility, the better individuals are inevitably educated into active participation in the collective task.

The reader may now be prepared to understand why the American faith in education has the appearance of being credulous and superstitious. The good average American usually wishes to accomplish exclusively by individual education a result which must be partly accomplished by national education. The nation, like the individual, must go to school; and the national school is not a lecture hall or a library.

Its schooling consists chiefly in experimental collective action aimed at the realization of the collective purpose. If the action is not aimed at the collective purpose, a nation will learn little even from its successes. If its action is aimed at the collective purpose, it may learn much even from its mistakes. No process of merely individual education can accomplish the work of collective education, because the nation is so much more than a group of individuals. Individuals can be "uplifted" without "uplifting" the nation, because the nation has an individuality of its own, which cannot be increased without the consciousness of collective responsibilities and the collective official attempt to redeem them. The processes of national and individual education should, of course, parallel and supplement each other. The individual can do much to aid national education by the single-minded and intelligent realization of his own specific purposes; but all individual successes will have little more than an individual interest unless they frequently contribute to the work of national construction. The nation can do much to aid individual education; but the best aid within its power is to offer to the individual a really formative and inspiring opportunity for public service. The whole round of superficial educational machinery—books, subsidies, resolutions, lectures, congresses—may be of the highest value, provided they are used to digest and popularize the results of a genuine individual and national educational experience, but when they are used, as so often at present, merely as a substitute for well-purposed individual and national action, they are precisely equivalent to an attempt to fly in a vacuum.

That the direct practical value of a reform movement may be equaled or surpassed by its indirect educational value is a sufficiently familiar idea—an idea admirably expressed ten years ago by Mr. John Jay Chapman in the chapter on "Education" in his "Causes and Consequences." But the idea in its familiar form is vitiated, because the educational effect of reform is usually conceived as exclusively individual. Its effect *must*, indeed, be considered wholly as an individual matter, just so long as reform is interpreted merely as a process of purification. From that point of view the collective purpose has already been fulfilled as far as it can be fulfilled by collective organization, and the *only* remaining method of social amelioration is that of the self-improvement of its constituent members. As President Nicholas Murray Butler of Columbia says, in his "True and False Democracy": "We must not lose sight of the fact that the corporate or collective responsibility which it (socialism) would substitute for individual initiative is only such corporate or collective responsibility as a group of these very same individuals could exercise. Therefore, socialism is primarily an attempt to overcome man's individual imperfections by adding them together, in the hope that they will cancel each other." But what is all

organization but an attempt, not to overcome man's individual imperfections by adding them together, so much as to make use of many men's varying individual abilities by giving each a sufficient sphere of exercise? While all men are imperfect, they are not all imperfect to the same extent. Some have more courage, more ability, more insight, and more training than others; and an efficient organization can accomplish more than a mere collection of individuals, precisely because it may represent a standard of performance far above that of the average individual. Its merit is simply that of putting the collective power of the group at the service of its ablest members; and the ablest members of the group will never attain to an individual responsibility commensurate with their powers, until they are enabled to work efficiently towards the redemption of the collective responsibility. The nation gives individuality an increased scope and meaning by offering individuals a chance for effective service, such as they could never attain under a system of collective irresponsibility. Thus under a system of collective responsibility the process of social improvement is absolutely identified with that of individual improvement. The antithesis is not between nationalism and individualism, but between an individualism which is indiscriminate, and an individualism which is selective.

II
CONDITIONS OF
INDIVIDUAL EMANCIPATION

It is, then, essential to recognize that the individual American will never obtain a sufficiently complete chance of self-expression, until the American nation has earnestly undertaken and measurably achieved the realization of its collective purpose. As we shall see presently, the cure for this individual sterility lies partly with the individual himself or rather with the man who proposes to become an individual; and under any plan of economic or social organization, the man who proposes to become an individual is a condition of national as well as individual improvement. It is none the less true that any success in the achievement of the national purpose will contribute positively to the liberation of the individual, both by diminishing his temptations, improving his opportunities, and by enveloping him in an invigorating rather than an enervating moral and intellectual atmosphere.

It is the economic individualism of our existing national system which inflicts the most serious damage on American individuality; and American individual achievement in politics and science and the arts will remain partially impoverished as long as our fellow-countrymen neglect or refuse systematically to regulate the distribution of wealth in the national interest. I am aware, of course, that the prevailing American conviction is absolutely contradictory of the foregoing assertion. Americans have always associated individual freedom with the unlimited popular enjoyment of all available economic opportunities. Yet it would be far more true to say that the popular enjoyment of practically unrestricted economic opportunities is precisely the condition which makes for individual bondage. Neither does the bondage which such a system fastens upon the individual exist only in the case of those individuals who are victimized by the pressure of unlimited economic competition. Such victims exist, of course, in large numbers, and they will come to exist in still larger number hereafter; but hitherto, at least, the characteristic vice of the American system has not been the bondage imposed upon its victims. Much more insidious has been the bondage imposed upon the conquerors and their camp-followers. A man's in-

dividuality is as much compromised by success under the conditions imposed by such a system as it is by failure. His actual occupation may tend to make his individuality real and fruitful; but the quality of the work is determined by a merely acquisitive motive, and the man himself thereby usually debarred from obtaining any edifying personal independence or any peculiar personal distinction. Different as American business men are one from another in temperament, circumstances, and habits, they have a way of becoming fundamentally very much alike. Their individualities are forced into a common mold, because the ultimate measure of the value of their work is the same, and is nothing but its results in cash.

Woodrow Wilson, in his first inaugural address, articulated the philosophy of the New Freedom. As in the case of Roosevelt and Croly, Wilson too affirmed the need to redefine the national purpose in keeping with the growth of large-scale industrial enterprise. And while Wilson may be more critical than the other two on the social consequences of bigness, he nonetheless in this selection refused to turn back the clock in the direction of atomization.

WOODROW WILSON: THE NEW FREEDOM*

MY FELLOW CITIZENS:

There has been a change of government. It began two years ago, when the House of Representatives became Democratic by a decisive majority. It has now been completed. The Senate about to assemble will also be Democratic. The offices of President and Vice-President have been put into the hands of Democrats. What does the change mean? That is the question that is uppermost in our minds to-day. That is the question I am going to try to answer, in order, if I may, to interpret the occasion.

It means much more than the mere success of a party. The success of a party means little except when the Nation is using that party for a large and definite purpose. No one can mistake the purpose for which the Nation now seeks to use the Democratic Party. It seeks to use it to interpret a change in its own plans and point of view. Some old things with which we had grown familiar, and which had begun to creep into the very habit of our thought and of our lives, have altered their aspect as we have latterly looked critically upon them, with fresh, awakened eyes; have dropped their disguises and shown themselves alien and sinister. Some new things, as we

look frankly upon them, willing to comprehend their real character, have come to assume the aspect of things long believed in and familiar, stuff of our own convictions. We have been refreshed by a new insight into our own life.

We see that in many things that life is very great. It is incomparably great in its material aspects, in its body of wealth, in the diversity and sweep of its energy, in the industries which have been conceived and built up by the genius of individual men and the limitless enterprise of groups of men. It is great, also, very great, in its moral force.

Nowhere else in the world have noble men and women exhibited in more striking forms the beauty and the energy of sympathy and helpfulness and counsel in their efforts to rectify wrong, alleviate suffering, and set the weak in the way of strength and hope. We have built up, moreover, a great system of government, which has stood through a long age as in many respects a model for those who seek to set liberty upon foundations that will endure against fortuitous change, against storm and accident. Our life contains every great thing, and contains it in rich abundance.

But the evil has come with the good, and much fine gold has been corroded. With riches has come inexcusable waste. We have squandered a great part of what we might have used, and have not stopped to conserve the exceeding

* Reprinted from *Senate Documents*, 63rd Cong., special sess. (Washington, D.C.: 1913), I, no. 3, 3–6.

bounty of nature, without which our genius for enterprise would have been worthless and impotent, scorning to be careful, shamefully prodigal as well as admirably efficient. We have been proud of our industrial achievements, but we have not hitherto stopped thoughtfully enough to count the human cost, the cost of lives snuffed out, of energies overtaxed and broken, the fearful physical and spiritual cost to the men and women and children upon whom the dead weight and burden of it all has fallen pitilessly the years through. The groans and agony of it all had not yet reached our ears, the solemn, moving undertone of our life, coming up out of the mines and factories and out of every home where the struggle had its intimate and familiar seat. With the great Government went many deep secret things which we too long delayed to look into and scrutinize with candid, fearless eyes. The great Government we loved has too often been made use of for private and selfish purposes, and those who used it had forgotten the people.

At last a vision has been vouchsafed us of our life as a whole. We see the bad with the good, the debased and decadent with the sound and vital. With this vision we approach new affairs. Our duty is to cleanse, to reconsider, to restore, to correct the evil without impairing the good, to purify and humanize every process of our common life without weakening or sentimentalizing it. There has been something crude and heartless and unfeeling in our haste to succeed and be great. Our thought has been "Let every man look out for himself, let every generation look out for itself," while we reared giant machinery which made it impossible that any but those who stood at the levers of control should have a chance to look out for themselves. We had not forgotten our morals. We remembered well enough that we had set up a policy which was meant to serve the humblest as well as the most powerful, with an eye single to the standards of justice and fair play, and remembered it with pride. But we were very heedless and in a hurry to be great.

We have come now to the sober second thought. The scales of heedlessness have fallen from our eyes. We have made up our minds to square every process of our national life again with the standards we so proudly set up at the beginning and have always carried at our hearts. Our work is a work of restoration.

We have itemized with some degree of particularity the things that ought to be altered and here are some of the chief items: A tariff which cuts us off from our proper part in the commerce of the world, violates the just principles of taxation, and makes the Government a facile instrument in the hands of private interests; a banking and currency system based upon the necessity of the Government to sell its bonds fifty years ago and perfectly adapted to concentrating cash and restricting credits; an industrial system which, take it on all its sides, financial as well as administrative, holds capital in leading strings, restricts the liberties and limits the opportunities of labor, and exploits without renewing or conserving the natural resources of the country; a body of agricultural activities never yet given the efficiency of great business undertakings or served as it should be through the instrumentality of science taken directly to the farm, or afforded the facilities of credit best suited to its practical needs; watercourses undeveloped, waste places unreclaimed, forests untended, fast disappearing without plan or prospect of renewal, unregarded waste heaps at every mine. We have studied as perhaps no other nation has the most effective means of production, but we have not studied cost or economy as we should either as organizers of industry, as statesmen, or as individuals.

Nor have we studied and perfected the means by which government may be put at the service of humanity, in safeguarding the health of the Nation, the health of its men and its women and its children, as well as their rights in the struggle for existence. This is no sentimental duty. The firm basis of government is justice, not pity. These are matters of justice. There can be no equality or opportunity, the first essential of justice in the body politic, if men and women and children be not shielded in their lives, their very vitality, from the consequences of great industrial and social processes which they can not alter, control, or singly cope with. Society must see to it that it does not itself crush or weaken or damage its own constituent parts. The first duty of law is to keep sound the society it serves. Sanitary laws, pure food laws, and laws determining conditions of labor which individuals are powerless to determine for themselves are intimate parts of the very business of justice and legal efficiency.

These are some of the things we ought to do, and not leave the others undone, the old-fashioned, never-to-be-neglected, fundamental safeguarding of property and of individual right. This is the high enterprise of the new day: To lift everything that concerns our life as a Nation to the light that shines from the hearthfire of every man's conscience and vision of the right. It is inconceivable that we should do this as partisans; it is inconceivable we should do it in ignorance of the facts as they are or in blind haste. We shall restore, not destroy. We shall deal with our economic system as it is and as it may be modified, not as it might be if we had a clean sheet of paper to write upon; and step by step we shall make it what it should be, in the spirit of those who question their own wisdom and seek counsel and knowledge, not shallow self-satisfaction or the excitement of excursions whither they can not tell. Justice, and only justice, shall alway be our motto.

And yet it will be no cool process of mere science. The Nation has been deeply stirred, stirred by a solemn passion, stirred by the knowledge of wrong, of ideals lost, of government too often debauched and made an instrument of evil. The feelings with which we face this new age of right and opportunity sweep across our heartstrings like some air out of God's own presence, where justice and mercy are reconciled and the judge and the brother are one. We know our task to be no mere task of politics but a task which shall search us through and through, whether we be able to understand our time and the need of our people, whether we be indeed their spokesmen and interpreters, whether we have the pure heart to comprehend and the rectified will to choose our high course of action.

This is not a day of triumph; it is a day of dedication. Here muster, not the forces of party, but the forces of humanity. Men's hearts wait upon us; men's lives hang in the balance; men's hopes call upon us to say what we will do. Who shall live up to the great trust? Who dares fail to try? I summon all honest men, all patriotic, all forward-looking men, to my side. God helping me, I will not fail them, if they will but counsel and sustain me!

CHAPTER EIGHTEEN

THE WILSONIAN DREAM
OF WORLD ORDER

Woodrow Wilson's importance in establishing the broad outlines of twentieth-century American foreign policy is only now, with the experience of World War II and a protracted Cold War, becoming fully understood. Taking the last five decades in historical perspective, one is struck by the fact of long-range continuity: a groping toward and gradual refinement of, the principle of collective security. Wilson can be credited with a bold departure. He led the United States away from its traditional role in international affairs, as symbolized by Washington's Farewell Address, and called for a counterconception in foreign policy: the preservation of world peace through a supranational organization when feasible and through regional mutual security pacts when not. The administrations of Wilson, Franklin D. Roosevelt, Truman, Eisenhower, and Kennedy have shared the same basic assumption that America must draw more closely together with Western European nations when faced by external threats. Whenever Western society was disrupted—whether by the Nazis in the 1930's and 1940's or by the Communists in more recent times—the policy sought was one of collective security. Wilson was one of the first to realize that, in an era of expanding economies and dynamic power blocs, the need for the imposition of stability was imperative. Whether his techniques following World War I were right or wrong is of less interest today than the fact that he believed the United States was menaced and felt involvement to be a necessary course.

When the war ended, Wilson made what at the time seemed to be a series of blunders, but which appear now as actions consistent with his larger vision. He angered the Republicans by announcing that he would attend the Peace Conference in person. This came after the Democratic defeat in the 1918 congressional elections, which the Republicans interpreted as a vote of no confidence. For Wilson, however, it was necessary to exert personal leadership at this time. A vindictive peace was not the answer; to ensure a lasting peace, he sought to steer the United States into participation in the League of Nations. America, he reasoned, must be made to see the importance of working with the rest of the world. In effect, Wilson was asking the American people to change one of their most basic conceptions, that of a policy of isolation.

Yet he overestimated the readiness of the American people to accept a new outlook, just as he overestimated, because of the cheering crowds he met in Europe, his ability to influence European statesmen to accept his views. Wilson insisted upon one point: the League must be included in the peace treaty, for only with the creation of the League could the treaty itself be made meaningful. Wilson was adamant; he would not compromise with the Senate and believed that public opinion would support him in this position.

But public opinion was largely apathetic, or was concerned more with domestic unrest than with the treaty. In some cases, however, hostility to his ideas was specific; the German-American and Irish-American groups, for example, expressed significant opposition. The latter group, in particular, had strong anti-British sentiments and criticized Wilson for not applying the self-determination principle to Ireland. Even many of the liberal journals did not go along with the President, arguing that the Treaty of Versailles was too vindictive. Perhaps most important, was the pervasive atmosphere of isolationism in America. The emergency over, people merely wanted to be left alone; they did not want to shoulder the responsibility of a world power. And these feelings Wilson did not fully appreciate or gauge, but thought instead that the people would stand behind him in any showdown with the Senate. He did not recognize the growing nationalistic appeal which struck such a sensitive nerve, as exemplified by the Palmer Raids and the attacks on labor. Idealism was quickly to become transformed into disillusionment.

The treaty itself, regardless of its merits, was bound to become a partisan issue, centering around Republican hostility to Wilson. Strong presidential leadership, the New Freedom domestic program, the fear of Wilson's seeking a third term, and the fact that he did not consult with Republicans all contributed to the bitterness against a "Wilsonian peace." The Republicans, with the 1920 election in mind, focused their opposition on the League. And this meant specifically that if the error of 1912 (a split in Republican ranks) was not to be repeated, the isolationist wing of the party had to be placated. There was no hope that the country at large would exert a moderating influence on party councils, for the fear prevailed that the irreconcilables would start a third party and thus ensure the continuation of the Democrats in office. The Democrats, on the other hand, were also not exempt from making political capital out of the League issue and Wilson's leadership. Partisan feelings ran high on both sides.

The fight, then, turned to the Senate, a body strongly desiring to assert its supremacy after several years of wartime presidential leadership. Trouble could be expected from the start; the Democrats did not even have a majority, much less the two-thirds support needed for ratification. On the Republican side, there was agreement that changes were necessary, particularly in order that the treaty could no longer be regarded as solely a Democratic measure. Nor were such reservations inspired simply from partisan considerations; there was a genuine fear of unrestricted immigration, lowered tariffs, and most important, the possibility that the United States—by Article 10—would be morally obligated to come to the aid of another nation without the consent of Congress. Three camps emerged within Republican ranks—mild and strong reservationists, and irreconcilables. The first group may well have supported the Democrats in voting down the strong reservations of Henry Cabot Lodge, thus making possible the passage of the treaty with minor changes. But Wilson made the critical mistake of refusing to cooperate with this group. The irreconcilables, or "bitter-enders," ensured the treaty's defeat through their destructive tactics and threat to bolt the party. Finally, there is the position associated with Lodge. It would be incorrect to make Lodge the whipping-boy in discussing the defeat of the League, for matters were too complex to permit such a black-and-white judgment. For one thing, Wilson's inflexibility must not be forgotten. For another, Lodge, unlike the irreconcilables, was not an isolationist. Moreover, he was sincere in his fear that American sovereignty might be jeopardized. But, in the last analysis, Lodge *was* also partisan and had an eye on the 1920 elections.

The Lodge side won; all sentiment to enter the League soon died, America was not yet ready to accept the principle of collective security. Woodrow Wilson had a prophetic vision of the course needed to ensure world peace, but he was ahead of his times.

Urging the adoption of the principle of collective security even before America entered the war, President Wilson, on January 22, 1917, sketched the blueprint for a League of Nations.

WOODROW WILSON: WORLD PEACE*

GENTLEMEN OF THE SENATE: On the eighteenth of December last I addressed an identic note to the governments of the nations now at war requesting them to state, more definitely than they had yet been stated by either group of belligerents, the terms upon which they would deem it possible to make peace. I spoke on behalf of humanity and of the rights of all neutral nations like our own, many of whose most vital interests the war puts in constant jeopardy. The Central Powers united in a reply which stated merely that they were ready to meet their antagonists in conference to discuss terms of peace. The Entente Powers have replied much more definitely and have stated, in general terms, indeed, but with sufficient definiteness to imply details, the arrangements, guarantees, and acts of reparation which they deem to be the indispensable conditions of a satisfactory settlement. We are that much nearer a definite discussion of the peace which shall end the present war. We are that much nearer the discussion of the international concert which must thereafter hold the world at peace. In every discussion of the peace that must end this war it is taken for granted that that peace must be followed by some definite concert of power which will make it virtually impossible that any such catastrophe should ever overwhelm us again. Every lover of mankind, every sane and thoughtful

man must take that for granted.

I have sought this opportunity to address you because I thought that I owed it to you, as the council associated with me in the final determination of our international obligations, to disclose to you without reserve the thought and purpose that have been taking form in my mind in regard to the duty of our Government in the days to come when it will be necessary to lay afresh and upon a new plan the foundations of peace among the nations.

It is inconceivable that the people of the United States should play no part in that great enterprise. To take part in such a service will be the opportunity for which they have sought to prepare themselves by the very principles and purposes of their polity and the approved practices of their Government ever since the days when they set up a new nation in the high and honourable hope that it might in all that it was and did show mankind the way to liberty. They cannot in honour withhold the service to which they are now about to be challenged. They do not wish to withhold it. But they owe it to themselves and to the other nations of the world to state the conditions under which they will feel free to render it.

That service is nothing less than this, to add their authority and their power to the authority and force of other nations to guarantee peace and justice throughout the world. Such a settlement cannot now be long postponed. It is right that before it comes this Government should frankly

* Reprinted from *Senate Document 685*, 64th Cong., 2nd sess. (Washington, D.C.: 1916–1917).

formulate the conditions upon which it would feel justified in asking our people to approve its formal and solemn adherence to a League for Peace. I am here to attempt to state those conditions.

The present war must first be ended; but we owe it to candour and to a just regard for the opinion of mankind to say that, so far as our participation in guarantees of future peace is concerned, it makes a great deal of difference in what way and upon what terms it is ended. The treaties and agreements which bring it to an end must embody terms which will create a peace that is worth guaranteeing and preserving, a peace that will win the approval of mankind, not merely a peace that will serve the several interests and immediate aims of the nations engaged. We shall have no voice in determining what those terms shall be, but we shall, I feel sure, have a voice in determining whether they shall be made lasting or not by the guarantees of a universal covenant; and our judgment upon what is fundamental and essential as a condition precedent to permanency should be spoken now, not afterwards when it may be too late.

No covenant of cooperative peace that does not include the peoples of the New World can suffice to keep the future safe against war; and yet there is only one sort of peace that the peoples of America could join in guaranteeing. The elements of that peace must be elements that engage the confidence and satisfy the principles of the American governments, elements consistent with their political faith and with the practical convictions which the peoples of America have once for all embraced and undertaken to defend.

I do not mean to say that any American government would throw any obstacle in the way of any terms of peace the governments now at war might agree upon, or seek to upset them when made, whatever they might be. I only take it for granted that mere terms of peace between the belligerents will not satisfy even the belligerents themselves. Mere agreements may not make peace secure. It will be absolutely necessary that a force be created as a guarantor of the permanency of the settlement so much greater than the force of any nation now engaged or any alliance hitherto formed or projected that no nation, no probable combination of nations could face or withstand it. If the peace presently to be made is to endure, it must be a peace made secure by the organized major force of mankind.

The terms of the immediate peace agreed upon will determine whether it is a peace for which such a guarantee can be secured. The question upon which the whole future peace and policy of the world depends is this: Is the present war a struggle for a just and secure peace, or only for a new balance of power? If it be only a struggle for a new balance of power, who will guarantee, who can guarantee, the stable equilibrium of the new arrangement? Only a tranquil Europe can be a stable Europe. There must be, not a balance of power, but a community of power; not organized rivalries, but an organized common peace.

Fortunately we have received very explicit assurances on this point. The statesmen of both of the groups of nations now arrayed against one another have said, in terms that could not be misinterpreted, that it was no part of the purpose they had in mind to crush their antagonists. But the implications of these assurances may not be equally clear to all,—may not be the same on both sides of the water. I think it will be serviceable if I attempt to set forth what we understand them to be.

They imply, first of all, that it must be a peace without victory. It is not pleasant to say this. I beg that I may be permitted to put my own interpretation upon it and that it may be understood that no other interpretation was in my thought. I am seeking only to face realities and to face them without soft concealments. Victory would mean peace forced upon the loser, a victor's terms imposed upon the vanquished. It would be accepted in humiliation, under duress, at an intolerable sacrifice, and would leave a sting, a resentment, a bitter memory upon which terms of peace would rest, not permanently, but only as upon quicksand. Only a peace between equals can last. Only a peace the very principle of which is equality and a common participation in a common benefit. The right state of mind, the right feeling between nations, is as necessary for a lasting peace as is the just settlement of vexed questions of territory or of racial and national allegiance.

The equality of nations upon which peace must be founded if it is to last must be an equality of rights; the guarantees exchanged must neither recognize nor imply a difference between big nations and small, between those that are powerful and those that are weak. Right must be based upon the common strength, not upon the individual strength, of the nations upon whose concert peace will depend. Equality of territory or of resources there of course cannot be; nor any other sort of equality not gained in the ordinary peaceful and legitimate development of the peoples themselves. But no one asks or expects anything more than an equality of rights. Mankind is looking now for freedom of life, not for equipoises of power.

And there is a deeper thing involved than even equality of right among organized nations. No peace can last, or ought to last, which does not recognize and accept the principle that governments derive all their just powers from the consent of the governed, and that no right anywhere exists to hand peoples about from sovereignty to sovereignty as if they were property. I take it for granted, for instance, if I may venture upon a single example, that statesmen everywhere are agreed that there should be a united, independent, and autonomous Poland, and that henceforth inviolable security of life, of worship, and of industrial and social development should be guaranteed to all peoples who have lived hitherto under the power of governments devoted to a faith and purpose hostile to their own.

I speak of this, not because of any desire to exalt an abstract political principle which has always been held very dear by those who have sought to build up liberty in America, but for the same reason that I have spoken of the other conditions of peace which seem to me clearly indispensable,—because I wish frankly to uncover realities. Any peace which does not recognize and accept this principle will inevitably be upset. It will not rest upon the affections or the convictions of mankind. The ferment of spirit of whole populations will fight subtly and constantly against it, and all the world will sympathize. The world can be at peace only if its life is stable, and there can be no stability where the will is in rebellion, where there is not tranquility of spirit and a sense of justice, of freedom, and of right.

So far as practicable, moreover, every great people now struggling towards a full development of its resources and of its powers should be assured a direct outlet to the great highways of the sea. Where this cannot be done by the cession of territory, it can no doubt be done by the neutralization of direct rights of way under the general guarantee which will assure the peace itself. With a right comity of arrangement no nation need be shut away from free access to the open paths of the world's commerce.

And the paths of the sea must alike in law and in fact be free. The freedom of the seas is the *sine qua non* of peace, equality, and cooperation. No doubt a somewhat radical reconsideration of many of the rules of international practice hitherto thought to be established may be necessary in order to make the seas indeed free and common in practically all circumstances for the use of mankind, but the motive for such changes is convincing and compelling. There can be no trust or intimacy between the peoples of the world without them. The free, constant, unthreatened intercourse of nations is an essential part of the process of peace and of development. It need not be difficult either to define or to secure the freedom of the seas if the governments of the world sincerely desire to come to an agreement concerning it.

It is a problem closely connected with the limitation of naval armaments and the cooperation of the navies of the world in keeping the seas at once free and safe. And the question of limiting naval armaments opens the wider and perhaps more difficult question of the limitation of armies and of all programmes of military preparation. Difficult and delicate as these questions are, they must be faced with the utmost candour and decided in a spirit of real accommodation if peace is to come with healing in its wings, and come to stay. Peace cannot be had without concession and sacrifice. There can be no sense of safety and equality among the nations if great preponderating armaments are henceforth to continue here and there to be built up and maintained. The statesmen of the world must plan for peace and nations must adjust and accommodate their policy to it as they have planned for war and made ready for pitiless contest and rivalry. The question of armaments, whether on land or sea, is the most immediately and intensely practical question connected with the future fortunes of nations and of mankind.

I have spoken upon these great matters without reserve and with the utmost explicitness because it has seemed to me to be necessary if the world's yearning desire for peace was anywhere to find free voice and utterance. Perhaps I am the only person in high authority amongst all the peoples of the world who is at liberty to speak and hold nothing back. I am speaking as an individual, and yet I am speaking also, of course, as the responsible head of a great government, and I feel confident that I have said what the people of the United States would wish me to say. May I not add that I hope and believe that I am in effect speaking for liberals and friends of humanity in every nation and of every programme of liberty? I would fain believe that I am speaking for the silent mass of mankind everywhere who have as yet had no place or opportunity to speak their real hearts out concerning the death and ruin they see to have come already upon the persons and the homes they hold most dear.

And in holding out the expectation that the people and Government of the United States will join the other civilized nations of the world in guaranteeing the permanence of peace upon such terms as I have named I speak with the greater boldness and confidence because it is clear to every man who can think that there is in this promise no breach in either our traditions or our policy as a nation, but a fulfilment, rather, of all that we have professed or striven for.

I am proposing, as it were, that the nations should with one accord adopt the doctrine of President Monroe as the doctrine of the world: that no nation should seek to extend its polity over any other nation or people, but that every people should be left free to determine its own polity, its own way of development, unhindered, unthreatened, unafraid, the little along with the great and powerful.

I am proposing that all nations henceforth avoid entangling alliances which would draw them into competitions of power, catch them in a net of intrigue and selfish rivalry, and disturb their own affairs with influences intruded from without. There is no entangling alliance in a concert of power. When all unite to act in the same sense and with the same purpose all act in the common interest and are free to live their own lives under a common protection.

I am proposing government by the consent of the governed; that freedom of the seas which in international conference after conference representatives of the United States have urged with the eloquence of those who are the convinced disciples of liberty; and that moderation of armaments which makes of armies and navies a power for order merely, not an instrument of aggression or of selfish violence.

These are American principles, American policies. We could stand for no others. And they are also the principles and policies of forward looking men and women everywhere, of every modern nation, of every enlightened community. They are the principles of mankind and must prevail.

The *New York Times*, strongly supporting Wilson on the League of Nations, called for a treaty with the means to enforce peaceful relations among nations. In July, 1919, it did not anticipate the difficulties standing in the way, and confidently predicted that the Senate would bow to the "irresistible force" of public opinion.

NEW YORK TIMES: PEACE WITH SAFEGUARDS*

The Council met with the purpose to end the war by a treaty of peace. As the work advanced the Council's view became clearer and broader, its purpose ripened into an aspiration, and it wrote a treaty which, if good faith carries hope to fulfillment, will secure the world in the enjoyment of peace. The spirit which guided the Council in its labors, the spirit of the Treaty and of the League covenant, could have no more lucid presentation than in the address of President Wilson to the Senate yesterday. His recital of the work done at Paris is like the story of a human soul rising from concern with grosser things to the higher heritage. . . . It was natural, it was inevitable, that in the beginning the thoughts of statesmen should run in the old channels, that their formulation of terms should incline to the old pattern. Following that ancient road the Council would have come, at the end, to another Treaty of Vienna, to a convention as vicious and unstable as that which the Congress of Berlin brought forth.

But new ideas were born, the American leaven had done its work. The nations had accepted Mr. Wilson's guiding principles of peace, the Council very early saw that those principles must become the soul of the Treaty. It saw something else, not less clearly. It saw that a treaty that merely ended the war and restored relations of nominal amity between the contending nations would not deliver the world out of the old order into the new. The President told the Senate that the statesmen of all belligerent countries were agreed that a League of Nations "must be created to sustain the settlements that would be effected." . . .

In that way all the statesmen of the Council came to see that the League was "not a counsel of perfection, but a council of necessity." Out of

that state of mind of the chief statesmen of Europe and America the League covenant came into being. Without it the Treaty of Versailles is no better, no sounder, no more enduring than hundreds of other treaties to which sovereigns or their envoys have affixed their names only to tear them to tatters or to see them torn as soon as "the chances of politics" again set passions free and summoned armed legions to the field. Without the covenant there is nothing to restrain Germany that was not in other treaties she has broken. Without it there is no possibility of extending protection over the people the war has set free from bondage and raised to the dignity of constituted nations. Without it there would have been no progress for history to record since the end of Napoleon's wars.

It is only in the United States that the covenant and the wisdom of the policy it embodies are called in question. The League of Nations is accepted as a new birth of freedom for the world by every responsible statesman of Europe, by the peoples of Europe, by the people of the United States, we may say by every statesman of the United States whose mind is free from the beclouding bias of some personal or partisan feeling. For a little time opposition will continue—in the Senate. It will give way, it must give way, the Treaty will be ratified, it must be ratified, because the people of the country will not permit it to be rejected or to be amended, since amendment is rejection. The address of the President yesterday compels ratification, it is an irresistible force which the Senate cannot withstand. Such a presentation of great principles as the President has made, with perfect straightforwardness and simplicity of manner, illuminating, as unassailable as the universally honored precepts of morality, has never failed to move profoundly the American people and to bring them to conviction and assent.

---

* Reprinted from *New York Times*, July 11, 1919, by permission.

Addressing the Senate on August 12, 1919, Henry Cabot Lodge viewed with alarm the prospect of America being drawn into the internal conflicts of other nations. While repudiating isolationism, Lodge nonetheless contended that the League covenant violated the sovereign rights of the United States and could not be accepted without significant modifications.

HENRY CABOT LODGE: OUR FIRST IDEAL IS OUR COUNTRY*

No revolutionary movement, no internal conflict, of any magnitude can fail to affect the peace of the world. The French Revolution, which was wholly internal at the beginning, affected the peace of the world to such an extent that it brought on a world war which lasted some 25 years. Can anyone say that our Civil War did not affect the peace of the world? At this very moment, who would deny that the condition of Russia, with internal conflicts raging in all parts of that great Empire, does not affect the peace of the world and therefore come properly within the jurisdiction of the league? "Any matter affecting the peace of the world" is a very broad statement which could be made to justify almost any interference on the part of the league with the internal affairs of other countries. That this fair and obvious interpretation is the one given to it abroad is made perfectly apparent in the direct and vigorous statement of M. Clemenceau in his letter to Mr. Paderewski, in which he takes the ground in behalf of the Jews and other nationalities in Poland that they should be protected, and where he says that the associated powers would feel themselves bound to secure guaranties in Poland "of certain essential rights which will afford to the inhabitants the necessary protection, whatever changes may take place in the internal constitution of the Polish Republic," he contemplates and defends interference with the internal affairs of Poland—among other things—in behalf of a complete religious freedom, a purpose with which we all deeply sympathize. These promises of the French prime minister are embodied in effective clauses in the treaties with Germany and with Poland and deal with the internal affairs of nations, and their execution is intrusted to the "principal allied and associated powers;" that is, to the United States, Great Britain, France, Italy, and Japan. This is a practical demonstration of what can be done under article 3 and under article 11 of the league covenant, and the authority which permits interference in behalf of religious freedom—an admirable object—is easily extended to the repression of internal disturbances, which may well prove a less admirable purpose. If Europe desires such an alliance or league with a power of this kind, so be it. I have no ob-

jection, provided they do not interfere with the American Continents or force us against our will but bound by a moral obligation into all the quarrels of Europe. If England, abandoning the policy of Canning, desires to be a member of a league which has such powers as this, I have not a word to say. But I object in the strongest possible way to having the United States agree, directly or indirectly, to be controlled by a league which may at any time, and perfectly lawfully and in accordance with the terms of the covenant, be drawn in to deal with internal conflicts in other countries, no matter what those conflicts may be. We should never permit the United States to be involved in any internal conflict in another country, except by the will of her people expressed through the Congress which represents them.

With regard to wars of external aggression on a member of the league, the case is perfectly clear. There can be no genuine dispute whatever about the meaning of the first clause of article 10. In the first place, it differs from every other obligation in being individual and placed upon each nation without the intervention of the league. Each nation for itself promises to respect and preserve as against external aggression the boundaries and the political independence of every member of the league. Of the right of the United States to give such a guaranty I have never had the slightest doubt, and the elaborate arguments which have been made here and the learning which has been displayed about our treaty with Granada, now Colombia, and with Panama, were not necessary for me, because, I repeat, there can be no doubt of our right to give a guaranty to another nation that we will protect its boundaries and independence. The point I wish to make is that the pledge is an individual pledge. We have, for example, given guaranties to Panama and for obvious and sufficient reasons. The application of that guaranty would not be in the slightest degree affected by ten or twenty other nations giving the same pledge, if Panama, when in danger, appealed to us to fulfill our obligation. We should be bound to do so without the slightest reference to the other guarantors. In article 10 the United States is bound on the appeal of any member of the league not only to respect but to preserve its independence and its boundaries, and that pledge, if we give it, must be fulfilled.

There is to me no distinction whatever in a treaty between what some persons are pleased to

---

* Reprinted from *Congressional Record*, 66th Cong., 1st sess. (Washington, D.C.: 1919–1920), pp. 3779–3784.

call legal and moral obligations. A treaty rests and must rest, except where it is imposed under duress and securities and hostages are taken for its fulfillment, upon moral obligations. No doubt a great power impossible of coercion can cast aside a moral obligation if it sees fit and escape from the performance of the duty which it promises. The pathway of dishonor is always open. I for one, however, can not conceive of voting for a clause of which I disapprove because I know it can be escaped in that way. Whatever the United States agrees to, by that agreement she must abide. Nothing could so surely destroy all prospects of the world's peace as to have any powerful nation refuse to carry out an obligation, direct or indirect, because it rests only on moral grounds. Whatever we promise we must carry out to the full, "without mental reservation or purpose of evasion." To me any other attitude is inconceivable. Without the most absolute and minute good faith in carrying out a treaty to which we have agreed, without ever resorting to doubtful interpretations or to the plea that it is only a moral obligation, treaties are worthless. The greatest foundation of peace is the scrupulous observance of every promise, express or implied, of every pledge, whether it can be described as legal or moral. No vote should be given to any clause in any treaty or to any treaty except in this spirit and with this understanding.

I return, then, to the first clause of article 10. It is, I repeat, an individual obligation. It requires no action on the part of the league, except that in the second sentence the authorities of the league are to have the power to advise as to the means to be employed in order to fulfill the purpose of the first sentence. But that is a detail of execution, and I consider that we are morally and in honor bound to accept and act upon that advice. The broad fact remains that if any member of the league suffering from external aggression should appeal directly to the United States for support the United States would be bound to give that support in its own capacity and without reference to the action of other powers, because the United States itself is abound, and I hope the day will never come when the United States will not carry out its promises. If that day should come, and the United States or any other great country should refuse, no matter how specious the reasons, to fulfill both in letter and spirit every obligation in this covenant, the United States would be dishonored and the league would crumble into dust, leaving behind it a legacy of wars. If China should rise up and attack Japan in an effort to undo the great wrong of the cession of the control of Shantung to that power, we should be bound under the terms of article 10 to sustain Japan against China, and a guaranty of that sort is never invoked except when the question has passed beyond the stage of negotiation and has become a question for the application of force. I do not like the prospect. It shall not come into existence by any vote of mine. . . .

It has seemed to me that the British delegation traveled a little out of the precincts of the peace conference when they undertook to explain the Monroe doctrine and tell the United States what it was and what it was not proposed to do with it under the new article. That, however, is merely a matter of taste and judgment. Their statement that the Monroe doctrine under this article, if any question arose in regard to it, would be passed upon and interpreted by the league of nations is absolutely correct. There is no doubt that this is what the article means. Great Britain so stated it, and no American authority, whether friendly or unfriendly to the league, has dared to question it. I have wondered a little why it was left to the British delegation to explain that article, which so nearly concerns the United States, but that was merely a fugitive thought upon which I will not dwell. The statement of M. Lausanne is equally explicit and truthful, but he makes one mistake. He says in substance that if we are to meddle in Europe, Europe can not be excluded from the Americas. He overlooks the fact that the Monroe doctrine also says: "Our policy in regard to Europe, which was adopted at an early stage of the wars which have so long agitated that quarter of the globe, nevertheless remains the same, which is not to interfere in the internal concerns of any of the powers."

The Monroe doctrine was the corollary of Washington's neutrality policy and of his injunction against permanent alliances. It reiterates and reaffirms the principle. We do not seek to meddle in the affairs of Europe and keep Europe out of the Americas. It is as important to keep the United States out of European affairs as to keep Europe out of the American Continents. Let us maintain the Monroe doctrine, then, in its entirety, and not only preserve our own safety, but in this way best promote the real peace of the world. Whenever the preservation of freedom and civilization and the overthrow of a menacing world conqueror summon us we shall respond fully and nobly, as we did in 1917. He who doubts that we should do so has little faith in America. But let it be our own act, and not done reluctantly by the coercion of other nations, at the bidding or by the permission of other countries.

Let me now deal with the article itself. We have here some protective coloration again. The Monroe doctrine is described as a "regional understanding," whatever that may mean. The boundaries between the States of the Union, I suppose, are "regional understandings," if anyone chooses to apply to them that somewhat swollen phraseology. But the Monroe doctrine is no more a regional understanding than it is an "international engagement." The Monroe doctrine was a policy declared by President Monroe. Its immediate purpose was to shut out Europe from interfering with the South American Republics, which the Holy Alliance designed to do. It was stated broadly, however, as we all know, and went much further than that. It was, as I have just said, the corollary of Washington's declaration against our interfering in European questions. It was so regarded by Jefferson at the time, and by John Quincy Adams, who formulated it, and by President Monroe, who declared it. It rested firmly on the great law of self-preservation, which is the basic principle of every independent State. It is not necessary to trace its history, or to point out the extensions which it has received, or its universal acceptance by all American statesmen without regard to party. All Americans have always been for it. They may not have known its details, or read all the many discussions in regard to it, but they knew that it was an American doctrine, and that, broadly stated, it meant the exclusion of Europe from interference with American affairs and from any attempt to colonize or set up new States within the boundaries of the American Continent. I repeat, it was purely an American doctrine, a purely American policy, designed and wisely designed for our defense. It has never been an "international engagement." No nation has ever formally recognized it. It has been the subject of reservation at international conventions by American delegates. It has never been a "regional understanding," or an understanding of any kind with anybody. It was the declaration of the United States of America, in their own behalf, supported by their own power. They brought it into being, and its life was predicated on the force which the United States could place behind it. Unless the United States could sustain it, it would die. The United States has supported it. It has lived—strong, efficient, respected. It is now proposed to kill it by a provision in a treaty for a league of nations.

The instant that the United States, who declared, interpreted, and sustained the doctrine, ceases to be the sole judge of what it means, that instant the Monroe doctrine ceases and disappears from history and from the face of the earth. I think it is just as undesirable to have Europe interfere in American affairs now as Mr. Monroe thought it was in 1823, and equally undesirable that we should be compelled to involve ourselves in all the wars and brawls of Europe. The Monroe doctrine has made for peace. Without the Monroe doctrine we should have had many a struggle with European powers to save ourselves from possible assault and certainly from the necessity of becoming a great military power, always under arms and always ready to resist invasion from States in our near neighborhood. In the interests of the peace of the world it is now proposed to wipe away this American policy, which has been a bulwark and a barrier for peace. With one exception it has always been successful, and then success was only delayed. When we were torn by civil war France saw fit to enter Mexico and endeavored to establish an empire there. When our hands were once free the empire perished, and with it the unhappy tool of the third Napoleon. If the United States had not been rent by civil war no such attempt would have been made, and nothing better illustrates the value to the cause of peace of the Monroe doctrine. Why, in the name of peace, should we extinguish it? Why, in the name of peace, should we be called upon to leave the interpretation of the Monroe doctrine to other nations? It is an American policy. It is our own. It has guarded us well, and I for one can never find consent in my heart to destroy it by a clause in a treaty and hand over its body for dissection to the nations of Europe. . . .

I have dwelt only upon those points which seem to me most dangerous. There are, of course, many others, but these points, in the interest not only of the safety of the United States but of the maintenance of the treaty and the peace of the world, should be dealt with here before it is too late. Once in the league the chance of amendment is so slight that it is not worth considering. Any analysis of the provisions of this league covenant, however, brings out in startling relief one great fact. Whatever may be said, it is not a league of peace; it is an alliance, dominated at the present moment by five great powers, really by three, and it has all the marks of an alliance. The development of international law is neglected. The court which is to decide disputes brought before it fills but a small place. The conditions for which this league really provides with the utmost care are political conditions, not judicial questions, to be reached by the executive council and the assembly, purely political bodies without any trace of a judicial character about them. Such being its machinery, the control being in the hands of political appointees whose votes will be controlled by interest and expediency, it exhibits that most marked characteristic of an alliance—that its decisions are to be carried out by force. Those articles upon which the whole structure rests are articles which provide for the use of force; that is, for war. This league to enforce peace does a great deal for enforcement and very little for peace. It makes more essential provisions looking to war than to peace for the settlement of disputes.

Article 10 I have already discussed. There is no question that the preservation of a State against external aggression can contemplate nothing but war. In article 11, again, the league is authorized to take any action which may be necessary to safeguard the peace of the world. "Any action" includes war. We also have specific provisions for a boycott, which is a form of economic warfare. The use of troops might be avoided, but the enforcement of a boycott would require blockades in all probability, and certainly a boycott in its essence is simply an effort to starve a people into submission, to ruin their trade, and, in the case of nations which are not self-supporting, to cut off their food supply. The misery and suffering caused by such a measure as this may easily rival that caused by actual war. Article 16 embodies the boycott and also, in the last paragraph, provides explicitly for war. We are told that the word "recommend" has no binding force; it constitutes a moral obligation; that is all. But it means that if we, for example, should refuse to accept the recommendation we should nullify the operation of article 16 and, to that extent, of the league. It seems to me that to attempt to relieve us of clearly imposed duties by saying that the word "recommend" is not binding is an escape of which no nation regarding the sanctity of treaties and its own honor would care to avail itself. The provisions of article 16 are extended to States outside the league who refuse to obey its command to come in and submit themselves to its jurisdiction—another provision for war.

Taken altogether, these provisions for war present what to my mind is the gravest objection to this league in its present form. We are told that of course nothing will be done in the way of warlike acts without the assent of Congress. If that is true let us say so in the covenant. But as it stands there is no doubt whatever in my mind that American troops and American ships may be ordered to any part of the world by nations other than the United States, and that is a proposition to which I for one can never assent. It must be made perfectly clear that no American soldiers, not even a corporal's guard, that no American sailors, not even the crew of a submarine, can ever be engaged in war or ordered anywhere except by the constitutional authorities of the United States. To Congress is granted by the Constitution the right to declare war, and nothing that would take the troops out of the country at the bidding or demand of other nations should ever be permitted except through congressional action. The lives of Americans must never be sacrificed except by the will of the American people expressed through their chosen Representatives in Congress. This is a point upon which no doubt can be permitted. American soldiers and American sailors have never failed the country when the country called upon them. They went in their hundreds of thousands into the war just closed. They went to die for the great cause of freedom and of civilization. They went at their service. We were late in entering the war. We made no preparation, as we ought to have done, for the ordeal which was clearly coming upon us; but we went and we turned the wavering scale. It was done by the American soldier, the American sailor, and the spirit and energy of the American people. They overrode all obstacles and all shortcomings on the part of the administration or of Congress and gave to their country a great place in the great victory. It was the first time we had been called upon to rescue the civilized world. Did we fail? On the contrary, we succeeded, succeeded largely and nobly, and we did it without any command from any league of nations. When the emergency came we met it, and we were able to meet it because we had built up on this continent the greatest and most powerful Nation in the world, built it up under our own policies, in our own way, and one great element of our strength was the fact that we had held aloof and had not thrust

ourselves into European quarrels; that we had no selfish interest to serve. We made great sacrifices. We have done splendid work. I believe that we do not require to be told by foreign nations when we shall do work which freedom and civilization require. I think we can move to victory much better under our own command than under the command of others. Let us unite with the world to promote the peaceable settlement of all international disputes. Let us try to develop international law. Let us associate ourselves with the other nations for these purposes. But let us retain in our own hands and in our own control the lives of the youth of the land. Let no American be sent into battle except by the constituted authorities of his own country and by the will of the people of the United States.

Those of us, Mr. President, who are either wholly opposed to the league, or who are trying to preserve the independence and the safety of the United States by changing the terms of the league, and who are endeavoring to make the league, if we are to be a member of it, less certain to promote war instead of peace have been reproached with selfishness in our outlook and with a desire to keep our country in a state of isolation. So far as the question of isolation goes, it is impossible to isolate the United States. I well remember the time, 20 years ago, when eminent Senators and other distinguished gentlemen who were opposing the Philippines and shrieking about imperialism sneered at the statement made by some of us, that the United States had become a world power. I think no one now would question that the Spanish war marked the entrance of the United States into world affairs to a degree which had never obtained before. It was both an inevitable and an irrevocable step, and our entrance into the war with Germany certainly showed once and for all that the United States was not unmindful of its world responsibilities. We may set aside all this empty talk about isolation. Nobody expects to isolate the United States or to make it a hermit Nation, which is a sheer absurdity. But there is a wide difference between taking a suitable part and bearing a due responsibility in world affairs and plunging the United States into every controversy and conflict on the face of the globe. By meddling in all the differences which may arise among any portion or fragment of humankind we simply fritter away our influence and injure ourselves to no good purpose. We shall be of far more value to the world and its peace by occupying, so far as possible, the situation which we have occupied for the last 20 years and by adhering to the policy of Washington and Hamilton, of Jefferson and Monroe, under which we have risen to our present greatness and prosperity. The fact that we have been separated by our geographical situation and by our consistent policy from the broils of Europe has made us more than any one thing capable of performing the great work which we performed in the war against

Germany, and our disinterestedness is of far more value to the world than our eternal meddling in every possible dispute could ever be.

Now as to our selfishness. I have no desire to boast that we are better than our neighbors, but the fact remains that this Nation in making peace with Germany had not a single selfish or individual interest to serve. All we asked was that Germany should be rendered incapable of again breaking forth, with all the horrors incident to German warfare, upon an unoffending world, and that demand was shared by every free nation and indeed by humanity itself. For ourselves we asked absolutely nothing. We have not asked any government or governments to guarantee our boundaries or our political independence. We have no fear in regard to either. We have sought no territory, no privileges, no advantages, for ourselves. That is the fact. It is apparent on the face of the treaty. I do not mean to reflect upon a single one of the powers with which we have been associated in the war against Germany, but there is not one of them which has not sought individual advantages for their own national benefit. I do not criticize their desires at all. The services and sacrifices of England and France and Belgium and Italy are beyond estimate and beyond praise. I am glad they should have what they desire for their own welfare and safety. But they all receive under the peace territorial and commercial benefits. We are asked to give, and we in no way seek to take. Surely it is not too much to insist that when we are offered nothing but the opportunity to give and to aid others we should have the right to say what sacrifices we shall make and what the magnitude of our gifts shall be. In the prosecution of the war we gave unstintedly American lives and American treasure. When the war closed we had 3,000,000 men under arms. We were turning the country into a vast workshop for war. We advanced ten billions to our allies. We refused no assistance that we could possibly render. All the great energy and power of the Republic were put at the service of the good cause. We have not been ungenerous. We have been devoted to the cause of freedom, humanity, and civilization everywhere. Now we are asked, in the making of peace, to sacrifice our sovereignty in important respects, to involve ourselves almost without limit in the affairs of other nations and to yield up policies and rights which we have maintained throughout our history. We are asked to incur liabilities to an unlimited extent and furnish assets at the same time which no man can measure. I think it is not only our right but our duty to determine how far we shall go. Not only must we look carefully to see where we are being led into endless disputes and entanglements, but we must not forget that we have in this country millions of people of foreign birth and parentage. . . .

I am as anxious as any human being can be to have the United States render every possible service to the civilization and the peace of mankind, but I am certain we can do it best by not putting ourselves in leading strings or subjecting our policies and our sovereignty to other nations. The independence of the United States is not only more precious to ourselves but to the world than any single possession. Look at the United States to-day. We have made mistakes in the past. We have had shortcomings. We shall make mistakes in the future and fall short of our own best hopes. But none the less is there any country to-day on the face of the earth which can compare with this in ordered liberty, in peace, and in the largest freedom? I feel that I can say this without being accused of undue boastfulness, for it is the simple fact, and in making this treaty and taking on these obligations all that we do is in a spirit of unselfishness and in a desire for the good of mankind. But it is well to remember that we are dealing with nations every one of which has a direct individual interest to serve, and there is grave danger in an unshared idealism. Contrast the United States with any country on the face of the earth to-day and ask yourself whether the situation of the United States is not the best to be found. I will go as far as anyone in world service, but the first step to world service is the maintenance of the United States. You may call me selfish, if you will, conservative or reactionary, or use any other harsh adjective you see fit to apply, but an American I was born, an American I have remained all my life. I can never be anything else but an American, and I must think of the United States first, and when I think of the United States first in an arrangement like this I am thinking of what is best for the world, for if the United States fails the best hopes of mankind fail with it. I have never had but one allegiance— I can not divide it now. I have loved but one flag and I can not share that devotion and give affection to the mongrel banner invented for a league. Internationalism, illustrated by the Bolshevik and by the men to whom all countries are alike provided they can make money out of them, is to me repulsive. National I must remain, and in that way I like all other Americans can render the amplest service to the world. The United States is the world's best hope, but if you fetter her in the interests and quarrels of other nations, if you tangle her in the intrigues of Europe, you will destroy her power for good and endanger her very existence. Leave her to march freely through the centuries to come as in the years that have gone. Strong, generous, and confident, she has nobly served mankind. Beware how you trifle with your marvelous inheritance, this great land of ordered liberty, for if we stumble and fall freedom and civilization everywhere will go down in ruin.

We are told that we shall "break the heart of the world" if we do not take this league just as it stands. I fear that the hearts of the vast majority of mankind would beat on strongly and steadily and without any quickening if the league were to perish altogether. If it should be effectively and beneficiently changed the people who would lie awake in sorrow for a single night could be easily gathered in one not very large room but those who would draw a long breath of relief would reach to millions.

We hear much of visions and I trust we shall continue to have visions and dream dreams of a fairer future for the race. But visions are one thing and visionaries are another, and the mechanical appliances of the rhetorician designed to give a picture of a present which does not exist and of a future which no man can predict are as unreal and short lived as the steam or canvas clouds, the angels suspended on wires and the artificial lights of the stage. They pass with the moment of effect and are shabby and tawdry in the daylight. Let us at least be real. Washington's entire honesty of mind and his fearless look into the face of all facts are qualities which can never go out of fashion and which we should all do well to imitate.

Ideals have been thrust upon us as an argument for the league until the healthy mind which rejects cant revolts from them. Are ideals confined to this deformed experiment upon a noble purpose, tainted, as it is, with bargains and tied to a peace treaty which might have been disposed of long ago to the great benefit of the world if it had not been compelled to carry this rider on its back? "Post equitem sedet atra cura," Horace tells us, but no blacker care ever sat behind any rider than we shall find in this covenant of doubt-ful and disputed interpretation as it now perches upon the treaty of peace.

No doubt many excellent and patriotic people see a coming fulfillment of noble ideals in the words "League for Peace." We all respect and share these aspirations and desires, but some of us see no hope, but rather defeat, for them in this murky covenant. For we, too, have our ideals, even if we differ from those who have tried to establish a monopoly of idealism. Our first ideal is our country, and we see her in the future, as in the past, giving service to all her people and to the world. Our ideal of the future is that she should continue to render that service of her own free will. She has great problems of her own to solve, very grim and perilous problems, and a right solution, if we can attain to it, would largely benefit mankind. We would have our country strong to resist a peril from the West, as she has flung back the German menace from the East. We would not have our politics distracted and embittered by the dissensions of other lands. We would not have our country's vigor exhausted, or her moral force abated, by everlasting meddling and muddling in every quarrel, great and small, which afflicts the world. Our ideal is to make her ever stronger and better and finer, because in that way alone, as we believe, can she be of the greatest service to the world's peace and to the welfare of mankind. [Prolonged applause in the galleries.]

The irreconcilable position was highly complex, containing several major strands. William E. Borah's speech in the Senate on November 19, 1919, revealed the dominant theme of isolationism: "America will live her own life." Also it showed at best two other concerns: a note of democratic idealism, insisting that the people had no "voice in this scheme for world peace," and a fear of the League as committing the United States to imperialistic ventures.

WILLIAM E. BORAH:
AMERICA WILL LIVE HER OWN LIFE*

Mr. President, I am not misled by the debate across the aisle into the view that this treaty will not be ratified. I entertain little doubt that sooner or later—and entirely too soon—the treaty will be ratified with the league of nations in it, and I am of the opinion with the reservations in it as they are now written. There may possibly be some change in verbiage in order that there may be a common sharing of parentage, but our friends across the aisle will likely accept the league of nations with the reservations in substance as now written. I think, therefore, this moment is just as appropriate as any other for me to express my final views with reference to the treaty and the league of nations. It is perhaps the last opportunity I shall have to state, as briefly as I may, my reasons for opposing the treaty and the league.

Mr. President, after Mr. Lincoln had been elected President, before he assumed the duties of the office and at a time when all indications were to the effect that we would soon be in the midst of civil strife, a friend from the city of Washington wrote him for instructions. Mr. Lincoln wrote back in a single line, "Entertain no

* Reprinted from *Congressional Record*, 66th Cong., 1st sess. (Washington, D.C.: 1919–1920), pp. 8781–8784.

compromise; have none of it." That states the position I occupy at this time and which I have, in an humble way, occupied from the first contention in regard to this proposal.

My objections to the league have not been met by the reservations. I desire to state wherein my objections have not been met. Let us see what our attitude will be toward Europe and what our position will be with reference to the other nations of the world after we shall have entered the league with the present reservations written therein. With all due respect to those who think that they have accomplished a different thing and challenging no man's intellectual integrity or patriotism, I do not believe the reservations have met the fundamental propositions which are involved in this contest.

When the league shall have been formed, we shall be a member of what is known as the council of the league. Our accredited representative will sit in judgment with the accredited representatives of the other members of the league to pass upon the concerns not only of our country but of all Europe and all Asia and the entire world. Our accredited representatives will be members of the assembly. They will sit there to represent the judgment of these 110,000,000 people—more then—just as we are accredited here to represent our constituencies. We can not send our representatives to sit in council with the representatives of other great nations of the world with mental reservations as to what we shall do in case their judgment shall not be satisfactory to us. If we go to the council or to the assembly with any other purpose than that of complying in good faith and in absolute integrity with all upon which the council or the assembly may pass, we shall soon return to our country with our self-respect forfeited and the public opinion of the world condemnatory.

Why need you gentlemen across the aisle worry about a reservation here or there when we are sitting in the council and in the assembly and bound by every obligation in morals, which the President said was supreme above that of law, to comply with the judgment which our representative and the other representatives finally form? Shall we go there, Mr. President, to sit in judgment, and in case that judgment works for peace join with our allies, but in case it works for war withdraw our cooperation? How long would we stand as we now stand, a great Republic commanding the respect and holding the leadership of the world, if we should adopt any such course?

So, sir, we not only sit in the council and in the assembly with our accredited representatives, but bear in mind that article 11 is untouched by any reservation which has been offered here: and with article 11 untouched and its integrity complete, article 10 is perfectly superfluous. If any war or threat of war shall be a matter of consideration for the league, and the league shall take such action as it deems wise to deal with it, what is the necessity of article 10? Will not external aggression be regarded as a war or threat of war? If the political independence of some nation in Europe is assailed will it be regarded as a war or threat of war? Is there anything in article 10 that is not completely covered by article 11?

It remains complete, and with our representatives sitting in the council and the assembly, and with article 11 complete, and with the assembly and the council having jurisdiction of all matters touching the peace of the world, what more do you need to bind the United States if you assume that the United States is a Nation of honor?

We have said, Mr. President, that we would not send our troops abroad without the consent of Congress. Pass by now for a moment the legal proposition. If we create executive functions, the Executive will perform those functions without the authority of Congress. Pass that question by and go to the other question. Our members of the council are there. Our members of the assembly are there. Article 11 is complete, and it authorizes the league, a member of which is our representative, to deal with matters of peace and war, and the league through its council and its assembly deals with the matter, and our accredited representative joins with the others in deciding upon a certain course, which involves a question of sending troops. What will the Congress of the United States do? What right will it have left, except the bare technical right to refuse, which as a moral proposition it will not dare to exercise? Have we not been told day by day for the last nine months that the Senate of the United States, a coordinate part of the treaty-making power, should accept this league as it was written because the wise men sitting at Versailles had so written it, and has not every possible influence and every source of power in public opinion been organized and directed against the Senate to compel it to do that thing? How much stronger will be the moral compulsion upon the Congress of the United States when we ourselves have indorsed the proposition of sending our accredited representatives there to vote for us?

Ah, but you say that there must be unanimous consent, and that there is vast protection in unanimous consent.

I do not wish to speak disparagingly; but has not every division and dismemberment of every nation which has suffered dismemberment taken place by unanimous consent for the last 300 years? Did not Prussia and Austria and Russia by unanimous consent divide Poland? Did not the United States and Great Britain and Japan and Italy and France divide China and give Shantung to Japan? Was that not a unanimous decision? Close the doors upon the diplomats of Europe, let them sit in secret, give them the material to trade on, and there always will be unanimous consent.

How did Japan get unanimous consent? I want to say here, in my parting words upon this proposition, that I have no doubt the outrage upon China was quite as distasteful to the President of the United States as it is to me. But Japan said: "I will not sign your treaty unless you turn over to me Shantung, to be turned back at my discretion," and you know how Japan's discretion operates with reference to such things. And so, when we are in the league, and our accredited representatives are sitting at Geneva, and a question of great moment arises, Japan, or Russia, or Germany, or Great Britain will say, "Unless this matter is adjusted in this way I will depart from your league." It is the same thing, operating in the same way, only under a different date and under a little different circumstances.

Mr. President, if you have enough territory, if you have enough material, if you have enough subject peoples to trade upon and divide, there will be no difficulty about unanimous consent.

Do our Democratic friends ever expect any man to sit as a member of the council or as a member of the assembly equal in intellectual power and in standing before the world with that of our representative at Versailles? Do you expect a man to sit in the council who will have made more pledges, and I shall assume made them in sincerity, for self-determination and for the rights of small peoples, than had been made by our accredited representative? And yet, what became of it? The unanimous consent was obtained nevertheless.

But take another view of it. We are sending to the council one man. That one man represents 110,000,000 people.

Here, sitting in the Senate, we have two from every State in the Union, and over in the other House we have Representatives in accordance with population, and the responsibility is spread out in accordance with our obligations to our constituency. But now we are transferring to one man the stupendous power of representing the sentiment and convictions of 110,000,000 people in tremendous questions which may involve the peace or may involve the war of the world.

However you view the question of unanimous consent, it does not protect us.

What is the result of all this? We are in the midst of all of the affairs of Europe. We have entangled ourselves with all European concerns. We have joined the alliance with all the European nations which have thus far joined the league, and all nations which may be admitted to the league. We are sitting there dabbling in their affairs and intermeddling in their concerns. In other words, Mr. President—and this comes to the question which is fundamental with me—we have forfeited and surrendered, once and for all, the great policy of "no entangling alliances" upon which the strength of this Republic has been founded for 150 years.

My friends of reservations, tell me where is the reservation in these articles which protects us against entangling alliances with Europe?

Those who are differing over reservations, tell me what one of them protects the doctrine laid down by the Father of his Country. That fundamental proposition is surrendered, and we are a part of the European turmoils and conflicts from the time we enter this league.

Let us not underestimate that. There has never been an hour since the Venezuelan difficulty that there has not been operating in this country, fed by domestic and foreign sources, a powerful propaganda for the destruction of the doctrine of no entangling alliances. . . .

Mr. President, there is another and even a more commanding reason why I shall record my vote against this treaty. It imperils what I conceive to be the underlying, the very first principles of this Republic. It is in conflict with the right of our people to govern themselves free from all restraint, legal or moral, of foreign powers. It challenges every tenet of my political faith. If this faith were one of my own contriving, if I stood here to assert principles of government of my own evolving, I might well be charged with intolerable presumption, for we all recognize the ability of those who urge a different course. But I offer in justification of my course nothing of my own save the deep and abiding reverence I have for those whose policies I humbly but most ardently support. I claim no merit save fidelity to American principles and devotion to American ideals as they were wrought out from time to time by those who built the Republic and as they have been extended and maintained throughout these years. In opposing the treaty I do nothing more than decline to renounce and tear out of my life the sacred traditions which throughout 50 years have been translated into my whole intellectual and moral being. I will not, I can not, give up my belief that America must, not alone for the happiness of her own people, but for the moral guidance and greater contentment of the world, be permitted to live her own life. Next to the tie which binds a man to his God is the tie which binds a man to his country, and all schemes, all plans, however ambitious and fascinating they seem in their proposal, but which would embarrass or entangle and impede or shackle her sovereign will, which would compromise her freedom of action, I unhesitatingly put behind me.

Sir, since the debate opened months ago those of us who have stood against this proposition have been taunted many times with being little Americans. Leave us the word American, keep that in your presumptuous impeachment, and no taunt can disturb us, no gibe discompose our purposes. Call us little Americans if you will, but leave us the consolation and the pride which the term American, however modified, still imparts. Take away that term and though you should coin in telling phrase your highest eulogy we would hurl it back as common slander. We have been ridiculed because, forsooth, of our limited vision. Possibly that charge may be true. Who is there here that can read the future? Time, and time alone, unerring and remorseless, will give us each our proper place in the affections of our country-men and in the esteem and commendation of those who are to come after us. We neither fear nor court her favor. But if our vision has been circumscribed it has at all times within its com-pass been clear and steady. We have sought nothing save the tranquillity of our own people and the honor and independence of our own Republic. No foreign flattery, no possible world glory and power have disturbed our poise or come between us and our devotion to the tradi-tions which have made us a people or the policies which have made us a Nation, unselfish and commanding. If we have erred we have erred out of too much love for those things which from childhood you and we together have been taught to revere—yes, to defend even at the cost of limb and life. If we have erred it is because we have placed too high an estimate upon the wis-dom of Washington and Jefferson, too exalted an opinion upon the patriotism of the sainted Lincoln. And blame us not therefore if we have, in our limited vision, seemed sometimes bitter and at all times uncompromising, for the things for which we have spoken, feebly spoken, the things which we have endeavored to defend, have been the things for which your fathers and our fathers were willing to die.

Senators, even in an hour so big with expect-ancy we should not close our eyes to the fact that democracy is something more, vastly more, than a mere form of government by which society is restrained into free and orderly life. It is a moral entity, a spiritual force, as well. And these are things which live only and alone in the atmosphere of liberty. The foundation upon which democracy rests is faith in the moral instincts of the people. Its ballot boxes, the franchise, its laws, and consti-tutions are but the outward manifestations of the deeper and more essential thing—a continuing trust in the moral purposes of the average man and woman. When this is lost or forfeited your outward forms, however democratic in terms, are a mockery. Force may find expression through in-stitutions democratic in structure equal with the simple and more direct processes of a single supreme ruler. These distinguishing virtues of a real republic you can not commingle with the discordant and destructive forces of the Old World and still preserve them. You can not yoke a government whose fundamental maxim is that of liberty to a government whose first law is that of force and hope to preserve the former. These things are in eternal war, and one must ultimately destroy the other. You may still keep for a time the outward form, you may still delude yourself, as others have done in the past, with appearances and symbols, but when you shall have committed this Republic to a scheme of world control based upon force, upon the combined military force of the four great nations of the world, you will have soon destroyed the atmosphere of freedom, of confidence in the self-governing capacity of the masses, in which alone a democracy may thrive.

We may become one of the four dictators of the world, but we shall no longer be master of our own spirit. And what shall it profit us as a Nation if we shall go forth to the dominion of the earth and share with others the glory of world control and lose that fine sense of confidence in the people, the soul of democracy? . . .

But your treaty does not mean peace—far, very far, from it. If we are to judge the future by the past it means war. Is there any guaranty of peace other than the guaranty which comes of the control of the war-making power by the people? Yet what great rule of democracy does the treaty leave unassailed? The people in whose keeping alone you can safely lodge the power of peace or war nowhere, at no time and in no place, have any voice in this scheme for world peace. Autocracy which has bathed the world in blood for centuries reigns supreme. Democracy is every-where excluded. This, you say, means peace.

Can you hope for peace when love of country is disregarded in your scheme, when the spirit of nationality is rejected, even scoffed at? Yet what law of that moving and mysterious force does your treaty not deny? With a ruthlessness unparal-leled your treaty in a dozen instances runs counter to the divine law of nationality. Peoples who speak the same language, kneel at the same an-cestral tombs, moved by the same traditions, ani-mated by a common hope, are torn asunder, broken in pieces, divided, and parceled out to antagonistic nations. And this you call justice. This, you cry, means peace. Peoples who have dreamed of independence, struggled and been patient, sacrificed and been hopeful, peoples who were told that through this peace conference they should realize the aspirations of centuries, have again had their hopes dashed to earth. One of the most striking and commanding figures in this war, soldier and statesman, turned away from the peace table at Versailles declaring to the world, "The promise of the new life, the victory of the great humane ideals for which the peoples have shed their blood and their treasure without stint, the fulfillment of their aspirations toward a new international order and a fairer and better world, are not written into the treaty." No; your treaty means injustice. It means slavery. It means war. And to all this you ask this Republic to become a party. You ask it to abandon the creed under which it has grown to power and accept the creed of autocracy, the creed of repression and force. . . .

Americanism shall not, can not, die. We may go back in sackcloth and ashes, but we will return to the faith of the fathers. America will live her own life. The independence of this Republic will have its defenders. Thousands have suffered and died for it, and their sons and daughters are not of the breed who will be betrayed into the hands of foreigners. The noble face of the Father of his Country, so familiar to every boy and girl, looking out from the walls of the Capitol in stern re-proach, will call those who come here for public service to a reckoning. The people of our beloved country will finally speak, and we will return to the policy which we now abandon. America dis- enthralled and free in spite of all these things will continue her mission in the cause of peace, of freedom, and of civilization.

Girding for the impending battle with the Senate over ratification of the Versailles Treaty, Wilson took to the road in the late summer of 1919 to carry his vision of world peace directly to the American people. "This was a war to make similar wars impossible," he asserted at St. Paul, Minnesota, "and merely to win this war and stop at that is to make it certain that we shall have to fight another and a final one."

WOODROW WILSON: THE DESTINY OF AMERICA*

Mr. Chairman, my fellow countrymen, I am very happy that the mayor sounded the note that he has just sounded, because by some sort of divination he realized what was in my heart to-night. I do not feel since I have left Washington this time that I am on an ordinary errand. I do not feel that I am on a political errand, even in the broad sense of that term. I feel rather that I am going about to hold counsel with my fellow countrymen concerning the most honorable and distinguished course which our great country can take at this turning point in the history of the world. And the mayor was quite right when he said that this is a conference concerning the true interpretation of the American spirit. I believe, I hope without an undue touch of national pride, that it is only the American spirit that can be the true mediator of peace.

The theme that I find uppermost in my thought to-night is this: We are all actuated, my fellow countrymen, by an intense consciousness and love of America. I do not think that it is fancy on my part; it is based upon long experience that in every part of the world I can recognize an American the minute I see him. Yet that is not because we are all of one stock. We are of more varied origins and stocks than any people in the world. We come from all the great races of the world. We are made up out of all the nations and peoples who have stood at the center of civilization. In this part of the country it is doubtful whether in some of our great cities 50 per cent of the people come of parents born in America. One of the somewhat serious jests which I allowed myself to indulge on the other side of the water was with my Italian colleagues when they were claiming the city of Fiume upon the Adriatic because of its Italian population, and other cities scattered here and there whose surrounding population was not Italian but in whom an Italian element played an important part. I said, "That is

not a sufficient argument for the extension of Italian sovereignty to these people, because there are more Italians in New York City than in any city in Italy, and I doubt if you would feel justified in suggesting that the sovereignty of Italy be extended over the city of New York." I advert to this, my fellow citizens, merely as one illustration, that could be multiplied a hundredfold, of the singular make-up of this great Nation.

I do not know how it happens that we are all Americans; we are so different in origin; we are so different in memories. The memory of America does not go very far back as measured by the distances of history, and great millions of our people carry in their hearts the traditions of other people, the traditions of races never bred in America; yet we are all unmistakably and even in appearance Americans, and nothing else. There is only one possible explanation for that, my fellow citizens, and that is that there is in the practice and in the tradition of this country a set of principles which, however imperfectly, get into the consciousness of every man who lives in this country.

One of the chief elements that make an American is this: In almost every other country there is some class that dominates, or some governmental authority that determines the course of politics, or some ancient system of land laws that limits the freedom of land tenure, or some ancient custom which ties a man into a particular groove in the land in which he lives. There is none of that in America. Every man in America, if he behaves himself, knows that he stands on the same footing as every other man in America, and, thank goodness, we are in sight of the time when every woman will know that she stands upon the same footing. We do not have to ask anybody's leave what we shall think or what we shall do or how we shall vote. We do not have to get the approval of a class as to our behavior. We do not have to square ourselves with standards that have been followed ever since our great-grandfathers. We are very much more interested in being great-grandfathers than in having had

---

* Reprinted from *Senate Document 120,* 66th Cong., 1st sess. (Washington, D. C.: 1919–1920), pp. 107–116.

great-grandfathers, because our view is to the future. America does not march, as so many other peoples march, looking back over its shoulder. It marches with its eyes not only forward, but with its eyes lifted to the distances of history, to the great events which are slowly culminating, in the Providence of God, in the lifting of civilization to new levels and new achievements. That is what makes us Americans.

And yet I was mistaken a moment ago when I said we are nothing else, because there are a great many hyphens left in America. For my part, I think the most un-American thing in the world is a hyphen. I do not care what it is that comes before the word "American." It may be a German-American, or an Italian-American, a Swedish-American, or an Anglo-American, or an Irish-American. It does not make any difference what comes before the "American," it ought not to be there, and every man who comes to take counsel with me with a hyphen in his conversation I take no interest in whatever. The entrance examination, to use my own parlance, into my confidence is, "Where do you put America in your thoughts? Do you put it first, always first, unquestionably first?" Then we can sit down together and talk, but not otherwise. Now, I want you distinctly to understand that I am not quarreling with the affectionate memories of people who have drawn their origin from other countries. I no more blame a man for dwelling with fond affection upon the traditions of some great race not bred in America than I blame a man for remembering with reverence his mother and his father and his forebears that bred him and that gave him a chance in the world. I am not quarreling with those affections; I am talking about purposes. Every purpose is for the future, and the future for Americans must be for America.

We have got to choose now, my fellow citizens, what kind of future it is going to be for America. I think that what I have said justifies me in adding that this Nation was created to be the mediator of peace, because it draws its blood from every civilized stock in the world and is ready by sympathy and understanding to understand the peoples of the world, their interests, their rights, their hopes, their destiny. America is the only Nation in the world that has that equipment. Every other nation is set in the mold of a particular breeding. We are set in no mold at all. Every other nation has certain prepossessions which run back through all the ramifications of an ancient history. We have nothing of the kind. We know what all peoples are thinking, and yet we by a fine alchemy of our own combine that thinking into an American plan and an American purpose. America is the only Nation which can sympathetically lead the world in organizing peace.

Constantly, when I was on the other side of the water, delegations representing this, that, and the other peoples of Europe or of Asia came to visit me to solicit the interest of America in their fortunes, and, without exception, they were able to tell me that they had kinsmen in America. Some of them, I am ashamed to say, came from countries I had never heard of before, and yet even they were able to point, not to a handful, not to a few hundreds, but to several thousand kinsmen in America. I never before knew that they came, but they are here and they are our interpreters, the interpreters on our behalf of the interests of the people from whom they sprang. They came to America as sort of advanced couriers of those people. They came in search of the Golden West. They came in search of the liberty that they understood reigned among that free and happy people. They were drawn by the lure of justice, by the lure of freedom, out of lands where they were oppressed, suppressed, where life was made impossible for them upon the free plane that their hearts had conceived. They said, "Yonder is our star in the west," and then the word went home, "We have found the land. They are a free people that are capable of understanding us. You go to their representatives in Paris and put your case before them, and they will understand." What a splendid thing that is, my fellow countrymen! I want you to keep this in your minds as a conception of the question that we are now called upon to decide.

To hear some men talk about the league of nations you would suppose that it was a trap set for America; you would suppose that it was an arrangement by which we entered into an alliance with other great, powerful nations to make war some time. Why, my fellow countrymen, it bears no resemblance to such description. It is a great method of common counsel with regard to the common interests of mankind. We shall not be drawn into wars; we shall be drawn into consultation, and we will be the most trusted adviser in the whole group. Consultation, discussion, is written all over the whole face of the covenant of the league of nations, for the heart of it is that the nations promise not to go to war until they have consulted, until they have discussed, until all the facts in the controversy have been laid before the court which represents the common opinion of mankind.

That is the league of nations. Nothing can be discussed there that concerns our domestic affairs. Nothing can be discussed there that concerns the domestic affairs of any other people, unless something is occurring in some nation which is likely to disturb the peace of the world, and any time that any question arises which is likely to disturb the peace of the world, then the covenant makes it the right of any member, strong or weak, big or little, of that universal concert of the nations to bring that matter up for clarification and discussion. Can you imagine anything more calculated to put war off, not only to put it off, but to make it violently improbable? When a man wants to fight he does not go and discuss the matter with the other fellow. He goes and hits him, and then somebody else has to come in and either join the fight or break it up. I used a very homely illustration the other night, which perhaps it may not be amiss for me to use again. I had two friends who were becoming more and more habitually profane. Their friends did not like it. They not only had the fundamental scruple that it was wrong, but they also thought, as I heard a very refined lady say, "It was not only wrong but, what was worse, it was vulgar." They did not like to see their friends adjourning all the rest of their vocabulary and using only those words. So they made them enter into a solemn agreement—I ought to say they lived in a large city—that they would not swear inside the corporate limits; that if they got in a state of mind which made it necessary to explode in profanity they would get out of town and swear.

The first time the passion came upon them and they recalled their promise they got sheepishly on a street car and made for the town limits, and I need hardly tell you that when they got there they no longer wanted to swear. They had cooled off. The long spaces of the town, the people going about their ordinary business, nobody paying any attention to them, the world seeming to be at peace when they were at war, all brought them to a realization of the smallness of the whole business, and they turned around and came into town again. Comparing great things with small, that will suffice as a picture of the advantage of discussion in international matters as well as in individual matters, because it was universally agreed on the other side of the water that if Germany had allowed the other Governments to confer with her 24 hours about the recent war, it could not have taken place. We know why. It was an unconscionable war. She did not dare discuss it. You can not afford to discuss a thing when you are in the wrong, and the minute you feel that the whole judgment of the world is against you, you have a different temper in affairs altogether.

This is a great process of discussion that we are entering into, and my point to-night—it is the point I want to leave with you—is that we are the people of all people in the world intelligently to discuss the difficulties of the nations which we represent, although we are Americans. We are the predestined mediators of mankind. I am not saying this in any kind of national pride or vanity. I believe that is mere historic truth, and I try to interpret circumstances in some intelligent way. If that is the kind of people we are, it must have been intended that we should make some use of the opportunities and powers that we have, and when I hear gentlemen saying that we must keep out of this thing and take care of ourselves I think to myself, "Take care of ourselves? Where did we come from? Is there nobody else in the world to take care of? Have we no sympathies that do not run out into the great field of human experience everywhere? Is that what America is, with her mixture of bloods?" Why, my fellow citizens, that is a fundamental misconception of what it is to be an American, and these gentlemen

are doing a harm which they do not realize. I want to testify to you here to-night, my fellow citizens, because I have the means of information, that since it has seemed to be uncertain whether we are going to play this part of leadership in the world or not, this part of leadership in accommodation, the old intrigues have stirred up in this country again. That intrigue which we universally condemn—that hyphen which looked to us like a snake, the hyphen between "German" and "American"—has reared its head again, and you hear the "his-s-s" of its purpose. What is that purpose? It is to keep America out of the concert of nations, in order that America and Germany, being out of that concert, may stand—in their mistaken dream—united to dominate the world, or, at any rate, the one assist the other in holding the nations of the world off while its ambitions are realized.

There is no conjecture about this, my fellow citizens. We know the former purposes of German intrigue in this country, and they are being revived. Why? We have not reduced very materially the number of the German people. Germany remains the great power of central Europe. She has more than 60,000,000 people now (she had nearly 70,000,000 before Poland and other Provinces were taken away). You can not change the temper and expectations of a people by five years of war, particularly five years of war in which they are not yet conscious of the wrong they did or of the wrong way in which they did it. They are expecting the time of the revival of their power, and along with the revival of their power goes their extraordinary capacity, their unparalleled education, their great capacity in commerce and finance and manufacture. The German bankers and the German merchants and the German manufacturers did not want this war. They were making conquest of the world without it, and they knew it would spoil their plans, not advance them; and it has spoiled their plans, but they are there yet with their capacity, with their conception of what it is to serve the world materially and so subdue the world psychologically. All of that is still there, my fellow countrymen, and if America stays out then the rest of the world will have to watch Germany and watch America, and when there are two dissociated powers there is danger that they will have the same purposes.

There can be only one intelligent reason for America staying out of this, and that is that she does not want peace, that she wants war sometimes and the advantage which war will bring her, and I want to say now and here that the men who think that by that thought they are interpreting America are making the sort of mistake upon which it will be useful for them to reflect in obscurity for the rest of their lives. This is a peaceful people. This is a liberty-loving people, and liberty is suffocated by war. Free institutions can not survive the strain of prolonged military administration. In order to live tolerable lives you must lift the fear of war and the practice of war from the lives of nations. America is evidence of the fact that no great democracy ever entered upon an aggressive international policy. I want you to know, if you will be kind enough to read the covenant of the league of nations—most of the people that are arguing against it are taking it for granted that you have never read it—take the pains to read it, and you will find that no nation is admitted to the league of nations that can not show that it has the institutions which we call free. Nobody is admitted except the self-governing nations, because it was the instinctive judgment of every man who sat around that board that only a nation whose government was its servant and not its master could be trusted to preserve the peace of the world. There are not going to be many other kinds of nations long, my fellow citizens. The people of this world—not merely the people of America, for they did the job long ago—have determined that there shall be no more autocratic governments.

And in their haste to get rid of one of them they set up another. I mean in pitiful Russia. I wish we could learn the lesson of Russia so that it would be burned into the consciousness of every man and woman in America. That lesson is that nobody can be free where there is not public order and authority. What has happened in Russia is that an old and distinguished and skillful autocracy has had put in its place an amateur autocracy, a little handful of men exercising without the slightest compunction of mercy or pity the bloody terror that characterized the worst days of the Czar. That is what must happen if you knock things to pieces. Liberty is a thing of slow construction. Liberty is a thing of universal cooperation. Liberty is a thing which you must build up by habit. Liberty is a thing which is rooted and grounded in character, and the reason I am so certain that the leadership of the world, in respect of order and progress, belongs to America is that I know that these principles are rooted and grounded in the American character. It is not our intellectual capacity, my fellow-citizens, that has given us our place in the world, though I rate that as high as the intellectual capacity of any other people that ever lived, but it is the heart that lies back of the man that makes America. Ask this question of yourselves. I have no doubt that this room is full of mothers and fathers and wives and sweethearts who sent their beloved young men to France. What did you send them there for? What made you proud that they were going? What made you willing that they should go? Did you think they were seeking to aggrandize America in some way? Did you think they were going to take something for America that had belonged to somebody else? Did you think that they were going in a quarrel which they had provoked and must maintain? The question answers itself. You were proud that they should go because they were going on an errand of self-sacrifice, in the interest of mankind. What a halo and glory surrounds those old men whom

we now greet with such reverence, the men who were the soldiers in our Civil War! They saved a Nation. Ah, when these youngsters grow old who have come back from the fields of France, what a halo will be around their brows! They saved the world. They are of the same stuff as those old veterans of the Civil War. Mind you, I was born and bred in the South, but I can pay that tribute with all my heart to the men who saved the Union. It ought to have been saved. It was the greatest thing that men had conceived up to that time. Now we come to a greater thing—to the union of great nations in conference upon the interests of peace. That is the fruitage, the fine and appropriate fruitage, of what these men achieved upon the fields of France.

I saw many fine sights in Paris, many gallant sights, many sights that quickened the pulse; but my pulse never beat so fast as when I saw groups of our boys swinging along the street. They looked as if they owned something, and they did. They owned the finest thing in the world, the thing that we are going to prove was theirs. They owned the ideals and conceptions that will govern the world. And on this errand that I am going about on I feel that I am doing what I can to complete what they so gallantly began. I should feel recreant, my fellow citizens, if I did not do all that is in my power to do to complete the ideal work which those youngsters so gallantly began.

This was a war to make similar wars impossible, and merely to win this war and stop at that is to make it certain that we shall have to fight another and a final one. I hear opponents of the league of nations say, "But this does not guarantee peace." No; nothing guarantees us against human passion and error, but I would like to put this business proposition to you: If it increases the probability of peace by, let us say, 10 per cent, do you not think it is worth while? In my judgment, it increases it about 99 per cent. Henceforth the genius of the world will be devoted to accommodating the counsels of mankind and not confusing them; not supplying heat but supplying light; not putting friction into the machine, but easing the friction off and combining the parts of the great machinery of civilization so that they will run in smooth harmony and perfection. My fellow citizens, the tasks of peace that are ahead of us are the most difficult tasks to which the human genius has ever been devoted. I will state the fundamental task, for it is the fundamental task. It is the relationship between those who toil with their hands and those who direct that toil. I will not say the relationship between capital and labor; that means something slightly different. I say the relationship between those who organize enterprise and those who make enterprise go by the skill and labor of their hands. There is at present, to say the least, a most unsatisfactory relationship between those two and we must devote our national genius to working out a method of association between the two which will make this Nation the nation to solve triumphantly and for all time the fundamental problem of peaceful production. You ask, "What has that got to do with the league of nations?" I dare say that you do not know because I have never heard anybody tell you that the great charter, the new international charter, of labor is in the treaty of peace and associated with the league of nations. A great machinery of consultation is set up there, not merely about international political affairs, but about standards of labor, about the relationships between managers and employees, about the standards of life and the conditions of labor, about the labor of women and of children, about the humane side and the business side of the whole labor problem. And the first conference is going to sit in Washington next month; not the conference which some of you may have heard of, which I have just called of our own people, but an international conference to consider the interests of labor all over the round world. I do not know—nobody knows—whether the Senate will have stopped debating by that time or not. I heard a Member of the Senate say that nobody knew that except God Almighty! But whether it has finished or not, the conference is going to sit, and if it has not finished, the only question that will be left unsettled is whether we are going to sit inside of it or outside of it. The conference at Paris voted, in their confidence in the American people, that the first meeting should be held in Washington and should be called by the President of the United States. They supposed in their innocence that the President of the United States represented the people of the United States. And in calling this conference, as I have called it, I am confident that I am representing the people of the United States. After I have bidden the delegates welcome, perhaps I can have a chair just outside the door and listen.

I am jesting, my fellow citizens, but there is a little sadness in the jest. Why do we wait to do a great thing? Why do we wait to fulfill the destiny of America? Why do we make it possible that anybody should think that we are not coming in now, but are going to wait later and come in with Germany? I suppose there is a certain intellectual excitement and pleasure in debate, but I do not experience any when great issues like this are pending, and I would be very sad, indeed, if I did not have an absolute, unclouded confidence of the result. I had the great good fortune to be born an American, I have saturated myself in the traditions of our country, I have read all the great literature that interprets the spirit of our country, and when I read my own heart with regard to these great purposes, I feel confident that it is a sample American heart. Therefore I have the most unbounded confidence in the result. All that is needed is that you should be vocal and audible. I know what you want. Say it and get it. I am your servant; all the men elected to go to Washington are your servants. It is not our privilege to follow our private convictions; it is our duty to represent your convictions and execute your purposes, and therefore all that is needed is a consciousness. Tell me that you do not want to do what I am urging and I will go home; but tell me, as your faces and your voices tell me, that you do want what I want, and I will be heartened for the rest of my journey, and I will say to the folks all the way from here to the Pacific, "Minnesota is up and on her tiptoes and behind you. Let's all of us get in the great team which is to redeem the destinies of mankind."

Our fathers of the revolutionary age had a vision, my fellow citizens. There were only 3,000,-000 Americans then, in a little strip of settlements on the Atlantic coast. Now the great body of American citizens extends from ocean to ocean, more than a hundred millions strong. These are the people of whom the founders of the Republic were dreaming, those great hosts of free men and women who should come in the future and who should say to all the world, "Here are the testaments of liberty. Here are the principles of freedom. Here are the things which we must do in order that mankind may be released from the intolerable things of the past." And there came a day at Paris when the representatives of all the great governments of the world accepted the American specifications upon which the terms of the treaty of peace were drawn. Shall we have our treaty, or shall we have somebody else's? Shall we keep the primacy of the world, or shall we abandon it?

This editorial from the *Nation* illustrates the liberal criticism of the League of Nations. Seeking perfection, many liberals went into opposition when they realized that the League's machinery was far from perfect. The *Nation* asked, "If the mouths of the Big Five must be held with bit and bridle, and the small Powers will not exercise any considerable influence, who, we may ask, is going to do the job?"

THE NATION: A COLOSSAL HUMBUG*

We refer to the League of Nations. President Wilson must wonder where to look for his friends. Lord Robert Cecil said the other day in an address to the International Brotherhood Congress that "it is not the League of Nations covenant itself but its underlying spirit that can save humanity and civilization," and further that "if we rely on the provisions of the covenant to preserve peace we shall be living in a fool's paradise."

These lukewarm observations once more raise the question, Just what will the League do and what will it not do? President Wilson goes about the country advertising its virtues in the pure vein of Dr. Dulcamara in the *Elisir d'Amore*. Meanwhile, Ian MacPherson, the British Chief Secretary for Ireland, says that "when Great Britain signed the armistice terms, she agreed to President Wilson's principles, including the right of self-determination for small nations, but she did not agree to the application of this principle within the British Empire." Some instinct told us that this was the case, even before we had it in black and white; but no matter, the point is that this seems to "let out" Ireland, Egypt, and India, league or no league. The President says with reference to Ireland that the League sets up a forum before which can be brought all claims for self-determination which are likely to affect the peace of the world. But the Irishman is not interested in forums; he carries his forum with him all the time. Where two or three are gathered together, there is the Irishman's forum. If the Irish question could be settled by wind-power, it would have disappeared long ago. Besides, there is a plenty of forums; there is a fine one at the Hague, not much used, and in shape to take on tenants at any time. As a forum, the League project seems superfluous.

And now, to confuse us further, comes Professor Gilbert Murray, saying that the League "does not put the world at the mercy of the Big Five; it is there already." We doubt this; we think that when the world gets around to it, it will succeed in convincing the Big Five to the contrary, with little trouble. "Without the League," says Professor Murray, "the Big Five would be so many robber chieftains." We agree

heartily; that is just what we think they are. We have hesitated to say it in those words, though they have often occurred to us, because we felt that we lacked authority; but the phraseology of the Regius Professor of Greek, the successor of Jowett and Bywater, is entitled to all our respect and shall have it—in this case, enthusiastically. But what pesters us is, how is the League of Nations going to convert and regenerate these robber chieftains and change their hearts? Perhaps Mr. Murray would say that it will not pretend to do anything so spectacular as that, but only disarm them and render them innocuous. Quite so; but just as we get our hopes sustained on that idea, along comes Lord Robert Cecil again and ruins them with a word—thus: "The composition of the league will be determined at the peace conference. Definitely untrustworthy and hostile States, e.g., Russia, should the Bolshevist government remain in power, should be excluded. Otherwise it is desirable not to be too rigid in scrutinizing qualifications, since the small powers will in any case not exercise any considerable influence."

If the mouths of the Big Five must be held with bit and bridle, and the small Powers will not exercise any considerable influence, who, we may ask, is going to do the job? It seems to us that Professor Murray and Lord Robert, between them—to say nothing of Mr. Wilson—have crosslifted the League into the limbo of improbability and fictitiousness and general scientific disrepute.

The future looks a little dark for China, too, in reference to Shantung; for while the Peace Conference could not go back on the sacredness of treaties (though, as we confessed in our last issue, at some length, we can not quite see how this contention is made out) the League of Nations will either start with a clean slate or else without any scruples; and China is to apply to the League for redress. We should like to be more optimistic about her chances than we are. It all comes of our inveterate habit of reading the foreign dispatches. Just as we are all comfortably warmed through with Mr. Wilson's rhetoric, and ready to take our ease in this best of all possible worlds, we pick up an evening edition and get a dash of cold water from Fiume or Hungary, or from Mr. Murray or Lord Robert Cecil, and we are in the dumps again and full of anxious questionings about what this League of Nations *will* really do, and whom, and how, and when, and we

* Reprinted from *Nation* (September 27, 1919), p. 424 by permission.

can not be sure of any answers, and our head gets thick and incompetent, and we are very unhappy. Such is the curse of an inquiring mind.

In our plight, however, we take a deal of comfort from the antics of our lively friends on the other side who have learned, apparently, that a bird in the hand is worth two in the bush, and that the League of Nations is a thing pre-eminently to be forestalled. From recent precedents we judge that the practical way is for some poet or piano-player to make sure he has national sentiment behind him, then to gather together an assortment of picturesque ragamuffins, march into the territory he wants, camp down on it, and stay. Fiume is a diverting spectacle, these days; all the more so because the Supreme Council has gently but firmly declined to burn its fingers on the uncommonly delicate problem involved. Nor can we quite see the League of Nations tackling it. What a mercy it is that Mr. Wilson's audiences are unimaginative and do not read the foreign press, for otherwise he would never finish his tour.

Then there is Danzig. The Fiume incident has evidently encouraged some virtuoso in that region to contemplate a similar raid on the newly-ac-

quired preserves of his professional *confrère* Paderewski. The news is in the papers, but as we go to press, the actual coup has not come off. Then there was the alert and thrifty move of little Rumania. The small Powers may not, as Lord Robert Cecil says, exercise much influence in the League of Nations, but outside it they sometimes exercise a good deal. Rumania exercised enough influence in Hungary, for instance, to carry off everything that lay handy, and the Supreme Council either could not or did not take any effective action. What the League could have done better in the premises, if it had been a going concern, is not clear; since the League and the Supreme Council are, for practical purposes, one and the same. These things conduce to skepticism. The late P. T. Barnum used to say that the American people enjoyed being humbugged, and he proposed to gratify them. They may have lost character since then, though Mr. Wilson, upon whose shoulders the mantle of the great showman has undoubtedly fallen, appears to think not. The popular success of the League project will determine whether he is right.

After the Senate had rejected the Versailles Treaty without reservations, President Wilson, in his last message to Congress, December 7, 1920, restated his belief that it was America's mission to preserve democracy in the world.

WOODROW WILSON: OUR DEMOCRATIC MISSION*

GENTLEMEN OF THE CONGRESS: When I addressed myself to performing the duty laid upon the President by the Constitution to present to you an annual report on the state of the Union, I found my thought dominated by an immortal sentence of Abraham Lincoln's, "Let us have faith that right makes might, and in that faith let us dare to do our duty as we understand it,"— a sentence immortal because it embodies in a form of utter simplicity and purity the essential faith of the nation, the faith in which it was conceived and the faith in which it has grown to glory and power. With that faith and the birth of a nation founded upon it came the hope into the world that a new order would prevail throughout the affairs of mankind, an order in which reason and right would take precedence of covetousness and force, and I believe that I express the wish and purpose of every thoughtful American when I say that this sentence marks for us in the plainest manner the part we should play alike in the arrangement of our domestic affairs and in our

exercise of influence upon the affairs of the world. By this faith, and by this faith alone, can the world be lifted out of its present confusion and despair. It was this faith which prevailed over the wicked force of Germany. You will remember that the beginning of the end of the war came when the German people found themselves face to face with the conscience of the world and realized that right was everywhere arrayed against the wrong that their government was attempting to perpetrate. I think, therefore, that it is true to say that this was the faith which won the war. Certainly this is the faith with which our gallant men went into the field and out upon the seas to make sure of victory.

This is the mission upon which democracy came into the world. Democracy is an assertion of the right of the individual to live and to be treated justly as against any attempt on the part of any combination of individuals to make laws which will overburden him or which will destroy his equality among his fellows in the matter of right or privilege, and I think we all realize that the day has come when democracy is being put upon its final test. The old world is just now suffering from a wanton rejection of the principle of

* Reprinted from *Congressional Record,* 66th Cong., 3rd sess. (Washington, D.C.: 1920–1921), p. 32.

democracy and a substitution of the principle of autocracy as asserted in the name but without the authority and sanction of the multitude. This is the time of all others when democracy should prove its purity and its spiritual power to prevail. It is surely the manifest destiny of the United States to lead in the attempt to make this spirit prevail.

There are two ways in which the United States can assist to accomplish this great object: First, by offering the example within her own borders of the will and power of democracy to make and enforce laws which are unquestionably just and which are equal in their administration,— laws which secure its full right to labor and yet at the same time safeguard the integrity of property, and particularly of that property which is devoted to the development of industry and the increase of the necessary wealth of the world. Second, by standing for right and justice as towards individual nations. The law of democracy is for the protection of the weak, and the influence of every democracy in the world should be for the protec-

tion of the weak nation, the nation which is struggling towards its right and towards its proper recognition and privilege in the family of nations. The United States can not refuse this rôle of champion without putting the stigma of rejection upon the great and devoted men who brought its government into existence and established it in the face of almost universal opposition and intrigue, even in the face of wanton force, as, for example, against the Orders in Council of Great Britain and the arbitrary Napoleonic Decrees which involved us in what we know as the War of 1812. I urge you to consider that the display of an immediate disposition on the part of the Congress to remedy any injustices or evils that may have shown themselves in our own national life will afford the most effectual offset to the forces of chaos and tyranny which are playing so disastrous a part in the fortunes of the free peoples of more than one part of the world. The United States is of necessity the sample democracy of the world, and the triumph of democracy depends upon its success.

CHAPTER NINETEEN

THE TWENTIES:
PROMISE OF ABUNDANCE

To its enthusiastic interpreters at the time, the decade of the 1920's represented the New Era when the benign managers of the American economic system, achieving ever greater efficiency and harnessing a multitude of new technical wonders, could bring to everyone within the nation an unparalleled abundance. And so, to a considerable degree, they did. Most farmers and some workers in depressed industries did not share the benefits of the New Era. But millions of city-dwellers—factory employees, white collar workers, professional men, and executives—did enjoy a burst of prosperity.

The great stockmarket crash of 1929 pricked the bubble. As abundance ebbed, leaving millions suffering privation, the twenties seemed no more than an unreal interlude or a cruel joke—an immoral jazz age, the era of the golden calf. Yet in many ways the New Era represented a step in development, not a hiatus, between the Progressive era and the New Deal.

The years after World War I brought problems for most Americans as they tried to adjust to the changes that the war had wrought. They sought new means to reach the age-old American end, the more abundant life. Despite all the newspaper excitement over the alleged debaucheries of the jazz age and the considerable shifts in moral standards that did take place, they adhered to the same basic moral verities as in the Progressive era, and for that matter, as in the ages of Lincoln and Jackson. A leading nonfiction bestseller was Bruce Barton's *The Man Nobody Knows*. While the book was written in the advertising man's booster jargon of the twenties, its main hero was Jesus, and a lesser hero was Lincoln.

One of the great national heroes of the twenties was Secretary of Commerce Herbert Hoover, a devoted Wilsonian, who, without doing too much violence to his ideology, could also be called a Jacksonian in spirit. Secretary Hoover set forth his credo in 1922 in a small book, *American Individualism*, which extolled the equality of opportunity which enabled Americans to succeed on their own merits, and the "rising vision of service" which led them to develop community responsibility rather than merely to seek "the acquisition and preservation of private property." Hoover's ideal means of action as Secretary of Commerce was in a way the opposite of Jackson's methods. President Jackson had been ready to use government as a negative force to prevent interference with free enterprise (small businesses). Secretary Hoover was ready to use government as a positive force to protect and strengthen small business. Essentially he was a Progressive (like President Wilson, one with brakes on) who carried into the 1920's the Progressive ideals of efficiency, scientific management, and the industrial laboratory.

Alfred E. Smith, the other leading Progressive of the 1920's, proved that a son of immigrants could voice emphatically the American credo. Smith like Hoover stood for efficiency. As Governor, Smith achieved a model reorganization of the governmental hodgepodge in the State of New York and fought successfully for better schools, good highways, and a modern park system.

While in the case of Secretary Hoover and Governor Smith Progressive action as well as the old ideology persisted, in Calvin Coolidge the American people had a President who could voice better than anyone else the old bucolic verities while standing firmly for the large scale industrial enterprise. Coolidge was not merely an historical accident, he was the logical man to be a highly popular president in the New Era. While he accepted the new mass-production order, he linked it with the old foundations through little homilies drawn from his Vermont boyhood—exhortations in which he fervently believed—urging his countrymen toward thrift, hard work, and respect for business. "The man who builds a factory builds a temple," Coolidge declared. "The man who works there worships there." It was the old Puritan ethic in homespun terms, sermons couched in the phrases of the "good old days," urging an acceptance of the new economic oligarchy. For millions of middle-class urban Americans only a generation or two away from rural backgrounds, there was a strong attraction in this country philosophy refurbished for the machine age.

The old verities had their greatest appeal among rural and small-town people who were not sharing the general prosperity and who had suffered from the changes that the war and the New Era had brought. Most of them in the North voted for Coolidge, but they felt bewildered, angry, and outnumbered, ready to express their resentment against city people and those who would overthrow Prohibition. To some of them there was a real relevance to the time-worn planks in Senator Robert M. La Follette's Progressive platform of 1924, which capitalized upon their yearning for the good times before the war. Unfortunately, some of these people resorted to techniques other than those of La Follette and tried to obtain by donning the bedsheet of the Ku Klux Klan what was beyond their grasp through the ballot. But they were largely ignored as well as outvoted; Sinclair Lewis had already written their requiem in *Main Street*.

In another novel, *Babbitt*, Lewis celebrated the new urban middle class. These were the beneficiaries of the glorious world of Hoover, Smith, and Coolidge. Arthur Link suggested that the middle class in the cities who had fought for power during the Progressive period thought they possessed power in the New Era.[1] One of the magazines they read, *The American*, which had earlier been devoted to muckraking, turned its attention to reciting the success stories of businessmen.

In schools and colleges, the old Progressive themes persisted. A generation of Wilsonian teachers and professors brought up a new generation to accept and support

---

[1] Arthur S. Link, "What Happened to the Progressive Movement in the 1920's?" *American Historical Review*, LXIV (July, 1959), 833–51.

collective security. A generation of former Bull Moosers helped prepare the way for a New Deal which went far beyond the New Nationalism and encompassed factors—especially a new relationship with organized labor—that the old Progressives would never have accepted. Above all, a new liberal national history, based largely on Progressive themes, was being fabricated by Vernon L. Parrington and Charles A. Beard, and, on a popular level, by Claude Bowers.

The Social Justice movement, as Link pointed out, continued to be exceedingly powerful. Enormous advances took place in regulatory city ordinances and state legislation, despite difficulties with the Supreme Court. The national budget increased only slightly (partly because of limitations imposed by Progressives in Congress), but state and local budgets soared as these governments assumed larger educational and welfare activities. Social work, especially that conducted by private charities, flourished; many social workers were swept into the new welfare capitalism and went to work for corporations like the Ford Motor Company or United States Steel.

Thus, in many ways, Progressivism, both in its strength and its shortcomings, carried over into the 1920's. Great innovations were taking place also. America was undergoing not only a technical revolution of the sort extolled by Earnest Elmo Calkins, but also was undergoing a moral revolution typified by the popular discovery (and garbling) of Freud's theories. Better schooling was bringing a more sophisticated and mature view of American society. The younger generation was growing up at the feet both of the former Progressives and of the new iconoclasts like Henry L. Mencken. Unlike both the Progressives and Mencken, when their time came they were ready to carry the country a considerable distance beyond both the Progressive period and the New Era. Along with the old, there was much that was new in their thinking, and the nation came to need the innovations. This generation was eager to see the promise of abundance of the 1920's affirmed in a more widespread, stable, and permanent prosperity.

Social scientists in the twenties intensified their efforts to gather and analyze facts and statistics as a means of understanding their times. Out of the data could come scientific solutions. Herbert Hoover commissioned two remarkable studies, a comprehensive survey, *Recent Social Trends,* not published until 1932, and a remarkable examination of the economy, *Recent Economic Changes,* completed before the great crash and published in 1929. Wesley C. Mitchell, one of the nation's greatest economists, concluded the study with a cogent over-all survey.

WESLEY C. MITCHELL: THE ECONOMY OF THE TWENTIES*

How the United States managed to attain a higher per capita income in 1922–1927 than ever before, though conditions in most other countries were not favorable, and though its basic industry, agriculture, was depressed, is the outstanding problem of the cycles of 1921–1924, 1924–1927 and 1927 to date.

* Reprinted from *Recent Economic Changes in the United States,* by the President's Conference on Unemployment, Herbert Hoover, Chairman. Copyright, 1929. McGraw-Hill Book Company, Inc. Used by permission.

. . . Since 1921, Americans have applied intelligence to the day's work more effectively than ever before. Thus the prime factor in producing the extraordinary changes in the economic fortunes of the European peoples during the nineteenth century is the prime factor in producing the prosperity of the United States in recent years. The old process of putting science into industry has been followed more intensively than before; it has been supplemented by tentative efforts to put science into business management, trade-union policy, and Government administration.

Concrete instances of technical improvements in many mining, metallurgical, and fabricating processes are given in the chapters on industry. The remarkable results achieved are demonstrated statistically from census data showing output per worker. Similar, though less striking, instances appear in the chapter on construction. Without help from any extraordinary invention, the railroads also have attained a higher level of operating efficiency. In farming there is an intriguing report of new machines and new methods coming into use. Here too, the record of average output per worker shows considerable gains.

All this means that since 1921 Americans have found ways of producing more physical goods per hour of labor than before. They have received larger average incomes because they have produced more commodities and services. That is true in the aggregate, although not all who have contributed to the increase in physical production have shared in the increase of real income. The important exceptions to the general rule will be discussed presently.

The reality of the gains made by improving the technique of farming, railroading, manufacturing, and building seems to be established beyond question. There is room for doubt only concerning the pace of recent progress in comparison with earlier spurts of technical improvement. . . . But doubts whether the rate of improvement in the past six years is unprecedented are not of great moment. It remains clear that the Industrial Revolution is not a closed episode; we are living in the midst of it, and the economic problems of to-day are largely problems of its making.

While the details of the latest technical advances always possess thrilling interest, perhaps there is more of promise for the future in the chapters on recent changes in economic policy. The efforts to apply scientific methods to such matters are in an early stage of development. The sciences which underlie these efforts—psychology, sociology, economics—are far less advanced than physics and chemistry. The experts who are making the applications—personnel managers, advertising specialists, sales directors, business economists and statisticians—are less rigorously trained than engineers. It is even harder to measure the results they achieve than to determine what difference a new machine makes in unit costs. Nor are business executives so generally convinced of the practical value of the rather intangible services which the new professions can render as they are of the indispensability of engineering advice. Yet it is conceivable that applications of the social sciences, now in their tentative stage, will grow into contributions of great moment to economic welfare. Certainly the chapters in this report on marketing, management and labor show that many enterprising business concerns and some enterprising trade unions are trying new policies, and often getting results which they deem good.

Perhaps none of the changes reported here will prove more important in the long run than the change in the economic theories on which the American Federation of Labor and certain outside unions are acting. That organizations of wage earners should grasp the relations between productivity and wages, and that they should take the initiative in pressing constructive plans for increasing efficiency upon employers, is not wholly without precedent; but the spread of such ideas and the vigor with which they are acted on by large organizations must startle those who have believed that trade unions are brakes upon economic progress.

Scarcely less significant is the report from the employing side. Our investigators believe that the art of business management turned a corner in 1921, cultivating since then more skillful understanding of the whole situation and nicer adjustment of means to the immediate environment. Numerous corporations and some trade associations are maintaining research bureaus of their own. Among the managerial devices experimented with, are co-ordinated staffs in place of one "big boss," bonus payments to executives and "incentive wages" for the rank and file, operating budgets, forecasts of business conditions, close inventory control, personnel management and employee representation. Most of these devices are attempts to understand and to utilize the psychological forces which control human behavior, or the economic forces which control business activity. "There is today not only more production per man, more wages per man and more horse power per man; there is also more management per man." Marketing—traditionally the part of business in which native shrewdness, experience and "personal magnetism" have been held all-important—even marketing is being permeated by applied psychology. Costly investigations of "consumer appeal," of advertising "pull," of "sales resistance"—the very terms would have been unintelligible to our fathers—show that sales managers are trying to base their planning upon factual studies of human behavior. And the rapid spread of chain stores and of installment selling show that marketing methods are no more standing still than is industrial technique.

By the side of these rather definite changes in trade-union and in business policy, we may set the influence of certain general ideas which have gained wide currency in the last few years.

First, there is the spirit of caution, manifested in minimizing future commitments, in hand-to-mouth buying by merchants, in efforts to keep down inventories or to pass the need for keeping large stocks on to the concern from which one buys. This lesson is taught afresh by every great crisis. The staggering financial losses of 1920–21 enforced the old moral emphatically; the sagging course of commodity prices has kept it in mind, and the increased operating efficiency of producers and railroads has made possible close scheduling of merchandise transactions. The Florida land boom and the stock-market adventure of

1928 indicate the course American business might have taken in the absence of all restraint. . . .

. . . belief in the economy of high wages has become prevalent among the abler business executives, much as belief in increasing productivity has become prevalent among the abler trade-union leaders. To find a market for the wares turned out by mass production and urged on consumers by national advertising, it is patently necessary to have corresponding purchasing power in the hands of consumers. Since studies of the national income have demonstrated that wages constitute by far the largest stream of personal income, it follows that wages per man—or rather, wages per family—must be increased as production is expanded. Perhaps most people would have accepted this argument in the abstract at any time in the last hundred years. But many employers in the past would have retorted with the assertion that high wages undermine the moral stamina of the masses. To-day such talk is far less common in the United States. Not only do many business executives admit the general principle that paying high wages is good policy; they are ready to assume what they consider their share of the responsibility for putting the principle into practice.

The share of Government in recent economic changes has not been made the subject of a separate chapter. But the service of one public agency, the Federal Reserve System, is treated in the chapter on banking, and the services of the Departments of Commerce, Agriculture, and Labor in collecting and diffusing knowledge are mentioned in several places. If the prime factor making for prosperity has been the application of intelligence to the day's work, then Government agencies must be credited with an indispensable, though indirect, part in what has been accomplished.

Further, our Federal Government has of late years manifested a more intelligent attitude toward problems of economic organization than it has manifested in the past. To treat business enterprises as agencies for performing social services, to facilitate their operations, and to hold them to this conception of their function, is a policy exceedingly difficult to carry out. It requires a delicate combination of constructive intervention at some points and of clearing away obstacles at other points. No one can say that this policy has become characteristic of Government in all of its dealings with business, any more than one can say that the doctrine of high wages is accepted by all employers, or the theory that increased productivity benefits labor is accepted by all trade-unionists. Yet no one who has watched Federal policy, as practiced by the numerous agencies which have to deal with economic issues, will question that a change has occurred. Efforts to check extortion have not ceased; but more regularly than in the past they are accompanied by active efforts to heighten the efficiency of what are judged to be legitimate enterprises. Farmers and exporters are not the only beneficiaries.

To repeat: all of the changes making for prosperity which have been recalled in this section, together with many others noted in preceding chapters, can be summed up under a single head—applying fresh intelligence to the day's work. From the use of abstruse researches in pure science to the use of broad economic conceptions and the use of common sense, the method of American progress in 1922–1928 has been the old method of taking thought. Peace let us turn our thoughts to common matters, the hard times of 1921 spurred our efforts, and the complicated consequences our efforts produced have kept us thinking.

. . . Scarcely less characteristic of our period than unit-cost reductions is the rapid expansion in the production and sale of products little used or wholly unknown a generation or even a decade ago. Among consumers' goods, the conspicuous instances are automobiles, radios and rayon. But the list includes also oil-burning furnaces, gas stoves, household electrical appliances in great variety, automobile accessories, antifreezing mixtures, cigarette lighters, propeller pencils, wrist watches, airplanes, and what not. Among producers' goods we have the truck and the tractor competing with the horse and the mule, reinforced concrete competing with brick and lumber, the high-tension line competing with the steam engine, fuel oil competing with coal, not to mention excavating machines, belt conveyors, paint sprayers, and "automatics" of many sorts competing with manual labor.

Changes in taste are in large part merely the consumers' response to the solicitation of novel products, effectively presented by advertising. But that is not all of the story; the consumer is free to choose what he likes among the vociferous offerings, and sometimes reveals traces of initiative. In what other terms can one explain the changes in diet pointed out in the first chapter? Americans are consuming fewer calories per capita; they are eating less wheat and corn but more dairy products, vegetable oils, sugar, fresh vegetables and fruit. More families than ever before are sending their sons and daughters to college—surely that is not a triumph of "high-powered" salesmanship. Young children, girls and women, are wearing lighter and fewer clothes. The short skirt, the low shoe, the silk or rayon stocking, "athletic" underwear, the soft collar, sporting suits and sporting goods, have an appeal which makers of rival articles have not been able to overcome. And, in a sense, every consumers' good, from college to candy, is a rival of every other consumers' good, besides being a rival of the savings bank.

"When the makers of one product get a larger slice of the consumer's dollar, the slices left for the makers of other products get smaller." This way of accounting for the hardships met by certain long-established industries in 1922–1927, such, for example, as the leather and woolen trades, is popular and sound, so far as it goes. But it does not take account of the fact that desire for new goods, or the pressure of installment purchases once made, may lead people to work harder or more steadily, and so get more dollars to spend. Presumably the enticements of automobiles and radios, of wrist watches and electric refrigerators, of correspondence courses and college, have steadied many youths, set many girls hunting for jobs and kept many fathers of families to the mark. Also a considerable part of the country's former bill for intoxicants has been available to spend in other ways. How much allowance we should make for these factors nobody knows. All one can say with assurance is that consumption per capita has increased in volume to match the increased per capita output of consumers' goods taken altogether. Yet the increase in consumption has not been rapid enough to prevent shifts in the kind of goods bought from pressing hard upon the makers of articles waning in popular favor.

So too in the realm of producers' goods. Despite the active building campaign, the lumber industry has had hard sledding. Coal mining has not prospered, and can attribute part of its difficulties to other fuels, water power, and more economical ways of burning coal itself. Breeders of draft animals have found their markets cut into by motor vehicles. Railways have lost traffic to trucks and omnibusses—though the loss in freight tonnage is held by Professor Cunningham to be less than the public supposes. Steam-engine builders have had to change their products or reduce their output. It is not necessary to multiply examples; most technical improvements reduce the demand for some other good, and so create difficulties for those who supply the latter.

. . . So far, the contrasts noted at the outset of this chapter between the economic fortunes of different income groups, different industries, and different sections of the United States in 1922–1927, have been traced to three factors—or rather to three great complexes of factors. (1) Foreign conditions on the whole have been none too favorable to American business, and they have been eminently unfavorable to American agriculture. Important branches of industry have enjoyed a large increase in foreign sales; but had Europe been prosperous, American prosperity would have been less "spotty" and more intense. (2) Such prosperity as we have enjoyed has been earned by many-sided and strenuous efforts, in which millions of people have shared, to improve our technical methods, our business management, our trade-union policy, and our Government administration. (3) While increasing efficiency has added to real income, it has put pressure, often rising to severe hardship, upon competitors, direct and indirect. The factory hand competing with the "automatic" machine, the horse farmer competing with the tractor farmer, the lumber industry competing with the cement industry, the New England cotton mill competing with the North Carolina cotton mill, the independent retailer competing with the chain store, the clothing trade competing with the makers of automobiles and radios for slices of the consumers' dollars, have had a hard time. . . .

HOW MATTERS STAND IN THE SPRING OF 1929

Forecasting the future is no part of the present task. But we should not close the record without noting that recent developments may appear less satisfactory in retrospect than they appear at present.

Even on the face of affairs, all is not well. Americans have seen more uniformly fortunate times: for example, in 1906, when the Secretary of the Treasury was praying that the country might be delivered from more prosperity. The condition of agriculture, the volume of unemployment, the textile trades, coal mining, the leather industries, present grave problems not only to the people immediately concerned, but also to their fellow citizens. How rapidly these conditions will mend, we do not know. Some may grow worse.

Nor can we be sure that the industries now prosperous will prolong indefinitely their recent record of stability. That we have not had a serious crisis since 1920 or a severe depression since 1921 is no guarantee that we shall be equally prudent, skillful and fortunate in the years to come. If we are to maintain business prosperity, we must continue to earn it month after month and year after year by intelligent effort. The incomes disbursed to consumers, and to wage earners in particular, must be increased on a scale sufficient to pay for the swelling volume of consumers' goods sent to market. The credit structure must be kept in due adjustment to the earnings of business enterprises. Security prices must not outrun prospective profits capitalized at the going rate of interest. Commodity stocks must be held in line with current sales. Overcommitments of all sorts must be avoided. The building of new industrial equipment must not be overrapid. These and the similar matters which might be mentioned present delicate problems of management which will find their practical solutions in the daily decisions of business executives. Perhaps errors are being kept within the limits of tolerance. Perhaps no serious setback will occur for years to come. But we are leaving 1921 well behind us, and there are signs that the caution inspired by that disastrous year is wearing thin.

Whether the recent rate of progress in the arts of industry and business can be maintained is another uncertainty. Past experience, as summed up in the introductory chapter, suggests that the pace will slacken presently, and that years may pass before we see such another well-maintained advance. But that is a matter in which experience is not a trustworthy guide. Scientific research, industrial invention and business pioneering all lead into the unknown. They are fascinating ventures which energetic minds will ever be trying, whether the tangible rewards prove great or small. All that is certain is that whatever progress in efficiency we continue to make must be won by the same type of bold and intelligent work that has earned our recent successes.

The twenties brought the advent of modern advertising, which burst upon readers luxuriantly and flamboyantly. The common man seems not to have been unduly concerned, but many intellectuals were indignant and derisive. Some of them were worried, because, like the advertising copywriters, they had been influenced by a psychologist, John B. Watson, in his book *Behaviorism,* who was proclaiming that what a man became was determined by the stimuli he received from his environment; only environment mattered. As for the advertising men, they were at pains to impress upon the public that their influence was of profound social benefit.

EARNEST ELMO CALKINS: ADVERTISING THE CIVILIZER*

A young man who had just joined the staff of one of the larger advertising agencies sought his boss in some perturbation. "I wish you would tell me the truth about this advertising business, chief. Is it all bunk?" To which his employer replied, "There is just as much bunk in advertising as there is in law or medicine, or for that matter, in literature and life, but it is never necessary to use bunk to practise advertising successfully."

That young man's state of mind was the natural result of his reading. He had been recruited from the profession of writing, and he still followed the animadversions of the ultra-intellectual world, which has lately concerned itself with the inconsistencies, the waste, and the smugness of advertising. In short, with the bunk. . . .

Then there are the fiction makers, with less restriction and more imagination. The younger men, most of them after brief experiences inside advertising organizations, have seized the excellent opportunity for satire which modern business affords, and we have Felix Reisenberg's *P. A. L.,* Will Irwin's *Lew Tyler's Wives,* Roger Burlingame's *You Too,* Scott Fitzgerald's *The Great Gatsby,* Christopher Morley's *Ginger Cubes,* Sinclair Lewis's *Babbitt,* Sherwood Anderson's *Story-teller's Story,* and *Bunk, Lottery,* and *Bread and Circuses* by William Woodward, all presenting advertising as a sort of gigantic conspiracy, fostered and maintained by highly paid advertising men whose interests, like those of the priests of ancient religions, lie in keeping up the great illusion, and who go about their work with their tongues in their cheeks. Sometimes the conspiracy is imagined as directed against the business man, but the popular conception is that the public is the victim, and that manufacturer and agent are working together to put something over. This something may be higher prices for worthless goods, creating unnecessary wants and desires, or exterminating a competitor making a better article at a lower price, but generally just misleading people with bunk about memory courses, or hair restorers, or correspondence universities. . . .

The slogan "It pays to advertise" acquired its currency from George M. Cohan's play. Admitting that advertising pays, whom does it pay? It pays the professional advertising man, beyond doubt. It also pays the manufacturer who uses it to increase his business. But the crucial question is, does it pay the public? Are the people as a whole better off for it? Is it a benefit to mankind? And who pays for it? Is it added to the cost of the goods? Would it be desirable, as writers have suggested, to remove advertising from our commercial fabric, and would we be better off without it?. . .

When I was a boy, about fifty years ago more or less, mother used to buy a bar of Castile soap half a yard long and four inches square and saw it up into cakes an inch thick. The cake was hard as Stonehenge, the corners sharper than a serpent's tooth. It took weeks of use to wear it down so that it comfortably fitted the hand.

To-day we have a cake of toilet soap—a great many of them, in fact—just the right shape to fit the hand, just as pure as Castile, scented if we like, tinted to match the bathroom decorations if we prefer, reasonable in price; and when we want another cake we go to the nearest grocery or drug store, and there it is.

And not only toilet soap. We have seen the evolution of shaving creams, safety razors, and tooth pastes, as well as soap powders, laundry chips, washing machines, vegetable shortenings, self-rising flours, electric sadirons, vacuum cleaners, hot-water taps, aluminum cooking utensils, refrigerators, kitchen cabinets—everything, in short, that constitutes the difference between our mothers' kitchens and our wives'.

The amount of sheer drudgery that has been taken out of housekeeping in fifty years can be realized only by comparison, by drawing the illuminating parallel. . . .

The amelioration that has come about in fifty years is due directly and indirectly to advertising. These things did not come into existence because women demanded them. Women did not know that they were possible. They exist because there was a method of distributing them, of teaching

* Reprinted from Earnest Elmo Calkins, *Business the Civilizer* (Boston: Atlantic Monthly Press, Little, Brown & Company, 1928), pp. 1–2, 12–13, 14–18 by permission.

possible buyers what a help they would be, of educating the housewife while offering her the means of applying what she learned, and of doing it on a large scale. And the strongest urge to invent desirable labor-saving devices has been this same possibility of distributing them—that is, selling enough of them to make it worth while.

Sometimes advertising supplies a demand, but in most cases it creates demand for things that were beyond even the imagination of those who would be most benefited by them. A woman knew the use of a broom, but she could not imagine a vacuum cleaner. Therefore she could not demand one, save with that vague unspoken desire which has existed from the beginning for some lightening of the terrible drudgery of keeping a house livable. The vacuum cleaner was introduced by educational advertising. The advertising was done partly by manufacturers anxious to sell vacuum cleaners, and partly by electric-light companies anxious to sell current. The spread of electrical housekeeping devices has followed the increase in the number of houses wired for electricity, and that too has been brought about by advertising, by the selfish desire to do more business, to sell more goods. But the result has been a public benefit, an increasing willingness to spend money to lighten the human burden, to cut down the waste of human energy spent in the operation of living.

No vacuum-cleaner factory could do business as a neighborhood proposition. Only a national market would furnish enough business to make the manufacture economically possible. And a national market is possible only through advertising. And that advertising must be educational. It must teach the sound economy of paying more to get the greater benefit. The woman's time and health and strength are worth more than the difference in cost between a broom and a cleaner. But not all of these improvements are in the vacuum-cleaner class. Most of them add nothing to the cost of upkeep. The greater number lower it. They teach the use of something better that costs less.

I do not think I am claiming too much in giving to advertising the credit of the great change in housekeeping that we have seen. I have had to observe it very closely for thirty years, and I have to some extent helped to bring it about. Some may be inclined to think it is due to the women's magazines. It is true that they have directed their editorial energies to the same ends and with remarkable results. But it should not be forgotten that it is advertising that makes such magazines possible. . . .

Advertising is not an end. It is a means to an end. So the question is not, Is advertising desirable, but Are those ends desirable, and is advertising too great a price to pay for them? To those who look upon advertising as merely the selfish effort of manufacturers to induce them to buy more goods it seems that the world could easily do without it. People say to themselves, "I do not want to be persuaded to buy more goods," and that should settle it. As far as they are concerned

advertising is unnecessary. For the manufacturer who uses it, advertising is a means of selling goods, but its present proportions are due not to the manufacturer's desire to sell goods, but to the real public need it supplies.

A familiar paradox is the man who tells you with much earnestness that he never reads advertising, and does not believe in it. And as he sits there he is dressed from head to foot in advertised goods. His office is equipped and his home is furnished with advertised goods. How did they get there? Because they were the things most accessible, the ones for sale in the stores where he bought, the ones the salesman showed him, and the ones that most exactly met his needs. It was not necessary for him to read the advertising. The advertising he did not read distributed the goods, brought them within his reach geographically and financially, and keeps them there for his benefit—better things than he could buy for the same money were it not for the tremendous savings that quantity production brings about. And most of them would not even exist, to say nothing of being distributed, if there had not been advertising.

But advertising adds to the cost of the goods! You still hear that. So does production add to the cost of the goods, and traveling salesmen, and retail stores, and jobbers' percentages. Everything that is done to a manufactured article and all handling of natural products must be added to the price that the customer pays. But nothing is so well established as the simple fact that the more you make the less the cost of each. And not only is cost of making lessened, but also the cost of selling, including cost of advertising. And the cost of selling can be and is lessened until the advertising costs nothing. Why does a tailor-made suit cost more than a ready-made? Why do custom-made shoes cost more than the product of the factories? It is difficult to prove these things by tables of statistics because prices of all things have advanced so in the years since the war.

But consider the motor car. Nearly everyone is interested in this product of advertising. Nearly everyone is aware of the continual improvement in the cars and the steady lowering of price, due to quantity production. Some are as much concerned over the congestion of motor cars as they are over the congestion of advertising. They feel that there is too much of both. Granted in both cases; but the only alternative is to turn back the page to mediæval times, when each village was self-contained, or forward to one of the many Utopias which promise enough of everything and not too much of anything.

The point is that we cannot eat our cake of accessible and convenient apparatus of living and still have our cake of freedom from advertising, freight trains, industrial villages, steel and cement construction, riveting hammers, congested highways, and the many other annoyances of a prosperous, material, and mercantile age.

The liveliest stir among well-informed people, and many who were less well-informed, was over the writings of Sigmund Freud. To the man on the street, Freud, who was in reality a strait-laced Viennese psychiatrist, stood for the loosening of the traditional moral bonds. This did take place to some extent, and it was done in the name of Freud. Freudism also influenced many American writers, especially Eugene O'Neill and William Faulkner. But of great ultimate importance, outlasting the popular furore over things Freudian and psychoanalytic, was the impact it had upon American psychiatry, which was dedicated not to license, but to bringing people to a better understanding, and thus more effective control, of their emotions.

CELIA BURNS STENDLER: AMERICA DISCOVERS FREUD*

AMERICA'S INTRODUCTION TO FREUDISM

While the years 1900 to 1925 have been designated as the span of time to be covered by this study, it has been difficult to find any mention of Freud during the first eight years of this period. Although there is some indication of an awareness of Freud as evidenced by such a remark as William James's that he was "aware of Freud in 1893,"[4] the leading psychologists in the country showed no recognition of the startling work being done in psychoanalysis abroad. Freud's first book with Breuer in 1895, *Studies in Hysteria,* called forth no comment in America, nor did writings on related subjects during the next fifteen years show any cognizance of his discoveries. J. J. Jastrow, of the University of Wisconsin, in his book, *The Subconscious,* published in 1906, discussed the theory of the subliminal self with no mention of Freud, nor did reviews by John B. Watson[5] or James R. Angell[6] criticize it in the light of the new evidence being presented on the other side of the Atlantic. C. K. Clarke, writing an article on psychiatric clinics of Germany[7] for the *American Journal of Insanity* in 1908 omitted any reference to Freud

or his followers. That the idea of the subconscious was beginning to worry psychologists, however, was evidenced by Hugo Munsterburg, Professor of Psychology at Harvard, who wrote a vigorous denial of the existence of the subconscious, giving a physiological explanation for the reproduction of names, etc., into the conscious, asserting it was simply a matter of connecting paths.[8]

To A. A. Brill must go the credit for being the first American champion of Freud in print. A New York physician interested in neuroses, he had gone abroad in 1907 and had studied under Freud. In 1908 he arranged to translate Freud's works—*Studies in Hysteria, The Interpretation of Dreams, The Psychopathology of Everyday Life, Three Contributions to the Theory of Sex,* and *Wit and Its Relation to the Unconscious.* Smith Ely Jelliffe accepted the small volumes on neuroses and sex for a new monograph series put out by the Journal for Nervous and Mental Diseases Society, and *Selected Papers on Hysteria and other Psychoneurosis,* finally appeared in 1912, but no American publisher was willing to take the risk of publishing *The Psychopathology of Everyday Life* until 1914.[9] Brill's first article on Freud appeared long before these translations were ready, however. In July, 1909, issue of *The American Journal of Insanity,* writing on "A Case of Schizophrenia," Brill described the treatment of several cases by Freud by the psychoanalytical method, and referred to the "new and invaluable psychology by Freud."[10] This journal in October of the same year published an article by Ernest Jones, of the University of Toronto, entitled, "Psycho-analytic Notes on a

* Reprinted from Celia Burns Stendler, "New Ideas for Old: How Freudism Was Received in the United States from 1900 to 1925," *Journal of Educational Psychology,* XXXVIII (April, 1947), 196–205 by permission.

[4] Jelliffe, Smith Ely, "Sigmund Freud and Psychiatry," *American Journal of Sociology,* Vol. 15, 1939.

[5] Watson, John B., Review of *The Subconscious* by J. H. Jastrow, *American Journal of Sociology,* 12, page 558–561, 1906–1907.

[6] Angell, James R., "In the Realm of the Subconscious" *Dial,* 41, 106–109, September 1, 1906.

[7] Clarke, C. K., "Notes on Some Psychiatric Clinics of German[y]," *American Journal of Insanity,* 65, 357–376, 1908–1909.

[8] Author not given, "A Psychologist's Denial of the Existence of the Subconscious," *Current Literature,* 47, 206–208, August, 1909.

[9] Brill, A. A., "Introduction and Development of Freud's Work in the United States," *American Journal Soc.,* 15, November, 1939.

[10] Brill, A. A., "A Case of Schizophrenia," *American Journal of Insanity,* 66, 52–69, July 1909.

Case of Hypomania" in which he gave accounts of cases treated by Freud, and stated, "The psycho-analytic methods developed by Freud in the past fifteen years have been singularly neglected by workers outside German-speaking countries as illustrated by the fact that no psycho-analytic, carried out in any country, has up to the present been published."[11]

Meanwhile, another champion had appeared in the person of G. Stanley Hall, of Clark University; and at his invitation Freud delivered a series of five lectures at Clark in September, 1909, where, apparently, he was very well received. Indeed, to quote his own account: "We found, to our great astonishment, that the unprejudiced men of that small but respected pedogogic-philosophical university, knew all the psycho-analytical writings and had honored them in their lectures to their students. Thus, even in prudish America, one could at least in academic circles, discuss freely and treat scientifically all those things that are regarded as offensive in life."[12] In true Freudian fashion, he attributed this freedom to the repression of the sex instinct, which intensifies interest in psychoanalysis!

The repercussions of this visit were distinctly favorable. Although the lectures themselves did not appear in an American magazine until April of the following year, loyal champions of Freudism began to break forth in print. J. J. Putnam, Harvard neurologist, was won over during this period, and wrote "Personal Impressions of Sigmund Freud and His Work, with Special Reference to His Recent Lectures at Clark University," in which he decried the fact that Freud's theories had been so long neglected, since they had a distinct message in dealing with the problem of adjustment to modern civilization.[13] Ernest Jones wrote two articles appearing in the early part of 1910, both favorable to Freud,[14] and, as evidence of the growing interest, Rudolph Archer reviewed in July, most of Freud's writings to date, ending with a plea for open-mindedness for this new school of psychology.[15]

The lay public (some of them) received its first written account of Freudism in two issues of *Current Literature* during 1911. Both articles were very favorable; one stated that this new doctrine would "go far to revolutionize all present psycho-logical conceptions,"[16] and the other described "remarkable discoveries in the pathology of mental ills by the distinguished Dr. Freud of Vienna."[17]

THE OPPOSITION MARSHALS ITS FORCES

It would appear, then, that up to the year 1913 Freud had a small number of ardent and vocal followers, and that, while opposition to his doctrines was referred to in some articles, this opposition did little or no writing. The year 1913 marked a change, however; the beginning of a storm which was to rage well into postwar World War I years. The early participants in the controversy, as might be expected, were the professional groups—doctors, psychiatrists, psychologists—whose interests were closely allied to this new field. There were several factors to account for the diversity of opinions, and the violence of them. One was the resistance to change—which accompanies every new movement in our culture and can probably only be explained by a tendency to inertia on the part of human beings; another might be termed vested interests, the fear that this new doctrine might eventually undermine the older schools; and a third, perhaps most important factor, was the blow to conventional morality dealt by Freud's treatment of sex.

Paul Carus, writing in 1913 for the *Monist,* a magazine devoted to the philosophy of science, was among the first to voice his doubts of Freud. He believed that the mistake made by the psycho-analyst was in "generalizing the lower tendency so as to cover the highest efflorescence of mental life," in other words, basing his whole psychology upon the erotic theory, and that "the success of the theory will last as long as the personality of the master holds the attention of the reading public."[18] Haberman was quoted in 1915 in an article entitled, "An American Expert's Indictment of Dream Analysis as Humbug," which self-explanatory title was followed in the same vein with statements such as this: "We must hold the entire 'sex' theory with its many ramifications as standing upon the same ground as the green cheese hypothesis of the composition of the moon."[19]

Southard, Woodworth, and Franklin—three prominent psychologists—scathingly denounced

[11] Jones, Ernest, "Psycho-analytic Notes on a Case of Hypomania," *American Journal of Insanity,* 66, 203–218, October, 1909.

[12] Freud, Sigmund, *Autobiography,* p. 950.

[13] Putnam, J. J., "Personal Impressions of Sigmund Freud and His Work," *Journal of Abnormal Psychology,* 1–26, December, 1909.

[14] Jones, Ernest, "The Oedipus-Complex as an Explanation of Hamlet's Mystery," *American Journal Psy.,* Jan. 1910. "Freud's Theory of Dreams," *American Journal Psy.,* 21, 283–308, April, 1910.

[15] Archer, Rudolph, *Recent Freudian Literature,* 22, 408–443, July, 1911.

[16] Archer, Rudolph, "Freud's Discovery of the Latest Chamber of the Soul," *Current Literature,* 50, 512–514, May, 1911.

[17] "A Medical Report from a New Psychoanalysis World," *Current Literature,* 50, 167–169, February, 1911.

[18] Carus, Paul, "Wrong Generalizations in Philosophy," *The Monist,* 23, 150–151, January, 1913.

[19] "An American Expert's Indictment of Dream Analysis as Humbug," *Current Literature,* 34–35, January, 1915.

Freudian practice in several issues of *The Nation* in 1916. Woodworth very cleverly attacked the doctrine of free association by showing that by tracing back the words 'Freudian principle' one ended up with irregular sex relations, thereby proving that Freud, according to his own theory, was "giving expression to a deep-seated wish, repressed by force of circumstances, for a career of unbridled lust." [20] C. Ladd Franklin was much more vehement. She related the case of a physician who practiced psychoanalysis, "who goes to work to discover whether his patients (they are most frequently young women) have symbolically married their fathers or not," and quoted a Harvard professor, who "when he discovered what was going on said: 'But this is a matter for the police court!' " [21]

On the other side, there were just as vigorous defenders of Freudism. F. B. Holt in his book *The Freudian Wish* expressed the belief that the Freudian view of the will could be of real service to ethics. [22] Alfred Kuttner, long a champion of psychoanalysis, wrote several articles for *New Republic* in 1914 and 1915, in which he ably and favorably discussed different aspects of the new psychology, and in the first of which he optimistically called Otto Rank's study of hero myths "the beginning of a change in the current attitude toward Freudian psychology." He commented to the effect that gross abuse of Freud was no longer considered altogether good form in neurological and psychological circles. [23]

FREUDISM IS PRESENTED TO THE LAY PUBLIC

The general public received its first presentation of these new doctrines in *Good Housekeeping* for February, 1915. Two characteristics of popularized Freudism are significant: first that psychoanalysis was presented as a cure-all for mental and certain physical disorders, and, secondly, that early presentations were deleted of sex. The closest references in the first article were rather ambiguous statements such as, "Soon the doctor was tracing the blow—back—to the struggles of a child to adjust itself and conform its love-life to the compulsions of the society into which it was growing up," and, again, "Not all our thought impulses are as harmless and innocent as those I've suggested . . . . they may come up out of our deeper selves . . . . and suggest desires, the grati-

fication of which would be highly agreeable, but which the morals of the community declare to be wrong, preposterous, unpermissible." [24]

This same author, in a subsequent issue of *Good Housekeeping* in 1915, gave a brief account of Freud's study of dreams, and quite boldly quoted Freud: "Every case of nervous invalidism not arising from a physical cause has its origin in some maladjustment of the sex life." He even referred to infantile sexuality and wound up with the sincere statement of his recognition of the "inadequacy of explanation, for it involves an intimate consideration of subjects perfectly legitimate and wholesome in themselves, but which, because of their relationships and associations in public thought, are not material for discussion in a journal of this kind." [25] Other writers, however, were not as daring, and as late as 1917, we find in the *Ladies Home Journal* such an enticing title as, "How We All Reveal Our Soul Secrets," dealing with the Freudian theory of forgetting, but with no mention of sex. [26]

INFLUENCE OF CHANGES IN THE SOCIAL SCENE

The trend toward more open discussion of sex, making popular presentation of Freudism possible (which in turn would help change further the current attitude toward sex) was speeded up by World War I, and gathered tremendous momentum in the years following. This period was characterized not only by great changes in political and economic life, but in manners and morals as well. A process already begun when war was declared, it was given tremendous impetus during the war by several factors: the prevailing eat-drink-and-be-merry philosophy, the development of a new code of morals by American soldiers in France, and the freedom of necessity granted to American women war-workers. With peace came the difficulty of adjustment and an attempt to find new values to fit a new way of life. An unmistakable trend toward a new philosophy of sex relations—a feeling that chastity and fidelity had been rated too highly was evident. Freudism, as interpreted for the public, taught new and disturbing things about life, advocated an uninhibited sex life, and encouraged the dogma that salvation lay in facing the facts of sex. This obsession with sex was revealed in the growth of 'confession' and 'sex' magazines, in the movies, and in the literature of the times. The flappers with their short skirts and rolled stockings, their cigarettes and flasks, their use of cosmetics, their abandon in

---

[20] Woodworth, R. S., "Followers of Freud and Jung," *Nation*, 103, 396 October 26, 1916.

[21] Franklin, C. Ladd, "Freudian Doctrines," *Nation*, 103, 373–374, October 18, 1916.

[22] Holt, F. B., *The Freudian Wish*, New York: Henry Holt and Co., 1915.

[23] Kuttner, Alfred, "The Freudian Theory," *New Republic*, 2, 182–183, March 20, 1915. "A Note on Forgetting," *New Republic*, 1, 15–17, November 28, 1914.

[24] MacFarlane, Peter Clark, "Diagnosis of Dreams," *Good Housekeeping*, 60, 125–133, February, 1915.

[25] *Op. cit*, 125–133.

[26] Tookey, John P., "How We All Reveal Our Soul Secrets," *Ladies Home Journal*, 34, November, 1917, p. 97.

dancing, seemed to typify the new spirit of the early 1920's.[27]

With such fruitful soil, it was only natural that Freudism should flourish, and in turn should contribute to the revolt against the accepted American moral order. However, during this next period several changes must be noted in the reception of psychoanalysis. We have seen that this new doctrine was first accepted and promoted by a group of pioneers, and generally ignored by the bulk of psychologists and doctors; that as these people recognized that Freudism was not going to die out in a day or even a year, but actually threatened established values, many began to oppose it, this opposition usually being on the grounds of Freudian over-emphasis of sex. Now by 1920, we find wider acceptance, but with many reservations of some of the tenets of Freudism, while earlier champions worked at refining and modifying the doctrine in the light of new evidence. G. Stanley Hall's autobiography, *Life and Confessions of a Psychologist,* which appeared in 1923, declared that the advent of Freudism marked the greatest epoch in the history of our science, but went on to criticize Freud's attempt to trace everything to one source.[28] Three years earlier Henry James had edited *Letters of William James,* and his statement, written following Freud's visit to Clark University: "I hope that Freud and his pupils will push their ideas to their utmost limits; they can't fail to throw light on human nature," probably had some effect on the critics of Freud, and although James in his letter went on to call Freud, "A man obsessed with fixed ideas," [29] the general implication, that there was something to Freud which James had recognized as early as 1909, may have influenced some of the loyal followers of James. McDougall referred to his opening "the doors of academic psychology just wide enough to admit some of the most fruitful conceptions of our time," [30] but he, too, questioned Freud's emphasis on sex.

POPULARIZATION OF FREUDISM

After World War I, however, another aspect entered into the picture. With the popularization of Freudism permissable because of the breakdown of traditional morality, together with the fact that Freudism had in it many elements of popular appeal (it catered to a natural curiosity about oneself and one could find in case studies experiences in common with one's own) we find the practice of psychoanalysis being taken up by 'quacks' and amateurs—often with dire results. Many sincere and honest people in the professional group who might otherwise have accepted much of Freudism failed to distinguish between what was real and what was faked, and judged the whole of the new doctrine in the light of the evils they saw around them. The increase in sexual license, the extreme cases of mental disorder brought about by amateur psychoanalysts— these they tended to generalize on and so condemned the whole doctrine. Edward Cowles writing for *Woman's Home Companion* in 1924 related the Frank's murder case in Chicago to the dangerous prevalence of the habit of self-analysis, and decried the existing obsession with sex.[31] An eminent New York psychologist, in a symposium on psychoanalysis at St. Mark's, called Freud's interpretation of the unconscious 'rotten' and attributed to it many of the evils of society.[32] Maxwell Bodenheim criticized, in *The Nation,* the Freudian influence on literature to the effect that "novels have become mere recitals of one man's affairs with different women," and attributed its success to the fact that those who accepted it "were longing for a diagrammed excuse for their sensual admirations." [33] A prominent New York neurologist (unnamed) asserted in *The New York Post* that a recent suicide was directly caused by Freudian studies—that psychoanalytical theories had unhinged the suicide's (a girl) mind.[34] *The Saturday Evening Post* in a particularly vicious satire attempted to show how the popularization of Freudism and its practice by amateurs was absurd[35]—a vicious satire because it made use of supposedly ignorant Negroes, leaving the reader with the impression that if Freudism appealed to the Negro, there must be something wrong with it.

The controversy between intellectuals as to the merits of Freud was somewhat abated during this period, although there were occasional flareups such as the one reported in *Forum* for March, 1925. George Sylvester Viereck, in an article entitled, "Is Psychoanalysis a Science?" [36], sum-

[27] Allen, Frederick Lewis, *Only Yesterday,* New York: Harper and Bros., 1931.

[28] Hall, G. Stanley, *Life and Confessions of a Psychologist,* New York: Appleton and Co., 1923, p. 409.

[29] James, Henry, *Letters of William James,* Boston: Atlantic Monthly Press, 1920, pp. 237–328.

[30] Ellis, Havelock, "A Tribute to Freud," *Forum,* 76, July, 1926, pp. 150–153.

[31] Cowles, Edward Spencer, "Dangerous Currents," *Woman's Home Companion,* 51, November, 1924, p. 4.

[32] *New York Times,* "Symposium on Psychoanalysis at St. Mark's," May 5, 1924.

[33] Bodenheim, Maxwell, "Psychoanalysis and American Fiction," *The Nation,* 114, July 7, 1922, pp. 683–684.

[34] *New York Post,* "Young Student Commits Suicide," January 4, 1922.

[35] Goodwin, Blanche, "Expression and the Freudian Complex," *Saturday Evening Post,* June 13, 1925, p. 70.

[36] Viereck, George Sylvester, "Is Psychoanalysis a Science?" *Forum,* 73, March, 1925, p. 302.

marized Freudism briefly, and stressed the contributions of Freud to knowledge about ourselves. This was followed by Aldous Huxley's *Our Contemporary Hocus-Pocus,* a bitter, scathing denunciation of Freud in which he analyzed psychoanalysis to show that it has all the qualifications of a pseudo-science ("one of the finest specimens ever devised"). He attributed its popularity to the fact that it required no special education, no remarkable intellect, and called Freud's interpretations of dreams 'obscene'[37]—a denunciation rather difficult to explain when one considers Huxley's novels!

With the popularization of knowledge came vehement protests from the Church and particularly from the Catholic Church. *The Catholic World* in 1923 ran several articles sharply criticizing Freudian doctrine for the application to normal minds of a method suitable only for the diseased and disordered, and even more strenuously objected to the usurpation by the psychoanalyst of the office of physician of the soul—an office reserved for the priest.[38] Another author pointed out the dangers to our morals from strict application of Freudism, and expressed his opinion that America suffered not from too much repression, but from too much self-indulgence.

The battle, however, was won. By 1925, although his concepts continued to be refined and modified, Freud had achieved a definite standing in professional circles. He was making his influence felt not only in medicine, psychology, education, literature, the drama and the arts, but such terms as 'repressed desires,' 'complexes' and 'inhibitions' had been added to the vocabulary of the average American.

How did the twenties affect most American people? A pair of sociologists, Robert S. and Helen Merrell Lynd, visited what seemed an average American city, Muncie, Indiana, spent months gathering data, and produced a vivid account, *Middletown.* It is like a doorway opening back into the New Era. The two sections that follow deal with two areas in which life had sharply changed for most people of "Middletown."

R. S. AND H. M. LYND:
THE NEW ERA IN MIDDLETOWN*

GETTING A LIVING

For both working and business class no other accompaniment of getting a living approaches in importance the money received for their work. It is more this future, instrumental aspect of work, rather than the intrinsic satisfactions involved, that keeps Middletown working so hard as more and more of the activities of living are coming to be strained through the bars of the dollar sign. Among the business group, such things as one's circle of friends, the kind of car one drives, playing golf, joining Rotary, the church to which one belongs, one's political principles, the social position of one's wife apparently tend to be scrutinized somewhat more than formerly in Middletown for their instrumental bearing upon the main business of getting a living, while, conversely, one's status in these various other activities tends to be much influenced by one's financial position. As vicinage has decreased in its influence upon the ordinary social contacts of this group, there appears to be a constantly closer relation between the solitary factor of financial status and one's social status. A leading citizen presented this matter in a nutshell to a member of the research staff in discussing the almost universal local custom of "placing" newcomers in terms of where they live, how they live, the kind of car they drive, and similar externals: "It's perfectly natural. You see, they know money, and they don't know you."

This dominance of the dollar appears in the apparently growing tendency among younger working class men to swap a problematic future for immediate "big money." Foremen complain that Middletown boys entering the shops today are increasingly less interested in being moved from job to job until they have become all-round skilled workers, but want to stay on one machine and run up their production so that they may quickly reach a maximum wage scale.

The rise of large-scale advertising, popular magazines, movies, radio, and other channels of increased cultural diffusion from without are rapidly changing habits of thought as to what things are essential to living and multiplying optional occasions for spending money. Install-

[37] Huxley, Aldous, *Our Contemporary Hocus-Pocus.*

* Reprinted from *Middletown* by Robert S. Lynd and Helen Merrell Lynd, copyright, 1929, by Harcourt, Brace & World, Inc.; renewed, 1957, by Robert S. Lynd and Helen Merrell Lynd. Reprinted by permission of the publishers.

[38] Bruckl, Charles, "Psychoanalysis," *The Catholic World,* Feb. 1923, p. 577.

ment buying, which turns wishes into horses overnight, and the heavy increase in the number of children receiving higher education, with its occasions for breaking with home traditions, are facilitating this rise to new standards of living. In 1890 Middletown appears to have lived on a series of plateaus as regards standard of living; old citizens say there was more contentment with relative arrival; it was a common thing to hear a remark that so and so "is pretty good for people in our circumstances." Today the edges of the plateaus have been shaved off, and every one lives on a slope from any point of which desirable things belonging to people all the way to the top are in view.

This diffusion of new urgent occasions for spending money in every sector of living is exhibited by such new tools and services commonly used in Middletown today, but either unknown or little used in the nineties, as the following:

IN THE HOME furnace, running hot and cold water, modern sanitation, electric appliances ranging from toasters to washing machines, telephone, refrigeration, green vegetables and fresh fruit all the year round, greater variety of clothing, silk hose and underwear, commercial pressing and cleaning of clothes, commercial laundering or use of expensive electrical equipment in the home, cosmetics, manicuring, and commercial hair-dressing.

IN SPENDING LEISURE TIME movies (attendance far more frequent than at earlier occasional "shows"), automobile (gas, tires, depreciation, cost of trips), phonograph, radio, more elaborate children's playthings, more club dues for more members of the family, Y.M.C.A. and Y.W.C.A., more formal dances and banquets, including a highly competitive series of "smartly appointed affairs" by high school clubs; cigarette smoking and expensive cigars.

IN EDUCATION high school and college (involving longer dependence of children), many new incidental costs such as entrance to constant school athletic contests.

In the face of these rapidly multiplying accessories to living, the "social problem" of "the high cost of living" is apparently envisaged by most people in Middletown as soluble if they can only inch themselves up a notch higher in the amount of money received for their work. Under these circumstances, why shouldn't money be important to people in Middletown? "The Bible never spoke a truer word," says the local paper in an editorial headed "Your Bank Account Your Best Friend," "than when it said: 'But money answereth all things.' . . . If it doesn't answer all things, it at least answers more than 50 per cent. of them." And again, "Of our happy position in world affairs there need be no . . . further proof than the stability of our money system." One leading Middletown business man summed up this trend toward a monetary approach to the satisfactions of life in addressing a local civic club when he said, "Next to the doctor we think of the banker

to help us and to guide us in our wants and worries today."

Money being, then, so crucial, how much money do Middletown people actually receive? The minimum cost of living for a "standard family of five" in Middletown in 1924 was $1,920.87. A complete distribution of the earnings of Middletown is not available. Twelve to 15 per cent. of those getting the city's living reported a large enough income for 1923 to make the filing of a Federal income tax return necessary. Of the 16,000-17,000 people gainfully employed in 1923—including, however, somewhere in the neighborhood of a thousand married women, some of whom undoubtedly made joint returns with their husbands—210 reported net incomes (i.e., minus interest, contributions, etc.) of $5,000 or over, 999 more net incomes less than $5,000 but large enough to be taxable after subtracting allowed exemptions ($1,000 if single, $2,500 if married, and $400 per dependent), while 1,036 more filed returns but were not taxable after subtracting allowed deductions and exemptions. The other 85-88 per cent. of those earning the city's living presumably received either less than $1,000 if single or less than $2,000 if married, or failed to make income tax returns. . . .

Thus this crucial activity of spending one's best energies year in and year out in doing things remote from the immediate concerns of living eventuates apparently in the ability to buy somewhat more than formerly, but both business men and working men seem to be running for dear life in this business of making the money they earn keep pace with the even more rapid growth of their subjective wants. A Rip Van Winkle who fell asleep in the Middletown of 1885 to awake today would marvel at the change as did the French economist Say when he revisited England at the close of the Napoleonic Wars; every one seemed to run intent upon his own business as though fearing to stop lest those behind trample him down. In the quiet county-seat of the middle eighties men lived relatively close to the earth and its products. In less than four decades, business class and working class, bosses and bossed, have been caught up by Industry, this new trait in the city's culture that is shaping the pattern of the whole of living. According to its needs, large numbers of people anxious to get their living are periodically stopped by the recurrent phenomenon of "bad times" when the machines stop running, workers are "laid off" by the hundreds, salesmen sell less, bankers call in loans, "credit freezes," and many Middletown families may take their children from school, move into cheaper homes, cut down on food, and do without many of the countless things they desire.

The working class is mystified by the whole fateful business. Many of them say, for instance, that they went to the polls and voted for Coolidge in November, 1924, after being assured daily by the local papers that "A vote for Coolidge is a vote for prosperity and your job"; puzzled as to why "times" did not improve after the overwhelming victory of Coolidge, a number of them asked the interviewers if the latter thought times would be better "after the first of the year"; the first of the year having come and gone, their question was changed to "Will business pick up in the spring?"

The attitude of the business men, as fairly reflected by the editorial pages of the press which today echo the sentiments heard at Rotary and the Chamber of Commerce, is more confident but confusing. Within a year the leading paper offered the following prescriptions for local prosperity: "The first duty of a citizen is to produce"; and later, "The American citizen's first importance to his country is no longer that of citizen but that of consumer. Consumption is a new necessity." "The way to make business boom is to buy." At the same time that the citizen is told to "consume" he is told, "Better start saving late than never. If you haven't opened your weekly savings account with some local bank, trust company, or building and loan, today's the day." Still within the same year the people of Middletown are told: "The only true prosperity is that for which can be assigned natural reasons such as good crops, a demand for building materials, . . . increased need for transportation," and ". . . advancing prices are due to natural causes which are always responsible for prices. . . . As all wealth comes from the soil, so does all prosperity, which is only another way of saying so does all business." But again, "natural causes" are apparently not the chief essential: "There can be no greater single contribution to the welfare of the nation than the spirit of hopefulness. . . . "[This] will be a banner year because the people believe it will be, which amounts to the determination that it shall be. . . ." Still another solution for securing "good times" appears: "The most prosperous town is that in which the citizens are bound most closely together. . . . Loyalty to the home town . . . is intensely practical. . . . The thing we must get into our heads about this out-of-town buying business is that it hurts the individual who does it and his friends who live here. Spending your money at home in the long run amounts practically to spending it upon yourself, and buying away from home means buying the comforts and luxuries for the other fellow." "A dollar that is spent out of town never returns." One looking on at this procedure may begin to wonder if the business men, too, are not somewhat bewildered.

Although neither business men nor working men like the recurring "hard times," members of both groups urge the maintenance of the present industrial system. The former laud the group leaders who urge "normalcy" and "more business in government and less government in business," while the following sentences from an address by a leading worker, the president of the Trades Council, during the 1924 political campaign, sets forth the same faith in "free competition" on the part of the working class: "The important issue is the economic issue. We can all unite on that. We want a return to active free competition, so that prices will be lower and a man can buy enough for himself and his family with the money he makes." Both groups, as they order a lay-off, cut wages to meet outside competition, or, on the other hand, vote for La Follette in the hope of his being able to "do something to help the working man," appear to be fumbling earnestly to make their appropriate moves in the situation according to the rules of the game as far as they see them; but both appear to be bound on the wheel of this modern game of corner-clipping production. The puzzled observer may wonder how far any of them realizes the relation of his particular move to the whole function of getting a living. . . .

INVENTIONS RE-MAKING LEISURE

Although lectures, reading, music, and art are strongly intrenched in Middletown's traditions, it is none of these that would first attract the attention of a newcomer watching Middletown at play.

"Why on earth do you need to study what's changing this country?" said a lifelong resident and shrewd observer of the Middle West. "I can tell you what's happening in just four letters: A-U-T-O!"

In 1890 the possession of a pony was the wildest flight of a Middletown boy's dreams. In 1924 a Bible class teacher in a Middletown school concluded her teaching of the Creation: "And now, children, is there any of these animals that God created that man could have got along without?" One after another of the animals from goat to mosquito was mentioned and for some reason rejected; finally, "The horse!" said one boy triumphantly, and the rest of the class agreed. Ten or twelve years ago a new horse fountain was installed at the corner of the Courthouse square; now it remains dry during most of the blazing heat of a Mid-Western summer, and no one cares. The "horse culture" of Middletown has almost disappeared. . . .

The first real automobile appeared in Middletown in 1900. About 1906 it was estimated that "there are probably 200 in the city and county." At the close of 1923 there were 6,221 passenger cars in the city, one for every 6.1 persons, or roughly two for every three families. Of these 6,221 cars, 41 per cent. were Fords; 54 per cent. of the total were cars of models of 1920 or later, and 17 per cent. models earlier than 1917. These cars average a bit over 5,000 miles a year. For some of the workers and some of the business class, use of the automobile is a seasonal matter, but the increase in surfaced roads and in closed cars is rapidly making the car a year-round tool for leisure-time as well as getting-a-living activities. As, at the turn of the century, business class people began to feel apologetic if they did not have a telephone, so ownership of an automobile has now reached the point of being an accepted essential of normal living.

Into the equilibrium of habits which constitutes for each individual some integration in living has come this new habit, upsetting old adjustments, and blasting its way through such accustomed and unquestioned dicta as "Rain or shine, I never miss a Sunday morning at church"; "A high school boy does not need much spending money"; "I don't need exercise, walking to the office keeps me fit"; "I wouldn't think of moving out of town and being so far from my friends"; "Parents ought always to know where their children are." The newcomer is most quickly and amicably incorporated into those regions of behavior in which men are engaged in doing impersonal, matter-of-fact things; much more contested is its advent where emotionally charged sanctions and taboos are concerned. No one questions the use of the auto for transporting groceries, getting to one's place of work or to the golf course, or in place of the porch for "cooling off after supper" on a hot summer evening; however much the activities concerned with getting a living may be altered by the fact that a factory can draw from workmen within a radius of forty-five miles, or however much old labor union men resent the intrusion of this new alternate way of spending an evening, these things are hardly major issues. But when auto riding tends to replace the traditional call in the family parlor as a way of approach between the unmarried, "the home is endangered," and all-day Sunday motor trips are a "threat against the church"; it is in the activities concerned with the home and religion that the automobile occasions the greatest emotional conflicts. . . .

Today a few plants close for one or two weeks each summer, allowing their workers an annual "vacation" without pay. Others do not close down, but workers "can usually take not over two weeks off without pay and have their jobs back when they return." Foremen in many plants get one or two weeks with pay. Of the 122 working class families giving information on this point, five families took one week off in 1923 and again in 1924, seven others took something over a week in each year, twelve took a week or more in only one of the two years. No others had as extensive vacations as these twenty-four, although other entire families took less than a week in one or both years, and in other cases some members of the families took vacations of varying lengths. Of the 100 families for whom income distribution was secured, thirty-four reported money spent on vacations; the amounts ranged from $1.49 to $175.00, averaging $24.12.

But even short trips are still beyond the horizon of many workers' families, as such comments as the following show: "We haven't had a vacation in five years. He got a day off to paint the house, and another year they gave him two hours off to get the deed to the house signed." "Never had a vacation in my life, honey!" "Can't afford one this year because we're repairing the house." "I don't know what a vacation is—I haven't had one for so long." "We like to get out in the car each week for half a day but can't afford a longer vacation."

But the automobile is extending the radius of those who are allowed vacations with pay and is putting short trips within the reach of some for whom such vacations are still "not in the dictionary." "The only vacation we've had in twenty years was three days we took off last year to go to Benton Harbor with my brother-in-law," said one woman, proudly recounting her trip. "We had two Fords. The women slept in the cars, the men on boards between the two running boards. Here's a picture of the two cars, taken just as the sun was coming up. See the shadows? And there's a *hill* back of them."

Like the automobile, the motion picture is more to Middletown than simply a new way of doing an old thing; it has added new dimensions to the city's leisure. To be sure, the spectacle-watching habit was strong upon Middletown in the nineties. Whenever they had a chance people turned out to a "show," but chances were relatively fewer. Fourteen times during January, 1890, for instance, the Opera House was opened for performances ranging from *Uncle Tom's Cabin* to *The Black Crook,* before the paper announced that "there will not be any more attractions at the Opera House for nearly two weeks." In July there were no "attractions"; a half dozen were scattered through August and September; there were twelve in October.

Today nine motion picture theaters operate from 1 to 11 P.M. seven days a week summer and winter; four of the nine give three different programs a week, the other five having two a week; thus twenty-two different programs with a total of over 300 performances are available to Middletown every week in the year. In addition, during January, 1923, there were three plays in Middletown and four motion pictures in other places than the regular theaters, in July three plays and one additional movie, in October two plays and one movie. . . .

The program of the five cheaper houses is usually a "Wild West" feature, and a comedy; of the four better houses, one feature film, usually a "society" film but frequently Wild West or comedy, one short comedy, or if the feature is a comedy, an educational film (e.g., *Laying an Ocean Cable* or *Making a Telephone*), and a news film. In general, people do not go to the movies to be instructed; the Yale Press series of historical films, as noted earlier, were a flat failure and the local exhibitor discontinued them after the second picture. As in the case of the books it reads, comedy, heart interest, and adventure compose the great bulk of what Middletown enjoys in the movies. Its heroes, according to the manager of the leading theater, are, in the order named, Harold Lloyd, comedian; Gloria Swanson, heroine in modern society films; Thomas

Meighan, hero in modern society films; Colleen Moore, ingénue; Douglas Fairbanks, comedian and adventurer; Mary Pickford, ingénue; and Norma Talmadge, heroine in modern society films. Harold Lloyd comedies draw the largest crowds. "Middletown is amusement hungry," says the opening sentence in a local editorial; at the comedies Middletown lives for an hour in a happy sophisticated make-believe world that leaves it, according to the advertisement of one film, "happily convinced that Life is very well worth living."

Next largest are the crowds which come to see the sensational society films. The kind of vicarious living brought to Middletown by these films may be inferred from such titles as: "*Alimony*—brilliant men, beautiful jazz babies, champagne baths, midnight revels, petting parties in the purple dawn, all ending in one terrific smashing climax that makes you gasp"; "*Married Flirts—Husbands:* Do you flirt? Does your wife always know where you are? Are you faithful to your vows? *Wives:* What's your hubby doing? Do you know? Do you worry? Watch out for *Married Flirts*." So fast do these flow across the silver screen that, e.g., at one time *The Daring Years, Sinners in Silk, Women Who Give,* and *The Price She Paid* were all running synchronously, and at another "*Name the Man*—a story of betrayed womanhood," *Rouged Lips,* and *The Queen of Sin*. While Western "action" films and a million-dollar spectacle like *The Covered Wagon* or *The Hunchback of Notre Dame* draw heavy houses, and while managers lament that there are too few of the popular comedy films, it is the film with burning "heart interest," that packs Middletown's motion picture houses week after week. Young Middletown enters eagerly into the vivid experience of *Flaming Youth:* "neckers, petters, white kisses, red kisses, pleasure-mad daughters, sensation-craving mothers, by an author who didn't dare sign his name; the truth bold, naked, sensational"—so ran the press advertisement—under the spell of the powerful conditioning medium of pictures presented with music and all possible heightening of the emotional content, and the added factor of sharing this experience with a "date" in a darkened room. Meanwhile, *Down to the Sea in Ships,* a costly spectacle of whaling adventure, failed at the leading theater "because," the exhibitor explained, "the whale is really the hero in the film and there wasn't enough 'heart interest' for the women."

Over against these spectacles which Middletown watches today stand the pale "sensations" of the nineties, when *Sappho* was the apogee of daring at the Opera House: "*The Telephone Girl*—Hurricane hits, breezy dialogue, gorgeous stage setting, dazzling dancing, spirited repartee, superb music, opulent costumes," *Over the Garden Wall, Edith's Burglar, East Lynne, La Bella Maria,* or *Women's Revenge, The Convict's Daughter, Joe, a Mountain Fairy, The Vagabond Heroine, Guilty Without Crime, The World Against Her* (which the baker pronounced in his diary, "good, but too solemn"), *Love Will Find a Way, Si. Plankard.*

These, it must be recalled, were the great days when *Uncle Tom's Cabin,* with "fifty men, women, and children, a pack of genuine bloodhounds, grandest street parade ever given, and two bands," packed the Opera House to capacity.

Actual changes of habits resulting from the week-after-week witnessing of these films can only be inferred. Young Middletown is finding discussion of problems of mating in this new agency that boasts in large illustrated advertisements, "Girls! You will learn how to handle 'em!" and "Is it true that marriage kills love? If you want to know what love really means, its exquisite torture, its overwhelming raptures, see ————." "Sheiks and their 'shebas,'" according to the press account of the Sunday opening of one film, ". . . sat without a movement or a whisper through the presentation. . . . It was a real exhibition of love-making and the youths and maidens of [Middletown] who thought that they knew something about the art found that they still had a great deal to learn." Some high school teachers are convinced that the movies are a powerful factor in bringing about the "early sophistication" of the young and the relaxing of social taboos. One working class mother frankly welcomes the movies as an aid in childrearing, saying, "I send my daughter because a girl has to learn the ways of the world somehow and the movies are a good safe way." The judge of the juvenile court lists the movies as one of the "big four" causes of local juvenile delinquency, believing that the disregard of group mores by the young is definitely related to the witnessing week after week of fictitious behavior sequences that habitually link the taking of long chances and the happy ending. While the community attempts to safeguard its schools from commercially intent private hands, this powerful new educational instrument, which has taken Middletown unawares, remains in the hands of a group of men—an ex-peanut-stand proprietor, an ex-bicycle racer and race promoter, and so on—whose primary concern is making money. . . .

Though less widely diffused as yet than automobile owning or movie attendance, the radio nevertheless is rapidly crowding its way in among the necessities in the family standard of living. Not the least remarkable feature of this new invention is its accessibility. Here skill and ingenuity can in part offset money as an open sesame to swift sharing of the enjoyments of the wealthy. With but little equipment one can call the life of the rest of the world from the air, and this equipment can be purchased piecemeal at the ten-cent store. Far from being simply one more means of passive enjoyment, the radio has given rise to much ingenious manipulative activity. In a count of representative sections of Middletown, it was found that, of 303 homes in twenty-eight blocks in the "best section" of town, inhabited almost entirely by the business class, 12 per cent. had radios; of 518 workers' homes in sixty-four blocks, 6 per cent. had radios.

As this new tool is rolling back the horizons of Middletown for the bank clerk or the mechanic sitting at home and listening to a Philharmonic concert or a sermon by Dr. Fosdick, or to President Coolidge bidding his father good night on the eve of election, and as it is wedging its way with the movie, the automobile, and other new tools into the twisted mass of habits that are living for the 38,000 people of Middletown, readjustments necessarily occur. Such comments as the following suggest their nature:

"I use time evenings listening in that I used to spend in reading."

"The radio is hurting movie going, especially Sunday evening." (From a leading movie exhibitor.)

"I don't use my car so much any more. The heavy traffic makes it less fun. But I spend seven nights a week on my radio. We hear fine music from Boston." (From a shabby man of fifty.)

"Sundays I take the boy to Sunday School and come straight home and tune in. I get first an eastern service, then a Cincinnati one. Then there's nothing doing till about two-thirty, when I pick up an eastern service again and follow 'em across the country till I wind up with California about ten-thirty. Last night I heard a ripping sermon from Westminster Church somewhere in California. We've no preachers here that can compare with any of them."

"One of the bad features of radio," according to a teacher, "is that children stay up late at night and are not fit for school next day."

"We've spent close on to $100 on our radio, and we built it ourselves at that," commented one of the worker's wives. "Where'd we get the money? Oh, out of our savings, like everybody else."

In the flux of competing habits that are oscillating the members of the family now towards and now away from the home, radio occupies an intermediate position. Twenty-five per cent. of 337 high school boys and 22 per cent. of 423 high school girls said that they listen more often to the radio with their parents than without them, and, as pointed out above, 20 per cent. of 274 boys in the three upper years of the high school answered "radio" to the question, "In what thing that you are doing at home this fall are you most interested?"—more than gave any other answer. More than one mother said that her family used to scatter in the evening—"but now we all sit around and listen to the radio."

Likewise the place of the radio in relation to Middletown's other leisure habits is not wholly clear. As it becomes more perfected, cheaper, and a more accepted part of life, it may cease to call forth so much active, constructive ingenuity and become one more form of passive enjoyment. Doubtless it will continue to play a mighty rôle in lifting Middletown out of the humdrum of every day; it is beginning to take over that function of the great political rallies or the trips by the trainload to the state capital to hear a noted speaker or to see a monument dedicated that a generation ago helped to set the average man in a wide place. But it seems not unlikely that, while furnishing a new means of diversified enjoyment, it will at the same time operate, with national advertising, syndicated newspapers, and other means of large-scale diffusion, as yet another means of standardizing many of Middletown's habits. Indeed, at no point is one brought up more sharply against the impossibility of studying Middletown as a self-contained, self-starting community than when one watches these space-binding leisure-time inventions imported from without— automobile, motion picture, and radio—reshaping the city.

The America of the twenties that is nostalgically remembered a generation later is less that of conventional, quiet Middletown than of the rambunctious, irreverent *American Mercury*. Its tart, iconoclastic editor, Henry L. Mencken, abetted by his co-editor, the critic George Jean Nathan, viewed the American scene with astringent wit that made mockery of the generally accepted conventions. In volume one, number one of the *American Mercury,* the editors set forth their policies and their prejudices.

H. L. MENCKEN AND G. J. NATHAN:
THE AIM OF THE *AMERICAN MERCURY**

The aim of THE AMERICAN MERCURY is precisely that of every other monthly review the world has ever seen: to ascertain and tell the truth. So far, nothing new. But the Editors cherish the hope that it may be possible, after all, to introduce some element of novelty into the execution of an enterprise so old, and upon that hope they found the magazine. It comes into being with at least one advantage over all its predecessors in the field of public affairs: it is entirely devoid of messianic passion. The Editors have heard no

* Reprinted from H. L. Mencken and G. J. Nathan, "The Aim of the *American Mercury*," *American Mercury,* I (1924), 27–30 by permission.

Voice from the burning bush. They will not cry up and offer for sale any sovereign balm, whether political, economic or aesthetic, for all the sorrows of the world. The fact is, indeed, that they doubt that any such sovereign balm exists, or that it will ever exist hereafter. The world, as they see it, is down with at least a score of painful diseases, all of them chronic and incurable; nevertheless, they cling to the notion that human existence remains predominantly charming. Especially is it charming in this unparalleled Republic of the West, where men are earnest and women are intelligent, and all the historic virtues of Christendom are now concentrated. The Editors propose, before jurisprudence develops to the point of prohibiting skepticism altogether, to give a realistic consideration to certain of these virtues, and to try to save what is exhilarating in them, even when all that is divine must be abandoned. They engage to undertake the business in a polished and aseptic manner, without indignation on the one hand and without too much regard for tender feelings on the other. They have no set program, either destructive or constructive. Sufficient unto each day will be the performance thereof.

As has been hinted, the Editors are not fond enough to believe in their own varieties of truth too violently, or to assume that the truth is ascertainable in all cases, or even in most cases. If they are convinced of anything beyond peradventure, it is, indeed, that many of the great problems of man, and particularly of man as a member of society, are intrinsically insoluble—that insolubility is as much a part of their essence as it is of the essence of squaring the circle. But demonstrating this insolubility thus takes on something of the quality of establishing a truth, and even merely arguing it gathers a sort of austere virtue. For human progress is achieved, it must be manifest, not by wasting effort upon hopeless and exhausting enigmas, but by concentrating effort upon inquiries that are within the poor talents of man. In the field of politics, for example, utopianism is not only useless; it is also dangerous, for it centers attention upon what ought to be at the expense of what might be. Yet in the United States politics remains mainly utopian—an inheritance, no doubt, from the gabby, gaudy days of the Revolution. The ideal realm imagined by an A. Mitchell Palmer, a King Kleagle of the Ku Klux Klan or a Grand Inquisitor of the Anti-Saloon League, with all human curiosity and enterprise brought down to a simple passion for the goose-step, is as idiotically utopian as the ideal of an Alcott, a Marx or a Bryan. THE AMERICAN MERCURY will devote itself pleasantly to exposing the nonsensicality of all such hallucinations, particularly when they show a certain apparent plausibility. Its own pet hallucination will take the form of an hypothesis that the progress of knowledge is less a matter of accumulating facts than a matter of destroying "facts". It will assume constantly that the more ignorant a man is the more he knows, positively and indignantly. Among the great leeches and barber-surgeons who profess to medicate the body politic, it will give its suffrage to those who admit frankly that all the basic diseases are beyond cure, and who consecrate themselves to making the patient as comfortable as possible.

In some of the preliminary notices of THE AMERICAN MERCURY, kindly published in the newspapers, apprehension has been expressed that the Editors are what is called Radicals, *i.e.,* that they harbor designs upon the Republic, and are bound by a secret oath to put down 100% Americanism. The notion is herewith denounced. Neither is a Radical, or the son of a Radical, or, indeed, the friend of any known Radical. Both view the capitalistic system, if not exactly amorously, then at all events politely. The Radical proposals to destroy it at one blow seem to them to be as full of folly as the Liberal proposals to denaturize it by arousing its better nature. They believe that it is destined to endure in the United States, perhaps long after it has broken up everywhere else, if only because the illusion that any bright boy can make himself a part of it remains a cardinal article of the American national religion—and no sentient man will ever confess himself doomed to life imprisonment in the proletariat so long as the slightest hope remains, in fact or in fancy, of getting out of it. Thus class consciousness is not one of our national diseases; we suffer, indeed, from its opposite—the delusion that class barriers are not real. That delusion reveals itself in many forms, some of them as beautiful as a glass eye. One is the Liberal doctrine that a prairie demagogue promoted to the United States Senate will instantly show all the sagacity of a Metternich and all the high rectitude of a Pierre Bayard. Another is the doctrine that a moron run through a university and decorated with a Ph.D. will cease thereby to be a moron. Another is the doctrine that J. P. Morgan's press-agents and dish-washers make competent Cabinet Ministers and Ambassadors. Yet another, a step further, is the doctrine that the interests of capital and labor are identical—which is to say, that the interests of landlord and tenant, hangman and condemned, cat and rat are identical. Such notions, alas, seem to permeate all American thinking, the shallowness of which has been frequently remarked by foreign observers, particularly in the Motherland. It will be an agreeable duty to track down some of the worst nonsense prevailing and to do execution upon it—not indignantly, of course, but nevertheless with a sufficient play of malice to give the business a Christian and philanthropic air.

II

That air, of course, will be largely deceptive, as it always is. For the second time the nobility and gentry are cautioned that they are here in the presence of no band of passionate altruists, consecrated to Service as, in the late Mr. Harding's poignant phrase, "the supreme commitment". The

Editors are committed to nothing save this: to keep to common sense as fast as they can, to belabor sham as agreeably as possible, to give a civilized entertainment. The reader they have in their eye, whose prejudices they share and whose woes they hope to soothe, is what William Graham Sumner called the Forgotten Man—that is, the normal, educated, well-disposed, unfrenzied, enlightened citizen of the middle minority. This man, as everyone knows, is fast losing all the rights that he once had, at least in theory, under American law. On the one hand he is beset by a vast mass of oppressive legislation issuing from the nether rabble of cowherds, lodge-joiners and Methodists, with Prohibition as its typical masterpiece. And on the other hand he is beset by increasing invasions of his freedom of opinion, the product of craven nightmares among the usurers, exploiters and other rogues who own and try to run the Republic. If, desiring to entertain a guest in the manner universal among civilized men, he procures a bottle or two of harmless wine, he runs a risk of being dragged to jail by official blackmailers and fined and lectured by some political hack in the robes of a Federal judge. And if, disgusted by the sordid tyranny and dishonesty of the government he suffers under, he denounces it righteously and demands a return to the Bill of Rights, he runs a grave risk of being posted as a paid agent of the Bolsheviki.

This Forgotten Man, when he is recalled at all, is thus recalled only to be placarded as infamous. The normal agencies for relieving psychic distress all pass him over. The Liberals have no comfort for him because he refuses to believe in their endless series of infallible elixirs; most of these very elixirs, in fact, only help to multiply his difficulties. And the Tories who perform in the great daily newspapers and in the Rotary Club weeklies and in the reviews of high tone— these prophets of normalcy can see in his discontent nothing save subversion and worse. There is no middle ground of consolation for men who believe neither in the Socialist fol-de-rol nor in the principal enemies of the Socialist fol-de-rol— and yet it must be obvious that such men constitute the most intelligent and valuable body of citizens that the nation can boast. The leading men of science and learning are in it. The best artists, in all the arts, are in it. Such men of business as have got any imagination are in it. It will be the design of THE AMERICAN MERCURY to bring, if not alleviation of their lot, then at least some solace to these outcasts of democracy. That they will ever actually escape from the morass in which they now wander so disconsolately is probably too much to hope. But at all events there is some chance of entertaining them to their taste while they flounder.

III

In the field of the fine arts THE AMERICAN MERCURY will pursue the course that the Editors have followed for fifteen years past in another place. They are asking various other critics to share their work and they will thus be able to cover a wider area than heretofore, but they will not deviate from their old program—to welcome sound and honest work, whatever its form or lack of form, and to carry on steady artillery practise against every variety of artistic pedant and mountebank. They belong to no coterie and have no aesthetic theory to propagate. They do not believe that a work of art has any purpose beyond that of being charming and stimulating, and they do not believe that there is much difficulty, taking one day with another, about distinguishing clearly between the good and the not good. It is only when theories begin to enter into the matter that counsels are corrupted—and between the transcendental, gibberishy theory of a Greenwich Village aesthete and the harsh, moral, patriotic theory of a university pedagogue there is not much to choose. Good work is always done in the middle ground, between the theories. That middle ground now lies wide open: the young American artist is quite as free as he needs to be. The Editors do not believe that he is helped by nursing and coddling him. If the obscure, inner necessity which moves him is not powerful enough to make him function unassisted, then it is not powerful enough to make a genuine artist of him. All he deserves to have is aid against the obscurantists who occasionally beset him—men whose interest in the fine arts, by some occult Freudian means, seems to be grounded upon an implacable hatred of everything that is free, and honest, and beautiful. It will be a pleasure to pursue such obscurantists to their fastnesses, and to work the *lex talionis* upon them. The business is amusing and now and then it may achieve some by-product of good.

The probable general contents of the magazine are indicated by this first number, but there will be no rigid formula, and a number of changes and improvements, indeed, are already in contemplation. In the department of *belles lettres* an effort will be made to publish one or two short stories in each issue, such occasional short plays as will merit print, some verse (but not much), and maybe a few other things, lying outside the categories. The essays and articles, it is hoped, will cover a wide range; no subject likely to be of interest to the sort of reader before described will be avoided, nor will there be any limitation upon the free play of opinion, so long as it is neither doctrinaire nor sentimental. To the departments already set up others may be added later on, but this is a matter that will have to determine itself. The Editors will welcome communications from readers, and those that seem to be of general interest will be printed, perhaps with editorial glosses. No effort will be made in the book reviews to cover all the multitude of books that come from the publishers every month. The reviews will deal only with such books as happen to attract the staff of reviewers, either by their virtues or by their defects. The dramatic reviews will, however, cover the entire range of the New York theatre.

In general THE AMERICAN MERCURY will live up to the adjective in its name. It will lay chief stress at all times upon American ideas, American problems and American personalities because it assumes that nine-tenths of its readers will be Americans and that they will be more interested in their own country than in any other. A number of excellent magazines are already devoted to making known the notions of the major and minor seers of Europe; at least half a dozen specialize in the ideas emanating from England alone. This leaves the United States rather neglected. It is, as the judicious have frequently observed, an immense country, and full of people. These people entertain themselves with a vast number of ideas and enterprises, many of them of an unprecedented and astounding nature. There are more political theories on tap in the Republic than anywhere else on earth, and more doctrines in aesthetics, and more religions, and more other schemes for regimenting, harrowing and saving human beings. Our annual production of messiahs is greater than that of all Asia. A single session of Congress produces more utopian legislation than Europe has seen since the first meeting of the English Witenagemot. To explore this great complex of inspirations, to isolate the individual prophets from the herd and examine their proposals, to follow the ponderous revolutions of the mass mind—in brief, to attempt a realistic presentation of the whole gaudy, gorgeous American scene—this will be the principal enterprise of THE AMERICAN MERCURY.

To John Dewey, the Vermont-reared philosopher of pragmatism, the 1920's brought fame as schools sought to follow his doctrine of "learning by doing"—education should promote adjustment to life. But the twenties were also a source of concern to Dewey as he saw the urban machine-age culture burying the type of community democracy which he had cherished.

JOHN DEWEY: THE ECLIPSE OF THE PUBLIC*

Optimism about democracy is to-day under a cloud. We are familiar with denunciation and criticism which, however, often reveal their emotional source in their peevish and undiscriminating tone. Many of them suffer from the same error into which earlier laudations fell. They assume that democracy is the product of an idea, of a single and consistent intent. Carlyle was no admirer of democracy, but in a lucid moment he said: "Invent the printing press and democracy is inevitable." Add to this: Invent the railway, the telegraph, mass manufacture and concentration of population in urban centers, and some form of democratic government is, humanly speaking, inevitable. Political democracy as it exists to-day calls for adverse criticism in abundance. But the criticism is only an exhibition of querulousness and spleen or of a superiority complex, unless it takes cognizance of the conditions out of which popular government has issued. All intelligent political criticism is comparative. It deals not with all-or-none situations, but with practical alternatives; an absolutistic indiscriminate attitude, whether in praise or blame, testifies to the heat of feeling rather than the light of thought.

American democratic polity was developed out of genuine community life, that is, association in local and small centers where industry was mainly agricultural and where production was carried on mainly with hand tools. It took form when English political habits and legal institutions worked under pioneer conditions. The forms of association were stable, even though their units were mobile and migratory. Pioneer conditions put a high premium upon personal work, skill, ingenuity, initiative and adaptability, and upon neighborly sociability. The township or some not much larger area was the political unit, the town meeting the political medium, and roads, schools, the peace of the community, were the political objectives. The state was a sum of such units, and the national state a federation—unless perchance a confederation—of states. The imagination of the founders did not travel far beyond what could be accomplished and understood in a congeries of self-governing communities. The machinery provided for the selection of the chief executive of the federal union is illustrative evidence. The electoral college assumed that citizens would choose men locally known for their high standing; and that these men when chosen would gather together for consultation to name some one known to them for his probity and public spirit and knowledge. The rapidity with which the scheme

* Reprinted from *The Public and Its Problems*, John Dewey, New York, 1927, Holt, Rinehart and Winston, Inc. By permission.

fell into disuse is evidence of the transitoriness of the state of affairs that was predicated. But at the outset there was no dream of the time when the very names of the presidential electors would be unknown to the mass of the voters, when they would plump for a "ticket" arranged in a more or less private caucus, and when the electoral college would be an impersonal registering machine, such that it would be treachery to employ the personal judgment which was originally contemplated as the essence of the affair. . . .

When the public is as uncertain and obscure as it is to-day, and hence as remote from government, bosses with their political machines fill the void between government and the public. Who pulls the strings which move the bosses and generates power to run the machines is a matter of surmise rather than of record, save for an occasional overt scandal.

Quite aside, however, from the allegation that "Big Business" plays the tune and pulls the strings to which bosses dance, it is true that parties are not creators of policies to any large extent at the present time. For parties yield in piece-meal accommodation to social currents, irrespective of professed principles. As these lines are written a weekly periodical remarks: "Since the end of the Civil War practically all the more important measures which have been embodied in federal legislation have been reached without a national election which turned upon the issue and which divided the two major parties." Reform of civil service, regulation of railways, popular election of senators, national income tax, suffrage for women, and prohibition are supported to substantiate the statement. Hence its other remark appears justified: "American party politics seem at times to be a device for preventing issues which may excite popular feeling and involve bitter controversies from being put up to the American people."

A negatively corroborating fact is seen in the fate of the Child Labor amendment. The need of giving to Congress power to regulate child labor, denied it by decisions of the Supreme Court, had been asserted in the platforms of all political parties; the idea was endorsed by the last three of the presidents belonging to the party in power. Yet so far, the proposed amendment to the constitution has not begun to secure the needed support. Political parties may rule, but they do not govern. The public is so confused and eclipsed that it cannot even use the organs through which it is supposed to mediate political action and polity.

The same lesson is taught by the breakdown of the theory of the responsibility of elected representatives to the electorate, to say nothing of their alleged liability to be called before the bar of the private judgment of individuals. It is at least suggestive that the terms of the theory are best met in legislation of the "pork-barrel" type. There a representative may be called to account for failure to meet local desire, or be rewarded for pertinacity and success in fulfilling its wishes. But only

rarely is the theory borne out in important matters, although occasionally it works. But the instances are so infrequent that any skilled political observer could enumerate them by name. The reason for the lack of personal liability to the electorate is evident. The latter is composed of rather amorphous groups. Their political ideas and beliefs are mostly in abeyance between elections. Even in times of political excitement, artificially accelerated, their opinions are moved collectively by the current of the group rather than by independent personal judgment. As a rule, what decides the fate of a person who comes up for election is neither his political excellence nor his political defects. The current runs for or against the party in power and the individual candidate sinks or swims as runs the current. At times there is a general consensus of sentiment, a definite trend in favor of "progressive legislation" or a desire for a "return to normalcy." But even then only exceptional candidates get by on any basis of personal responsibility to the electorate. The "tidal wave" swamps some; the "landslide" carries others into office. At other times, habit, party funds, the skill of managers of the machine, the portrait of a candidate with his firm jaw, his lovely wife and children, and a multitude of other irrelevancies, determine the issue. . . .

The questions of most concern at present may be said to be matters like sanitation, public health, healthful and adequate housing, transportation, planning of cities, regulation and distribution of immigrants, selection and management of personnel, right methods of instruction and preparation of competent teachers, scientific adjustment of taxation, efficient management of funds, and so on. These are technical matters, as much so as the construction of an efficient engine for purposes of traction or locomotion. Like it they are to be settled by inquiry into facts; and as the inquiry can be carried on only by those especially equipped, so the results of inquiry can be utilized only by trained technicians. What has counting heads, decision by majority and the whole apparatus of traditional government to do with such things? Given such considerations, and the public and its organization for political ends is not only a ghost, but a ghost which walks and talks, and obscures, confuses and misleads governmental action in a disastrous way.

Personally I am far from thinking that such considerations, pertinent as they are to administrative activities, cover the entire political field. They ignore forces which have to be composed and resolved before technical and specialized action can come into play. But they aid in giving definiteness and point to a fundamental question: What, after all, is the public under present conditions? What are the reasons for its eclipse? What hinders it from finding and identifying itself? By what means shall its inchoate and amorphous estate be organized into effective political action relevant to present social needs and opportunities? . . .

Our concern at this time is to state how it is

that the machine age in developing the Great Society has invaded and partially disintegrated the small communities of former times without generating a Great Community. The facts are familiar enough; our especial affair is to point out their connections with the difficulties under which the organization of a democratic public is laboring. For the very familiarity with the phenomena conceals their significance and blinds us to their relation to immediate political problems. . . .

In general, the non-political forces are the expressions of a technological age injected into an inherited political scheme which operates to deflect and distort their normal operation. The industrial and commercial relations that created the situation of which the war is a manifestation are as evident in small things as great. They were exhibited, not only in the struggle for raw materials, for distant markets, and in staggering national debts, but in local and unimportant phenomena. Travelers finding themselves away from home could not get their letters of credit cashed even in countries not then at war. Stockmarkets closed on one hand, and profiteers piled up their millions on the other. One instance may be cited from domestic affairs. The plight of the farmer since the war has created a domestic political issue. A great demand was generated for food and other agricultural products; prices rose. In addition to this economic stimulus, farmers were objects of constant political exhortation to increase their crops. Inflation and temporary prosperity followed. The end of active warfare came. Impoverished countries could not buy and pay for foodstuffs up to even a pre-war level. Taxes were enormously increased. Currencies were depreciated; the world's gold supply centered here. The stimulus of war and of national extravagance piled up the inventories of factories and merchants. Wages and the prices of agricultural implements increased. When deflation came it found a restricted market, increased costs of production, and farmers burdened with mortgages lightly assumed during the period of frenzied expansion.

This instance is not cited because it is peculiarly important in comparison with other consequences which have happened, especially in Europe. It is relatively insignificant by contrast with them, and in contrast with the arousal of nationalistic sentiments which has everywhere taken place since the war in so-called backward countries. But it shows the ramifying consequences of our intricate and interdependent economic relations, and it shows how little prevision and regulation exist. The farming population could hardly have acted with knowledge of the consequences of the fundamental relations in which they were implicated. They could make a momentary and improvised response to them, but they could not manage their affairs in controlled adaptation to the course of events. They present themselves as hapless subjects of overwhelming operations with which they were hardly acquainted and over which they had no more control than over the vicissitudes of climate.

The illustration cannot be objected to on the ground that it rests upon the abnormal situation of war. The war itself was a normal manifestation of the underlying unintegrated state of society. The local face-to-face community has been invaded by forces so vast, so remote in initiation, so far-reaching in scope and so complexly indirect in operation, that they are, from the standpoint of the members of local social units, unknown. Man, as has been often remarked, has difficulty in getting on either with or without his fellows, even in neighborhoods. He is not more successful in getting on with them when they act at a great distance in ways invisible to him. An inchoate public is capable of organization only when indirect consequences are perceived, and when it is possible to project agencies which order their occurrence. At present, many consequences are felt rather than perceived; they are suffered, but they cannot be said to be known, for they are not, by those who experience them, referred to their origins. It goes, then, without saying that agencies are not established which canalize the streams of social action and thereby regulate them. Hence the publics are amorphous and unarticulated.

There was a time when a man might entertain a few general political principles and apply them with some confidence. A citizen believed in states' rights or in a centralized federal government; in free trade or protection. It did not involve much mental strain to imagine that by throwing in his lot with one party or another he could so express his views that his belief would count in government. For the average voter to-day the tariff question is a complicated medley of infinite detail, schedules of rates specific and *ad valorem* on countless things, many of which he does not recognize by name, and with respect to which he can form no judgment. Probably not one voter in a thousand even reads the scores of pages in which the rates of toll are enumerated and he would not be much wiser if he did. The average man gives it up as a bad job. At election time, appeal to some time-worn slogan may galvanize him into a temporary notion that he has convictions on an important subject, but except for manufacturers and dealers who have some interest at stake in this or that schedule, belief lacks the qualities which attach to beliefs about matters of personal concern. Industry is too complex and intricate.

Again the voter may by personal predilection or inherited belief incline towards magnifying the scope of local governments and inveigh against the evils of centralization. But he is vehemently sure of social evils attending the liquor traffic. He finds that the prohibitory law of his locality, township, county or state, is largely nullified by the importation of liquor from outside, made easy by modern means of transportation. So he becomes an advocate of a national amendment giving the central government power to regulate the manufacture and sale of intoxicating drinks. This brings in its train a necessary extension of federal officials and powers. Thus to-day, the south, the traditional home of the states' rights doctrine, is the chief supporter of national prohibition and Volstead Act. It would not be possible to say how many voters have thought of the relation between their professed general principle and their special position on the liquor question: probably not many. On the other hand, life-long Hamiltonians, proclaimers of the dangers of particularistic local autonomy, are opposed to prohibition. Hence they play a tune *ad hoc* on the Jeffersonian flute. Gibes at inconsistency are, however, as irrelevant as they are easy. The social situation has been so changed by the factors of an industrial age that traditional general principles have little practical meaning. They persist as emotional cries rather than as reasoned ideas.

The same criss-crossing occurs with reference to regulation of railways. The opponent of a strong federal government finds, being a farmer or shipper, that rates are too high; he also finds that railways pay little attention to state boundaries, that lines once local are parts of vast systems and that state legislation and administration are ineffectual for his purpose. He calls for national regulation. Some partisan of the powers of the central government, on the other hand, being an investor in stocks and bonds, finds that his income is likely to be unfavorably affected by federal action and he promptly protests against the vexatious tendency to appeal to national aid, which has now become in his eyes a foolish paternalism. The developments of industry and commerce have so complicated affairs that a clear-cut, generally applicable, standard of judgment becomes practically impossible. The forest cannot be seen for the trees nor the trees for the forest.

A striking example of the shift of the actual tenor of doctrines—that is, of their consequences in application—is presented in the history of the doctrine of Individualism, interpreted to signify a minimum of governmental "interference" with industry and trade. At the outset, it was held by "progressives," by those who were protesting against the inherited régime of rules of law and administration. Vested interests, on the contrary, were mainly in favor of the old status. To-day the industrial-property régime being established, the doctrine is the intellectual bulwark of the standpatter and reactionary. He it is that now wants to be let alone, and who utters the war-cry of liberty for private industry, thrift, contract and their pecuniary fruit. In the United States the name "liberal," as a party designation, is still employed to designate a progressive in political matters. In most other countries, the "liberal" party is that which represents established and vested commercial and financial interests in protest against governmental regulation. The irony of history is nowhere more evident than in the reversal of the practical meaning of the term "liberalism" in spite of a literal continuity of theory.

Political apathy, which is a natural product of the discrepancies between actual practices and traditional machinery, ensues from inability to identify one's self with definite issues. These are hard to find and locate in the vast complexities of current life. When traditional war-cries have lost their import in practical policies which are consonant with them, they are readily dismissed as bunk. Only habit and tradition, rather than reasoned conviction, together with a vague faith in doing one's civic duty, send to the polls a considerable percentage of the fifty per cent. who still vote. And of them it is a common remark that a large number vote against something or somebody rather than for anything or anybody, except when powerful agencies create a scare. The old principles do not fit contemporary life as it is lived, however well they may have expressed the vital interests of the times in which they arose. Thousands feel their hollowness even if they cannot make their feeling articulate. The confusion which has resulted from the size and ramifications of social activities has rendered men skeptical of the efficiency of political action. Who is sufficient unto these things? Men feel that they are caught in the sweep of forces too vast to understand or master. Thought is brought to a standstill and action paralyzed. Even the specialist finds it difficult to trace the chain of "cause and effect"; and even he operates only after the event, looking backward, while meantime social activities have moved on to effect a new state of affairs.

Similar considerations account for depreciation of the machinery of democratic political action in contrast with a rising appreciation of the need of expert administrators. For example, one of the by-products of the war was the investment of the government at Muscle Shoals for the manufacture of nitrogen, a chemical product of great importance to the farmer, as well as to armies in the field. The disposition and utilization of the plant have become matters of political dispute. The questions involved, questions of science, agriculture, industry and finance, are highly technical. How many voters are competent to measure all the factors involved in arriving at a decision? And if they were competent after studying it, how many have the time to devote to it? It is true that this matter does not come before the electorate directly, but the technical difficulty of the problem is reflected in the confused paralysis of the legislators whose business it is to deal with it. The confused situation is further complicated by the invention of other and cheaper methods of producing nitrates. Again, the rapid development of hydro-electric and super-power is a matter of public concern. In the long run, few questions exceed it in importance. Aside from business corporations which have a direct interest in it and some engineers, how many citizens have the data or the ability to secure and estimate the facts involved in its settlement? One further illustration: Two things which intimately concern a local public are street-railway transportation and the marketing of food products. But the history of municipal politics shows in most cases a flare-up of intense interest followed by a period of indifference. Results come home to the masses of the people.

But the very size, heterogeneity and mobility of urban populations, the vast capital required, the technical character of the engineering problems involved, soon tire the attention of the average voter. I think the three instances are fairly typical. The ramification of the issues before the public is so wide and intricate, the technical matters involved are so specialized, the details are so many and so shifting, that the public cannot for any length of time identify and hold itself. It is not that there is no public, no large body of persons having a common interest in the consequences of social transactions. There is too much public, a public too diffused and scattered and too intricate in composition. And there are too many publics, for conjoint actions which have indirect, serious and enduring consequences are multitudinous beyond comparison, and each one of them crosses the others and generates its own group of persons especially affected with little to hold these different publics together in an integrated whole. . . .

The new era of human relationships in which we live is one marked by mass production for remote markets, by cable and telephone, by cheap printing, by railway and steam navigation. Only geographically did Columbus discover a new world. The actual new world has been generated in the last hundred years. Steam and electricity have done more to alter the conditions under which men associate together than all the agencies which affected human relationships before our time. There are those who lay the blame for all the evils of our lives on steam, electricity and machinery. It is always convenient to have a devil as well as a savior to bear the responsibilities of humanity. In reality, the trouble springs rather from the ideas and absence of ideas in connection with which technological factors operate. Mental and moral beliefs and ideals change more slowly than outward conditions. If the ideals associated with the higher life of our cultural past have been impaired, the fault is primarily with them. Ideals and standards formed without regard to the means by which they are to be achieved and incarnated in flesh are bound to be thin and wavering. Since the aims, desires and purposes created by a machine age do not connect with tradition, there are two sets of rival ideals, and those which have actual instrumentalities at their disposal have the advantage. Because the two are rivals and because the older ones retain their glamor and sentimental prestige in literature and religion, the newer ones are perforce harsh and narrow. For the older symbols of ideal life still engage thought and command loyalty. Conditions have changed, but every aspect of life, from religion and education to property and trade, shows that nothing approaching a transformation has taken place in ideas and ideals. Symbols control sentiment and thought, and the new age has no symbols consonant with its activities. Intellectual instrumentalities for the formation of an organized public are more inadequate than its overt means. The ties which hold men together in action are numerous, tough and subtle. But they are invisible and intangible. We have the physical tools of communication as never before. The thoughts and aspirations congruous with them are not communicated, and hence are not common. Without such communication the public will remain shadowy and formless, seeking spasmodically for itself, but seizing and holding its shadow rather than its substance. Till the Great Society is converted into a Great Community, the Public will remain in eclipse. Communication can alone create a great community. Our Babel is not one of tongues but of the signs and symbols without which shared experience is impossible.

CHAPTER TWENTY

THE NEW DEALERS: GOVERNMENT INTERVENTION IN THE ECONOMY

The challenge of the Great Depression of the 1930's brought a new relationship between the government and the business community. In the Progressive era, government became an arbiter, a sort of policeman to regulate conflicting economic forces, especially to restrain large enterprise from engulfing small business. Then came World War I when the government for the first time undertook to manage the whole economy both in industry and agriculture, regulating some prices and wages, stimulating production of needed goods, and stifling production of nonessentials. In the 1920's, the government ended most of its economic management, but continued its regulatory functions in mild form. Overall it tried to stimulate prosperity through benign methods with which businessmen, if they wished, could voluntarily cooperate. "The business of the government is business," said President Calvin Coolidge. Then came the Great Depression, not too serious in the first year after the stockmarket crash of 1929, but increasing in severity until, by December, 1932, one wage-earner out of four was out of work and nearly one farmer in four had lost his farm. Millions of others teetered on the brink of total disaster. President Herbert Hoover sought at first by minor voluntary methods to stem the depression, then as it worsened he resorted to more drastic measures reminiscent of the way in which the government had intervened in the economy during World War I, but he depended upon voluntary cooperation by business and agriculture rather than compulsion. He denounced those who favored carrying government intervention to the point of compulsion.

In March, 1933, when President Franklin D. Roosevelt was inaugurated, he and his advisers undertook to bring speedy recovery to a nation seriously demoralized and despairing. What could the New Dealers do? How far were they willing to go? Roosevelt's own ideological background was almost identical to that of Hoover. Both had been young Progressives, admirers of Theodore Roosevelt's New Nationalism; both had become devoted followers of Woodrow Wilson; and both had been vigorous administrators in Washington during World War I. Like Hoover, therefore, Roosevelt was ready to apply to the depression methods similar to those with which Progressives had marshalled the economy during the war. Like Hoover, Roosevelt was ready to label these measures as voluntary— but in contrast to Hoover he was ready to put into them in fact the teeth of compulsion. Voluntary methods had not worked very well.

The New Deal unfolded thus at the outset, but forces and factors in the depression decade were so different from those in earlier periods that the New Deal necessarily came to embody a good deal more than a resurgence of Progressivism and the Progressive policies during the war. The selections that follow delineate several types of thinking that came to be important and the conservative response to them. Roosevelt planned at the outset to undertake a speedy recovery program and then to obtain a number of more permanent reforms to make further depressions less likely. Recovery did not come as speedily as he wished, and to his surprise he became the target of increasing hostility from the business community. In turn, Roosevelt depended more and more upon a political coalition of farmers and working people. The New Deal came to emphasize reforms that would improve the lot of the underprivileged, and in economic matters it came to involve the assumption of a new and lasting obligation on the part of the government to promote prosperity. Partly through large-scale spending, the government came to be an actively intervening force and controlling factor in the economy far more than ever before in peacetime. Around this point swirled much of the political debate of the New Deal era as it still does today. These selections need not stimulate the reader to choose sides, but they should help him understand the issues that were involved as the American system of government once again underwent major change.

President Roosevelt's first inaugural address, delivered March 4, 1933, was enthusiastically acclaimed by almost all groups of the American people. To a remarkable degree it helped inspire confidence among them. In retrospect, it is interesting to analyze as the beginning of the New Deal and as a statement of how far Roosevelt was prepared to go in meeting the emergency if more moderate expedients failed.

FRANKLIN D. ROOSEVELT: FIRST INAUGURAL ADDRESS*

I am certain that my fellow Americans expect that on my induction into the Presidency I will address them with a candor and a decision which the present situation of our Nation impels. This is preeminently the time to speak the truth, the whole truth, frankly and boldly. Nor need we shrink from honestly facing conditions in our country today. This great Nation will endure as it has endured, will revive and will prosper. So, first of all, let me assert my firm belief that the only thing we have to fear is fear itself—nameless, unreasoning, unjustified terror which paralyzes needed efforts to convert retreat into advance. In every dark hour of our national life a leadership of frankness and vigor has met with that understanding and support of the people themselves which is essential to victory. I am convinced that you will again give that support to leadership in these critical days.

In such a spirit on my part and on yours we face our common difficulties. They concern, thank God, only material things. Values have shrunken to fantastic levels; taxes have risen; our ability to pay has fallen; government of all kinds is faced by serious curtailment of income; the means of exchange are frozen in the currents of trade; the withered leaves of industrial enterprise lie on every side; farmers find no markets for their produce; the savings of many years in thousands of families are gone.

More important, a host of unemployed citizens face the grim problem of existence, and an equally great number toil with little return. Only a foolish optimist can deny the dark realities of the moment.

Yet our distress comes from no failure of substance. We are stricken by no plague of locusts. Compared with the perils which our forefathers

* Reprinted from *The Public Papers and Addresses of Franklin D. Roosevelt*, edited by Samuel I. Rosenman. Copyright 1938 by Franklin Delano Roosevelt. Reprinted by permission of Random House, Inc.

conquered because they believed and were not afraid, we have still much to be thankful for. Nature still offers her bounty and human efforts have multiplied it. Plenty is at our doorstep, but a generous use of it languishes in the very sight of the supply. Primarily this is because rulers of the exchange of mankind's goods have failed through their own stubbornness and their own incompetence, have admitted their failure, and have abdicated. Practices of the unscrupulous money changers stand indicted in the court of public opinion, rejected by the hearts and minds of men.

True they have tried, but their efforts have been cast in the pattern of an outworn tradition. Faced by failure of credit they have proposed only the lending of more money. Stripped of the lure of profit by which to induce our people to follow their false leadership, they have resorted to exhortations, pleading tearfully for restored confidence. They know only the rules of a generation of self-seekers. They have no vision, and when there is no vision the people perish.

The money changers have fled from their high seats in the temple of our civilization. We may now restore that temple to the ancient truths. The measure of the restoration lies in the extent to which we apply social values more noble than mere monetary profit.

Happiness lies not in the mere possession of money; it lies in the joy of achievement, in the thrill of creative effort. The joy and moral stimulation of work no longer must be forgotten in the mad chase of evanescent profits. These dark days will be worth all they cost us if they teach us that our true destiny is not to be ministered unto but to minister to ourselves and to our fellow men.

Recognition of the falsity of material wealth as the standard of success goes hand in hand with the abandonment of the false belief that public office and high political position are to be valued only by the standards of pride of place and personal profit; and there must be an end to a conduct in banking and in business which too often has given to a sacred trust the likeness of callous and selfish wrongdoing. Small wonder that confidence languishes, for it thrives only on honesty, on honor, on the sacredness of obligations, on faithful protection, on unselfish performance; without them it cannot live.

Restoration calls, however, not for changes in ethics alone. This Nation asks for action, and action now.

Our greatest primary task is to put people to work. This is no unsolvable problem if we face it wisely and courageously. It can be accomplished in part by direct recruiting by the Government itself, treating the task as we would treat the emergency of a war, but at the same time, through this employment, accomplishing greatly needed projects to stimulate and reorganize the use of our natural resources.

Hand in hand with this we must frankly recognize the overbalance of population in our industrial centers and, by engaging on a national scale in a redistribution, endeavor to provide a better use of the land for those best fitted for the land. The task can be helped by definite efforts to raise the values of agricultural products and with this the power to purchase the output of our cities. It can be helped by preventing realistically the tragedy of the growing loss through foreclosure of our small homes and our farms. It can be helped by insistence that the Federal, State, and local governments act forthwith on the demand that their cost be drastically reduced. It can be helped by the unifying of relief activities which today are often scattered, uneconomical, and unequal. It can be helped by national planning for and supervision of all forms of transportation and of communications and other utilities which have a definitely public character. There are many ways in which it can be helped, but it can never be helped merely by talking about it. We must act and act quickly.

Finally, in our progress toward a resumption of work we require two safeguards against a return of the evils of the old order: there must be a strict supervision of all banking and credits and investments, so that there will be an end to speculation with other people's money; and there must be provision for an adequate but sound currency.

These are the lines of attack. I shall presently urge upon a new Congress, in special session, detailed measures for their fulfillment, and I shall seek the immediate assistance of the several States.

Through this program of action we address ourselves to putting our own national house in order and making income balance outgo. Our international trade relations, though vastly important, are in point of time and necessity secondary to the establishment of a sound national economy. I favor as a practical policy the putting of first things first. I shall spare no effort to restore world trade by international economic readjustment, but the emergency at home cannot wait on that accomplishment.

The basic thought that guides these specific means of national recovery is not narrowly nationalistic. It is the insistence, as a first consideration, upon the interdependence of the various elements in and parts of the United States—a recognition of the old and permanently important manifestation of the American spirit of the pioneer. It is the way to recovery. It is the immediate way. It is the strongest assurance that the recovery will endure.

In the field of world policy I would dedicate this Nation to the policy of the good neighbor—the neighbor who resolutely respects himself and, because he does so, respects the rights of others—the neighbor who respects his obligations and respects the sanctity of his agreements in and with a world of neighbors.

If I read the temper of our people correctly, we now realize as we have never realized before our interdependence on each other; that we cannot merely take but we must give as well; that if we are to go forward, we must move as a trained and loyal army willing to sacrifice for the good of a common discipline, because without such discipline no progress is made, no leadership becomes effective. We are, I know, ready and willing to submit our lives and property to such discipline, because it makes possible a leadership which aims at a larger good. This I propose to offer, pledging that the larger purposes will bind upon us all as a sacred obligation with a unity of duty hitherto evoked only in time of armed strife.

With this pledge taken, I assume unhesitatingly the leadership of this great army of our people dedicated to a disciplined attack upon our common problems.

Action in this image and to this end is feasible under the form of government which we have inherited from our ancestors. Our Constitution is so simple and practical that it is possible always to meet extraordinary needs by changes in emphasis and arrangement without loss of essential form. That is why our constitutional system has proved itself the most superbly enduring political mechanism the modern world has produced. It has met every stress of vast expansion of territory, of foreign wars, of bitter internal strife, of world relations.

It is to be hoped that the normal balance of Executive and legislative authority may be wholly adequate to meet the unprecedented task before us. But it may be that an unprecedented demand and need for undelayed action may call for temporary departure from that normal balance of public procedure.

I am prepared under my constitutional duty to recommend the measures that a stricken Nation in the midst of a stricken world may require. These measures, or such other measures as the Congress may build out of its experience and wisdom, I shall seek, within my constitutional authority, to bring to speedy adoption.

But in the event that the Congress shall fail to take one of these two courses, and in the event that the national emergency is still critical, I shall not evade the clear course of duty that will then confront me. I shall ask the Congress for the one remaining instrument to meet the crisis—broad Executive power to wage a war against the emergency, as great as the power that would be given to me if we were in fact invaded by a foreign foe.

For the trust reposed in me I will return the courage and the devotion that befit the time. I can do no less.

We face the arduous days that lie before us in the warm courage of national unity; with the clear consciousness of seeking old and precious moral values; with the clean satisfaction that comes from the stern performance of duty by old and young alike. We aim at the assurance of a rounded and permanent national life.

We do not distrust the future of essential democracy. The people of the United States have not failed. In their need they have registered a mandate that they want direct, vigorous action. They have asked for discipline and direction under leadership. They have made me the present instrument of their wishes. In the spirit of the gift I take it.

In this dedication of a Nation we humbly ask the blessing of God. May He protect each and every one of us. May He guide me in the days to come.

As the New Deal began to unfold, it bore certain similarities, both in personnel and ideas, to the earlier New Freedom. Max Lerner in 1933 drew a balance sheet of comparisons and contrasts and in footnotes added in 1939 recorded two afterthoughts.

MAX LERNER: THE NEW FREEDOM AND THE NEW DEAL*

Twenty years have passed since Woodrow Wilson in 1912, on the threshold of the presidency and at the height of his powers, wrote his whole social credo into the campaign speeches gathered in this book. As the most open and defiant indictment that anyone in high public office has up to now made of the American plutocracy, the book has ranked as a cross between a classic and a museum piece, equally notable for the clangor of its sentences and the slightness of its results.

Wilson had, along with his iron-principled Calvinism, a sort of literary sensitiveness. He was forever sniffing the breezes of public opinion, forever finding "something new astir in the air." "We stand in the presence of a revolution," he announced to one audience, "not a bloody revolution—America is not given to the spilling of blood—but a silent revolution." Today when we are again talking of silent revolutions, the New Deal sends us not unnaturally back to the New

---

* Reprinted from Max Lerner, *Ideas Are Weapons* (New York: Viking Press, 1939), pp. 113–16 by permission.

Freedom, in a quest partly for origins but mainly for perspective.

The New Freedom was more than the phrase of a college professor turned politician. It was a fleeting gleam of vision caught by a whole generation of a way of escape from the intolerable oppression of the vested interests. Wilson was astute enough to snare the vision and to attach to it his political fortunes; he was phrase-maker enough to invest it with a moral fervor against which even the skeptical reader of today will not be immune. The formula that he evolves in these speeches is simple enough: smash the trusts, destroy special privilege, restore competition, let the full light of publicity beat in on all the activities of business and government. And the strategy for effecting the return of this primitive economic democracy? "The way to resume is to resume," says Wilson, quoting Horace Greeley. Amazingly simple. Yet it elected a President and stirred his generation. In its day it was held to be desperately radical. But Wilson's radicalism was of the sort that took itself out mainly in after-dinner eloquence. "I do not say this," he warns, after one of his attacks on the plutocracy, "with the slightest desire to create any prejudice against wealth; on the contrary, I should be ashamed of myself if I excited class feeling of any kind."

Others of Wilson's time—Veblen, La Follette, Brandeis, and even the muckraking group—had gone far beyond him in making the age realistically aware of the power and the threat of the huge corporations. What Wilson did was to translate this awareness into terms of political thinking, and keep it from finding too dangerous an outlet in class feeling. Not for nothing had he read Burke and Bagehot and Gladstone. He saw the corporations as another government, superimposed upon and often displacing the regular government. The threat that he chose to see was the threat to the English ideal of political freedom. And his proud phrase, "Freemen need no guardians," was simply a diluted version of "Britons never shall be slaves." It would operate as cogently against government control as against plutocratic domination.

This is why in all fairness to Franklin Roosevelt—and despite certain gracious acknowledgements that he makes to his old chief in his own book of speeches, Looking Forward—the New Deal as a program must be clearly dissociated from Wilson's New Freedom. In fact, in the matter of control, the present Roosevelt stands in a more direct line of descent, in thought as well as in blood, from Theodore Roosevelt, who called specifically for monopoly control and for a differentiation between good trusts and bad trusts. Wilson's thought never departed essentially from the old competitive ideal of nineteenth-century England.

To say, as do some critics of the New Deal, that Roosevelt's recovery program is merely Wilsonian liberalism transferred to the present situation is to stretch the much abused term "liberalism" beyond all recognition. In place of laissez-faire we have a vigorous economic constructivism, in place of "government by discussion" we have a semi-dictatorship, instead of leaving freemen to their own desires and devices we regulate them through a highly centralized economic government in Washington, instead of the new freedom we have an approach to the corporate state.[2] The Wilson of these speeches would have been entirely out of sympathy with the New Deal. "I don't want a smug lot of experts to sit down behind closed doors in Washington and play Providence to me"—these words of his could be used to great advantage today by the coal and steel operators and by Henry Ford.

Despite these differences there is a real historical continuity between the New Freedom and the New Deal. Franklin Roosevelt has said of Wilson: "The problem he saw so clearly is left with us as a legacy." What he is referring to is "the concentration of financial power." It is the problem of an outward-moving finance capitalism which in Wilson's day had taken the form of enslaving the industrial system by monopoly and in Roosevelt's day has led to complete industrial collapse. Wilson's brilliant and yet somehow platitudinous phrases were the product of an era which could still personify the evil forces to be overthrown; Roosevelt's concrete administrative bulletins are an index of the agony of the capitalist state. But the two are bound in a real community by the fact that each represents for his own period the interests and the attitudes of the small man and his revolt against the dominance of the big fellow. And as both leaders set themselves to fight Big Business, so have they been loathed and feared by Big Business. The bitterness with which Wall Street hated Wilson on his entrance into office, even threatening to pull a panic on him, is matched only by the bitterness with which the captains of industry have been sabotaging the Recovery Act.

But the dialectic of history moves forward and carries with it the ironic compulsion of events. The Wilson who sat for eight years in the White House was a different Wilson from the one who had toured the country radiating moral energy. He never made any efforts to smash the trusts, but contented himself with establishing the Federal Reserve System and the Federal Trade Commission; his "government by discussion" turned into a uniquely despotic presidency; and his ideals of freedom were sadly squeezed out in the war which he had sought to avoid entering. The irony of the historical perspective that Wilson's later experience affords is that Little Business, which knows how to fight Big Business when the interests of the two diverge, knows also how to unite with Big Business against a common enemy. Wilson was led to draw his thunder,

---

[2] I now believe (1939) that some of the phrases in this sentence were overstrong. But I have allowed them to stand unchanged.

leaving the field to the Morgans and Palmers; Roosevelt may find on the other hand that only increasing coercion applied to labor as well as to capital can bring recovery and order.[2] In either case they strengthened capitalism in the very process of fighting it. For Roosevelt today,

as for Wilson in its earlier phase, capitalism plays the role of Brahma in Emerson's poem: "When me they fly, I am the wings."

1933

President Roosevelt's closest adviser during the early New Deal, Raymond Moley, outlined in 1934 three main lines of thought among the New Dealers and demonstrated how they diverged and intertwined. In the years since, Moley looked back upon the New Deal more critically, but reiterated the main points of this analysis. Newspapers frequently called Roosevelt's advisers the Brains Trust.

RAYMOND MOLEY: THERE ARE THREE BRAINS TRUSTS*

EXPERTS INVITED TO CONFER

. . . there is no single, cohesive Brains Trust. The term is applied loosely to many people and accurately to no group at all.

Long before the embattled Democracy in Chicago selected Mr. Roosevelt as its candidate, he asked the assistance of three men whom he jocularly called "The Privy Council." They were Samuel I. Rosenman, counsel to the Governor; Basil O'Connor, Mr. Roosevelt's former law partner, and myself. O'Connor and I regarded Rosenman as our chief and our means of contact with Mr. Roosevelt.

Louis Howe, all through this period giving his energy unsparingly to the pre-convention fight, advised us when time permitted. As I have learned through the years, his advice is always worth considering, and is often brilliantly right.

It was my task during the Spring of 1932 to seek out people expert in various subjects relating to policy. I would invite them to meet with Mr. Roosevelt in the Executive Mansion at Albany. In his study there, in the quiet of the evening, after his work as Governor of New York was completed and dinner was out of the way, the visitors would set forth to him their ideas on public questions. . . .

Of the great number of people who came for these meetings, the majority came only once because their contribution was highly specialized and one discussion was sufficient. A few, however,

showed such a diverse knowledge of national economic problems that they gradually assumed a sort of permanent membership in the group. The most notable of these were Professor Tugwell, Professor Berle and General Johnson. The group thus completed was what Jimmy Kieran, a newspaper man, called the "brains trust," in September, 1932.

Sometimes this small group met with Mr. Roosevelt alone in the book-lined study at Albany. But more frequently, our function was to question and discuss the ideas of the others who were brought there. These others were by no means always professors. There were lawyers, business men, engineers, editors, doctors, farm experts and social workers. We questioned them, tried to test out their suggestions and to develop these suggestions whenever they seemed practicable.

Our group met frequently, too, in a suite of rooms that we had taken at the Roosevelt Hotel in New York. Hundreds of people came there to talk over ideas with us. These rooms were, in fact, the first place where ideas were sifted. We met almost continuously in an attempt to extract, from the flood of suggestions on economic rehabilitation that were current that year, those that might have substance.

From the very beginning, Mr. Roosevelt established the principle that a campaign for the Presidency involves two things: A vital organization of experienced politicians to gather delegates, to organize members of the party, to send out speakers, and to perform the other functions so necessary to a campaign; and, separate from the campaign organization, a policy group reporting to the candidate and concerned only with the questions of national policy. Mr. Roosevelt determined that the two groups should be kept separate, each reporting directly to him. This distinction is important. It is of the essence that those concerned with policy should not be in any

---

[2] Here too I have allowed the sentence to stand, although I now think I misjudged the trend of the New Deal with regard to labor. The argument that follows, however, I still believe to be valid.

* Reprinted from *Today*, I (April 11, 1934), 3–4, 23 by permission.

way influenced by the exigencies of the campaign itself, particularly the raising of money from contributors. . . .

This period of the New Deal might be appropriately called the phase of economics. We were all trying to help Mr. Roosevelt answer the questions in the minds and voices of the American people. "Why are we in this jam?" "What can the government do to help us?" It was a challenge to modern economic science. We felt that if economics could not answer this, it ought to quit its pretensions. Mr. Roosevelt carried this challenge of the American people, through us, squarely to the economists of the United States.

This was the reason for the existence of the Brains Trust, and when the need for this kind of a group service passed, the dissolution of the original Brains Trust took place.

THE LAW-MAKING PHASE BEGINS

Immediately after the election, the work of law-making, the second phase of the New Deal, began. It ran through to the end of the One Hundred Days' Congress in June. But in the interregnum between the election and the inauguration, all energies were bent to a consideration of the means by which the promises of the campaign might be fulfilled by the actual making of laws.

During this period, the task at hand had grown far too great for any small group. My function ceased to be that of collaborator of a group and became that of a general helper for Mr. Roosevelt. . . .

We realized that no little group is wise enough or resourceful enough to formulate policies. The strands of policy must come from all directions and it is only the President who is able to bind these strands together into a unified policy.

After the inauguration, moreover, many of those who originally had helped were appointed to specific jobs. They found the requirements of these jobs so demanding that their contacts with other aspects of legislative and administrative policy became less and less frequent.

At this time there entered a new sort of expert worker. The science of law and legislation became more and more important. Those most useful to Mr. Roosevelt consisted not only of experts in economics, but lawyers and legislators. Scores of members of the Senate and the House, whose names are now familiar to the country, gave assistance to the President, as well as other advisers who contributed to the work of formulating legislation. Berle, Tugwell and Johnson all performed extraordinarily valuable services; Tugwell in cooperation with Henry Morgenthau, Jr., in assisting the responsible members of Congress in formulating the agricultural legislation; Berle in connection with railroads and general bankruptcy legislation; Johnson in a number of ways, finally culminating in his creation almost single-handed of the National Industrial Recovery Act. But it is only fair to say here that

when the practical business of putting ideas into laws began, Congressmen and Senators became the dominating factors in the business of giving advice.

With the coming of the third phase of the New Deal, that of administering the laws in which the policies had been embodied, Tugwell, Berle and Johnson were thoroughly immersed in specific and separate tasks.

THE ORIGINAL TRUST VANISHES

It is absurd to continue to talk about the activities of the original Brains Trust at any time after March 4, 1933. It vanished. If it has any meaning now, it applies only to a habit of mind of the President's which has properly been characterized by the free use of men of expertness in various fields of human knowledge.

Romanticists still speak of a unified group; but any one who has viewed the development of the New Deal will see not one group, but a vast number of individuals, possessing varying points of view and lending service to the President in innumerable ways.

Roughly speaking, the many people who have participated in the giving of advice and service may be divided into three schools of thought. There are three Brains Trusts, in this new sense of the term. The New Deal, far from being the result of an economic policy advocated by any one of these, is rather a coordination of these three distinct points of view.

In one Brains Trust there are those who believe that the economic betterment of the people of the country depends upon an inflationary or reflationary monetary policy. Important among those who have held this point of view are Professors Warren, Fisher and Rogers. Their concern is in the readjustment of money and credit in order to provide a just means of compensation for the decline of prices and the increasing burden of debt throughout the country, particularly among the farmers. They believe, if I understand them correctly, that to relieve this burden of debt will restore a general degree of prosperity that will carry on the individualistic economics of the past.

Included in this group, of course, are innumerable people—some as naively simple in their economic views as was Bryan. Some of them talk of salvation through a currency based on foot-pounds of human energy; others, of a currency based on undeveloped natural resources; still others, of any one of a dozen varieties of plans of this nature. But it is only fair to say that the men who have been mentioned in this group advocate, in the large, simply a permanently managed currency in order that the stability of prices and debts may be maintained.

During the campaign, I observed a reluctance on the part of the group who were helping to formulate policies—and this applies particularly to Berle, Tugwell and Johnson—to place much dependence upon an exclusively monetary policy.

They believed that the way to economic justice was a much more complicated way than the one suggested by Professors Warren and Rogers. As the President developed his monetary policy, however, it was apparent that it was only one aspect of an infinitely broader and more complex policy.

The second school of thought—and the most luminous exponents of this point of view in the past generation were Justice Brandeis and Senators LaFollette and Borah—are those who believe in the strict regulation of business, the protection of the small unit, the enforcement of the anti-trust laws and the formulation of new regulatory measures such as the Securities Act and the Stock Exchange bill. In some respects this Brains Trust is legalistic. Those most eminent in its councils are lawyers—such as Professor Felix Frankfurter and a number of younger men, largely trained in the Harvard Law School and who, in many instances, have served as secretaries to various justices of the Supreme Court. Thomas G. Corcoran, James M. Landis and Benjamin V. Cohen are notable in this group.

REGULATION STILL NEEDED

In general, those in this second Brains Trust do not believe that government is yet able to relax its regulatory function and to sit down in partnership with big business. They say that big business is possessed of more individuals of ability than government. The broad implications of their position are easy to see. They believe that with a leverage of regulatory measures and a few individuals concentrated in the Interstate Commerce Commission, the Federal Trade Commission, the Department of Justice and elsewhere, the vast industries of the country can be regulated by legal definitions of conduct. These men are essentially individualists. They hope for a continuation of an individualistic society under strict governmental rules.

The third Brains Trust, with which Professors Tugwell, Berle and General Johnson may be more completely identified, believes, within certain limits, that the government ought to go beyond the negative process of telling business what it ought not to do, and sit down with business and agriculture and attempt to provide a cooperative means of solving their problems. This is the basic idea embodied in the NRA and the AAA.

This idea of "partnership" does not mean a regimentation of our economic life, in the sense that timid Tories would imply. But it does mean that in a nation, the parts of which are interdependent and in a national economy which depends upon the balancing of one part against another, there must be intelligence and direction of thinking. It is this idea behind the NRA and the AAA, which, to my mind, are the most permanently valuable contributions of the New Deal.

It is to be taken for granted that these groups are not mutually exclusive. They are all part of a general picture. The genius of Roosevelt is that he has so adapted the suggestions of them all that they fit into one harmonious picture. For example, it is not inflation that he has created in his monetary policy, it is a currency managed from the center of things. Recognizing the necessary place of the idea of regulation, advocated by the second school of thought, he has properly insisted upon the application of restrictive measures such as the Securities Act and the Stock Exchange bill. And finally, in addition to the creation of the NRA and the AAA, he has applied the third idea of a broad national planning of our economic life. A conspicuous example of this is the planned project in the entire Tennessee Valley.

Thus the New Deal follows the single pattern of no one of these groups. There are three Brains Trusts in policy, and no Brains Trust in actual fact.

The President has utilized the thinking and expert service of many schools of thought, shaping them all into a single pattern. This, it seems to me, is the essence of statesmanship. Those who have been close to the making of this policy have profound admiration for the skill with which the President has created a new synthesis out of many old strands.

To say that this formulation into a single policy of elements that came from many schools of thought in America and from generations of governmental development in states, cities and the nation, is a thing borrowed from abroad, is to assert nonsense. In the two years that have passed since the first policy meetings, I have been present at scores of conferences, not only among the various people who have assisted, but in their contacts with the President. I have never yet heard a person, outside of one evangelistic crackpot who called himself "head of the American Reds," mention the possibility of the adaptation of a policy now in operation in any other country to the uses of this country. The people at these conferences did not talk of Fascism or of Communism. They talked of the United States.

A GROTESQUE CHARGE

There is something grotesque in a recent statement in a financial publication that the young "Brains Trusters" who formulated the Securities Act were trying to regiment this country. If whoever wrote this statement had been present when these men were engaged in arguing the traditional American rights of small business as against those who believed in a controlled monopoly, he would never have uttered such a fallacy. If he had heard the argument as between those who favored the retention of the gold standard and those who believed in reflation, his fear of a concerted effort to destroy values would certainly have been less articulate.

Despite hysterical efforts to inflame the public against attempts to establish competence and expertness in public office, there should be some recognition of the fact that the President's dependence upon expertness is a commendable sign in the history of American politics. The thing that the President is insisting upon (and this has been the test of every individual who has con-tributed to furthering his purpose) is that those who serve the public should serve it with one interest in view—the much-abused, elusive but fundamental abstraction known as the public interest.

Only a man who was not doctrinaire and who was moderate could successfully synthesize a program like the New Deal and steer its course between the extremes of right and left. This, asserted Archibald MacLeish, a noted poet who became an important New Deal administrator, explained much of the emotional appeal of Roosevelt.

ARCHIBALD MacLEISH: PREFACE TO AN AMERICAN MANIFESTO*

Let no man miss the point of Mr. Roosevelt's hold upon the minds of the citizens of this republic. Men's minds are fired by Mr. Roosevelt because they are sick to nausea of the rich bankers and their economists upon the one side and the great revolutionaries and their economists upon the other, repeating over and over that the world is ruled by incontrovertible economic laws which it is not only blasphemy but idiocy to oppose, and which lead inevitably to certain fixed and inescapable conclusions. It is not the first time the world has been told it existed in a closed system of which the rules were comprehensible only to the doctors. And from the human point of view it is almost irrelevant whether or not Mr. Roosevelt's particular attempt to break out of the cage is successful. What is important is the attempt—and the reaction to that attempt on the part of the people of this nation. It is only to the free, inventive gestures of the human soul that men wholly and believingly respond. They will, in a crisis, rise against arrogance. They may, for a time, fight from hatred. But only to hope will they give themselves entirely. And only writers writing out of hope can lead them to anything more permanent than the barricades.

By 1934, powerful attacks were already being launched against the New Deal by those who claimed that it menaced the traditional relationships between the government and the economy. In *The Challenge to Liberty,* former President Herbert Hoover warned that the regimentation being imposed by the New Deal could lead to the destruction of American liberty. Part of his arguments follow.

HERBERT HOOVER: THE CONSEQUENCES TO LIBERTY OF CONTINUED REGIMENTATION*

The most gigantic step morally, spiritually, economically, and governmentally that a nation can take is to shift its fundamental philosophic and social ideas. The entry upon such a movement presents the most fateful moment in the history of a people.

But before entering upon the subject of the further and broader consequences of National Regimentation or the adoption of other social philosophies in American life, I shall clear the road of some unrelated subjects.

I am not here discussing any of the current measures except so far as our present experience of them illustrates the effect which they have upon Liberty. Although I hold that emer-

* Reprinted from Archibald MacLeish, "Preface to an American Manifesto," *A Time to Speak* (Boston: Houghton Mifflin Company, 1941), p. 17 by permission.

* Reprinted with the permission of Charles Scribner's Sons from *The Challenge to Liberty* by Herbert Hoover. Copyright 1934 Curtis Publishing Co., Copyright 1934 Charles Scribner's Sons; renewal copyright © 1962 Herbert Hoover.

465

gency neither necessitates nor justifies departures from fundamental liberties—and incidentally will in the end retard recovery itself through disturbance of confidence in the future—I am not here dealing with temporary actions as such. Overshadowing temporary actions, whether wise or unwise, is the far larger issue. An emergency program for recovery is one thing, but to implant a new social philosophy in American life in conflict with the primary concepts of American Liberty is quite another thing.

We are told today by men high in our government both legislative and administrative that the social organization which we have developed over our whole history is "outworn" and "must be abandoned." We have been told that it has "failed." We are told of "outworn traditions," that we have come to the "end of an era," that we are passing through a "bloodless revolution." We are also told that the American System "is in ruins," that we must "build on the ruins of the past a new structure." It is advocated now that many of the emergency measures shall be "consolidated" and made "permanent." We should therefore earnestly and dispassionately examine what the pattern of this transformation of the economic, social, and governmental system is to be, and what the ultimate effect of its continuance would be upon our national life.

Among the important measures of government, both in the present Administration and in the last, are a large number devoted to relief of distress, both personal and institutional; the expansion of public works; revisions of the older laws regulating business; the reinforcement of State regulation by Federal acts; and the support of co-operative action among the citizens by temporary use of Federal credit. Many of the additional measures undertaken in these directions during the past months are admirable if properly administered.

Proper action in relief of distress is inherent in the social vision of the true American System. No American should go hungry or cold if he is willing to work. Under our system relief is first the obligation of the individual to his neighbors, then of institutions, then of local communities, and then of the State governments. The moment the need exceeds the honest capacities of the local agencies, then they must have support of the Federal Government as the final reservoir of national strength.

This includes an indirect relief through public works, direct relief when all other measures have failed, and proper support to financial institutions when failures will reduce large numbers to destitution. We may not approve the current methods of applying relief. We may feel that some of these methods undermine State and local responsibility; that they are wasteful or futile or alive with corruption. We may fear that they may be misused, by subversion of the electorate through partisan organization, to create future artillery against the walls of Liberty. But even so,

these are correctable abuses and lesser questions, evanescent in the long view of national life.

The depression has brought to the surface a number of weaknesses and abuses in the economic system. I deal elsewhere more fully with the whole subject of abuse of Liberty. For this immediate discussion I may state that reform and revision of our older regulatory laws in banking, commodity and stock markets, transportation, utilities and natural resource industries are absolutely necessary. So long as these revisions conform to the conditions of Liberty there can be no difference of opinion except as to method. All reform entails some degree of experiment. I have no fear of experiments which take account of experience, do not remake the errors of history, and do not set out to experiment with the principles of Liberty. We may feel that some reform measures do not reach to the heart of the problems they undertake to solve; that they are in part punitive rather than constructive; that they are in part impractical of producing the desired result; that in attempting to suppress a dozen scoundrels they are retarding the normal and active flow of economic life among a thousand honest men, and are thus retarding recovery from the depression. But we must remember that reform is a hard horse to ride in the blinding storm of world war liquidation.

There have run through all the dissertations of the past months the slogans and promise of "National Planning," "Planned Economy" or "Permanent Planning."[1] Obviously these phrases have been given a new meaning. They do not mean mere charts and blueprints. They mean execution as well. They do not mean only the planning and executing of the normal functions of government. Obviously there is included also regimentation of industry and agriculture, management of currency and credit, government competition with business, management of foreign trade, and many other activities, all to be definitely dictated by officials acting from Washington. That is the coercive execution of plans for the daily economic and social lives of the people.

We have been engaged in planning, and the execution of plans, within the proper functions of government ever since the first days of George Washington's administration. We have planned and executed public school systems, safeguards to public health, conservation of national resources, the reclamation of desert lands, vast

---

[1] It has been said that statesmanship often consists of presenting old forms under new names. But modern social agitation seems to have reversed this procedure to presenting new forms of their own coinage under familiar terms. This use of the term "national planning" is not alone in this advent. To it may be added the new meanings given such terms as "Capitalism," "Liberalism," "Democratic Processes," "Sound Money," *"Laissez Faire,"* "Rugged Individualism," "Regulation," "Control," "Readjustment," "Co-operation," and "Emergency."

river and harbor development, a magnificent system of highways and public buildings, the creation of parks, the beautification of cities, and a thousand other activities in every state, town, and village. We have planned and executed laws controlling semi-monopolies and maintenance of competition. We have set up the Federal Reserve System, the Land Banks, the Home Loan Banks. We planned and built the Panama Canal. The government has co-operated with the people in planning and executing a great system of railways, of airways, of merchant marine. It has gone further. The government through its constituted officials has co-operated in furthering great social activities, by determining facts and by assisting organizations to make plans for social advancement, to create standards, to co-ordinate thought and stimulate effort.

Nor have our non-governmental activities been without plan and execution by the people themselves, as witness the gigantic physical equipment of the nation and its intellectual progress. If this vast achievement was not the result of conscious planning, then it is eloquent proof that these things come spontaneously out of our American System.

No civilization has hitherto ever seen such a growth of voluntary associative activities in every form of planning, co-ordination and co-operation of effort, the expression of free men. It comes naturally, since the whole system builded on Liberty is a stimulant to plan and progress. The unparalleled rise of the American man and woman was not alone the result of riches in lands, forests, or mines; it sprang from ideals and philosophic ideas out of which plans, and the execution of them, are stimulated by the forces of freedom.

The assertion is made that these Regimentations or National Planning are merely extended co-operation. Civilization dawned when the first group of men acted in co-operation, and men have ever since divided over how far they should be forced to group action or whether they should join of their own free will. Our American civilization is based upon the maximum of free will in an ordered Liberty. Aside from the very philosophy of Liberty, the practicalities are that when free men come together in economic life they pool a wealth of practical experience and conscientious responsibility. They are compelled to find workable methods of co-operation. Over every deliberation hangs the sobering threat of personal loss for a wrong decision. There is no one to whom the cost of error may be passed. But under coercive co-operation by government, the final determination of method for the joint action is made not by men of large experience in practical affairs, but by government agents—often by men wholly lacking in both vision and ability. The bureaucrat is above accountability so long as his political support holds. Co-operation appraises its methods and consequences step by step and pays its bills as it goes. Bureaucracy rushes headlong

into visions of the millennium and sends the bill to the Treasury.

The methods of planning progress cannot be through governmental determination of when and how much a factory may be operated, what the farmer may plant or sell, or any other of the processes of regimentation. The forces of true co-operation may be less immediate in their results than coercion, but they are more permanent, for they do not wither the real impulses of progress and they do not atrophy the responsibility of the citizen.

There are transcendent obstacles to the successful working of these ideas of coercive National Planning or National Regimentation of our economic and social life. The first is the inability to command the omniscient genius required to plan and co-ordinate and direct the operation of the economic and social machine. This is true even if the government enjoyed the powers of complete dictatorship as in the cases of Fascism and Communism. The second and higher obstacle is created when these ideas are mixed with democracy, for they are based upon wholly different conceptions of human rights which instantly clash.

There arise from this mixture conflicts and interferences which will undermine Liberty by rendering its economic system only partly operative, and they do not give any other system a fair trial. The mixture automatically destroys confidence in the future, which is the essential of our system, and that at once delays initiative and new enterprise. It produces astonishing effects, from the behavior of men part free, which thwart the hoped-for results. It develops surprising conflicts between the regiments created, because of the inability of any human mind to co-ordinate such vast plans and activities. Complete dictatorship is of course abolition of representative government, but even partial regimentation raises at once conflicts which are destructive to it. One result is to drive unceasingly for more drastic steps. Our American System cannot be made to work part free and part regimented. It is a new form of an old conflict. No system can be part dictatorship and part democracy.

We may confirm these observations if we examine actual results of the operations now in progress and if we examine their tendencies toward the future.

As I have said, the first necessity of this program of National Planning or National Regimentation, whatever may be the name we apply to it, is obviously a vast concentration of political and economic authority in the Executive. All these plans and regiments must be invented. Their execution must be commanded, administered, and enforced by a delegated somebody. Thus overhanging all these organisms of "managed currency," "regimented industry," "government operation," and "regimented agriculture" is the most vital of questions: Who is to invent? Who is to manage? Who is to command these regiments?

And above all, who is to co-ordinate their activities?

It is not enough to answer, "the Government," "the State," or "the Executive." This direction ultimately must be reposed in government bureaus and they are comprised of human beings with dictatorial powers over us all.

These proposals necessitate that a large part of leadership and managerial responsibility and authority in business and agriculture is to be wrenched from the hands of those who have risen to leadership by success and skill in each specialized calling, and placed in the hands of those who appear to merit political power. An enormous extension of bureaucracy is inevitable. Already a host of new government bureaus and nearly two thousand commissions have been established with authority over every trade, and in nearly every town and village. We have witnessed this host of government agents spread out over the land, limiting men's honest activities, conferring largess and benefits, directing, interfering, disseminating propaganda, spying on, threatening the people and prosecuting for a new host of crimes. It is pertinent therefore to inquire shortly into the course and characteristics of bureaucracy, for in the end that is the agency that will rule over us.

No one with a day's experience in government fails to realize that in all bureaucracies there are three implacable spirits—self-perpetuation, expansion, and an incessant demand for more power. These are human urges and are supported by a conviction, sometimes justified, that they know what is good for us. Nevertheless, these spirits are potent and possess a dictatorial complex. They lead first to subversive influence in elections. They drive always to extension of powers by interpretation of authority, and by more and more legislation. Power is the father of impatience with human faults, and impatience breeds arrogance. In their mass action, they become the veritable exponents of political tyranny. . . .

We can test the ability to dictate the economic life of the people, and above all to co-ordinate these regiments, by observing some of the contradictory, conflicting, and confusing results which we have experienced already in the past months. At the same time we can indicate the surprising effects of human behavior in the mixture of Regimentation with freedom.

Inescapably there is conflict between the idea of the commanders of one regiment that artificial price-rises will increase business activity and employment, and thereby consumption of goods; and the idea of another regimental command that, in order to increase consumption and employment, prices must be kept down.

There are conflicts between artificial price-increases undertaken to restore agriculture to parity with other industry, and those taken to increase prices of the things the farmer buys. Separated from the drought, the result has added practically nothing to agriculture. There is contradiction in destroying food when people are in want. There is direct conflict between the policy of eliminating marginal agriculture on the one hand, and on the other hand, the policy of maintaining marginal production by subsidies and by the expansion of production through reclamation.

Through regimentation of employers, employees, and consumers there are conflicts as to who is to bear the cost of these artificial price-rises. The consequent struggles between employers and employees have resulted in more days' labor lost in nine months through strikes than in the whole of the previous three years. The consumer regiments set their buying resistance against the producers, so that consumption slackens and surpluses increase. This is especially evident in perishable agricultural products where the processing tax, by decreasing consumption, has in effect forced back at least part of the tax to the farmer instead of adding it to the consumer.

There is the conflict between lenders and borrowers as to who shall take the risk of unstable currencies, the result of which is to continue unemployment in the durable goods industries. There is a conflict between government absorption of capital by taxes and borrowings from the common pool for the purpose of giving employment, and its urging of private industry to secure from the depleted pool the capital with which it might give employment. There is conflict of plans, on one hand, that the people should spend a larger part of the current income, and steps on the other hand, which frighten them to restrict spendings.

There is a conflict between maintaining anti-trust laws and the setting of monopoly under the codes, one result of which is to squeeze out the smaller business and another result is to increase prices and the cost of living and thus to promote strikes to equate wages. There is at least incompatibility between a system which makes its progress through invention and improvement, and governmental action which creates drags upon the competition which alone inspires them. There is inherent conflict between the theory of government limitation of private production, and the government going into business where there is already ample production. There is a conflict between attempts to move industry to the rural districts and the tendency of production to move to urban areas because of fixed regional wages.

Industry is further confused by the government's payment of higher wages for relief than that fixed in the codes. There is inconsistency between commanding increased wages, shorter hours and greater employment in industry, and cuts and dismissals in government service. There is contradiction between repudiation of government obligations under contracts and the insistence by the law that private contracts be observed. There is inconsistency between the stern reprimand for incapacity and dishonesty in administration of industry and the inevitable outbreak of waste, corruption, and spoils where government goes into business.

There is conflict between the theory of one regiment holding to lower tariffs, and to the lending of government money to promote trade, and the theory of another regiment which increases the tariffs and puts on import quotas and currency wars that restrict trade. There is inconsistency between the government denunciation of private lenders of money to foreign countries, and the government itself lending them money.

These are but part of the catalogue, but sufficient for examples.

These are not surprising results, for they represent in part the inability of men to know the destiny of economic forces, artificially created, even if it is all planned in advance; they represent in part the inability of any government to coordinate these artificial forces when set in motion. They represent also another phase of equal importance, and that is the effect of partial regimentation of the economic system. So long as it is partial, human behavior still controls some elements in the individual's interest, and he uses them. And because of all these difficulties there arises an insistent demand for more power, and the danger of further and further assumption of it.

Such is the march of regimentation. The effect upon our liberties needs no amplification.

The seeking of opportunities for expending huge sums of public money, upon the theory that this will prime the economic pump, ignores the fact that the priming water is an exhaustion of the living water of the public credit. And even beyond that, it enfeebles the power delivered to the pump through stifling confidence and enterprise. Its costs in huge budget deficits must ultimately necessitate huge increase in taxes or the manipulation of either currency or credit or all three. Government postponement of paying for these unprecedented expenditures by expanding bank credits and then borrowing the expansion has implications which no one can foresee. But so far no nation or individual has been able to squander itself into prosperity. So far as history shows, every such borrowing government has had to repay either by a mortgage on the social development of the next generation, or by desperate measures of repudiation through inflation in its own generation. Either leads to devastating invasions of Liberty. . . .

Many of the critics of the New Deal held that its economic regulations were contrary to the Constitution, and in 1935–1936 the Supreme Court seemed to agree with them. In the Schechter or "Sick Chicken" case, decided in May, 1935, the justices by a nine to nothing vote held that the code system of the National Recovery Administration involved an unconstitutional delegation of power from Congress to the executive branch of the government, and that provisions concerning the wholesale poultry business in the New York area were beyond the powers given Congress to regulate interstate commerce. Government attorneys had cited evidence to indicate that most of the poultry sold in New York came from outside of the state, and that the price of poultry established in New York affected poultry prices nationally. They had also cited precedents in support of their argument that the poultry code did not go beyond what the Supreme Court had earlier established as the power of Congress over interstate commerce. The decision was delivered by Chief Justice Charles Evans Hughes.

SCHECHTER POULTRY CORPORATION *v.* UNITED STATES*

HUGHES, C. J. Petitioners were convicted in the District Court of the United States for the Eastern District of New York on eighteen counts of an indictment charging violations of what is known as the "Live Poultry Code," and on an additional count for conspiracy to commit such violations. . . .

The defendants are slaughterhouse operators. . . . A. L. A. Schechter Poultry Corporation and

Schechter Live Poultry Market are corporations conducting wholesale poultry slaughterhouse markets in Brooklyn, New York City. Defendants ordinarily purchase their live poultry from commission men at the West Washington Market in New York City or at the railroad terminals serving the City, but occasionally they purchase from commission men in Philadelphia. They buy the poultry for slaughter and resale. After the poultry is trucked to their slaughterhouse markets in Brooklyn, it is there sold, usually within twenty-

* Reprinted from 295 U.S. 495 (1935).

four hours, to retail poultry dealers and butchers who sell directly to consumers. The poultry purchased from defendants is immediately slaughtered, prior to delivery, by shochtim in defendants' employ. Defendants do not sell poultry in interstate commerce.

The "Live Poultry Code" was promulgated under section 3 of the National Industrial Recovery Act. That section authorizes the President to approve "codes of fair competition."

Of the eighteen counts of the indictment upon which the defendants were convicted, aside from the count for conspiracy, two counts charged violation of the minimum wage and maximum hour provisions of the Code, and ten counts were for violation of the requirement (found in the "trade practice provisions") of "straight killing." The charges in the ten counts, respectively, were that the defendants in selling to retail dealers and butchers had permitted "selections of individual chickens taken from particular coops and half coops."

Of the other six counts, one charged the sale to a butcher of an unfit chicken; two counts charged the making of sales without having the poultry inspected or approved in accordance with regulations or ordinances of the City of New York; two counts charged the making of false reports or the failure to make reports relating to the range of daily prices and volume of sales for certain periods; and the remaining count was for sales to slaughterers or dealers who were without licenses required by the ordinances and regulations of the City of New York.

First. Two preliminary points are stressed by the Government with respect to the appropriate approach to the important questions presented. We are told that the provision of the statute authorizing the adoption of codes must be viewed in the light of the grave national crisis with which Congress was confronted. Undoubtedly, the conditions to which power is addressed are always to be considered when the exercise of power is challenged. Extraordinary conditions may call for extraordinary remedies. But the argument necessarily stops short of an attempt to justify action which lies outside the sphere of constitutional authority. Extraordinary conditions do not create or enlarge constitutional power. The Constitution established a national government with powers deemed to be adequate, as they have proved to be both in war and peace, but these powers of the national government are limited by the constitutional grants. Those who act under these grants are not at liberty to transcend the imposed limits because they believe that more or different power is necessary. Such assertions of extraconstitutional authority were anticipated and precluded by the explicit terms of the Tenth Amendment,—"The powers not delegated to the United States by the Constitution, nor prohibited by it to the States, are reserved to the States respectively, or to the people."

The further point is urged that the national crisis demanded a broad and intensive cooperative effort by those engaged in trade and industry, and that this necessary cooperation was sought to be fostered by permitting them to initiate the adoption of codes. But the statutory plan is not simply one for voluntary effort. It does not seek merely to endow voluntary trade or industrial associations or groups with privileges or immunities. It involves the coercive exercise of the lawmaking power. The codes of fair competition, which the statute attempts to authorize, are codes of laws. If valid, they place all persons within their reach under the obligation of positive law, binding equally those who assent and those who do not assent. Violations of the provisions of the codes are punishable as crimes.

Second. The question of the delegation of legislative power. . . .

. . . Section 3 of the Recovery Act is without precedent. It supplies no standards for any trade, industry or activity. It does not undertake to prescribe rules of conduct to be applied to particular states of fact determined by appropriate administrative procedure. Instead of prescribing rules of conduct, it authorizes the making of codes to prescribe them. For that legislative undertaking, section 3 sets up no standards, aside from the statement of the general aims of rehabilitation, correction and expansion described in section one. In view of the scope of that broad declaration, and of the nature of the few restrictions that are imposed, the discretion of the President in approving or prescribing codes, and thus enacting laws for the government of trade and industry throughout the country, is virtually unfettered. We think that the code-making authority thus conferred is an unconstitutional delegation of legislative power.

Second. The question of the application of the provisions of the Live Poultry Code to intrastate transactions. This aspect of the case presents the question whether the particular provisions of the Live Poultry Code, which the defendants were convicted for violating and for having conspired to violate, were within the regulating power of Congress.

These provisions relate to the hours and wages of those employed by defendants in their slaughterhouses in Brooklyn and to the sales there made to retail dealers and butchers.

(1) Were these transactions *"in"* interstate commerce? Much is made of the fact that almost all the poultry coming to New York is sent there from other States. But the code provisions, as here applied, do not concern the transportation of the poultry from other States to New York, or the transactions of the commission men or others to whom it is consigned, or the sales made by such consignees to defendants. When defendants had made their purchases, whether at the West Washington Market in New York City or at the railroad terminals serving the City, or elsewhere, the poultry was trucked to their slaughterhouses in Brooklyn for local disposition. The interstate transactions in relation to that poultry then ended. Defendants held the poultry at their slaughter-

house markets for slaughter and local sale to retail dealers and butchers who in turn sold directly to consumers. Neither the slaughtering nor the sales by defendants were transactions in interstate commerce.

The undisputed facts thus afford no warrant for the argument that the poultry handled by defendants at their slaughterhouse markets was in a "*current*" or "*flow*" of interstate commerce and was thus subject to congressional regulation. The mere fact that there may be a constant flow of commodities into a State does not mean that the flow continues after the property has arrived and has become commingled with the mass of property within the State and is there held solely for local disposition and use. So far as the poultry here in question is concerned, the flow in interstate commerce had ceased. The poultry had come to a permanent rest within the State. It was not held, used, or sold by defendants in relation to any further transactions in interstate commerce and was not destined for transportation to other states. Hence, decisions which deal with a stream of interstate commerce—where goods come to rest within a State temporarily and are later to go forward in interstate commerce—and with the regulations of transactions involved in that practical continuity of movement, are not applicable here.

(2) Did the defendants' transactions directly "*affect*" interstate commerce so as to be subject to federal regulation? The power of Congress extends not only to the regulation of transactions which are part of interstate commerce, but to the protection of that commerce from injury.

In determining how far the federal government may go in controlling intrastate transactions upon the ground that they "affect" interstate commerce, there is a necessary and well-established distinction between direct and indirect effects. The precise line can be drawn only as individual cases arise, but the distinction is clear in principle. Direct effects are illustrated by the railroad cases we have cited, as *e.g.*, the effect of failure to use prescribed safety appliances on railroads which are the highways of both interstate and intrastate commerce, injury to an employee engaged in interstate transportation by the negligence of an employee engaged in an intrastate movement, the fixing of rates for intrastate transportation which unjustly discriminate against interstate commerce. But where the effect of intrastate transactions upon interstate commerce is merely indirect, such transactions remain within the domain of state power. If the commerce clause were construed to reach all enterprises and transactions which could be said to have an indirect effect upon interstate commerce, the federal authority would embrace practically all the activities of the people and the authority of the State over its domestic concerns would exist only by sufferance of the federal government. Indeed, on such a theory, even the development of the State's commercial facilities would be subject to federal control.

The distinction between direct and indirect effects has been clearly recognized in the application of the Anti-Trust Act. Where a combination or conspiracy is formed, with the intent to restrain interstate commerce or to monopolize any part of it, the violation of the statute is clear. But where that intent is absent, and the objectives are limited to intrastate activities, the fact that there may be an indirect effect upon interstate commerce does not subject the parties to the federal statute, notwithstanding its broad provisions.

While these decisions related to the application of the federal statute, and not to its constitutional validity, the distinction between direct and indirect effects of intrastate transactions upon interstate commerce must be recognized as a fundamental one, essential to the maintenance of our constitutional system. Otherwise as we have said, there would be virtually no limit to the federal power and for all practical purposes we should have a completely centralized government. We must consider the provisions here in question in the light of this distinction.

The question of chief importance relates to the provisions of the Code as to the hours and wages of those employed in defendants' slaughterhouse markets. It is plain that these requirements are imposed in order to govern the details of defendants' management of their local business. The persons employed in slaughtering and selling in local trade are not employed in interstate commerce. Their hours and wages have no direct relation to interstate commerce. The question of how many hours these employees should work and what they should be paid differs in no essential respect from similar questions in other local businesses which handle commodities brought into a State and there dealt in as a part of its internal commerce. This appears from an examination of the considerations urged by the Government with respect to conditions in the poultry trade. Thus, the Government argues that hours and wages affect prices; that slaughterhouse men sell at a small margin above operating costs; that labor represents 50 to 60 per cent of these costs; that a slaughterhouse operator paying lower wages or reducing his cost by exacting long hours of work, translates his saving into lower prices; that this results in demands for a cheaper grade of goods; and that the cutting of prices brings about demoralization of the price structure. Similar conditions may be adduced in relation to other businesses. The argument of the Government proves too much. If the federal government may determine the wages and hours of employees in the internal commerce of a State, because of their relation to cost and prices and their indirect effect upon interstate commerce, it would seem that a similar control might be exerted over other elements of cost, also affecting prices, such as the number of employees, rents, advertising, methods of doing business, etc. All the processes of production and distribution that enter into cost could likewise be controlled. If the cost of doing an intrastate business is in itself the permitted object of federal control, the extent of the regulation of cost would be a question of discretion and not of power.

The Government also makes the point that efforts to enact state legislation establishing high labor standards have been impeded by the belief that unless similar action is taken generally, commerce will be diverted from the States adopting such standards, and that this fear of diversion has led to demands for federal legislation on the subject of wages and hours. The apparent implication is that the federal authority under the commerce clause should be deemed to extend to the establishment of rules to govern wages and hours in intrastate trade and industry generally throughout the country, thus overriding the authority of the States to deal with domestic problems arising from labor conditions in their internal commerce.

It is not the province of the Court to consider the economic advantages or disadvantages of such a centralized system. It is sufficient to say that the Federal Constitution does not provide for it. Our growth and development have called for wide use of the commerce power of the federal government in its control over the expanded activities of interstate commerce, and in protecting that commerce from burdens, interferences, and conspiracies to restrain and monopolize it. But the authority of the federal government may not be pushed to such an extreme as to destroy the distinction, which the commerce clause itself establishes, between commerce "among the several States" and the internal concerns of a State. The same answer must be made to the contention that is based upon the serious economic situation which led to the passage of the Recovery Act,—the fall in prices, the decline in wages and employment, and the curtailment of the market for commodities. Stress is laid upon the great importance of maintaining wage distributions which would provide the necessary stimulus in starting "the cumulative forces making for expanding commercial activity." Without in any way disparaging this motive, it is enough to say that the recuperative efforts of the federal government must be made in a manner consistent with the authority granted by the Constitution.

We are of the opinion that the attempt through the provisions of the Code to fix the hours and wages of employees of defendants in their intrastate business was not a valid exercise of federal power.

On both the grounds we have discussed, the attempted delegation of legislative power, and the attempted regulation of intrastate transactions which affect interstate commerce only indirectly, we hold the code provisions here in question to be invalid and that the judgment of conviction must be reversed.

Justice CARDOZO delivered a concurring opinion with which Justice STONE concurred.

The Supreme Court decision invalidating the N.R.A. codes gave promise that the larger part of the New Deal program of economic regulation might also be invalidated. And, indeed, in the next eighteen months, the Court did hold several other pieces of legislation, including the Agricultural Adjustment Administration processing tax, to be unconstitutional. At the same time, it denied similar regulatory powers over the economy to the states. This was the preface to President Roosevelt's struggle in 1937 to enlarge the membership of the Supreme Court, the "Court Packing Plan." Roosevelt lost the struggle, but perhaps coincidentally the Court, early in 1937, took a far broader view of the power of Congress to regulate interstate commerce.

On May 31, 1935, before these events had unfolded, Roosevelt delivered a lengthy extemporaneous talk to the newspapermen at a press conference upon the nature of the New Deal recovery program and the significance of the Supreme Court decision. Contrary to many newspaper accounts, he delivered it in a good-natured fashion.

FRANKLIN D. ROOSEVELT: THE HORSE-AND-BUGGY DEFINITION OF INTERSTATE COMMERCE*

THE PRESIDENT: What is the news?
Q. (*Francis Stephenson*) That's what we want.

* Reprinted from Franklin D. Roosevelt, *Public Papers and Addresses* (New York: Random House, 1938), 1935 volume, pp. 200–221 by permission.

THE PRESIDENT: Have you any questions to ask?
Q. What did you do yesterday outside of seeing Mr. Richberg?
THE PRESIDENT: I saw lots of people. I telephoned to a lot more, and I am continuing to do it.

Q. Do you care to comment any on the N.R.A.?

THE PRESIDENT: Well, Steve, if you insist. That's an awful thing to put up to a fellow at this hour of the morning just out of bed. Suppose we make this background and take some time because it is an awfully big subject to cover, and it is just possible that one or two of you may not have read the whole twenty-eight or twenty-nine pages of the Supreme Court decision.

I have been a good deal impressed by—what shall I call it?—the rather pathetic appeals that I have had from all around the country to do something. They are very sincere as showing faith in the Government. They are so sincere that you feel in reading them—and so far there have been somewhere between two and three thousand by letter and telegram and I haven't seen this morning's mail yet—so sincere that you feel the country is beginning to realize that something in the long run has to be done. And they are all hoping that something will be done right away.

I think probably the best way to illustrate it is to read you just a few telegrams that came out of this huge pile. They are all from business men, every one. I took out only the telegrams from business men. And they illustrate pretty well that the information that they have received since Monday through the press and through the radio has failed to explain to them the implications of the Supreme Court's decision. In other words, they are groping, and they have not yet had information from either the press or the radio or from me, which would put this situation in plain, lay language.

Well, for instance, here is one from Indiana. A State association of small—well, they are drug-store people. They start off: "We commend you for what you have done to protect the small business man from ruthless destructive trade practices. We hope you will continue your sincere efforts to the end that Constitutional legislation be enacted that will save the small business man from eventual extinction."

. . . Here is one from Galveston, Texas: "We feel that some law meeting the objections of the Supreme Court should be passed immediately to take the place of N.R.A. If this cannot be done by Federal law then think you should urge all States to pass laws to take care of this." That is another suggestion. That is the forty-eight-States man. . . . And so forth and so on.

I suppose there are several thousand along the same line, mainly from business men.

Now, coming down to the decision itself. What are the implications? For the benefit of those of you who haven't read it through I think I can put it this way: the implications of this decision are much more important than almost certainly any decision of my lifetime or yours, more important than any decision probably since the Dred Scott case, because they bring the country as a whole up against a very practical question. That is in spite of what one gentleman said in the paper this morning, that I resented the

decision. Nobody resents a Supreme Court decision. You can deplore a Supreme Court decision, and you can point out the effect of it. You can call the attention of the country to what the implications are as to the future, what the results of that decision are if future decisions follow this decision. . . .

Since 1885 the Court in various decisions has enlarged on the definition of interstate commerce —railroad cases, coal cases and so forth and so on. It was clearly the opinion of the Congress before this decision and the opinion of various attorneys-general, regardless of party, that the words "interstate commerce" applied not only to an actual shipment of goods but also to a great many other things that affected interstate commerce. . . .

The whole tendency over these years has been to view the interstate commerce clause in the light of present-day civilization. The country was in the horse-and-buggy age when that clause was written and if you go back to the debates on the Federal Constitution you will find in 1787 that one of the impelling motives for putting in that clause was this: There wasn't much interstate commerce at all—probably 80 or 90 percent of the human beings in the thirteen original States were completely self-supporting within their own communities. . . .

They had in those days no problems relating to employment. They had no problems relating to the earning capacity of people—what the man in Massachusetts earned, what his buying power was. Nobody had ever thought of what the wages were or the buying capacity in the slave-holding States of the South. There were no social questions in those days. The question of health on a national basis had never been discussed. The question of fair business practices had never been discussed. The word was unknown in the vocabulary of the Founding Fathers. The ethics of the period were very different from what they are today. If one man could skin a fellow and get away with it, why, that was all right.

In other words, the whole picture was a different one when the interstate commerce clause was put into the Constitution from what it is now. Since that time, because of the improvement in transportation, because of the fact that, as we know, what happens in one State has a good deal of influence on the people in another State, we have developed an entirely different philosophy.

The prosperity of the farmer does have an effect today on the manufacturer in Pittsburgh. The prosperity of the clothing worker in the city of New York has an effect on the prosperity of the farmer in Wisconsin, and so it goes. We are interdependent—we are tied in together. And the hope has been that we could, through a period of years, interpret the interstate commerce clause of the Constitution in the light of these new things that have come to the country. It has been our hope that under the interstate commerce clause we could recognize by legislation and by judicial decision that a harmful practice in one section of the country could be prevented on the theory that it was doing harm to another section of the country. That was why the Congress for a good many years, and most lawyers, have had the thought that in drafting legislation we could depend on an interpretation that would enlarge the Constitutional meaning of interstate commerce to include not only those matters of direct interstate commerce, but also those matters which indirectly affect interstate commerce.

The implication, largely because of what we call obiter dicta in this opinion, the implication of this opinion is that we have gone back, that the Supreme Court will no longer take into consideration anything that indirectly may affect interstate commerce. That hereafter they will decide the only thing in interstate commerce over which they can permit the exercise of Federal jurisdiction is goods in transit plus, perhaps, a very small number of transactions which would directly affect goods in transit.

Furthermore, they say on page 19, "(1) Were these transactions 'in' interstate commerce? Much is made of the fact that almost all the poultry coming to New York is sent there from other States" . . . "When defendants had made their purchases, whether at the West Washington Market in New York City or at the railroad terminals serving the City, or elsewhere, the poultry was trucked to their slaughter houses in Brooklyn for local disposition. The interstate transactions in relation to that poultry then ended."

Then to come to the next point, they take one very interesting stand; first they talk about necessary and well-established distinctions between the direct and indirect effects. They quote a number of cases and finally come down to the quotation from *Industrial Association vs. United States* at the top of page 23: "The alleged conspiracy and the acts here complained of, spent their intended and direct force upon a local situation—for building is as essentially local as mining, manufacturing or growing crops—and if, by a resulting diminution of the commercial demand, interstate trade was curtailed either generally or in specific instances, that was a fortuitous consequence so remote and indirectly as plainly to cause it to fall outside the reach of the Sherman Act."

Now that is interesting because the implication is this: We have in this country about five major human activities. One is transportation and that is not listed here.

The other four are: first, construction. I suppose the theory is that the building, even though the materials come from other States and none of the materials come from the locality of the building, that the building is part of the land and therefore that nothing entering into the erection of that building can have anything to do with the interstate commerce clause of the Constitution.

The next, the third large occupation, is mining—that is to say the taking of coal, oil or copper or anything else out of the ground. The implication there is that no matter where the coal or oil or copper goes it cannot be considered to have any relationship to interstate commerce because it came out of one place. It was a part of a place or locus.

Another great occupation is manufacturing. The implication is that if I manufacture at Hyde Park, New York, let us say, a national article such as a national brand of tooth paste or a national brand of automobiles while I only sell a few tubes of tooth paste or four or five cars in the place of manufacture at Hyde Park, and sell the rest in interstate commerce, the actual manufacturing itself seems to be so closely tied to the actual factory, that it does not make any difference where the goods go and therefore the interstate commerce clause of the Constitution cannot apply to any of the elements of the manufacturing at that place, either to materials that may come from other States, to the working conditions that obtain in the factory, to the wages paid or to the unfair practices that I as a manufacturer may be engaged in.

An then finally you have a fifth great occupation of human life—the growing of crops. It evidently does not make any difference, after I grow my wheat, whether it is put in an elevator in a different State, perhaps to be commingled with other wheat and sold in Liverpool, or New York or Germany or in any other State of the Union—it does not make any difference. The fact is that the wheat was grown in one place, and therefore the growing of crops cannot be considered in any shape, manner or form as coming under the interstate commerce clause of the Constitution. Perhaps wheat actually in transit under this decision may come under it. But it could not if it were in storage, for example in a bin, because there it would be tied to a definite locality.

And so it does bring us up rather squarely as to the big issue in the country and as to how we are going to solve it. The big issue is this: Does this decision mean that the United States Government has no control over any national economic problem?

The simple example is crop adjustment. Are we going to take the hands of the Federal Government completely off any effort to adjust the growing of national crops, and go right straight back to the old principle that every farmer is a lord of his own farm and can do anything he wants, raise anything, any old time, in any quantity, and sell any time he wants? You and I know perfectly well that if we completely abandon crop control—I don't care whether it is the present method or, let us say, the McNary-Haugen method, because, after all, that is a Federal method, too—if we are to abandon Federal relationship to any national crop, we shall again have thirty-six-cent wheat. You can't stop it. Under present world conditions we will have five-cent cotton. That is obvious.

And then you come down to the next series of things—manufacturing. We have tried to improve the economic conditions of certain forms of manufacturing. I am not talking about the social conditions now. I am talking about the economic conditions, giving to manufacturers a chance to eliminate things that we have nationally concluded are not fair. For example, the chain stores going into little communities or big communities all over the country and starting a system of loss leaders. Of course anybody who does his own marketing, and all you ladies of the press will appreciate this, knows perfectly well that where there is the loss-leader system and you are trying to get along on a budget, you are going to look into the chain-store window and see what the loss leader is each day. You may get a can of peas for fourteen cents instead of eighteen cents; naturally you wait and buy the loss leader. The chain store can afford to put out loss leaders; but the independent grocery store cannot.

A number of States—and here we come down to the last question—have attempted to take away the privileges or the advantages that come to very large nationwide businesses, by imposing special taxes on chain stores, but only a few States have succeeded in doing it. And that is a very good illustration of the difficulty of correcting economic conditions by forty-eight separate actions.

We attempted to do it in the codes by getting industry itself to formulate codes that would eliminate loss leaders. They did, and as a result the wave of bankruptcies of small stores which was under way throughout the country two years ago was stopped. And the volume of telegrams that has come in today leads one to believe that they again face, a great many of them, bankruptcies, or at least they think they do.

The other example is that of a department store which puts in a book department and sells all the latest detective stories that retail ordinarily at $1.50—I ought to know because I read them— for ninety cents. Up to the time that their code went through, bankruptcies of small book stores throughout the country where these practices were engaged in were increasing. They were being put out of business because they could not afford to sell $1.50 books for ninety cents. The big department stores could afford to do it, because people who went into that department to save sixty cents on a detective story undoubtedly bought a good many other things in that department store, and the store was able to make up the loss.

Now all that seems to be "out of the window." We made a very sincere effort to eliminate things that were called unfair trade practices not only because they were hurting little fellows, but also because they were giving advantages to people with lots of capital or with nationwide systems— advantages over smaller men or local men. It seemed to be going pretty well. It was done under the general theory that, because these goods came from every part of the United States, there was a rather direct implication that they affected the internal commerce of the United States as a whole, and therefore came under the interstate commerce clause.

Then we come down to the mines. There have been a number of cases about mines, but the implication in this quotation is that mines and mining do not come under interstate commerce. It is purely a local thing no matter where the copper or the oil or coal goes. It is rather interesting, I think, that there are former decisions of the Supreme Court which have held much more liberally in labor cases, in mining cases where people were trying to get an injunction against labor. In those cases the Supreme Court has tended to approve mining injunctions on the ground that the coal was going to go into interstate commerce.

This case, however, seems to be a direct reversal in saying that where you try to improve the wages and hours of miners, the coal suddenly becomes a purely local intrastate matter and you can't do anything about it. Of course, here the shoe is on the other foot.

Those are the important human occupations affected by this decision, the mining and manufacturing and growing of crops—the important ones.

Well, what does it do? It seems to me it brings—oh, I suppose you will want to say an issue. I accept the word "issue" on one condition; and that is that you make it very clear that it is not a partisan issue. It is infinitely deeper than any partisan issue; it is a national issue. Yes, and the issue is this—going back to these telegrams that I have been reading to you: Is the United States going to decide, are the people of this country going to decide that their Federal Government shall in the future have no right under any implied power or any court-approved power to enter into a solution of a national economic problem, but that that national economic problem must be decided only by the States?

The other part of it is this: Shall we view our social problems—and in that I include employment of all kinds—shall we view them from the same point of view or not; that the Federal Government has no right under this or following opinions to take any part in trying to better national social conditions? Now that is flat and that is simple!

If we accept the point of view that under no interpretation of the Constitution can the Federal Government deal with construction matters, mining matters (which means everything that comes out of the ground), manufacturing matters or agricultural matters, but that they must be left wholly to the States, the Federal Government must abandon any legislation. Thus we go back automatically to the fact that there will be not merely thirteen Governments as there were in 1789 at a time where none of these questions existed in the country—but we will go back to a Government of forty-eight States.

Or we can go ahead with every possible effort to make national decisions based on the fact that forty-eight sovereignties cannot agree quickly enough or practically enough on any solution for a national economic problem or a national social problem.

When I was in Albany I had the desire of getting through the Legislature on two or three occasions certain bills relating to the improvement of factory conditions and the improvement of labor conditions, and people came to me and said, "If those bills go through we are going to move into Pennsylvania."

That gave to the Chief Executive of one State serious concern. Should he force the legislation and let these factories move out of this State into a State that didn't have any restrictions and didn't have nearly as advanced social legislation; or should he go in and leave certain evils just as they were? In other words, by the returning of all these powers exclusively to the States you will unavoidably develop sectionalism. Just imagine what will happen in the case of the cotton textile industry—the problem of the differential in wage between New England and the South. Less than two years ago that differential was more than five dollars a week in favor of the South. Under the code system it has been cut to two and a half dollars; and in all human probability if we had gone on under code methods, the differential would gradually have been cut still further. They were actually working on an additional cut in the labor differential in the cotton textile industry. That, of course, we have had to stop.

We come down, in passing, to the question of whether they can now live up to these codes. We hope so—surely. Everybody hopes that the wage agreements and codes will be lived up to, and every effort should be made to have people in every industry live up to the codes. I sincerely hope that everybody will live up to them.

On the other hand, as President, naturally, I have to think of what is going to happen to the country if people, some people, do not live up to them. You go back to the same old 90 percent and 10 percent we have talked about so often. There are, let's say, 100 of us in this room who are making cotton textiles. Each one owns a mill and out of the 100 there are three or four, that is all, who see an advantage to be gained—an immediate advantage of quick profit. So they cut their wages, and increase their hours, and go ahead with the stretch-out system beyond the code allowance. What is going to happen to us? . . .

You and I know human nature. Fundamentally it comes down to this. In the long run can voluntary processes on the part of business bring about the same practical results that were attained under N.R.A.? I mean the good results. Of course there have been some bad ones. But I mean the good results. Can it be done by voluntary action on the part of business? Can we go ahead as a Nation with the beautiful theory, let us say, of some of the press, "At last the rule of Christ is restored. Business can do anything it wants and business is going to live up to the golden rule so marvelously that all of our troubles are ended." It is a school of thought that is so delightful in its naïveté.

And so we are facing a very, very great national non-partisan issue. We have got to decide one way or the other. I don't mean this summer or winter or next fall, but over a period, perhaps, of five years or ten years we have got to decide: whether we are going to relegate to the forty-eight States practically all control over economic conditions—not only State economic conditions but national economic conditions; and along with that whether we are going to relegate to the States all control over social and working conditions throughout the country regardless of whether those conditions have a very definite significance and effect in other States outside of the individual States. That is one side of the picture. The other side of the picture is whether in some way we are going to turn over or restore to—whichever way you choose to put it—turn over or restore to the Federal Government the powers which exist in the national Governments of every other Nation in the world to enact and administer laws that have a bearing on, and general control over, national economic problems and national social problems.

That actually is the biggest question that has come before this country outside of time of war, and it has to be decided. And, as I say, it may take five years or ten years.

This N.R.A. decision—if you accept the obiter dicta and all the phraseology of it—seems to be squarely on the side of restoring to the States forty-eight different controls over national economic and social problems. This is not a criticism of the Supreme Court's decision; it is merely pointing out the implications of it.

In some ways it may be the best thing that has happened to this country for a long time that such a decision has come from the Supreme Court, because it clarifies the issue. If the press and the radio of this country can make that issue perfectly clear, it will be doing a very great service. The telegrams that I have been reading to you, suggesting every kind of method of overcoming the decision, will not continue to come in, because all except a very few of them suggest remedies which are wholly outside of the opinion of the Supreme Court. In other words, they are in violation of that opinion—nine suggested remedies out of ten are in violation of the strict interpretation of that opinion.

I think it is perfectly proper to say further that the implications of this decision could, if carried to their logical conclusion, strip the Federal Government of a great many other powers. . . .

Your next implication relates to certain things that we believe are within the Federal power. They have not been definitely outlawed by this decision; but the decision raises a very great question about them. The Securities Act of 1933, for example, was intended to prevent nationally the issuing of securities to the investing or speculating public under false pretenses. The Act required that, through a central Federal organization, securities that were proposed to be issued should have the full truth stated about them.

That is all there was to it—it was a Truth in Securities Act and it has been working very well. However, securities, I suppose, like a crop or like manufactured goods, can be held to be issued in one place and bought by the public in one place, and are therefore wholly intrastate.

It does not make any difference whether the securities afterward go into forty-eight States or not. The issuance and buying in one State, like a crop or a factory product, have no character of interstate commerce about them under this decision.

In the same way the decision raises a question with respect to the Stock Exchange Act. After all, a stock exchange is just a building in one place—in one city. There are a good many of them scattered throughout the country. They sell various forms of securities, but each one is attached to the ground like wheat or cotton—like coal or anything else. The decision raises a question about that.

Then you come to the A.A.A. itself. I have discussed that. The question is raised by this decision as to whether the Federal Government has any constitutional right to do anything about any crop in the United States; and it suggests by implication that forty-eight States should each have their own crop laws.

You see the implications of the decision. That is why I say it is one of the most important decisions ever rendered in this country. And the issue is not going to be a partisan issue for a minute. The issue is going to be whether we go one way or the other. Don't call it right or left; that is just first-year high-school language, just about. It is not right or left—it is a question for national decision on a very important problem of Government. We are the only Nation in the world that has not solved that problem. We thought we were solving it, and now it has been thrown right straight in our faces. We have been relegated to the horse-and-buggy definition of interstate commerce. . . .

Neither Roosevelt's most enthusiastic supporters nor his most dire critics had much notion early in the New Deal what the outcome of the new experiences would be by the 1940's and thereafter. In later years, the new economic policies were to be summed up in the popular mind by the term "Keynesian." How these policies developed and what they were has been explained in simple language by an economist, John Kenneth Galbraith.

JOHN KENNETH GALBRAITH: THE NEW RELATIONSHIP OF THE STATE TO THE ECONOMY*

. . . One can only suppose that in 1929 the fates undertook, after great deliberation, to shake the confidence of the people of the United States in their economy. Nothing could have been more ingeniously or more elaborately designed to achieve this result. There was the shock effect—the sudden dramatic collapse in the stock-market values with which the lives and fortunes of thousands of innocents, who only then became aware of their innocence, had become entwined. This was followed by the inexorable decline in output, values and employment which, in a little more than two years, cut the value of national production almost in half and left twelve million workers—ten and a half million more than in 1929—without jobs and mostly without reliable means of support. Those who still had jobs lived in the penetrating fear that their turn would be next. Meanwhile hundreds of thousands of well-to-do citizens either made a sudden and irretrievable descent into poverty or dwelt in the cold fear that they soon would. It would have added to the security of the country if businessmen and bankers had escaped the debacle. But their well-publicized plight suggested, all too plainly, that they too had no formula for contending with capitalism when the latter was on shipwreck tack. The broken banker was as commonplace a figure in the news as the unemployed worker, and a much less reassuring one. The economy was the impartial destroyer of all.

When there was nothing else to hope for, it could still be hoped that the depression would be temporary. A rhythm of good times and bad was the minimum promise of the competitive model. To this shaky standard the defenders of the system repaired in droves. Then, the most malicious act of all, the depression was made to last ten years. The very notion that depressions in the United States were self-correcting—that there were corners that would be turned—became a national jest. As if to sharpen the point, a

---

* Reprinted from John Kenneth Galbraith, *American Capitalism, The Concept of Countervailing Power* (Revised Edition; Boston: Houghton, Mifflin Company, 1956), pp. 64–68, 76–83 by permission.

modest recovery prior to the summer of 1937, which however had left between seven and eight million still unemployed, was followed by a slump in production that was even sharper than the one following 1929. The Great Depression of the thirties never came to an end. It merely disappeared in the great mobilization of the forties. For a whole generation it became the normal aspect of peacetime life in the United States—the thing to be both feared and expected.

Measured by its continuing imprint on actions and attitudes, the depression clearly stands with the Civil War as one of the two most important events in American history since the Revolution. For the great majority of Americans World War II, by contrast, was an almost casual and pleasant experience. Several million found jobs who had doubted whether they might ever find jobs again. Hundreds of thousands of others escaped the routines of middle-class employments, their boredom with which they had concealed even from themselves. Men and women who had never supposed that society would entrust them with responsibility found themselves discharging important tasks with a competence of which they alone had been previously aware. Only a minority experienced the nagging homesickness, the fear, the physical suffering and the mutilation and death which is the less pleasant destiny of the fighting soldier in wartime. Because they were a minority the war left no lasting imprint. The depression which afflicted a great majority of the people did.

The depression not only contributed deeply to the insecurity with which Americans viewed their economy. It also had an important bearing on economic behavior. In the years following World War II the fear of a recurrence of depression was without question a dominant factor in the calculations of a large proportion of all businessmen. The convention, so scrupulously observed by the business community, which bans the public expression of fear of economic collapse lest to express fear be to invite the fact, concealed much of this alarm. Nonetheless, when *Fortune* magazine in 1946 asked some 15,000 leading business executives in confidence whether they expected an "extended major depression with large-scale unemployment in the next ten years"—a phrasing that was not designed to minimize the scope of the contemplated disaster—fifty-eight per cent of those replying said they did. Of the remainder only twenty-eight per cent said they did not.[1] In these same years labor was preoccupied with measures to maintain the level of employment and farmers with support prices that would provide shelter in a slump. Even the radicals had long ceased to talk about the inequality or exploitation under capitalism or its "inherent contradictions." They stressed only the utter unreliability of its performance.

These attitudes have since changed. With prosperity and the passage of time the fear of depression has been somewhat dulled. In 1949 and again in 1954 there were minor setbacks, which were first viewed as the beginning of a new disaster but from which there was a prompt recovery. These provided more reassurance. The convention which requires businessmen and politicians who are in office to say that all will always be well—that at any time prosperity is assured—has brought a rich yield of optimism. This too has had an effect.

It has been the custom of economists to take people, and their attitudes, aspirations, hopes and fears, as given and much the same from one generation to the next. It seems certain that changes in these attitudes are of deep importance. . . .

II

By the mid-thirties, the layman—whether worker, businessman, farmer or unemployed—had undoubtedly reached his own conclusions concerning American capitalism. Asked were its norm an equilibrium of stable prices and full employment, the conclusion of the competitive model, he would have recommended his interrogator to the care of a good doctor. But, as ideas to be influential need the support of experience, so experience needs interpretation by ideas. Only then does it become the basis for generalization, for a theory. The Great Depression might, conceivably, have remained the great accident if ideas had not again intervened. These, in their mature form, made depression, or its counterpart inflation, the normal behavior pattern of uninhibited and unmanaged capitalism. While this discouraging analysis carried with it a remedy —a remedy that was received with profound enthusiasm by many economists and much of the public at large—the remedy was unorthodox and disturbing. It is only partial comfort for a patient, who is being told he is chronically ill, to learn that there are violent and painful cures for his disease.

The ideas which interpreted the depression, and which warned that depression or inflation might be as much a part of the free-enterprise destiny as stable full employment, were those of John Maynard Keynes. A case could easily be made by those who make such cases, that his were the most influential social ideas of the first half of the century. A proper distribution of emphasis as between the role of ideas and the role of action might attribute more influence on modern economic history to Keynes than to Roosevelt. Certainly his final book, *The General Theory of Employment, Interest and Money,* shaped the course of events as only the books of three earlier economists—Smith's *Wealth of Nations,* Ricardo's *Principles of Political Economy* and Marx's *Capital*—have done. . . .

The time has now come to consider the politi-

---

[1] *Fortune,* February 1947, p. 34. The rest declined to say.

cal consequences of Keynes for, more than any man of the century, he reformulated attitudes on the agitated question of the relation of the state to the economy.

The United States, in the thirties, was urgently in need of a new theory of the relation of government to economic life. The American political parties had long been in the habit of assuming full responsibility for economic well-being and of campaigning with promises of prosperity for all. The inconsistency of these promises, which Republicans and Democrats had made with equal fervor, with the role assigned to the state by the competitive model was untroublesome so long as there was reasonable prosperity in any event. It was bound to be troublesome to a party which was forced to contend with a serious depression. The New Deal came to power on the usual promises and with little clearer view than predecessor administrations of how the government might intervene to bring prosperity.

It was inevitable that the attention of liberals in a liberal administration would be directed toward the structure of the economy. The preconceptions of the competitive model guided their thinking in this direction. Implicit in the rise of big business was the possibility that it had created a structure that departed so far from the competitive model that it could not work. Two courses of action were open. The incentives which, under the competitive model, were presumed to guide businessmen to a socially desirable behavior could be replaced by some kind of central guidance which would get the desired results. Perhaps businessmen could be brought together under the aegis of government and be told, or made to agree, to increase employment and stabilize wages and prices. Or, alternatively, perhaps private incentives could be rehabilitated by remaking business enterprise so that it conformed more closely to the preconceptions of the model.

Both enterprises involved the most serious difficulties. The first, which was given a trial run in the NRA, suffered from a grievous unclarity of both methods and goals. The self-interest of the businessman dictated the particular low level of employment he was offering and investment he was making in 1933. This simple fact was not altered by bringing him together with other businessmen under the supervision of a Code Authority. It seems improbable that much would have been accomplished had he been ordered directly by government to increase employment and investment outlays at his own cost and contrary to his own assessment of interest.

To remake the economy in accordance with the requirements of the competitive model was obviously a time-consuming enterprise. To take time out to break up large corporate units and re-establish the competition of the model was hardly in keeping with the temper of a country which found depression tiresome and which was not noted for its patience. To the extent that it was contemplated in the later years of the New

Deal it was as a decidedly long-run reform. There remained in 1933 only the possibility of abandoning capitalism entirely. This was a project which raised the question of alternatives concerning which only a handful of Communists were in any way clear. It is hardly surprising that the early days of the New Deal were distinguished in American history for their foggy semanticism—for meaningless or incomprehensible talk about social planning, guided capitalism and industrial self-government. When stumped by a problem the American liberal rarely admits defeat. He takes the offensive with words.

It was Keynes who provided the escape from the dilemma—and the words. It would be hard, at first glance, to imagine a formula that was better designed for the American scene. The depression was overwhelmingly the important problem. The notion of an excess of savings or a deficiency of investment[10] defined the nature of the government intervention. By public borrowing or expenditure, or the appropriate changes in taxation, the government could make up for the deficiency in private spending. By so doing it could return the economy to full employment and keep it there. To the naked eye, the scope of private business decision remained as before. General Motors still decided what cars to produce, what prices to charge, how to advertise and sell them, when to build a new assembly plant and how many workers to employ. It merely sold more cars because employees on public works projects became customers for secondhand Chevrolets, their foremen for new ones and the contractor for a Buick.

The government had always taxed: to reduce taxes and so release income for spending or, perhaps, to adjust taxes to fall more heavily on income that was likely to end up as redundant saving involved no radical departure. The government had always spent. To spend for the express purpose of absorbing savings and raising the level of output and employment in the economy, if novel, was far from revolutionary. The government borrowed for at least part of this expenditure. But the debt so created was the counterpart of private debt that would have been created had private investment absorbed the excess of savings. In any case one strong wing of the Keynesian thought assumed (and the assumption has not yet been entirely abandoned) that periods of unemployment and of inflation would alternate at convenient intervals. Since the formula for periods of inflation seemed to be the simple obverse of that for unemployment—higher taxes, especially on income to be spent, diminished public spending and a budget surplus—the debts of one period would be liquidated by the excess revenues of the next. The budget would be

---

[10] More awkwardly but more accurately, of efforts to save and intentions to invest. By frustrating these efforts and intentions, changes in total output keep savings and investment as Keynes defines them always equal.

balanced in accordance with all the canons of fiscal orthodoxy. It was only necessary that a little time elapse.

V

Liberals almost spontaneously adopted the Keynesian formula. They were also puzzled by the reluctance of conservatives, especially businessmen, to embrace it. Here was protection from the overwhelming threat of depression, the only threat of potentially revolutionary proportions seemingly faced by capitalism. The businessman remained undisturbed in his prerogatives as an owner and manager and had the promise of better business to boot. What could he lose?

With time there has been some explicit and a great deal of implicit acceptance of the Keynesian formula by American businessmen. However, as often happens, it encountered the sharp cleavage which exists in our attitude toward technological and social change. If a man seeks to design a better mousetrap he is the soul of enterprise; if he seeks to design a better society he is a crackpot. For those who mistrust social change it was not an argument that profits might be increased, even that disaster might be avoided. They were opposed to change and they could not be bought. They were men of principle.

There were also more positive grounds for business opposition to Keynes than liberals have been inclined to suppose. The Keynesian system, though it perhaps involved a less than revolutionary change in the relation of the government to the economy, implied, nonetheless, an important one. For a doctrine that excluded government it substituted one that made government indispensable. Keynes was sufficiently unpalatable when he made depression and inflation not adventitious or war-induced misfortunes but normal occurrences. He went on to make government the indispensable partner of business. In failing to recognize the prestige that goes with power and decision-making in American life, American liberals failed to recognize that, for some businessmen, the Keynesian remedy was at least as damaging as the depression it presumed to eliminate. Even though the businessman might profit in a narrow pecuniary sense from the new role of government there was no chance that his prestige would survive intact. Where, in economic life, people had previously looked upon business decisions as the ones that had shaped their destiny, now they would have regard for government decisions as well, or instead. Those of an Assistant Secretary of the Treasury on interest rates were now of more importance than those of any banker. Those of a regional administrator of public works on investment attained a significance greater than those of a corporation president. To share the prestige of decision-making is to lose prestige. The Keynesian remedies thus represented an assault on a valued possession. Those who were losers could hardly be expected to embrace the ideas that brought this loss. Much of their dissatisfaction was expressed in personal terms—it was directed against the Administration and against the public servants who implemented the new ideas. But a good deal was directed at Keynes. His American followers, taking at face value our conventional disavowal of any interest in power, failed to understand the discontent over its impairment.

The Keynesian system also, though unobtrusively, opened the way for a large expansion of government services and activities. This was the result of a new and very important concept of social waste which followed in its train. If the normal tendency of the economy is toward full employment, then the use of labor and other economic resources by government is at the expense of their use by the private economy. Dams and post offices are built at the cost of private consumption or investment. If there is full employment in the first place, something must be given up. But if employment is chronic, the dams and post offices require no sacrifice of private production or consumption. The labor, plants and materials that are used would otherwise have been unemployed. They are wasted if someone does not employ them. Again ideas had produced a topsy-turvy world. Government spending, long the mark of profligacy, was now sanctioned in the sacred name of avoiding waste. It was inevitable also that wild men would draw from this paradox, and the substantial truths on which it is built, a sanction for any and all expenditures at any and all times. Here was further discomfort for the conservative.

The Keynesian ideas had other new, heterodox and even threatening corollaries. Thrift, an ancient and once an absolute virtue, was brought into question; it suffered from the guilt of association with redundant saving and depression. A doctrine which cast doubt on so conventional a good was bound to be suspect. We commonly bring a deep theological conviction to the defense of our chosen principles. Those who dissent are not wrong, they are evil. Nothing could better prove that a man was secretly in the service of the devil or communism than that he should raise his voice against thrift.

Finally the new doctrine raised uncomfortable questions concerning both income distribution and profits. Say's Law provided a highly satisfactory defense of incomes and profits even when these were generous. They might not be deserved but, since they were either spent or saved and promptly invested, they did not impair the functioning of the economy. On the contrary they benefited it. The pressure to consume is least urgent on high personal incomes and high profits; there is the greatest chance of saving from such income and, when invested, this provides the factories, machinery, utilities and motive power by which future production is increased.

Once saving and the certainty of its utilization in investment became suspect, this defense of high personal incomes and high profits dissolved. More than that, such income became subject to a new attack. If these were the incomes whence the most saving came, it was by these that depressions were caused. By leveling off high incomes and profits one could reduce the amount of savings that had to be offset by investment at full employment. This would promote economic stability.

In the decade following World War II business profits were exceedingly handsome—several times what they were before or even during the war. The question of the fairness of these profits and the resulting personal incomes—the question of whether someone was getting more than he deserved—was hardly raised. This was the ancient objection to high profits but it is so no longer.

Envy in our time is confined to the contemplation of the privileges or possessions of others of nearly equal income. The postwar attack on profits, as avowed, was almost exclusively on their alleged contribution to instability. It was widely asserted that high profits were the feature of the boom which, if uncurbed, would cause the bust. This also was the handiwork of Keynes.

The disagreements arising out of Keynes' proposals should not be magnified. He was not a divisive figure; on the contrary his work was solidly in the Anglo-American tradition of compromise which seeks progress by reconciling the maximum number of conflicts of interest. But it is also easy to see how his formula, and the speed with which it was accepted, provided its own ground for uneasiness. . . .

CHAPTER TWENTY-ONE

ROOSEVELT:
FROM ISOLATIONISM
TO THE UNITED NATIONS

One of the most sudden and profound revolutions in American thinking came between 1937 and 1945 when the United States, with the overwhelming approval of the American people, abandoned its deep-seated isolationism and assumed leadership in establishing a new international organization, the United Nations, to maintain the peace through collective security. It was the catalyst of Nazi and Japanese aggression that wrought the change; unfolding Russian policies in the years beginning with 1945 caused it to take directions unforeseen earlier.

This remarkable change from isolationism to collective security is easily obscured by the hectic events in which it took place: the rise of Hitler and outbreak of war in Europe, the bitter debate between isolationists and interventionists, the events leading up to Pearl Harbor, and the conduct of a grueling global war. In these selections, the emphasis is not upon these events, vital as they were, but upon the policy question of collective security put back into its contemporary setting.

The United States, which had rallied to President Wilson's challenge to "make the world safe for democracy," had, in an almost accidental fashion, failed in the 1920's to go into the League of Nations. The League floundered and undoubtedly would have floundered even if the United States had been a full member. As it was, most Americans, by the 1930's, felt that the League was a failure, and that the true interests of the United States required the nation to remain isolated from world politics. In actual fact, the United States was not functioning much differently from the other great powers, placing its internal problems and national interests first but also making its weight felt in international affairs.

By 1937, crises were developing both in Europe where Hitler was becoming dominant and in Asia where Japan was plunging into China. President Roosevelt, a strong leader in foreign policy, was deeply committed to keeping the United States out of war. He was therefore looking for some plan which would further the cause of world peace. It was at this point, in October, 1937, that he delivered his famous speech in which he suggested the possibility of quarantining an aggressor. Dorothy Borg's analysis of it (from which some of the supporting evidence has been deleted) indicated the uncertain way in which the nation began to move toward the catastrophe of World War II.

DOROTHY BORG: NOTES ON ROOSEVELT'S "QUARANTINE" SPEECH*

The "quarantine" speech which President Roosevelt made at Chicago on October 5, 1937, is generally assumed to have been a landmark in our foreign policy, showing the point at which the President made a definite decision to take a strong stand against the Axis Powers. It is also widely supposed that, because of evidence at every hand of the country's hostility to the speech, Mr. Roosevelt, quite justifiably, felt compelled to relinquish his determination to deal firmly with the totalitarian states. Yet the further one examines these assumptions, the more they seem to invite rethinking.

I

Turning to the speech itself, the most popular interpretations are that the President was announcing that he had decided: to reverse his foreign policy, abandoning the isolationism of our neutrality legislation for a Wilsonian type of collective security; or to use sanctions against Japan to stop the hostilities in China; or to initiate forthwith a program for the application of sanctions against future aggressors—meaning the Axis Powers. However, a consideration of the events surrounding the speech, and of its text, suggests that the President was probably only engaging in a groping and intermittent effort, which he had been making for some time to find some sort of a plan which would avert war between the dictatorships and the democracies. If so, the "quarantine" speech should not be regarded as an indication that, in the autumn of 1937, Mr. Roosevelt resolved to embark upon some strong and specific policy toward the Axis countries but rather as indicating that he was still pursuing a variety of nebulous schemes for warding off catastrophe.

In order to discuss further both the popular interpretations of the speech and the interpretation just advanced, it is necessary first to look at the two areas where the material lies which make more detailed discussion possible: the President's search for a program to avoid war and the story of the writing of the Chicago address.

As the international crisis deepened in the 1930's, Mr. Roosevelt was intensely concerned over the aggression of the Axis nations. In keeping with a pattern he tended to follow almost instinctively, he seems to have felt that, if he advanced notions of his own about possible means of meeting the crisis, he might stimulate others to build on his suggestions until a solution was found. His first great effort to dramatize the concept of searching for a program to stabilize the world situation was made in connection with the Buenos Aires Conference of 1936. It will be recalled that this conference was convened at his suggestion to strengthen the Inter-American peace system. However, both the President and Secretary Hull proclaimed over and over again that the purpose of the conference was not just to work out a scheme for the maintenance of peace in the Americas but to evolve a program, which, speaking in general terms, could be copied by the rest of the world. And it was precisely to draw the attention of as many people as possible to the universal significance of the proceedings at Buenos Aires that Mr. Roosevelt made his own dramatic trip to the conference.

Two features of the developments at Buenos Aires have a special significance in connection with later efforts to formulate a program to deal with the problem of war and peace.[1] One was the over-all character of the Buenos Aires agreements. The sixty-seven agreements arrived at by the Conference constituted a comprehensive plan divorced from any commitments to sanctions. They emphasized the value of a so-called constructive approach to peace, by which was meant an attempt to settle the underlying causes of friction that give rise to wars. They also emphasized the need to develop machinery to adjust disputes by peaceful means or, if this proved impossible, to limit hostilities once they occurred.

The second significant factor was the discussion about plans for organizing, in wartime, the countries that were not parties to the dispute. One

---

* Reprinted from Dorothy Borg, "Notes on Roosevelt's 'Quarantine' Speech," *Political Science Quarterly*, LXXII (September, 1957), 405–13, 416–17, 418–23, 424–26, 427–28, 430–33 by permission.

[1] Stenographic report of the conference in *The Inter-American Conference for the Maintenance of Peace, Proceedings* (Buenos Aires, 1937); *Report of Delegation of the United States to the Inter-American Conference for the Maintenance of Peace* (Washington, 1937), Department of State Conference Series 33.

idea was that an arrangement should be made so that these nations would adopt a collective neutrality that went further than anything as yet embodied in the Inter-American peace system. This view was vigorously pushed by Secretary Hull in his famous Eight Pillars of Peace speech delivered at the outset of the Conference.[2] It was incorporated in the draft convention presented to the Conference by the United States Delegation; for the convention would have committed neutral American countries, in case of war between two or more American republics, to apply laws comparable to the neutrality legislation existing in the United States.[3] While the United States proposal was not adopted, the determination to develop the concept of collective neutrality in the Americas remained a fixed part of our policy.

Another idea was that there should be what, for lack of a better term, may be called a collective nonbelligerency. This concept became a center of discussion at Buenos Aires because the Central American nations introduced a draft treaty based on a plan, advanced by Uruguay during the First World War, for the creation by the American states of a moral front which would adopt measures, such as the severance of diplomatic relations, that were noncoercive but not neutral.[4] In the process of watering down the Central American draft the closeness of this type of a collective nonbelligerency and a common neutrality was underscored. The purpose of both was to have the nations, not parties to the conflict, form a community for their own protection and to influence the course of the hostilities. (It was thought that a collective neutrality could, if necessary, be manipulated to favor one side or the other, as was indeed done after the outbreak of war in Europe.)[5] Moreover both the ideas of collective neutrality and of collective nonbelligerency were regarded as preventive in that, if either were incorporated in an agreement, they would serve to deter would-be aggressors.

Following the Buenos Aires Conference, the President continued to look for a program to relieve the international tension, suggesting frequently that the nations of the world might get together to work out something comparable to the achievements reached at Buenos Aires. Secretary Hull spoke similarly, both men often stressing the noncoercive character of the Buenos Aires agreements. When, for example, Prime Minister King of Canada visited Washington in the spring of 1937, Mr. Hull told him that, in his estimation, the only way of stopping the drift toward war was for England to seek the coöperation of other European countries in developing a constructive and comprehensive scheme for the stabilization of peace like the Buenos Aires program.[6] The President himself discussed at length with Mr. King the possibility of calling an international conference to set up a new world organization which would seek to maintain peace by peaceful means rather than by economic or military sanctions.[7] He suggested that new methods of achieving peace be tried such as "going after the root causes of war" so as to establish a "collective security based on the removal of war causes." Also wars should be prevented or cured by "public opinion" not by "penalty". A few weeks later the President talked along similar lines to Norman Davis, who was about to leave on a mission to Europe, indicating that Mr. Davis might explore some of these ideas with European statesmen informally.[8]

At the same time the President was groping for other means of getting the dictatorships and the democracies to make a concerted effort to ensure peace. Even before the Buenos Aires Conference, Mr. Roosevelt had spoken to friends of the possibility of stopping the trend toward war by some dramatic action such as inviting the heads of the big European nations to a meeting on board a battleship at sea where they would evolve some plan for a "lasting peace" to be achieved without commitments to coercion.[9] Word of the President's scheme reached the *New York Times* which printed a front-page article under a streaming headline: "ROOSEVELT IF ELECTED MAY CALL KINGS, DICTATORSHIPS AND PRESIDENTS TO GREAT POWER CONFERENCE".[10]

The net result of all this talk of a program to resolve the existing crisis was that, by the

[2] *Peace and War: United States Foreign Policy, 1931–41* (Washington, 1943), p. 342; *The Memoirs of Cordell Hull* (New York, 1948), I, 498.

[3] *Documents on International Affairs, 1936* (London, 1937), p. 77.

[4] Martin, Percy Alvin, *Latin America and the War* (Baltimore, 1925), pp. 361 *et seq.*, 381. *Inter-American Conference for the Maintenance of Peace, Proceedings*, pp. 138, 221, 739.

[5] Bemis, Samuel Flagg, *The Latin American Policy of the United States* (New York, 1943), p. 287, chapter xxi. Welles, Sumner, *The Time for Decision* (New York, 1944), p. 204.

[6] The memorandum of this conversation was an unusually comprehensive statement of Mr. Hull's views and was sent to the President. See *Foreign Relations of the United States, 1937*, I, 641, and Hull, *Memoirs*, I, 546. Even after the outbreak of the Sino-Japanese war, Mr. Hull was urging Japan to join the United States in the leadership of a peace movement based on the Buenos Aires agreements. See *Foreign Relations of the United States: Japan, 1931–41*, p. 331.

[7] *F.D.R.: His Personal Letters, 1928–45* (New York, 1947), I, 664. Based on notes of their discussion written by Mr. King while talking with the President and shown to the latter.

[8] Memorandum by Mr. Davis on telephone conversation with the President on March 19. Davis files.

[9] Hull, *Memoirs*, I, 546.

[10] August 26, 1936, story by Arthur Krock.

spring of 1937, there were repercussions even in the European dictatorships. Mussolini, in a highly publicized interview, virtually invited the President to take the initiative in bringing the statesmen of the world together to settle some of the outstanding causes of tension.[11] Hitler was rumored to have said that he would attend a conference for the improvement of the international situation if Mr. Roosevelt convened it.[12]

Perhaps encouraged by signs of possible coöperation from the Axis nations, Mr. Roosevelt, in the spring and summer of 1937, tried to take some concrete steps toward a general international agreement that would make for peace.[13] Norman Davis, on his trip to Europe in May, had long conversations on this subject with various European statesmen, primarily British and French—conversations of which he kept detailed records that have turned up in his files.[14] Mr. Davis spoke first with Mr. Spinasse, then French Minister of National Economy, and with Anthony Eden. All agreed that a comprehensive program should be developed that would tackle the three most important sources of the growing international crisis: political and economic conditions and the race in armaments. It was assumed that the United States would have to take the initiative in starting such a program but that President Roosevelt would want to limit himself to economic and disarmament problems, leaving the European Powers to settle their political controversies among themselves. In the end it was agreed that some plan might be launched, probably by calling a large international conference, in a few months—possibly September.

When Mr. Davis approached Neville Chamberlain, the latter proved to be more than sympathetic to the idea that the dictatorships and the democracies should try to adjust their differences but considerably less interested in the American concept of bringing this about through a comprehensive program undertaken by many nations. Mr. Chamberlain thought it impractical "to do everything at once" and declared that, in his opinion, political appeasement would have to precede economic appeasement and the limitation of armaments. He told Mr. Davis that the British government was doing what it could toward a "beginning of political appeasement" and had just instructed its Ambassador in Berlin to impress upon Hitler that the British wanted to establish "more friendly relations and a sound basis for

peace" as soon as they were convinced that Germany genuinely desired the same thing. Mr. Davis indicated that he was quite in favor of England's trying to reach an understanding with Germany; he only wondered whether tackling the problem of peace on a wider scale could await the outcome of Britain's efforts. In addition Mr. Davis raised the question of the possibility of Mr. Chamberlain's coming to the United States to talk with the President directly.

The President decided, after Mr. Davis' return home, to go on from where the latter had left off. Early in June, Mr. Davis wrote the Prime Minister, in the strictest secrecy, that Mr. Roosevelt would like him to visit the White House around late September.[15] The President, he explained, was ready to make arrangements immediately to have an agenda drawn up for their meeting. Mr. Davis stated also that he thought England and America should pave the way for a "broader move" to ensure peace and hoped that, within a few months, it would be possible to start a "concerted and comprehensive effort to achieve economic rehabilitation, financial stability, a limitation of armaments and peace." The Prime Minister replied that he did not believe the time ripe for a meeting with the President.[16] The British government was, he asserted, still trying to open talks with the Germans and these might provide a "valuable indication" of the direction in which it might be possible to advance, thereby serving as a useful preliminary to discussions between himself and Mr. Roosevelt.

The President was, however, too intent upon his course to drop matters here. At the end of July he wrote personally to the Prime Minister saying that he appreciated his desire to make such progress as was possible along other lines but nevertheless would like suggestions for steps that might be taken to expedite their meeting.[17] Mr. Chamberlain did not answer until two months later when he informed Mr. Roosevelt that he had no suggestions to make.[18] The international situation, he declared, was changing so quickly that any plans were likely to be obsolete almost as soon as they were made. While the tension in Europe was easing somewhat, things were still a "long way from the resumption of cordial relations between the totalitarian states and the democracies."

It was precisely at the time that the Prime Minister rejected the President's second invitation to open discussions that Mr. Roosevelt delivered the "quarantine" speech. Presumably he felt that, if an advance toward peace was to be

---

[11] *Foreign Relations of the United States, 1937*, I, 655.

[12] *Ibid.*, pp. 29, 638, 640, 649.

[13] Apparently in March, Secretary Morgenthau told Mr. Chamberlain that the United States wanted to help in finding some way of preventing the outbreak of war. For correspondence on this see *ibid.*, I, 98–106.

[14] The following accounts of Mr. Davis' conversations are all based upon his memoranda.

[15] Davis files. Draft in Roosevelt files, P.S.F. Great Britain, 1933–38, Box 7.

[16] *Ibid.*

[17] *Foreign Relations of the United States, 1937*, I, 113.

[18] *Ibid.*, p. 131.

made, he would have to try some method less dependent upon Mr. Chamberlain's initiative. Perhaps it was to encourage others to supply the necessary impetus that the President renewed his efforts to dramatize publicly the idea of searching for a plan to avert war. Parts of the "quarantine" speech (for reasons that will be clearer later) appear to have constituted one of these efforts. Another effort was started on the day following the "quarantine" speech when Sumner Welles wrote a memorandum for the President outlining a new peace program.

So much has been written about Mr. Welles's scheme that it does not seem necessary to do more than recall its essentials.[19] Mr. Welles believed that it would be easier to get the democracies and dictatorships together to seek a solution of political, economic and armament problems if they first succeeded in reaching an understanding on less explosive issues. He therefore suggested trying to achieve a general agreement on questions such as the fundamental rules which ought to govern international behavior. The President himself proposed holding a dramatic meeting of diplomatic representatives accredited to Washington, in the White House on Armistice Day, at which he would read a message designed to set in motion procedures leading to an agreement of the kind Mr. Welles envisaged. Mr. Welles thereupon put his scheme into more concrete form but the entire matter was dropped before Armistice Day because of Secretary Hull's objections. It was revived, however, in early January 1938 when it was hoped that it would, among other matters, lend support to Great Britain's continued attempt to arrive at an understanding with Germany.[20] Perhaps the best-known part of the story is that which deals with the submission of the Welles plan to Mr. Chamberlain; the latter's rejection of it during Mr. Eden's absence from England; and Mr. Eden's successful efforts to get the Prime Minister to reverse his stand around the middle of January. In the end the matter was dropped for a number of reasons but in Hyde Park files there are revised drafts with notations by Mr. Roosevelt which show that the President and Mr. Welles continued working on the scheme until at least mid-February.[21]

It would seem therefore that the President was searching for a program to reduce the danger of war over a period which started considerably before and continued for some time after the "quarantine" speech. The programs that Mr. Roosevelt acted upon differed in many respects but all aimed at getting the various conflicting nations to coöperate in the interests of peace at the least by entering into some sort of initial agreement. The emphasis was mainly on a constructive approach to maintain peace. But it was also on arrangements which were designed: to prevent the outbreak of war by providing for a collective neutrality or nonbelligerency, the mere threat of which would act as a restraint upon aggression; or to make possible the use of pressure, through such a neutrality or nonbelligerency, in case hostilities could not be averted.

This then was Mr. Roosevelt's search for a plan which could be used to cope with the international situation. The story of the writing of the speech starts with Mr. Hull. The Secretary, on learning that the President was to make an extensive trip in late September, urged him to deliver an address, in some large mid-western city, for the purpose—according to Mr. Hull's own account—of counteracting the growing trend toward isolationism throughout the country.[22] One may take for granted that Mr. Hull also believed that an expression of the moral outrage felt in the United States against the Axis nations would be welcome at home and have a salutary effect abroad. Mr. Roosevelt, no doubt wholly in sympathy with the Secretary's views on this matter, at once agreed and asked Mr. Hull and Norman Davis to furnish him with the necessary material. . . .

No doubt some of the reasons for thinking that the popular interpretations of the "quarantine" speech should be reconsidered are already evident. Nevertheless it seems desirable to discuss briefly these interpretations and the conclusion advanced here, one by one.

1. Those who believe the President planned the speech as an announcement of a decision to revert to the type of collective security embodied in the League Covenant rely mainly on two arguments: that the tone of the address was so threatening it must have been designed to indicate a drastic move of this kind; that the speech conspicuously emphasized the idea of nations maintaining peace by a "concerted effort".

But the tone of the speech existed in the original memoranda where it was clearly not meant to go beyond fulfilling Mr. Hull's purpose of awakening the American people to the dangers of isolationism and voicing moral indignation at the destructiveness of the Axis countries. It might be argued, as already suggested, that Mr. Roosevelt strengthened the meaning of the original in places but he does not seem to have sharpened the tone of the draft as a whole and, in one very important instance, he moderated it. The passage of the Davis text which Mr. Roosevelt discarded and replaced with his "quarantine" statement could certainly be construed as a warning that, if pushed too far, the United States would fight. The first version was even stronger, for it included,

---

[19] *Ibid.*, pp. 665–670. Mr. Welles's own accounts of his plan are in *The Time for Decision*, p. 64, and *Seven Decisions That Shaped History* (New York, 1950), chapter i. See also discussion in *The Challenge to Isolation* by William L. Langer and S. Everett Gleason (New York, 1952), p. 22.

[20] *Foreign Relations of the United States, 1938,* I, 115–126.

[21] Roosevelt files, P.S.F. State—1938.

[22] Hull, *Memoirs,* I, 544–545.

"We recognize, however, that a policy of peace at any price will not ensure peace. . . . This nation was born fighting for certain principles which our forebears considered to be of greater value than life itself. . . ." President Roosevelt may have seen the initial draft but, even if he did not, the interpretation to which the revision opened itself could scarcely have escaped him and it seems probable that he omitted it as too menacing.[28] This thesis is further supported by the fact that the one paragraph (referred to earlier) which the President did not use out of the memoranda sent from Washington had similar overtones.

The reference to a "concerted effort" was also in the drafts forwarded from Washington and, read in context, clearly meant that peace-loving nations should coöperate to arouse the conscience of the world to ensure the maintenance of high moral standards in the conduct of international relations. The presence of this theme is indeed not surprising, for, of all themes, it was most frequently used by Mr. Hull at this time and was also often employed by the President.

2. The idea that the "quarantine" speech was an advance notice of a declaration of sanctions against Japan resulted, to a large extent, from the circumstances under which the speech was given. The day after Mr. Roosevelt's appearance at Chicago, the League of Nations blamed Japan for the hostilities which had started in China in July and called for a conference of the Nine Power Treaty nations. Within a matter of hours, the State Department endorsed the League's position. The fact that these events happened hard upon each other gave rise to the belief that they were all part of one piece of political strategy which would culminate in the Nine Power nations adopting sanctions against Japan. However, we know today that there was no such direct connection between the President's Chicago address and the League's actions. And there is no convincing evidence to suggest that the President had decided to use coercive measures against Japan. . . .

3. There is a contemporary record which suggests that the President planned the "quarantine" speech to introduce a program involving sanctions against future aggressors (meaning the Axis states) which he expected to launch immediately after his return from Chicago. Secretary Ickes, in his diary entry of September 19, 1937, described a talk with the President in which the latter said he was considering addressing a letter to all the countries of the world, except possibly the "three bandit nations", proposing that all peace-loving peoples isolate those who invaded the rights of others. "What he had in mind," Mr. Ickes wrote, "is to cut off all trade with any such nation."[31] According to the Secretary, Mr. Roosevelt said further that his proposal would not apply to the current situations in Spain and China, as what had been done could not be undone; that he wanted to "evolve a new policy for the future." Mr. Ickes himself commented that "of course, if he should do this, it would be a warning to the nations that are today running amuck." The Secretary wrote further that Mr. Roosevelt asked him whether he should send this letter before or after his trip out west, to which Mr. Ickes replied that he should wait until his return.

It would seem, however, that Mr. Roosevelt could not have settled upon this plan more than momentarily, for he appears to have been considering a variety of other schemes with equal seriousness. Just before his talk with Secretary Ickes, the President told two other members of the Cabinet—Hull and Morgenthau—that he was thinking of publicly declaring his readiness to act as a clearing house for peace—a suggestion which on the surface does not sound the same as the one discussed with Mr. Ickes. Further, the day after his talk with Mr. Ickes, the President told Mr. Morgenthau that he had dropped the idea of making such a public declaration and had decided to do nothing that would call for any response or action from any quarter, the whole thing being a matter of long-term education. It should also be recalled that at this time the President was considering still another course, not having as yet received a response from Prime Minister Chamberlain to his proposal for opening discussions which were partly intended to lead to an agreement between the democracies and the Axis countries. Moreover it is clear that he did not abandon the desire to get the democracies and totalitarian states together, for he started working on the Welles plan only three days after his Chicago speech.

4. The theory that the "quarantine" speech was not a vital landmark in Mr. Roosevelt's foreign policy but part of a groping attempt to find some means of forestalling war is based on various pieces of evidence (some already mentioned) including Mr. Roosevelt's own statements.

Immediately after the delivery of the "quarantine" speech, Mr. Roosevelt went to Cardinal Mundelein's house in Chicago where they had a long talk which was—and has remained—confidential. However, there appears in the Roosevelt files a letter written, on the following day, by Cardinal Mundelein to the Apostolic Delegate to the United States which says in part: "Yesterday

---

[28] The original version of this memorandum is in the Davis files and is marked "N.Y. September 17, 1937" with a further notation, "Phoned to Mr. Dunn." Presumably the State Department suggested the changes which appeared in the revised version in the Roosevelt files.

[31] This statement leaves open to question whether Mr. Roosevelt actually stated he had in mind cutting off all trade with the aggressor or whether Mr. Ickes thought that was what the President had in mind. The document which indicates most clearly that one of the President's ideas was to find some means of using coöperative economic pressures is cited in footnote 34.

the President of the United States delivered here in Chicago a strong and important address which may affect the future peace and tranquility of the world. Afterwards, in my own house, he continued discussion of the subject to which he had given considerable thought. He asked me whether he might invite participation of the Holy See in the movement and, as it is for the purpose of establishing permanent peace in a war-torn world, I answered him that I thought he should. . . .

"His plan does not contemplate either military or naval action against the unjust aggressor nation, nor does it involve 'sanctions' as generally understood but rather a policy of isolation, severance of ordinary communications in a united manner by all the governments of the pact." [32]

The rest of the letter indicated that the President hoped such a movement for the creation of a "permanent peace" would arrest the wave of lawlessness already submerging parts of the world.

About two weeks after the "quarantine" speech, Norman Davis, who was about to leave for the Brussels Conference where he was to represent the United States, went to see the President for oral instructions.[33] Mr. Davis' notes show that Mr. Roosevelt used language similar to that of the "quarantine" speech and of his talk with Cardinal Mundelein. They state that the President remarked that, if all other procedures failed at Brussels, the countries wanting to stop the Sino-Japanese conflict and safeguard themselves from its consequences—"or in other words the so-called neutral nations"—should "band together for their own protection against this contagion." The other Powers might, for example, give China every facility for acquiring arms; or an alternative might be for "the neutrals to ostracize Japan, break off relations."

Side by side with his notes on this interview, there is, in Mr. Davis' files, a paper marked: "Handed to me by President as of possible use". This contains what must be an excerpt from an article or book which says, in substance, that the Inter-American principle of neutral coöperation, short of force, would seem to offer a useful formula for the United States in the existing situation; and it urges the President to apply this formula so as to develop a "constructive program" in which a group of neutrals, acting in common, might make their influence felt.

It would seem therefore that, immediately after delivering his address at Chicago, Mr. Roosevelt spoke to Cardinal Mundelein, not as though he had just proclaimed some drastic policy, but as though, as in the past, he were throwing out the germ of an idea with the hope that it might grow. From the tenor of his remarks and the paper he gave Mr. Davis, it appears likely that the President thought the Inter-American

concepts of collective neutrality or nonbelligerency contained the seeds of some method for dealing with the world-wide situation. He suggested that "so-called neutrals" might develop a common program but he seems to have been very vague about the nature of that program. It was not to involve military action nor "'sanctions' as generally understood". But it might include, among other matters, the "severance of ordinary communications in a united manner" or a "break-off" of relations. Perhaps in talking to Cardinal Mundelein, Mr. Roosevelt had in mind the possibility of developing a plan which would provide for the creation, under certain circumstances, of a moral front limited to such matters as the severance of diplomatic relations—a plan which, it might be added, would seem to furnish appropriate grounds for an appeal to the Pope. Or perhaps he was looking for a scheme which would, if necessary, permit the extension of the concepts of collective neutrality or nonbelligerency so that they might embrace a wide range of pressures up to and including economic pressures.[34] The mere existence of arrangements of this character was, as stated earlier, regarded as likely to discourage aggression so that they might be considered as a sound basis for the establishment of a "permanent peace". It is just possible that the President also thought some technique might be developed whereby if "neutrals" exercised pressures, which were not regarded as sanctions in the ordinary sense but as measures taken for their own protection against the contagion of war, they would avoid the risk of having to resort to military action inherent in systems like that of the League.[35]

Somewhat curiously, in addition to Cardinal Mundelein's letter and Mr. Davis' notes, a document which has long been familiar to historians seems to support the idea that the President had no definite policy at this stage but was contemplating a variety of possibilities including ways of embroidering on the Inter-American system. This document is a transcript of the off-the-record press conference he held the day after he spoke at Chicago.[36] It is usually assumed that Mr. Roosevelt, anxious to avoid being questioned, was deliberately confusing in his answers to the correspondents; but it seems quite possible that the President's replies were meant to be taken at their face value.

The reporters, over and over again, asked the

[34] The President must have mentioned a plan including economic pressures to Clark Eichelberger in early July 1937. In mid-July Mr. Eichelberger sent the President a memorandum based on a talk which they had had some two weeks earlier. . . .

[35] Based partly on a remark to this effect said to have been made by Mr. Roosevelt some months later. (Talks with John M. Blum who is working on a book with Mr. Morganthau based on the latter's diaries.)

[36] *The Public Papers and Addresses of Franklin D. Roosevelt, 1937*, pp. 414–425.

[32] Roosevelt files.

[33] Davis files.

President to define the meaning of his Chicago address and especially of the word "quarantine." The President stuck to the following explanation of the speech as whole: "P: . . . the lead is in the last line, 'America actively engages in the search for peace.' I can't tell you what the methods will be. We are looking for some way to peace. . . .

Q: Foreign papers put it as an attitude without a program. . . .

P: It is an attitude and it does not outline a program; but it says we are looking for a program. . . ."[37]

To me it would seem that throughout the period, before and after the "quarantine" speech, Mr. Roosevelt was moved by a deep inner feeling that it must be possible to find a formula which would avoid as unthinkable a catastrophe as another world war. In retrospect it may look to many as though nothing could have averted tragedy short of a clear-cut and determined policy against the Axis. But the chances are that the Chicago speech reflected no such policy. What governed Mr. Roosevelt's behavior could be fully understood only by a grasp of the whole history of the times illuminated by that rarest of things, a wise and informed feeling for the President's personality. Nevertheless one influence is blatantly obvious, namely, the political situation in the United States, a matter which prompted the rest of these notes.

II

The second assumption referred to at that outset is that Mr. Roosevelt, with full justification, felt that the American people wholly repudiated the "quarantine" speech and that he therefore abandoned his decision to adopt a firm policy against the Axis Powers. If Mr. Roosevelt made no such decision, obviously he did not abandon it. But this does not rule out the possibility that the President, Mr. Hull, and others in the Administration believed that the country almost uniformly rejected the speech and were influenced by their belief. Indeed there is a good deal to suggest that this was the case. Sumner Welles has described the President as "dismayed by the widespread violence of the attacks" following his appearance at Chicago.[38] Mr. Hull has stated in his *Memoirs* that the "reaction against the quarantine idea was quick and violent" and set back by many months the Administration's efforts to educate public opinion away from isolationism.[39] Judge Rosen-

man has likewise spoken of the nation's response to the speech as "quick and violent—and nearly unanimous."[40] The effect of this evaluation of the country's attitude upon the Administration's policy is inevitably an elusive matter. But certainly during the main international event that followed—that is, the Brussels Conference—the Administration's policy was exceedingly cautious, and cables from Washington to Norman Davis, during his conduct of the negotiations at Brussels, are marked by a worried preoccupation with public opinion at home.[41] As will be seen later, Mr. Roosevelt himself introduced this note of concern in his original instructions to Mr. Davis.

However, even a limited look (such as that which follows) at the kind of material—mainly leading newspapers and weeklies—which the Administration must have used to assess the popular reaction to the "quarantine" speech raises a question which may well be worth more intensive study.[42] Were the President and those around him, in fact, justified in concluding that the country reacted with speed, vehemence and solidarity against the speech; or were they perhaps so responsive to the criticisms of certain isolationists that they equated these with the opinions of the country as a whole?

A reading of a group of leading publications, of the type that members of the Administration must have seen, shows that the controversy over the "quarantine" speech lasted until the end of the Brussels Conference in late November. Because the speech was immediately followed by the League's denunciation of Japan and its call for a Nine Power Conference, and because we supported the League's action, many believed that these events had been planned to introduce a new, forceful foreign policy which would be fully revealed at Brussels.

In this group of publications, estimates of the country's reaction to the speech went through two phases. Pierrepont Moffat, writing in his diary, described the initial phase—the immediate response to the speech—as a "burst of applause".[43] A similar impression was recorded in comment after comment in the publications surveyed. On

1937, that a meeting of State Department officials was being held on that day in the Secretary's office when the ticker service brought in the text of the President's Chicago address. "The Secretary was delighted at the speech," Mr. Moffat wrote, "and the majority thought it would be strongly approved by the public." See *The Moffat Papers* (Cambridge, 1956), p. 153.

[40] Rosenman, *op.cit.*

[41] Statement based on a study of our Far Eastern policy during this period which the writer is making.

[42] There do not seem to be any polls that show any particular shift in opinion right after the "quarantine" speech. See *Public Opinion, 1935-1946* (Princeton, 1951) which includes exact dates on which polls were issued. . . .

[43] *The Moffat Papers*, p. 155.

---

[37] *Ibid.*, p. 429.

[38] Welles, *Seven Decisions That Shaped History*, p. 13. See also p. 73 and Welles, *The Time for Decision*, p. 63.

[39] Hull, *Memoirs*, I, 545. One cannot help wondering whether the severely critical attitude which Mr. Hull is known to have developed toward the "quarantine" speech did not arise only after he saw the attacks in the isolationist press. Pierrepont Moffat recorded in his diary on October 5,

October 6, the *New York Times* printed excerpts from sixteen editorials from all parts of the country and indicated their trend in its headline: "ROOSEVELT SPEECH WIDELY APPROVED".[44] . . .

The marked tendency to agree that the initial response to the speech was positive disappeared in the second phase. Fundamentally, the question was whether the American people were initially enthusiastic about the speech largely because they were glad to have the President openly express disapproval of the Axis Powers; and, if so, whether their enthusiasm had changed after the idea became widespread that the "quarantine" speech would be translated into strong action against Japan at the Brussels Conference. Publications, such as *Newsweek,* felt that, influenced by increasing cries of alarm from leading isolationists, the tide of opinion soon began to turn.[48] Publications like *Time,* on the other hand, believed that popular sentiment remained firmly behind the President.[49] Most of the comments in other publications ranged between these extremes. In general they agreed that the original enthusiasm for the speech had been tempered by anxiety that, at the Brussels Conference, Mr. Roosevelt's new foreign policy would not stop short of war. This was by no means intended, however, to imply that the country would not support punitive measures against Japan, including economic sanctions. For the view was constantly expressed that boycotts, embargoes, etc. against the Japanese would not involve military action. In short, it would seem that the feeling in this group of journals was that the "quick" reaction to the "quarantine" speech, far from being hostile, was decidedly favorable, and it would seem that, in the long run, their opinions differed too widely to justify any definite conclusion. . . .

If the editorial opinions of [many] newspapers suggest considerable evidence of support for the "quarantine" speech, so, it should be added, did the President's mail. The great majority of the letters on the Chicago address, which fill several boxes in the Hyde Park files, are messages of appreciation, often written with deep emotion.

The other side of the coin is the nature of the opposition to the speech and its influence upon the Administration including the President. The two hostile papers in Mr. [Lawrence] Kramer's study were the *Chicago Tribune* and a Hearst publication. Nothing demonstrated the attitude of the *Tribune* better than its account of Mr. Roosevelt's appearance at Chicago on October 5. It described thousands of Chicagoans turning out to greet the President, expecting to hear a message of peace, and being plunged by his words into a "world-hurricane of war fright." Throughout October and November the *Tribune* harped upon two themes: that a "quarantine" must mean economic sanctions and economic sanctions must

mean war; that we were merely puppets of the British, serving as saviors of their Empire in the Far East.

The same themes were emphasized by the Hearst press. But Mr. Hearst went much further. He issued a questionnaire to members of Congress which, leading off from the "quarantine" speech, asked whether we should take sides in the Sino-Japanese conflict or steer clear of all wars. The answers were published in a series of articles which began on October 17 and ran for about two weeks. The introduction stated that Congressmen from the "Atlantic to the Pacific, from Canada to the Gulf" had "roared back their determination for today, to-morrow, and forever to keep the United States out of foreign wars."

Many of the published replies came from important political leaders, mainly well-known isolationists.[58] Senator Borah said he was utterly opposed to the United States participating in sanctions against Japan which would be "just the same as initiating war". Senator Vandenberg declared that any move toward naming aggressors, using sanctions, etc., would lead us in the direction of entangling alliances—the one thing we were determined to avoid. Senator George of Georgia wrote that he would not, under any circumstances, favor action which might risk war with Japan. Senator Richard Russell asserted that, instead of policing the world to maintain peace, we should rely upon our neutrality legislation to "quarantine" us against war. Senator La Follette stated that he was opposed to anything which, by implication or otherwise, might ultimately require the United States to use force.

The statement which received the widest publicity was that issued by Hiram Johnson on October 19, the eve of Norman Davis' departure for Brussels.[59] Speaking of the coming conference, the Senator said, "We want no union with welching nations who will . . . tell us we must lead mankind to save the world." Mr. Davis, he insisted, would not be going to Europe unless an agreement had been reached in advance between England and the United States. Mr. Roosevelt had no right to make a mystery of what he meant by a "quarantine" and, unless he intended nothing but words, the inevitable result would be war.

Even a cursory look at the record shows that the Administration observed Mr. Hearst's tactics closely from the outset. At his press conference on October 6, Mr. Roosevelt made some remarks about excerpts from editorials around the country, presumably those in the *New York Times.* He failed, however, to mention that they were mostly in his favor but concentrated instead upon the editorial written by—to use his own words—"the old man of the seas—old man Hearst." This, he declared, was "the silliest ever . . . perfectly terrible—awful. Says it means this is getting us into

---

[44] P. 17.

[48] December 20, p. 11.

[49] November 1, p. 17.

[58] The references in this paragraph are to articles printed on October 17 and 18.

[59] *San Francisco Examiner,* October 20, p. 1.

war and a lot more of that." A few days later, Mr. Ickes recorded in his diary that the Hearst press was after Mr. Roosevelt "full cry" for his Chicago address and that the President had said he wanted to remind Hearst that he had been responsible for an absolutely unjustifiable war with Spain.[60] At about the same time, Pierrepont Moffat noted in his diary that Hearst was "alleged to be about to start a campaign against the idea of a 'quarantine' ".[61] When the campaign got underway, Mr. Roosevelt clearly showed his concern. On the day Norman Davis sailed, the President issued a statement which was generally accepted as a reply to Senator Johnson's attack.[62] Obviously addressing himself to the accusation that we had an understanding with the British, Mr. Roosevelt asserted that we were "of course" entering the Nine Power Conference without any prior commitments. He also emphasized that the purpose of the meeting was to seek a *peaceable* solution of the Sino-Japanese conflict. Off the record, the President dictated some instructions to guide

Mr. Davis in his relations with the British.[63] The British Cabinet, these said, must recognize that there was such a thing as American public opinion. Mr. Davis must make clear, "at every step", that the United States would neither take the lead at Brussels nor be made a "tail to the British kite as is now being charged by the Hearst press and others."

There can be little doubt therefore that the "quarantine" speech provoked a barrage from prominent isolationists and that this barrage had its effect upon the Administration. There can also be little doubt that considerable evidence of approval of the speech came to the attention of the Administration but was not accepted as weighing substantially in the balance. Perhaps an extensive study would reveal a wider tide of opinion against the address to support the Administration's view. But until such a study is made, it seems pertinent to continue asking whether the Administration's judgment was not unduly governed by its sensitivity to the attacks of leading isolationists.

Norman Davis and Secretary of State Cordell Hull sent two memoranda to President Roosevelt, which served as a draft of the collective security speech. Roosevelt inserted the famous passage:

"It seems to be unfortunately true that the epidemic of world lawlessness is spreading.

"When an epidemic of physical disease starts to spread the community approves and joins in a quarantine of the patients in order to protect the health of the community against the spread of the disease."

The occasion for the speech, delivered October 5, 1937, was the dedication of a bridge over the Chicago River.

FRANKLIN D. ROOSEVELT: THE "QUARANTINE" SPEECH*

I am glad to come once again to Chicago and especially to have the opportunity of taking part in the dedication of this important project of civic betterment.

On my trip across the continent and back I have been shown many evidences of the result of common sense cooperation between municipalities and the Federal Government, and I have been greeted by tens of thousands of Americans who have told me in every look and word that their material and spiritual well-being has made great strides forward in the past few years.

And yet, as I have seen with my own eyes, the prosperous farms, the thriving factories and the busy railroads, as I have seen the happiness and security and peace which covers our wide land, almost inevitably I have been compelled to contrast our peace with very different scenes being enacted in other parts of the world.

It is because the people of the United States under modern conditions must, for the sake of their own future, give thought to the rest of the world, that I, as the responsible executive head of the Nation, have chosen this great inland city and this gala occasion to speak to you on a subject of definite national importance.

The political situation in the world, which of

---

[60] Ickes, *Secret Diary*, II, 227.

[61] *The Moffat Papers*, p. 155.

[62] *New York Times*, October 20, p. 15.

* Reprinted with permission of the Macmillan Company from *Public Papers and Addresses* by Franklin D. Roosevelt. Copyright 1941 by Franklin D. Roosevelt.

---

[63] *Foreign Relations of the United States, 1937*, IV, 85. The memorandum was also sent to Ambassador Bingham in London who conveyed its contents to Mr. Eden (*ibid.*, p. 114).

late has been growing progressively worse, is such as to cause grave concern and anxiety to all the peoples and nations who wish to live in peace and amity with their neighbors.

Some fifteen years ago the hopes of mankind for a continuing era of international peace were raised to great heights when more than sixty nations solemnly pledged themselves not to resort to arms in furtherance of their national aims and policies. The high aspirations expressed in the Briand-Kellogg Peace Pact and the hopes for peace thus raised have of late given way to a haunting fear of calamity. The present reign of terror and international lawlessness began a few years ago.

It began through unjustified interference in the internal affairs of other nations or the invasion of alien territory in violation of treaties; and has now reached a stage where the very foundations of civilization are seriously threatened. The landmarks and traditions which have marked the progress of civilization toward a condition of law, order and justice are being wiped away.

Without a declaration of war and without warning or justification of any kind, civilians, including vast numbers of women and children, are being ruthlessly murdered with bombs from the air. In times of so-called peace, ships are being attacked and sunk by submarines without cause or notice. Nations are fomenting and taking sides in civil warfare in nations that have never done them any harm. Nations claiming freedom for themselves deny it to others.

Innocent peoples, innocent nations, are being cruelly sacrificed to a greed for power and supremacy which is devoid of all sense of justice and humane considerations.

To paraphrase a recent author "perhaps we foresee a time when men, exultant in the technique of homicide, will rage so hotly over the world that every precious thing will be in danger, every book and picture and harmony, every treasure garnered through two millenniums, the small, the delicate, the defenseless—all will be lost or wrecked or utterly destroyed."

If those things come to pass in other parts of the world, let no one imagine that America will escape, that America may expect mercy, that this Western Hemisphere will not be attacked and that it will continue tranquilly and peacefully to carry on the ethics and the arts of civilization.

If those days come "there will be no safety by arms, no help from authority, no answer in science. The storm will rage till every flower of culture is trampled and all human beings are leveled in a vast chaos."

If those days are not to come to pass—if we are to have a world in which we can breathe freely and live in amity without fear—the peace-loving nations must make a concerted effort to uphold laws and principles on which alone peace can rest secure.

The peace-loving nations must make a concerted effort in opposition to those violations of treaties and those ignorings of humane instincts which today are creating a state of international anarchy and instability from which there is no escape through mere isolation or neutrality.

Those who cherish their freedom and recognize and respect the equal right of their neighbors to be free and live in peace, must work together for the triumph of law and moral principles in order that peace, justice and confidence may prevail in the world. There must be a return to a belief in the pledged word, in the value of a signed treaty. There must be recognition of the fact that national morality is as vital as private morality.

A bishop wrote me the other day: "It seems to me that something greatly needs to be said in behalf of ordinary humanity against the present practice of carrying the horrors of war to helpless civilians, especially women and children. It may be that such a protest might be regarded by many, who claim to be realists, as futile, but may it not be that the heart of mankind is so filled with horror at the present needless suffering that that force could be mobilized in sufficient volume to lessen such cruelty in the days ahead. Even though it may take twenty years, which God forbid, for civilization to make effective its corporate protest against this barbarism, surely strong voices may hasten the day."

There is a solidarity and interdependence about the modern world, both technically and morally, which makes it impossible for any nation completely to isolate itself from economic and political upheavals in the rest of the world, especially when such upheavals appear to be spreading and not declining. There can be no stability or peace either within nations or between nations except under laws and moral standards adhered to by all. International anarchy destroys every foundation for peace. It jeopardizes either the immediate or the future security of every nation, large or small. It is, therefore, a matter of vital interest and concern to the people of the United States that the sanctity of international treaties and the maintenance of international morality be restored.

The overwhelming majority of the peoples and nations of the world today want to live in peace. They seek the removal of barriers against trade. They want to exert themselves in industry, in agriculture and in business, that they may increase their wealth through the production of wealth-producing goods rather than striving to produce military planes and bombs and machine guns and cannon for the destruction of human lives and useful property.

In those nations of the world which seem to be piling armament on armament for purposes of aggression, and those other nations which fear acts of aggression against them and their security, a very high proportion of their national income is being spent directly for armaments. It runs from thirty to as high as fifty percent. We are fortunate. The proportion that we in the United States spend is far less—eleven or twelve percent.

How happy we are that the circumstances of the moment permit us to put our money into bridges and boulevards, dams and reforestation, the conservation of our soil and many other kinds of useful works rather than into huge standing armies and vast supplies of implements of war.

I am compelled and you are compelled, nevertheless, to look ahead. The peace, the freedom and the security of ninety percent of the population of the world is being jeopardized by the remaining ten percent who are threatening a breakdown of all international order and law. Surely the ninety percent who want to live in peace under law and in accordance with moral standards that have received almost universal acceptance through the centuries, can and must find some way to make their will prevail.

The situation is definitely of universal concern. The questions involved relate not merely to violations of specific provisions of particular treaties; they are questions of war and of peace, of international law and especially of principles of humanity. It is true that they involve definite violations of agreements, and especially of the Covenant of the League of Nations, the Briand-Kellogg Pact and the Nine Power Treaty. But they also involve problems of world economy, world security and world humanity

It is true that the moral consciousness of the world must recognize the importance of removing injustices and well-founded grievances; but at the same time it must be aroused to the cardinal necessity of honoring sanctity of treaties, of respecting the rights and liberties of others and of putting an end to acts of international aggression.

It seems to be unfortunately true that the epidemic of world lawlessness is spreading.

When an epidemic of physical disease starts to spread, the community approves and joins in a quarantine of the patients in order to protect the health of the community against the spread of the disease.

It is my determination to pursue a policy of peace. It is my determination to adopt every practicable measure to avoid involvement in war. It ought to be inconceivable that in this modern era, and in the face of experience, any nation could be so foolish and ruthless as to run the risk of plunging the whole world into war by invading and violating, in contravention of solemn treaties, the territory of other nations that have done them no real harm and are too weak to protect themselves adequately. Yet the peace of the world and the welfare and security of every nation, including our own, is today being threatened by that very thing.

No nation which refuses to exercise forbearance and to respect the freedom and rights of others can long remain strong and retain the confidence and respect of other nations. No nation ever loses its dignity or its good standing by conciliating its differences, and by exercising great patience with, and consideration for, the rights of other nations.

War is a contagion, whether it be declared or undeclared. It can engulf states and peoples remote from the original scene of hostilities. We are determined to keep out of war, yet we cannot insure ourselves against the disastrous effects of war and the dangers of involvement. We are adopting such measures as will minimize our risk of involvement, but we cannot have complete protection in a world of disorder in which confidence and security have broken down.

If civilization is to survive the principles of the Prince of Peace must be restored. Trust between nations must be revived.

Most important of all, the will for peace on the part of peace-loving nations must express itself to the end that nations that may be tempted to violate their agreements and the rights of others will desist from such a course. There must be positive endeavors to preserve peace.

America hates war. America hopes for peace. Therefore, America actively engages in the search for peace.

State Department dispatches and memoranda recorded European reaction to the "Quarantine" speech. The following are a sample:

EUROPEAN REACTION TO THE "QUARANTINE" SPEECH*

THE CHARGÉ IN FRANCE (WILSON)
TO THE SECRETARY OF STATE

Paris, October 6, 1937—9 p.m.
[Received October 6—8:15 p.m.]
1404. Delbos sent for me this afternoon. He said that he wanted to ask me to inform my Government that President Roosevelt's speech yesterday at Chicago had caused the utmost satisfaction to the French Government and people. He said that the speech was "magnificent" and that it was "an act" of the highest importance. He said that he of course understood perfectly that the speech did not mean that the United States was going to throw itself into the middle of European disputes but that even if the speech

* Reprinted from *Foreign Relations of the United States . . . 1937* (Washington, D.C.: Government Printing Office, 1954), I, 132–33, 138–39, 151.

stood alone and was not followed up by any action it should prove of tremendous assistance to the cause of peace in Europe. He said that not only the subject matter of the speech but also the time of its delivery was most important: it had been delivered at a time when France and England were striving to the best of their abilities to deal with the blackmailing tactics of the dictators and to prevent them from creating a situation which might prove disastrous to the peace of the world. It had been delivered upon the eve of the preparation of the Italian reply to the Franco-British note proposing conversations on the Spanish question and it could not fail to make a deep impression upon the two dictators. . . .

MEMORANDUM BY THE UNDER SECRETARY OF STATE (WELLES) OF A CONVERSATION WITH THE GERMAN AMBASSADOR (DIECKOFF)

[Extract]

[WASHINGTON,] October 11, 1937.

The Ambassador then referred to the President's Chicago speech. He said that he was very interested to know the exact interpretation which he should give to it. I said that it seemed to me hardly necessary for me to attempt to interpret the President's speech inasmuch as it was in my judgment a speech which spoke for itself, but that I felt the Ambassador might wish to give particular emphasis in his own consideration of the speech to the last paragraph thereof. I said that the President sincerely believed that all of the difficult problems with which the countries of the world were today confronted could be solved through a spirit of friendly cooperation and by recognition of each other's difficulties, and that no permanent solution could ever be found through force. I said that the President further believed that the Government of the United States should work actively towards peace inasmuch as a continuation of the policies of force undertaken by certain governments of the world would in all likelihood bring about a state of affairs which would jeopardize the interests of all peace-loving nations, and that it was therefore imperative for all countries "actively to work for peace."

The Ambassador said that this was exactly the view which he himself had taken of the speech; that he had so informed his Government; and that he again had to express his regret that the press in Germany, as well as a portion of the press in the United States, should, through erroneous and exaggerated interpretations of the President's statements, endeavor to create further ill-will between the two peoples. He reminded me, very significantly I thought, that throughout the past years the German Government had declared its belief that the restitution of German colonies was necessary for the solution of the German problem. The German Government had at the same time repeatedly made it known publicly that it did not intend to seek colonial restoration through force but through negotiation and by peaceful methods. He stated that I should remember—and I told him that I did clearly remember—that when the German Government had taken unilateral action to abrogate certain provisions of the Versailles Treaty, such action had always been taken within its own territory and for the sole purpose of restoring to the German people their own unimpaired national sovereignty. He reminded me that Germany had never expressed a determination to regain the Polish Corridor through force nor any other of its former continental territory of which it had been deprived by the Versailles Treaty.

I said to the Ambassador that I was very glad to recognize the complete accuracy of what he said, and that I believed that the influence of Germany towards a solution of international problems by negotiation would be a powerful factor in the cause of peace in the world today. . . .

THE AMBASSADOR IN POLAND (BIDDLE) TO PRESIDENT ROOSEVELT

[Extract]

WARSAW, October 27, 1937.

MY DEAR MR. PRESIDENT: Your magnificent Chicago address created a profound impression throughout Europe. Those nations who enjoy a clear conscience in their conduct of foreign policy greeted your words with genuine enthusiasm, and have received a marked stimulation. On the other hand, as Colonel Beck, Polish Minister for Foreign Affairs, confidentially imparted to me, it has served as a "Stop, Look, and Listen" sign for potential aggressors. He gave every evidence of being profoundly impressed by your statements, and felt that you had, as usual, wisely taken occasion to bring our people to a genuine sense of the realistic—to face the situation as it actually existed throughout the world today. At the same time, the speech, in Colonel Beck's opinion, undoubtedly represented an expression on your part of the difficulties entailed in pursuing a policy of isolation, under current world conditions. Hence, it appeared to him that in your drive for peace, you had wished it to be known that the United States was interested, and would henceforth evince more active interest in the maintenance of the principles contained in treaties to which the United States was a part.

During the 1930's, public opinion polls became increasingly popular, and several polling organizations regularly took samples of attitudes toward foreign affairs. Measuring the pollsters' election forecasts against election results, the margin of error was perhaps as much as 6 per cent. On foreign policy questions, the answers ran so overwhelmingly one way or the other that they can be considered a good indication of what the general public thought. From these polls, Jerome S. Bruner synthesized trends in opinion from the mid-thirties into the war years.

JEROME S. BRUNER:
PUBLIC OPINION POLLS ON FOREIGN POLICY*

. . . Our overall attitude toward the great foreign powers [in the mid-thirties] was more that of passive indifference than anything else. America was large enough to fill most of our minds. Interest in other countries, though in many cases it suffered from distortion, was not great. . . .

And so we faced the events that led to war. First came the Spanish Civil War—full dress rehearsal. In May, 1937, 79 per cent of the public felt that it made no difference to them which side won. Nearly two years later, in December, 1938, when the Civil War had almost run its grisly course, 60 per cent were still indifferent about its outcome. The remaining minority was split three to one in favor of the Republic. After two years, then, only four in every ten Americans had taken sides. Far from wanting to give aid, only 17 per cent of the voting public favored any changes in the Neutrality Act which might allow us to send arms to the Loyalists. Spain was not the spark to set America off. Matters had not yet come close enough to home.

Spain was no special case. We were not ready to face the facts of Europe. The context from which our opinions took life was still streaked with the hatred of war. The answer to the following question is characteristic of our thinking in the mid-thirties: "If one foreign nation insists upon attacking another, should the United States join with other nations to compel it to stop?" Does it seem out of character now that only slightly more than a quarter of us were prepared to see the United States join in sanctions against aggressor nations? And of that minority who favored American intervention at that date, over two-thirds would have confined our activities to the non-military!

The fact of the matter is, that of all the alternative ways of assuring our future national security, we were prepared to accept none of them. We did not want to arm; that smacked too much of war. We did not want to join the League, even

if the League proved that it could work successfully. We did not even believe, in 1937, that the dissolution of the League would make any difference to the future peace of the world. We did not believe that it was the President's responsibility to try to interfere with the armament race going on in Europe. That was our feeling in 1937. It was also our opinion in pre-war 1939.

Looking back, there is something nightmarish about our reluctance to take action. We knew that Europe was heading for a showdown, that war was looming. We were refusing to take sides in the Spanish Civil War, but two-thirds of us were answering "yes" to the question, "Do you think there will be another World War?" By the time we reached Munich, hardly more than a third of the nation thought that war in Europe could be put off for another year. The pact at Munich only reinforced our conviction that a European war was in the offing. Chamberlain may have believed Hitler when he said, "I have no more territorial ambitions in Europe." America did not. Less than one in ten were fooled.

One myth had been shattered. We knew that there would be war. But our blindness was too comforting to abandon. Yes, said America, war there will be, but not for us. That was the last barrier between inaction and action. In the relatively serene days of 1936, scarcely a third of the country thought that if there were another war the United States would become involved in it. It was not until four months after the fall of France that the figure rose to the level of a majority.

Had we not been conditioned by our history to such a strong faith in our impregnability, in our geographical isolation, in the inherent stability of things political, perhaps we might have abandoned the notion that war did not threaten us. Because we did not see our own danger, we did not feel that the problems brewing in Europe needed a solution here. Why get entangled gratuitously in an affair which can only hurt one?

And then war came. When it did, American sympathies were unerring. There had never been anything wrong with our sympathies where Germany was concerned. We hated the tyranny of fascism as we hated all tyranny. In spite of the

* Reprinted from Jerome S. Bruner, *Mandate from the People* (New York: Duell, Sloan and Pearce, 1944), pp. 18–27 by permission. Copyright, 1944, by Jerome S. Bruner.

best effort of the German Propaganda Ministry and its American outlets, no doubts about war guilt clouded the American mind. The overwhelming majority of the American people saw no justification in Hitler's claims to Danzig and the Polish Corridor; we were fed up with appeasement. The fateful week of September 1, 1939, saw eight in every ten Americans place the blame for the war squarely on Germany.

But sympathy is not action. After Poland we still did not want to get into the war. Yet gradually, step by step, public thinking was changing.

What changed it? Certainly not Pearl Harbor alone. Was it a sense of military or economic expediency? Was it plain fright at what might come after a Nazi victory? Or was it a growth of ideological insight, a growth of understanding of the world's essential interdependence?

The answer to these questions contains the key to our *actions* in international affairs. Our sympathies will always be for the democracies, for the weak against the strong, for the oppressed against the oppressor. The world knows that. What it does not know is why we act on the basis of our sympathies when we do act, and why we do not.

The problem of causation here is complex. It helps to simplify it if one narrows the discussion to a single case. Consider, as such a case, the matter of America's aid-to-Britain policy. From May, 1940, to November, 1941, the number of people in the United States who were willing to aid Britain even if it involved the risk of getting into the war, doubled—from a third of the country to some seven in every ten Americans. . . .

Why the shift? One clue: the really big swing toward aiding England coincides with the period during which the Wehrmacht demonstrated its lightning-like striking power to the world; opinion shifted from 35 per cent in May, 1940, favoring aid to England even if it meant risking war, to 60 per cent four months later. This was the Period of Threat. For the first time since the last war, our sense of security, hitherto so unshaken, was given a crucial jolt. This was the period during which we became convinced that America would have to enter the war.

And so the first, and obvious, answer is that our taste for action catches up with our sympathies when we see our stakes in the proceedings. Thus, the more we felt the threat of Germany, the greater became our willingness to help Britain.

Look inside the heads of those who favored and those who opposed aid to Britain. You find the adherents of aid are preoccupied with the dangers of German domination. They fear *we* will be attacked, dominated, robbed of our freedom. The opponents of aid are no less patriotic. To them, there is no threat, so why risk a war by aiding Britain? . . .

There is a second condition which influenced our policy of aiding Britain. We knew by the late winter of 1940 that, eventually, we would have to fight. To fight we would need arms—enormous quantities of them. If England had looked like a beaten man by the winter of 1940, there would

have been agitation in this country for withholding aid so that we might make ourselves stronger. Our concern was self-defense. Lindbergh and others among the isolationists tried to convince the public that the British were whipped, that our problem was to arm America. If they had succeeded, England might truly have been defeated. For, . . . our desire to aid the British was firmly linked with our estimate of whether Britain was strong enough to help us—strong enough in short, to defeat the Nazis.

Thus far little has been said about Britain's war aims as a factor in hastening American intervention. Britain's ideological position in the war enlisted our sympathies; it did not, of itself, lead us into action. Certainly Britain's stated war aims had little to do with our willingness to aid her. In the crucial months during which we were rapidly becoming convinced that England must be helped, opinion on the nature of Britain's war aims changed not one whit. . . .

Put it this way. Britain's war aims did not tip the balance of action. Yet had Britain not been ideologically what she is, nothing would have tipped it. From that point of view our action had its origin in sympathy; its catalyst was self-interest. Aristotle might have put it this way: ideology in American opinion is a material cause, self-interest an efficient cause of action. Ideological kinship was only one factor in the equation. Sympathy for England's plight during the blitz was another. . . .

The best summary of why Americans grew to the belief that we must run the risk of getting into war by aiding England is presented by Americans themselves. In June, 1941, when the trend toward helping England had become well established, people who felt that we should aid England at the risk of war and those who were against such risks were asked for their reasons. Two facts emerged. First, the majority of people who favored an aid-to-Britain policy did so for hardheaded, realistic, selfish reasons. Second, the non-interventionist sentiment was based primarily on traditional pacifist appeals that were applicable to any war at any time. But let the people speak for themselves.

OF THOSE WHO FAVORED AID TO BRITAIN

5% pointed to the economic advantages to us of an English victory

9% talked about the ideological stakes in an English victory

68% noted the military advantages of a "help Britain" policy, and

17% gave other, miscellaneous reasons

OF THOSE WHO OPPOSED AID TO BRITAIN

2% mentioned uncertain or questionable British war aims

9% felt that aid was contrary to our economic self-interest

18% contended that American isolation was the best policy for us

19% pointed to the military disadvantages of aiding Britain

27% based their position on a belief in pacifism as the best policy

25% gave other, miscellaneous reasons

The case of England is not something special. It stands as an illustration of our hard-headedness in international affairs.

As we have gone deeper into war, have sensed its danger, our ardor for working with other nations against the common threat has increased. We have come a long way since 1936. But if we feel more strongly that we must stick together with our Allies, it is not the result of a new political philosophy of internationalism. The case of aid-to-Britain is applicable too to our new internationalism. If we have become convinced that our future security lies in a policy of collaboration with other countries, it is because of solicitude for our own security, not out of sympathy for others.

Our desires for action have changed much; our understanding of ideology has not. We have not repented for old sins. We still think we were right. The difference is that the conditions which held in 1935 are no longer considered the conditions of the world today. Three years before Pearl Harbor only some two in every ten Americans, and these mainly the better educated, were willing to admit our failure to participate in the League as a cause of the European crisis. Six months before Pearl Harbor the percentage was virtually unchanged. One year after Pearl Harbor the same opinion prevailed. We prefer instead the simple "devil theory" of war: the greed of Hitler and Mussolini caused it. But that is the past. The present is different.

Today, we feel less secure, less isolated geographically. We know now that the safest protection is joint protection, collective security. But that is not, of itself, a new philosophy of internationalism. We still do not believe that there is something about internationalism which makes it *inherently* better than nationalism. Circumstances and not a change of heart have guided us.

What are we fighting for? People answer readily that we are fighting for freedom, liberty, and democracy. They say it with the sincerity of people who believe it. It is difficult to get behind the meaning of these words. It does no good to ask people what they mean. They have lived with the words so long that they can't define them any more. They feel them now as they have always felt them before—in the fringe of consciousness. The words are no longer revolutionary. They stand for the things we have had and want to keep. The same words were used by Americans in 1918, in 1898. They mean the same thing today.

But behind the words there is something else. We are not fighting for freedom and democracy and liberty because we want those symbols to be realized *everywhere*. We would be a happy nation if the world could exist as a free, equal, and democratic family. . . .

The fall of France in the summer of 1940 led the United States to provide aid to the besieged British that was little short of open war against the Nazis. In his annual message to Congress of January 6, 1941, President Roosevelt called for a lend-lease program to increase the flow of supplies to the British. Moreover, he strongly set forth his view that the security of the United States was involved in the struggle against the Axis and enunciated as war aims the "Four Freedoms."

FRANKLIN D. ROOSEVELT: "WE LOOK FORWARD TO A WORLD FOUNDED UPON FOUR . . . FREEDOMS"*

I address you, the Members of the Seventy-seventh Congress, at a moment unprecedented in the history of the Union. I use the word "unprecedented," because at no previous time has American security been as seriously threatened from without as it is today. . . .

What I seek to convey is the historic truth that the United States as a nation has at all times maintained clear, definite opposition, to any attempt to lock us in behind an ancient Chinese wall while the procession of civilization went past. Today, thinking of our children and of their children, we oppose enforced isolation for ourselves or for any other part of the Americas. . . .

Even when the World War broke out in 1914, it seemed to contain only small threat of danger to our own American future. But, as time went

* Reprinted with permission of the Macmillan Company from *Public Papers and Addresses* by Franklin D. Roosevelt. Copyright 1941 by Franklin D. Roosevelt.

on, the American people began to visualize what the downfall of democratic nations might mean to our own democracy.

We need not overemphasize imperfections in the Peace of Versailles. We need not harp on failure of the democracies to deal with problems of world reconstruction. We should remember that the Peace of 1919 was far less unjust than the kind of "pacification" which began even before Munich, and which is being carried on under the new order of tyranny that seeks to spread over every continent today. The American people have unalterably set their faces against that tyranny.

Every realist knows that the democratic way of life is at this moment being directly assailed in every part of the world—assailed either by arms, or by secret spreading of poisonous propaganda by those who seek to destroy unity and promote discord in nations that are still at peace.

During sixteen long months this assault has blotted out the whole pattern of democratic life in an appalling number of independent nations, great and small. The assailants are still on the march, threatening other nations, great and small.

Therefore, as your President, performing my constitutional duty to "give to the Congress information of the state of the Union," I find it, unhappily, necessary to report that the future and the safety of our country and of our democracy are overwhelmingly involved in events far beyond our borders.

Armed defense of democratic existence is now being gallantly waged in four continents. If that defense fails, all the population and all the resources of Europe, Asia, Africa and Australasia will be dominated by the conquerors. Let us remember that the total of those populations and their resources in those four continents greatly exceeds the sum total of the population and the resources of the whole of the Western Hemisphere—many times over.

In times like these it is immature—and incidentally, untrue—for anybody to brag that an unprepared America, single-handed, and with one hand tied behind its back, can hold off the whole world.

No realistic American can expect from a dictator's peace international generosity, or return of true independence, or world disarmament, or freedom of expression, or freedom of religion—or even good business.

Such a peace would bring no security for us or for our neighbors. "Those, who would give up essential liberty to purchase a little temporary safety, deserve neither liberty nor safety."

As a nation, we may take pride in the fact that we are soft-hearted; but we cannot afford to be soft-headed.

We must always be wary of those who with sounding brass and a tinkling cymbal preach the "ism" of appeasement.

We must especially beware of that small group of selfish men who would clip the wings of the American eagle in order to feather their own nests.

I have recently pointed out how quickly the tempo of modern warfare could bring into our very midst the physical attack which we must eventually expect if the dictator nations win this war.

There is much loose talk of our immunity from immediate and direct invasion from across the seas. Obviously, as long as the British Navy retains its power, no such danger exists. Even if there were no British Navy, it is not probable that any enemy would be stupid enough to attack us by landing troops in the United States from across thousands of miles of ocean, until it had acquired strategic bases from which to operate.

But we learn much from the lessons of the past years in Europe—particularly the lesson of Norway, whose essential seaports were captured by treachery and surprise built up over a series of years.

The first phase of the invasion of this Hemisphere would not be the landing of regular troops. The necessary strategic points would be occupied by secret agents and their dupes—and great numbers of them are already here, and in Latin America.

As long as the aggressor nations maintain the offensive, they—not we—will choose the time and the place and the method of their attack.

That is why the future of all the American Republics is today in serious danger.

That is why this Annual Message to the Congress is unique in our history.

That is why every member of the Executive Branch of the Government and every member of the Congress faces great responsibility and great accountability.

The need of the moment is that our actions and our policy should be devoted primarily—almost exclusively—to meeting this foreign peril. For all our domestic problems are now a part of the great emergency.

Just as our national policy in internal affairs has been based upon a decent respect for the rights and the dignity of all our fellow men within our gates, so our national policy in foreign affairs has been based on a decent respect for the rights and dignity of all nations, large and small. And the justice of morality must and will win in the end.

Our national policy is this:

First, by an impressive expression of the public will and without regard to partisanship, we are committed to all-inclusive national defense.

Second, by an impressive expression of the public will and without regard to partisanship, we are committed to full support of all those resolute peoples, everywhere, who are resisting aggression and are thereby keeping war away from our Hemisphere. By this support, we express our determination that the democratic cause shall prevail; and we strengthen the defense and the security of our own nation.

Third, by an impressive expression of the public will and without regard to partisanship, we are committed to the proposition that principles of morality and considerations for our own security will never permit us to acquiesce in a peace dictated by aggressors and sponsored by appeasers. We know that enduring peace cannot be bought at the cost of other people's freedom.

In the recent national election there was no substantial difference between the two great parties in respect to that national policy. No issue was fought out on this line before the American electorate. Today it is abundantly evident that American citizens everywhere are demanding and supporting speedy and complete action in recognition of obvious danger. . . .

I also ask this Congress for authority and for funds sufficient to manufacture additional munitions and war supplies of many kinds, to be turned over to those nations which are now in actual war with aggressor nations.

Our most useful and immediate role is to act as an arsenal for them as well as for ourselves. They do not need man power, but they do need billions of dollars worth of the weapons of defense.

The time is near when they will not be able to pay for them all in ready cash. We cannot, and we will not, tell them that they must surrender, merely because of present inability to pay for the weapons which we know they must have.

I do not recommend that we make them a loan of dollars with which to pay for these weapons—a loan to be repaid in dollars.

I recommend that we make it possible for those nations to continue to obtain war materials in the United States, fitting their orders into our own program. Nearly all their matériel would, if the time ever came, be useful for our own defense.

Taking counsel of expert military and naval authorities, considering what is best for our own security, we are free to decide how much should be kept here and how much should be sent abroad to our friends who by their determined and heroic resistance are giving us time in which to make ready our own defense.

For what we send abroad, we shall be repaid within a reasonable time following the close of hostilities, in similar materials, or, at our option, in other goods of many kinds, which they can produce and which we need.

Let us say to the democracies: "We Americans are vitally concerned in your defense of freedom. We are putting forth our energies, our resources and our organizing powers to give you the strength to regain and maintain a free world. We shall send you, in ever-increasing numbers, ships, planes, tanks, guns. This is our purpose and our pledge."

In fulfillment of this purpose we will not be intimidated by the threats of dictators that they will regard as a breach of international law or as an act of war our aid to the democracies which dare to resist their aggression. Such aid is not an act of war, even if a dictator should unilaterally proclaim it so to be.

When the dictators, if the dictators, are ready to make war upon us, they will not wait for an act of war on our part. They did not wait for Norway or Belgium or the Netherlands to commit an act of war.

Their only interest is in a new one-way international law, which lacks mutuality in its observance, and, therefore, becomes an instrument of oppression. . . .

In the future days, which we seek to make secure, we look forward to a world founded upon four essential human freedoms.

The first is freedom of speech and expression—everywhere in the world.

The second is freedom of every person to worship God in his own way—everywhere in the world.

The third is freedom from want—which, translated into world terms, means economic understandings which will secure to every nation a healthy peacetime life for its inhabitants—everywhere in the world.

The fourth is freedom from fear—which, translated into world terms, means a world-wide reduction of armaments to such a point and in such a thorough fashion that no nation will be in a position to commit an act of physical aggression against any neighbor—anywhere in the world.

That is no vision of a distant millennium. It is a definite basis for a kind of world attainable in our own time and generation. That kind of world is the very antithesis of the so-called new order of tyranny which the dictators seek to create with the crash of a bomb.

To that new order we oppose the greater conception—the moral order. A good society is able to face schemes of world domination and foreign revolutions alike without fear.

Since the beginning of our American history, we have been engaged in change—in a perpetual peaceful revolution—a revolution which goes on steadily, quietly adjusting itself to changing conditions—without the concentration camp or the quick-lime in the ditch. The world order which we seek is the cooperation of free countries, working together in a friendly, civilized society.

This nation has placed its destiny in the hands and heads and hearts of its millions of free men and women; and its faith in freedom under the guidance of God. Freedom means the supremacy of human rights everywhere. Our support goes to those who struggle to gain those rights or keep them. Our strength is our unity of purpose.

To that high concept there can be no end save victory.

Illustrative of the vehement isolationist objections to President Roosevelt's collective security policies are these excerpts from a national radio address that Senator Hiram W. Johnson of California delivered on May 31, 1941.

SENATOR HIRAM W. JOHNSON: "PEACE ITSELF IS WAR IN MASQUERADE . . ."*

Good evening, ladies and gentlemen. I am very proud to be speaking tonight under the auspices of the America First Committee. I remember the long fights upon the so-called neutrality bills. When the first one was before the Senate I made some remarks which I prefaced by a little couplet from Dryden. This was as follows:
"Such subtle covenants shall be made
Till peace itself is war in masquerade."
I early sensed from occasional newspapers, different correspondents, and columnists, whither we were drifting. The little couplet I often had in mind, and during the few years that have intervened its truth became more apparent. I have lived to see my utterances in opposition to war justified. It's true that today insidiously the propaganda has crept upon all of us, and finally we see it so deftly administered that like a rare anesthetic it almost overcomes us. In the shock of the poison the jingle has ever been in my mind—
"Such subtle covenants shall be made
Till peace itself is war in masquerade."
As we look back we can realize how gradual was the development; how artfully planned, until now we stand aghast on the very brink of war.

At the very commencement of the remarks I made in the speech referred to, I said: "At the outset, Mr. President, I wish to say I am not a Nazi-ist, I am not a Fascist, thank God, I am not a Communist, and I do not believe, to employ a much misused word, in the ideology of any one of those particular groups. I belong to nothing of that sort; I abhor them all. I detest dictators, whether they are actual or potential, and wherever they may be."

And time has intensified this opinion. . . .

Shall this great, peace-loving country that is not a party to the war, that had naught to do with its original declaration, be pitchforked into the brutal conflict from which we have nothing to expect, and everything to lose? It is asserted that we must take sides with all the gruesome horrors in defense of one belligerent, or else we'll be seized by the other and subjected to the most awful indignities.

Bluntly, frankly, the issue at stake here is whether we'll go to war. On the one side are a smattering of good citizens, the vociferous little puppets of J. P. Morgan and Co., a large part of the press, practically all the columnists, the newspaper correspondents, all crying for war with Germany and against Hitler; on the other side is the great inarticulate mass of citizens like you and me, of Americans who love their country, whose thoughts are ever first for it, and who, at all hazards, will protect it.

Judging from the newspapers these last named are in the woeful minority, but we, whose correspondence is large, know that the exact opposite is true. We, who are only Americans, with no other thought than the preservation of America, pray God to help us do that which would be for the best interests and welfare of America. . . .

The ordinary man listening to [President Roosevelt's most recent] speech will conclude that we must be prepared to send men required to meet the Nazi in Africa, in Egypt, at the Suez Canal, and the Near East, to take Dakar, the Azores, and the Cape Verde Islands, to say nothing of the war we must carry on in continental Europe for the purpose of rescuing the oppressed nations there, and above all, for the rescue of Great Britain. What a stupendous task he maps out for America. It may become necessary that we should fight nearly all of the nations of the earth, and that we should conquer them, but God forbid. And, above all, we should know, and have the right to know, if this is the program of our President.

But, what will become of our United States of America while we are pursuing these Herculean tasks. We have seen, little by little, power concentrated in one man's hands. We have soothed our perturbed spirits by pretending that those powers were needed to be thus concentrated in order to meet the crisis, but when you are meeting crises on practically all lands of every continent, what will become, the ordinary citizen will ask, of the good old United States. It is no reply to talk in generalities, and in enigmas of sacrifices that must be made. What is to become of your Government, Mr. American? Is it not plain that all this fighting on every shore, and in practically every country will mean but one thing, perhaps, the destruction of a dictatorship in other lands, but the certainty of the creation of a dictatorship in our own. You may live under a

* Reprinted from *Vital Speeches of the Day,* VII (June 15, 1941), 514–17.

beneficent despot the rest of your days if you desire. I prefer the good old American way, and I will protest and fight to the bitter end. You cannot with this plan that apparently is mapped out for you, escape a dictatorship and perhaps worse. If ever there was a time in the history of this country when it is the duty of Americans to stand forth and be men it is now. It will soon be too late, and then the outstretched hands of liberty may no longer join yours.

The propaganda is abroad today in far greater volume than ever before. We were subject during the last war to it, and the books which have been written since by the men who were guilty of it have exposed it. The same technique, though immensely improved, has been adopted now, and every man in this country feeling an inferiority complex, and subject to the dictates of the English, is in favor of it. Not only that, but whole flocks of titled Englishmen and English women, have gone about our country lecturing and wheedling us into war. The British Ambassador himself set a bad example as openly he has gone from city to city in its behalf. Societies under all sorts of names have been formed. Where the money comes from to support all of these the ordinary citizen can only guess, but it has been spent without stint during the past 10 days. Full-page advertisements have been carried by our newspapers calling upon authoritative action and citizens to contribute. In this country I would not shut off a single one of these people because of the precious regard I have for the right of free speech but when an invidious epithet is applied to Colonel Lindbergh, and pious Philadelphia closes its halls to him, I think that it is quite time that America cries out against this sort of thing.

Now I am fully aware that to speak this way opens me to the charge of Nazi, and, because it is viler, of being a copperhead, but some of us were made of such stuff that we won't be frightened, nor cajoled when the liberties that are ours—the sacred, personal liberties, are attacked. All of our precious civil liberties will be lost in the mad adventure and the fantastic enterprise. It is only a step now to forbid free speech in this country, and the minority of our citizens who are so enthusiastic for Britain would justify it, and perhaps the concentration camp would follow; but there are some of us who laugh at a concentration camp and who are old enough to spend the rest of their days in one laughing.

The four liberties for which the President so eloquently appealed, and which Anthony Eden so weakly reechoed, would have but a sorry chance of existence if we would march our armies from Greenland's icy mountains to India's coral strand. . . .

Dictatorship and war together marched very early in [the Roosevelt administration], and have led us step by step, along the dangerous road until today we can reach out and touch it, and its fury burns into our very souls. Dismayed, betrayed, we reel and stagger as we realize that the subtle plan is about to flower. The masquerade is over and we now know that God had no place amongst them. . . .

The Japanese attack upon Pearl Harbor followed by Hitler's declaration of war upon the United States brought the nation into instant leadership of the forces warring against the Axis. Increasingly, as Bruner pointed out, most Americans came to feel that the United States must participate permanently in collective security programs if World War III were to be avoided. Both Democrats and Republicans in Congress voted for a resolution looking toward this end. Secretary of State Cordell Hull returned from Moscow in 1943, enthusiastic because of Russian willingness to participate in a collective security organization which, Hull asserted, would end the age-old competitiveness of alliances and spheres of influence. At Dumbarton Oaks, an estate in Washington, D. C., American delegates met in August, 1944, with delegates from Great Britain, Russia, and China to draft plans for the new international organization. President Roosevelt's extemporaneous remarks to the delegates as they met were an indication of the prevalent optimism and of the goals the organization was expected to achieve.

FRANKLIN D. ROOSEVELT:
REMARKS TO THE DELEGATES AT DUMBARTON OAKS*

Gentlemen, this is an informal occasion. I have not prepared any speech. This is merely a feeling on my part that I would like to shake hands with you. I should like to be able to go out to Dumbarton Oaks, to take a part in your discussions.

A conference of this kind always reminds me of an old saying of a gentleman called Alfred E. Smith, who used to be Governor of New York. He was very, very successful in settling any problem between capital and labor, or anything that had to do with the State government in which there was a controversy. He said if you can get the parties into one room with a big table and make them take their coats off and put their feet up on the table, and give each one of them a good cigar, you can always make them agree. Well, there was something in the idea.

You have a great responsibility. In a way, it is a preliminary responsibility. But after all we learn from experience, and what I hope is that in planning for the peace that is to come we will arrive at the same good cooperation and unity of action as we have in the carrying on of the war. It is a very remarkable fact that we have carried on this war with such great unanimity.

I think that often it comes down to personalities. When, back in 1941, at the time of the Atlantic Charter, just for example, I did not know Mr. Churchill at all well. I had met him once or twice very informally during the first World War. I did not know Mr. Eden. But up there in the North Atlantic—three or four days together, with our two ships lying close together—

we got awfully fond of each other. I got to know him, and he got to know me. In other words, we met, and you cannot hate a man that you know well.

Later on Mr. Molotov came here and we had a grand time together. Then during the following year, at Tehran, the Marshal and I got to know each other. We got on beautifully. We cracked the ice, if there ever was any ice; and since then there has been no ice. And that's the spirit in which I know you are going about your work.

I was just talking with the Secretary of War, Mr. Stimson. He was saying that one of the tasks we face in making this conference of ours—and the successor conferences—something that will last, last a long time. He said that unfortunately in Germany the young people, the young Nazis, favor an idea which will be dangerous to the peace of the world just as long as they have anything to say about it. The prisoners of 17, 18, 20 that we are capturing now—both the French front and the Soviet front—these German prisoners of that age are even worse in their Nazism than the prisoners of 40 or 45. And, therefore, as long as these young men have anything to say about it, the peril of Nazism will always be before us.

And we have got to make not merely a peace but a peace that will last, and a peace in which the larger nations will work absolutely in unison in preventing war by force. But the four of us have to be friends, conferring all the time—the basis of getting to know each other—'putting their feet up on the table'.

And so I am very hopeful that it can be done because of the spirit that has been shown in the past in getting together for the winning of the war. But that is the spirit that we have learned so well in the last few years. It is something new, this close relationship between the British Em-

* Reprinted from *Department of State Bulletin*, XI (August 27, 1944), 197.

pire and the United States. This great friendship between the Russian people and the American people—that is new. Let's hang on to both friendships, and by spreading that spirit around the world we may have a peaceful period for our grandchildren to grow up in.

All I can do is to wish you every possible success in this great task that you have undertaken. It will not be a final task, but at least it gives us something to build on, so that we can accomplish the one thing that humanity has been looking forward to for a great many hundreds of years.

It is good to see you. Good luck.

The degree to which almost all segments of the nation had been won over to the concepts of collective security was dramatized on January 10, 1945. Senator Arthur H. Vandenberg of Michigan, once a confirmed isolationist, arose on the floor of the Senate to deliver a momentous address in favor of the new doctrines.

ARTHUR H. VANDENBERG: "WE CANNOT TOLERATE UNILATERAL PRIVILEGE IN A MULTILATERAL PEACE."*

There are critical moments in the life of every nation which call for the straightest, the plainest and the most courageous thinking of which we are capable. We confront such a moment now. It is not only desperately important to America. It is important to the world. It is important not only to this generation which lives in blood. It is important to future generations if they shall live in peace.

No man in his right senses will be dogmatic in his viewpoint at such an hour. A global conflict which uproots the earth is not calculated to submit itself to the domination of any finite mind. The clash of rival foreign interests, which have motivated wars for countless centuries, are not likely suddenly to surrender to some simple man-made formula, no matter how nobly meditated. . . .

We not only have two wars to win; we also have yet to achieve such a peace as will justify this appalling cost. Here again an even more difficult unity is indispensable. Otherwise we shall look back upon a futile, sanguinary shambles and —God save the mark! We shall be able to look forward only to the curse of World War Number Three. . . .

Yet it cannot be denied that our Government has not spoken out—to our own people or to our allies—in any such specific fashion as have the others. It cannot be denied, as a result, that too often a grave melancholy settles upon some sectors of our people. It cannot be denied that citizens, in increasing numbers, are crying "What are we fighting for?" It cannot be denied that our silence—at least our public and official silence—has multiplied confusion at home and abroad. It cannot be denied that this confusion threatens our unity—yes, Mr. President, and already hangs like a cloud over Dumbarton Oaks. . . .

In a word, the first thing we must do is to reassert, in high places, our American faith in these particular elemental objectives of the so-called "Atlantic Charter." . . .

That's the indispensable point. These basic pledges cannot now be dismissed as a mere nautical nimbus. They march with our armies. They sail with our fleets. They fly with our eagles. They sleep with our martyred dead. The first requisite of honest candor, I respectfully suggest, is to relight this torch.

The next thing we need to do, Mr. President, if I may be so bold, in this spirit of honest candor, is to appeal to our Allies, in the name of reason, to frankly face the post-war alternatives which are available to them, and to us, as a means to preserve tomorrow's peace for them and for us.

There are two ways to do it. One way is by exclusive individual action in which each of us tries to look out for himself. The other way is by joint action in which we undertake to look out for each other.

The first way is the old way which has twice taken us to Europe's interminable battlefields within a quarter century. The second way is the new way in which our present fraternity of war becomes a new fraternity of peace. I do not believe that either we or our Allies can have it both ways. They serve to cancel out each other. We cannot tolerate unilateral privilege in a multilateral peace. Yet that seems to be the fatalistic trend today. I think we must make our choice. I think we need to make it wholly plain to our major Allies that they, too, must make their choice.

I hasten to make my own personal viewpoint clear. I have always been frankly one of those

* Reprinted from *Vital Speeches of the Day,* XI (February 1, 1945), 226-31.

who has believed in our own self-reliance. I still believe that we can never again—regardless of collaborations—allow our national defense to deteriorate to anything like a point of impotence. But I do not believe that any nation hereafter can immunize itself by its own exclusive action.

STRESSES NEW ROLE OF WAR

Since Pearl Harbor, World War Number Two has put the gory science of mass murder into new and sinister perspective. Our oceans have ceased to be moats which automatically protect our ramparts. Flesh and blood now compete unequally with winged steel. War has become an all-consuming juggernaut. If World War Number Three ever unhappily arrives, it will open new laboratories of death too horrible to contemplate. I propose to do everything within my power to keep those laboratories closed for keeps.

I want maximum American cooperation, consistent with legitimate American self-interest, with constitutional process, and with collateral events that warrant it, to make the basic idea of Dumbarton Oaks succeed. I want a new dignity and a new authority for international law. I think American self-interest requires it. But, Mr. President, this also requires wholehearted reciprocity.

In honest candor I think we should tell other nations that this glorious thing we contemplate is not and cannot be one-sided. I think we must say again that unshared idealism is a menace which we could not underwrite in the post-war world.

Now, I am not so impractical as to expect any country to act on any final motive other than self-interest. I know of no reason why it should. That is what nations are for. I certainly intend that intelligent and loyal American self-interest shall be just as vigilantly and vigorously guarded as is amply obvious, from time to time, in their own behalf by the actions of our allies. The real question always becomes just this— where does real self-interest lie?

Here we reach the core of the immediate problem. Without remotely wanting to be invidious, I use one of many available examples. I would not presume to use it except that it ultimately involves us. Russia's unilateral plan appears to contemplate the engulfment, directly or indirectly of a surrounding circle of buffer states, contrary to our conception of what we thought we were fighting for in respect to the rights of small nations and a just peace. Russia's announced reason is her insistent purpose never again to be at the mercy of another German tyranny. That is a perfectly understandable reason. The alternative is collective security.

ALTERNATIVES FOR MOSCOW

Now, which is better, in the long view, from a purely selfish Russian standpoint? To forcefully surround herself with a cordon of unwillingly controlled or partitioned states, thus affronting the opinions of mankind, as a means of post-war protection against a renaissance of German aggression, or to win the priceless asset of world confidence in her by embracing the alternative; namely, full and whole-hearted cooperation with a reliance on a vital international organization in which all of us shall honorably participate to guarantee that Axis aggression shall never rise again?

Well—at that point, Russia, or others like her, in equally honest candor, has a perfect right to reply and say this to us—"where is there any such alternative reliance until we know what the United States will do? How can you expect us to rely on an enigma?"

Now we are getting somewhere: Fear of reborn German aggression in years to come is at the base of most of our contemporary frictions. It is a perfectly human and understandable fear on the part of all neighboring nations which German militarism has twice driven to the Valley of the Shadow within one generation.

Fear of reborn German aggression in years to come is the cause assigned to unilateral plans for Russian post-war expansion. Fear of reborn German aggression is the reason assigned to the proposed partition of Poland. Fear of reborn German aggression gave birth to the Anglo-Soviet agreement of 1942; the Soviet-Czechoslovak agreement of 1943; the Franco-Soviet treaty of 1944, and similar unilateral and bilateral actions inevitably yet to come. Fear of reborn German aggression is our apple of discord.

This second World War plagues the earth chiefly because France and Britain did not keep Germany disarmed, according to contract, after World War No. 1. In other words, when we deal with Europe's fear—her justified fear—of another rebirth of German military tyranny in some future post-war era, we are at the heart of the immediate problem which bedevils our Allied relationships.

I propose that we meet this problem conclusively and at once. There is no reason to wait.

America has this same self-interest in permanently and conclusively and effectively disarming Germany and Japan. It is simply unthinkable that America, or any other member of the United Nations, would allow this Axis calamity to reproduce itself again.

Whether we Americans do, or do not, agree upon all the powers that shall reside in an ultimate international council to call upon us for joint military action in behalf of collective security, surely we can agree that we do not want an instant's hesitation or an instant's doubt about our military cooperation in the peremptory use of force, if needed, to keep Germany and Japan permanently demilitarized. Such a crisis would be the lengthened shadow of the present war. It would be a direct epilogue of the present war. It should be handled as this present war is handled.

IMMEDIATE TREATY URGED

There should be no need to refer any such action back to Congress any more than Congress would expect to pass upon battle plans today. The Commander in Chief should have instant power to act, and he should act. I know of no reason why a hard-and-fast treaty between the major Allies should not be signed today to achieve this dependable end. We need not await the determination of our other post-war relationships.

This problem—this menace—stands apart by itself. Regardless of what our later decision may be, in respect to the power that shall be delegated to the President to join our military force with others in a new Peace League—no matter what limitations may command themselves to our ultimate judgments in this regard—I am sure we can agree that there should be no limitations when it comes to keeping the Axis out of piracy for keeps. . . .

Because they were engaged in a desperate struggle against the Axis, the Americans envisaged their primary collective security problem in the years following the war as being the prevention of the resurgence of Germany and Japan. President Roosevelt was himself aware that the fate of the peace depended upon cordial relations between the United States and Russia, and he had received reports of Russian uncooperativeness from the Commanding General of the United States Military Mission and the Ambassador to Moscow. In view of what was to develop in the future, it is instructive to examine the discussions among Roosevelt, Churchill, and Stalin concerning voting in the Security Council of the proposed United Nations organization. The following are minutes kept by Charles Bohlen at the Yalta Conference.

YALTA CONFERENCE: THE WORLD SECURITY ORGANIZATION*

TRIPARTITE DINNER MEETING, FEBRUARY 4, 1945, 8:30 P.M., LIVADIA PALACE

Top Secret

Subject: Voice of Smaller Powers in Postwar Peace Organization.

Before dinner and during the greater part of the dinner the conversation was general and personal in character. Marshal Stalin, the President and the Prime Minister appeared to be in very good humor throughout the dinner. No political or military subjects of any importance were discussed until the last half hour of the dinner when indirectly the subject of the responsibility and rights of the big powers as against those of the small powers came up.

MARSHAL STALIN made it quite plain on a number of occasions that he felt that the three Great Powers which had borne the brunt of the war and had liberated from German domination the small powers should have the unanimous right to preserve the peace of the world. He said that he could serve no other interest than that of the Soviet state and people but that in the international arena the Soviet Union was prepared to pay its share in the preservation of peace. He said that it was ridiculous to believe that Albania would have an equal voice with the three Great Powers who had won the war and were present at this dinner. He said some of the liberated countries seemed to believe that the Great Powers had been forced to shed their blood in order to liberate them and that they were now scolding these Great Powers for failure to take into consideration the rights of these small powers.

MARSHAL STALIN said that he was prepared in concert with the United States and Great Britain to protect the rights of the small powers but that he would never agree to having any action of any of the Great Powers submitted to the judgment of the small powers.

THE PRESIDENT said he agreed that the Great Powers bore the greater responsibility and that the peace should be written by the Three Powers represented at this table.

THE PRIME MINISTER said that there was no question of the small powers dictating to the big powers but that the great nations of the world

* Reprinted from *Foreign Relations of the United States. Diplomatic Papers. The Conferences at Malta and Yalta, 1945* (Washington, D.C.: Government Printing Office, 1955), pp. 589–90, 660–67, 711–12.

should discharge their moral responsibility and leadership and should exercise their power with moderation and great respect for the rights of the smaller nations. . . .

THE PRIME MINISTER, referring to the rights of the small nations, gave a quotation which said: "The eagle should permit the small birds to sing and care not wherefor they sang." . . .

THIRD PLENARY MEETING, FEBRUARY 6, 1945, 4 P.M., LIVADIA PALACE

Top Secret

Subjects: 1. World Security Organization . . . .

THE PRESIDENT inquired whether the committee of Foreign Ministers had anything to report to the Conference. . . .

MR. STETTINIUS [the Secretary of State] . . . said that . . . they would like to have some more time before reporting on reparations and the relationship of the French zone [of occupation of Germany] to the control commission.

THE PRIME MINISTER said that . . . in regard to the French zone he felt that the importance of France in the future had been enhanced by the [two year] limitation which the President yesterday had placed on the length of time United States forces might stay in Europe. He said that Great Britain would not be strong enough alone to guard the Western approaches to the Channel.

THE PRESIDENT said that he had spoken on the basis of present conditions and he felt public opinion in the United States would be prepared to support an international organization along the lines of Dumbarton Oaks and that this might change their attitude in regard to the question of troops. The President then added that he felt the Conference should now proceed to the consideration of the United States proposal in regard to Dumbarton Oaks. He felt strongly that all the nations of the world shared a common desire to see the elimination of war for at least fifty years. He said he was not so optimistic as to believe in eternal peace, but he did believe fifty years of peace were feasible and possible. He said that since neither he, Marshal Stalin, nor the Prime Minister had been present at Dumbarton Oaks he would ask the Secretary of State (Mr. Stettinius) who had been chairman of that conference to explain the United States position on the question of voting in the Security Council.

MR. STETTINIUS then read the following statement of the American position on voting in the Council:

"1. *Review of Status of this Question.*

"It was agreed at Dumbarton Oaks that certain matters would remain under consideration for future settlement. Of these, the principal one was that of voting procedure to be followed in the Security Council.

"At Dumbarton Oaks, the three Delegations thoroughly explored the whole question. Since that time the matter has received continuing intensive study by each of the three Governments.

"On December 5, 1944, the President sent to Marshal Stalin and to Prime Minister Churchill a proposal that this matter be settled by making Section C, Chapter VI of the Dumbarton Oaks proposals read substantially as follows:

'C. *Voting*

'1. Each member of the Security Council should have one vote.

'2. Decisions of the Security Council on procedural matters should be made by an affirmative vote of seven members.

'3. Decisions of the Security Council on all other matters should be made by an affirmative vote of seven members including the concurring votes of the permanent members; provided that, in decisions under Chapter VIII, Section A and under the second sentence of paragraph 1 of Chapter VIII, Section C, a party to a dispute should abstain from voting.'

"2. *Analysis of the American Proposal.*

"(*a*) We believe that our proposal is entirely consistent with the special responsibilities of the great powers for the preservation of the peace of the world. In this respect our proposal calls for unqualified unanimity of the permanent members of the Council on all major decisions relating to the preservation of peace, including all economic and military enforcement measures.

"(*b*) At the same time our proposal recognizes the desirability of the permanent members frankly stating that the peaceful adjustment of any controversy which may arise is a matter of general world interest in which any sovereign member state involved should have a right to present its case.

"We believe that unless this freedom of discussion in the Council is permitted, the establishment of the World Organization which we all so earnestly desire in order to save the world from the tragedy of another war would be seriously jeopardized. Without full and free discussion in the Council, the Organization, even if it could be established, would be vastly different from the one we have contemplated.

"The paper which we have placed before the other two delegations sets forth the text of the provisions which I have read and lists specifically those decisions of the Council which, under our proposals, would require unqualified unanimity and, separately, those matters in the area of discussion and peaceful settlement in which any party to a dispute would abstain from casting a vote.

"3. *Reasons for the American Position.*

"From the point of view of the United States Government there are two important elements in the matter of voting procedure.

"First, there is the necessity for unanimity among the permanent members for the preservation of the peace of the world.

"Second, it is of particular importance to the people of the United States, that there be provision for a fair hearing for all members of the organization, large and small.

"We believe that the proposals submitted by the President to Marshal Stalin and Prime Minister Churchill on December 5 of last year provide a reasonable and just solution and satisfactorily combine these two main considerations.

"It is our earnest hope that our two great Allies will find it possible to accept the President's proposal." . . .

MR. MOLOTOV said that the Soviet Government attached great importance to the question of voting in the Security Council and, therefore, he wished to study the United States proposal and in particular the effect of the drafting change and would be ready to discuss the question tomorrow.

THE PRIME MINISTER stated that the British Government had given the most careful consideration to the United States proposals. He had not agreed with the original proposals made at Dumbarton Oaks since he was anxious that the realities of the situation of the Three Great Powers should be considered, but in studying the President's latest proposal his anxieties on that score had been removed. He could thus say that on behalf of the British Commonwealth of Nations, the Empire and, he believed, the Self-Governing Dominions the President's new proposals were entirely satisfactory. He said that in the last resort world peace depended on the friendship and cooperation of the three Governments, but that the British Government would consider that they were committing an injustice if reservation were not made for free statement of their grievances by small countries. The matter looks as though the Three Great Powers were trying to rule the world, whereas, our desires are to save the world and save it from a repetition of the horrors of this war. He said he felt that the Three Major Powers should make a proud submission. He said that he had looked into the whole matter as it would affect British interests and would give an illustration of why the British Government does not think the President's proposal would bring any harm to British interests. He said, for example, if China should raise the question of the return of Hongkong under the President's proposal, both China and Great Britain would be precluded from voting in regard to the methods of settlement of this controversy, as listed in the five points of the analysis read by Mr. Stettinius. In the last analysis Great Britain would be protected against any decision adverse to her interests by the exercise of the veto power under paragraph 3 of Mr. Stettinius' analysis. . . .

THE PRESIDENT then said that he recalled that in the Tehran Declaration the Three Powers had stated: "We recognize fully the supreme responsibility resting upon us and all the nations to make a peace which will command good will from the overwhelming masses of the peoples of the world. . . ."

THE PRESIDENT added that he thought this Declaration was pertinent to the discussion in progress.

THE PRIME MINISTER said that since he saw no reason to fear the United States proposals he was glad to associate the British Government with them. He added that because of our great power, which is still protected by the veto if we do not agree, we should allow others to be heard.

MARSHAL STALIN said that he would like to have this document to study, since only hearing it orally it was impossible to catch all of the implications. He said that the Dumbarton Oaks proposals already give the right of discussion in the assembly, but he did not believe that any nation would be satisfied with expressing its opinion. They would want some decision. He said that if Mr. Churchill thought that China after raising the question of Hongkong would be satisfied with merely expressing her opinion, he was mistaken since China would want a decision. The same was true of Egypt in the possible question of the Suez Canal. He added that it was not a question of one power or three powers desiring to be masters of the world since he felt that the Dumbarton Oaks organization put a brake on that. He said that he would like to ask for further clarification on what powers Mr. Churchill had in mind when he spoke of a desire to rule the world. He said that he was sure Great Britain had no such desire, nor did the United States and that that left only the U. S. S. R.

THE PRIME MINISTER replied that he had spoken of the three Great Powers who could collectively place themselves so high over the others that the whole world would say these three desired to rule.

MARSHAL STALIN then said ironically that it looks as though two Great Powers have already accepted a document which would avoid any such accusation but that the third has not yet signified its assent. He then went on to say that in his opinion there was a more serious question than the voting procedure or the question of the domination of the world. They all knew that as long as the three of them lived none of them would involve their countries in aggressive actions, but after all, ten years from now none of them might be present. A new generation would come into being not knowing the horrors of the present war. He felt that there was, therefore, an obligation to create for the future generation such an organization as would secure peace for at least fifty years. He said the main thing was to prevent quarrels in the future between the three Great Powers and that the task, therefore, was to secure their unity for the future. The covenant of the new World Organization should have this as its primary task. He said the greatest danger was conflict between the three Great Powers represented here, but that if unity could be preserved there was little danger of the renewal of German aggression. He said, therefore, a covenant must be worked out which would prevent conflicts between the three Great Powers. Marshal Stalin apologized for not having had an opportunity for studying in detail the

Dumbarton Oaks proposals. He said he had been busy on other matters. He said that as he understood it, there were two categories of disputes involved in Mr. Stettinius' explanation: (1) conflicts which would require the application of sanctions, economic, political or military, and (2) conflicts which could be settled by peaceful means. He said in regard to the first the permanent members had a right to vote even if they were parties to such disputes. Under the second category, however, in conflicts susceptible to settlement by peaceful means, the parties in dispute would not be allowed to vote. He added that we Russians were being accused of spending too much time on the technique of voting, which he admitted. But they attached great importance to this question since all decisions were made by votes and they were interested in the decisions, not in the discussions. He said, for example, if China or Egypt raised complaints against England they would not be without friends or protectors in the assembly.

Both the PRIME MINISTER and MR. STETTINIUS pointed out that under the United States proposal the power of the World Organization could not be directed against any of the permanent members.

MARSHAL STALIN said that he was afraid that any conflict might break the unity of our united front.

THE PRIME MINISTER replied that he saw the force of that argument, but he did not believe that the world organization would eliminate disputes between powers and that would remain the function of diplomacy.

MARSHAL STALIN said that his colleagues in Moscow could not forget the events of December 1939 during the Finnish war when at the instiga-

tion of England and France the League of Nations expelled the Soviet Union from the League and mobilized world opinion against the Soviet Union, even going so far as to speak of a crusade.

THE PRIME MINISTER answered that at that time the British and French Governments were very angry at the Soviet Union and in any event any such action was impossible under the Dumbarton Oaks proposals.

MARSHAL STALIN said he was not thinking of expulsion but of the question of the mobilization of opinion against one country.

THE PRIME MINISTER answered that he thought this might happen to any nation, but he doubted very much if either the President or Marshal Stalin would lead a savage attack against Great Britain and he felt this applied also to the other two countries.

THE PRESIDENT then said that he felt that the unity of the Great Powers was one of our first aims and that the United States policy promoted rather than impaired this aim. He said that should there unfortunately be any differences between the Great Powers, and there might well be, this fact would become fully known to the world no matter what voting procedure was adopted. In any event, there was no method of preventing discussions of differences in the assembly. He said that full and friendly discussions in the Council would in no sense promote disunity, but on the contrary, would serve to demonstrate the confidence which the Great Powers had in each other and in the justice of their own policies. . . .

[At a session the next day, Molotov asserted that the "Soviet Government felt that these proposals fully guaranteed the unity of the Great Powers in the matter of preservation of peace," and that it would accept them.]

Within a few days after the Yalta Conference, the Russians began disregarding various agreements they had made there and acting toward the Americans with truculence. President Roosevelt, disturbed, sent a firm message to Stalin. Nevertheless in a speech Roosevelt was preparing at the time of his death to have been delivered on April 13, 1945, he called upon the American people to undertake the responsibility of preserving the peace.

FRANKLIN D. ROOSEVELT: "GREAT POWER INVOLVES GREAT RESPONSIBILITY"*

. . . Today we have learned in the agony of war that great power involves great responsibility. Today we can no more escape the consequences

of German and Japanese aggression than could we avoid the consequences of attacks by the Barbary Corsairs a century and a half before.

We, as Americans, do not choose to deny our responsibility.

Nor do we intend to abandon our determination that, within the lives of our children and our

* Reprinted from *New York Times*, April 14, 1945.

508

children's children, there will not be a third world war.

We seek peace—enduring peace. More than an end to war, we want an end to the beginnings of all wars—yes, an end to this brutal, inhuman, and thoroughly impractical method of settling the differences between governments. . . .

The only limit to our realization of tomorrow will be our doubts of today. Let us move forward with strong and active faith.

CHAPTER TWENTY-TWO

THE FORTIES:
PROSPERITY AND INFLATION

The close of World War II marked the beginning of a new era in the American economy, one whose central features are still unfolding in the 1960's. This basic change was from an economy of scarcity to one of abundance. When the war ended in 1945, America had not yet abandoned its depression outlook or frame of reference. Few people at that time spoke of economic growth, and fewer still expected postwar prosperity. Instead, it was widely held that another depression was just around the corner. Even official sources, such as Office of War Mobilization reports, predicted rough times. Thus an examination of the mid-1940's, culminating with the election of 1948, reveals how America first faced the problems of a full economy. Many of the issues now familiar to Americans, such as the wage-price spiral and the growth of large unions, were present at that time. To understand the 1960's, one must see the way business, labor, and the government faced the new era of abundance when it first arose.

In the fall of 1945, when the country was rushing to reconvert to a peacetime economy, something totally unexpected happened: there was inflation rather than deflation, and the labor force and productive capacity were unable to catch up with demand. At this time President Harry S. Truman sought to remove government regulations slowing down reconversion, but also insisted that the effect of decontrolling on prices and wages be noninflationary. There was general acceptance of the first of these two goals, speedy reconversion, but serious differences existed over how inflation should be combatted. Many critics of the Truman administration had one simple answer: immediate and total decontrolling of prices. Whatever the disagreements, reconversion itself went more successfully than after World War I.

Then came the inflationary spiral. Confronted by scarcities, consumers had accumulated ample savings to bid up the price of goods. After four years of war, the mood of the country was to make up for lost time. An even more important source of inflation, however, centered around the postwar relations of labor and capital. The workers were not happy at the prospect of suffering a wage cut or losing their lucrative overtime pay. They strongly felt that current profits justified higher wages. Management, on the other hand, moved in the opposite direction, arguing that labor had already become too powerful. In November, 1945, the Labor-Management Conference, in its inability to reach an agreement, provided a portent of the coming difficulties between employers and workers. The year 1946 saw major strikes in key industries. Walter Reuther, leader of the United Automobile Workers, demanded that General Motors open its books to see whether a wage increase was justified. General Motors refused, and for a short time it appeared that Truman would support the union. But the President backed down. Truman also took a compromise position on the steel strike of 1946. Going against the advice of Chester Bowles, head of the Office of Price Administration, Truman permitted a $5.00 per ton increase in steel to match the wage hike. And in April, John L. Lewis called a coal strike which threatened to tie up the entire economy.

The public, angry at the ensuing inflation and fearful of work stoppages, adopted a militantly antilabor position. Truman reflected this anger (to the extent even that Senator Robert A. Taft assailed his stand as too tough) when a railroad strike seemed likely to occur in the midst of the coal strike. Stating that the army would take over the railroads, Truman successfully prevented the strike. His solution to strikes in basic industries was to draft the workers and give corporate profits to the government, a remedy opposed by liberals and conservatives alike. As this antilabor sentiment built up, conservatives took the offensive and demanded the removal of all price controls. Holding that controls perpetuated the black market and stifled full production, business groups campaigned for major limitations at the end of June, 1946. Senator Taft, spokesman for the business community, amended the bill on controls to provide for a "reasonable" profit on the items covered. This created a real bone of contention since even accountants could not determine what was a reasonable profit. With the old act about to terminate, Truman vetoed the new measure and thereby ended price controls. For nearly four weeks, with controls off, prices soared on such basic commodities as meat. Finally, Congress gave the President a stronger bill than the one he vetoed, and controls were temporarily restored. Yet, by keeping meat off the market, stockmen forced Truman to rescind meat controls in October. After the 1946 elections, all controls were removed except those on rents—and even here Congress permitted increases of 15 per cent. The over-all result was a staggering increase in prices, at the rate of 3 per cent per month.

The nation blamed the Democrats for inflation and promptly elected a Republican Eightieth Congress. The complex problems of inflation and economic growth were now to be met through an orthodox laissez faire attitude. Taft summed up the feeling when, in discussing meat prices, he suggested that people "Eat less." The domestic record of this Congress was directed to three goals: curb labor unions, cut social welfare expenditures, and enact taxation legislation beneficial to upper income groups. The lines were clearly drawn for the 1948 presidential campaign with inflation as the central issue. Truman stood virtually alone in sensing the changing mood of the electorate. He was confident that the American people were ready to reject laissez faire in favor of the Fair Deal. Faced with defections on the right and left in his own party as well as the selection of liberal candidates by the Republicans, Truman nonetheless remained undaunted. He waged a vigorous whistlestop campaign throughout the country, calling for increased welfare spending, repeal of the Taft-Hartley Act, and civil rights legislation. In the election, Truman defeated Dewey by more than two million votes, and the Democrats resumed control of Congress. The trying period of postwar adjustment drew to a close, but the problems of economic growth and inflation still remained largely unsolved.

This Bureau of the Budget report outlines the first stages of the postwar anti-inflation fight. Recognizing the conflicting tendencies of the process of decontrol and price stabilization, it states the Truman administration's case for retaining certain controls.

BUREAU OF THE BUDGET:
THE FIGHT AGAINST WARTIME INFLATION*

During the war, consumers' incomes had risen sharply, whereas the supply of goods available for purchase had increased much less rapidly: the supply of many consumer durables either declined or ceased altogether to be available. While increased tax payments, bond purchase campaigns, and voluntary savings served to absorb a substantial portion of the expansion in consumer incomes, imbalance between purchasing power and the supply of goods was sufficiently great to create dangerous inflationary possibilities.

Prior to the end of the war, there was no unanimity of agreement that such inflationary pressures would continue long beyond the attainment of victory. Some observers felt that the very sharp drop in Federal expenditures to be expected after VJ-day would result in serious deflation and that as a consequence unemployment would be the Nation's major problem. Others, recalling that during World War I price inflation had been far more severe after the end of hostilities than during the war, argued that consumers' purchasing power would for some time exceed the supply of available goods and that the danger of inflation would continue for an extended period.

The Government, in view of these two possibilities, prepared to combat both deflation and inflation. Plans for public works and the maintenance of consumer purchasing power were discussed. Chief emphasis was placed, however, on ways and means of combating inflation. The Baruch-Hancock Report had suggested that the problem would be one of controlling prices and President Roosevelt in his Budget message in January 1945 had said: "When war production is extensively reduced some of the controls which were needed in an all-out war economy can be relaxed, although other controls must be continued to assure necessary war production and orderly reconversion. For example, we must avoid speculation in inventories such as contributed to the inflation after the last war. The fact that many businesses and individuals have ample funds for a buying spree necessitates caution in relaxing controls. The balance between incomes, savings and expenditures will still be precarious during the reconversion period. It will therefore be necessary to retain the machinery for allocation and

price controls as long as certain materials and finished goods are in short supply." [44]

The situation after VJ-day was one of high-wage levels though somewhat reduced from wartime peaks, combined with favorable employment conditions, continuing large Federal expenditures, vast pent-up demands for many classes of goods, and very large liquid savings in the hands of individuals as well as business corporations. In view of the long time lag before the desired goods could appear on the markets in significant volume, the danger of an upward spiral of prices was very real. The Office of Price Administration had prepared to handle these problems well before VJ-day. Price control during the reconversion period, and until the Price Control Act came before Congress for renewal, was to be within the framework of administration and policy developed during the war.

Among the demands made by business groups in 1944 and early 1945 for adequate Government preparation for reconversion, requests for enunciation of a price control policy were frequent and insistent. The task was essentially that of reviewing and making the necessary adjustments in the price ceilings of products which were on the market in 1941–42 but which were not being manufactured for some time before the end of the war. It was necessary also to determine price ceilings for new products, a more difficult task but one with which OPA had acquired considerable experience. It was essential that the pricing program be developed so that these commodities would flow into the civilian market in maximum volume as quickly as possible after the end of war production. While the administrative burden was heavy, the number of commodities involved in the reconversion pricing program was relatively small and their production was highly concentrated in a small group of large firms.

The Office of Price Administration had given some attention to the problem of reconversion pricing since the last half of 1943; intensively so in the middle of 1944 when partial reconversion seemed probable.[45] The specific policy to be followed was, however, not announced until

---

* Reprinted from The Bureau of the Budget, *United States at War*, in *Historical Reports on War Administration* (Washington, D.C.: 1947), I, 492–97.

[44] *The Budget of the U. S. Government, Fiscal Year ending June 30, 1946*, p. xxiii.

[45] Office of Price Administration, *11th Quarterly Report*, pp. 5–7.

May 1945. Under the program, prices on reconversion products were set at 1941–42 levels with adjustments for legitimate increase in costs to be made upon application. Such adjustments would cover increased costs by the use of industry-wide formulae or in the case of smaller firms, on an individual basis.[46] There were, however, larger issues involving the entire framework of economic stabilization which required administrative action.

The problem of controlling prices after VJ-day differed sharply from the task in the war period. On the one hand, the decision to eliminate a maximum number of controls over production meant that price stabilization could find only limited support in that direction. On the other hand, President Truman had early indicated his agreement with the popular desire to return to free collective bargaining in labor relations at the earliest possible opportunity. If such release of controls was to mean a sharp rise in hourly wage levels, as did prove to be the case, inflationary pressures would be expanded. Such increase would be reflected in higher costs to consumers, increasing the cost of living. The task was thus one of reconciling the objective of continuing price control with the desire to eliminate or the impracticability of continuing other controls which over the war period had proven essential supports of the anti-inflationary effort.

On August 18, the President issued an Executive order "providing for assistance to expand production and continued stabilization of the national economy during the transition from war to peace, and for the orderly modification of wartime controls over prices, wages, materials, and facilities".[47]

By this order the whole process of decontrol—of removing wartime restrictions—became subject to the requirements of the stabilization program. The objectives of the Government were stated as the removal of price, wage, production, and other controls, and the restoration of collective bargaining and the free market. These were to be accomplished "without endangering the stability of the economy."

The Price Administrator was specifically instructed to "take all necessary steps to assure that the cost of living and the general level of prices shall not rise". Such price increases as might be approved for designated reasons were not to cause increases at later levels of production or distribution. Wage increases might be made by industry without approval of NWLB or the Director of the Economic Stabilization if such increases were not to be used to seek an increase in price ceilings or to increase the cost to the Government of products produced under Government contract. Wage increases to correct maladjustments and inequities might be approved by NWLB when such "in-

terfered with the effective transition to a peacetime economy" but such increases when involving a change in a price ceiling were subject to the approval of the Director of Economic Stabilization.

This policy was clarified and strengthened October 30 by the President in an address to the Nation and with the simultaneous release of an Executive order.[48] By this order wage increases were to be approved by the Stabilization Administrator when NWLB found: (a) that total wage increases since January 1941 were not equal to the percentage increase in the cost of living from that date to September 1945; (b) where such increases were required to correct industry or area inequities; (c) and where such increases were found "necessary to insure full production in an industry, designated by the Stabilization Administrator, which is essential to reconversion and in which existing rates or salaries are inadequate to the recruitment of needed manpower."

In support of this stabilization program, certain controls over production were necessary. While an early complete disappearance of WPB's controls over industry had been anticipated, the importance to the price control program of an adequate supply of low price consumer goods forced reconsideration of the Government's postwar role in allocating scarce materials to such essential civilian items. With WPB's Chairman convinced that such a function was beyond WPB's powers, the issue was taken by the Director of OWMR to the President for settlement. In a letter to Krug, the President, while agreeing on the desirability of a quick removal of controls, urged the temporary retention of such controls as were needed to prevent or break bottlenecks in the production of low-priced goods. In consequence, when an effective date was set for the termination of the War Production Board, the creation of the Civilian Production Administration was also announced,[49] that new organization to take over the administration of some 60 orders in such fields as textiles and construction.

The task of reconciling labor's demands for higher wages with the economic stabilization program presented many great difficulties. Wage stabilization was essential to the program since it was to be expected that most employers would demand increases in price ceilings adequate to cover any production costs arising from increased wages. Although the Administration at various times suggested the feasibility and desirability of raising wages out of anticipated profits, strenuous employer resistance was met. The resultant labor-management conflicts, when expressed as work stoppages, were a stumbling block to smooth and expeditious reconversion.

The problem presented serious administrative difficulties. During the war period NWLB had

---

[46] Office of Price Administration, *14th Quarterly Report*, pp. 2–4; 15th Quarterly Report, p. 5.

[47] Executive Order No. 9599, Aug. 18, 1945, 10 *Federal Register* 10155.

[48] Executive Order No. 9651, Oct. 30, 1945, 10 *Federal Register* 13487.

[49] Executive Order No. 9638, Oct. 4, 1945, 10 *Federal Register* 12591.

administered the wage stabilization program with marked success. Its accomplishment had rested very largely upon labor's adherence to the no-strike pledge at the beginning of the war and continued for the duration. It had consequently expired on VJ-day and the Board was in no position to take on new cases after that date. Although President Roosevelt in his Budget message in January 1945, had said, "We must also see to it that our administrative machinery for the adjustment of labor disputes is ready for the strains of the reconversion period" and urged that wartime lessons be applied in working out a long-range labor policy, nothing had been accomplished.[50]

President Truman made some effort to continue NWLB as an effective wage control organization. He requested labor to accept NWLB's jurisdiction and decisions and to continue the no-strike pledge until a labor-management conference could be convened to develop new machinery for maintaining industrial peace. In his Executive order of August 18, he directed that "disputes which would interrupt work contributing to the production of military supplies or interfere with effective transition to a peacetime economy are disputes which interrupt work contributing to the effective prosecution of the war." These efforts were not rewarded with success.

Organized labor had during the war years to a substantial degree, sacrificed the peculiarly favorable opportunities to obtain large wage increases which were inherent in the tight labor market situation. The sacrifice was not an easy one to make and labor had grown restive over the war period, resentful of the wartime restraints of the no strike pledge and the little steel formula, fearful of reduced weekly earnings as a result of the loss of overtime pay. In consequence, VJ-day was followed by an upsurge of work stoppages and strikes, despite the fact that public opinion strongly disapproved of such interferences with the progress of reconversion.

The lack of preparations which might have made of NWLB a useful postwar device to meet these problems was the result of labor's desire to escape all the wartime restrictions of Government intervention in collective bargaining, a desire with which industry appeared to be in substantial sympathy and which had previously been shared by Government officials including the members of NWLB. Thus, NWLB had not concerned itself with preparing for a role in the transition period but solely with making plans for finishing its backlog of work and then liquidating. By the time the threat of labor stoppages to reconversion had become clear, these

steps had so weakened NWLB that its members felt it necessary to advise the President that it could not function effectively to handle the crisis. Without the no-strike pledge or some similar agreement on the part of labor to abide by NWLB rulings, the Government had only the device of plant seizure under the Smith-Connally Act with which to meet work stoppages. Consequently, NWLB proceeded with its plans to liquidate, announcing in October that it intended to dissolve at the end of the year. The President, meanwhile, had requested that the Board set up a successor organization for the purpose of administering the wage stabilization program. The National Wage Stabilization Board, organized similarly to the National War Labor Board, was formed to begin operations the following year.[51]

Though it then had the administrative machinery to approve wage increases, the Administration was faced with the necessity of developing quickly new policy with which to meet the threat of labor strikes in cases where labor-management disagreements could not be settled by collective bargaining. Such policy and accompanying machinery was hoped for as a product of the National Labor-Management Conference which the President called early in November. No formula or agreement whereby industrial disputes might be settled within the framework of announced economic stabilization policy was forthcoming, however.

Meanwhile, as a stop-gap device the President set up fact-finding boards to handle the most pressing of the industrial disputes, at the same time requesting Congress action to bestow on such boards legislative sanction and authority. These boards had, in fact, no authority save only agreement by the two parties to accept them as arbitrators. Their awards did, however, carry the prestige of coming from a Presidential board and consequently carried with them considerable pressure for acceptance on both parties. In any case, the issue was what action OPA would take to cover the increased labor costs which might result from awards of increased wages. That agency attempted insofar as possible to obtain the absorption of such cost increases by the intermediary stages in the flow of products to ultimate consumers and thus prevent or at least reduce the impact upon the cost of living. This absorption policy met strenuous opposition on the part of the affected industries, particularly wholesale and retail merchants, and became a basic issue in the controversy over the extension of the Price Control Act.

---

[50] *The Budget of the U. S. Government, Fiscal Year ending June 30, 1946*, pp. xx–xxi.

[51] Executive Order No. 9672, Dec. 31, 1945, 11 *Federal Register* 221–4.

James E. Murray of Montana, introducing the Full Employment Bill in the Senate, January 22, 1945, presented the argument for strong federal action to iron out the business cycle, prevent inflation, and encourage economic growth. Arguing from New Deal and Keynesian principles, Murray declared that a comprehensive program must be devised to insure full employment. The bill, then, sought to establish the principle that government must assume responsibility for a smoothly functioning economic system.

JAMES E. MURRAY: THE PROMISE OF FULL EMPLOYMENT*

Mr. President, in the history of the world, the struggle for existence has manifested itself in economic systems that have been constantly changing. At one time western civilization was based upon the feudal manor. Then came the city and the development of handicraft industry. Then came the industrial revolution, and with it the economic system of free enterprise and the political system which we call democracy.

In America private enterprise and political democracy have developed and flourished side by side. They have contributed more to human welfare and human happiness than any previous system. The American people, therefore, want to preserve this system. They want it further strengthened and perfected so as to usher in a still greater future for our country. They know that no economic system can survive by remaining static. Times and conditions change, and our lives must change with them.

Our free-enterprise system has been subject to many improvements. Since the beginning of the twentieth century, we have enacted minimum-wage laws, we have reduced working hours, we have created unemployment compensation benefits, we have provided old-age benefits, we have guaranteed the right of collective bargaining for labor, we have corrected abuses in the security market and provided protection to investors. We have made it possible for millions of farmers to cooperate among themselves and with their Government in matters of land use, soil conservation, production, and prices. When these laws were first proposed they were attacked and it was charged that they would undermine our system. But after these laws were put in operation they were recognized as necessary to the strengthening of business enterprise, and today no one would dare to propose their repeal.

While we have been improving and strengthening our economic system of free enterprise throughout the years, we have as yet been unable to control the violent economic fluctuations which have resulted in periodic mass unemployment. . . .

Expansion is the essence of our capitalist system. But today, when there is no longer any frontier in the geographical sense, we must think of strengthening our free competitive economy by expanding it from within. Today our new frontier is in our back yard in every State and city of the country. Today we must again attempt to foster economic expansion through wise laws, just as we did when we enacted the Homestead Act and the other measures which helped develop the West.

If, after the war, we fail to expand, America will once again be visited with another great depression. And another serious depression would mean millions of disillusioned and jobless men would have little interest in the maintenance of a system which offers so little in the way of good living conditions. It would give birth to strong political pressures against such a system.

There are some in this country who have lost faith in capitalism. It is up to us in the Congress to stop this trend. I have a stubborn and abiding faith in the principle of private competitive enterprise and in the necessity of making our system work. I have confidence that we can succeed in finding a way to eliminate its principal weakness —periodic mass unemployment.

The full employment bill which we are proposing here today is a bill to help make free enterprise work. For unless we make it work, unless we can make it operate so as to avoid the wild fluctuations that have characterized our economy in past years, capitalism will be threatened in America and throughout the world. Already, before the war, three of the largest nations in the world had abandoned it, and many other nations were preparing to emulate their action.

There are some today who dread lest America be converted to socialism, communism, fascism, or some other ism such as those that have taken root in other countries. I say to them—let us make our system of private competitive enterprise work so well here in America that other countries will seek to imitate us. Other nations follow our lead in technology—in mass production methods of making steel and of fabricating automobiles and airplanes. Why should we not progress to the point where they will imitate us in the field of economics also?

Why can we not take the lead in remedying the weaknesses that have developed in our capi-

---

* Reprinted from *Congressional Record*, 79th Cong., 1st sess. (Washington, D.C.: 1945, pp. 380–83.

talist system? Why can we not set an example here for all the peoples of the world by affording the fullest possible opportunity and encouragement for private initiative and ending chronic unemployment? Why can we not demonstrate to the world that it is possible to have the highest standard of living without abandoning our cherished political freedoms? . . .

The bill declares that it is the policy of the United States to foster free competitive enterprise and to assure the existence at all times of sufficient employment opportunities for all Americans who have finished their schooling and who do not have full-time home and family responsibilities. The bill recognizes that these Americans are entitled to opportunities for "useful, remunerative, regular, and full-time employment."

The right to a job does not mean guaranteeing John Jones a given job carrying a set salary and a definite social standing. It is not the aim of the bill to provide specific jobs for specific individuals. However, I believe nobody will deny that our economic system of free enterprise must offer opportunities for jobs for all who are able and want to work. Our American system owes no man a living but it does owe every man an opportunity to make a living. That is the proper interpretation of the "right to work."

Full employment is not a static condition. It depends upon changing national trends, population growth, changes in school age or retirement age, the number of persons serving in the armed forces, the number of hours worked, and similar factors which change the size of the labor force.

Furthermore, full employment does not mean that there should be at any given time no unemployment at all. Our economic system requires flexibility, which means that at all times a minimum amount of unemployment is unavoidable. Technological advances, the desire to shift to other work, seasonal changes in production, or other circumstances cause what is known among economists as short-run frictional unemployment. As conditions change, the volume of this relatively small amount of frictional unemployment will also change.

The responsibility of the Government with regard to full employment is clearly stated in the bill. I quote from the declaration of policy, as set forth in the bill: "In order to assist industry, agriculture, labor, and State and local governments in achieving continuing full employment, it is the responsibility of the Federal Government to pursue such consistent and openly arrived at economic policies and programs as will stimulate and encourage the highest feasible levels of employment through private and other non-Federal investment and expenditure.

"To the extent that continuing full employment cannot otherwise be achieved, it is the further responsibility of the Federal Government to provide such volume of Federal investment and expenditure as may be needed to assure continuing full employment. . . ."

There are some who think that the major emphasis in our post-war economy must be upon Government expenditures. There are others who say that this means deficit financing, and that deficit financing would lead to a planned economy or to national bankruptcy. They, in turn, propose that the Government do everything in its power to give a green light to business and heighten the confidence of private investors so that the major emphasis in the post-war period would be upon increased capital outlays of private enterprise.

It is my own personal opinion—and I have stated this before on the floor of the Senate— that the royal road to prosperity is high wages, low prices, and a tax system that is unequivocally based upon the ability to pay and the encouragement to produce. It is my belief that in this way, with only moderate Government expenditures for desirable Government services, we could achieve a more equitable distribution of the national income. It is my conviction that this improved distribution of the national income would give us an unprecedented expansion in consumers' expenditures and a vigorous, though not excessive, expansion in the capital outlays of business.

But my personal opinion on how the national economy might best be balanced is not relevant to the question of how it would be balanced under this bill. The specific National Budget that would result in any given period would be determined, not by the operations of any one individual or any one group, but on the basis of that active interplay between all groups and all our political leaders which is the very essence of the democratic process in our democratic America.

NEED FOR ACTION

A few weeks ago, Dr. Gallup's interviewers went around the country asking people whether they thought that there would be enough jobs after the war. Sixty-eight percent thought that there would not be enough jobs. The younger people of the country were even more pessimistic than their elders; 73 percent of those between 20 and 30 years of age thought that the outlook was black.

What Senator would stand up and say that the people of this country are mistaken in their beliefs? Who is there who, on the basis of what has thus far been done in the field of post-war planning, would be willing to predict that there will be jobs for all after this war?

We all know that during the war we have transformed our economy into an economic skyscraper of breath-taking magnitude.

We all know that when war-production contracts are withdrawn, the danger will be that the entire edifice will topple over.

We all know that while the end of the war may bring with it 6 to 18 months of an inflationary boom, the long-term threat is a deflationary collapse.

Unless an economic substitute is found for war contracts, we face mass unemployment in this country of a magnitude which could easily surpass anything that was dreamed of during the last depression. Thus far, we have not found that substitute.

This country cannot afford again to go into a depression such as we experienced in the 1930's. It would be extremely dangerous to do so. Mass unemployment would mean discontent, disunity, and an irreparable loss to our Nation in terms of both physical wealth and moral well-being.

Still more appalling, an unemployment crisis in America would spread like wildfire throughout the world. It would give us dumping, higher tariffs, export subsidies, blocked currencies, and every other new and old type of economic warfare. And this, I submit, would inevitably wreck our plans for an effective international security organization, turn back the clock of progress, and plunge us into another holocaust of blood, suffering, and chaos.

We here in Congress have it in our power to take effective action now to reassure the people of America that mass unemployment shall not happen again.

We have it in our power to make full employment the cardinal principle in our domestic economic policy.

We have it in our power to make full employment in America the keystone of our economic relations with the other countries of the world. . . .

Every two decades, for the past 100 years, we have been plagued by a boom and a major depression; and every decade has brought forth new explanations as to the causes of the business cycle and new remedies. But there is one fact upon which all are agreed, namely, that fear of a depression tends to lead us inevitably into a depression. When business, agriculture and labor fear unemployment, they make plans to adjust themselves to unemployment. When their daily actions are based upon such plans, then we are doomed to have unemployment.

Whatever program we adopt, therefore, let us act without delay.

Let us have courage and be decisive in our efforts. Let us not be swayed by fear of our inability to determine our own destiny.

Let us not wait until millions of men are walking the streets looking for work before we do something about post-war employment.

Let us act now, through the regular legislative processes as set forth in our Constitution, to provide our businessmen, our farmers, and workers, and, above all, our 11,000,000 soldiers and sailors, with confidence in the future of American enterprise and American democracy.

Addressing the principal opponent of price controls, the National Association of Manufacturers, Chester Bowles contended that these controls would in no way interfere with increased production. Bowles, head of the Office of Price Administration, believed that controls could not be removed until supply caught up with demand, otherwise, "to remove them before competitive conditions are again established is to invite inflationary chaos."

CHESTER BOWLES: WHAT PRICE INFLATION?*

I am very glad of an opportunity to appear before the annual meeting of the National Association of Manufacturers. I have always found here a friendly atmosphere and a willingness to discuss any public policy in a constructive atmosphere of give and take.

The whole country is deeply concerned in the program of inflation control about which you have asked me to speak today. Businessmen are concerned. Farmers are concerned. The workers in our factories are concerned. And so are the great mass of our people which cannot readily be fitted into any group.

There are many audiences before which I appear where the support of our program is heartfelt and vigorous. Last night I spoke before several hundred businessmen at a dinner given by the Business Council. Next week I will appear at the annual dinner of the Ohio Grange, an organization representing thousands of farmers which has also pledged its all-out support to the OPA's price control program.

Here in this meeting of the NAM I am face to face with a group whose leaders have gone on record during the last 18 months in vigorous opposition to what we have done and to what we are now doing.

Only the leaders of the National Retail Dry Goods Association and the leaders of the Association of Real Estate Boards have equalled the

---

* Reprinted from *Vital Speeches of the Day*, XII (January 1, 1946), pp. 173–75.

vigor with which the National Association of Manufacturers heads are opposing the stabilization control program through which inflation thus far has been kept in check.

I must point out that this opposition to effective price control is a departure from the original NAM stand when wartime price controls were first proposed.

In 1941 when price and rent control legislation was under discussion, the stand of the NAM was clear cut. Mr. Noel Sargent, who was then your secretary, testified before a congressional committee that firm controls on prices were an absolute essential to meet the inflationary circumstances created by war. In many respects his recommendations went beyond the actual program which your Government has put into effect.

I am told that Mr. Sargent's testimony was a major factor in securing the passage of the original price control act.

But more recently your position has changed. To some degree in 1943 and increasingly in 1944 and 1945 you have swung into sharp opposition to effective price control.

Obviously today we are in disagreement. Obviously we cannot both be right. One of us must be wrong.

Let me emphasize my own feeling of deep humility with which I approach the problems which confront us. I have been wrong on occasion in the past and like most human beings I shall probably be wrong on occasion in the future. I do not want to appear dogmatic or above all to create the impression that I think I have all the answers.

In that spirit I should like to analyze the stand of your association on this question of price and rent control. At the outset I believe it is a proper question to ask what would have happened if the nation had followed the advice of the NAM leaders in 1944 and 1945.

Before Congress eighteen months ago and again last spring NAM officials advocated amendments to the act which in my opinion would have made effective price control absolutely impossible.

But for the sake of clarifying the point, let's accept the view of those who claimed that these changes would have increased prices only 10 per cent each year. Even though we accept this viewpoint the result would have been a 30 billion dollar increase in the cost of fighting the war—a sum only 2 billion less than the cost of the entire World War I. At the same time Mr. and Mrs. long-suffering American consumer would have found 36 billion dollars added to their cost of living. In other words, even relying on the most optimistic estimates put forward by the proponents of the NAM sponsored amendments, the nation has already saved 66 billion dollars by not taking your leaders advice.

But these figures are in my opinion only a portion of what your official proposal would have actually cost our nation.

Those of us who have been entrusted with the task of wartime price control have long recognized the fact that controlled inflation is an idle dream. One man's price may be the cost of a thousand other firms.

There is no organization big enough or smart enough or efficient enough to handle the vast deluge of price adjustments which would result from any such concept. There could be only one result and that is higher and still higher prices each feeding on itself with the beginning of an inflationary spiral which would soon be out of control.

As I analyze the NAM's position on price control, it seems clear that the opposition of your leaders stems from a conviction that these controls tend to hold down production. Certainly there was no indication of this during the war years. This is perfectly clear from the record.

Both industrial and farm production during the years of effective price control have risen to record levels. They have gone far beyond even our most ardent hopes. American management and American labor in their all out war effort have hurried the day of victory and have amazed our enemies as well as our allies.

Today it is generally recognized that inflationary pressures are at record levels. Liquid assets are at an all time high. Savings have increased from pre-war levels by 145 billions of dollars. Currency in circulation is almost five times as great as before the war.

The stock market has been booming merrily upward. As in 1929 taxi drivers, barbers, and elevator boys are providing inside information on just what selections are apt to rise the fastest. The dope sheets coming from Wall Street anticipate higher and still higher prices. The real estate market is starting to skyrocket.

What, under such circumstances, would happen to prices if the nation now accepted the advice which Mr. Robert R. Wason, chairman of the NAM Reconversion Council and Mr. John Airey, chairman of the NAM War Controls Termination Committee offered to Congress on November 7. This NAM recommendation called for the elimination of all price controls by the fifteenth day of February. What, for instance, would happen to food prices?

Those of you who are in the candy business know that cocoanut, which OPA decontrolled some thirty days ago, has quadrupled in price. Many grades of furs, from which price controls were removed during the fall months, have more than doubled. Your wife will tell you that some grades of oranges, lemons, and grapefruit moved up 50 to 100 percent in the first few days following the action by OPA in removing the price restrictions.

If this occurred on food products which seemed to be in adequate supply, what would happen to meat, vegetables, milk, cereals, and all the other dozens of food products which are in more scarce supply?

If the nation accepted the advice of your

leaders to drop price control 60 days from now, what would happen to clothing prices? Right now the apparel situation is tighter than it has been since the beginning of the war.

Our veterans in search of their first outfit of "civvies" are forced to walk from store to store and even then often fail to secure the clothing to fit their needs. All authorities agree that this shortage is likely to continue for a great many months to come.

If we accepted your official recommendation of the early removal of all price control, what would the public be asked to pay for automobiles, refrigerators, washing machines and vacuum cleaners. Some say that competition would take care of all that. I can only say that this expectance is not in line with the facts.

The original requests of OPA by manufacturers were for increases ranging from 25 percent to 55 percent. On October 26 and 27 orders were taken for 300,000 Ford cars, one-third of the entire 1941 production—with no questions asked on prices or trade-ins.

If the nation accepted the official NAM recommendation, what would happen to the price of building materials? During the period of the first World War, the cost of lumber, soil pipe, brick, and other essential building materials tripled. Today the housing shortage is infinitely greater. Under the best of circumstances I am told that only 500,000 homes can be built in 1946.

This will be meagre relief to the 3,401,000 families, a major portion of them young married veterans, who will be forced to live with relatives, or otherwise double up during the coming year. If we removed price controls, is there any limit to the heights to which building materials would move in 1946? Certainly not judging from what occurred 25 years ago.

If we accepted the official advice of the NAM what would happen to rents? We could not remove price controls without removing rent controls. We know that in the period of the last war 90 percent of the entire increase in rents occurred not during the war itself but after the Armistice. In view of the critical housing shortage, could we expect any greater restraint on the part of our landlords today?

Finally if we accepted the advice of your leaders what would happen to wages? Today most of you gentlemen feel that the demands of the labor groups are excessive. If controls were ripped off as you propose, if rents were allowed to shoot upward, if food and apparel prices were allowed to boom, labor would very properly intensify its demands for higher and still higher pay checks.

History has proven that in a race between prices and wages, prices invariably go up faster. Under such circumstances, however, our workers would have but one defense, and that would be to get what they could as fast as they could get it in the hope of keeping their incomes within speaking distance of the rising cost of living.

Organized labor could at least make an effort to keep its earnings in line with increasing living costs. But how about the millions of workers, farmers, and people living on fixed incomes who have no strong unions to protect them? What would happen to them as prices and rents shot upwards?

Finally how about the businessmen if the nation accepted the official advice of the NAM? Prices that skyrocket invariably collapse. How would our businessmen, particularly our small businessmen, fare as inventories were thrown on the market for any price they would buy and as the inevitable drop in purchasing power dried up their sales?

We had 106,000 bankruptcies following the collapse after the inflationary rise in 1919 and 1920. If we ripped off our inflation controls today could we expect anything less in 1947?

Your leaders say they fear inflation as much as I do. They agree with me that production, production, and still more production is the only final cure for the inflationary danger.

But it is their claim that price control interferes with production, and that if price controls were removed the whole situation would take care of itself. The record has proven them emphatically wrong in the past. The record indicates that their claim is equally wrong today.

Last week the President's report stated reconversion has been achieved at record speed. Manufacturers of automobiles, washing machines, electric refrigerators, and other reconversion products, reporting to the Civilian Production Administration estimated their volume of sales by June 1946 at from 75 percent to 300 percent above 1939 levels—all under OPA price controls.

Retail sales today, again under the very price controls which your leaders claim make all out production impossible, are breaking every record.

Admittedly, price control has never been painless. Admittedly, it can never be painless. Obviously, there have been some delays, some fumbling, some outright mistakes. Everyday we are moving to correct these mistakes and to eliminate hardship to the fullest extent of our ability.

Business is restless. Business has had its fill of wartime regimentation and red tape. Very properly, business is anxious to get back to a free economy with Government interference reduced to a minimum.

Believe me, there is no one in America as anxious to get rid of price controls as I. I cordially dislike the job I have. I would like nothing better than to drop it tomorrow.

Price control should and must be removed as rapidly as supply conditions permit. Barring continued labor management difficulties, the production estimates for 1946 indicate that in industry after industry during the next 12 months we will find supply and demand coming into balance. As that occurs, I assure you that your Government will move promptly to eliminate the last vestige of price restrictions in those industries. But to remove them before competitive conditions are again established is to invite inflationary chaos.

Gentlemen, the recommendation of your leaders for the removal of price control in 60 days is reckless in the extreme. Just how high prices would go I do not know. But at the best it is a risky, reckless, gambling policy which in all likelihood would produce a national disaster.

The everyday people of America are looking forward eagerly to good jobs, steady jobs at higher wages—to a high sustained level of farm income—to good profits for our businessmen—to the development of a land of peace and abundance where every man may raise his family in an atmosphere of economic security and with steadily increasing standard of living.

Today the entire country, with very few exceptions, believes that our capitalistic free enterprise system continues to be our best hope of achieving this future. But we must face the fact that this deep seated confidence and belief in our free enterprise system is largely confined to America. In practically every European country, capitalism has ceased to be even a source of controversy. In country after country we find the left wingers advocating communism while the right wingers advocate various forms of a socialistic state.

I have great faith in our ability to make our free enterprise system work here in America. But would this system, in spite of its great achievements, and its deep seated roots in the traditions and thinking of our country, survive the bitter disillusionment which would surely develop if the inflationary forces are allowed to take hold? Frankly, gentlemen, I am very skeptical.

Let's make no mistake about it. The everyday people in this country are wholeheartedly behind this program of inflation control. Our farmers are behind it. Our workers are behind it. The consuming public is behind it. And tens of thousands of businessmen, large and small, many of them members of the NAM, are also behind it.

The urge to strip off price controls now (or let us say on February 15th), and to let the devil take the hindmost, comes with relatively few exceptions from business and business association leaders. As I have pointed out the leaders of the NAM have been among the most outspoken.

The dizzy inflation which could so readily develop in the absence of OPA controls on prices and rents would, I repeat, not be accepted lying down by the great masses of our people. It is for this reason that I firmly believe that the stand which your leaders have taken represents a most dangerous threat to the future health and success of our entire free enterprise system.

Gentlemen, I might have come to you today and made a pleasant easy speech about the inflationary dangers and our efforts to combat them. But such a speech would have failed dismally to meet the basic issue.

These are critical times and I believe we are all entitled to frank statements and blunt opinions. Your leaders are on record in favor of a course of action which I believe to be utterly foolhardy and dangerous. I would have failed to meet my public responsibilities if I did not state to you my own sharp disagreement with them.

Let me emphasize that I accept fully the great sincerity and patriotism with which Mr. Mosher, and other leaders of your organization, have stated their views. I hope you will accept with equal readiness the sincerity with which I have tried to state the facts as I see them.

Let me take this occasion to ask your organization to reexamine its position. You supported price control in 1941. If you will but look at the facts of the present inflationary situation, it seems to me you must support price control now.

In spite of whatever disagreement there may be between some of us, let us never forget that we are all working wholeheartedly and humbly for the same goal—a country of peace, abundance, and prosperity—for all of our people of all races, of all groups—whoever they may be, wherever they may live.

In the heated Senate debate over the continuation of price controls, Edward H. Moore of Oklahoma attacked the Office of Price Administration as undermining the capitalist system. Speaking on June 27, 1946, Moore not only maintained that OPA stifled production and brought on inflation, but he sought to identify supporters of OPA with the totalitarian views of German and Italian fascism.

EDWARD H. MOORE:
PRICE CONTROLS MEAN A CONTROLLED ECONOMY*

Price controls mean a controlled economy. A controlled economy is wrong in principle and will not work under our American system.

No man in America or no set of men can enforce price control, whatever the law may be and regardless of how many snoopers and inspectors and FBI men are loosed upon the people. The enforcement of price controls is as impossible as the enforcement of prohibition. The American people are not ready for regimentation. I have said on numerous occasions, and I want to say it again, that had price controls been removed on VJ-day we would today be experiencing a flood of production that would already have leveled prices off to prewar relationships. Instead, we still experience shortages in practically every field of consumer goods, and we are now going into a period of severe food shortages for the rest of 1946 and for 1947, and until the Congress has the good judgment to take the Government out of business and to return business to private industry, we shall continue to experience such shortages. Price control means that the Government is in charge of every industrial effort in this country. By the manipulation of price control, the inexperienced experimenters determine the destiny of every industry, business, and industrial activity in America. Such is inherent in price control and a controlled economy. . . .

Mr. President, provision has been made for a Decontrol Board appointed by the President, the members of which are to be confirmed by the Senate, and are to receive a salary, I believe, of $12,000 a year, with full power and authority to employ clerical staffs, assistants, and do other things which are inherent in a bureaucracy. What is to be done? It has been said by the proponents of the measure that persons may petition the Administrator and make a showing before him that the supply of a certain commodity or article is equal to the demand. The language of the statute uses the word "shall." Does not the language in all similar statutes use the word "shall"? An appeal may be made from the decision rendered in connection with all matters, and all actions are to be under the rules and regulations prescribed by the Administrator. My belief, Mr. President, is that there will be no decontrol. I believe that the entire proposal is quite agreeable to the advocates of the extension of OPA, including the Political Action Committee, the CIO, and all similar organizations of whom many persons are afraid. They are all pleased with the bill, and I believe that the President will sign it. Statements about the President vetoing it are all bunk. They are made only to fool the people. I am not at all impressed by them. There is only one answer, namely, to take all authority away from the OPA and turn it back to the people.

Mr. President, relief with respect to individual prices has been almost as difficult to obtain from OPA as has industry-wide relief. A few relief applications have been granted. Political strategy demands that prices here and there be raised. Moreover, there is that class of price increase which constitutes pure favoritism of one competitor as against another. Of course, favoritism may be exercised in many instances. Some persons like it. There may be some engaged in industry who are doing well, but they are generally those who are favorites of the officials. A condition of that kind is always the product of unrestrained and uncontrolled political, economic, or social power, and no legislative restraints will effectively prevent the dispensing of favoritism.

Deputy OPA Administrator Baker told the Senate Banking and Currency Committee on April 17 that applications for individual relief passed through 187 separate stages of processing before reaching a final conclusion.

It would be very fine for a man living in Colorado or in Oklahoma, for example, to come to Washington and file an application for relief. All he would need to do would be to come to Washington and pay $15 a day for a room, if he could find one, and wait around until the whole matter had gone through 187 separate stages of processing before reaching a final conclusion.

Mr. President, I have said that Deputy OPA Administrator Baker told the committee on Banking and Currency that applications for individual relief passed through 187 separate stages of processing before reaching a final conclusion.

He hastened to say, however, that this had been cut down to 78 steps and hoped that it could

* Reprinted from *Congressional Record*, 79th Cong., 2nd sess. (Washington, D.C.: 1947), pp. 7617–18.

be cut down some more. In the face of this admitted intolerable condition, Mr. Porter, at the same time, had the effrontery to tell the committee that all the OPA wanted out of the committee was "more appropriations." That statement appears in the record of the committee hearings. Mr. Porter stated that all the OPA wanted was "more appropriations." There are many persons who would like to see the OPA given such appropriations. We have seen evidences of that fact during the past few days. Mr. Porter stated further: "Only one amendment we ask to the existing law and that is one granting us the power to control commercial rents."

A controlled economy leads to an authoritarian psychology which results in the oppression and destruction of individual rights and liberties under a gestapo system. The oppressive and arbitrary action of OPA officials is a story so repugnant and so rotten that it is hard to believe that such could happen within the confines of a constitutional government such as we have in America.

In Oklahoma it is estimated that 15 percent of all grocers have been deprived from selling or handling sugar, for periods ranging from 30 days to the duration of rationing, because of errors or mistakes in following OPA regulations. In some instances, the penalty was imposed as a result of selling some item for 1 cent above the ceiling. This travesty upon justice and freedom has been perpetrated on the retailers throughout the length and breadth of this country. The OPA gestapo has instilled fear in the hearts of every merchant of America. The price control law and its administration is rapidly destroying respect for all law and order. We must be prepared to suffer the consequences in the years to come. . . .

No doubt, every Member of this Congress, both in the House and the Senate, has had brought to his attention as I have, dozens of examples of the arbitrary tyranny of OPA underlings. We have been too prone to dismiss them as isolated cases and as a mere incident of wartime controls. We should understand that it is the aggregate of such activities that is destroying constitutional government in America and we in Congress, if we fail to act, must accept the responsibility for the consequences. When centralized government plans and executes the orders, rules and regulations under which wages, work, prices, and production of 140,000,000 Americans

shall be controlled, it naturally leads to a government by dictation.

I have often said, and I say it again, because the evidence is so convincing that there is no escape from the conclusion, that a large segment of those supporting the OPA has in view the single purpose of permanently continuing a governmentally controlled economy. I know that there are Members of the Senate who will take issue with that statement, but let me read what Mrs. Eleanor Roosevelt had to say in her daily column of April 30, 1946: "It has been a long fight to put the control of our economic system in the hands of the Government where it can be administered in the interests of the people as a whole. Now, Congress, under the influence of powerful lobbies, is rapidly trying to return control to big business."

Is there a Member of the Congress, save possibly one, who would care to defend such a philosophy?

Compare Mrs. Roosevelt's statement with that of a leading Fascist of the Mussolini regime, as found in Mr. Mario Palmieri's book, The Philosophy of Fascism: "We see thus the Fascist State resolutely enter the economic field to dictate what shall be from now on the relationship between capital and labor, employer and employee, landowner and farm land, industrialist and worker."

Compare, also, Mrs. Roosevelt's statement with the announcement of Hitler of October 18, 1936, in which he advised the German people that he had appointed Hermann Goering to control and direct, on behalf of the Government, the economic life of the German Nation.

OPA's propaganda for self-perpetuation is confined to two propositions: First, that it has held the line; and, second, that without OPA price controls we will have runaway inflation.

I was very glad to hear our majority leader say yesterday morning that he indulged himself in no wild predictions as to what would happen if price controls were released.

If it can be shown beyond any reasonable doubt that both these propositions are fallacious and, on the contrary, prices are high and shortages exist because of OPA, then certainly, no one who believes in our form of constitutional government and the freedoms guaranteed under it would argue for a continuation of this agency.

President Truman repeatedly asserted that anti-inflation measures were essential to the successful conduct of United States foreign policy. In an address to the American Society of Newspaper Editors, April 17, 1948, he stated a theme that later ran through his campaign for election: the need to check inflation because America was "the chief support of those people of the world who are seeking to rebuild their civilization in accordance with the principles of democracy and freedom."

HARRY S. TRUMAN: "OUR FOREIGN POLICY DEPENDS . . . UPON THE . . . STABILITY OF OUR DOMESTIC ECONOMY"*

I am going to talk to you about inflation.

All of us have the foreign situation very much in our minds these days. This is proper, for we must devote a great deal of thought to our foreign relations if we are to succeed in working out the difficult international problems facing us. But we cannot afford to neglect our problems at home.

The success of our foreign policy depends to a very large extent upon the strength and stability of our domestic economy. The plain fact is, however, that our economy is in serious danger as a result of high prices and inflation.

Inflation may seem to you to be an old story. But there are some men in this country—men who happen to be in influential positions—who still fail to understand or who deliberately ignore the gravity of the situation and the need for forthright measures to meet it. They have tinkered with the problem of inflation—they have even taken some feeble steps in the right direction. But they have taken other steps in the wrong direction—steps that have made the problem much worse.

For my part, I believe that inflation is so grave a menace to this country and to the world that I do not propose to let it be forgotten.

I believe that the Government has a clear-cut responsibility to deal with high prices. I believe that we know what measures the Government should take. I cannot sit by silently while inflation continues to creep up on the American people.

The basic facts which make this problem of such fundamental importance are plain. The world stands now at one of the decisive points in history. Emerging from the most terrible of all wars, people all over the earth are fixing anew the pattern of civilization.

By virtue of the strength with which we have been blessed, the United States is the chief support of those people of the world who are seeking to rebuild their civilization in accordance with the principles of democracy and freedom. The heart of our support is economic assistance. To be effective, it must be coupled with sufficient military strength to give the free peoples of the world some sense of security while they rebuild.

These requirements must be met in large part from the production of American mines and factories and farms. Thus, a strong American economy is the bedrock upon which rest the hopes for establishing a peace of free men in the world. Without it we can provide neither aid, nor leadership, nor example.

The strength and vitality of our economy are being undermined by inflation. High prices are now working real hardship upon most American families. If unchecked, inflation will bring on economic consequences which will hurt every one of us.

This is not a new situation, but it is getting worse.

I have been calling attention to the hardships and dangers of high prices for a long time. I have repeatedly urged businessmen to exercise voluntary restraint in setting prices. Many of them have courageously done what they could to hold prices down. But they are not strong enough to stem the tide, and prices have continued to rise.

By last fall, it had become clear that we could not place our main reliance on voluntary methods. On November 17th, I presented to the Congress a ten-point legislative program for dealing with inflation. This program has not been enacted. And prices have continued to rise.

The program which I presented to the Congress was sound and necessary last November. It is still sound and it is even more necessary now.

The total demand for goods is still outrunning production. Competition for scarce items is still pushing prices up. Employment is at record levels, but the real purchasing power of most of our people is still losing ground to inflation.

In February, there was a break in the market for wheat, corn and other agricultural products. But agricultural prices did not drop for long, and they did not drop very far. The prices paid by housewives were affected hardly at all. The general level of prices has remained well above the already excessive level which prevailed in 1947.

And now there are new factors that have made the outlook for inflation considerably worse.

Some key prices have been increased, un-

* Reprinted from *Vital Speeches of the Day,* XIV (May 1, 1948), 418, 420–421.

wisely and unnecessarily. The outstanding case was, of course, the increase in some important steel prices. I believe that the businessmen who made these increases did not consider their far-reaching effect on the rest of the economy.

They made the regrettable decision to increase prices even though they were already making record profits. In the face of these actions, other businessmen, with a greater regard for the public welfare, have fought a losing battle to keep their prices down.

In addition to these price increases, inflation has been encouraged by some unnecessary interruptions to production. The outstanding example, of course, was the work stoppage in the coal industry. The serious effect of the loss of coal production shows the narrow margin of supply on which we are operating, and how quickly shortages of base materials can cripple our entire economy.

Another new factor making for inflation is the bill recently enacted by the Congress reducing Government revenues by $5 billion. This is also dangerous from the standpoint of the Government's financial stability, because it is likely to result in a deficit in the next fiscal year.

It is also dangerous from the standpoint of high prices, for the additional billions of dollars of purchasing power will not be accompanied by any significant increase in production. It means simply that more dollars will be bidding for the same goods, and prices will be bid up accordingly. Furthermore, by eliminating the Government's surplus of receipts over expenditures, the tax reduction bill will remove the most important single factor which has helped to hold prices in check during recent months.

At the same time that taxes are being reduced, we are undertaking a program of assistance to foreign countries. We are also considering certain necessary additions to our national defense program. Both of these programs are of utmost importance, and we must have them. But they will result in strains on the parts of our economy, which can add to inflation if we do not have the proper controls.

In considering the effects of these programs, it is extremely important to realize that we now have practically no slack in our economy. We have substantially full employment. Factories already are operating at top capacity. We cannot increase our plant capacity rapidly. We have only the normal growth in the labor force to count on for new manpower.

Under these circumstances, new demands for materials and production necessarily have a direct and telling effect on prices—unless the proper anti-inflationary steps are taken.

It is apparent, when all these factors are considered, that the danger of inflation has not diminished in the last few months. On the contrary, the need for the legislation I requested is even more urgent.

It seems to me that the basic question is clear.

It is whether we take action in time to do some good or whether we delay until a crisis is upon us. It is simply a matter of taking out insurance before the house catches fire.

If the cost of living continues to climb, wages and prices will continue to chase each other upward. The unhealthy boom will impose further hardships upon those who fall behind in the race. The greater the inflation and the longer it lasts, the greater the danger that it will end in unemployment, business distress, and a recession or depression.

It is of little significance that no one can forecast the exact time when this will happen. The important point is that we cannot afford to let it happen at all.

Since I addressed the Congress one month ago today on the need for prompt action on the European Recovery Program, and on universal training and selective service, there has been a greatly increased interest by our citizens in national defense and in our foreign policy. This interest has been reflected by the enactment of the legislation to aid European recovery. But our domestic economy has been dangerously neglected. It should be neglected no longer.

I believe that the anti-inflation program I recommended to the Congress last November should be enacted at once. That program is balanced and well-rounded. It includes measures to reduce the excessive amounts of money and credit which are lifting prices. It includes measures to see that scarce goods are distributed fairly and to their most important uses. It includes measures to deal directly with specific high prices.

All these measures are reasonable and practical. They attack inflation in a direct manner. They offer a complete and consistent program to strike at the heart of the problem of high prices.

The measures I proposed are designed to hold prices down while keeping production up, and increasing it as rapidly as possible. They are designed to stop runaway prices, so that great numbers of American families will not be priced out of the market for things they need. These measures are designed to insure that scarce goods are not wasted, but are used where they will be of the greatest benefit.

I wish to emphasize that the situation has already been made more difficult by delay. Additional delay will only add to the danger.

The American people must not be misled by those who oppose a reasonable anti-inflation program and a reasonable defense program. It has been said that the present Administration is trying to create an economic crisis or an international crisis. The exact opposite is the truth. We are striving to avoid an economic crisis by protecting our prosperity while we still have it. We are striving to avoid a war crisis by being firm before it is too late.

The welfare of our own people, and the effectiveness of our foreign policy, and the strength of our defenses all depend on our prosperity. Only if we preserve the soundness of our economy, through prompt and adequate measures to control inflation, can we contribute our full share to a peace in which freedom and democracy will be secure.

I believe that the people of the United States understand that we have a great opportunity and a great responsibility to lead the world through these changing and difficult times. I believe that our people have faith, the wisdom and the unselfish devotion to the common good to take whatever actions are necessary to meet that responsibility.

We can succeed if we act courageously and act in time.

Senator Taft, at the Union League Club in Philadelphia, warned that "our gallivanting President" was creating a regimented society. This speech in January, 1948, anticipated the Republican position in the coming election: the Truman program would destroy free enterprise, enhance the power of labor, and appease communism.

ROBERT A. TAFT: "THE PRESIDENT WOULD DESTROY OUR FREE ECONOMY . . ."*

President Truman has opened his campaign for nomination and election. He is traveling through the country with a fifteen-car train at the expense of the voters. He is blackguarding Congress at every whistle station in the West for the simple reason that Congress happens to differ with him in his whole philosophy of government.

I have repeatedly set forth the constructive accomplishments of this first Republican Congress in sixteen years in reducing expenses, reducing taxes, eliminating war regulations, establishing equality and justice in labor relations, reorganizing the armed forces and reversing the foreign policy of the Administration toward communism.

But today I want you to look at the program of President Truman. I want you to consider where we would be today if we did not have the Eightieth Congress prepared to resist the feeble spurs which our gallivanting President says he would like to apply. I want you to consider what this country would be like if Congress followed his advice, or if he should be re-elected in November with a Congress of his own choosing.

The President's program would create a nation completely regimented, choked by taxation, under the complete domination of centralized bureaucracy and arbitrary union leadership.

In 1946 the people became so indignant with government regulation that President Truman himself, prior to the election, abolished rationing and meat control, and abolished most price controls before the Republican Congress could take office. Yet, within a year, he demanded from Congress, and still demands on his Western trip, complete authority to re-establish OPA, to re-establish WPB, to re-establish the War Labor Board, to ration every housewife.

He wants power to fix prices and wages and regulate all phases of industry in his own arbitrary selection and discretion. He says he wants selective controls to be selected by him, but experience has shown that once any important commodity is placed under regulation, the regulation must extend to every related commodity. We have the greatest production and the highest standard of living of any country in the world without controls.

The President would destroy our free economy and adopt those controls which in every country in Europe have so reduced production that our taxpayers are paying seven billions dollars a year today to help support them. If such controls were effective they would decrease production, but they would be no more effective than they were after the war. They would fail because vast shortages and black markets would develop in every city and on every farm.

Federal bureaus would be regulating every one of a billion transactions a day in the United States. They would tell the farmer how to run his farm, the businessman how to run his business and the housewife how to run her kitchen.

The President would not stop there. He has repeatedly recommended the socialization and the nationalization of medicine. He wants five billion dollars more taxes to be paid into Washington so that a Federal bureau may employ all the doctors in the United States to give free medical care to all the people of the United States. He would destroy the freedom of the medical profession and make every doctor an employe of the Federal Government.

---

* Reprinted from *Vital Speeches of the Day,* XIV (January 15, 1948), 199–201.

Federal bureaus with thousands of employes would have to keep track of millions of medical services, make regulations telling every family when it could have a doctor, what kind of medicine it could have, and every detail of medical care for children. In Great Britain the book of regulations is an inch thick.

What does the President want in labor relations? He has told the unions in the West that he is opposed to the Taft-Hartley law and that the unions' only remedy lies in November, 1948. In vetoing the law, he attacked every feature which tended to impose any responsibility on unions or restore equality in the administration of the law by the National Labor Relations Board.

We can only conclude that he would repeal the law and restore labor union officers to their former position, where there was no recourse against their arbitrary actions either by the employer, by the public or by the labor union members themselves.

In the passage of that law, we deprived labor of no rights. We require the employer to recognize the union and bargain only with a representative of a majority of the employees on an equal basis across the table. We base our law on free collective bargaining with the right to strike for better hours, wages or working conditions.

The President would restore the days when every small employer was at the mercy of a labor-union officer, no matter how arbitrary. He would restore the days of secondary boycotts and jurisdictional strikes. The number of strikes has been cut in half under the present law, and millions of workmen and their wives bless the day when they are no longer forced to quit their jobs in the arbitrary discretion of unreasonable men.

The President's program does not stop at this point. He is in favor of vastly increased spending by the Federal Government. I have never heard of a spending project which has invoked his opposition. No matter how wild the proposal, he will endorse it. He is traveling through the country promising every group and every state and every community money from the Federal Treasury to support its favorite projects.

Here in Washington, he and the Democratic minority in Congress have opposed every effort of the Republican Congress to cut the expenditures of the Federal Government. Today he is deriding Congress because it has some sense of responsibility to the taxpayers, which he entirely lacks.

Here in Washington we are still fighting the New Deal. While there is a Republican Congress, the President still appoints more than a million employes. Hundreds of Federal bureaus and thousands of press agents are busy propagandizing for their own pet spending, and against every effort of Congress to hold them in restraint.

If any bureau is cut, word goes out through the country to cut off that project or those employes who have the most popular appeal in order that Congress may be subjected to popular pressure to restore the cut which has been made. But the personnel sitting at the desks in Washington continues to increase.

The President favors every project for spending money abroad. He favors every recommendation of the Defense Department. If Congress carried out the recommendations of his famous New Deal message of January, 1948, the Federal budget would be sixty billion dollars instead of forty.

If the President had his way, there would be an immediate increase in taxes in every category. Since the wealthy already pay a greater part of their income in taxes most of the new burden would fall on the middle and lower incomes. Thus socialized medicine is to be financed by a 3 or 4 per cent payroll tax, tough on the lower income employes.

The President vetoed three tax reduction bills, although the money was not necessary for the current expenses of the Government. Like every true New Dealer, he wants a lot of extra money in the Treasury, because he expects to find a way to spend it.

On top of all the other control and taxation he would impose on the American people universal compulsory military training. There can hardly be a greater limitation of individual liberty than it is to take a million boys a year—and perhaps a million girls—for an entire year from their homes and families, their education or their occupation, upset their normal approach to life at an impressionable age, and subject them to the training and indoctrination considered advisable by some military bureau in Washington.

We can be sure that under President Truman that bureau would be infected with New Deal doctrines as it was during the war, and the youth of this country would be trained to a military approach to all questions. It would be literally the regimentation of our children.

Furthermore, there is every sign that the President would return to the same soft policy toward communism which was followed by his predecessor, the policy which placed Russia in the powerful position it occupies today, and introduced Communist influence into every labor union and Government department.

In the President's speech at Chicago, he showed a complete misconception of the dangers of communism. He opposed all legislation to check the spread of communism in the United States. The only remedy he can think of is the passage of social-welfare laws, price-control laws and a planned economy. He doesn't seem to realize that communism is an organized, worldwide conspiracy directed from Russia and using every means, legal and illegal, to extend its influence and power in the United States.

Certainly, we cannot make it a crime to be a Communist, but we can legislate against every activity which goes beyond the Constitutional protection.

We are all in favor of social-welfare legislation. I have drafted and supported proposals for Federal aid to education, to housing and to health. I am for these measures because I want constantly to improve the condition of the American people.

But this program is a pretty slow method of meeting the crusading campaign of communism today. This is the kind of talk which the New Dealers engaged in while they encouraged the spread of communism throughout the world and in the American Government itself.

For fourteen years the New Deal has been apologizing for conditions in this country and advocating the adoption of Socialist and social-welfare measures invented in Europe where they have usually failed.

We want a government which will tell the world what our system has accomplished, not what it has failed to accomplish. That kind of government can prove to the world that American principles have already produced a higher standard of living and a greater production than any socialistic country has ever seen.

The President attacks the Republican Congress because it has not enacted as much legislation relating to civil rights and housing and education and health as he recommends. The Republicans have been in power a little over a year and they have made extensive studies and progress in every one of these fields even if the exact remedies advocated by the President have not been adopted.

It hardly lies in the mouth of the President to accuse them of failure. The New Deal has been in power for fourteen years. It has boasted of its interest in social-welfare legislation. It has promised the people social security and free lunches, and yet today the President admits that it has utterly failed in its much vaunted programs to improve housing, education and health.

Every one of these subjects is complicated and difficult and requires careful study to work out the proper relationship between the Federal Government and local communities. The New Dealer always tries to give complete power to some Washington bureau to tell the states and localities how to run their programs and direct the lives of the people who may get the benefit of Federal assistance.

Look at their program for nationalized medicine. We Republicans are working out constructive programs which retain local control and responsibility, retain the freedom of the medical profession, retain the freedom of the people themselves to live their own lives.

It is to the credit of Congress that we are determined to develop the right method of working out these programs in a manner consistent with liberty and equal justice, and local home rule.

The President talks of his farm program. The Senate created a committee which studied and developed a farm program before we ever heard from the President. He never had a farm program until we wrote one, and he has none now. It is easy enough to state general principles of dealing with agriculture, but hard indeed to get general agreement on details. Our program is contained in a bill to be considered by the Senate next week.

If the President had his way, we would return to a regimented agriculture with full power to the Government to limit production and tell every farmer what he can plant and what he can't plant. Here again, we are trying to work out stability for farm prices with little Federal control or limitations on production.

If the President were re-elected with a Congress of his own choosing, that would be indeed a rubber-stamp Congress. In his blanket condemnation of Congress, we see his determination to write the Congressional program. It is an effort not only to condemn this Congress, but to discredit the institution of Congress. It is an attack on the principle of representative government itself.

As such, it gives aid and comfort to all those who want to destroy representative government as do the Communists, Fascists and every believer in a totalitarian state. The institution of Congress, the direct representatives of the people, is the great bulwark of liberty. Where legislatures have been suppressed by a strong executive, freedom has died.

There would be little left to that bulwark of liberty under a President whose attitude toward the people's representatives is that exhibited in the recent performance on the West Coast.

The President has chosen to veto the most constructive measures adopted by this Congress, in labor legislation, and taxation and scientific research. Many are urging that Congress stay here to deal with those important problems which are still before the American people. There is little use in our working day and night to complete constructive programs when we have a President whose attitude towards Congress and its philosophy is that of President Truman.

There is little use remaining here to face the vetoes of a man who does not understand the difference between American principles of free government and communism, who does not understand the threat of totalitarian control. We had better adjourn now and appeal to the people in November for a vote of confidence in the election of a President who will cooperate in our programs.

Our only hope of winning the great ideological war today is to elect an Administration which abhors regulation and spending and Federal power, which believes in liberty, equality and justice, which believes in the success of the American system, which is prepared to spread American philosophy throughout the world, to meet the Communist crusade with an American faith.

We did it after 1776, and we can do it again. Under such an Administration alone can we hope for continued progress in the United States; under such an administration alone can we hope for peace and security throughout the world.

At the height of the 1948 campaign, Truman, in a stump speech at Denver, charged the Republican party with being dominated by Wall Street. Reviewing the record of the Eightieth Congress, he placed the blame for inflation, inadequate housing, and other problems squarely on Republican shoulders. In contrast, he continued, the nation needs a strong federal government to make effective strides in conservation, public power, and economic growth.

HARRY S. TRUMAN:
WHAT DID THE REPUBLICAN CONGRESS DO?*

Every time I come out this way I feel again the tremendous vitality of the West. That feeling comes not only from magnificent scenery and bracing air. It comes from talking to the vigorous and confident people who live here.

This is a straight-from-the-shoulder country, and it has produced a great breed of fighting men. I am going to call upon your fighting qualities. For you and I have a fight on our hands—a fight for the future of this country and for the welfare of the people of the United States.

The other day a cartoonist for a Republican newspaper drew a cartoon of me that I enjoyed. He showed me dressed up as Paul Revere, riding through a Colonial town yelling to the townspeople: "Look out, the Republicans are coming."

That was a good cartoon. There's a lot of truth in it. But it's not quite accurate. What I am really telling you is not that the Republicans are coming but that they are here. They have been in Washington for the last two years, in the form of the notorious Republican Eightieth Congress.

Today I want to talk to you about what that Republican Congress has been doing to you, to your families and to your country.

Understand me, when I speak of what the Republicans have been doing I'm not talking about the average Republican voter. Nobody knows better than I that, man for man, individually, most Republicans are fine people. But there's a big distinction between the individual Republican voter and the policies of the Republicans as a party.

Something happens to Republican leaders when they get control of the Government or even of a part of the Government—something that shocks and dismays many of their own loyal supporters.

Republicans in Washington have a habit of becoming curiously deaf to the voice of the people. They have a hard time hearing what the ordinary people of the country are saying. But they have no trouble at all hearing what Wall Street is saying. They are able to catch the slightest whisper from big business.

When I talk to you here today about Republicans, I am talking about the party that gets most of its campaign funds from Wall Street. I am talking about the party that gave us the phony boom of the Nineteen Twenties and the Hoover depression that followed. I am talking to you about the party that gave us the Republican Eightieth Congress.

The Republican party today is controlled by silent and cunning men who have a dangerous lust for power and privilege. These men are now reaching out for control of the country and its resources.

It is your votes which will decide whether or not they have their way; that is why I have come here today.

I want you to know the facts.

I repeat: the most reactionary elements in the country today are backing the Republican party in its effort to take over your Government on Election Day.

If they succeed, I predict that they will try to turn back the clock to the day when the West was an economic colony of Wall Street.

On Election Day this year, your choice will not be merely between political parties. You will be choosing a way of life for the years ahead. This is a fateful election. On it will depend your standard of living and the economic independence of your community.

You can choose to be governed by Republican puppets of big business—the same breed that gave you the worst depression in our history.

Or you can choose to be governed by Democratic servants of the people, who are pledged to work for the increasing welfare of the people.

Some of you may feel that I am attacking the leaders of the Republican party pretty sharply. I am, I have good reasons for it—reasons like the obstacles placed in the way of conservation of our natural resources; reasons like the housing conditions in this country; reasons like the high cost of living; reasons that are close to your hearts, and to mine.

You people out here have been thinking about these problems. You have a right to know what

* Reprinted from *Vital Speeches of the Day,* XIV (October 1, 1948), 738–40.

your Government is going to do about them.

Let's go into them. Let's see where the Republicans stand on these vital issues, and where the Democratic party stands.

We all know that the housing situation in this country is a national disgrace. It is almost unbelievable that we should have made so little progress in providing decent housing conditions for millions of American families.

From the first day of the Republican Eightieth Congress, there was a housing bill before it which would meet the problem. That bill was a full scale program to provide housing for all our people and not just for those who can pay high prices. But the Republicans refused to act.

The situation became worse and more desperate. Veterans' groups, labor groups, Mayors of cities, Governors of states, pleaded with the Republicans to pass the housing bill. They still did nothing.

The Republican stand on housing was clearly exposed last July, when I called the Congress into special session and demanded again that they enact housing legislation. The bill was ready. It has been studied and discussed a thousand times. It was supposed to be non-partisan.

But what happened? There was a certain real estate lobby which had its high-priced agents operating in Washington. These men, representing big real estate interests, were in close touch with Republican leaders, the Republican leadership in the House of Representatives cracked the whip, and the Republican Senate killed the non-partisan housing bill.

This was no accident. It was Republican policy. In 1947 Senator Taft joined with two Democratic Senators in introducing the housing bill. But in 1948 he voted against the bill with his own name on it.

Why did the Republicans kill the bill? The answer is plain. They wanted to leave housing under the control of profiteering big business. There is a lot of money to be made out of providing houses for the people if private interests are allowed to exact exorbitant profits from the people.

Have you felt the pinch of the housing shortage? Put the blame where it belongs.

And remember, if the Republicans were to come into power for the next four years, the future of American housing would be in the hands of the same men who killed the housing bill—the men who obey the lobbyists of the selfish interests.

Let's talk about high prices. I know you are deeply troubled by them. Well, put the blame where it belongs—on the leaders of the Republican party. The Republican record in dealing with inflation is typical.

When I called the Republican Congress into special session this year and asked them for price control measures, they said that my request was made for political purposes. They used that

as an excuse and did nothing about prices. They consistently forgot that I had called a special session of the same Congress in 1947 and asked for price control. And 1947 was not an election year.

If they had put into effect the controls I asked for, the prices on such things as meat, milk, steel and automobiles would have been stabilized or reduced.

The Republicans could easily have taken this issue out of politics merely by doing something about it. But they did nothing.

I have been talking about the conservation of our economic well-being. Now I come to a particular phase of that conservation that has special interest for you of the West. You live in a region whose whole future depends on its wise use of the rich resources that nature has provided.

Early in this century a unique Republican President, Theodore Roosevelt, fought for conservation, only to be repudiated by his own party.

All through the Republican Administration from 1921 to 1933 big business pressure groups prevented adequate conservation measures from being put into effect. They wanted quick profits, the easy way, and so Western forests were logged off and left barren. Range lands were grazed off and ruined. Farm land was worked to the point where its fertility was gone. Precious water ran unused past barren land. There was no soil conservation program, no range conservation program.

The nation lost tremendous quantities of its most valuable resources. The West continued to bow to Wall Street—furnishing raw materials at low prices and buying back finished goods at high prices.

Then in 1933 came the Democratic Administration of Franklin Roosevelt.

Under his leadership conservation was made a living reality. You know better than anyone how much it has meant to the West.

The Democratic Administration won its fight for conservation and for Western development against the bitter opposition of Wall Street. You of the West see the results of our victory every day. You see those results in bigger and better crops; in new industries; in the growing national parks and forest and the tourists who visit them; in the rising standards of living of the peoples of the West, and in the stronger economy of the whole nation.

But we still have a long way to go. We are still using our timber faster than we grow it. Thousands of acres of land are still being washed away every year. Disastrous floods are still frequent, conservation in the West is of first importance to the whole country.

In the face of all this, what did the Republican Congress do?

Remember, the record of that Congress is the actual test of the attitude of the Republican leadership toward the people.

The Republicans in the Congress consistently

tried to cut the ground from under our conservation program. Last year, the Republican-dominated House of Representatives voted to cut the agricultural conservation program in half in 1947, and end it entirely in 1948.

The Democrats in the Senate led, and finally won, a fight to save the life of the program. They saved it, but they could not completely restore it. The program was seriously damaged by the Republican Eightieth Congress.

Here is a significant fact. Nineteen forty-seven was the first year in a decade and a half that the Republicans had control of Congress. And that was the first year in which the Congress took a step backward in the spiral of soil conservation since that program was begun.

The first time the Republicans had a chance they began to undermine conservation.

Now let's look at another subject that is closely bound up with your future—the industrial development of the West.

I know that all of you recognize the importance of creating new industries in this region, using the resources of the West so as to reduce your industrial dependence on the East.

For my part, I am convinced that rapid and sound industrial development in the West will make a vital contribution to the living standards and well-being not only of the people of the West but of the entire nation. The heart of the Western industrial development program is hydroelectric power. Coupled with irrigation projects and flood control, electric power is of fundamental importance to your future.

The Democratic party for the past fifteen years has been energetically developing the great dams, irrigation projects and power systems which have contributed so much to the prosperity of the West.

But as soon as the Republican party gained control of the Congress it began to tear down the whole Western development program. The Republicans slashed funds right and left. They cut back projects to bring water to the land and electric power to industry.

Right here in this state the Colorado-Big Thompson project is under way. It is an inspiring project, involving the transfer of water from one side of the Continental Divide to the other. The Republican Congress sharply reduced the funds for that project. When I pointed out the danger of that action and requested them to restore those funds, they refused.

Wherever you turn, no matter what the field of activity, you find the same story. In the light of the evidence, I say flatly that the Republican leaders have been working against the interest of the people. They have been the eager agents of the big business lobbies and the most reactionary elements in American economic life.

In the last sixteen years, Democratic Administrations have built a firm foundation for a new and greater West.

We restored grazing lands for the sustained production of live stock. Millions of cattle and sheep feed today where only prairie dogs and rattlesnakes existed before.

We restored forests for a sustained yield of timber. Trees stand for the future where exploiters have been kept out.

We established a sound conservation policy to prevent land erosion and restore the fertility of the soil.

We built the Federal system of hydroelectric and irrigation projects which are now providing water for more than 5,000,000 irrigated acres in the West and for better living for millions of people.

We have been leading the fight for decent housing, effective reduction of the cost of living, and a rise in living standards—all for a better nation of happier people.

That is the Democratic record—a record of which I am exceedingly proud.

There is more to do, much more. What we have done so far is only the beginning. This is no time to permit your progress to be checked, when you can foresee great new developments of your agriculture, your industry and your commerce, if you have the aid and support of the Federal Government.

Your need is to insure the election of an Administration pledged to give you that aid and support—a Democratic Administration.

There is a hard fight ahead. We shall have to fight the slick political propaganda of the special interests and the Republican leadership.

We shall have to fight the millions of dollars that Wall Street is pouring into the treasury of the Republican party.

We shall have to fight the Republican undercover sabotage of the West.

But we of the Democratic party are eager for that fight. We believe that we owe to future generations the bequest of a strong America, mighty in its resources and wise in its use of them.

We are fairly determined to leave after us a land that is better than we found it.

CHAPTER TWENTY-THREE

MEETING THE THREAT
OF NUCLEAR WAR

The world that emerged after the triumphant conclusion of World War II was far different from that which most Americans had envisaged. The prime problem did not become the prevention of Germany and Japan from rising again as military powers as had been expected. Rather it was to contain the militant force of a former ally, Soviet Russia, and, after 1949, of a China that was newly Communistic. Far from being the world Secretary Hull had predicted in which alliances and spheres of influence would be outmoded, the world became one in which the United States and its allies had to maintain strong counterforce against the Communist power. For several years the main weapon, perhaps the ultimate weapon, in this counterforce was the atomic bomb with which the United States had so spectacularly ended the war against Japan. But in 1949, Russia set off its first nuclear explosion and began building its own arsenal of nuclear weapons. Both sides developed hydrogen bombs and powerful intercontinental missiles with which to launch them. Both sides came to possess the force to inflict upon the other damage far greater than any ever known in history, indeed perhaps the capacity to wipe out all mankind.

From the outset, the United States had expressed its willingness to negotiate a treaty with Russia which would, as Secretary of War Henry L. Stimson proposed in 1945, "control and limit the use of the atomic bomb as an instrument of war and so far as possible . . . direct and encourage the development of atomic power for peaceful and humanitarian purposes." In 1946, the United States proposed to the United Nations a system of international control of atomic energy, including thoroughgoing inspection. When the system went into operation, the United States would destroy its stockpile of atomic bombs. Russia refused all American proposals. Nevertheless, in the late 1950's and into the 1960's, Russia did engage in endless, seemingly fruitless negotiations with the United States looking toward the possible control of nuclear weapons. Meanwhile, the world lived in the shadow of what was often referred to as a nuclear balance of terror. The most serious continuing problem facing the government of the United States was countering the Communist challenge, and one of the most critical aspects of this challenge was negotiating to try to decrease the threat of nuclear war.

531

Two vital decisions faced the Secretary of War and the President of the United States in the spring of 1945: what use should be made of the atomic bomb, assuming that it would work, and what provision should be made thereafter to control the destructive force of atomic energy? Less than two years later, Henry L. Stimson, who had served as Secretary of War, explained how and why he made the recommendations he did to the President concerning the function of the bomb.

HENRY L. STIMSON:
THE DECISION TO USE THE ATOMIC BOMB*

. . . The policy adopted and steadily pursued by President Roosevelt and his advisers was a simple one. It was to spare no effort in securing the earliest possible successful development of an atomic weapon. The reasons for this policy were equally simple. The original experimental achievement of atomic fission had occurred in Germany in 1938, and it was known that the Germans had continued their experiments. In 1941 and 1942 they were believed to be ahead of us, and it was vital that they should not be the first to bring atomic weapons into the field of battle. Furthermore, if we should be the first to develop the weapon, we should have a great new instrument for shortening the war and minimizing destruction. At no time, from 1941 to 1945, did I ever hear it suggested by the President, or by any other responsible member of the government, that atomic energy should not be used in the war. All of us of course understood the terrible responsibility involved in our attempt to unlock the doors to such a devastating weapon; President Roosevelt particularly spoke to me many times of his own awareness of the catastrophic potentialities of our work. But we were at war, and the work must be done. I therefore emphasize that it was our common objective, throughout the war, to be the first to produce an atomic weapon and use it. The possible atomic weapon was considered to be a new and tremendously powerful explosive, as legitimate as any other of the deadly explosive weapons of modern war. The entire purpose was the production of a military weapon; on no other ground could the wartime expenditure of so much time and money have been justified. The exact circumstances in which that weapon might be used were unknown to any of us until the middle of 1945, and when that time came, as we shall presently see, the military use of atomic energy was connected with larger questions of national policy.

The extraordinary story of the successful development of the atomic bomb has been well told elsewhere. As time went on it became clear that the weapon would not be available in time for use in the European Theater, and the war against Germany was successfully ended by the use of what are now called conventional means. But in the spring of 1945 it became evident that the climax of our prolonged atomic effort was at hand. By the nature of atomic chain reactions, it was impossible to state with certainty that we had succeeded until a bomb had actually exploded in a full-scale experiment; nevertheless it was considered exceedingly probable that we should by midsummer have successfully detonated the first atomic bomb. This was to be done at the Alamogordo Reservation in New Mexico. It was thus time for detailed consideration of our future plans. What had begun as a well-founded hope was now developing into a reality.

On March 15, 1945 I had my last talk with President Roosevelt. . . .

This conversation covered the three aspects of the question which were then uppermost in our minds. First, it was always necessary to suppress a lingering doubt that any such titanic undertaking could be successful. Second, we must consider the implications of success in terms of its long-range postwar effect. Third, we must face the problem that would be presented at the time of our first use of the weapon, for with that first use there must be some public statement.

I did not see Franklin Roosevelt again. The next time I went to the White House to discuss atomic energy was April 25, 1945, and I went to explain the nature of the problem to a man whose only previous knowledge of our activities was that of a Senator who had loyally accepted our assurance that the matter must be kept a secret from him. Now he was President and Commander-in-Chief, and the final responsibility in this as in so many other matters must be his. President Truman accepted this responsibility with the same fine spirit that Senator Truman had shown before in accepting our refusal to inform him.

I discussed with him the whole history of the project. We had with us General Groves, who explained in detail the progress which had been made and the probable future course of the work.

* Reprinted from Henry L. Stimson, "The Decision to Use the Atomic Bomb," *Harper's Magazine*, CXCIV (February, 1947), 98–102, 104–7 by permission.

I also discussed with President Truman the broader aspects of the subject, and the memorandum which I used in this discussion is again a fair sample of the state of our thinking at the time.

MEMORANDUM DISCUSSED WITH PRESIDENT TRUMAN APRIL 25, 1945

1. Within four months we shall in all probability have completed the most terrible weapon ever known in human history, one bomb of which could destroy a whole city.

2. Although we have shared its development with the U.K., physically the U.S. is at present in the position of controlling the resources with which to construct and use it and no other nation could reach this position for some years.

3. Nevertheless it is practically certain that we could not remain in this position indefinitely.

a. Various segments of its discovery and production are widely known among many scientists in many countries, although few scientists are now acquainted with the whole process which we have developed.

b. Although its construction under present methods requires great scientific and industrial effort and raw materials, which are temporarily mainly within the possession and knowledge of U.S. and U.K., it is extremely probable that much easier and cheaper methods of production will be discovered by scientists in the future, together with the use of materials of much wider distribution. As a result, it is extremely probable that the future will make it possible for atomic bombs to be constructed by smaller nations or even groups, or at least by a larger nation in a much shorter time.

4. As a result, it is indicated that the future may see a time when such a weapon may be constructed in secret and used suddenly and effectively with devastating power by a wilful nation or group against an unsuspecting nation or group of much greater size and material power. With its aid even a very powerful unsuspecting nation might be conquered within a very few days by a very much smaller one. . . .[1]

5. The world in its present state of moral advancement compared with its technical development would be eventually at the mercy of such a weapon. In other words, modern civilization might be completely destroyed.

6. To approach any world peace organization of any pattern now likely to be considered, without an appreciation by the leaders of our country of the power of this new weapon, would seem to be unrealistic. No system of control heretofore considered would be adequate to control this menace. Both inside any particular coun-

try and between the nations of the world, the control of this weapon will undoubtedly be a matter of the greatest difficulty and would involve such thoroughgoing rights of inspection and internal controls as we have never heretofore contemplated.

7. Furthermore, in the light of our present position with reference to this weapon, the question of sharing it with other nations and, if so shared, upon what terms, becomes a primary question of our foreign relations. Also our leadership in the war and in the development of this weapon has placed a certain moral responsibility upon us which we cannot shirk without very serious responsibility for any disaster to civilization which it would further.

8. On the other hand, if the problem of the proper use of this weapon can be solved, we would have the opportunity to bring the world into a pattern in which the peace of the world and our civilization can be saved.

9. As stated in General Groves' report, steps are under way looking towards the establishment of a select committee of particular qualifications for recommending action to the executive and legislative branches of our government when secrecy is no longer in full effect. The committee would also recommend the actions to be taken by the War Department prior to that time in anticipation of the postwar problems. All recommendations would of course be first submitted to the President.

The next step in our preparations was the appointment of the committee referred to in paragraph (9) above. This committee, which was known as the Interim Committee, was charged with the function of advising the President on the various questions raised by our apparently imminent success in developing an atomic weapon. I was its chairman, but the principal labor of guiding its extended deliberations fell to George L. Harrison, who acted as chairman in my absence. It will be useful to consider the work of the committee in some detail. Its members were the following, in addition to Mr. Harrison and myself:

James F. Byrnes (then a private citizen) as personal representative of the President.

Ralph A. Bard, Under Secretary of the Navy.

William L. Clayton, Assistant Secretary of State.

Dr. Vannevar Bush, Director, Office of Scientific Research and Development, and president of the Carnegie Institution of Washington.

Dr. Karl T. Compton, Chief of the Office of Field Service in the Office of Scientific Research and Development, and president of the Massachusetts Institute of Technology.

Dr. James B. Conant, Chairman of the National Defense Research Committee, and president of Harvard University.

The discussions of the committee ranged over the whole field of atomic energy, in its political, military, and scientific aspects. That part of its

---

[1] A brief reference to the estimated capabilities of other nations is here omitted; it in no way affects the course of the argument.

work which particularly concerns us here relates to its recommendations for the use of atomic energy against Japan, but it should be borne in mind that these recommendations were not made in a vacuum. The committee's work included the drafting of the statements which were published immediately after the first bombs were dropped, the drafting of a bill for the domestic control of atomic energy, and recommendations looking toward the international control of atomic energy. The Interim Committee was assisted in its work by a Scientific Panel whose members were the following: Dr. A. H. Compton, Dr. Enrico Fermi, Dr. E. O. Lawrence, and Dr. J. R. Oppenheimer. All four were nuclear physicists of the first rank; all four had held positions of great importance in the atomic project from its inception. At a meeting with the Interim Committee and the Scientific Panel on May 31, 1945 I urged all those present to feel free to express themselves on any phase of the subject, scientific or political. Both General Marshall and I at this meeting expressed the view that atomic energy could not be considered simply in terms of military weapons but must also be considered in terms of a new relationship of man to the universe.

On June 1, after its discussions with the Scientific Panel, the Interim Committee unanimously adopted the following recommendations:

(1) The bomb should be used against Japan as soon as possible.

(2) It should be used on a dual target—that is, a military installation or war plant surrounded by or adjacent to houses and other buildings most susceptible to damage, and

(3) It should be used without prior warning [of the nature of the weapon]. One member of the committee, Mr. Bard, later changed his view and dissented from recommendation (3).

In reaching these conclusions the Interim Committee carefully considered such alternatives as a detailed advance warning or a demonstration in some uninhabited area. Both of these suggestions were discarded as impractical. They were not regarded as likely to be effective in compelling a surrender of Japan, and both of them involved serious risks. Even the New Mexico test would not give final proof that any given bomb was certain to explode when dropped from an airplane. Quite apart from the generally unfamiliar nature of atomic explosives, there was the whole problem of exploding a bomb at a predetermined height in the air by a complicated mechanism which could not be tested in the static test of New Mexico. Nothing would have been more damaging to our effort to obtain surrender than a warning or a demonstration followed by a dud—and this was a real possibility. Furthermore, we had no bombs to waste. It was vital that a sufficient effect be quickly obtained with the few we had.

The Interim Committee and the Scientific Panel also served as a channel through which suggestions from other scientists working on the atomic project were forwarded to me and to the President. Among the suggestions thus forwarded was one memorandum which questioned using the bomb at all against the enemy. On June 16, 1945, after consideration of that memorandum, the Scientific Panel made a report, from which I quote the following paragraphs: "The opinions of our scientific colleagues on the initial use of these weapons are not unanimous: they range from the proposal of a purely technical demonstration to that of the military application best designed to induce surrender. Those who advocate a purely technical demonstration would wish to outlaw the use of atomic weapons, and have feared that if we use the weapons now our position in future negotiations will be prejudiced. Others emphasize the opportunity of saving American lives by immediate military use, and believe that such use will improve the international prospects, in that they are more concerned with the prevention of war than with the elimination of this special weapon. We find ourselves closer to these latter views; *we can propose no technical demonstration likely to bring an end to the war; we see no acceptable alternative to direct military use.* [Italics mine]

"With regard to these general aspects of the use of atomic energy, it is clear that we, as scientific men, have no proprietary rights. It is true that we are among the few citizens who have had occasion to give thoughtful consideration to these problems during the past few years. We have, however, no claim to special competence in solving the political, social, and military problems which are presented by the advent of atomic power."

The foregoing discussion presents the reasoning of the Interim Committee and its advisers. I have discussed the work of these gentlemen at length in order to make it clear that we sought the best advice that we could find. The committee's function was, of course, entirely advisory. The ultimate responsibility for the recommendation to the President rested upon me, and I have no desire to veil it. The conclusions of the committee were similar to my own, although I reached mine independently. I felt that to extract a genuine surrender from the Emperor and his military advisers, they must be administered a tremendous shock which would carry convincing proof of our power to destroy the Empire. Such an effective shock would save many times the number of lives, both American and Japanese, that it would cost.

The facts upon which my reasoning was based and steps taken to carry it out now follow.

U.S. POLICY TOWARD JAPAN IN JULY 1945

The principal political, social, and military objective of the United States in the summer of 1945 was the prompt and complete surrender of

Japan. Only the complete destruction of her military power could open the way to lasting peace.

Japan, in July 1945, had been seriously weakened by our increasingly violent attacks. It was known to us that she had gone so far as to make tentative proposals to the Soviet government, hoping to use the Russians as mediators in a negotiated peace. These vague proposals contemplated the retention by Japan of important conquered areas and were therefore not considered seriously. There was as yet no indication of any weakening in the Japanese determination to fight rather than accept unconditional surrender. If she should persist in her fight to the end, she had still a great military force. . . .

As we understood it in July, there was a very strong possibility that the Japanese government might determine upon resistance to the end, in all the areas of the Far East under its control. In such an event the Allies would be faced with the enormous task of destroying an armed force of five million men and five thousand suicide aircraft, belonging to a race which had already amply demonstrated its ability to fight literally to the death.

The strategic plans of our armed forces for the defeat of Japan, as they stood in July, had been prepared without reliance upon the atomic bomb, which had not yet been tested in New Mexico. We were planning an intensified sea and air blockade, and greatly intensified strategic air bombing, through the summer and early fall, to be followed on November 1 by an invasion of the southern island of Kyushu. This would be followed in turn by an invasion of the main island of Honshu in the spring of 1946. The total U. S. military and naval force involved in this grand design was of the order of 5,000,000 men; if all those indirectly concerned are included, it was larger still.

We estimated that if we should be forced to carry this plan to its conclusion, the major fighting would not end until the latter part of 1946, at the earliest. I was informed that such operations might be expected to cost over a million casualties, to American forces alone. Additional large losses might be expected among our allies, and, of course, if our campaign were successful and if we could judge by previous experience, enemy casualties would be much larger than our own.

It was already clear in July that even before the invasion we should be able to inflict enormously severe damage on the Japanese homeland by the combined application of "conventional" sea and air power. The critical question was whether this kind of action would induce surrender. It therefore became necessary to consider very carefully the probable state of mind of the enemy, and to assess with accuracy the line of conduct which might end his will to resist.

With these considerations in mind, I wrote a memorandum for the President, on July 2, which I believe fairly represents the thinking of the American government as it finally took shape in action. This memorandum was prepared after discussion and general agreement with Joseph C. Grew, Acting Secretary of State, and Secretary of the Navy Forrestal, and when I discussed it with the President, he expressed his general approval. . . .

In this lengthy memorandum, Stimson warned that Japanese resistance to an invasion was likely to be extreme, and recommended sending a strong warning to Japan of the fate that faced it before the invasion was undertaken.

It is important to emphasize the double character of the suggested warning. It was designed to promise destruction if Japan resisted, and hope, if she surrendered.

It will be noted that the atomic bomb is not mentioned in this memorandum. On grounds of secrecy the bomb was never mentioned except when absolutely necessary, and furthermore, it had not yet been tested. It was of course well forward in our minds, as the memorandum was written and discussed, that the bomb would be the best possible sanction if our warning were rejected.

THE USE OF THE BOMB

The adoption of the policy outlined in the memorandum of July 2 was a decision of high politics; once it was accepted by the President, the position of the atomic bomb in our planning became quite clear. I find that I stated in my diary, as early as June 19, that "the last chance warning . . . must be given before an actual landing of the ground forces in Japan, and fortunately the plans provide for enough time to bring in the sanctions to our warning in the shape of heavy ordinary bombing attack and an attack of S-1." S-1 was a code name for the atomic bomb.

There was much discussion in Washington about the timing of the warning to Japan. The controlling factor in the end was the date already set for the Potsdam meeting of the Big Three. It was President Truman's decision that such a warning should be solemnly issued by the U.S. and the U.K. from this meeting, with the concurrence of the head of the Chinese government, so that it would be plain that *all* of Japan's principal enemies were in entire unity. This was done, in the Potsdam ultimatum of July 26, which very closely followed the above memorandum of July 2, with the exception that it made no mention of the Japanese Emperor.

On July 28 the Premier of Japan, Suzuki, rejected the Potsdam ultimatum by announcing that it was "unworthy of public notice." In the face of this rejection we could only proceed to demonstrate that the ultimatum had meant exactly what it said when it stated that if the Japanese continued the war, "the full application of our military power, backed by our resolve, will mean the inevitable and complete destruction of the Japanese armed forces and just as inevitably the utter devastation of the Japanese homeland."

For such a purpose the atomic bomb was an eminently suitable weapon. The New Mexico test occurred while we were at Potsdam, on July 16. It was immediately clear that the power of the bomb measured up to our highest estimates. We had developed a weapon of such a revolutionary character that its use against the enemy might well be expected to produce exactly the kind of shock on the Japanese ruling oligarchy which we desired, strengthening the position of those who wished peace, and weakening that of the military party.

Because of the importance of the atomic mission against Japan, the detailed plans were brought to me by the military staff for approval. With President Truman's warm support I struck off the list of suggested targets the city of Kyoto. Although it was a target of considerable military importance, it had been the ancient capital of Japan and was a shrine of Japanese art and culture. We determined that it should be spared. I approved four other targets including the cities of Hiroshima and Nagasaki.

Hiroshima was bombed on August 6, and Nagasaki on August 9. These two cities were active working parts of the Japanese war effort. One was an army center; the other was naval and industrial. Hiroshima was the headquarters of the Japanese Army defending southern Japan and was a major military storage and assembly point. Nagasaki was a major seaport and it contained several large industrial plants of great wartime importance. We believed that our attacks had struck cities which must certainly be important to the Japanese military leaders, both Army and Navy, and we waited for a result. We waited one day.

Many accounts have been written about the Japanese surrender. After a prolonged Japanese cabinet session in which the deadlock was broken by the Emperor himself, the offer to surrender was made on August 10. It was based on the Potsdam terms, with a reservation concerning the sovereignty of the Emperor. While the Allied reply made no promises other than those already given, it implicitly recognized the Emperor's position by prescribing that his power must be subject to the orders of the Allied Supreme Com-

mander. These terms were accepted on August 14 by the Japanese, and the instrument of surrender was formally signed on September 2, in Tokyo Bay. Our great objective was thus achieved, and all the evidence I have seen indicates that the controlling factor in the final Japanese decision to accept our terms of surrender was the atomic bomb.[2]

The two atomic bombs which we had dropped were the only ones we had ready, and our rate of production at the time was very small. Had the war continued until the projected invasion on November 1, additional fire raids of B-29's would have been more destructive of life and property than the very limited number of atomic raids which we could have executed in the same period. But the atomic bomb was more than a weapon of terrible destruction; it was a psychological weapon. In March 1945 our Air Force had launched its first great incendiary raid on the Tokyo area. In this raid more damage was done and more casualties were inflicted than was the case at Hiroshima. Hundreds of bombers took part and hundreds of tons of incendiaries were dropped. Similar successive raids burned out a great part of the urban area of Japan, but the Japanese fought on. On August 6 one B-29 dropped a single atomic bomb on Hiroshima. Three days later a second bomb was dropped on Nagasaki and the war was over. So far as the Japanese could know, our ability to execute atomic attacks, if necessary by many planes at a time, was unlimited. As Dr. Karl Compton has said, "it was not one atomic bomb, or two, which brought surrender; it was the experience of what an atomic bomb will actually do to a community, *plus the dread of many more,* that was effective."

The bomb thus served exactly the purpose we intended. The peace party was able to take the path of surrender, and the whole weight of the Emperor's prestige was exerted in favor of peace. When the Emperor ordered surrender, and the small but dangerous group of fanatics who opposed him were brought under control, the Japanese became so subdued that the great undertaking of occupation and disarmament was completed with unprecedented ease. . . .

As I read over what I have written, I am aware that much of it, in this year of peace, may have a harsh and unfeeling sound. It would perhaps be possible to say the same things and say them more gently. But I do not think it would be wise. As I look back over the five years of my service as Secretary of War, I see too many stern and heartrending decisions to be willing to pretend that war is anything else than what it is. The face of war is the face of death; death is an inevitable part of every order that a wartime leader gives. The decision to use the atomic bomb was a

[2] Report of United States Strategic Bombing Survey, "Japan's Struggle to End the War"; "If the Atomic Bomb Had Not Been Used," by K. T. Compton, *Atlantic Monthly,* December 1946; unpublished material of historical division, War Department Special Staff, June, 1946.

decision that brought death to over a hundred thousand Japanese. No explanation can change that fact and I do not wish to gloss it over. But this deliberate, premeditated destruction was our least abhorrent choice. The destruction of Hiroshima and Nagasaki put an end to the Japanese war. It stopped the fire raids, and the strangling blockade; it ended the ghastly specter of a clash of great land armies.

In this last great action of the Second World War we were given final proof that war is death.

War in the twentieth century has grown steadily more barbarous, more destructive, more debased in all its aspects. Now, with the release of atomic energy, man's ability to destroy himself is very nearly complete. The bombs dropped on Hiroshima and Nagasaki ended a war. They also made it wholly clear that we must never have another war. This is the lesson men and leaders everywhere must learn, and I believe that when they learn it they will find a way to lasting peace. There is no other choice.

The destruction at Hiroshima and Nagasaki not only helped shock Japan into surrender, but also shocked the world. In later years, the shock remained in part because so much damage had been done by two relatively small bombs that possessed only a fraction of the destructive force of succeeding bombs. Some of the shock resulted from the frightful suffering of the victims at Hiroshima. This suffering was not greatly different from that inflicted by the more conventional explosive bombs, the fire bombs, and the rockets that rained upon civilians throughout World War II. But somehow Hiroshima came to symbolize the horrors of modern warfare. Although Americans could cite Secretary Stimson's reasoning in justification of Hiroshima or could point to the atrocities the Axis countries had inflicted, many of them nevertheless tended to feel a burden of guilt for what had happened.

THE UNITED STATES STRATEGIC BOMBING SURVEY: THE DESTRUCTION AT HIROSHIMA AND NAGASAKI*

... On 6 August and 9 August 1945, the first two atomic bombs to be used for military purposes were dropped on Hiroshima and Nagasaki respectively. One hundred thousand people were killed, 6 square miles or over 50 percent of the built-up areas of the two cities were destroyed. The first and crucial question about the atomic bomb thus was answered practically and conclusively; atomic energy had been mastered for military purposes and the overwhelming scale of its possibilities had been demonstrated. A detailed examination of the physical, economic, and morale effects of the atomic bombs occupied the attention of a major portion of the Survey's staff in Japan in order to arrive at a more precise definition of the present capabilities and limitations of this radically new weapon of destruction.

Eyewitness accounts of the explosion all describe similar pictures. The bombs exploded with a tremendous flash of blue-white light, like a giant magnesium flare. The flash was of short duration and accompanied by intense glare and

heat. It was followed by a tremendous pressure wave and the rumbling sound of the explosion. This sound is not clearly recollected by those who survived near the center of the explosion, although it was clearly heard by others as much as fifteen miles away. A huge snow-white cloud shot rapidly into the sky and the scene on the ground was obscured first by a bluish haze and then by a purple-brown cloud of dust and smoke.

Such eyewitness accounts reveal the sequence of events. At the time of the explosion, energy was given off in the forms of light, heat, radiation, and pressure. The complete band of radiations, from X- and gamma-rays, through ultraviolet and light rays to the radiant heat of infra-red rays, travelled with the speed of light. The shock wave created by the enormous pressures built up almost instantaneously at the point of explosion but moved out more slowly, that is at about the speed of sound. The superheated gases constituting the original fire ball expanded outward and upward at a slower rate.

The light and radiant heat rays accompanying the flash travelled in a straight line and any opaque object, even a single leaf of a vine, shielded objects lying behind it. The duration of the flash was only a fraction of a second, but it was sufficiently intense to cause third degree

* Reprinted from The United States Strategic Bombing Survey, *Summary Report (Pacific War)* (Washington, D.C.: Government Printing Office, 1946), pp. 22–25.

burns to exposed human skin up to a distance of a mile. Clothing ignited, though it could be quickly beaten out, telephone poles charred, thatchroofed houses caught fire. Black or other dark-colored surfaces of combustible material absorbed the heat and immediately charred or burst into flames; white or light-colored surfaces reflected a substantial portion of the rays and were not consumed. The heavy black clay tiles which are an almost universal feature of the roofs of Japanese houses bubbled at distances up to a mile. Test of samples of this tile by the National Bureau of Standards in Washington indicates that temperatures in excess of 1,800° C. must have been generated in the surface of the tile to produce such an effect. The surfaces of granite blocks exposed to the flash scarred and spalled at distances up to almost a mile. In the immediate area of ground zero (the point on the ground immediately below the explosion), the heat charred corpses beyond recognition.

Penetrating rays such as gamma-rays exposed X-ray films stored in the basement of a concrete hospital almost a mile from ground zero. Symptoms of their effect on human beings close to the center of the explosion, who survived other effects thereof, were generally delayed for two or three days. The bone marrow and as a result the process of blood formation were affected. The white corpuscle count went down and the human processes of resisting infection were destroyed. Death generally followed shortly thereafter.

The majority of radiation cases who were at greater distances did not show severe symptoms until 1 to 4 weeks after the explosion. The first symptoms were loss of appetite, lassitude and general discomfort. Within 12 to 48 hours, fever became evident in many cases, going as high as 104° to 105° F., which in fatal cases continued until death. If the fever subsided, the patient usually showed a rapid disappearance of other symptoms and soon regained his feeling of good health. Other symptoms were loss of white blood corpuscles, loss of hair, and decrease in sperm count.

Even though rays of this nature have great powers of penetration, intervening substances filter out portions of them. As the weight of the intervening material increases the percentage of the rays penetrating goes down. It appears that a few feet of concrete, or a somewhat greater thickness of earth, furnished sufficient protection to humans, even those close to ground zero, to prevent serious after effects from radiation.

The blast wave which followed the flash was of sufficient force to press in the roofs of reinforced-concrete structures and to flatten completely all less sturdy structures. Due to the height of the explosion, the peak pressure of the wave at ground zero was no higher than that produced by a near-miss of a high-explosive bomb, and decreased at greater distances from ground zero. Reflection and shielding by intervening hills and structures produced some unevenness in the pattern. The blast wave, however, was of far greater extent and duration than that of a high-explosive bomb and most reinforced-concrete structures suffered structural damage or collapse up to 700 feet at Hiroshima and 2,000 feet at Nagasaki. Brick buildings were flattened up to 7,300 feet at Hiroshima and 8,500 feet at Nagasaki. Typical Japanese houses of wood construction suffered total collapse up to approximately 7,300 feet at Hiroshima and 8,200 feet at Nagasaki. Beyond these distances structures received less serious damage to roofs, wall partitions, and the like. Glass windows were blown out at distances up to 5 miles. The blast wave, being of longer duration than that caused by high-explosive detonations, was accompanied by more flying debris. Window frames, doors, and partitions which would have been shaken down by a near-miss of a high-explosive bomb were hurled at high velocity through those buildings which did not collapse. Machine tools and most other production equipment in industrial plants were not directly damaged by the blast wave, but were damaged by collapsing buildings or ensuing general fires. . . .

The Survey has estimated that the damage and casualties caused at Hiroshima by the one atomic bomb dropped from a single plane would have required 220 B–29s carrying 1,200 tons of incendiary bombs, 400 tons of high-explosive bombs, and 500 tons of anti-personnel fragmentation bombs, if conventional weapons, rather than an atomic bomb, had been used. One hundred and twenty-five B–29s carrying 1,200 tons of bombs would have been required to approximate the damage and casualties at Nagasaki. This estimate presupposed bombing under conditions similar to those existing when the atomic bombs were dropped and bombing accuracy equal to the average attained by the Twentieth Air Force during the last 3 months of the war.

As might be expected, the primary reaction of the populace to the bomb was fear, uncontrolled terror, strengthened by the sheer horror of the destruction and suffering witnessed and experienced by the survivors. Prior to the dropping of the atomic bombs, the people of the two cities had fewer misgivings about the war than people in other cities and their morale held up after it better than might have been expected. Twenty-nine percent of the survivors interrogated indicated that after the atomic bomb was dropped they were convinced that victory for Japan was impossible. Twenty-four percent stated that because of the bomb they felt personally unable to carry on with the war. Some 40 percent testified to various degrees of defeatism. A greater number (24 percent) expressed themselves as being impressed with the power and scientific skill which underlay the discovery and production of the atomic bomb than expressed anger at its use (20 percent). In many instances, the reaction was one of resignation. . . .

The following is the account of a girl who was attending junior college in Hiroshima when the atomic bomb exploded.

ATSUKO TSUJIOKA: A RECOLLECTION OF HIROSHIMA*

Ah, that instant! I felt as though I had been struck on the back with something like a big hammer, and thrown into boiling oil. For some time I was unconscious. When I abruptly came to again, everything around me was smothered in black smoke; it was all like a dream or something that didn't make sense. My chest hurt, I could barely breathe, and I thought 'This is the end!' I pressed my chest tightly and lay face down on the ground, and ever so many times I called for help. . . .

Through a darkness like the bottom of Hell I could hear the voices of the other students calling for their mothers. I could barely sense the fact that the students seemed to be running away from that place. I immediately got up, and without any definite idea of escaping I just frantically ran in the direction they were all taking. As we came close to Tsurumi Bridge a red hot electric wire wrapped itself around both my ankles. I don't know how but I managed to pull it off, and as though I were moving in a dream I reached the end of the bridge. By this time everything had long since changed to white smoke. The place where I had been working was Tanaka-cho, a little more than 600 yards from the center of the explosion. Although I should have been at a place straight in from Tsurumi Bridge, I seem to have been blown a good way to the north, and I felt as though the directions were all changed around.

At the base of the bridge, inside a big cistern that had been dug out there, was a mother weeping and holding above her head a naked baby that was burned bright red all over its body, and another mother was crying and sobbing as she gave her burned breast to her baby. In the cistern the students stood with only their heads above the water and their two hands, which they clasped as they imploringly cried and screamed, calling their parents. But every single person who passed was wounded, all of them, and there was no one to turn to for help. The singed hair on people's heads was frizzled up and whitish, and covered with dust—from their appearance you couldn't believe that they were human creatures of this world. Looking at these people made me think suddenly 'It can't be possible that I—.' I looked at my two hands and found them covered with blood, and from my arms something

that looked like rags was hanging and inside I could see the healthy-looking flesh with its mingled colors of white, red and black. Shocked, I put my hand into my *mompei* [slacks] pocket to get out my handkerchief, but there was no handkerchief, nor pocket either. And my *mompei* were also burned off below my hips. I could feel my face gradually swelling up, but there was nothing I could do about it, and when some of my friends suggested that we try to return to our homes in the suburbs, I set out with them. As we walked along, fires were blazing high on both sides of us, and my back was painfully hot. From inside the wreckage of the houses we would hear screaming voices calling "Help!" and then the flames would swallow up everything. A child of about six, all covered with blood, holding a kitchen pot in his arms, was facing a burning house, stamping his feet and screaming something. . . .

Luckily there were some kind soldiers from a medical unit there, and they carried me up the hill to a place where I could lie down. There they gave me first aid treatment right away. It seemed that I had received a terrific blow on the back of my head, and there were fragments of roof tile left there. They pulled these out and bandaged the wound for me. . . .

My father and four or five of our neighbors were searching around for me day after day and finally on the evening of the third day they discovered me in one corner of the barracks at the foot of Futaba Hill. On my blouse there was sewn a name-tag that my father had written for me; the letters had been burned out just as though that part of the cloth had been eaten away by moths, and it was by this that they were able to find me.

"Atchan. This is Father."

When he said that, I was so happy that I couldn't say a word—I could only nod my head. My swollen eyes wouldn't open, so I couldn't see my father's face. This is how I was rescued.

Even now the scars of those wounds remain over my whole body. On my head, my face, my arms, my legs and my chest. As I stroke these blackish-red raised scars on my arms, and every time I look in a mirror at this face of mine which is not like my face, and think that never again will I be able to see my former face and that I have to live my life forever in this condition, it becomes too sad to bear. At the time I lost hope for the future. . . . But with human beings, it isn't only a beautiful outward appearance that is good. True beauty, worthy of a human being,

* Reprinted from Arata Osada, ed., *Children of the A-Bomb* (First English language edition: Tokyo: Uchida Rokakuho Publishing House, 1959. Abridged American edition: New York: G. P. Putnam's Sons, 1963) by permission.

takes away an ugly appearance and makes it into a splendid one. . . .

It is my hope that in the future such a tragic event as this will never make a second appearance in this world. And I want things to work out so that atomic energy will be the power which will give birth to a peaceful world. I believe there is no necessity for mankind to experience directly such suffering.

Since the surrender of Japan, it has been the policy of the United States government to try to arrive at agreements which will eliminate fissionable weapons. However, the United States would not agree to Russian demands for atomic disarmament without inspection. "If we accepted the Russian position [of 1946]," President Truman wrote in his *Memoirs,* "we would be deprived of everything except their promise to agree to controls. Then, if the Russians should launch an atomic armament race, our present advantage and security gained by our discovery and initiative would be wiped out." As it was, President Truman soon found himself engaged in a race to keep the United States ahead of the Soviet Union.

HARRY S. TRUMAN· THE RACE FOR THE HYDROGEN BOMB*

In all my dealings with the Atomic Energy Commission I made it a practice to conclude each discussion with the admonition that we must keep ahead. But our monopoly came to an end sooner than the experts had predicted. An atomic explosion took place in Russia in August 1949.

The intelligence experts had different opinions about it, but in general none of them had looked for the Russians to detonate any atomic device before 1952. Fortunately, the Long Range Detection System of the Air Force had become fully developed in early 1949, and it was through this network that we were able to learn, in surprising detail, that an atomic explosion, not under our control, had taken place. . . .

The Government of the United States was not unprepared for the Russian atomic explosion. There was no panic, and there was no need for emergency decisions. This was a situation that we had been expecting to happen sooner or later. To be sure, it came sooner than the experts had estimated, but it did not require us to alter the direction of our program. . . .

One of the positive effects of this development was to spur our laboratories and our great scientists to make haste on hydrogen bomb research. By the early fall of 1949, development of the "super"—the thermonuclear or hydrogen—bomb had progressed to the point where we were almost ready to put our theories into practice. I believed that anything that would assure us the lead in the field of atomic energy development for de-

fense had to be tried out, but a most complicated and baffling problem had arisen, and the alternatives were a long way from clear-cut.

The first problem was to decide how much of the AEC's energies and resources should be devoted to an early test that might show us whether or not the H-bomb would work. In order to do this, uranium now going into A-bomb production would have to be diverted. But how far could a program now working so successfully (the uranium-plutonium process) be cut back for tests on a method that might fail?

Everything pertaining to the hydrogen bomb was at this time still in the realm of the uncertain. It was all theory and assumption. Even the scientists and the Commission were divided. And, in addition, the questions with which we were concerned related not only to matters of scientific knowledge but also to our defense strategy and our foreign policy. All of these had to be weighed.

On the AEC, Chairman David Lilienthal, Sumner Pike, and Robert Bacher favored a policy of going slow on the hydrogen bomb. Gordon Dean and Lewis Strauss, however, saw no reason for any delay and wanted to go ahead at once with a test program.

The Commission gave me a full account of its differences of opinion, and individual members expressed their own views in separate letters. I once again sought the advice of the Special Committee of the National Security Council, with Dean Acheson, Louis Johnson, and David Lilienthal as members.

"I have recently received," I wrote this committee on November 10, "a report by the Chairman of the Atomic Energy Commission which raises the question as to whether the United States

* Reprinted from Harry S. Truman, *Memoirs* (Garden City, N.Y.: Doubleday & Company, 1956), II, 306–15 by permission. Copyright, 1956, Time Inc.

should proceed with the construction of 'super' atomic weapons. This question involves consideration not only of the factors presented by the Atomic Energy Commission in its report but also political and military factors of concern to the Departments of State and Defense.

"To assist me in reaching a decision with respect to this vital question, I am therefore designating the Secretary of State, the Secretary of Defense and the Chairman of the Atomic Energy Commission as a special committee of the National Security Council to advise me on this problem. I suggest that each member of the committee provide from his agency appropriate staff officers to prepare under your supervision the necessary studies. I desire that the committee analyze all phases of the question including particularly the technical, military and political factors, and make recommendations as to whether and in what manner the United States should undertake the development and possible production of 'super' atomic weapons. Included in these recommendations, I should like to have the advice of the Council as to whether and when any publicity should be given this matter. . . ."

On January 31, 1950, at twelve-thirty, the Special Committee came to the White House with their report. It was a unanimous recommendation signed by all three members—Dean Acheson, Louis Johnson, and David Lilienthal, and the gist of their recommendation was this: that I should direct the AEC to take whatever steps were necessary to determine whether we could make and set off a hydrogen weapon. Concurrently with this, the Special Committee recommended a re-examination of our foreign policy and our strategic plans, both diplomatic and military.

I approved these recommendations and issued a public statement:

"It is part of my responsibility as Commander-in-Chief of the armed forces to see to it that our country is able to defend itself against any possible aggressor.

"Accordingly, I have directed the Atomic Energy Commission to continue its work on all forms of atomic weapons, including the so-called hydrogen or super-bomb.

"Like all other work in the field of atomic weapons, it is being and will be carried forward on a basis consistent with the overall objectives of our program for peace and security.

"This we shall continue to do until a satisfactory plan for international control of atomic energy is achieved. We shall also continue to examine all those factors that affect our program for peace and this country's security."

On February 24, about a month later, the Secretary of Defense and the Joint Chiefs of Staff submitted a recommendation to step up our program sharply by "immediate implementation of all-out development of hydrogen bombs and means for their production and delivery."

The military chiefs were going on the assumption that the test of the H-bomb would be successful and that for this reason they recommended authorization to plan for full-scale production of facilities, equipment, and appropriate carriers.

I referred this proposal for examination to the Special Committee of the National Security Council, which made a thorough study of all phases of the situation and on March 9 brought me a detailed report. In this I was informed that, according to my directive of January 31 (to the Atomic Energy Commission), the scientists at Los Alamos had turned their maximum efforts to a research and development program that would enable us to test a thermonuclear weapon as soon as possible, and that they were now of the opinion that a test of the first step in the process could take place sometime in 1951.

If the first step succeeded, then the entire process might be ready for testing by late 1952. The Special Committee reported that after a careful examination of all the facts it had been concluded that "there are no known additional steps which might be taken for further acceleration of the test program."

With these conclusions reached, it was now necessary to decide whether the AEC should proceed with its plans for the production of materials needed for thermonuclear weapons on the assumption that the tests would be successful.

There were many considerations involved, including the expense. The tests would cost an estimated ninety-five million dollars, and the diversion of parts of the U-235 bomb program would cost considerably more. The plants for the production, the main substance needed for the hydrogen bomb, would take, even on a modest scale, two hundred million dollars as a start. There would also be about one hundred million dollars involved in development programs that were less directly related to the making of the bomb.

It is obvious that a great many facts had to be studied in order to make a decision like this. Still, it is the President's responsibility to draw all ideas and all the obtainable facts together and balance them. He cannot allow himself to be swayed in any one direction. He must balance the military with the foreign policy, and both with the nation's economy.

Studying the report of the Special Committee, I had noted that the production facilities for one of the components could also be used for our current atomic program and in other fields of defense production. Thus there would not be a total loss even if it turned out that the process failed to work. This, however, was still the big "IF."

Later in 1950 and in early 1951, Dr. Ulam and Dr. Teller, at Los Alamos, made new discoveries that changed the picture. But in March 1950 it was still to be proved that the fusing of a light atom like hydrogen could be achieved.

These were the circumstances at the time. Nevertheless, on March 10 additional emphasis was given to the H-bomb research by my declaring it to be "of the highest urgency," and I directed the Commission to plan at once for quantity production. Then, once we knew that the H-bomb was feasible, production on it should get under way as soon as possible.

As a result of this decision, the huge Savannah River project of the Atomic Energy Commission was started, and other expansions were made in the AEC plant facilities.

Meanwhile, the State Department policy planners and the planners in the Defense Department had been hard at work on the re-evaluation of our objectives which I had asked them to make in the directive of January 31, and I received from the two departments a first draft of their conclusions on April 7.

The report began with an analysis of the world situation. It pointed out that within the past thirty-five years the world had gone through two world wars, had seen two major revolutions, in Russia and in China, had witnessed the passing of five empires and the drastic decline of two major imperial systems, the French and the British. These events had basically altered the historical distribution of power until now there were only two major centers of power remaining, the United States and the Soviet Union.

The United States, the report continued, had its fundamental purpose clearly defined. The Preamble to the Constitution of the United States lists the aims of the American people in simple words that cannot be misunderstood: ". . . to form a more perfect Union, establish Justice, insure domestic Tranquillity, provide for the common defense, promote the general Welfare, and secure the Blessings of Liberty to ourselves and our Posterity."

In short, our fundamental aim was and is to assure the integrity and vitality of the free society we live in, a society that is based upon the dignity and worth of the individual.

The fundamental design of the Soviet Union, on the other hand, is a world dominated by the will of the Kremlin. Whether we like it or not, this makes the United States the principal target of the Kremlin—the enemy that must be destroyed or subverted before the Soviets can achieve their goal.

The danger spots in the situation were discussed, and close attention was given to the effect of Russian atomic strength, as it was likely to develop over the next few years.

Our foreign policy aimed at building up rapidly the combined political, economic, and military strength of the free world.

The power of the atom is of key importance in a search for a peaceful world. With its vast potentialities for power development, the atom can bring welfare and prosperity to a world at peace. On the other hand, in a world that is close to the brink of war as ours has been for the past few years, the atom's power in the wrong hands can spell disaster. In the right hands, however, it can be used as an overriding influence against aggression and reckless war, and for that reason I have always insisted that, within the

resources of a balanced security system and a balanced economy, we stay ahead of all the world in atomic affairs.

The development of the hydrogen bomb was one direction in which we held our commanding lead. But we were also able to adapt the A-bomb to new uses, even to the point where it became possible to build atomic cannons, to put atomic warheads on guided missiles and atomic-powered units into submarines. . . .

Thermonuclear power developments were moving on, in spite of unavoidable delays by material shortages. A crucial test came off successfully in March 1951 at Eniwetok. This was a tremendously important event, for it proved that the scientific calculations were correct, and with that knowledge in hand it now became possible to make further definite plans. Major progress was made shortly thereafter at a planning conference at Princeton, New Jersey, in June 1951, where the most important idea that was presented had to do with a novel plan for producing the hydrogen bomb in quantity.

On June 12 Gordon Dean brought me a full report of this meeting and of the program that was agreed upon. He said that if I approved this program now, we could expect our first full-size thermonuclear test by early fall of 1952, and I took Dean's report with me for further study.

A week later he got my approval to go ahead.

One complication with this H-bomb test that we did not anticipate at the time was the combination of weather and American politics. When the fall of 1952 rolled around and preparations seemed near completion, the Atomic Energy Commission called for a weather forecast for the Eniwetok test site so that they could fix the exact date for the test. The weather in that part of the Pacific is such that in the fall only one or two days each month will give ideal conditions, and the best date for the test, it turned out, was November 1, only three days before the election.

Gordon Dean came to me and said that he and some of the other AEC Commissioners felt that it might perhaps not be desirable to set off the first full-scale H-bomb test so near to the election date. They were of the opinion that the explosion would surely not remain a secret and that it might be judged a political maneuver. I asked Gordon Dean if he knew of any other suitable date and what it would cost to postpone the test shot. He told me. I then instructed him to forget politics and hold the test on whatever date weather conditions would be most favorable. I think he knew what my answer was going to be before he came, for more than once he had heard me say that political considerations should never be tolerated in the nation's atomic program.

The first test of a hydrogen bomb, which was set off on November 1, 1952, was a dramatic success. So powerful was the explosion that an entire island was blown away and a huge crater left in the coral. It was an awesome demonstration of the new power, and I felt that it was important that the newly elected President should be fully informed about it. And on the day after the election I requested the Atomic Energy Commission to arrange to brief President-elect Eisenhower on the results of the test as well as on our entire nuclear program.

At the time the new administration took over, the nation had been through nearly seven and a half years of the atomic age. We had invested seven billion dollars in research and development in nuclear energy. By 1953 the nation had a stockpile of atomic bombs, together with the means for delivering these bombs to the target. It also had a growing arsenal of tactical weapons using atomic warheads, a submarine under construction powered by atomic energy, and a successfully tested hydrogen bomb and facilities for its production. By 1953 atomic energy had been applied successfully in the fields of medicine and biology, and research was being pushed still further for economically feasible peacetime uses. Furthermore, we had taken the leadership in proposing United Nations control of atomic power. In the interest of peace, we kept pressing for international control in the face of obstructive resistance of the Russians.

It is to the scientists, the members of the Commission, and the dedicated workers in laboratories and in factories to whom all credit must go. The roster of the membership of the Atomic Energy Commission, its staff and its advisory groups, reads like a list of the best men who have been attracted to public service. Some of them were subjected to harassment and abuse because they spoke their minds and refused to play politics with the program, but these are the men who keep democracy in the lead.

In this list of atomic developments, I have put the peaceful uses and the military uses side by side. It is a matter of practical necessity in the kind of world in which we live today that we gave priority to security, but I have always had the profound hope that atomic energy would one day soon serve its rightful purpose—the benefit of all mankind.

I would have been more than happy if our plan for international control had been carried out and if *all* efforts of the world's scientists could have been bent toward finding ways and means to make the atom serve man's wants and needs. It will always remain my prayer that the world will come to look upon the atom as a source of useful energy and a source of important healing power, and that there will never again be any need to invoke the terrible destructive powers that lie hidden in the elements.

Only a few months after the United States exploded a hydrogen bomb, the Russians also successfully tested one. President Dwight D. Eisenhower warned the American people that the physical security of the nation had "almost totally disappeared before the long-range bomber and the destructive power of a single bomb." Since the same destructive force could threaten Russia, there seemed some possibility that the new Russian leaders who had succeeded Stalin might be receptive to disarmament proposals. At a "summit conference" at Geneva on July 21, 1955, President Eisenhower laid before Chairman Nikolai Bulganin of the Russian Council of Ministers and Nikita Khrushchev proposals for disarmament and aerial inspection. Nothing came of the proposals.

DWIGHT D. EISENHOWER: DISARMAMENT PROPOSALS: STATEMENT ON DISARMAMENT PRESENTED AT THE GENEVA CONFERENCE*

MR. CHAIRMAN, GENTLEMEN:

Disarmament is one of the most important subjects on our agenda. It is also extremely difficult. In recent years the scientists have discovered methods of making weapons many, many times more destructive of opposing armed forces—but also of homes, and industries and lives—than ever known or even imagined before. These same scientific discoveries have made much more complex the problems of limitation and control and reduction of armament.

After our victory as Allies in World War II, my country rapidly disarmed. Within a few years our armament was at a very low level. Then events occurred beyond our borders which caused us to realize that we had disarmed too much. For our own security and to safeguard peace we needed greater strength. Therefore we proceeded

* Reprinted from *Public Papers of the Presidents . . . : Dwight D. Eisenhower . . . 1955* (Washington, D.C.: Government Printing Office, 1959), pp. 713–16.

to rearm and to associate with others in a partnership for peace and for mutual security.

The American people are determined to maintain and if necessary increase this armed strength for as long a period as is necessary to safeguard peace and to maintain our security.

But we know that a mutually dependable system for less armament on the part of all nations would be a better way to safeguard peace and to maintain our security.

It would ease the fears of war in the anxious hearts of people everywhere. It would lighten the burdens upon the backs of the people. It would make it possible for every nation, great and small, developed and less developed, to advance the standards of living of its people, to attain better food, and clothing, and shelter, more of education and larger enjoyment of life.

Therefore the United States government is prepared to enter into a sound and reliable agreement making possible the reduction of armament. I have directed that an intensive and thorough study of this subject be made within our own government. From these studies, which are continuing, a very important principle is emerging to which I referred in my opening statement on Monday.

No sound and reliable agreement can be made unless it is completely covered by an inspection and reporting system adequate to support every portion of the agreement.

The lessons of history teach us that disarmament agreements without adequate reciprocal inspection increase the dangers of war and do not brighten the prospects of peace.

Thus it is my view that the priority attention of our combined study of disarmament should be upon the subject of inspection and reporting. Questions suggest themselves.

How effective an inspection system can be designed which would be mutually and reciprocally acceptable within our countries and the other nations of the world? How would such a system operate? What could it accomplish?

Is certainty against surprise aggression attainable by inspection? Could violations be discovered promptly and effectively counteracted?

We have not as yet been able to discover any scientific or other inspection method which would make certain of the elimination of nuclear weapons. So far as we are aware no other nation has made such a discovery. Our study of this problem is continuing. We have not as yet been able to discover any accounting or other inspection method of being certain of the true budgetary facts of total expenditures for armament. Our study of this problem is continuing. We by no means exclude the possibility of finding useful checks in these fields.

As you can see from these statements, it is our impression that many past proposals of disarmament are more sweeping than can be insured by effective inspection.

Gentlemen, since I have been working on this memorandum to present to this Conference, I have been searching my heart and mind for something that I could say here that could convince everyone of the great sincerity of the United States in approaching this problem of disarmament.

I should address myself for a moment principally to the Delegates from the Soviet Union, because our two great countries admittedly possess new and terrible weapons in quantities which do give rise in other parts of the world, or reciprocally, to the fears and dangers of surprise attack.

I propose, therefore, that we take a practical step, that we begin an arrangement, very quickly, as between ourselves—immediately. These steps would include:

To give to each other a complete blueprint of our military establishments, from beginning to end, from one end of our countries to the other; lay out the establishments and provide the blueprints to each other.

Next, to provide within our countries facilities for aerial photography to the other country—we to provide you the facilities within our country, ample facilities for aerial reconnaissance, where you can make all the pictures you choose and take them to your own country to study, you to provide exactly the same facilities for us and we to make these examinations, and by this step to convince the world that we are providing as between ourselves against the possibility of great surprise attack, thus lessening danger and relaxing tension. Likewise we will make more easily attainable a comprehensive and effective system of inspection and disarmament, because what I propose, I assure you, would be but a beginning.

Now from my statements I believe you will anticipate my suggestion. It is that we instruct our representatives in the Subcommittee on Disarmament in discharge of their mandate from the United Nations to give priority effort to the study of inspection and reporting. Such a study could well include a step by step testing of inspection and reporting methods.

The United States is ready to proceed in the study and testing of a reliable system of inspections and reporting, and when that system is proved, then to reduce armaments with all others to the extent that the system will provide assured results.

The successful working out of such a system would do much to develop the mutual confidence which will open wide the avenues of progress for all our peoples.

The quest for peace is the statesman's most exacting duty. Security of the nation entrusted to his care is his greatest responsibility. Practical progress to lasting peace is his fondest hope. Yet in pursuit of his hope he must not betray the trust placed in him as guardian of the people's security. A sound peace—with security, justice, wellbeing, and freedom for the people of the world—*can* be achieved, but only by patiently and thoughtfully following a hard and sure and tested road.

Despite the disappointing reception of his proposals, President Eisenhower continued to wage "a war for peace." On August 21, 1957, he authorized including a suspension of nuclear tests among the disarmament proposals being made by the United States. After a Russian rebuff on August 28, he reiterated his proposals. Finally, in the spring of 1958, Khrushchev announced unilaterally that Russia would cease nuclear tests. President Eisenhower declared that the United States also would stop testing on a year-to-year basis, providing Russia would negotiate a control agreement and seriously discuss disarmament.

DWIGHT D. EISENHOWER:
PROPOSAL TO SUSPEND NUCLEAR TESTS*

In our efforts with our allies to reach a sound and early agreement with the Soviet Union on a first-step disarmament program, I have authorized the Secretary of State to make a significant change in our proposals in the United Nations Disarmament Sub-Committee now meeting in London.

Pursuant to this authorization the Secretary of State has instructed the Chairman of our delegation in London to inform the Sub-Committee today that we will be willing as part of our proposal for a first-step disarmament agreement to include a suspension of testing of nuclear weapons for a period up to two years under certain conditions and safeguards. These include Soviet acceptance of the United States position that, within that period, there will be initiated a permanent cessation of production of fissionable materials for weapons purposes and installation of inspection systems to insure performance.

The delegations of Canada, France and the United Kingdom join us in presenting this proposal which should be a major step toward reaching a sound and safeguarded first-step arms control agreement.

I sincerely hope that the Soviet Union will now join us and our Western colleagues in agreeing to our disarmament proposals, including the cessation of production of fissionable materials for weapons purposes.

Until such a first-step arms control agreement comes into force, the United States will, of course, conduct such nuclear testing as our security requires.

DWIGHT D. EISENHOWER: REPLY TO SOVIET UNION'S
ATTACK ON THE DISARMAMENT PROPOSALS*

It is deeply disappointing to all true lovers of peace that the Soviet Union should have already attacked, with such scornful words, the proposals which Canada, France, the United Kingdom and the United States are putting forward at the United Nations Disarmament Subcommittee in London. It is noteworthy that this attack coincides with the boastful statement by the Soviet Union that they have made advances in the development of means for bringing mass destruction to any part of the world.

The Western Powers at London are completing their presentation of a rounded and interdependent first-stage proposal which, among other things, would, on a supervised and safeguarded basis,

(a) provide a measure of protection against massive attack;

(b) suspend for two years the further testing of nuclear weapons;

(c) seek that outer space shall be used only for peaceful, not military, purposes;

(d) provide a date after which no fissionable material will be produced for weapons purposes and existing nuclear weapons stockpiles will begin to be reduced by transfers for peaceful purposes;

(e) begin a reduction of armed forces and armaments.

It would be tragic if these important first-stage proposals, fraught with such significance for the peace of the world, were rejected by the Soviet Union even before they could have been seriously

* Reprinted from *Public Papers of the Presidents . . . : Dwight D. Eisenhower . . . 1957* (Washington, D.C.: Government Printing Office, 1958), p. 627.

* Reprinted from *Public Papers of the Presidents . . . : Dwight D. Eisenhower . . . 1957* (Washington, D.C.: Government Printing Office, 1958), pp. 635–36.

studied and before the Western presentation is complete. Such a Soviet attitude would condemn humanity to an indefinite future of immeasurable danger.

So far as the United States is concerned, we shall never renounce our efforts to find ways and means to save mankind from that danger and to establish a just and lasting peace.

While the United States in good faith abstained from nuclear testing and preparations for tests (which would take months), negotiations with the Soviet Union went on endlessly and fruitlessly. Suddenly in September, 1961, Khrushchev announced that Russia was undertaking a series of tests of unprecedented scale. President John F. Kennedy called upon him to agree to an immediate test ban. When Khrushchev refused, Kennedy ordered resumption of underground tests and in March, 1962, announced his reluctant decision to resume tests in the atmosphere.

JOHN F. KENNEDY: "THE UNITED STATES MUST MAINTAIN . . . EFFECTIVE . . . NUCLEAR WEAPONS"*

Seventeen years ago, man unleashed the power of the atom. He thereby took into his mortal hands the power of self-extinction. Throughout the years that have followed, under three successive Presidents, the United States has sought to banish this weapon from the arsenals of individual nations. . . .

But until mankind has banished both war and its instruments of destruction, the United States must maintain an effective quantity and quality of nuclear weapons, so deployed and protected as to be capable of surviving any surprise attack and devastating the attacker. Only through such strength can we be certain of deterring a nuclear strike, or an overwhelming ground attack, upon our forces and allies.

Only through such strength can we in the free world—should that deterrent fail—face the tragedy of another war with any hope of survival. And that deterrent strength, if it is to be effective and credible when compared with that of any other nation, must embody the most modern, the most reliable and the most versatile nuclear weapons our research and development can produce.

The testing of new weapons and the effects is necessarily a part of that research and development process. Without tests—to experiment and verify—progress is limited. A nation which is refraining from tests obviously cannot match the gains of a nation conducting tests. And when all nuclear powers refrain from testing, the nuclear arms race is held in check.

But on Sept. 1 of last year, while the United States and the United Kingdom were negotiating

in good faith at Geneva, the Soviet Union callously broke its moratorium with a two-month series of more than forty nuclear tests.

Preparations for these tests had been secretly under way for many months. Accompanied by new threats and new tactics of terror, these tests—conducted mostly in the atmosphere—represented a major Soviet effort to put nuclear weapons back into the arms race.

Once it was apparent that new appeals and proposals were to no avail, I authorized on Sept. 5 a resumption of United States nuclear tests underground, and I announced on Nov. 2—before the close of the Soviet series—that preparations were being ordered for a resumption of atmospheric tests, and that we would make whatever tests our security required in the light of Soviet gains.

This week, the National Security Council has completed its review of this subject. The scope of the Soviet tests has been carefully reviewed by the most competent scientists in the country. The scope and justification of proposed American tests have been carefully reviewed, determining which experiments can be safely deferred, which can be deleted, which can be combined or conducted underground, and which are essential to our military and scientific progress.

Careful attention has been given to the limiting of radioactive fall-out, to the future course of arms control diplomacy, and to our obligations to other nations.

Every alternative was examined. Every avenue of obtaining Soviet agreement was explored. We were determined not to rush into imitating their tests. And we were equally determined to do only what our own security required us to do. Although the complex preparations have continued at full speed while these facts were being

* Reprinted from *New York Times,* March 3, 1962.

uncovered, no single decision of this Administration has been more thoroughly or more thoughtfully weighed.

Having carefully considered these findings—having received the unanimous recommendations of the pertinent department and agency heads—and having observed the Soviet Union's refusal to accept any agreement which would inhibit its freedom to test extensively after preparing secretly—I have today authorized the Atomic Energy Commission and the Department of Defense to conduct a series of nuclear tests—beginning when our preparations are completed, in the latter part of April and to be concluded as quickly as possible (within two or three months) —such series, involving only those tests which cannot be held underground, to take place in the atmosphere over the Pacific Ocean.

The tests are to be conducted under conditions which restrict the radioactive fall-out to an absolute minimum, far less than the contamination created by last fall's Soviet series. . . .

Nevertheless, I find it deeply regrettable that any radioactive material must be added to the atmosphere—that even one additional individual's health may be risked in the foreseeable future. And however remote and infinitesimal those hazards are judged to be, I still exceedingly regret the necessity of balancing these hazards against the hazards to hundreds of millions of lives which would be created by any relative decline in our nuclear strength.

In the absence of a major shift in Soviet policies, no American President—responsible for the freedom and safety of so many people—could in good faith make any other decision. . . .

Had the Soviet tests of last fall reflected merely a new effort in intimidation and bluff, our security would not have been affected. But in fact they also reflected a highly sophisticated technology, the trial of novel designs and techniques, and some substantial gains in weaponry. . . .

In short, last fall's tests, in and by themselves, did not give the Soviet Union superiority in nuclear power. They did, however, provide the Soviet laboratories with a mass of data and experience on which, over the next two or three years, they can base significant analyses, experiments and extrapolations, preparing for the next test series, which would confirm and advance their findings.

And I must report to you in all candor that further Soviet series, in the absence of further Western progress, could well provide the Soviet Union with a nuclear attack and defense capability so powerful as to encourage aggressive designs. Were we to stand still while the Soviets surpassed us—or even appeared to surpass us—the free world's ability to deter, to survive and to respond to an all-out attack would be seriously weakened.

The fact of the matter is that we cannot make similar strides without testing in the atmosphere as well as underground. For, in many areas of nuclear weapons research, we have reached the point where our progress is stifled without experiments in every environment.

While we will be conducting far fewer tests than the Soviets, with far less fall-out, there will still be those in other countries who will urge us to refrain from testing at all.

Perhaps they forget that this country long refrained from testing, and sought to ban all tests, while the Soviets were secretly preparing new explosions. Perhaps they forget the Soviet threats of last autumn and their arbitrary rejection of all appeals and proposals, from both the United States and the United Nations.

But those free people who value their freedom and their security, and look to our relative strength to shield them from danger—those who know of our good faith in seeking an end to testing and an end to the arms race—will, I am confident, want the United States to do whatever it must do to deter the threat of aggression.

If they felt we could be swayed by threats or intimidation—if they thought we could permit a repetition of last summer's deception—then surely they would lose faith in our will and wisdom as well as our weaponry.

I have no doubt that most of our friends around the world have shared my hope that we would never find it necessary to test again—and my own belief that, in the long run, the only real security in this age of nuclear peril rests not in armament but in disarmament.

But I am equally certain that they would insist on our testing once that is deemed necessary to protect free world security. They know we are not deciding to test for political or psychological reasons—and they also know that we cannot avoid testing for political or psychological reasons.

The leaders of the Soviet Union are also watching this decision. Should we fail to follow the dictates of our own security, they will chalk it up, not to good will, but to a failure of will—not to a confidence in Western superiority, but to our fear of world opinion, the very world opinion for which they showed such contempt.

They could well be encouraged by such signs of weakness to seek another period of no testing without controls—another opportunity for stifling our progress while secretly preparing, on the basis of last fall's experiments, for the new test series which might alter the balance of power.

With such a one-sided advantage, why would they change their strategy, or refrain from testing, merely because we refrained? Why would they want to halt their drive to surpass us in nuclear technology? And why would they ever consider accepting a true test ban or mutual disarmament?

Our reasons for testing and our peaceful intentions are clear—so clear that even the Soviets could not objectively regard our resumption of tests, following their own resumption of tests, as provocative or preparatory for war. On the contrary, it is my hope that the prospects for peace may actually be strengthened by this decision— once the Soviet leaders realize that the West will no longer stand still, negotiating in good faith, while they reject inspection and are free to prepare for further tests.

As new disarmament talks approach, the basic lesson of some three years and 353 negotiating sessions in Geneva is this—that the Soviets will not agree to an effective ban on nuclear tests as long as a new series of offers and prolonged negotiations, or a new uninspected moratorium, or a new agreement without controls, would enable them once again to prevent the West from testing while they prepare in secret.

But inasmuch as this choice is now no longer open to them, let us hope that they will take a different attitude on banning nuclear tests—that they will prefer to see the nuclear arms race checked instead of intensified, with all the dangers that that intensification brings: The spread of nuclear weapons to other nations; the constant increase in world tensions; the steady decrease in all prospects for disarmament; and, with it, a steady decrease in the security of us all.

If the Soviets should change their position, we will have an opportunity to learn it immediately. On the 14th of March, in Geneva, Switzerland, a new eighteen-power conference on disarmament will begin. A statement of agreed principles has been worked out with the Soviets and endorsed by the United Nations.

In the long run, it is the constructive possibilities of this conference—and not the testing of new destructive weapons—on which rest the hope of all mankind. However dim those hopes may sometimes seem, they can never be abandoned. And however far-off most steps toward disarmament appear, there are some that can be taken at once.

The United States will offer at the Geneva conference—not in the advance expectation they will be rejected, and not merely for purposes of propaganda—a series of concrete plans for a major "breakthrough to peace." We hope and believe that they will appeal to all nations opposed to war.

They will include specific proposals for fair and enforceable agreements: To halt the production of fissionable materials and nuclear weapons and their transfer to other nations, to convert them from weapon stockpiles to peaceable use, to destroy the warheads and the delivery systems that threaten man's existence, to check the danger of surprise and accidental attack, to reserve outer space for peaceful use, and progressively to reduce all armed forces in such a way as ultimately to remove forever all threats and thoughts of war.

And of greatest importance to our discussion tonight, we shall, in association with the United Kingdom, present once again our proposals for a separate comprehensive treaty—with appropriate arrangements for detection and verification—to halt permanently the testing of all nuclear weapons, in every environment: in the air, in outer space, underground and underwater. New modifications will also be offered in the light of new experience.

The essential arguments and facts relating to such a treaty are well known to the Soviet Union. There is no need for further repetition, propaganda or delay. The fact that both sides have decided to resume testing only emphasizes the need for new agreement, not new arguments.

And before charging that this decision shatters all hope for agreement, the Soviets should recall that we were willing to work out with them, for joint submission to the U. N., an agreed statement of disarmament principles at the very time their autumn tests were being conducted. And Mr. Khrushchev knows, as he said in 1960, that any nation which broke the moratorium could expect other nations to be forced, and I quote, "to take the same road."

Our negotiators will be ready to talk about this treaty even before the conference on March 14th—and they will be ready to sign well before the date on which our tests are ready to begin. That date is still nearly two months away.

If the Soviet Union should now be willing to accept such a treaty, sign it before the latter part of April, and apply it immediately—if all testing can thus be actually halted—then the nuclear arms race would be slowed down at last, the security of the United States and its ability to meet its commitments would be safeguarded and there would be no need for our tests to begin.

But this must be a fully effective treaty. We know now enough about broken negotiations, secret preparations and the advantage gained from a long test series never to offer again an uninspected moratorium. . . .

. . . our ultimate objective is not to test for the sake of testing. Our real objective is to make our own tests unnecessary, to prevent others from testing, to prevent the nuclear arms race from mushrooming out of control, to take the first steps toward general and complete disarmament.

And that is why, in the last analysis, it is the leaders of the Soviet Union who must bear the heavy responsibility of choosing, in the weeks that lie ahead, whether we proceed with these new steps—or proceed with new tests. . . .

It is our hope and prayer that these grim, unwelcome tests will never have to be made— that these deadly weapons will never have to be fired—and that our preparations for war will bring about the preservation of peace.

Our foremost aim is the control of force, not the pursuit of force, in a world made safe for mankind. But whatever the future brings, I am sworn to uphold and defend the freedom of the American people—and I intend to do whatever must be done to fulfill that solemn obligation.

Even after Russia had resumed nuclear tests, she continued to discuss the limitation of armaments with the United States. Month after month, these negotiations produced nothing but discouraging news. Nevertheless, John J. McCloy, who had been the President's Advisor on Disarmament among numerous other high offices he had held, could also see some significant fields of mutual interest between the United States and Russia.

JOHN J. McCLOY: BALANCE SHEET ON DISARMAMENT*

I have discussed some discouraging prospects for disarmament. . . . But we should not dwell exclusively on the discouraging factors; there are basic fields of mutual interest which must also be examined and appraised. One can reasonably assume that both the leaders and the peoples of the Soviet Union and the United States are convinced of the necessity of avoiding a nuclear war. Despite loose statements and conjectures on both sides, the leaders of each country have facts available to them which bear conclusive evidence that "victory" in a serious thermonuclear exchange is a highly questionable concept.

Thus the fundamental common interest is the elimination of this threat of destruction. Some Soviet leaders continue to contend that if an all-out nuclear war should occur, capitalism would be destroyed while the Soviet Union would merely be damaged. Apart from purely ideological reasoning, they have made some attempt to base this conclusion on concrete military grounds, placing emphasis on such factors as the distribution of population in the Soviet Union, its lesser reliance on communications, and similar matters. Others in the Soviet Union have been more realistic in assessing the possibility of mutual destruction. If the responsible Soviet leadership were frank with itself and the Russian people, it would acknowledge destruction on an unacceptable scale as a certainty rather than a possibility.

It may be argued that the tone of some Soviet predictions about the outcome of an all-out nuclear war might mean that the Soviet Union has not abandoned the possibility of embarking on such a war as an instrument of policy, feeling that perhaps out of the ashes it might construct a Communist world. Though my belief in the sincere desire of the Soviet leaders for disarmament was shaken by the manner in which the Soviet Union conducted the test-ban negotiations, and by its resumption of tests, I do not share that view. I believe the Soviet leaders who hold the chief positions of responsibility recognize the true facts. A thermonuclear exchange would involve complete destruction of the Soviet standard of living, built up so painfully since 1917. If the leaders are well informed, and I believe they are, they know that conjecture as to which would survive better, capitalism or Communism, is simply silly. What would be left after such a war would not be recognizable either as Communism or capitalism. Such survivors as there were would have to find a new name for the primitive system by which they would conduct their struggle to recover. Another consideration which must be in the minds of the Soviet leaders is the horrifying thought of a Soviet Union, terribly crippled, living next to a relatively undamaged China with a population of about 700,000,000.

Granted that the Soviet Union may be willing to accept a higher level of risk of war than is the United States, nevertheless, in my judgment, the facts greatly favor the view that, in so far as they understand the risks in any particular step they may be contemplating, and in so far as they can control the situation, the Soviet leaders wish to avoid general nuclear war, if only for selfish reasons.

A second area of mutual interest which arises from the common desire to avoid a nuclear war must be the prevention of any such war by accident, miscalculation or failure of communication. Soviet discussions of this problem have at times tended to be heavily tinged with propaganda aimed at the West's defense arrangements; thus they have often discussed the problems solely in terms of a possible Western mistake or accident. Moreover, the conceptual approach to this problem which they adopt publicly—namely, that measures short of radical or complete disarmament are of marginal or temporary value in meeting the dangers confronting mankind—has been pushed to the extreme. It has appeared to inhibit their discussion of the more immediate measures aimed at reducing these dangers. Finally, they are most sensitive about the possibilities— as they see them—that measures to reduce the chances of war by accident or miscalculation might seriously infringe upon the secrecy surrounding their military establishment, which they cling to as an alleged strategic asset.

Nevertheless, there does seem to be an increasing recognition on their part, as there has been on the part of the United States, of the increased danger involved in the growth of nuclear

* Reprinted from John J. McCloy, "Balance Sheet on Disarmament," *Foreign Affairs*, XL (April, 1962), 347–58 by permission.

549

stockpiles and more particularly in the growth of complex and extensive systems for the delivery of nuclear weapons. They seem aware, too, of the resulting heavier responsibility imposed upon the principal nuclear powers, pending the adoption of a disarmament agreement, to minimize the dangers either by unilateral action or by multilateral agreement.

The revolution in weapons development has resulted in the creation of delivery systems with fantastic rates of speed. Certain missiles that might be used in case of war have a speed of around 16,000 miles per hour, which would mean a delivery time of only about one-half hour between the Soviet Union and the United States; and missile-launching submarines will provide almost no warning time at all. As a counter, defensive systems are being developed with such quick reaction times as to give real meaning to the term "war by accident, miscalculation or failure of communication." Indeed, it is questionable whether the human mind can encompass all the problems involved in controlling these devices even without a war. It is not inconceivable that we could blow ourselves up without help from the Russians; and vice versa. Thus, the arms race has an impressive way of building its own tensions. The Government of the United States is aware of these dangers and is spending a very great amount of time, effort and money in attempting to devise ways to reduce them. It is to be hoped devoutly that there is a similar effort in the U.S.S.R.

Another common desire is to prevent any third country from provoking a nuclear war. In concrete terms, this expresses itself principally in the Soviet Union's concern about the acquisition of an independent nuclear capability by Germany and (judging the situation objectively) by Communist China. For then both these powers would have the ability to involve the United States and the Soviet Union—Germany through its alliance with the United States, Red China through an attack upon some vital American interest which would call forth an American reaction, which, in turn, would require Soviet assistance to Communist China (at least in the present state of the alliance). The Soviets could reasonably conclude that the acquisition of nuclear weapons by West Germany and by Communist China, or indeed by anyone else, would substantially take out of their control the decision of whether or not to go to war. In somewhat different degree, the same danger exists for us.

From such information as we possess, Communist China intends to become a nuclear power and there are strong indications that its leaders will not be bound by any commitments the Soviet Union may make to others in regard to disarmament. The true attitude of Communist China may be "a mystery wrapped in an enigma," but the auguries for its good will in international affairs at the moment hardly seem propitious. For one thing, the Red Chinese leaders may not share the same sober feelings that many of the Soviet leaders have about the effects of a nuclear war. Certainly no far-reaching agreements on disarmament can be undertaken without having in mind the position of Red China. If we question the willingness of the Soviet Union to submit disputes in which it has an interest to determination by an international institution, our reservations must be even greater about Red China's willingness to do so in similar situations.

Whenever Red China was brought up in the course of our discussions on the test ban, the usual Soviet retort was, "What about France?" That France is presumably a long way from an ability to make and deliver a significant number of bombs did not deflect the question. The fact remains, however, that although France's desire to become a nuclear power has quite different implications than does Red China's, the French position has not been helpful to the general cause of disarmament. It has contributed to a plurality of nuclear power which involves the danger that the employment of nuclear weapons may be irresponsible. But Red China's possession of the bomb is clearly a greater threat—a view with which, I have the impression, Moscow would agree.

The Soviet interest in avoiding an extension of nuclear weapons to additional countries coincides to a substantial degree with our own. The United States policy, as expressed in our national legislation, is directed against a proliferation of nuclear weapons. The United States Program of September 25, 1961, includes as one of its important measures a provision that states owning nuclear weapons would not relinquish control of them to any nation not already owning them nor transmit to any such nation information or material necessary for their manufacture.

The similarity of American and Soviet interests in this regard should not be overestimated. The geographic and political relationship between the United States and the other members of NATO is quite different from the geographic relationship between the U.S.S.R. and the other Warsaw Pact nations. The President of the United States indicated in Ottawa that our relationship with our Allies would have to be taken into account in determining the physical disposition and political control of nuclear weapons that are available for the area covered by the NATO treaty. In this connection, there is substantially more security to be derived from having nuclear weapons under the control of NATO than independent of its control. If the U.S.S.R. is seriously concerned to see that these weapons are disposed and controlled so as to eliminate the danger that any nation at present without them could one day start a war which would engulf the world, then a real mutuality of interest exists.

The fourth area of mutual interest is economic. It would be advantageous to the Soviet Union, one would think, to be free of the economic burden of the arms race and thus be able to devote all its economic resources to fulfilling its long-range plans for internal improvement. According to the best estimates, it is at present spending considerably more than 10 percent of its gross national product for defense purposes.

In the United States we devote just under 10 percent of our gross national product (which is about twice as large as the Soviet G.N.P.) to defense. Furthermore, in the United States a smaller proportion of the working population is dependent upon defense for employment than is the case in the Soviet Union. However, statistics do not fully reflect the great concentration of capital, energy, thought and skills which are devoted directly or indirectly to armaments in the United States. Admittedly, this concentration has a deep impact on our economy and it is not going to be a simple matter to switch the human and physical resources involved to purely peacetime pursuits. Advance planning will be required at all levels of government and on the part of business and labor if we are to make appropriate provision for the maintenance and growth of aggregate demand and if we are to master the structural problems which would be involved in the process of conversion.

In the United States serious studies have already been instituted in this field. Like other nations, we have many unmet needs, public and private, and with imagination and determination they can be translated into economic demand once we are free to turn our backs on the production of weapons of destruction. It is enough to think simply of the unsatisfied needs in the fields of education, natural resources, urban renewal, transportation and social welfare to realize what a vast economic interest we really have in disarmament. And beyond these domestic needs are the almost inexhaustible requirements of the underdeveloped countries of the world.

In the past, moreover, this country has moved successfully from mobilization to demobilization more rapidly and completely than any other country of comparable size. Going back to the time of the Rush-Bagehot Agreements, which initiated the demilitarization of the Canadian-United States border, down to the demobilization and disarmament after both World Wars, the record of the United States in actually carrying out disarmament compares most favorably with that of any other country. Under present circumstances the problems may be more complicated, but there is no basis for Soviet contentions that the United States does not genuinely seek disarmament because of its concern for economic consequences. If anti-capitalistic propaganda is not swallowed in this respect, the over-all economic benefits of disarmament are seen as a definite field of common interest between ourselves and the Soviet Union. Indeed, it is to be hoped that the Soviet leaders are as clear on this point as our own leaders are.

Just as there are underlying points of mutual interest, so there are underlying points of divergence, and if we are to be realistic some of these must be identified here, even though most of them are only too well known.

For some years the stated policy of the United States has been to maintain a decisive military superiority over the U.S.S.R. and our responsible government officials have made it quite clear that we do have a substantial superiority in nuclear weapons and the means of delivering them. In the last few years the Soviet Union has taken the position that it possesses a military superiority. It has based this contention mainly upon its superiority in propulsion, as evidenced by its larger satellites, though other items have also been stressed. Clearly, a situation in which each of the two most powerful nations in the world is committed to the proposition that it must retain a decisive military superiority over the other does not create a climate conducive to the negotiation of a far-reaching disarmament agreement.

A second underlying obstacle, already mentioned, is created by the Soviet attitude toward inspection and controls. The Joint Statement of Agreed Principles included an agreement upon the need for a control system capable of assuring all parties that obligations undertaken as part of a disarmament agreement are being faithfully fulfilled. The Soviet Union, however, refused to accept what the United States believes to be an inherent and essential element in this concept, namely, that whenever an agreement stipulates that only certain levels of forces and armaments are to be retained, the control organization shall have the authority to verify that these levels are not exceeded. That is, verification of compliance must consist not only in assurance that specified units have been demobilized and specified weapons destroyed, but also that what remains is not in excess of agreed limits. Therefore, the control organization must have the right of free access to search for clandestine facilities.

In the discussions on this point, the Soviet representatives usually stated the Soviet position in purely semantic terms. They insisted that the Soviet Union could agree only to inspection and control over disarmament, not control over armament; therefore, they said, the inspector could verify only the dismantling of arms. The difference, of course, goes much deeper than semantics, indicating a fundamental difference in attitude. This was sharply brought out in the letters exchanged between Mr. Zorin and myself on September 20 and 21, 1961.

The United States is a free society, and within certain well-defined limits it has very little to hide from an international inspector. This is not to say that it does not have important installations and devices to guard, or that it would enjoy having a burdensome system of inspections imposed upon it. The fact remains that an effective inspectorate would be tolerable and would be accepted provided there was a reciprocal means of determining what was going on in the Soviet Union.

The Soviet Union, on the other hand, is a closed

society. Its claim that the American insistence on inspection and control is designed merely to create a cover for espionage is nonsense. It is a fact, however, that an international inspectorate, operating freely within the Soviet territory, would run counter to the concept of Soviet secrecy as a military and political asset. It must be ascertained to what degree the Soviet leadership can be persuaded that secrecy, far from being a military asset, can constitute a real military danger. Secrecy breeds suspicion and distrust. Since we do not know the facts and since we receive repeated intimations of fantastic new Soviet weapons we naturally seek to arm more intensively than ever, perhaps even to a degree which is unnecessary. The disposition is to credit fearsome rumors and to redouble our own efforts to improve our weapons.[4] It would be immeasurably healthier for both of us if this secrecy were to be diluted.

In the view of the Soviet leaders, an international inspector may also represent a threat to the insularity and secrecy which form part of the Soviet and Russian way of life. The Russian aversion to foreign intrusion is traditional, at least in certain parts of the country and in certain strata of society; it far antedates 1917. It has been diminished somewhat in the past few years, but it still plays a role as part of the control which the Party exercises over the people. Vast areas of government operations are simply not known to the masses of the Soviet people or to the peoples of the world. Any external inspection might be considered as endangering the government's control.

The American and Soviet approaches diverge again in the attitude of the U.S.S.R. and other Communist countries toward the use of threats of force, indirect aggression and subversion as means of overthrowing free societies. We have felt bound to set up counter forces to meet this form of aggression, but we would be quick to abandon them if the threat were removed. If significant progress is to be made toward disarmament, the dangerous distinction between just and unjust wars must certainly be abandoned. We cannot be asked to disband the means of self-defense, while the Communists seek to exempt certain kinds of conflict from the process of international settlement. The same is true of attempts from abroad to bring about changes within a free country by force of arms. It is hard to see how we can reach the goal of a secure world in which there no longer is need for national armed forces and armaments so long as the Communist leadership sets the destruction of free governments as a basic aim, in achieving which it feels justified in using any method, including force.

Nor is it easy to be trustful of a nation whose leaders insist that our American society is about to crumble away and who say openly that they will do all in their power to accelerate the process. This is not our concept of peaceful coexistence. For example, Mr. Khrushchev's speech of January 6, 1961, to the Communist leaders assembled in Moscow, does not create confidence among those societies whose collapse he declared to be the chief objective of Soviet policy, and who are called upon, at the same time, to agree to wide areas of disarmament.

There is, finally, another respect in which the attitude of the U.S.S.R., and to some degree of the United States as well, must undergo a change if disarmament negotiations in Geneva or elsewhere are to succeed. The Joint Statement of September 20, 1961, is quite clear that progress toward general and complete disarmament is closely linked with improvement in the international machinery for peaceful settlement of disputes. One side of the coin cannot be dealt with successfully without the other.

In recent years many disarmament negotiations have proceeded on the assumption that a system of inspection which gave promise of detecting violations would be sufficient by itself to assure compliance with whatever agreement might be reached. On this assumption, the only penalty for violating a disarmament agreement would be the cancellation of the agreement, with the consequent threat of the resumption of the arms race and perhaps the condemnation of public opinion throughout the world.

This assumption may be valid for some first steps in the disarmament process, particularly if, as proposed in the Statement of Principles, disarmament proceeds through stages subject to balanced, phased and safeguarded measures. There will come a point, however, where a control system which merely reports a violation is not adequate. Precisely when this point will be reached cannot be stated with certainty in the absence of actual experience with institutions for control; but clearly it will not be long deferred. Indeed, the greater the degree of disarmament achieved, the greater might be the temptations for a potential violator to transgress the agreement and the greater the risks presented to all those who were complying with it in good faith. It would not, for example, take many hidden megaton bombs to constitute a most formidable threat against any nation or group of nations which had already disposed of its own weapons. In the kingdom of the blind, the one-eyed man is king. Nations cannot be expected to pass this point in disarming, to give up the means of defending themselves against aggression, unless they can be assured that there exists the machinery to guard against illegal accumulations of arms.

---

[4] An example of this was the increased effort to produce I.C.B.M.'s in the United States as the result of what now seems to have been an exaggerated estimate in 1959 of the number of such operational missiles which the Soviets would shortly possess.

But, as indicated earlier, the necessity for effective control machinery is only one reason why international institutions must be strengthened as steps are taken toward total and universal disarmament. They must not merely be able to enforce disarmament agreements; they must be strengthened to the point where they are capable of bringing about just settlements of international disputes, including adjustments which are necessary and appropriate in a changing world. This poses fundamental questions for both the Soviet Union and the United States, indeed for all countries, Communist and non-Communist alike; and they must be faced and dealt with if we are to advance far on the disarmament road.

It was not intended by the Joint Statement of Agreed Principles merely to introduce meaningless words and generalities into the future disarmament discussions in referring to the need of improved machinery for the adjudication of international disputes and the maintenance of peace. In due course, specific proposals implementing these principles will have to be made. This will require the application of the best minds and statesmanship. It will demand common effort and thought on the part of all the nations, for the interests of all are involved. The hope of reaching the objective of general and complete disarmament is dependent upon having specific plans for improved methods of keeping the peace which will keep pace with specific plans for general disarmament.

All this having been said, however, the exigency of the situation in which the world finds itself is such, the danger of nuclear war by miscalculation, accident or design is so great, that we cannot wait until all obstacles have been eliminated before taking steps to reduce tensions and control the armaments which in themselves generate tensions. These steps must be taken whether they be classed as disarmament measures, test bans, arms control, arms limitation or the improvement of means for settling international disputes. The immediate need is to deflect downward the intensity of the present arms race. Each step that increases confidence will not only permit us to edge out from under the danger now hanging over us but to move toward a condition of mutual trust on which far broader measures may be based.

And now what is the over-all balance between these positive and negative factors? President Kennedy said in his address to Congress on January 11 [, 1962]: "World order will be secured only when the whole world has laid down these weapons which seem to offer present security but threaten our future survival. That Armistice Day seems very far away." However, he also went on to say: "But the world was not meant to be a prison in which man awaits his execution. Nor has mankind survived the tests and trials of thousands of years to surrender everything—including his existence."

It does indeed seem true that before the world lays down its arms in reliance on a secure international order many years may have passed. Nevertheless, the positive elements in the present world situation which have been pointed out here do give hope that progress can be made toward the goal. Statesmen should not find the obstacles in the way insuperable. To say this does not imply that threats of inevitable destruction will stampede either side into taking reckless risks with disarmament. Yet the very obstacles—the tensions, the diverse ideologies, the fears, the suspicions—act as a stimulant to action. Were not the dangers so real and the obstacles to their removal so great we would not be concentrating so much attention on disarmament.

Even the resumption of large-scale testing of which the Soviet Union was guilty, like the actual or threatened resumption of large-scale testing by others in retaliation, may finally impel both sides, at long last, to agree on an effective test ban. In the same way, the heavy tensions of the Berlin crisis, induced on the one hand by the Soviet Union's threat of unilateral action and on the other by the realization that the West will certainly resist by force the impairment of its rights in Berlin, produce a powerful urge to action.

The United States now has a plan for the achievement of general and complete disarmament which is realistic and balanced. The Joint Statement of Agreed Principles, to which the Soviet Union subscribed, envisages the intermediate measures to be implemented on the way to the ultimate goal. It commits both countries to continue their efforts until the total program has been achieved. The Soviet Union is committed, to the same degree as is the United States, to a program by which war shall no longer be an instrument for settling international problems and in which the twin requisites—reliable procedures for the peaceful settlement of disputes and effective measures for maintaining peace—go hand in hand with disarmament. . . .

CHAPTER TWENTY-FOUR

THE SIXTIES:
NEW FRONTIER

As the United States entered the 1960's, new domestic issues came to the forefront, and the burden of trying to solve them fell upon a new generation. In the campaign of 1960, two candidates for president, John F. Kennedy and Richard M. Nixon, both in their forties and both of whom had been in college during the New Deal, debated these issues. There were the familiar problems of combatting inflation and balancing (or not balancing) the budget, but commingled with them was intense discussion of the need for greater national growth. A more rapid rate of growth, it was argued, was imperative if the nation were to continue to compete successfully with the Soviet Union. At home, more rapid growth could provide the additional income to finance urban renewal, better schools, better transportation systems, better social security programs, and better conservation and development of national resources. Neither Kennedy nor Nixon questioned the need for more rapid economic growth, but in the debates Kennedy seemed readier to undertake drastic steps to obtain it; Nixon seemed more concerned with preventing inflation and balancing the federal budget.

After his inauguration, President Kennedy proceeded cautiously toward his avowed goals—his New Frontier program—in a fashion calculated not to alienate businessmen. Most businessmen were unwilling to accept the new economic ideas that lay behind talk of national growth, and many of them were deeply suspicious of any Democratic president. Kennedy as a young Congressman had worked vigorously on behalf of the social and economic welfare of his constituents, most of whom were Boston laboring people; but also as Senator from Massachusetts, he had obtained a lengthy and impressive array of legislation of benefit to the businessmen of his state and all of New England. As President, he was equally ready to work on behalf of both the underprivileged and the businessmen. Yet in the second year of his administration, he had a dramatic clash with business in trying to prevent further inflation.

In 1962, a Professor of Industrial Management and Economics at Massachusetts Institute of Technology, Edwin Kuh, analyzed for British readers the economic course of the Kennedy administration down to that time.

EDWIN KUH: ECONOMIC PROBLEMS
OF THE KENNEDY ADMINISTRATION*

The Economic Fates have been kind to President Kennedy so that looking backward over the first year in office provides grounds for genuine satisfaction. The toughest problems lie ahead, with no strong reason to expect the quick success that has come Kennedy's way until now. At the moment Kennedy took office the recession which so much aided his election in 1960 obligingly came to an end. While Kennedy cannot take credit for the brevity of the downturn, since most of the policy actions taken had their effect much later, he did take energetic fiscal policy steps to promote a rapid recovery. Indeed, a rate of growth in Gross National Product of 11 per cent. occurred during his first year of office and a realistic 8 per cent. estimate has been forecast for 1962 by his Council of Economic Advisers.

The really tough problems, ones painfully familiar to the British by name at least, concern the development of policies to cope with economic growth, full employment, inflation, and the balance of payments. Although the names are familiar in Britain, the solutions and political environment are less so. The major obstacles to success are political, since the fundamental economic potential of the United States is extremely high. Onerous political constraints consist of the inheritance of a basic political conservatism and a widely held set of beliefs about the role of Government, the Federal Budget, and inflation.

THE POLITICAL NEED FOR ECONOMIC GROWTH

Accelerated long-term economic growth is a central concern of the Kennedy Administration, yet no dramatic actions are contemplated. Why economic growth is thought to be important can be readily stated, and the desire for more growth does not just depend upon a juvenile desire to match mere percentages generated by the Soviet *bloc*. Rather, it depends upon the political difficulties of redistributing income between the public and private sectors. To put the matter most simply, if the United States grows at an average of 2 per cent. a year about $10 billion of additional resources become available per year and when it grows 4 per cent. a year $20 billion of additional resources become available. It is politically more feasible to acquire a given fraction of additional resources from the increment to output than it is to shift resources to the Government by increasing taxes or reducing certain subsidies out of a constant or slowly rising level of income. Indeed, what are considered vital

national concerns of United States policy, particularly Foreign Aid, are especially affected by actually attained rates of growth. When tax yields increase rapidly, more funds will be made available for these activities. Foreign Aid is considered more important by the White House than by Congress so that when tax yields out of a given tax structure are low because income is low, there is an inclination for Congress to cut back especially heavily on Foreign Aid as well as domestic welfare expenditures. Hence, financing two of the Administration's important programmes depends critically upon a rapid rate of growth.

It is a fallacy of Kenneth Galbraith's *The Affluent Society* that economic growth is incidental since what really should be done is to put resources into the under-financed sector of the economy, Government. But redistribution is extraordinarily difficult so that the thesis propounded by Galbraith on growth is inconsistent, a matter on which Ambassador Galbraith can ruminate in India. Furthermore, and this should not cause surprise, not everybody drives Cadillacs in the United States. Today about 30 per cent. of families have an income of $1,000 or less per person. While the welfare implications are altogether different for this group than for the most poverty-stricken parts of the globe, it is really stretching things to consider these people as full participants in the affluence of the United States economy.

Before describing policy measures designed to speed the growth process, it is important to distinguish two aspects of economic growth. The first aspect concerns the full utilisation of existing resources and will be more fully discussed when we turn to the employment problem. The second aspect is the most fundamental and least understood—the rate of increase of output when labour and/or capital are both fully employed. Both aspects interact, since a high level of unemployment and output well below its potential level cause low levels of investment and thus inhibit the long-run full employment rate of growth. Furthermore, unless there is full employment, strong pressure is generated for work-spreading and restrictive labour practices. When unemployment is pervasive trade union leaders press for a much shorter work week than they would press for under conditions of full employment. Emphasis in recent labour negotiations has switched to restrictive job security protection rather than wage increases, a development that could seriously impede other efforts to accelerate growth. Exhortation will not be enough—unless we have a high employment economy, potential output gains from productivity increases will be lost through the reduction in hours worked.

The first and foremost area in which long-term growth can be speeded is in the accumula-

* Reprinted from Edwin Kuh, "Economic Problems of the Kennedy Administration," *The Political Quarterly*, XXXIII (April–June, 1962), 183–95 by permission.

tion of fixed assets. Last year the Kennedy Administration proposed investment incentives that would particularly benefit industrial firms purchasing fixed assets in amounts exceeding their depreciation allowances. The original proposal met so much opposition from Congress that since then it has been considerably diluted for presentation to this year's session. The proposal now before Congress provides tax rebates of 8 per cent. of gross investment outlays, a much less potent incentive than the earlier proposals. It is unlikely that major new efforts will be made to increase the proportion of plant and equipment investment to G.N.P., which is now well below the post-Second World War high of about 12 per cent. If the Government succeeds in consistently maintaining a high level of aggregate demand, the desire of business to expand capacity might increase the potential rate of growth substantially above the present 3½ per cent. per year long-term average.

Other measures to increase the long-term rate of growth include assistance to education. Last year Congress was requested to appropriate Federal funds to help primary and elementary schools but failed to take action because the tradition of almost complete state independence in this area would be threatened and because of the parochial school issue, one of the most divisive quarrels on the American political scene. A high rate of growth is needed to generate the additional funds that Congress will be willing to devote to these efforts because of current budgetary procedures and beliefs. Even should the funds become available, political barriers surely will restrict the amount of additional funds that could be devoted to this form of growth and welfare outlay, although possibilities for Federal support to university education are much better.

It is important to realise that education and welfare are inextricably linked, especially that of minority groups, Negroes, and Puerto Ricans, who are among the most poorly educated groups in the United States. Lower income *per capita* in the Southern states compared to those in the North handicaps both races. The relation of education to technological advance and individual welfare has much broader implications. A steadily decreasing fraction of the work force, today less than half the total, is factory labour as clerical and technical skills become more important. The magnitude of the change becomes dramatically apparent when it is realised that United States manufacturing industry produced 43 per cent. more output in 1960 than in 1950, yet the number of production workers was about the same in both years, while non-production labour had increased by more than 50 per cent. Accelerated concern about education originates in part from the need for improved quality of training to keep pace with the growing requirements of modern technology. This means that (quite apart from discrimination) the typically more poorly educated

Negroes are only eligible for the lowest-paying jobs. Hence their long-term welfare depends crucially upon an improvement in education open to them.

THE OPPOSITION TO PLANNING

One ingredient of growth recently much discussed in the United Kingdom has been French-style planning of the past ten or fifteen years, that has met with so much apparent success. This is unlikely to take place in the United States. Indeed, the ideological objection to planning in the United States is intense, contrasting with the hard-headed insistence that countries receiving United States aid must do a great deal of planning. Most specific Government intervention in the private economy is *ad hoc,* dictated by political and economic emergencies of the past and cherished by various political forces in the present. Agricultural and shipping subsidies offer obvious examples. However, Congress is extremely jealous of its control over these activities so that systematic Government planning, primarily in the area of investment, is most improbable. This innovation would tend to upset "Government by Pressure Group," which is such an integral part of the American scene. Government by pressure group in practice means that various coalitions representing the basis of political power must be formed to obtain the passage of economic legislation. A major overhaul of the Government connections with specific economic activities would require a radical change in the present orientation of political power.

In substance then, the principal effort of the Kennedy Administration to increase growth is a mild shift in the distribution of income to capitalists as an inducement to expand capital formation. The Administration hopes that substantial investment will be forthcoming, which will provide increased income to offset the adverse effects of the changed income distribution. At the same time legislation to close tax "loopholes" especially favourable to upper income groups is part of the same tax programme. The relation between welfare and growth in the United States is stressed much more by the Democrats than income redistribution as an alternative route to assisting low income groups.

THE EISENHOWER LEGACY

One of the principal bequests to Kennedy from the Eisenhower Administration was a slack economy. Not only was the economy in recession when Kennedy came to office but—a fact which greatly perturbed many onlookers—the minimum level of unemployment reached in the early 1960 cyclical peak was alarmingly high. During the 1950s the minimum level of unemployment reached in each successive boom was higher than its predecessor. In 1952 minimum unemployment rates were 3 per cent., in 1956 a minimum figure of 4 per cent. was achieved, while Eisenhower's terminal boom year unemployment rate of 5 per cent. occurred early in 1960. A deduction of 1½ or 2½ per cent. is needed to adjust United States unemployment statistics to a comparable United Kingdom figure. In addition, most measures of aggregate capacity utilisation indicate that excessive spare plant and equipment existed even at the peak level of output during the 1959 boom. As a last fact in the catalogue of Eisenhower macroeconomics, each recovery was shorter than its predecessor, the 1958–60 recovery lasting only about twenty-six months. The rate of growth in output tapered off strongly in the last half of the Eisenhower Administration, a fact reflected in the increasingly under-utilised resources, equipment and plant on the one hand, and labour on the other. Unemployment exerts a strong influence on the welfare of minority groups. Negro unemployment rates are typically twice that of whites, not just because there is discrimination, although this is certainly a part of the explanation, but also because Negro employment is heavily concentrated in unskilled job categories which in the United States are subject to the greatest unemployment.

Another measure of employment presents a more sombre picture, that of part-time unemployment (*i.e.*, under-employment), calculated in terms of equivalent full-time unemployment, is also included in the unemployment statistics. This resulted in the total figure reaching 10 per cent. in the recent recession, and 12 per cent. in 1958.

Had the Eisenhower Administration been more willing to use stronger fiscal policy to combat unemployment, the Kennedy Administration would not be faced with its present severe problem. But Eisenhower was most strongly influenced by George Humphrey, his Treasury Secretary, and other fiscal arch-conservatives. In their eyes, a balanced budget is a good thing and an unbalanced budget a fearsome evil. Equally important, "Big Government" is the enemy, that is, government expenditure as such is to be feared. While he was President and even afterward, Eisenhower would repeatedly issue warnings about the burdens being created for our grandchildren whenever the national debt was increased, forgetting perhaps that the parents of these grandchildren might be out of a job because of this solicitude, largely unfounded, for the unborn generations. Despite the mythology of the balanced budget, in part based upon the analytically erroneous view that budget deficits by themselves cause inflation, Eisenhower acted much as his successor when faced with a recession. The 1957/58 recession was accompanied by the largest peace-time budget deficits on record, an occurrence which depended heavily upon the built-in stabilisers, *i.e.*, declines in tax receipts and increases in unemployment benefits when the level of income declines.

MILITARY AND SPACE-RESEARCH EXPENDITURES

The parallel between actions by Eisenhower and Kennedy is indeed remarkably close. When Sputnik was launched in 1957, coincidental with the start of the second Eisenhower recession, the Government stepped up expenditures designed to meet the Russian advance in part because it was realised that additional expenditures would hasten economic recovery. National Defence expenditures went up by 5 per cent. and outlays on space research and development also were rapidly expanded. Some economic commentators believe that the earlier cut-backs in these very expenditures intended to balance the budget, helped to trigger off the recession in 1957. We have just witnessed similar actions by Kennedy who, "aided" this time by the Berlin crisis, stepped up military outlays in the budget for the 1962 fiscal year by $7 billion. The two post-recession budgets are also destined to behave in much the same way. The Eisenhower budget went from a deficit of $12 billion in fiscal year 1958/59 to a surplus of $1 billion in the next year. Kennedy's budget is going from a milder deficit of $7 billion projected for the current fiscal year (1961/62) to a hoped-for small surplus, which more likely will be a small deficit, during the next fiscal year.

Recalling that the Eisenhower legacy of a soggy economy probably required larger fiscal deficits than would have been necessary had the economy been kept at a higher average level of activity, one might infer that Kennedy is a fiscal conservative although perhaps less doctrinaire and more flexible than his predecessor. Within the present Administration, the Secretary of the Treasury, Douglas Dillon, and William MacChesney Martin, who heads the Federal Reserve System, represent the spokesmen for a cautious course of action although neither one is a victim of the crude fiscal policy fallacies. As a result of a cautious outlook reinforced by a conservative Congress, as well as extreme, perhaps excessive, concern over the balance of payments problem, Kennedy has insisted on presenting a balanced budget for the fiscal year 1963. It seems that Kennedy is willing to take more energetic fiscal policy actions towards achieving full employment than Eisenhower, although it is highly significant that the balance of payments problem and preoccupation with price level stability still lead to a rather moderate policy. Recent requests to Congress for strictly limited discretionary Executive control over personal taxes and public works outlays in order to control cyclical fluctuations would mark a new departure in American fiscal policy, although it is doubtful that Congress will accept the proposed transfer of the power to tax. Even though the Economic Message indicates that unemployment should hit 4 per cent. by the middle of 1963, expert observers of the United States economic scene seriously doubt that unemployment will dip much below 5 per cent. If a dispassionate observer were obliged to distinguish between the two administrations in fiscal policy terms, he might perhaps say that Kennedy favours a provisional minimum 4 per cent. level of unemployment but seems willing to settle for 4½–5 per cent., whereas Eisenhower would be willing to run the country at a level ½–1 per cent. greater. There has been some change but no revolutionary transformation in outlook.

THE BUDGET

The Federal Budget reveals the aspirations of the Executive and the views of Congress. The dominant fact is the Cold War, which leaves little room for other outlays. Almost two-thirds of the United States budget is devoted to national defence, international affairs, and the space programme. Only 6 per cent. of the proposed budget is scheduled for health, education, and welfare, an amount equal to $5.1 billion. 16 per cent. is devoted to payments on the legacies from past wars, namely, interest on the Government debt, and the care of veterans. Social security and unemployment insurance outlays derived from self-contained funds, which do not appear in the regular Federal budget, amount to over $18 billion a year. This type of financing does not appear to be notably more regressive than social security benefits in Great Britain, which are heavily financed out of excise taxes. Far and away the biggest increases over the preceding fiscal year (July 1960–June 1961) came in the defence area.

Should peace break out, would changes in current heavy economic dependence on military outlays cause a disastrous slump? Almost certainly not, although tough problems of reallocating resources would accompany any abrupt major change in expenditure patterns. Massive, sudden reductions in military outlays under the most optimistic peacemongering assumptions appear most improbable. Slashes in military outlays of $6 or $7 billion per year ought to be readily absorbed, amounting to less than 1½ per cent. of current Gross National Product. Cuts of this magnitude accompanied by tax cuts of similar amount could be digested without severe consequences. Actual cuts of $2½ billion to $3½ billion for a period of, say, ten years seem much more likely. Furthermore, general disarmament would require elaborate, costly detection and inspection apparatus so that massive economic disruption can pretty well be discounted. This is not to deny, as ex-President Eisenhower solemnly warned in his farewell address, that strong vested interests in high military outlays pose a serious political problem.

Campaign oratory aside, the principal Federal Government function is defence, and welfare is secondary. Local governments, on the other hand, have had primary responsibility for welfare measures. This division of power creates a serious problem. Individual states have extremely unequal ability and willingness to levy taxes, the wealthier states having twice as much income *per capita* as the poorer ones. As a consequence the Federal Government has increasingly taken on the task of redistribution, through grants-in-aid and other means. The much-discussed underrepresentation of the urban areas existing at both federal and state levels of government reinforces difficulties of inter-state inequality of income.

Six to nine months from now the present Administration could face its first really tough economic decision. At that time, according to Administration estimates, it is predicted that the rate of increase in output will diminish, yet unemployment might remain well above the Administration target of 4 per cent. Will the Administration evade the issue in order to promote price stability, or will it be willing to run some political and economic risks to decrease unemployment? In the American context it seems that unemployment has not been a dominant political concern when it is stationary, even though at a relatively high level, while output is increasing and prosperity is widespread. Should this surmise about political attitudes prove correct, it may be much easier to keep unemployment 1 per cent. above what it ought to be according to professed Administration desires and thus diminish expected price level increases.

THE BALANCE OF PAYMENTS

The main Administration worry about price stability concerns the balance of payments, a problem that would have the highest priority in the British context, but in the American milieu it perhaps deserves to be, as it is in this paper, placed last on the list. In the last five years the United States stock of monetary gold has declined from about $22 billion to $17 billion, while at the same time short-term liabilities owed foreigners have also increased rapidly. The day when the almighty dollar was almighty has passed. In part because it had been an article of faith for so long that the dollar was supreme, worries over the new style dollar problem appear to be quite excessive. Some of these fears are similar to those about sterling in the United Kingdom—a dollar is a dollar and should its parity rate change, this action would be looked upon as a destructive blow to prestige. Substitute the word sterling for dollar and one finds similar widely held views expressed in Great Britain. Banter as one will about this belief, the fact remains that if the Kennedy Administration were to revalue the dollar downward relative to currencies like the German mark or the Swiss franc it would prove a major political liability, given the present temper of the country. Hence the cautious voice of Mr. Dillon, who stands as the guardian of the gold stock, is respectfully heeded in these matters.

Just what is the nature of the present "dollar problem"? To deal with this exceedingly complicated problem here will necessitate severe over-simplification because of the pressure of space. The United States position can most accurately be assessed in terms of the "basic deficit" which consists of receipts and payments on current account for goods and services, United States payments for foreign assistance and military expenditure, and long-term capital movements. In short, it is the balance of payments exclusive of highly volatile, short-term capital movements which recently have been so important. The deficit on the basic balance of payments accounts averaged $1.4 billion in 1951–55 and $2.2 billion in 1955–60. Currently, total payments are at a rate of $25 billion to $30 billion a year. This deficit has been a healthy development because such a disproportionate quantity of the world's gold resources flowed to the United States during the 1930s and 1940s. As the recovery problems of Europe diminished, the demand for dollars decreased so that the deficit, leading to a reallocation of reserves away from the United States can be viewed as not only natural but a desirable turn of events. However, when the dollar becomes a speculative currency, it must be a matter of concern for responsible officials. Thus the basic deficit has not been overwhelming, although its continuation at present rates would lead either to a devaluation or emergency measures to forestall a devaluation or general currency realignment within the next five years. What must be stressed, however, is that the basic balance of payments deficit is small enough compared to total payments of around $30 billion a year so that steps to rectify it need not be extreme. It is possible that the mild measures so far proposed by the Kennedy Administration, including tied foreign aid and reductions in fringe military costs, will go a fair way toward reducing or eliminating the basic deficit.

THE UNITED STATES AS INTERNATIONAL BANKER

The role of international banker requires a tremendous amount of what bankers like to call "internal discipline." Translated into ordinary language, "internal discipline" more often than not means unemployment to curb price increases and imports. The United States has had this status thrust upon itself as the importance of United States international trade and aid increased and that of sterling diminished. Both are now the so-called "key currencies" which between them finance most world trade. If the United States is to continue as banker, it must have the support of other world banking centres, including those in England and on the Continent. In particular, there must be a substantial willing-ness to devise various monetary measures that will make ample liquidity available to forestall speculative flights from the dollar. If international trade were the paramount concern of the United States in the way that it must be in the United Kingdom, the United States would have less power to exert pressure on the orthodox monetary economists whose views are so influential in Europe. While the International Monetary Fund has recently reached an agreement which would supplement the international financial resources in a way which would help prevent a run on the dollar in future years, these provisions are unlikely to prove adequate. Further international monetary co-operation seems essential.

Hence the United States balance of payments problem can be restated in the following way. As a matter of public policy the United States desires to transfer big amounts of long-term capital and government outlays but it is not generating a sufficient, even though large, surplus on current account to effectuate the transfer. At the same time, the welfare content of international trade is inconsequential for the United States. Trade is only about 5 per cent. of our national output so that even should the terms of trade move strongly against the United States, the real income effects would be negligible. The relative unimportance of trade provides the United States with a strong bargaining weapon which it need use only in dire circumstances. Since the United States is, so to speak, more important to world trade than world trade is to it, the time may come when this bargaining advantage will be used to insist upon an international payments scheme which would remove or reduce the primary responsibility for the maintenance of international liquidity.

THE UNITED STATES AND THE COMMON MARKET

The United States has undertaken several measures to meet the balance of payments problem. Most dramatic of all international trade measures has been Kennedy's recent tariff-cutting proposals. These could lead to a drastic reduction in American tariffs on manufactured goods in return for similar concessions by the Common Market countries. The reasons for this international trade programme are complex. First of all, there exists a real concern that a high external tariff barrier by the European Economic Community would lead to a curtailment of United States exports to these rapidly growing markets and, at the same time, would encourage the flow of private capital into the Common Market by American manufacturers as well as American security holders. Euphoria would also be abundant if President Kennedy could only export one of his major domestic political problems, the overflowing farm surpluses, by continuing to export large quantities of United States foodstuffs to the Continent. In addition, a lowering of tariffs all around would open up markets to those parts of the world excluded from the European Economic Community, as well as the United States, by present tariff and trade restrictions.

It is not clear from publicly available evidence that the United States balance of payments will be materially improved by a major reduction in tariffs, certainly not initially. Persistence of high unemployment levels would make lowering tariffs very hard indeed in a country with strong protectionist elements. A conflict can arise between full employment and the international trade balance since extremely full employment is likely to be associated with rapidly rising prices and real demand for imports, both adversely affecting the trade balance. Yet a reduction in tariffs is politically most feasible when employment is at high levels. When foreigners are selling goods in the United States while American factories and workers are idle, most American politicians uninitiated to the charmed circle of True Believers in Free Trade are prone to take a critical outlook on tariff cutting.

PRICE STABILITY

The final resolution of the United States payments problem will be strongly influenced by relative desires to increase prices and unit costs. Great Britain and the United States until recently were among those countries with the more rapid price and unit cost increases. Important European trading countries had price-rises too, but much more rapid increases in productivity than the United States and Great Britain so that their unit costs fell relatively. If the German and French inflations continue, external payment pressures on both the United States and Britain to enforce domestic price-level stability will tend to diminish. But if one believes that national institutions and attitudes towards price-level increases are deeply ingrained and subject only to slow change, one would then predict that Germany, Switzerland, Belgium, and Italy will be among those countries with the lowest domestic price increases and that Great Britain and the United States, and possibly France, will be among those countries with the greatest price rise. In such circumstances, the present relatively favourable position of the United States and Great Britain will evaporate. For the United States at least, it could mean that a minor currency readjustment will prove desirable, say 10 per cent. against the German mark, to indicate a roughly reasonable sort of magnitude. Such an action would, if it became necessary, be politically difficult for Kennedy to undertake. The real question is, would he be willing to do this if it were called for or instead use unemployment to regain external balance. In attenuated form the payments-employment dilemma has already diminished the vigour of a strong full-employment policy. If there is a difference between Republican and Democratic philosophies, it ought to be revealed should this particular issue come to the fore, which is not at all certain. This could turn out to be the second critical economic test facing President Kennedy.

Politics and the balance of payments get mixed up in some rather peculiar ways. For instance, the United States has reached an agreement with West Germany whose terms oblige the West Germans to purchase half a billion dollars a year of NATO arms in the United States, a move which goes quite a distance toward reducing the "basic deficit" of the United States. One wonders sometimes how much additional diplomatic strength Western Germany has acquired, beyond its substantial legitimate amount, as a result of its willingness to alleviate the United States balance of payments problem.

THE PRESIDENT A MODERATE CONSERVATIVE

The preceding commentary on the major economic policy problems of the Kennedy Administration has these common factors. First, the potentialities for rapid and widespread economic expansion are great. The balance of payments need not be a fundamental restriction upon the freedom of action of the United States. Secondly, however, strongly conservative political beliefs do put inhibitions on actions which would "risk the stability of the dollar" or lead to price-level increases of any sizeable magnitude. Thirdly, the particular form of federalism in the United States has reserved much welfare and educational duties for the individual states, although since the 1930s the Federal Government has become much more active in these areas. Several decades hence, when historians evaluate the Kennedy record, they are unlikely to view his economic policies as departing substantially from the preceding Republican Administration. While moderately conservative himself, the President is much less conservative than the Congress facing him. Only when the popular economic thinking is stripped of the budget-balancing ideology and is willing to accept the fact that some moderate inflation is a necessary price to pay for high-level employment, will a Democratic Administration be distinguishable from a Republican Administration. This particular new frontier looks as though it will remain unsullied for quite a long time to come.

On February 2, 1961, only a few days after his inauguration, President Kennedy sent Congress a special message outlining immediate measures to end a mild recession and a long-range course of action to increase economic growth. The sections on economic growth follow.

JOHN F. KENNEDY:
PROGRAM FOR ECONOMIC RECOVERY AND GROWTH*

TO THE CONGRESS OF THE UNITED STATES:

I.

Our Goals and Problems

America has the human and material resources to meet the demands of national security and the obligations of world leadership while at the same time advancing well-being at home. But our nation has been falling further and further short of its economic capabilities. In the past seven years, our rate of growth has slowed down disturbingly. In the past 3½ years, the gap between what we can produce and what we do produce has threatened to become chronic. And in the past year, our economic problem has been aggravated by recession and by loss of gold. I shall shortly send to the Congress a separate message dealing with our international balance of payments and gold position.

The nation cannot—and will not—be satisfied with economic decline and slack. The United States cannot afford, in this time of national need and world crisis, to dissipate its opportunities for economic growth. We cannot expect to make good in a day or even a year the accumulated deficiencies of several years. But realistic aims for 1961 are to reverse the downtrend in our economy, to narrow the gap of unused potential, to abate the waste and misery of unemployment, and at the same time to maintain reasonable stability of the price level. For 1962 and 1963 our programs must aim at expanding American productive capacity at a rate that shows the world the vigor and vitality of a free economy. These are not merely fond hopes, they are realistic goals. We pledge and ask maximum effort for their attainment.

I am proposing today measures both to alleviate the distress arising from unsatisfactory performance of the economy and to stimulate economic recovery and growth. If economic developments in the first quarter of this year indicate that additional measures are needed, I will promptly propose such measures.

---

* Reprinted from *Public Papers of the Presidents . . . John F. Kennedy . . . 1961* (Washington, D.C.: Government Printing Office, 1962), pp. 41–43, 51–53.

The Present Situation and Outlook. The potential of the American economy is constantly expanding. The labor force is rising by 1.5 percent per year. Output per man rises annually by 2 percent as a result of new and better plant and equipment, modern technology, and improved human skills. These increases in manpower and productivity provide the base for a potential annual growth of 3.5 percent in the nation's total output. This is not high enough. Our potential growth rate can and should be increased. To do so, we propose to expand the nation's investments in physical and human resources, and in science and technology.

But in recent years the economy has not realized even its present possible growth. From the peak of the business cycle in the second quarter of 1953 to the top of the anemic recovery seven years later, gross national product grew only at an annual rate of 2.5 percent. The failure to use our full capacity is the urgent economic problem of the day.

In 1960, the American economy produced $503 billion of output when it was capable of producing at least $535 billion. In the fourth quarter of 1960, actual output could have been 8 percent higher than it was. More than a million and a half unemployed—over one-third of all unemployed—could have had jobs. Twenty billion dollars more personal income could have been earned in 1960. Corporate profits could have been $5 billion higher. All this could have been accomplished with readily available manpower, materials and machines—without straining productive capacity and without igniting inflation.

The performance of the economy in 1960 was not only well below its full capacity; it also fell short of the modest levels expected by the previous Administration.

Adjusting all figures to the same statistical basis, the Budget projections last January were based on a 1960 national output of $513 billion. In October, output for the year was still expected to exceed $508 billion, implying a rate of at least $521 billion in the fourth quarter. The actual figure turned out to be $503 billion both for the year as a whole and for the last quarter.

Even when the recession ends and economic activity begins to expand again, the problem of unused potential will remain. Even if we were to achieve the $515 billion output projected for 1961 in connection with last month's Budget Message, the gap between potential and actual output would continue to grow and unemployment would hover between 6 and 7 percent of the labor force throughout the year. Under these circumstances, the expectation of minor improvements in business conditions during the next year provides no basis for complacency, no excuse for inaction. And—speaking out of realism, not pessimism—we cannot rule out the possibility of further deterioration if we fail to act.

An unbalanced economy does not produce a balanced budget. The Treasury's pocketbook suffers when the economy performs poorly. Lower incomes earned by households and corporations are reflected in lower Federal tax receipts. Assistance to unemployed workers and the costs of other measures for alleviation of economic distress are certain to rise as business declines. That is why recession—as our $12.4 billion deficit in the fiscal year 1959 recently reminded us—forces the budget into imbalance. That is why the prospect of surpluses in the Federal budgets for fiscal 1961 and fiscal 1962 is fading away.

GENERAL FISCAL POLICY AND THE BUDGET. The Federal Budget can and should be made an instrument of prosperity and stability, not a deterrent to recovery. This Administration is pledged to a Federal revenue system that balances the budget over the years of the economic cycle—yielding surpluses for debt retirement in times of high employment that more than offset the deficits which accompany—and indeed help overcome—low levels of economic activity in poor years.

If this economy were operating at full potential, the existing Federal revenue system would yield more than $90 billion in fiscal year 1962, instead of the $82.3 billion now estimated, producing a large budget surplus, and permitting retirement of national debt as well as the further development of Federal programs to meet urgent national needs. Debt retirement at high employment contributes to economic growth by releasing savings for productive investment by private enterprise and State and local governments.

The programs I am now proposing will not by themselves unbalance the budget which was earlier submitted, but are designed to fulfill our responsibility to alleviate distress and speed recovery—both through benefits directly available to needy persons and through desirable fiscal effects on the economy. They will sustain consumer spending and increase aggregate demand now when the economy is slack. Many of these expenditures will automatically cease when high employment and production are restored.

Other measures contained in this message propose necessary uses of national economic capacity and tax revenue for our long-range growth, and are essential even in the absence of a recession. They are proposed because the country needs them, can afford them, and would indeed be poorer without them.

AGRICULTURE. Recession in agriculture has been chronic since the early Fifties. Falling farm income has been a drag on the industrial economy, while economic slack has restricted the job openings which might have eased the adjustment process in agriculture. The marginal or displaced farmer is most painfully aware of the interdependence of agriculture and industry. Restoration of the economy as a whole to satisfactory and rising levels of performance is an important prerequisite to restoring farm prices and income to their rightful levels. The American farmer should receive for his managerial skills, his labor, and his capital investment returns that are similar to those received for comparable human talents and resources in other types of enterprise. To this end the Administration will recommend further specific measures in a separate message on agriculture to be submitted to the Congress at an early date. . . .

III.
Promotion of Economic Growth and Price Stability

I have emphasized that the solution to our economic problem requires a program that goes well beyond anti-recession measures, important as these are to the relief of distress and the reversal of economic decline. Equally important are measures for the longer pull to restore our economy to its full potential and to accelerate economic growth. Fortunately, the measures to overcome recession, to take up the slack, and to speed growth all reinforce each other.

Today, most industries have the facilities to produce well above current levels. They lack only customers. As a nation, we lose not only $30 to $40 billion of production per year. We also lose the vital incentives which capacity operation gives for expansion and modernization of plant and equipment. The measures I have proposed to reduce unemployment and stimulate markets will help to restore these incentives for economic growth.

1. SPECIAL TAX INCENTIVES TO INVESTMENT. Expansion and modernization of the nation's productive plant is essential to accelerate economic growth and to improve the international competitive position of American industry. Embodying modern research and technology in new facilities will advance productivity, reduce costs, and market new products. Moreover, an early stimulus to business investment will promote recovery and increase employment.

Among the reforms of the Federal tax system which I expect to propose at a later date is a modification of the income tax laws to provide additional incentives for investment in plant and equipment. To avoid a net revenue loss, I will also recommend measures to remove several unwarranted special tax benefits, and to improve tax compliance and administration. It should be possible to reform the tax system to stimulate economic growth, without reducing revenues and without violating the basic principles of fairness in taxation.

2. INVESTMENT IN HUMAN RESOURCES. Another fundamental ingredient of a program to accelerate long-run economic growth is vigorous improvement in the quality of the Nation's human resources. Modern machines and advanced technology are not enough, unless they are used by a labor force that is educated, skilled and in good health. This is one important reason why, in the legislative programs that I will submit in the days to come, I will emphasize so strongly programs to raise the productivity of our growing population, by strengthening education, health, research and training activities.

3. INVESTMENT IN NATURAL RESOURCES. The economic growth of the United States has been favored by an abundant supply of natural resources of almost every sort. But resource needs and supplies are not static. As our needs mount, as past reserves are depleted, and as technological requirements change, we must constantly develop new supplies if growth is not to be inhibited.

Exhaustion of low-cost domestic mineral deposits is a growing problem which calls for technological advance and new national long-range minerals policy.

Our water resources programs, including flood control, irrigation, navigation, watershed development, water pollution control—and above all, water desalinization—require priority attention. In addition, we need to develop sound and uniform standards for sharing costs between Federal, State, and local governments.

Improvement of our forest resources will require expanded Government credit sources for the development of woodland properties, more research on forest management, additional funds for cooperative forest programs, acceleration of the national forest program, and improvement of grazing resources.

Also essential to economic growth are long-range energy resource development and accelerated programs for economical production of energy from nuclear sources, including nuclear fusion. We must begin now also to plan for regional cooperative pooling of electrical power. Both efficiency and growth goals will be served if we interconnect our hydroelectric and thermal power resource plants.

4. PRODUCTIVITY AND PRICE STABILITY. Rapid technological change is resulting in serious employment dislocations, which deny us the full stimulus to growth which advancing technology makes possible. Labor and industry have demonstrated cooperative initiative in working out solutions in specific plants and industries. Government action is also necessary, not only to maintain an environment favorable to economic growth, but also to deal with special problems in communities and industries suffering from economic dislocations and to help those who through unemployment are bearing an unfair share of the burden of technological change.

I have dealt with some of these problems elsewhere in this message, in connection with unemployment insurance, aid to depressed areas, and efforts to broaden the services of the United States Employment Service.

Government can help further by encouraging labor and management to find ways to smooth the adjustment to technological change and thus to maintain and re-enforce the favorable attitude toward economic progress that characterizes American business and labor alike. Accordingly, I shall issue an executive order establishing the President's Advisory Committee on Labor-Management Policy, with members drawn from labor, management, and the public. The Committee is directed to advise the President with respect to actions that may be taken by labor, management, and the public which will promote free and responsible collective bargaining, industrial peace, sound wage policies, sound price policies and stability, a higher standard of living, increased productivity, and America's competitive position in world markets. It will consider national manpower needs and the special benefits and problems created by automation and other technological advances. I look to the Committee to make an important contribution to labor-management relations and an understanding of their importance to the stability of prices and the health of the economy.

The course of the American price level depends in substantial measure on wage and price decisions of labor and management. This dependence grows in importance as the economy moves toward full employment. All of us must now be conscious of the need for policies that enable American goods to compete successfully with foreign goods. We cannot afford unsound wage and price movements which push up costs, weaken our international competitive position, restrict job opportunities, and jeopardize the health of our domestic economy.

Price stability will also be aided by the adoption of a tax incentive plan mentioned earlier, which will encourage a higher rate of business investment in improved plants and equipment.

Price increases for many products and services have occurred because these industries have lagged behind in the march of productivity and technological advance. Indeed, in the present economic situation, a stepping-up of productivity improvement throughout the economy would contribute to the achievement of price stability.

We must not as a nation come to accept the proposition that reasonable price stability can be achieved only by tolerating a slack economy, chronic unemployment, and a creeping rate of growth.

Neither will we seek to buy short-run economic gains by paying the price of excessive increases in the cost of living. Always a cruel tax upon the weak, inflation is now the certain road to a balance of payments crisis and the disruption of the international economy of the Western World.

Inflation has no single cause. There have been times in the postwar period when prices rose sharply in response to a rate of total spending in excess of our capacity to produce. The government will not contribute to this process, and we shall use the powerful tools of fiscal and monetary policy to arrest any such movement if it should threaten in the year ahead. Some price increases, particularly among the consumer services, have been caused by the failure of productive resources to move promptly in response to basic shifts in the pattern of demand. We shall seek means to encourage the movement of manpower and capital into sectors of expanding demand.

Conclusion

I have sought in this message to propose a program to restore momentum to the American economy. I have recommended measures designed to set us firmly on the road to full recovery and sustained growth. But if these measures prove to be inadequate to the task, I shall submit further proposals to the Congress within the next 75 days. We will do what needs to be done to fulfill the high promise of the American economy.

Nikita Khrushchev entered the discussion of national growth by boasting that the Soviet Union would outproduce the United States by 1970. President Kennedy took the occasion of his press conference of June 28, 1961, to reply.

JOHN F. KENNEDY: "WE CAN MAINTAIN OUR PRODUCTIVE DEVELOPMENT AND ALSO OUR SYSTEM OF FREEDOM"*

. . . Chairman Khrushchev has compared the United States to a wornout runner living on its past performance and stated that the Soviet Union would out-produce the United States by 1970.

Without wishing to trade hyperbole with the Chairman, I do suggest that he reminds me of the tiger hunter who has picked a place on the wall to hang the tiger's skin long before he has caught the tiger. This tiger has other ideas.

Premier Khrushchev states that the Soviet Union is only 44 years old but his country is far older than that, and it is an interesting fact that in 1913, according to the best calculations I can get from governmental and private sources, the Russian gross national product was 46 percent of the United States gross national product.

Interestingly enough, in 1959 it was 47 percent. Because, while the Soviet Union was making progress and improving the material standards of her people in the ensuing years, so was the tired-out runner, and, on a per capita basis, the Soviet product in 1959 was only 39 percent of ours.

If both countries sustain their present rate of growth, 3½ percent in the United States and 6 percent in the Soviet Union, Soviet output will not reach two-thirds of ours by 1970 and our rate will be far easier to sustain or improve than the Soviet rate, which starts from a lower figure.

Indeed, if our growth rate is increased to even

4½ percent, which is well within our capability, it is my judgment that the Soviet Union will not outproduce the United States at any time in the twentieth century.

This faster growth rate is a primary object of the various measures I've submitted and will submit in the future, tax incentives, education, resource development, research, area redevelopment, and all the rest.

Mr. Khrushchev obviously sees the future differently than we do and he has urged his people to work hard to develop that future. We in the United States must work hard, too, to realize our potential.

But I believe that we can maintain our productive development and also our system of freedom. We invite the U.S.S.R. to engage in this competition which is peaceful and which could only result in a better living standard for both of our people.

In short, the United States is not such an aged runner and, to paraphrase Mr. Coolidge, "We do choose to run." . . .

Q. Mr. President, you said that if the United States can attain a rate of growth of 4½ percent, that Russia will not catch up with us in the twentieth century. What is our rate of growth now, sir?

THE PRESIDENT. Well, culling it from 1953 to today, it's about 3½ percent.

[16.] Q. What are we doing to attain a rate of growth?

THE PRESIDENT. Well, we're going to have a sharp—from the recession of 1960, winter of '61, we ought to have a substantial rate of increase. The big problem will be to sustain it over a period of time and that will require—I mentioned some

---

* Reprinted from *Public Papers of the Presidents . . . John F. Kennedy . . . 1961* (Washington, D.C.: Government Printing Office, 1962), pp. 478, 481–82.

of the things—a tax system which provides a stimulation to growth, education, and research, also the development of the natural resources of this country and also monetary and fiscal policies which will recognize the necessity of preventing a recurrence of these successive dips.

Now we had a recession in '54, we had a recession in '58, we had a recession in '60. The '60 recession came right on the heels of the '58 recession. Two of the reasons why it may have contributed—it was the movement from a $12 billion deficit in '58–59 to a prospective $4 billion surplus, which was a change of more than $16 billion in the potential receipts of the Government, which did have a restraining influence on the recovery.

Secondly, of course, the long-term interest rates were extremely high. Now we have to—the Federal Reserve will meet with Mr. Martin frequently. It's a very uncertain science, but we have to figure out what steps we can take—with this free economy—that will provide not only a recovery now, and we hope a reduced unemployment rate, but will also sustain it, not just through '62 but over a period of time. That we have to do if we're going to defeat Mr. Khrushchev, but it's within our potential and, therefore, I think, my judgment is that if the United States considers this problem and the people of the United States and the Government working together attempt to master this uncertain science in a more precise way, that we will remain not only ahead on a per capita basis but also on a national income basis in this century.

We have to recognize, of course, that the Soviet Union is working extremely hard and enjoys some advantages in being able to mobilize its resources for this purpose in the sense that a totalitarian society enjoys that advantage. What we wish was that they would do it under a system of freedom, but that is their decision.

In keeping with his concern to prevent renewed inflation, President Kennedy urged the United Steelworkers not to make demands upon the steel companies that could send prices spiraling. When David J. McDonald, President of the Steelworkers, sent assurances of his cooperation, Kennedy replied, September 14, 1961:

JOHN F. KENNEDY: THE IMPORTANCE OF PRICE STABILITY*

Dear Mr. McDonald:

I appreciate very much your letter of September 8 in which you pledge the cooperation of the Steelworkers Union in the negotiations next year with the steel industry, to make sure that full weight and recognition is given to the public interest.

I am sure that you agree with me that the public interest requires responsible price and wage policies in this basic industry and throughout the American economy. The Steelworkers Union can make a significant contribution to the public interest by following, in the forthcoming negotiations, policies that will ensure that their collective bargaining proposals are fashioned so that, in meeting the needs of workers in the industry, the interests of stockholders are safeguarded and the public interest in price stability is protected. This implies a labor settlement within the limits of advances in productivity and price stability.

No one, including workers in the industry, can profit by inflation and by advances in the cost of living. Nor can America as a whole maintain its position in the world if our balance of payments is jeopardized by price and wage policies that make our goods less competitive in the world markets. The whole nation has benefited from the price stability in steel for the last three years. We count on all concerned to maintain this stability.

I am confident that on the basis of your letter, we can rely upon the leadership and members of the Steelworkers Union to act responsibly in the wage negotiations next year in the interests of all of the American people.

Sincerely,

JOHN F. KENNEDY

* Reprinted from *Public Papers of the Presidents . . . John F. Kennedy . . . 1961* (Washington, D.C.: Government Printing Office, 1962), pp. 604–5.

When the United Steelworkers signed a contract in the spring of 1962 that was noninflationary, the tacit assumption was that the steel companies would not raise their prices. Several days later, United States Steel announced increases of approximately 3.5 per cent, and the President brought heavy pressure on the company to force it to rescind its increases. A *New York Times* team of reporters subsequently reconstructed the events of the three days that followed.

WALLACE CARROLL, *ET AL.*: STEEL: A 72-HOUR DRAMA*

WASHINGTON, April 22—It was peaceful at the White House on the afternoon of Tuesday, April 10—so peaceful, that the President of the United States thought he might have time for a nap or a little relaxed reading.

Just to be sure, he called his personal secretary, Mrs. Evelyn Lincoln, and asked what the rest of the day would bring.

"You have Mr. Blough at a quarter to six," said Mrs. Lincoln.

"Mr. Blough?" exclaimed the President.

Yes, said Mrs. Lincoln.

There must be a mistake, thought the President. The steel negotiations had been wound up the previous week.

"Get me Kenny O'Donnell," he said.

But there had been no mistake—at least not on the part of Kenneth P. O'Donnell, the President's appointment secretary.

Whether Mr. Blough—Roger I. Blough, chairman of the board of United States Steel Corporation—had made a mistake was a different question.

For when he walked into the President's office two hours later with the news that his company had raised the price of steel, he set off seventy-two hours of activity such as he and his colleagues could not have expected.

During those seventy-two hours, four antitrust investigations of the steel industry were conceived, a bill to roll back the price increases was seriously considered, legislation to impose price and wage controls on the steel industry was discussed, agents of the Federal Bureau of Investigation questioned newspaper men by the dawn's early light, and the Defense Department —biggest buyer in the nation—began to divert purchases away from United States Steel.

Also in those seventy-two hours—and this was far more significant—the Administration maintained its right to look over the shoulders of capital and labor when they came to the bargaining table and its insistence that any agreement they reached would have to respect the national interest.

And in those seventy-two hours, new content and meaning were poured into that magnificent abstraction, "the Presidency," for the historically minded to argue about as long as men remained interested in the affairs of this republic.

A full and entirely accurate account of those seventy-two hours may never be written. The characters were many. They moved so fast that no one will be able to retrace all of what they did.

Understandably, industry participants—facing official investigation now—would not talk much. Nor were Government participants willing to tell all.

Nevertheless, a team of New York Times reporters undertook to piece the tale together while memories were fresh.

Here is what they learned.

Early on that afternoon of April 10, Roger Blough had met with his colleagues of United States Steel's executive committee in the board room on the twentieth floor at 71 Broadway, New York. Three of the twelve members were absent, but Leslie B. Worthington, president of the company, and Robert C. Tyson, chairman of the finance committee, were there.

For several months these men had been giving out hints, largely overlooked in Washington, that the company would have to raise prices to meet increasing costs.

The Kennedy Administration had pressed for no increase in prices last fall, and there had been no increase. It had pressed again for a modest wage contract this year, and a modest contract had been signed a few days earlier. The Administration expected no price increase now.

The company's executive committee reviewed the situation. The sales department had concurred in a recommendation to increase prices by $3\frac{1}{2}$ per cent—about $6 on top of the going average of $170 a ton.

Mr. Blough had taken soundings within the company on the public relations aspects. Everyone realized that the move would not win any popularity prize, but the committee voted unanimously to go ahead.

With the decision made, Mr. Blough took a plane to Washington. Word was telephoned to the White House that he wanted to see the President and had something "important" to say about steel.

* Reprinted from *The New York Times*, April 23, 1962. Copyright by The New York Times. Reprinted by permission.

A few minutes after 5:45 the President received him in his oval office, motioned him to a seat on a sofa to his right and made himself comfortable in his rocking chair.

With little preliminary, Mr. Blough handed the President a four-page mimeographed press release that was about to be sent to newspaper offices in Pittsburgh and New York.

The President read:

"Pittsburgh, Pa., April 10—For the first time in nearly four years United States Steel today announced an increase in the general level of its steel prices."

Mr. Kennedy raced through the announcement. Then he summoned Arthur J. Goldberg, the Secretary of Labor. Minutes later Mr. Goldberg reached the President's office from the Labor Department four blocks away.

Grimly, the President gave the paper to Mr. Goldberg and said it had been distributed to the press. Mr. Goldberg skimmed over it and asked Mr. Goldberg [Blough] what was the point of the meeting, since the price decision had been made.

Mr. Blough replied that he thought he should personally inform the President as a matter of courtesy. Mr. Goldberg retorted it was hardly a courtesy to announce a decision and confront the President with an accomplished fact.

In the half-hour discussion that followed President Kennedy seems to have kept his temper. But Mr. Goldberg lectured Mr. Blough with some heat. The price increase, the Secretary said, would jeopardize the Government's entire economic policy. It would damage the interests of United States Steel itself. It would undercut responsible collective bargaining. Finally he said, the decision could be viewed only as a double-cross of the President because the company had given no hint of its intentions while the Administration was urging the United Steelworkers of America to moderate its wage demands.

Mr. Blough, a former high school teacher turned lawyer and company executive, defended himself and the company in a quiet voice.

When he had gone President Kennedy called for the three members of his Council of Economic Advisers. Dr. Walter W. Heller, the chairman, a lean and scholarly looking man, came running from his office across the street. Dr. Kermit Gordon followed in three minutes. James Tobin, the third member, hurried back to his office later in the evening.

Into the President's office came Theodore C. Sorensen, the White House special counsel, Mr. O'Donnell and Andrew T. Hatcher, acting press secretary in the absence of Pierre Salinger, who was on vacation.

Now the President, who usually keeps his temper under rein, let go. He felt he had been double-crossed—deliberately. The office of the President had been affronted. The national interest had been flouted. . . .

It was clear that the Administration would fight. No one knew exactly what could be done, but from that moment the awesome power of the Federal Government began to move.

To understand the massive reaction of the Kennedy Administration, a word of background is necessary.

Nothing in the range of domestic economic policy had brought forth a greater effort by the Administration than the restraint it sought to impose on steel prices and wages.

Starting last May the Administration worked on the industry, publicly and privately, not to raise its prices when wages went up in the fall. And when the price line held, the Administration turned its efforts to getting an early and "noninflationary" wage contract this year.

Above all, the Administration constantly tried to impress on both sides that the national interest was riding on their decisions. A price increase or an inflationary wage settlement, it argued, would set off a new wage-price spiral that would stunt economic growth, keep unemployment high, cut into export sales, weaken the dollar and further aggravate the outflow of gold.

On Friday and Saturday, April 6 and 7, the major steel companies had signed the new contract. President Kennedy had hailed it as "noninflationary." Privately, some steel leaders agreed with him.

Thus, the President confidently expected that the companies would not increase prices. And the standard had been set, he hoped, for other industries and unions.

This was the background against which the group in the President's office went to work.

By about 8 P.M. some decisions had been reached.

President Kennedy would deliver the first counter-attack at his news conference scheduled for 3:30 the following afternoon.

Messrs. Goldberg, Heller and Sorensen would gather material for the President's statement. Other material of a statistical nature would be prepared in a longer-range effort to prove the price increase was unjustified.

While the discussion was going on, the President called his brother, Robert F. Kennedy, the Attorney General; Secretary of Defense Robert S. McNamara, and the Secretary of the Treasury, Douglas Dillon, who had just arrived in Hobe Sound, Fla., for a short vacation.

At his home on Hillbrook Lane, Senator Estes Kefauver of Tennessee, chairman of the Senate Antitrust Subcommittee, was getting ready to go out for the evening. The phone rang. It was the President. Would Senator Kefauver publicly register "dismay" at the price increase and consider an investigation?

The Senator certainly would. He promised an investigation. So did the Justice Department.

In the President's office, meanwhile, there had been some talk of what could be done to keep other steel companies from raising prices. Most of the discussion centered on the economic rebuttal of the case made by United States Steel.

Mr. Goldberg and Dr. Heller decided to pool resources. Mr. Goldberg called Hyman L. Lewis, chief of the Office of Labor Economics of the Bureau of Labor Statistics, and asked him to assemble a crew.

Mr. Lewis reached three members of the bureau—Peter Henle, special assistant to the Commissioner of Labor Statistics; Arnold E. Chase, chief of the Division of Prices and Cost of Living, and Leon Greenberg, chief of the Productivity Division.

He told them what was wanted and asked them to go to Dr. Heller's office in the old State Department Building.

Dr. Heller who had been working on the problem in his office, hurried off after a few minutes to the German Ambassador's residence on Foxhall Road.

The Ambassador was giving a dinner, a black tie affair, in honor of Prof. Walter Hallstein, president of the European Common Market. The guests were well into the meal when Dr. Heller arrived, looking, as one of the guests remarked, like Banquo's ghost in a tuxedo.

Back at the White House the President had also changed to black tie. The members of Congress and their wives were coming to his annual reception at 9:45. Ruefully, the President recalled that the news of the Cuban disaster had arrived during his reception in 1961.

"I'll never hold another Congressional reception," he remarked.

But as he and Mrs. Kennedy received the leaders of Congress and their wives, he easily relaxed into small talk.

What did the men think, he asked, of the break with tradition by making this a black tie, instead of a white tie, affair? Republicans and Democrats unanimously favored the change. Many of the younger members of Congress, they pointed out, did not have a white tie and all that went with it.

With the party spread through three rooms, no one could tell how many times Mr. Kennedy slipped out to talk about steel. The President stayed until 12:08 A.M. Then he retired.

By that time, the White House staff, the Council of Economic Advisers and the Departments of Labor, Justice, Defense, Commerce and The Treasury were all at work on the counterattack.

WEDNESDAY

Midnight had struck when Walter Heller, still in black tie, returned to his office from the German Embassy. With him, also in black tie, came another dinner guest, George W. Ball, Under Secretary of State.

Dr. Heller's two colleagues in the Council of Economic Advisers, Dr. Gordon and Dr. Tobin, were already there. So were the four men from the Bureau of Labor Statistics.

At about 2:45 A.M. the four men from the Bureau of Labor Statistics left the session. Their assignment from then on was to bring up to date a fact book on steel put out by the Eisenhower Administration two years ago.

The idea was to turn it into a kind of "white paper" that would show that the price increase was unjustified.

Toward 4 o'clock Dr. Heller and Dr. Tobin went home for two or three hours' sleep. Dr. Gordon [sic].

As the normal working day began, President Kennedy held a breakfast meeting at the White House with Vice President Johnson; Secretary of State Dean Rusk (who played no part in the steel crisis); Secretary Goldberg; Mr. Sorensen; Myer Feldman, Mr. Sorensen's deputy; Dr. Heller and Andrew Hatcher.

The meeting lasted an hour and forty-five minutes. Mr. Goldberg and Dr. Heller reported on the night's work. Mr. Sorensen was assigned to draft the President's statement on steel for the news conference. Mr. Goldberg gave him a two-page report from the Bureau of Labor Statistics headed:

"Change in Unit Employment Costs in the Steel Industry 1958 to 1961."

It said in part:

"While employment costs per hour of all wage and salaried employes in the basic iron and steel industry rose from 1958 to 1961, there was an equivalent increase in output per man-hour.

"As a result, employment costs per unit of steel output in 1961 was essentially the same as in 1958."

The latter sentence was quoted that afternoon in the President's statement.

During the morning the President had called Secretary Dillon in Florida and discussed with him the Treasury's work on tax write-offs that would encourage investment in more modern plant and machinery. The two decided that the course would not be altered.

Secretary of Commerce Luther H. Hodges, who was about to testify before a House Maritime subcommittee [sic]. After giving his testimony Secretary Hodges spent most of the day on the phone to business men around the country.

In Wall Street that morning United States Steel shares opened at 70¾, up 2¾ from the day before. But on Capitol Hill the company's stock was down.

Senator Mike Mansfield, the majority leader, called the price increase "unjustified." Speaker John W. McCormack said the company's action was "shocking," "arrogant," "irresponsible." Senator Hubert H. Humphrey, the Democratic whip, spoke of "an affront to the President."

Senator Albert Gore of Tennessee suggested a law that would empower the courts to prohibit price increases in basic industries such as steel until there had been a "cooling-off period."

Representative Emanuel Celler of Brooklyn, chairman of the House Antitrust subcommittee, scheduled a broad investigation of the steel industry. So did Senator Kefauver.

The pressures on United States Steel were beginning to mount. But now some of the other titans of the industry began to fall in line behind Big Steel.

As the President came out of the White House shortly before noon to go to the airport where he was to welcome the Shah of Iran, he was shown a news bulletin. Bethlehem Steel, second in size only to United States Steel, had announced a price increase.

Others followed in short order—Republic, Jones and Laughlin, Youngstown and Wheeling. And Inland, Kaiser and Colorado Fuel & Iron said they were "studying" the situation.

When he faced the newsmen and television cameras at 3:30, President Kennedy spoke with cold fury. The price increase, he said, was a "wholly unjustifiable and irresponsible defiance of the public interest." The steel men had shown "utter contempt" for their fellow citizens.

He spoke approvingly of the proposed investigations. But what did he hope to accomplish that might still save the Administration's broad economic program?

In his conference statement the President had seemed to hold out no hope that the price increases could be rolled back. If the increases held, what imminent comfort could there be in possible antitrust decrees that would take three years to come from the courts?

Actually, the possibility of making United States Steel retract the increase had been considered early in the consultation.

Drs. Heller and Gordon, and possibly some of the other economists, had argued that the principal thrust of the Administration's effort should be to convince one or two significant producers to hold out. In a market such as steel, they said, the high-priced sellers would have to come down if the others did not go up.

This suggested a line of strategy that probably proved decisive.

As one member of the Big Twelve after another raised prices, only Armco, Inland, Kaiser, C F & I and McLouth remained holding the line. These five hold-outs represented 14 per cent of total industry capacity, or 17 per cent of the capacity of the Big Twelve.

Everything pointed to Inland as the key to the situation.

Inland Steel Corporation with headquarters in Chicago is a highly efficient producer. It could make a profit at lower prices than those of some of the bigger companies. And any company that sold in the Midwest, such as United States Steel, would feel Inland's price competition.

Moreover, there was a tradition of public service at Inland. Clarence B. Randall, a former chairman of the board, had served both the Eisenhower and Kennedy Administrations. (But he played no part in this crisis.)

Joseph Leopold Block, Inland's present chairman, who was in Japan at the moment, had been a member of President Kennedy's Labor-Management Advisory Committee.

At 7:45 that Wednesday morning, Philip D. Block Jr., vice chairman of Inland, was called to the telephone in his apartment at 1540 North Lake Shore Drive in Chicago.

"Hello, P. D.," said Edward Gudeman, Under Secretary of Commerce, a former schoolmate and friend of Mr. Block's, calling from Washington.

"What do you think of this price increase of United States Steel's?"

Mr. Block said he had been surprised.

"I didn't ask P. D. what Inland might do," said Mr. Gudeman several days later. "I didn't want them to feel that the Administration was putting them on the spot. I just wanted him to know how we felt and to ask his consideration."

Inland officials agreed to consider. They said they had not been coaxed or threatened by any of the officials who called them.

The approach, which seems to have developed rather spontaneously in many of the calls that were made to business men, was to ask their opinion, state the Government's viewpoint, and leave it at that.

But there also were calls with a more pointed aim—to steel users, asking them to call their steel friends and perhaps even issue public statements.

Another call to Inland was made by Henry H. Fowler, Under Secretary of the Treasury and Acting Secretary in Mr. Dillon's absence.

After Mr. Kennedy's afternoon news conference Mr. Fowler called John F. Smith Jr., Inland's president. Like other Treasury officials who telephoned other business men, Mr. Fowler talked about the effect of a steel price increase on imports and exports and the further pressure it would place on the balance of payments.

A third call went to Inland that day. It was from Secretary Goldberg to Leigh B. Block, vice president for purchasing.

Both Inland and Government officials insist that there was no call from the White House or from any Government office to Joseph Block in Japan.

Though no concrete assurance was asked or volunteered in these conversations, the Administration gathered assurance that Inland would hold the line for at least another day or two.

Next came Armco, sixth largest in the nation. Walter Heller had a line into that company. So did others. Calls were made. And through these channels the Administration learned that Armco was holding off for the time being, but there would be no public announcement one way or the other.

Meanwhile, Mr. Gudeman had called a friend in the upper reaches of the Kaiser Company. Secretary McNamara had called a number of friends, one of them at Allegheny-Ludlum, a large manufacturer of stainless.

How many calls were made by President Kennedy himself cannot be told. But some time during all the activity he talked to Edgar Kaiser, chairman of Kaiser Steel, in California.

According to one official who was deeply involved in all this effort, the over-all objective was to line up companies representing 18 per cent of the nation's capacity. If this could be done, according to friendly sources in the steel industry, these companies with their lower prices soon would be doing 25 per cent of the business. Then Big Steel would have to yield.

Parallel with this "divide-and-conquer" maneuver, the effort moved forward on the antitrust line.

During the morning someone had spotted in the newspapers a statement attributed to Edmund F. Martin, president of Bethlehem Steel. Speaking to reporters on Tuesday after a stockholders' meeting in Wilmington, Del., Mr. Martin was quoted as having said:

"There shouldn't be any price rise. We shouldn't do anything to increase our costs if we are to survive. We have more competition both domestically and from foreign firms."

If Mr. Martin had opposed a price rise on Tuesday, before United States Steel announced its increase, and if Bethlehem raised its prices on Wednesday after that announcement, his statement might prove useful in antitrust proceedings. It could be used to support a Government argument that United States Steel, because of its bigness, exercised an undue influence over other steel producers.

At about 6 o'clock Wednesday evening, according to officials of the Justice Department, Attorney General Kennedy ordered the Federal Bureau of Investigation to find out exactly what Martin had said.

At about this same time, Paul Rand Dixon, chairman of the Federal Trade Commission, told reporters that his agency had begun an informal investigation to determine whether the steel companies had violated a consent decree of June 15, 1951.

That decree bound the industry to refrain from collusive price fixing or maintaining identical delivered prices. It provided penalties running up to $5,000 a day.

Meanwhile, more calls were going out from Washington.

The Democratic National Committee called many of the Democratic Governors and asked them to do two things:

First, to make statements supporting the President and, second, to ask steel producers in their states to hold the price line.

Among those called were David L. Lawrence of Pennsylvania, Richard J. Hughes of New Jersey and Edmund G. Brown of California. But the National Committee said nothing in its own name. The smell of "politics" was not to be allowed to contaminate the Administration's efforts.

Another call was made by Robert V. Roosa, an Under Secretary of the Treasury, to Henry Alexander, chairman of Morgan Guaranty Trust Company in New York. Morgan is represented on United States Steel's board of directors and is widely considered one of the most powerful influences within the company.

Thus by nightfall on Wednesday—twenty-four hours after Mr. Blough's call on the President—the Administration was pressing forward on four lines of action:

First, the rallying of public opinion behind the President and against the companies.

Second, divide-and-conquer operation within the steel industry.

Third, antitrust pressure from the Justice Department, the Federal Trade Commission, the Senate and the House.

Fourth, the mobilization of friendly forces within the business world to put additional pressure on the companies.

That night at the White House the Kennedys gave a state dinner for the visiting Shah and his Empress.

In a toast to his guests, President Kennedy, a man seemingly without a care in the world, observed that he and the Shah shared a common "burden." Each of them had made a visit to Paris and each of them might as well have stayed at home, for the Parisians had eyes only for their wives.

When the guests had gone, the President put in a call to Tucson, Ariz. It came through at 12:15 A.M.

THURSDAY

Archibald Cox, the Solicitor General, had left by plane on Wednesday afternoon for Tucson, where he was to make two speeches to the Arizona Bar.

On arriving at his hotel that night, he received a message to call the President. When he called he was asked what suggestions did he have for rolling back steel prices?

Mr. Cox had been chairman of the Wage Stabilization Board during the Korean War and had worked with young Senator Kennedy on statements about steel prices and strikes of the past.

After the call, Mr. Cox stayed up all night, thinking and making notes, mostly about legislation. From past experience Mr. Cox had concluded that the antitrust laws could not cope with the steel problem and that special legislation would be necessary.

Mr. Cox made his two speeches, flew back to Washington and stayed up most of that night working on the legislative draft.

But Mr. Cox was not the only one at work on the steel problem in the early hours of Thursday.

At 3 A.M. Lee Linder, a reporter in the Philadelphia bureau of the Associated Press, was awakened by a phone call. It was the F.B.I. At first Mr. Linder thought he was being fooled. Then he determined that the call was genuine. The agents asked him a question or two and then told him:

"We are coming right out to see you."

Mr. Linder had been at the stockholders' meeting of Bethlehem Steel in Wilmington on Tuesday and had quoted Mr. Martin about the undesirability of a price increase. Bethlehem Steel later called the quotation incorrect.

The agents were checking on that quotation. Mr. Linder said later that he had given them the same report he had written for The Associated Press.

At 6:30 A.M. James L. Parks Jr. of The Wilmington Evening Journal arrived at his office. Two F. B. I. agents were waiting for him. He had talked to Mr. Martin after the meeting, together with Mr. Linder and John Lawrence of The Wall Street Journal. Later in the day the Federal agents interviewed Mr. Lawrence.

This descent of the F.B.I. on the newsmen was the most criticized incident in the seventy-two frenzied hours.

Republicans, who had kept an embarrassed silence up to this point, pounced on this F.B.I. episode. Representative William E. Miller of upstate New York, chairman of the Republican National Committee, compared it to the "knock on the door" techniques of Hitler's Gestapo.

In Chicago, as the day progressed, Philip Block and two other high officials of Inland reached a decision: prices would not be raised. They called Joseph Block in Kyoto. He concurred and they agreed to call a directors' meeting to ratify their decision the next morning.

No announcement was to be made until the morning and no one in Washington was told.

Back in Washington, the President was holding an early meeting in the Cabinet Room at the White House. Present were:

Attorney General Kennedy; Secretaries McNamara, Goldberg, Hodges; Under Secretary of the Treasury Fowler; Mr. Dixon, chairman of the Federal Trade Commission; Dr. Heller and Mr. Sorensen.

Roger Blough was scheduled to hold a televised news conference in New York at 3:30 that afternoon. The White House meeting decided that the Administration should put in a speedy rebuttal to his case for United States Steel.

Secretary Hodges had long-scheduled engagements that day in Philadelphia and New York. It was decided that he would hold a news conference in New York at 5 P.M. and try to rebut Mr. Blough point by point.

Meanwhile two of the most secret initiatives of the entire seventy-two hours had been set in motion.

The first involved a newspaperman—Charles L. Bartlett, the Washington correspondent of The Chattanooga Times. All Mr. Bartlett would say later was:

"I helped two friends get in touch with each other again."

One friend was President Kennedy—Mr. Bartlett and his wife are members of the Kennedy social set. The other friend was an officer of United States Steel. His identity has not been definitely established, but Mr. Bartlett knows Mr. Blough.

What came of this effort to reopen "diplo-matic relations" is not known, although at least one Cabinet member thought it was useful. What came of the second secret initiative, however, can be reported.

At noon or earlier on Thursday President Kennedy phoned Clark Clifford, a Washington lawyer who had first come to national prominence as counsel for President Truman.

Secretary Goldberg, said the President, knew the officers of United States Steel very well and could, of course, talk to them on behalf of the Administration. But Mr. Goldberg, he went on, was known to the steel men mainly as an adversary.

For years he had been the counsel for the steel workers' union and one of their chief strategists in negotiations with the company. In view of this would Mr. Clifford, familiar as he was with the outlook of corporation executives through his law work, join Mr. Goldberg in speaking to United States Steel?

Mr. Clifford agreed, flew to New York and met Mr. Blough. He presented himself as a friend of the disputants, but he made clear that he was in 100 per cent agreement with the President. His purpose, he said, was to see if a tragic mistake could be rectified. The mistake, he left no doubt, was on the company's side.

For fourteen months, he continued, President Kennedy and Mr. Goldberg had worked for healthy conditions in the steel industry. They had tried to create an atmosphere of cooperation in the hope of protecting the national interest. Now all this was gone.

The President, he went on, believed there had been a dozen or more occasions when the company's leaders could easily have told him that despite all he had done they might have to raise prices. But they never had told him. The President, to put it bluntly, felt double-crossed.

What Mr. Blough said in reply could not be learned. But he indicated at the end that he would welcome further talks and he hoped Mr. Clifford would participate in them. Mr. Clifford returned to Washington the same day.

Secretary Hodges, meanwhile, arrived at the University Club in New York at about 3:40, ten minutes after Mr. Blough had begun his news conference.

While Mr. Hodges shaved and changed his shirt, his assistant, William M. Ruder, tried to take notes on Mr. Blough's broadcast, but the static he heard sounded like the Grand Central shuttle.

The Blough news conference was held in the ground floor auditorium at 71 Broadway.

"Let me say respectfully," Mr. Blough began, "that we have no wish to add acrimony or misunderstanding."

On several occasions, he said, he had made it clear that United States Steel was in a cost-price torque that could not be tolerated forever, that a company without profits is a company that cannot modernize, and that the price increase would add "almost negligibly" to the cost of other products—$10.64 for the steel in a standard automobile, 3 cents for a toaster.

One question and answer in the fifty-eight-minute session caught the ears of people in Washington: Could United States Steel hold its new price if Armco and Inland stood pat?

"It would definitely affect us," conceded Mr. Blough. "I don't know how long we could maintain our position."

A half-hour after Mr. Blough finished, Secretary Hodges held his news conference in the Empire State Building.

But the words that probably hit Big Steel the hardest came that day from two Pennsylvania Republicans—Representatives William W. Scranton, the party's candidate for Governor, and James E. Van Zandt, the candidate for Senator.

"The increase at this time," they wired Mr. Blough, "is wrong—wrong for Pennsylvania, wrong for America, wrong for the free world. The increase surely will set off another round of inflation. It will hurt people most who can least afford to be hurt."

Meanwhile, Justice Department agents appeared at the headquarters of United States Steel, Bethlehem, Jones & Laughlin and other companies and served subpoenas for documents bearing on the price increase and other matters.

And at 7 P.M. Attorney General Kennedy announced that the Justice Department had ordered a grand jury investigation of the increase.

By that time, President and Mrs. Kennedy were getting ready for another state dinner with the Shah and Empress—this time at the Iranian Embassy.

FRIDAY

The first big news of the day came from Kyoto, Japan. Joseph Block, Inland's chairman, had told a reporter for the Chicago Daily News:

"We do not feel that an advance in steel prices at this time would be in the national interest."

That news heartened the Administration but it did not stop planning or operations. Nor did Inland's official announcement from Chicago at 10:08 A.M., Washington time, that it would hold the price line.

At 10:15 Solicitor General Cox met in Mr. Sorensen's office with representatives of the Treasury, Commerce and Labor Departments, Budget Bureau and Council of Economic Advisers.

The discussion was on emergency wage-price legislation of three broad kinds:

First, ad hoc legislation limited to the current steel situation; second, permanent legislation imposing some mechanism on wages and prices in the steel industry alone, and third, permanent legislation for steel and other basic industries, setting up "fact-finding" procedures.

At 11:45 Secretary McNamara said at his news conference that the Defense Department had ordered defense contractors to shift steel purchases to companies that had not raised prices.

Later in the day the department awarded to the Lukens Steel Company, which had not raised prices, a contract for more than $5,000,000 worth of a special armor plate for Polaris-missile submarines.

At 12:15 President Kennedy and most of the Thursday group met again in the Cabinet Room. It was estimated at that time that the price line was being held on 16 per cent of the nation's steel capacity.

Inland had announced. Armco had decided to hold but not announce. Kaiser's announcement came in while the meeting was on. This might be enough to force the bigger companies down again, but the sentiment of the meeting was that the retreat would not come soon.

Accordingly, preparations continued for a long struggle. Lists of directors of the companies that were holding the line were distributed, and each man present was asked to call men he knew.

Notably absent from this meeting was Secretary Goldberg. He was on his way to New York with Mr. Clifford in a Military Air Transport plane.

A secret rendezvous had been arranged with Mr. Blough and some of the other leaders of United States Steel at the Carlyle Hotel.

At this meeting, as in Mr. Clifford's talk with Mr. Blough on the previous day, no demands or threats or promises came from the Government side.

The discussion seems to have been a general one about what lay ahead. The outlook, said Mr. Clifford, was "abysmal."

United States Steel, he contended, had failed to weigh the consequences of its action. If it held this position, its interest and those of the industry would inevitably be damaged, and the nation as a whole would suffer.

While the talk was going on, Mr. Blough was called to the phone. Then Mr. Goldberg was called. Each received the same message. Bethlehem Steel had rescinded the price increase—the news had come through at 3:20 P.M.

President Kennedy heard the news while flying to Norfolk for a week-end with the fleet. It was unexpected.

The Administration had made no special effort with Bethlehem. To this day, officials here are uncertain what did it.

Among other things, Bethlehem's officials were struck by the Inland and Kaiser announcement that morning. Inland posed direct competition to Bethlehem's sales in the Midwest—the largest steel market—and Kaiser posed it on the West Coast.

Further, special questions were raised by the Pentagon's order to defense industries to shift their steel buying to mills that did not raise prices. What did this mean for Bethlehem's vast operations as a ship builder?

Whatever the compelling factors were, Bethlehem's decision brought the end of the battle clearly in sight. The competitive situation was such that United States Steel's executive committee was not called into session to reverse its action of the previous Tuesday. The company's officers acted on their own.

The big capitulation came at 5:28. Mrs. Barbara Gamarekian, a secretary in the White House press office, was checking the Associated Press news ticker. And there was the announcement—United States Steel had pulled back the price increase.

Mrs. Gamarekian tore it off and ran into the office of Mr. Sorensen, who was on the phone to the acting press secretary, Mr. Hatcher, in Norfolk.

"Well," Mr. Sorensen was saying, "I guess there isn't anything new."

Mrs. Gamarekian put the next bulletin under his eye.

"Wait a minute!" shouted Mr. Sorensen.

Mr. Hatcher gave the news to the President as he came off the nuclear submarine, Thomas A. Edison, in Norfolk.

It was just seventy-two hours since Roger Blough had dropped in on Mr. Kennedy.

President Kennedy's extraordinary intervention in the economy brought a stinging protest from the Senate-House Republican leadership of Congress. On April 19, 1962, the bloc issued the following statement:

SENATE-HOUSE REPUBLICAN LEADERSHIP: "SHOULD A PRESIDENT . . . BLACKJACK ANY SEGMENT OF OUR FREE SOCIETY INTO LINE?"*

We, the members of the Joint Senate-House Republican Leadership, deplore the necessity for issuing this statement, but the issues involved are too compelling to be ignored.

Beyond the administrative operations of the Federal Government, it is a proper function of a President, in fact it is a duty, to help American private enterprise maintain a stable economy. In our free society he must usually find his way by persuasion and the prestige of his office.

Last week President Kennedy made a determination that a 3½ per cent increase [in the price of steel would] throw the American economy out of line on several fronts. In the next twenty-four hours the President directed or supported a series of Governmental actions that imperiled basic American rights, went far beyond the law, and were more characteristic of a police state than a free government.

We, the members of the Joint Senate-House Republican Leadership, believe that a fundamental issue has been raised: should a President of the United States use the enormous powers of the Federal Government to blackjack any segment of our free society into line with his personal judgment without regard to law?

Nine actions which followed President Kennedy's press conference of Wednesday, April 11, were obviously a product of White House direction or encouragement and must be considered for their individual and cumulative effect. They were:

1. The Federal Trade Commission publicly suggested the possibility of collusion, announced an immediate investigation and talked of $2,000 a day penalties.

2. The Justice Department spoke threateningly of anti-trust violations and ordered an immediate investigation.

3. Treasury Department officials indicated they were at once reconsidering the planned increase in depreciation rates for steel.

4. The Internal Revenue Service was reported making a menacing move toward U. S. Steel's incentive benefits plan for its executives.

5. The Senate Antitrust and Monopoly subcommittee began subpoenaing records from twelve steel companies, returnable May 14.

6. The House Antitrust subcommittee announced an immediate investigation with hearings opening May 2.

7. The Justice Department announced it was ordering a grand jury investigation.

8. The Department of Defense, seemingly ignoring laws requiring competitive bidding, publicly announced it was shifting steel purchases to companies that had not increased prices, and other Government agencies were directed to do likewise.

9. The F.B.I. began routing newspaper men out of bed at 3:00 A.M. on Thursday, April 12, in line with President Kennedy's press conference

---

* Reprinted from the Senate-House Republican Leadership (Senate members: Everett M. Dirksen, Thomas H. Kuchel, Bourke B. Hickenlooper, and Leverett Saltonstall; House members: William E. Miller, Charles A. Halleck, Leslie C. Arends, John W. Byrnes, Charles B. Hoeven, and Clarence J. Brown), *The New York Times,* April 20, 1962.

assertion that "we are investigating" a statement attributed to a steel company official in the newspapers.

'NAKED POLITICAL POWER'

Taken cumulatively these nine actions amount to a display of naked political power never seen before in this nation.

Taken singly these nine actions are punitive, heavy-handed and frightening.

Although the President at his press conference made it clear that "price and wage decisions in this country . . . are and ought to be freely and privately made," there was nothing in the course of action which he pursued that supported this basic American doctrine.

Indeed, if big government can be used to extra-legally reverse the economic decisions of one industry in a free economy, then it can be used to reverse the decisions of any business, big or small, of labor, of farmers, in fact, of any citizen.

Most disturbing in its implications was the use of the F.B.I. Since the days of our founding fathers, this land has been the haven of millions who fled from the feared knock on the door in the night.

We condone nothing in the actions of the steel companies except their right to make an economic judgment without massive retaliation by the Federal Government.

Temporarily President Kennedy may have won a political victory, but at the cost of doing violence to the fundamental precepts of a free society.

This nation must realize that we have passed within the shadow of police state methods. We hope that we never again step into those dark regions whatever the controversy of the moment, be it economic or political.

Speaking before the United States Chamber of Commerce on April 30, 1962, President Kennedy emphasized his wish for cordial cooperation between government and business. At the same session, Richard Wagner, President of the Chamber of Commerce, presented the businessmen's point of view.

RICHARD WAGNER: "BOTH BUSINESS AND LABOR [SHOULD] REMAIN FREE TO MAKE THEIR OWN DECISIONS"*

Recently we have witnessed a most unusual and mistaken interpretation of fact. By reason of the dramatic incident involved in the steel wage-price relationships, many people have been led to believe that inflationary pressures in this country are created by business and its so-called greedy desire for profit. Nothing could be further from the truth.

Steel had already been subjected to three increases in wage costs as well as increases in other costs without an increase in price. Other businesses have had similar experiences and have not added these increased costs to prices, because some of them did not want to increase inflationary conditions of the country, and others did not put them on prices because the market would not accept an increase.

Of course there have been increases in prices, but the fact is that corporate earnings over all have been on a constant decline in relation to the general economy during the past twelve years.

We in business deplore inflationary pressures. We would much prefer conditions permitting reductions in prices, but, lacking adequate earnings and adequate depreciation provisions in the tax code, this has not been possible.

Earnings are not adequate because too much is siphoned off for spending programs in this country at all government levels and for increases to labor which are in excess of gains in productivity. Government intervention in price decisions in industry presupposes that this may be balanced by Government intervention in the determination of the price of labor.

It is a challenge to business leadership to make certain that both business and labor will remain free to make their own decisions without government intervention. . . .

In this great Constitution Hall it is perhaps most appropriate that we talk for a few minutes about our leadership responsibility in helping to prevent further erosion of what are termed checks and balances. . . .

Over the past several generations you and I know that there has been an erosion of some of these checks and balances with more and more power being invested in the executive, with more and more of the judicial function being absorbed by administrative bureaus and agencies, and with more and more intervention in the affairs of the states and local governments which

---

* Reprinted from *The New York Times*, May 1, 1962.

were to have the right to all powers not specifically vested in the Federal Government.

We should make it clear, however, that we do not believe that there are in high places in our Government, in the Executive branch, or the legislative branch, or the judicial branch, any coterie trying to drive us toward totalitarianism.

But we should remember that dictators in other lands usually come to power under accepted constitutional procedures established as a result of the erosion of sound constitutional principles. We should make certain that there is no further erosion of sound principles in this country so that it will not be possible some day for anyone to take over the reins of power under dictatorship.

On an over-all basis we in business in our leadership efforts should not resort to name-calling. There are many matters in which we agree with this or any other Administration, such as foreign commerce, defense, balance of payments, and the like.

We should work objectively with all departments of Government in these matters and keep the lines of communication wide open. We should never, however, bury our principles in matters in which we are in complete disagreement, but here too our approach should be an objective one in an effort to present and persuade others to our viewpoint.

Once again expounding the economic policies of the New Frontier, President Kennedy, speaking at Yale University where he received an honorary degree on June 11, 1962, urged the American people to reappraise their economic beliefs in the light of modern needs.

JOHN F. KENNEDY: "WHAT IS AT STAKE . . . IS . . . THE PRACTICAL MANAGEMENT OF A MODERN ECONOMY"*

. . . I am very glad to be here, and as a new member of the club I have been checking to see what earlier links existed between the institution of the Presidency and Yale. I found that a member of the Class of 1878, William Howard Taft, served one term in the White House as preparation for becoming a member of this faculty. And a graduate of 1804, John C. Calhoun, regarded the Vice Presidency, quite naturally, as too lowly a status for a Yale alumnus and became the only man in history to ever resign that office.

Calhoun in 1804 and Taft in 1878 graduated into a world very different from ours today. They and their contemporaries spent entire careers, stretching over forty years, in grappling with a few dramatic issues on which the nation was sharply and emotionally divided—issues that occupied the attention of a generation at a time: the national bank, the disposal of the public lands, nullification or union, freedom or slavery, gold or silver.

Today these old sweeping issues have largely disappeared. The central domestic problems of our time are more subtle and less simple. They relate not to basic clashes of philosophy of ideology, but to ways and means of reaching common goals—to research for sophisticated solutions to complex and obstinate issues.

The world of Calhoun, the world of Taft, had its own hard problems and notable challenges.

But its problems are not our problems. Their age is not our age. As every past generation has had to disenthrall itself from an inheritance of truisms and stereotypes, so in our time we must move on from the reassuring repetition of stale phrases to a new, difficult but essential confrontation with reality.

For the great enemy of the truth is very often not the lie—deliberate, contrived and dishonest—but the myth—persistent, persuasive and unrealistic.

Too often we hold fast to clichés of our forebears. We enjoy the comfort of opinion without the discomfort of thought.

Mythology distracts us everywhere—in government as in business, in politics as in economics, in foreign affairs as in domestic affairs.

But today I want to particularly consider the myth and reality in our national economy.

In recent months many have come to feel as I do that the dialogue between the parties—between business and government—between the Government and the public—is clogged by illusion and platitude and fails to reflect the true realities of contemporary American society.

I speak of these matters here at Yale because of the self-evident truth that a great university is always enlisted against the spread of illusion and on the side of reality.

No one has said it more clearly than your President Griswold:

"Liberal learning is both a safeguard against false ideas of freedom and a source of true ones."

Your role as university men, whatever your

* Reprinted from *The New York Times,* June 12, 1962.

calling, will be to increase each new generation's grasp of its duties.

There are three great ideas of our domestic affairs in which, today, there is a danger that illusion may prevent effective action.

They are:

First, the question of the size and shape of government's responsibilities; secondly, the question of public fiscal policy; and third, the matter of confidence—business confidence, or public confidence—or simply confidence in America.

I want to talk about all three and I want to talk about them carefully and dispassionately—and I emphasize that I am concerned here not with political debate but with ways to separate false problems from real ones.

If a contest in angry argument were forced upon it, no Administration could shrink from response, and history does not suggest that American Presidents are totally without resources in an engagement forced upon them because of hostility in one sector of society.

But in the wider national interest we need not partisan wrangling but common concentration on common problems. I came here to this distinguished university to ask you to join in this great task.

Let us take first the question of the size and the shape of government. The myth is that government is big, and bad—and steadily getting bigger and worse.

Obviously this myth has some excuse for existence. It is true that in recent history each new Administration has spent much more money than its predecessors.

Thus President Roosevelt outspent President Hoover and, with allowances for the special case of the second World War, President Truman outspent President Roosevelt.

Just to prove that this was not a partisan matter, President Eisenhower then outspent President Truman by the handsome figure of $182,-000,000,000. It is even possible, some think, that this trend may continue.

But does it follow from this that big government is growing relatively bigger? It does not. For the fact is for the last fifteen years the Federal Government, and also the Federal debt, and also the Federal bureaucracy, have grown less rapidly than the economy as a whole.

If we leave defense and space expenditures aside, the Federal Government since the Second World War has expanded less than any other major section of our national life; less than industry; less than commerce; less than agriculture; less than higher education, and very much less than the noise about big government.

The truth about big government is the truth about any great activity: it is complex. Certainly it is true that size brings dangers, but it is also true that size can bring benefits.

Here at Yale, which has contributed so much to our national progress in science and medicine, it may be proper for me to mention one great and little noticed expansion of government which has brought strength to our whole society: the new role of our Federal Government as the major patron of research in science and in medicine.

Few people realize that in 1961, in support of all university research in science and medicine, $3 out of every $4 came from the Federal Government. I need hardly point out that this has taken place without undue enlargement of government control; that American scientists remain second to none in their independence and in their individualism.

I am not suggesting that Federal expenditure cannot bring on some measure of control. The whole thrust of Federal expenditures in agriculture has been related by purpose and design to control, as a means of dealing with the problems created by our farmers and our growing productivity. Each sector, my point is, of activity must be approached on its own merits and in terms of specific national needs.

Generalities in regard to Federal expenditures, therefore, can be misleading. Each case—science, urban renewal, agriculture, natural resources—each case must be determined on its merits if we are to profit from our unrivaled ability to combine the strength of public and private purposes.

Next, let us turn to the problem about fiscal myths. Here the myths are legion and the truth hard to find. But let me take as a prime example the problem of the Federal budget.

We persist in measuring our Federal fiscal integrity today by the conventional, or administrative, budget with results which would be regarded as absurd in any business firm, in any country of Europe, or in any careful assessment of the reality of our national finances.

The administrative budget has sound administrative uses. But for wider purposes it is less helpful. It omits our special trust funds and the effect they have on our economy. It neglects changes in assets or inventories. It cannot tell a loan from a straight expenditure. And worst of all it cannot distinguish between operating expenditures and long-term investments.

This budget in relation to the great problems of Federal fiscal policy, which are basic to our country in 1962, is not simply irrelevant; it can be actively misleading. And yet there is a mythology that measures all our national soundness or unsoundness on the single simple basis of this same annual administrative budget.

If our Federal budget is to serve not the debate but the country, we must find ways of clarifying this area of discourse.

Still in the area of fiscal policy, let me say a word about deficits. The myth persists that Federal deficits create inflation, and budget surpluses prevent it.

Yet sizable budget surpluses after the war did not prevent inflation, and persistent deficits for the last several years have not upset our basic price stability.

Obviously, deficits are sometimes dangerous—

and so are surpluses. But honest assessment plainly requires a more sophisticated view than the old and automatic cliché that deficits automatically bring inflation.

There are myths also about our public debt. It is widely supposed that this debt is growing at a dangerously rapid rate. In fact, both the debt per person and the debt as a proportion of our Gross National Products have declined sharply since the end of the second World War.

In absolute terms, the national debt since the end of World War II has increased only 8 per cent while private debt was increasing 305 per cent and the debt of state and local governments on whom people frequently suggest we should place additional burden—the debt of state and local government has increased 378 per cent.

Moreover, debts public and private are neither good nor bad in and of themselves. Borrowing can lead to overextension and collapse—but it can also lead to expansion and strength. There is no single simple slogan in this field that we can trust.

Finally, I come to the problem of confidence. Confidence is a matter of myth and also a matter of truth—and this time let me take the truth of the matter first.

It is true and of high importance that the prosperity of this country depends on the assurances that all major elements within it will live up to their responsibilities.

If business were to neglect its obligations to the public; if labor were blind to all public responsibility; above all, if Government were to abandon its obvious—and statutory—duty of watchful concern for our economic health—and any of these things should happen—then confidence might well be weakened and the danger of stagnation would increase.

This is the true issue of confidence.

But there is also the false issue—and in its simplest form it is the assertion that any and all unfavorable turns of the speculative wheel—however temporary and however plainly speculative in character—are the result of—and I quote—a lack of confidence in the national Administration.

This, I must tell you, while comforting, is not wholly true. Worse, it obscures the reality which is also simple. The solid ground of mutual confidence is the necessary partnership of government with all of the sectors of our society in the steady quest for economic progress.

Corporate plans are not based on a political confidence in party leaders but on an economic confidence in the nation's ability to invest and produce and consume.

Business had full confidence in the Administration in power in 1929, 1954, 1958 and 1960. But this was not enough to prevent recession when business lacked full confidence in the economy. What matters is the capacity of the nation as a whole to deal with its economic problems and its opportunities.

The stereotypes I have been discussing distract our attention and divide our efforts. These stereotypes do our nation a disservice not just because they are exhausted and irrelevant, but above all because they are misleading—because they stand in the way of the solution of hard and complicated facts.

It is not new that past debates should obscure present realities. But the damage of such a false dialogue is greater today than ever before simply because today the safety of all the world—the very future of freedom—depends as never before upon the sensible and clear-headed management of the domestic affairs of the United States.

The real issues of our time are rarely as dramatic as the issues of Calhoun's. The differences today are usually matters of degree. And we cannot understand and attack our contemporary problems in 1962 if we are bound by traditional labels and worn-out slogans of an earlier era.

But the unfortunate fact of the matter is that our rhetoric has not kept pace with the speed of social and economic change. Our political debate, our public discourse on current domestic and economic issues, too often bears little or no relation to the actual problems the United States faces.

What is at stake in our economic decisions today is not some grand warfare of rival ideologies which will sweep the country with passion but the practical management of a modern economy. What we need are not labels and cliches but more basic discussion of the sophisticated and technical questions involved in keeping a great economic machinery moving ahead.

The national interest lies in high employment and steady expansion of output and stable prices and a strong dollar. The declaration of such an objective is easy. The attainment in an intricate and interdependent economy and world is a little more difficult. To attain them we require not some automatic response but hard thought.

Let me end by suggesting a few of the real questions on our national agenda.

First, how can our budget and tax policies supply adequate revenues and preserve our balance-of-payments position without slowing up our economic growth?

Two, how are we to set our interest rates and regulate the flow of money in ways which will stimulate the economy at home without weakening the dollar abroad? Given the spectrum of our domestic and international responsibilities, what should be the mix between fiscal and monetary policies?

Let me give several examples from my experience with the complexity of these matters, and how political labels and ideological approaches are irrelevant to the solutions.

Last week a distinguished graduate of this school, Senator [William] Proxmire [Democrat of Wisconsin] of the Class of 1938, who is ordinarily regarded as a liberal Democrat, suggested that we should follow in meeting our economic problems a stiff fiscal policy with emphasis on budget balance and an easy monetary policy with low interest rates in order to keep our economy going.

In the same week the Bank for International Settlements in Basle, Switzerland, a conservative organization representing the central bankers of Europe, suggested that the appropriate economic policy in the United States should be the very opposite—that we should follow a flexible budget policy as in Europe, with deficits when the economy is down, and a high monetary policy on interest rates, as in Europe, in order to control inflation and protect gold.

Both may be right or wrong. It will depend on many different factors. The point is that this is basically an administrative or executive problem in which political labels or cliches do not give us a solution.

A well-known business journal this morning, as I journeyed to New Haven, raised the prospects that a further budget deficit would bring inflation and encourage the flow of gold. We have had several budget deficits beginning with $12,500,000,000 deficit in '58. And it is true that in the fall of 1960 we had a gold dollar loss running at $5,000,000,000 annually.

This would seem to prove the case that a deficit produces inflation and that we lose gold. Yet there was no inflation following the deficit of 1958 nor has there been inflation since then. Our wholesale price and index since 1958 has remained completely level in spite of several deficits, because the loss of gold has been due to other reasons—price instability, relative interest rates, relative export-import balances, national security expenditures—all the rest.

Let me give you a third and final example. At the World Bank meeting in September, a number of American bankers attending predicted to their European colleagues that because of the fiscal 1962 budget deficit there would be a strong inflationary pressure on the dollar and a loss of gold.

Their predictions of inflation were shared by many in business and helped push the market up. The recent reality of non-inflation helped bring it down.

We have had no inflation because we have had other factors in our economy that have contributed to price stability. I do not suggest that the Government is right and they are wrong. The fact of the matter is, in the Federal Reserve Board and in the Administration this fall, a similar view was held by many well-informed and disinterested men—that inflation was the major problem that we would face in the winter of 1962. But it was not.

What I do suggest is that these problems are endlessly complicated. And yet they go to the future of this country and its ability to prove to the world what we believe it must prove. I am suggesting that the problems of fiscal and monetary policy in the Sixties as opposed to the kinds of problems we faced in the Thirties demand

subtle challenges for which technical answers—not political answers—must be provided.

These are matters upon which government and business may, and in many cases will, disagree. They are certainly matters that government and business should be discussing in the most sober, dispassionate and careful way if we are to maintain the kind of vigorous economy upon which our country depends.

How can we develop and sustain strong and stable world markets for basic commodities without unfairness to the consumer and without undue stimulus to the producer?

How can we generate the buying power which can consume what we produce on our farms and in our factories?

How can we take advantage of the miracles of automation with the great demand that it will put upon high-skilled labor and yet offer employment to the half a million of unskilled school dropouts every year who enter the labor market—8,000,000 of them in the Nineteen Sixties?

How do we eradicate the barriers which separate substantial minorities of our citizens from access to education and employment on equal terms with the rest?

How, in sum, can we make our free economy work at full capacity, that is, provide adequate profits for enterprise and adequate wages for labor and adequate utilization of plant and opportunity for all?

These are the problems that we should be talking about, that the political parties and the various groups in our country should be discussing. They cannot be solved by incantations from the forgotten past.

But the example of Western Europe shows that they are capable of solution. That government, and many of them are conservative governments, prepared to face technical problems without ideological preconceptions, can coordinate the elements of a national economy and bring about growth and prosperity—a decade of them.

Some conversations I have heard in our country sound like old records, long-playing, left over from the middle Thirties. The debate of the Thirties had its great significance and produced great results. But it took place in a different world with different needs and different tasks. It is our responsibility today to live in our own world, and to identify the needs and discharge the tasks of the Nineteen Sixties.

If there is any current trend toward meeting present problems with old clichés, this is the moment to stop it—before it lands us all in the bog of sterile acrimony.

Discussion is essential, and I am hopeful that the debate of recent weeks, though up to now somewhat barren, may represent the start of a serious dialogue of the kind which has led in Europe to such fruitful collaboration among all the elements of economic society and to a decade of unrivaled economic progress.

But let us not engage in the wrong argument at the wrong time, between the wrong people in the wrong country, while the real problems of our time grow and multiply, fertilized by our neglect.

Nearly 150 years ago Thomas Jefferson wrote:

"The new circumstances under which we are placed call for new words, new phrases, and the transfer of old words to new objects."

That is truer today than it was in the time of Jefferson, because the role of this country is so vastly more significant.

There is a show in England called "Stop the World, I Want to Get Off." You have not chosen to exercise that option. You are part of the world, and you must participate in these days of our years in the solution of the problems that pour upon us, requiring the most sophisticated and technical judgment.

And, as we work in concert to meet the authentic problems of our time, we will generate a vision and an energy which will demonstrate anew to the world the superior vitality and the strength of the free society.

INDEX

Representatives, and responsibility to the public, 453
Reservations, and League of Nations, 415–420
Rice, George, 299–306
Roosevelt, Eleanor, 522
Roosevelt, Franklin D., 457–465, 472–477, 483–493, 497–499, 502–503, 505–509, 532
Roosevelt, Theodore, 390–401

Sandys, George, 11
Schurz, Carl, 173, 218, 288, 378–380
Science, impact on industry, 434–435, 436
Seapower, importance of, 368–372
Seas, freedom of, 413–414
Seward, William H., 176–177, 214, 231–236
Slack economy, under Eisenhower, 556–557
Slavery: Bible and, 190–191, 193–194, 209–210; conditions under, 197–199; law and, 191–192, 201; opposition to, 190–197; philosophic critique of, 199–203; philosophic defense of, 203–212
Social Darwinism, 147

Social status, function of economic status, 444
Socialism, Populist attitude toward, 348–349, 350
Sons of Liberty, 62–63
Stamp Act crisis, 61–62
Standard of living, Chicago in 1880's, 315–323
Steel price rise, 566–573; criticism of Kennedy's response, 573–575
Stewardship, doctrine of, 306–309
Stoddard, John, and qualities of leadership, 34–36
Stone, Samuel, 33–34
Suffrage, and Negroes, 268–273
Sumner, Charles, 253
Sumptuary orientation, and Progressivism, 389
Supreme Court, 120–142, 237–238, 256, 469–477

Taft, William Howard, 394–395, 396
Taxation, and the American Revolution, 55–63
Tennent, Gilbert, 28, 34
Testing nuclear weapons, reasons for resumption, 546–548
Texas, annexation of, 172, 182–186
Tramps and vagabonds, significance of 347–348

Treaty of Versailles, 414
Truman, Harry S., 510, 511, 513, 523–525, 532–533, 535–536, 540–543
Tugwell, Rexford G., 463, 464

United Nations, sentiment on formation, 502–509
Urbanization, trend toward, 310–334

Vallandigham, Clement, 261
Values, transformation called for, 402–406
Veto in United Nations, preliminary discussions on, 505–508
Virginia: during Reconstruction, 284–285; seventeenth-century colony, 11–27
Voting, and American Revolution, 52–53

Washington, George, 74–75
Webster, Daniel, 145
Weld, Theodore Dwight, 190, 191, 194, 197–199
Welles, Sumner, 486, 489, 494
Whitefield, George, 44–47
Winthrop, John, 2–11

Yerkes, Charles T., 325

37